Lecture Notes in Artificial Intelligence 2250

Subseries of Lecture Notes in Computer Science
Edited by J. G. Carbonell and J. Siekmann

Lecture Notes in Computer Science
Edited by G. Goos, J. Hartmanis, and J. van Leeuwen

Springer
Berlin
Heidelberg
New York
Barcelona
Hong Kong
London
Milan
Paris
Tokyo

Robert Nieuwenhuis   Andrei Voronkov (Eds.)

Logic for Programming, Artificial Intelligence, and Reasoning

8th International Conference, LPAR 2001
Havana, Cuba, December 3-7, 2001
Proceedings

Series Editors

Jaime G. Carbonell, Carnegie Mellon University, Pittsburgh, PA, USA
Jörg Siekmann, University of Saarland, Saarbrücken, Germany

Volume Editors

Robert Nieuwenhuis
Technical University of Catalonia, Department of Software
Jordi Girona 1, 08034 Barcelona, Spain
E-mail: roberto@lsi.upc.es

Andrei Voronkov
University of Manchester, Department of Computer Science
Kilburn Building, Oxford Road, Manchester M13 9PL, UK
E-mail: voronkov@cs.man.ac.uk

Cataloging-in-Publication Data applied for

Die Deutsche Bibliothek - CIP-Einheitsaufnahme

Logic for programming, artificial intelligence, and reasoning : 8th international conference ; proceedings / LPAR 2001, Havana, Cuba, December 3 - 7, 2001. Robert Nieuwenhuis ; Andrei Voronkov (ed.). - Berlin ; Heidelberg ; New York ; Barcelona ; Hong Kong ; London ; Milan ; Paris ;Tokyo : Springer, 2001
(Lecture notes in computer science ; Vol. 2250 : Lecture notes in artificial intelligence)
ISBN 3-540-42957-3

CR Subject Classification (1998): I.2.3, F.3, F.4.1, D.2.4

ISBN 3-540-42957-3 Springer-Verlag Berlin Heidelberg New York

Springer-Verlag Berlin Heidelberg New York
a member of BertelsmannSpringer Science+Business Media GmbH

http://www.springer.de

Printed in Germany

Typesetting: Camera-ready by author, data conversion by PTP-Berlin, Stefan Sossna
Printed on acid-free paper SPIN: 10845965 06/3142 5 4 3 2 1 0

Preface

This volume contains the papers presented at the Eighth International Conference on Logic for Programming, Artificial Intelligence and Reasoning (LPAR 2001), held on December 3-7, 2001, at the University of Havana (Cuba), together with the Second International Workshop on Implementation of Logics.

There were 112 submissions, of which 19 belonged to the special submission category of experimental papers, intended to describe implementations or comparisons of systems, or experiments with systems. Each submission was reviewed by at least three program committee members and an electronic program committee meeting was held via the Internet. The high number of submissions caused a large amount of work, and we are very grateful to the other 31 PC members for their efficiency and for the quality of their reviews and discussions.

Finally, the committee decided to accept 40 papers in the theoretical category, and 9 experimental papers. In addition to the refereed papers, this volume contains an extended abstract of the invited talk by Frank Wolter. Two other invited lectures were given by Matthias Baaz and Manuel Hermenegildo.

Apart from the program committee, we would also like to thank the other people who made LPAR 2001 possible: the additional referees; the Local Arrangements Chair Luciano García; Andrés Navarro and Òscar Güell, who ran the internet-based submission software and the program committee discussion software at the LSI Department lab in Barcelona; and Bill McCune, whose program committee management software was used.

October 2001

Robert Nieuwenhuis
Andrei Voronkov

Conference Organization

Program Chairs

Robert Nieuwenhuis (Technical University of Catalonia)
Andrei Voronkov (University of Manchester)

Program Committee

Franz Baader (Technische Universität Dresden)
Maurice Bruynooghe (Katholieke Universiteit Leuven)
Jan Van den Bussche (Limburgs Universitair Centrum)
Thierry Coquand (Göteborgs Universitet)
Patrick Cousot (ENS Paris)
Nachum Dershowitz (Tel-Aviv University)
Jürgen Dix (University of Manchester)
Thomas Eiter (Technische Universität Wien)
Javier Esparza (University of Edinburgh)
Alan Frish (University of York)
Harald Ganzinger (Max-Planck Institut, Saarbrücken)
Georg Gottlob (Technische Universität Wien)
Jean Goubault-Larrecq (ENS de Cachan)
John Harrison (Intel Research)
Neil Immerman (University of Massachusetts)
Neil Jones (Københavns Universitet)
Jean-Pierre Jouannaud (CNRS)
Deepak Kapur (University of New Mexico)
Hans Kleine Büning (Universität Paderborn)
Maurizio Lenzerini (Università di Roma "La Sapienza")
Giorgio Levi (Università di Pisa)
Fabio Massacci (Università di Siena)
Tobias Nipkow (Technische Universität München)
Mitsuhiro Okada (Keio University)
Leszek Pacholski (Wroclawski Uniwersytet)
Michel Parigot (Université Paris 7)
Frank Pfenning (Carnegie Mellon University)
Maarten de Rijke (Universiteit van Amsterdam)
Natarajan Shankar (SRI International)
Wolfgang Thomas (RWTH Aachen)
Moshe Vardi (Rice University)

Local Organization

Luciano Garcia (Universidad de la Habana)

List of Referees

Maria Alpuente
Gianluca Amato
Ofer Arieli
Roberto Bagnara
Richard Banach
Chitta Baral
Gertrud Bauer
Peter Baumgartner
Robert Baumgartner
Chantal Berline
Gerd Beuster
Piero Bonatti
Julian Bradfield
Stefan Brass
Antonio Brogi
Chad Brown
Marco Cadoli
Diego Calvanese
Iliano Cervesato
Kaustuv Chaudhuri
Henry Chinaski
Carl Christian Frederiksen
Roy Crole
Steven Dawson
Emmanuel De Mot
Giuseppe De Giacomo
Alvaro del Val
Giorgio Delzanno
Bart Demoen
Agostino Dovier
Lyndon Drake
Uwe Egly
Amy Felty
Chris Fermueller
Maurizio Gabbrielli
Didier Galmiche
Paul Gastin
Juergen Giesl
Enrico Giunchiglia
Roberta Gori
Martin Grohe
Michael Hanus
James Harland
Juan Heguiabehere
Tamir Heyman
Thomas Hillenbrand
Martin Hofmann
Tetsuo Ida
Tomi Janhunen
David Janin
Gerda Janssens
A. John Power
Hirofumi Katsuno
Andrzej Kisielewicz
Felix Klaedtke
Gerwin Klein
Christoph Koch
Michael Kohlhase
Ralf Kuester
Orna Kupferman
Gerhard Lakemeyer
Javier Larrosa
Paolo Liberatore
Christof Loeding
Christoph Lueth
Thomas Lukasiewicz
Monika Maidl
Henning Makholm
Pascal Manoury
Victor Marek
Ian Miguel
Torben Mogensen
Peter Møller Neergaard
Sara Negri
Hans de Nivelle
Damian Niwinski
Kazuhiro Ogata
Nikolay Pelov
Jens Peter Secher
Axel Polleres
David Pym
Riccardo Rosati
Paul Roziere
Harald Ruess
Salvatore Ruggieri
Tatiana Rybina
David Rydeheard
Ken Satoh
Ulrike Sattler
Francesco Scarcello
Andrea Schalk
Torsten Schaub
Francesca Scozzari
Dietmar Seipel
Dan Sheridan
Viorica Sofronie-Stokkermans
Chin Soon Lee
Colin Sterling
Frieder Stolzenburg
Terry Swift
Kazushige Terui
Sven Thiel
Michael Thielscher
Ashish Tiwari
Hans Tompits
Iddo Tzameret
Christian Urban
Bert Van Nuffelen
Wim Vanhoof
Helmut Veith
Sofie Verbaeten
Luca Vigano
Uwe Waldmann
Toby Walsh
Igor Walukiewicz
Markus Wenzel
Emil Weydert
Stefan Woehrle
Frank Wolter

Conferences Preceding LPAR 2001

RCLP'90, Irkutsk, Soviet Union
RCLP'91, Leningrad, Soviet Union, aboard the ship "Michail Lomonosov"
LPAR'92, St. Petersburg, Russia, aboard the ship "Michail Lomonosov"
LPAR'93, St. Petersburg, Russia
LPAR'94, Kiev, Ukraine, aboard the ship "Marshal Koshevoi"
LPAR'99, Tbilisi, Republic of Georgia
LPAR 2000, Reunion Island, France

Table of Contents

Session 6. Automated Theorem Proving

Session 7. Non-classical Logics

Session 8. Types

Session 9. Experimental Papers

Session 10. Foundations of Logic

Session 11. CSP and SAT

Session 12. Non-monotonic Reasoning

Session 13. Semantics

Session 14. Experimental Papers

Session 15. Termination

Session 16. Knowledge-Based Systems

Session 17. Analysis of Logic Programs

Session 18. Databases and Knowledge Bases

Session 19. Termination

Session 20. Program Analysis and Proof Planning

Monodic Fragments of First-Order Temporal Logics: 2000–2001 A.D.

Ian Hodkinson[1], Frank Wolter[2], and Michael Zakharyaschev[3]

[1] Department of Computing, Imperial College,
180 Queen's Gate, London SW7 2BZ, U.K.
imh@doc.ic.ac.uk

[2] Institut für Informatik, Universität Leipzig,
Augustus-Platz 10-11, 04109 Leipzig, Germany
wolter@informatik.uni-leipzig.de

[3] Department of Computer Science, King's College,
Strand, London WC2R 2LS, U.K.
mz@dcs.kcl.ac.uk

Abstract. The aim of this paper is to summarize and analyze some results obtained in 2000–2001 about decidable and undecidable fragments of various first-order temporal logics, give some applications in the field of knowledge representation and reasoning, and attract the attention of the 'temporal community' to a number of interesting open problems.

1 Introduction

Temporal logic has found numerous applications in computer science, ranging from the traditional and well-developed fields of program specification and verification [45,42,43], temporal databases [20,21,3,50,30], and distributed and multi-agent systems [27], to more recent uses in knowledge representation and reasoning [6,7,10,49,60]. This is true of both propositional and first-order temporal logic. However, the mainstream of theoretical studies in the discipline has mostly been restricted to the propositional case—witness the surveys [26,51], or the two-volume monograph [28,30] where only one chapter is devoted to first-order temporal logics.

The reason for this seems clear. Though some axiomatizations of first-order temporal logics are known (e.g., [48] presents axiomatizations for first-order logics with Until and Since over the class of all linear flows and over the rationals), a series of incompleteness theorems [1,4,28,31,44,53,54], started by unpublished results of Scott and Lindström in the 1960s, show that many of the first-order temporal logics most useful in computer science are not even recursively enumerable. But in contrast to classical first-order logic, where the early undecidability results of Turing and Church stimulated research and led to a rich and profound theory concerned with classifying fragments of first-order logic according to their decidability (see, e.g., [13]), for a long time there were few if any serious attempts to convert the 'negative' results in first-order temporal logic into a classification

R. Nieuwenhuis and A. Voronkov (Eds.): LPAR 2001, LNAI 2250, pp. 1–23, 2001.

problem. Apparently, the extremely weak expressive power of the temporal formulas required to prove undecidability left no hope that any useful decidable fragments located 'between' propositional and first-order temporal logics could ever be found.

A certain breakthrough has been recently achieved in [35,61], where the so-called *monodic fragment* of first-order temporal and modal logics was shown to have much better computational behavior. In monodic formulas, the scope of temporal operators is restricted only to subformulas with at most one free variable. The idea to consider them came from knowledge representation, where a number of decidable description logics with modal, temporal, dynamic, and similar operators were constructed [49,9,56,60]. It turned out that if these operators are applicable only to concepts (i.e., unary predicates) or subsumptions (closed formulas) of a decidable description logic, then the resulting hybrid logic is usually decidable as well; but applications of temporal operators to roles (i.e., binary predicates) lead to undecidable logics [57].

The aim of this paper is to survey the rapidly growing body of results, obtained since 2000, about decidable and undecidable fragments of various first-order temporal logics. We will describe some applications in knowledge representation and reasoning. We also include some interesting open problems, which we hope will attract the attention of the 'temporal community' in both logic and computer science.

2 First-Order Logics of Linear and Branching Time

2.1 Linear Time

Denote by $\mathcal{QTL}$ the *first-order temporal language* constructed in the standard way from the following alphabet:

- *predicate symbols* $P_0, P_1, \ldots$, each of which is of some fixed arity,
- *individual variables* $x_0, x_1, \ldots$,
- *individual constants* $c_0, c_1, \ldots$,
- the *booleans* $\wedge$, $\neg$,
- the *universal quantifier* $\forall x$ for each individual variable x,
- the *temporal operators* $\mathcal{S}$ (Since) and $\mathcal{U}$ (Until).

Note that the language contains neither equality nor function symbols.

We will use the following standard abbreviations:

$$\exists x\varphi = \neg\forall x\neg\varphi \qquad \Diamond_F\varphi = \top\mathcal{U}\varphi$$
$$\Box_F\varphi = \neg\Diamond_F\neg\varphi \qquad \Box_F^+\varphi = \varphi\wedge\Box_F\varphi$$
$$\Diamond_F^+\varphi = \varphi\vee\Diamond_F\varphi \qquad \bigcirc\varphi = \bot\mathcal{U}\varphi$$

where $\top$ and $\bot$ are the boolean constants 'truth' and 'falsehood', respectively. Thus, $\Diamond_F$ can be read as 'some time in the future', $\Box_F^+$ as 'from now on', and $\bigcirc$ as 'at the next moment' or 'tomorrow'.

$\mathcal{QTL}$ is interpreted in *first-order temporal models* of the form $\mathfrak{M} = \langle \mathfrak{F}, D, I \rangle$, where $\mathfrak{F} = \langle W, < \rangle$ is a strict linear order representing the intended *flow of time*, D is a non-empty set, the *domain* of $\mathfrak{M}$, and I is a function associating with every moment of time $w \in W$ a first-order structure

$$I(w) = \left\langle D, P_0^{I(w)}, \ldots, c_0^{I(w)}, \ldots \right\rangle,$$

the *state* of $\mathfrak{M}$ at moment w. Here, for each i, $P_i^{I(w)}$ is a predicate on D of the same arity as P_i (for a propositional variable p_i, the predicate $p_i^{I(w)}$ is simply true or false), and $c_i^{I(w)}$ is an element of D. We require that $c_i^{I(w)} = c_i^{I(v)}$ for any $w, v \in W$—i.e., that constants are 'rigid'.

An *assignment in D* is a function $\mathfrak{a}$ from the set *var* of individual variables to D. We extend $\mathfrak{a}$ to constants via $\mathfrak{a}(c) = c^{I(w)}$ for any $w \in W$; this is well-defined. The *truth-relation* $(\mathfrak{M}, w) \models^{\mathfrak{a}} \varphi$ (or simply $w \models^{\mathfrak{a}} \varphi$, if $\mathfrak{M}$ is understood) in the model $\mathfrak{M}$ under the assignment $\mathfrak{a}$ is now defined inductively in the usual way:

- $w \models^{\mathfrak{a}} P_i(y_1, \ldots, y_\ell)$ iff $P_i^{I(w)}(\mathfrak{a}(y_1), \ldots, \mathfrak{a}(y_\ell))$ is true in $I(w)$, where the y_i are variables or constants;
- $w \models^{\mathfrak{a}} \varphi \land \psi$ iff $w \models^{\mathfrak{a}} \varphi$ and $w \models^{\mathfrak{a}} \psi$;
- $w \models^{\mathfrak{a}} \neg\psi$ iff $w \not\models^{\mathfrak{a}} \psi$;
- $w \models^{\mathfrak{a}} \forall x \psi$ iff $w \models^{\mathfrak{b}} \psi$ for every assignment $\mathfrak{b}$ in D that may differ from $\mathfrak{a}$ only on x;
- $w \models^{\mathfrak{a}} \varphi \mathcal{S} \psi$ iff there is $v < w$ such that $v \models^{\mathfrak{a}} \psi$ and $u \models^{\mathfrak{a}} \varphi$ for every u in the interval $(v, w) = \{u \in W : v < u < w\}$;
- $w \models^{\mathfrak{a}} \varphi \mathcal{U} \psi$ iff there is $v > w$ such that $v \models^{\mathfrak{a}} \psi$ and $u \models^{\mathfrak{a}} \varphi$ for every $u \in (w, v)$.

For a class $\mathcal{F}$ of strict linear orders, we let $QTL(\mathcal{F})$, 'the *temporal logic of $\mathcal{F}$*', denote the set of $\mathcal{QTL}$-formulas that are true at all times in all models based on flows of time in $\mathcal{F}$ under all assignments. $QTL_{fin}(\mathcal{F})$ consists of the $\mathcal{QTL}$-formulas that are valid in all models based on flows of time in $\mathcal{F}$ and having *finite domains.*

Remark 1. In this paper we consider only models with *constant domains.* Satisfiability in models with expanding domains is known to be reducible to satisfiability in models with constant domains; see, e.g., [61].

2.2 Branching Time

There are a number of approaches to constructing temporal logics based on the branching time paradigm; see, e.g., [16,26,64,30]. Many of the resulting languages turn out to be fragments of the language we call here $\mathcal{QPCTL}^*$, *quantified* $\mathcal{CTL}^*$ *with past operators.* It is obtained by extending the vocabulary of $\mathcal{QTL}$ with a unary *path quantifier* A, which can be applied to arbitrary formulas. We let $\mathsf{E}\varphi$ abbreviate $\neg\mathsf{A}\neg\varphi$.

Important sublanguages of $\mathcal{QPCTL}^*$ are:

- $\mathcal{QCTL}^*$, that is $\mathcal{QPCTL}^*$ without the past operator $\mathcal{S}$;
- $\mathcal{QCTL}^*_F$, that is $\mathcal{QCTL}^*$ in which the binary operator $\mathcal{U}$ is replaced with the unary operator $\Box_F$ 'always in the future';
- $\mathcal{QPCTL}$, the fragment of $\mathcal{QPCTL}^*$ in which the path quantifiers and temporal operators occur only in the form $\mathsf{E}(\psi_1\mathcal{U}\psi_2)$, $\mathsf{E}(\psi_1\mathcal{S}\psi_2)$, $\mathsf{A}(\psi_1\mathcal{U}\psi_2)$, or $\mathsf{A}(\psi_1\mathcal{S}\psi_2)$.

A *tree* is a strict partial order $\mathfrak{F} = \langle W, < \rangle$ such that for all $w \in W$, the set $\{v \in W : v < w\}$ is well-ordered by $<$. A *full branch* of $\mathfrak{F}$ is a maximal linearly-ordered subset of W. An ω*-tree* is a tree whose full branches, ordered by $<$, are all order-isomorphic to $\langle \mathbb{N}, < \rangle$. $\mathcal{QPCTL}^*$ (as well as its sublanguages) is interpreted in structures of the form $\mathfrak{M} = \langle \mathfrak{F}, \mathcal{H}, D, I \rangle$, where $\mathfrak{F} = \langle W, < \rangle$ is an ω-tree, $\mathcal{H}$ is a set (*bundle*) of full branches in $\mathfrak{F}$ with $\bigcup \mathcal{H} = W$, D is a non-empty set called the *domain* of $\mathfrak{M}$, and I is again a function associating with every $w \in W$ a first-order structure $I(w)$ with domain D. Constants are again rigid. We call $\mathfrak{M}$ a *bundled tree model,* and the branches in the bundle $\mathcal{H}$ are called *histories.* In the case when $\mathcal{H}$ contains all full branches in $\mathfrak{F}$, we say that $\mathfrak{M}$ is a *full tree model,* or simply a *tree model.*

Assignments $\mathfrak{a}$ in D are defined as in the linear case. The *truth-relation* $(\mathfrak{M}, h, w) \models^{\mathfrak{a}} \varphi$, for $w \in h \in \mathcal{H}$ (or simply $(h, w) \models^{\mathfrak{a}} \varphi$ if $\mathfrak{M}$ is understood), is defined as follows:

- $(h, w) \models^{\mathfrak{a}} P_i(y_1, \ldots, y_\ell)$ iff $P_i^{I(w)}(\mathfrak{a}(y_1), \ldots, \mathfrak{a}(y_\ell))$ is true in $I(w)$, where the y_i are variables or constants;
- $(h, w) \models^{\mathfrak{a}} \forall x \psi$ iff $(h, w) \models^{\mathfrak{b}} \psi$ for every assignment $\mathfrak{b}$ in D that may differ from $\mathfrak{a}$ only on x;
- $(h, w) \models^{\mathfrak{a}} \varphi \mathcal{S} \psi$ iff there is $v < w$ such that $(h, v) \models^{\mathfrak{a}} \psi$ and $(h, u) \models^{\mathfrak{a}} \varphi$ for every $u \in (v, w)$;
- $(h, w) \models^{\mathfrak{a}} \varphi \mathcal{U} \psi$ iff there is $v \in h$ such that $v > w$, $(h, v) \models^{\mathfrak{a}} \psi$ and $(h, u) \models^{\mathfrak{a}} \varphi$ for every $u \in (w, v)$;
- $(h, w) \models^{\mathfrak{a}} \mathsf{A}\psi$ iff for all $h' \in \mathcal{H}$ such that $w \in h'$ we have $(h', w) \models^{\mathfrak{a}} \psi$,

plus the standard clauses for the booleans.

For any of the branching time languages $\mathcal{L}$ introduced above, denote by BL (L) the set of all $\mathcal{L}$-formulas that are true at all points in all histories under every assignment in every bundled (respectively, full) tree model. Thus, $BQPCTL^*$ is the set of $\mathcal{QPCTL}^*$-formulas valid in bundled tree models, while $QPCTL^*$ is the set of $\mathcal{QPCTL}^*$-formulas valid in all tree models.

Remark 2. The logic $BQPCTL^*$ is the first-order version of bundled Ockhamist logic; cf. e.g. [30]. In the computer science literature, $\mathcal{QCTL}^*$ often denotes only the set of *state* (i.e., history-independent) $\mathcal{QCTL}^*$*-formulas.* However, this makes no difference as far as decidability is concerned, because a *path* (history-dependent) *formula* φ is satisfiable iff the state formula $\mathsf{E}\varphi$ is satisfiable.

Satisfiability in bundled tree models can be reduced to satisfiability in full tree models. Indeed, given a $\mathcal{QPCTL}^*$-formula φ, let q be a propositional variable not occurring in φ, and denote by $\varphi^{\uparrow}$ the result of replacing each subformula of φ of the form $\mathsf{A}\psi$ by

$$\mathsf{A}(\Diamond_F \Box_F q \to \psi).$$

Then we have the following:

Proposition 1 ([36]). *φ is satisfiable in a bundled tree model iff $\mathsf{E}\Diamond_F\Box_F q \wedge \varphi^{\uparrow}$ is satisfiable in a full tree model.*

Example 1 in Section 3.2 illustrates the difference between satisfiability in bundled and full tree models.

3 Who Needs Decidable First-Order Temporal Logics?

As was mentioned in the introduction, temporal logic has a wide range of applications in various fields of computer science and artificial intelligence. Here we give just two examples from knowledge representation in AI, where the standard requirements of KR formalisms are *effectiveness and practical implementability.* We show how to embed the KR systems into first-order temporal logic; this will be used in Section 7 to obtain decidability results.

3.1 Temporal Description Logics

Classical description logic is a family of KR formalisms intended for dealing with conceptual knowledge about *static* application domains (see, e.g., [18] and references therein). In a description logic, knowledge is represented by means of subsumption relations between complex concepts and instance assertions between objects and concepts. For example, in the logic $\mathcal{ALC}$ of [14], complex concepts are composed from a countably infinite set $A_1, A_2, \ldots$ of atomic concepts (unary predicates) by means of the boolean operators $\sqcap$ and $\neg$ and the quantifiers $\forall R$ and $\exists R$, where R is a role name (binary predicate) from a countably infinite set of role names. Concepts are evaluated in $\mathcal{ALC}$-models

$$I = \langle \Delta, A_1^I, \ldots, R_1^I, \ldots, a_1^I, \ldots \rangle,$$

where Δ is a non-empty set, the A_i^I are subsets of Δ, the R_i^I subsets of $\Delta \times \Delta$, and the a_i^I are members of Δ interpreting the object names a_i of $\mathcal{ALC}$. The value C^I of a complex concept C is defined inductively, the only non-trivial clause being the following:

– $(\exists R.C)^I = \{x \in \Delta : \exists y \in \Delta\ (xR^I y \wedge y \in C^I)\}$.

We say that C_1 *subsumes* C_2 in I, $I \models C_1 \sqsubseteq C_2$ in symbols, if $C_1^I \subseteq C_2^I$. We say that an object name a is an *instance* of C in I, $I \models a : C$ in symbols, if $a^I \in C^I$. For example, the subsumption

$$\mathsf{Person} \sqcap \exists \mathsf{lives\_in}.\mathsf{Bavaria} \sqsubseteq \mathsf{Person} \sqcap \forall \mathsf{drinks}.\mathsf{Beer}$$

says that every person living in Bavaria drinks only beer, while the assertion

$$John : \exists \mathsf{drinks}.\mathsf{Whiskey}$$

claims that John drinks whiskey (and possibly some other liquids).

To represent *dynamic* conceptual knowledge bases, description logics have been extended by means of temporal operators; see, e.g., [49,9,60,7]. On the semantical level, such an extension is quite straightforward. Models for temporal description logics are obtained from first-order temporal models by taking I to be a function associating with every time point $w \in W$ not a first-order model but an $\mathcal{ALC}$-model $I(w) = \left\langle \Delta, A_1^{I(w)}, \ldots, R_1^{I(w)}, \ldots, a_1^{I(w)}, \ldots \right\rangle$, where $a_i^{I(w)} = a_i^{I(v)}$ for all $v, w \in W$.

On the syntactic side, we can obtain a hierarchy of temporalized description logics by allowing applications of temporal operators to various syntactic entities of $\mathcal{ALC}$. We can apply them to concepts, as in

$$\mathsf{Ordered\_object} \sqsubseteq \bigcirc \bigcirc \mathsf{Delivered\_object}$$

('each ordered object will be delivered in two days'), or

$$\mathsf{Mortal} = \mathsf{Living\_being} \sqcap (\mathsf{Living\_being}\ \mathcal{U}\ \Box_F \neg \mathsf{Living\_being})$$

('mortals are living beings which eventually die'). We can also apply them to subsumption relations, as in

$$\Box_F \Diamond_F \neg(\mathsf{Living\_being} \sqsubseteq \bot)$$

('living beings will never die out completely'). If time is branching, we can also say

$$\mathsf{E}\Box_F(\mathsf{Ordered\_object} \sqsubseteq \bigcirc \mathsf{Delivered\_object})$$

('it is possible that every ordered object is always delivered in one day'), or

$$\mathsf{Ordered\_object} \sqsubseteq \mathsf{A} \bigcirc \mathsf{Delivered\_object}$$

('an ordered object must be delivered the next day').

The maximal language $\mathcal{DPCTL}^*$ ($\mathcal{Q}$ for 'quantified' is replaced by $\mathcal{D}$ for 'description') that we consider in this paper allows applications of the temporal operators and path quantifiers to both concepts and subsumption relations.[1] More precisely, if C and D are concepts then $C\mathcal{U}D$, $C\mathcal{S}D$, $\mathsf{E}C$ and $\mathsf{A}C$ are also concepts. Atomic $\mathcal{DPCTL}^*$-formulas are of the form $a : C$, aRb, and $C \sqsubseteq D$, where C, D are $\mathcal{DPCTL}^*$-concepts, R is a role name, and a, b are object names. Complex formulas are composed from atomic ones using the booleans, $\mathcal{S}$, $\mathcal{U}$, and A.

The semantics of $\mathcal{DPCTL}^*$ should be clear. First, given a bundled tree model $\mathfrak{M} = \langle \mathfrak{F}, \mathcal{H}, \Delta, I \rangle$, we define the extension $C^{I(h,w)}$ of a concept C relative to a history h and a moment w in h. This is done by induction as follows (we list only the interesting clauses):

[1] We could, of course, allow for temporalized roles as well. However, the obtained temporal description logics would be undecidable; see [60] for more information.

- $A^{I(h,w)} = A^{I(w)}$, for all concept names A;
- $(\exists R.C)^{I(h,w)} = \{x \in \Delta : \exists y\ (xR^{I(w)}y \wedge y \in C^{I(h,w)})\}$;
- $x \in (C_1 \mathcal{U} C_2)^{I(h,w)}$ iff there exists $v \in h$ such that $w < v$, $x \in C_2^{I(h,v)}$ and $x \in C_1^{I(h,u)}$ for all $u \in (w, v)$;
- $x \in (\mathsf{E}C)^{I(h,w)}$ iff there exists $h' \in \mathcal{H}$ such that $w \in h'$ and $x \in C^{I(h',w)}$.

The truth-relation $(\mathfrak{M}, h, w) \models \varphi$ (or $(h, w) \models \varphi$ for short) is now defined as in the first-order case. We give only the truth-conditions for atomic formulas:

- $(h, w) \models C_1 \sqsubseteq C_2$ iff $C_1^{I(h,w)} \subseteq C_2^{I(h,w)}$;
- $(h, w) \models a : C$ iff $a^{I(w)} \in C^{I(h,w)}$;
- $(h, w) \models aRb$ iff $a^{I(w)} R^{I(w)} b^{I(w)}$.

The other temporal description logics we are interested in are fragments of $\mathcal{DPCTL}^*$. For example, $\mathcal{DTL}$ is the linear time fragment of $\mathcal{DPCTL}^*$ obtained by omitting the path quantifiers. $\mathcal{DCTL}_F^*$ is the future fragment of $\mathcal{DPCTL}^*$ in which $\mathcal{U}$ is replaced with $\Box_F$. $\mathcal{DPCTL}$ is obtained by restricting the application of temporal operators and path quantifiers to concepts and formulas by allowing only the patterns $\mathsf{A}(E_1 \mathcal{U} E_2)$, $\mathsf{E}(E_1 \mathcal{U} E_2)$, $\mathsf{A}(E_1 \mathcal{S} E_2)$, and $\mathsf{E}(E_1 \mathcal{S} E_2)$.

All these logics can be regarded as fragments of first-order temporal logic having the object names $a, b, \ldots$ as their constants. Indeed, fix two different individual variables, say, x, y. The translation R_i^T of a role name R_i is the formula $R(x, y)$ with two free variables x, y. The translation C^T of a concept C is a formula with one free variable x defined by taking

$$A_i^T = A_i(x) \qquad (\neg C)^T = \neg C^T$$
$$(C \sqcap D)^T = C^T \wedge D^T \qquad (C_1 \mathcal{U} C_2)^T = C_1^T \mathcal{U} C_2^T$$
$$(\exists R.C)^T = \exists y\,(R^T \wedge C^T\{y/x\}) \qquad (\mathsf{A}C)^T = \mathsf{A}C^T$$

and similarly for $\mathcal{S}$ and E. The translation φ^T of a $\mathcal{DPCTL}^*$-formula φ is a sentence defined as follows:

$$(C \sqsubseteq D)^T = \forall x\ (C^T \to D^T) \qquad (a : C)^T = C^T\{a/x\}$$
$$(aRb)^T = R^T\{a/x, b/y\} \qquad (\varphi \wedge \psi)^T = \varphi^T \wedge \psi^T,$$
$$(\neg\varphi)^T = \neg\varphi^T \qquad (\mathsf{A}\varphi)^T = \mathsf{A}\varphi^T$$

and similarly for the other temporal operators. It is readily checked that a $\mathcal{DPCTL}^*$-formula φ is satisfiable iff its first-order translation φ^T is satisfiable.

3.2 Spatio-Temporal Logics

Our second example is a family of logics devised in [59,62] for qualitative representation and reasoning about spatial regions moving in time. The logics are obtained by combining (propositional) temporal logics with the region connection calculus RCC-8.

Recall that RCC-8 contains eight binary relations between regions in topological spaces: DC (disconnection), EQ (equality), PO (partial overlap), EC (external connection), TTP (tangential proper part), NTTP (non-tangential proper part), and the inverses of the last two. Boolean operations are allowed on these relations. See, e.g., [47,24,25,11,58].

The intended semantics of RCC-8 is as follows. Region variables $X, Y, \ldots$ are interpreted as regular closed sets in a topological space $\langle T, \mathbb{I} \rangle$. Here, $\mathbb{I}$ is the interior operator on the universe T, and $\mathbb{C}$ is the corresponding closure operator. A regular closed set $S \subseteq T$ is one satisfying $S = \mathbb{C}\mathbb{I}S$. Given such an interpretation (or assignment) of the region variables, we then put

$$
\begin{array}{ll}
\mathsf{DC}(X,Y) & \text{iff } \neg\exists x\; x \in X \cap Y, \\
\mathsf{EQ}(X,Y) & \text{iff } \forall x\; (x \in X \leftrightarrow x \in Y), \\
\mathsf{PO}(X,Y) & \text{iff } \exists x\; (x \in \mathbb{I}X \cap \mathbb{I}Y) \wedge \exists x\; (x \in \mathbb{I}X \cap -Y) \wedge \exists x\; (x \in -X \cap \mathbb{I}Y), \\
\mathsf{EC}(X,Y) & \text{iff } \exists x\; (x \in X \cap Y) \wedge \neg\exists x\; (x \in \mathbb{I}X \cap \mathbb{I}Y), \\
\mathsf{TPP}(X,Y) & \text{iff } \forall x\; (x \in -X \cup Y) \wedge \exists x\; (x \in X \cap -\mathbb{I}Y) \wedge \exists x\; (x \in -X \cap Y), \\
\mathsf{TPPi}(X,Y) & \text{iff } \mathsf{TPP}(Y,X), \\
\mathsf{NTPP}(X,Y) & \text{iff } \forall x\; (x \in -X \cup \mathbb{I}Y) \wedge \exists x\; (x \in -X \cap Y), \\
\mathsf{NTPPi}(X,Y) & \text{iff } \mathsf{NTPP}(Y,X).
\end{array}
$$

The maximal spatio-temporal language $\mathcal{SPCTL}^*$ ($\mathcal{S}$ for 'spatial') that we consider in this paper is defined as follows. *Region terms* are constructed from region variables by means of the boolean operators, $\mathcal{S}, \mathcal{U}$, and A. *Atomic formulas* are of the form $R(t_1, t_2)$, where t_1, t_2 are region terms and R an RCC-8 relation. Complex *formulas* are constructed from atomic ones using the booleans, $\mathcal{S}$, $\mathcal{U}$, and A. (E continues to abbreviate $\neg\mathsf{A}\neg$.) In this language, we can speak about the temporal development of relations between regions, as in

$$\mathsf{E}\Box_F \mathsf{TPP}(\mathit{Kosovo},\ \mathit{Yugoslavia}) \wedge \mathsf{E} \bigcirc \mathsf{EC}(\mathit{Kosovo},\ \mathit{Yugoslavia})$$

('it is possible that Kosovo will always be part of Yugoslavia and also possible that already in one year Kosovo will be a neighbor of Yugoslavia'). We can also speak about the dynamics of regions themselves. For example,

$$\Box_F(\mathsf{NTPP}(EU, \bigcirc EU) \vee \mathsf{TPP}(EU, \bigcirc EU)),$$

interpreted in discrete flows of time, means that the EU will never contract. As an example of a more complex statement, consider

$$\mathsf{DC}(\mathit{Russia}\ \mathcal{S}\ \mathit{Russian\_Empire}, \mathit{Russia}\ \mathcal{S}\ \mathit{Germany}),$$

which can be used to say that the part of Russia that has remained Russian since 1917 is not connected to the part of Germany (Königsberg) that became Russian after the Second World War.

Models for $\mathcal{SPCTL}^*$ are obtained from first-order temporal models by associating via I with every moment w not a first-order structure but a topological space together with an assignment $\mathfrak{a}_w$ for the region variables. Thus, $I(w)$ is a triple of the form $\langle T, \mathbb{I}, \mathfrak{a}_w \rangle$, where $\mathfrak{a}_w$ maps each region variable X to a regular closed subset of T. (Note that region variables are not rigid.)

Now define the *value* $t^{I(h,w)}$ of a region term t relative to a history h and a moment $w \in h$, as follows (we list only some clauses):

$$\begin{aligned}
X^{I(h,w)} &= \mathfrak{a}_w(X),\\
(\neg t)^{I(h,w)} &= \mathbb{CI}(T - t^{I(h,w)}),\\
(t_1 \sqcap t_2)^{I(h,w)} &= \mathbb{CI}(t_1^{I(h,w)} \cap t_2^{I(h,w)}),\\
(t_1 \mathcal{U} t_2)^{I(h,w)} &= \mathbb{CI}\{x : \exists v > w \, (v \in h \ \wedge x \in t_2^{I(h,v)} \wedge \forall u \in (w,v)\ x \in t_1^{I(h,u)})\},\\
(\mathsf{E}t)^{I(h,w)} &= \mathbb{CI}\{x : \exists h' \in \mathcal{H} \, (w \in h' \wedge x \in t^{I(h',w)})\}.
\end{aligned}$$

The right-hand side is always prefixed by $\mathbb{CI}$ because spatial regions are interpreted as regular closed sets.

The truth-relation $(h,w) \models \varphi$ is now defined in the obvious manner. For example, $(h,w) \models \mathsf{DC}(t_1,t_2)$ iff $\mathsf{DC}(t_1^{I(h,w)}, t_2^{I(h,w)})$ holds in $\langle T, \mathbb{I} \rangle$.

Example 1. Let φ be the conjunction of the following three $\mathcal{SPCTL}^*$-formulas:

$$\mathsf{P}(\mathit{Kosovo}, \mathit{Yugoslavia})$$
$$\mathsf{A}\Diamond_F \Box_F \mathsf{EC}(\mathit{Kosovo}, \mathit{Yugoslavia})$$
$$\mathsf{A}\Box_F(\mathsf{P}(\mathit{Kosovo}, \mathit{Yugoslavia}) \rightarrow \mathsf{E} \bigcirc \mathsf{P}(\mathit{Kosovo}, \mathit{Yugoslavia}))$$

The first formula means that at present Kosovo is part of Yugoslavia. The second says that in all possible histories, there'll be a time starting from which Kosovo will be externally connected to Yugoslavia. And the last formula claims that in all possible histories, it is always the case that if Kosovo is part of Yugoslavia then it is still possible that it will remain in Yugoslavia at least one more day. Clearly, φ is satisfiable in a bundled tree model but not in a full tree model.

Consider the following fragments of $\mathcal{SPCTL}^*$:

- $\mathcal{SCTL}^*_F$—the fragment without past operators and with $\Box_F$ instead of $\mathcal{U}$;
- $\mathcal{SCTL}^*_\bigcirc$—the fragment without past operators in which region terms are constructed using the booleans and $\bigcirc$ only;
- $\mathcal{STL}$—the fragment of $\mathcal{SPCTL}^*$ without path quantifiers;
- $\mathcal{STL}_\bigcirc$—the fragment of $\mathcal{STL}$ in which region terms are constructed using the boolean operators and $\bigcirc$.

It is not clear whether the full language $\mathcal{SPCTL}^*$ or its 'linear fragment' $\mathcal{STL}$ can be embedded into first-order temporal logics, because we have to deal with arbitrary topological spaces and infinite intersections and unions of sets. However, in some cases topological spaces induced by rather simple Kripke frames are enough. This is so for the languages $\mathcal{SCTL}^*_\bigcirc$ and $\mathcal{STL}_\bigcirc$. As for $\mathcal{SPCTL}^*$ and $\mathcal{STL}$, in many applications it is sufficient to consider satisfiability in models where every region can have only *finitely many* states—the so-called *FSA-models*. (FSA stands for the 'finite state assumption'.) In all these cases, the satisfiability problem for spatio-temporal formulas can be (polynomially) reduced to satisfiability of first-order temporal formulas with *only one individual variable*. This (rather non-trivial) reduction can be found in [62,29].

4 Natural Borders of Decidability

The following theorems indicate some limits beyond which one cannot hope to find decidable fragments of first-order temporal logics.

Given a first-order temporal language $\mathcal{TL}$ and $\ell < \omega$, we denote by $\mathcal{TL}^\ell$ the *ℓ-variable fragment* of $\mathcal{TL}$ (i.e., every formula in $\mathcal{TL}^\ell$ contains at most ℓ distinct individual variables). And by $\mathcal{TL}^{mo}$ we denote the *monadic fragment* of $\mathcal{TL}$ (i.e., the set of formulas which contain only unary predicates and propositional variables). Both the two-variable and the monadic fragments of classical (non-temporal) first-order logic are known to be decidable and have the finite model property; see [13] and references therein. The computational behavior of the corresponding fragments of first-order temporal logics turns out to be quite different.

Theorem 1 ([35]). *Let $\mathfrak{F}$ be either $\{\langle \mathbb{N}, < \rangle\}$ or $\{\langle \mathbb{Z}, < \rangle\}$. Then*

$$\mathcal{QTL}^2 \cap \mathcal{QTL}^{mo} \cap QTL(\mathfrak{F})$$

is not recursively enumerable.

Theorem 2 ([35]). *Let $\mathcal{F}$ be one of the following classes of temporal frames: $\{\langle \mathbb{N}, < \rangle\}$, $\{\langle \mathbb{Z}, < \rangle\}$, the class of all strict linear orders. Then*

$$\mathcal{QTL}^2 \cap \mathcal{QTL}^{mo} \cap QTL_{fin}(\mathcal{F})$$

is not recursively enumerable.

Another well-behaved fragment of classical predicate logic is the *guarded fragment* of [5]. The corresponding fragment $\mathcal{TGF}$ of first-order temporal logic is the smallest set of $\mathcal{QPCTL}^*$-formulas such that:

- every atomic formula is in $\mathcal{TGF}$;
- if φ and ψ are in $\mathcal{TGF}$, then so are $\varphi \wedge \psi$, $\neg\varphi$, $\varphi \mathcal{S} \psi$, $\varphi \mathcal{U} \psi$, and $\mathsf{A}\varphi$;
- if $\overline{x}, \overline{y}$ are tuples of variables, $G(\overline{x}, \overline{y})$ is an atomic formula, $\varphi(\overline{x}, \overline{y}) \in \mathcal{TGF}$, and every free variable occurring in $\varphi(\overline{x}, \overline{y})$ occurs in $G(\overline{x}, \overline{y})$ as well, then $\forall \overline{y}\, (G(\overline{x}, \overline{y}) \to \varphi(\overline{x}, \overline{y}))$ is in $\mathcal{TGF}$.

The set $\mathcal{TGF}$ is called the *guarded fragment* of the first-order temporal language. Again in contrast to the case of classical predicate logic, we have the following:

Theorem 3 ([35]). *Let $\mathfrak{F} \in \{\langle \mathbb{N}, < \rangle, \langle \mathbb{Z}, < \rangle\}$. Then $QTL(\mathfrak{F}) \cap \mathcal{QTL}^2 \cap \mathcal{TGF}$ is not recursively enumerable.*

The computational behavior of branching time logics is even worse:

Theorem 4 ([36]). *The one-variable fragments of $QCTL^*_F$ and $BQCTL^*_F$ are undecidable.*

Remark 3. A more general version of this result can be formulated in terms of products of propositional modal logics; see [29] and references therein. Namely, there is no decidable set L of formulas such that

$$\mathsf{K} \times \mathsf{CTL}^*_F \subseteq L \subseteq \mathsf{S5} \times \mathsf{CTL}^*_F.$$

The same holds for the propositional bundled case as well.

Problem 1. Which fragments of $BQPCTL^*$ and $QPCTL^*$ are recursively enumerable?

5 Decidable Fragments

The negative results of the previous section can be 'explained' by the fact that all the undecidable fragments there are in a sense 'three-dimensional', which is often a cause of bad computational properties. The three-variable fragment of classical first-order logic is undecidable even without equality [41], and products of three propositional modal logics are usually undecidable [34]. In Theorems 1, 2, and 3, the linear time operator $\mathcal{U}$ can be applied to formulas with two free variables, and so we can quantify in three 'dimensions': one temporal and two domain. In Theorem 4 we also have quantification in three dimensions: temporal operators, path quantifiers and the domain quantification.

The following definition of [35,61] suggests a way to avoid this kind of interaction.

Definition 1 (monodic formulas). Let $\mathcal{QPCTL}^*_1$ be the set of all $\mathcal{QPCTL}^*$-formulas φ such that any subformula of φ of the form $\psi_1\mathcal{U}\psi_2$, $\psi_1\mathcal{S}\psi_2$, or $\mathsf{A}\psi$ has at most one free variable. Such formulas φ will be called *monodic.* In other words, monodic formulas allow quantification into temporal contexts only with one free variable. $\mathcal{QPCTL}_1$, $\mathcal{QTL}_1$, and $\mathcal{TGF}_1$ denote the corresponding fragments of $\mathcal{QPCTL}$, $\mathcal{QTL}$, and $\mathcal{TGF}$ respectively.

Of course the monodic fragments of the logics under consideration are still undecidable, simply because they contain full first-order logic. However, the monodic fragments of $QTL(\langle\mathbb{N},<\rangle)$ and $QTL(\langle\mathbb{Z},<\rangle)$ become recursively enumerable: see [63] for axiomatizations.

Problem 2. Are the monodic fragments of other temporal logics considered in this paper (finitely) axiomatizable—in particular, the monodic fragments of $QCTL$ and $QPCTL^*$?

We now provide some general conditions under which fragments of the monodic temporal logics are decidable. To simplify presentation, we will assume that our languages contain no individual constants.

Fix a $\mathcal{QPCTL}_1^*$-formula φ. Denote by $sub_1\varphi$ the closure under (single) negation of the set of all subformulas of φ that contain at most one free variable. Let x be a variable not occurring in φ. Put

$$sub_x\varphi = \{\psi\{x/y\} : \psi(y) \in sub_1\varphi\}.$$

By a *type* for φ we mean any boolean-saturated subset t of $sub_x\varphi$: that is,

- $\psi \wedge \chi \in t$ iff $\psi \in t$ and $\chi \in t$, for every $\psi \wedge \chi \in sub_x\varphi$;
- $\neg\psi \in t$ iff $\psi \notin t$, for every $\neg\psi \in sub_x\varphi$.

For every $\mathcal{QPCTL}_1^*$-formula $\psi(x)$ starting with $\mathcal{U}$, $\mathcal{S}$, or A, and having one free variable x, we reserve a unary predicate $P_\psi(x)$. Similarly, for every sentence ψ of this form we fix a propositional variable p_ψ. These predicates and variables are called the *surrogates* of the original formulas. We denote by $\overline{\varphi}$ the result of replacing in φ all its subformulas starting with $\mathcal{U}$, $\mathcal{S}$, or A by their surrogates. Thus, $\overline{\varphi}$ is a formula of classical first-order logic. For a φ-type t, we write $\overline{t}$ for $\{\overline{\psi} : \psi \in t\}$; we identify $\overline{t}$ with its conjunction $\bigwedge \overline{t}$.

A set S of φ-types is called (*finitely*) *realizable* if the sentence

$$\alpha_S \quad = \quad \bigwedge_{t \in S} \exists x\, \overline{t}(x) \quad \wedge \quad \forall x \bigvee_{t \in S} \overline{t}(x)$$

is satisfiable (in a finite model).

Theorem 5 (criterion 1: linear case [35]). *Let $\mathcal{L}' \subseteq \mathcal{QTL}_1$.*

(i) *Let $\mathcal{F}$ be any of the following classes of flows of time:*

- $\{\langle \mathbb{N}, < \rangle\}$,
- $\{\langle \mathbb{Z}, < \rangle\}$,
- $\{\langle \mathbb{Q}, < \rangle\}$,
- *the class of all finite strict linear orders,*
- *any first-order-definable class of strict linear orders.*

Suppose there is an algorithm that decides for any $\mathcal{L}'$-formula φ whether an arbitrarily-given set of φ-types is realizable. Then the satisfiability problem for $\mathcal{L}'$-sentences in models based on flows of time in $\mathcal{F}$ is decidable.

(ii) *Let $\mathcal{F}^+$ range over the classes of flows of time above and $\{\langle \mathbb{R}, < \rangle\}$, and suppose that finite realizability is decidable for sets of types of formulas in $\mathcal{L}'$. Then the satisfiability problem for $\mathcal{L}'$-sentences in models based on flows of time in $\mathcal{F}$ and having finite domains is decidable.*

The proof of part (i) of the theorem uses *quasimodels*. A quasimodel of φ over a flow of time $\mathfrak{F} = \langle W, < \rangle$ consists of an assignment of a realizable set of types S_w to each $w \in W$, the sequence $\langle S_w : w \in W \rangle$ having certain specified properties. The existence of a quasimodel for φ can be expressed by a sentence σ_φ of monadic second-order logic, which can be effectively constructed from φ so long as it is decidable whether an arbitrary set of φ-types is realizable. It is shown that φ is satisfiable in a model with flow of time $\mathfrak{F}$ iff there exists a quasimodel for φ over $\mathfrak{F}$. Thus, φ has a model with flow of time $\mathfrak{F}$ iff $\mathfrak{F} \models \sigma_\varphi$. If $\mathfrak{F}$ is $\{\langle \mathbb{N}, < \rangle\}$, $\{\langle \mathbb{Z}, < \rangle\}$, or $\{\langle \mathbb{Q}, < \rangle\}$, this last statement is decidable by results of [15,46]. The other cases can now be obtained by reduction. Part (ii) is proved differently, since the full monadic second-order theory of $\langle \mathbb{R}, < \rangle$ is undecidable. The proof adapts the argument of the second part of [17]: see [35] for details.

As a consequence of Theorem 5 we obtain, for example, the following results, where $\mathcal{F}$ and $\mathcal{F}^+$ have the same meaning as above.

Theorem 6. *The following fragments are decidable:*

$$\begin{array}{ll} QTL(\mathcal{F}) \cap \mathcal{QTL}^1, & QTL_{fin}(\mathcal{F}^+) \cap \mathcal{QTL}^1, \\ QTL(\mathcal{F}) \cap \mathcal{QTL}^2_1, & QTL_{fin}(\mathcal{F}^+) \cap \mathcal{QL}^2_1, \\ QTL(\mathcal{F}) \cap \mathcal{QTL}^{mo}_1, & QTL_{fin}(\mathcal{F}^+) \cap \mathcal{QTL}^{mo}_1, \\ QTL(\mathcal{F}) \cap \mathcal{TGF}_1, & QTL_{fin}(\mathcal{F}^+) \cap \mathcal{TGF}_1. \end{array}$$

The corresponding loosely guarded and fluted fragments are decidable as well (for definitions see [61]).

Problem 3. Does Theorem 6 hold for $QTL(\langle \mathbb{R}, < \rangle)$?

Problem 4. What is the computational complexity of the decision problem for the above fragments as well as other decidable fragments mentioned in this paper?

It follows from the proof of Theorem 5 in [35] for the flow of time $\langle \mathbb{N}, < \rangle$ that $QTL(\langle \mathbb{N}, < \rangle) \cap \mathcal{L}'$ is in EXPSPACE whenever the problem of whether a set of φ-types, for an $\mathcal{L}'$-formula φ, is realizable is decidable in EXPSPACE (in the length of φ). Conversely, it is proved in [29] that $QTL(\langle \mathbb{N}, < \rangle) \cap \mathcal{QTL}^1$ is EXPSPACE-hard. It follows, for example, that the satisfiability problem for $\mathcal{QTL}^{mo}_1$-formulas in models based on $\langle \mathbb{N}, < \rangle$ is EXPSPACE-complete.

According to Theorem 4, the results above do not generalize to $\mathcal{QPCTL}^*$, since already the one-variable fragment of $\mathcal{QCTL}^*_F$ is undecidable. However, as soon as we restrict ourselves to $\mathcal{QPCTL}$, we obtain the following:

Theorem 7 (criterion 2: branching case [36]). *Let $\mathcal{L}' \subseteq \mathcal{QPCTL}_1$ and suppose that there is an algorithm that decides for any $\mathcal{L}'$-formula φ whether an arbitrarily-given set of φ-types is realizable. Then satisfiability of $\mathcal{L}'$-formulas is decidable for both bundled and full tree models.*

The proof is again via quasimodels and embedding into monadic second-order logic.

As a consequence we obtain

Theorem 8. *The fragments*

$$QPCTL \cap \mathcal{QPCTL}_1^2, \quad QPCTL \cap \mathcal{QPCTL}_1^{mo}, \quad QPCTL \cap \mathcal{TGF}_1,$$

as well as their bundled versions are decidable.

Another way to obtain decidable fragments in the branching time case is to restrict further the formulas that can have free variables. Denote by $\mathcal{QCTL}_\bigcirc^*$ the fragment of $\mathcal{QCTL}_1^*$ in which only $\bigcirc$ may be applied to formulas with one free variable (the other operators $\mathcal{U}$, E and A may be applied only to sentences). Then we have:

Theorem 9 (criterion 3: branching case [36]). *Let $\mathcal{L}' \subseteq \mathcal{QCTL}_\bigcirc^*$ and suppose that there is an algorithm that decides for any $\mathcal{L}'$-formula φ whether an arbitrarily-given set of φ-types is realizable. Then satisfiability of $\mathcal{L}'$-formulas in bundled trees models is decidable.*

Here the proof uses quasimodels and a mosaic technique.

Therefore, we also obtain

Theorem 10. *The fragments*

$$BQCTL^* \cap (\mathcal{QCTL}_\bigcirc^*)^2, \quad BQCTL^* \cap (\mathcal{QCTL}_\bigcirc^*)^{mo}, \quad BQCTL^* \cap \mathcal{TGF}_\bigcirc$$

are decidable.

Problem 5. Does Theorem 10 hold for the unbundled case?

Problem 6. Are there any interesting languages between $\mathcal{QCTL}_\bigcirc^*$ and $\mathcal{QCTL}^*$ for which Theorem 10 holds? In particular, does it hold for the fragment of those $\mathcal{QCTL}^*$-formulas in which $\mathcal{U}$ can be applied to formulas with one free variable but A only to closed formulas? Does it hold for the fragment of those $\mathcal{QCTL}^*$-formulas in which $\bigcirc$ and E can be applied to formulas with one free variable but $\mathcal{U}$ only to closed formulas?

6 Adding Equality

So far we have considered first-order temporal languages *without equality and function symbols.* A natural question is whether our decidability results concerning the class of monodic formulas can be generalized to the languages with these ingredients.

It is not hard to see (cf. [63]) that adding function symbols quickly destroys the nice properties of monodic formulas. For example, the set of one-variable formulas with one function symbol that are valid in models based on $\langle \mathbb{N}, < \rangle$ is not recursively enumerable.

Let us now consider the language $\mathcal{QTL}$ extended with equality (but not function symbols). This language will be denoted by $\mathcal{QTL}^=$. The following negative result can be proved by reduction of the validity problem for first-order formulas in finite structures.

Theorem 11 ([61]). *The set of monodic $\mathcal{QTL}^{=}$-formulas that are valid in all temporal models based on $\langle \mathbb{N}, < \rangle$ is not recursively enumerable, and so not recursively axiomatizable.*

Recently, this result was generalized to fragments that are decidable without equality:

Theorem 12 ([22]). *The set of two-variable monodic formulas in $\mathcal{QTL}_1^{=}$ that are valid in models based on $\langle \mathbb{N}, < \rangle$ is not recursively enumerable.*

The guarded fragment (and extensions like the loosely guarded, packed, and clique-guarded [33] fragments) are more robust under addition of equality:

Theorem 13 ([37]). *$QTL^{=}(\mathcal{F}) \cap \mathcal{QTL}_1 \cap \mathcal{TGF}$ and $QTL^{=}_{fin}(\mathcal{F}^{+}) \cap \mathcal{QTL}_1 \cap \mathcal{TGF}$ are decidable, where $\mathcal{F}, \mathcal{F}^{+}$ are as in theorem 5.*

The reason for this robustness is that the models of guarded sentences are closed under disjoint unions. The same property was used in [60] to show that various temporalized description logics with number restrictions and nominals are decidable.

7 Applications

The results obtained for monodic fragments of first-order temporal logics can be applied to both temporal description logics and spatio-temporal logics.

7.1 Temporal Description Logics

Observe that the translation φ^T (defined in Section 5) of any $\mathcal{DTL}$-formula φ lies in the two-variable fragment of the monodic fragment of $\mathcal{QTL}$.[2] Hence, we obtain the following results; cf. [60].

Theorem 14. *Suppose that $\mathcal{F}$ is a class of strict linear orders. If satisfiability of $\mathcal{QTL}_1 \cap \mathcal{QTL}^2$-formulas in models based on flows of time in $\mathcal{F}$ is decidable, then satisfiability of $\mathcal{DTL}$-formulas in $\mathcal{F}$ is decidable as well.*

This decidability result extends to temporalized description logics based on more expressive description logics than $\mathcal{ALC}$. For example, one can take instead of $\mathcal{ALC}$ the description logic $\mathcal{CI}$ corresponding to propositional dynamic logic with converse (see [60]) or the description logic $\mathcal{DLR}$ of [19] which contains n-ary roles. The resulting temporalized description logics are suitable for temporal conceptual modelling [8].

The situation is quite different in the branching case. One can show (see [29] for details) that the one-variable fragment of $\mathcal{QCTL}_F^*$ is embeddable into $\mathcal{DCTL}_F^*$. Hence we obtain from Theorem 4:

[2] Note that we would not obtain monodic formulas if temporal operators were applied to roles. This is another explanation of the bad behavior of temporal description logics with temporalized roles.

Theorem 15. *Satisfiability of $\mathcal{DCTL}_F^*$-formulas is undecidable both in bundled and full ω-trees.*

To obtain positive results in the branching case, we can employ Theorem 8. The translation φ^T of any $\mathcal{DPCTL}$-formula φ belongs to $\mathcal{QPCTL}_1 \cap \mathcal{QPCTL}^2$. So we have:

Theorem 16. *Satisfiability of $\mathcal{DPCTL}$-formulas is decidable both in bundled and full ω-trees.*

7.2 Spatio-Temporal Logics

We now apply the results about first-order temporal logics to spatio-temporal logics. Consider first the linear case.

Theorem 17 ([59]). *Suppose satisfiability of the one-variable fragment of $\mathcal{QTL}$ in the class $\mathcal{F}$ of linear flows of time is decidable. Then satisfiability of $\mathcal{STL}_{\bigcirc}$-formulas in $\mathcal{F}$ is decidable.*

Problem 7. Is the satisfiability problem for arbitrary $\mathcal{STL}$-formulas in models based on $\langle \mathbb{N}, < \rangle$ and other flows of time decidable?

The difficulty here is that the application of temporal operators different from $\bigcirc$ corresponds on the semantic side to possibly infinite intersections and unions of sets. These are not respected by the embeddings into first-order temporal logics. However, as far as we are satisfied with FSA-models (in which each region may have only finitely many states), we can reduce the satisfiability problem to satisfiablity of one-variable first-order formulas in models with *finite* domains. We then obtain:

Theorem 18 ([62]). *Suppose that satisfiability of the one-variable fragment of $\mathcal{QTL}$ in models based on flows of time from a class $\mathcal{F}$ and having finite domains is decidable. Then satisfiability of $\mathcal{STL}$-formulas in FSA-models based on flows of time in $\mathcal{F}$ is decidable as well. This applies, in particilar, to all classes $\mathcal{F}^+$ mentioned in Theorem 5 (ii).*

The branching case is again different because we can encode the one-variable fragment of $\mathcal{QCTL}_F^*$ in $\mathcal{SCTL}_F^*$, even if we confine ourselves to discrete topological spaces. Thus we obtain from Theorem 4:

Theorem 19 ([36]). *Satisfiability of $\mathcal{SCTL}_F^*$-formulas is undecidable for both bundled and full ω-trees, even for models based on discrete topological spaces.*

$\mathcal{SCTL}_{\bigcirc}^*$ can be embedded into the one-variable fragment of $\mathcal{QCTL}_{\bigcirc}^*$. So we obtain from Theorem 10:

Theorem 20 ([36]). *Satisfiability of $\mathcal{SCTL}_{\bigcirc}^*$-formulas in bundled ω-trees is decidable.*

8 Practical Reasoning Algorithms

Two kinds of 'practical' algorithms have been proposed for logics related to monodic fragments of first-order temporal logics. [52,40] develop tableau-based decision procedures for temporal description logics which combine standard tableaux for description logics with Wolper's [55] tableau for propositional temporal logic. An interesting aspect of those tableau calculi is that they are based on the same idea as the model-theoretic decidability proofs. Instead of constructing models directly, they construct quasimodels in which the states are locally saturated sets of (partial) types. A tableau calculus for temporal description logics with *expanding domains* is implemented in [32]. Those algorithms are easily modified to obtain an algorithm deciding the future-fragment of $QTL(\langle \mathbb{N}, < \rangle) \cap \mathcal{QTL}^1$.

The second approach employs the resolution method. [23] provides a clausal temporal resolution calculus which is complete for those formulas of the future fragment of $QTL(\langle \mathbb{N}, < \rangle) \cap \mathcal{QTL}_1$ in which only $\bigcirc$ is applied to open formulas (other temporal operators may be applied only to sentences).

9 Expressive Completeness

The temporal language $\mathcal{QTL}$ provides only 'implicit' access to time. Quantification over points in time in the sense of first-order logic is not permitted, and the only means of expressing temporal properties is by the operators Since and Until. A common alternative is to reason about time explicitly, using first-order logic. Following this approach in the propositional case yields monadic first-order logic interpreted in strict linear orders, while in the predicate case it leads to a two-sorted first-order language, called '$\mathcal{TS}$' in what follows, one sort of which refers to points in time and the other to the first-order domain (see, e.g., [2,3, 20,21]).

The alphabet of $\mathcal{TS}$ consists of:

- an infinite set of individual variables $x_0, x_1, \ldots$, and a set of constants $c_0, c_1, \ldots$ of domain sort,
- an infinite set of individual variables $t_0, t_1, \ldots$ of temporal sort,
- the binary predicate symbol $<$ of sort 'temporal $\times$ temporal',
- predicate symbols $P_0, P_1, \ldots$ of sort 'temporal $\times$ domain^n', $n < \omega$.

Formulas of $\mathcal{TS}$ are defined inductively:

- $t_i < t_j$ is an (atomic) formula, for temporal variables t_i, t_j;
- $P(t, y_1, \ldots, y_n)$ is an (atomic) formula, for a predicate symbol P of sort temporal $\times$ domain^n, a temporal variable t, and domain variables or constants $y_1, \ldots, y_n$;
- if φ and ψ are formulas and v is a (temporal or domain) variable, then $\neg\varphi$, $\varphi \wedge \psi$, and $\forall v \varphi$ are formulas.

$\mathcal{TS}$ is interpreted in standard first-order temporal models $\mathfrak{M} = \langle \mathfrak{F}, D, I \rangle$, where $\mathfrak{F} = \langle W, < \rangle$ is a flow of time (i.e., a strict linear order), D is a non-empty set, the *domain* of $\mathfrak{M}$, and I is a function associating with every moment of time $w \in W$ a first-order structure

$$I(w) = \left\langle D, P_0^{I(w)}, \dots, c_0^{I(w)}, \dots \right\rangle,$$

in which, for each i, $P_i^{I(w)}$ is a predicate on D of arity n whenever P_i is of arity $n+1$, and $c_i^{I(w)} \in D$. We require again that $c_i^{I(w)} = c_i^{I(w')}$ for all $w, w' \in W$.

An *assignment* in $\mathfrak{M}$ is a function $\mathfrak{a} = \mathfrak{a}_1 \cup \mathfrak{a}_2$ such that $\mathfrak{a}_1$ associates with every temporal variable t a moment of time $\mathfrak{a}_1(t) \in W$ and $\mathfrak{a}_2$ associates with every domain variable x an element $\mathfrak{a}_2(x)$ of D. We extend $\mathfrak{a}$ canonically to constants as before.

The truth relation $\mathfrak{M} \models^{\mathfrak{a}} \varphi$ is defined inductively as follows:

- $\mathfrak{M} \models^{\mathfrak{a}} t_i < t_j$ iff $\mathfrak{a}_1(t_i) < \mathfrak{a}_1(t_j)$;
- $\mathfrak{M} \models^{\mathfrak{a}} P(t, y_1, \dots, y_n)$ iff $\langle \mathfrak{a}_2(y_1), \dots, \mathfrak{a}_2(y_n) \rangle \in P^{I(\mathfrak{a}_1(t))}$, for any constants or domain variables $y_1, \dots, y_n$;
- the standard clauses for the booleans;
- $\mathfrak{M} \models^{\mathfrak{a}} \forall v \varphi$ iff $\mathfrak{M} \models^{\mathfrak{b}} \varphi$ for every assignment $\mathfrak{b}$ that may differ from $\mathfrak{a}$ only on v.

It should be clear that the temporal operators $\mathcal{U}$ and $\mathcal{S}$ of $\mathcal{QTL}$ are expressible in $\mathcal{TS}$. Formally, suppose that each n-ary predicate symbol Q_i of $\mathcal{QTL}$ is associated with the $(n+1)$-ary predicate symbol P_i of $\mathcal{TS}$. Also fix a temporal variable t. Define a translation $\dagger$ from $\mathcal{QTL}$ into $\mathcal{TS}$ by taking

$$\begin{aligned}
Q_i(x_1, \dots, x_n)^\dagger &= P_i(t, x_1, \dots, x_n), \\
(\varphi \wedge \psi)^\dagger &= \varphi^\dagger \wedge \psi^\dagger, \\
(\neg \varphi)^\dagger &= \neg(\varphi^\dagger), \\
(\forall x \varphi)^\dagger &= \forall x(\varphi^\dagger), \\
(\psi \mathcal{U} \varphi)^\dagger &= \exists t'(t < t' \wedge \varphi^\dagger\{t'/t\} \wedge \forall t''(t < t'' < t' \to \psi^\dagger\{t''/t\})), \\
(\psi \mathcal{S} \varphi)^\dagger &= \exists t'(t' < t \wedge \varphi^\dagger\{t'/t\} \wedge \forall t''(t' < t'' < t \to \psi^\dagger\{t''/t\})),
\end{aligned}$$

where t' and t'' are new temporal variables.

The meaning of the translation $\dagger$ can be explained as follows. Suppose that $\mathfrak{M} = \langle \mathfrak{F}, D, I \rangle$ is a $\mathcal{TS}$-model and that $\mathfrak{a} = \mathfrak{a}_1 \cup \mathfrak{a}_2$ is an assignment in $\mathfrak{M}$. Let $\mathfrak{N} = \langle \mathfrak{F}, D, J \rangle$ be a $\mathcal{QTL}$-model, and $\mathfrak{b}$ an assignment in $\mathfrak{N}$. We say that $\langle \mathfrak{M}, \mathfrak{a} \rangle$ and $\langle \mathfrak{N}, \mathfrak{b} \rangle$ are *equivalent* if $P_i^{I(w)} = Q_i^{J(w)}$ for all w, i, and $\mathfrak{a}_2 = \mathfrak{b}$.

Lemma 1. *Suppose that $\langle \mathfrak{M}, \mathfrak{a} \rangle$ and $\langle \mathfrak{N}, \mathfrak{b} \rangle$ are equivalent. Then for every $\mathcal{QTL}$-formula φ, we have $\langle \mathfrak{N}, \mathfrak{a}(t) \rangle \models^{\mathfrak{b}} \varphi$ iff $\mathfrak{M} \models^{\mathfrak{a}} \varphi^\dagger$.*

The proof is an easy induction on φ.

On the other hand, there are $\mathcal{TS}$-formulas that are not expressible in $\mathcal{QTL}$ over any interesting class of flows of time. For example, the $\mathcal{TS}$-sentence

$$\exists t_1 \exists t_2 (t_1 < t_2 \wedge \forall x (P(t_1, x) \leftrightarrow P(t_2, x)))$$

cannot be expressed in $\mathcal{QTL}$ over the flow of time $\langle \mathbb{Q}, < \rangle$, nor over the class of finite linear flows [39,2,3]. Recall that in the propositional case, both languages are known to have the same expressive power over most classes of flows of time—i.e., the temporal propositional language is *expressively complete*, see [38,28]. It turns out, however, that $\mathcal{QTL}$ and $\mathcal{QTL}_1$ are expressively complete for some natural fragments of $\mathcal{TS}$.

Definition 2. *Let $\mathcal{TS}_{1t}$ (respectively, $\mathcal{TS}_{1x}$) consist of all $\mathcal{TS}$-formulas φ with no subformulas of the form $\forall x \psi$ ($\forall t \psi$) where ψ has more than one free temporal (respectively, domain) variable. Let $\mathcal{TS}_1 = \mathcal{TS}_{1t} \cap \mathcal{TS}_{1x}$.*

Note that for every $\mathcal{QTL}$-formula φ, we have $\varphi^\dagger \in \mathcal{TS}_{1t}$, and for every $\varphi \in \mathcal{QTL}_1$ we have $\varphi^\dagger \in \mathcal{TS}_1$.

Let $\mathcal{F}$ be a class of flows of time, $\mathcal{L}' \subseteq \mathcal{QTL}$, and $\mathcal{L}'' \subseteq \mathcal{TS}$. We say that $\mathcal{L}'$ is *expressively complete* for $\mathcal{L}''$ over $\mathcal{F}$ if for every $\varphi \in \mathcal{L}''$ with at most one free temporal variable, there exists a formula $\widehat{\varphi} \in \mathcal{L}'$ such that $(\widehat{\varphi})^\dagger$ and φ are equivalent in all models based on flows of time in $\mathcal{F}$.

Theorem 21 ([35]). *Let $\mathcal{F}$ be the class of all dedekind-complete linear flows of time ($\mathcal{F}$ contains, for example, $\langle \mathbb{N}, < \rangle$, $\langle \mathbb{Z}, < \rangle$, $\langle \mathbb{R}, < \rangle$, and all finite linear orders). Then*

1. *$\mathcal{QTL}$ is expressively complete for $\mathcal{TS}_{1t}$ over $\mathcal{F}$,*
2. *$\mathcal{QTL}_1$ is expressively complete for $\mathcal{TS}_1$ over $\mathcal{F}$.*

The proof uses Kamp's theorem ([38]; see also [28, chapters 9–12]) that the propositional temporal logic with $\mathcal{S}$ and $\mathcal{U}$ is expressively complete for monadic first-order logic over $\mathcal{F}$. The required $\widehat{\varphi}$ can be constructed effectively from φ.

For a class $\mathcal{H}$ of flows of time, denote by $TS(\mathcal{H})$ the set of all $\mathcal{TS}$-sentences that are true in all models based on frames in $\mathcal{H}$, and by $TS_{fin}(\mathcal{H})$ the set of $\mathcal{TS}$-sentences true in all models based on frames in $\mathcal{H}$ and having finite domains. Given a set $\mathcal{QTL}' \subseteq \mathcal{QTL}_1$, let

$$\mathcal{TS}' = \{\varphi \in \mathcal{TS}_1 : \widehat{\varphi} \in \mathcal{QTL}'\},$$

where $\widehat{\varphi}$ is as above. Since $\widehat{\varphi}$ can be constructed effectively from φ, by Lemma 1 and Theorem 21 we obtain the following:

Theorem 22. *Suppose that every $\mathfrak{F} \in \mathcal{H}$ be dedekind-complete, and let $\mathcal{QTL}' \subseteq \mathcal{QTL}_1$. If the fragment $QTL(\mathcal{H}) \cap \mathcal{QTL}'$ is decidable, then the fragment $TS(\mathcal{H}) \cap \mathcal{TS}'$ is decidable. If the fragment $QTL_{fin}(\mathcal{H}) \cap \mathcal{QTL}'$ is decidable, then the fragment $TS_{fin}(\mathcal{H}) \cap \mathcal{TS}'$ is decidable.*

This can be combined with Theorem 6 to obtain decidable fragments of $\mathcal{TS}$.

Problem 8. Extend the above results to cover branching time.

See [28] for information about expressive completeness for propositional temporal logics over branching time.

Acknowledgements. The work of the first and third authors was partially supported by UK EPSRC grant GR/R45369/01 "Analysis and mechanisation of decidable first-order temporal logics." The work of the second author was supported by Deutsche Forschungsgemeinschaft (DFG) grant Wo583/3-1.

References

1. M. Abadi. The power of temporal proofs. In *Proc. Symp. on Logic in Computer Science*, pages 176–186, Ithaca, 1979.
2. S. Abiteboul, L. Herr, and J. van den Bussche. Temporal connectives versus explicit timestamps in temporal query languages. In J. Clifford and A. Tuzhilin, editors, *Recent Advances in Temporal Databases*, pages 43–57. Springer, 1995.
3. S. Abiteboul, L. Herr, and J. van den Bussche. Temporal versus first-order logic in query temporal databases. In *ACM Symposium on Principles of Database Systems*, pages 49–57, Montreal, Canada, 1996.
4. H. Andréka, I. Németi, and I. Sain. Completeness problems in verification of programs and program schemes. In *Mathematical Foundations of Computer Science 1979*, Lecture Notes in Computer Science. Springer-Verlag, 1979.
5. H. Andréka, J. van Benthem, and I. Németi. Modal languages and bounded fragments of predicate logic. *Journal of Philosophical Logic*, 27:217–274, 1998.
6. A. Artale and E. Franconi. A computational account for a description logic of time and action. In *Proceedings of the fourth Conference on Principles of Knowledge Representation and Reasoning*, pages 3–14, Montreal, Canada, 1994. Morgan Kaufmann.
7. A. Artale and E. Franconi. Temporal description logics. In *Handbook of Time and Temporal Reasoning in Artificial Intelligence.* MIT Press, 2001. To appear.
8. A. Artale, E. Franconi, M. Mosurovic, F. Wolter, and M. Zakharyaschev. The $\mathcal{DLR}_{\mathcal{US}}$ temporal description logic. In D. McGuinness, P. Patel-Schneider, C. Goble and R. Möller, editors, *Proceedings of the 2001 Description Logic Workshop (DL-2001)*, Stanford, pages 96–105, 2001.
9. F. Baader and A. Laux. Terminological logics with modal operators. In *Proceedings of the 14th International Joint Conference on Artificial Intelligence*, pages 808–814, Montreal, Canada, 1995. Morgan Kaufmann.
10. F. Baader and H.J. Ohlbach. A multi-dimensional terminological knowledge representation language. *Journal of Applied Non-Classical Logic*, 5:153–197, 1995.
11. B. Bennett, A. Cohn, and A. Isli. A logical approach to incorporating qualitative spatial reasoning into GIS. In *Proceedings the International Conference on Spatial Information Theory (COSIT)*, pages 503–504, 1997.
12. J. van Benthem. Dynamic bits and pieces. Technical Report LP–97–01, ILLC, University of Amsterdam, 1997.
13. E. Börger, E. Grädel, and Yu. Gurevich. *The Classical Decision Problem.* Perspectives in Mathematical Logic. Springer, 1997.
14. R. Brachman and J. Schmolze. An overview of the KL-ONE knowledge representation system. *Cognitive Science*, 9:171–216, 1985.
15. J. Büchi. On a decision method in restricted second order arithmetic. In *Logic, Methodology, and Philosophy of Science: Proc. 1960 Intern. Congress*, pages 1–11. Stanford University Press, 1962.
16. J. Burgess. Logic and time. *Journal of Symbolic Logic*, 44:566–582, 1979.

17. J. Burgess and Yu. Gurevich. The decision problem for linear temporal logic. *Notre Dame J. Formal Logic*, 26(2):115–128, 1985.
18. D. Calvanese, G. De Giacomo, M. Lenzerini, and D. Nardi. Reasoning in expressive description logics. In A. Robinson and A. Voronkov, editors, *Handbook of Automated Reasoning*, pages 1581–1634. Elsevier Science Publishers B.V., 2001.
19. D. Calvanese, M. Lenzerini, and D. Nardi. Unifying class-based representation formalisms. Journal of Artificial Intelligence Research, 11: 199–240, 1999
20. J. Chomicki. Temporal query languages: a survey. In D. Gabbay and H.J. Ohlbach, editors, *Temporal Logic, First International Conference*, pages 506–534, Montreal, Canada, 1994. Springer-Verlag.
21. J. Chomicki and D. Niwinski. On the feasibility of checking temporal integrity constraints. *Journal of Computer and Systems Sciences*, 51:523–535, 1995.
22. A. Degtyarev, M. Fisher, and A. Lisitsa. Equality and monodic first-order temporal logic. *Studia Logica*, 2001. (To appear.)
23. A. Degtyarev and M. Fisher. Towards First-Order Temporal Resolution. In F. Baader, G. Brewka and T. Eiter, editors, *KI 2001: Advances in Artificial Intelligence*, volume 2174 of *LNCS*, pages 18–32. Springer, 2001.
24. M. Egenhofer and R. Franzosa. Point-set topological spatial relations. *International Journal of Geographical Information Systems*, 5:161–174, 1991.
25. M. Egenhofer and D. Mark. Naive geography. In A. Frank and W. Kuhn, editors, *Spatial Information Theory: a theoretical basis for GIS*, volume 988 of *Lecture Notes in Computer Science*, pages 1–16. Springer-Verlag, Berlin, 1995.
26. E. Emerson. Temporal and modal logic. In J. van Leeuwen, editor, *Handbook of Theoretical Computer Science*, pages 996–1076, 1990.
27. R. Fagin, J. Halpern, Y. Moses, and M. Vardi. *Reasoning about Knowledge.* MIT Press, 1995.
28. D. Gabbay, I. Hodkinson, and M. Reynolds. *Temporal Logic: Mathematical Foundations and Computational Aspects, Volume 1.* Oxford University Press, 1994.
29. D. Gabbay, A. Kurucz, F. Wolter, and M. Zakharyaschev. *Many-Dimensional Modal Logics: Theory and Applications.* Elsevier, 2002.
30. D. Gabbay, M. Reynolds, and M. Finger. *Temporal Logic: Mathematical Foundations and Computational Aspects, Volume 2.* Oxford University Press, 2000.
31. J. Garson. Quantification in modal logic. In D. Gabbay and F. Guenthner, editors, *Handbook of Philosophical Logic*, volume 2, pages 249–307. Kluwer Academic Publishers, 1984.
32. C. Günsel and M. Wittmann. Towards an implementation of the temporal description logic $\mathcal{TL}_{\mathcal{ALC}}$. In D. McGuinness, P. Patel-Schneider, C. Goble and R. Möller, editors, *Proceedings of the 2001 Description Logic Workshop (DL-2001)*, Stanford, pages 162–169, 2001.
33. E. Grädel. Decision procedures for guarded logics. In *Automated Deduction—CADE-16, Proceedings of the 16th International Conference on Automated Deduction*, volume 1632 of *LNCS*, pages 31–51. Springer, 1999.
34. R. Hirsch, I. Hodkinson, and A. Kurucz. On modal logics between $\mathsf{K} \times \mathsf{K} \times \mathsf{K}$ and $\mathsf{S5} \times \mathsf{S5} \times \mathsf{S5}$. *Journal of Symbolic Logic*, 2001. (In press.)
35. I. Hodkinson, F. Wolter, and M. Zakharyaschev. Decidable fragments of first-order temporal logics. *Annals of Pure and Applied Logic*, 106:85–134, 2000.
36. I. Hodkinson, A. Kurucz, F. Wolter, and M. Zakharyaschev. Decidable and undecidable fragments of first-order logics of branching time. Manuscript, 2001.
37. I. Hodkinson. Monodic packed fragment with equality is decidable. *Studia Logica*, 2001. (To appear.)

38. H. Kamp. *Tense Logic and the Theory of Linear Order.* Ph.D. Thesis, University of California, Los Angeles, 1968.
39. H. Kamp. Formal properties of 'now'. *Theoria*, 37:237–273, 1971.
40. C. Lutz, H. Sturm, F. Wolter, and M. Zakharyaschev. Tableaux for temporal description logic with constant domains. In *Proceedings of the 1st International Joint Conference on Automated Reasoning, IJCAR 2001*, pages 121–136, LNAI 2083. Springer-Verlag, 2001.
41. R. Maddux. The equational theory of CA_3 is undecidable. *Journal of Symbolic Logic*, 45:311–316, 1980.
42. Z. Manna and A. Pnueli. *The temporal logic of reactive and concurrent systems.* Springer-Verlag, 1992.
43. Z. Manna and A. Pnueli. *Temporal Verification of Reactive Systems: Safety.* Springer–Verlag, 1995.
44. S. Merz. Decidability and incompleteness results for first-order temporal logics of linear time. *Journal of Applied Non-classical Logic*, 2, 1992.
45. A. Pnueli. Applications of temporal logic to the specification and verification of reacrive systems, a survey of current trends. In *Current Trends in Concurrency*, Lecture Notes in Computer Science, pages 510–584. Springer-Verlag, 1986.
46. M. Rabin. Decidability of second order theories and automata on infinite trees. *Trans. Amer. Math. Soc.*, 141:1–35, 1969.
47. D. Randell, Z. Cui, and A. Cohn. A spatial logic based on regions and connection. In *Proceedings of the 3rd International Conference on Knowledge Representation and Reasoning*, pages 165–176. Morgan Kaufmann, 1992.
48. M. Reynolds. Axiomatizing first-order temporal logic: Until and Since over linear time. *Studia Logica*, 57:279–302, 1996.
49. K. Schild. Combining terminological logics with tense logic. In *Proceedings of the 6th Portuguese Conference on Artificial Intelligence*, pages 105–120, Porto, 1993.
50. A. Sernadas. Temporal aspect of logical procedure definition. *Information Systems*, 5:167–187, 1980.
51. C. Stirling. Modal and temporal logics. In D. Gabbay, S. Abramsky, and T. Maibaum, editors, *Handbook of Logic in Computer Science*, volume 2, pages 478–551. Clarendon Press, Oxford, 1992.
52. H. Sturm and F. Wolter. A tableau calculus for temporal description logic: the expanding domain case. *Journal of Logic and Computation*, 2001. (In press.)
53. A. Szalas. Concerning the semantic consequence relation in first-order temporal logic. *Journal of Theoretical Computer Science*, 47:329–334, 1986.
54. A. Szalas and L. Holenderski. Incompleteness of first-order temporal logic with until. *Theoretical Computer Science*, 57:317–325, 1988.
55. P. Wolper. The tableau method for temporal logic: an overview. *Logique et Analyse*, 28:119–152, 1985.
56. F. Wolter and M. Zakharyaschev. Satisfiability problem in description logics with modal operators. In A.G. Cohn, L. Schubert, and S.C. Shapiro, editors, *Proceedings of the sixth Conference on Principles of Knowledge Representation and Reasoning, KR'98, Trento, Italy*, pages 512–523, Montreal, Canada, 1998. Morgan Kaufmann.
57. F. Wolter and M. Zakharyaschev. Modal description logics: modalizing roles. *Fundamenta Informaticae*, 39:411–438, 1999.
58. F. Wolter and M. Zakharyaschev. Spatial reasoning in RCC-8 with Boolean region terms. In W. Horn, editor, *Proceedings of the fourteenth European Conference on Artificial Intelligence, ECAI 2000, Berlin, Germany*, pages 244–248. IOS Press, 2000.

59. F. Wolter and M. Zakharyaschev. Spatio-temporal representation and reasoning based on RCC-8. In *Proceedings of the seventh Conference on Principles of Knowledge Representation and Reasoning, KR2000, Breckenridge, USA*, pages 3–14, Montreal, Canada, 2000. Morgan Kaufmann.
60. F. Wolter and M. Zakharyaschev. Temporalizing description logics. In D. Gabbay and M. de Rijke, editors, *Frontiers of Combining Systems II*, pages 379–401. Studies Press/Wiley, 2000.
61. F. Wolter and M. Zakharyaschev. Decidable fragments of first-order modal logics. *Journal of Symbolic Logic*, 2001. (In press).
62. F. Wolter and M. Zakharyaschev. Qualitative spatio-temporal representation and reasoning: a computational perspective. In G. Lakemeyer and B. Nebel, editors, *Exploring Artificial Intelligence in the New Millenium*, Morgan Kaufmann, 2001.
63. F. Wolter and M. Zakharyaschev. Axiomatizing the monodic fragment of first-order temporal logic. *Annals of Pure and Applied Logic*, 2001. (In press).
64. A. Zanardo. Branching-time logic with quantification over branches: the point of view of modal logic. *Journal of Symbolic Logic*, 61:1–39, 1996.

On Bounded Specifications

Orna Kupferman[1]* and Moshe Y. Vardi[2]**

[1] Hebrew University, School of Engineering and Computer Science, Jerusalem 91904, Israel
orna@cs.huji.ac.il, http://www.cs.huji.ac.il/ orna

[2] Rice University, Department of Computer Science, Houston, TX 77251-1892, U.S.A.
vardi@cs.rice.edu, http://www.cs.rice.edu/ vardi

Abstract. *Bounded model checking* methodologies check the correctness of a system with respect to a given specification by examining computations of a bounded length. Results from set-theoretic topology imply that sets in Σ^ω that are both open and closed (*clopen sets*) are precisely bounded sets: membership of a word in a clopen set can be determined by examining a bounded prefix of it. Clopen sets correspond to specifications that are both safety and co-safety. In this paper we study bounded specifications from this perspective. We consider both the linear and the branching frameworks. In the linear framework, we show that when clopen specifications are given by word automata or temporal logic formulas, we can identify a bound and translate the specification to bounded formalisms such as cycle-free automata and bounded LTL. In the branching framework, we show that while clopen sets of trees with infinite branching degrees may not be bounded, we can extend the results from the linear framework to clopen specifications given by tree automata or temporal logic formulas, even for trees with infinite branching degrees. There, we can identify a bound and translate clopen specifications to cycle-free automata and modal logic. Finally, we show how our results imply that the bottom levels of the μ-calculus hierarchy coalesce.

1 Introduction

Today's rapid development of complex and safety-critical systems requires reliable verification methods. In model checking, we verify that a system meets a desired property by checking that a mathematical model of the system meets a formal specification that describes the property [CGP99]. For example, we can view computations of a nonterminating system $\mathcal{S}$ as infinite words over an alphabet Σ (typically, $\Sigma = 2^{AP}$, where AP is the set of the system's atomic propositions). Then, $\mathcal{S}$ induces a language $\mathcal{L}(\mathcal{S}) \subseteq \Sigma^\omega$. Similarly, we can view a property ψ of the system as a language $\mathcal{L}(\psi) \subseteq \Sigma^\omega$ of all the computations that satisfy ψ. Verification that $\mathcal{S}$ satisfies ψ can then be reduced to checking that $\mathcal{L}(\mathcal{S}) \subseteq \mathcal{L}(\psi)$ [Kur94,VW94].

Of special interest are properties asserting that the system always stays within some allowed region in which nothing "bad" happens. For example, we may want to assert that every message received was previously sent. Such properties of systems are called

* Supported in part by BSF grant 9800096.

** Supported in part by NSF grants CCR-9700061, CCR-9988322, IIS-9908435, IIS-9978135, and EIA-0086264 by BSF grant 9800096, and by a grant from the Intel Corporation.

R. Nieuwenhuis and A. Voronkov (Eds.): LPAR 2001, LNAI 2250, pp. 24–38, 2001.

safety properties. Intuitively, a property ψ is a safety property if every violation of ψ occurs after a finite execution of the system. In our example, if in a computation of the system a message is received without previously being sent, this occurs after some finite execution of the system [Kin94].

Model checking of general properties considers infinite computations. Indeed, $\mathcal{L}(\mathcal{S})$ and $\mathcal{L}(\psi)$ are languages in Σ^ω, and checking whether $\mathcal{L}(\mathcal{S}) \subseteq \mathcal{L}(\psi)$ involves a search for bad cycles [VW94]. A symbolic implementation of such a search may be very expensive [HKSV97,BGS00]. On the other hand, model checking of safety properties involves a search for finite bad prefixes. Therefore, such a search considered only finite computations and is much simpler than general model-checking search [KV99]. The simplicity of the search for finite bad prefixes has motivated the development of *bounded model checking* methodologies, which consider computations of a bounded length. For example, in *SAT-based* model checking, we generate a propositional formula φ_k, for a fixed $k \geq 0$, such that φ_k is satisfiable iff the property is violated by a prefix of length k of some computation [BCC+99,BCRZ99]. In *symbolic trajectory evaluation* (STE), we try to falsify the correctness of a computation by referring only to a bounded prefix of it. The method is sound but not complete: we may terminate with no answer to the model-checking problem [SB95]. While it is possible to extend both SAT-based model checking and STE to handle ω-regular properties[1], the key idea of bounded model-checking methodologies is to reason about prefixes of a bounded length.

Recall that if a safety property is violated, then there is a finite prefix along which the violation has occurred. While we know that such a bad prefix exists, we cannot in general bound its length a-priori. Moreover, it may be that no such bound exists. For example, no bound exists for the safety property *Gp* (p is always true). Indeed, for every $k \geq 0$, the prefix p^k can be extended to a computation that satisfies *Gp* and can also be extended to a computation that does not satisfy *Gp*. We say that a property ψ is *bounded* if there is $k \geq 0$ such that for every computation π, the satisfaction of ψ in π can be determined by observing only the prefix of length k of π. It is clear that all bounded properties are also safety properties, but, as *Gp* demonstrates, safety is not a sufficient condition to boundedness.

The recent developments in bounded model checking have led to growing interest in bounded properties and their power. Motivated by these developments, we set out to characterize the expressive power of bounded properties. The initial goal of this research was to lift results about *bounded sets* in set-theoretic topology to results about bounded properties. Several basic topological notions have natural meaning in the context of formal languages and have been useful in studying the latter [HR86]. In particular, the study of the *Borel hierarchy* in set-theoretic topology was helpful to the study of the various types of automata on infinite words, whose acceptance conditions can be classified in terms of their location in the Borel hierarchy [Lan69,Tho90].

Let us first review some of the relevant terminology from set-theoretic topology. Consider a set X and a distance function $d : X \times X \to \mathbb{R}$ between the elements of X. For an element $x \in X$ and $\gamma \geq 0$, let $K(x, \gamma)$ be the set of elements x' such that

[1] In SAT-based model checking, it is possible to reason about cycles of a bounded length [BCCZ99], and in STE it is possible to combine several checks in order to reason about cycles [Yan00].

$d(x, x') \leq \gamma$. Consider a set $S \subseteq X$. An element $x \in S$ is called an *interior element* of S if there is $\gamma > 0$ such that $K(x, \gamma) \subseteq S$. The set S is *open* if all the elements in S are interior. A set S is *closed* if $X \setminus S$ is open. So, a set S is open if every element in S has a nonempty "neighborhood" contained in S, and a set S is closed if every element not in S has a nonempty neighborhood whose intersection with S is empty. A set that is both open and close is called a *clopen* set.

A *Cantor space* consists of $X = D^\omega$, for some finite D, and d defined by $d(w, w') = \frac{1}{2^n}$, where n is the first position where w and w' differ. Thus, elements of X can be viewed as infinite words over D and two words are close to each other if they have a long common prefix. If $w = w'$, then $d(w, w') = 0$. It is known that clopen sets in Cantor space are *bounded*, where a set S is bounded if it is of the form $W \cdots D^\omega$ for some finite set $W \subseteq D^*$. Hence, clopen sets in our Cantor space correspond exactly to the bounded properties we are looking for: each clopen language $L \subseteq \Sigma^\omega$ has a bound $k \geq 0$ such that membership in L can be determined by the prefixes of length k of words in Σ^ω.

What are these clopen sets in Σ^ω? It turns out that topology has an answer to this question as well [MP89,Gum93]: recall that a language $L \subseteq \Sigma^\omega$ is a *safety* language[2] iff every $w \notin L$ has a *bad prefix* $x \in \Sigma^*$ such that for all $y \in \Sigma^\omega$, we have $x \cdot y \notin L$. A language $L \subseteq \Sigma^\omega$ is a *co-safety* language[3] iff $\Sigma^\omega \setminus L$ is a safety language. Equivalently, L is co-safety iff every $w \in L$ has a *good prefix* $x \in \Sigma^*$ such that for all $y \in \Sigma^\omega$, we have $x \cdot y \in L$. It is not hard to see that a language $L \subseteq \Sigma^\omega$ is co-safety iff L is an open set in our Cantor space. To see that, consider a word w in a co-safety language L, and let x be a good prefix of w. All the words w' with $d(w, w') \leq \frac{1}{2^{|x|}}$ have x as their prefix, so they all belong to L. For the second direction, consider a word w in an open set L, and let $\gamma > 0$ be such that $K(w, \gamma) \subseteq L$. The prefix of w of length $\lfloor \log \frac{1}{\gamma} \rfloor$ is a good prefix for L. It follows that the clopen sets in Σ^ω, namely the bounded properties we are after, are exactly these properties that are both safety and co-safety!

While topology immediately solved our initial question about bounded properties (c.f., [Sta97]), it has led to many new questions. The properties we are interested in are not general subsets of Σ^ω. Rather, they are ω-regular, given by an automaton or a temporal-logic formula. Can we make use of this extra structure? For example, can we identify a bound for a given clopen property? Can we identify a tight bound? Once we found a bound k, can we translate clopen properties to formalisms that refer to the prefix of length k only? (We call such formalisms *bounded formalisms*.) What would be the blow-up of such a translation? Also, sometime we want to verify branching temporal properties (that is, properties that describe the whole computation tree of a system, and not its individual computations) [Lam80,EH86]. Can we extend the results from the linear framework to the branching one?

So, the enhanced goal of this research has become the study of clopen ω-regular linear and branching properties. We start with the linear framework. We first show that for an ω-regular clopen language $L \subseteq \Sigma^\omega$, we can identify a bound. We describe two incomparable bounds. The first refers to the deterministic automaton for L and the

[2] The definition of safety we consider here is given in [AS85], it coincides with the definition of limit closure defined in [Eme83], and is different from the definition in [Lam85], which also refers to the property being closed under stuttering.

[3] The term used in [MP92] is *guarantee* language.

second refers to the nondeterministic automata for L and $\Sigma^\omega \setminus L$. Using the bound, we translate L to bounded formalisms, specifically, to a cycle-free automaton and to an LTL formula whose only temporal operator is X ("next"), and we study the blow up of these translations. In particular, we show that the translation of a clopen LTL formula to a formula whose only temporal operator is X is tightly exponential (that is, exponential in both the upper and lower bound senses).

We then turn to the branching framework. The definition of safety and co-safety properties can be easily extended to the branching framework [BFG$^+$91,KV99,MT01]. Let $\tau(\Sigma, \Upsilon)$ be the set of Σ-labeled trees with directions in Υ; that is, the trees are prefix-closed subsets of Υ^*, and each node of the tree is labeled by a letter from Σ. Intuitively, a language $L \subseteq \tau(\Sigma, \Upsilon)$ is a safety language if every tree not in L has a bad prefix (which is a tree of a finite height) all of whose extensions are not in L. A clopen tree language is a language that is both safety and co-safety. We show that a distinction should be made between trees of finite branching degrees and trees with possibly infinite branching degrees. For the first type of trees, we can prove boundedness using the same considerations as in the linear framework. On the other hand, for trees with infinite branching degrees, it is not true that general clopen tree properties are bounded! Nevertheless, when the clopen tree languages are ω-regular[4], it is possible extend the results from the linear framework to both types of trees: we are able to identify a bound and to translate clopen properties to cycle-free tree automata[5]. To obtain our result, we use *symmetric nondeterministic automata* as a novel automata-theoretic tool (symmetry has been previously applied only to alternating automata). The advantage of working with nondeterministic automata is the ability to use pumping arguments.

The understanding that ω-regular clopen tree languages are bounded enables us to show that the bottom levels of the μ-calculus expressiveness hierarchy coalesce. The *μ-calculus* is an expressive and important specification language in which formulas are built from Boolean operators, next-times modalities, and least and greatest fixed-point operators [Koz83]. μ-calculus formulas are classified according to their *alternation depth*, which is the maximal number of alternations between nested least and greatest fixed-point operators. From a practical point of view, the classification is important, as the alternation depth is the major factor in the complexity of μ-calculus model checking [EL86]. A more refined classification also distinguishes between formulas in which the outermost fixed-point operator in the nested chain is a least fixed-point operator (Σ_i formulas, where i is the alternation depth) and formulas where it is a greatest fixed-point operator (Π_i formulas). *Modal Logic* (ML) consists of μ-calculus formulas with no fixed-point operators. The μ-calculus is more expressive than ML, and in fact, it

[4] A tree language is ω-regular if it can be recognized by a tree automaton. When the language contains trees with infinite branching degrees, the automata are *amorphous*, capable of handling infinite branching degrees. Several types of amorphous automata are studies in the literature. In particular, in *symmetric automata* [JW95,Wil99a], the transition function describes universal and existential requirements on the successors of the current node, it is independent of the branching degree, and can handle trees with an infinite branching degree.

[5] We assume that Υ is known; thus finite branching degrees are bounded by $|\Upsilon|$. We could have considered also trees with finite but unbounded branching degrees. As we note in the sequel, general clopen properties of such trees may not be bounded, yet ω-regular properties of such trees are bounded.

is possible to decide, given a μ-calculus formula, whether it has and equivalent ML formula [Ott99]. Moreover, it was recently proved that the μ-calculus hierarchy is strict (i.e., there is no $d \geq 1$ such that all μ-calculus formulas can be translated to formulas of alternation depth d) [Bra98]. For several hierarchies in computer science, even strict ones, it is possible to show local *coalescence*, where membership in some class of the hierarchy and in its complementary class implies membership in a lower class. For example, the equation RE$\cap$co-RE=Recursive implies a coalescence at the bottom of the arithmetical hierarchy.[6] It is shown in [BM78] that if a property describing classes of structures can be expressed both as a least fixed-point and a greatest fixed-point of a first-order formula, then it is equivalent to a first-order formula with no fixed points. Since first-order formulas that are preserved under bisimulation are equivalent to ML formulas [BB93,Ben91], the result in [BM78] implies a coalescence at the bottom of the μ-calculus expressiveness hierarchy, namely $\Sigma_1 \cap \Pi_1 = ML$. Using the fact that μ-calculus formulas of alternation depth 1 induce either safety or co-safety symmetric languages, we are able to get a constructive proof to the above coalescence, and to extend it to finite structures.[7]

Due to lack of space, some of the proofs are missing. The full version of the paper can be found at the author's URLs.

2 Preliminaries

2.1 Safety and Co-safety Languages

Consider a language $L \subseteq \Sigma^\omega$ of infinite words over the alphabet Σ. A finite word $x \in \Sigma^*$ is a *bad prefix* for L if for all $y \in \Sigma^\omega$, we have $x \cdot y \notin L$. Thus, a bad prefix is a finite word that cannot be extended to an infinite word in L. Note that if x is a bad prefix, then all the finite extensions of x are also bad prefixes. We say that a bad prefix x is *minimal* if all the strict prefixes of x are not bad. A language L is a *safety* language iff every $w \notin L$ has a finite bad prefix. For a safety language L, we denote by $\mathit{bad\_pref}(L)$ the set of all bad prefixes for L.

For a language $L \subseteq \Sigma^\omega$, we use $\mathit{comp}(L)$ to denote the complement of L; i.e., $\mathit{comp}(L) = \Sigma^\omega \setminus L$. We say that a language $L \subseteq \Sigma^\omega$ is a *co-safety* language iff $\mathit{comp}(L)$ is a safety language. Equivalently, L is co-safety iff every $w \in L$ has a *good prefix* $x \in \Sigma^*$ such that for all $y \in \Sigma^\omega$, we have $x \cdot y \in L$. For a co-safety language L, we denote by $\mathit{good\_pref}(L)$ the set of good prefixes for L. Note that $\mathit{good\_pref}(L) = \mathit{bad\_pref}(\mathit{comp}(L))$.

For a set Υ of directions, an *Υ-tree* is a nonempty set $T \subseteq \Upsilon^*$, where for every $x \cdot \upsilon \in T$ with $x \in \Upsilon^*$ and $\upsilon \in \Upsilon$, we have $x \in T$. The elements of T are called *nodes*, and the empty word ε is the *root* of T. For every $x \in T$, the nodes $x \cdot \upsilon \in T$ where $\upsilon \in \Upsilon$ are the *children* of x. A node with no children is a *leaf*. The *degree* of a node x, denoted $\mathit{deg}(x)$, is the number of children x has. Note that $\mathit{deg}(x) \leq |\Upsilon|$. We assume that Υ is

[6] On the other hand, the analogous coalescence for the polynomial hierarchy is not known. It is a major open question whether NP$\cap$co-NP=PTIME [GJ79]

[7] The result in [BM78] appeals to the Compactness Theorem, so it is not constructive and does not carry over to finite structures.

finite or $\Upsilon = \mathbb{N}$, in which case we may have nodes with an infinite degree. The *height* of a tree T is the length (possibly ∞) of the longest node in T. Note that when $\Upsilon = \mathbb{N}$, there may be infinite trees with a finite height. A tree is *leafless* iff it has no leaves. Note that a tree may be infinite and still have leaves. A *path* π of a tree T is a set $\pi \subseteq T$ such that $\varepsilon \in \pi$ and for every $x \in \pi$, either x is a leaf, or there exists a unique $v \in \Upsilon$ such that $x \cdot v \in \pi$. For an integer d, a *d-Υ-cone* is an Υ-tree all of whose paths are finite and have leaves in Υ^d. An Υ-cone is a d-Υ-cone for some d. For a tree T with a finite height, an *extension* of T is a tree T' such that $T \subseteq T'$ and every node $z \in T' \setminus T$ has a leaf x of T for which $z = x \cdot y$ for some $y \in \Upsilon^+$.

Given a finite set Σ, a *Σ-labeled Υ-tree* is a pair $\langle T, V\rangle$ where T is an Υ-tree and $V : T \to \Sigma$ maps each node of T to a letter in Σ. We use $\tau(\Sigma, \Upsilon)$ to denote the set of all Σ-labeled leafless Υ-trees. For a language $L \subseteq \tau(\Sigma, \Upsilon)$, we use $comp(L)$ to denote the complement of L; i.e., $comp(L) = \tau(\Sigma, \Upsilon) \setminus L$.

Consider an Υ-tree $T \subseteq \Upsilon^*$. A prefix of T is a nonempty prefix-closed subset of T with a finite height. A prefix of a tree $\langle T, V\rangle \in \tau(\Sigma, \Upsilon)$ is a Σ-labeled Υ-tree $\langle P, V\rangle$, where P is a prefix of T. An *extension* of $\langle P, V\rangle$ is a tree $\langle T', V'\rangle \in \tau(\Sigma, \Upsilon)$ such that T' is an extension of P, and V and V' agree on the labels of the nodes in P. We say that a language $L \in \tau(\Sigma_\Upsilon)$ is a safety language if every tree $\langle T, V\rangle \notin L$ has a prefix $\langle P, V\rangle$ all whose extensions are not in L. The prefix $\langle P, V\rangle$ is then a *bad prefix* for L. Dually, $L \in \tau(\Sigma, \Upsilon)$ is co-safety if every tree $\langle T, V\rangle$ in L has a prefix $\langle P, V\rangle$ all whose extensions are in L. The prefix $\langle P, V\rangle$ is then a *good prefix* for L. Note that, as in the linear case, $L \subseteq \tau(\Sigma, \Upsilon)$ is co-safety iff $comp(L)$ is safety. A *cone prefix* is a prefix which is a cone. Since prefixes have a finite height, it is easy to see that each bad prefix induces a bad cone prefix, and similarly for good prefixes.

In both the linear and the branching frameworks, we say that a language is *clopen* if it is both safety and co-safety (or, equivalently, if both L and $comp(L)$ are safety.) Note that the set of clopen languages is closed under complementation. For a temporal logic formula ψ, we say that ψ is a *safety formula* iff the set of words/trees that satisfy ψ is a safety language. Similarly, ψ is a *co-safety formula* iff this set is a co-safety language, or, equivalently, $\neg\psi$ is a safety formula. For an LTL formula ψ over a set AP of atomic propositions, let $\|\psi\|$ denote the set of computations in $(2^{AP})^\omega$ that satisfy ψ. Similarly, for a CTL* formula over AP, and a set Υ of directions, let $\|\psi\|_\Upsilon$ denote the set of computation trees in $\tau((2^{AP}), \Upsilon)$ that satisfy ψ. We say that ψ is a *safety formula* iff $\|\psi\|_\Upsilon$ is a safety language for all Υ. Also, ψ is a *co-safety formula* iff $\|\psi\|_\Upsilon$ is a co-safety language for all Υ or, equivalently, $\neg\psi$ is a safety formula.

2.2 Automata

Let Σ be a finite alphabet. For a word $w = \sigma_0 \cdot \sigma_1 \cdots$ over Σ and integers i and j, we use $w[i, \ldots, j]$ to denote the infix (possibly prefix of suffix) $\sigma_i \cdots \sigma_j$ of w. A *looping word automaton* is $\mathcal{A} = \langle \Sigma, Q, \delta, Q_0\rangle$, where Σ is the input alphabet, Q is a finite set of states, $\delta : Q \times \Sigma \to 2^Q$ is a transition function, and $Q_0 \subseteq Q$ is a set of initial states. The set Q contains a state q_{acc} designated as an *accepting sink*. If $|Q_0| = 1$ and δ is such that for every $q \in Q$ and $\sigma \in \Sigma$, we have that $|\delta(q, \sigma)| \leq 1$, then $\mathcal{A}$ is a *deterministic* automaton.

Given an input word $w = \sigma_0 \cdot \sigma_1 \cdots$ in Σ^ω, a *run* of $\mathcal{A}$ on σ is a function $r : \mathbb{N} \to Q$ where $r(0) \in Q_0$ and for every $i \geq 0$, either $r(i) = q_{acc}$ or $r(i+1) \in \delta(r(i), \sigma_i)$; i.e., the run starts in one of the initial states and obeys the transition function. Once the run reaches the accepting sink, its continuation is not important. Note that a nondeterministic automaton can have many runs on σ. In contrast, a deterministic automaton has a single run on σ. An automaton $\mathcal{A}$ accepts an input word w iff there exists a run of $\mathcal{A}$ on w.

Amorphous tree automata run on Σ-labeled Υ-trees. A *looping tree automaton* is $\mathcal{A} = \langle \Sigma, \Upsilon, Q, \delta, Q_0 \rangle$, where Σ, Q, and Q_0, are as in Büchi word automata (in particular, Q contains an accepting sink q_{acc}), and $\delta : Q \times \Sigma \times \{1, \ldots, |\Upsilon|\} \to 2^{Q^*}$ is a (nondeterministic) transition function, with $\delta(q, \sigma, k) \subseteq Q^k$. When Υ is infinite and $k = \mathbb{N}$, the tuples in Q^k are represented in some succinct way. We will return to this point shortly. Intuitively, in each of its transitions, $\mathcal{A}$ splits into several copies. Each copy proceeds to a subtree of the current node. A k-tuple $\langle q_1, q_2, \ldots, q_k \rangle \in \delta(q, \sigma, k)$ means that if $\mathcal{A}$ is now in state q and it reads a node of degree k labeled by σ, then a possible transition is one in which the copy that proceeds to direction leftmost subtree moves to state q_1, the copy that proceeds to the subtree near the leftmost one moves to state state q_1, and so on. A *run* of $\mathcal{A}$ on an input Σ-labeled Υ-tree $\langle T, V \rangle$ is a Q-labeled Υ tree $\langle T, r \rangle$ such that $r(\varepsilon) \in Q_0$ and for every $x \in T$ with successors $x \cdot v_1, x \cdot v_2, \ldots, x \cdot v_{deg(x)}$ in T, either $r(x) = q_{acc}$ or $\langle r(x \cdot v_1), r(x \cdot v_2), \ldots, r(x \cdot v_{deg(x)}) \rangle \in \delta(r(x), V(x), deg(x))$. If, for instance, $\Upsilon = \{0, 1\}$, $r(0) = q_2$, $V(0) = a$, $deg(x) = 2$, and $\delta(q_2, a, 2) = \{\langle q_1, q_2 \rangle, \langle q_4, q_5 \rangle\}$, then either $r(0 \cdot 0) = q_1$ and $r(0 \cdot 1) = q_2$, or $r(0 \cdot 0) = q_4$ and $r(0 \cdot 1) = q_5$. An automaton $\mathcal{A}$ accepts $\langle T, V \rangle$ iff there exists an run of $\mathcal{A}$ on $\langle T, V \rangle$.

Recall that amorphous automata are capable of reading trees with infinite branching degrees. For that, the tuples in the transition function are described in some succinct way. To handle trees with arbitrary branching degree, we introduce here *symmetric* nondeterministic looping automata, which are the nondeterministic counterpart of symmetric alternating looping automata [JW95,Wil99a]. In a symmetric looping automaton $\mathcal{A} = \langle \Sigma, Q, \delta, Q_0 \rangle$, the state space is $Q = 2^S$ for some set S of *underlying states*, and the transition function $\delta : Q \times \Sigma \to 2^{Q \times Q}$ maps a state and a letter to sets of pairs $\langle S_U, S_E \rangle$ of subsets of S. The set $S_U \subseteq S$ is the *universal set* and it describes the underlying states that should be members in all the successor states. The set $S_E \subseteq S$ is the *existential set* and it describes underlying states each of which has to be a member in at least one successor state. Formally, the tuples induced by $\delta(q, \sigma)$ are $\langle S_1, \ldots, S_k \rangle$ for an arbitrary k (possibly $k = \omega$), such that there is $\langle S_U, S_E \rangle$ in $\delta(q, \sigma)$ such that for all $1 \leq i \leq k$ we have $S_U \subseteq S_i$ and for all $s \in S_E$ there is $1 \leq i \leq k$ such that $s \in S_i$. Runs of symmetric automata are then defined as runs of usual nondeterministic automata, by means of the tuples induced by the transition function. A language is *symmetric* if there is a nondeterministic symmetric automaton recognizing it[8].

We now define a bounded form of automata. These are automata that essentially read only a bounded prefix of their input. A word automaton $\mathcal{A}$ is a *cycle-free* automaton if it contains no cycles. Formally, $\mathcal{A}$ is cycle free if for all runs r of $\mathcal{A}$ and two positions $i, j \geq 0$, either $r(i) \neq r(j)$ or $r(i) = q_{acc}$. When $\mathcal{A}$ is a tree automaton, it is cycle free if for all runs $\langle T, r \rangle$ of $\mathcal{A}$ and two nodes $x, y \in T$ such that x is a prefix of y, we have

[8] Readers familiar with alternating automata can see that symmetric nondeterministic looping automata are essentially symmetric alternating looping automata with transitions in DNF.

$r(x) \neq r(y)$ or $r(x) = q_{acc}$. The *diameter* of a deterministic cycle-free word automaton $\mathcal{A}$, denoted $diameter(\mathcal{A})$, is the length of the longest path from the initial state of $\mathcal{A}$ to the accepting sink of $\mathcal{A}$.

The language $\mathcal{L}(\mathcal{A})$ is the set of words/trees accepted by $\mathcal{A}$. We say that an automaton $\mathcal{A}$ is a clopen automaton if $\mathcal{L}(\mathcal{A})$ is clopen. As shown in [AS87,BFG+91,Sis94, KV99], looping automata recognize safety languages. Moreover, if a safety language L is recognized by an automaton $\mathcal{A}$ with an acceptance condition such as Büchi, Rabin, etc., then L is also recognized by the looping automaton obtained by ignoring the acceptance condition. It follows that every safety ω-regular word language can be recognized by a looping automaton. Note that looping word automata can be determinized by an application of the standard *subset construction* [RS59], thus a safety ω-regular word language can be recognized by a deterministic looping word automaton.

3 Clopen Properties: The Linear Framework

In this section we study linear clopen properties. We first give a direct proof, independent of set-theoretic topology, that linear clopen properties are bounded. We then consider ω-regular clopen properties, obtain two bounds for them, and consider their translation to bounded formalisms.

Consider a clopen language $L \subseteq \Sigma^\omega$. For a finite word $x \in \Sigma^*$, we say that x is *determined* with respect to L if x is a bad or a good prefix for L. Accordingly, x is *undetermined* with respect to L if there are $y \in \Sigma^\omega$ and $z \in \Sigma^\omega$ such that $x \cdot y \in L$ and $x \cdot z \notin L$.

Lemma 1. *If $L \subseteq \Sigma^\omega$ is clopen, then every word $w \in \Sigma^\omega$ has only finitely many prefixes that are undetermined with respect to L.*

We say that a clopen language L is *bounded* if there are only finitely many words in Σ^* that are undetermined with respect to L. For an integer k, we say that L is *bounded by k* if all the words $x \in \Sigma^*$ such that $|x| \geq k$ are determined with respect to L. Note that each bounded language L has an integer k such that L is bounded by k.

Theorem 1. [Sta97] *All clopen languages $L \subseteq \Sigma^\omega$ are bounded.*

Proof: Assume by way of contradiction that there is a clopen language $L \subseteq \Sigma^\omega$ that is not bounded. Thus, there are infinitely many $x \in \Sigma^*$ such that x is undetermined with respect to L. Since Σ is finite and the set of undetermined words is prefix closed, it follows, by König's Lemma, that there is an infinite word in Σ^ω all of whose prefixes are undetermined. This, however, contradicts Lemma 1. □

As discussed in Section 1, the clopen requirement is essential. Indeed, the language induced by the safety property *Gp* is not bounded, and so is the language induced by the co-safety property $F\neg p$.

Theorem 1 applies to languages L that are not necessarily ω-regular. We now show that when L is ω-regular, it is possible to obtain a bound for L. We first present a bound that refer to this deterministic automaton, and then use some observations about automata to present a bound that refer to the nondeterministic automata for L and $comp(L)$.

For a clopen ω-regular language L, let $det(L)$ be the size of the minimal deterministic looping automaton that recognizes L. Note that deterministic looping automata can be minimized in a way that is analogous to way deterministic automata on finite words are minimized. Furthermore, there is unique minimal deterministic automaton for L.

Lemma 2. *All minimal deterministic looping automata that recognize a clopen language are cycle free.*

So, the minimal deterministic looping automaton that recognizes a clopen language L is cycle free. Thus, we can talk about diameters of clopen ω-regular languages and define $diameter(L)$ as the diameter of the minimal automaton for L.

Lemma 3. *A clopen ω-regular language $L \subseteq \Sigma^\omega$ is bounded by $diameter(L)$.*

It follows that a clopen ω-regular language $L \subseteq \Sigma^\omega$ is bounded by $diameter(L)$ and can be recognized by a cycle-free automaton with $det(L)$ states. The weakness of these immediate bounds is that they refer to a deterministic automaton for L, which may be exponentially bigger than a nondeterministic automaton for it. We now show it is possible to obtain a bound of a clopen ω-regular language that refers to nondeterministic automata for L and $comp(L)$.

For safety language L, the *in index* of L, denoted $in\_index(L)$, is the minimal number of states that a nondeterministic looping automaton recognizing L has. Similarly, the *out index* of a co-safety language L, denoted $out\_index(L)$, is the minimal number of states that a nondeterministic looping automaton recognizing $comp(L)$ has. If L is clopen, we also refer to the *index* of L, denoted $index(L)$, which is the product of the in and out indices of L.

Lemma 4. *A clopen ω-regular language $L \subseteq \Sigma^\omega$ is bounded by $index(L)$.*

Theorem 2. *If an ω-regular language $L \subseteq \Sigma^\omega$ is clopen, then there is a cycle-free nondeterministic word automaton of size $in\_index(L) \cdot index(L)$ that recognizes L.*

Since LTL formulas can be translated to nondeterministic Büchi word automata with an exponential blow up [VW94], it follows from Theorem 2 that clopen LTL formulas can be translated to nondeterministic cycle-free automata with an exponential blow up. LTL formulas can also be translated to alternating Büchi word automata, with only a linear blow up [Var96]. Can clopen LTL formulas then be translated to alternating cycle-free automata with a linear blow up? In Theorem 3 below we answer this question to the negative. The idea is that a cycle-free automaton, even an alternating one, needs to visit k different states in order to read the k-th letter of the input.

Theorem 3. *The translation of clopen LTL formulas or clopen alternating word automata to to nondeterministic or alternating cycle-free word automata is tightly exponential.*

The translation of LTL formulas or alternating word automata to nondeterministic word automata involves an exponential blow up [MH84,VW94]. Hence, the cost of cycle-freeness is reflected only in the exponent, which can be three times larger in the cycle-free case. We note that, as with the translation of LTL formulas to nondeterministic automata, the exponential blow up refers to the worst case, and it does rarely appear in practice.

It is shown in [KV99] that the blow-up going from a co-safety LTL formula to a nondeterministic word automaton recognizing its good prefixes involves a doubly exponential blow up. Thus, for every n, there is a co-safety formula ψ of size $O(n)$ such that the minimal automaton for $good\_pref(\psi)$ has $2^{2^{O(n)}}$ states. The proof in [KV99] can be extended to ψ that is clopen. Hence, while we are able to translate a clopen LTL formula to a cycle-free automaton with an exponential blow up, we cannot expect an exponential translation of clopen LTL formulas to a cycle-free automaton for its good prefixes.

Bounded LTL is a fragment of the linear temporal logic LTL in which the only temporal operator is X ("next"). Since nondeterministic cycle-free word automata can be linearly translated to bounded LTL [Wil99b], it follows that clopen LTL formulas can be exponential translated to bounded LTL.

4 Clopen Properties: The Branching Framework

In this section we study clopen branching properties. We first restrict attention to the case Υ is finite. We show that in this case, we can prove boundedness using the same considerations as in the linear framework. On the other hand, when Υ is infinite and the trees may have infinite branching degrees, it is not true that general clopen tree properties are bounded. We then show that for clopen ω-regular tree languages, it is possible extend the results from the linear framework to both types of trees: we are able to identify a bound and to translate clopen properties to cycle-free tree automata.

Consider a clopen language $L \subseteq \tau(\Sigma, \Upsilon)$. For a Σ-labeled Υ-tree $\langle P, V\rangle$ with a finite height, we say that $\langle P, V\rangle$ is *determined* with respect to L if it is a bad or a good prefix for L. Accordingly, $\langle P, V\rangle$ is *undetermined* with respect to L if there are extensions $\langle T_1, V_1\rangle$ and $\langle T_2, V_2\rangle$ of $\langle P, V\rangle$ such that $\langle T_1, V_1\rangle \in L$ and $\langle T_2, V_2\rangle \notin L$. We say that a clopen language $L \in \tau(\Sigma, \Upsilon)$ is *bounded* if there are only finitely many integers $d \geq 0$ for which there is a Σ-labeled d-Υ-cone that is undetermined with respect to L. For an integer k, we say that L is *bounded by* k if all the Σ-labeled d-Υ-cones, with $d \geq k$, are determined with respect to L.

Lemma 5. *If $L \subseteq \tau(\Sigma, \Upsilon)$ is clopen, then every tree in $\tau(\Sigma, \Upsilon)$ has only finitely many cone prefixes that are undetermined with respect to L.*

When Υ is finite, König's Lemma can be applied, as in Section 3, in order to prove that clopen tree languages are bounded.

Theorem 4. *Let Υ be a finite set of directions. All clopen languages $L \subseteq \tau(\Sigma, \Upsilon)$ are bounded.*

We now turn to consider $\mathbb{N}$-trees. Recall that $\mathbb{N}$-trees may have nodes with an infinite degree. While Lemma 5 does not depend on Υ being finite, the finiteness of Υ is crucial for the application of König's Lemma in the proof of Theorem 4. In fact, as we prove in Theorem 5 below, it is not true that all clopen languages in $\tau(\Sigma, \mathbb{N})$ are bounded.

Theorem 5. *There is a clopen language in $\tau(\Sigma, \mathbb{N})$ that is not bounded.*

Proof: Consider the language $L \subseteq \tau(\{0,1\}, \mathbb{N})$, where $\langle T, V\rangle \in L$ iff either $deg(\varepsilon) = \infty$, or there is a node x with $|x| \leq deg(\varepsilon)$ and $V(x) = 1$. Thus, L contains exactly all $\{0,1\}$-labeled $\mathbb{N}$-trees in which, if the root has a finite degree k, then a node labeled 1 is reachable within k steps. It is not hard to see that L is clopen: if $\langle T, V\rangle \notin L$, its $deg(\varepsilon)$-$\mathbb{N}$-cone prefix is a bad prefix. Also, if $\langle T, V\rangle \in L$, either its 1-$\mathbb{N}$-cone prefix or its $deg(\varepsilon)$-$\mathbb{N}$-cone prefix is a good prefix. Now, for every a candidate bound k for L, the tree $\langle T, V\rangle$ with $deg(\varepsilon) = k+1$ and $V(x) = 0$ for all $x \in T$ has an undetermined k-$\mathbb{N}$-cone prefix. Hence, L is not bounded.[9] □

The language L examined in Theorem 5 is quite unnatural. In practice, we are concerned with ω-regular languages. In Section 3 we show that in the linear framework, ω-regularity enables us to identify a bound for the clopen language. We now show that in the branching framework ω-regularity enables us not only to identify a bound but also to handle $\mathbb{N}$-trees, where the branching degree is infinite or finite but unbounded. We first need some notations.

A *frontier* of an Υ-tree T is a set $E \subseteq T$ of nodes such that for every path $\pi \subseteq T$, we have $|\pi \cap E| = 1$. For a node x and a frontier E, we say that $x \leq E$ if x is a prefix of some node in E. A *roof* of a frontier E is a set E' such that every node in E has a strict prefix in E'. For a Σ-labeled Υ-tree $\langle T, V\rangle$, a frontier E of T and a roof E' of E, the tree $\langle T^{E\leftarrow E'}, V^{E\leftarrow E'}\rangle$ is obtained from $\langle T, V\rangle$ by pumping the difference between E' and E infinitely often. Note that a node $x \in E$ may have several prefixes in E'. Let $up(x)$ be the longest prefix of x in E'. When we pump the difference between E' and x, we refer to $up(x)$. Formally, for $x \in E$, we define $pump(x, E)$ as the set of all words $y_0 \cdot y_1 \cdots y_n \in \Upsilon^*$, with $n \geq 1$, such that $y_0 = x$, for all $0 < i < n-1$ we have $up(y_i) \cdot y_{i+1} \in E$, and $up(y_{n-1}) \cdot y_n \leq E$. Note that since E is a frontier, every word $z \in \Upsilon^*$ is a member of $pump(x, E)$ for at most one $x \in E$, in which case it has a single partition to $y_0 \cdot y_1 \cdots y_n$ as above. Accordingly, for $z \in pump(x, E)$, we can define $tail(z)$ as $up(x) \cdot y_n$. Now,

$$T^{E\leftarrow E'} = \bigcup_{x \in E} \{z : z \text{ is a prefix of } x\} \cup pump(x, E),$$

and

$$V^{E\leftarrow E'}(z) = \begin{cases} V(z) & \text{if } z \leq E, \\ V(tail(z)) & \text{if } z \in pump(x, E) \text{ for } x \in E. \end{cases}$$

For simplicity, we denote $\langle T^{E\leftarrow E'}, V^{E\leftarrow E'}\rangle$ by $\langle T, V\rangle^{E\leftarrow E'}$.

When the clopen language L is ω-regular, we can talk about the size of the nondeterministic automaton that accepts L [10]. We say that L is *strongly* ω-regular if both L and

[9] Note that L is bounded by the size of the set Υ of directions (in the theorem, L is defined with respect to Υ-trees with $\Upsilon = \mathbb{N}$, thus $|\Upsilon|$ is infinite and L is unbounded). So, when defined with respect to Υ-trees with a finite Υ, the language L is bounded. Also, note that it is the unboundedness of Υ, rather than its infiniteness, that makes L unbounded.

[10] It is possible to extend also the bound based on the diameter of L to the branching framework. The extension, however, is very technical and not very enlightening.

$comp(L)$ are ω-regular. When Υ is finite, all ω-regular languages are strongly ω-regular. Since amorphous automata are not closed under complementation, not all ω-regular languages in $\tau(\Sigma, \mathbb{N})$ are strongly ω-regular. In order to talk about the in and out indices of a clopen tree language, we restrict attention to strongly ω-regular languages. It can be shown that the set of symmetric looping nondeterministic automata that recognize clopen languages is closed under complementation, thus, in particular, our results apply to symmetric clopen languages.

Lemma 6. *A strongly ω-regular clopen language $L \subseteq \tau(\Sigma, \Upsilon)$ is bounded by $index(L)$.*

Proof: Assume by way of contradiction that there is a d-Υ-cone $\langle P, V\rangle$ such that $d \geq index(L)$ and $\langle P, V\rangle$ is undetermined. Thus, there are extensions $\langle T_1, V_1\rangle$ and $\langle T_2, V_2\rangle$ of $\langle P, V\rangle$ such that $\langle T_1, V_1\rangle \in L$ and $\langle T_2, V_2\rangle \notin L$. Let $\mathcal{A}_1$ and $\mathcal{A}_2$ be nondeterministic looping automata such that $\mathcal{L}(\mathcal{A}_1) = L$, $\mathcal{L}(\mathcal{A}_2) = comp(L)$, and $\mathcal{A}_1$ and $\mathcal{A}_2$ have $in\_index(L)$ and $out\_index(L)$ states, respectively. By the above, there are accepting runs $\langle T_1, r_1\rangle$ and $\langle T_2, r_2\rangle$ of $\mathcal{A}_1$ and $\mathcal{A}_2$ on $\langle T_1, V_1\rangle$ and $\langle T_2, V_2\rangle$, respectively. Both T_1 and T_2 have P as their d-Υ-cone prefix. Since $d \geq in\_index(L) \cdot out\_index(L)$, every path $\pi \subseteq P$ has two nodes x_1 and x_2 such that x_1 is a strict prefix of x_2, $r_1(x_1) = r_1(x_2)$, and $r_2(x_1) = r_2(x_2)$. Thus, both runs repeat their state at x_1 and x_2. The set of nodes x_2 as above is a frontier E and the set of nodes x_1 as above is a roof E' of E. Consider the tree $\langle P, V\rangle^{E \leftarrow E'}$. The accepting run of $\mathcal{A}_1$ on $\langle T_1, V_1\rangle$ induces an accepting run of $\mathcal{A}_1$ on $\langle P, V\rangle^{E \leftarrow E'}$. Formally, the tree $\langle P, r_1\rangle^{E \leftarrow E'}$ is an accepting run of $\mathcal{A}_1$ on $\langle P, V\rangle^{E \leftarrow E'}$. Similarly, the accepting run of $\mathcal{A}_2$ on $\langle T_2, V_2\rangle$ induces an accepting run of $\mathcal{A}_2$ on $\langle P, V\rangle^{E \leftarrow E'}$. It follows that $\langle P, V\rangle^{E \leftarrow E'}$ is accepted by both $\mathcal{A}_1$ and $\mathcal{A}_2$, contradicting the fact that $\mathcal{L}(\mathcal{A}_2) = comp(\mathcal{L}(\mathcal{A}_1))$. □

Theorem 6. *If a strongly ω-regular language $L \subseteq \tau(\Sigma, \Upsilon)$ is clopen, then there is a cycle-free nondeterministic tree automaton of size $in\_index(L) \cdot index(L)$ that recognizes L. If L is symmetric, so is the cycle-free automaton.*

The proof of Theorem 3 can be adapted to the branching case, where the specification language is CTL. The upper bound follows from the exponential translation of CTL to Büchi tree automata [VW86]. For the lower bound, the same example as the linear case works (with the specification being universally quantified). Hence we have the following.

Theorem 7. *The translation of clopen CTL formulas and clopen alternating tree automata to nondeterministic or alternating cycle-free tree automata is tightly exponential.*

5 Clopen μ-Calculus Specifications

The *propositional μ-calculus* is a propositional modal logic augmented with least and greatest fixed-point operators [Koz83]. Specifically, we consider a μ-calculus where formulas are constructed from Boolean propositions with Boolean connectives, the temporal operators EX ("exists next") and AX ("for all next"), as well as least (μ) and greatest (ν) fixed-point operators. We assume that μ-calculus formulas are written in positive normal form (negation only applied to atomic propositions constants and variables). We classify formulas according to the nesting of fixed-point operators in them. Several versions to such a classification can be found in the literature [EL86,Niw86,Bra98]. Intuitively, the class Σ_i contains all Boolean and modal combinations of formulas in which there are at most $i-1$ alternations of μ and ν, with the external fixed-point being a μ. Similarly, the class Π_i contains all Boolean and modal combinations of formulas in which there are at most i alternations of μ and ν, with the external fixed-point being a ν. *Modal logic* (ML) is a branching temporal logic in which the only temporal operators are EX and AX. Note that ML coincides with Σ_0 and Π_0. The problem of deciding whether a μ-calculus formula has an equivalent ML formula can be decided in exponential time [Ott99].

We now relate the bottom of the μ-calculus hierarchy to safety and co-safety languages.

Lemma 7. *All Π_1 formulas induce symmetric safety languages, and all Σ_1 formulas induce symmetric co-safety languages.*

In particular, since Σ_1 formulas induce ω-regular languages, whatever we say in this section about μ-calculus, is valid for trees with arbitrary branching degree.

Lemma 8. *A nondeterministic symmetric cycle-free automaton can be translated to an ML formula with a linear blow up.*

Lemmas 7 and 8 together imply that the levels at the bottom of the μ-calculus expressiveness hierarchy coalesce.

Theorem 8. *If $\psi \in \Sigma_1 \cap \Pi_1$, then $\psi \in ML$. The translation of $\Sigma_1 \cap \Pi_1$ to ML is tightly exponential.*

It can be shown that the pumping argument used in the proof of Lemma 6 can yield finitely-generated trees, which are trees that are generated by unfolding finite graphs. This can be used to show that Theorem 8 holds even if we restrict attention to finite structures. It is an interesting open question whether Theorem 8 can be generalized to a characterization of $\Sigma_i \cap \Pi_i$, for $i > 1$.

Acknowledgment. We thank Vaughan Pratt for very helpful explanations about clopen sets in Cantor spaces.

References

[AS85] B. Alpern and F.B. Schneider. Defining liveness. *IPL*, 21:181–185, 1985.

[AS87] B. Alpern and F.B. Schneider. Recognizing safety and liveness. *Distributed computing*, 2:117–126, 1987.

[BB93] J. Benthem and J. Bergstra. Logic of transition systems. Technical Report P9308, Programing research group, University of Amsterdam, 1993.

[BCC+99] A. Biere, A. Cimatti, E.M. Clarke, M. Fujita, and Y. Zhu. Symbolic model checking using SAT procedures instead of BDDs. In *Proc. 36th DAC*, pp. 317–320, 1999.

[BCCZ99] A. Biere, A. Cimatti, E.M. Clarke, and Y. Zhu. Symbolic model checking without BDDs. In *TACAS*, LNCS 1579, 1999.

[BCRZ99] A. Biere, E.M. Clarke, R. Raimi, and Y. Zhu. Verifying safety properties of a PowerPC[tm] microprocessor using symbolic model checking without BDDs. In *Proc. 11th CAV*, LNCS 1633, pp. 172–183, 1999.

[Ben91] J. Benthem. Languages in actions: categories, lambdas and dynamic logic. *Studies in Logic*, 130, 1991.

[BFG+91] A. Bouajjani, J.-C. Fernandez, S. Graf, C. Rodriguez, and J. Sifakis. Safety for branching semantics. In *Proc. 18th ICALP*, LNCS, pp. 76–92, 1991.

[BGS00] R. Bloem, H.N. Gabow, and F. Somenzi. An algorithm for strongly connected component analysis in $n \log n$ symbolic steps. In *FMCAD*, LNCS 1954, pp. 37-54, 2000.

[BM78] J. Barwise and Y.N. Moschovakis. Global inductive definability. *Journal of Symbolic Logic*, 43(3):521–534, 1978.

[Bra98] J.C. Bradfield. The modal μ-calculus alternation hierarchy is strict. *Theoretical Computer Science*, 195(2):133–153, March 1998.

[CGP99] E.M. Clarke, O. Grumberg, and D. Peled. *Model Checking*. MIT Press, 1999.

[EH86] E.A. Emerson and J.Y. Halpern. Sometimes and not never revisited: On branching versus linear time. *JACM*, 33(1):151–178, 1986.

[EL86] E.A. Emerson and C.-L. Lei. Efficient model checking in fragments of the propositional μ-calculus. In *Proc. 1st LICS*, pp. 267–278, 1986.

[Eme83] E.A. Emerson. Alternative semantics for temporal logics. *Theoretical Computer Science*, 26:121–130, 1983.

[GJ79] M. Garey and D. S. Johnson. *Computers and Intractability: A Guide to the Theory of NP-completeness*. W. Freeman and Co., San Francisco, 1979.

[Gum93] H.P. Gumm. Another glance at the Alpern-Schneider characterization of safety and liveness in concurrent executions. *IPL*, 47:291–294, 1993.

[HKSV97] R.H. Hardin, R.P. Kurshan, S.K. Shukla, and M.Y. Vardi. A new heuristic for bad cycle detection using BDDs. In *Proc. 9th CAV*, LNCS 1254, pp. 268–278, 1997.

[HR86] H.J. Hoogeboom and G. Rozenberg. Infinitary languages: basic theory and applications to concurrent systems. In *Proc. Advanced School on Current Trends in Concurrency*, LNCS 224, pp. 266–342, 1986.

[JW95] D. Janin and I. Walukiewicz. Automata for the modal μ-calculus and related results. In *Proc. 20th MFCS*, LNCS, pp. 552–562, 1995.

[Kin94] E. Kindler. Safety and liveness properties: A survey. *EATCS*, 53:268 – 272, 1994.

[Koz83] D. Kozen. Results on the propositional μ-calculus. *TCS*, 27:333–354, 1983.

[Kur94] R.P. Kurshan. *Computer Aided Verification of Coordinating Processes*. Princeton Univ. Press, 1994.

[KV99] O. Kupferman and M.Y. Vardi. Model checking of safety properties. In *Proc. 11th CAV*, LNCS 1633, pp. 172–183, 1999.

[KVW00] O. Kupferman, M.Y. Vardi, and P. Wolper. An automata-theoretic approach to branching-time model checking. *JACM*, 47(2):312–360, March 2000.

[Lam80] L. Lamport. Sometimes is sometimes "not never" - on the temporal logic of programs. In *Proc. 7th POPL*, pp. 174–185, 1980.

[Lam85] L. Lamport. Logical foundation. In *Distributed systems - methods and tools for specification*, LNCS 190, 1985.

[Lan69] L.H. Landweber. Decision problems for ω–automata. *Mathematical Systems Theory*, 3:376–384, 1969.

[MH84] S. Miyano and T. Hayashi. Alternating finite automata on ω-words. *Theoretical Computer Science*, 32:321–330, 1984.

[MP89] Z. Manna and A. Pnueli. The anchored version of the temporal framework. In *Linear time, branching time, and partial order in logics and models for concurrency*, LNCS 345, pp. 201–284, 1989.

[MP92] Z. Manna and A. Pnueli. *The Temporal Logic of Reactive and Concurrent Systems: Specification.* , Berlin, January 1992.

[MT01] P. Manolios and R. Trefler. Safety and liveness in branching time. In *Proc. 16th LICS*, 2001.

[Niw86] D. Niwiński. On fixed point clones. In *Proc. 13th ICALP*, LNCS 226, pp. 464–473, 1986.

[Ott99] M. Otto. Eliminating recursion in the μ-calculus. In *Proc. 16th STACS*, LNCS 1563, pp. 531–540, 1999.

[RS59] M.O. Rabin and D. Scott. Finite automata and their decision problems. *IBM Journal of Research and Development*, 3:115–125, 1959.

[SB95] C.J.H. Seger and R.E. Bryant. Formal verification by symbolic evaluation of partially-ordered trajectories. *Formal Methods in System Design*, 6:147–189, 1995.

[Sis94] A.P. Sistla. Safety, liveness and fairness in temporal logic. *Formal Aspects of Computing*, 6:495–511, 1994.

[Sta97] L. Staiger. ω-languages. *Handbook of Formal Languages*, pp. 339–388, 1997.

[Tho90] W. Thomas. Automata on infinite objects. *Handbook of Theoretical Computer Science*, pp. 165–191, 1990.

[Var96] M.Y. Vardi. An automata-theoretic approach to linear temporal logic. In *Logics for Concurrency: Structure versus Automata*, LNCS 1043, pp. 238–266, 1996.

[VW86] M.Y. Vardi and P. Wolper. Automata-theoretic techniques for modal logics of programs. *Journal of Computer and System Science*, 32(2):182–221, April 1986.

[VW94] M.Y. Vardi and P. Wolper. Reasoning about infinite computations. *Information and Computation*, 115(1):1–37, November 1994.

[Wil99a] T. Wilke. CTL$^+$ is exponentially more succinct than CTL. In *Proc. 19th FST&TCS*, 1738, pp. 110–121, 1999.

[Wil99b] T. Wilke. Classifying discrete temporal properties In *Proc. 16th STACS*, LNCS 1563, pp. 32-46, 1999.

[Yan00] J. Yang. A theory for generalized symbolic trajectory evaluation. In *Symposium on Symbolic Trajectory Evaluation*, Chicago, July 2000.

Improving Automata Generation for Linear Temporal Logic by Considering the Automaton Hierarchy

K. Schneider

University of Karlsruhe, Department of Computer Science
Institute for Computer Design and Fault Tolerance
P.O. Box 6980, 76128 Karlsruhe, Germany
email: Klaus.Schneider@informatik.uni-karlsruhe.de
http://goethe.ira.uka.de/~schneider

Abstract. We present new algorithms to translate linear time temporal logic (LTL) formulas with past operators to equivalent ω-automata. The resulting automata are given in a symbolic representation that directly supports symbolic model checking. Furthermore, this has the advantage that the translations run in linear time wrt. the length of the input formula. To increase the efficiency of the model checking, our translations avoid as far as possible the introduction of computationally expensive fairness constraints, or at least replace them by simpler reachability constraints. Using the well-known automaton hierarchy, we show that our improvements are complete. Finally, we show how large parts of the formulas can be translated to the simpler logic CTL, which accelerates the LTL model checking by orders of magnitude which is shown by experimental results.

1 Introduction

The reactive behavior of concurrent systems can be conveniently specified with temporal logics [10] like CTL [5], LTL [24], and CTL* [11]. These logics have a different expressiveness and also very different verification procedures: CTL* model checking can be easily reduced to LTL model checking [12], LTL model checking in turn is reduced to nonemptiness problems of ω-automata, and CTL model checking is reduced to model checking of the alternation-free μ-calculus. While symbolic CTL model checking is very efficient [3], some authors complain about the hard restrictions of CTL [17,26], and therefore tend to use the more comfortable logics LTL and CTL* [35]. All modern model checking tools therefore support LTL.

Verification procedures for LTL seem, however, not to be as powerful as those for CTL [6,33]. Usually, the given LTL formulas are translated to equivalent ω-automata whose emptiness is then to be checked. Similar to the verification procedures, there are two different approaches to these translations: procedures that construct the automata explicitly like [19,34,23,15,9,31,13,38,14], and others that derive a symbolic description of the automata like [3,6,18,29,8]. The latter have the advantage that they run with linear runtime and memory requirements wrt. the length of the formulas. Moreover, they can be directly used for symbolic model checking.

All of the mentioned translation procedures construct special ω-automata, usually *generalized Büchi automata* (a special form of Streett automata [32]). The acceptance

R. Nieuwenhuis and A. Voronkov (Eds.): LPAR 2001, LNAI 2250, pp. 39–54, 2001.

of these automata is defined by a set of sets of states $\{Q_1, \ldots, Q_n\}$: an infinite input sequence is accepted by such an automaton iff there is a run through the state transition system that visits each Q_i infinitely often. In the following, the Q_i's are called *fairness constraints* (as usual in CTL model checking). It is well-known that the verification of such fairness constraints requires a nested fixpoint iteration which makes them hard to verify[1], especially in symbolic model checking [25,1].

In this paper, we reconsider the translation procedures as given in [3,6,18,29], and show that these procedures can be significantly improved. The problem with these procedures is that each temporal future operator (except for the next-time operator) of the considered LTL formula induces a fairness constraint during the translation. It is well-known that the translation of *arbitrary* temporal formulas is not possible without fairness constraints. Nevertheless, there are a lot of specifications, including all *safety and liveness properties* [20], that can be translated to simpler classes of ω-automata (whose acceptance condition does not require fairness constraints). Consequently, some of the fairness constraints introduced by the procedures [3,6,18,29] are unnecessary, and others (still used by [8]) can be replaced with simpler constraints.

We therefore present two powerful improvements of the symbolic translation procedures that still retain the linear runtime of the translation. The first improvement is based on exploiting the monotonicity of logical operators and therefore allows one to *neglect the introduction of those fairness constraints that stem from positive/negative occurrences of weak/strong temporal operators*. This is already used in [8] and in most of the explicit translation procedures, but not in [3,6,18,29]. The second improvement allows one to *replace some of the remaining fairness constraints by simpler reachability constraints*. This improvement can be used as long as only strong temporal future operators are nested into each other, followed by only nestings of weak temporal future operators. To the best of our knowledge such an improvement has not been used so far. Based on these improvements, we define new subclasses of LTL that can be translated without fairness constraints at all, i.e., either without any constraints, or with only reachability constraints.

Beneath the translations of subclasses of LTL to corresponding automaton classes, we also consider a combination with the methods presented in [26,27]. These procedures allows one to translate large parts of the LTL formulas to CTL, thus bridging the gap between LTL and CTL. We have implemented all translation procedures in a front-end for the SMV model checker family [21,22,4], which yields a new verification tool for LTL specifications that outperforms the direct use of these tools. The tool has been completely written in Java, so that it is platform-independent and can be freely accessed under `http://goethe.ira.uka.de/~schneider/my_tools`.

The paper is organized as follows: In the next section, we define the syntax and the semantics of the temporal logic that is used in the paper. After this, we define our *new temporal logics in correspondence to the well-known automaton hierarchy*. In section 4, we review the translation procedures of [3,6,29]. In section 5, we present our improvements and hence, the first variant of our new translation procedures. We then combine all

[1] The best known algorithm [7] for checking a μ-calculus formula Φ in a finite state system with $|\mathcal{S}|$ states and $|\mathcal{R}|$ transitions is of order $O((|\mathcal{S}|\,|\Phi|)^{\mathsf{ad}(\Phi)-1}\,|\mathcal{R}|\,|\Phi|)$, where $\mathsf{ad}(\Phi)$ is the alternation depth of Φ. Fairness constraints increase the alternation depth to $\mathsf{ad}(\Phi) = 2$.

our improvements in section 6. We also show there how parts of the LTL formulas can be directly translated to CTL to further increase the efficiency. Experimental results that prove the power of our improvements are finally given in section 7. Due to lack of space, we do not list proofs; however, we note that most parts of the translation procedures have been checked with the HOL [16] proof assistant, and a more detailed description of the algorithms together with proofs can be found in [28].

Some recent work can be combined with the translations presented here: [13] and [31] list different sets of rewrite rules to simplify LTL formulas before translating them to automata. Moreover, [2] presents symbolic procedures for checking nonemptiness of weak and terminal Büchi-automata (which are called $\mathsf{NDet}_{\mathsf{FG}}$ and $\mathsf{NDet}_{\mathsf{F}}$ below), which yields a perfect back-end for our translations.

2 Syntax and Semantics of $\mathcal{L}_\omega$

We first define an extended temporal logic $\mathcal{L}_\omega$ (as did many authors like [37] before) to present our translations in a single formalism.

Definition 1 (Syntax of $\mathcal{L}_\omega$). *The following mutually recursive definitions introduce the set of $\mathcal{L}_\omega$ formulas over a given finite set of variables $\mathcal{V}$:*

- *each variable is a $\mathcal{L}_\omega$ formula, i.e., $\mathcal{V} \subseteq \mathcal{L}_\omega$*
- $\neg\varphi$, $\varphi \vee \psi \in \mathcal{L}_\omega$ *if* $\varphi, \psi \in \mathcal{L}_\omega$
- $\mathsf{X}\varphi$, $\overleftarrow{\mathsf{X}}\varphi$, $[\varphi\ \underline{\mathsf{U}}\ \psi]$, $[\varphi\ \overleftarrow{\underline{\mathsf{U}}}\ \psi] \in \mathcal{L}_\omega$, *if* $\varphi, \psi \in \mathcal{L}_\omega$
- *Given a finite set of variables Q with $Q \cap \mathcal{V} = \{\}$, a propositional formula $\Phi_\mathcal{I}$ over $Q \cup \mathcal{V}$, a propositional*[2] *formula $\Phi_\mathcal{R}$ over $Q \cup \mathcal{V} \cup \{\mathsf{X}v \mid v \in Q \cup \mathcal{V}\}$, and a $\mathcal{L}_\omega$ formula $\Phi_\mathcal{F}$ over $Q \cup \mathcal{V}$, then $\mathcal{A}_\exists(Q, \Phi_\mathcal{I}, \Phi_\mathcal{R}, \Phi_\mathcal{F})$ is a $\mathcal{L}_\omega$ formula.*

The above logic is based on the usual temporal future time operators X and $[\cdot\ \underline{\mathsf{U}}\ \cdot]$, and their corresponding past time operators $\overleftarrow{\mathsf{X}}$ and $[\cdot\ \overleftarrow{\underline{\mathsf{U}}}\ \cdot]$. Moreover, it uses ω-automata as temporal operators to receive the full power of ω-regular languages. Note, that arbitrary $\mathcal{L}_\omega$ formulas are allowed as acceptance conditions in the automata expressions, which might be unusual, but simplifies the following explanations.

The semantics is given wrt. Kripke structures $\mathcal{K} = (\mathcal{I}, \mathcal{S}, \mathcal{R}, \mathcal{L}, \mathcal{F})$: $\mathcal{S}$ is a finite set of states, $\mathcal{R} \subseteq \mathcal{S} \times \mathcal{S}$ is the transition relation, and $\mathcal{L} : \mathcal{S} \to 2^\mathcal{V}$ is a labeling function that maps a state $s \in \mathcal{S}$ to the set of variables $\mathcal{L}(s) \subseteq \mathcal{V}$ that hold on s. $\mathcal{I} \subseteq \mathcal{S}$ is the set of initial states, and $\mathcal{F} = \{F_1, \ldots, F_f\}$ is a finite set of sets of states F_i that are called fairness constraints. A path through $\mathcal{K}$ is a function $\pi : \ \to \mathcal{S}$ such that $\forall t.(\pi^{(t)}, \pi^{(t+1)}) \in \mathcal{R}$ holds. A path π is fair iff π visits every $F_i \in \mathcal{F}$ infinitely often.

$\mathcal{A}_\exists(Q, \Phi_\mathcal{I}, \Phi_\mathcal{R}, \Phi_\mathcal{F})$ is an (existential) automaton formula that describes an ω-automaton in a symbolic manner: Q is the set of state variables, so the set of states corresponds with the powerset of Q. We identify any set $\vartheta \subseteq Q \cup \mathcal{V} \cup \{\mathsf{X}v \mid v \in Q \cup \mathcal{V}\}$ with a propositional interpretation that exactly assigns the variables of ϑ to true. With this view, the formula $\Phi_\mathcal{I}$ describes the set of the initial conditions: These are the sets $\vartheta \subseteq Q \cup \mathcal{V}$ that satisfy $\Phi_\mathcal{I}$. Similarly, $\Phi_\mathcal{R}$ describes the set of transitions. Intuitively, an existential automaton formula $\mathfrak{A}$ holds on a path π iff there is an accepting run for the trace $\mathcal{L}(\pi^{(0)})$, $\mathcal{L}(\pi^{(1)})$, ..., through $\mathfrak{A}$. To define this formally, we

[2] For variables v, we often treat $\mathsf{X}v$ as a normal variable for propositional evaluations.

define the Kripke structure $\mathcal{K}_{\mathfrak{A}} = (\mathcal{I}_{\mathfrak{A}}, \mathcal{S}_{\mathfrak{A}}, \mathcal{R}_{\mathfrak{A}}, \mathcal{L}_{\mathfrak{A}}, \{\})$ for an automaton formula $\mathfrak{A} = \mathcal{A}_{\exists}(Q, \Phi_{\mathcal{I}}, \Phi_{\mathcal{R}}, \Phi_{\mathcal{F}})$ with $\mathcal{S}_{\mathfrak{A}} := 2^{Q \cup \mathcal{V}}$, $\mathcal{I}_{\mathfrak{A}} := \{\vartheta \subseteq Q \cup \mathcal{V} \mid \vartheta \models \Phi_{\mathcal{I}}\}$, $\mathcal{R}_{\mathfrak{A}} := \{(\vartheta_0, \vartheta_1) \subseteq (Q \cup \mathcal{V}) \times (Q \cup \mathcal{V}) \mid \vartheta_0 \cup \{\mathsf{X}v \mid v \in \vartheta_1\} \models \Phi_{\mathcal{R}}\}$, and $\mathcal{L}_{\mathfrak{A}}(s) := s$. Note that $\mathcal{K}_{\mathfrak{A}}$ is independent of the acceptance condition $\Phi_{\mathcal{F}}$; the effect of $\Phi_{\mathcal{F}}$ is considered in the definition of the semantics below:

Definition 2 (Semantics of $\mathcal{L}_\omega$). *Given a structure $\mathcal{K} = (\mathcal{I}, \mathcal{S}, \mathcal{R}, \mathcal{L}, \mathcal{F})$, a fair path π through $\mathcal{K}$, and a number $t \in$, the semantics of $\mathcal{L}_\omega$ formulas is recursively defined as follows:*

- $(\mathcal{K}, \pi, t) \models x$ *iff* $x \in \mathcal{L}(\pi^{(t)})$ *for each variable* x
- $(\mathcal{K}, \pi, t) \models \neg\varphi$ *iff not* $(\mathcal{K}, \pi, t) \models \varphi$
- $(\mathcal{K}, \pi, t) \models \varphi \vee \psi$ *iff* $(\mathcal{K}, \pi, t) \models \varphi$ *or* $(\mathcal{K}, \pi, t) \models \psi$
- $(\mathcal{K}, \pi, t) \models \mathsf{X}\varphi$ *iff* $(\mathcal{K}, \pi, t+1) \models \varphi$
- $(\mathcal{K}, \pi, t) \models \overleftarrow{\mathsf{X}}\varphi$ *iff* $t = 0$ *or* $t > 0$ *and* $(\mathcal{K}, \pi, t-1) \models \varphi$
- $(\mathcal{K}, \pi, t) \models [\varphi \ \underline{\mathsf{U}}\ \psi]$ *iff there is a* $\delta \geq t$ *such that* $(\mathcal{K}, \pi, \delta) \models \psi$ *and for all* x *with* $t \leq x < \delta$, *we have* $(\mathcal{K}, \pi, x) \models \varphi$
- $(\mathcal{K}, \pi, t) \models [\varphi \ \overleftarrow{\underline{\mathsf{U}}}\ \psi]$ *iff there is a* $\delta \leq t$ *such that* $(\mathcal{K}, \pi, \delta) \models \psi$ *and for all* x *with* $\delta < x \leq t$, *we have* $(\mathcal{K}, \pi, x) \models \varphi$
- *Given* $\mathfrak{A} = \mathcal{A}_{\exists}(Q, \Phi_{\mathcal{I}}, \Phi_{\mathcal{R}}, \Phi_{\mathcal{F}})$ *with Kripke structure* $\mathcal{K}_{\mathfrak{A}} = (\mathcal{I}_{\mathfrak{A}}, \mathcal{S}_{\mathfrak{A}}, \mathcal{R}_{\mathfrak{A}}, \mathcal{L}_{\mathfrak{A}}, \{\})$, *we define* $(\mathcal{K}, \pi, t) \models \mathfrak{A}$ *iff there is fair path* ξ *through*[3] $\mathcal{K} \times \mathcal{K}_{\mathfrak{A}}$ *such that (1)* $\forall x.\mathsf{fst}(\xi^{(x)}) = \pi^{(x+t)}$, *(2)* $\mathsf{snd}(\xi^{(0)}) \in \mathcal{I}_{\mathfrak{A}}$, *and (3)* $(\mathcal{K} \times \mathcal{K}_{\mathfrak{A}}, \xi, 0) \models \Phi_{\mathcal{F}}$ *holds.*[4]

φ is generally valid if $(\mathcal{K}, \pi, t) \models \varphi$ holds on every path of every structure $\mathcal{K}$ for any position t. φ is initially valid if $(\mathcal{K}, \pi, 0) \models \varphi$ holds on every path of every structure $\mathcal{K}$.

Except for the automaton formulas, the above definition is done in the standard way and can be found in many related papers. Note that $\mathsf{snd}(\xi^{(0)})$ must be an initial state of $\mathcal{K}_{\mathfrak{A}}$, but $\mathsf{fst}(\xi^{(0)})$ is simply $\pi^{(t)}$ and not necessarily an initial state of $\mathcal{K}$.

Moreover, we use the following standard abbreviations: $\mathsf{G}a = \neg[1\ \underline{\mathsf{U}}\ (\neg a)]$, $\mathsf{F}a = [1\ \underline{\mathsf{U}}\ a]$, $[a\ \mathsf{U}\ b] = [a\ \underline{\mathsf{U}}\ b] \vee \mathsf{G}a$, $\overleftarrow{\underline{\mathsf{X}}}a = \neg\overleftarrow{\mathsf{X}}\neg a$, $\overleftarrow{\mathsf{G}}a = \neg[1\ \overleftarrow{\underline{\mathsf{U}}}\ (\neg a)]$, $\overleftarrow{\mathsf{F}}a = [1\ \overleftarrow{\underline{\mathsf{U}}}\ a]$, and $[a\ \overleftarrow{\mathsf{U}}\ b] = [a\ \overleftarrow{\underline{\mathsf{U}}}\ b] \vee \overleftarrow{\mathsf{G}}a$. We distinguish between strong and weak variants of temporal operators by underlining the strong variant (a strong variant requires that the event that is waited for actually will occur or has occurred, or in case of $\overleftarrow{\underline{\mathsf{X}}}$ that really a previous point of time exists). Moreover, we introduce further Boolean operators as $\varphi \wedge \psi := \neg(\neg\varphi \vee \neg\psi)$, $\varphi \rightarrow \psi := \neg\varphi \vee \psi$, and $(\varphi = \psi) := (\varphi \rightarrow \psi) \wedge (\psi \rightarrow \varphi)$, with priorities $= \preceq \rightarrow \preceq \vee \preceq \wedge \preceq$ 'unary operators' ($\bigwedge_{i=0}^{n}$ and $\bigvee_{i=0}^{n}$ are also unary).

As an important notation, we write $\Phi\langle\varphi\rangle_x$ to denote that the variable x is replaced in Φ by the formula φ. This notation for substitution will be important in the following. Finally, we denote the length of a formula Φ, i.e., the number of its operators as $|\Phi|$.

3 A Hierarchy of Temporal Logics

Several acceptance conditions are distinguished for defining different classes of ω-automata [36,32]. Acceptance conditions of the form $\mathsf{G}\varphi_0$, $\mathsf{F}\varphi_0$, $\bigwedge_{i=0}^{n}(\mathsf{G}\varphi_i \vee \mathsf{F}\psi_i)$,

[3] Products of structures are defined in the usual way (see e.g., [27]).

[4] We assume the following definitions: $\mathsf{fst}((a,b)) = a$ and $\mathsf{snd}((a,b)) = b$.

$\mathsf{FG}\varphi_0$, $\mathsf{GF}\varphi_0$, and $\bigwedge_{i=0}^{n}(\mathsf{FG}\varphi_i \vee \mathsf{GF}\psi_i)$ determine the automaton classes $\mathsf{(N)Det_G}$, $\mathsf{(N)Det_F}$, $\mathsf{(N)Det_{Prefix}}$, $\mathsf{(N)Det_{FG}}$, $\mathsf{(N)Det_{GF}}$, $\mathsf{(N)Det_{Streett}}$, respectively, where all subformulas φ_i and ψ_i are propositional. Det_κ and NDet_κ denote thereby the sets of deterministic and nondeterministic ω-automata with acceptance condition of type κ. The expressiveness of these classes can be illustrated as follows, where $\mathcal{C}_1 \precapprox \mathcal{C}_2$ means that for any automaton in $\mathcal{C}_1$, there is an equivalent one in $\mathcal{C}_2$. Moreover, we define $\mathcal{C}_1 \approx \mathcal{C}_2 := \mathcal{C}_1 \precapprox \mathcal{C}_2 \wedge \mathcal{C}_2 \precapprox \mathcal{C}_1$ and $\mathcal{C}_1 \precnapprox \mathcal{C}_2 := \mathcal{C}_1 \precapprox \mathcal{C}_2 \wedge \neg(\mathcal{C}_1 \approx \mathcal{C}_2)$.

$$\begin{array}{ccccccc}
\mathsf{Det_F} & & & \mathsf{Det_{GF}} & & & \mathsf{Det_{Streett}} \\
& \precnapprox & \mathsf{Det_{Prefix}} & \precnapprox & \precnapprox & \mathsf{NDet_{GF}} & \approx \\
\mathsf{Det_G} & \precnapprox & & \precnapprox\ \mathsf{Det_{FG}} & \precnapprox & & \approx\ \mathsf{NDet_{Streett}} \\
\approx & & & \approx & & & \\
\mathsf{NDet_G} & & & \mathsf{NDet_F} & \approx\ \mathsf{NDet_{Prefix}} & \approx & \mathsf{NDet_{FG}}
\end{array}$$

The above automaton hierarchy is closely related to the Borel hierarchy of topology [32]. As can be seen, it consists of six different classes, and each class has a deterministic representative. It can be shown that the nonemptiness problem for all automaton classes except for $\mathsf{(N)Det_{GF}}$ and $\mathsf{(N)Det_{Streett}}$ can be reduced to the alternation-free μ-calculus, whereas $\mathsf{(N)Det_{GF}}$ and $\mathsf{(N)Det_{Streett}}$ require μ-calculus formulas of alternation-depth 2. This is not only a theoretical issue, since the alternation-depth dramatically influences the runtime of the verification procedure (it reflects the number of nested fixpoint iterations of the model checking procedure).

Manna and Pnueli were the first who investigated a temporal logic hierarchy in analogy to the above automaton hierarchy [20]. However, they only considered very restricted normal forms, namely formulas that are obtained by replacing the subformulas φ_i and ψ_i in the acceptance conditions of the automata with formulas that contain only Boolean and past temporal operators. In the following definition, we present a completely new definition of a temporal logic hierarchy with syntactically much richer temporal logics. One can even show [28] that the future time fragments of these logics are as expressive as the logic themselves, so that past operators can be eliminated.

Definition 3 (Temporal Borel Classes). *We define the logics* TL_κ *for* $\kappa \in \{\mathsf{G}, \mathsf{F}, \mathsf{Prefix}, \mathsf{FG}, \mathsf{GF}, \mathsf{Streett}\}$ *by the following grammar rules, where* TL_κ *is the set of formulas that can be derived from the nonterminal* P_κ *(*$\mathcal{V}$ *represents any variable* $v \in \mathcal{V}$*):*

<table>
<tr><td>$P_{\mathsf{G}} ::= \mathcal{V} \mid \neg P_{\mathsf{F}} \mid P_{\mathsf{G}} \wedge P_{\mathsf{G}} \mid P_{\mathsf{G}} \vee P_{\mathsf{G}}$
$\mid \overleftarrow{\mathsf{X}} P_{\mathsf{G}} \mid [P_{\mathsf{G}}\ \overleftarrow{\mathsf{U}}\ P_{\mathsf{G}}]$
$\mid \underline{\overleftarrow{\mathsf{X}}} P_{\mathsf{G}} \mid [P_{\mathsf{G}}\ \underline{\overleftarrow{\mathsf{U}}}\ P_{\mathsf{G}}]$
$\mid \mathsf{X} P_{\mathsf{G}} \mid [P_{\mathsf{G}}\ \mathsf{U}\ P_{\mathsf{G}}]$</td><td>$P_{\mathsf{F}} ::= \mathcal{V} \mid \neg P_{\mathsf{G}} \mid P_{\mathsf{F}} \wedge P_{\mathsf{F}} \mid P_{\mathsf{F}} \vee P_{\mathsf{F}}$
$\mid \overleftarrow{\mathsf{X}} P_{\mathsf{F}} \mid [P_{\mathsf{F}}\ \overleftarrow{\mathsf{U}}\ P_{\mathsf{F}}]$
$\mid \underline{\overleftarrow{\mathsf{X}}} P_{\mathsf{F}} \mid [P_{\mathsf{F}}\ \underline{\overleftarrow{\mathsf{U}}}\ P_{\mathsf{F}}]$
$\mid \mathsf{X} P_{\mathsf{F}} \mid [P_{\mathsf{F}}\ \underline{\mathsf{U}}\ P_{\mathsf{F}}]$</td></tr>
<tr><td colspan="2">$P_{\mathsf{Prefix}} ::= P_{\mathsf{G}} \mid P_{\mathsf{F}} \mid \neg P_{\mathsf{Prefix}} \mid P_{\mathsf{Prefix}} \wedge P_{\mathsf{Prefix}} \mid P_{\mathsf{Prefix}} \vee P_{\mathsf{Prefix}}$</td></tr>
<tr><td>$P_{\mathsf{GF}} ::= P_{\mathsf{Prefix}}$
$\mid \neg P_{\mathsf{FG}} \mid P_{\mathsf{GF}} \wedge P_{\mathsf{GF}} \mid P_{\mathsf{GF}} \vee P_{\mathsf{GF}}$
$\mid \overleftarrow{\mathsf{X}} P_{\mathsf{GF}} \mid \underline{\overleftarrow{\mathsf{X}}} P_{\mathsf{GF}} \mid \mathsf{X} P_{\mathsf{GF}}$
$\mid [P_{\mathsf{GF}}\ \overleftarrow{\mathsf{U}}\ P_{\mathsf{GF}}] \mid [P_{\mathsf{GF}}\ \underline{\overleftarrow{\mathsf{U}}}\ P_{\mathsf{GF}}]$
$\mid [P_{\mathsf{GF}}\ \mathsf{U}\ P_{\mathsf{GF}}] \mid [P_{\mathsf{GF}}\ \underline{\mathsf{U}}\ P_{\mathsf{F}}]$</td><td>$P_{\mathsf{FG}} ::= P_{\mathsf{Prefix}}$
$\mid \neg P_{\mathsf{GF}} \mid P_{\mathsf{FG}} \wedge P_{\mathsf{FG}} \mid P_{\mathsf{FG}} \vee P_{\mathsf{FG}}$
$\mid \overleftarrow{\mathsf{X}} P_{\mathsf{FG}} \mid \mathsf{X} P_{\mathsf{FG}} \mid \underline{\overleftarrow{\mathsf{X}}} P_{\mathsf{FG}}$
$\mid [P_{\mathsf{FG}}\ \overleftarrow{\mathsf{U}}\ P_{\mathsf{FG}}] \mid [P_{\mathsf{FG}}\ \underline{\overleftarrow{\mathsf{U}}}\ P_{\mathsf{FG}}]$
$\mid [P_{\mathsf{FG}}\ \underline{\mathsf{U}}\ P_{\mathsf{FG}}] \mid [P_{\mathsf{G}}\ \mathsf{U}\ P_{\mathsf{FG}}]$</td></tr>
<tr><td colspan="2">$P_{\mathsf{Streett}} ::= P_{\mathsf{GF}} \mid P_{\mathsf{FG}} \mid \neg P_{\mathsf{Streett}} \mid P_{\mathsf{Streett}} \wedge P_{\mathsf{Streett}} \mid P_{\mathsf{Streett}} \vee P_{\mathsf{Streett}}$</td></tr>
</table>

TL_G is the set of formulas where each occurrence of a weak/strong temporal future operator is positive/negative, and similarly, each occurrence of a weak/strong temporal future operator in TL_F is negative/positive. Hence, both logics are dual to each other, which means that one contains the negations of the other one. $\mathsf{TL}_\mathsf{Prefix}$ is the Boolean closure of TL_G (and TL_F). The logics TL_GF and TL_FG are constructed in the same way as TL_G and TL_F; there are two differences: (1) these logics allow occurrences of $\mathsf{TL}_\mathsf{Prefix}$ where otherwise variables would have been required in TL_G and TL_F, and (2) there are additional 'asymmetric' grammar rules. It can be easily proved that TL_GF and TL_FG are also dual to each other, and their intersection strictly contains $\mathsf{TL}_\mathsf{Prefix}$. Finally, $\mathsf{TL}_\mathsf{Streett}$ is the Boolean closure of TL_GF (and TL_FG).

Note that the 'asymmetric' grammar rules of the logics TL_GF and TL_FG can be eliminated due to the following equivalences: $[\varphi\ \underline{\mathsf{U}}\ \psi] = [\varphi\ \mathsf{U}\ \psi] \wedge \mathsf{F}\psi$ and $[\varphi\ \mathsf{U}\ \psi] = [\varphi\ \underline{\mathsf{U}}\ \psi] \vee \mathsf{G}\varphi$. In the following, we therefore neglect these asymmetric grammar rules to simplify the remaining considerations[5].

For the completeness of the logics TL_κ, we note that the logics TL_κ (syntactically) strictly contain the logics defined in [20] that are known to be complete with respect to counter-free Det_κ automata. Hence, it is possible to translate any counter-free Det_κ automaton to an equivalent TL_κ formula, the other direction is proved in the following.

4 The Basic Translation to ω-Automata

Translations from temporal logics to equivalent ω-automata have been intensively studied. Common to most procedures is the consideration of the truth values of all subformulas of the given formula. In particular, one considers the set of *elementary subformulas* of a given formula Φ which is essentially the set of all subformulas of Φ that start with a temporal operator. The states of the ω-automaton that is to be constructed consist then of the truth values of these elementary formulas: If Φ has the elementary formulas $\{\varphi_1, \ldots, \varphi_n\}$, we need n state variables $\{q_1, \ldots, q_n\}$ to encode the state set, and therefore already see where the exponential blow-up of the automaton comes from. Clearly, for any run through the automaton, we want that $q_i = \varphi_i$ holds. For this reason, the transition relation of the automaton must respect the semantics of the temporal operators that occur in φ_i. The following theorem shows however that it is not enough to only follow the recursion laws of the operators:

Theorem 1. *Given a formula Φ with some occurrences of a variable x, and propositional formulas φ and ψ, the following equations are valid :*

$$\mathcal{A}_\exists(\{q\}, 1, \mathsf{X}q = \varphi, \Phi\langle q\rangle_x) = \Phi\langle \overleftarrow{\mathsf{X}}\varphi\rangle_x \vee \Phi\langle \underline{\overleftarrow{\mathsf{X}}}\varphi\rangle_x$$

$$\mathcal{A}_\exists(\{q\}, 1, \mathsf{X}q = \psi \vee \varphi \wedge q, \Phi\langle \psi \vee \varphi \wedge q\rangle_x) = \Phi\langle[\varphi\ \overleftarrow{\mathsf{U}}\ \psi]\rangle_x \vee \Phi\langle[\varphi\ \underline{\overleftarrow{\mathsf{U}}}\ \psi]\rangle_x$$

$$\mathcal{A}_\exists(\{q\}, 1, q = \psi \vee \varphi \wedge \mathsf{X}q, \Phi\langle q\rangle_x) = \Phi\langle[\varphi\ \mathsf{U}\ \psi]\rangle_x \vee \Phi\langle[\varphi\ \underline{\mathsf{U}}\ \psi]\rangle_x$$

As strong and weak operators fulfill exactly the same recursion laws, they can not be distinguished by transition relations alone. The next theorem shows that we can select the strong or the weak variant by either adding suitable initialization conditions or fairness constraints (for past and future operators, respectively).

[5] A simple rewriting procedure would however blow-up the formula which is not necessary when the translation procedures directly support the full logics [28].

Theorem 2 (Translating Temporal Logic to ω-Automata). *Given a formula Φ, a variable x, and propositional formulas φ and ψ, the following equations are valid:*

$$
\begin{aligned}
\Phi\langle \overleftarrow{\mathsf{X}}\varphi\rangle_x &= \mathcal{A}_\exists\left(\{q\}, q, \mathsf{X}q = \varphi, \Phi\langle q\rangle_x\right)\\
\Phi\langle \underline{\overleftarrow{\mathsf{X}}}\varphi\rangle_x &= \mathcal{A}_\exists\left(\{q\}, \neg q, \mathsf{X}q = \varphi, \Phi\langle q\rangle_x\right)\\
\Phi\langle[\varphi\ \overleftarrow{\mathsf{U}}\ \psi]\rangle_x &= \mathcal{A}_\exists\left(\{q\}, q, \mathsf{X}q = \psi \vee \varphi \wedge q, \Phi\langle \psi \vee \varphi \wedge q\rangle_x\right)\\
\Phi\langle[\varphi\ \underline{\overleftarrow{\mathsf{U}}}\ \psi]\rangle_x &= \mathcal{A}_\exists\left(\{q\}, \neg q, \mathsf{X}q = \psi \vee \varphi \wedge q, \Phi\langle \psi \vee \varphi \wedge q\rangle_x\right)\\
\Phi\langle \mathsf{X}\varphi\rangle_x &= \mathcal{A}_\exists\left(\{q\}, 1, q = \mathsf{X}\varphi, \Phi\langle q\rangle_x\right)\\
\Phi\langle[\varphi\ \mathsf{U}\ \psi]\rangle_x &= \mathcal{A}_\exists\left(\{q\}, 1, q = \psi \vee \varphi \wedge \mathsf{X}q, \Phi\langle q\rangle_x \wedge \mathsf{GF}[\varphi \rightarrow q]\right)\\
\Phi\langle[\varphi\ \underline{\mathsf{U}}\ \psi]\rangle_x &= \mathcal{A}_\exists\left(\{q\}, 1, q = \psi \vee \varphi \wedge \mathsf{X}q, \Phi\langle q\rangle_x \wedge \mathsf{GF}[q \rightarrow \psi]\right)
\end{aligned}
$$

There is a subtlety concerning the X operator: If φ contains occurrences of input variables, the transition relation of the automaton refers to the next input, which is normally not allowed for automata[6]. Theorem 2 can already be used to translate any temporal logic formula Φ to an equivalent ω-automaton $\mathfrak{A}_\Phi$, if the laws are applied in a bottom-up traversal over the syntax tree of Φ to abbreviate any elementary formula by a propositional one [29].

Theorem 3 (Basic Translation). *Given any formula $\Phi \in \mathsf{LTL}$, the laws given in theorem 2 can be used to compute an equivalent* $\mathsf{NDet}_{\mathsf{Streett}}$ *automaton $\mathfrak{A}$ in time $O(|\Phi|)$.*

A machine-checked proof of the above theorem can be found in [29]; the sources are available in the newest HOL98 distributions. Although the automaton may have in the worst case $O(2^{|\Phi|})$ states, we still compute it in linear time, since we use a *symbolic representation*, that is directly usable for symbolic model checking.

5 Improving the Basic Translation

5.1 Exploiting the Monotonicity of Temporal Operators

Reconsider the translation procedure of the previous section: If we omit the fairness constraints, then we leave it unspecified whether the operator that is on top of the abbreviated formula was a weak or a strong one: For example, the automaton formula $\mathcal{A}_\exists\left(\{q\}, 1, q = \psi \vee \varphi \wedge \mathsf{X}q, \Phi\langle q\rangle_x\right)$ is equivalent to $\Phi\langle[\varphi\ \mathsf{U}\ \psi]\rangle_x \vee \Phi\langle[\varphi\ \underline{\mathsf{U}}\ \psi]\rangle_x$ (cf. theorem 1). Our aim is therefore to find a simple condition so that $\Phi\langle[\varphi\ \mathsf{U}\ \psi]\rangle_x \vee \Phi\langle[\varphi\ \underline{\mathsf{U}}\ \psi]\rangle_x = \Phi\langle[\varphi\ \mathsf{U}\ \psi]\rangle_x$ holds. As $p \vee q = q$ is equivalent to $p \rightarrow q$, it follows that we must find a criterion for Φ so that $\Phi\langle[\varphi\ \underline{\mathsf{U}}\ \psi]\rangle_x \rightarrow \Phi\langle[\varphi\ \mathsf{U}\ \psi]\rangle_x$ holds. As $[\varphi\ \underline{\mathsf{U}}\ \psi] \rightarrow [\varphi\ \mathsf{U}\ \psi]$ holds, this means in turn that we must study the monotonicity of temporal/Boolean operators (we define the partial order $\varphi \preceq \psi$ as $\models \mathsf{G}[\varphi \rightarrow \psi]$).

It is not difficult to prove that all of our temporal operators are monotonic in all arguments. For example, $\mathsf{G}[\underline{\alpha} \rightarrow \alpha]$, and $\mathsf{G}[\underline{\beta} \rightarrow \beta]$ implies $\mathsf{G}\left([\underline{\alpha}\ \underline{\mathsf{U}}\ \underline{\beta}] \rightarrow [\alpha\ \underline{\mathsf{U}}\ \beta]\right)$. Hence, checking the monotonicity of a temporal formula $\Phi\langle\varphi\rangle_x$ in the argument x reduces to checking whether φ occurs only under an even or odd number of negations. To be precise and concise, we use the notion of positive/negative occurrences in a temporal logic formula: An occurrence is positive/negative iff it appears under an even/odd number of negation symbols (we exclude implications and equivalences at the moment). It is straightforward to prove the following theorem:

[6] The alternative $\Phi\langle \mathsf{X}\varphi\rangle_x = \mathcal{A}_\exists\left(\{q_0, q_1\}, 1, (q_0 = \varphi) \wedge (q_1 = \mathsf{X}q_0), \Phi\langle q_1\rangle_x\right)$ circumvents this.

function $\mathsf{TopProp}_\sigma(\Phi)$
case Φ **of**
$\mathsf{is\_prop}(\Phi)$: **return** $\mathcal{A}_\exists(\{\}, 1, 1, \{\}, \Phi)$;
$\neg\varphi$: $\mathcal{A}_\exists(\mathcal{Q}_\varphi, \mathcal{I}_\varphi, \mathcal{R}_\varphi, \mathcal{F}_\varphi, \varphi') \equiv \mathsf{TopProp}_{\neg\sigma}(\varphi)$;
return $\mathcal{A}_\exists(\mathcal{Q}_\varphi, \mathcal{I}_\varphi, \mathcal{R}_\varphi, \mathcal{F}_\varphi, \neg\varphi')$;
$\varphi \wedge \psi$: $\mathcal{A}_\exists(\mathcal{Q}_\Phi, \mathcal{I}_\Phi, \mathcal{R}_\Phi, \mathcal{F}_\Phi, \varphi' \wedge \psi') \equiv \mathsf{TopProp}_\sigma(\varphi) \times \mathsf{TopProp}_\sigma(\psi)$;
return $\mathcal{A}_\exists(\mathcal{Q}_\Phi, \mathcal{I}_\Phi, \mathcal{R}_\Phi, \mathcal{F}_\Phi, \varphi' \wedge \psi')$;
$\varphi \vee \psi$: $\mathcal{A}_\exists(\mathcal{Q}_\Phi, \mathcal{I}_\Phi, \mathcal{R}_\Phi, \mathcal{F}_\Phi, \varphi' \wedge \psi') \equiv \mathsf{TopProp}_\sigma(\varphi) \times \mathsf{TopProp}_\sigma(\psi)$;
return $\mathcal{A}_\exists(\mathcal{Q}_\Phi, \mathcal{I}_\Phi, \mathcal{R}_\Phi, \mathcal{F}_\Phi, \varphi' \vee \psi')$;
$\mathsf{X}\varphi$: $\mathcal{A}_\exists(\mathcal{Q}_\varphi, \mathcal{I}_\varphi, \mathcal{R}_\varphi, \mathcal{F}_\varphi, \varphi') \equiv \mathsf{TopProp}_\sigma(\varphi)$; $q = \mathsf{new\_var}$;
return $\mathcal{A}_\exists(\mathcal{Q}_\varphi \cup \{q\}, \mathcal{I}_\varphi, \mathcal{R}_\varphi \wedge (q = \mathsf{X}\varphi'), \mathcal{F}_\varphi, q)$;
$[\varphi \ \mathsf{U}\ \psi]$: $\mathcal{A}_\exists(\mathcal{Q}_\Phi, \mathcal{I}_\Phi, \mathcal{R}_\Phi, \mathcal{F}_\Phi, \varphi' \wedge \psi') \equiv \mathsf{TopProp}_\sigma(\varphi) \times \mathsf{TopProp}_\sigma(\psi)$;
$q = \mathsf{new\_var}$; $\mathcal{R}_q = [q = \psi' \vee \varphi' \wedge \mathsf{X}q]$;
$\mathcal{F}_q$ = **if** σ **then** $\{\}$ **else** $\{\mathsf{GF}[\varphi' \rightarrow q]\}$;
return $\mathcal{A}_\exists(\mathcal{Q}_\Phi \cup \{q\}, \mathcal{I}_\Phi, \mathcal{R}_\Phi \wedge \mathcal{R}_q, \mathcal{F}_\Phi \cup \mathcal{F}_q, q)$;
$[\varphi \ \underline{\mathsf{U}}\ \psi]$: $\mathcal{A}_\exists(\mathcal{Q}_\Phi, \mathcal{I}_\Phi, \mathcal{R}_\Phi, \mathcal{F}_\Phi, \varphi' \wedge \psi') \equiv \mathsf{TopProp}_\sigma(\varphi) \times \mathsf{TopProp}_\sigma(\psi)$;
$q = \mathsf{new\_var}$; $\mathcal{R}_q = [q = \psi' \vee \varphi' \wedge \mathsf{X}q]$;
$\mathcal{F}_q$ = **if** σ **then** $\{\mathsf{GF}[q \rightarrow \psi']\}$ **else** $\{\}$;
return $\mathcal{A}_\exists(\mathcal{Q}_\Phi \cup \{q\}, \mathcal{I}_\Phi, \mathcal{R}_\Phi \wedge \mathcal{R}_q, \mathcal{F}_\Phi \cup \mathcal{F}_q, q)$;
$\overleftarrow{\mathsf{X}}\varphi$: $\mathcal{A}_\exists(\mathcal{Q}_\varphi, \mathcal{I}_\varphi, \mathcal{R}_\varphi, \mathcal{F}_\varphi, \varphi') \equiv \mathsf{TopProp}_\sigma(\varphi)$; $q = \mathsf{new\_var}$;
return $\mathcal{A}_\exists(\mathcal{Q}_\varphi \cup \{q\}, \mathcal{I}_\varphi \wedge q, \mathcal{R}_\varphi \wedge (\mathsf{X}q = \varphi'), \mathcal{F}_\varphi, q)$;
$\underline{\overleftarrow{\mathsf{X}}}\varphi$: $\mathcal{A}_\exists(\mathcal{Q}_\varphi, \mathcal{I}_\varphi, \mathcal{R}_\varphi, \mathcal{F}_\varphi, \varphi') \equiv \mathsf{TopProp}_\sigma(\varphi)$; $q = \mathsf{new\_var}$;
return $\mathcal{A}_\exists(\mathcal{Q}_\varphi \cup \{q\}, \mathcal{I}_\varphi \wedge \neg q, \mathcal{R}_\varphi \wedge (\mathsf{X}q = \varphi'), \mathcal{F}_\varphi, q)$;
$[\varphi \ \overleftarrow{\mathsf{U}}\ \psi]$: $\mathcal{A}_\exists(\mathcal{Q}_\Phi, \mathcal{I}_\Phi, \mathcal{R}_\Phi, \mathcal{F}_\Phi, \varphi' \wedge \psi') \equiv \mathsf{TopProp}_\sigma(\varphi) \times \mathsf{TopProp}_\sigma(\psi)$;
$q = \mathsf{new\_var}$; $r_q = \psi' \vee \varphi' \wedge q$; $\mathcal{R}_q = [\mathsf{X}q = r_q]$;
return $\mathcal{A}_\exists(\mathcal{Q}_\Phi \cup \{q\}, \mathcal{I}_\Phi \wedge q, \mathcal{R}_\Phi \wedge \mathcal{R}_q, \mathcal{F}_\Phi, r_q)$;
$[\varphi \ \underline{\overleftarrow{\mathsf{U}}}\ \psi]$: $\mathcal{A}_\exists(\mathcal{Q}_\Phi, \mathcal{I}_\Phi, \mathcal{R}_\Phi, \mathcal{F}_\Phi, \varphi' \wedge \psi') \equiv \mathsf{TopProp}_\sigma(\varphi) \times \mathsf{TopProp}_\sigma(\psi)$;
$q = \mathsf{new\_var}$; $r_q = \psi' \vee \varphi' \wedge q$; $\mathcal{R}_q = [\mathsf{X}q = r_q]$;
return $\mathcal{A}_\exists(\mathcal{Q}_\Phi \cup \{q\}, \mathcal{I}_\Phi \wedge \neg q, \mathcal{R}_\Phi \wedge \mathcal{R}_q, \mathcal{F}_\Phi, r_q)$;
end case
end function

Fig. 1. Improving the Translation from Temporal Logic to ω-Automata by Considering the Monotonicity of Operators

Theorem 4 (Translation to ω-Automata wrt. Positive/Negative Occurrences). *Given a formula Φ, a variable x, and propositional formulas φ and ψ. Then the following equation is generally valid, provided that any occurrence of x in Φ is positive:*

$$\Phi\langle[\varphi\ \mathsf{U}\ \psi]\rangle_x = \mathcal{A}_\exists(\{q\}, 1, q = \psi \vee \varphi \wedge \mathsf{X}q, \Phi\langle q\rangle_x)$$

If, on the other hand, any occurrence of x in Φ is negative, then the following holds:

$$\Phi\langle[\varphi\ \underline{\mathsf{U}}\ \psi]\rangle_x = \mathcal{A}_\exists(\{q\}, 1, q = \psi \vee \varphi \wedge \mathsf{X}q, \Phi\langle q\rangle_x)$$

Hence, fairness constraints need not be generated for positive/negative occurrences of weak/strong temporal future operators. This improves the translations of [3,6,18,29], however, [8] already uses this improvement. An algorithm is given in Figure 1, where σ

denotes the signum of the occurrence. For convenience, we extended automaton formulas in the algorithm by an additional argument for the constraints: $\mathcal{A}_\exists(\mathcal{Q}, \mathcal{I}, \mathcal{R}, \mathcal{F}, \Phi) = \mathcal{A}_\exists\left(\mathcal{Q}, \mathcal{I}, \mathcal{R}, \Phi \wedge \bigwedge_{\xi \in \mathcal{F}} \xi\right)$, and $\mathcal{A}_\exists(Q_1, \mathcal{I}_1, \mathcal{R}_1, \mathcal{F}_1, \Phi_1) \times \mathcal{A}_\exists(Q_2, \mathcal{I}_2, \mathcal{R}_2, \mathcal{F}_2, \Phi_2)$ is defined as $\mathcal{A}_\exists(Q_1 \cup Q_2, \mathcal{I}_1 \wedge \mathcal{I}_2, \mathcal{R}_1 \wedge \mathcal{R}_2, \mathcal{F}_1 \cup \mathcal{F}_2, \Phi_1 \wedge \Phi_2)$.

Theorem 5 (Correctness of $\mathsf{TopProp}_\sigma(\Phi)$). *For any $\Phi \in \mathsf{LTL}$ and the automaton formula $\mathcal{A}_\exists(\mathcal{Q}, \mathcal{I}, \mathcal{R}, \mathcal{F}, \Phi_0) = \mathsf{TopProp}_\sigma(\Phi)$ obtained by the algorithm given in Figure 1, we have the following facts:*

(1) $\mathsf{TopProp}_\sigma(\Phi)$ *runs in time* $O(|\Phi|)$.
(2) Φ_0 *is propositional.*
(3) *Each* ξ_i *is of the form* $\mathsf{GF}\xi_i'$ *where* ξ_i' *is propositional.*
(4) *For* $\sigma = 1$, *the equation* $\Phi = \mathcal{A}_\exists(\mathcal{Q}, \mathcal{I}, \mathcal{R}, \mathcal{F}, \Phi_0)$ *is initially valid.*
(5) *For* $\sigma = 0$, *the equation* $\neg\Phi = \mathcal{A}_\exists(\mathcal{Q}, \mathcal{I}, \mathcal{R}, \mathcal{F}, \neg\Phi_0)$ *is initially valid.*

5.2 Considering Finite Intervals of Interest

We have seen above that the basic translation as given in Section 4 can be improved by exploiting the monotonicity of operators. This allows one to avoid the introduction of fairness constraints for all positive/negative occurrences of weak/strong operators. As a second improvement, we will now show that in the remaining situations, the operator strength can often be fixed by a simpler *reachability constraint* of the form $\mathsf{F}\varphi$ instead of a more expensive fairness constraint $\mathsf{GF}\varphi$.

The key is thereby the following: Assume Φ contains only positive/negative occurrences of strong/weak temporal future operators. For any path π with $(\mathcal{K}, \pi, 0) \models \Phi$, we must evaluate the subformulas of Φ *for only finitely many points of time*, i.e., all models of Φ do only depend on a finite prefix. Hence, it is not necessary to define state variables q_φ and q_ψ such that the equations $q_\varphi = \varphi$ and $q_\psi = \psi$ hold *for all points of time*. Instead, it is completely sufficient that these equations hold long enough, i.e., for some finite interval. The key to our next improvement is therefore the following lemma:

Lemma 1 (Solutions of $q = \psi \vee \varphi \wedge \mathsf{X}q$). *Given that the formula $\mathsf{G}[q = \psi \vee \varphi \wedge \mathsf{X}q]$ initially holds, then the following equations initially holds:*

$$\mathsf{G}\left[(\mathsf{F}(q \rightarrow \psi)) \rightarrow \left(\overleftarrow{\mathsf{G}}(q = [\varphi\ \underline{\mathsf{U}}\ \psi])\right)\right] \qquad \mathsf{G}[(\neg\mathsf{F}(q \rightarrow \psi)) \rightarrow (\mathsf{G}(q = [\varphi\ \mathsf{U}\ \psi]))]$$

This lemma is used as follows: Whenever a state variable q always satisfies the fixpoint equation $q = \psi \vee \varphi \wedge \mathsf{X}q$, and at some point of time $\mathsf{F}(q \rightarrow \psi)$ holds, then it follows that q is uniquely defined up to this point of time, since $q = [\varphi\ \underline{\mathsf{U}}\ \psi]$ holds up to this point of time. Hence, we can still abbreviate an elementary subformula $[\varphi\ \underline{\mathsf{U}}\ \psi]$ with a new state variable q by adding the equation $q = \psi \vee \varphi \wedge \mathsf{X}q$ to the transition relation. At the end of the interval I where we need to evaluate $[\varphi\ \underline{\mathsf{U}}\ \psi]$, we demand that $\mathsf{F}(q \rightarrow \psi)$ must hold (this can always be demanded, since $\mathsf{F}([\varphi\ \underline{\mathsf{U}}\ \psi] \rightarrow \psi)$ is generally valid).

It remains to define for each subformula the maximal point of time, where it must be evaluated. It is to be noted that nestings of temporal operators extend these intervals, since at the end of the interval of the outermost operator, we need to evaluate the inner ones. An algorithm that keeps track of this, is given in Figure 2.

function $\mathsf{BorelFG}_\sigma(\Phi)$
  case Φ **of**
  $\mathsf{is\_prop}(\Phi)$: **return** $\mathcal{A}_\exists(\{\}, 1, 1, \{\}, \Phi)$;
  $\neg\varphi$: $\mathcal{A}_\exists(\mathcal{Q}_\varphi, \mathcal{I}_\varphi, \mathcal{R}_\varphi, \mathcal{F}_\varphi, \varphi') \equiv \mathsf{BorelFG}_{\neg\sigma}(\varphi)$;
    return $\mathcal{A}_\exists(\mathcal{Q}_\varphi, \mathcal{I}_\varphi, \mathcal{R}_\varphi, \mathcal{F}_\varphi, \neg\varphi')$;
  $\varphi \wedge \psi$: $\mathcal{A}_\exists(\mathcal{Q}_\Phi, \mathcal{I}_\Phi, \mathcal{R}_\Phi, \mathcal{F}_\Phi, \varphi' \wedge \psi') \equiv \mathsf{BorelFG}_\sigma(\varphi) \times \mathsf{BorelFG}_\sigma(\psi)$;
    return $\mathcal{A}_\exists(\mathcal{Q}_\Phi, \mathcal{I}_\Phi, \mathcal{R}_\Phi, \mathcal{F}_\Phi, \varphi' \wedge \psi')$;
  $\varphi \vee \psi$: $\mathcal{A}_\exists(\mathcal{Q}_\Phi, \mathcal{I}_\Phi, \mathcal{R}_\Phi, \mathcal{F}_\Phi, \varphi' \wedge \psi') \equiv \mathsf{BorelFG}_\sigma(\varphi) \times \mathsf{BorelFG}_\sigma(\psi)$;
    return $\mathcal{A}_\exists(\mathcal{Q}_\Phi, \mathcal{I}_\Phi, \mathcal{R}_\Phi, \mathcal{F}_\Phi, \varphi' \vee \psi')$;
  $\mathsf{X}\varphi$: $\mathcal{A}_\exists(\mathcal{Q}_\varphi, \mathcal{I}_\varphi, \mathcal{R}_\varphi, \mathcal{F}_\varphi, \varphi') \equiv \mathsf{BorelFG}_\sigma(\varphi)$; $q = \mathsf{new\_var}$;
    if $\mathcal{F}_\varphi \neq \{\}$ **then** $\mathcal{F}_\varphi := \{\mathsf{X} \bigwedge_{\xi \in \mathcal{F}_\Phi} \xi\}$ **end**;
    return $\mathcal{A}_\exists(\mathcal{Q}_\varphi \cup \{q\}, \mathcal{I}_\varphi, \mathcal{R}_\varphi \wedge (q = \mathsf{X}\varphi'), \mathcal{F}_\varphi, q)$;
  $[\varphi\ \mathsf{U}\ \psi]$: $\mathcal{A}_\exists(\mathcal{Q}_\Phi, \mathcal{I}_\Phi, \mathcal{R}_\Phi, \mathcal{F}_\Phi, \varphi' \wedge \psi') \equiv \mathsf{BorelFG}_\sigma(\varphi) \times \mathsf{BorelFG}_\sigma(\psi)$;
    $q = \mathsf{new\_var}$; $\mathcal{R}_q = [q = \psi' \vee \varphi' \wedge \mathsf{X}q]$;
    $\mathcal{F}_q$ = **if** σ **then** $\{\}$ **else** $\left\{\mathsf{F}\left[(\varphi' \to q) \wedge \bigwedge_{\xi \in \mathcal{F}_\Phi} \xi\right]\right\}$;
    return $\mathcal{A}_\exists(\mathcal{Q}_\Phi \cup \{q\}, \mathcal{I}_\Phi, \mathcal{R}_\Phi \wedge \mathcal{R}_q, \mathcal{F}_q, q)$;
  $[\varphi\ \underline{\mathsf{U}}\ \psi]$: $\mathcal{A}_\exists(\mathcal{Q}_\Phi, \mathcal{I}_\Phi, \mathcal{R}_\Phi, \mathcal{F}_\Phi, \varphi' \wedge \psi') \equiv \mathsf{BorelFG}_\sigma(\varphi) \times \mathsf{BorelFG}_\sigma(\psi)$;
    $q = \mathsf{new\_var}$; $\mathcal{R}_q = [q = \psi' \vee \varphi' \wedge \mathsf{X}q]$;
    $\mathcal{F}_q$ = **if** σ **then** $\left\{\mathsf{F}\left[(q \to \psi') \wedge \bigwedge_{\xi \in \mathcal{F}_\Phi} \xi\right]\right\}$ **else** $\{\}$;
    return $\mathcal{A}_\exists(\mathcal{Q}_\Phi \cup \{q\}, \mathcal{I}_\Phi, \mathcal{R}_\Phi \wedge \mathcal{R}_q, \mathcal{F}_q, q)$;
  $\overleftarrow{\mathsf{X}}\varphi$: $\mathcal{A}_\exists(\mathcal{Q}_\varphi, \mathcal{I}_\varphi, \mathcal{R}_\varphi, \mathcal{F}_\varphi, \varphi') \equiv \mathsf{BorelFG}_\sigma(\varphi)$; $q = \mathsf{new\_var}$;
    return $\mathcal{A}_\exists(\mathcal{Q}_\varphi \cup \{q\}, \mathcal{I}_\varphi \wedge q, \mathcal{R}_\varphi \wedge (\mathsf{X}q = \varphi'), \mathcal{F}_\varphi, q)$;
  $\underline{\overleftarrow{\mathsf{X}}}\varphi$: $\mathcal{A}_\exists(\mathcal{Q}_\varphi, \mathcal{I}_\varphi, \mathcal{R}_\varphi, \mathcal{F}_\varphi, \varphi') \equiv \mathsf{BorelFG}_\sigma(\varphi)$; $q = \mathsf{new\_var}$;
    return $\mathcal{A}_\exists(\mathcal{Q}_\varphi \cup \{q\}, \mathcal{I}_\varphi \wedge \neg q, \mathcal{R}_\varphi \wedge (\mathsf{X}q = \varphi'), \mathcal{F}_\varphi, q)$;
  $[\varphi\ \overleftarrow{\mathsf{U}}\ \psi]$: $\mathcal{A}_\exists(\mathcal{Q}_\Phi, \mathcal{I}_\Phi, \mathcal{R}_\Phi, \mathcal{F}_\Phi, \varphi' \wedge \psi') \equiv \mathsf{BorelFG}_\sigma(\varphi) \times \mathsf{BorelFG}_\sigma(\psi)$;
    $q = \mathsf{new\_var}$; $r_q = \psi' \vee \varphi' \wedge q$; $\mathcal{R}_q = [\mathsf{X}q = r_q]$;
    return $\mathcal{A}_\exists(\mathcal{Q}_\Phi \cup \{q\}, \mathcal{I}_\Phi \wedge q, \mathcal{R}_\Phi \wedge \mathcal{R}_q, \mathcal{F}_\Phi, r_q)$;
  $[\varphi\ \underline{\overleftarrow{\mathsf{U}}}\ \psi]$: $\mathcal{A}_\exists(\mathcal{Q}_\Phi, \mathcal{I}_\Phi, \mathcal{R}_\Phi, \mathcal{F}_\Phi, \varphi' \wedge \psi') \equiv \mathsf{BorelFG}_\sigma(\varphi) \times \mathsf{BorelFG}_\sigma(\psi)$;
    $q = \mathsf{new\_var}$; $r_q = \psi' \vee \varphi' \wedge q$; $\mathcal{R}_q = [\mathsf{X}q = r_q]$;
    return $\mathcal{A}_\exists(\mathcal{Q}_\Phi \cup \{q\}, \mathcal{I}_\Phi \wedge \neg q, \mathcal{R}_\Phi \wedge \mathcal{R}_q, \mathcal{F}_\Phi, r_q)$;
  end case
end function

Fig. 2. Considering Finite Intervals of Interest

Theorem 6 (Correctness of $\mathsf{BorelFG}_\sigma(\Phi)$). *For any $\Phi \in \mathsf{TL}_{\mathsf{FG}}$ and the automaton formula $\mathcal{A}_\exists(\mathcal{Q}, \mathcal{I}, \mathcal{R}, \mathcal{F}, \Phi_0) = \mathsf{BorelFG}_\sigma(\Phi)$ obtained by the algorithm of Figure 2, the following holds:*

(1) $\mathsf{BorelFG}_\sigma(\Phi)$ *runs in time* $O(|\Phi|)$.
(2) Φ_0 *is propositional.*
(3) *Each $\xi \in \mathcal{F}$ can be derived from the nonterminal C_{F} by the following grammar:*

$$P_{\mathsf{Prop}} ::= \mathcal{V} \mid \neg P_{\mathsf{Prop}} \mid P_{\mathsf{Prop}} \wedge P_{\mathsf{Prop}} \mid P_{\mathsf{Prop}} \vee P_{\mathsf{Prop}} \mid P_{\mathsf{Prop}} \to P_{\mathsf{Prop}}$$
$$C_{\mathsf{F}} ::= \mathsf{F} P_{\mathsf{Prop}} \mid \mathsf{F}(P_{\mathsf{Prop}} \wedge C_{\mathsf{F}}) \mid \mathsf{X} C_{\mathsf{F}} \mid C_{\mathsf{F}} \wedge C_{\mathsf{F}}$$

(4) *For $\sigma = 1$, the equation $\Phi = \mathcal{A}_\exists(\mathcal{Q}, \mathcal{I}, \mathcal{R}, \mathcal{F}, \Phi_0)$ is initially valid.*
(5) *For $\sigma = 0$, the equation $\neg\Phi = \mathcal{A}_\exists(\mathcal{Q}, \mathcal{I}, \mathcal{R}, \mathcal{F}, \neg\Phi_0)$ is initially valid.*

For example, the formula $[[\varphi\ \underline{\mathsf{U}}\ \psi]\ \underline{\mathsf{U}}\ \gamma]$ is translated by introducing new state variables p,q with appropriate transition relations and the reachability constraint $\mathcal{F} = \{\mathsf{F}\,[(q \to \gamma) \wedge \mathsf{F}(p \to \psi)]\}$. For the proof of the above theorem, we used initially valid formulas of the following form to establish the invariants:

$$\left(\begin{array}{l}\mathsf{G}(\varphi \to \varphi_0) \wedge \mathsf{G}\left(\zeta_\varphi \to \overleftarrow{\mathsf{G}}\,[\varphi_0 = \varphi]\right) \wedge \\ \mathsf{G}(\psi \to \psi_0) \wedge \mathsf{G}\left(\zeta_\psi \to \overleftarrow{\mathsf{G}}\,[\psi_0 = \psi]\right) \wedge \\ \mathsf{G}\,[q = \psi_0 \vee \varphi_0 \wedge \mathsf{X}q] \to \mathsf{G}\left(\mathsf{F}\,([q \to \psi_0] \wedge \zeta_\varphi \wedge \zeta_\psi) \to \overleftarrow{\mathsf{G}}\ (q = [\varphi\ \underline{\mathsf{U}}\ \psi])\right)\end{array}\right)$$

The above formula is used in the induction step for $[\varphi\ \underline{\mathsf{U}}\ \psi]$. ζ_φ and ζ_ψ are thereby the reachability constraints that have been obtained from the translation of the subformulas φ and ψ. Due to the definition of $\mathsf{TL}_{\mathsf{FG}}$, we always have the monotonicity conditions $\mathsf{G}(\varphi \to \varphi_0)$ and $\mathsf{G}(\psi \to \psi_0)$, so that the conjunction of the transition relation with $q = \psi_0 \vee \varphi_0 \wedge \mathsf{X}q$ will fix q as desired whenever $\mathsf{F}\,([q \to \psi_0] \wedge \zeta_\varphi \wedge \zeta_\psi)$ holds.

5.3 Translation by Closures

The automaton obtained by the function BorelFG does not right fall into one of the automaton classes. However, it is easily seen that we can reduce it to either a NDet_F or an $\mathsf{NDet}_{\mathsf{FG}}$ automaton. For reasons of efficiency[7], we choose the latter class for a further translation. This further translation is based on a simple bottom-up rewriting with the equations of the following lemma:

Lemma 2 (Closures of $\mathsf{NDet}_{\mathsf{FG}}$). *Given a propositional formula φ, and $\mathsf{NDet}_{\mathsf{FG}}$ automata $\mathfrak{A}_\Phi = \mathcal{A}_\exists\,(Q_\Phi, \Phi_\mathcal{I}, \Phi_\mathcal{R}, \mathsf{FG}\Phi_\mathcal{F})$ and $\mathfrak{A}_\Psi = \mathcal{A}_\exists\,(Q_\Psi, \Psi_\mathcal{I}, \Psi_\mathcal{R}, \mathsf{FG}\Psi_\mathcal{F})$ with $Q_\Phi \cap Q_\Psi = \{\}$, the following equations are generally valid:*

- $\mathsf{F}\varphi = \mathcal{A}_\exists\,(\{q\}, \neg q, [\neg q \wedge \neg\varphi \wedge \neg\mathsf{X}q] \vee [\neg q \wedge \varphi \wedge \mathsf{X}q] \vee [q \wedge \mathsf{X}q]\,, \mathsf{FG}q)$
- $\mathsf{F}\,(\varphi \wedge \mathfrak{A}_\Phi) = \mathcal{A}_\exists \left(\begin{array}{l} Q \cup \{p\}, \neg p \vee \Phi_\mathcal{I}, \\ [\neg p \wedge \neg\mathsf{X}p] \vee \\ [\neg p \wedge \mathsf{X}\,(p \wedge \Phi_\mathcal{I} \wedge \varphi)] \vee \\ [p \wedge \Phi_\mathcal{R} \wedge \mathsf{X}p]\,, \\ \mathsf{FG}(p \wedge \Phi_\mathcal{F}) \end{array}\right)$
- $\mathsf{X}\,[\mathfrak{A}_\Phi] = \mathcal{A}_\exists \left(\begin{array}{l} Q \cup \{p\}, \neg p, \\ [\neg p \wedge \mathsf{X}p \wedge \mathsf{X}\Phi_\mathcal{I}] \vee [p \wedge \Phi_\mathcal{R} \wedge \mathsf{X}p]\,, \\ \mathsf{FG}\Phi_\mathcal{F} \end{array}\right)$
- $\varphi \wedge \mathfrak{A}_\Phi = \mathcal{A}_\exists\,(Q_\Phi, \Phi_\mathcal{I} \wedge \varphi, \Phi_\mathcal{R}, \mathsf{FG}\Phi_\mathcal{F})$
- $\mathfrak{A}_\Phi \wedge \mathfrak{A}_\Psi = \mathcal{A}_\exists\,(Q_\Phi \cup Q_\Psi, \Phi_\mathcal{I} \wedge \Psi_\mathcal{I}, \Phi_\mathcal{R} \wedge \Psi_\mathcal{R}, \mathsf{FG}(\Phi_\mathcal{F} \wedge \Psi_\mathcal{F}))$

The above equations are not hard to prove. The reader is asked to draw the transition systems to convince himself/herself of the correctness. *Using* BorelFG *and the above closures, we can now translate any* $\mathsf{TL}_{\mathsf{FG}}$ *formula to an equivalent* $\mathsf{NDet}_{\mathsf{FG}}$ *automaton with linear runtime and memory requirements (cf. Figure 3).*

---

[7] We only need the conjunction of automata, and never the disjunction. As $\mathsf{FG}\varphi \wedge \mathsf{FG}\psi = \mathsf{FG}\,(\varphi \wedge \psi)$ is valid, we can easily compute the conjunction of $\mathsf{NDet}_{\mathsf{FG}}$ automata, which is not so simple for NDet_F automata.

6 The Final Translation

The algorithms of the previous sections already allow us to efficiently translate any $\mathsf{TL}_{\mathsf{FG}}$ formula to an equivalent $\mathsf{NDet}_{\mathsf{FG}}$ automaton with only linear runtime and memory requirements. This is important since each formula that can be translated to the alternation-free μ-calculus has an equivalent $\mathsf{TL}_{\mathsf{FG}}$ formula, since it can be translated to $\mathsf{NDet}_{\mathsf{FG}}$. Therefore, with symbolic model checking, these formulas can be more efficiently checked than arbitrary LTL formulas, and our experiments show that the verification procedures are almost comparable to CTL model checking (see also [33]).

The translation procedure for $\mathsf{TL}_{\mathsf{FG}}$ can also be used to enhance the translation of arbitrary LTL formulas. To see this, it is convenient to use the notion of *templates*: Φ is a template of Ψ, if Ψ can be obtained from Φ by replacing some occurrences of variables in Φ with some other formulas (Φ matches with Ψ). It is straightforward to compute from any temporal logic formula Φ the largest template that belongs to $\mathsf{TL}_{\mathsf{FG}}$. To perform this computation, we simply traverse the syntax tree of Φ and abbreviate any subformula that violates the grammar rules of $\mathsf{TL}_{\mathsf{FG}}$ by a new state variable by application of TopProp to that subformula (having this view, TopProp is also an extraction procedure that extracts the largest propositional template). The resulting function TopFG is very similar to TopProp, and also runs in linear time [28].

Theorem 7 (Algorithm TopFG). *There is an algorithm TopFG such that for any temporal logic formula $\Phi \in \mathsf{LTL}$, and the automaton formula $\mathcal{A}_\exists(\mathcal{Q},\mathcal{I},\mathcal{R},\mathcal{F},\Phi_0) = \mathsf{TopFG}_\sigma(\Phi)$, the following holds:*

(1) *$\mathsf{TopFG}_\sigma(\Phi)$ runs in time $O(|\Phi|)$.*
(2) *If $\sigma = 1$ holds, we have $\Phi_0 \in \mathsf{TL}_{\mathsf{FG}}$, otherwise, we have $\Phi_0 \in \mathsf{TL}_{\mathsf{GF}}$.*
(3) *Each $\xi \in \mathcal{F}$ is of the form $\mathsf{GF}\xi'$ where ξ' is propositional.*
(4) *For $\sigma = 1$, the equation $\Phi = \mathcal{A}_\exists\left(\mathcal{Q},\mathcal{I},\mathcal{R},\Phi_0 \wedge \bigwedge_{\xi\in\mathcal{F}} \xi\right)$ is initially valid.*
(5) *For $\sigma = 0$, the equation $\neg\Phi = \mathcal{A}_\exists\left(\mathcal{Q},\mathcal{I},\mathcal{R},\neg\Phi_0 \wedge \bigwedge_{\xi\in\mathcal{F}} \xi\right)$ is initially valid.*

Given any formula $\Phi \in \mathsf{LTL}$, we can therefore apply the function TopFG to extract the largest template of Φ that belongs to $\mathsf{TL}_{\mathsf{FG}}$. This template is then translated by BorelFG and the closure equations to an equivalent $\mathsf{NDet}_{\mathsf{FG}}$ automaton (without fairness constraints). Note that TopFG still introduces fairness constraints, but BorelFG does not.

This translation procedure can be further improved. To explain this, we need to note that the final automaton problems can be reduced to fair CTL model checking problems due to the following lemma, where E is the existential path quantifier ($\mathsf{E}\varphi$ holds on a state s if there is a fair path starting in s that satisfies φ):

Lemma 3 (Reducing ω-Automata Model Checking to CTL Model Checking). *Given an automaton formula $\mathfrak{A} = \mathcal{A}_\exists(\mathcal{Q},\mathcal{I},\mathcal{R},\mathcal{F})$ so that $\mathcal{F}$ does not contain past temporal operators. Then, the following is equivalent for any structure $\mathcal{K}$, and any state s of $\mathcal{K}$:*

- $(\mathcal{K}, s) \models \mathsf{E}\mathcal{A}_\exists(\mathcal{Q},\mathcal{I},\mathcal{R},\mathcal{F})$
- *there is a $\vartheta \subseteq \mathcal{Q} \cup \mathcal{V}$ such that $(\mathcal{K} \times \mathcal{K}_{\mathfrak{A}}, (s,\vartheta)) \models \mathcal{I} \wedge \mathsf{E}\mathcal{F}$ and $\mathcal{L}(s) = \vartheta \cap \mathcal{V}$*

```
function Automaton(OnlyMono, useBorel, toCTL, Φ)
  if OnlyMono then return TopProp₁(Φ) end;
  A∃ (Q0, I0, R0, F0, Φ0) ≡ TopFG₁(Φ);
  if useBorel then // translate to reachability automaton
    A∃ (Q1, I1, R1, F1, Φ1) ≡ BorelFG₁(Φ0);
    I1 := I1 ∧ Φ1;
    Φ1 := ⋀_{ξ∈F1} ξ;
  else // extract top-level TL_PE formula
    A∃ (Q1, I1, R1, Φ1) ≡ TopPE₁(Φ0);
  end;
  // in any case, we now have Φ1 ∈ TL_PE
  if toCTL then // translate to CTL
    Φ2 := LeftCTL2CTL(Φ1);
    return A∃ (Q0 ∪ Q1, I0 ∧ I1, R0 ∧ R1, F0, Φ2);
  else // apply closure theorems
    A∃ (Q2, I2, R2, Φ_FG) ≡ close(Φ1);
    return A∃ (Q0 ∪ Q1 ∪ Q2, I0 ∧ I1 ∧ I2, R0 ∧ R1 ∧ R2, F0, Φ_FG);
end function
```

Fig. 3. The Final Translation from LTL to ω-Automata or CTL Model Checking

Hence a reduction to the standard automaton classes is not necessary. *Instead, a reduction to an 'ω-automaton' $\mathcal{A}_\exists(\mathcal{Q},\mathcal{I},\mathcal{R},\mathcal{F})$ would be sufficient so that $\mathsf{E}\mathcal{F}$ can be easily translated to a* CTL *formula.* For our model checking tool, this view offers another alternative to the translation to simple ω-automata that is already contained in the algorithm of Figure 3: Using $OnlyMono = 1$ will simply call TopProp for the translation. Otherwise, we extract the largest template Φ_0 of Φ that belongs to $\mathsf{TL}_{\mathsf{FG}}$. Using the flag *useBorel*, we then have the choice to either apply BorelFG to compute an automaton $\mathcal{A}_\exists(\mathcal{Q}_1,\mathcal{I}_1,\mathcal{R}_1;\mathcal{F}_1,\Phi_1)$ where Φ_1 is propositional and the constraints of $\mathcal{F}_1$ obey the grammar rules of theorem 6, or to reduce Φ_1 to an automaton $\mathcal{A}_\exists(\mathcal{Q}_1,\mathcal{I}_1,\mathcal{R}_1,\Phi_1)$ where Φ_1 belongs to the following logic $\mathsf{TL}_{\mathsf{PE}}$:

Definition 4 (The Linear Time Fragment of $\mathsf{LeftCTL}^*$ **[26]).** *We define the logics* $\mathsf{TL}_{\mathsf{PE}}$ *and* $\mathsf{TL}_{\mathsf{PA}}$ *by the following grammar rules, where* $\mathsf{TL}_{\mathsf{PE}}$ *and* $\mathsf{TL}_{\mathsf{PA}}$ *are the sets of formulas that can be derived from the nonterminals* P_{PE} *and* P_{PA}*, respectively, where the rules of* P_{Prop} *are given in theorem 6:*

$$\begin{array}{ll} P_{\mathsf{PA}} ::= \mathcal{V} & P_{\mathsf{PE}} ::= \mathcal{V} \\ \quad \mid \neg P_{\mathsf{PE}} \mid P_{\mathsf{PA}} \wedge P_{\mathsf{PA}} \mid P_{\mathsf{PA}} \vee P_{\mathsf{PA}} & \quad \mid \neg P_{\mathsf{PA}} \mid P_{\mathsf{PE}} \wedge P_{\mathsf{PE}} \mid P_{\mathsf{PE}} \vee P_{\mathsf{PE}} \\ \quad \mid \mathsf{X}P_{\mathsf{PA}} \mid \mathsf{G}P_{\mathsf{PA}} \mid \mathsf{F}P_{\mathsf{Prop}} & \quad \mid \mathsf{X}P_{\mathsf{PE}} \mid \mathsf{G}P_{\mathsf{Prop}} \mid \mathsf{F}P_{\mathsf{PE}} \\ \quad \mid [P_{\mathsf{PA}}\ \underline{\mathsf{U}}\ P_{\mathsf{Prop}}] \mid [P_{\mathsf{PA}}\ \mathsf{U}\ P_{\mathsf{Prop}}] & \quad \mid [P_{\mathsf{Prop}}\ \underline{\mathsf{U}}\ P_{\mathsf{PE}}] \mid [P_{\mathsf{Prop}}\ \mathsf{U}\ P_{\mathsf{PE}}] \end{array}$$

Obviously, we have $\mathsf{TL}_{\mathsf{PE}} \subseteq \mathsf{TL}_{\mathsf{FG}}$ and $\mathsf{TL}_{\mathsf{PA}} \subseteq \mathsf{TL}_{\mathsf{GF}}$, and both inclusions are strict. It is therefore possible to modify our function BorelFG to a new procedure TopPE that does not abbreviate all temporal operators until a propositional formula is obtained, but only those that violate the grammar rules of $\mathsf{TL}_{\mathsf{PE}}$ and $\mathsf{TL}_{\mathsf{PA}}$, respectively.

The reason why we want to extract the largest $\mathsf{TL}_{\mathsf{PE}}$ template of a $\mathsf{TL}_{\mathsf{FG}}$ formula is that in [26], it has been shown that all formulas of the form $\mathsf{E}\Phi$ with $\Phi \in \mathsf{TL}_{\mathsf{PE}}$ can be translated to CTL. Note further that the reachability constraints generated by BorelFG do also belong to $\mathsf{TL}_{\mathsf{PE}}$. Therefore, after the application of either BorelFG or $\mathsf{TL}_{\mathsf{PE}}$, we have the choice to either translate by means of closure theorems or by a translation to CTL. This is controlled by the remaining flag *toCTL*.

7 Experimental Results

The presented translation procedures have been implemented in ML as a plug-in for the theorem prover HOL [16] and as a Java Applet that can be accessed[8] via a WWW browser with a Java virtual machine. Some experiments have already been made that have clearly shown that the presented translation procedures often outperform existing tools. To illustrate this with a practical example, we consider the verification of the arbitration process given in [30]. The specification we verified for this arbitration process is the following property that assures that no process is indefinitely ignored [30]:

$$\underbrace{\mathsf{G}\left[\left(\bigvee_{j=1}^{n} \alpha_j\right) \rightarrow \mathsf{XF} f_A\right]}_{\text{termination of access}} \wedge \underbrace{\mathsf{G}\left[\bigwedge_{j=1}^{n} \left(\varrho_j \rightarrow [\varrho_j \,\mathsf{U}\, \alpha_j]\right)\right]}_{\text{persistent requests}} \rightarrow \underbrace{\mathsf{G}\bigwedge_{j=1}^{n} \mathsf{F}\left[\varrho_j \rightarrow \alpha_j\right]}_{\text{fairness}}$$

We have checked this specification using different translation procedures. The memory consumptions and runtime requirements on a Pentium-III@450MHz with 256 MBytes main memory with CMU-SMV 2.4.3 as backend model checker are given in Figure 4.

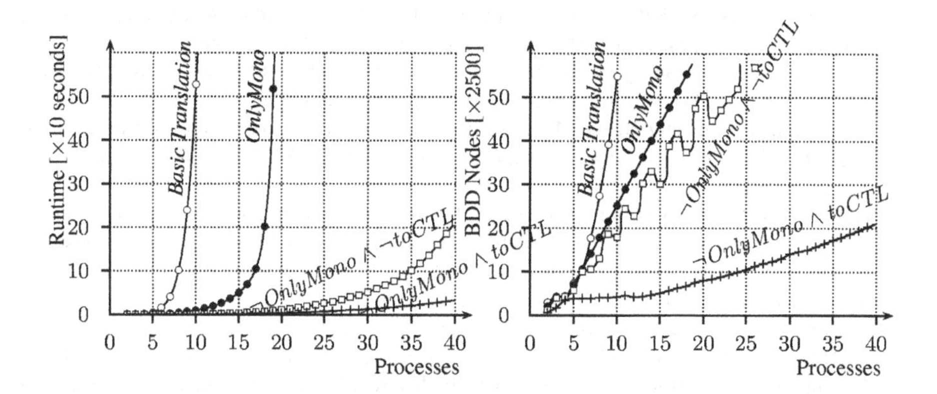

Fig. 4. Experimental data for the verification of the arbitration process

The above results have been obtained by optimized variable orderings. The basic translation introduces $2n + 4$ fairness constraints for n processes, while TopProp will only generate three, and using *useBorel* even none (note that the negation of the specification is translated). Note that all the LTL model checkers of the SMV family, i.e., CMU-SMV [21,6], CADENCE-SMV [22], and NuSMV [4] only use – beneath some other

[8] http://goethe.ira.uka.de/~schneider/my_tools/TempLogicTool

improvements, different from the ones presented here – the basic translation of theorem 3.

We have had similar experiences with other experiments (we checked over 10000 randomly generated LTL formulas with up to 100 operators). We therefore claim that our translations outperform state-of-the-art symbolic model checking tools for LTL.

References

1. R. Bloem, H. Gabow, and F. Somenzi. An algorithm for strongly connected component analysis in $n \log(n)$ symbolic steps. In *International Conference on Formal Methods in Computer Aided Design (FMCAD), LNCS 1954*, pp. 37–54. Springer Verlag, 2000.
2. R. Bloem, K. Ravi, and F. Somenzi. Efficient decision procedures for model checking of linear time logic properties. In *Conference on Computer Aided Verification (CAV), LNCS 1633*, Trento, Italy, 1999. Springer-Verlag.
3. J. Burch, E. Clarke, K. McMillan, D. Dill, and L. Hwang. Symbolic Model Checking: 10^{20} States and Beyond. *Information and Computing*, 98(2):142–170, June 1992.
4. A. Cimatti, E. Clarke, F. Giunchiglia, and M. Roveri. NuSMV: A new symbolic model verifier. In *Conference on Computer Aided Verification (CAV), LNCS 1633*, pp. 495–499, Trento, Italy, 1999. Springer-Verlag.
5. E. Clarke and E. Emerson. Design and Synthesis of Synchronization Skeletons using Branching Time Temporal Logic. In *Workshop on Logics of Programs, LNCS 131*, pp. 52–71, Yorktown Heights, New York, May 1981. Springer-Verlag.
6. E. Clarke, O. Grumberg, and K. Hamaguchi. Another look at LTL model checking. In *Conference on Computer Aided Verification (CAV), LNCS 818*, pp. 415–427, Standford, California, USA, June 1994. Springer-Verlag.
7. R. Cleaveland and B. Steffen. A linear-time model checking algorithm for the alternation-free μ-calculus. *Formal Methods in System Design*, 2(2):121–147, April 1993.
8. J.-M. Couvreur. On-the-fly verification of linear temporal logic. In *FM'99 - Formal Methods, LNCS 1708*, pp. 233–252, Toulouse, France, 1999. Springer Verlag.
9. M. Daniele, F. Giunchiglia, and M. Vardi. Improved automata generation for linear temporal logic. In *Conference on Computer Aided Verification (CAV), LNCS 1633*, Trento, Italy, 1999. Springer-Verlag.
10. E. Emerson. Temporal and Modal Logic. In J. van Leeuwen, editor, *Handbook of Theoretical Computer Science*, volume B, pp. 996–1072, Amsterdam, 1990. Elsevier Science Publishers.
11. E. Emerson and J. Halpern. "sometimes" and "not never" revisited: On branching versus linear time temporal logic. *Journal of the ACM*, 33(1):151–178, January 1986.
12. E. Emerson and C.-L. Lei. Modalities for model checking: Branching time strikes back. In *ACM Symposium on Principles of Programming Languages*, pp. 84–96, New York, 1985.
13. K. Etessami and G. Holzmann. Optimizing Büchi automata. In *International Conference on Concurrency Theory, LNCS 1877*, pp. 153–168. Springer Verlag, 2000.
14. P. Gastin and D. Oddoux. Fast LTL to Büchi automata translation. In *Conference on Computer Aided Verification (CAV), LNCS 2102*, pp. 53–65, Paris, France, 2001. Springer Verlag.
15. R. Gerth, D. Peled, M. Vardi, and P. Wolper. Simple on-the-fly automatic verification of linear temporal logic. In *Protocol Specification, Testing, and Verification (PSTV)*, Warsaw, June 1995. North-Holland.
16. M. Gordon and T. Melham. *Introduction to HOL: A Theorem Proving Environment for Higher Order Logic*. Cambridge University Press, 1993.
17. S. Johnson, P. Miner, and A. Camilleri. Studies of the single pulser in various reasoning systems. In *International Conference on Theorem Provers in Circuit Design (TPCD), LNCS 901*, pp. 126–145, Bad Herrenalb, Germany, September 1994. Springer-Verlag.

18. Y. Kesten, A. Pnueli, and L. Raviv. Algorithmic verification of linear temporal logic specifications. In *Automata, Languages and Programming (ICALP), LNCS 1443*, Aalborg, Denmark, 1998. Springer Verlag.
19. O. Lichtenstein and A. Pnueli. Checking that finite state concurrent programs satisfy their linear specification. In *ACM Symposium on Principles of Programming Languages (POPL)*, pp. 97–107, New York, January 1985. ACM.
20. Z. Manna and A. Pnueli. A hierarchy of temporal properties. In *ACM Symposium on Principles of Distributed Computing*, pp. 377–408, 1990.
21. K. McMillan. *Symbolic Model Checking*. Kluwer Academic Publishers, Norwell Massachusetts, 1993.
22. K. McMillan. Cadence SMV, http://www-cad.eecs.berkeley.edu/~kenmcmil, 2000.
23. M.Y.Vardi and P. Wolper. Reasoning about infinite computations. *Information and Computation*, 115(1):1–37, 1994.
24. A. Pnueli. The temporal logic of programs. In *Symposium on Foundations of Computer Science*, volume 18, pp. 46–57, New York, 1977. IEEE.
25. K. Ravi, R. Bloem, and F. Somenzi. A comparative study of symbolic algorithms for the computation of fair cycles. In *International Conference on Formal Methods in Computer Aided Design (FMCAD), LNCS 1954*. Springer Verlag, 2000.
26. K. Schneider. CTL and equivalent sublanguages of CTL*. In *IFIP Conference on Computer Hardware Description Languages and their Applications (CHDL)*, pp. 40–59, Toledo,Spain, April 1997. IFIP, Chapman and Hall.
27. K. Schneider. Model checking on product structures. In *Formal Methods in Computer-Aided Design, LNCS 1522*, pp. 483–500, Palo Alto, USA, November 1998. Springer Verlag.
28. K. Schneider. *Exploiting Hierarchies in Temporal Logics, Finite Automata, Arithmetics, and μ-Calculus for Efficiently Verifying Reactive Systems*. Habilitation Thesis. University of Karlsruhe, 2001.
29. K. Schneider and D. Hoffmann. A HOL conversion for translating linear time temporal logic to ω-automata. In *Higher Order Logic Theorem Proving and its Applications, LNCS 1690*, pp. 255–272, Nice, France, September 1999. Springer Verlag.
30. K. Schneider and V. Sabelfeld. Introducing mutual exclusion in Esterel. In *Andrei Ershov Third International Conference Perspectives of Systems Informatics, LNCS 1755*, pp. 445–459, Akademgorodok, Novosibirsk, Russia, July 1999. Springer Verlag.
31. F. Somenzi and R. Bloem. Efficient Büchi automata from LTL formulae. In *Conference on Computer Aided Verification, LNCS 1633*, pp. 247–263, Trento, Italy, 2000. Springer-Verlag.
32. W. Thomas. Automata on infinite objects. In J. van Leeuwen, editor, *Handbook of Theoretical Computer Science*, vol. B, pp. 133–191, Amsterdam, 1990. Elsevier Science Publishers.
33. M. Vardi. Branching vs. linear time: Final showdown. In *Tools and Algorithms for the Construction and Analysis of Systems, LNCS 2031*, pp. 1–22, Genova, Italy, 2001. Springer Verlag.
34. M. Vardi and P. Wolper. An automata-theoretic approach to automatic program verification. In *IEEE Symposium on Logic in Computer Science*, pp. 332–344. IEEE Computer Society Press, June 1986.
35. W. Visser, H. Barringer, D. Fellows, G. Gough, and A. Williams. Efficient CTL* model checking for analysis of rainbow designs. In *Conference on Correct Hardware Design and Verification Methods*, Montreal, Canada, October 1997. IFIP WG 10.5, Chapman and Hall.
36. K. Wagner. On ω-regular sets. *Information and control*, 43:123–177, 1979.
37. P. Wolper. Temporal logic can be more expressive. *Information and Control*, 56:72–99, 1983.
38. P. Wolper. Constructing automata from temporal logic formulas: A tutorial. In *Summer School on Formal Methods in Performance Analysis, LNCS 2090*, pp. 261–277. Springer Verlag, 2001.

Local Temporal Logic Is Expressively Complete for Cograph Dependence Alphabets*

Volker Diekert[1] and Paul Gastin[2]

[1] Inst. für Informatik, Universität Stuttgart, Breitwiesenstr. 20-22, D-70565 Stuttgart
diekert@informatik.uni-stuttgart.de
[2] LIAFA, Université Paris 7, 2, place Jussieu, F-75251 Paris Cedex 05
Paul.Gastin@liafa.jussieu.fr

Abstract. Recently, local logics for Mazurkiewicz traces are of increasing interest. This is mainly due to the fact that the satisfiability problem has the same complexity as in the word case. If we focus on a purely local interpretation of formulae at vertices (or events) of a trace, then the satisfiability problem of linear temporal logics over traces turns out to be PSPACE–complete. But now the difficult problem is to obtain expressive completeness results with respect to first order logic.
The main result of the paper shows such an expressive completeness result, if the underlying dependence alphabet is a cograph, i.e., if all traces are series parallel graphs. Moreover, we show that this is the best we can expect in our setting: If the dependence alphabet is not a cograph, then we cannot express all first order properties.

Keywords. Temporal logics, Mazurkiewicz traces, concurrency

1 Introduction

Trace theory, initiated in computer science by Mazurkiewicz [12] is one of the most popular settings to study concurrency. The behavior of a concurrent process is not represented by a string, but more accurately by some labelled partial order.

A suitable way for a formal specification of concurrent systems is given by temporal logic formulae which in turn have a direct (either global or local) interpretation for Mazurkiewicz traces. It is therefore no surprise that temporal logics for traces have received quite an attention, see [1,13,14,15,16,18]. In [17] it was shown that the basic (global) linear temporal logic with future tense operators and with past tense constants is expressively complete with respect to the first order theory of finite and infinite traces (*real traces*). In [3] we have obtained the same result but without any past tense modalities by quite different proof techniques (which will be used here again). This positive result has solved a long standing open question [6,17]. The price of this logic is an extremely difficult satisfiability problem, it has been shown to be non-elementary

* Partial support of EC-FET project IST-1999-29082 (ADVANCE), CEFIPRA-IFCPAR Project 2102-1 (ACSMV) and PROCOPE project 00269SD (MoVe) is gratefully acknowledged.

R. Nieuwenhuis and A. Voronkov (Eds.): LPAR 2001, LNAI 2250, pp. 55–69, 2001.

by Walukiewicz [20]. The main reason for this difficulty is the global interpretation of a formula which makes it necessary to speak about configurations, i.e., we give an interpretation of a formula for a trace with respect to some finite prefix – and the prefix structure of a trace is much more complicated than in the case of linear orders (words). If we give a local interpretation such that each formula can be evaluated at a single vertex (or event), then we obtain logics where the satisfiability problem is still in PSPACE. This is in particular the case for the logic TLC, which has been introduced by Alur et al. in [1]. The logic has been extended and studied in detail by Henriksen in [8,9]. The logic TLC uses an existential version of the until–operator, which is not expressible in first order, in general (Section 5). On the other hand, it seems also too weak to express all first order properties for all dependence alphabets.

In our paper, we shall use a universal version of the until–operator, which, by its very definition, is first order definable. The main result of our paper shows that we obtain a local logic which is expressively complete, if the underlying dependence graph is a cograph, i.e., every trace is a series parallel graph (or N–free). This result is robust, the same holds for TLC or other variants how to define a semantics to the until– operator. Moreover, we show that cographs are in some sense the limit where we can expect such a positive result. As long as we use no past tense modalities we cannot specify all first order properties by our logic, whether or not the until is existential or universal or whether we have both options. Our main theorems (Thms. 2, 3) are therefore *if-and-only-if* statements.

In the final section we will see that a universal until does not change complexity issues very much. The satisfiability problem of TLC augmented by this operator can still be solved in PSPACE.

For lack of space, we cannot give full proofs in this extended abstract.

2 Preliminaries

We briefly recall some notions concerning Mazurkiewicz traces. For the background we refer to [4]. A *dependence alphabet* is a pair (Σ, D) where the alphabet Σ is a finite set and the dependence relation $D \subseteq \Sigma \times \Sigma$ is reflexive and symmetric. The *independence relation* I is the complement of D. For $A \subseteq \Sigma$, we denote $I(A) = \{b \in \Sigma \mid (a,b) \in I \text{ for all } a \in A\}$ the set of letters independent from A and we let $D(A) = \Sigma \setminus I(A)$ be the set of letters depending on (some action in) A.

A *real Mazurkiewicz trace* is (an isomorphism class of) a labelled partial order $t = [V, \leq, \lambda]$ where V is a set of vertices, $\lambda : V \to \Sigma$ is the labelling, $\leq$ is a partial order over V satisfying the following conditions: For all $x \in V$, the downward set $\{y \in V \mid y \leq x\}$ is finite, $(\lambda(x), \lambda(y)) \in D$ implies $x \leq y$ or $y \leq x$, and $x \lessdot y$ implies $(\lambda(x), \lambda(y)) \in D$, where $\lessdot \, = \, < \setminus <^2$ is the direct successor relation in the Hasse diagram of t.

The *alphabet* of the trace t is the set $\mathrm{alph}(t) = \lambda(V) \subseteq \Sigma$ and its *alphabet at infinity* $\mathrm{alphinf}(t)$ is the set of letters occurring infinitely often in t. The set of all traces is denoted by $\mathbb{R}(\Sigma, D)$ or simply by $\mathbb{R}$. A trace t is called *finite*, if V is finite. For $t = [V, \leq, \lambda] \in \mathbb{R}$, we define $\min(t) \subseteq V$ as the set of all minimal vertices of t. We can read $\min(t) \subseteq \Sigma$ also as the set of labels of the minimal vertices of t. It will always be clear from the context what we actually mean. If t is finite, we define $\max(t) \subseteq V$ as the set of all maximal vertices of t and we also use $\max(t) \subseteq \Sigma$ for the set of labels of the maximal vertices of t. Note that $\max(t)$ is only defined when t is a finite trace, though the definition would make sense also for infinite traces.

We define the concatenation of two traces $t_1 = [V_1, \leq_1, \lambda_1] \in \mathbb{R}$ and $t_2 = [V_2, \leq_2, \lambda_2] \in \mathbb{R}$ verifying $\text{alphinf}(t_1) \times \text{alph}(t_2) \subseteq I$ by $t_1 \cdot t_2 = [V, \leq, \lambda]$ where $V = V_1 \cup V_2$ (assuming w.l.o.g. that $V_1 \cap V_2 = \emptyset$), $\lambda = \lambda_1 \cup \lambda_2$ and $\leq$ is the transitive closure of the relation $\leq_1 \cup \leq_2 \cup (V_1 \times V_2 \cap \lambda^{-1}(D))$. The set of finite traces becomes a monoid which is denoted by $\mathbb{M}(\Sigma, D)$ or simply by $\mathbb{M}$. The empty trace $1 = (\emptyset, \emptyset, \emptyset)$ is the unit element. Also, if $A \subseteq \Sigma$, we let $\mathbb{R}_A = \{x \in \mathbb{R} \mid \text{alph}(x) \subseteq A\}$ and $\mathbb{M}_A = \mathbb{M} \cap \mathbb{R}_A$. We also define $\mathbb{M}^+ = \mathbb{M} \setminus \{1\}$ and $\mathbb{M}_A^+ = \mathbb{M}^+ \cap \mathbb{M}_A$.

Our main results concern dependence alphabets which are cographs. According to standard graph theoretical notions, a dependence alphabet is called a *cograph*, if it belongs to the smallest class of graphs which contains singletons and which is closed under the operations of disjoint union and complementation. Clearly, (Σ, D) is a cograph if and only if the *independence alphabet* (Σ, I) is a cograph. It is well-known that an undirected graph is a cograph if and only if it does not contain any P_4 (a line of 4 vertices) as an induced subgraph [2]. It turns out that (Σ, D) is a cograph if and only if all $t \in \mathbb{M}(\Sigma, D)$ are *series parallel graphs*, i.e., we can build up the trace starting with letters by taking serial and parallel products. In particular, every such trace is N–free, i.e., whenever there are four vertices a, b, c, d with $a < b$, $c < b$, and $c < d$, then there is at least one more ordering between them.

We shall use the algebraic notion for recognizability: Let $h : \mathbb{M} \to S$ be a morphism to some finite monoid S. For $x, y \in \mathbb{R}$, we say that x and y are h-similar, denoted by $x \sim_h y$ if either $x, y \in \mathbb{M}$ and $h(x) = h(y)$ or x and y have infinite factorizations in non-empty finite traces $x = x_1 x_2 \cdots$, $y = y_1 y_2 \cdots$ with $x_i, y_i \in \mathbb{M}^+$ and $h(x_i) = h(y_i)$ for all i. We denote by $\approx_h$ the transitive closure of $\sim_h$ which is therefore an equivalence relation. Since S is finite, this equivalence relation is of finite index with at most $|S|^2 + |S|$ equivalence classes. A real trace language $L \subseteq \mathbb{R}$ is *recognized* by h if it is saturated by $\sim_h$, i.e., $x \in L$ implies $[x]_{\approx_h} \subseteq L$ for all $x \in \mathbb{R}$.

Let $L \subseteq \mathbb{R}$ be recognized by a morphism $h : \mathbb{M} \to S$ and $A \subseteq \Sigma$. Then, $L \cap \mathbb{M}_A$ and $L \cap \mathbb{R}_A$ are recognized by the restriction $h\restriction_{\mathbb{M}_A}$.

A finite monoid S is *aperiodic*, if there is some $n \geq 0$ such that $s^n = s^{n+1}$ for all $s \in S$. A real trace language $L \subseteq \mathbb{R}$ is *aperiodic* if it is recognized by some morphism to some finite and aperiodic monoid. We denote by $\text{AP}(\Sigma, D)$ or simply by AP the set of aperiodic languages $L \subseteq \mathbb{R}(\Sigma, D)$. If $A \subseteq \Sigma$, we use the notation AP_A for the aperiodic languages over $\mathbb{R}_A$.

In the following we shall use the well-known equivalence between first-order definability and aperiodic languages. The first order theory of traces is given by the syntax of $\mathrm{FO}_\Sigma(<)$:

$$\varphi ::= P_a(x) \mid x < y \mid \neg\varphi \mid \varphi \vee \varphi \mid (\exists x)\varphi,$$

where $a \in \Sigma$ and $x, y \in \mathrm{Var}$ are first order variables. Given a trace $t = [V, \leq, \lambda]$ and a valuation σ of the free variables into the vertices, the semantics is obtained by interpreting the predicate $P_a(x)$ by $\lambda(\sigma(x)) = a$ and the relation $<$ as the strict partial order relation of the trace t. Then we can say whether or not $t, \sigma \models \varphi$. If φ is a sentence, i.e., a closed formula, then we define the language $\mathcal{L}(\varphi) = \{t \in \mathbb{R} \mid t \models \varphi\}$. We say that a trace language $L \subseteq \mathbb{R}$ is expressible in $\mathrm{FO}_\Sigma(<)$ if there exists some sentence $\varphi \in \mathrm{FO}_\Sigma(<)$ such that $L = \mathcal{L}(\varphi)$. We denote by $\mathrm{FO}_{(\Sigma,D)}(<)$ the set of real trace languages $L \subseteq \mathbb{R}(\Sigma, D)$ such that for some sentence $\varphi \in \mathrm{FO}_\Sigma(<)$ we have $L = \mathcal{L}(\varphi)$

Theorem 1 ([6,5]). *A language $L \subseteq \mathbb{R}(\Sigma, D)$ is expressible in $\mathrm{FO}_\Sigma(<)$ if and only if it is aperiodic, i.e., $\mathrm{FO}_{(\Sigma,D)}(<) = \mathrm{AP}(\Sigma, D)$.*

We say that a first order formula is in $\mathrm{FO}^n_\Sigma(<)$ if it uses at most n first order variables (it may use each variable several times).

3 Local Temporal Logics for Traces

In this section, we introduce the *local temporal logic* over traces and its semantics. We restrict ourselves to future modalities (partly for lack of space), but of course, dual past tense modalities can also be defined and whenever we state that a fragment is in $\mathrm{FO}_\Sigma(<)$, then the fragment augmented by the dual past tenses will have the same property. In the next sections we specialize the logics by considering various subsets of the modalities. We say that a temporal logic over traces is *local* if it is evaluated at the vertices of the trace as for first order formulae. This is in contrast with global temporal logic formulae that are evaluated at global configurations of the trace, i.e., at finite prefixes of the trace.

For global formulae, we say that a trace is a model of a formula if it satisfies the formula at the empty configuration. There is no such canonical way to interpret a formula at some trace without fixing some vertex since there is no canonical vertex in the trace where to start the evaluation of the formula. Natural vertices are the minimal ones but a trace may have several minimal vertices. We have chosen to introduce initial formulae to address this problem. There are other possibilities, like adding a unique minimal dummy, but then the logic becomes more expressive and we are mainly interested in expressive completeness (with respect to first-order) for a weak fragment of our logic.

We start with the definition of (*internal*) formulae that are evaluated at vertices. The syntax of $\mathrm{LocTL}^{\mathsf{i}}_\Sigma(\mathsf{EX}, \mathsf{U}, \mathsf{EU})$ is given by

$$\varphi ::= \bot \mid a \in \Sigma \mid \neg\varphi \mid \varphi \vee \varphi \mid \mathsf{EX}\,\varphi \mid \varphi\,\mathsf{U}\,\varphi \mid \varphi\,\mathsf{EU}\,\varphi.$$

The symbol $\bot$ means *false*, $\mathsf{EX}\,\varphi$ claims that φ holds for some immediate successor of the current vertex; $\varphi\,\mathsf{U}\,\psi$ is a *universal* until claiming that ψ holds for some vertex above the current one and that φ holds for all vertices in between; on the contrary, $\varphi\,\mathsf{EU}\,\psi$ is an *existential* until claiming the existence of some path starting at the current vertex in the Hasse diagram of the trace where φ holds until ψ does. Formally, the semantics is inductively given as follows. Let $t = [V, \leq, \lambda] \in \mathbb{R}$ and let $x \in V$ (we also write $x \in t$).

$$
\begin{array}{ll}
t, x \models a & \text{if } \lambda(x) = a \\
t, x \models \neg\varphi & \text{if } t, x \not\models \varphi \\
t, x \models \varphi \vee \psi & \text{if } t, x \models \varphi \text{ or } t, x \models \psi \\
t, x \models \mathsf{EX}\,\varphi & \text{if } \exists y,\ x \lessdot y \text{ and } t, y \models \varphi \\
t, x \models \varphi\,\mathsf{U}\,\psi & \text{if } \exists z,\ x \leq z \text{ and } t, z \models \psi \text{ and } t, y \models \varphi, \forall x \leq y < z \\
t, x \models \varphi\,\mathsf{EU}\,\psi & \text{if } \exists x = y_0 \lessdot \cdots \lessdot y_n, \text{ with } t, y_n \models \psi \text{ and } t, y_i \models \varphi, \forall 0 \leq i < n
\end{array}
$$

We define $\top = \neg\bot$, hence $\top$ means *true*. We derive some more operators from the above ones. Eventually φ claims the existence of some vertex where φ holds above the current one: $\mathsf{F}\,\varphi = \top\,\mathsf{U}\,\varphi = \top\,\mathsf{EU}\,\varphi$. Its dual operator, always φ, means that φ holds at all positions above the current one: $\mathsf{G}\,\varphi = \neg\,\mathsf{F}\,\neg\varphi$.

The initial formulae $\mathrm{LocTL}_\Sigma(\cdots)$ are defined by the syntax

$$\alpha ::= \bot \mid \mathsf{EM}\,\varphi \mid \neg\alpha \mid \alpha \vee \alpha$$

where $\varphi \in \mathrm{LocTL}^{\mathrm{i}}_\Sigma(\cdots)$. Intuitively, $\mathsf{EM}\,\varphi$ means that φ holds at some minimal vertex. Formally, the semantics is given by

$$
\begin{array}{ll}
t \models \mathsf{EM}\,\varphi & \text{if } \exists x \in \min(t) \text{ with } t, x \models \varphi \\
t \models \neg\alpha & \text{if } t \not\models \alpha \\
t \models \alpha \vee \beta & \text{if } t \models \alpha \text{ or } t \models \beta
\end{array}
$$

The dual $\mathsf{AM}\,\varphi = \neg\,\mathsf{EM}\,\neg\varphi$ means that φ holds for all minimal vertices. One can show that each initial formula is equivalent to a finite disjunction of formulae of the form $\mathsf{AM}\,\varphi \wedge \bigwedge_{a\in A} \mathsf{EM}\,a$ with $\varphi \in \mathrm{LocTL}^{\mathrm{i}}_\Sigma(\cdots)$ and $A \subseteq \Sigma$.

An initial formula $\alpha \in \mathrm{LocTL}_\Sigma(\cdots)$ defines the language $\mathcal{L}(\alpha) = \{t \in \mathbb{R} \mid t \models \alpha\}$ and we say that a trace language $L \subseteq \mathbb{R}$ is expressible in $\mathrm{LocTL}_\Sigma(\cdots)$ if there exists an initial formula $\alpha \in \mathrm{LocTL}_\Sigma(\cdots)$ such that $L = \mathcal{L}(\alpha)$. We denote by $\mathrm{LocTL}_{(\Sigma,D)}(\cdots)$ the set of languages over $\mathbb{R}(\Sigma, D)$ that are expressible by some local temporal formula using the modalities $(\cdots)$.

With local temporal formulae, we can express various alphabetic properties.

$$
\begin{array}{lcl}
(a \in \min) & = & \mathsf{EM}\,a \\
(a \in \mathrm{alph}) & = & \mathsf{EM}\,\mathsf{F}\,a \\
(a \in \mathrm{alphinf}) & = & \mathsf{EM}(\mathsf{F}\,a \wedge \mathsf{G}(a \Rightarrow \mathsf{EX}\,\mathsf{F}\,a))
\end{array}
$$

It is clear from the semantics of EX and U that all trace languages expressible in $\mathrm{LocTL}_\Sigma(\mathsf{EX}, \mathsf{U})$ are also expressible in $\mathrm{FO}_\Sigma(<)$, and even in $\mathrm{FO}^3_\Sigma(<)$. This is however not true in general for the existential until EU as shown in the next example.

if for all

Note that if two traces t_1 and t_2 have the same minimal letters and for all minimal letters the corresponding upper sets in t_1 and t_2 are the same, then the two traces cannot be distinguished by any formula in $\mathrm{LocTL}_\Sigma(\mathsf{EX}, \mathsf{U}, \mathsf{EU})$. The following example for such a situation has been taken from Walukiewicz [21]:

$$t_1 = \left(\begin{array}{ccccccc} a & \to & b & \to & c & \to & b \quad \cdots \\ & & \uparrow & & & & \\ d & \to & c & & & & \end{array}\right) \qquad t_2 = \left(\begin{array}{ccccccc} a & \to & b & & & & \\ & & \downarrow & & & & \\ d & \to & c & \to & b & \to & c \quad \cdots \end{array}\right)$$

Since t_1 and t_2 are clearly distinguishable in $\mathrm{FO}_\Sigma(<)$, we deduce that a pure future local temporal logic cannot be expressively complete for $\mathrm{FO}_\Sigma(<)$ as soon as (Σ, D) is not a cograph. Note that it is easy to distinguish t_1 from t_2 if we allow some past tense modalities or if we introduce a dummy minimal vertex. One can also show that the language $ad(bc)^* \subseteq \mathbb{M}$ of finite traces is first order but cannot be expressed in $\mathrm{LocTL}_\Sigma(\mathsf{EX}, \mathsf{U}, \mathsf{EU})$.

We are interested in the expressive completeness of pure future local temporal logics. The simple example above shows that we can restrict our study to traces defined by a dependence alphabet that are cographs.

The following lemma shows that we can *localize* initial formulae.

Lemma 1. *Let* $\alpha \in \mathrm{LocTL}_\Sigma(\mathsf{EX}, \mathsf{U}, \mathsf{EU})$ *be an initial formula. There exists an internal formula* $\mathrm{loc}(\alpha) \in \mathrm{LocTL}^{\mathrm{i}}_\Sigma(\mathsf{EX}, \mathsf{U})$ *such that for all* $t = t_1 t_2 \in \mathbb{R}$ *and* $x \in \max(t_1)$ *with* $\min(t_2) \subseteq D(\lambda(x))$, *we have* $t_2 \models \alpha$ *if and only if* $t, x \models \mathrm{loc}(\alpha)$. *The same holds for the fragment* $\mathrm{LocTL}_\Sigma(\mathsf{EX}, \mathsf{U})$.

Proof. Clearly, we have $\mathrm{loc}(\alpha \vee \beta) = \mathrm{loc}(\alpha) \vee \mathrm{loc}(\beta)$ and $\mathrm{loc}(\neg\alpha) = \neg\mathrm{loc}(\alpha)$. The interesting case is $\mathsf{EM}\,\varphi$ where $\varphi \in \mathrm{LocTL}^{\mathrm{i}}$. We have, $\mathrm{loc}(\mathsf{EM}\,\varphi) = \mathsf{EX}(\varphi)$. □

4 Universal Until

In this section, we consider the fragment of the local temporal logic using next and the *universal* until, only. We give the following characterization of the expressive completeness of $\mathrm{LocTL}_\Sigma(\mathsf{EX}, \mathsf{U})$ with respect to $\mathrm{FO}_\Sigma(<)$.

Theorem 2. *Let* (Σ, D) *be a dependence alphabet. Then we have the equality* $\mathrm{LocTL}_{(\Sigma,D)}(\mathsf{EX}, \mathsf{U}) = \mathrm{FO}_{(\Sigma,D)}(<)$ *if and only if* (Σ, D) *is a cograph.*

We have seen in the previous section that $\mathrm{LocTL}_\Sigma(\mathsf{EX}, \mathsf{U})$ is not expressively complete, if (Σ, D) is not a cograph. Conversely, for all dependence alphabets, we already know that $\mathrm{LocTL}_{(\Sigma,D)}(\mathsf{EX}, \mathsf{U}) \subseteq \mathrm{FO}^3_{(\Sigma,D)}(<)$ and that first order languages coincide with aperiodic languages (Theorem 1). Hence, in order to get the converse inclusion, we will prove that $\mathrm{AP} \subseteq \mathrm{LocTL}_{(\Sigma,D)}(\mathsf{EX},\mathsf{U})$, if (Σ, D) is a cograph.

Before going into the proof, we derive an immediate corollary. It is well-known that for words, all first order languages can be expressed with only 3 first order variables. This result has been extended to traces by Walukiewicz [22]. In the special case of (Σ, D) being a cograph, we get this result as a trivial consequence of Theorem 2.

Corollary 1. *If (Σ, D) is a cograph, then* $\mathrm{FO}_\Sigma(<) = \mathrm{FO}^3_\Sigma(<)$.

If (Σ, D) is a cograph, then either Σ is a singleton, or Σ is the disjoint union of two non empty sets $\Sigma = A \cup B$ with either $A \times B \subseteq I$ or $A \times B \subseteq D$. We consider these three cases in turn.

Assume that $\Sigma = \{a\}$. Then, traces over Σ coincide with words over Σ and the semantics of EX and U coincide with the semantics of the usual *next* and *until* modalities over words. Therefore, by Kamp's classical theorem [11,7] we obtain the claim in this case.

Next, we consider the case where the alphabet is the disjoint union of two independent subset. This means $\mathbb{R}(\Sigma, D) = \mathbb{R}_A \times \mathbb{R}_B$ is a direct product.

Proposition 1. *Assume that $\Sigma = A \cup B$ with $A \times B \subseteq I$. If we have both* $\mathrm{AP}_A \subseteq \mathrm{LocTL}_A(\mathsf{EX},\mathsf{U})$ *and* $\mathrm{AP}_B \subseteq \mathrm{LocTL}_B(\mathsf{EX},\mathsf{U})$*, then* $\mathrm{AP}_\Sigma \subseteq \mathrm{LocTL}_{(\Sigma,D)}(\mathsf{EX},\mathsf{U})$.

The last case and the most interesting one is when the dependence alphabet is the disjoint union of two fully dependent subsets: $\Sigma = A \cup B$ with $A \cap B = \emptyset$ and $A \times B \subseteq D$. In this case, the trace monoid $\mathbb{M}$ is the free product of the monoids $\mathbb{M}_A$ and $\mathbb{M}_B$.

Proposition 2. *Assume that $\Sigma = A \cup B$ with $A \cap B = \emptyset$ and $A \times B \subseteq D$. If we have both* $\mathrm{AP}_A \subseteq \mathrm{LocTL}_A(\mathsf{EX},\mathsf{U})$ *and* $\mathrm{AP}_B \subseteq \mathrm{LocTL}_B(\mathsf{EX},\mathsf{U})$*, then* $\mathrm{AP}_\Sigma \subseteq \mathrm{LocTL}_{(\Sigma,D)}(\mathsf{EX},\mathsf{U})$.

Our proof is inspired by a technique introduced by Wilke [23] in order to show that aperiodic languages over words are expressible in LTL. This method was then extended in order to cope with traces: We have shown in [3] that the most natural global temporal logic over traces is expressively complete with respect to $\mathrm{FO}_\Sigma(<)$.

We use several splittings of languages in products. We shall use the following composition lemmas to get the expressibility of the products from the expressibility of their components. We assume until the end of this section that $\Sigma = A \cup B$ with $A \cap B = \emptyset$ and $A \times B \subseteq D$.

Lemma 2. *Let $L \subseteq \mathbb{R}_A$ be a language expressible in* $\mathrm{LocTL}_A(\mathsf{EX},\mathsf{U})$*. Then, the language* $(L \cap \mathbb{M}_A^+) \cdot (\min \subseteq B)$ *is expressible in* $\mathrm{LocTL}_\Sigma(\mathsf{EX},\mathsf{U})$.

Lemma 3. *Let* $\alpha \in \mathrm{LocTL}_A(\mathsf{EX},\mathsf{U})$*. The language* $(\max \subseteq B) \cdot \mathcal{L}_A(\alpha)$ *is definable in* $\mathrm{LocTL}_\Sigma(\mathsf{EX},\mathsf{U})$ *by the formula*

$$\Big((\mathrm{alph} \subseteq A) \wedge \alpha\Big) \vee \Big((\mathrm{alphinf} \subseteq A) \wedge \mathsf{EM}\big(\mathsf{F}(B \wedge \neg\, \mathsf{EX}\,\mathsf{F}\,B \wedge \mathrm{loc}(\alpha))\big)\Big).$$

Lemma 4. *Let $L \subseteq \mathbb{R}$ be a language expressible in* $\mathrm{LocTL}_\Sigma(\mathsf{EX},\mathsf{U})$. *Then, the language* $(L \cap (\max \subseteq B)) \cdot \mathbb{R}_A$ *is expressible in* $\mathrm{LocTL}_\Sigma(\mathsf{EX},\mathsf{U})$.

We consider the set $\Delta = \mathbb{M} \cup ((\mathrm{alphinf} \not\subseteq A) \cap (\mathrm{alphinf} \not\subseteq B))$. Note that Δ is expressible in $\mathrm{LocTL}_\Sigma(\mathsf{EX},\mathsf{U})$ since it is characterized by alphabetic information. Each trace $x \in \Delta$ has a unique (finite or infinite) factorization $x = x_1 x_2 \cdots$ in non-empty finite traces alternating $\mathbb{M}_A^+$ and $\mathbb{M}_B^+$.

Let $h : \mathbb{M} \to S$ be a morphism into some finite aperiodic monoid S. Let $T = h(\mathbb{M}^+)$ and let $e : T^* \to S$ be the evaluation morphism. Using the unique factorization of elements $x \in \Delta$, we can define a mapping $\sigma : \Delta \to T^\infty$ by $\sigma(x) = h(x_1)h(x_2)\cdots$. This mapping σ allows to reduce our problem to words over the alphabet T.

Lemma 5. *Let $L \subseteq \mathbb{R}$ be recognized by h. Then, $L \cap \Delta = \sigma^{-1}(K)$ for some language $K \in T^\infty$ expressible in* $\mathrm{LTL}_T(\mathsf{XU})$.

Proof. Let $K = [\sigma(L \cap \Delta)]_{\approx_e}$. By definition, K is recognized by the evaluation morphism e into the aperiodic monoid S. Hence K is an aperiodic word language over T. Since, by Kamp's Theorem on words, $\mathrm{AP}_T = \mathrm{FO}_T(<) = \mathrm{LTL}_T(\mathsf{XU})$, we deduce that K is expressible in $\mathrm{LTL}_T(\mathsf{XU})$. Therefore, it remains to show that $L \cap \Delta = \sigma^{-1}(K)$. The inclusion $L \cap \Delta \subseteq \sigma^{-1}(K)$ is clear.

For the converse inclusion, let $y \in \sigma^{-1}(K)$. There exists $x \in L \cap \Delta$ such that $\sigma(x) \approx_e \sigma(y)$. Note that x is finite iff y is finite and in this case $h(x) = e(\sigma(x)) = e(\sigma(y)) = h(y)$. Therefore, $y \approx_h x \in L$ and we deduce $y \in L$. Assume now that x and y are both infinite. Using the following claim we also have $y \approx_h x$ and we deduce as above that $y \in L$.

Claim: Let $x = x_1 x_2 \cdots \in \mathbb{R}$ and $y = y_1 y_2 \cdots \in \mathbb{R}$ with $x_i, y_i \in \mathbb{M}^+$. If $h(x_1)h(x_2)\cdots \approx_e h(y_1)h(y_2)\cdots$, then $x \approx_h y$. □

In order to make use of the previous lemma, we need to lift through σ^{-1} an LTL formula over T to some local temporal formula. This is the purpose of the next lemma.

Lemma 6. *Let $f \in$* $\mathrm{LTL}_T(\mathsf{XU})$. *There exists a formula $\widetilde{f} \in$* $\mathrm{LocTL}_\Sigma(\mathsf{EX},\mathsf{U})$ *such that $\mathcal{L}(\widetilde{f}) = \sigma^{-1}(\mathcal{L}(f))$.*

Proof. The lemma is shown by structural induction on the formula f. First, $\widetilde{\bot} = \bot$, $\widetilde{\varphi \vee \psi} = \widetilde{\varphi} \vee \widetilde{\psi}$, and $\widetilde{\neg\varphi} = \Delta \wedge \neg\widetilde{\varphi}$. Now, it can be shown that $\widetilde{\varphi \,\mathsf{XU}\, \psi}$ equals

$$\Delta \wedge \mathsf{EM}\Big(((A \wedge \mathsf{EX}\, A) \vee (B \wedge \mathsf{EX}\, B) \vee \mathrm{loc}(\widetilde{\varphi}))\,\mathsf{U}\,(((A \wedge \mathsf{EX}\, B) \vee (B \wedge \mathsf{EX}\, A)) \wedge \mathrm{loc}(\widetilde{\psi}))\Big)$$

It remains to deal with the case $f = s$ with $s \in T$. We have $\mathcal{L}(s) = sT^\infty$ and

$$\sigma^{-1}(sT^\infty) = \Delta \cap \Big((h^{-1}(s) \cap \mathbb{M}_A^+)(\min \subseteq B) \cup (h^{-1}(s) \cap \mathbb{M}_B^+)(\min \subseteq A)\Big).$$

The language $h^{-1}(s) \cap \mathbb{M}_A^+$ is recognized by $h \restriction_{\mathbb{M}_A}$ and is therefore an aperiodic language over $\mathbb{R}_A$. Since we have assumed $\text{AP}_A \subseteq \text{LocTL}_A(\mathsf{EX}, \mathsf{U})$, the language $h^{-1}(s) \cap \mathbb{M}_A^+$ is expressible in $\text{LocTL}_A(\mathsf{EX}, \mathsf{U})$. Using Lemma 2, we deduce that $(h^{-1}(s) \cap \mathbb{M}_A^+)(\min \subseteq B)$ is expressible in $\text{LocTL}_\Sigma(\mathsf{EX}, \mathsf{U})$. Similarly, $(h^{-1}(s) \cap \mathbb{M}_B^+)(\min \subseteq A)$ is expressible in $\text{LocTL}_\Sigma(\mathsf{EX}, \mathsf{U})$ and we deduce that $\sigma^{-1}(sT^\infty)$ is expressible in $\text{LocTL}_\Sigma(\mathsf{EX}, \mathsf{U})$. □

Now, we have all we need in hand to prove the main result of this section.

Proof of Proposition 2 Let $L \subseteq \mathbb{R}$ be recognized by the morphism h. Since $\mathbb{R} = \Delta \cup (\text{alphinf} \subseteq A) \cup (\text{alphinf} \subseteq B)$, we have

$$L = (L \cap \Delta) \cup (L \cap (\text{alphinf} \subseteq A)) \cup (L \cap (\text{alphinf} \subseteq B)).$$

From Lemmas 5 and 6, we deduce that $L \cap \Delta$ is expressible in $\text{LocTL}_\Sigma(\mathsf{EX}, \mathsf{U})$.

One can show that the language $L \cap (\text{alphinf} \subseteq A)$ is a finite union of products $(L_1 \cap (\max \subseteq B)) \cdot (L_2 \cap \mathbb{R}_A)$, where L_1 and L_2 are languages recognized by h.

Since $(\max \subseteq B) \subseteq \mathbb{M} \subseteq \Delta$, we have $L_1 \cap (\max \subseteq B) = (L_1 \cap \Delta) \cap (\max \subseteq B)$. Now, L_1 is recognized by h and using Lemmas 5 and 6, we deduce that $L_1 \cap \Delta$ is expressible in $\text{LocTL}_\Sigma(\mathsf{EX}, \mathsf{U})$. Finally, from Lemma 4 we deduce that $(L_1 \cap (\max \subseteq B)) \cdot \mathbb{R}_A$ is expressible in $\text{LocTL}_\Sigma(\mathsf{EX}, \mathsf{U})$.

Now, L_2 is recognized by h. Hence, $L_2 \cap \mathbb{R}_A$ is recognized by $h \restriction_{\mathbb{M}_A}$ and is therefore an aperiodic language over $\mathbb{R}_A$. Since we have assumed $\text{AP}_A \subseteq \text{LocTL}_A(\mathsf{EX}, \mathsf{U})$, $L_2 \cap \mathbb{R}_A$ is also expressible in $\text{LocTL}_A(\mathsf{EX}, \mathsf{U})$. Using Lemma 3, we deduce that $(\max \subseteq B) \cdot (L_2 \cap \mathbb{R}_A)$ is expressible in $\text{LocTL}_\Sigma(\mathsf{EX}, \mathsf{U})$.

Finally, the product $(\max \subseteq B) \cdot \mathbb{R}_A$ is unambiguous, hence we have

$$(L_1 \cap (\max \subseteq B)) \cdot (L_2 \cap \mathbb{R}_A) = (L_1 \cap (\max \subseteq B)) \cdot \mathbb{R}_A \cap (\max \subseteq B) \cdot (L_2 \cap \mathbb{R}_A).$$

We deduce that $(L_1 \cap (\max \subseteq B)) \cdot (L_2 \cap \mathbb{R}_A)$ is expressible in $\text{LocTL}_\Sigma(\mathsf{EX}, \mathsf{U})$. Therefore, $L \cap (\text{alphinf} \subseteq A)$ is expressible in $\text{LocTL}_\Sigma(\mathsf{EX}, \mathsf{U})$. □

5 Existential Until

In this section, we consider the fragment of the local temporal logic using next and the *existential* until only. We prove the following characterization.

Theorem 3. *Let (Σ, D) be a dependence alphabet. Then we have the equality $\text{LocTL}_{(\Sigma,D)}(\mathsf{EX}, \mathsf{EU}) = \text{FO}_{(\Sigma,D)}(<)$ if and only if (Σ, D) is a cograph.*

We have seen in Section 3 that $\text{LocTL}_\Sigma(\mathsf{EX}, \mathsf{EU})$ is not expressively complete, if (Σ, D) is not a cograph. Conversely, The proofs of Propositions 1 and 2 can be carried out with slight modifications using the existential until instead of the universal until. Therefore, we get $\text{FO}_{(\Sigma,D)}(<) = \text{AP} \subseteq \text{LocTL}_{(\Sigma,D)}(\mathsf{EX}, \mathsf{EU})$ if (Σ, D) is a cograph. The difficulty with the existential until is that we do not get the converse inclusion for free as with the universal until. Indeed, the semantics of existential until is given by a monadic second order formula since it claims the

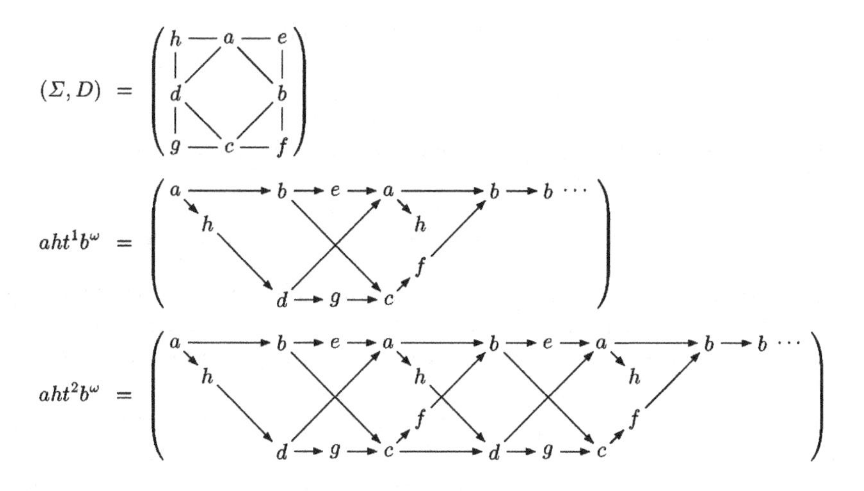

Fig. 1. The dependence alphabet (Σ, D) and some traces.

existence of some path in the trace. This MSO formula can be expressed in first order, if (Σ, D) is a cograph. This is certainly not true for arbitrary dependence alphabet as shown by the following example.

Consider the dependence alphabet (Σ, D) depicted in Figure 1. Let $t = bdegachf \in \mathbb{M}$ and let $\varphi = (a \vee b \vee c \vee d)\ \mathsf{EU}\ \mathsf{G}\, b$. Then, it is easy to verify that $aht^n b^\omega \models \mathsf{EM}\,\varphi$ if and only if n is even. Now, the trace language t^* is aperiodic. Therefore, the language aht^*b^ω is aperiodic as well and we have $aht^*b^\omega \cap \mathcal{L}(\mathsf{EM}\,\varphi) = ah(t^2)^*b^\omega$ which is not aperiodic. Since aperiodic languages are closed under intersection, we deduce that $\mathcal{L}(\mathsf{EM}\,\varphi)$ is not aperiodic. Therefore, $\mathrm{LocTL}_{(\Sigma,D)}(\mathsf{EU}) \nsubseteq \mathrm{FO}_{(\Sigma,D)}(<)$ for the dependence alphabet of Figure 1.

The key result for showing that $\mathrm{LocTL}_{(\Sigma,D)}(\mathsf{EX}, \mathsf{EU}) \subseteq \mathrm{FO}_{(\Sigma,D)}(<)$, if the dependence alphabet is a cograph, is to express in $\mathrm{FO}_\Sigma(<)$ the existence of a path satisfying some first order formula. Let $\varphi(z)$ be a first order formula with z as only free variable and let $C \subseteq \Sigma$. We define the formula $\mathrm{Path}_C^\varphi(x,y)$ by

$$(\forall x \le z \le y,\ \lambda(z) \in C) \text{ and}$$
$$(\exists x = z_1 \lessdot \cdots \lessdot z_n = y, \text{ with } \varphi(z_k) \text{ for all } 1 \le k \le n).$$

Lemma 7. *If (Σ, D) is a cograph, then the formula $\mathrm{Path}_C^\varphi(x,y)$ can be expressed in first order.*

Proof. If (Σ, D) is a cograph, then either Σ is a singleton, or Σ is the disjoint union of two non empty sets $\Sigma = A \cup B$ with either $A \times B \subseteq I$ or $A \times B \subseteq D$. We consider these three cases in turn.

First, assume that $\Sigma = \{a\}$ is a singleton, then

$$\mathrm{Path}_a^\varphi(x,y) = x \le y \wedge \forall x \le z \le y,\ (\lambda(z) = a) \wedge \varphi(z).$$

Next, Assume that $\Sigma = A \cup B$ with $A \times B \subseteq I$. Then, we have

$$\mathrm{Path}^{\varphi}_{A \cup B}(x, y) = \mathrm{Path}^{\varphi}_{A}(x, y) \vee \mathrm{Path}^{\varphi}_{B}(x, y).$$

Finally, we consider the more interesting case $\Sigma = A \cup B$ with $A \cap B = \emptyset$ and $A \times B \subseteq D$. Then, we have

$$\mathrm{Path}^{\varphi}_{A \cup B}(x, y) = \mathrm{Path}^{\varphi}_{A}(x, y) \vee \mathrm{Path}^{\varphi}_{B}(x, y) \vee (\Phi(x, y) \wedge \Psi(x, y))$$

where the formulae $\Phi(x, y)$ and $\Psi(x, y)$ are defined below. We give simultaneously pictures that should help understanding the formulae. The vertical lines in the pictures indicate a separation between factors from $\mathbb{M}^{+}_{A}$ and factors from $\mathbb{M}^{+}_{B}$.

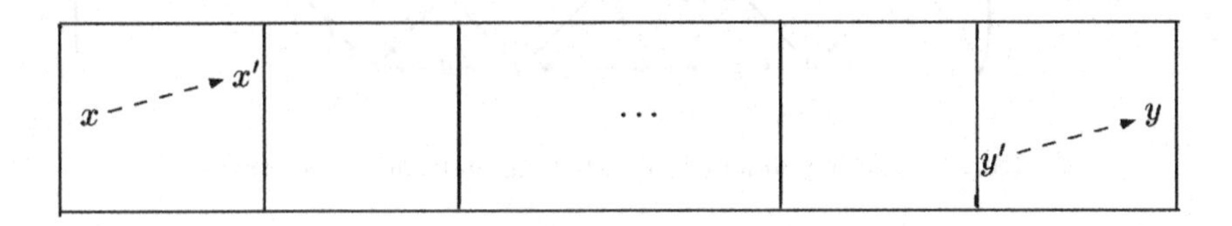

$$\Phi(x, y) = \exists x \le x' < y' \le y, \begin{pmatrix} \forall x \le u \le x',\ (\lambda(u) \in A \Leftrightarrow \lambda(x) \in A) \\ \wedge\ \forall x' \lessdot u,\ (\lambda(u) \in A \Leftrightarrow \lambda(x) \notin A) \\ \wedge\ (\mathrm{Path}^{\varphi}_{A}(x, x') \vee \mathrm{Path}^{\varphi}_{B}(x, x')) \\ \wedge\ \forall y' \le u \le y,\ (\lambda(u) \in A \Leftrightarrow \lambda(y) \notin A) \\ \wedge\ \forall u \lessdot y',\ (\lambda(u) \in A \Leftrightarrow \lambda(y) \notin A) \\ \wedge\ (\mathrm{Path}^{\varphi}_{A}(y', y) \vee \mathrm{Path}^{\varphi}_{B}(y', y)) \end{pmatrix}$$

and

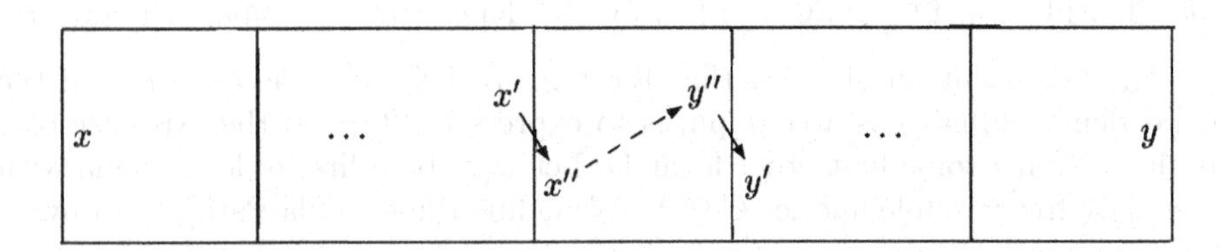

$$\Psi(x, y) = \forall x \le x' < y' \le y, \begin{pmatrix} (\lambda(x') \in A \Leftrightarrow \lambda(y') \in A) \\ \wedge\ \exists x' < u < y',\ (\lambda(u) \in A \Leftrightarrow \lambda(x') \notin A) \\ \wedge\ \forall x' < u < y',\ (\lambda(u) \in A \Leftrightarrow \lambda(x') \notin A) \end{pmatrix}$$
$$\Rightarrow \left(\exists x' \lessdot x'' \le y'' \lessdot y',\ \mathrm{Path}^{\varphi}_{A}(x'', y'') \vee \mathrm{Path}^{\varphi}_{B}(x'', y'')\right)$$

□

From this lemma, we immediately deduce the desired result.

Proposition 3. *If the dependence alphabet is a cograph, then the existential modality* EU *can be expressed in* $\mathrm{FO}_{\Sigma}(<)$.

Proof. Follows directly from the Lemma 7 since we have

$$t, x \models \varphi \,\mathsf{EU}\, \psi \text{ iff } t, x \models \psi \text{ or } \exists y, \mathrm{Path}^{\varphi}_{\Sigma}(x, y) \text{ and } \exists z,\ y \lessdot z \text{ and } t, z \models \psi$$

The logic TLC introduced in [1] uses EX, EU, the dual past modalities EY and ES and two additional modalities $\mathsf{Eco}\,\varphi$ claiming that φ holds for some vertex that is concurrent with the current one; and $\mathsf{EG}\,\varphi$ claiming the existence of some maximal path starting from the current vertex such that φ holds everywhere along this path. EY and Eco are clearly first order modalities, while ES and EG are in general only (monadic) second order. But, using the technique of Lemma 7 and Proposition 3 one can show that ES and EG are expressible in first order, if the dependence alphabet is a cograph.

Proposition 4. *Let (Σ, D) be a dependence alphabet which is a cograph. Then,* $\mathrm{TLC}(\Sigma, D) \subseteq \mathrm{FO}_{(\Sigma,D)}(<)$.

6 Complexity

In this section, we show that the satisfiability problem for local temporal logics is PSPACE-complete. The PSPACE-hardness is a consequence of the PSPACE-hardness for words. For TLC the inclusion in PSPACE has been shown in [1]. In order to prove that our problem is still in PSPACE, we have to deal with the universal until–operator which we have introduced here. For this, we associate with each initial formula α an alternating automaton that accepts all the linearizations of the traces that model α. Here, we describe the construction for the pure future local temporal logic $\mathrm{LocTL}_{\Sigma}(\mathsf{EX}, \mathsf{U})$. We assume the reader is familiar with alternating automata and the usual translation from LTL formulae to alternating automata [19].

Let $\alpha \in \mathrm{LocTL}_{\Sigma}(\mathsf{EX}, \mathsf{U})$. Without loss of generality, we assume that the negations in α are only over formulae of the form $\mathsf{EM}\,\varphi$ or b or $\mathsf{EX}\,\varphi$ or $\varphi \,\mathsf{U}\, \psi$. We construct an alternating automaton $\mathcal{A}_\alpha$ as follows. The set of states is $Q \cup \overline{Q}$ where

$$\begin{aligned} Q = \{\xi \mid\ & \xi \text{ is a subformula of } \alpha \text{ of the form } \mathsf{EM}\,\varphi \text{ or } b \text{ or } \mathsf{EX}\,\varphi \text{ or } \varphi \,\mathsf{U}\, \psi\} \\ \cup\ & \{(D(B), \mathsf{EM}\,\varphi) \mid \mathsf{EM}\,\varphi \text{ is a subformula of } \alpha,\ B \subseteq \Sigma \\ & \qquad \text{and } \Sigma \setminus D(B) \neq \emptyset\} \\ \cup\ & \{(D(a), D(B), \mathsf{EX}\,\varphi) \mid \mathsf{EX}\,\varphi \text{ is a subformula of } \alpha,\ a \in \Sigma,\ B \subseteq \Sigma, \\ & \qquad \{a\} \cup B \text{ connected and } D(a) \setminus D(B) \neq \emptyset\} \\ \cup\ & \{(D(A), D(B), \varphi \,\mathsf{U}\, \psi) \mid \varphi \,\mathsf{U}\, \psi \text{ is a subformula of } \alpha,\ A, B \subseteq \Sigma, \\ & \qquad A \cup B \text{ connected and } D(A) \setminus D(B) \neq \emptyset\} \end{aligned}$$

and $\overline{Q} = \{\neg p \mid p \in Q\}$. The set of positive boolean combinations of states is denoted $\mathbb{B}^+(Q \cup \overline{Q})$. The initial state is $\alpha \in \mathbb{B}^+(Q \cup \overline{Q})$. We define the extended transition function $\delta : \mathbb{B}^+(Q \cup \overline{Q}) \times \Sigma \to \mathbb{B}^+(Q \cup \overline{Q})$ as follows.

$\delta(f \vee g, a) = \delta(f, a) \vee \delta(g, a)$, for $f, g \in \mathbb{B}^+(Q)$.

$\delta(f \wedge g, a) = \delta(f, a) \wedge \delta(g, a)$, for $f, g \in \mathbb{B}^+(Q)$.

$$\delta(\mathsf{EM}\,\varphi,a)=\begin{cases}\quad\delta(\varphi,a) & \\ \vee\,(D(a),\mathsf{EM}\,\varphi) & \text{if } D(a)\neq\Sigma.\end{cases}$$

$$\delta((D(B),\mathsf{EM}\,\varphi),a)=\begin{cases}\quad(D(B)\cup D(a),\mathsf{EM}\,\varphi) & \text{if } D(B)\cup D(a)\neq\Sigma\\ \vee\,\delta(\varphi,a) & \text{if } a\notin D(B).\end{cases}$$

$$\delta(b,a)=\begin{cases}\top & \text{if } a=b,\\ \bot & \text{if } a\neq b.\end{cases}$$

$$\delta(\mathsf{EX}\,\varphi,a)=(D(a),\emptyset,\mathsf{EX}\,\varphi).$$

$$\delta((D(A),D(B),\mathsf{EX}\,\varphi),a)=$$
$$\begin{cases}\quad(D(A),D(B)\cup D(a),\mathsf{EX}\,\varphi) & \text{if } a\in D(A)\cup D(B) \text{ and}\\ & \quad D(A)\setminus(D(B)\cup D(a))\neq\emptyset\\ \vee\,(D(A),D(B),\mathsf{EX}\,\varphi) & \text{if } a\notin D(A)\cup D(B),\\ \vee\,\delta(\varphi,a) & \text{if } a\in D(A)\setminus D(B).\end{cases}$$

$$\delta(\varphi\,\mathsf{U}\,\psi,a)=\delta(\psi,a)\vee(\delta(\varphi,a)\wedge(D(a),\emptyset,\varphi\,\mathsf{U}\,\psi)).$$

$$\delta((D(A),D(B),\varphi\,\mathsf{U}\,\psi),a)=$$
$$\begin{cases}\quad(D(A),D(B)\cup D(a),\varphi\,\mathsf{U}\,\psi) & \text{if } a\in D(A)\cup D(B) \text{ and}\\ & \quad D(A)\setminus(D(B)\cup D(a))\neq\emptyset\\ \vee\,(D(A),D(B),\varphi\,\mathsf{U}\,\psi) & \text{if } a\notin D(A)\cup D(B),\\ \vee\,\delta(\varphi,a)\wedge(D(A)\cup D(a),D(B),\varphi\,\mathsf{U}\,\psi) & \text{if } a\in D(A)\setminus D(B),\\ \vee\,\delta(\psi,a) & \text{if } a\in D(A)\setminus D(B).\end{cases}$$

$$\delta(\neg p,a)=\widetilde{\delta(p,a)},\ \text{for } p\in Q;$$

where $\widetilde{f\vee g}=\widetilde{f}\wedge\widetilde{g}$ and $\widetilde{f\wedge g}=\widetilde{f}\vee\widetilde{g}$, for $f,g\in\mathbb{B}^+(Q)$; and $\widetilde{p}=\neg p$ and $\widetilde{\neg p}=p$ for $p\in Q$. The actual transition function of $\mathcal{A}_\alpha$ is the restriction of δ to $(Q\cup\overline{Q})\times\Sigma$.

The states in Q represent obligations that the word has to fulfill in order to be accepted, hence an infinite branch looping on such a state should not be accepted. Therefore, the co-Büchi acceptance condition is given by the set Q. Note that the alternating automaton defined above is *very weak*. Hence, each infinite branch in the run of the alternating automaton is ultimately constant and the co-Büchi acceptance condition Q is equivalent with the Büchi acceptance condition $\overline{Q}$.

Proposition 5. *The automaton $\mathcal{A}_\alpha$ accepts the word language*

$$\mathcal{L}(\mathcal{A}_\alpha)=\{w\in\Sigma^\infty\mid[w]\models\alpha\},$$

where $[w]$ denotes the trace associated with the word $w\in\Sigma^\infty$.

Let $N(\Sigma,D)=1+|\{(D(A),D(B))\mid A,B\subseteq\Sigma, A\cup B \text{ connected and } D(A)\setminus D(B)\neq\emptyset\}|$. The number of states of the automaton $\mathcal{A}_\alpha$ is $|Q\cup\overline{Q}|\leq 2N(\Sigma,D)|\alpha|$. Note that when the dependence relation is full, that is, when traces are actually words, then $N(\Sigma,D)=2$ and the size of our automaton does not depend on the size of the alphabet. In this case, we essentially get the usual construction for LTL formulae over words.

In fact, we shall use a slightly better parameter. Decompose (Σ, D) into its connected components such that (Σ, D) is a disjoint union of connected graphs (Σ_i, D_i) for $1 \leq i \leq k$. Let $M = \max_{1 \leq i \leq k} N(\Sigma_i, D_i)$. Using this parameter M we can state.

Theorem 4. *Let M be defined as above and let M be bounded by some constant which is not part of the input. Then the satisfiability problem for the local logic* $\mathrm{LocTL}_{\Sigma}(\mathsf{EX}, \mathsf{U})$ *is PSPACE-complete.*

Proof. The PSPACE-hardness follows from the word case. The PSPACE algorithm reduces the satisfiability problem in a first phase to a conjunction of satisfiability problems, one for each connected component of (Σ, D). Then we can check emptiness for the alternating automata according to the construction in Proposition 5. Checking emptiness for an alternating automaton can be done in PSPACE with respect to the size the automaton. □

The construction of an alternating automaton associated with a local temporal logic formula can be carried out for the *existential* until EU and the operator EG from TLC. Also, we can extend the construction for the past modalities EY, S and ES and for the operator Eco from TLC is we use two-ways alternating automata. Since the emptiness problem for two-ways alternating automata is also PSPACE-complete [10], we get a similar result for the local temporal logic using all operators. This extends the result in [1] concerning TLC.

7 Conclusion

We have defined a basic and natural local logic for Mazurkiewicz traces which is expressively complete with respect to first order if and only if the dependence alphabet is a cograph, i.e., all traces are series parallel graphs. The main open problem remains to define a (natural) local logic which yields expressive completeness for more general (best for all) dependence alphabets, and such that the satisfiability problem is in PSPACE or at least elementary.

There is a proposal by Walukiewicz [21] for a local logic for traces, but his focus is on monadic second order logic and based on a μ–calculus, so it is of quite different spirit.

References

1. R Alur, D. Peled, and W. Penczek. Model-checking of causality properties. In *Proceedingss of the Tenth IEEE Symposium on Logic in Computer Science (LICS'95)*, pages 90–100, 1995.
2. D.G. Corneil, H. Lerchs, and L.S. Burlingham. Complement reducible graphs. *Discrete Applied Mathematics*, 3:163–174, 1981.
3. V. Diekert and P. Gastin. LTL is expressively complete for Mazurkiewicz traces. In *Proceedings of ICALP 2000*, number 1853 in Lecture Notes in Computer Science, pages 211–222. Springer Verlag, 2000.

4. V. Diekert and G. Rozenberg, editors. *The Book of Traces.* World Scientific, Singapore, 1995.
5. W. Ebinger and A. Muscholl. Logical definability on infinite traces. *Theoretical Computer Science*, 154:67–84, 1996.
6. W. Ebinger. *Charakterisierung von Sprachklassen unendlicher Spuren durch Logiken.* Dissertation, Institut für Informatik, Universität Stuttgart, 1994.
7. D. Gabbay, A. Pnueli, S. Shelah, and J. Stavi. On the temporal analysis of fairness. In *Conference Record of the 12th ACM Symposium on Principles of Programming Languages*, pages 163–173, Las Vegas, Nev., 1980.
8. J. G. Henriksen. An expressive extension of TLC. In *Proceedings of ASIAN'99*, number 1742 in Lecture Notes in Computer Science, pages 126–138. Springer Verlag, 1999.
9. J. G. Henriksen. *Logic and Automata for Verification: Expressiveness and Decidability Issues.* PhD thesis, Dept. of Comp. Sci., University of Aarhus, 2000.
10. T. Jiang and B. Ravikumar. A note on the space complexity of some decision problems fir finite automata. *Information Processing Letters*, 40:25–31, 1991.
11. J. A. W. Kamp. *Tense Logic and the Theory of Linear Order.* PhD thesis, University of California, Los Angeles, Calif., 1968.
12. A. Mazurkiewicz. Concurrent program schemes and their interpretations. DAIMI Rep. PB 78, Aarhus University, Aarhus, 1977.
13. M. Mukund and P. S. Thiagarajan. Linear time temporal logics over Mazurkiewicz traces. In *Proceedings of the 21th MFCS, 1996*, number 1113 in Lecture Notes in Computer Science, pages 62–92. Springer Verlag, 1996.
14. P. Niebert. A ν-calculus with local views for sequential agents. In *Proceedings of the 20th MFCS, 1995*, number 969 in Lecture Notes in Computer Science, pages 563–573. Springer Verlag, 1995.
15. W. Penczek. Temporal logics for trace systems: On automated verification. *International Journal of Foundations of Computer Science*, 4:31–67, 1993.
16. R. Ramanujam. Locally linear time temporal logic. In *Proceedings of LICS'96*, Lecture Notes in Computer Science, pages 118–128, 1996.
17. P.S. Thiagarajan and I. Walukiewicz. An expressively complete linear time temporal logic for Mazurkiewicz traces. In *Proceedings of LICS'97*, 1997.
18. P. S. Thiagarajan. A trace based extension of linear time temporal logic. In *Proceedings of LICS'94*, pages 438–447, 1994.
19. M. Vardi. An automata-theoretic approach to linear temporal logic. In *Logics for Concurrency: Structure versus Automata,* number 1043 in Lecture Notes in Computer Science, pages 238–266. Springer Verlag, 1996.
20. I. Walukiewicz. Difficult configurations – on the complexity of LTrL. In *Proceedings of ICALP'98*, number 1443 in Lecture Notes in Computer Science, pages 140–151. Springer Verlag, 1998.
21. I. Walukiewicz. Local logics for traces. *Journal of Automata, Languages and Combinatorics*, 2001. To appear.
22. I. Walukiewicz. Private communication, 2001.
23. Th. Wilke. Classifying discrete temporal properties. In *Proceedings of STACS'99*, number 1563 in Lecture Notes in Computer Science, pages 32–46. Springer Verlag, 1999.

Games and Model Checking for Guarded Logics

Dietmar Berwanger and Erich Grädel

Mathematische Grundlagen der Informatik
RWTH Aachen

Abstract. We investigate the model checking problems for guarded first-order and fixed point logics by reducing them to parity games. This approach is known to provide good results for the modal μ-calculus and is very closely related to automata-based methods. To obtain good results also for guarded logics, optimized constructions of games have to be provided.
Further, we study the structure of parity games, isolate 'easy' cases that admit efficient algorithmic solutions, and determine their relationship to specific fragments of guarded fixed point logics.

1 Introduction

Guarded logics are fragments of first-order logic, second-order logic, or fixed point logics defined by restricting quantification so that, semantically speaking, each subformula can simultaneously refer only to elements that are 'very close together' or 'guarded'. The main motivation for the investigation of guarded logics was to explain the good algorithmic and model-theoretic properties of propositional *modal* logics (in a broad sense, including verification logics like CTL and the modal μ-calculus) and to generalize them to a richer setting. The goal was to define natural and expressive logics that could be used on relational structures of arbitrary vocabulary and still would retain convenient features of modal logic, such as the characterization via an appropriate notion of bisimulation, the applicability of automata-based methods, and the good balance between expressiveness and algorithmic manageability (see [13]).

Syntactically, guarded logics are based on a restriction of first-order quantification to the form $\exists \boldsymbol{y}(\alpha(\boldsymbol{x},\boldsymbol{y}) \wedge \psi(\boldsymbol{x},\boldsymbol{y}))$ or $\forall \boldsymbol{y}(\alpha(\boldsymbol{x},\boldsymbol{y}) \rightarrow \psi(\boldsymbol{x},\boldsymbol{y}))$ where quantifiers may range over a tuple $\boldsymbol{y}$ of variables, but are 'guarded' by a formula α that must contain all the free variables of the formula ψ that is quantified over. The guard formulae are of a simple syntactic form (in the basic version, they are just atoms). Depending on the conditions imposed on guard formulae, one has logics with different levels of 'guardedness'. In this paper we consider guarded fragments of first-order logic and least fixed point logic with two notions of guardedness.

While model-theoretic properties and satisfiability algorithms for guarded logics have already been studied rather extensively (see, e.g., [1,8,11,12,15]), the model checking problem has not yet received as much attention. In [9] a guarded variant of Datalog, called Datalog LITE, has been introduced which is shown

R. Nieuwenhuis and A. Voronkov (Eds.): LPAR 2001, LNAI 2250, pp. 70–84, 2001.

to admit efficient query evaluation (linear time in the query length and the size of the database). Datalog LITE is equivalent, via efficient translations, to the alternation-free portion of the guarded fixed point logic μGF so we have efficient model checking for an interesting part of μGF. Guarded logics have also been related to the complexity of query evaluation, in particular for conjunctive queries (see [7,10]). However, a systematic and comprehensive study of the complexity of model checking problems for guarded logics has not been done yet. In this paper, we attack this problem by developing the game approach to model checking for these logics.

It is well-known that model checking problems for almost any logic can be cast as strategy problems for the appropriate evaluation games (also called Hintikka games). That is, a sentence ψ is true in a structure $\mathfrak{A}$ if and only if Verifier (alias Player 0, alias Eloise) has a winning strategy in the associated Hintikka game $\mathcal{G}(\mathfrak{A}, \psi)$. For *first-order logic*, evaluation games are well-founded (i.e., all plays are finite) and the strategy problem can be solved in linear time in the size of the game. For fixed point logics, the appropriate evaluation games are *parity games.* These are infinite games where each position is assigned a natural number, called its priority, and the winner of an infinite play is determined according to whether the least priority seen infinitely often during the play is even or odd. It is open whether winning sets and winning strategies for parity games can be computed in polynomial time. The best algorithms known today are polynomial in the size of the game, but exponential with respect to the number of priorities. Competitive model checking algorithms for the modal μ-calculus work by solving the strategy problem for the associated parity game (see e.g. [18]).

The reason for the good model checking properties of *guarded logics* is that the associated evaluation games remain small. Indeed, guarded quantification limits the number of possible moves in the evaluation games and thus leads to smaller game graphs. We analyze the translation from guarded formulae to evaluation games and determine the complexity of the resulting games in terms of structural parameters of formulae and input structures. As a consequence *guarded fixed point logics* admit efficient model checking if and only if parity games can be efficiently solved. While we do not know whether this is possible in general, we analyze the structure of parity games and isolate 'easy' cases that admit efficient solutions. With this analysis, we also try to make precise some of the game theoretic intuitions that underly algorithmic approaches to automata and model checking problems. We link these 'easy games' to logic and thus obtain efficient model checking algorithms for fragments of guarded fixed point logic.

2 Guarded Logics

Definition 1. The *guarded fragment* GF of first-order logic is defined inductively as the closure of atomic formulae (in a relational vocabulary, with equality) under Boolean connectives and the following quantification rule: For every formula $\psi(\boldsymbol{x}, \boldsymbol{y}) \in$ GF and every atom $\alpha(\boldsymbol{x}, \boldsymbol{y})$ such that $\{y : y \text{ in } \boldsymbol{y}\} \cup \text{free}(\psi) \subseteq$

free(α), the formulae $\exists \boldsymbol{y}(\alpha(\boldsymbol{x},\boldsymbol{y}) \wedge \psi(\boldsymbol{x},\boldsymbol{y}))$ and $\forall \boldsymbol{y}(\alpha(\boldsymbol{x},\boldsymbol{y}) \rightarrow \psi(\boldsymbol{x},\boldsymbol{y}))$ also belong to GF. The semantics is the usual one for first-order logic.

Here, free(ψ) means the set of free variables of ψ. An atom $\alpha(\boldsymbol{x},\boldsymbol{y})$ that relativizes a quantifier as in the quantification rule for GF is the *guard* of the quantifier. We sometimes use the notation $(\exists \boldsymbol{y} \,.\, \alpha)\psi$ and $(\forall \boldsymbol{y} \,.\, \alpha)\psi$ for guarded formulae.

Guarded fixed point logic. The natural fixed point extension of GF is μGF and was introduced in [15]. It relates to GF in the same way as the modal μ-calculus relates to propositional modal logic and as least fixed point logic LFP (popular in finite model theory) relates to first-order logic FO.

Definition 2. μGF extends GF by the following rules for constructing fixed point formulae: Let T be a k-ary relation symbol, $\boldsymbol{x} = x_1, \dots, x_k$ a k-tuple of distinct variables, and $\psi(T, \boldsymbol{x})$ a formula that contains only positive occurrences of T, no free first-order variables other than $x_1, \dots, x_k$, and where T is not used in guards. Then we can build the formulae

$$[\mathrm{LFP}\; T\boldsymbol{x} \,.\, \psi](\boldsymbol{x}) \qquad \text{and} \qquad [\mathrm{GFP}\; T\boldsymbol{x} \,.\, \psi](\boldsymbol{x}).$$

The semantics of the fixed point formulae is the usual one: Given a structure $\mathfrak{A}$ providing interpretations for all free second-order variables in ψ, except T, we have $\mathfrak{A} \models [\mathrm{LFP}\; T\boldsymbol{x} \,.\, \psi(T,\boldsymbol{x})](\boldsymbol{a})$ iff $\boldsymbol{a}$ is contained in the least fixed point of the monotone operator mapping each $T \subseteq A^k$ to $\psi^{\mathfrak{A}}(T) := \{\boldsymbol{a} \in A^k : \mathfrak{A} \models \psi(T, \boldsymbol{a})\}$, and similarly for GFP and greatest fixed points.

It is clear that μGF generalizes the modal μ-calculus L_μ and also the μ-calculus with inverse modalities. Hence the algorithmic problems for μGF, even for formulae with two variables, are at least as hard as for L_μ.

Note that there are two important syntactic restrictions for μGF: Fixed point variables may not be used in guards and fixed point formulae may not contain parameters, i.e., other free variables than those used for constructing the fixed point. These restrictions on μGF are essential. Relaxing either of them would make the logic lose its desirable properties (decidability, closure under guarded bisimulation, tree model property). Hence μGF is contained in the *parameter-free fragment* of the least fixed point logic, which behaves somewhat differently than full LFP. For instance, while the expression complexity and combined complexity of LFP formulae of bounded width (even for width 2) is PSPACE-complete if parameters are allowed, the same problems for parameter-free formulae can be solved in NP $\cap$ co-NP (see [4,14,22]).

Clique guarded logics. In GF and μGF only atomic formulae can be used as guards. For some applications this is too restrictive (for instance, temporal operators like **until** cannot be expressed). There exist more general notions of guardedness that lead to more expressive guarded logics but preserve most of their desirable model-theoretic and algorithmic properties. The most powerful and arguably also the most natural of these extensions are the clique guarded logics.

Definition 3. Let $\mathfrak{A} = (A, R_1, \ldots, R_m)$ be a relational structure. A set $X \subseteq B$ is *guarded* in $\mathfrak{A}$ if $X = \{a\}$ or if there is a tuple $\boldsymbol{a} \in R_i$ (for some $i \leq m$) such that $X = \{a : a \text{ in } \boldsymbol{a}\}$. A set $X \subseteq A$ is *clique guarded* in $\mathfrak{A}$ if for any two elements a, a' of X there exists a guarded set containing both a and a'. (To put it differently, X induces a clique in the Gaifman graph of $\mathfrak{A}$). A tuple $\boldsymbol{a} \in A^k$ is (clique) guarded if $\boldsymbol{a} \in X^k$ for some clique guarded set X.

Note that for each finite vocabulary τ and each $k \in \mathbb{N}$, there is a positive, existential first-order formula $clique(x_1, \ldots, x_k)$ such that, for every τ-structure $\mathfrak{A}$ and every k-tuple $\boldsymbol{a} \in A^k$, $\mathfrak{A} \models clique(\boldsymbol{a}) \iff \boldsymbol{a}$ is clique guarded in $\mathfrak{A}$.

Definition 4. The *clique guarded fragment* CGF of first-order logic and the *clique guarded fixed point logic* μCGF are defined in the same way as GF and μGF, but with the *clique*-formulae as guards. Hence, the quantification rule for CGF and μCGF is the following: If $\psi(\boldsymbol{x}, \boldsymbol{y})$ is a formula of CFG or μCGF, then

$$\exists \boldsymbol{y}(clique(\boldsymbol{x}, \boldsymbol{y}) \wedge \psi(\boldsymbol{x}, \boldsymbol{y})) \quad \text{and} \quad \forall \boldsymbol{y}(clique(\boldsymbol{x}, \boldsymbol{y}) \rightarrow \psi(\boldsymbol{x}, \boldsymbol{y}))$$

belong to CGF, provided that $\text{free}(\psi) \cup \{y : y \text{ in } \boldsymbol{y}\} \subseteq \text{free}(clique)$.

In practice, one will not want to spell out the clique-formulae explicitly. One possibility is not to write them down at all, i.e., to take the usual (unguarded) first-order syntax and to change the semantics of quantifiers so that only clique guarded tuples are considered. Another common option is to use as guards any formula implying a clique formula, i.e., any of the form $\gamma(\boldsymbol{x}, \boldsymbol{y}) := \exists \boldsymbol{z} \beta(\boldsymbol{x}, \boldsymbol{y}, \boldsymbol{z})$ where β is a conjunction of atoms such that each pair of variables from $\text{free}(\gamma)$ occurs together in at least one conjunct of β. As we want our complexity results to be as powerful as possible, we do not take into account the length of clique guards at all. See [12] for background on clique guarded logics and their relations to other notions such as the *loosely guarded* or *packed* fragments.

Normal forms and alternation depth. We will always assume that fixed point formulae are in *negation normal form*, i.e., that negations apply to atoms only and that formulae are *well-named*, i.e., every fixed point variable is bound only once and the free second-order variables are distinct from fixed point variables. We write $D_\psi(T)$ for the unique subformula in ψ of form $[\text{FP}\, T\boldsymbol{x} \,.\, \varphi(T, \boldsymbol{x})]$ (here and in the following FP means either LFP or GFP). For technical reasons, we finally assume that each fixed point variable T occurs in $D_\psi(T)$ only inside the scope of a quantifier. This is a common assumption that does not affect the expressive power.

We say that T depends on T', if it occurs free in $D_\psi(T')$. The transitive closure of this dependency relation is called the *dependency order*, denoted by $\sqsubset_\psi$. The *alternation level* $\text{al}_\psi(T)$ of T in ψ is the maximal number of alternations between least and greatest fixed point variables on the $\sqsubset_\psi$-paths descending from T. The *alternation depth* $\text{ad}(\psi)$ of a fixed point sentence ψ is the maximal alternation level of its fixed point variables.

3 Evaluation Games for Guarded Logics

Parity games are two-player games of possibly infinite duration. We describe a parity game formally by a labelled graph $\mathcal{G} = (V, V_0, E, \Omega)$ over a finite set of *positions* V with a designated subset V_0, an irreflexive edge relation E representing the possible *moves*, and a labelling function $\Omega : V \to \mathbb{N}$ that assigns to each position a *priority*. The number of different priorities used in the game is the *index* of $\mathcal{G}$.

A *play* of $\mathcal{G}$ is a path $v_0, v_1, \ldots$ formed by the two players starting from a given position v_0. If the current position v belongs to V_0, Player 0 chooses a move $(v, w) \in E$ and the play proceeds from w. Otherwise, her opponent, Player 1, chooses the move. When no moves are available at the current position, the player who has to choose loses. In case this never occurs the play goes on infinitely and the winner is established by looking at the sequence $\Omega(v_0), \Omega(v_1), \ldots$ If the least priority appearing infinitely often in this sequence is even, Player 0 wins the play, otherwise Player 1 wins.

Let $V_1 := V \setminus V_0$ be the set of positions where Player 1 moves. A *positional strategy* for Player i in $\mathcal{G}$ is a function $f : V_i \to V$ which indicates a choice $(v, f(v)) \in E$ for every position $v \in V_i$. (It is called positional, because it does not depend on the history of the play, but only on the current position.) A strategy for a player is *winning* from position v_0 if the indicated choices allow him to win every play starting from v_0. We say a strategy is winning on a set W if it is winning from each position in W. The Forgetful Determinacy Theorem for parity games [5] states that these games are always determined (i.e. from each position one of the players has a winning strategy) and in fact, positional strategies always suffice.

Theorem 1 (Forgetful Determinacy). *In any parity game the set of positions can be partitioned into two sets W_0 and W_1 such that Player 0 has a positional winning strategy on W_0 and Player 1 has a positional winning strategy on W_1.*

We call W_0 and W_1 the *winning sets* of Player 0 and, respectively, Player 1 and the pair (W_0, W_1) the *winning partition* or *solution* of $\mathcal{G}$. Since positional strategies are small objects and since it can be efficiently checked whether a strategy is winning, it can be decided in NP ∩ co-NP whether a given position in a parity games is a winning position for Player 0. In fact, it is known [17] that the problem is in UP ∩ co-UP. The best known deterministic algorithms to compute winning partitions of parity games have running times that are polynomial with respect to the size of the game graph, but exponential with respect to the index of the game [18].

Theorem 2. *The winning partition of a parity game $\mathcal{G} = (V, V_0, E, \Omega)$ of index d can be computed in space $O(d \cdot |E|)$ and time*

$$O\left(d \cdot |E| \cdot \left(\frac{|V|}{\lfloor d/2 \rfloor}\right)^{\lfloor d/2 \rfloor}\right).$$

Game semantics for fixed point formulae. Consider a finite structure $\mathfrak{A}$ and a guarded fixed point sentence ψ which we assume to be well-named and in negation normal form.

The model checking game $\mathcal{G}(\mathcal{A}, \psi)$ is a parity game whose positions are pairs (φ, ρ) such that φ is a subformula of ψ, and ρ is an assignment from the free first-order variables of φ to elements of $\mathfrak{A}$. The initial position is the pair $(\psi, \emptyset)$.

Verifier (Player 0) moves at positions associated to disjunctions and to formulae starting with an existential quantifier. From a position $(\varphi \vee \vartheta, \rho)$ she moves to either (φ, ρ) or (ϑ, ρ). From a position $((\exists \boldsymbol{y} \,.\, \alpha)\varphi, \rho)$ Verifier can move to any position (φ, ρ') such that ρ' is the restriction to free(φ) of an assignment $\rho^+ : \text{free}(\alpha) \to A$ with $\rho^+ \supseteq \rho$ and $\mathfrak{A} \models \alpha[\rho^+]$. In addition, Verifier is supposed to move at atomic false positions, i.e., at positions (φ, ρ) such that φ is a literal $x = y$, $x \neq y$, $R\boldsymbol{x}$, or $\neg R\boldsymbol{x}$ (where R is *not* a fixed point variable) and $\mathfrak{A} \models \neg\varphi[\rho]$. However, positions associated with literals do have no successors, so Verifier loses at atomic false positions.

Dually, Falsifier (Player 1) moves at conjunctions and universal quantifications, and loses at atomic true positions. In addition there are positions associated with fixed point formulae and with fixed points atoms. At these positions there is a unique move (by Falsifier, say) to the formula defining the fixed point. For a more formal definition, recall that as ψ is well-named there is for any fixed point variable T in ψ a unique subformula $[\text{FP } T\boldsymbol{x} \,.\, \varphi(T, \boldsymbol{x})](\boldsymbol{x})$. From position $([\text{FP } T\boldsymbol{x} \,.\, \varphi(T, \boldsymbol{x})](\boldsymbol{x}), \rho)$ Falsifier moves to the pair (φ, ρ), and from $(T\boldsymbol{y}, \rho)$ he moves to the position $(\varphi(T, \boldsymbol{x}), \rho')$ with $\rho'(\boldsymbol{x}) = \rho(\boldsymbol{y})$.

In the simple case where we do not have fixed points (i.e., we deal with formulae from GF or CGF), the game is just the guarded version of the usual Hintikka game for first-order logic. In particular, it is well-founded, and it should be obvious that Verifier has a winning strategy for $\mathcal{G}(\mathfrak{A}, \psi)$ iff $\mathfrak{A} \models \psi$. Next, we consider the case of a formula with just one least fixed point. From a position $([\text{LFP } T\boldsymbol{x} \,.\, \varphi(T, \boldsymbol{x})](\boldsymbol{x}), \rho)$ the Verifier tries to establish that $\rho(\boldsymbol{x})$ enters T at stage α of the fixed point induction defined by φ. The game goes to (φ, ρ) and from there, as φ is a guarded first-order formula, Verifier can either win the φ-game in a finite number of steps, or she can force it to a position $(T\boldsymbol{y}, \rho')$ where $\rho'(\boldsymbol{y})$ enters the fixed point at some stage $\beta < \alpha$. The game then resumes at a position associated with φ. As any descending sequence of ordinals is finite, Verifier will win the game in a finite number of steps. If the formula is not true, then Falsifier can either win in a finite number of steps or force the play to go through infinitely many positions of form $T\boldsymbol{y}$. Hence, these positions should be assigned priority 1 (and all other positions higher priorities) so that such a play will be won by Falsifier. For GFP-formulae the situation is reversed. Verifier wants to force an infinite play, going infinitely often through positions $T\boldsymbol{y}$, so GFP-atoms are assigned priority 0.

In the general case, we have a formula ψ with nested least and greatest fixed points and on an infinite play of $\mathcal{G}(\mathfrak{A}, \psi)$ one may see different fixed point variables infinitely often. But then one of these variables is the smallest with respect to the dependency order $\sqsubset_\psi$. It can be shown that $\mathfrak{A} \models \psi$ iff this smallest variable is a GFP-variable (provided players play optimally).

Hence, the priority labelling should assign even priorities to GFP-atoms and odd priorities to LFP-atoms. Further, if $T \sqsubset_\psi T'$ and T, T' are fixed point variables of different kind, then T-atoms should get lower priority than T'-atoms.

As the index of a parity game is the main source of difficulty in computing winning sets, the number of different priorities should be kept as small as possible. We avoid the factor 2 appearing in common constructions of this kind by adjusting the definition of alternation level and alternation depth, setting $\mathrm{al}^*_\psi(T) := \mathrm{al}_\psi(T) + 1$ if $\mathrm{al}_\psi(T)$ is even (odd) and T is an LFP (GFP) variable. In the other cases, $\mathrm{al}^*_\psi(T) = \mathrm{al}_\psi(T)$. Finally let $\mathrm{ad}^*(\psi)$ be the maximal value of $\mathrm{ad}^*_\psi(T)$ for the fixed point variables in ψ.

Definition 5. The priority labelling Ω on positions of $\mathcal{G}(\mathfrak{A}, \psi)$ is defined by

$$\Omega(\psi, \rho) = \begin{cases} \mathrm{al}^*_\psi(T) & \text{if } \varphi = T\boldsymbol{x} \text{ and } T \text{ is a fixed point variable} \\ \mathrm{ad}^*_\psi & \text{otherwise.} \end{cases}$$

This completes the definition of the game $\mathcal{G}(\mathcal{A}, \psi)$. Note that the priority labelling satisfies the properties explained above, and that the index of $\mathcal{G}(\mathcal{A}, \psi)$ is at most $\mathrm{ad}(\psi) + 1$.

The proof that the game is correct is similar to the proofs for model checking games for the μ-calculus (see e.g. [16,21]). For details taking into account the optimizations made here, see [2].

Proposition 1. *Let ψ be a guarded fixed point sentence from μGF or μCGF, and let $\mathfrak{A}$ be a relational structure. $\mathfrak{A} \models \psi$ if and only if Player 0 has a winning strategy for the parity game $\mathcal{G}(\mathcal{A}, \psi)$.*

4 The Complexity of Model Checking

The reduction scheme in the previous section provides a model checking technique for guarded fixed point logics: Given $(\mathfrak{A}, \psi)$, construct the corresponding game $\mathcal{G}(\mathfrak{A}, \psi)$ and check whether Player 0 has a winning strategy. The complexity of this algorithm is determined by the complexity of the reduction and the complexity of solving the resulting parity game. In this section we discuss the construction of the game $\mathcal{G}(\mathcal{A}, \psi)$ for different kinds of guarded formulae and determine the size of the game. The general algorithmic results on parity games, yield complexity results for our model checking problems. In the last section, we will then look more closely at the structure of games.

We can measure the complexity in terms of different parameters of the given formula and the given finite structure. Relevant notions, besides formula length, are the closure $\mathrm{cl}(\psi)$ of ψ, which is just the set of its subformulae, and the *width*, which is the maximal number of free variables in subformulae, i.e. $\mathrm{width}(\psi) := \max\{|\mathrm{free}(\varphi)| : \varphi \in \mathrm{cl}(\psi)\}$. The size of a finite relational structure

$\mathfrak{A} = (A, R_1, \ldots, R_m)$ is defined as $\|\mathfrak{A}\| = |A| + \sum_{i=1}^{m} r_i |R_i|$ where r_i is the arity of R_i (i.e., the number of structure elements plus the sum of the length of all tuples in its relations).

Model checking GF and μGF. It is obvious that GF generalizes propositional modal logic ML. The model checking problem for ML is PTIME-complete [14] and can be solved in time $O(\|\mathfrak{A}\| \cdot |\psi|)$. Both results extend to GF.

Proposition 2. *Given a sentence $\psi \in \mu$GF and a finite structure $\mathfrak{A}$, the associated parity game $\mathcal{G}(\mathfrak{A}, \psi)$ can be constructed in time $O(\|\mathfrak{A}\| \cdot |\psi|)$.*

Proof. In the construction of the parity game $\mathcal{G}(\mathfrak{A}, \psi) = (V, V_0, E, \Omega)$ we can restrict V to the positions (φ, ρ) that are reachable from the initial position $(\psi, \emptyset)$. The construction of the game is straightforward, we just have to estimate its size. It suffices to prove that $|E| = O(\|\mathfrak{A}\| \cdot |\psi|)$.

Let $H(\psi)$ be the syntax tree of ψ, with back edges from fixed point atoms $T\boldsymbol{x}$ to the defining formula $\varphi(T, \boldsymbol{x})$. Obviously, $H(\psi)$ has less than $|\psi|$ nodes and edges.

We claim that for every edge $\varphi \to \varphi'$ of $H(\psi)$ there exist at most $\|\mathfrak{A}\|$ edges of form $(\varphi, \rho) \to (\varphi', \rho')$ in the game graph $\mathcal{G}(\mathfrak{A}, \psi)$. We consider several cases.

First, let $\varphi = (Q\boldsymbol{x} \,.\, \alpha)\varphi'$. In that case an edge $(\varphi, \rho) \to (\varphi, \rho')$ can exist only if there exists an assignment ρ^+ such that $\mathfrak{A} \models \alpha[\rho^+]$ and ρ, ρ' are the restrictions of ρ^+ to the free variables of φ and φ', respectively. As guards are atomic formulae the number of assignments satisfying a guard is bounded by $\|\mathfrak{A}\|$.

In all other cases, i.e. if φ is not a quantified formula, then for any fixed φ and ρ there are at most two edges $(\varphi, \rho) \to (\varphi', \rho')$. Hence it suffices to show that for each such $\varphi \in H(\psi)$ there exist at most $\|\mathfrak{A}\|$ reachable positions (φ, ρ) in the game graph. Recall that fixed point variables occur inside their defining formulae only under the scope of a quantifier. If φ is not inside a quantifier, only the position $(\varphi, \emptyset)$ is reachable. Otherwise there is a uniquely determined least subformula of ψ that strictly contains φ and has the form $(Q\boldsymbol{y} \,.\, \alpha)\vartheta$. Then a position (φ, ρ) is reachable if and only if (ϑ, ρ) is reachable. Note that ϑ and α are uniquely determined by φ, and the position (ϑ, ρ) is reachable only if $\mathfrak{A} \models \alpha[\rho^+]$ where $\rho^+ \supseteq \rho$. By the same argument as above it follows that the number of reachable positions (φ, ρ) is bound by $\|\mathfrak{A}\|$. This completes the proof.

According to Theorem 2, we obtain the following complexity bounds for model checking μGF via the associated parity game.

Theorem 3. *Given a structure $\mathfrak{A}$ and a μGF-sentence ψ of alternation depth d the model checking problem $\mathfrak{A} \models \psi$ can be solved in space $O(d \cdot \|\mathfrak{A}\| \cdot |\psi|)$ and time*

$$O\left(d^2 \cdot \left(\frac{\|\mathfrak{A}\| \cdot |\psi|}{\lfloor (d+1)/2 \rfloor}\right)^{\lfloor (d+3)/2 \rfloor}\right).$$

It is instructive to compare these results to the case of unguarded formulae. Note that even though there is no explicit restriction on the width (or equivalently, the number of first-order variables) in GF or μGF, the width is implicitly bounded by the arity of the relation symbols. (On graphs, for instance, GF and μGF are really two-variable logics). For a meaningful comparison of the size of evaluation games and the model checking complexity for GF/μGF with FO/LFP (or with clique guarded logics, see below) one should bound the width of these formulae.

On a coarse level, if one just considers membership and completeness in major complexity classes, then modal logic ML, bounded-variable first-order logics, and GF are on the same level, with model checking problems that are PTIME-complete. For fixed-point logics, a similar picture emerges: L_μ, bounded-width parameter-free LFP, and μGF have model checking problems that are in UP $\cap$ co-UP and hard for PTIME.

However, a more detailed analysis reveals differences that are quite relevant for practical algorithms. Even for bounded-variable fragments FO^k of first-order logic the size of the corresponding model checking game is $O(|A|^k|\psi|)$, as in general, all possible assignments $\rho : \{x_1, \ldots, x_k\} \to A$ need to be taken into account. Hence, the model checking games (and the complexity) of bounded-variable logics are often quite substantially larger than for guarded logics. We will see that the complexity of clique guarded logic is between these two.

Model checking CGF **and** μCGF**.** By the definition of clique guardedness, for a tuple $\boldsymbol{x}$ of variables appearing free in a subformula of ψ, the value of any assignment $\rho(\boldsymbol{x})$ induces a clique in the Gaifman graph of $\mathfrak{A}$. The number and size of cliques in this graph can be bound by parameters derived from its tree decompositions.

Definition 6. A *tree decomposition* of width l of some structure $\mathcal{B}$ is a tree labelled with subsets of at most $l+1$ elements of B, called *blocks*, such that (1) every strictly guarded set in $\mathcal{B}$ is included in some block and (2) for any element $a \in B$ the set of blocks which contain b is connected. The *tree width* of $\mathcal{B}$ is the minimal width of a tree decomposition of $\mathcal{B}$.

Lemma 1. *Given a structure $\mathfrak{A}$ of tree width l, the number of clique guarded assignments in $\mathfrak{A}$ for a tuple of k variables is bounded by $c_k(\mathfrak{A}) := (l+1)^k \cdot |\mathfrak{A}|$.*

Proof. Let T be a tree decomposition of width l of the structure $\mathfrak{A}$ and thus also of its Gaifman graph. A simple graph theoretic argument [12] shows that cliques are not disbanded by tree decompositions, that is, every clique of the Gaifman graph is contained in some decomposition block. Consequently, every clique guarded set in $\mathfrak{A}$, in particular $\rho(\boldsymbol{x})$, is contained in some block of T. Since we can assume without loss that $|T| \leq |A|$, the number of clique guarded k-tuples in $\mathfrak{A}$, and with it the number of clique guarded assignments, is bounded by $(l+1)^k \cdot |A|$.

By a similar analysis as in the case of μGF we obtain the following estimates.

Proposition 3. *Given a μCGF-sentence ψ of width k and a finite structure $\mathfrak{A}$ of tree width l, the associated parity game $\mathcal{G}(\mathfrak{A}, \psi)$ can be constructed in time $O(c_k(\mathfrak{A}) \cdot |\mathrm{cl}(\psi)|)$.*

Theorem 4. *For a structure $\mathfrak{A}$ and a μCGF sentence ψ of width k and alternation depth d the model checking problem can be solved in space $O(d \cdot c_k(\mathfrak{A}) \cdot |\mathrm{cl}(\psi)|)$ and time*

$$O\left(d^2 \cdot \left(\frac{c_k(\mathfrak{A}) \cdot |\mathrm{cl}(\psi)|}{\lfloor (d+1)/2 \rfloor}\right)^{\lfloor (d+3)/2 \rfloor}\right).$$

For unguarded sentences, corresponding complexity expressions are obtained by replacing $c_k(\mathfrak{A})$ with the number of possible assignments in that case, $|\mathfrak{A}|^k$. If the tree width l of $\mathfrak{A}$ is small compared to $|\mathfrak{A}|$ this value is be much higher than $c_k(\mathfrak{A}) = (l+1)^k \cdot |\mathfrak{A}|$. Especially, for a fixed clique guarded sentence ψ, the size of the game $\mathcal{G}(\mathfrak{A}, \psi)$ for structures $\mathfrak{A}$ of bounded tree width grows linearly with the size of $\mathfrak{A}$, while it grows polynomially with degree k when ψ is unguarded.

However, in the case of unbounded width the model checking problem for CGF and μCGF ar as hard as for FO and LFP. To prove this, one takes input structures with a complete binary guard relation, so that all tuples in the structure become clique guarded. Similar observations apply to expression complexity and to other guarded logics (like loosely guarded or packed fragments).

Proposition 4. *The model checking problems for* CGF *and* μCGF *of unbounded width are* PSPACE*-complete and* EXPTIME*-complete, respectively.*

5 Easy Games and Tractable Fixed Point Formulae

In the previous section we established complexity results for model checking problems based on complexity bounds for the associated parity games as given by Theorem 2. These complexity bounds take into account worst-case scenarios as, for example, that the underlying game graph is strongly connected and that each player can force the play to reach almost any priority. However, for model checking games resulting from specific classes of formulae or structures such assumptions may be overly pessimistic and better heuristics apply. By looking more closely at the structure of parity games, we can isolate easy cases of games and obtain classes of formulae for which the associated parity games can be solved efficiently, in subquadratic time with regard to their size.

De-tangling the game. An obvious approach to complex problems is by decomposition into independent simpler subproblems. In the context of games subproblems correspond to subgames. A *subgame* of a parity game $\mathcal{G}$ is a game $\mathcal{G}\restriction_U$ obtained by restricting $\mathcal{G}$ to the positions of some subset $U \subseteq V$. The subgame induced by the set of all positions reachable from a node v in $\mathcal{G}$ is called *rooted* at v and denoted by $\mathcal{G}\restriction_v$. We say a subgame $\mathcal{H}$ of $\mathcal{G}$ is *stable*, if the winning set of each player in $\mathcal{H}$ is a subset of its winning set in $\mathcal{G}$.

Clearly, in any game the rooted subgames are stable. Given a parity game $\mathcal{G}$, let $\mathcal{H}$ be a rooted subgame. Note that there may be different positions v, w such that $\mathcal{H} = \mathcal{G}\restriction_v = \mathcal{G}\restriction_w$. In that case we say that v and w are *entangled.* The entanglement relation is an equivalence on game positions. Let us call its classes the *tangles* of $\mathcal{G}$. In particular, we call the class of v with $\mathcal{G}\restriction_v = \mathcal{H}$ the *root tangle* of $\mathcal{H}$. Via their root tangle the rooted subgames of $\mathcal{G}$ are in one-to-one correspondence to the tangles of $\mathcal{G}$. We call a tangle that induces a rooted subgame in $\mathcal{G}$ a *leaf* tangle. Observe that the tangles of a game are precisely the strongly connected components of the underlying graph. Over these the reachability relation in $\mathcal{G}$ induces a partial ordering with the root tangle of $\mathcal{G}$ as the greatest element and the leaf tangles as least elements.

Towards a divide-and-conquer approach, we are interested in subproblems which are independent, so that the global solution can easily be recomposed from the partial solutions. Suppose that, in order to solve $\mathcal{G}$, some rooted strict subgame $\mathcal{G}\restriction_U$ was already solved. At this point it would not help to solve the subgame induced by the unresolved positions $\mathcal{G}\restriction_{V\setminus U}$, which is it not necessarily stable. Instead, we can first propagate the solutions found for U into $V \setminus U$ by including in the winning set W_0 of Player 0 every position from V_0 with some successor already in W_0 and those positions from V_1 with all successors already in W_0; for Player 1 we can proceed dually. Let P be the set of positions assigned to winning sets by iterating the above process. Then the subgame $\mathcal{G}\restriction_{V\setminus(U\cup P)}$ induced by the unresolved positions is stable.

This suggests a heuristics for solving a parity game that starts by solving the leaf tangles and then, after propagating their solutions, applies recursively to the subgame induced by the unresolved positions. In a concrete implementation, this heuristics relies on three algorithms.

(1) A *decomposition procedure* which computes and updates the strongly connected components of the game graph to provide a list of its leaf tangles.
(2) A *tangle-solver* for solving the games induced by the leaf tangles.
(3) A *propagator* that evaluates the obtained partial solutions and passes a new stable subgame to the next recursion step.

For an efficient implementation, the game graph can initially be decomposed into its strongly connected components by using Tarjan's algorithm which works in time linear in the number of edges. Subsequently, this decomposition can be updated dynamically by removing a component after each call of the tangle-solver and refining the decomposition order for every batch of positions removed from the original game by the propagator. By adapting an algorithm from [3] the time for this operation can be linearly bounded by the number of removed edges, so the global algorithm will not spend more than linear time in the decomposition procedure. Also the propagator can be written such that it visits every edge of the game graph at most once. Thus, the above heuristics leads to an algorithm which spends only linear time in the decomposition and the propagation procedures.

Proposition 5. *The winning partition of a parity game can be computed efficiently if an efficient tangle-solver is available.*

Well-founded games. A tangle is *trivial*, if it consists of a single position. If all tangles in a game are trivial, the game graph is acyclic and the solution of the leaf tangles propagate all the way up to the root. Such games are called *well-founded*, and it is folklore that they can be solved efficiently.

Proposition 6. *Any well-founded game can be solved in linear time.*

For instance, given a well-founded game $\mathcal{G} = (V, V_0, E)$ we can write in time $O(|E|)$ a propositional Horn formula $\psi_{\mathcal{G}}$ consisting of the clauses $u \leftarrow v$ for all edges $(u, v) \in E$ with $u \in V_0$, and the clauses $u \leftarrow v_1 \wedge \cdots \wedge v_m$ for all nodes $u \in V - V_0$ where $uE = \{v_1, \ldots, v_m\}$. The minimal model of $\psi_{\mathcal{G}}$ is precisely the winning set W_0. In fact for well-founded games, the above heuristics yields a linear time decision procedure which coincides with the known linear time algorithm for solving propositional Horn formulae.

Corollary 1. *For a structure $\mathfrak{A}$ and a* CGF*-sentence ψ of width k, the model checking problem can be solved in time $O(c_k(\mathfrak{A}) \cdot |\text{cl}(\psi)|)$. If $\psi \in$ GF the problem can be solved in time $O(\|\mathfrak{A}\| \cdot |\psi|)$.*

Dull versus lively games. Given a game, an i-loop is a simple cycle in the game graph with the least occurring priority i. Let the *range* of a tangle T be the set of priorities i for which T contains an i-loop. We say a tangle is *dull* if all priorities in its range are of the same parity. A game is dull if all its tangles are so, otherwise it is called *lively.* Note that whenever a tangle is not trivial, then its range contains the least priority occurring in it. Thus, any nontrivial tangle T which is dull in a game $\mathcal{G}$ can be decided by checking whether the least occurring priority is even. If this is the case, Player 0 wins from each position in $\mathcal{G}\restriction_T$, otherwise he loses. Using this tangle-solver with our heuristics we can solve dull games in linear time.

Theorem 5. *Any dull game $\mathcal{G} = (V, V_0, E, \Omega)$ can be solved in time $O(|V|+|E|)$.*

The problem of establishing the winner of a parity game is algorithmically equivalent to the emptiness problem for nondeterministic parity automata over *trees.* In [20] Kupferman, Vardi, and Wolper show that the latter problem reduces to the 1-letter emptiness problem of alternating automata over *words.* In this framework, dull games correspond to so-called weak automata. Kupferman, Vardi, and Wolper show that the 1-letter emptiness problem for weak alternating word automata can be solved in linear time, thus proving that model checking for alternation-free L_μ-formulae can be performed in linear time. Here, we will generalize this result to alternation-free guarded formulae, i.e., formulae of alternation depth 1. Towards this, let us establish a connection between the alternation depth of a formula and the range of the tangles in the associated game. Let T be a tangle in a model checking game $\mathcal{G}(\mathfrak{A}, \psi)$. We say that a fixed point variable X is *alive* in T if the tangle contains some position $(X\boldsymbol{x}, \beta)$.

Lemma 2. *In any nontrivial tangle of $\mathcal{G}(\mathfrak{A}, \psi)$ the set of alive fixed point variables has a unique minimal element w.r.t. $\sqsubset_\psi$.*

Proof. Consider a play π cycling in T from some position $v = (X\boldsymbol{x}, \beta)$ back to itself. By a straightforward induction, we can verify that for each fixed point variable Y seen along π, $D_\psi(Y)$ is a subformula of $D_\psi(X)$ and X appears free in $D_\psi(Y)$. Hence, $X \sqsubset_\psi Y$ for all fixed point variables Y on π. As T is strongly connected, for any variable $Y \in T$ there is a play cycling through X and Y.

Observe that in a model checking game the range of a tangle T consists of the priorities of all alive fixed point variables. Thus, if all these variables depend on some fixed point variable X, the range of T is included in $\{\Omega(Y) : X \sqsubset_\psi Y\}$. By definition, in an alternation-free formula ψ there are no dependencies between variables of different kind. Accordingly, the priorities associated to any two alive variables are of the same parity. It follows that there are no alternating priorities in the range of any tangle of a model checking game $\mathcal{G}(\mathfrak{A}, \psi)$.

Proposition 7. *Alternation-free fixed point formulae lead to dull games.*

Corollary 2. *For a structure* $\mathfrak{A}$ *and an alternation-free* μCGF*-sentence* ψ *of width* k*, model checking can be performed in time* $O(c_k(\mathfrak{A}) \cdot |\mathrm{cl}(\psi)|)$*. In particular, if* $\psi \in \mu$GF *the problem can be solved in time* $O(\|\mathfrak{A}\| \cdot |\psi|)$.

The result for alternation-free μGF has been proved by a different method in [9].

Solitaire games. For arbitrary games, the number of alternating priorities in the range of a tangle or, more generally, its index, is not bounded. To our present knowledge, this index appears as a significant source of complexity in all decision procedures for parity games. Typically, the worst-case running time of such a procedure grows exponentially with (a constant fraction of) the index. One reason for this difficulty may be that even if a player has a winning strategy in a game, he cannot tell in which priority the play will finally be trapped. In general, the opponent may be able to choose at any point between different, though hostile, loops and thus continually trade against the first player's strategy. The costs of a search for a trap where all this trading is ineffective can be quite high in terms of complexity.

In the case of dull games considered above, this difficulty is circumvented by restricting the trading range as much as possible. Thus, each player knows that the only way to win is by attracting its opponent into a loop of the right priority in which the game can be kept infinitely. Another approach to avoid the difficulties caused by trading priorities consists in allowing only one player to move in the cyclic parts of the game.

Definition 7. A game is *solitaire* if all nontrivial moves are performed by the same player. A game is *nested solitaire* if all its tangles are solitaire games.

Notice that a positional strategy can be presented as a solitaire game. In the automata-theoretic view a solitaire game corresponds to a *deterministic* parity tree automaton whose emptiness problem is linear time reducible to the nonemptiness problem of a one-letter nondeterministic parity word automaton. This problem was known to be solvable in time $O((n + m)d)$ for an automaton with n states, m transitions and d even priorities. Recently, King, Kupferman, and Vardi [19] presented an algorithm which solves this problem in time $O((n+m)\log d)$. Via the aforementioned equivalence their result applies to solitaire games also.

Proposition 8. *The winner of a solitaire game* $\mathcal{G} = (V, V_0, E, \Omega)$ *of index* d *can be established in time* $O\big(\log d \cdot (|V| + |E|)\big)$.

However, for deciding the winner of a *nested* solitaire game, our heuristics relies on the computation of the entire winning partition of leaf tangles. It is not clear whether the algorithm of King, Kupferman, and Vardi can be extended to a fast solver for games that consist of solitaire tangles but are not solitaire themselves. To solve the leaf tangles of such games we will therefore use another approach.

Let $\mathcal{H}$ be a solitaire game on a tangle with all positions belonging to Player 0. She wins from a position if she can reach an even loop. Let the even priorities in the range of $\mathcal{H}$ be $\{i_1, \ldots, i_d\}$. To determine the winning partition of $\mathcal{H}$ we can proceed as follows.

Decompose $\mathcal{H}$ into d copies $\mathcal{H}_1, \ldots, \mathcal{H}_d$ where $\mathcal{H}_j$ is the subgame of $\mathcal{H}$ induced by the positions of priority at least i_j. Transform $\mathcal{H}_j$ into a dull game by assigning to all positions of priority greater than i_j some higher, odd priority. Now solve every $\mathcal{H}_j$ as a dull game. Note that, if the copy of a position v in $\mathcal{H}_j$ is winning for Player 0, then v is also winning in $\mathcal{H}$. Thus, the union of winning sets in the copies $\mathcal{H}_j$ yields, by propagation, the winning set of Player 0 in $\mathcal{H}$.

This procedure reduces the solution of a solitaire tangle game to the solution of d dull games. By embedding the algorithm into our decomposition and propagation scheme we obtain a solver for nested solitaire games.

Theorem 6. *A nested solitaire parity game* $\mathcal{G} = (V, V_0, E, \Omega)$ *of index* d *can be solved in time* $O\big(d \cdot (|V| + |E|)\big)$.

Solitaire formulae. Given that nested solitaire games can be treated efficiently, the question arises whether these games correspond to a natural fragment of fixed point logic. Note that in a model checking game, Player 0 makes choices at positions corresponding to disjunctions or existential quantifications, whereas Player 1 makes nontrivial choices at conjunctions and universal quantifications. To make sure that all tangles in a game are (nested) solitaire we thus have to restrict the use of one of these pairs of operators. The radical approach would be to remove $\wedge$ and $\forall$ (or, equivalently, $\vee$ and $\exists$). We thus would obtain a fragment whose model checking games are solitaire which, however, is not very expressive. A more liberal approach is to restrict the syntax as follows.

Definition 8. The *solitaire fragment* of μCGF consist of those formulae where negation and universal quantification apply to closed formulae only and conjunctions to pairs of formulae of which at least one is closed.

Recall that a fixed point formula is *closed* if it contains no free fixed point variables. By Lemma 2, positions with closed subformulae are not entangled with any other positions. Consequently, the model checking games of solitaire μCGF-formulae are nested solitaire games. We remark that the solitaire fragment of the modal μ-calculus has already been studied under the name L_2 in [6].

Proposition 9. *The model checking problem for a structure* $\mathfrak{A}$ *and a solitaire* μCGF*-sentence* ψ *of width* k *and alternation depth* d*, can be solved in time* $O\left(d \cdot c_k(\mathfrak{A}) \cdot |\mathrm{cl}(\psi)|\right)$. *In particular, for* $\varphi \in \mu$GF *the problem can be solved in time* $O\left(d \cdot \|\mathfrak{A}\| \cdot |\psi|\right)$.

References

[1] H. Andréka, J. van Benthem, and I. Németi, *Modal languages and bounded fragments of predicate logic*, Journal of Philosophical Logic, 27 (1998), 217–274.

[2] D. Berwanger, *Games and model checking for guarded logics.* Diploma thesis, RWTH Aachen, 2000.

[3] R. Bloem, H. Gabow, and F. Somenzi, *An algorithm for strongly connected component analysis in $n \log n$ symbolic steps*, in Formal Methods in Computer Aided Design, LNCS Nr. 1954 (2000), 37–54.

[4] S. Dziembowski, *Bounded-variable fixpoint queries are PSPACE-complete*, Computer Science Logic CSL 96. LNCS Nr. 1258 (1996), 89–105.

[5] A. Emerson and C. Jutla, *Tree automata, mu-calculus and determinacy*, in Proc. 32nd IEEE Symp. on Foundations of Computer Science, 1991, 368–377.

[6] A. Emerson and C. Jutla and A. P. Sistla, *On model checking for the μ-calculus and its fragments*, Theoretical Computer Science 258 (2001), 491–522.

[7] J. Flum, M. Frick, and M. Grohe, *Query evaluation via tree-decompositions*, in Database Theory - ICDT 2001, LNCS Nr. 1973 (2001), 22–38.

[8] H. Ganzinger, C. Meyer, and M. Veanes, *The two-variable guarded fragment with transitive relations*, in Proc. 14th IEEE Symp. on Logic in Computer Science, 1999, 24–34.

[9] G. Gottlob, E. Grädel, and H. Veith, *Datalog LITE: A deductive query language with linear time model checking*, ACM Transactions on Computational Logic, (to appear).

[10] G. Gottlob, N. Leone, and F. Scarcello, *Robbers, marshals, and guards: Game theoretic and logical characterizations of hypertree width*, in Proc. 20th ACM Symp. on Principles of Database Systems, 2001, 195–201.

[11] E. Grädel, *On the restraining power of guards*, Journal of Symbolic Logic, 64 (1999), 1719–1742.

[12] E. Grädel, *Guarded fixed point logics and the monadic theory of countable trees*, to appear in Theoretical Computer Science, (2001).

[13] E. Grädel, *Why are modal logics so robustly decidable?*, in Current Trends in Theoretical Computer Science. Entering the 21st Century, G. Paun, G. Rozenberg, and A. Salomaa, eds., World Scientific, 2001, 393–498.

[14] E. Grädel and M. Otto, *On logics with two variables*, Theoretical Computer Science, 224 (1999), 73–113.

[15] E. Grädel and I. Walukiewicz, *Guarded fixed point logic*, in Proc. 14th IEEE Symp. on Logic in Computer Science, 1999, 45–54.

[16] B. Herwig, *Zur Modelltheorie von L_μ*. Dissertation, Universität Freiburg, 1989.

[17] M. Jurdzinski, *Deciding the winner in parity games is in UP $\cap$ Co-UP.*, Information Processing Letters, 68 (1998), 119–124.

[18] M. Jurdziński, *Small progress measures for solving parity games*, Proceedings of STACS 2000, LNCS Nr. 1770 (2000), 290–301.

[19] V. King, O. Kupferman, and M. Vardi, *On the complexity of parity word automata*, in Proceedings of FOSSACS 2001, LNCS Nr. 2030 (2001), 276–286.

[20] O. Kupferman, M. Vardi, and P. Wolper, *An automata-theoretic approach to branching-time model checking*, Journal of the ACM, 47 (2000), 312–360.

[21] C. Stirling, *Bisimulation, model checking and other games.* Notes for the Mathfit instructional meeting on games and computation. Edinburgh, 1997.

[22] M. Vardi, *On the complexity of bounded-variable queries*, in Proc. 14th ACM Symp. on Principles of Database Systems, 1995, 266–267.

Computational Space Efficiency and Minimal Model Generation for Guarded Formulae*

Lilia Georgieva[1], Ullrich Hustadt[2], and Renate A. Schmidt[1]

[1] Department of Computer Science, University of Manchester
Manchester M13 9PL, United Kingdom, {georgiel,schmidt}@cs.man.ac.uk
[2] Department of Computer Science, University of Liverpool
Liverpool L69 7ZF, United Kingdom, U.Hustadt@csc.liv.ac.uk

Abstract. This paper describes a number of hyperresolution-based decision procedures for a subfragment of the guarded fragment. We first present a polynomial space decision procedure of optimal worst-case space and time complexity for the fragment under consideration. We then consider minimal model generation procedures which construct all and only minimal Herbrand models for guarded formulae. These procedures are based on hyperresolution, (complement) splitting and either model constraint propagation or local minimality tests. All the procedures have concrete application domains and are relevant for multi-modal and description logics that can be embedded into the considered fragment.

1 Introduction

The guarded fragment (GF) is a generalisation of the modal fragment of first-order logic. The fragment was introduced in an attempt to explain the good model-theoretic and proof-theoretic properties of modal logics, including the decidability of the satisfiability problem [1]. A variety of decision procedures for the fragment and its extensions have been developed, which utilise different techniques such as ordered resolution, model-theoretic constructions, alternating automata or embedding into second-order logic [7,9,12,13]. However, the devised decision procedures have some drawbacks. In particular, they exhibit at least double exponential worst-case time and space complexity [7,12] which is in contrast to the low complexity of the satisfiability problem of basic modal logic. Moreover, extensions of the guarded fragment with transitivity or number restrictions lead to undecidability [10], even though modal logics extended with transitivity or number restrictions are decidable. This shows that the guarded fragment as a whole is too general and expressive and cannot thoroughly explain the good computational properties of modal logics and related description logics. A natural question arises whether there are more restricted, but yet expressive fragments which provide more suitable logics and for which there are

* The authors thank Peter Baumgartner for drawing our attention to Niemelä's work and raising the question of the computational complexity of minimal model generation. The work of the first and third authors is supported by EPSRC Research Grant GR/M36700.

R. Nieuwenhuis and A. Voronkov (Eds.): LPAR 2001, LNAI 2250, pp. 85–99, 2001.

algorithms with better worst-case complexity and that possibly employ inference techniques similar to those prominently used for modal and description logics. Such a subfragment, called GF1$^-$, is identified by Lutz, Sattler and Tobies [18], who describe a tableaux procedure which decides GF1$^-$ and prove that under certain assumptions the satisfiability problem of GF1$^-$ is PSPACE-complete.

Our investigations are situated in the framework of resolution which is well-studied and well-mechanised. In previous work [11] we describe a hyperresolution decision procedure for GF1$^-$ and certain generalisations of GF1$^-$, which also include formulae outside the guarded and loosely guarded fragment. This procedure polynomially simulates the tableaux procedure for GF1$^-$ of [18] and forms a generalisation of the selection-based resolution procedure which polynomially simulates tableaux procedures for modal logics and description logics [8, 15]. However, in the worst case the procedure has double exponential space complexity.

The first part of this paper describes a resolution decision procedure for GF1$^-$ with optimal space complexity (Section 3). This procedure is based on the hyperresolution decision procedure of [11] and uses the so-called trace technique [21] which is utilised in PSPACE tableaux procedures for description (and modal) logics. The presentation of the algorithm is sufficiently detailed and preserves the essential structure of the main inference loop found in state-of-the-art theorem provers such as Gandalf, OTTER, SPASS and Vampire, and is thus easily implementable.

The second part of the paper considers the problem of generating minimal Herbrand models for GF1$^-$ (Section 4). The generation of minimal (Herbrand) models has been shown to be useful in a number of applications [2,4] and we believe that modal logics and generalisations like GF1$^-$ could provide expressive languages for the specification of related applications in the area of multi-agent systems [19].

There are various approaches to generating minimal Herbrand models with hyperresolution [5,6,14,20] which, with the exception of [6], have been applied only to propositional clause sets. We focus on two of these approaches. The first is based on an extension of our resolution-based decision procedure for GF1$^-$ [11] by a model constraint propagation rule which ensures that only minimal models are generated. This generalises the approach and results of Bry and Yahya [6]. The second approach avoids the need for model constraints by using a variant of a local minimality test proposed by Niemelä [20]. Unfortunately, Niemelä's approach requires that the complement of a Herbrand model is finite, which is not the case for GF1$^-$. We show how this problem can be solved, and discuss and compare the space and time complexity of procedures based on these two approaches to minimal model generation for GF1$^-$.

Both minimal Herbrand model generation approaches are applicable to the clausal class $\mathcal{PVD}$ [16] and to all modal and description logics that can be embedded into GF1$^-$, the description logic $\mathcal{ALC}$, and the modal logic $K_{(m)}(\cap, \cup, \smile)$, which is defined over families of binary relations closed under intersection, union and converse [8].

2 Preliminaries

The notational convention is as follows. We denote first-order variables by x, y, z, terms by s, t, u, constants by a, b, functions by f, g, h, predicate symbols by P, Q, G, atoms by A, A_1, A_2, literals by L, clauses by C, formulae by φ, ϕ, ψ, ϑ, and sets of clauses by N. An over-line indicates a sequence. If $\overline{s} = (s_1, \ldots, s_n)$ then $\overline{f(\overline{s})}$ denotes a sequence of terms of the form $f_k(s_1, \ldots, s_n)$.

Let each predicate symbol G be associated with a unique grouping (i, j) where i, $j > 0$. Then: (i) If φ is an atomic formula, φ is in GF1$^-$. (ii) If φ is in GF1$^-$ and G has grouping (i, j), then $\exists\overline{y}\,(G(\overline{x},\overline{y}) \wedge \varphi(\overline{y}))$, $\forall\overline{y}\,(G(\overline{x},\overline{y}) \rightarrow \varphi(\overline{y}))$, $\exists\overline{x}\,(G(\overline{x},\overline{y}) \wedge \varphi(\overline{x}))$, and $\forall\overline{x}\,(G(\overline{x},\overline{y}) \rightarrow \varphi(\overline{x}))$ are GF1$^-$ formulae provided $\overline{x}$ is an sequence of variables of length i, $\overline{y}$ is a sequence of variables of length j, and $\overline{x} \cap \overline{y} = \emptyset$. Repetitions and permutations of variables are allowed. The atoms $G(\overline{x},\overline{y})$ are called *guards.* (iii) $\top$ and $\bot$ are in GF1$^-$. And, (iv) GF1$^-$ is closed under Boolean connectives. If $\overline{s}$ and $\overline{t}$ are arbitrary sequences of terms of length i and j, then $\mathcal{G}(\overline{s},\overline{t})$ represents both $G(\overline{s},\overline{t})$ and $G(\overline{t},\overline{s})$.

The procedures described in this paper are based on the resolution decision procedure for GF1$^-$ presented in [11]. It proceeds as follows. First a given GF1$^-$ formula is transformed (by a polynomial time algorithm) into a set of clauses, which have the following forms.

$Q_\varphi(\overline{a})$	
$\neg Q_\varphi(\overline{x}) \vee \neg P(\overline{x})$	if $\varphi = \neg P(\overline{x})$
$\neg Q_\varphi(\overline{x}) \vee \neg \mathcal{G}(\overline{x},\overline{y}) \vee Q_\psi(\overline{y})$	if $\varphi = \forall\overline{y}\,(\mathcal{G}(\overline{x},\overline{y}) \rightarrow \psi(\overline{y}))$
$\neg Q_\varphi(\overline{x}) \vee \mathcal{G}(\overline{x}, \overline{f(\overline{x})})$ $\neg Q_\varphi(\overline{x}) \vee Q_\psi(\overline{f(\overline{x})})$	if $\varphi = \exists\overline{y}\,(\mathcal{G}(\overline{x},\overline{y}) \wedge \psi(\overline{y}))$
$\neg Q_\varphi(\overline{z}) \vee Q_\psi(\overline{x})$ $\neg Q_\varphi(\overline{z}) \vee Q_\phi(\overline{y})$	if $\varphi = \psi(\overline{x}) \wedge \phi(\overline{y})$, $\overline{z} = \overline{x} \cup \overline{y}$
$\neg Q_\varphi(\overline{z}) \vee Q_\psi(\overline{x}) \vee Q_\phi(\overline{y})$	if $\varphi = \psi(\overline{x}) \vee \phi(\overline{y})$, $\overline{z} = \overline{x} \cup \overline{y}$

Here, $\overline{f(\overline{x})}$ is a sequence of (distinct) Skolem terms introduced for the sequence of existentially quantified variable $\overline{y}$ in $\exists\overline{y}\,(\mathcal{G}(\overline{x},\overline{y}) \wedge \psi(\overline{y}))$.

Second, a hyperresolution calculus is used to determine satisfiability of the clause set. The calculus, denoted by $\mathsf{R}^{\mathsf{hyp}}$, uses the following expansion rules:

Deduce: $\dfrac{N}{N \cup \{C\}}$ where C is a resolvent or a factor.

Splitting: $\dfrac{N \cup \{C_1 \vee C_2\}}{N \cup \{C_1\} \mid N \cup \{C_2\}}$ where C_1 and C_2 are variable disjoint.

The resolution and factoring inference rules are:

Hyperresolution: $\dfrac{C_1 \vee A_1 \quad \ldots \quad C_n \vee A_n \quad \neg A_{n+1} \vee \ldots \vee \neg A_{2n} \vee D}{(C_1 \vee \ldots \vee C_n \vee D)\sigma}$

where (i) σ is the most general unifier such that $A_i\sigma = A_{n+i}\sigma$ for every i, $1 \leq i \leq n$, and (ii) $C_i \vee A_i$ and D are positive clauses, for every i, $1 \leq i \leq n$. The right most premise in the rule is referred to as the *negative* premise and all other premises are referred to as *positive* premises.

Factoring: $$\frac{C \vee A_1 \vee A_2}{(C \vee A_1)\sigma}$$
where σ is the most general unifier of A_1 and A_2.

A *derivation* in $\mathsf{R}^{\mathsf{hyp}}$ from a set of clauses N is a finitely branching, ordered tree T with root N and nodes are sets of clauses. The tree is constructed by applications of the expansion rules to the leaves. We assume that no hyperresolution or factoring inference is computed twice on the same branch of the derivation. Any path $N(= N_0), N_1, \dots$ in a derivation T is called a *closed branch* in T iff the clause set $\bigcup_j N_j$ contains the empty clause, otherwise it is called an *open branch.* We call a branch B in a derivation tree *complete* (with respect to $\mathsf{R}^{\mathsf{hyp}}$) iff no new successor nodes can be added to the endpoint of B by $\mathsf{R}^{\mathsf{hyp}}$, otherwise it is called an *incomplete branch.* A derivation is *complete* iff all of its branches are either closed or complete. A derivation T is a *refutation* iff every path $N(= N_0), N_1, \dots$ in it is a closed branch, otherwise it is called an *open derivation.* A *branch selection function* is a function, mapping an open derivation tree to one of its open branches. A derivation T from N is called *fair* if for any path $N(= N_0), N_1, \dots$ in T, with *limit* $N_\infty = \bigcup_j \bigcap_{k \geq j} N_k$, it is the case that each clause C that can be deduced from non-redundant premises in N_∞ is contained in some N_j. Note that for a finite path $N(= N_0), N_1, \dots N_n$, the limit N_∞ is equal to N_n.

Theorem 1 ([3]). *Let T be a fair derivation from a set N of clauses. Then: (i) If $N(= N_0), N_1, \dots$ is a path with limit N_∞, N_∞ is saturated up to redundancy. (ii) N is satisfiable if and only if there exists a path in T with limit N_∞ such that N_∞ is satisfiable. (iii) N is unsatisfiable if and only if for every path $N(= N_0), N_1, \dots$ the clause set $\bigcup_j N_j$ contains the empty clause.*

We restrict our attention to derivations generated by strategies such that the positive premises of any hyperresolution step are positive ground unit clauses. For GF1$^-$ this can be achieved by performing suitable splitting and factoring inferences before hyperresolution inferences. Since we are able to prove termination of any such derivation for the clausal set rendered by formulae in GF1$^-$, any such strategy is fair.

Theorem 2 ([11]). *Let φ be a GF1$^-$ formula and let N be the corresponding clause set. Then: (i) Any $\mathsf{R}^{\mathsf{hyp}}$ derivation from N terminates. (ii) φ is unsatisfiable iff all branches in any complete $\mathsf{R}^{\mathsf{hyp}}$ derivation with root N are closed.*

We now recall the definitions of some notions from [11] (which are closely related to notions introduced in [18]). By the *class of GF1$^-$ clause sets* we mean the class of all clause sets N for which a GF1$^-$ formula φ exists such that N is the clausal form of φ as described above. Let N be a GF1$^-$ clause set. A function symbol f_k is said to be *associated with* a predicate symbol Q iff N contains a definitional clause of the form $\neg Q(\overline{x}) \vee \mathcal{G}(\overline{x}, \overline{f(\overline{x})})$ in which f_k occurs. A set $\{t_1, \dots, t_n\}$ (or sequence $\overline{t} = (t_1, \dots, t_n)$) of ground terms is called a *uni-node* iff either each t_i, $1 \leq i \leq n$, is a constant, or there exists a predicate symbol Q and a sequence of ground terms $\overline{s}$, such that each t_i, $1 \leq i \leq n$, has the form $f_k(\overline{s})$, where f_k is a function symbol associated with Q. A uni-node X_2 is called a *direct successor* of a uni-node X_1 iff there is a predicate symbol Q such that for each element t of X_2 there is a function symbol f_k, associated with Q, and $t = f_k(\overline{s})$, where $\overline{s}$ is a sequence of precisely the elements of X_1. A set (or sequence) of ground terms is called a *bi-node* iff it can be presented as a union $X_1 \cup X_2$ of two non-empty disjoint uni-nodes X_1 and X_2 such that X_2 is a direct successor of X_1. A ground literal is a *uni-node* (*bi-node*) iff the set of its arguments is a uni-node (bi-node). A clause is a *uni-node* (*bi-node*) iff the set of the arguments of all literals in it is a uni-node (bi-node). The *successor relation* on uni-nodes is the transitive closure of the direct successor relation. (See [11] for examples.)

3 A Space Efficient Resolution Decision Procedure

Due to space restrictions we only describe the modifications necessary to turn the main procedure of a standard saturation based theorem prover with splitting [22] into a space efficient decision procedure for GF1$^-$ and stipulate the main results.

The procedure exploits the tree structure of uni-nodes induced by bi-nodes of the form $\mathcal{G}(\overline{s}, \overline{t})$. With each uni-node $\overline{s}$ we can associate all unit clauses of the form $Q(\overline{s})$. Then, inferences never involve premises $Q(\overline{s})$ and $Q'(\overline{t})$ associated with distinct uni-nodes $\overline{s}$ and $\overline{t}$. Thus, the sets of clauses associated with different uni-nodes can be investigated independently of each other in a depth-first manner. This is sometimes called the *trace technique*. However, similar as for the modal logic KB or description logics with inverse roles, clauses associated with a uni-node $\overline{t}$ can be used to derive additional clauses associated with a uni-node $\overline{s}$ such that $\overline{t}$ is a direct successor of $\overline{s}$. This suggests a way of investigating the uni-nodes of the tree structure that minimises the space required to store the uni-node clauses associated with the nodes and goes as follows.

Suppose we are currently investigating a uni-node $\overline{s}$. We first try to derive all uni-node clauses associated with $\overline{s}$. If one or more of these clauses is a non-unit clause, we apply the splitting rule which generates additional branches in the derivation tree. If we derive a contradiction, then the current branch is closed and we backtrack to an alternative open branch. If no open branch exists, then the clause set and also the GF1$^-$ formula under consideration are unsatisfiable. If we do not derive a contradiction, then we continue by deriving all bi-nodes of the form $\mathcal{G}(\overline{s}, \overline{f(\overline{s})})$ providing us with the information of which direct successors of $\overline{s}$ exist. We continue by investigating each of these successor nodes independently. Using the clauses stemming from the existentially and universally quantified formulae of the GF1$^-$ formula under consideration we first establish an initial set of clauses associated with a particular successor node $\overline{f(\overline{s})}$. We then recursively call the main procedure for this initial set of clauses. The recursive call can lead to three different results. First, we may derive a contradiction by an application of positive hyperresolution to the clauses associated with one of the uni-nodes. Again, the current branch of the derivation is closed and we move to an alternative open branch of the derivation (no investigation of other successor nodes of $\overline{s}$ is necessary). Second, we may not derive a contradiction, but while considering

Procedure 1 Space efficient resolution decision procedure

```
Procedure ResolutionProver(s̄, US, WO)
local N, NEW, R, Given, Flag, t̄;
begin
  while (US ≠ ∅ and (⊥ ∉ US or not StackEmpty(Stack))) do
    if (⊥ ∈ US) then
      (Stack, US, WO) := backtrack(Stack, US, WO)
    else
      (N, Flag, US) := choose(US, WO);
      if (Flag ∈ {BOOLEAN, DEFAULT, UNI-NODE, UNIV}) then
        (Given, N) := PickAndDelete(N);
        if (Splittable(Given)) then
          NEW := FirstSplitCase(Given);
          Stack := push(Stack, SecondSplitCase(Given))
        else
          WO := WO ∪ Given;
          NEW := inf(Given, WO);
        (NEW, WO, US) := ired(NEW, WO, US);
        US := US ∪ NEW
      else (* Flag ∈ {EXIST, BI-NODE} *)
        (R, US, WO) := InvestigateAllSuccessors(s̄, N, Flag, US, WO);
        if (restart(t̄) ∈ R) then return(R)
  return(US)
end
```

$\overline{f(\overline{s})}$ we derive some additional clause associated with $\overline{s}$. In this case we delete the clauses associated with the successor node $\overline{f(\overline{s})}$, backtrack to the node $\overline{s}$, add the newly derived clause, and restart the investigation of this node. The node $\overline{f(\overline{s})}$ will then be revisited later. This has been referred to as the *reset-restart* technique [18]. Third, we may neither derive a contradiction nor additional information about a predecessor node. Then we can delete all clauses associated with $\overline{f(\overline{s})}$ and turn to some other successor node $\overline{g(\overline{s})}$. If there is no other successor node, then the clause set is satisfiable.

The main procedure ResolutionProver presented in Procedure 1 follows the search strategy just outlined. ResolutionProver operates on two sets of clauses $\mathcal{US}$ and $\mathcal{WO}$ (the set of *usable clauses* and the set of *worked-off clauses*). The set $\mathcal{WO}$ contains all the clauses that have already been used as (positive) premises in inference steps (or can never be used as positive premises) and the set $\mathcal{US}$ contains all the clauses that still need to be considered as (positive) premises. Let N denote the clauses obtained from a given $\mathrm{GF1}^-$ formula φ. Initially $\mathcal{US}$ is the singleton set $\{Q_\varphi(\overline{a})\}$ while $\mathcal{WO}$ is $N - \{Q_\varphi(\overline{a})\}$.

The procedure proceeds in a while-loop which terminates if either the set $\mathcal{US}$ is empty or $\mathcal{US}$ contains the empty clause and there are no more alternative open branches in the derivation tree generated by applications of the splitting rule that can be considered. In the while-loop we choose some of the clauses from $\mathcal{US}$, perform the inferences possible with these clauses and update $\mathcal{US}$ and $\mathcal{WO}$ accordingly. Note that ResolutionProver takes as an additional argument a

Procedure 2 The procedure choose for guarded formulae

Procedure choose($\mathcal{US}$, $\mathcal{WO}$)
local $N, \mathcal{G}, Q, Q', C, \overline{t}, \overline{x}, \overline{f(\overline{x})}$;
begin
  if ($Q(\overline{t}) \in \mathcal{US}$ for some Q, not newly introduced, and $Q(\overline{t})$ is a uni-node) **then**
    return($\{Q(\overline{t})\}$, UNI-NODE, $\mathcal{US} - \{Q(\overline{t})\}$)
  else if ($Q(\overline{t}) \in \mathcal{US}$ where $\neg Q(\overline{x}) \vee \neg \mathcal{G}(\overline{x}, \overline{y}) \vee Q'(\overline{y}) \in \mathcal{WO}$) **then**
    return($\{Q(\overline{t})\}$, UNIV, $\mathcal{US} - \{Q(\overline{t})\}$)
  else if ($Q(\overline{t}) \in \mathcal{US}$ where $\neg Q(\overline{x}) \vee C$ is a Boolean definitional clause in $\mathcal{WO}$) **then**
    return($\{Q(\overline{t})\}$, BOOLEAN, $\mathcal{US} - \{Q(\overline{t})\}$)
  else if ($C \in \mathcal{WO}$ where C is ground, but non-unit) **then**
    return($\{C\}$, BOOLEAN, $\mathcal{US} - \{C\}$)
  else if ($Q(\overline{t}) \in \mathcal{US}$ where $\neg Q(\overline{x}) \vee \mathcal{G}(\overline{x}, \overline{f(\overline{x})}) \in \mathcal{WO}$) **then**
    $N := \{Q(\overline{t}) \in \mathcal{US} \mid \neg Q(\overline{x}) \vee \mathcal{G}(\overline{x}, \overline{f(\overline{x})}) \in \mathcal{WO}$ or $\neg Q(\overline{x}) \vee Q'(\overline{f(\overline{x})}) \in \mathcal{WO}\}$;
    return(N, EXIST, $\mathcal{US} - N$)
  else if ($\mathcal{G}(\overline{s}, \overline{t}) \in \mathcal{US}$ for some $\mathcal{G}$, not newly introduced, and $\mathcal{G}(\overline{s}, \overline{t})$ is a bi-node) **then**
    return($\{\mathcal{G}(\overline{s}, \overline{t})\}$, BI-NODE, $\mathcal{US}$)
  else if (C is some (arbitrary) clause in $\mathcal{WO}$) **then**
    return($\{C\}$, DEFAULT, $\mathcal{US} - \{C\}$)
end

sequence of terms $\overline{t}$ which is the uni-node the procedure is currently working on. The uni-node the procedure ResolutionProver is initially working on will be $\overline{a}$.

The procedure choose selects the clauses which will be the next to serve as one of the premises of $\mathsf{R}^{\mathsf{hyp}}$, it is a so-called *clause selection function.* Normally, it selects one clause according to some heuristic taking the 'complexity' and 'age' of clauses into account. Instead the modified version of choose presented in Procedure 2 chooses a set of clauses in a way that allows us to take advantage of the trace technique. For this purpose we have to delay the consideration of clauses related to existentially quantified formulae until all other clauses have been dealt with. To ensure this, choose not only selects potential positive premises accordingly, but also passes information about the corresponding negative premises back to the main procedure in the form of a flag. In all cases, except if the value of the flag is 'BI-NODE', choose also returns the set $\mathcal{US}$ from which the chosen clauses have been removed.

Three additional procedures used by ResolutionProver are PickAndDelete, inf, and ired. Given a set N of clauses the procedure PickAndDelete selects a clause C from a set N of clauses according to some appropriate heuristic and returns it together with $N - \{C\}$. The actual inferences by hyperresolution and factoring[1] are performed by the procedure inf. Tautologies and subsumed clauses are removed from the sets $\mathcal{NEW}$, $\mathcal{WO}$, and $\mathcal{US}$ by the procedure ired.

If choose returns the flag value 'EXIST' or 'BI-NODE', then the investigation of the current uni-node is complete and we are about to turn to its successor

[1] For completeness we do not need factoring for $\mathrm{GF1}^-$ clause sets because all derived non-unit clauses are ground and can be split.

Procedure 3 Investigation of all successor nodes

```
Procedure InvestigateAllSuccessors(t̄, N, Flag, US, WO)
local AUXUS, AUXWO, B, G, NEW, R, UNIVS, Given, Q, Q', s̄;
begin
  AUXUS := US ∪ N;
  AUXWO := WO;
  if (Flag ∈ EXIST) then
    while (N ≠ ∅) do
      (Given, N) := PickAndDelete(N);
      WO := WO ∪ {Given};
      NEW := inf(Given, WO);
    (NEW, WO, US) := ired(NEW, WO, US);
    US := US ∪ NEW;
  UNIVS := {Q(t̄) ∈ US ∪ WO | ¬Q(x̄) ∨ ¬G(x̄, ȳ) ∨ Q'(ȳ) ∈ WO};
  B := {G(t̄, s̄) | G(t̄, s̄) ∈ US ∪ WO and G(t̄, s̄) is a bi-node};
  while (B ≠ ∅ and ⊥ ∉ US) do
    (Given, B) := PickAndDelete(B);
    (R, US) := InvestigateOneSuccessor(t̄, US, WO, UNIVS, Given);
    if (restart(s̄) ∈ R) then
      if (depth(s̄) = depth(t̄)) then
        US := AUXUS ∪ R − {restart(s̄)};
        WO := AUXWO;
        B := ∅;
        R := ∅;
      else
        B := ∅;
  return(R, US, WO)
end
```

nodes, which is done by the procedure InvestigateAllSuccessors in Procedure 3. To do this, we first have to establish which successor nodes exist for the current uni-node. If the value of the flag is 'EXIST', then the set of selected clauses returned by choose contains all the unit clauses which can be resolved with clauses stemming from existentially quantified subformulae of φ to generate clauses of the form $\mathcal{G}(\bar{t}, \bar{s})$ and $Q_\psi(\bar{s})$ where $\bar{s}$ is a direct successor of $\bar{t}$. These clauses are computed and added to $\mathcal{US}$. Besides clauses of the form $Q_\psi(\bar{s})$ which already provide information about the successor node $\bar{s}$, additional information can be derived using unit clauses $Q_\vartheta(\bar{t})$ together with $\mathcal{G}(\bar{t}, \bar{s})$ and $\neg Q_\vartheta(\bar{x}) \vee \neg\mathcal{G}(\bar{x}, \bar{y}) \vee Q_\phi(\bar{y})$. We compute the set of all these unit clauses and assign it to $\mathcal{UNIVS}$ and we also compute the set of all bi-nodes of the form $\mathcal{G}(\bar{t}, \bar{s})$ and assign it to $\mathcal{B}$. As described in the outline of the search strategy of the main procedure, we want to investigate the successor nodes independently of each other. Therefore, we consider each element of $\mathcal{B}$ using the procedure InvestigateOneSuccessor presented in Procedure 4. InvestigateOneSuccessor adds the element of $\mathcal{B}$ to the set $\mathcal{WO}$ to form the set $\mathcal{WO}'$ and uses it and the clauses in $\mathcal{UNIVS}$ to compute additional uni-node clauses associated with the successor node it investigates and stores them in $\mathcal{NEW}$. If we already derive the empty clause at this point, then

Procedure 4 Investigation of a single successor node

Procedure InvestigateOneSuccessor($\bar{t}$, $\mathcal{US}$, $\mathcal{WO}$, $\mathcal{UNIVS}$, Binode)
local $\mathcal{WO}'$, $\mathcal{NEW}$, $\mathcal{R}$, Given, $\bar{s}$;
begin
  $\mathcal{WO}' := \mathcal{WO} \cup \{\text{Binode}\}$;
  $\mathcal{NEW} := \emptyset$;
  while ($\mathcal{UNIVS} \neq \emptyset$ and $\bot \notin \mathcal{US}$) **do**
    (Given, $\mathcal{UNIVS}$) := PickAndDelete($\mathcal{UNIVS}$);
    $\mathcal{NEW}$:= inf(Given, $\mathcal{WO}$);
    ($\mathcal{NEW}$, $\mathcal{WO}'$, $\mathcal{US}$) := ired($\mathcal{NEW}$, $\mathcal{WO}'$, $\mathcal{US}$);
  if ($\bot \in \mathcal{NEW}$) **then**
    return($\{\bot\}, \mathcal{US} \cup \mathcal{NEW}$)
  else if ($Q_\vartheta(\bar{s}) \in \mathcal{NEW}$ such that $\bar{s}$ is not a successor of $\bar{t}$) **then**
    return($\{Q_\psi(\bar{s}) \mid Q_\psi(\bar{s}) \in \mathcal{NEW}\} \cup \{\text{restart}(\bar{s})\}, \mathcal{US}$)
  else
    $\bar{s}$:= SuccessorOf($\bar{t}$, Binode);
    $\mathcal{R} := \{Q(\bar{s}) \mid Q(\bar{s}) \in \mathcal{US}\}$;
    $\mathcal{NEW} := \mathcal{NEW} \cup \mathcal{R}$;
    $\mathcal{US} := \mathcal{US} - \mathcal{R}$;
    $\mathcal{R}$:= ResolutionProver($\bar{s}$, $\mathcal{NEW}$, $\mathcal{WO}'$);
    if (restart($\bar{s}$) $\in \mathcal{R}$) **then return**($\mathcal{R}$, $\mathcal{US}$) **else return**($\emptyset$, $\mathcal{US} - \{\text{Binode}\}$)
end

InvestigateOneSuccessor returns the set $\mathcal{US}$ containing the empty clause to the main procedure which will conclude that the clause set under consideration is unsatisfiable. If we do not derive a contradiction, but additional information about a node $\bar{s}$ which is not a successor of $\bar{t}$, the uni-node under investigation by the main procedure, then we return the additional information to InvestigateAllSuccessors together with an instruction to restart the investigation for $\bar{s}$. This instruction is encoded in a special unit clause restart($\bar{s}$) that we add to the result returned. Otherwise, we determine the successor node $\bar{s}$ of $\bar{t}$ by using the function SuccessorOf, collect the information about $\bar{s}$ contained in $\mathcal{US}$ in $\mathcal{R}$, add the clauses in $\mathcal{R}$ to $\mathcal{NEW}$ and delete them from $\mathcal{US}$, and call the main procedure ResolutionProver with parameters $\bar{s}$, $\mathcal{NEW}$, and $\mathcal{WO}'$. The important point here is that the set of usable clauses on which ResolutionProver will work only contains uni-nodes associated with $\bar{s}$.

Theorem 3. *The following holds for the refined decision procedure: (i) The procedure* choose *ensures a fair selection of positive premises. (ii) The refined decision procedure is sound. (iii) The refined decision procedure is complete.*

In general the space requirement of the refined decision procedure is still exponential in the size of the given $GF1^-$ formula. To achieve the polynomial space bound we have to assume that either (i) the predicates have bounded arity, or (ii) that each subformula of a $GF1^-$ formula has a bounded number of free variables. These assumptions have been made in [12] in order to establish that the satisfiability problem of the guarded fragment is complete for exponential time and are weaker than the ones made in [18].

Theorem 4. *Under one or both of the assumptions (i) and (ii) the refined procedure decides the satisfiability of GF1$^-$ formulae in polynomial space.*

There are three important points worth noting. (i) Even with either, or both, of the assumptions made above a standard saturation theorem prover based on $\mathsf{R}^{\mathsf{hyp}}$ would require exponential space, that is, the modifications described in this section are essential for Theorem 4. (ii) Since the procedure deletes clauses which are not redundant by the standard definition, the set of positive ground unit clauses it keeps, does not necessarily form a Herbrand model of the clause set N at any point in the derivation. (iii) While our procedure imposes a certain order on the selection of clauses, this order still provides flexibility for further refinement and heuristics. In particular, all the standard heuristics used in tableaux decision procedures for description logics can still be utilised. On the other hand most of the heuristics found in resolution theorem provers will provide little guidance due to the particular normal form used.

4 Generating Minimal Herbrand Models

A *Herbrand interpretation* is a set of ground atoms. By definition a ground atom A is *true* in the interpretation H if $A \in H$ and it is *false* in H if $A \notin H$, $\top$ is true in all interpretations and $\bot$ is false in all interpretations. A literal $\neg A$ is true in H iff A is false in H. A clause C is true in an interpretation H iff for all ground substitutions σ there is a literal L in $C\sigma$ which is true in H. A set N of clauses is true in H iff all clauses in N are true in H. If a set N of clauses is true in an interpretation H then H is referred to as a *Herbrand model* of N. An interpretation H is a *minimal Herbrand model* for a set N of clauses iff H is a Herbrand model of N and for no Herbrand model H' of N, $H' \subset H$ holds.

A clause C is *range restricted* iff the set of variables in the positive part of C is a subset of the variables of the negative part of C. This means that a positive clause is range restricted only if it is a ground clause. A clause set is range restricted iff it contains only range restricted clauses.

Lemma 1. *Let N be the clausal form of a GF1$^-$ formula φ. Then, any clause in N and any clause derived from N by $\mathsf{R}^{\mathsf{hyp}}$ is range restricted.*

For range restricted clauses, the open branches of a complete derivation tree T constructed by a $\mathsf{R}^{\mathsf{hyp}}$ derivation for N describe Herbrand models in a very simple way. These models are finite for any subclass of the class of range-restricted clause sets which is decidable by $\mathsf{R}^{\mathsf{hyp}}$, for example the class of GF1$^-$ clause sets. Let $[\![B]\!]$ denote the set of positive ground unit clauses in the limit N_∞ of a branch B of a (complete or incomplete) derivation tree T for a clause set N.

Theorem 5 ([11]). *Let N be the clausal form of a GF1$^-$ formula φ, and let N_∞ be the limit of any branch B in an $\mathsf{R}^{\mathsf{hyp}}$ derivation tree with root N. If N_∞ does not contain the empty clause, then $[\![B]\!]$ is a finite (Herbrand) model of N.*

We refer to $[\![B]\!]$ as a (partial Herbrand) model for N represented by the open branch B.

Theorem 6 (Minimal model completeness [6]). *Let N be a satisfiable set of range restricted clauses, and let T be any complete* $\mathsf{R}^{\mathsf{hyp}}$ *derivation tree constructed from N. For every minimal model H there is an open branch B in T such that $[\![B]\!]$ coincides with the ground atoms in H.*

As GF1$^-$ clause sets are range restricted it follows immediately that for every minimal model H there is an open branch B in a derivation from a GF1$^-$ clause set N such that $[\![B]\!]$ coincides with the ground atoms in H. However, not every model computed with $\mathsf{R}^{\mathsf{hyp}}$ is a minimal model of the input set.

One way to ensure that only minimal models are generated is the use of model constraints. If $[\![B]\!] = \{A_1, \ldots, A_n\}$ is the finite Herbrand model of an open branch B, then let $\overline{[\![B]\!]}$ denote the clause $\neg A_1 \vee \ldots \vee \neg A_n$. The clause $\overline{[\![B]\!]}$ is called a *model constraint.* Suppose B is an open, complete branch in a derivation and we add $\overline{[\![B]\!]}$ to a branch B' distinct from B. If B' would otherwise generate a model $[\![B']\!]$ which is a superset of $[\![B]\!]$, then we will now be able to derive a contradiction using $\overline{[\![B]\!]}$. Because $[\![B]\!]$ may not be a minimal model, it is not enough to add a model constraint to branches which are incomplete with respect to $\mathsf{R}^{\mathsf{hyp}}$ (i.e. branches which can be further expanded by the application of an $\mathsf{R}^{\mathsf{hyp}}$ inference rule). A model constraint also needs to be added to branches complete with respect to $\mathsf{R}^{\mathsf{hyp}}$. In this case, adding the model constraint $\overline{[\![B]\!]}$ to the leaf of a complete branch B' may change the status of B' from complete to incomplete, and it is possible to perform a single additional hyperresolution inference which closes B'. Some additional bookkeeping is necessary to ensure that a model constraint generated by a branch B is propagated only once. We achieve this by introducing the concept of a *finished branch.* A branch is *finished* once its model constraint has been added to all relevant branches of the derivation.

Formally, we extend our calculus by the following *model constraint propagation* rule. We use the notation $\mathsf{R}^{\mathsf{hyp}}_{\mathsf{min}}$ to refer to the calculus based on factoring, hyperresolution, splitting, and model constraint propagation.

Model constraint propagation: Let B be an open, non-finished branch which is complete with respect to $\mathsf{R}^{\mathsf{hyp}}$. Then add the clause $\overline{[\![B]\!]}$ to all leaves of branches in the derivation tree which are incomplete with respect to $\mathsf{R}^{\mathsf{hyp}}_{\mathsf{min}}$ or are marked finished. We say the model constraint propagation rule *is applied to B*. Once the rule has been applied, B will be marked *finished.*

The rule ensures that the model constraint is propagated to all relevant branches. Since the model constraint propagation rule can only be applied to branches which are not marked as finished and a branch is marked finished immediately after the model propagation rule has been applied to it, the rule is applied at most once to any branch in the derivation tree.

Theorem 7. *Let φ be a GF1$^-$ formula and let N be the corresponding clause set. Then: (i) Any* $\mathsf{R}^{\mathsf{hyp}}_{\mathsf{min}}$ *derivation from N terminates. (ii) φ is unsatisfiable iff all branches in any completed* $\mathsf{R}^{\mathsf{hyp}}_{\mathsf{min}}$ *derivation tree with root N are closed.*

Theorem 8. *Let N be the clausal form of a GF1$^-$ formula φ. Then: (i) If $[\![B]\!]$ is the set of positive ground unit clauses in the limit of an open branch in an* $\mathsf{R}^{\mathsf{hyp}}_{\mathsf{min}}$

derivation tree from N, $[\![B]\!]$ *forms a minimal Herbrand model for N. (ii)* $\mathsf{R}^{\mathsf{hyp}}_{\mathsf{min}}$ *generates only minimal Herbrand models for N. (iii)* $\mathsf{R}^{\mathsf{hyp}}_{\mathsf{min}}$ *generates all minimal Herbrand models for N, and does so only once.*

$\mathsf{R}^{\mathsf{hyp}}_{\mathsf{min}}$ is generally sound and complete. For range restricted clauses, the previous theorem is true as well. But $\mathsf{R}^{\mathsf{hyp}}_{\mathsf{min}}$ is, of course, not a decision procedure for the class of range restricted clauses, for example, it does not terminate on this simple clause set: $\{P(a), \neg P(x) \vee P(f(x))\}$.

The calculus above supports arbitrary branch selection functions and clause selection functions provided that derivations are fair. However, branch selection and clause selection functions have an impact on the performance of an implementation, and developing good strategies is crucial for practical applications.

The minimal model generation procedure of Bry and Yahya [6] can be viewed as a refinement of $\mathsf{R}^{\mathsf{hyp}}_{\mathsf{min}}$ with an additional rule, the *complement splitting* rule, and with a particular branch selection function which always selects the left-most open branch in a derivation tree.

Complement splitting: $\dfrac{N \cup \{C_1 \vee C_2\}}{N \cup \{C_1, \neg C_2\} \quad | \quad N \cup \{C_2\}}$

where C_2 is a ground clause.

The complement splitting rule can be seen as variant of the folding down rule [17] or as a combination of the cut rule (applied to C_2), clause reduction (replacing $C_1 \vee C_2$ by C_1 in the presence of $\neg C_2$), and subsumption deletion (removing $C_1 \vee C_2$ in the presence of C_2). Complement splitting ensures that the first (and left most) completed open branch B determines a minimal model. The model constraint propagation rule then adds the model constraint $\overline{[\![B]\!]}$ to all leaves of branches to the right of the current branch. Subsequent models generated are always minimal, and only constraints of minimal models are propagated. Hence, there is no need for the marking scheme of $\mathsf{R}^{\mathsf{hyp}}_{\mathsf{min}}$ which ensures that the model constraint propagation rule is applied only once to a branch.

The Bry-Yahya procedure is sound and complete, and for range restricted clauses the set of generated models is exactly the set of minimal Herbrand models of the input set [6]. Thus clearly, this approach is also applicable to $\mathrm{GF1}^-$.

A disadvantage of $\mathsf{R}^{\mathsf{hyp}}_{\mathsf{min}}$ and the Bry-Yahya procedure are their worst-case space requirement. Let φ be a $\mathrm{GF1}^-$ formula of size n and let N be the corresponding set of clauses. Let $\epsilon_2(n)$ denote n^{n^n}. Since we have to maintain a complete representation of the models during the derivation, the space optimisation techniques described in Section 3 cannot be applied here. Ignoring the model constraints, the space required to maintain the essential information on a branch, in other words, the clauses in the leaf of the branch, is bounded by $O(n^2\epsilon_2(n))$ which is also the space required to store a Herbrand model of N, while the number of branches is bounded by $O(2^{\epsilon_2(n)})$. Since a model constraint contains the negation of each atom occurring in a Herbrand model, the space required for a model constraint is again bounded by $O(n^2\epsilon_2(n))$. In the worst case, each branch generates a model constraint which is propagated to all the remaining branches. Thus, in the worst case, a minimal model generation procedure based on $\mathsf{R}^{\mathsf{hyp}}_{\mathsf{min}}$ stores all the essential information for all the branches in the derivation plus all the model constraints propagated to all branches in space bounded by $O(2^{\epsilon_2(n)}(n^2\epsilon_2(n) + 2^{\epsilon_2(n)}n^2\epsilon_2(n)))$. This gives a triple exponential space bound. Using the Bry-Yahya approach we can discard a branch once it has been closed or has produced a minimal model and its model constraint has been propagated, and only for minimal models do we generate and keep model constraints. This brings the space requirement down to $O(n^2\epsilon_2(n) + \binom{\epsilon_2(n)}{\lfloor\epsilon_2(n)/2\rfloor}n^2\epsilon_2(n))$. This is an improvement over the general $\mathsf{R}^{\mathsf{hyp}}_{\mathsf{min}}$ procedure, although it is still triple exponential. Likewise, the time complexity of $\mathsf{R}^{\mathsf{hyp}}_{\mathsf{min}}$ derivations is a triple exponential function.

A way of reducing the space requirement of minimal model generation is by adopting the approach of Niemelä [20] which is based on the following observation. Given a (finite) set H of positive ground atoms (or unit clauses) define: $\neg H = \{\neg A \mid A \in H\}$ and $\overline{H} = \bigvee_{A\in H} \neg A$. Let N be a set of clauses and U be the set of all atoms over the Herbrand universe of N. Let H be a finite Herbrand model of N. Then H is a minimal Herbrand model of N iff $MMT(N, H) = N \cup \neg(U - H) \cup \{\overline{H}\}$ is unsatisfiable. This minimality test is called *groundedness test*. Thus, we can use $\mathsf{R}^{\mathsf{hyp}}$ to enumerate all models of a GF1$^-$ clause set N and also use $\mathsf{R}^{\mathsf{hyp}}$ to test each model H for minimality by testing $MMT(N, H)$ for unsatisfiability. This approach has been applied and refined in [2,5]. A practical problem from our perspective is that these approaches have been described for propositional or ground clause logic only. In this case, the set U, and therefore $U - H$, are always finite. In the case of GF1$^-$, the Herbrand universe of GF1$^-$ clause sets is infinite in general and thus, U and $U - H$ can be infinite sets. However, we observe that in the case of an $\mathsf{R}^{\mathsf{hyp}}$ derivation from $MMT(N, H)$, the clauses in $\neg(U - H)$ have only the effect of deriving a contradiction in any clause set N' derivable from N which contains a positive unit clause not in H. Since H itself is finite, this effect is straightforward to implement.

Procedure 5 defines a minimal model generation procedure MMG using this variant of Niemelä's groundedness test. Like $\mathsf{ResolutionProver}$, MMG operates on the same two sets of clauses $\mathcal{US}$ and $\mathcal{WO}$. Since for the groundedness test we need the initial set of clauses, MMG takes as additional arguments the original sets of usable and worked-off clauses ($\mathcal{IUS}$ and $\mathcal{IWO}$). In its incarnation as groundedness test, procedure MMG requires the Herbrand model H it has to check for minimality as an argument. The last parameter of MMG (i.e. Flag) distinguishes whether MMG operates as the minimal model generator (when the value of Flag is *true*) or as the groundedness test procedure (when the value of Flag is *false*). Applied to a set N of clauses obtained from a GF1$^-$ formula φ, initially $\mathcal{US}$ is the singleton set $\{Q_\varphi(\overline{a})\}$ and $\mathcal{WO}$ is $N - \{Q_\varphi(\overline{a})\}$, and the call $\mathsf{MMG}(\mathcal{US}, \mathcal{WO}, \mathcal{US}, \mathcal{WO}, \emptyset, \text{true})$ will print out all minimal Herbrand models of N.

In the procedure MMG, $\mathsf{choose'}$ selects an arbitrary clause (according to some heuristic) and returns it together with the set of usable clauses from which the

Procedure 5 Minimal model generation procedure

```
Procedure MMG(US, WO, IUS, IWO, H, Flag)
local NEW, C_mc, Given
begin
  repeat
    while (US ≠ ∅ and (⊥ ∉ US or not StackEmpty(Stack))) do
      if (⊥ ∈ US) then
        (Stack, US, WO) := backtrack(Stack, US, WO)
      else
        (Given, US) := choose'(US, WO);
        if (Splittable(Given)) then
          NEW := FirstSplitCase(Given);
          Stack := push(Stack, SecondSplitCase(Given))
        else
          WO := WO ∪ {Given};
          NEW := inf(Given, WO);
        if (not Flag and ∃A : A ∈ PGUC(NEW) ∧ A ∉ H) then
          US := US ∪ {⊥}
        else
          (NEW, WO, US) := ired(NEW, WO, US);
          US := US ∪ NEW
    C_mc := ⋁_{A∈PGUC(WO)} ¬A;
    if (Flag and ⊥ ∈ MMG(IUS ∪ {C_mc}, IWO, ∅, ∅, PGUC(WO), false)) then
      print(PGUC(WO));
      US := US ∪ {⊥}
    else
      return(US)
  until (StackEmpty(Stack))
end
```

chosen clause has been removed and $\mathsf{PGUC}(N)$ is a function returning the set of all positive ground unit clauses occurring in a clause set N.

We assume that once a minimal model has been generated and printed, we can discard it from the memory. Similar to the Bry-Yahya approach, MMG only needs to store one branch at a time. However, it does not need to store any model constraints. Instead we need some additional space for the minimality test. Again, during the minimality test we only have to store one branch of the derivation and, in addition, the model we test for minimality. For a $\mathrm{GF1}^-$ formula of size n, this brings the space requirement down to $O(n^2\epsilon_2(n))$, which is a considerable improvement (by one exponent). An upper bound of the time complexity is $O((2^{2\epsilon_2(n)}+1)n^2\epsilon_2(n))$, although we believe that improvements of the search strategy during the minimality tests and a closer analysis can improve this bound. So, for $\mathrm{GF1}^-$ MMG is a minimal model generator of double exponential space and triple exponential time complexity.

The complexity bounds do not improve under assumptions like the ones we made in Section 3 where we assumed bounds on either the arity of predicate symbols or the number of free variables in subformulae of $\mathrm{GF1}^-$ formulae.

References

1. H. Andréka, I. Németi, and J. van Benthem. Modal languages and bounded fragments of predicate logic. *J. Philos. Logic*, 27(3):217–274, 1998.
2. C. Aravindan and P. Baumgartner. Theorem proving techniques for view deletion in databases. *Journal of Symbolic Computation*, 29(2):119–147, 2000.
3. L. Bachmair, H. Ganzinger, and U. Waldmann. Superposition with simplification as a decision procedure for the monadic class with equality. In *Proc. KGC'93*, vol. 713 of *LNCS*, pp. 83–96. Springer, 1993.
4. P. Baumgartner, P. Fröhlich, U. Furbach, and W. Nejdl. Semantically guided theorem proving for diagnosis applications. In *Proc. IJCAI'97*, pp. 460–465. Morgan Kaufmann, 1997.
5. P. Baumgartner, J. Horton, and B. Spencer. Merge path improvements for minimal model hyper tableaux. In *Proc. TABLEAUX'99*, vol. 1617 of *LNAI*. Springer, 1999.
6. F. Bry and A. Yahya. Positive unit hyperresolution tableaux for minimal model generation. *J. Automated Reasoning*, 25(1):35–82, 2000.
7. H. de Nivelle and M. de Rijke. Deciding the guarded fragments by resolution. To appear in J. Symbolic Computat., 2001.
8. H. de Nivelle, R. A. Schmidt, and U. Hustadt. Resolution-based methods for modal logics. *Logic J. IGPL*, 8(3):265–292, 2000.
9. H. Ganzinger and H. de Nivelle. A superposition decision procedure for the guarded fragment with equality. In *Proc. LICS'99*, pp. 295–303. IEEE Computer Society Press, 1999.
10. H. Ganzinger, C. Meyer, and M. Veanes. The two-variable guarded fragment with transitive relations. In *Proc. LICS'99*, pp. 24–34. IEEE Computer Society, 1999.
11. L. Georgieva, U. Hustadt, and R. A. Schmidt. Hyperresolution for guarded formulae. In *Proc. of FTP'2000*, pp. 101–112. Univ. Koblenz-Landau, 2000.
12. E. Grädel. On the restraining power of guards. *J. Symbolic Logic*, 64:1719–1742, 1999.
13. E. Grädel and I. Walukiewicz. Guarded fixed point logic. In *Proc. LICS'99*, pp. 45–54. IEEE Computer Society Press, 1999.
14. R. Hasegawa, H. Fujita, and M. Koshimura. Efficient minimal model generation using branching lemmas. In *Proc. CADE-17*, LNAI, pp. 184–199. Springer, 2000.
15. U. Hustadt and R. A. Schmidt. Using resolution for testing modal satisfiability and building models. To appear in *J. Automated Reasoning*, 2001.
16. A. Leitsch. Deciding clause classes by semantic clash resolution. *Fundamenta Informatica*, 18:163–182, 1993.
17. R. Letz and G. Stenz. Model elimination and connection tableau procedures. In A. Robinson and A. Voronkov, eds., *Handbook of Automated Reasoning*, pp. 2017–2116. Elsevier, 2001.
18. C. Lutz, U. Sattler, and S. Tobies. A suggestion of an n-ary description logic. In *Proc. DL'99*, pp. 81–85. Linköping University, 1999.
19. J.-J. Ch. Meyer, W. van der Hoek, and B. van Linder. A logical approach to the dynamics of commitments. *Artificial Intelligence*, 113(1–2):1–40, 1999.
20. I. Niemelä. A tableau calculus for minimal model reasoning. In *Proc. TABLEAUX'96*, vol. 1071 of *LNAI*, pp. 278–294. Springer, 1996.
21. M. Schmidt-Schauß and G. Smolka. Attributive concept descriptions with complements. *J. Artificial Intelligence*, 48:1–26, 1991.
22. C. Weidenbach. SPASS: Combining superposition, sorts and splitting. In A. Robinson and A. Voronkov, eds., *Handbook of Automated Reasoning*, pp. 1967–2015. Elsevier, 2001.

Logical Omniscience and the Cost of Deliberation

Natasha Alechina and Brian Logan

School of Computer Science and IT,
University of Nottingham,
Nottingham NG8 1BB, UK,
{nza,bsl}@cs.nott.ac.uk

Abstract. Logical omniscience is a well known problem which makes traditional modal logics of knowledge, belief and intentions somewhat unrealistic from the point of view of modelling the behaviour of a resource bounded agent. We propose two logics which take into account 'deliberation time' but use a more or less standard possible worlds semantics with classical possible worlds.

1 Introduction

There has been considerable recent interest in *agent-based systems*, systems based on autonomous software and/or hardware components which perceive their environment and act in that environment in pursuit of their goals. The paradigmatic example of an agent is an autonomous robot situated in a physical environment, but there are other kinds of agents, including software agents whose environment is the Internet and synthetic characters in games and computer entertainments. Agents integrate a range of (often relatively shallow) competences, e.g., goals and reactive behaviour, emotional state and its effect on behaviour, natural language, memory and inference. As such they are central to the study of many problems in Artificial Intelligence, including modelling human mental capabilities (e.g., emotions) and performing complex tasks (e.g., those combining perception, planning, and opportunistic plan execution).

An agent can be viewed as a mapping from percepts to actions (see Fig. 1). The agent constantly monitors its environment and selects actions which allow it to achieve its goals given the current state of the environment. For example, a robot with the goal of delivering a package to an office at the end of the hall may modify its path to avoid someone who has just stepped out of an office half way down the hall.

An agent consists of three main components (e.g., [9]):

- the *agent program* implements a mapping from percepts to actions (this is sometimes called the action selection function or action composition);
- the *agent state* includes all the internal representations on which the agent program operates (this may include representations of the agent's environment and goals, the plans it has for achieving those goals, which parts of the plan have been executed and so on); and

R. Nieuwenhuis and A. Voronkov (Eds.): LPAR 2001, LNAI 2250, pp. 100–109, 2001.

– the *agent architecture*, a (possibly virtual) machine that makes the percepts from the agent's sensors available to the agent program, runs the agent program, updates the agent state, and executes the primitive action(s) chosen by the agent program.

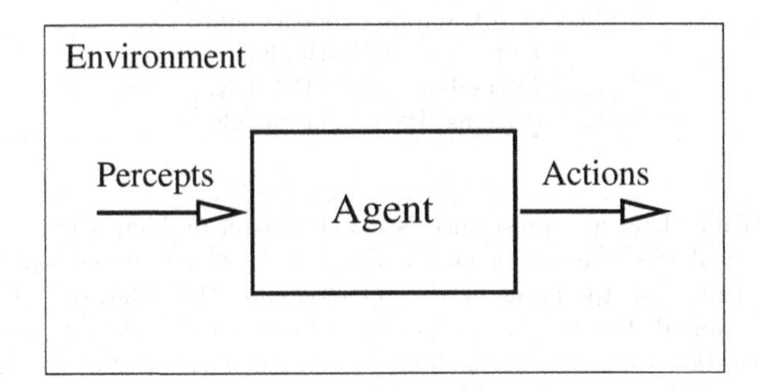

Fig. 1. An agent

Our main concern is with the agent architecture. The architecture defines the atomic operations of the agent program, and implicitly defines the components of the agent. Building a successful agent system consists largely in finding the correct architecture. There is no one correct architecture for all problems; the correct architecture depends on the task and environment.

A major focus of research in intelligent agents has therefore been to understand the implications of different agent architectures. One way to do this is empirically, by building a range of agent systems with differing architectures and conducting controlled experiments (often using simulations) to assess the relative advantages and disadvantages of each architecture. Such experiments allow the agent designer to learn more about the behaviour of a proposed system, and the agent researcher to probe the relationships between agent architectures, environments and behaviour [10]. However, conducting experiments, even in simulation, is time consuming and costly. Existing work on agent simulation is largely ad-hoc, with little re-use of simulation components and scenarios, and often fails to distinguish clearly between models of the agent and the test environment, and between these models and the simulations themselves. Agent and environment models and the simulation mechanisms are typically developed and implemented from scratch for each project or application. This limits the re-use of test scenarios, makes it difficult to reproduce previous experimental results and makes it difficult to compare architectures and implementations.

Another approach is to prove properties of the agent architecture. This means that we formalise a particular architecture in some logic and prove theorems about agent behaviour resulting from the architecture, for example: an agent with architecture X will solve a given problem faster than an agent with architecture Y; an agent with architecture Z will not be able to solve a given problem, or will not be able to solve it before the environment changes and the solution becomes irrelevant.

However most logical approaches to reasoning about agents are based on idealisations which make reasoning about agent architectures problematic. Chief among those is *logical omniscience.* The concept of logical omniscience was introduced by Hintikka in [4] and is usually defined as the agent knowing all logical tautologies and all the consequences of its knowledge. For example, the influential Belief, Desire, Intention (BDI) framework of Georgeff and Rao [8] models agents as logically omniscient. However, logical omniscience is problematic when attempting to build realistic models of agent behaviour, as closure under logical consequence implies that deliberation takes no time. If processes within the agent such as belief revision, planning and problem solving are modelled as derivations in a logical language, such derivations require no investment of computational resources by the agent. To return to the example of the package delivery robot above, when the robot becomes aware of an obstacle in the hall (e.g., from sonar data) it instantaneously revises its beliefs to update its representation of the world, making decisions about whether the obstacle is real or the result of noisy sensor data, and instantaneously decides which steps in its current plan need to be revised and derives a new plan to avoid the obstacle.

There is a significant body of work which has addressed the problem of logical omniscience from a number of different perspectives including: limiting the agent's deductive capabilities by introducing non-classical worlds in the possible worlds semantics [7,3]; distinguishing between beliefs which can be ascribed to the agent and the agent's actual beliefs [6]; and explicitly incorporating the notion of resources [1,13].

In this paper, we propose an alternative approach which incorporates a notion of 'delayed belief'. This has some similarities to the notion of resources in [1,13] but our approach is developed within the context of standard possible worlds semantics. We believe that this makes it more transparent and computationally tractable. In section 2 we develop the notion of delayed belief and define two logics which formalise this notion. We prove that both logics have complete and sound axiomatisations and are decidable. In section 3 we briefly survey related work and point out similarities and differences with our approach. In section 4 we outline some open problems and sketch a program of further work.

2 Delayed Belief

In this section we consider two logics, $L_{\Delta}^{\equiv}$ and $L_{\Delta}^{\rightarrow}$. Both logics contain an operator $\Box$ which can be interpreted as standing for belief or knowledge[1]. These logics are our first attempt to incorporate the notion of computational cost (time) in reasoning about the agent's beliefs or knowledge. In $L_{\Delta}^{\equiv}$, if at the current moment an agent believes ϕ, then after a fixed delay Δ it will believe in all propositions

[1] Or any other propositional attitude where closure under logical equivalence or consequence could be expected from an ideally rational and computationally unbounded agent, but not from a realistic agent.

equivalent to ϕ. In $L^{\rightarrow}_{\Delta}$, after the same delay it will believe in all consequences of its beliefs at the previous step. The intuition underlying this notion of delayed belief is that an agent is able to draw inferences but needs time to derive consequences of its beliefs, so it does not believe the consequences *instantaneously.*

In both logics, none of the principles usually identified with logical omniscience (see for example [12]) is valid:

$\models \Box\phi \land \Box(\phi \rightarrow \psi) \rightarrow \Box\psi$ (the agent's beliefs are closed under modus ponens)
$\models \phi \Longrightarrow \models \Box\phi$ (the agent believes all tautologies)
$\models \phi \rightarrow \psi \Longrightarrow \models \Box\phi \rightarrow \Box\psi$ (the agent believes all logical consequences of its beliefs)
$\models \phi \equiv \psi \Longrightarrow \models \Box\phi \equiv \Box\psi$ (if ϕ and ψ are logically equivalent, the agent believes ϕ if and only if it believes ψ)
$\models \Box\phi \land \Box\psi \rightarrow \Box(\phi \land \psi)$ (the agent's beliefs are closed under conjunctions)
$\models \Box\phi \rightarrow \Box(\phi \lor \psi)$ (the agents beliefs are closed under weakening)
$\models \neg(\Box\phi \land \Box\neg\phi)$ (the agent's beliefs are consistent).

The logics $L^{\equiv}_{\Delta}$ and $L^{\rightarrow}_{\Delta}$ contain an operator Δ which stands for 'After a delay'. We make several simplifying assumptions concerning Δ. We assume that the world (atomic facts) does not change while the agent is deriving consequences of its beliefs (during the delay). We also assume that although new beliefs can be added, no beliefs can be removed from the agent's belief set. These are very strong assumptions. We discuss possible ways of overcoming them in Section 4.

2.1 $L^{\equiv}_{\Delta}$

The language of both logics $L^{\equiv}_{\Delta}$ and $L^{\rightarrow}_{\Delta}$ consists of a set *Prop* of propositional variables $p, q, r, p_1, \ldots$, usual boolean connectives $\neg, \land, \rightarrow, \ldots$ and two unary modalities: $\Box$ which could be informally read as 'Believes' and Δ, standing for 'After a delay'. A well formed formula is defined as usual: $p|\neg\phi|\phi \land \psi|\Box\phi|\Delta\phi$ however we require that $\Box\phi$ is a well formed formula only if ϕ does not contain $\Box$ and Δ. We denote the set of all well formed formulas as *Form*. We denote the set of formulas which do not contain $\Box$ and Δ as *NonModForm*.

Definition 1. *The models of $L^{\equiv}_{\Delta}$ are structures of the form $M = \langle W, V, R, \delta\rangle$ where W is a non-empty set of possible worlds, $V : Prop \longrightarrow 2^W$ assigns subsets of W to propositional variables, $R \subseteq W \times NonModForm$ is a relation used to interpret $\Box$ and $\delta : W \longrightarrow W$ is a function (a sort of successor function) which is used to describe the next state of the world (after a delay) and interpret Δ. The satisfaction relation of a formula being true in a world in a model ($M, w \in W \models \phi$) is as follows:*

$M, w \models p \Longleftrightarrow w \in V(p);$
$M, w \models \neg\phi \Longleftrightarrow M, w \not\models \phi;$
$M, w \models \phi \land \psi \Longleftrightarrow M, w \models \phi$ and $M, w \models \psi;$
$M, w \models \Box\phi \Longleftrightarrow R(w, \phi);$
$M, w \models \Delta\phi \Longleftrightarrow M, \delta(w) \models \phi;$

There are two conditions on δ:

Frozen world. *For every $p \in Prop$, $w \in V(p) \iff \delta(w) \in V(p)$*

Equivalences. *For every $\phi \in NonModForm$, if $R(w, \phi)$ or there exists a formula ψ such that $R(w, \psi)$ and $\vdash \phi \equiv \psi$ in classical propositional logic, then $R(\delta(w), \phi)$.*

The notions of $L^{\equiv}_{\Delta}$-valid and satisfiable formulas are standard: a formula ϕ is $L^{\equiv}_{\Delta}$-satisfiable if there exists an $L^{\equiv}_{\Delta}$-model M and a world w such that $M, w \models \phi$. A formula ϕ is $L^{\equiv}_{\Delta}$-valid ($\models \phi$) if all worlds in all models satisfy ϕ.

Consider the following axiom system (we will refer to it as $L^{\equiv}_{\Delta}$, too, in the light of the completeness theorem which follows):

Cl Classical propositional logic;
A1 $\phi \equiv \Delta\phi$ for all $\phi \in NonModForm$;
A2 $\Delta\phi \vee \Delta\neg\phi$
A3 $\neg\Delta(\phi \wedge \neg\phi)$
A4 $\Delta(\phi \rightarrow \psi) \rightarrow (\Delta\phi \rightarrow \Delta\psi)$
MP If ϕ and $\phi \rightarrow \psi$ derive ψ
R1 If $\phi \equiv \psi$ derive $\Box\phi \rightarrow \Delta\Box\psi$
R2 If ϕ derive $\Delta\phi$

We say that ϕ is derivable in $L^{\equiv}_{\Delta}$ if there is a sequence of formulas $\phi_1, \ldots, \phi_n$, each of which is either an instance of an axiom schema from $L^{\equiv}_{\Delta}$ or is obtained from the previous formulas using the inference rules of $L^{\equiv}_{\Delta}$, and $\phi_n = \phi$.

Theorem 1. *$L^{\equiv}_{\Delta}$ is complete and sound, namely $\vdash_{L^{\equiv}_{\Delta}} \phi \iff \models_{L^{\equiv}_{\Delta}} \phi$*

Proof. First we give a proof of soundness: $\vdash_{L^{\equiv}_{\Delta}} \phi \Longrightarrow \models_{L^{\equiv}_{\Delta}} \phi$. All instances of the axiom schemas are obviously valid. **A1** expresses the fact that the world is 'frozen' as far as non-modal statements are concerned. **A2**-**A4** state that after a delay the world is still a classical boolean universe.

Note that $\neg(\Delta\phi \wedge \Delta\neg\phi)$ follows from **A3, A4**, $\Box\phi \rightarrow \Delta\Box\phi$ follows from **R1** and $\Delta\neg\Box\phi \rightarrow \neg\Box\phi$ follows from the previous formulas.

Next we need to show that if the premises of the rules are valid, then the conclusions are. Rule **R1** expresses the main point of $L^{\equiv}_{\Delta}$: if an agent believes ϕ and ϕ is equivalent to ψ, then after a delay the agent believes ψ. This follows from the second condition on δ. **R2** states that after a delay all tautologies are still valid.

Next we prove completeness: $\models_{L^{\equiv}_{\Delta}} \phi \Longrightarrow \vdash_{L^{\equiv}_{\Delta}} \phi$. We show that for every ϕ if $\nvdash_{L^{\equiv}_{\Delta}} \neg\phi$ then ϕ is satisfiable, that is $\not\models_{L^{\equiv}_{\Delta}} \neg\phi$.

Assume that ϕ is an $L^{\equiv}_{\Delta}$-consistent formula. In a standard way, we can show that ϕ can be extended to a maximally consistent set of formulas w_{ϕ}, which is a consistent set closed under $L^{\equiv}_{\Delta}$ derivability and containing either ψ or $\neg\psi$ for each $\psi \in Form$. We construct a model $M^{canonical}$ (M^c for short) satisfying ϕ as follows:

W^c is the set of all maximally consistent sets; we also require that each world is unique, in other words there are no copies of the same set;

$w \in V^c(p) \Longleftrightarrow p \in w$;
$R^c(w, \psi) \Longleftrightarrow \Box\psi \in w$;
$\delta^c(w) = \{\psi | \Delta\psi \in w\}$. In other words, $\forall \psi \in Form(\Delta\psi \in w \Longleftrightarrow \psi \in \delta(w))$.

In order to complete the proof, we need to show:

Truth Lemma: for every $\psi \in Form$ and every $w \in W^c$, $M^c, w \models \psi \Longleftrightarrow \psi \in w$.
Correctness of δ^c: for every $w \in W^c$, $\delta^c(w)$ is unique and is a maximally consistent set.
Frozen world: for every $p \in Prop$, $w \in V^c(p) \Longleftrightarrow \delta^c(w) \in V^c(p)$.
Equivalences: For every $\phi \in NonModForm$, if $R^c(w, \phi)$ or there exists a formula ψ such that $R^c(w, \psi)$ and $\vdash \phi \equiv \psi$ in classical propositional logic, then $R^c(\delta(w), \phi)$.

From the Truth Lemma, it follows that ϕ is true in w_ϕ, hence ϕ is satisfiable.
The proofs of these statements are given below.

Truth lemma. The proof goes by induction on subformulas of ψ. It is very easy for $\psi = p | \neg\psi_1 | \psi_1 \wedge \psi_2$.
Suppose $\psi = \Delta\psi_1$. Then $M^c, w \models \Delta\psi_1 \Longleftrightarrow M^c, \delta^c(w) \models \psi_1 \Longleftrightarrow \psi_1 \in \delta^c(w)$ (induction hypothesis) $\Longleftrightarrow \Delta\psi_1 \in w$ (definition of δ^c).
Suppose $\psi = \Box\psi_1$. Then $M^c, w \models \Box\psi_1 \Longleftrightarrow R^c(w, \psi_1) \Longleftrightarrow \Box\psi_1 \in w$ (definition of R^c).
Correctness of δ^c. Consistency of $\delta^c(w)$ follows from **A3**. Maximality follows from **A2, A4** and **R2**. Uniqueness follows from the fact that each $w' \in W^c$ is unique.
Frozen world $w \in V^c(p) \Longleftrightarrow p \in w \Longleftrightarrow \Delta p \in w$ (**A1**) $\Longleftrightarrow p \in \delta^c(w) \Longleftrightarrow \delta^c(w) \in V^c(p)$.
Equivalences. Suppose $R^c(w, \phi)$. Then $\Box\phi \in w$. By **R2**, $\Delta\Box\phi \in w$. By definition of δ^c, $\Box\phi \in \delta^c(w)$. Hence $R^c(\delta^c(w), \phi)$.
Suppose there exists a formula ψ such that $R^c(w, \psi)$ and $\phi \equiv \psi$ is provable in classical propositional logic and hence in $L_\Delta^\equiv$. Then $\Box\psi \in w$ and $\Delta\Box\phi \in w$ by **R2**. This implies $\Box\phi \in \delta^c(w)$ so $R^c(\delta^c(w), \phi)$.

2.2 $L_\Delta^\rightarrow$

It is easy to modify $L_\Delta^\equiv$ so that an agent, instead of being able to derive all formulas equivalent to its beliefs, after a delay can derive all *consequences* of its beliefs.

Definition 2. *A model for $L_\Delta^\rightarrow$ is defined in the same way as a model for $L_\Delta^\equiv$, but replacing the* **Equivalences** *condition with the following stronger condition:*

Consequences. *For every $\phi \in NonModForm$, if $R(w, \phi)$ or there exists a formula ψ such that $R(w, \psi)$ and $\vdash \psi \rightarrow \phi$in classical propositional logic, then $R(\delta(w), \phi)$.*

Theorem 2. *The following axiom system is sound and complete for $L_\Delta^\rightarrow$: the axioms and rules for $L_\Delta^\equiv$ plus*

R3 *If* $\phi \to \psi$ *derive* $\Box\phi \to \Delta\Box\psi$

(Note that **R1** *becomes derivable).*

The proof is very similar to the proof of completeness and soundness of $L_{\Delta}^{\equiv}$.

Both logics $L_{\Delta}^{\equiv}$ and $L_{\Delta}^{\rightarrow}$ are decidable and have the bounded model property. Before proving this, we need a simple lemma. Below, $Subf(\phi)$ denotes the set of all subformulas of ϕ, and $ModSubf(\phi) = \{\psi \in Subf(\phi) : \Box\psi \in Subf(\phi)\}$ are modal subformulas of ϕ.

Lemma 1. *For every* $\phi \in Form$, *and every two* $L_{\Delta}^{\equiv}$ *(*$L_{\Delta}^{\rightarrow}$*) models* $M_1 = \langle W_1, V_1, R_1, \delta_1 \rangle$ *and* $M_2 = \langle W_2, V_2, R_2, \delta_2 \rangle$, *if* $W_1 = W_2$, $\delta_1 = \delta_2$, V_1 *and* V_2 *agree on* $p \in Prop \cap Subf(\phi)$ *and* R_1 *and* R_2 *agree on* $\psi \in ModSubf(\phi)$, *then for every* w,

$$M_1, w \models \phi \Longleftrightarrow M_1, w \models \phi$$

Proof. The proof is just a simple induction on subformulas of ϕ.

Let us call the number of nestings of Δ operator in ϕ *Δ-depth of ϕ*, $d(\phi)$. More precisely,

$d(p) = 0$ for $p \in Prop$;
$d(\neg\psi) = d(\psi)$;
$d(\Box\psi) = d(\psi)$;
$d(\psi_1 \wedge \psi_2) = max(d(\psi_1), d(\psi_2))$;
$d(\Delta\psi) = d(\psi) + 1$.

Clearly $d(\phi) \leq |\phi|$ where $|\phi|$ is the size (number of subformulas) of ϕ. So the result below is better than usual results for modal logics obtained by filtrations which produce models of size less or equal to $2^{|\phi|}$.

Theorem 3. $L_{\Delta}^{\equiv}$ *and* $L_{\Delta}^{\rightarrow}$ *have the bounded model property, that is, if a formula* ϕ *is satisfiable then it has a model where the set of worlds is less or equal to* $d(\phi)$ *(hence less or equal to* $|\phi|$*).*

Proof. The proof is similar for both logics. We can show that if a formula ϕ of Δ-depth $d(\phi) = k$ is satisfied in a world w of a model M then it is satisfied in a model M' where the set of worlds contains only w and the worlds reachable from w in k δ-steps, i.e. $W' = \{w, \delta(w), \delta(\delta(w)), \ldots, \delta^k(w)\}$. Obviously W' is of size at most $d(\phi)$ even if W is infinite ($|W'|$ could be less than k if for some $m < k, \delta^m(w) = \delta^{m+1}(w)$).

The proof that $M, w \models \phi \Longleftrightarrow M', w \models \phi$ is standard (see for example [11], Lemma 2.8) and is omitted here.

Theorem 4. *The satisfiability problem for* $L_{\Delta}^{\equiv}$ *and* $L_{\Delta}^{\rightarrow}$ *is decidable.*

Proof. Suppose we would like to check whether a formula ϕ is satisfiable in $L_{\Delta}^{\equiv}$ ($L_{\Delta}^{\rightarrow}$). By the previous theorem, it suffices to check whether ϕ is satisfiable in any $L_{\Delta}^{\equiv}$ ($L_{\Delta}^{\rightarrow}$) model of size less or equal to $|\phi|$. The set of models of size less or equal to $|\phi|$ is strictly speaking infinite since R is defined on the set of all formulas which is infinite, so there are infinitely many models of a fixed finite size which differ in R. However, by the previous lemma the only part of R in every model which really matters for checking whether ϕ is satisfied or not is the part dealing with all subformulas of ϕ of the form $\Box\psi$. There are only finitely many different relations R with respect to the set $ModSubf(\phi)$, so we need to check only finitely many cases. Being an $L_{\Delta}^{\equiv}$ ($L_{\Delta}^{\rightarrow}$) model is a decidable property since the equivalence relation (consequence relation) on classical propositional formulas is decidable.

3 Related Work

In this section, we briefly survey previous approaches to the problem of logical omniscience and point out similarities and differences with our approach.

Hintikka [4,5] and Rantala [7] saw the problem of logical omniscience mostly as a result of unrealistic principles in a formal model of knowledge. The solution they favoured was to make the principles invalid by changing the possible worlds semantics so that logically equivalent formulas do not necessarily hold in the same sets of possible worlds. This was achieved by introduction of 'impossible worlds' ([7]) where classical logic does not hold. Similar in spirit is the work of Fagin et al. [3] where possible worlds model a flavour of relevance logic. There again classical logical omniscience does not hold, although the agents are perfect reasoners in a weaker logic. Levesque [6] makes an important distinction between the beliefs which the agent actually has (explicit beliefs) and beliefs which can be attributed to it. The explicit beliefs do not conform to the principle of logical omniscience. Levesque's approach involves using incomplete worlds (situations). A similar but simpler and more intuitive semantics for explicit beliefs was proposed by Fagin et al. [2]. Elgot-Drapkin & Perlis [1] and Weyhrauch et al. [13] take a different approach which is concerned more with modelling the bounded resources which prevent the agent from deriving all consequences from its beliefs rather than modelling its irrationality or lack of awareness.

Our motivation is closer to the bounded-resources approach of Elgot-Drapkin and Perlis and Weyhrauch et al., in that we would like to model a rational but resource-bounded agent. However, our solution is in a traditional possible worlds setting rather than in a complex first-order theory of resources or step-logic. Unlike many other epistemic logic approaches, we distinguish between beliefs at the current moment and beliefs after the reasoner had time to consider their consequences, rather than distinguishing between implicit and explicit beliefs.

4 Discussion and Further Work

The logics $L_{\Delta}^{\equiv}$ and $L_{\Delta}^{\rightarrow}$ are simple and have attractive formal properties. However, they are far from what we actually would like to achieve. We describe them here as a proof of concept, which requires further elaboration to achieve a realistic model of agent behaviour. In this section, we briefly outline some of the ways in which the approach presented above could be extended.

First of all, we would like to make the connection between delay time and computational effort involved in deducing a formula more explicit. Although nestings of the delay operator Δ can express some of the intuitions (e.g $\Box\phi \wedge \Delta\Box(\phi \rightarrow \psi) \rightarrow \Delta\Delta\Box\psi$), it may be useful to introduce finer structure on what kind of derivations can be made after a fixed amount of time. For example, after a single unit of delay we could add all statements derivable from current beliefs in one application of an inference rule. Another possibility is to add extra expressive power to the language to allow us to explicitly mention moments of time as in [1] or available resources (e.g., inference rules) as in [13].

Another serious limitation of $L_{\Delta}^{\equiv}$ and $L_{\Delta}^{\rightarrow}$ is that we assume that the world does not change while the agent is reasoning and that the agent never has to revise its beliefs. This could be overcome by explicitly tagging particular beliefs with moments of time.

For some applications, the agent's inability to reason about its beliefs is a limitation. For example, an agent should be able to realise that it does not know whether ϕ and attempt to derive it (see [1] for more examples).

The logics we proposed only consider deductive reasoning, not default reasoning or planning. However, we believe that our approach can be extended to other kinds of deliberation.

References

[1] Elgot-Drapkin, J. J., Perlis, D.: Reasoning situated in time I: Basic concepts. *Journal of Experimental and Theoretical Artificial Intelligence*, 2:75–98, 1990.

[2] Fagin, R., Halpern, J. Y.: Belief, awareness, and limited reasoning. In *Proceedings of the Ninth International Joint Conference on Artificial Intelligence (IJCAI-85)*, pages 480–490, 1985.

[3] Fagin, R., Halpern, J. Y., Vardi, M. V.: A non-standard approach to the logical omniscience problem. *Artificial Intelligence*, 79(2):203–240, 1996.

[4] Hintikka, J.: *Knowledge and belief.* Cornell University Press, Ithaca, NY, 1962.

[5] Hintikka, J.: Impossible possible worlds vindicated. *Journal of Philosophical Logic*, 4:475–484, 1975.

[6] Levesque, H. J.: A logic of implicit and explicit belief. In *Proceedings of the Fourth National Conference on Artificial Intelligence, AAAI-84*, pages 198–202. AAAI, 1984.

[7] Rantala, V.: Impossible worlds semantics and logical omniscience. *Acta Philosophica Fennica*, 35:106–115, 1982.

[8] Rao, A. S., Georgeff, M. P.: Modeling rational agents within a BDI-architecture. In *Proceedings of the Second International Conference on Principles of Knowledge Representation and Reasoning (KR'91)*, pages 473–484, 1991.

[9] Russell, S., Norvig, P.: *Artificial Intelligence: a modern approach.* Prentice Hall, 1995.

[10] Scheutz, M., Logan, B.: Affective vs. deliberative agent control. In *Proceedings of the AISB'01 Symposium on Emotion, Cognition and Affective Computing*, pages 1–10. AISB, The Society for the Study of Artificial Intelligence and the Simulation of Behaviour, March 2001.

[11] van Benthem, J.: *Modal logic and classical logic.* Bibliopolis, 1983.
[12] van der Hoek, W., van Linder, B., Meyer, J-J. Ch.: An integrated modal approach to rational agents. In Wooldridge, M. and Rao, A. editors, *Foundations of Rational Agency*, pages 133–168. Kluwer Academic, Dordrecht, 1999.
[13] Weyhrauch, R. W., Cadoli, M., Talcott, C. L.: Using abstract resources to control reasoning. *Journal of Logic, Language and Information*, 7(1):77–101, 1998.

Local Conditional High-Level Robot Programs

Sebastian Sardiña

Department of Computer Science
University of Toronto
Toronto, Canada M5S 1A4
ssardina@cs.toronto.edu,
http://www.cs.toronto.edu/ ssardina

Abstract. When it comes to building robot controllers, high-level programming arises as a feasible alternative to planning. The task then is to verify a high-level program by finding a legal execution of it. However, interleaving offline verification with execution in the world seems to be the most practical approach for large programs and complex scenarios involving information gathering and exogenous events.
In this paper, we present a mechanism for performing local lookahead for the Golog family of high-level robot programs. The main features of such mechanism are that it takes sensing seriously by constructing conditional plans that are ready to be executed in the world, and it mixes perfectly with an account of interleaved perception, planning, and action. Also, a simple implementation is developed.

1 Motivation

In general terms, this paper is concerned with how to conveniently specify the behavior of an intelligent agent or robot living in an incompletely known dynamic world. One popular way of specifying the behavior of an agent is through planning — the generation of a sequence of actions achieving or maintaining a set of goals. To cope with incomplete knowledge, some sort of sensing behavior is usually assumed [1,2], resulting in conditional or contingency plans [3,4,5], where branches are executed based on the outcome of perceptual actions or sensors. The task of a conditional planner is to find a tree-structured plan that accounts for and handles all eventualities, in advance of execution.

However this type of conditional planning is computationally difficult and impractical in many robot domains. The non-conditional planning problem is already highly intractable, and taking sensing into account only makes it worse.

High-level logic programming languages like Golog [6] and ConGolog [7] offer an interesting alternative to planning in which the user specifies not just a goal, but also constraints on how it is to be achieved, perhaps leaving small subtasks to be handled by an automatic planner. In that way, a high-level program serves as a "guide" heavily restricting the search space. By a high-level program, we mean one whose primitive instructions are domain-dependent actions of the robot, whose tests involve domain-dependent fluents affected by these actions, and whose code may contain nondeterministic choice points.

R. Nieuwenhuis and A. Voronkov (Eds.): LPAR 2001, LNAI 2250, pp. 110–124, 2001.

Instead of looking for a legal sequence of actions achieving some goal, the task now is to find a sequence that constitutes a legal execution of a high-level program. Originally, Golog and ConGolog programs were intended to be solved offline, that is, a complete solution was obtained before committing even to the first action. Also, sensing behavior was not considered so that the approach to uncertainty resembles more that of conformant planners [8]. While Lakemeyer [9] suggested an extension of Golog to handle sensing and contingent plans, De Giacomo and Levesque [10] provided an account of interleaved perception, planning, and action [11,12] for ConGolog programs.

In this paper, we propose to combine both improvements by suggesting a method of executing high-level robot programs that is both conditional (in the sense of Lakemeyer) and local (in the sense of De Giacomo and Levesque.) The advantages are twofold. First, we can expect to deal with much larger programs, assuming planning is locally restricted. Second, the offline verification of subtasks will handle sensing and provide contingent solutions. Although this may seem initially a trivial intersection of the two pieces, it is not. For one, sGolog semantics is given as a macro expansion while an incremental execution is defined with a single-step semantics. Furthermore, sGolog does not handle ConGolog constructs, namely those for concurrency and reactive behavior, which we do not want to give up.

The rest of the paper is organized as follows: in the next two sections, we give brief introductions to the situation calculus, high-level programs, and their executions. Section 4 is devoted to our approach to offline verification of programs. In Section 5, we develop a simple and provably sound Prolog implementation. We draw conclusions and discuss future lines of research in Section 6.

2 Situation Calculus and Programs

In this section, we start by explaining the situation calculus dialect on which all the high-level approach is based on, and after that, we informally show what high-level programs look like.

The situation calculus is a second order language specifically designed for representing dynamically changing worlds [13,14]. We will not go over it here except to note the following components: there is a special constant S_0 used to denote the *initial situation* where no actions have yet occurred; there is a distinguished binary function symbol *do* where $do(a, s)$ denotes the successor situation to s resulting from performing action a; relations whose truth values vary from situation to situations are called *fluents*, and are denoted by predicate/function symbols taking a situation term as their last argument; there is a special predicate $Poss(a, s)$ used to state that action a is executable in situation s. Depending on the type of action theory used we may have other predicates and axioms to state what are the sensing results of special sensing actions [4] or the outcomes of onboard sensors [2] at some situation. Finally, by a history σ we mean a sequence of pairs (a, μ) where a is a primitive action and μ encodes the sensing results at that point.[1] A formula $Sensed[\sigma]$ in the language can be defined stating the sensing results of history σ. Lastly, $end[\sigma]$ stands for the situation term corresponding to history σ. Informally, while $Sensed[\sigma]$ extracts from σ all the sensing information already gathered, $end[\sigma]$ extracts the sequence of actions already performed.

On top of the situation calculus, we can define logic-based programming languages like Golog [6] and ConGolog [7], which, in addition to the primitive actions of the situation calculus, allow the definition of complex actions. Indeed, Golog offers all the control structures known from conventional programming languages (e.g., sequence, iteration, conditional, etc.) plus some nondeterministic constructs. It is due to these last control structures that programs do not stand for complete solutions, but only for sketches of them whose gaps have to be filled later, usually at execution time. ConGolog extends Golog to accommodate concurrency and interrupts. As one may expect, both Golog and ConGolog rely on an underlying situation calculus axiomatization to describe how the world changes as the result of available actions, i.e. a theory of action. For instance, *basic action theories* [15] or the more general *guarded action theories* [2] may be used for that propose.

To informally introduce the syntax and some of the common constructs of these programming languages, we show next a possible ConGolog program for a version of the well-known airport problem [4,9,16]. Suppose that the ultimate goal of an agent is to board its plane. For that, she first needs to get to the airport, go to the right airline terminal, and once there, she has to get to the correct gate, and finally board her plane. In addition, she probably wants to buy something to read and drink before boarding the plane. The following may be a ConGolog control program for such agent:

proc *catch_plane*1
  $(\pi a.a)^*$; at(airport)?;
  (goto(term1) | goto(term2));
  (buy(magazine) | buy(paper));
  if *gate* $\geq$ 90 **then** { goto(gate); buy(coffee) } **else**
    { buy(coffee); goto(gate) }
  board_plane;
end_proc

where $\delta_1; \delta_2$ stands for sequence of programs δ_1 and δ_2; $\pi x.\delta(x)$ for nondeterministic choice of argument x; $\delta_1|\delta_2$ for nondeterministic selection between programs δ_1 and δ_2; and δ^* for nondeterministic iteration of program δ (zero, one, or more times). Finally, action (ϕ)? checks that condition ϕ holds. As it is easy to observe, the above program has many gaps due to nondeterministic points that need to be resolved by an automated planner. For example, the first two complex actions $(\pi a.a)^*; at(airport)$? require the agent to select some number of actions (pick up the car key, get in the car, drive to the airport, etc.) so that after their execution

[1] The outcome of a itself in basic theories, or the values of all sensors in guarded theories.

she would eventually be at the airport. As the reader may have noticed, that particular sub-task is very similar to classical planning.[2] Once in the airport, the agent has to decide whether to head to terminal 1 or 2 (another gap to be filled) and, after that, whether to buy a magazine or a newspaper. Finally, she would buy something to drink and board the airplane. However, in case the gate number is 90 or up, it is preferable to buy coffee at the gate, otherwise it is better to buy coffee before going to the gate.

3 Incremental Execution of Programs

Finding a legal execution of high-level programs is at the core of the whole approach. Indeed, a sequence of action standing for a program execution will be taken as the ultimate agent behavior. Originally, Golog and ConGolog programs were conceived to be executed (verified) offline. In other words, we look for a sequence of actions $[a_1, ..., a_m]$ such that $Do(\delta, s, do([a_1, ..., a_m], S_0))$[3] is entailed by the specification, where $Do(\delta, s, s')$ is intended to say that situation s' represents a legal execution of program δ from the initial situation s. Once a sequence like that is found, the agent is supposed to execute it one action at a time. Clearly, this type of execution remains infeasible for large programs and precludes both runtime sensing information and reactive behavior. To deal with these drawbacks, De Giacomo and Levesque [10] provided a formal notion of interleaved planning, sensing, and action [11,12] which we support for cognitive robotic applications. In their account, they make use of two predicates defined in [7] in order to give a single-step semantics to ConGolog programs:

- $Trans(\delta, s, \delta', s')$ is meant to say that program δ in situation s may legally execute one step, ending in situation s' with program δ' remaining;
- $Final(\delta, s)$ is meant to say that program δ may legally terminate in situation s.

Both predicates are defined inductively for each language construct. As an example, we list the axioms corresponding to the nondeterministic choice of program and sequence:[4]

$$\begin{aligned}
Trans(\delta_1|\delta_2, s, \delta', s') &\equiv Trans(\delta_1, s, \delta', s') \vee Trans(\delta_2, s, \delta', s') \\
Trans(\delta_1;\delta_2, s, \delta', s') &\equiv Trans(\delta_1, s, \delta', s'') \wedge \delta' = (\delta''; \delta_2) \vee \\
&\qquad Final(\delta_1, s) \wedge Trans(\delta_2, s, \delta', s') \\
Final(\delta_1|\delta_2, s) &\equiv Final(\delta_1, s) \vee Final(\delta_2, s) \\
Final(\delta_1;\delta_2, s) &\equiv Final(\delta_1, s) \wedge Final(\delta_2, s)
\end{aligned}$$

From now on, we use *Axioms* to refer to the set of axioms defining the underlying theory of action, the axioms for *Trans* and *Final*, and those needed

[2] In fact, one would prefer to avoid this kind of sub-tasks and write more detailed programs since the search space required for such sub-tasks will be huge.

[3] $do([a_1, ..., a_m], S_0))$ denotes the situation term $do(a_m, do(a_{m-1}, ..., do(a_1, S_0))...)$.

[4] From now on, we assume all free variables are universally quantified.

for the encoding of programs as first-order terms (see [7].) Also, $Trans^*$ stands for the second-order definition of the transitive closure of $Trans$.

Definition 1. *An online execution of a program δ_0 starting from a history σ_0 is a sequence $(\delta_0, \sigma_0), \ldots, (\delta_n, \sigma_n)$, such that for $i = 0, .., n-1$:*

$$Axioms \cup Sensed[\sigma_i] \models Trans(\delta_i, end[\sigma_i], \delta_{i+1}, end[\sigma_{i+1}])$$

$$\sigma_{i+1} = \begin{cases} \sigma_i, & \text{if } end[\sigma_{i+1}] = end[\sigma_i] \\ \sigma_i \cdot (a, \mu), & \text{if } end[\sigma_{i+1}] = do(a, end[\sigma_i]) \\ & \text{and } \mu \text{ is the sensing outcomes after } a \end{cases}$$

Furthermore, the online execution is successful if:

$$Axioms \cup Sensed[\sigma_n] \models Final(\delta_n, end[\sigma_n])$$

Among other things, with an online (incremental) execution, it is possible to gather information after each transition. However, given that an incremental execution requires committing in the world at each step and programs may contain nondeterministic points, some lookahead mechanism is required to avoid unsuccessful (dead-end) executions. To that end, in [10] a new language construct Σ, the search operator, is provided as a local controlled form of offline verification where the amount of lookahead to be performed is under the control of the programmer. As with all the other language constructs, a single-step semantics for it can be defined such that $\Sigma\delta$ selects from all possible transitions of (δ, s) those for which there exists a sequence of further transitions leading to a final configuration (δ', s'). Formally,

$$\begin{aligned} Final(\Sigma\delta, s) &\equiv Final(\delta, s) \\ Trans(\Sigma\delta, s, \delta', s') &\equiv \exists\gamma, \gamma', s''.\delta' = \Sigma\gamma \land Trans(\delta, s, \gamma, s') \land \\ &\qquad Trans^*(\gamma, s', \gamma', s'') \land Final(\gamma', s'') \end{aligned}$$

Nonetheless, we recognize some important limitations of this search operator. In particular, we are concerned with its limitation to explicitly handle sensing and the fact that it does not generate solutions that are ready to be carried out by the agent. This is because search only calculates the next "safe" action the agent should commit to, even though there may be a *complete* (conditional) course of action to follow. What we propose here is a new search operator which overcomes both issues.

3.1 Offline Verification with Sensing

As already noted, one way to cope with incomplete information, especially when sensors are cheap and accurate, or effectors are costly, is by gaining new information through sensing and adopting a contingent planning strategy. Consider a revised version of the airport example in which the agent does not know the gate number, but can learn it by examining the departure screen at the right terminal.

```
proc catch_plane2
    (πa.a)*; at(airport)?;
    (goto(term1) | goto(term2));
    watch_screen;          /* Sensing Action! */
    (buy(magazine) | buy(paper));
    if gate ≥ 90 then { goto(gate); buy(coffee) } else
                      { buy(coffee); goto(gate) }
    board_plane;
end_proc
```

Conformant planning (like [8]), the development of non-conditional plans that do not rely on sensory information, cannot generally solve our example because there is no linear course of action that solves the program under any possible outcome of the sensing action *watch_screen*. It should be clear then that neither Golog nor ConGolog would find any successful offline execution for *catch_plane*2. An online execution, however, would adapt the sequence depending on the information observed on the boarding panel.

In [9], it was argued that, yet, "*there is a place for offline interpretation of programs with sensing.*" In fact, Lakemeyer suggested an extension of Golog, namely sGolog, that handles sensing actions offline by computing conditional plans instead of linear ones. These plans are represented - in the language - by *conditional action trees* (CATs) terms of the form $a \cdot c_1$ or $[\phi, c_1, c_2]$, where a is an action term, ϕ is a formula, and c_1 and c_2 are two CATs. Roughly, an sGolog solution for our airport example would look as follows:

$$\begin{aligned} c = {} & goto(airport) \cdot goto(term2) \cdot watch\_screen \cdot buy(paper) \\ & \cdot [gate \geq 90, goto(gate) \cdot buy(coffee) \cdot board\_plane, \\ & \qquad buy(coffee) \cdot goto(gate) \cdot board\_plane] \end{aligned}$$

sGolog extends Golog's $Do(\delta, s, s')$ to $Do_s(\delta, s, c)$ which expands into a formula of the situation calculus augmented by a set of axioms Ax_{CAT} for dealing with CAT terms. $Do_s(\delta, s, c)$ may be read as "executing the program δ in situation s results in CAT c." It is worth noting that although sGolog is able to build conditional plans as the above one, it requires programs to use a special action *branch_on*(ϕ) to state where to split and how. Intuitively, a *branch_on*(ϕ) tells the planner that it should split w.r.t. the condition $\phi(s)$. In that sense, the above CAT c is not a seen as a legal solution for program *catch_plane*2, but it is a legal one for the following version of it:

```
proc catch_plane2b
    (πa.a)*; at(airport)?;
    (goto(term1) | goto(term2));
    watch_screen;               /* Sensing Action! */
    (buy(magazine) | buy(paper)); branch_on(gate ≥ 90);
    if gate ≥ 90 then { goto(gate); buy(coffee) } else
                      { buy(coffee); goto(gate) }
    board_plane;
end_proc
```

From now on, we denote by δ^- to the program δ with all its "*branch_on*" actions suppressed (e.g., $catch\_plane2b^- = catch\_plane2$).

4 Conditional Lookahead

Lakemeyer argued that many programs with a moderate number of sensing actions can very well be handled with his approach. Even though we are skeptical about doing full offline execution of any (large) program, we consider his argument a much more plausible one if offline execution were restricted to local places in a program. In what follows, we define a new search construct providing a local lookahead mechanism that takes potential sensing behavior seriously and fits smoothly with the incremental execution scheme from Section 3. We begin by defining a subset of useful high-level programs.

Definition 2. *A Golog program δ is a conditional program plan (CPP) if*

- $\delta = nil$, *i.e., δ is the empty program;*
- $\delta = A$, *A is an action term;*
- $\delta = (A; \delta_1)$, *A is an action term, and δ_1 is a CPP;*
- $\delta =$ **if** ϕ **then** δ_1 **else** δ_2, *ϕ is a fluent formula, and δ_1, δ_2 are CPPs.*

Under our approach, CPPs will play the role of conditional-plan solutions. Notice they are no more than regular *deterministic* high-level programs where only sequence of actions and conditional splitting (branching) are allowed. It is easy to state an axiom defining the relation *condPlan*(δ), which, informally, holds only when δ is a CPP.

Next, we introduce a two-place function *run*–our version of Lakemeyer's *cdo* function–which takes a CPP δ and a situation s, and returns a situation which is obtained from s using the actions along a path in δ.[5] Briefly, *run* follows a certain branch in the CPP depending on the truth value of the branch-conditions.

$$
\begin{aligned}
run(nil, s) &= s \\
run(a, s) &= do(a, s) \\
run((a; \delta), s) &= run(\delta, do(a, s)) \\
\phi(s) \supset run(\text{if } \phi \text{ then } \delta_1 \text{ else } \delta_2, s) &= run(\delta_1, s) \\
\neg\phi(s) \supset run(\text{if } \phi \text{ then } \delta_1 \text{ else } \delta_2, s) &= run(\delta_2, s)
\end{aligned}
$$

Lastly, predicate *knowHow*(δ, s) is intended to mean that "we know how to execute δ starting at situation s." By this we mean that at every branching point in the CPP δ, the branch-formula is known to be true or false. In order to enforce this restriction, programs would generally have some sensing behavior that will guarantee that each formula in a CPP will be known. A high-level description of the corresponding axioms for *run* is the following:

[5] A CPP can be easily seen as a tree with actions and conditional splittings as nodes.

$$\begin{aligned}
knowHow(nil, s) &\equiv TRUE \\
knowHow(a, s) &\equiv TRUE \\
knowHow((a;\delta), s) &\equiv knowHow(\delta, do(a, s)) \\
knowHow(\text{if } \phi \text{ then } \delta_1 \text{ else } \delta_2, s) &\equiv Kwhether(\phi, s) \wedge \\
&\quad \phi(s) \supset knowHow(\delta_1, s) \wedge \\
&\quad \neg\phi(s) \supset knowHow(\delta_2, s)
\end{aligned}$$

Observe that the last axiom makes use of predicate $Kwhether(\phi, s)$ defined in [17], which gives us a solution to knowledge in the situation calculus. Relation $Kwhether(\phi, s)$ is intended to say that the condition ϕ will be eventually known (true or false) in situation s.[6] Although it is possible to use more general definitions of "knowing how to execute a program" we stick to the above one for the the sake of simplicity.

We now have all the machinery needed to define our new mechanism of controlled lookahead. Namely, we introduce a conditional search operator Σ_c that, instead of only returning the next action to be performed, it computes a whole (remaining) CPP that solves the original program and is ready to be executed online. To that end, we define *Final* and *Trans* for the new operator. For *Final*, we have that $(\Sigma_c\delta, s)$ is a final configuration if (δ, s) itself is.

$$Final(\Sigma_c\delta, s) \equiv Final(\delta, s)$$

For *Trans*, a configuration $(\Sigma_c\delta, s)$ can evolve to (δ', s) if δ' is a CPP that the agent knows how to execute from s, and such that *every possible and complete* path through δ' represents a successful execution of the original program δ.

$$\begin{aligned}
Trans(\Sigma_c\delta, s, \delta', s') \equiv{}& s' = s \wedge condPlan(\delta') \wedge knowHow(\delta', s) \wedge \\
& \exists\delta''.Trans^*(\delta, s, \delta'', run(\delta', s)) \wedge Final(\delta'', run(\delta', s))
\end{aligned}$$

While the first line defines what the "form" of a legal solution is, the second one makes the connection between the CPP δ' and the original program δ. Notice we want this sentence to be true in every interpretation, and, therefore, the sequence of actions produced by $run(\delta', s)$ must always correspond to a (complete) sequence of transitions for δ. This is very important since not every CPP will be acceptable, but only the ones that are "hidden" in δ. It is important to remark that different interpretations could lead to different "runs" and transitions.

From now on, we assume the above two axioms for Σ_c, together with the axioms for *run*, *condPlan* and *knowHow*, are all included into the already mentioned set of axioms *Axioms*. If, for example, we execute $\Sigma_c catch\_plane2$ we get that

$$Axioms \cup Sensed[\sigma_0] \models Trans(\Sigma_c catch\_plane2, S_0, \delta', S_0)$$

where

[6] See [17] for a complete coverage of knowledge and sensing in the situation calculus.

$$\delta' = goto(airport); goto(term2); watch\_screen; buy(paper); \\ \text{if } gate \geq 90 \text{ then } \{goto(gate); buy(coffee); board\_plane\} \\ \text{else } \{buy(coffee); goto(gate); board\_plane\}$$

In this case, $run(\delta', S_0)$ would have two different interpretations w.r.t. the set $Axioms \cup Sensed[\sigma_0]$. In the models where $gate \geq 90$, function $run(\delta', S_0)$ denotes the situation

$$do([goto(airport), goto(term2), watch\_screen, \\ buy(paper), goto(gate), buy(coffee), board\_plane], S_0)$$

On the contrary, in those models where $gate < 90$, function $run(\delta', S_0)$ denotes the situation term

$$do([goto(airport), goto(term2), watch\_screen, \\ buy(paper), buy(coffee), goto(gate), board\_plane], S_0)$$

The point is that, in either case, $run(\delta', S_0)$ is supported by the original program $catch\_plane2$.

By inspecting the above $Trans$ axiom for Σ_c, one can see that Σ_c performs no action step, but calculates a remaining program δ' (in particular, a CPP one) that is ready to be executed online, and that has previously considered how future sensing will be managed. This implies that the final sequence of actions will eventually depend on the future sensing outcomes; in our example, after committing to action $watch\_screen$. Furthermore, the CPP returned has already solved all nondeterministic points in the original program as well as all concurrency involved on it. In some sense, Σ_c can be visualized as an operator that transforms an arbitrary complex ConGolog program into a simple and deterministic CPP without requiring it to know in advance how future sensing will turn out.

The following are some useful properties of Σ_c.

Property 1

$$Trans((\Sigma_c\delta_1)|(\Sigma_c\delta_2), s, \delta', s') \equiv Trans(\Sigma_c(\delta_1|\delta_2), s, \delta', s')$$

i.e., search distributes over the nondeterministic choice of program. An interesting example comes up with programs $\delta_1 = (a; \phi; b)$ and $\delta_2 = (a; \neg\phi; c)$. Even though not trivial to see, the CPP $\delta' = (a; \text{if } \phi \text{ then } b \text{ else } c)$ is a solution for both $\Sigma_c(\delta_1|\delta_2)$ and $(\Sigma_c\delta_1)|(\Sigma_c\delta_2)$. The former case is easy; the latter, though, involves realizing that, in the interpretation where ϕ holds, the program $\Sigma_c\delta_1$ is the one that performs the transition and a "run" of δ' is action a followed by action b. However, in the interpretation where $\neg\phi$ holds, the program chosen for the transition is $\Sigma_c\delta_2$, and a "run" of δ' is action a followed by action c.

Property 2

$$Trans(\Sigma_c\delta, s, \delta', s') \supset Final(\Sigma\delta, s) \vee \exists\delta''.s''.Trans(\Sigma\delta, s, \delta'', s'')$$

This means that whenever there is a transition w.r.t. Σ_c, there is also a transition w.r.t. Σ. However, the converse does not apply.

Property 3

$$Trans(\Sigma_c(\delta_1;\delta_2), s, \delta, s) \equiv \exists\delta_1'.Trans(\Sigma_c\delta_1, s, \delta_1', s) \wedge$$
$$\exists\delta^*.Trans(\Sigma_c\delta_2, run(\delta_1', s), \delta^*, run(\delta_1', s)) \wedge ext_{CPP}(\delta_1', \delta, \delta^*, s)$$

i.e., a solution for $\delta_1;\delta_2$ can be seen as some solution for δ_1 extended, at each leaf, with a conditional plan that solves δ_2. Relation $ext_{CPP}(\delta', \delta, \delta^*, s)$ is the analogous one to sGolog's $ext(c', c, c^*, s)$. Informally, $ext_{CPP}(\delta', \delta, \delta^*, s)$ means that CPP δ is obtained by extending the CPP δ' with the CPP δ^* after executing δ' from situation s. The axioms for such relation can be obtained by a straightforward reformulation of *ext*'s axioms given in [9].

Property 4

$$Trans(\Sigma_c\delta, s, \delta', s') \supset Final(\delta, s) \vee$$
$$\exists\delta'', s'', \delta^*, s^*.Trans(\delta, s, \delta'', s'') \wedge Trans(\Sigma_c\delta'', s'', \delta^*, s^*)$$

This property is closely related to Property 2 for Σ given in [10]. Intuitively, search can be seen as performing one single step while propagating itself to the program that remains after such step.

It is not surprising that sGolog solutions are solutions under conditional search as well. To show that, we make use of a one-place function $CATtoCPP$ that takes a CAT and returns its analogous CPP. We will refer with $Ax_{CATtoCPP}$ to the set of axioms defining such function.

Theorem 1. *Let δ be a sGolog program, and let σ be some history the agent has already committed to. Then, the set of axioms $Axioms \cup Sensed[\sigma] \cup Ax_{CAT} \cup Ax_{CATtoCPP}$ entails the following sentence:*

$$Do_s(\delta, end[\sigma], c) \supset Trans(\Sigma_c\delta^-, end[\sigma], CATtoCPP(c), end[\sigma])$$

The opposite, though, does not hold, because conditional search is more general than sGolog in that it allows for splittings *at any point*. In contrast, and as already stated, sGolog splits only at the points explicitly stated by the user via the special action *branch_on*. As a matter of fact, the CAT c of Section 3.1 is a solution for *catch_plane2b*, but not for *catch_plane2*. On the other hand, program δ' above *is indeed a solution* for (Σ_c*catch_plane2*) itself, since Σ_c need not be told where to split.[7]

4.1 Restricted Conditional Search

We finish this section by noting that it is easy to slightly modify our axioms to define a restricted version of Σ_c, say Σ_{cb}, such that splittings in CPPs occurs *only* where the programmer has explicitly said so via a special action $branch\_on(\phi)$

[7] However, under Σ_c, there may be strange solutions due to naive and useless splittings (e.g., splittings w.r.t. tautologies are always allowed.)

(as done in sGolog.) The main motivation for defining Σ_{cb} is to provide a simple and clear semantics to our implementation.

We then make use of a special action $branch\_on(\phi)$, whose "effect" is to introduce a new conditional construct into the solution, i.e., into the CPP. Fortunately, we can achieve this by simply treating $branch\_on(\phi)$ as a normal primitive action that is always possible. Intuitively, a transition on a branch action is used to leave a "mark" in the situation term so as to force a conditional splitting at that point. Given that, at planning time, the branch action will be added to the situation term (as done with any other primitive action), we should guarantee that it has no effect on any of the domains fluents. In other words, every fluent in the domain should have the same (truth) value before and after a branch action.

In addition, we change the last axiom of function run to the following one:

$$\phi(s) \supset run(\text{if } \phi \text{ then } \delta_1 \text{ else } \delta_2\text{,s}) = do(branch\_on(\phi), run(\delta_1, s))$$
$$\neg\phi(s) \supset run(\text{if } \phi \text{ then } \delta_1 \text{ else } \delta_2\text{,s}) = do(branch\_on(\phi), run(\delta_2, s))$$

Now, a "run" of the program leaves a "mark" on the situation term, namely a $branch\_on(\phi)$ action term, to account for a conditional splitting.

It worth observing that, by using the same $Trans$ and $Final$ axioms given for Σ_c, all conditional constructs in the CPP solution are now required to perfectly coincide with the branch statements mentioned in the program. Finally, it is very important to remark that a branch action will never be mentioned in any CPP δ' obtained by search. In that sense, a $branch\_on(\phi)$ action can be viewed as a (meta-level) action whose direct effects are seen only at "planning time."

It is not difficult to prove that all four properties listed for Σ_c are properties of Σ_{cb} as well.[8] What is more important, it can be proved that Σ_{cb} and sGolog are equivalent for Golog programs. In addition, all solutions of Σ_{cb} are also solutions of Σ_c. We will refer with $Axioms'$, instead of $Axioms$, when using the modified axioms of Σ_{cb}.

Theorem 2. *Let δ_1 be an sGolog program and δ_2 a ConGolog one. Let σ be some history the agent has already committed to. Then, the set of axioms $Axioms' \cup Sensed[\sigma] \cup Ax_{CAT} \cup Ax_{CATtoCPP}$ entails the following sentence:*

$$Do_s(\delta_1, end[\sigma], c) \equiv Trans(\Sigma_{cb}\delta_1, end[\sigma], CATtoCPP(c), end[\sigma])$$

Furthermore, if $Axioms' \cup Sensed[\sigma] \models Trans(\Sigma_{cb}\delta_2, end[\sigma], \delta', s')$, then

$$Axioms \cup Sensed[\sigma] \models Trans(\Sigma_c\delta_2^-, end[\sigma], \delta', s')$$

Once again, the restricted version of search is not interesting in terms of the specification itself, as it is less general than Σ_c; but it is convenient in terms of implementation issues as we will see in the following section.

[8] Nonetheless we should replace $\Sigma\delta$ by $\Sigma\delta^-$ in Property 2; for, branch actions make no sense in the scope of Σ.

5 A Simple Implementation

In this section, we show a simple Prolog implementation of the restricted conditional search construct Σ_{cb} under two main assumptions borrowed from [9]: (i) only the truth value of relational fluents can be sensed; (ii) whenever a *branch_on*(P) action is reached, where P is a fluent, both truth values are conceivable for P. Assumption (ii) allows us to safely use hypothetical reasoning on the two possible truth values of P. For that, we use two auxiliary actions *assm*(P) and *assm*(*neg*(P)) whose only effect is to turn P true and false respectively. We also assume the following code is already available:

1. A set of `trans/4` and `final/2` clauses constituting a correct implementation of *Trans* and *Final* predicates for all ConGolog constructs (see [7,18]);
2. A set of clauses implementing the underlying theory of action used. In particular, this set will include facts of the form `action(`a`)` and `fluent(`f`)` defining each action name a and each fuent name f respectively;
3. A set of `kwhether/2` clauses implementing predicate $Kwhether(P, s)$. For basic action theories, we can make a simplification by checking whether the fluent in question was sensed earlier and not changed since then [9]. For guarded theories, where inertia law may not apply, one may check that the fluent can be regressed up to a situation where a sensing axiom is applicable.

With all these assumptions, the restricted search implementation arises as a nice, but still not trivial, mixture between the implementation of sGolog and the one for ConGolog. The reader will quickly notice that the code below reuses the clauses for *Trans* and *Final* of all the other constructs. Besides, it is independent of the background theory used, in particular independent on how sensing is modeled, as long as the above requirements are met.[9]

```
trans(searchcr(E),S,CPP,S):- build_cpp(E,S,CPP).
trans(branch_on(P),S,[],[branch_on(P)|S]).

build_cpp(E,S,[])       :- final(E,S).
build_cpp([E1|E2],S,C):- E2\=[], !, build_cpp(E1,S,C1),
                         ext_cpp(E2,S,C1,C).
build_cpp(branch_on(P),S,if(P,[],[])):- !, kwhether(P,S).
build_cpp(E,S,C)        :- trans(E,S,E1,[branch_on(P)|S]),
                           build_cpp([branch_on(P)|E1],S,C).
build_cpp(E,S,C)        :- trans(E,S,E1,S), build_cpp(E1,S,C).
build_cpp(E,S,[A|C])   :- trans(E,S,E1,[A|S]), fluent(P),
                           A\=branch_on(P), build_cpp(E1,[A|S],C).

/* ext_cpp(E,S,C,C1) recursively descends  the CPP C. On a         */
/* leaf, build_cpp/3 is used to extend the branch wrt program E.*/
ext_cpp(E,S,[A|C],[A|C2]):- action(A), ext_cpp(E,[A|S],C,C2).
```

[9] For legibility, we keep the translation between the theory and Prolog implicit.

```
ext_cpp(E,S,if(P,C1,C2),if(P,C3,C4)):-
 ext_cpp(E,[assm(P)|S],C1,C3), ext_cpp(E,[assm(neg(P))|S],C2,C4).
ext_cpp(E,S,[],C):- build_cpp(E,S,C). /* leaf of CPP */
```

Roughly speaking, `build_cpp`(δ, s, C) builds a CPP C for program δ at situation term s by calling `trans/4` to obtain a single step, and `ext_cpp/4` to extend intermediate already-computed CPPs. Relying on the correctness of `trans/4`, `final/2`, and `kwhether/2`, it is possible to show that the above program, which we will refer as P, is occur-check and floundering free [19].

Lemma 1. *Let δ be a ground ConGolog program term, and let s be a ground situation term. Then, the goal $G =$*`build_cpp`*(δ, s, C) is occur-check and floundering free w.r.t. program P, assuming a correct implementation of* `trans/4`, `final/2`, `action/1`, `fluent/1`, *and* `kwhether/2`. [10]

Finally, we show that whenever the above implementation succeeds, a conditional program plan supported by the specification as a legal solution of both Σ_{cb} and Σ_c is returned (by binding variable P below.) In contrast, whenever the implementation finitely fails, we can only guarantee that the specification of Σ_{cb} supports no solution at all.

Theorem 3. *Let δ be a ground program term without mentioning search, and let σ be a history. Let G be the goal* `trans`*$(searchcr(\delta), end[\sigma], P, S)$. If G succeeds with computed answer $P = \delta', S = s'$, then δ' is a CPP, $s' = end[\sigma]$, and*

$$Axioms' \cup Sensed[\sigma] \models Trans(\Sigma_{cb}\delta, end[\sigma], \delta', s')$$
$$Axioms \cup Sensed[\sigma] \models Trans(\Sigma_c\delta^-, end[\sigma], \delta', s')$$

On the other hand, whenever G finitely fails, then

$$Axioms' \cup Sensed[\sigma] \models \forall\delta', s'.\neg Trans(\Sigma_{cb}\delta, end[\sigma], \delta', s')$$

It is worth noting that our results rely heavily on the implementation of `trans/4`, `final/2`, and `kwhether/2`. In particular, in order to assure correctness for the first two predicates, we may need to impose extra conditions on both programs and histories (e.g., see just-in-time histories and programs in [10,18].)

Finally, we conjecture that it is possible to develop a better, and yet implementable, splitting strategy that does not rely on the user, and hence, does not use any special branching action. A plausible approach may be to split whenever the interpreter finds a condition ϕ that is not known at planning time. Clearly, this means that at least one fluent mentioned in ϕ is unknown; if the fluent will be known due to future sensing, we should branch w.r.t. to it. Observe that we should not only consider the conditions mentioned in the program, but all the formulas required to evaluate a transition (such as the actions' preconditions.) One point in favor of this strategy is that it is always sound w.r.t. Σ_c, due to the

[10] In reality, the program used will be P union the code for `trans/4`, `final/2`, `kwhether/2`, and the one implementing the underlying theory of action.

fact that Σ_c allows for any branching at any point, even for naive and unnecessary ones. Put differently, any solution reported by Prolog will be supported by the specification. On the other hand, it is not totally clear whether we can capture the branching power of Σ_c completely. Furthermore, this strategy will require considerable more computational effort during the search. Despite this difficulties, we think these ideas deserve future attention in pursuit of a more flexible and practical implementation.

6 Conclusions and Further Research

In this article, we have developed a new local lookahead construct for the Golog family of robot programs. The new construct provides local offline verification with sensing of ConGolog programs, produces complete conditional plans, and moreover, it mixes well with an interleaved account of execution. In some sense, the work here shows how easily one can extend Golog and ConGolog, together with their implementations, to handle *local contingent planning*. Proofs and more technical details can be found in an extended version of this paper [20].

Many problems remain open. First, it would be interesting to investigate some principled way of interleaving search in high-level programs since that determines how realistic, practical, and complete our programs are. Second, there is much to say regarding the relation between our search and the original one in [10]. For instance, neither subsumes completely the other. Nonetheless, it can be shown that, in some interesting cases, the original search Σ would actually execute an "implicit" CPP which Σ_c would support as a solution. Third, as already said, we would like to investigate some principled way of branching that does not rely on the user and still be implementable. Last, but not least, our approach may suggest the construction of more general (robot) plans than CPPs (in the sense of [4,21,22].) Indeed, solutions where the length of a branch is finite, but not bounded, cannot be captured with our conditional construct, but would be captured with a more general framework using loops (e.g., the cracking eggs example in [4].) There seems to be, however, a natural tradeoff between the expressivity in the theory and its corresponding computational complexity.

Acknowledgements. I am grateful to Hector Levesque for many helpful discussions and comments. Thanks also to Gerhard Lakemeyer for an early discussion on the subject of this paper, and to the anonymous referees for their valuable suggestions.

References

1. Baral, C., Son, T.C.: Approximate reasoning about actions in presence of sensing and incomplete information. In Maluszynski, J., ed.: International Logic Programming Symposium (ILSP' 97), Port Je erson, NY, MIT Press (1997) 387–401
2. De Giacomo, G., Levesque, H.: Projection using regression and sensors. In: Proceedingsof the Sixteenth International Joint Conference on Artificial Intelligence (IJCAI), Stockholm, Sweden (1999) 160–165

3. Etzioni, O., Hanks, S., Weld, D.: An approach to planning with incomplete information. In: Proceedings of 3rd International Conference on Knowledge Representation and Reasoning. (1992)
4. Levesque, H.: What is planning in the presence of sensing? In: The Proceedings of the Thirteenth National Conference on Artificial Intelligence, AAAI-96, Portland, Oregon, American Association for Artificial Intelligence (1996) 1139–1146
5. Peot, M.A., Smith, D.E.: Conditional nonlinear planning. In: Proceedings of the First International Conference on AI Planning Systems, College Park, Maryland (1992) 189–197
6. Levesque, H., Reiter, R., Lesperance, Y., Lin, F., Scherl, R.: GOLOG: A logic programming language for dynamic domains. Journal of Logic Programming **31** (1997) 59–84
7. De Giacomo, G., Lespérance, Y., Levesque, H.: ConGolog, a concurrent programming language based on the situation calculus. Artificial Intelligence **121** (2000) 109–169
8. Smith, D., Weld, D.: Conformat graphplan. In: Proceedings of AAAI-98. (1998)
9. Lakemeyer, G.: On sensing and off-line interpreting in Golog. In: Logical Foundations for Cognitive Agents, Contributions in Honor of Ray Reiter. Springer, Berlin (1999) 173–187
10. De Giacomo, G., Levesque, H.: An incremental interpreter for high-level programs with sensing. In Levesque, H.J., Pirri, F., eds.: Logical Foundation for Cognitive Agents: Contributions in Honor of Ray Reiter. Springer, Berlin (1999) 86–102
11. Kowalski, R.A.: Using meta-logic to reconcile reactive with rational agents. In Apt, K.R., Turini, F., eds.: Meta-Logics and Logic Programming. MIT Press (1995) 227–242
12. Shanahan, M.: What sort of computation mediates best between perception and action? In Levesque, H., Pirri, F., eds.: Logical Fundations for Cognitive Agents: Contributions in Honor of Ray Reiter. Springer-Verlag (1999) 352–368
13. McCarthy, J., Hayes, P.J.: Some philosophical problems from the standpoint of artificial intelligence. Machine Intelligence **4** (1969) 463–502
14. Reiter, R.: Knowledge in Action. Logical Foundations for Specifying and Implementing Dynamical Systems. MIT Press (2001)
15. Reiter, R.: The frame problem in the situation calculus: A simple solution (sometimes) and a completeness result for goal regression. In Lifschitz, V., ed.: Artificial Intelligence and Mathematical Theory of Computation: Papers in Honor of John McCarthy. Academic Press, San Diego, CA (1991) 359–380
16. Lifschitz, V., McCain, N., Remolina, E. Tacchella, A.: Getting to the airport: The oldest planning problem in AI. Logic-Based Artificial Intelligence (2000) 147–165
17. Scherl, R., Levesque, H.: The frame problem and knowledge-producing actions. In: Proceedings of AAAI-93. (1993) 689–695
18. De Giacomo, G., Levesque, H.J., Sardiña, S.: Incremental execution of guarded theories. ACM Transactions on Computational Logic (TOCL) **2** (2001) To appear.
19. Apt, K.R., Pellegrini, A.: On the occur-check free prolog program. ACM Toplas **16** (1994) 687–726
20. Sardiña, S.: Local conditional high-level robot program (extended version). http://www.cs.toronto.edu/~ssardina/papers/lchlrp-ext.ps (2001)
21. Smith, D.E., Williamson, M.: Representation and evaluation of plans with loops. In: Working Notes of the AAAI Spring Symposium on Extended Theories of Actions. Formal Theory and Practical Applications., Stanford, CA (1995)
22. Lin, S.H., Dean, T.: Generating optimal policies for high-level plan. In Ghallab, M., Milani, A., eds.: New Directions in AI Planning. IOS Press (1996) 187–200

A Refinement Theory that Supports Reasoning about Knowledge and Time for Synchronous Agents

Kai Engelhardt, Ron van der Meyden, and Yoram Moses

[1] School of Computer Science and Engineering
The University of New South Wales, Sydney 2052, Australia
[kaie|meyden]@cse.unsw.edu.au
[2] Department of Electrical Engineering
Technion, Haifa, Israel
moses@ee.technion.ac.il

Abstract. An expressive semantic framework for program refinement that supports both temporal reasoning and reasoning about the knowledge of multiple agents is developed. The refinement calculus owes the cleanliness of its decomposition rules for all programming language constructs and the relative simplicity of its semantic model to a rigid synchrony assumption which requires all agents and the environment to proceed in lockstep. The new features of the calculus are illustrated in a derivation of the two-phase-commit protocol.

1 Introduction

The knowledge-based approach to the design and analysis of distributed systems, introduced by Halpern and Moses [13] involves the use of modal logics of knowledge. One of the key contributions of this approach is the notion of knowledge-based programs [9,8], that is, programs with formulas in the logic of knowledge as tests in conditional constructs. Such programs contain statements of the form "if you know that ϕ then do A else B". Knowledge-based programs provide abstractions of distributed programs that allow for perspicuous descriptions of how agents' actions are related to their, typically incomplete, state of information about their environment. While knowledge-based programs provide a useful type of high level specification for distributed systems, they have a number of limitations, such as their failure to abstract actions, the fact that they sometimes permit as implementations only programs of unacceptably high computational complexity, and the lack of a formal development framework [23,14, 7]. These limitations have led us to seek to develop a more general framework that enhaces knowledge-based programs in order to overcome their limitations. Our more general framework is in the form of a *refinement calculus*. Refinement calculi [1,19,20] are formalizations of the ubiquitous stepwise refinement method of program construction [26]. They view programs and specifications as having the same semantic type, and guide top-down development by a set of rules. One begins with a specification and transforms it to an implementation by means of a sequence of correctness preserving refinement steps according to those rules.

R. Nieuwenhuis and A. Voronkov (Eds.): LPAR 2001, LNAI 2250, pp. 125–141, 2001.

The initial focus in this area has been on sequential programs and atemporal assertions.

Recently, the scope of refinement calculi has been broadened to overcome both limitations. Some calculi have distributed or parallel systems as domain [2, 3], others admit the expressive power of temporal logics [24, 15].

The refinement calculus we are developing is aimed at supporting development of distributed systems using the insights afforded by the knowledge-based approach, but without suffering the limitations of knowledge-based programs. Some of the key ingredients of the calculus were introduced in previous papers. In order to address the problem that knowledge-based programs sometimes have only implementations of high computational complexity, [6] generalised multi-agent epistemic logics [13] to the Logic of Local Propositions (LLP), which enables knowledge-based program-like specifications having a broader range of implementations. Since reasoning about distributed systems frequently involves temporal considerations, a refinement calculus incorporating linear time temporal logic assertions was developed in [25]. The logic of local propositions and the temporal refinement calculus were amalgamated in [7], yielding the first refinement calculus that supports assertional reasoning about knowledge and time.

The calculus of [7] is restricted to a single agent interacting with its environment. The present paper presents the next step towards our aim, by extending the single agent calculus to one with multiple agents. We restrict ourselves to a program operator for agent parallelism which amounts to insisting that all agents and even the environment proceed in lockstep. While we will ultimately be interested in more flexible forms of agent interaction, this operator has the benefit of admitting some perspicuous refinement rules, and is already rich enough to capture some interesting examples that exercise key features of our knowledge-based refinement approach. In particular, we demonstrate how it can be used for the top down development of an atomic commitment protocol in the presence of process crashes. This provides an informative case study for our broader program.

The paper is structured as follows. Section 2 summarizes the framework presented in [7] and how it is extended to the synchronous multi-agent case. We first define an assertion language that adapts the LLP semantics to the richer temporal setting required for reasoning about multi-agent programs. Then we present the syntax and semantics of our multi-agent programming and specification language. Section 3 defines the refinement relation we use for this class of programs and develops a number of refinement rules valid for this relation, including the abovementioned decomposition rules. Section 4 illustrates the use of the new rules in a derivation of the two-phase-commit protocol. Section 5 concludes and indicates where we intend to go from here.

2 Programming with Assertions about Knowledge and Time

2.1 Semantic Domain

In [7] we presented a semantic framework that is extended here from the single-agent case to the synchronous multi-agent case. Further motivation for this general line of work can be found in [8].

Let $n \in \mathbb{N}$ be a number of *agents*, traditionally named $1, \ldots, n$. Let L_e be a set of possible states for the environment and, for $i \in \{1, \ldots, n\}$, let L_i be a set of possible local states for agent i. We take $\mathcal{G} = (\times_{i=1}^{n} L_i) \times L_e$ to be the set of *global states.* Let A_i and A_e be nonvoid sets of *actions* for agent i and for the environment, respectively. (These sets usually contain a special *null action* Λ.) A *joint action* is an $(n+1)$-tuple $(a_1, \ldots, a_n, a_e) \in \mathcal{A} = (\times_{i=1}^{n} A_i) \times A_e$. A *run* over $\mathcal{G}$ and $\mathcal{A}$ is a pair $r = (h, \alpha)$ of infinite sequences: a *state history* $h : \mathbb{N} \longrightarrow \mathcal{G}$, and an *action history* $\alpha : \mathbb{N} \longrightarrow \mathcal{A}$. Intuitively, for $c \in \mathbb{N}$, $h(c)$ is the global state of the system at time c and $\alpha(c)$ is the joint action occurring at time c. (We say more about the transition relation connecting states and actions later.) A *system* over $\mathcal{G}$ and $\mathcal{A}$ is a set of runs over $\mathcal{G}$ and $\mathcal{A}$, intuitively representing all possible histories. A pair (r, c) consisting of a run r (in system S) and a time $c \in \mathbb{N}$ is called a *point (in S)*. We write Points(S) for the set of points of S. Let *Prop* be a set of propositional variables. An *interpretation* of a system S is a mapping $\pi : Prop \longrightarrow 2^{\text{Points}(S)}$ associating a set of points with each propositional variable.[1] Intuitively, proposition $p \in Prop$ is true exactly at the points contained in $\pi(p)$. An *interpreted system (over $\mathcal{G}$ and $\mathcal{A}$)* is a pair $\mathfrak{I} = (S, \pi)$ where S is a system over $\mathcal{G}$ and $\mathcal{A}$ and π is an interpretation of S.

The structure in the above definitions supports the following notions used to define an agent's knowledge. We say two points $(r, c), (r', c')$ in a system S are *i-indistinguishable*, denoted $(r, c) \sim_i (r', c')$, if the agent i's local components of the global states at these points are equal, i.e., the ith projection of $h(c)$ and $h'(c')$ are equal, where $r = (h, \alpha)$ and $r' = (h', \alpha')$. A set P of points of S is *i-local* if it is closed under $\sim_i$, in other words, when for all pairs of points $(r, c), (r', c')$ of S, if $(r, c) \in P$ and $(r, c) \sim_i (r', c')$ then $(r', c') \in P$. Intuitively, i-local sets of points correspond to properties that agent i is able to determine entirely on the basis of its local state. If π and π' are interpretations and $p \in Prop$, then π' is said to be a *p-variant* of π, denoted $\pi \simeq_p \pi'$, if π and π' differ at most in the value of p. If, additionally, $\pi'(p)$ is i-local, then π' is said to be an *i-local p-variant* of π, denoted $\pi \simeq_p^i \pi'$. If $\mathfrak{I} = (S, \pi)$ and $\mathfrak{I}' = (S', \pi')$ are two interpreted systems over $\mathcal{G}$ and $\mathcal{A}$, then $\mathfrak{I}'$ is said to be a *p-variant (i-local p-variant)* of $\mathfrak{I}$, denoted $\mathfrak{I} \simeq_p \mathfrak{I}'$ (resp. $\mathfrak{I} \simeq_p^i \mathfrak{I}'$), if $S = S'$ and $\pi \simeq_p \pi'$ (resp. $\pi \simeq_p^i \pi'$).

2.2 An Assertion Language for Knowledge and Time

The assertion language $\mathcal{L}$ we use in this paper resembles S5 with two additions: (a) restricted monadic second order quantification for each of the agent's local

[1] Some standard treatments such as [8] interpret propositions over sets of global states so that $\pi : Prop \rightarrow 2^{\mathcal{G}}$. This could easily be done for this paper, with practically no changes to the resulting framework.

predicates and (b) operators from the linear time temporal logic LTL [18]. Its syntax is given by:

$$\mathcal{L} \ni \phi ::= p \mid \neg\phi \mid \phi \wedge \phi \mid \mathsf{Nec}\,\phi \mid \forall p\,(\phi) \mid \forall_i p\,(\phi) \mid \bigcirc\phi \mid \phi\,\mathsf{U}\,\phi \mid \ominus\phi \mid \phi\,\mathsf{S}\,\phi$$

where $p \in \mathit{Prop}$ and $i \in \{1,\ldots,n\}$. Intuitively, $\mathsf{Nec}\,\phi$ says that ϕ is true at all points in the interpreted system, and its dual $\mathsf{Poss}\,\phi = \neg\,\mathsf{Nec}\,\neg\phi$ states that ϕ is true at some point. The formula $\forall p\,(\phi)$ says that ϕ is true for all assignments of a proposition (set of points) to the propositional variable p. Formula $\forall_i p\,(\phi)$ says the same, except that the assignments to p must be i-local. We write $\exists_i p\,(\phi)$ for its dual $\neg\forall_i p\,(\neg\phi)$. The remaining connectives have their standard interpretations from linear time temporal logic: $\bigcirc$ ("next"), U ("until"), $\ominus$ ("previously") and S ("since"). We employ parenthesis to indicate aggregation and use standard abbreviations such as *true*, *false*, $\vee$, $\exists p\,(.)$, and definable future time operators such as $\Box$ ("henceforth") and $\Diamond$ ("eventually"), as well as their past time counterparts $\boxminus$ ("until now") and $\diamondminus$ ("once").

Formulae of $\mathcal{L}$ are interpreted at a point (r,c) of an interpreted system $\mathfrak{I} = (S,\pi)$ by means of the satisfaction relation $\models$, defined inductively by:

- $\mathfrak{I},(r,c) \models p$ iff $(r,c) \in \pi(p)$;
- $\mathfrak{I},(r,c) \models \neg\phi$ iff $\mathfrak{I},(r,c) \not\models \phi$;
- $\mathfrak{I},(r,c) \models \phi \wedge \psi$ iff $\mathfrak{I},(r,c) \models \phi$ and $\mathfrak{I},(r,c) \models \psi$;
- $\mathfrak{I},(r,c) \models \mathsf{Nec}\,\phi$ iff $\mathfrak{I},(r',c') \models \phi$, for all $(r',c') \in \mathrm{Points}(S)$;
- $\mathfrak{I},(r,c) \models \forall p\,(\phi)$ iff $\mathfrak{I}',(r,c) \models \phi$ for all $\mathfrak{I}'$ such that $\mathfrak{I} \simeq_p \mathfrak{I}'$;
- $\mathfrak{I},(r,c) \models \forall_i p\,(\phi)$ iff $\mathfrak{I}',(r,c) \models \phi$ for all $\mathfrak{I}'$ such that $\mathfrak{I} \simeq_p^i \mathfrak{I}'$;
- $\mathfrak{I},(r,c) \models \bigcirc\phi$ iff $\mathfrak{I},(r,c+1) \models \phi$;
- $\mathfrak{I},(r,c) \models \phi\mathsf{U}\psi$ iff there exists a $d \geq c$ such that $\mathfrak{I},(r,d) \models \psi$ and $\mathfrak{I},(r,e) \models \phi$ for all e with $c \leq e < d$;
- $\mathfrak{I},(r,c) \models \ominus\phi$ iff $c > 0$ and $\mathfrak{I},(r,c-1) \models \phi$;
- $\mathfrak{I},(r,c) \models \phi\mathsf{S}\psi$ iff there exists a $d \leq c$ such that $\mathfrak{I},(r,d) \models \psi$ and $\mathfrak{I},(r,e) \models \phi$ for all e with $d < e \leq c$.

Let $\phi \in \mathcal{L}$ and let $\mathcal{S}$ be a set of interpreted systems. We say that ϕ *is valid in* $\mathcal{S}$, and write $\mathcal{S} \models \phi$, if ϕ is satisfied at all points of all interpreted systems in $\mathcal{S}$.

It is possible to express in $\mathcal{L}$ many operators from the literature on reasoning about knowledge. For example, consider the standard knowledge operator K_i, defined by $\mathfrak{I},(r,c) \models K_i\phi$ if $\mathfrak{I},(r',c') \models \phi$ for all points (r',c') of $\mathfrak{I}$ such that $(r,c) \sim_i (r',c')$. The formula $K_i\phi$ is expressible as $\exists_i p\,(p \wedge \mathsf{Nec}(p \to \phi))$, where p does not occur freely in ϕ. This characterization of knowledge motivates a weaker notion, that of an i-local condition p that is sound for ϕ, i.e., satisfies $\mathsf{Nec}(P \to \phi)$. This weaker notion (which we apply in Section 4), helps to overcome some of the complexity and proof-theoretic limitations of knowledge-based programs. We refer to [6] for further examples and discussion.

2.3 A Programming Language with Quantification over Local Propositions

In this section we define our wide spectrum programming language, and discuss its semantics. We also define a refinement relation on programs.

Syntax. Let CT be a set of *constraint tags* and let $PV, PV_1, \ldots, PV_n$ be mutually disjoint sets of *program variables.* For each $i \in \{1, \ldots, n\}$ define a syntactic category Prg_i of *(sequential) programs* for agent i by:

$$Prg_i \ni P_i ::= \epsilon \mid Z \mid a \mid P_i * P_i \mid P_i + P_i \mid P_i^\omega \mid \exists_i p\,(P_i) \mid [\phi, \phi]^X \mid [\phi]^X \mid \{\phi\}_C$$

where $Z \in PV_i$, $a \in A_i$, $p \in Prop$, $\phi \in \mathcal{L}$, $X \in CT$, and $C \subseteq CT$. The very similar syntactic category Prg of *n-agent programs* is formally defined by:

$$Prg \ni P ::= \epsilon \mid Z \mid (\|_{i=1}^n P_i) \mid P * P \mid P + P \mid P^\omega \mid \exists_i p\,(P) \mid [\phi, \phi]^X \mid [\phi]^X \mid \{\phi\}_C$$

where $Z \in PV$, $P_i \in Prg_i$, $p \in Prop$, $\phi \in \mathcal{L}$, $X \in CT$, and $C \subseteq CT$. The intuitive meaning of these constructs is the same for both levels of the language. The symbol ϵ denotes the *empty program*, which takes no time to execute, and has no effects. Program variables Z are placeholders used to allow substitution of programs. Note that a sequential program for agent i may refer directly to actions a of agent i, but the actions of the environment are left implicit. The operation "$*$" represents *sequential composition.* The symbol "+" denotes nondeterministic choice, while P^ω denotes zero or more (possibly infinitely many) repetitions of program P. The construct $\exists_i p\,(P)$ can also be understood as a kind of nondeterministic choice: it states that P runs with respect to some assignment of an i-local proposition to the propositional variable p. The last three constructs are similar to constructs found in refinement calculi. Intuitively, the *specification* $[\phi, \psi]^X$ stands for any program that, if started at a point satisfying ϕ, eventually terminates at a point satisfying ψ.[2] The *coercion* $[\phi]^X$ is a program that takes no time to execute, but expresses a constraint on the surrounding program context: this must guarantee that ϕ holds at this location. The constraint tag X in specifications and coercions acts as a label that allows references by other pieces of program text. Specifically, this is done in the *assertion statements*, which have the form $\{\phi\}_C$ and act as program annotations: such a statement takes no time to execute, and, intuitively, asserts that ϕ can be proved to hold at this program location, with the proof depending only on concrete program fragments, and on specification and coercion statements whose tags are in C. We may omit the constraint tags when there is no need to make such references.

In local programs "$*$" binds tighter than "+", which in turn binds tighter than (the necessarily n-agent) "$\|$". Also in n-agent programs "$*$" binds tighter than "+" but both bind less tightly than "$\|$". We employ parentheses to indicate aggregation wherever necessary and tend to omit "$*$" near coercions and assertions. We use **if**^{X} ϕ **then** P **else** Q **fi** as abbreviation for $[\phi]^X * P + [\neg\phi]^X * Q$.

Semantics. Our semantics will treat programs as specifications of certain sets of run segments in a system, intuitively, the sets of run segments that can be

[2] In refinement calculi, such statements are typically associated with *frame variables*, representing the variables allowed to change during the execution — we could add these, but omit them for brevity.

viewed as having been generated by executing the program. We note that the semantics presented in this section treats assertions $\{\phi\}_C$ as equivalent to the null program ϵ — the role of assertions in the framework will be explained in Section 3.1.

Execution Trees. We first define execution trees, which represent all unfoldings of the nondeterminism in a program. It is convenient to represent these trees as follows. An *n-ary tree domain* is a prefix-closed subset of the set $\{0, \ldots, n-1\}^* \cup \{0, \ldots, n-1\}^\omega$. In particular, each nonvoid tree domain contains the empty sequence λ. Let A be a set. An *A-labelled n-ary tree* is a function T from an n-ary tree domain D to A. The *nodes* of T are the elements of D. The node λ is called the *root* of T. If $l \in D$ we call $T(l)$ the *label* at node l. If $l \in D$ then the *children of l in T* are the nodes of T (if any) of the form $l \cdot i$ where $i \in \{0, \ldots, n-1\}$. Finite maxima in the prefix order on D are called *leaves* of T.

An *execution tree for agent i* is a Prg_i-labelled binary tree, subject to the following constraints on the nodes l:

1. If l is labelled by ϵ, a program variable $Z \in PV$, a specification $[\phi, \psi]^X$, a coercion $[\phi]^X$, or an assertion $\{\phi\}_C$, then l is a leaf.
2. If l is labelled by a basic action $a \in A_i$, then l is also a leaf.
3. If l is labelled by $\exists_i p\,(P)$ then l has exactly one child $l \cdot 0$, labelled by P.
4. If l is labelled by $P * Q$ or $P + Q$ then l has exactly two children $l \cdot 0$, $l \cdot 1$, labelled by P and Q respectively.
5. If l is labelled by P^ω then l has exactly two children, $l \cdot 0$, $l \cdot 1$, labelled by ϵ and $P * (P^\omega)$, respectively.

With each program $P_i \in Prg_i$ we associate a particular execution tree, T_{P_i}, namely the unique execution tree for agent i labelled with P_i at the root λ. An *n-agent execution tree* is a $Prg \cup \bigcup_{i=1}^n Prg_i$-labelled n-ary tree, subject to the same constraints on the nodes l as if it were an execution tree for some agent, except for condition 2, which is replaced by:

2' If l is labelled by $(\|_{i=1}^n P_i)$ then l has exactly n children $l \cdot 0, \ldots, l \cdot (n-1)$, labelled by $P_1, \ldots, P_n$ respectively. For each $i \in \{1, \ldots, n\}$ the subtree rooted at $l \cdot (i-1)$ is an execution tree for agent i.

With each n-agent program $P \in Prg$ we associate a particular execution tree, namely the unique n-agent execution tree labelled with P at the root λ.

Interval Sets. We now define the semantic constructs specified by programs. An *interval in a system S* is a triple $r[c, d]$ consisting of a run r of S and two elements c and d of $\mathbb{N}_+ = \mathbb{N} \cup \{\infty\}$ such that $c \leq d$. We say that the interval is *finite* if $d < \infty$. A set I of intervals is *run-unique* if $r[c, d], r[c', d'] \in I$ implies $c = c'$ and $d = d'$. An *interpreted interval set over S* (or *iis* for short) is a pair (π, I) consisting of an interpretation π of S and a run-unique set I of intervals over S.

We will view programs as specifying, or executing over, iis, by means of certain mappings from execution trees to iis. To facilitate the definition in the case of sequential composition, we introduce a shorthand for the two sets obtained by splitting each interval in a given set I of run-unique intervals of S in two. Say that $f : I \longrightarrow \mathbb{N}_+$ *divides* I whenever $c \leq f(r[c,d]) \leq d$ holds for all $r[c,d] \in I$. Given some f dividing I, we write $f_{\blacktriangleleft}(I)$ for the set of intervals $r[f(r[c,d]),d]$ such that $r[c,d] \in I$. Analogously, we write $f_{\blacktriangleright}(I)$ for $\{ r[c, f(r[c,d])] \mid r[c,d] \in I \}$.

Embeddings. Let S be a system, let (π, I) be an iis w.r.t. S, and let $P_i \in Prg_i$ be a sequential program for agent i. A function θ mapping each node l of T_{P_i} to an iis $(\pi_\theta(l), I_\theta(l))$ is an *embedding* of T_{P_i} in (π, I) w.r.t. S whenever the following conditions are satisfied:

1. $\theta(\lambda) = (\pi, I)$.
2. If l is labelled ϵ or $\{\phi\}_C$, then $c = d$ for all $r[c,d] \in I_\theta(l)$.
3. If l is labelled a for some $a \in A_i$, then, for all $(h,\alpha)[c,d] \in I_\theta(l)$, if $c < \infty$ then both $d = 1 + c$ and the ith projection of $\alpha(c)$ is a.
4. If l is labelled $[\phi, \psi]^X$, then, for all $r[c,d] \in I_\theta(l)$, if $c < \infty$ and $(S, \pi_\theta(l)), (r,c) \models \phi$, then both $d < \infty$ and $(S, \pi_\theta(l)), (r,d) \models \psi$.
5. If l is labelled $[\phi]^X$, then $c < \infty$ implies that $c = d$ and $(S, \pi_\theta(l)), (r,c) \models \phi$, for all $r[c,d] \in I_\theta(l)$.
6. If l is labelled $\exists_i p\,(Q)$ then $\pi_\theta(l) \simeq_p^i \pi_\theta(l \cdot 0)$ and $I_\theta(l \cdot 0) = I_\theta(l)$.
7. If l is labelled $Q_1 + Q_2$, then $\pi_\theta(l \cdot 0) = \pi_\theta(l \cdot 1) = \pi_\theta(l)$ and $I_\theta(l)$ is the disjoint union of $I_\theta(l \cdot 0)$ and $I_\theta(l \cdot 1)$.
8. If l is labelled $Q_1 * Q_2$, then $\pi_\theta(l \cdot 0) = \pi_\theta(l \cdot 1) = \pi_\theta(l)$ and there is an f dividing $I_\theta(l)$ such that $I_\theta(l \cdot 0) = f_{\blacktriangleright}(I_\theta(l))$ and $I_\theta(l \cdot 1) = f_{\blacktriangleleft}(I_\theta(l))$.
9. If l is labelled Q^ω then $\pi_\theta(l \cdot 0) = \pi_\theta(l \cdot 1) = \pi_\theta(l)$ and $I_\theta(l)$ is the disjoint union of $I_\theta(l \cdot 0)$ and $I_\theta(l \cdot 1)$ (as in case 7) and, for all $r[c,d] \in I_\theta(l)$:
   $d = \bigsqcup \{ d' \mid r[c',d'] \in I_\theta(l \cdot m)$ for some leaf $l \cdot m$ of T_P below $l \}$.

We write $S, (\pi, I) \Vdash_\theta P_i$ whenever θ is an embedding of T_{P_i} in (π, I) w.r.t. S. Say that P_i *occurs over* (π, I) *w.r.t.* S and write $S, (\pi, I) \Vdash P_i$ if there exists a θ such that $S, (\pi, I) \Vdash_\theta P_i$. (See [7] for further motivation on the definitions for single agent related notions.)

Let $P \in Prg$. A function θ mapping each node l of T_P to an iis $(\pi_\theta(l), I_\theta(l))$, respectively, is an *embedding* of T_P in (π, I) w.r.t. S whenever the above conditions with the following replacement for condition 3 are satisfied:

3' If l is labelled by $(\|_{i=1}^n P_i)$ then $\theta(l \cdot (i-1)) = \theta(l)$ and $S, \theta(l \cdot (i-1)) \Vdash P_i$ for all $i \in \{1, \ldots, n\}$.

Analogously to the single-agent case, we write $S, (\pi, I) \Vdash_\theta P$ whenever θ is an embedding of T_P in (π, I) w.r.t. S. Say that P *occurs over* (π, I) *w.r.t.* S and write $S, (\pi, I) \Vdash P$ if there exists a θ such that $S, (\pi, I) \Vdash_\theta P$.

3 Refinement

The semantics presented above is a straightforward generalization of the semantics of [7] which corresponds to the special case $n = 1$. That paper also contains an example illustrating the need for sets of intervals instead of single intervals in the definition of program semantics. In the context of knowledge-based programs, the need for sets (in that case of runs, not intervals) has been observed by Moses in his thesis [21] and is discussed by Halpern [12].

Traditionally, a program P refines another program Q whenever the use of P does not lead to an observation which is not also an observation of Q [10]. A refinement relation of this type, when it is transitive and preserved under program composition, allows us to start with a high level specification and derive a concrete implementation through a sequence of refinement steps. The properties of the refinement relations then guarantee that the final stage of the derivation refines the initial stage.

The standard approach to define a refinement relation based on our semantics is to identify the notion of observation with occurrence, that is to say that P *refines* Q, denoted $P \sqsubseteq Q$, when for all systems S and iis (π, I) over S, if $S, (\pi, I) \Vdash P$ then $S, (\pi, I) \Vdash Q$. While having both desired properties, this refinement notion is insensitive to assertion statements because the semantics cannot distinguish between programs that differ only in their assertions. Assertions are meant to play an important role in our refinement rules: they should allow us to specify assumptions about the context a program fragment is used in.

3.1 The role of assertions

We now briefly summarize the role of assertions $\{\phi\}_C$ in the framework and define the associated semantic notions. The reader is referred to [25] for a more detailed explanation of these ideas in a simpler setting and to [7] for additional refinement rules.

Constraint erasure. In order to capture constraint dependencies, we firstly define for each program P and constraint tag set $C \subseteq CT$ a program $P^{[C]}$ that is the same as P, except that only constraints whose tags are in C are enforced: all other constraints are relaxed. We formally obtain $P^{[C]}$ from P by replacing each occurrence of a coercion $[\phi]^X$ where $X \notin C$ by ϵ, and also replacing each occurrence of a specification $[\phi, \psi]^X$ where $X \notin C$ in P by $[\mathit{false}, \mathit{true}]^X$ in $P^{[C]}$.

Program validity. Secondly, we may now define a program (regardless of whether it is a sequential program or an n-agent program) P to be *valid* with respect to a set of interpreted systems $\mathcal{S}$ (and write $\models_{\mathcal{S}} P$ for this) when for all assertions $\{\phi\}_C$ in P, all interpreted systems $(S, \pi) \in \mathcal{S}$ and all run-unique interval sets I over S, all embeddings θ of $T_{P^{[C]}}$ into $S, (I, \pi)$ have the property that for all $i \in \{1, \ldots, n\}$ and nodes l of $T_{P_i^{[C]}}$ labelled with $\{\phi\}_C$, we have $S, \theta_i(l) \Vdash [\phi]$. Thus, validity can be understood as a kind of generalized partial correctness. We define validity with respect to a set of interpreted systems $\mathcal{S}$ to allow assumptions concerning the environment to be modelled, e.g., $\mathcal{S}$ might be the set of all interpreted systems in which actions have specific intended interpretations. We give an example of this in Section 4.

Justification transformations. To define a refinement notion that only allows one to derive valid programs from valid programs, we first need to define a technical notion. A *justification transformation* is a mapping $\eta : CT \longrightarrow 2^{CT}$ that satisfies $X \in \eta(X)$ for all $X \in CT$. In some definitions in the sequel we make liberal use of the pointwise extension of justification transformations: $\eta(C) = \bigcup_{X \in C} \eta(X)$. For instance, the result of applying a justification transformation η to a program P is the program $P\eta$ obtained by replacing each instance of an assertion $\{\phi\}_C$ in P by the assertion $\{\phi\}_{\eta(C)}$.

The *composition* of two justification transformations, η and η', is defined by $\eta \circ \eta' = \lambda X : CT.\eta'(\eta(X))$.

The identity justification transformation $\lambda X : CT.\{X\}$ is denoted by ι. We will also represent justification transformations using expressions of the form $X \hookrightarrow D$, where $X \in CT$ and $D \subseteq CT$. Such an expression denotes the justification transformation that is everywhere as ι, except for on X, which is mapped to $\{X\} \cup D$.

Valid refinement. Let $\mathcal{S}$ be a set of interpreted systems, let η be a justification transformation and let P and Q be sequential programs for agent i. We say that *P validly refines Q in $\mathcal{S}$ under η*, and write $P \leq^{\mathcal{S}}_{\eta} Q$, if for all programs $R \in Prg$ and program variables $Z \in PV_i$, if $R[^Q/_Z]$ is valid with respect to $\mathcal{S}$ then $R\eta[^P/_Z]$ is valid with respect to $\mathcal{S}$, and for all $(S, \pi) \in \mathcal{S}$ and run-unique interval sets I over S, if $S, (\pi, I) \Vdash R\eta[^P/_Z]$ then $S, (\pi, I) \Vdash R[^Q/_Z]$.

An analogous definition fixes the notion of an n-agent program P validly refining $Q \in Prg$. The only other change in the previous paragraph is that program variable Z must now be drawn from PV.

3.2 Valid Refinement Rules

We now present a number of rules concerning valid refinement that are sound with respect to the semantics just presented, making no attempt at completeness. We focus on rules concerning n-agent programs, and refer to [7] for additional rules concerning the sequential programs, which are also sound in the framework of the present paper. Formally, most rules should come in two versions: one for sequential programs and one for n-agent programs, but in many cases the two will be identical but for typing of the components, so we generally omit the distinction.

Two rules are essential ingredients of any refinement calculus. Valid refinement must be transitive and the program constructs must be monotone w.r.t. the valid refinement order. These two rules make it possible for refinement to be broken down into a sequence of steps that operate on small program fragments.

$$\frac{P \leq^{\mathcal{S}}_{\eta} Q, \quad Q \leq^{\mathcal{S}}_{\eta'} R}{P \leq^{\mathcal{S}}_{\eta \circ \eta'} R} \quad \textbf{trans}$$

$$\frac{P \leq^{\mathcal{S}}_{\eta} Q}{R\eta[^P/z] \leq^{\mathcal{S}}_{\eta} R[^Q/z]} \quad \textbf{mon}$$

One advantage of our model is that specifications can be split using any of the composition operators $+$, $*$, and $\|$.

$$\frac{\mathcal{S} \models \psi_1 \vee \psi_2 \rightarrow \psi}{[\phi, \psi_1]^{X_1} + [\phi, \psi_2]^{X_2} \leq^{\mathcal{S}}_{X \hookrightarrow \{X_1, X_2\}} [\phi, \psi]^X} \quad \textbf{+-spec}$$

$$\frac{\mathcal{S} \models \phi \rightarrow \phi_1 \vee \phi_2, \quad \mathcal{S} \models \psi_1 \vee \psi_2 \rightarrow \psi}{\textbf{if}^{X_1}\ \phi_1\ \textbf{then}\ [\phi_1, \psi_1]^{X_2}\ \textbf{else}\ [\phi_2, \psi_2]^{X_3}\ \textbf{fi} \leq^{\mathcal{S}}_{X \hookrightarrow \{X_1, X_2, X_3\}} [\phi, \psi]^X} \quad \textbf{if-spec}$$

$$[\phi, \phi']^{X_1} * [\phi', \psi]^{X_2} \leq^{\mathcal{S}}_{X \hookrightarrow \{X_1, X_2\}} [\phi, \psi]^X \quad \textbf{*-spec}$$

$$\frac{\mathcal{S} \models \phi \rightarrow \bigwedge_{i=1}^{n} \phi_i, \quad \mathcal{S} \models \bigwedge_{i=1}^{n} \psi_i \rightarrow \psi}{(\|_{i=1}^{n} [\phi_i, \psi_i]^{X_i}) \leq^{\mathcal{S}}_{X \hookrightarrow \{X_1, \ldots, X_n\}} [\phi, \psi]^X} \quad \textbf{\|-spec}$$

The execution of many distributed programs can be meaningfully split into several *phases*. Specifying, or reasoning about, such programs is potentially simplified if one can do so on a phase-by-phase basis. Instead of reasoning about the parallel composition of local programs each of which comprises of a sequence of phases, it is usually much easier to reason about the sequential composition of several global phases, each of which is an n-agent program. Such phased reasoning would be supported by a rule of the form

$$(\|_{i=1}^{n} (P_i * Q_i)) \leq^{\mathcal{S}}_{\iota} (\|_{i=1}^{n} P_i) * (\|_{i=1}^{n} Q_i)$$

Refinement rules reflecting this proof principle do not hold without side conditions on $(\|_{i=1}^{n} P_i)$, $(\|_{i=1}^{n} Q_i)$, and $\mathcal{S}$ (though the converse holds unconditionally.) One such condition is that all the intervals in the iis over $\mathcal{S}$ over which some P_i occurs have the same length.[3] Say that a program P *has length* l *in* $\mathcal{S}$ whenever, for each $(S, \pi) \in \mathcal{S}$, for each run-unique set I of intervals over S, if $S, (\pi, I) \Vdash P$, interval $r[c, d] \in I$, and c is finite, then $l = d - c$. We say that P *has constant length in* $\mathcal{S}$ if there exists $l \in \mathbb{N}_+$ such that P has length l in $\mathcal{S}$.

$$\frac{\text{all } P_i \text{ have the same length in } \mathcal{S}}{(\|_{i=1}^{n} (P_i * Q_i)) \leq^{\mathcal{S}}_{\iota} (\|_{i=1}^{n} P_i) * (\|_{i=1}^{n} Q_i)} \quad \textbf{\|-distribute-*}$$

Having constant length is a semantic condition. A sufficient (but not necessary) syntactic condition is that the program does not contain any specification statement, iteration, or choice. This can be relaxed in various ways. For instance,

[3] Another such side condition in the literature is that each phase is *communication-closed* [5]. This means that there is no communication across phase boundaries. The communication-closed layers rule is tailored to an asynchronous setting, rather than our synchronous framework.

choice $P + Q$ itself is not problematic if both P and Q have the same length in $\mathcal{S}$. Similarly, iteration P^ω has constant length if P does and the number of iteration is fixed, e.g., in the style of a **for**-loop.

4 Example: Two-Phase Commit

To illustrate our framework we consider a problem from the area of distributed databases. Two- and three-phased commit protocols have previously been considered (though less formally) from a knowledge-based perspective in [11, 22, 16].

Problem. Suppose n agents collaborate on a database transaction. After each of the agents has done its share of the transaction, they want to come to an agreement on whether to commit the transaction for later use of the result by other transactions. Each agent can be assumed to have formed an initial vote but not yet made a final decision. All that remains to be done is to ensure that no two agents make different decisions. The only faults considered in this example are crashes — communication is assumed reliable. The presentation is inspired by [4, 17].

Informal specification. The requirements on an atomic commitment protocol are typically stated as follows:

1. All agents that reach a decision reach the same one.
2. If an agent decides to commit, then all agents voted to commit.
3. If there are no failures and all agents voted to commit, then the decision reached is to commit.

Algorithm. The standard solution to this problem is called *two-phase commit (2PC)*. One distinguished agent, say, agent 1, collects the other agents' votes. If all votes (including agent 1's) are "commit" then agent 1 tells all other agents to commit, otherwise, to abort. Note that "otherwise" could also mean that some agent crashed before being able to communicate its vote to agent 1.

The first phase thus consists of all agents telling agent 1 their individual votes and, if they are in favour of aborting, deciding to do so. In the second phase the agents learn (if they haven't done so already because their vote was "abort") what to decide.

Assumptions about $\mathcal{S}$. Agent i's vote is modeled as the value of a local Boolean variable, v_i, which is either *true* (for "commit") or *false* (for "abort"). Agent i's decision d_i has one more option, it could also be $\perp$ (for "undecided"). Agents never change their initially held votes. Initially, agents are undecided. Once they decide, they cannot change their decision. Each agent $i = 2, \ldots, n$ has a three-valued variable c_i in which it can receive a message from agent 1. Agent 1 also has a set of three-valued variables $m_2, \ldots, m_n$ in which it receives information from the other agents concerning their vote.[4] Initially, each m_i has value $\perp$.

Agents have available the following actions. The environment is used to model the fact that all these actions have a non-deterministic effect on the state. When an action is performed, it either has its intended effect on the state, or (at the discretion of the

[4] One could of course, use a richer modelling of communication, such as message buffers, but this simple approach suffices for our illustrative purposes.

environment) the agent crashes, and the action has no effect on the state. Once an agent has crashed, it is crashed at all subsequent states, so its actions have no effect. We describe just the intended effects below. All agents can perform the null action Λ, which has no effect. Each agent i also has the action $dcd_i(v)$, where v is a truth value, the intended effect of which is to set d_i equal to v. In addition to these actions, agent 1 can perform the action $bcst_1(v)$, where v is a truth value. The action $bcst_1(v)$ has the intended effect of setting all the variables c_i equal to the value of v. Each agent i can perform the action $snd_{i,1}(v)$, where v is a truth value. The intended effect of this is to set agent 1's variable m_i equal to v.

The environment has a set of actions $crash(F)$, where F is a subset of $\{1,\ldots,n\}$, which it uses to crash the agents in F, making the proposition $\dagger_i$ true for agents $i \in F$. Initially, $\dagger_i$ is false. Crashes are non-recoverable: once it has perfomed $crash(F)$, the environment always performs $crash(F')$ for some superset F' of F, so that once crashed, an agent $i \in F$ remains crashed (and the proposition $\dagger_i$ remains true.)

Due to space restrictions, we restrict ourselves to this rather informal description of $\mathcal{S}$. One of the strengths of the full calculus is that each formal description of the set of target systems generates a set of tailor-made refinement rules. (See [7] for some detail.)

4.1 Sketch of a 2PC protocol derivation

The point of departure of this derivation is an assertion followed by a single specification. The assertion expresses that this program should only be used in contexts that guarantee that the program is started in an initial state. The specification statement expresses that the program should take the agents from an initial state to a state satisfying the informal specification above. The precondition of the initial specification expresses that no agent has received a message and that no agent has decided. Let us abbreviate: *none voted* $\mathrm{NV} = \bigwedge_{i=2}^{n}(m_i = \bot)$, *none received broadcast* $\mathrm{NB} = \bigwedge_{i=2}^{n}(c_i = \bot)$, and *none decided* $\mathrm{ND} = \bigwedge_{i=1}^{n}(d_i = \bot)$.

$$\mathrm{Init} = \mathrm{NV} \wedge \mathrm{NB} \wedge \mathrm{ND} \ .$$

Note that we do not assume that all agents are alive. The postcondition of the initial specification is $\exists d\,(\Psi)$ where

$$\Psi = \bigwedge_{i=1}^{n}(d_i \neq \neg d) \wedge (d \rightarrow \mathrm{AC}) \wedge (\mathrm{AC} \wedge \mathrm{NF} \rightarrow \bigwedge_{i=1}^{n} d_i) \ .$$

In the postcondition, each of the three conjuncts corresponds to one of the informal requirements stated above. One of the first refinement steps will split the specification into two phases. The challenge there is to find a good intermediate assertion. To motivate our choice of intermediate assertion, we note the following informal argument. Intuitively, we would like the first phase of the protocol to consist of each agent informing the coordinator of its vote, so that by the end of the first phase, assuming there have been no failures, if all agents vote to commit then by the end of the first phase the coordinator knows this. That is, we would like to make true the formula $\mathrm{NF} \wedge \mathrm{AC} \rightarrow K_1\mathrm{AC}$, in which we employ the abbreviations *none failed* $\mathrm{NF} = \bigwedge_{i=1}^{n}\neg\dagger_i$ and *all commited* $\mathrm{AC} = \bigwedge_{i=1}^{n} v_i$ true. Recall from the discussion above that $K_1\mathrm{AC}$ is equivalent to $\exists_1 p\,(p \wedge \mathsf{Nec}(p \rightarrow \mathrm{AC}))$, i.e., the agent knows that AC if some sound 1-local test p for AC is true. This motivates rewriting the intermediate assertion as the following slightly stronger formula

$$\Phi = (\mathrm{NF} \wedge \mathrm{AC} \rightarrow p) \wedge (p \rightarrow \mathrm{AC}) \wedge \mathrm{ND}$$

where we have dropped the necessity operator, because the formula as a whole will be implicitly given a neccessity-like force by placing it in a specification construct. To capture that the proposition p in the intermediate assertion is required to be 1-local, we add a quantifier as the first refinement step.

$$
\begin{array}{ll}
& \{\text{Init}\}_{\{Z\}} * [\text{Init}, \exists d\,(\Psi)]^X \\
\geq_\iota^S & \text{(instance of axiom: } \exists_i p\,(P) \leq_\iota^S P\text{, for } p \text{ not free in } P\text{)} \\
& \exists_1 p\left(\{\text{Init}\}_{\{Z\}} * [\text{Init}, \exists d\,(\Psi)]^X\right) \\
\geq_{X \hookrightarrow \{Y\}}^S & (*\textbf{-spec}) \\
& \exists_1 p\left(\{\text{Init}\}_{\{Z\}} * [\text{Init}, \Phi]^X * [\Phi, \exists d\,(\Psi)]^Y\right)
\end{array}
$$

For the moment, let us treat the two phases separately, beginning with the first. After this first phase the obvious candidate expression for p is the *accumulated vote* AV $=(v_1 \wedge \bigwedge_{i=2}^n (m_i = \mathit{true}))$.

$$
\begin{array}{ll}
& \{\text{Init}\}_{\{Z\}} * [\text{Init}, \Phi]^X \\
\geq_{X \hookrightarrow \{X'\}} & \text{(instance of axiom: } [\phi, \psi']^Y\, [\psi]^X \leq_{Y \hookrightarrow \{X\}}^S [\phi, \psi]^Y\text{)} \\
& \{\text{Init}\}_{\{Z\}} * [\text{Init}, \Phi[^{\text{AV}}/_p]]^X * [\Phi]^{X'} \\
\geq_\iota^S & \text{(specification consequence)} \\
& [\text{Init}, \Phi[^{\text{AV}}/_p]]^X * \left\{\Phi[^{\text{AV}}/_p]\right\}_{\{Z,X\}} * [\Phi]^{X'}
\end{array}
$$

To apply the parallel decomposition rule $\|$**-spec** one has to show that in $\mathcal{S}$ the conjunction of the local postconditions implies the original n-agent postcondition $\Phi[^{\text{AV}}/_p]$, which, in this instance, is straightforward. To abbreviate the connection between crashes, messages, and votes, let us employ the abbreviation $\text{CMV}_i = ((\dagger_i \rightarrow (m_i = \perp)) \wedge (\neg\dagger_i \rightarrow (m_i = v_i)))$.

$$
\begin{array}{ll}
\geq_\iota^S & (\|\textbf{-spec}) \\
& ([\text{Init}, d_1 = \perp]^X \parallel \|_{i=2}^n [\text{Init}, \text{CMV}_i \wedge (d_i = \perp)]^X) \left\{\Phi[^{\text{AV}}/_p]\right\}_{\{Z,X\}} [\Phi]^{X'} \\
\geq_\iota^S & \text{(exploit } \mathcal{S} \text{ to implement local specifications with basic actions)} \\
& (A \parallel \|_{i=2}^n\, \mathit{snd}_{i,1}(v_i)) \left\{\Phi[^{\text{AV}}/_p]\right\}_{\{Z,X\}} [\Phi]^{X'}
\end{array}
$$

Let us now consider the development of the second phase of the program. The intuition here is that the coordinator broadcasts its knowledge of the outcome of the vote and then decides. Each remaining agent i has two options: either it already voted to abort, and thus knows that the only possible decision is to abort, or it voted to commit and has to wait for the broadcast message from agent 1 before it decides according to that message. Consequently the next refinement step is another sequential decomposition. The intermediate assertion $\Phi' = \bigwedge_{i=1}^n \phi_i'$ states that, unless agent 1 failed, each uncrashed agent received the broadcast prospective decision:

$$\phi_1' = (d_1 = \perp) \wedge \bigwedge_{i=2}^n ((\dagger_1 \vee \dagger_i \rightarrow c_i = \perp) \wedge (\neg(\dagger_1 \vee \dagger_i) \rightarrow c_i = p))$$

It also states that each uncrashed agent $i = 2, \ldots, n$ that voted to abort decided so already:

$$\phi'_i = (\dagger_i \vee v_i \rightarrow (d_i = \bot)) \wedge (\neg(\dagger_i \vee v_i) \rightarrow \neg d_i)$$

The derivation proper follows.

$$\begin{array}{ll} & [\Phi]^{X'} * [\Phi, \exists d\,(\Psi)]^{Y} \\ \geq^{\mathcal{S}}_{Y \hookrightarrow \{Y'\}} & \quad (*\textbf{-spec}) \\ & [\Phi]^{X'} * [\Phi, \Phi']^{Y} * [\Phi', \exists d\,(\Psi)]^{Y'} \\ \geq^{\mathcal{S}}_{\iota} & \quad \text{(introduce assertion)} \\ & [\Phi]^{X'} * \{\Phi\}_{\{X'\}} * [\Phi, \Phi']^{Y} * [\Phi', \exists d\,(\Psi)]^{Y'} \\ \geq^{\mathcal{S}}_{\iota} & \quad \text{(specification consequence)} \\ & [\Phi]^{X'} * [\Phi, \Phi']^{Y} * \{\Phi'\}_{\{X',Y\}} * [\Phi', \exists d\,(\Psi)]^{Y'} \end{array}$$

Let us focus on the first half of the second phase and proceed by parallel decomposition.

$$\begin{array}{ll} & [\Phi]^{X'} * [\Phi, \Phi']^{Y} \\ \geq^{\mathcal{S}}_{\iota} & \quad (\|\textbf{-spec}) \\ & [\Phi]^{X'} * \|_{i=1}^{n} [\Phi, \phi'_i]^{Y} \\ \geq^{\mathcal{S}}_{\iota} & \quad (n-1 \text{ times } \textbf{if-spec}) \\ & [\Phi]^{X'} \left([\Phi, \phi'_1]^{Y} \;\|\; \|_{i=2}^{n} \,\textbf{if}^{\,Y} \neg v_i \;\textbf{then}\; [\neg v_i \wedge \Phi, \phi'_i]^{Y} \;\textbf{else}\; [v_i \wedge \Phi, \phi'_i]^{Y} \;\textbf{fi}\right) \\ \geq^{\mathcal{S}}_{\iota} & \quad \text{(exploit } \mathcal{S} \text{ to implement specifications by basic actions)} \\ & [\Phi]^{X'} \left(\mathit{bcst}_1(p) \;\|\; \|_{i=2}^{n} \,\textbf{if}^{\,Y} \neg v_i \;\textbf{then}\; \mathit{dcd}_i(\mathit{false}) \;\textbf{else}\; \Lambda \;\textbf{fi}\right) \end{array}$$

In the second half of the second phase all uncrashed yet undecided agents decide.

$$\begin{array}{ll} & [\Phi', \exists d\,(\Psi)]^{Y'} \\ \geq^{\mathcal{S}}_{\iota} & \quad \text{(strengthen postcondition)} \\ & [\Phi', \Psi[^{p}/_{d}]]^{Y'} \\ \geq^{\mathcal{S}}_{\iota} & \quad (\|\textbf{-spec}) \\ & \|_{i=1}^{n} [\Phi', (d_i \neq \neg p) \wedge (p \rightarrow \mathrm{AC}) \wedge (\mathrm{AC} \wedge \mathrm{NF} \rightarrow d_i)]^{Y'} \\ \geq^{\mathcal{S}}_{\iota} & \quad (n-1 \text{ times } \textbf{if-spec}) \\ & [\Phi', (d_1 \neq \neg p) \wedge (p \rightarrow \mathrm{AC}) \wedge (\mathrm{AC} \wedge \mathrm{NF} \rightarrow d_1)]^{Y'} \;\| \\ & \|_{i=2}^{n} \,\textbf{if}^{\,Y'} \neg d_i \;\textbf{then}\; [\neg d_i \wedge \Phi', (d_i \neq \neg p) \wedge (\mathrm{AC} \wedge \mathrm{NF} \rightarrow d_i)]^{Y'} \\ & \qquad\qquad \textbf{else}\; [(d_i \neq \mathit{false}) \wedge \Phi', (d_i \neq \neg p) \wedge (\mathrm{AC} \wedge \mathrm{NF} \rightarrow d_i)]^{Y'} \;\textbf{fi} \\ \geq^{\mathcal{S}}_{\iota} & \quad \text{(exploit } \mathcal{S} \text{ to implement a specification by a basic action)} \\ & \mathit{dcd}_1(p) \;\|\; \|_{i=2}^{n} \,\textbf{if}^{\,Y'} \neg d_i \;\textbf{then}\; \Lambda \;\textbf{else}\; \mathit{dcd}_i(c_i) \;\textbf{fi} \end{array}$$

Finally, we have to tie the phases together and get rid of the local propositional quantifier.

$$
\begin{array}{ll}
& \{\mathrm{Init}\}_{\{Z\}} * [\mathrm{Init}, \exists d\,(\Psi)]^{X} \\
\geq_\iota^S & \text{(by the above and } \mathbf{mon}) \\
& \exists_1 p \begin{pmatrix} (\Lambda \parallel \|_{i=2}^n\, snd_{i,1}(v_i)) * \{\Phi[^{\mathrm{AV}}/_p]\}_{\{Z,X\}} * [\Phi]^{X'} * \\ (bcst_1(p) \parallel \|_{i=2}^n\, \mathbf{if}^{\,Y} \neg v_i \mathbf{\ then\ } dcd_i(\mathit{false}) \mathbf{\ else\ } \Lambda \mathbf{\ fi}) * \\ (dcd_1(p) \parallel \|_{i=2}^n\, \mathbf{if}^{\,Y'} \neg d_i \mathbf{\ then\ } \Lambda \mathbf{\ else\ } dcd_i(c_i) \mathbf{\ fi}) \end{pmatrix}
\end{array}
$$

This leaves us with a program that is concrete except for the coercion defining p. This can the be eliminated by pushing the existential quantifier first around this coercion, then inside it, and noting that what results is a tautology, so the coercion can be eliminated.

$$
\begin{array}{ll}
\geq_\iota^S & (p \text{ not free in parts of the program}) \\
& (\Lambda \parallel \|_{i=2}^n\, snd_{i,1}(v_i)) * \{\Phi[^{\mathrm{AV}}/_p]\}_{\{Z,X\}} * \\
& \exists_1 p \begin{pmatrix} [\Phi]^{X'} * (bcst_1(p) \parallel \|_{i=2}^n\, \mathbf{if}^{\,Y} \neg v_i \mathbf{\ then\ } dcd_i(\mathit{false}) \mathbf{\ else\ } \Lambda \mathbf{\ fi}) * \\ (dcd_1(p) \parallel \|_{i=2}^n\, \mathbf{if}^{\,Y'} \neg d_i \mathbf{\ then\ } \Lambda \mathbf{\ else\ } dcd_i(c_i) \mathbf{\ fi}) \end{pmatrix} \\
\geq_\iota^S & \text{(instance of axiom: } [\exists_i p\,(\mathsf{Nec}(\phi \equiv p))]^X\,(P[^\phi/_p]) \leq_\iota^S \exists_i p\,(P)) \\
& (\Lambda \parallel \|_{i=2}^n\, snd_{i,1}(v_i))\, \{\Phi[^{\mathrm{AV}}/_p]\}_{\{Z,X\}}\, [\exists_1 p\,(\mathsf{Nec}(p \equiv \mathrm{AV}))]^V\, [\Phi[^{\mathrm{AV}}/_p]]^{X'} \\
& (bcst_1(\mathrm{AV}) \parallel \|_{i=2}^n\, \mathbf{if}^{\,Y} \neg v_i \mathbf{\ then\ } dcd_i(\mathit{false}) \mathbf{\ else\ } \Lambda \mathbf{\ fi}) * \\
& (dcd_1(\mathrm{AV}) \parallel \|_{i=2}^n\, \mathbf{if}^{\,Y'} \neg d_i \mathbf{\ then\ } \Lambda \mathbf{\ else\ } dcd_i(c_i) \mathbf{\ fi}) \\
\geq_\iota^S & \text{(all variables in AV are 1-local in } \mathcal{S}\text{, eliminate coercion)} \\
& (\Lambda \parallel \|_{i=2}^n\, snd_{i,1}(v_i)) * \{\Phi[^{\mathrm{AV}}/_p]\}_{\{Z,X\}} * [\Phi[^{\mathrm{AV}}/_p]]^{X'} * \\
& (bcst_1(\mathrm{AV}) \parallel \|_{i=2}^n\, \mathbf{if}^{\,Y} \neg v_i \mathbf{\ then\ } dcd_i(\mathit{false}) \mathbf{\ else\ } \Lambda \mathbf{\ fi}) * \\
& (dcd_1(\mathrm{AV}) \parallel \|_{i=2}^n\, \mathbf{if}^{\,Y'} \neg d_i \mathbf{\ then\ } \Lambda \mathbf{\ else\ } dcd_i(c_i) \mathbf{\ fi}) \\
\geq_{X' \hookrightarrow \{Z,X'\}} & \text{(eliminate coercion)} \\
& (\Lambda \parallel \|_{i=2}^n\, snd_{i,1}(v_i)) * \\
& (bcst_1(\mathrm{AV}) \parallel \|_{i=2}^n\, \mathbf{if}^{\,Y} \neg v_i \mathbf{\ then\ } dcd_i(\mathit{false}) \mathbf{\ else\ } \Lambda \mathbf{\ fi}) * \\
& (dcd_1(\mathrm{AV}) \parallel \|_{i=2}^n\, \mathbf{if}^{\,Y'} \neg d_i \mathbf{\ then\ } \Lambda \mathbf{\ else\ } dcd_i(c_i) \mathbf{\ fi})
\end{array}
$$

We have now arrived at a concrete program implementing the specification for agent i. While sketchy and a little tedious, the derivation does serve to highlight a number of key features of the framework: the role of reasoning using assertions and coercions, and the use of i-locality assumptions to arrive at conclusions about agents' knowledge.

$$
\begin{array}{ll}
\geq_\iota^S & \text{(twice } \|\textbf{-distribute-}* \text{ using that all basic actions have length 1)} \\
& (\Lambda * bcst_1(\mathrm{AV}) * dcd_1(\mathrm{AV})) \parallel \\
& \|_{i=2}^n \begin{pmatrix} snd_{i,1}(v_i) * \mathbf{if}^{\,Y} \neg v_i \mathbf{\ then\ } dcd_i(\mathit{false}) \mathbf{\ else\ } \Lambda \mathbf{\ fi} * \\ \mathbf{if}^{\,Y'} \neg d_i \mathbf{\ then\ } \Lambda \mathbf{\ else\ } dcd_i(c_i) \mathbf{\ fi} \end{pmatrix} \\
\geq_\iota^S & \text{(exploit } \mathcal{S} \text{ to merge the two conditionals)} \\
& (\Lambda * bcst_1(\mathrm{AV}) * dcd_1(\mathrm{AV})) \parallel \\
& \|_{i=2}^n (snd_{i,1}(v_i) * \mathbf{if}^{\,Y} \neg v_i \mathbf{\ then\ } dcd_i(\mathit{false}) * \Lambda \mathbf{\ else\ } \Lambda * dcd_i(c_i) \mathbf{\ fi})
\end{array}
$$

□

Observe that the program obtained is only one of many possible implementations of the specification w.r.t. $\mathcal{S}$. Another — in a sense the weakest — program satisfying the specification is one in which there is no attempt made to have agents abort when they know that this is what the decision is going to be but another agent has failed. At the other end of the spectrum, one could implement the specification by 3-phase commit, that is, an extension of 2PC that ensures that no uncrashed agent will block.

5 Conclusion and Future Work

We have sketched the main features of an extension of our compositional refinement calculus to multiple agents. It incorporates an assertion language strong enough to express temporal and epistemic notions. The example sketched in Section 4 was chosen to illustrate the use of the new rules, not those carried over from the single-agent calculus.

In future work, we plan to explore variants of the framework with less rigidly synchronous and fully asynchronous semantics.

Acknowledgment

Manuel Chakravarty provided valuable comments on a draft of this paper.

References

1. R.-J. Back and J. von Wright. *Refinement Calculus: A Systematic Introduction.* Graduate Texts in Computer Science. Springer-Verlag, 1998.
2. R. R. J. Back and K. Sere. Stepwise refinement of parallel algorithms. *Science of Computer Programming*, 13:133–180, 1990.
3. R. R. J. Back and Q. Xu. Refinement of fair action systems. *Acta Informatica*, 35(11):131–165, 1998.
4. P. A. Bernstein, V. Hadzilacos, and N. Goodman. *Concurrency Control and Recovery in Database Systems.* Addison-Wesley, 1987.
5. T. Elrad and N. Francez. Decomposition of distributed programs into communication-closed layers. *Science of Computer Programming*, 2(3):155–173, Dec. 1982.
6. K. Engelhardt, R. van der Meyden, and Y. Moses. Knowledge and the logic of local propositions. In I. Gilboa, editor, *Theoretical Aspects of Rationality and Knowledge, Proceedings of the Seventh Conference (TARK 1998)*, pages 29–41. Morgan Kaufmann, July 1998.
7. K. Engelhardt, R. van der Meyden, and Y. Moses. A program refinement framework supporting reasoning about knowledge and time. In J. Tiuryn, editor, *Foundations of Software Science and Computation Structures*, volume 1784 of *LNCS*, pages 114–129. Springer-Verlag, Mar. 2000.
8. R. Fagin, J. Y. Halpern, Y. Moses, and M. Y. Vardi. *Reasoning About Knowledge.* MIT-Press, 1995.
9. R. Fagin, J. Y. Halpern, Y. Moses, and M. Y. Vardi. Knowledge-based programs. *Distributed Computing*, 10(4):199–225, 1997.

10. P. H. B. Gardiner and C. C. Morgan. A single complete rule for data refinement. *Formal Aspects of Computing*, 5(4):367–382, 1993.
11. V. Hadzilacos. A knowledge-theoretic analysis of atomic commitment protocols. In *Proceedings 6th ACM Symposium on Principles of Database Systems*, pages 129–134, 1987.
12. J. Y. Halpern. A note on knowledge-based programs and specifications. *Distributed Computing*, 13(3):145–153, 2000.
13. J. Y. Halpern and Y. Moses. Knowledge and common knowledge in a distributed environment. *Journal of the ACM*, 37(3):549–587, July 1990.
14. J. Y. Halpern and Y. Moses. Using counterfactuals in knowledge-based programming. In I. Gilboa, editor, *Theoretical Aspects of Rationality and Knowledge, Proceedings of the Seventh Conference (TARK 1998)*, pages 97–110, San Francisco, California, July 1998. Morgan Kaufmann.
15. I. Hayes. Separating timing and calculation in real-time refinement. In J. Grundy, M. Schwenke, and T. Vickers, editors, *International Refinement Workshop and Formal Methods Pacific 1998*, Discrete Mathematics and Theoretical Computer Science, pages 1–16. Springer-Verlag, 1998.
16. W. Janssen. Layers as knowledge transitions in the design of distributed systems. In U. H. Engberg, K. G. Larsen, and A. Skou, editors, *Proceedings of the Workshop on Tools and Algorithms for the Construction and Analysis of Systems, TACAS* (Aarhus, Denmark, 19–20 May, 1995), number NS-95-2 in Notes Series, pages 304–318, Department of Computer Science, University of Aarhus, May 1995. BRICS.
17. N. A. Lynch. *Distributed Algorithms.* Morgan Kaufmann, 1996.
18. Z. Manna and A. Pnueli. *The Temporal Logic of Reactive and Concurrent Systems: Specification.* Springer-Verlag, 1992.
19. C. C. Morgan. *Programming from Specifications.* Prentice Hall, 1990.
20. J. M. Morris. A theoretical basis for stepwise refinement and the programming calculus. *Science of Computer Programming*, 9(3):287–306, Dec. 1987.
21. Y. Moses. *Knowledge in a distributed environment.* PhD thesis, Stanford University, 1986.
22. Y. Moses and O. Kislev. Knowledge-oriented programming. In *Proceeding of the 12th Annual ACM Symposium on Principles of Distributed Computing (PODC 93)*, pages 261–270, New York, USA, Aug. 1993. ACM Press.
23. B. Sanders. A predicate transformer approach to knowledge and knowledge-based protocols. In *Proceeding of the 10th Annual ACM Symposium on Principles of Distributed Computing (PODC 91)*, pages 217–230, 19–21 Aug. 1991.
24. M. Utting and C. Fidge. A real-time refinement calculus that changes only time. In H. Jifeng, J. Cooke, and P. Wallis, editors, *BCS-FACS Seventh Refinement Workshop.* Springer-Verlag, 1996.
25. R. van der Meyden and Y. Moses. On refinement and temporal annotations. In M. Joseph, editor, *Formal Techniques in Real-Time and Fault-Tolerant Systems, 6th International Symposium, FTRTFT 2000 Pune, India, September 20–22, Proceedings*, volume 1926 of *LNCS.* Springer-Verlag, 2000.
26. N. Wirth. Program development by stepwise refinement. *Communications of the ACM*, 14:221–227, 1971.

Proof and Model Generation with Disconnection Tableaux

Reinhold Letz and Gernot Stenz

Institut für Informatik
Technische Universität München
D-80290 Munich, Germany
{letz,stenzg}@in.tum.de

Abstract. We present the disconnection tableau calculus, which is a free-variable clausal tableau calculus where variables are treated in a non-rigid manner. The calculus essentially consists of a single inference rule, the so-called linking rule, which strongly restricts the possible clauses in a tableau. The method can also be viewed as an integration of the linking rule as used in Plaisted's linking approach into a tableau format. The calculus has the proof-theoretic advantage that, in the case of a satisfiable formula, one can characterise a model of the formula, a property which most of the free-variable tableau calculi lack. In the paper, we present a rigorous completeness proof and give a procedure for extracting a model from a finitely failed branch.

1 Introduction

In the last years considerable progress has been made in the development of tableau-based proof systems for automated deduction. While the tableau framework always was very influential in proof theory and in the development of logics, particularly non-classical ones, it had almost no influence on automated deduction in classical logic. This changed about ten years ago, when it was recognised that it is more natural to view automated deduction calculi like model elimination or the connection method as particular refinements of the tableau calculus. The central new feature of those refinements is the active use of connections as a control mechanism for guiding the proof search. This view had a very fruitful effect on the research in the area. In the meantime, many proof systems developed in automated deduction have been reformulated in tableau style. Furthermore, new calculi have been developed which are based on tableaux and integrate connections in different manners. Currently, some of the most powerful theorem proving systems are based on tableaux with connections.

The main objective in the use of connections is to avoid the blind application of the γ-rule used in Smullyan's tableau system [Smu68]. Instead one uses the substitutions that are induced by the connections in the formula. Since, in general, such substitutions are not ground, this requires the introduction of free variables in tableaux. The question then is how to treat these free variables? The overwhelming majority of the developed free-variable tableau calculi (e.g.,

R. Nieuwenhuis and A. Voronkov (Eds.): LPAR 2001, LNAI 2250, pp. 142–156, 2001.

[Fit96],[LMG94]) treat free variables as *rigid* in the sense that a free variable x is just treated as a placeholder for a single yet unknown (ground) term t. And during the tableau construction this term is successively approximated by applying substitutions to the variable x. The resulting tableau calculi are *destructive* [Let99] in the sense that they not only have expansion inferences as in Smullyan's system but also modification inferences. The negative side-effect is that these calculi lack a fundamental property of Smullyan's tableau method, namely, the possibility of branch saturation. But branch saturation is one of the most appealing features of traditional tableau calculi, since it permits the extraction of models for certain satisfiable formulae. With the new calculi, model generation is impossible. Also, the decision power of free-variable tableau systems is significantly weakened. [1] These negative consequences of free-variable tableau calculi have not sufficiently been recognised so far.

In [Bil96], an alternative clausal free-variable framework is presented, the *disconnection method.* In its tableau format, the method treats a free variable not as rigid but as universally quantified wrt. the respective clause in the tableau. Unfortunately, in [Bil96] many questions concerning the properties of the method remain unanswered. So the completeness proof is only sketched and the problem of model generation is not addressed. In the current paper we give a rigorous presentation of the *disconnection tableau calculus*, as we term it. This includes an elaborated completeness proof. The main emphasis of this paper is on issues of model generation. We develop some new concepts like an *instance-preserving enumeration* of a tableau branch and its associated *Herbrand path*, which permit the convenient extraction of Herbrand models from open saturated tableau branches. As we will demonstrate, these concepts permit a compact representation of Herbrand models.

The paper is organised as follows. Following this introduction, Section 2 motivates the disconnection calculus, defines the required notation and provides an intuitive as well as a formal description of the disconnection calculus. Then, in Section 3 we show how the branch saturation property of our calculus can be used to extract models from saturated branches. Subsequently, the completeness of the disconnection calculus can be proven in a straightforward manner in Section 4. Section 5 shows how the calculus can be strengthened wrt. deductive power and, finally, in Section 6 we give an assessment of our work and address future perspectives.

2 The Disconnection Tableau Calculus

The disconnection tableau calculus was first developed in [Bil96]. Essentially, this proof system can be viewed as an integration of Plaisted's *clause linking* method [PL92] into a tableau control structure. Therefore, in order to comprehend the

[1] For example, Fitting's free-variable tableaux [Fit96] provide no decision procedure for the Bernays-Schoenfinkel class [DG79], unless very rough external criteria like maximal path lengths are used, whereas with a slight modification Smullyan's original tableau method decides the class (see [Let99]).

disconnection tableau calculus, it is instructive to first briefly review the most important features of the clause linking method. This method is in the spirit of the first theorem proving procedures developed in the sixties, which where direct applications of Herbrand's approach to proving the completeness of first-order logic (see [DP60]). Such *Herbrand procedures* consist of two subprocedures, a generator for sets of ground instances and a propositional decision procedure. For some decades this methodology was not pursued in automated deduction, mainly because no guided method of ground instance generation existed. The linking mechanism (and its hyperlinking variant) integrate *unification* into the process of ground instantiation, thus making the ground instantiation more controlled.

Before describing the proof method, we need to introduce some terminology. As usual, a *literal* is an atomic formula or a negated atomic formula. A *clause* is a finite set of literals; occasionally, we will also display clauses as disjunctions of literals. A *literal occurence* is any pair $\langle c, l \rangle$ where c is a clause, l is a literal, and $l \in c$.

Definition 1 (Link, linking instance). *Given two literal occurences $\langle c, l \rangle$ and $\langle c', \neg l' \rangle$, if there is a unifier σ of l and $\neg l'\tau$ where τ is a renaming of c' such that $c'\tau$ is variable-disjoint from c, then the set $\ell = \{\langle c, l \rangle, \langle c', \neg l' \rangle\}$ is called a* connection *or* link *(between the clauses c and c'). The clause $c\sigma$ is a* linking instance *of c wrt. the connection ℓ.* [2]

Instead of guessing arbitrary ground instances of clauses as in the theorem proving procedures of the sixties, one can restrict oneself to linking instances (or hyperlinking instances) wrt. the connections in the iteratively increasing clause set. Additionally, from time to time, the current clause set is tested for propositional unsatisfiability. Before this test, the clause set is *grounded*, i.e., all variables are replaced by one and the same constant. If the unsatisfiability test succeeds, then this obviously demonstrates the unsatisfiability of the original clause set.

One of the strengths of the clause linking method is that it avoids the so-called *duplication problem* in resolution, which means that the unresolved parts of a parent clause c are duplicated over and over again in resolvents derived from c. One of the main weaknesses of the clause linking method is that the propositional decision procedure is separated from the generation of the linking instances. And the interfacing problem between the two subroutines may lead to tremendous inefficiencies. The disconnection tableau method provides an intimate integration of the two subroutines. This is achieved by embedding the linking process into a tableau guided control structure. As a result of this embedding, no separate propositional decision procedure is needed and the number of produced linking instances can be significantly reduced. For describing the disconnection tableau method, we need the following notions.

[2] There is also a *hyperlinking* variant, which requires that *each* literal l_i in the clause c has a link with substitution σ_i; the hyperlinking variant of c is $c\sigma$ where σ is the composition of the substitutions σ_i.

Definition 2 (Path). *A* path through *a clause set S is any total mapping $P : S \to \bigcup S$ with $P(c) \in c$, i.e., a set containing exactly one literal occurence $\langle c, l \rangle$ for every $c \in S$. The* set of literals *of P is the set of all l such that $\langle c, l \rangle$ in P. A path P is* complementary *if it contains two literal occurences of the form $\langle c, l \rangle$ and $\langle c', \neg l \rangle$, otherwise P is called* consistent *or* open.

Definition 3 (Tableau). *A* tableau *is a (possibly infinite) downward tree with literal labels at all tree nodes except the root. Given a clause set S, a* tableau for *S is a tableau in which, for every tableau node N, the set of literals $c = l_1, \ldots, l_m$ at the immediate successor nodes $N_1, \ldots, N_m$ of N is an instance of a clause in S; for every N_i $(1 \leq i \leq m)$, c is called* the clause *of N_i. With every tableau node N_i the literal occurence $\langle c, l_i \rangle$ will be associated. Furthermore, a* branch *of a tableau T is any maximal sequence $B = N_1, N_2, N_3, \ldots$ of nodes in T such that N_1 is an immediate successor of the root node and any N_{i+1} is an immediate successor of N_i. With every branch B we will associate a path P_B, viz., the set of literal occurences associated with the nodes in B.*

The specific feature of Billon's disconnection tableau calculus [Bil96] is that it starts the construction of a tableau wrt. to a path through the set S of input clauses, which we call the *initial path* P_S. P_S can arbitrarily chosen but remains fixed throughout the entire tablau construction. The disconnection tableau calculus consists of a single complex inference rule, the so-called *linking rule.*

Definition 4 (Linking rule). *Given an initial path P_S and a tableau branch B with two literal occurrences $\langle c, l \rangle$ and $\langle c', \neg l' \rangle$ in $P_S \cup P_B$, such that $\ell = \{\langle c, l \rangle, \langle c', \neg l' \rangle\}$ is a connection with unifier σ, then*

1. *expand the branch B with a linking instance wrt. ℓ of one of the two clauses, say, with $c\sigma$,*
2. *below the node labeled with $l\sigma$, expand the branch with a linking instance wrt. ℓ of $c'\sigma$.*

In other terms, we perform a clause linking step and attach the coupled linking instances below the leaf node of the current tableau branch. Afterwards, the respective connection must not be used any more below the node on any extension of B, thus "disconnecting" the connected literals. This last feature explains the naming disconnection tableau calculus for the proof method.

As branch closure condition, the standard tableau closure condition is not sufficient, but the same notion as employed in the clause linking method can be used.

Definition 5 (Closure). *A tableau branch B is* closed *if its associated path is complementary. B is* closed wrt. a term t, t-closed *for short, if B becomes closed when all the variables in the literals on B are substituted by the term t. B is* universally closed, $\forall$-closed *for short, if B is t-closed for any term t; if B is not $\forall$-closed it is called* open.

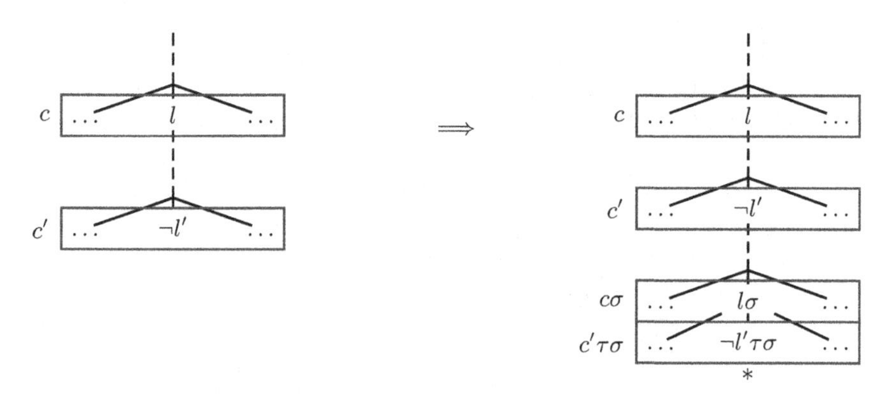

Fig. 1. Illustration of a linking step.

That is, a branch of a tableau is ∀-closed if it contains two literals l and k such that $l\theta$ is the complement of $k\theta$ where θ is a substitution identifying all variables in the tableau. Applied to the tableau in Figure 1, this means that after the linking step at least the middle branch is ∀-closed, as indicated with an asterisk.

The *disconnection tableau calculus* then simply consists of the linking rule plus a rule for the selection of an initial path applicable merely once at the beginning of the proof construction. The calculus is sound and complete for any initial path selection, i.e., a clause set S is unsatisfiable if and only if, for any initial path P_S, there exists a finite disconnection tableau T for S and P_S such that all branches of T are ∀-closed (or t-closed for an arbitrary term t). Both notions of closure can be used, but using t-closure may lead to shorter proofs if the respective term is selected in a fortunate manner. We will present all our results for the weaker notion of ∀-closure, since then they automatically hold for the t-closure case.

Definition 6 (Disconnection tableau sequence). *Given a set of clauses S and an initial path P_S through S, a* disconnection tableau sequence *for S and P_S is any (possibly infinite) sequence $\mathcal{T} = T_0, T_1, T_2, \ldots$ satisfying the following properties:*

- *T_0 is the trivial tableau consisting just of the root node,*
- *any T_{i+1} in $\mathcal{T}$ can be obtained from T_i by application of a linking step.*

Any tableau in $\mathcal{T}$ is called a disconnection tableau *for S and P_S.*

Figure 2 displays a ∀-closed disconnection tableau for the clause set consisting of the transitivity clause $\{P(x,z), \neg P(x,y), \neg P(x,z)\}$, and the three unit clauses $\{P(c,b)\}$, $\{P(a,b)\}$, and $\{\neg P(a,c)\}$. As usual, upper-case letters denote predicate symbols, lower-case letters from the end of the alphabet like x, y, z denote variables, the other function symbols. The selected initial path passes through every clause at the first literal position. In the figure, we have shown the set of input clauses, with the initial path marked, in a box at the beginning of the actual tableau. We have also depicted the connections as arcs, and immediately before every linking instance c in the tableau we have annotated from which connection c derives.

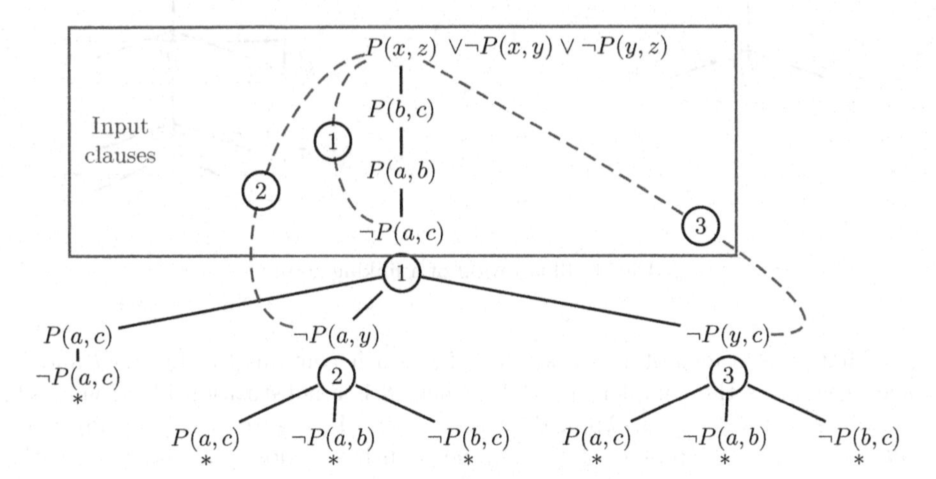

Fig. 2. A $\forall$-closed disconnection tableau.

As usual, a pure calculus is nothing without refinements. The most important of these for the disconnection tableau calculus is the following.

Definition 7 (Variant freeness). *A disconnection tableau T is* variant-free *if, for no node N with clause c in T, there exists an ancestor node N' in T with clause c' such that c and c' are* variants *of each other, i.e., c can be obtained from c' by renaming its variables. (It should be noted that this restriction does not extend to the initial path.)*

With this refinement the disconnection framework can be used for proving the satisfiability of certain clause sets, and from the respective tableau a model for S can be extracted, as we shall demonstrate in the next section. In the following, we assume all disconnection tableaux to be variant free. In order to illustrate the decision power of the disconnection calculus, we give a very simple satisfiable clause sets, which is very hard for other calculi. For example, none of the generally successful theorem provers based on resolution or model elimination terminate. The clause set is displayed on the left-hand side of Figure 3. It is obtained from the clause set displayed in Figure 2 by two simple modifications. First, we have exchanged the positions of the constants b and c in the unit clause $P(b,c)$, which makes the set satisfiable. Furthermore, we have switched the signs of the literals, which does evidently not change the logic. [3]

[3] But it significantly changes the behaviour of resolution systems, for example. Without the second modification, since the set is Horn, we can use unit resolution, which terminates on this set.

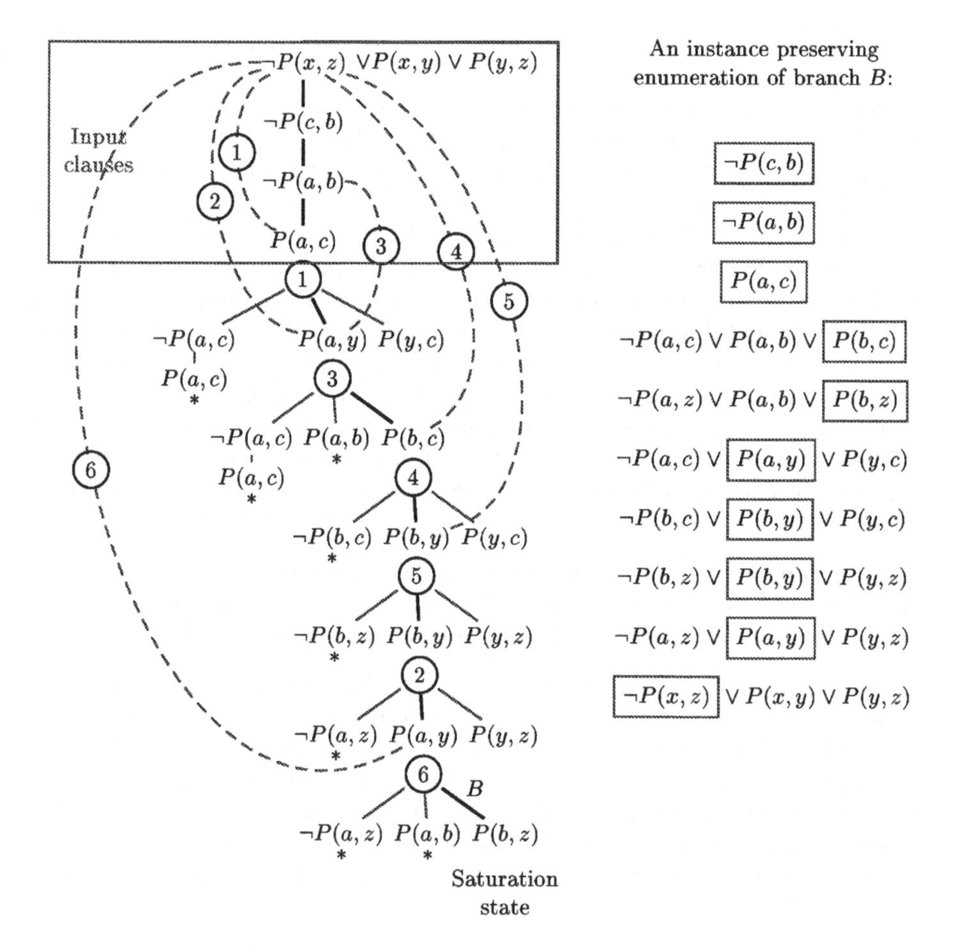

Fig. 3. A saturated open branch and an instance-preserving enumeration.

When considering the branch B in the tableau, we observe that any further linking step on B produces a variant of a clause already on the branch. This proves the satisfiability of the set of input clauses. In fact, the disconnection tableau method is a decision procedure for the class of finite clause sets without function symbols of arity > 0, which corresponds to the Bernays-Schoenfinkel class [DG79].

3 Model Extraction from Disconnection Tableaux

In [Bil96] only a sketch of a completeness proof is given and the problem of extracting a model from the failed construction of a $\forall$-closed tableau is left open. In this paper, we address both topics. We present a full and self-contained completeness proof which is different from the approach in [Bil96]. For example, we do not need auxiliary concepts like the *connective depth* as used in [Bil96]. Furthermore, we show how a Herbrand model can be extracted from such a failed tableau construction. Since the completeness proof uses the model property, we start with the part concerned with model generation.

We employ the following notions. The *Herbrand set* S^* of a set of clauses S is defined as usual, i.e., a clause c is in S^* if and only if c is a ground instance of a clause in S wrt. the Herbrand universe of S. As usual, a *Herbrand interpretation* for S can be viewed as a set I of literals containing, for each atom A in the Herbrand base of S, exactly one of A or $\neg A$. The set I is a *Herbrand model* for S if there is a path P through the Herbrand set S^* of S such that the set of literals in P is a subset of I. For completeness and model generation, it is even more elegant to work with *partial* Herbrand interpretations and models. Any subset I of an Herbrand interpretation for S is called a *partial Herbrand interpretation.* I is a *partial Herbrand model* for S if all Herbrand interpretations for S which are supersets of I are Herbrand models for S. Obviously, the following proposition holds.

Proposition 1. *The set of literals I_P of any consistent path P through the Herbrand set S^* of a set of clauses S is a partial Herbrand model for S, and any partial Herbrand interpretation $I \supseteq I_P$ is a partial Herbrand model for S.*

An appealing feature of the disconnection tableau calculus is that it provides us with a natural representation of partial Herbrand models for any saturated tableau branch B which is not $\forall$-closed or t-closed. Under certain circumstances this representation may be more compact than just explicitly specifying a partial Herbrand model as a set of ground literals. The idea which permits such a representation is to enumerate the literal occurences of a branch in an order which respects the instance relation of the contained clauses. This is formalised with the following notions.

Definition 8. *Given any set of literal occurences P, an* instance-preserving enumeration of P *is any sequence $E = L_1, L_2, L_3, \ldots$ in which exactly the elements of P occur and in such an order that, for any $L_i = \langle c_i, l_i \rangle$ and $L_j = \langle c_j, l_j \rangle$, when c_i is a proper instance of c_j, then $i < j$. Let, furthermore, S^* be the Herbrand set of the clauses occuring in P. Then, with any instance-preserving enumeration E of P, we associate a path P^* through S^* as follows: a literal occurence $\langle c, l \rangle$ is in P^* if and only if there is a literal occurence $L_k = \langle c_k, l_k \rangle$ in E and there is no $L_j = \langle c_j, l_j \rangle$ with $j < k$ in E such that c is an instance of c_j; we term L_k* the minimal matcher *in E of the clause c. The path P^* is called* the Herbrand path *of E and an* Herbrand path *of P.*

In case the Herbrand path P^* of such an enumeration E is consistent, then the set of literals of P^* is a partial Herbrand model. As an example, consider the sequence E of literal occurences displayed on the right-hand side of Figure 3. E is an instance-preserving enumeration of the open tableau branch on the left-hand side. The set of literals of its Herbrand path is

$$\{\neg P(c,b), \neg P(a,b), P(a,c), P(b,c), P(b,a), P(b,b), P(a,a), \neg P(c,a), \neg P(c,c)\}$$

which is an Herbrand interpretation for S. This technique has similarities with Baumgartner's exception rule [Bau00] and with Peltier's method [Pel99] of annotating clauses with equational constraints. However, due to lack of space we cannot present a detailed comparison in this paper.

For the generation of models, we have to formalise the notion of a tableau which cannot be $\forall$-closed. In contrast to tableau calculi like connection tableaux [LMG94] or Fitting's free-variable tableaux [Fit96], the disconnection tableau calculus is *nondestructive*, i.e., any inference step performs just an expansion of the previous tableau and any tableau of a disconnection tableau sequence $\mathcal{T}$ contains all tableaux with smaller indices in the sequence as initial segments. This permits that we can form the union $\bigcup\mathcal{T}$ of all tableaux in $\mathcal{T}$. In the case of a finite sequence, $\bigcup\mathcal{T}$ is just the last element in the sequence. In general, $\bigcup\mathcal{T}$ may be an infinite tableau. We call $\bigcup\mathcal{T}$ *the* tableau of the sequence $\mathcal{T}$.

Definition 9 (Saturation). *A branch B in a (possibly infinite) tableau T is called* saturated *if B is open and cannot be extended in a variant-free manner by the linking rule. The tableau $\bigcup\mathcal{T}$ of a disconnection tableau sequence $\mathcal{T}$ is called* saturated *if either all its branches are closed or it has a saturated branch.*

As a final preparation of the main result of this section, we mention the following straightforward property of disconnection tableaux.

Lemma 1. *Let B be a saturated branch in a disconnection tableau. If B contains a node N_1 with literal l and clause c and a node N_2 with literal $\neg l'$ and clause c' such that $\ell = \{\langle c, l\rangle, \langle c', \neg l'\rangle\}$ is a connection with unifier σ which is no renaming substitution, then B must contain a linking instance of c or c' wrt. ℓ.*

Proposition 2 (Model characterisation). *Given a branch B of the tableau of a disconnection tableau sequence for a clause set S and an initial path P_S, let P be the path associated with B. If B is saturated, then the set of literals I of any Herbrand path P^* of $P \cup P_S$ is a partial Herbrand model for S.*

Proof. First, we show that P^* is a consistent Herbrand path through S^*. Assume, indirectly, that P^* is not. This means that P^* contains two literal occurences $\langle c, l\rangle$ and $\langle c', \neg l\rangle$. Since P^* is the Herbrand path of an instance-preserving enumeration E of $P \cup P_S$, $P \cup P_S$ must contain two literal occurences which are more general than $\langle c, l\rangle$ and $\langle c', \neg l\rangle$, respectively. We select their minimal matchers $o_1 = \langle c_1, k\rangle$ and $o_2 = \langle c_2, \neg k'\rangle$ in E. Obviously, k and k' must be unifiable. Let σ be a most general unifier of k and $k'\tau$ where $c_2\tau$ is a variant of c_2 which is variable-disjoint from c_1. Either σ is a renaming substitution. In this case B would be $\forall$-closed, which contradicts our assumption. Or, σ is no renaming substitution. Then we can apply Lemma 1 which assures that a proper instance c_3 of c_1 or c_2 must be on the branch B and c_3 is a linking instance of that clause wrt. the connection $\{o_1, o_2\}$. Then c_3 is a matcher of c or c', but this contradicts our selection of o_1 and o_2 as minimal matchers of c and c', respectively. Since we have considered all cases, P^* must be a consistent Herbrand path through S^*. Therefore, by Proposition 1, the set of literals I of P^* is a partial Herbrand model for S. □

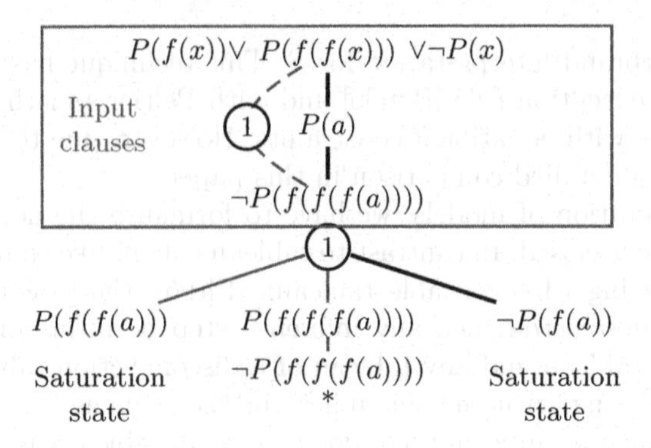

Fig. 4. A saturated open disconnection tableau for a clause set with an infinite Herbrand universe.

In principle, this result suffices for the explicit extraction of Herbrand models as sets of ground literals from saturated branches. But, in certain cases, a finite branch can even represent an infinite Herband model. As an example, consider the saturated tableau in Figure 4 and its right-most branch. The enumeration

$$\neg P(f(f(f(a)))),\ \neg P(f(a)),\ P(a),\ P(f(f(x)))$$

of this branch represents an infinite Herbrand model for the respective clause set S, viz.,

$$\{\neg P(f(f(f(a)))), \neg P(f(a)), P(a)\} \cup \{P(f(f(\mathfrak{s}))) : \mathfrak{s} \neq f(a)\}$$

where $\mathfrak{s}$ ranges over the Herbrand universe of S. From every finite enumeration, one can compute such a schematic expression with instantiation exceptions. Many important questions concerning Herbrand models can be solved efficiently in this framework.

Given an finite enumeration E of a saturated branch B in a disconnection tableau for a clause set S and any literal l, then the following problems (among others) can be decided in time polynomial in the size of E and l, even if the Herband universe of S is infinite:

1. is an instance of l in the partial Herbrand model I represented by E,
2. are all instances of l in I,
3. compute a schematic expression of all instances of l in I.

This shows the potential of the framework for the extraction and representation of models. We should emphasise, however, that this approach does not subsume the term schematisation concepts developed, e.g., in [Sal92,HG97].

4 Completeness of the Disconnection Tableau Calculus

With the model characterisation proposition at hand, the completeness of the disconnection tableau calculus can be recognised with a technique which is more traditional for tableaux. The key approach is to use a *systematic* or *fair* inference strategy [Smu68]. In general, the disconnection tableau calculus is nondeterministic. An *inference strategy* makes the tableau construction deterministic for any input set. Formally, an inference strategy $\mathfrak{f}$ is a mapping which associates with every clause set S a disconnection tableau sequence $\mathcal{T}$ for S. We call $\bigcup \mathcal{T}$ *the* tableau for S and $\mathfrak{f}$.

In detail, an inference strategy has to deal with the following three kinds of indeterminisms:

1. the selection of the initial path,
2. the selection of the next branch B to be expanded,
3. the selection of the next linking step to be performed on B.

Definition 10 (Fairness). *An inference strategy $\mathfrak{f}$ is called* systematic *or* fair *if, for any clause set, the tableau for S and $\mathfrak{f}$ is saturated.*

Obviously, there are fair inference strategies for the disconnection tableau calculus. It can easily be checked that the following describes such a fair strategy.

Example 1 (A fair inference strategy).

1. For the initial path: select the first literal in each clause,
2. for branch selection: choose the left-most open branch B,
3. for link selection: from all links on B where the sum of the depths[4] of the connected nodes is minimal, select the one where the depth of the upper node is minimal.

Proposition 3 (Completeness). *If S is an unsatisfiable clause set and $\mathfrak{f}$ is a fair inference strategy, then the tableau T for S and $\mathfrak{f}$ is a finite $\forall$-closed disconnection tableau for S.*

Proof. First, we show that every branch of T is $\forall$-closed. Assume not, then, because of the fairness of the strategy $\mathfrak{f}$, T would be saturated and contain a saturated branch. Then, by Proposition 2, S would be satisfiable, contradicting our assumption. The $\forall$-closedness entails the finiteness of every branch. Since T is finitely branching, by König's Lemma, it must be finite. □

5 Refinements

Our research regarding the disconnection tableau calculus was not for theoretical purposes only. There also exists an implementation of the disconnection tableau calculus, which was presented in [LS01]. When designing a new calculus for implementation in a powerful theorem prover, it is impossible to ignore the successful paradigms developed in the field of automated theorem proving

[4] The *depth* of a tableau node is the number of its ancestor nodes.

over the recent decades. Therefore, when new issues such as proof length and redundancy elimination came into focus also from a practical point of view, we incorporated a number of completeness preserving refinements into the calculus that are described in the aforementioned paper.

These refinements include different variations of subsumption, a strong unit theory element and several deletion strategies for redundancy elimination. For lack of space, however, we cannot describe these refinements here in depth or give proof of their preserving the completeness of the disconnection calculus.

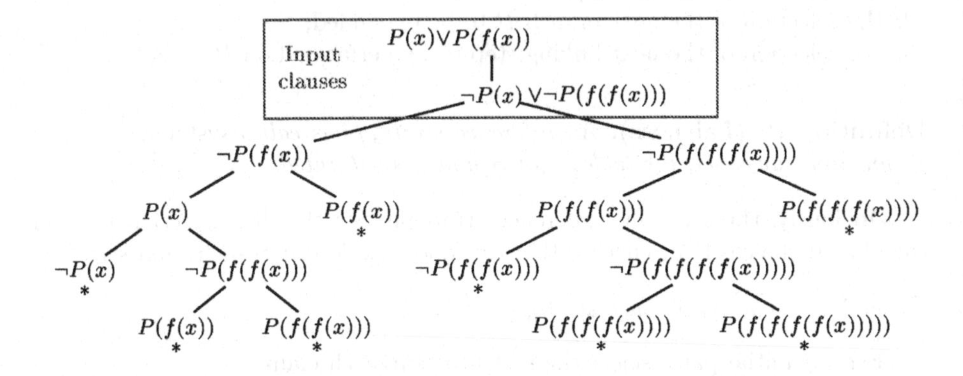

Fig. 5. ∀-closed plain disconnection tableau.

Here, we will concentrate on one particular facet of these refinements. One inherent characteristic of plain tableau calculi is that they are inherently cut-free. This property may lead to the generation of large proofs containing many redundant inferences and these redundancies also occur when searching for models. The standard approach for solving this problem is the use of *lemmas* or *controlled cuts* [LMG94].

The following example demonstrates the possibility of introducing unit lemmas, which simulate certain atomic cut steps. Figure 5 shows a ∀-closed plain disconnection tableau for the unsatisfiable clause set

$$S = \{\{P(x), P(f(x))\}, \{\neg P(x), \neg P(f(f(x)))\}\}.$$

The structure of the subtableau below the node $\neg P(f(x))$ strongly resembles the structure of the subtableau below the node $\neg P(f(f(f(x))))$, which indicates that a part of the proof might be redundant. If we look at the tableau in Figure 6, we see that this redundancy indeed exists and how, by the use of *folding up* and *unit simplification*, we can avoid this redundancy. Folding up works as follows. Assume a subtableau T with root literal l is ∀-closed without refering to literals on the branch above l. This amounts to the generation of a new unit lemma, namely, the complement of $l\sigma$ where σ identifies all variables in l—just taking the complement of l would be unsound because of the branch closure condition, which identifies all variables. This feature is a special case of the so-called *folding up* procedure [LMG94]. In the example, the new unit lemma $P(f(x))$ is inserted at the root of the tableau after closure step 4.

Unit simplification allows the immediate closure of a branch if it contains a literal k which can be unified with the complement of the literal in an input unit clause or a unit lemma. Unit simplification is used to close the right-most branch of the tableau in Figure 6, thus eliminating the entire right subtableau.

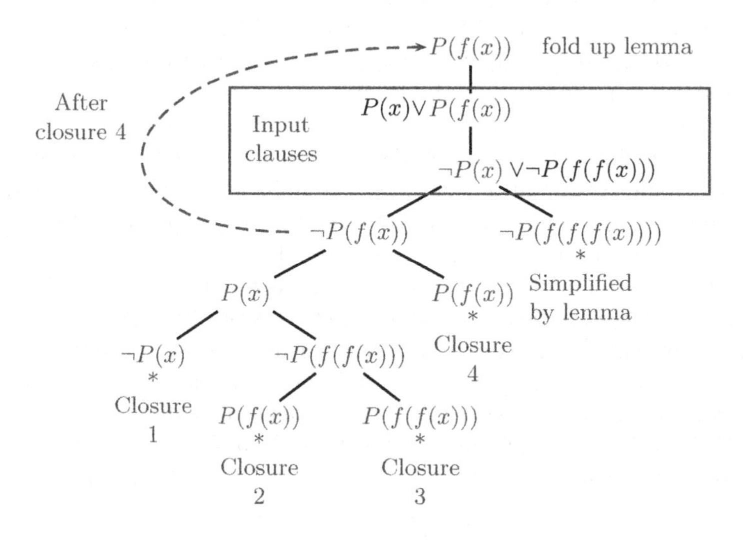

Fig. 6. ∀-closed disconnection tableau with unit lemmas.

It is the use of refinements like the ones described above that turns the implementation of a calculus into a potentially successful proof procedure. It must be noted, however, that the disconnection calculus is not compatible with certain refinements or is only compatible with weakened forms of those refinements. Examples for such refinements are hyperlinking or goal orientation. Goal orientation may be introduced into the proof procedure to a certain degree by adjusting the weighting and selection functions, but the fairness condition required to sustain the branch saturation property prevents us from exploiting goal orientation to the full.

6 Conclusions and Further Work

In this paper, we have presented the disconnection tableau calculus, a promising framework for proof and model finding in automated reasoning. We have given rigorous self-contained proofs of completeness and model generation. In order to make the calculus practically relevant, we have shown how the special handling of unit clauses can be integrated into the framework. Proof-theoretically, the disconnection framework has a number of advantages. Like Plaisted's linking method, the disconnection approach avoids the duplication problem inherent in calculi like resolution. Furthermore, it is branch saturating and combines the appealing properties of traditional tableau methods wrt. model generation with a controlled method of generating clause instances purely guided by connections.

As future promising research directions we would like to mention the following three issues. First, it is absolutely necessary to integrate an efficient equality handling into the framework. In [Bil96], a method was briefly sketched which is a form of paramodulation adapted to the tableau framework. Since we have no structural tableau restrictions (like, e.g., the connectedness condition in connection tableau) which are incompatible with orderings, even the integration of an ordered equality handling is possible [BG98].

A further interesting research line would be to consider the integration of term schematisation techniques [Sal92,HG97] into the disconnection tableau framework, which would require an extension of the unification procedure. Such techniques would permit a further condensation of the representation of models.

Finally, it could be interesting to envisage the generation of finite general (i.e., non-Herbrand) models. The current methods for the generation of general finite models like *Finder* [Sla94] or *Mace* [McC94] work by a more or less blind identification of terms. Since the literals and terms on a (non-saturated) branch of a disconnection tableau often induce certain promising identifications of terms, it seems promising to integrate such a subcomponent into a disconnection tableau prover. With such a subcomponent, the decision power of the system could significantly be improved.

References

[Bau00] Peter Baumgartner. FDPLL – A First-Order Davis-Putnam-Logeman-Loveland Procedure. In David McAllester, editor, *CADE-17 – The 17th International Conference on Automated Deduction*, volume 1831 of *Lecture Notes in Artificial Intelligence*, pages 200–219. Springer, 2000.

[BG98] Leo Bachmair and Harald Ganzinger. Equational reasoning in saturation-based theorem proving. In Wolfgang Bibel and Peter H. Schmidt, editors, *Automated Deduction: A Basis for Applications. Volume I, Foundations: Calculi and Methods*, pages 353–398. Kluwer Academic Publishers, Dordrecht, 1998.

[Bil96] Jean-Paul Billon. The disconnection method: a confluent integration of unification in the analytic framework. In P. Migliolo, U. Moscato, D. Mundici, and M. Ornaghi, editors, *Proceedings of the 5th International Workshop on Theorem Proving with analytic Tableaux and Related Methods (TABLEAUX)*, volume 1071 of *LNAI*, pages 110–126, Berlin, May15–17 1996. Springer.

[DG79] Burton Dreben and Warren D. Goldfarb. *The Decision Problem: Solvable Classes of Quantificational Formulas.* Addison-Wesley Publishing Company, Reading, MA, 1979.

[DP60] Martin Davis and Hilary Putman. A computing procedure for quantification theory. *Journal of the ACM*, 7(3):201–215, July 1960.

[Fit96] Melvin C. Fitting. *First-Order Logic and Automated Theorem Proving.* Springer, second edition, 1996.

[HG97] Miki Hermann and Roman Galbavý. Unification of infinite sets of terms schematized by primal grammars. *Theoretical Computer Science*, 176(1–2):111–158, April 1997.

[Let99] Reinhold Letz. First-Order Tableaux Methods. In M. D'Agostino, D. Gabbay, R. Hähnle, and J. Posegga, editors, *Handbook of Tableau Methods*, pages 125–196. Kluwer, Dordrecht, 1999.

[LMG94] R. Letz, K. Mayr, and C. Goller. Controlled integration of the cut rule into connection tableau calculi. *Journal of Automated Reasoning*, 13(3):297–337, December 1994.

[LS01] Reinhold Letz and Gernot Stenz. DCTP: A Disconnection Calculus Theorem Prover. In Rajeev Goré, Alexander Leitsch, and Tobias Nipkow, editors, *Proceedings of the International Joint Conference on Automated Reasoning (IJCAR-2001), Siena, Italy*, volume 2083 of *LNAI*, pages 381–385. Springer, Berlin, June 2001.

[McC94] William McCune. A Davis-Putnam program and its application to finite first-order model search: quasigroup existence problems. Technical Memorandum ANL/MCS-TM-194, Argonne National Laboratories, IL/USA, September 1994.

[Pel99] Nicolas Peltier. Pruning the search space and extracting more models in tableaux. *Logic Journal of the IGPL*, 7(2):217–251, 1999.

[PL92] David A. Plaisted and Shie-Jue Lee. Eliminating duplication with the hyperlinking strategy. *Journal of Automated Reasoning*, 9(1):25–42, 1992.

[Sal92] Gernot Salzer. The unification of infinite sets of terms and its applications. In A. Voronkov, editor, *Proceedings of the International Conference on Logic Programming and Automated Reasoning (LPAR'92)*, volume 624 of *LNAI*, pages 409–420, St. Petersburg, Russia, July 1992. Springer Verlag.

[Sla94] John Slaney. FINDER: Finite domain enumerator. In Alan Bundy, editor, *Proceedings of the 12th International Conference on Automated Deduction*, volume 814 of *LNAI*, pages 798–801, Berlin, June/July 1994. Springer.

[Smu68] Raymond Smullyan. *First-Order Logic.* Springer, 1968.

Counting the Number of Equivalent Binary Resolution Proofs

Joseph D. Horton*

Faculty of Computer Science, University of New Brunswick
P.O. Box 4400, Fredericton, New Brunswick, Canada E3B 5A3
jdh@unb.ca, http://www.cs.unb.ca

Abstract. A binary resolution proof is represented by a binary resolution tree (brt) with clauses at the nodes and resolutions being performed at the internal nodes. A rotation in a brt can be performed on two adjacent internal nodes if the result of reversing the order of the resolutions does not affect the clause recorded at the node closer to the root. Two brts are said to be rotationally equivalent if one can be obtained from the other by a sequence of rotations. Let $c(T)$ be the number of brts rotationally equivalent to T. It is shown that if T has n resolutions, all on distinct atoms, and m merges or factors between literals, then

$$c(T) \geq 2^{2n-\Theta(m \log(n/m))}$$

Moreover $c(T)$ can be as large as $n!/(m+1)$. A-ordering, lock resolution and the rank/activity restriction avoid calculating equivalent brts.
A dynamic programming polynomial-time algorithm is also given to calculate $c(T)$ if T has no merges or factors.

1 Introduction

Binary resolution [8] is a commonly used technique in automated reasoning. There are many different ways to represent a binary resolution proof. The first method is to make a list of the clauses needed in whatever one is trying to prove, and record whether each clause is an input clause, or is produced by resolving two previous clauses in the list. As the order in which many of the resolutions steps are performed is not important, many effectively identical proofs would be considered to be different if a proof were only considered to be a list.

A better method is to consider a proof to be a binary tree, where the child of two nodes is the result of resolving the clauses at the parent nodes. Here the binary resolution tree (brt) of [6,10] is used to represent such proofs. Many resolution-based automated reasoners construct proofs that can be effectively represented by brts. Every clause produced is the result of a brt, and such a reasoner can be considered to be producing brts rather than clauses.

Binary resolution sometimes is associative. For some clauses A, B and D, $(A *_c B) *_e D = A *_c (B *_e D)$. Resolution on an atom p is denoted by the

* Research supported by a grant from NSERC of Canada

R. Nieuwenhuis and A. Voronkov (Eds.): LPAR 2001, LNAI 2250, pp. 157–171, 2001.

operation $*_p$. Thus it is possible to change the order of the resolutions in the brt and produce essentially equivalent proofs. The clauses produced along the way are different, so that as lists of clauses, the proofs could look quite different. This *associative redundancy* of binary resolution is studied in [10,6], where equivalent brts are said to be rotationally equivalent. If a redundant brt is produced whose result is not the empty clause, then a clause is produced which is not needed.

Binary resolution has *commutative redundancy* also, which is much easier to handle. Because $A *_c B = B *_c A$ for all clauses A and B which can be resolved, resolution procedures only perform one of these resolutions. One common way to avoid the duplication is to order the clauses into a "waiting" list, select each one at a time as a "given" clause, resolve the given clause with any former given clause which has been retained, and put the resulting clauses into the waiting list. In this way, each pair of clauses is chosen only once. Assuming that clause A is chosen before clause B, the pair $\{A, B\}$ is resolved only when B is the chosen clause, and not when A is the chosen clause. If a procedure does not avoid this commutative redundancy, then each brt with n resolutions can be constructed in 2^n different ways. By deleting identical clauses using forward subsumption, such a procedure produces each brt in two ways. Hence most clauses, except some near the end, would be produced twice, so that such a procedure would be half as fast as an equivalent procedure which avoids commutative redundancy. Avoiding commutative redundancy thus speeds up a procedure by a factor of nearly two.

How much can one speed up a reasoner by removing associative redundancy? One way to estimate this speedup is to count the number of equivalent proofs that would be produced by a procedure that does not avoid associative redundancy, which calculates all the equivalent brts. The number of equivalent proofs is typically exponential, but this does not imply that the speedup is exponential. The number of equivalent proofs under commutative redundancy is 2^n, where n is the number of resolutions, but the speedup factor is only 2. It is conjectured in the last section that the speedup factor is usually about the nth root of the number of equivalent proofs.

An automated binary resolution procedure generally produces multiple brts that are redundant because of associativity. Once produced, the extra brts are typically removed by subsumption. The rank/activity restriction of [6] combined with a fair resolution procedure (any allowed resolution is eventually performed) constructs exactly one brt from each equivalence class. The rank/activity restriction avoids precisely the associative redundancy of resolution.

Variants of resolution that order the literals with a clause, such as ordered resolution [7,3] or lock resolution [1], also avoid constructing equivalent brts, but these procedures do not produce brts in all equivalence classes. Nevertheless this is a possible explanation of why they are relatively fast procedures.

Associative redundancy is more difficult to deal with than commutative redundancy partly because resolution always commutes but does not always associate. If two of the clauses have a common literal, and it is one of the resolved literals, then in one order of the resolutions it can be merged and then resolved away, but with the other order it is left in the result. For example: $(ace *_c b\bar{c}e) *_e d\bar{e} = abd$, but $ace *_c (b\bar{c}e *_e d\bar{e}) = abde$.

In this paper it is shown that if a brt contains n internal nodes and m mergings of literals, then the number of brts equivalent to a given brt is $c(T) \geq 2^{2n-\Theta(m \log(n/m))}$, and can be as great as $n!/(m+1)$. Deleting identical clauses allows one to construct a number of equivalent brts equal to the number of nodes which can be rotated to the root of the brt. In clause tree terms, this is the number of internal atom nodes which are not internal to a merge path. Supposing that m is not too big, then the r/a restriction saves a factor of between about 4 and n on the number of resolutions performed, and hence indicates that the above procedures which order the literals of clauses should run 4 times faster than otherwise equivalent procedures.

As only the structure of the proofs are important in this paper, it can be assumed for the most part that all atoms are ground atoms. Also one can consider in any given proof that each resolution is done on a different atom from all the other resolution in the proofs. These assumptions prevent consideration of improvements to the proof by inserting different factoring operations, or different merges. Indeed factors are often called merges thruout this paper. However the results of this paper apply to first order logic without these restrictions just as well as to propositional logic.

The second section gives background concerning brts and clause trees [5]. Clause trees are another method of considering binary resolution proofs, and are essential for understanding the results in this paper. Section 3 considers the extreme cases for the number of equivalent brts when there are no merges of literals in the proofs. Section 4 gives a dynamic programming algorithm to calculate the exact number of brts equivalent to a given brt without any merges. Section 5 considers the extreme cases when the proof is allowed to have merges. Section 6 lists some open questions.

2 Background

The reader is assumed to be familiar with the standard notions of binary resolution [2]. Resolution proofs can be represented by the following type of proof tree.

Definition 1. *A* binary resolution tree, *or* brt *on a set $\mathcal{S}$ of input clauses is a binary tree where each node N in the tree is labeled by a* clause label, *denoted $cl(N)$. The clause label of a leaf node is an instance of a clause in $\mathcal{S}$, and the clause label of a non-leaf is the resolvent of the clause label of its parents. A non-leaf node is also labeled by an* atom label, *$al(N)$, equal to the atom resolved upon. The clause label of the root is called the* result *of the tree, $result(T)$. A* sub-brt *of a brt T is a brt which consists of a node of T together with all its ancestor nodes, induced edges and their labels.*

For the brt in Figure 1, $\mathcal{S} = \{\{b,e\},\{\bar{e},f\},\{\bar{a},\bar{b},c\},\{a,\bar{b},d\},\{c,\bar{d}\}\}$. The result of the brt is the clause $\{c,f\}$. The order of the parents of a node is not defined, thereby avoiding commutative redundancy.

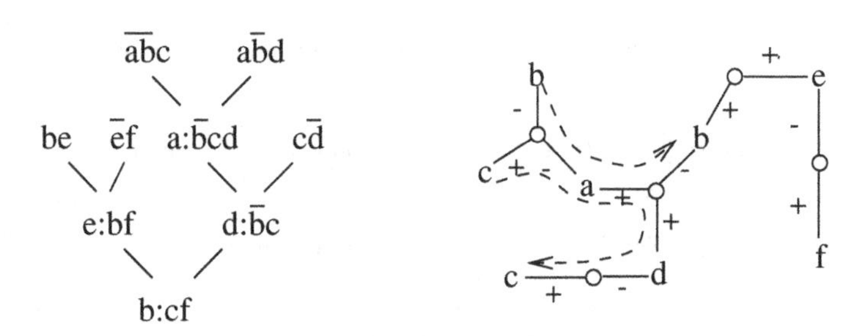

Fig. 1. A binary resolution tree and a corresponding clause tree

Merging literals during the construction of a proof is only done immediately after a resolution, at the first possible opportunity. This differs from [10] where factoring was delayed as long as possible instead. Either way there is no need to have nodes for factoring, as it always appears as part of a resolution step. Forcing factoring to be done early agrees better with what some automated reasoning procedures do. To avoid some trivial paths, in both brts and in clause trees defined below, all general factors of the input clauses are assumed to be available.

The *resolution mapping* ρ at an internal node in a brt maps each resolved literal to the atom resolved upon, and maps each unresolved literal c to the occurrence of $c\theta$ in the resolvent, where θ is the product of the unifications used in the resolution and any required factoring operations. Let the nodes $(N_0, \ldots, N_n)$ occur in a brt T such that N_0 is a leaf whose clause label contains a literal a, and for each $i = 1, \ldots, n$, N_{i-1} is a parent of N_i. Let ρ_i be the resolution mapping from the parents of N_i to N_i. Also let $\rho_i \ldots \rho_2\rho_1 a$ occur in $cl(N_i)$, so that a is not resolved away at any N_i. Suppose N_n either is the root of T, or has a child N such that $\rho_n \ldots \rho_1 a$ is resolved upon. Then $P = (N_0, \ldots, N_n)$ is the *history path* for a. The history path is said to *close* at N if N exists. However N is not considered to be on the history path. The resolution mapping tells what happens to each literal in a given resolution step, and the history path tells what happens to it from the leaf where it is introduced to the node where it is resolved away.

The application of associativity requires two adjacent nodes to be rotated in a brt, reversing the order of the resolutions, and still produce the same resulting clause at the lower node. This rotation is similar to the rotation performed in AVL-trees when rebalancing.

Operation 1 (edge rotation) *Let T be a binary resolution tree with an edge (C, E) between internal nodes such that C is the parent of E and C has two parents A and B. Further, assume that no history path through A closes at E. Then the result of a* rotation *on this edge is the binary resolution tree T' defined by resolving $cl(B)$ and $cl(D)$ on $al(E)$ giving $cl(E)$ in T' and then resolving $cl(E)$ with $cl(A)$ on $al(C)$ giving $cl(C)$ in T'. Any history path closed at C in T is closed at C in T'; similarly any history path closed at E in T is closed at E in T'. Also, the child of E in T, if it exists, is the child of C in T'. (See Figure 2).*

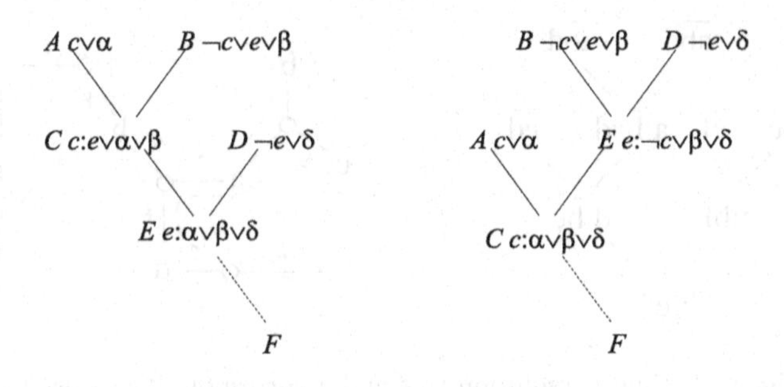

Fig. 2. A binary tree rotation

A rotation may introduce tautologies to clause labels of internal nodes. For instance, if $al(C)$ occurs in $cl(D)$ then $cl(E)$ in T' may be tautological. However the clause label of the root is not changed.

Lemma 1. *Given a binary resolution tree T with an internal node C and its child E, the rotation of edge (C, E) generates a new binary resolution tree and $cl(C) = cl(E)$ up to variable renaming.*

Rotations are invertible; after a rotation, no history path through D closes at C, so another rotation at (E, C) can be done, which generates the original tree again. Two binary resolution trees are *rotationally equivalent* if one can be generated from the other by a sequence of rotations. Rotation equivalence is an equivalence relation. Rotation equivalence captures precisely the associative redundancy of binary resolution.

In a brt, the atom being resolved upon labels the nodes instead of the edges as is usually done in proof trees [2,4]. In the equivalent proofs studied in this paper, what is constant between them is what instances of input literals merge and resolve together. Which history paths close together is the important thing. Rotations do not affect what literal instances merge and resolve.

It is possible that a brt has two sub-brts which are isomorphic, in that the subtrees are isomorphic, and the atom and clause labels of corresponding nodes are the same. A theorem prover could thus have two different nodes with a common parent, and the proof found would become an acyclic directed graph (dag) instead of a tree.

Binary resolution proofs can also be represented by an entirely different tree structure, the clause tree, introduced in [5]. Conceptually, a clause tree represents a clause together with a proof from a set of input clauses. An input clause is represented by a complete bipartite graph $K_{1,n}$ or claw, in which the leaves correspond to the atoms of the literals of the clause, modified by the sign on the edge connecting the leaf to the central vertex. Such a clause tree is said to be *elementary*. A new clause tree can be built by resolving two complementary literals from different elementary clause trees. Identify the two leaves, so the resolved literal becomes an internal node of the tree, thereby building a clause tree with leaves still corresponding to the other literals of the clauses. Thus leaves of the clause tree correspond to the literals of the clause. If there are two leaves with unifiable or identical literals, then two unifiable or identical literals occur in the clause. Merging two such literals is represented in the clause tree by applying a substitution if necessary, and choosing a *merge path* from the leaf corresponding to the removed literal to the other leaf corresponding to the now identical literal.

The above discussion suggests a procedural definition, by giving the operations to construct clause clause trees, as in [5]. Here the definition is structural.

Definition 2 (Clause Tree). *$\mathcal{T} = (N, E, L, M)$ is a clause tree on a set S of input clauses if:*

1. *(N, E) as a graph is an unrooted tree.*
2. *L is a labeling of the nodes and edges of the tree. $L : N \cup E \to S \cup A \cup \{+, -\}$, where A is the set of instances of atoms in S. Each node is labeled either by a clause in S and called a clause node, or by an atom in A and called an atom node. Each edge is labeled $+$ or $-$.*
3. *No atom node is incident with two edges labeled the same.*
4. *Each edge $e = \{a, c\}$ joins an atom node a and a clause node c; it is associated with the literal $L(e)L(a)$.*
5. *For each clause node c, $\{L(a, c)L(a) | \{a, c\} \in E\}$ is an instance of $L(c)$. A path $(v_0, e_1, v_1, \ldots, e_n, v_n)$ where $0 \leq i \leq n$, $v_i \in N$ and $e_j \in E$ where $1 \leq j \leq n$ is a* merge path *if $L(e_1)L(v_0) = L(e_n)L(v_n)$. Path $(v_0, \ldots, v_n)$* precedes *($\prec$) path $(w_0, \ldots, w_m)$ if $v_n = w_i$ for some $i = 1, \ldots, m-1$.*
6. *M is the set of chosen merge paths such that:*
   a) the tail of each is a leaf (called a closed *leaf),*
   b) the tails are all distinct and different from the heads, and
   c) the relation $\prec$ on M can be extended to a partial order, that is, does not contain a cycle.

An *open leaf* is an atom node leaf that is not the tail of any chosen merge path. The set the literals at the open leaves of a clause tree $\mathcal{T}$ is called the *clause* of $\mathcal{T}$, $cl(\mathcal{T})$, and is identical to the clause at the root of a corresponding brt.

Some relationships between brts and clause trees are discussed in [10]. Among them are: internal nodes of brts correspond to atom nodes of the clause tree; leaves of a brt correspond to clause nodes of the clause tree; a history path in a brt corresponds to an edge of a clause tree. See Figure 1 to see a clause tree that corresponds to a brt.

In this paper we disallow merge paths of length two since they correspond to factoring an input clause. Any most general factor of an input clause is allowed to form an elementary clause tree instead.

When a merge path is chosen between two open leaves, there is no reason to choose one direction over the other, unless one specifies some arbitrary heuristic. The corresponding proofs remain exactly the same. One can define a *path reversal* operation which changes the clause tree except that one merge path runs in the opposite direction, which may cause some other merge paths to be modified somewhat. Then two clause trees are said to be *reversal equivalent* if there is a sequence of path reversals which transform one tree to the other. Perhaps a better alternative, developed in [9] in a slightly different context and put into general clause trees in [5], is the foothold restriction, which can be used to make an arbitrary choice that is consistent regardless of the order of the resolutions.

Since both clause trees and brts are simply ways to write down resolution proofs, they are also equivalent to each other. The rotational equivalence classes of brts are in one-to-one correspondence with the reversal equivalence classes of clause trees [10].

3 Proofs without Merges

A resolution proof that does not contain any step in which two literals merge, or factor, corresponds to a clause tree with no chosen merge paths. The resolutions can be done in any order. Such proofs have been considered in several ways. Given a set S of clauses, it is known that the following statements are equivalent: S has an input refutation; S has a unit refutation; the set of factors of S contains a relative Horn subset which is unsatisfiable. These are equivalent to S admitting a clause tree without merge paths [5]. If there are n resolutions, then there are $n!$ different proofs, written as a sequence of resolutions, for which every resolution is relevant to the proof. The clause tree corresponding to these proofs is unique, since there are no merge paths to be reversed. Many brts, all rotationally equivalent, can correspond to these proofs, as a sequence of resolutions, yet each brt may correspond to many of these proofs.

Given a brt T with n atom nodes, let $c(T)$ be the number of brts rotationally equivalent to T. Similarly define the number of brts corresponding to a given clause tree $\mathcal{T}$ to be $c(\mathcal{T})$.

Theorem 2. *If T is a mergeless brt with n internal nodes, so that it corresponds to a mergeless clause tree $\mathcal{T}$, then*

$$C_n \leq c(\mathcal{T}) \leq n!$$

where $C_n = ((2n)!/(n!(n+1)!)$ is the nth Catalan number. These bounds are tight.

Proof. Once the order of the n resolutions is determined, so is the brt. Therefore $c(\mathcal{T}) \leq n!$, the number of possible orderings of the resolutions. If $\mathcal{T}$ is a(n extended) claw $K_{n,1}$, then T itself is a linear binary tree, with every resolution being between an input unit clause and the "central" clause. The resolutions can be done in any order, so the number of equivalent brts is $n!$. See Figure 3.

If $\mathcal{T}$ is a path, see Figure 4, then the corresponding brt T can be shaped like any binary tree with n internal nodes. Let $f(n)$ be the number of brts corresponding to a clause tree which is a path, containing n internal atom nodes. Assume that the kth internal atom node corresponds to the last resolution. Removing the atom node breaks the path into two clause trees which are paths themselves,

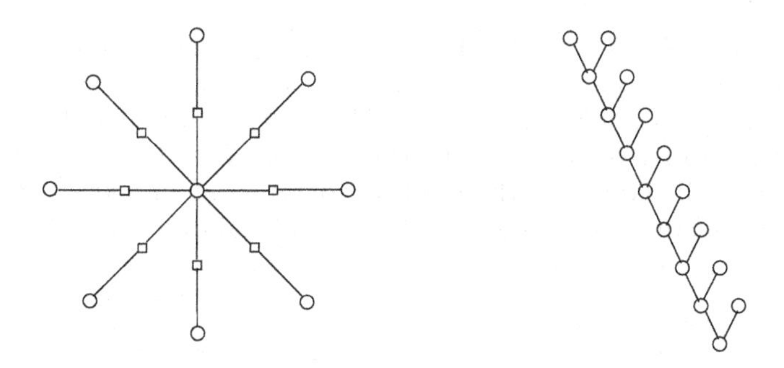

Fig. 3. A clause tree maximizing the number of equivalent brts, with shape of corresponding brt.

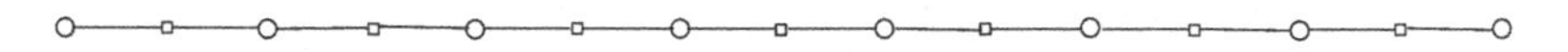

Fig. 4. A clause tree minimizing the number of equivalent brts.

one with $k-1$ internal atom nodes and the other with $n-k$. The number of brts then is $f(k-1)f(n-k)$. Summing over all the choices of internal atom nodes, any of which can be the last resolution, $f(n) = \sum_{k=1}^{n} f(k-1)f(n-k)$. The solution to this recurrence is well-known to be $f(n) = C_n$. Therefore the lower bound is tight.

Lastly we prove the lower bound. Assume that $c(\mathcal{T}^*) \geq C_k$ if $\mathcal{T}^*$ has $k < n$ internal atom nodes. Let the internal atom nodes of $\mathcal{T}$ be $\{a_1, a_2, \ldots, a_n\}$. For each atom node a_i, let the subtrees determined by breaking $\mathcal{T}$ at the atom node a_i be $\mathcal{T}_i$ and $\mathcal{T}_i'$. Assume that $\mathcal{T}_i$ has no more internal atom nodes than $\mathcal{T}_i'$, and that this number is b_i. Thus the number of internal atom nodes in $\mathcal{T}_i'$ is $n-1-b_i \geq b_i$. Then

$$c(\mathcal{T}) \geq \sum_{i=1}^{n} C_{b_i} C_{n-1-b_i} \equiv f(\mathcal{T}) \tag{1}$$

The function f defined in equation (1) is a lower bound on $c(\mathcal{T})$ which can be calculated from the shape of $\mathcal{T}$. We show that if $\mathcal{T}$ has a node of degree 3, then we can find another clause tree with n internal atom nodes for which this lower bound f is smaller.

Note that

$$\frac{C_k}{C_{k-1}} = \frac{(2k)!}{k!(k+1)!} \frac{(k-1)!k!}{(2k-2)!} = \frac{(2k)(2k-1)}{k(k+1)} = 4 - 6/(k+1) \tag{2}$$

This ratio increases with k. But the product $C_k C_{n-1-k}$ decreases as k increases for a fixed n, as long as $2k < n$, since

$$\frac{C_{k-1}C_{n-k}}{C_k C_{n-1-k}} = \frac{(4-6/(n-k+1))}{(4-6/(k+1))} > 1 \tag{3}$$

It follows that the product $C_k C_{n-1-k}$ is minimized when $k = \lfloor (n-1)/2 \rfloor$.

Suppose that T has a node c of degree 3 or more. Rename the atom nodes of T such that a_1 and a_2 are the two atom nodes adjacent to c which make b_1 and b_2 are as small as possible, with $b_1 \leq b_2$. Then b_1 is the number of internal atom nodes in the subtree obtained by deleting a_1 from T and does not contain the clause node c. Similarly b_2 is the number of internal atom nodes in the subtree obtained by deleting a_2 from T and does not contain the clause node c. Thus $b_1 \leq b_2 < n - 2 - b_1 - b_2$.

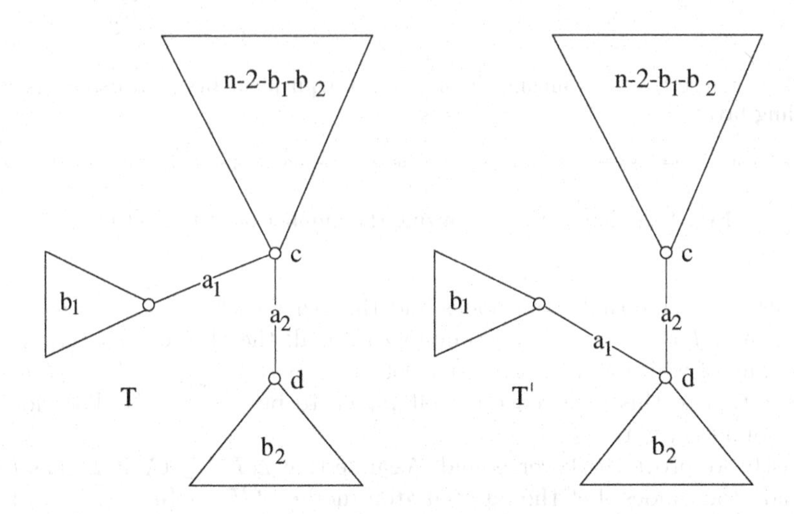

Fig. 5. The construction to show the lower bound

We modify T to make a new clause tree T' by detaching a_1 from c, and re-attaching it to the other clause node d adjacent to a_2. See Figure 5. Let b_i' be defined for T' in the same way as b_i is defined for T. Thus b_i' is the number of internal atom nodes in the smaller clause tree obtained by deleting a_i from T'. Then $b_i = b_i'$ except for $i = 2$. For this case $b_2' = min\{b_1+b_2+1, n-2-b_1-b_2\} > b_2$. By equation (3), $f(T') < f(T)$. Thus f is minimized only for clause trees with all nodes of degree less than 3, that is, only for paths. For a path the value of f from equation (1) is exactly $C_n = \sum C_i C_{n-1-i}$.□

4 A Polynomial Algorithm to Count Mergeless Proofs

Given a mergeless clause tree T, it is possible to count in polynomial time the exact number of corresponding brts. The algorithm uses dynamic programming. Given a specific clause node c of T, let $f(c, h, T)$ be the number of brts corresponding to T in which the leaf node corresponding to c occurs at height h. Once $f(c, h, T)$ is known for any specific c and all $h = 1, \ldots, n$, one can calculate $c(T)$ by summing $f(c, h, T)$ over all values for h. If T contains zero atom nodes and one clause node c, then $f(c, 0, T) = 1$ and $f(c, k, T) = 0$ for $k > 0$.

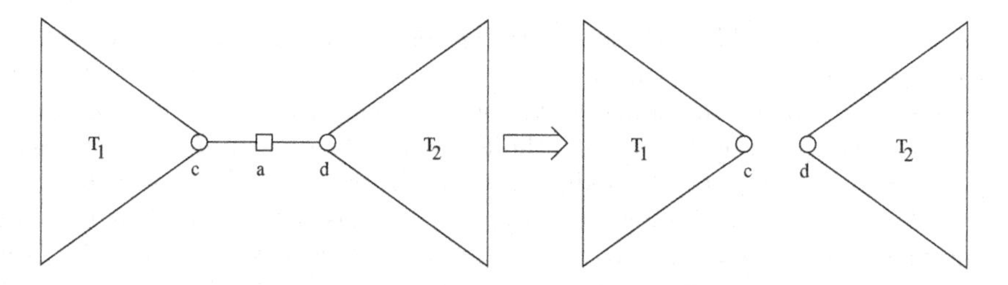

Fig. 6. Breaking the clause tree

Next we need a recursive formula for $f(c, h, \mathcal{T})$. Let a be an atom node adjacent to c, with d being the other clause node adjacent to a. Deleting a, and its incident edges, breaks $\mathcal{T}$ into two smaller clause trees $\mathcal{T}_1$ containing c and $\mathcal{T}_2$ containing d. See Figure 6.

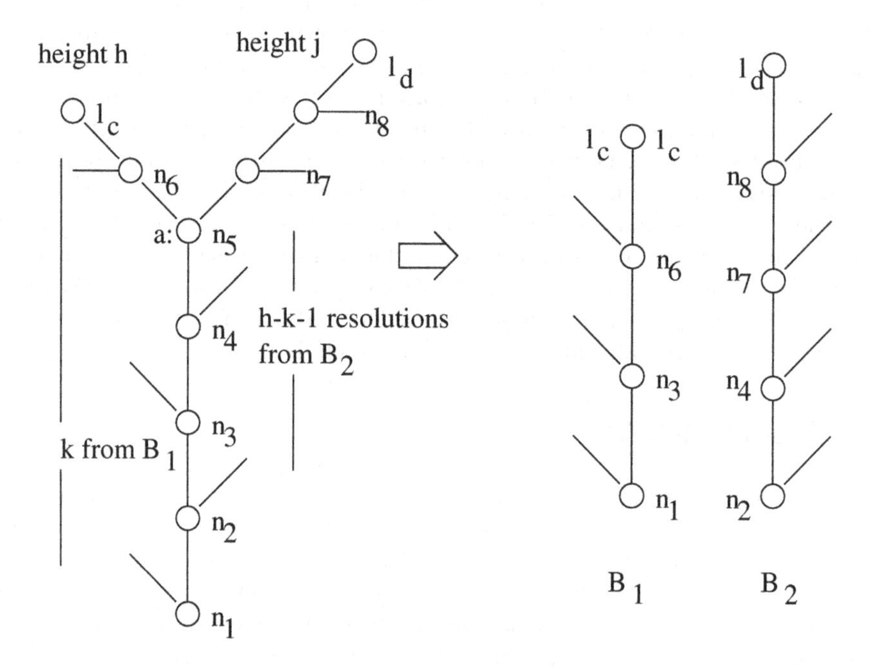

Fig. 7. Breaking the brt

Consider any brt B corresponding to $\mathcal{T}$. Let the leaf l_c corresponding to c be at height h in B. Consider the path from this leaf to the root. It must contain the node at which the resolution corresponding to a is done. Suppose that it contains k nodes at which other resolutions from $\mathcal{T}_1$ are done. Then it has $h - k - 1$ nodes at which resolutions from $\mathcal{T}_2$ are done, excluding the resolution corresponding to a. If one were to remove the nodes corresponding to atom nodes of $\mathcal{T}_2$ and reconnect this path from l_c to the root, then the result would be a brt B_1 corresponding to $\mathcal{T}_1$ in which the leaf corresponding to c would be at height k. Similarly removing the nodes corresponding to atom nodes of $\mathcal{T}_1$ would leave a brt B_2 corresponding to $\mathcal{T}_2$, with the leaf corresponding to d being at height $j \geq h-k-1$. See Figure 7. Looking at the path from l_c to the root in B again, the nodes from B_1 can be inserted anywhere on this path, as long as they are below the node corresponding to a. The number of ways in which the nodes from $\mathcal{T}_1$ can be placed is $\binom{h}{k}$. Summing over the possible values of k,

$$f(c,h,\mathcal{T}) = \sum_{k=0}^{h-1}(\binom{h}{k} f(c,k,\mathcal{T}_1) \sum_{j \geq h-k-1} f(d,j,\mathcal{T}_2))$$

The values of f can be calculated using dynamic programming. Let the clause tree be rooted at some clause node, complete with child/parent and ancestor/descendant relationships. Suppose that we evaluate f for each subtree rooted at any clause node c. To evaluate f for c, first all the values of f for all immediate descendant clause nodes must be known, for the subtree rooted at that clause node. Then the recursion formula must be applied for each of the atom node children of c, so that the formula, for each possible value of h, is applied up to $degree(c)$ times at c. The recursion formula must be applied once for each internal atom node of $\mathcal{T}$, for values of h up to the number of internal atom nodes below the parent clause node of the atom node in the rooted $\mathcal{T}$.

The internal summation for $\mathcal{T}_2$ can be found for all the values of h in linear time. Thus the values of f can be calculated in time quadratic in h for any given c and $\mathcal{T}$, assuming that the values of F are known for the subtrees and the nodes c and d. The set of recursions need to be calculated once for each atom node of $\mathcal{T}$. Hence the whole calculation can be done in cubic time.

5 Proofs with Merges

If the proof includes merging or factoring of literals, then the above arguments are not valid. Each merge requires that some of the resolutions be performed before the resolution of the merged literal. Hence the number of equivalent proofs is smaller for the same number of resolution steps. A single merge can reduce the number of equivalent brts considerably. In the case of a single merge in a proof, the number is divided by approximately the number of internal atom nodes on the merge path in the clause tree. If the merge were just within an input clause, it does not change the number of equivalent brts at all. It is assumed that merges always occur between literals from different input clauses, specifying that different occurrences of a given input clause are considered to be different input clauses. Moreover we assume that no two distinct literals from the same occurrence of a clause are merged with the same literal of another clause. In a clause tree this means that two merge paths with the same head cannot have their tails being adjacent to the same clause node, because this implies that the two literals of one input clause are factored.

The following theorem defines a lower bound on $c(\mathcal{T})$, denoted by $lb(n,m)$, which is a product of Catalan numbers.

Theorem 3. *Let T is a brt with n internal nodes and m merges, so that it corresponds to a clause tree $\mathcal{T}$ with m merge paths. Also let $n = \sum_{i=0}^{m} n_i$ such that $n_i = \lfloor n/(m+1) \rfloor$ or $n_i = \lfloor n/(m+1) \rfloor + 1$. Then*

$$c(\mathcal{T}) \geq \prod_{i=0}^{m} C_{n_i} \equiv lb(n,m)$$

Moreover this bound is tight.

Proof. First we demonstrate the extreme case. Let $n = k(m+1)$. Let brt T correspond to a clause tree $\mathcal{T}$ whose internal atom nodes $a_1, a_2, \ldots, a_n$ all lie in order on a single path. Thus all the nodes of $\mathcal{T}$ form a path except possibly for atom nodes which are leaves. Let $\mathcal{T}$ have m merge paths $P_1, P_2, \ldots, P_m$. Let the heads of the paths be spaced out almost equally along the path, with the head of path P_i at atom node a_{ki+1}, and the tail of P_i adjacent to the clause node adjacent to a_1 and not between a_1 and a_2. See Figure 8.

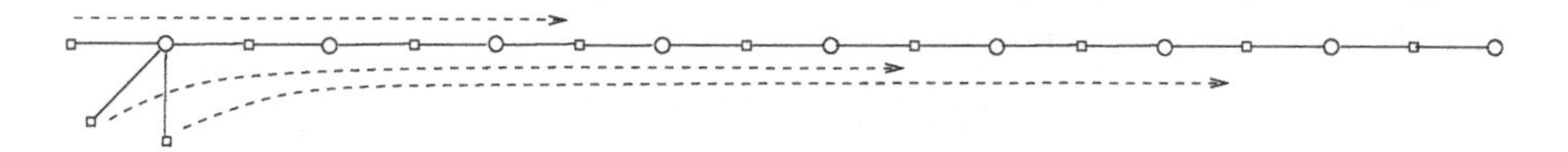

Fig. 8. An example of the lower bound, with $c(\mathcal{T}) = (C_2)^4$.

Let n_i be the interior node of the brt T corresponding to the interior atom node a_i of the clause tree $\mathcal{T}$. The resolutions corresponding to $a_1, \ldots, a_k$ must all occur before the resolution of a_{k+1}, and so $n_1, \ldots, n_k$ form a sub-brt $T_1$of T. Because $\mathcal{T}$ is effectively a path, the root of T_1 is a parent of n_{k+1}. By the results of the previous section, there are C_k brts rotationally equivalent to T_1. Similarly the resolutions corresponding to $a_{k+1}, \ldots, a_{2k}$ must all occur before the resolution of a_{2k+1}, and again these resolutions can be organized in C_k ways. The nodes $n_1, \ldots, n_{2k}$ must form a sub-brt T_2 of T, and the root of T_2 must be a parent of n_{2k+1}. The number of brts rotationally equivalent to T_2 equals the product of the number of ways that the nodes $n_{k+1}, \ldots n_{2k}$ can be organized and the number of brts rotationally equivalent to T_1, that is $(C_k)^2$. Continuing in this way, for $j = 1, \ldots, m$, nodes $n_1, \ldots, n_{kj}$ form a sub-brt T_j which is rotationally equivalent to $(C_k)^j$ brts. Then $T_m = T$, and is equivalent to $(C_k)^m$ brts.

Next we prove the lower bound. Consider the set A of interior atom nodes of $\mathcal{T}$ that are not interior nodes of any merge path. They may be heads of merge paths. Consider $\mathcal{C} = \mathcal{T} - A$, $\mathcal{T}$ with the nodes of A and their incident edges deleted. $\mathcal{C}$ consists of a set of $k \leq m$ component clause trees which are subtrees of $\mathcal{T}$. Some of these trees may consist of a single isolated clause node. Let the nontrivial component clause trees be $\mathcal{T}_i$ with n_i internal atom nodes and m_i

merge paths. Note that for each non-trivial component clause tree $\mathcal{T}_i$, the head of at least one merge path with internal atom nodes in it has as its head an atom node from A. Exclude these merge paths from being chosen merge paths of the $\mathcal{T}_i$. Also consider the clause tree $\mathcal{D}$ obtained from $\mathcal{T}$ by contracting all the edges of $\mathcal{C}$. $\mathcal{D}$ is a mergeless clause tree with, say, n_0 internal atom nodes. Note that $\sum_{i=0}^{k} n_i = n$ and $\sum_{i=1}^{k} m_i \leq m - k$.

Let C_i be a brt corresponding to $\mathcal{C}_i$, and D a brt corresponding to $\mathcal{D}$. Then build a brt from D by replacing each leaf of D which corresponds to a contracted $\mathcal{C}_i$, by C_i. The resulting brt corresponds to $\mathcal{T}$. Moreover the result is different if any of the component brts are changed. Thus

$$c(\mathcal{T}) \geq c(\mathcal{D}) \prod_{i=1}^{k} c(\mathcal{C}_i) \geq C_{n_0} \prod_{i=1}^{k} lb(n_i, m_i)$$

Each $lb(n_i, m_i)$ is a product of Catalan numbers. By the observation after equation 3 that the product $C_k C_{h-k}$ is minimized when $k = h/2$ or $k = (h-1)/2$ for a fixed h, the product of all the Catalan numbers is minimized when the subscripts are as equal as possible. One can also see that maximizing the number of factors minimizes the product, by considering adding a factor of C_0 to the product if there is not a factor for each merge path.□

Let $n = (m+1)k$. Because $C_k = \Theta((4^k)/(k^{1.5})) = 2^{2k - \Theta(\log k)}$, and $C_n \geq (C_k)^{(m+1)}$, it follows that

$$c(T) \geq 2^{2n - \Theta(m \log(n/m))}$$

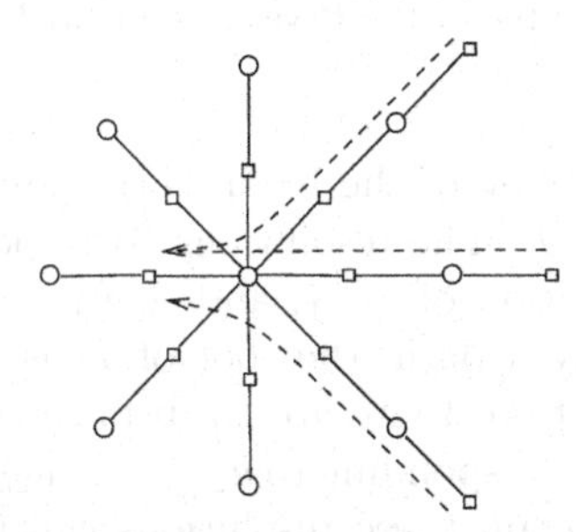

Fig. 9. A clause tree with merges and many equivalent brts.

The upper bound on the number of equivalent brts when merge paths are allowed does decrease when merge paths are allowed, but not very much. I do not have a proof of an upper bound significantly better than $n!$, but it is no less than $n!/(m+1)$. Consider the same clause tree as in the mergeless case, the claw if you like, and add m merge paths, all with the same head, h, from tails $t_1, t_2, \ldots, t_m$ attached at m distinct clause nodes, and not the central clause node. The m atom nodes internal to the merge paths must resolve before the atom node at the head. This decreases the number of brts by a factor of $m+1$. See Figure 9. Is this clause tree is the extreme case?

6 Open Questions and Discussion

A natural question to ask, is whether there is a polynomial-time algorithm to count the number of equivalent brts with n internal nodes and m merges? If we cannot count them, or alternatively show that this is a difficult question, then our understanding of binary resolution is limited.

More important is asking the equivalent questions for dags. Dags are what binary resolution theorem provers usually produce as proofs. Can one count the number of rotationally equivalent binary resolution dags, with or without merges? Can one put bounds on the number of such dags? Maybe this is a very difficult question.

Perhaps more interesting question is: Given a brt, what is the smallest equivalent dag? Goerdt [4] has shown that there are unsatisfiable sets of clauses such that the smallest non-regular (an atom label does not occur twice on one branch of the brt) refutation is exponentially bigger that the smallest refutation. Since the smallest refutation brt is regular, indeed surgically minimal, for any unsatisfiable set of clauses [10], the smallest brt must be exponentially larger than the smallest dag. I do not know whether the smallest rotationally equivalent dag is typically, commonly or only rarely much smaller than the smallest brt.

The previous question leads to another. Is there some other reasonable definition of equivalence for dags? Using clause trees, one can do more than just path reversals to get more proofs which are almost equivalent. One has the operations of surgery and supplanting. Surgery is not always reversible, so this is not a strict equivalence relation, yet a refutation always transforms to a refutation, and even non-refutations may transform to a refutation.

I wanted to determine the size of these equivalence classes in order to prove that a procedure that avoids producing redundant brts, would be significantly faster than an otherwise equivalent procedure which produces all the brts in an equivalence class. As it is obvious that the classes were exponentially large, I thought that the speedup would also be exponential. Only later did I realize that one should take the nth root of the count to estimate the speedup.

Consider a tree which represents the ways in which a given brt can be calculated. Each node in the tree represents a partial proof (minimal set of brts from which the result of the proof can be derived). The root represents the single clause which is the result of the proof. Each edge corresponds to doing a single step (resolution), with the node closer to the root containing the result of the resolution of two of the clauses from the further node, and all the other clauses from the further node. Each leaf has all the input clauses used in the proof. Every leaf is of height n; the number of leaves is the number of equivalent proofs. For each internal node of the tree, a procedure which avoids associative redundancy only does a resolution on a single edge leading to it, whereas a procedure which keeps all associative redundancy, even if it removes all identical clauses, does every resolution in this tree eventually. Thus the speedup of avoiding the associative redundancy is the average degree of the nodes in this tree. If the tree were regular, the average degree is the nth root of the number of equivalent brts. Since the tree is clearly not regular, this estimate is not rigorous. The leaves are of degree one, and the degree typically increases as one approaches the root, which suggests that the average degree is less than the nth root. On the contrary, one must consider these trees over all brts which are produced. The leaves occur in many of these trees for many different brts, and what one should average over is the number of ways in which each brt can be constructed in one step. This number is the number of internal atom nodes which are not interior nodes of chosen merge paths, and typically increases as one considers larger brts. Because there are more larger brts, I believe that the average speedup is at least 4, maybe even proportional to the size of the resulting proof, but this must be verified experimentally.

The problem to get an exact count in polynomial time intrigued me because the obvious dynamic programming algorithm is not polynomial. The solution using clause trees shows the effectiveness of clause trees as a tool to think about binary resolution.

Thanks are due to the anonymous referees for suggesting improvements to the paper.

References

1. R. S. Boyer. *Locking: a Restriction of Resolution.* PhD thesis, University of Texas at Austin, 1971.
2. Chin-Liang Chang and Richard Char-Tung Lee. *Symbolic Logic and Mechanical Theorem Proving.* Academic Press, New York and London, 1973.
3. Hans de Nivelle. Resolution games and non-liftable resolution orderings. *Collegium Logicum, Annals of the Kurt Gödel Society*, 2:1–20, 1996.
4. Andreas Goerdt. Regular resolution versus unrestricted resolution. *SIAM Journal on Computing*, 22:661–683, 1993.
5. J. D. Horton and B. Spencer. Clause trees: a tool for understanding and implementing resolution in automated reasoning. *Artificial Intelligence*, 92:25–89, 1997.
6. J. D. Horton and B. Spencer. Rank/activity: a canonical form for binary resolution. In C. Kirchner and H. Kirchner, editors, *Automated Deduction — CADE-15*, LNAI 1421:412–426, Lindau, Germany, July 1998. Springer.
7. J. Reynolds. Seminar notes. Stanford University, Palo Alto, California, 1965.
8. J. A. Robinson. A machine-oriented logic based on the resolution principle. *J. ACM*, 12:23–41, 1965.
9. Bruce Spencer. Avoiding duplicate proofs with the foothold refinement. *Annals of Mathematics and Artificial Intelligence*, 12:117–140, 1994.
10. Bruce Spencer and J. D. Horton. Efficient algorithms to detect and restore minimality, an extension of the regular restriction of resolution. *Journal of Automated Reasoning*, 25:1–34, 2000.

Splitting through New Proposition Symbols

Hans de Nivelle

Max Planck Institut für Informatik
Stuhlsatzenhausweg 85
66123 Saarbrücken, Germany
nivelle@mpi-sb.mpg.de

Abstract. The splitting rule is a tableau-like rule, that is used in the resolution context. In case the search state contains a clause $C_1 \vee C_2$, which has no shared variables between C_1 and C_2, the prover splits the search state, and tries to refute C_1 and C_2 separately.
Instead of splitting the state of the theorem prover, one can create a new proposition symbol α, and replace $C_1 \vee C_2$ by $C_1 \vee \alpha$ and $\neg\alpha \vee C_2$. In the first clause α is the least preferred literal. In the second clause α is selected. In this way, nothing can be done with C_2 as long as C_1 has not been refuted.
This way of splitting simulates search state splitting only partially, because a clause that inherits from $C_1 \vee \alpha$ cannot subsume or simplify a clause that does not inherit from C_1. With search state splitting, a clause that inherits from C_1 can in principle subsume or simplify clauses that do not derive from C_1. As a consequence, splitting through new symbols is less powerfull than search state splitting. In this paper, we present a solution for this problem.

1 Introduction

It is an empirical fact that methods with state splitting are better on propositional problems than resolution-like methods. When there are variables, state splitting becomes difficult due to the fact that it is necessary to maintain shared variables between states. It seems reasonable to keep as much as possible from state splitting, but avoiding the problems with shared variables.

The *splitting rule* is the following rule: Suppose that the search state of a resolution theorem prover contains a clause $C_1 \vee C_2$, where both C_1 and C_2 are non-trivial and have no variables in common. In that case the prover splits its search state into two states, one for C_1 and one for C_2. When properly applied, the splitting rule can improve the chance of finding a proof significantly. In addition to increased efficiency when finding a proof, the splitting rule increases the chance of finding a saturation. This is due to the fact that C_1 or C_2 may backward subsume clauses that are not subsumed by $C_1 \vee C_2$. Similarly it may be possible to derive an equality from C_1 or C_2 that simplifies the search state significantly, but which could not be derived from $C_1 \vee C_2$.

Some resolution decision procedures rely on the splitting rule. Examples are the procedure for E^+ of [FLTZ93] and [dN94], and the procedure for the 2-variable fragment of [dNPH01].

R. Nieuwenhuis and A. Voronkov (Eds.): LPAR 2001, LNAI 2250, pp. 172–185, 2001.

The splitting rule is practically useful, but difficult to implement in the resolution context. Currently (2001), Spass ([Wb01]) is the only implementation of resolution with search state splitting. It is not practical to make two copies of the search state. Therefore splitting has to be implemented through backtracking. The system deletes $C_1 \vee C_2$ from the search state, and replaces it by C_1. After that, search continues until either a saturation or a proof is found. If it finds a saturation then the system can terminate. If the empty clause is derived, then the system has to backtrack to the point on which C_1 was introduced, and replace it by C_2. In order to be able to restore the search state, the theorem prover has to do a complex administration. In particular, when a clause is deleted because it subsumed or rewritten, it has to be be done in such a way that it can be restored.

Because of these implementation difficulties, some resolution provers implement the following approximation: If the clause $C_1 \vee C_2$ can be split, then it can be replaced by the two clauses $C_1 \vee \alpha$ and $\neg\alpha \vee C_2$. Here α is a new propositional atom. It is ensured that α ist the least preferred literal in $C_1 \vee \alpha$, and that $\neg\alpha$ is selected in $\neg\alpha \vee C_2$. The only way in which $\neg\alpha \vee C_2$ can be used is by resolving it with a clause in which α is maximal. Such a clause will be derived only when C_1 is refuted. This way of splitting has been implemented in the Saturate System ([GNN98]), and in Vampire ([RV01]). We call this way of splitting *splitting through new symbols.*

Structural clause transformations ([NW01], [BFL94]) are closely related to splitting through new symbols. Assume that $F_1 \vee F_2$ is *antiprenexed*, i.e. that quantifiers are factored inwards as much as possible. In that case, every free variable of F_1 or F_2 is a free variable of both F_1 and F_2. A structural clause transformation would replace $F_1 \vee F_2$ by $F_1 \vee \alpha(\overline{x})$ and $\forall x(\alpha(\overline{x}) \rightarrow F_2)$. Here $\overline{x}$ are the free variables of F_2 and α is a new predicate symbol. In case F_1 and F_2 have no shared variables, symbol α will be propositional.

Unfortunately, splitting through new symbols only partially simulates search state splitting, because the new symbols hinder backward subsumption and simplification. Every clause that inherits from C_1 contains the literal α. Because of this, it cannot simplify or subsume a clause that does not inherit from C_1. This makes that splitting through new symbols fails to have one of the major advantages of splitting. In this paper, we give the following solution for this problem: If there are two clauses $C_1 \vee \alpha$ and D, and C_1 subsumes D, then we replace D by $\neg\alpha \vee D$. In this way D is switched off, until α has been derived.

Simplification can be handled in the same way. Suppose that C_1 can simplify the clause D_1 into D_2, but that the prover has the clause $C_1 \vee \alpha$ instead of C_1 in its search state. Then D_1 is replaced by $D_2 \vee \alpha$, and $\neg\alpha \vee D_1$. Doing this, the simplification D_2 is available on the current branch, and D_1 is switched off until α has been derived. We give an example:

Example 1. Suppose that one wants to refute the following clause set

$$p(0), \quad \neg p(s^{16}(0)), \quad s(s(X)) \approx X \vee s(Y) \approx Y,$$

and assume that one is using the Knuth-Bendix order. The equalities in the last clause are uncomparable under the Knuth-Bendix order, so both equalities have to be used for paramodulation.

The last clause can be split into $s(s(X)) \approx X$ and $s(Y) \approx Y$. Splitting results in the following two states, both of which have a trivial refutation using simple rewriting and one resolution step. The states are:

$$p(0), \quad \neg p(s^{16}(0)), \quad s(s(X)) \approx X,$$

and

$$p(0), \quad \neg p(s^{16}(0)), \quad s(Y) \approx Y.$$

Instead of search state splitting, one can split through a new symbol. Using α as new symbol, the last clause can be replaced by

$$s(s(X)) \approx X \vee \alpha \text{ and } \neg\alpha \vee s(Y) \approx Y.$$

After that, α can be derived by iterated paramodulation from $s(s(X)) \approx X \vee \alpha$. When this is done, $s(Y) \approx Y$ becomes available again. This equality will simplify $\neg p(s^{16}(0))$ into $\neg p(0)$.

In Example 1, splitting through new symbols is better than no splitting at all, but it is still not as good as state splitting. In the first search state, $s(s(X)) \approx X$ can simplify $\neg p(s^{16}(0))$ into $\neg p(0)$. However $s(s(X)) \approx X \vee \alpha$ cannot simplify $\neg p(s^{16}(0))$, because of the extra literal α.
In the following example, we use extended backward simplification:

Example 2. With extended backward simplification, Example 1 is handled as follows: After the split, the search state consists of the clauses

$$p(0), \quad \neg p(s^{16}(0)), \quad s(s(X)) \approx X \vee \alpha, \quad \neg\alpha \vee s(X) \approx X.$$

With $s(s(X)) \approx X \vee \alpha$, the clause $\neg p(s^{16}(0))$ is simplified into

$$\neg p(s^{14}(0)) \vee \alpha \text{ and } \neg\alpha \vee \neg p(s^{16}(0)).$$

Seven more rewrites result in

$$\neg p(0) \vee \alpha \text{ and } \neg\alpha \vee \neg p(s^{16}(0)).$$

Now the complete search state consists of the clauses

$$p(0), \quad \neg p(0) \vee \alpha, \quad s(s(X)) \approx X \vee \alpha,$$

$$\neg\alpha \vee \neg p(s^{16}(0)), \quad \neg\alpha \vee s(X) \approx X.$$

The first two clauses resolve into the clause α. After that, the two last clauses resolve with α, which results in the clauses

$$\neg p(s^{16}(0)) \text{ and } s(X) \approx X.$$

Now $\neg p(s^{16}(0))$ is simplified into $\neg p(0)$, which resolves with $p(0)$ into the empty clause.

In order to handle cases where more than one splitting symbol is missing, it is necessary to extend the clause format. Suppose that C_1 subsumes C_2, but the search state contains $C_1 \vee \alpha \vee \beta$. In that case C_2 has to be restored, when either of α or β is derived. One could obtain this by replacing C_2 by $\neg\alpha \vee C_2$ and $\neg\beta \vee C_2$. However, when there are many splitting symbols, this would result in too many copies. For this reason, it is better to extend the clause format by allowing negated disjunctions of splitting symbols. Using the extension, C_2 can be replaced by $\neg(\alpha \vee \beta) \vee C_2$. Each of the symbols α or β can restore C_2. Note that only a minor extension of the clause format is needed. Negated disjunctions need to be added only for splitting symbols, not for usual atoms. Both the positive disjunctions of splitting literals, and the negative disjunctions can be easily represented by bit strings, so they can be manipulated very efficiently.

If one does not want to extend the clause format, it is also possible to replace C_2 by

$$\neg\, \gamma \vee C_2, \neg\alpha \vee \gamma, \neg\beta \vee \gamma,$$

where γ is a new literal. However we think that it is better to make a small extension to the clause format.

In the next section we formally define search state splitting, and we give a couple of variants of splitting through new propositional symbols. After that, in Section 3, we prove a general completeness result, that is general enough to prove completeness of all types of splitting, combined with all restrictions of resolution.

2 Splitting through New Symbols

We first define two variants of the splitting rule, usual splitting and extended splitting. It is possible to add the negation of one of the branches in the other branch. This is called *extended splitting*. Extended splitting is possible because $C_1 \vee C_2$ is logically equivalent with $C_1 \vee (C_2 \wedge \neg C_1)$.

Definition 1. *Let C be a clause, not the empty clause. Let A be a literal in C. The* component *of A in C is the smallest subset C_1 of C, s.t*

- *$A \in C_1$, and*
- *if literals B_1, B_2 have some variables in common, $B_1 \in C_1$, $B_2 \in C$, then $B_2 \in C_1$.*

Write $C = C_1 \vee C_2$, where C_2 are the literals of C that are not in C_1. If C_2 is non-empty, then clause $C_1 \vee C_2$ can be split. Write Γ for the remaining clauses in the search state of the theorem prover.

- Splitting *is obtained by replacing the search state $\Gamma, C_1 \vee C_2$ by two search states Γ, C_1 and Γ, C_2.*
- Extended splitting *is defined by replacing the search state by the two search states Γ, C_1 and $\Gamma, \neg C_1, C_2$. In the second proof state, variables in $\neg C_1$ have to be Skolemized.*

The original search state is refuted if both of the split search states are refuted. The original search state has a saturation if one of the split search states has a saturation.

Note that our definition implies that C_1 cannot be split another time. It is possible however that C_2 can be split another time. In practive, one does not always split when it is possible, because search state splitting is costly. Spass uses heuristics to decide whether or not a possible split should take place, and whether extended or simple splitting should be used. Typically both components need to contain non-propositional, positive literals. It is reported in [Wb01] that extended splitting is not always better than non-extended splitting. See [Wb01] for details. Next we define splitting through new symbols. We do this in two ways. The first way is the way that we described in the introduction. The second way tries to reduce the number of splitting symbols by exploiting dependencies between them. We call this splitting with *literal suppression.*

Definition 2. *We first define splitting without literal suppression. Let $C_1 \vee C_2$ be a clause that can be split.*

- *Non-extended splitting replaces the clause by*

$$C_1 \vee \beta, \quad \neg\beta \vee C_2.$$

- *Extended splitting replaces the clause by*

$$C_1 \vee \beta, \quad \neg\beta \vee C_2, \quad \neg\beta \vee \neg C_1.$$

  The negation of C_1 has to be Skolemized.

If some clause has more than one split clause among its parents, it will contain more than one splitting symbol. If one would split such a clause using Definition 2, then one more splitting symbol will be added. The following way of splitting makes it possible to drop other splitting atoms when a clause is split, that already contains splitting atoms.

Definition 3. *Let $C_1 \vee C_2 \vee \alpha_1 \vee \cdots \vee \alpha_p$ be a clause that can be split, where $\alpha_1, \ldots, \alpha_p$ $p \geq 0$ are positive splitting symbols, resulting from earlier splits. We define splitting with* symbol suppression.

- *Simple splitting replaces the clause by*

$$C_1 \vee \beta, \quad \neg\beta \vee C_2 \vee \alpha_1 \vee \cdots \vee \alpha_p,$$

$$\neg\alpha_1 \vee \beta, \ldots, \neg\alpha_p \vee \beta.$$

- *Extended splitting replaces the clause by*

$$C_1 \vee \beta, \quad \neg\beta \vee C_2 \vee \alpha_1 \vee \cdots \vee \alpha_p, \quad \neg\beta \vee \neg C_1 \vee \alpha_1 \vee \cdots \vee \alpha_p,$$

$$\neg\alpha_1 \vee \beta, \cdots, \neg\alpha_p \vee \beta.$$

It may seem that the effect of splitting with literal suppression can be also obtained by splitting $C_1 \vee C_2 \vee \alpha_1 \vee \cdots \vee \alpha_p$ into $C_1 \vee \beta$ and $\neg\beta \vee C_2 \vee \alpha_1 \vee \cdots \vee \alpha_p$. However if the first clause resolves with a clause containing some of the α_i, then both the α_i and β have to be kept in the resulting clause. If one has literal supression, then any clause of form $D \vee \alpha_{i_1} \vee \cdots \vee \alpha_{i_k} \vee \beta$ can be simplified into $D \vee \beta$, due to presence of the $\neg\alpha_i \vee \beta$ clauses.

For all four ways of splitting, it can be easily verified that the clauses resulting from the split imply the original clause. This does not imply completeness for the case where splitting is done eagerly, but it does imply that splitting with fresh literals can be done finitely often without losing completeness.

We will now prove that the four ways of splitting are sound. We do this by proving that in each case there exists a first order formula F, which can be substituted for β, such that the resulting clauses become logical consequences of the original clause. This makes the splitting rules provably sound in higher order logic. This makes it possible to verify resolution proofs that use splitting through new symbols, see [dN01]. In first order logic, the splitting rules are satisfiability preserving. Instead of substituting F for β, one can extend the interpretation with β, and copy the truth value for β from F.

Theorem 1. *For all four ways of splitting, there exists a formula F which can be substituted for β, s.t. the resulting clauses are logical consequences of the original clause.*

Proof.

- First we consider splitting without literal suppression. For non-extended splitting, one can simply take

$$\beta := C_2.$$

For extended splitting, one can take

$$\beta := \neg C_1 \wedge C_2.$$

- Next we consider splitting with literal suppression. For non-extended splitting, one can take

$$\beta := C_2 \vee \alpha_1 \vee \cdots \vee \alpha_p.$$

Substituting in the formulas that result from the split, gives

$$C_1 \vee (C_2 \vee \alpha_1 \vee \cdots \vee \alpha_p),$$

$$\neg(C_2 \vee \alpha_1 \vee \cdots \vee \alpha_p) \vee C_2 \vee \alpha_1 \vee \cdots \vee \alpha_p,$$

$$\neg\alpha_1 \vee (C_2 \vee \alpha_1 \vee \cdots \vee \alpha_p), \ldots, \neg\alpha_p \vee (C_2 \vee \alpha_1 \vee \cdots \vee \alpha_p).$$

The first formula equals $C_1 \vee C_2 \vee \alpha_1 \vee \cdots \vee \alpha_p$. The other formulae are tautologies.

In the case of extended splitting with literal suppression, one can take

$$\beta := (\neg C_1 \wedge C_2) \vee \alpha_1 \vee \cdots \vee \alpha_p.$$

Substituting in the formulas, resulting from the split, gives

$$C_1 \vee (\neg C_1 \wedge C_2) \vee \alpha_1 \vee \cdots \vee \alpha_p,$$
$$\neg((\neg C_1 \wedge C_2) \vee \alpha_1 \vee \cdots \vee \alpha_p) \vee C_2 \vee \alpha_1 \vee \cdots \vee \alpha_p,$$
$$\neg((\neg C_1 \wedge C_2) \vee \alpha_1 \vee \cdots \vee \alpha_p) \vee \neg C_1 \vee \alpha_1 \vee \cdots \vee \alpha_p,$$
$$\neg\alpha_1 \vee (\neg C_1 \wedge C_2) \vee \alpha_1 \vee \cdots \vee \alpha_p, \cdots, \neg\alpha_p \vee (\neg C_1 \wedge C_2) \vee \alpha_1 \vee \cdots \vee \alpha_p.$$

It is easily checked that all of these formulas are tautologies or logical consequences of $C_1 \vee C_2 \vee \alpha_1 \vee \cdots \vee \alpha_p$.

3 A Meta Calculus

We prove a general completeness result, which applies to all splitting strategies described so far. We do not want the result to be restricted to one calculus, or to one type of redundancy. The completeness result has to be applicable to all resolution decision procedures that need the splitting rule, and also to other refinements of resolution, that are used for full first order.

One could try to give separate completeness proofs for the various calculi, but this is too complicated. The completeness proofs are rather heterogeneous. Some of them rely on the completeness of the superposition calculus ([BG01]), others are based on the resolution game ([dN94]) or lock resolution. ([B71])

In order to obtain a general completeness result, we define a *meta calculus* which extends some refinement of resolution (called *calculus* here) by adjoining the splitting atoms to it. We then prove relative completeness: Every derivation, that fulfills certain conditions, will either derive the empty clause, or construct in the limit a saturation of the original calculus.

The rules of the meta calculus are obtained by modifying the rules of the original calculus. When a rule of the original calculus is applied on clauses containing splitting symbols, the resulting clause inherits the splitting symbols from the parents in the meta calculus. Redundancy in the meta calculus is obtained by combining the redundancy of the original calculus with propositional implication on the splitting symbols.

It is necessary to keep the splitting symbols apart from the calculus literals. Using the propositional redundancy techniques in full generality on all literals would result in incompleteness.

Definition 4. *We identify a calculus $\mathcal{C}$ by its derivation rules and its redundancy rules. A* calculus *is characterized by an ordered tuple $\mathcal{C} = (A, D, R, e)$ in which*

- *A is the set of clauses,*
- *$D \subseteq A^* \times A$ is the set of derivation rules,*
- *$R \subseteq A^* \times A$ is the set of redundancy rules. R must be* reflexive *and* transitive. *Reflexive means that $R(a, a)$ for all $a \in A$. Transitive means that $R(a_1, \ldots, a_n, a)$ and $R(b_1, \ldots, b_{i-1}, a, b_{i+1}, \ldots, b_m, b)$ imply*

  $$R(b_1, \ldots, b_{i-1}, a_1, \ldots, a_n, b_{i+1}, \ldots, b_m, b).$$
- *$e \in A$ is the empty clause of $\mathcal{C}$.*

In examples, clauses of $\mathcal{C}$ will be between square brackets, to stress that we see them as closed objects. For example, if one would have ordinary resolution with subsumption, one would have

$$([p(X) \vee q(X)], [\neg p(X) \vee r(Y)]; [q(X) \vee r(Y)]) \in D,$$

$$([p(X,Y) \vee p(Y,X) \vee r(X,Y)]; [p(X,X) \vee r(X,X)] \in D.$$

In R, one would have

$$([p(X) \vee q(X)]; [p(0) \vee q(0)]) \in R,$$

$$([p(X)]; [p(f(X))]) \in R.$$

The calculus $\mathcal{C}$ is considered on the predicate level. Clauses are not replaced by their ground instances. However, since the clauses of $\mathcal{C}$ are closed objects, the meta calculus is a propositional calculus.

All natural redundancy criteria are transitive, because they are based on implication and on some ordering conditions.

There is no need to specify what the splitting rules of $\mathcal{C}$ exactly are. The reason for this fact is that, as far as completeness is concerned, splitting can be handled by redundancy. When a clause $C_1 \vee C_2$ is split into C_1 and C_2, both of the components subsume the original clause.

The method can handle any form of splitting, as long as the clauses obtained by splitting subsume the split clause. We are not concerned about soundness in this section. The soundness of most of the possible ways of splitting has been proven in Theorem 1.

Definition 5. *A* saturated set *is a set $M \subseteq A$, such that for each set of clauses $a_1, \ldots, a_n \in M$, $(n \geq 0)$ and clause $a \in A$, for which*

$$D(a_1, \ldots, a_n, a),$$

there are clauses $b_1, \ldots, b_m \in M$, $(m \geq 0)$ such that

$$R(b_1, \ldots, b_m, a).$$

A set $M \subseteq A$ is a saturation *of some set of initial clauses I if M is a saturated set, and for each $a \in I$, there are clauses $a_1, \ldots, a_m \in M$, such that $R(a_1, \ldots, a_m, a)$.*

We use the letter M for saturations, because they play the role of models. If the calculus $\mathcal{C}$ is complete, then M (in principle) represents a model of the clauses it contains.

We now extend calculus $\mathcal{C}$ with splitting atoms:

Definition 6. *Let $\mathcal{C} = (A, D, R, e)$ be a calculus. Let $(\Sigma, \prec)$ be a well-ordered set of propositional atoms, non-overlapping with any object in A. Clauses of the* extended *calculus $\mathcal{C}^{\Sigma}$ have form*

$$(\neg\sigma_1 \vee \cdots \vee \neg\sigma_p) \vee a \vee \tau.$$

It must be the case that $a \in A$. *It is possible that* $a = e$. *Each* σ_i $(1 \leq i \leq p)$ *is a disjunction of splitting literals. If* $p > 0$, *then the clause is blocked by the sequence* $(\neg\sigma_1, \ldots, \neg\sigma_p)$. *If* $p = 0$, *then the clause is not blocked. When the clause is not blocked, we write* $a \vee \tau$ *instead of* $(\ ) \vee a \vee \tau$.

The τ *is a disjunction of splitting atoms, representing the splitting context. We assume that* τ *is sorted by* $\prec$, *with the maximal atom first, and that repeated splitting atoms are deleted. If* τ *is empty, we omit it from the clause.*
Similarly we write $(\neg\sigma_1 \vee \cdots \vee \neg\sigma_p) \vee \tau$ *instead of* $(\neg\sigma_1 \vee \cdots \vee \neg\sigma_p) \vee e \vee \tau$.
The empty clause of the extended calculus is the clause

$$(\ ) \vee e \vee \bot,$$

where $\bot$ *is the empty disjunction.*

Next we define the rules of the calculus $\mathcal{C}^{\Sigma}$.

Definition 7. *The derivation rules* D^{Σ} *of the extended calculus are defined as follows:*

CONTEXT: *If* $D(a_1, \ldots, a_n, a)$ *in the original calculus* $\mathcal{C}$, *then for all splitting contexts* $\tau_1, \ldots, \tau_n$,

$$D^{\Sigma}(a_1 \vee \tau_1, \ldots, a_n \vee \tau_n, a \vee (\tau_1 \vee \cdots \vee \tau_n)\ ).$$

On clauses that are not blocked, we simply apply the rules of $\mathcal{C}$. *The splitting contexts of the parents are collected into the splitting context of the new clause.*

RESTORE: *Let*

$$c = (\neg\sigma_1 \vee \cdots \vee \neg\sigma_p) \vee a \vee \tau$$

be a blocked $\mathcal{C}^{\Sigma}$*-clause with* $p > 0$. *For each* i, $1 \leq i \leq p$, *let the clause* c_i *have form* $\alpha_i \vee \tau_i$. *(It consists only of splitting atoms) It must be the case that* α_i *is the maximal splitting atom of the clause* $\alpha_i \vee \tau_i$. *If each* α_i *occurs in* σ_i, *then we put* $D^{\Sigma}(c, c_1, \ldots, c_p, d)$ *for the* $\mathcal{C}^{\Sigma}$*-clause*

$$d = a \vee (\tau \vee \tau_1 \vee \cdots \vee \tau_p).$$

Definition 8. *The redundancy rule* R^{Σ} *is defined as follows: Assume that*

$$R(a_{1,1}, \ldots, a_{1,m_1}, b_1), \ldots, R(a_{k,1}, \ldots, a_{k,m_k}, b_k)$$

in the original calculus $\mathcal{C}$. *If*

$$\neg a_{1,1} \vee \cdots \vee \neg a_{1,m_1} \vee b_1, \ldots, \neg a_{k,1} \vee \cdots \vee \neg a_{k,m_k} \vee b_k,\ c_1, \ldots, c_n \models c$$

in propositional logic, treating the clauses $a_{i,j}$, b_i $(1 \leq i \leq k,\ 1 \leq j \leq m_i)$ *as propositional atoms, then*

$$R^{\Sigma}(c_1, \ldots, c_n, c).$$

What this rule says is that the calculus $\mathcal{C}^\Sigma$ inherits the redundancy from $\mathcal{C}$ through propositional implication on the splitting literals. We give a couple of examples in order to show that Definition 8 does what it is supposed to do:

Example 3. We show how R^Σ handles subsumption. Let $\mathcal{C}$ be the simple resolution calculus. Clause $p(X) \vee q(X)$ subsumes $p(s(X)) \vee q(s(X))$.
Then $[p(X) \vee q(X)]$ makes $[p(s(X)) \vee q(s(X))]$ redundant in R^Σ, because

$$\neg[p(X) \vee q(X)] \vee [p(s(X)) \vee q(s(X))], [p(X) \vee q(X)] \models [p(s(X)) \vee q(s(X))].$$

Similarly $[p(X) \vee q(X)] \vee \alpha$ makes $[p(s(X)) \vee q(s(X))] \vee \alpha$ redundant, because of the propositional implication

$$\neg[p(X) \vee q(X)] \vee [p(s(X)) \vee q(s(X))],\ [p(X) \vee q(X)] \vee \alpha \models$$

$$[p(s(X)) \vee q(s(X))] \vee \alpha.$$

In the presence of $[p(X) \vee q(X)] \vee \alpha$, it is possible to replace $[p(s(X)) \vee q(s(X))]$ by $\neg\alpha \vee [p(s(X)) \vee q(s(X))]$, because $[p(X) \vee q(X)] \vee \alpha$ and $\neg\alpha \vee [p(s(X)) \vee q(s(X))]$ make $[p(s(X)) \vee q(s(X))]$ redundant in R^Σ. This fact follows from the following propositional implication

$$\neg[p(X) \vee q(X)] \vee [p(s(X)) \vee q(s(X))],$$

$$[p(X) \vee q(X)] \vee \alpha,\ \neg\alpha \vee [p(s(X)) \vee q(s(X))] \models [p(s(X)) \vee q(s(X))].$$

The following example demonstrates how R^Σ handles simplification:

Example 4. If $\mathcal{C}$ is the superposition calculus, then the clauses

$$c_1 = [s(X) \approx X] \vee \alpha \text{ and } c_2 = [t(Y) \approx Y] \vee \beta$$

can simplify $d = [p(s(X), t(Y))]$ into

$$d_1 = [p(X, Y)] \vee \alpha \vee \beta \text{ and } d_2 = \neg(\alpha \vee \beta) \vee [p(s(X), t(Y))].$$

In order to justify this simplification, we need to show that c_1, c_2, d_1, d_2 make d redundant in $\mathcal{C}^\Sigma$. This follows from the implication

$$\neg[s(X) \approx X] \vee \neg[t(Y) \approx Y] \vee \neg[p(X, Y)] \vee [p(s(X), t(Y))],$$

$$[s(X) \approx X] \vee \alpha,\ [t(Y) \approx Y] \vee \beta,$$

$$[p(X, Y)] \vee \alpha \vee \beta, \neg(\alpha \vee \beta) \vee [p(s(X), t(Y))] \models$$

$$[p(s(X), t(Y))].$$

The following example shows how Definition 8 handles splitting through fresh literals.

Example 5. Suppose we want to split $p(X) \vee q(Y)$. Both $p(X)$ and $q(Y)$ make $p(X) \vee q(Y)$ redundant in the original calculus $\mathcal{C}$. Because of the implication

$$\neg[p(X)] \vee [p(X) \vee q(Y)],\ \neg[q(Y)] \vee [p(X) \vee q(Y)],$$
$$[p(X)] \vee \alpha,\ \neg\alpha \vee [q(Y)] \ \models$$
$$[p(X) \vee q(Y)],$$

the clauses $p(X) \vee \alpha$ and $\neg\alpha \vee q(Y)$ make $p(X) \vee q(Y)$ redundant in R^{Σ}.

The last example gives a simplification that is allowed by Definition 8:

Example 6. Suppose there is a clause

$$(\neg\sigma_1 \vee \cdots \vee \neg\sigma_p) \vee a \vee \tau,$$

and one of the splitting symbols in τ occurs in one of the σ_i. Call this splitting atom α. Then the clause can be replaced by

$$(\neg\sigma_1 \vee \cdots \vee \neg\sigma_i' \vee \cdots \vee \neg\sigma_p) \vee a \vee \tau.$$

where σ_i' is obtained by deleting α from σ_i. If σ_i' is empty, then the clause can be removed completely.

It is clear that all variants of Definition 2 and Definition 3 can be handled, because the clauses resulting from the split logically imply the original clause.

Definition 9. *A saturated set $M^{\Sigma} \subseteq A^{\Sigma}$ of $\mathcal{C}^{\Sigma}$ is defined as follows:*

- *For each clause c, which is derivable by rule CONTEXT from clauses $c_1, \ldots, c_n \in M^{\Sigma}$, there are clauses $d_1, \ldots, d_m \in M^{\Sigma}$, such that*
$$R^{\Sigma}(d_1, \ldots, d_m, c).$$
- *For each clause c, which is derivable by rule RESTORE from clauses $c_1, \ldots, c_n \in M^{\Sigma}$, there are clauses $d_1, \ldots, d_m \in M^{\Sigma}$ that do not contain negative Σ-literals, and*
$$R^{\Sigma}(d_1, \ldots, d_m, c)$$

A set $M^{\Sigma} \subseteq A^{\Sigma}$ is a saturation of some set of initial clauses $I^{\Sigma} \subseteq A^{\Sigma}$ if it is a saturated set of $\mathcal{C}^{\Sigma}$ and for each $c \in I^{\Sigma}$, there are $d_1, \ldots, d_m \in M^{\Sigma}$, such that

$$R^{\Sigma}(d_1, \ldots, d_m, c).$$

It is necessary to restrict R^{Σ} in the definition of a saturated set, because the full combination of D^{Σ} and R^{Σ} would have been incomplete, even when $\mathcal{C}$ is complete.

Theorem 2. *If $\mathcal{C}^{\Sigma}$ has a saturation that does not contain the empty clause, then $\mathcal{C}$ has a saturation not containing the empty clause.*

Proof. Let M^Σ be a saturation of $\mathcal{C}^\Sigma$.

We construct an interpretation $M = M_1 \cup M_2$, s.t. M_1 consists of Σ-atoms, M_2 consists of clauses from A, and all clauses of M^Σ are true in M. A clause $(\neg\sigma_1 \vee \cdots \vee \neg\sigma_p) \vee a \vee \tau$ is true in M, if one of the following holds:

- For one of the σ_i, none of the literals in σ_i occurs in M_1.
- There are clauses $a_1, \ldots, a_m \in M_2$, that make a redundant in the original calculus.
- One of the symbols of τ occurs in M_1.

First put

$$C_1 = \{c \in M^\Sigma \mid c \text{ has form } (\ ) \vee e \vee \tau\}.$$

These are the clauses containing only positive atoms from Σ. Next put

$$C_2 = \{c \in M^\Sigma \mid c \text{ has form } (\ ) \vee a \vee \sigma \text{ and } a \neq e\}.$$

We construct the set M_1 from a sequence $\Sigma_0, \Sigma_1, \ldots$ The set of symbols Σ is well-ordered by $\prec$. Let k_1 be the ordinal length of $\prec$ on Σ. Write σ_λ for the λ-th element of Σ, based on $\prec$.

- For a limit ordinal λ, put $\Sigma_\lambda = \bigcup_{\mu<\lambda} \Sigma_\mu$. This implies that $\Sigma_0 = \{\ \}$.
- For a successor ordinal $\lambda + 1$, put $\Sigma_{\lambda+1} = \Sigma_\lambda \cup \{\sigma_\lambda\}$ if there is a clause of the form $(\sigma_\lambda \vee \tau) \in C_1$, in which σ_λ is $\prec$-maximal and $\sigma_\lambda \vee \tau$ is false in Σ_λ. If there is no such clause, then put $\Sigma_{\lambda+1} = \Sigma_\lambda$.
- Finally put $M_1 = \Sigma_{k_1}$.

Each clause C_1 is true in M_1 and for each symbol $\sigma \in M_1$ there is a clause $c \in C_1$, such that σ is the maximal literal in c, and σ is the unique true literal of c.
M_2 is constructed essentially similar to M_1, but there is no need to do an iteration, because every clause contains at most one clause from A. Let

$$M_2 = \{a \mid (\ ) \vee a \vee \tau \in C_2, \text{ and } \tau \text{ is false in } M_1\}.$$

We want to show that all clauses in M^Σ are true in M. For the clauses of C_1 and C_2, this is immediate. For the remaining clauses, we use the following argument: Let c be a clause of form

$$(\neg\sigma_1 \vee \cdots \vee \neg\sigma_p) \vee a \vee \tau,$$

with $p > 0$. Suppose that all σ_i are true in M_1. For each σ_i, there is a symbol $\alpha_i \in \Sigma$, such that $\alpha_i \in M_1$. There must be clauses

$$\alpha_1 \vee \tau_1, \ldots, \alpha_p \vee \tau_p,$$

s.t. each α_i is maximal in $\alpha_i \vee \tau_i$, and each τ_i is false in M_1. By rule RESTORE, one can derive

$$d = a \vee (\tau \vee \tau_1 \vee \cdots \vee \tau_p).$$

There are clauses $b_1, \ldots, b_m \in C_1 \cup C_2$, which are true in M, s.t.

$$D^{\Sigma}(b_1, \ldots, b_m, d).$$

Because of this, d must be true in M. Since none of the τ_i is true, $a \vee \tau$ must be true in M. This makes

$$(\neg\sigma_1 \vee \cdots \vee \neg\sigma_p) \vee a \vee \tau$$

true.

It remains to show that M_2 is a saturated set of $\mathcal{C}$ and that M_2 does not contain e. Clearly, by the way M_2 is constructed, $e \notin M_2$.

Suppose that there are clauses $a_1, \ldots, a_n \in M_2$ from which an inference $R(a_1, \ldots, a_n, a)$ is possible. There are clauses $a_1 \vee \tau_1, \ldots, a_n \vee \tau_n \in M^{\Sigma}$ for which the τ_i are false. By rule CONTEXT, it is possible to derive

$$a \vee (\tau_1 \vee \cdots \vee \tau_n).$$

If we can prove that this clause is true in M, then we are ready, because then a must be true. If a is true there must be clauses in M_2, that make it redundant.

Because M^{Σ} is a saturated set of $\mathcal{C}^{\Sigma}$, there are clauses $d_1, \ldots, d_m \in M^{\Sigma}$, which make $a \vee (\tau_1 \vee \cdots \vee \tau_n)$ redundant. The clauses $d_1, \ldots, d_m$ are true in M. By definition of redundancy, there exist $\mathcal{C}$-clauses

$$a_{1,1}, \ldots, a_{1,m_1}, b_1, \ldots, a_{k,1}, \ldots, a_{k,m_k}, b_k,$$

such that

$$R(a_{1,1}, \ldots, a_{1,m_1}, b_1), \ldots, R(a_{k,1}, \ldots, a_{k,m_k}, b_k),$$

and

$$\neg a_{1,1} \vee \cdots \vee \neg a_{1,m_1} \vee b_1, \ldots, \neg a_{k,1} \vee \cdots \vee \neg a_{k,m_k} \vee b_k,$$
$$d_1, \ldots, d_m \models a \vee (\tau_1 \vee \cdots \vee \tau_n)$$

in propositional logic.

We know already that the clauses $d_1, \ldots, d_m$ are true in M. The other clauses $\neg a_{j,1} \vee \cdots \vee \neg a_{j,m_j} \vee b_j$ $(1 \leq j \leq k)$ are true by the fact that R is a transitive relation. From this it follows that $a \vee (\tau_1 \vee \cdots \vee \tau_n)$ is true.

4 Conclusions

We have presented a way for simulating search state splitting by splitting through new symbols. The method preserves redundancy elimination, what is particularly important if one is looking for a saturated set.

In our method negative splitting literals are always selected, so that they block the clause. In [RV01], an interesting alternative was introduced: Simply use an A-order which makes both the positive and the negative splitting atom minimal. In this way, different splitting branches are explored in parallel. Different branches cannot interact, because any inference between clauses of the form $C_1 \vee \alpha$ and $C_2 \vee \neg\alpha$ will result in a tautology. It would be interesting to see if our method of redundancy elimination could be combined with this style of splitting.

Acknowledgements. The author became aware of the problem with splitting through proposition symbols after a discussion with Ullrich Hustadt. Harald Ganzinger read a draft version. The present presentation has benefitted from his comments.

References

[BFL94] Baaz, M., Fermüller, C. Leitsch, A.: A non-elementary speed up in proof length by structural clause form transformation, In LICS 94.

[BG01] Bachmair, L., Ganzinger, H.: Resolution Theorem Proving, pp. 19–99, in the Handbook of Automated Reasoning, **2001**, Edited by A. Robinson and A. Voronkov, Elsevier Science, Amsterdam, the Netherlands.

[B71] Boyer, R.S.: Locking: A Restriction of Resolution (Ph. D. Thesis). University of Texas at Austin, (1971).

[FLTZ93] Fermüller, C., Leitsch, A., Tammet, T., Zamov, N.: Resolution Methods for the Decision Problem. LNCS 679, Springer Verlag Berlin Heidelberg New York, (1993).

[GNN98] Ganzinger, H., Nieuwenhuis, R., Nivela, P., The Saturate System, `www.mpi-sb.mpg.de/SATURATE/Saturate.html`, **1998**.

[GdN99] Ganzinger, H., de Nivelle, H.: A superposition procedure for the guarded fragment with equality. LICS **14**, IEEE Computer Society Press, (1999), 295–303.

[HdNS00] Hustadt, U., de Nivelle, H., Schmidt, R.: Resolution-Based Methods for Modal Logics, Journal of the IGPL **8-3**, (2000), 265-292.

[dN94] de Nivelle, H.: Resolution Games and Non-Liftable Resolution Orderings, in Computer Science Logic **1994**, Selected Papers, (1995) pp. 279–293, LNCS 933, Springer Verlag.

[dN00] de Nivelle, H.: Deciding the E^+-Class by an A Posteriori, Liftable Order. Annals of Pure and Applied Logic **104-(1-3)**, (2000), pp. 219–232, Elsevier Science, Amsterdam.

[dNPH01] de Nivelle, H., Pratt-Hartmann, I.: A Resolution-Based Decision Procedure for the Two-Variable Fragment with Equality, Proceedings IJCAR **2001**, Springer Verlag (2001), 211-225.

[NR01?] de Nivelle, H., de Rijke, M.: Deciding the Guarded Fragments by Resolution, to appear in the Journal of Symbolic Computation.

[dN01] de Nivelle, H.: Translation of Resolution Proofs into Higher Order Natural Deduction, **2001**, unpublished, to appear.

[NW01] Nonnengart, A., Weidenbach, C.: Computing Small Clause Normal Forms, pp. 335–370, in the Handbook of Automated Reasoning, **2001**, Edited by A. Robinson and A. Voronkov, Elsevier Science, Amsterdam, the Netherlands.

[RV01] Riazanov, A., Voronkov, A.: Splitting Without Backtracking, Preprint of the Department of Computer Science, University of Manchester, CSPP-10.

[Wb01] Weidenbach, C.: SPASS: Combining Superposition, Sorts and Splitting, pp. 1967–2012, in the Handbook of Automated Reasoning, **2001**, Edited by A. Robinson and A. Voronkov, Elsevier Science, Amsterdam, the Netherlands.

Complexity of Linear Standard Theories*

Christopher Lynch and Barbara Morawska

Department of Mathematics and Computer Science Box 5815, Clarkson University, Potsdam, NY 13699-5815, USA, clynch,morawskb@clarkson.edu

Abstract. We give an algorithm for deciding E-unification problems for linear standard equational theories (linear equations with all shared variables at a depth less than two) and varity 1 goals (linear equations with no shared variables). We show that the algorithm halts in quadratic time for the non-uniform E-unification problem, and linear time if the equational theory is varity 1. The algorithm is still polynomial for the uniform problem. The size of the complete set of unifiers is exponential, but membership in that set can be determined in polynomial time. For any goal (not just varity 1) we give a NEXPTIME algorithm.

1 Introduction

Automated Deduction problems frequently involve the use of equational logic. Usually, it is necessary to solve some kind of equational unification problem[1]. These problems can take three forms. The simplest is the word problem, where one must decide if two given terms are equivalent modulo an equational theory. A more difficult problem is the problem of deciding E-unification, i.e., deciding if there is a substitution that will make two terms equivalent modulo an equational theory. Finally, it is also sometimes necessary to solve an E-unification problem, which means to find a generating set of all the substitutions which make two terms equivalent modulo an equational theory.

All of these problems are undecidable in general. However, it is possible that an E-unification problem might be decidable in the equational theory of interest. Therefore, an important goal is to classify the equational theories and unification problems for which these problems can be solved. If a problem is decidable, it is also desirable to know the complexity of the problem. In particular, it would be especially useful to classify equational theories in a syntactic way, such that the decidability and complexity of these problems are easily known just by examining the equational theory.[1] This paper makes progress in that direction.

For a long time, one such syntactic class has been known: the class of ground equations (no variables). The word problem in this class is decidable in time $O(n \cdot lg(n))$[11]. The problem of deciding E-unification is NP complete.[12]. Shallow theories are an extension of ground theories, where no variable in an equation

* This work was supported by NSF grant number CCR-9712388 and ONR grant number N00014-01-1-0435. .

[1] When we refer to an equational theory, we mean a finite presentation of the theory.

R. Nieuwenhuis and A. Voronkov (Eds.): LPAR 2001, LNAI 2250, pp. 186–200, 2001.

occurs at a depth greater than one. This class was identified and shown decidable in [4], and also studied in [3,18]. For shallow theories, the word problem is decidable in polynomial time, deciding E-unification is NP-complete, and the number of E-unifiers in a minimal complete set of unifiers is simply exponential. See [18] for a simple proof.

In linear standard theories[8,18], both sides of each equation are linear, which means that no variable occurs twice on a side, and variables that are shared by both sides of the equation appear at depth 1 or 0 on both sides. Notice that non-shared variables may appear at any depth. The E-unification problem for this class has been shown to be decidable, but no complexity results are known, even for the word problem. The minimal complete set of E-unifiers has been shown to be finite, but a bound is not known. Similar results exist for standard theories[18] and semilinear theories[9].

In this paper we give a new technique for finding decidability and complexity results for E-unification problems. The technique is based on a simple algorithm, given by goal-directed inference rules. We consider linear standard theories. In particular, we examine the E-unification problem for goals of varity 1, which means that no variable occurs more than once in the goal. This problem is simpler than the general E-unification problem, but more difficult than the word problem, so all the complexity results we obtain apply directly to the word problem. We make a distinction between uniform and non-uniform E-unification problems. In the uniform problem, the input contains the goal and the equational theory, while the non-uniform problem is parameterized by the equational theory, and the input just contains the goal. We show that the complexity of the non-uniform E-unification problem is quadratic. Furthermore, if no variable occurs more than once in any equation of the equational theory, then the complexity is linear. Even in the uniform problem the complexity is still polynomial.

We show several other results. We define a set of terms, polynomial in size such that every term in the range of a substitution in the complete set of E-unifiers belongs to that set of terms. Using that and the polynomial complexity result, we get some other results that are independent of our algorithm. We show how to construct a complete set of E-unifiers whose size is at most simply exponential. We also show that it is not possible to do better, because we show an example of a ground theory where the varity 1 E-unification problem has a simply exponential minimal complete set of E-unifiers. Even though the complete set of E-unifiers we construct is exponential, we show that membership in that set can be decided in polynomial time.

Finally, we examine the general E-unification problem for linear standard theories, i.e., now the goal is unrestricted. In this case, we show that E-unification is decidable in NEXPTIME. The size of a minimal complete set is at most doubly exponential, but each term appearing in the range of a substitution in that set has linear depth. It is known that E-unification is NP hard, because of the NP completeness result for ground theories. So there is a gap here to be filled.

We would like to give some flavor of our results. The first thing we do in this paper is to give a goal-directed inference procedure. We prove that the procedure is sound and complete for any linear theory and varity 1 goal. This inference system has interest on its own. It is similar to the inference procedure for Syntactic Theories[10]. However, our inference procedure does not require the theory to be syntactic. The problem of Eager Variable Elimination is an open problem for the inference procedure for Syntactic Theories and other related inference systems[6,10,15]. We solve it in our context, given the restriction on theories and goals. The only other procedure known to us where Eager Variable Elimination has been shown to preserve completeness is in [17]. It is an important problem to solve because it adds determinism to the procedure.

After proving the completeness of the inference rules for linear theories, we tailor them for linear standard theories. First we show that when an inference rules is applied to a varity 1 goal, it remains varity 1. In other words, no variables are shared among goal equations, and they can each be considered separately. We also give a polynomial size set of terms and show that every equation generated is made up of these terms. The inference rules may seem arbitrary, but they were designed to allow these two results, which were difficult to obtain for theories containing collapse axioms (see Section 3). Since no variable occurs more than once in a subgoal, Variable Elimination does not applies. Therefore, there are no inference rules that combine goal equations. This means that each inference rule can be written as a Horn Clause, with the premise of the inference rule at the head and its conclusion as the body. Since we know that only polynomially many terms can appear in the inference, we know we only need polynomially many instances of the Horn clause, and our complexity results follow from the fact that Horn Clause implication is decidable in linear time[5]. This process is similar to what is done in stably local theories[16,2,7]. Results about the size of the complete set of E-unifiers and the general E-unification problem for linear standard theories follow from these results. All missing proofs, lemmas and definitions can be found in [13].

2 Preliminaries

We use standard definitions as in [1].

Given a unification problem we can either solve the unification problem or decide the unification problem. Given a goal G and a set of equations E, to *solve* the unification problem means to find a complete set of E-unifiers of G. To *decide* the unification problem simply means to answer true or false as to whether G has an E-unifier. In this paper, we consider both of these problems.

We say that a term t (or an equation or a set of equations) has *varity* n if each variable in t appears at most n times. An equation $s \approx t$ is linear if s and t are both of varity 1. Note that the equation $s \approx t$ is then of varity 2, but it might not be of varity 1. A set of equations is *linear* if each equation in the set is linear. For example, the axioms of group theory $(\{f(x, f(y, z)) \approx f(f(x, y), z), f(w, e) \approx w, f(u, i(u)) \approx e$. are of varity 2.

If G is a set of equations then we define a *path* in G to be a sequence of equations $u_1 \approx v_1, \cdots u_n \approx v_n$ from G, such that for all j, $1 \leq j \leq n$, $u_j \approx v_j \in G$

or $v_j \approx u_j \in G$, and for all i, $1 \leq i < n$, $Vars(v_i) \cap Vars(u_{i+1}) \neq \emptyset$. In addition, we require that if $u \approx v$ is in G but $v \approx u$ is not, then they cannot both appear in the path. We call the path a *cycle* if $Vars(u_1) \cap Vars(v_n) \neq \emptyset$. For example, the sequence $f(x_1, x_2) \approx g(x_3), f(x_3, x_4) \approx g(x_5), f(x_6, x_5) \approx g(x_2)$ is a cycle. Note that a single equation $u \approx v$ forms a cycle if u and v have any variables in common. If G has a cycle, we say that G is cyclic.

3 Inference Rules

We give a set of inference rules for finding a complete set of E-unifiers of a goal G, and later we prove that for a linear equational theory E, every goal G of varity 1 and substitution θ such that $E \models G\theta$ can be converted into a *normal form* which determines a substitution more general than θ. The inference rules decompose an equational proof by choosing a potential step in the proof and leaving what is remaining when that step is removed.

We define *solved equations* recursively. An equation $x \approx t$ in a goal $x \approx t \cup G$ is *solved* if x does not appear in an unsolved equation in $G - \{x \approx t\}$. Then x is called a *solved variable.* We define the *unsolved part of* G to be the set of all equations in G that are not solved.

As in Logic Programming, we have a selection rule. For each goal G, we don't-care nondeterministically select a unsolved equation $u \approx v$ from G. We say that $u \approx v$ is *selected in* G. If all equations in G are solved, then nothing is selected, G is in normal form and a most general E-unifier can be easily determined.

The inference rules are given in Figure 1. Except for Mutate, these are the usual inference rules for syntactic unification. We assume that the equational theory is consistent, i.e., that it has no equations of the form $t \approx x$ with $x \notin t$. Therefore, in the Mutate-2 rule, $f(s_1, \cdots, s_p)$ must contain x. In that case, we call $f(s_1, \cdots, s_p) \approx x$ a *collapse axiom.* So, Mutate-2 and Mutate-3 are only applicable in theories containing collapse axioms.

The Mutate-1 rule is so-called because it is similar to the inference rule Mutate that is used in the inference procedure for Syntactic Theories[10]. The rule assumes that there is an equational proof of the goal equation with at least one step at the root. If one of the equations in this proof is $s \approx t$ then that breaks up the proof at the root into two separate parts. We see from the inference rules that this rule is applicable if the last step at the root is not a collapse axiom with a variable on the right hand side. Otherwise, Mutate-2 or Mutate-3 will apply. Mutate-2 is applicable if there is a step at the root that is not a collapse axiom with a variable on the right hand side. Otherwise, Mutate-3 is applicable.

Notice that the Mutate-1 rule decomposes $f(t_1, \cdots, t_n) \approx f(v_1, \cdots, v_n)$. The Mutate Rule for Syntactic Theories also decomposes $u \approx s$. However, that is only complete for Syntactic Theories. Our inference procedure is not just for Syntactic theories, and decomposing $u \approx s$ is not complete in our case.

We will write $G \longrightarrow G'$ to indicate that G goes to G' by one application of an inference rule. Then $\stackrel{*}{\longrightarrow}$ is the reflexive, transitive closure of $\longrightarrow$.

Decomposition:

$$\frac{\{f(s_1,\cdots,s_n) \approx f(t_1,\cdots,t_n)\} \cup G}{\{s_1 \approx t_1,\cdots,s_n \approx t_n\} \cup G}$$

Mutate 1:

$$\frac{\{u \approx f(v_1,\cdots,v_n)\} \cup G}{\{u \approx s, t_1 \approx v_1,\cdots,t_n \approx v_n\} \cup G}$$

where $s \approx f(t_1,\cdots,t_n) \in E$. [a] [b]

Mutate 2:

$$\frac{\{u \approx v\} \cup G}{\{u \approx s, t_1 \approx s_1,\cdots,t_p \approx s_p, x \approx v\} \cup G}$$

where $s \approx f(t_1,\cdots,t_p), f(s_1,\cdots,s_p) \approx x \in E$.

Mutate 3:

$$\frac{\{f(u_1,\cdots,u_m) \approx v\} \cup G}{\{u_1 \approx s_1,\cdots,u_m \approx s_m, x \approx v\} \cup G}$$

where $f(s_1,\cdots,s_m) \approx x \in E$.

Variable Elimination:

$$\frac{\{x \approx t\} \cup G \cup H}{\{x \approx t\} \cup G[x \mapsto t] \cup H}$$

where $x \in G$, G is unsolved, and H is solved.

Orient:

$$\frac{\{t \approx x\} \cup G}{\{x \approx t\} \cup G}$$ where t is not a variable.

Trivial:

$$\frac{\{t \approx t\} \cup G}{G}$$

[a] To be exact, $s \approx t$ is renamed to have no variables in common with the goal.

[b] For simplicity, we assume that E is closed under symmetry.

Fig. 1. The inference rules

We want our inference rules to be applied deterministically or don't-care nondeterministically whenever possible. Therefore, we allow the Trivial, Orient and Variable Elimination rules to be performed eagerly. It is usual in inference systems for the Trivial and Orient rules to be performed eagerly. However, it is an open question in many inference systems whether the Variable Elimination rule can be applied eagerly. Since we restrict our inference rules to the case where E is linear and G is of varity 1, we can prove the completeness when Variable Elimination is performed eagerly. Eager inferences are a form of determinism, because when inferences are performed eagerly, that means that there is no need to backtrack and try other rules.

Inferences must be performed on a selected equation. This selection is a source of don't-care non-determinism in our procedure. However, there are still some sources of don't-know nondeterminism. If Decomposition and a Mutate rule (or two different Mutate rules) are both applicable to the selected equation, we don't know which one to do, and therefore have to try them both. Similarly, there may be more than one equation we can use in order to perform a Mutate rule on the selected equation. In that case, we must also try all the possibilities.

We will prove that the above inference rules solve a goal G by transforming it into normal forms representing a complete set of E-unifiers of G.

In order for the final result of the procedure to determine a unifier, it must not be cyclic. We will consider a goal G of varity 1 and a set of linear equations. Since G is of varity 1, it is not cyclic. We show that property is preserved.

Lemma 1. *Suppose that E is linear and $G \longrightarrow H$. If G is of varity 2, each term in G is of varity 1 and G is not cyclic, then H is of varity 2, each term in H is of varity 1 and H is not cyclic.*

A goal G is in *normal form* if the equations of G are all of the form $x \approx t$, where x is a variable, and the equations of G can be arranged in the form $\{x_1 \approx t_1, \cdots, x_n \approx t_n\}$ such that for all $i \leq j$, x_i is not in t_j. Then define θ_G to be the substitution $[x_1 \mapsto t_1][x_2 \mapsto t_2]\cdots[x_n \mapsto t_n]$. θ_G is a most general E-unifier of G. Notice that if a noncyclic goal has no selected equation, then the goal is in normal form, since Variable Elimination is applied eagerly.

4 A Bottom Up Inference System

In order to prove the completeness of this procedure, we first define an equational proof using Congruence and Equation Application rules. We prove that this equational proof is equivalent to the usual definition of equational proof, which involves Reflexivity, Symmetry, Transitivity and Congruence.

We will define a bottom-up inference system for ground terms, using the following rules of inference from a set of equations closed under symmetry:

$$\text{Congruence:} \quad \frac{s_1 \approx t_1 \cdots s_n \approx t_n}{f(s_1, \cdots, s_n) \approx f(t_1, \cdots, t_n)}$$

$$\text{Equation Application:} \quad \frac{u \approx s \quad t \approx v}{u \approx v},$$

if $s \approx t$ is a ground instance of an equation in E.

For Congruence $n \geq 0$. In the special case where $n = 0$, f is a constant.

We define $E \vdash u \approx v$ if there is a proof of $u \approx v$ using the Congruence and Equation Application rules. If π is a proof, then $|\pi|_E$ is the ordered pair (m, n), where m is the number of Equation Application steps in π and n is the number of Congruence steps. These ordered pairs are compared lexicographically, and addition is defined by components, i.e., $(m, n) + (p, q) = (m+n, p+q)$. $|u \approx v|_E$ is the pair (m, n), which is the minimum $|\pi|_E$ such that π is a proof of $u \approx v$.

We need to prove that $\{u \approx v \mid E \vdash u \approx v\}$ is closed under Reflexivity, Symmetry and Transitivity Also, we need to prove that certain rotations of a proof can be done without making the proof any larger (see [13]).

Theorem 1. *If u and v are ground and $E \models u \approx v$, then $E \vdash u \approx v$.*

5 Completeness

In this section, we will state the completeness of the inference rules given in Figure 1, where E is linear, and G is of varity 1. See [13] for the proof. First we define a measure on the equations in the goal, which will be used in the completeness proof.

Definition 1. *Let E be an equational theory and G be a goal. Let θ be a substitution such that $E \models G\theta$. We will define a measure μ, parameterized by θ and G. Let m (resp. q) be the sum of all the first (resp. second) components of $|u\theta \approx v\theta|_E$, where $u \approx v$ is an unsolved equation of G. Let n be the number of unsolved variables in G. Let p be the number of equations of the form $t \approx x$, where x is a variable and t is not. Then Define $\mu(G, \theta)$ to be the quadruple (m, n, q, p). We will compare these quadruples lexicographically.*

Now we come to the completeness theorem, which says that every E-unifier can be gotten from our algorithm. The proof of the theorem shows that if there is a goal which is not in normal form, then an inference can be performed to reduce the measure of the goal. Variable Elimination, Orient and Trivial always reduce the measure of the goal.

Theorem 2. *Suppose that E is an equational theory, G is a set of goal equations, E is linear, G is of varity 2, every term in G is varity 1, G is not cyclic, and θ is a ground substitution. If $E \models G\theta$ then there exists a goal H in normal form such that $G \stackrel{*}{\longrightarrow} H$ and $\theta_H \leq_E \theta[Var(G)]$.*

Corollary 1. *Suppose that E is an equational theory, G is a set of goal equations, E is linear, G is of varity 1, and θ is a ground substitution. If $E \models G\theta$ then there exists a goal H such that $G \stackrel{*}{\longrightarrow} H$ and $\theta_H \leq_E \theta[Var(G)]$.*

6 Linear Standard Theories

In this section we consider Linear Standard (LS) theories.

Definition 2. *An equation $u \approx v$ is LS if u and v are linear, and every variable that is shared by u and v is at depth 1 or 0 in u and also at depth 1 or 0 in v. A set of equations E is LS if every equation in E is LS.*

For example, $f(g(h(x_1)), x_2, h(g(x_3)), x_4) \approx k(x_2, x_4, k(x_5, a, x_6))$ is LS. So is the the collapsing equation $f(x) \approx x$. Some examples that are not LS are $f(x, x) \approx g(a)$ and $f(x, f(y)) \approx g(y)$. The first one is not LS because $f(x, x)$ is not linear. The second one is not LS, because y appears on both sides, but is at depth 2 on the right side.

Throughout this section, we will refer to equational theories E that are LS and goals G that are varity 1. We consider the E-unification problem for such theories and goals. For simplicity, since no variable is repeated in a goal, we will consider goals consisting of a single equation, because each equation can be E-unified separately, and the results can be combined.

We have defined inference rules for linear theories, and shown their completeness and soundness. For LS theories and varity 1 goals, we will derive an algorithm that always halts, and show therefore that this kind of E-unification is decidable, and then analyze its complexity.

In our completeness result, we proved that Variable Elimination and Orient and Trivial can be performed eagerly. Therefore, we will refer to Mutate+ inference rules (Mutate 1+, Mutate 2+ and Mutate 3+). These inference rule will consist of Mutate, plus some eager Variable Eliminations.

Mutate 1+:

$$\frac{\{u \approx f(v_1, \cdots, v_n)\} \cup G}{\{u \approx s\sigma, t_1 \approx v_1, \cdots, t_n \approx v_n\} \cup G}$$

where $s \approx f(t_1, \cdots, t_n) \in E$ and $\sigma = \{t_j \mapsto v_j \mid t_j \in Vars, 1 \leq j \leq n\}$.

Mutate 2+:

$$\frac{\{u \approx v\} \cup G}{\{u \approx s\sigma, t_1 \approx s_1, \cdots, t_i \approx v, \cdots, t_p \approx s_p, x \approx v\} \cup G}$$

where $s \approx f(t_1, \cdots, t_p), f(s_1, \cdots, s_p) \approx x \in E$, $s_i = x$, and $\sigma = \{t_j \mapsto s_j \mid t_j \in Vars, 1 \leq j \leq n\}$.

Mutate 3+:

$$\frac{\{f(u_1, \cdots, u_m) \approx v\} \cup G}{\{u_1 \approx s_1, \cdots, u_i \approx v, \cdots, u_m \approx s_m, x \approx v\} \cup G}$$

where $f(s_1, \cdots, s_m) \approx x \in E$ and $s_i = x$.

Next we prove that the property that the unsolved part of a goal is varity 1 is preserved by the inference rules. Recall that this means that no variable is repeated anywhere else in the entire goal.

Lemma 2. *Let G be a goal such that the unsolved part of G is of varity 1, and E is LS. Suppose $G \longrightarrow G'$. Then the unsolved part of G' is of varity 1.*

Furthermore, suppose that no variable appears more than twice in G, and any variable y that does appear twice in G appears in a term t in a solved equation of the form $x \approx t$ with x a variable from E. Then the same thing is true in G'

Corollary 2. *Suppose E is LS. If G is of varity 1, and $G \xrightarrow{*} G'$, then the unsolved part of G' is of varity 1. Furthermore, the Variable Elimination rule is not used in the derivation of G', except as part of a Mutate+ inference rule.*

Next, we give a description of what terms can appear in a derivation. First we give a recursive definition of a *decomposition* of an equation $u \approx v$

Definition 3. Decomposition *of an equation $u \approx v$ is defined recursively as*

1. *$u \approx v$ is a* decomposition of $u \approx v$.
2. *If $s \approx t$ is a decomposition of $u \approx v$ then $t \approx s$ is a* decomposition of $u \approx v$.
3. *If $f(u_1, \cdots, u_n) \approx f(v_1, \cdots, v_n)$ is a decomposition of $u \approx v$ then $u_i \approx v_i$ is a* decomposition of $u \approx v$ *for all i, $1 \leq i \leq n$.*

For example, the equation $f(g(x), h(y)) \approx f(g(h(a)), f(z))$ has four decompositions. They are $f(g(x), h(y)) \approx f(g(h(a)), f(z))$, $g(x) \approx g(h(a))$, $h(y) \approx f(z)$ and $x \approx h(a)$. Notice that if $s \approx t$ is a decomposition of $u \approx v$ then there exists a position i such that $u|_i = s$ and $v|_i = t$, or $v_| = s$ and $u|_i = t$.

Decompositions of the goal can appear in a derivation. We need some more definitions before we can say what else can appear in a derivation.

Definition 4. – *$St(t)$ is the set of all subterms of t. $St(s \approx t) = St(s) \cup St(t)$. $St(E) = \bigcup\{St(e) \mid e \in E\}$.*
- *$Pr(t)$ is the set of all proper subterms of t. $Pr(s \approx t) = Pr(s) \cup Pr(t)$. $Pr(E) = \bigcup\{Pr(e) \mid e \in E\}$.*
- *$Im(t)$ is the set of all immediate subterms of t, i.e., $t_i \in Im(f(t_1, \cdots, t_n))$ for all i, $1 \leq i \leq n$.*
- *$Ren(t)$ is the set of all renamings(variants) of t*

Some instances of terms can appear in the derivation, called shallow instances, because only the shared shallow variables are instantiated.

Definition 5. *$s \in Sh(t, E, u)$ (s is a shallow (t, E)* instance *of u) if there is a variant $u' \approx v'$ of an equation $u \approx v \in E$ and a substitution σ such that*

1. *The domain of σ is the set of all shared variables in $u' \approx v'$.*
2. *$Ran(\sigma) \subseteq Im(t) \cup Ren(Pr(E))$.*
3. *$s = u'\sigma$.*

$s \in Sh(t, E)$ if there is a u such that $s \in Sh(t, E, u)$.

For example, suppose that t is $f(h(x, y), f(c, d))$, and E is $\{g(h(x, y), z, w) \approx f(z, w), h(f(a, x), y) \approx f(y, g(a, a, b))\}$. Then $g(h(x', y'), z', w')$ and $g(h(x', y'), h(x, y), f(a, x''))$ are both shallow (t, E) instances of $g(h(x, y), z, w)$.

The next definition shows what can appear in a derivation.

Definition 6. – *$s \in Der(E,e)$ if there is a t in $St(e)$ with a symbol from E as its top symbol, such that $s \in Im(t) \cup Ren(St(E)) \cup Sh(t,E)$.*
– *$s \approx s' \in Der(E,e)$ if s and s' are in $Der(E,e)$.*
– *$G \in Der(E,e)$ if every $s \approx s' \in G$ is in $Der(E,e)$.*

We need a small proposition about this definition.

Proposition 1. *Let $s \in Der(E,e)$. There there is a $t \in St(e)$ such that $Im(s) \subseteq Im(t) \cup Ren(Pr(E))$.*

From Proposition 1, we see that all immediate subterms (and therefore all subterms) of a term in $Der(E,e)$ are also in $Der(E,e)$.

We prove that only those kinds of equations can appear in a derivation.

Lemma 3. *Let E be LS. Let G be varity 1 and $G \in Der(E,e)$. Suppose $G \longrightarrow G'$. Then $G' \in Der(E,e)$.*

Corollary 3. *Suppose E is LS. If e is of varity 1, and $e \stackrel{*}{\longrightarrow} G'$, then $G' \in Der(E,e)$.*

We get a better complexity result when the equations of E are varity 1.

Lemma 4. *Let E be varity 1. Let G be varity 1. Suppose $G \longrightarrow G'$. Suppose that every side of an equation in G is in $Ren(St(E)) \cup Im(t)$ for some $t \in St(e)$. Furthermore, suppose that each equation in G is a Decomposition or one side is in $Ren(St(E))$. Then G' has those same properties.*

Corollary 4. *Suppose E and G are varity 1. If $e \stackrel{*}{\longrightarrow} G'$, Then every side of an equation in G is in $Ren(St(E)) \cup Im(t)$ for some $t \in St(e)$. Also, each equation in G is a Decomposition or one side is in $Ren(St(E))$.*

Since we have shown that Variable Elimination is not applicable, all of our inference rules can be expressed as Horn clauses, where the head of the clause is the selected literal, and the body is the result of the inference on the selected literal. In fact the variables which are introduced in the body of the Horn clause can be skolemized, again because of the fact that the Variable Elimination rule is not applicable. We define a Skolem function Sk which turns a variable into a constant, i.e., $Sk(t) = t\theta$, where $\theta = \{x \mapsto c \mid x \in Vars(t)\}$. Note that every variable maps to the same constant, since the constant is not important. We also add Horn clauses to eliminate solved variables. Therefore, the inference rules are expressed by the following Horn clauses.

Decomposition, Orient and Trivial are expressed as:

$$f(x_1, \cdots, x_n) \approx f(y_1, \cdots, y_n) \leftarrow x_1 \approx y_1, \cdots, x_n \approx y_n$$

$$c \approx y \leftarrow y \approx c$$

$$x \approx x \leftarrow$$

The Mutate 1+ rule is:

$$y \approx f(x_1, \cdots, x_n) \leftarrow (y \approx s\sigma, t_1 \approx x_1, \cdots, t_n \approx x_n)\theta$$

where $s \approx f(t_1, \cdots, t_n) \in E$, $\sigma = \{t_j \mapsto x_j \mid s_j \in Vars, 1 \leq j \leq n\}$, and $\theta = \{x' \mapsto c \mid x' \in Vars(s \approx f(t_1, \cdots, t_n)\}$.

The Mutate 2+ rule is:

$$y \approx z \leftarrow (y \approx s\sigma, t_1 \approx s_1, \cdots, t_i \approx z, \cdots, t_p \approx s_p, x \approx z)\theta$$

where $s \approx f(t_1, \cdots, t_p), f(s_1, \cdots, s_p) \approx x \in E$, $s_i = x$, $\sigma = \{t_j \mapsto s_j \mid s_j \in Vars, 1 \leq j \leq n\}$, and $\theta = \{x' \mapsto c \mid x' \in Vars(s \approx f(t_1, \cdots, t_p)) \cup Vars(f(s_1, \cdots, s_p) \approx x)$.

The Mutate 3+ rule is:

$$f(x_1, \cdots, x_m) \approx y \leftarrow (x_1 \approx s_1, \cdots, x_i \approx v, \cdots, x_m \approx s_m, x \approx v)\theta$$

where $f(s_1, \cdots, s_m) \approx x \in E$, $s_1 = x$, and $\theta = \{x' \mapsto c \mid x' \in Vars(f(s_1, \cdots, s_m) \approx x)\}$.

We also add an inference rule to remove solved variables:

$$c \approx y \leftarrow$$

Therefore, each equational theory E determines a particular set of Horn clauses. Let us denote this set of Horn clauses as $HC(E)$. Note that the equality in these Horn clauses is now interpreted just as a binary predicate symbol with no special meaning. We have the following result:

Theorem 3. *Let e be a goal of varity 1 and E be LS. Then e is E-unifiable if and only if there is an SLD derivation of $Sk(e)$ in $HC(E)$.*

Corollary 5. *Let e be a goal of varity 1 and E be LS. Then e is E-unifiable if and only if $HC(E) \models Sk(e)$*

We notice that only certain ground instances will arise in the SLD refutation. Let $HC(e, E)$ be the set of all instances of $HC(E)$ such that the head of the clause is in $Sk(Der(E, e))$. Then we have the following theorem:

Theorem 4. *Let e be a goal of varity 1 and E be LS. Then e is E-unifiable if and only if there is an SLD derivation of $Sk(e)$ in $HC(e, E)$.*

Corollary 6. *Let e be a goal of varity 1 and E be LS. Then e is E-unifiable if and only if $HC(e, E) \models Sk(e)$*

Finally we have the decidability and complexity theorem of E-unification for varity 1 goals in LS theories.[2]

Theorem 5. *Suppose that E is LS and e is varity 1. Then*

1. *It is decidable in polynomial time whether e is E-unifiable.*
2. *If E is considered constant, then it is decidable in $O(|e|^2)$ whether e is E-unifiable.*
3. *If E is considered constant, and all equations in E are varity 1, then it is decidable in $O(|e|)$ whether e is E-unifiable.*

[2] Note: $|e|$ refers to the size of e (number of symbols).

7 Most General E-Unifiers

In this section we extend our results on LS theories and varity 1 goals to examine how efficient it is to compute a complete set of E-unifiers. First, we show that, there is a complete set of unifiers such that the range of every substitution in the set only contains terms from $Der(E, e)$. This result, along with the polynomial time algorithm for deciding E-unifiability leads us to all the rest of the results of the section, which are independent of the algorithm we have given.

We show that there is a complete set of E-unifiers no bigger than simply exponential. However, we give an example of a ground theory where the size of the minimal complete set of E-unifiers is simply exponential. So the bound is tight. Even though the size can be exponential, it still has some nice properties. We define a complete set of E-unifiers $CSU_E(u \approx v)$, and show that given a substitution σ, it can be decided in polynomial time whether $\sigma \in CSU_E(u \approx v)$.

Using those results, we finally move to the general E-unification problem for LS theories. In other words, we no longer restrict ourselves to varity 1 goals. We give a NEXPTIME algorithm for deciding unifiability. It is known that E-unification is NP hard, even for ground theories[18]. This leaves us with a gap for the actual complexity of the problem. The complete set of E-unifiers that we construct may be doubly exponential in size. However, all terms appearing in a substitution in the complete set of E-unifiers have depth linear in the maximum of the depths of the terms in the goal and the equational theory.

First we show that it is decidable in polynomial time if σ is an E-unifier of $u \approx v$ We will define $Gr(u \approx v)$ to be an instance of $u \approx v$ such that each variable in $u \approx v$ is replaced by a different new constant.

Theorem 6. *Let E be LS. Then it is decidable in polynomial time whether σ is an E-unifier of $u \approx v$.*

The next result in this section refers to the earlier completeness results.

Theorem 7. *Suppose E is LS and $u \approx v$ is of varity 1. Then there is a complete set of E-unifiers Θ of $u \approx v$ such that if $\sigma \in \Theta$ then $Ran(\sigma) \subseteq Der(E, e)$.*

Using that result, we can show that there is a complete set of E-unifiers with at most simply exponentially many members.

Theorem 8. *If E is LS and $u \approx v$ is varity 1 then there is a simply exponential size complete set of E-unifiers of $u \approx v$.*

There are goals which have simply exponential sized minimal complete sets of E-unifiers, even in ground theories, so this is a tight bound.

Theorem 9. *There is a ground theory E and a goal $u \approx v$ of varity 1, such that every minimal complete set of E-unifiers of $u \approx v$ has exponentially many members.*

A complete set of E-unifiers of $u \approx v$ can be described as follows: $CSU_E(u \approx v) = \{\sigma \mid Dom(\sigma) = Vars(u \approx v), Ran(\sigma) \subseteq Der(E, e)$, and σ is an E-unifier of $u \approx v$ $\}$. We can decide in polynomial time whether a given σ is a member of $CSU_E(u \approx v)$.

Theorem 10. *Let E be LS, and e be varity 1. Let σ be a substitution. Then it is decidable in polynomial time if $\sigma \in CSU_E(e)$*

Finally, we move to the most general case of E-unification, where E is LS but the goal e is not necessarily varity 1. It can be in any form.

Theorem 11. *Let E by LS and e be a goal. Then*

1. *E-unification for e is decidable in NEXPTIME.*
2. *There is a complete set, Θ, of E-unifiers of e which is of doubly exponential size.*
3. *Every term appearing in the range of a substitution of Θ has depth linear in the maximum depth of the terms in E and e.*

8 Conclusion

This paper presents a new technique for showing decidability and complexity results for E-unification problems. It makes it easy to analyze what forms of subgoals will arise from the initial goal equation. That can give useful information used to make the procedure halt, and then an examination of what kinds of equations are generated allows us to determine the complexity.

One application of the results of this paper is for approximating E-unification problems. For any theory and goal, we can rename all the variables in the theory and goal to new variables until they are varity 1.[3] As we showed, a linear time algorithm can be run on the new problem, and if the algorithm says "not E-unifiable", then that is also true of the initial E-unification problem. This is useful in the context of automated deduction problems that require lots of E-unification, and would allow a quickly discarding many E-unification problems.

There are some relationships with some of our other papers. In [15], we gave a goal directed inference system for E-unification in a similar style. The method of showing soundness and completeness in that paper is similar to the method in this paper. However, this time the inference system is different, and the Eager Variable Elimination rules make the proof more difficult. That paper had no decidability or complexity results.

Another recent work of ours[14] also develops decidability and complexity results for a class of equational theories and goals of varity 1. However, the class of problems in that paper is not a syntactic class, and the complexity results are not as good. We have actually shown in this paper that Linear Standard theories are in that class, because any E-unification problem whose goal contains only subterms of E or general terms will have a complete set of E-unifiers, such that the range of every substitution in the complete set only contains goal terms.

We would also like to compare our work to other recent works, which show E-unification decidable for syntactic classes such as linear standard theories.[4,3,8, 18,9]. There are three basic approaches to the problem: saturation based theorem

[3] This is more renaming than necesary, because it removes all variables shared by both sides of an equation.

proving methods like completion[18,9], tree automata techniques[3,8], and goal-directed inference rule methods[4]. Actually, [9] shows a relationship between their saturation methods and tree automata techniques. The methods of [4] are quite different from ours, even though they both use goal directed inference rule methods. One difference is that [4] saturate E by completion-like inference rules to make it syntactic. We do not do that, since our inference procedure is not limited to Syntactic Theories. In fact, all of the methods except ours pre-process E using something like completion. Therefore our method benefits from a memoization technique (as opposed to dynamic programming) that the other methods may not benefit from. On the other hand, there is one thing that all the methods share in common. They all are based on the fact that only certain terms will appear during the procedure.

Most of those other techniques have been used to show decidability results. Complexity results and bounds on the size of the minimal complete set of unifiers are not usually addressed. However, these issues are addressed quite nicely for shallow theories in [18]. The main benefit of our paper is to focus more on complexity. Our quadratic bound is interesting, because the results on shallow theories give a polynomial bound for the word problem, but not the exact polynomial. We suspect that the techniques used in this paper to analyze complexity could be used in other methods. We also discuss E-unification for varity 1 goals. There is a mention of E-unification for varity 1 goals in shallow linear theories in [9], where they give a simple decidability result using tree automata.

Since we reduced our E-unification problem to a Horn clause implication problem, and then showed only certain instances of the Horn Clauses are necessary for the derivation, it is natural to ask whether these Horn clauses are stably local[7], i.e. if variables only need to be substituted by terms appearing in the theory and goal. The presented Horn clause theory is not stably local, but if the single variables appearing in the horn clause were replaced by all possible terms of the form $f(x_1, \cdots, x_n)$, then the theory would be stably local. The initial equational theory is not stably local, because the shallow instances take us out of the set of subterms, and also because the shared variables may need to unify with terms that are not even in $Der(E, e)$.

We plan to extend the algorithm and techniques presented in this paper to get other decidability and complexity results. We would like to know what other classes can be shown decidable and efficient using this method. We have already started analyzing other syntactic forms of linear theories. But we also will consider non-linear theories. We left a gap in the complexity results for general E-unification of linear standard theories, which needs to be filled. Also, we are interested in finding better ways of approximating equational theories. Finally, there should be a closer examination of the relationship between our goal-directed method and the saturation-based and tree automata methods. Can our complexity techniques be used there? Maybe all these methods are encodings of the same process.

References

1. F. Baader and T. Nipkow. *Term Rewriting and All That.* Cambridge, 1998.
2. D. Basin and H. Ganzinger. Automated complexity analysis based on ordered resolution. In *J. Association for Computing Machinery* 48(1), 70-109, 2001.
3. H. Comon. Sequentiality, second order monadic logic and tree automata. In *Proceedings 10th IEEE Symposium on Logic in Computer Science, LICS'95*, IEEE Computer Society Press, 508-517, 1995.
4. H. Comon, M. Haberstrau and J.-P. Jouannaud. Syntacticness, Cycle-Syntacticness and shallow theories. In *Information and Computation* 111(1), 154-191, 1994.
5. W. Dowling and J. Gallier. Linear-time algorithms for testing the satisfiability of propositional horn formulae. In *Journal of Logic Programming 3*, 267-284, 1984.
6. J. Gallier and W. Snyder. Complete sets of transformations for general E-unification. In *TCS*, vol. 67, 203-260, 1989.
7. H. Ganzinger. Relating Semantic and Proof-Theoretic Concepts for Polynomial Time Decidability of Uniform Word Problems. In *Proceedings 16th IEEE Symposium on Logic in Computer Science, LICS'2001*, Boston, 2001.
8. F. Jacquemard. Decidable approximations of term rewriting systems. In H. Ganzinger, ed., *Rewriting Techniques and Applications, 7th International Conference, RTA-96*, Vol. 1103 of LNCS, Springer, 362-376, 1996.
9. F. Jacquemard, Ch. Meyer, Ch. Weidenbach. Unification in Extensions of Shallow Equational Theories. In T. Nipkow, ed., *Rewriting Techniques and Applications, 9th International Conference, RTA-98*, Vol. 1379, LNCS, Springer, 76-90, 1998.
10. C. Kirchner. Computing unification algorithms. In *Proceedings of the Fourth Symposium on Logic in Computer Science*, Boston, 200-216, 1990.
11. D. Kozen. Complexity of finitely presented algebras. In *Proc. 9th STOC*, 164-177, 1977.
12. D. Kozen. Positive first order logic is NP-complete. *IBM Journal of Res. Developp.*, 25(4):327-332, July 1981.
13. C. Lynch and B. Morawska. Complexity of Linear Standard Theories. `http://www.clarkson.edu/ clynch/papers/standard_full.ps/`, 2001.
14. C. Lynch and B. Morawska. Decidability and Complexity of Finitely Closable Linear Equational Theories. In R. Goré, A. Leitsch and T. Nipkow, eds., *Automated Reasoning. First International Joint Conference, IJCAR 2001*, Vol. 2083 of LNAI, 499-513, Springer, 2001.
15. C. Lynch and B. Morawska. Goal Directed E-Unification. In *RTA 12*, ed. A. Middeldorp, LNCS vol. 2051, 231-245, 2001.
16. D. McAllester. Automated Recognition of Tractability in Inference Relations. In *Journal of the ACM*, vol.40(2) , pp. 284-303, 1993.
17. A. Middeldorp, S. Okui, T. Ida. Lazy Narrowing: Strong Completeness and Eager Variable Elimination. In *Theoretical Computer Science* 167(1,2), pp. 95-130, 1996.
18. R. Nieuwenhuis. Basic paramodulation and decidable theories. (Extended abstract), In *Proceedings 11th IEEE Symposium on Logic in Computer Science, LICS'96*, IEEE Computer Society Press, 473-482, 1996.

Herbrand's Theorem for Prenex Gödel Logic and Its Consequences for Theorem Proving*

Matthias Baaz, Agata Ciabattoni**, and Christian G. Fermüller

Technische Universität Wien, Austria

Abstract. Herbrand's Theorem for $G^{\triangle}_{\infty}$, i.e., Gödel logic enriched by the projection operator $\triangle$ is proved. As a consequence we obtain a "chain normal form" and a translation of prenex $G^{\triangle}_{\infty}$ into (order) clause logic, referring to the classical theory of dense total orders with endpoints. A chaining calculus provides a basis for efficient theorem proving.

1 Introduction

Fuzzy logic formalizes reasoning in the context of vague (imprecise) information. (See the introduction of [21].) Automated reasoning in first order fuzzy logic(s) is a big and important challenge. Among the three fundamental fuzzy logics — Lukasiewicz logic L, Product logic P, and Gödel logic G_∞ — only G_∞ (also called "intuitionistic fuzzy logic"[26]) is recursively axiomatizable (see [21]). In fact, even Gödel logic is incomplete if either certain "0-1-relativizations" are added to the language (see [4]) or the topological structure of the truth value is changed (see [8]). In any case, in contrast to propositional logics, efficient proof search at the (general) first order level seems to be beyond the current state of the art, if possible at all. Thus it is reasonable to consider natural, non-trivial fragments.

Here we focus on the *prenex* fragment of $G^{\triangle}_{\infty}$; i.e., G_∞ enriched by the relativisation operator $\triangle$. $\triangle$ allows to make "fuzzy" statements "crisp" by mapping $\triangle P$ to the distinguished truth value 1 if the value of P equals 1, and to 0 otherwise. (See [4,11] and Section 2, below, for more information about $\triangle$.)

We demonstrate (in Section 3) that Herbrand's Theorem holds for $G^{\triangle}_{\infty}$. This has important consequences not only from a theoretical point of view, but also for automated proof search. Indeed, we will use Herbrand's Theorem to show (in Section 5) that all prenex formulas P from $G^{\triangle}_{\infty}$ can be translated faithfully and efficiently (in linear time) into corresponding sets of "order clauses". The latter are classical clauses with predicate symbols $<$ and $\leq$ interpreted as total dense orders (strict and reflexive, respectively). "Chaining calculi" for efficient deduction in such a context have been introduced (among others) in [13,14]. We will focus on one of these calculi (in Sections 6) and argue (in Section 7) that it is a suitable basis for handling translated formulas from prenex $G^{\triangle}_{\infty}$; in particular for the *monadic* fragment of prenex $G^{\triangle}_{\infty}$, which we will also show to be undecidable. See [20] for another approach applying chaining techniques to deduction in many-valued logics.

* Partly supported by the Austrian Science Fund under grant P–12652 MAT

** Research supported by EC Marie Curie fellowship HPMF–CT–1999–00301

R. Nieuwenhuis and A. Voronkov (Eds.): LPAR 2001, LNAI 2250, pp. 201–216, 2001.

Another consequence of Herbrand's Theorem for $G_\infty^\triangle$ is the existence of a "chain normal form" for prenex formulas. This is investigated in Section 4.

2 Preliminaries

First-order Gödel logics G_∞, sometimes also called intuitionistic fuzzy logic [26] or Dummett's *LC* (eg. in [1,19], referring to [16]), arises from intuitionistic logic by adding the axiom of linearity $(P \supset Q) \vee (Q \supset P)$ and the axioms $\forall x(P(x) \vee Q^{(x)}) \supset (\forall x P(x)) \vee Q^{(x)}$ and $\exists x(P(x) \vee Q^{(x)}) \supset (\exists x P(x)) \vee Q^{(x)}$ ($\vee$-shift), where the notation $A^{(x)}$ indicates that x does not occur free in A. Semantically Gödel logic is viewed as infinite-valued logic with the real interval $[0,1]$ as set of truth values[1] .

An *interpretation* $\mathcal{I}$ consists of a non-empty *domain* D and a *valuation function* $\mathrm{val}_\mathcal{I}$ that maps constants and object variables to elements of D and n-ary function symbols to functions from D^n into D. $\mathrm{val}_\mathcal{I}$ extends in the usual way to a function mapping all terms of the language to an element of the domain. Moreover, $\mathrm{val}_\mathcal{I}$ maps every n-ary predicate symbol p to a fuzzy relation, i.e., a function from D^n into $[0,1]$. The truth-value of an atomic formula (*atom*) $A = p(t_1, \ldots, t_n)$ is thus defined as

$$\mathrm{val}_\mathcal{I}(A) = \mathrm{val}_\mathcal{I}(p)(\mathrm{val}_\mathcal{I}(t_1), \ldots, \mathrm{val}_\mathcal{I}(t_n)).$$

For the truth constants $\bot$ and $\top$ we have $\mathrm{val}_\mathcal{I}(\bot) = 0$ and $\mathrm{val}_\mathcal{I}(\top) = 1$.

The semantics of propositional connectives is given by

$$\mathrm{val}_\mathcal{I}(P \supset Q) = \begin{cases} 1 & \text{if } \mathrm{val}_\mathcal{I}(P) \leq \mathrm{val}_\mathcal{I}(Q) \\ \mathrm{val}_\mathcal{I}(Q) & \text{otherwise}, \end{cases}$$
$$\mathrm{val}_\mathcal{I}(P \wedge Q) = \min(\mathrm{val}_\mathcal{I}(P), \mathrm{val}_\mathcal{I}(Q))$$
$$\mathrm{val}_\mathcal{I}(P \vee Q) = \max(\mathrm{val}_\mathcal{I}(P), \mathrm{val}_\mathcal{I}(Q)).$$

$\neg A$ and $A \leftrightarrow B$ are abbreviations for $A \supset \bot$ and $(A \supset B) \wedge (B \supset A)$, respectively.

To assist a concise formulation of the semantics of quantifiers we define the *distribution* of a formula P and a free variable x with respect to an interpretation $\mathcal{I}$ as $\mathrm{Distr}_\mathcal{I}(P(x)) \stackrel{\text{def}}{=} \{\mathrm{val}_{\mathcal{I}'}(P(x)) \mid \mathcal{I}' \sim_x \mathcal{I}\}$, where $\mathcal{I}' \sim_x \mathcal{I}$ means that $\mathcal{I}'$ is exactly as $\mathcal{I}$ with the possible exception of the domain element assigned to x. The semantics of quantifiers is given by the infimum and supremum of the corresponding distribution:

$$\mathrm{val}_\mathcal{I}((\forall x)P(x)) = \inf \mathrm{Distr}_\mathcal{I}(P(x)) \quad \mathrm{val}_\mathcal{I}((\exists x)P(x)) = \sup \mathrm{Distr}_\mathcal{I}(P(x)).$$

Following [4] we extend G_∞ with the "projection modalities" $\triangledown$ and $\triangle$:

$$\mathrm{val}_\mathcal{I}(\triangledown P) = \begin{cases} 1 & \text{if } \mathrm{val}_\mathcal{I}(P) = 0 \\ 0 & \text{if } \mathrm{val}_\mathcal{I}(P) \neq 0 \end{cases} \qquad \mathrm{val}_\mathcal{I}(\triangle P) = \begin{cases} 1 & \text{if } \mathrm{val}_\mathcal{I}(P) = 1 \\ 0 & \text{if } \mathrm{val}_\mathcal{I}(P) \neq 1 \end{cases}$$

A formula P is called *valid* in $G_\infty^\triangle$ — we write: $\models_{G_\infty^\triangle} P$ — if $\mathrm{val}_\mathcal{I}(P) = 1$ for all interpretations $\mathcal{I}$.

Whereas $\triangledown P$ can already be defined in G_∞ as $\neg P$, the extension including $\triangle$, called $G_\infty^\triangle$ here, is strictly more expressive. $\triangle$ allows to recover classical reasoning inside "fuzzy reasoning" in a very simple and natural manner: If all atoms are prefixed

[1] For more information about Gödel logic—its winding history, importance, variants, alternative semantics and proof systems—see, e.g., [1,2,4,5,7,8,9,10,11,12,16,17,18,21,22,26].

by $\triangle$ then $G^{\triangle}_{\infty}$ coincides with classical logic. However, the expressive power of $\triangle$ goes much beyond this. In particular, observe that $\triangle\exists x P(x) \supset \exists x \triangle P(x)$ is not valid in $G^{\triangle}_{\infty}$. In fact, as shown in [4], $G^{\triangle}_{\infty}$ is not even recursively axiomatizable if a certain "relativization operator" is present. (The recursive axiomatizability of $G^{\triangle}_{\infty}$ itself still seems to be an open problem; compare [4].) This motivates the interest in fragments of $G^{\triangle}_{\infty}$ in the context of effective theorem proving. A natural (syntactically simple) and non-trivial (see below) fragment of $G^{\triangle}_{\infty}$ is *prenex* $G^{\triangle}_{\infty}$, i.e., all quantifiers in a formula are assumed to occur at the left hand side of the formula.

Remark 1. Whereas the prenex fragment of intuitionistic logic is PSPACE-complete [15], prenex $G^{\triangle}_{\infty}$ is undecidable. In fact, we will show in Section 7 that prenex $G^{\triangle}_{\infty}$ is already undecidable for signatures with only *monadic* predicate symbols and no function symbols. On the other hand — like in intuitionistic logic — quantifiers cannot be shifted arbitrarily in G_{∞} and $G^{\triangle}_{\infty}$. In other words, arbitrary formulas cannot be reduced to provably equivalent prenex formulas (in contrast to classical logic).

3 Herbrand's Theorem

In this section we show how to effectively associate with each prenex formula P of $G^{\triangle}_{\infty}$ a propositional (variable free) formula P^* which is valid if and only if P is valid.

Definition 2. *Let* $\mathsf{Q}_1 y_1 \ldots \mathsf{Q}_n y_n P$*, with* $\mathsf{Q}_i \in \{\forall, \exists\}$ *be a (prenex) formula, where* P *is quantifier free. Its* Skolem form*, denoted by* $\exists \overline{x} P^F(\overline{x})$[2]*, is obtained by rewriting* $\exists \overline{z} \forall u Q(\overline{z}, u)$ *to* $\exists \overline{z} Q(\overline{z}, f(\overline{z}))$ *as often as possible.*

Lemma 3. *Let* P *be a quantifier free formula:*

$$\models_{G^{\triangle}_{\infty}} \mathsf{Q}_1 y_1 \ldots \mathsf{Q}_n y_n P(y_1, \ldots, y_n) \;\Rightarrow\; \models_{G^{\triangle}_{\infty}} \exists \overline{x} P^F(\overline{x}).$$

Proof. Follows from the usual laws of quantification. □

Let P be a formula. The *Herbrand universe* $U(P)$ of P is the set of all *ground* terms (those with no variables) which can be constructed from the set of function symbols occurring in P. To prevent $U(P)$ from being finite or empty we add a constant and a function symbol of positive arity if no such symbols appear in P. The *Herbrand base* $\mathcal{B}(P)$ is the set of atoms constructed from the predicate symbols in P and the terms of the Herbrand universe. A *Herbrand expansion* of P is a disjunction of instances of P where free variables are replaced with terms in $U(P)$.

Remark 4. We make use of the fact that the truth-value of any formula P of $G^{\triangle}_{\infty}$ under a given interpretation only depends on the ordering of the respective values of atoms occurring in P.

Lemma 5. *Let* P *be a quantifier-free formula. If* $\models_{G^{\triangle}_{\infty}} \exists \overline{x} P(\overline{x})$ *then there exist tuples* $\overline{t_1}, \ldots \overline{t_n}$ *of terms in* $U(P)$*, such that* $\models_{G^{\triangle}_{\infty}} \bigvee_{i=1}^{n} P(\overline{t_i})$.

[2] The notation hides the fact that the Skolem form also depends on the quantifier prefix. However, below, the context will always provide the relevant information.

Proof. Let $A_1, A_2, \ldots$ be a non-repetitive enumeration of (the infinite set) $\mathcal{B}(P)$. We construct a "semantic tree" T; i.e., a systematic representation of all possible order types of interpretations. T is a rooted tree whose nodes appear at levels. Each node at level ℓ is labelled with an expression, called *constraint*, of form

$$c_\ell^\pi \stackrel{\text{def}}{=} 0 \bowtie_0 A_{\pi(1)} \bowtie_1 \ldots \bowtie_{\ell-1} A_{\pi(\ell)} \bowtie_\ell 1,$$

where $\bowtie$ is either $=$ or $<$ and π is a permutation of $\{1, \ldots, \ell\}$. We say that an interpretation $\mathcal{I}$ of $P(\overline{x})$ *fulfills* the constraint c_ℓ^π if

$$0 \bowtie_0 \text{val}_\mathcal{I}(A_{\pi(1)}) \bowtie_1 \ldots \bowtie_{\ell-1} \text{val}_\mathcal{I}(A_{\pi(\ell)}) \bowtie_\ell 1$$

holds. We say that the constraint $c_{\ell+1}^{\pi'} \stackrel{\text{def}}{=} 0 \bowtie_0 A_{\pi'(1)} \bowtie_1 \ldots \bowtie_\ell A_{\pi'(\ell+1)} \bowtie_{\ell+1} 1$ *extends* c_ℓ^π if every interpretation fulfilling $c_{\ell+1}^{\pi'}$ also fulfills c_ℓ^π.

T is constructed inductively as follows:

- The root of T is at level 0 and is labelled with the constraint $0 < 1$.
- Let ν be a node at level ℓ with label c_ℓ^π. If for all interpretations $\mathcal{I}$ that fulfill c_ℓ^π we have $\text{val}_\mathcal{I}(P(\overline{t})) = 1$ for some instance $P(\overline{t})$ of $P(\overline{x})$, where the atoms of $P(\overline{t})$ are among $A_1, \ldots, A_\ell$, then ν is a leaf node of T. Otherwise, for each constraint $c_{\ell+1}^{\pi'}$ that extends c_ℓ^π a successor node ν' labelled with this constraint is appended to ν (at level $\ell + 1$).

Observe that for all interpretations $\mathcal{I}$ of $\mathcal{B}(P)$ there is branch of T such that $\mathcal{I}$ fulfills all constraints at all nodes of this branch. Two cases arise:

1. T is finite. Let $\nu_1, \ldots, \nu_m$ be the leaf nodes of T. Then $\models_{\text{G}_\infty^\triangle} \bigvee_{i=1}^m P(\overline{t_i})$, where $P(\overline{t_i})$ is an instance of $P(\overline{x})$ such that $\text{val}_\mathcal{I}(P(\overline{t_i})) = 1$ for all interpretations $\mathcal{I}$ that fulfill the constraint at ν_i.
2. T is infinite. By König's lemma, T has an infinite branch. This implies that there is an interpretation $\mathcal{I}$ such that $\text{val}_\mathcal{I}(P(\overline{t_i})) < 1$ for every tuple $\overline{t_i}$ of terms of $U(P)$. Now we use the following

   Claim. For every propositional formula P of $\text{G}_\infty^\triangle$ and interpretation $\mathcal{I}$ such that $\text{val}_\mathcal{I}(P) < 1$, one can find an interpretation $\mathcal{I}^c$ such that $\text{val}_{\mathcal{I}^c}(P) < c$, for an arbitrary constant $0 < c < 1$.

   The claim is easily proved by structural induction on P. It follows that there is an interpretation $\mathcal{I}'$ with $\text{val}_{\mathcal{I}'}(\exists\overline{x}P(\overline{x})) < 1$. This contradicts the assumption that $\models_{\text{G}_\infty^\triangle} \exists\overline{x}P(\overline{x})$. □

The following lemma establishes sufficient conditions for a logic to allow *reverse Skolemization*. By this we mean the re-introduction of quantifiers in Herbrand expansions. Here, by a *logic* $\mathcal{L}$ we mean a set of formulas that is closed under modus ponens, generalization and substitutions (of both formulas and terms). We call a formula P *valid* in $\mathcal{L}$ — and write: $\models_\mathcal{L} P$ — if $P \in \mathcal{L}$.

Lemma 6. *Let $\mathcal{L}$ be a logic satisfying the following properties:*

1. $\models_\mathcal{L} Q \vee P \Rightarrow \models_\mathcal{L} P \vee Q$ *(commutativity of* $\vee$*)*
2. $\models_\mathcal{L} (Q \vee P) \vee R \Rightarrow \models_\mathcal{L} Q \vee (P \vee R)$ *(associativity of* $\vee$*)*
3. $\models_\mathcal{L} Q \vee P \vee P \Rightarrow \models_\mathcal{L} Q \vee P$ *(idempotency of* $\vee$*)*
4. $\models_\mathcal{L} P(y) \Rightarrow \models_\mathcal{L} \forall x[P(x)]^{(y)}$
5. $\models_\mathcal{L} P(t) \Rightarrow \models_\mathcal{L} \exists x P(x)$

6. $\models_{\mathcal{L}} \forall x(P(x) \vee Q^{(x)}) \Rightarrow \models_{\mathcal{L}} (\forall x P(x)) \vee Q^{(x)}$
7. $\models_{\mathcal{L}} \exists x(P(x) \vee Q^{(x)}) \Rightarrow \models_{\mathcal{L}} (\exists x P(x)) \vee Q^{(x)}$.

Let $\exists \overline{x} P^F(\overline{x})$ be the Skolem form of $\mathsf{Q}_1 y_1 \ldots \mathsf{Q}_n y_n P(y_1, \ldots, y_n)$. For all tuples of terms $\overline{t_1}, \ldots, \overline{t_m}$ of the Herbrand universe of $P^F(\overline{x})$

$$\models_{\mathcal{L}} \bigvee_{i=1}^{m} P^F(\overline{t_i}) \Rightarrow \models_{\mathcal{L}} \mathsf{Q}_1 y_1 \ldots \mathsf{Q}_n y_n P(y_1, \ldots, y_n).$$

Proof. To re-introduce quantifiers we proceed as follows. Every instance of a Skolem term $s = f(t'_1, \ldots, t'_k)$ in $\bigvee_{i=1}^{m} P^F(\overline{t_i})$ is replaced by a new variable x_s. We denote the resulting formula by $\bigvee_{i=1}^{m} P^F(\overline{t_i})[\overline{s}/\overline{x_s}]$. Let $\mathcal{V}_{SK}$ be the set of such new variables. We define $x_s \leq x_t$ iff either s is a subterm of t or $s = f(t_1, \ldots, t_a)$ and $t = g(t'_1, \ldots, t'_b)$ and $a \leq b$.

Starting with the innermost quantifier occurrence Q_n we re-introduce all quantifiers in k steps from $k = n$ down to $k = 1$. We use $\overline{\mathsf{Q}}P_i^{(k)}$ to denote the result of applying the substitutions from step n down to $k+1$ to the disjunct $P^F(\overline{t_i})[\overline{s}/\overline{x_s}]$ and prefixing it with $\mathsf{Q}_{k+1} y_{k+1} \ldots \mathsf{Q}_n y_n$. m_k is the number of disjuncts remaining before step k is applied.

If $\mathsf{Q}_k y_k = \exists y_k$: Re-substitute y_k for the variable $z_s \in \mathcal{V}_{SK}$ that occurs in $\overline{\mathsf{Q}}P_j^{(k)}$ at the positions where s has replaced y_k in $P^F(\overline{t_j})$. By hypothesis 5 we obtain

$$\models_{\mathcal{L}} \exists y_k \Big(\bigvee_{i=1}^{i=j-1} \overline{\mathsf{Q}}P_i^{(k)} \vee \overline{\mathsf{Q}}P_j^{(k)}[y_k/z] \vee \bigvee_{i=j}^{i=m_k} \overline{\mathsf{Q}}P_i^{(k)} \Big)$$

By hypotheses 1, 2, and 7 one has

$$\models_{\mathcal{L}} \Big(\bigvee_{i=1}^{i=j-1} \overline{\mathsf{Q}}P_i^{(k)} \vee \exists y_k \overline{\mathsf{Q}}P_j^{(k)}[y_k/z] \vee \bigvee_{i=j}^{i=m_k} \overline{\mathsf{Q}}P_i^{(k)} \Big)$$

This is repeated for all m_k disjuncts until $\exists y_k$ is re-introduced everywhere.

If $\mathsf{Q}_k y_k = \forall y_k$: First eliminate redundant copies of identical disjuncts. This can be done by hypotheses 1, 2 and 3. Observe that, by the special form of Skolem terms, any *maximal* variable $z_s \in \mathcal{V}_{SK}$ can now occur only in a single disjunct $\overline{\mathsf{Q}}P_j^{(k)}$. Analogously to the case above, we can apply hypotheses 1, 2, 4 and 6 to re-introduce Q_k and shift it to the appropriate disjunct to obtain:

$$\models_{\mathcal{L}} \Big(\bigvee_{i=1}^{i=j-1} \overline{\mathsf{Q}}P_i^{(k)} \vee \forall y_k \overline{\mathsf{Q}}P_j^{(k)}[y_k/z] \vee \bigvee_{i=j}^{i=m_k} \overline{\mathsf{Q}}P_i^{(k)} \Big)$$

This is repeated for all m_k disjuncts until $\forall y_k$ is re-introduced everywhere.

Finally, $\models_{\mathcal{L}} \mathsf{Q}_1 y_1 \ldots \mathsf{Q}_n y_n P(y_1, \ldots, y_n)$ follows from contracting identical disjuncts (i.e., applying hypotheses 1, 2, and 3). □

Corollary 7. *Let $\exists \overline{x} P^F(\overline{x})$ be the Skolem form of $\mathsf{Q}_1 y_1 \ldots \mathsf{Q}_n y_n P(y_1, \ldots, y_n)$. For all tuples $\overline{t_1}, \ldots \overline{t_m}$ of terms of the Herbrand universe of $P^F(\overline{x})$:*

$$\models_{\mathsf{G}_\infty^\Delta} \bigvee_{i=1}^{m} P^F(\overline{t_i}) \Rightarrow \models_{\mathsf{G}_\infty^\Delta} \mathsf{Q}_1 y_1 \ldots \mathsf{Q}_n y_n P(y_1, \ldots, y_n).$$

Corollary 8. *Let P be a quantifier free formula of $\mathrm{G}_\infty^\triangle$:*

$$\models_{\mathrm{G}_\infty^\triangle} \exists\overline{x}P^F(\overline{x}) \;\Rightarrow\; \models_{\mathrm{G}_\infty^\triangle} \mathrm{Q}_1y_1\ldots\mathrm{Q}_ny_nP(y_1,\ldots,y_n).$$

Proof.

$\models_{\mathrm{G}_\infty^\triangle} \exists\overline{x}P^F(\overline{x})$

$\Rightarrow \models_{\mathrm{G}_\infty^\triangle} \bigvee_{i=1}^n P^F(\overline{t_i})$ for appropriate $\overline{t_1},\ldots,\overline{t_m}$ by Lemma 5

$\Rightarrow \models_{\mathrm{G}_\infty^\triangle} \mathrm{Q}_1y_1\ldots\mathrm{Q}_ny_nP(y_1,\ldots,y_n)$ by Corollary 7 □

Proposition 9. *For all formulas P and Q of $\mathrm{G}_\infty^\triangle$*

1. $\models_{\mathrm{G}_\infty^\triangle} P \Leftrightarrow \models_{\mathrm{G}_\infty^\triangle} \triangle P$
2. $\models_{\mathrm{G}_\infty^\triangle} \triangle(P\vee Q) \Leftrightarrow \models_{\mathrm{G}_\infty^\triangle} (\triangle P\vee\triangle Q)$.

Theorem 10. *Let P be a quantifier-free formula of $\mathrm{G}_\infty^\triangle$ and $\mathrm{Q}_i\in\{\forall,\exists\}$*

$$\models_{\mathrm{G}_\infty^\triangle} \mathrm{Q}_1y_1\ldots\mathrm{Q}_ny_nP(y_1,\ldots,y_n)$$

if and only if there exist tuples $\overline{t_1},\ldots\overline{t_m}$ of terms of the Herbrand universe of $\exists\overline{x}P(\overline{x})$, such that

$$\models_{\mathrm{G}_\infty^\triangle} \bigvee_{i=1}^m \triangle P^F(\overline{t_i}).$$

Proof.

$(\Rightarrow)$ $\models_{\mathrm{G}_\infty^\triangle} \mathrm{Q}_1y_1\ldots\mathrm{Q}_ny_nP(y_1,\ldots,y_n)$

$\Rightarrow \models_{\mathrm{G}_\infty^\triangle} \exists\overline{y}P^F(\overline{y})$ by Lemma 3

$\Rightarrow \models_{\mathrm{G}_\infty^\triangle} \bigvee_{i=1}^m P^F(\overline{t_i})$ by Lemma 5

$\Rightarrow \models_{\mathrm{G}_\infty^\triangle} \triangle(\bigvee_{i=1}^m P^F(\overline{t_i}))$ by Proposition 9.1

$\Rightarrow \models_{\mathrm{G}_\infty^\triangle} \bigvee_{i=1}^m \triangle P^F(\overline{t_i})$ by Proposition 9.2

$(\Leftarrow)$ $\models_{\mathrm{G}_\infty^\triangle} \bigvee_{i=1}^m \triangle P^F(\overline{t_i})$

$\Rightarrow \models_{\mathrm{G}_\infty^\triangle} \triangle(\bigvee_{i=1}^m P^F(\overline{t_i}))$ by Proposition 9.2

$\Rightarrow \models_{\mathrm{G}_\infty^\triangle} \bigvee_{i=1}^m P^F(\overline{t_i})$ by Proposition 9.1

$\Rightarrow \models_{\mathrm{G}_\infty^\triangle} \mathrm{Q}_1y_1\ldots\mathrm{Q}_ny_nP(y_1,\ldots,y_n)$ by Corollary 7 □

Remark 11. For G_∞ (without $\triangle$), an alternative proof of Herbrand's theorem can be obtained using the analytic calculus *HIF* ("Hypersequent calculus for Intuitionistic Fuzzy logic") introduced in [12].

Corollary 12. *Let P be a quantifier-free formula of $\mathrm{G}_\infty^\triangle$:*

$$\models_{\mathrm{G}_\infty^\triangle} \mathrm{Q}_1y_1\ldots\mathrm{Q}_ny_nP(y_1,\ldots,y_n) \quad\Leftrightarrow\quad \models_{\mathrm{G}_\infty^\triangle} \mathrm{Q}_1y_1\ldots\mathrm{Q}_ny_n \triangle P(y_1,\ldots,y_n).$$

Proof.

$\models_{\mathrm{G}_\infty^\triangle} \mathrm{Q}_1y_1\ldots\mathrm{Q}_ny_nP(y_1,\ldots,y_n)$

$\Leftrightarrow \models_{\mathrm{G}_\infty^\triangle} \bigvee_{i=1}^m \triangle P^F(\overline{t_i})$ for appropriate $\overline{t_1}\ldots\overline{t_n}$ by Theorem 10

$\Leftrightarrow \models_{\mathrm{G}_\infty^\triangle} \mathrm{Q}_1y_1\ldots\mathrm{Q}_ny_n \triangle P(y_1,\ldots,y_n)$ by Corollary 7 and Lemma 3 □

4 A Chain Normal Form for Prenex $G_\infty^\triangle$

We define a normal form for formulas P of prenex $G_\infty^\triangle$, that is based on the fact that the truth-value of P under a given interpretation only depends on the ordering of the respective values of atoms occurring in P. We exploit the fact that the corresponding order relation is expressible in $G_\infty^\triangle$. (This is not true for G_∞.) More formally, we use

$$\begin{array}{lll} P \lessdot Q & \text{as an abbreviation for} & \neg\triangle(Q \supset P), \text{ and} \\ P \equiv_\triangle Q & \text{as an abbreviation for} & \triangle(P \supset Q) \wedge \triangle(Q \supset P). \end{array}$$

These formulas express strict linear order and equality, respectively, in the following sense. For every interpretation $\mathcal{I}$ of $G_\infty^\triangle$ one has

$$\begin{array}{lll} \mathrm{val}_\mathcal{I}(P \lessdot Q) & \text{iff} & \mathrm{val}_\mathcal{I}(P) < \mathrm{val}_\mathcal{I}(Q), \text{ and} \\ \mathrm{val}_\mathcal{I}(P \equiv_\triangle Q) & \text{iff} & \mathrm{val}_\mathcal{I}(P) = \mathrm{val}_\mathcal{I}(Q). \end{array}$$

Definition 13. *Let P be a quantifier-free formula of $G_\infty^\triangle$ and $A_1, \dots, A_n$ the atoms occurring in P except $\bot$ and $\top$. A $\triangle$-chain over P is any formula of the form*

$$(\bot \bowtie_0 A_{\pi(1)}) \wedge (A_{\pi(1)} \bowtie_1 A_{\pi(2)}) \wedge \cdots \wedge (A_{\pi(n-1)} \bowtie_{n-1} A_{\pi(n)}) \wedge (A_{\pi(n)} \bowtie_n \top)$$

where π is a permutation of $\{1, \dots, n\}$, $\bowtie_i$ is either $\lessdot$ or $\equiv_\triangle$, and at least one of the $\bowtie_i$'s stands for $\lessdot$.

Every $\triangle$-chain describes a possible ordering of the values of atoms of P. By $\xi(P)$ we denote the set of all $\triangle$-chains over P. For any $C \in \xi(P)$, we define

$$\{P\}^C \stackrel{\text{def}}{=} \begin{cases} \top & \text{if } \mathrm{val}_\mathcal{I}(P) = 1 \\ \bot & \text{if } \mathrm{val}_\mathcal{I}(P) < 1 \end{cases}$$

for all interpretations $\mathcal{I}$ that satisfy the ordering conditions expressed by C. Observe that $\{P\}^C$ is always defined.

Proposition 14. *For all quantifier free formulas P, Q and F of $G_\infty^\triangle$*

$$\models_{G_\infty^\triangle} P \leftrightarrow Q \Rightarrow \models_{G_\infty^\triangle} F[P] \leftrightarrow F[Q],$$

where $F[Q]$ denotes the formula arising from $F[P]$ by replacing some occurrences of the subformula P by Q.

Lemma 15. *For every quantifier free formula P and $\triangle$-chain $C \in \xi(P)$*

$$\models_{G_\infty^\triangle} C \supset (\triangle P \leftrightarrow \{P\}^C).$$

Proof. By induction on the structure of P using the following tautologies of $G_\infty^\triangle$:

$$\begin{array}{ll} (P \lessdot Q) \supset \triangle((P \supset Q) \leftrightarrow \top) & (Q \lessdot P) \supset \triangle((P \supset Q) \leftrightarrow Q) \\ (P \equiv_\triangle Q) \supset \triangle((P \supset Q) \leftrightarrow \top) & (P \lessdot Q) \supset \triangle((P \vee Q) \leftrightarrow Q) \\ (Q \lessdot P) \supset \triangle((P \vee Q) \leftrightarrow P) & (Q \equiv_\triangle P) \supset \triangle((P \vee Q) \leftrightarrow P) \\ (P \lessdot Q) \supset \triangle((P \wedge Q) \leftrightarrow P) & (Q \lessdot P) \supset \triangle((P \wedge Q) \leftrightarrow Q) \\ (Q \equiv_\triangle P) \supset \triangle((P \wedge Q) \leftrightarrow P) & (P \lessdot \top) \supset \triangle(\triangle P \leftrightarrow \bot) \\ (P \equiv_\triangle \top) \supset \triangle(\triangle P \leftrightarrow \top) & \end{array}$$

as well as $\models_{G_\infty^\triangle} \triangle(P \leftrightarrow Q) \supset (\triangle P \leftrightarrow \triangle Q)$ together with Proposition 14. □

Lemma 16. *For every quantifier free formula P and $C \in \xi(P)$*

$$\models_{G^{\triangle}_{\infty}} (C \wedge \triangle P) \leftrightarrow (C \wedge \{A\}^{C}).$$

Proof. It is easy to check that $\models_{G^{\triangle}_{\infty}} (P_1 \wedge P_2) \wedge (P_1 \supset (P_2 \leftrightarrow P_3)) \supset (P_1 \wedge P_3)$. We instantiate the above formula by setting $P_1 = C$, $P_2 = \triangle P$ and $P_3 = \{P\}^C$. By using Lemma 15 we obtain $\models_{G^{\triangle}_{\infty}} (C \wedge \triangle P) \supset (C \wedge \{P\}^C)$. The converse implication follows analogously. □

Theorem 17. *For every quantifier free formula P there exists $\Gamma(P) \subseteq \xi(P)$ such that*

$$\models_{G^{\triangle}_{\infty}} \triangle P \leftrightarrow \bigvee_{C \in \Gamma(P)} C$$

Proof. First note that $\models_{G^{\triangle}_{\infty}} \bigvee_{C \in \xi(P)} C$. Therefore we have

$$\models_{G^{\triangle}_{\infty}} \triangle P \leftrightarrow [(\bigvee_{C \in \xi(P)} C) \wedge \triangle P].$$

By moving $\triangle P$ into the disjunction and using Lemma 16, one obtains

$$\models_{G^{\triangle}_{\infty}} \triangle P \leftrightarrow [\bigvee_{C \in \xi(P)} (C \wedge \{P\}^C]$$

The claim follows by Proposition 14 since for every $C \in \xi(P))$ we have either $\models_{G^{\triangle}_{\infty}} (C \wedge \{P\}^C) \leftrightarrow (C \wedge \top)$ or $\models_{G^{\triangle}_{\infty}} (C \wedge \{P\}^C) \leftrightarrow (C \wedge \bot)$. □

Remark 18. A related normal form has been introduced for propositional Gödel logic without $\triangle$ in [11]. There, the total order of the truth values is expressed using the formulas $A \leftrightarrow B$ and $A \prec B$, where the latter abbreviates $(A \supset B) \wedge ((B \supset A) \supset A)$.

As a corollary to this normal form theorem and Herbrand's theorem (Theorem 10) we obtain:

Corollary 19. *Let P be a quantifier-free formula of $G^{\triangle}_{\infty}$. There exist tuples of terms $\overline{t_1}, \ldots, \overline{t_n}$ of the Herbrand universe of P,*

$$\models_{G^{\triangle}_{\infty}} Q_1 y_1 \ldots Q_n y_n P(y_1, \ldots, y_n) \Leftrightarrow \models \bigvee_{i=1}^{n} \bigvee_{C \in \Gamma(P^F)} C[^{\overline{t_i}}/_{\overline{y_i}}]$$

where $C[^{\overline{t_i}}/_{\overline{y_i}}]$ is the chain obtained by substituting $\overline{t_i}$ for $\overline{y_i}$.

5 Translation into Order Clauses

The chain normal form for prenex formulas P of $G^{\triangle}_{\infty}$, introduced in Section 4 above, can be used to reduce the validity problem for P into the problem of detecting unsatisfiability of a corresponding set of "order clauses" with respect to the (classical) theory of dense total orders with endpoints 0 and 1. However, the computation of the chain normal form is quite inefficient in general. Therefore we use properties of $\triangle$ to introduce also a "definitional normal form", similar to the one for classical or intuitionistic logic (see, e.g., [6]).

Definition 20. *For any formula F of form $F_1 \circ F_2$, where $\circ \in \{\wedge, \vee, \supset\}$, let*

$$\mathrm{df}(F) \stackrel{\mathrm{def}}{=} [p_F(\overline{x}) \equiv_{\triangle} (p_{F_1}(\overline{x_1}) \circ p_{F_2}(\overline{x_2}))]$$

where p_F, p_{F_1}, p_{F_2} are new predicate symbols and $\overline{x}, \overline{x_1}, \overline{x_2}$ are the tuples of variables occurring in F, F_1, F_2, respectively. If F is of form $\triangle F_1$ then

$$\mathrm{df}(F) \stackrel{\mathrm{def}}{=} [p_F(\overline{x}) \equiv_{\triangle} \triangle p_{F_1}(\overline{x_1})].$$

If F is atomic then $p_F(\overline{x})$ is used as an alternative denotation for $F(\overline{x})$.

For any quantifier free formula P the definitional normal form *is defined as*

$$\mathrm{DEF}(P) \stackrel{\mathrm{def}}{=} [(\bigwedge_{F \in \mathrm{nasf}(P)} \mathrm{df}(F)) \supset \triangle p_P(\overline{x})]$$

where $\mathrm{nasf}(P)$ *denotes the set of all non-atomic subformulas of P, $\overline{x}$ is the tuple of variables occurring in P, and p_P is a new predicate symbol.*

Remark 21. Certain optimizations, using tautologies of $G^{\triangle}_{\infty}$, will lead to shorter definitional normal forms in general. However, in any case the logical complexity (i.e. the number of connectives) of $\mathrm{DEF}(P)$ is *linear* in the logical complexity of P.

Lemma 22. *For all quantifier free formulas P of $G^{\triangle}_{\infty}$:*

$$\models_{G^{\triangle}_{\infty}} \exists \overline{x} P(\overline{x}) \;\Leftrightarrow\; \models_{G^{\triangle}_{\infty}} \exists \overline{x} \mathrm{DEF}(P(\overline{x})).$$

Proof. By Corollary 12, $\models_{G^{\triangle}_{\infty}} \exists \overline{x} P(\overline{x})$ iff $\models_{G^{\triangle}_{\infty}} \exists \overline{x} \triangle P(\overline{x})$. For every interpretation $\mathcal{I}$: $\mathrm{val}_{\mathcal{I}}(A \equiv_{\triangle} B) = 1$ if $\mathrm{val}_{\mathcal{I}}(A) = \mathrm{val}_{\mathcal{I}}(B)$ and $\mathrm{val}_{\mathcal{I}}(A \equiv_{\triangle} B) = 0$, otherwise. Consequently, the proof proceeds exactly as in the case for classical logic (see [24,6]). I.e., for all non-atomic quantifier free formulas $F(\overline{x})$, one can show by induction on the complexity of F that $\mathrm{val}_{\mathcal{I}}(\mathrm{df}(F(\overline{x}))) = 1$ iff $\mathrm{val}_{\mathcal{I}}(F(\overline{x})) = \mathrm{val}_{\mathcal{I}}(p_F(\overline{x}))$. □

We translate prenex $G^{\triangle}_{\infty}$-formulas into sets of clauses of the following form.

Definition 23. *Let the sign $\lhd$ stands for either $<$ or $\leq$. An* inequality *is an expression of form $s \lhd t$, where $s, t \in T(\mathbf{F}, \mathcal{X})$, i.e., the set of all terms over function symbols $\mathbf{F}$ (including constants) and variables $\mathcal{X}$. An* (order) clause *is a finite set of inequalities.*

Definition 24. *By a* dense total order $\mathcal{O}$ *we mean a (classical) interpretation of the signature* $<$, $\leq$, *and* $\mathbf{F}$, *where* $<$ *is interpreted as strict and dense total (linear) order over the elements assigned to* $T(\mathbf{F}, \mathcal{X})$ *and* $\leq$ *is interpreted as the reflexive closure of* $<$. *If also the* endpoint *axioms* $\forall x(0 \leq x)$, $\forall x(x \leq 1)$, *and* $0 < 1$ *are satisfied we call* $\mathcal{O}$ *a* DTOE*-model. A set of order clauses* $\mathcal{S}$ *is* DTOE-satisfiable *if* $\mathcal{S}$ *has a dense total order with endpoints* 0 *and* 1, *respectively, as model.*

In the following we also allow equalities $s = t$ to occur in clauses. However, a clause of form $\{s = t\} \cup C$ is considered here as an abbreviation for the two clauses $\{s \leq t\} \cup C$ and $\{t \leq s\} \cup C$.

Remark 25. In implementing the proof procedure, equalities can and should be handled more efficiently than indicated above. In particular, combinations of chaining and superposition along the line of [13,14] should be applied.

Definition 26. *We define sets of clauses that correspond to the various forms of formulas of type* $\mathrm{df}(F)$*:*

$$\mathrm{cl}(A \equiv_\triangle (B \wedge C)) \stackrel{\mathrm{def}}{=} \{\{A \leq B\}, \{A \leq C\}, \{A = B, A = C\}\}$$
$$\mathrm{cl}(A \equiv_\triangle (B \vee C)) \stackrel{\mathrm{def}}{=} \{\{B \leq A\}, \{C \leq A\}, \{A = B, A = C\}\}$$
$$\mathrm{cl}(A \equiv_\triangle (B \supset C)) \stackrel{\mathrm{def}}{=} \{\{1 \leq A, A = C\}, \{B \leq C, A = C\}, \{1 \leq A, C < B\}\}$$
$$\mathrm{cl}(A \equiv_\triangle \triangle B) \stackrel{\mathrm{def}}{=} \{\{A < 1, 1 \leq B\}, \{B < 1, 1 \leq A\}\}$$

where A, B *and* C *are atoms, considered as terms.*

The clause form *for formulas* $\exists \overline{x} P(\overline{x})$ *is given by*

$$\mathrm{CF}^{\mathrm{d}}(\exists \overline{x} P(\overline{x})) \stackrel{\mathrm{def}}{=} \{\{p_P(\overline{x}) < 1\}\} \cup \bigcup_{F \in \mathrm{nasf}(P)} \mathrm{cl}(\mathrm{df}(F))$$

To define the alternative clause normal form $\mathrm{CF}^{\mathrm{c}}(\exists \overline{x} P(\overline{x}))$ *based on chains, let* $[A \lessdot B]^{\#} \stackrel{\mathrm{def}}{=} \{B \leq A\}$ *and* $[A \equiv_\triangle B]^{\#} \stackrel{\mathrm{def}}{=} \{A < B, B < A\}$.

$$\mathrm{CF}^{\mathrm{c}}(\exists \overline{x} P(\overline{x})) \stackrel{\mathrm{def}}{=} \{\{ \bigcup_{A \bowtie_i B \; in \; C} [A \bowtie_i B]^{\#}\} \mid C \in \Gamma(P)\}$$

where $\Gamma(P)$ *is the subset of* $\xi(P)$ *given by Theorem 17.*

Lemma 27. *For every interpretation* $\mathcal{I}$ *there is a* DTOE*-model* $\mathcal{O}_\mathcal{I}$*, such that for all non-atomic* F*:* $val_\mathcal{I}(\mathrm{df}(F)) = 1$ *iff* $\mathcal{O}_\mathcal{I}$ *satisfies* $\mathrm{cl}(\mathrm{df}(F))$*; and vice versa.*

Proof. We only present the case for $F = [A \equiv_\triangle (B \wedge C)]$. The other cases are similar. We have:

$$\begin{aligned} \mathrm{val}_\mathcal{I}(A \equiv_\triangle (B \wedge C)) = 1 &\Leftrightarrow \mathrm{val}_\mathcal{I}(A) = \min\{\mathrm{val}_\mathcal{I}(B), \mathrm{val}_\mathcal{I}(C)\} \\ &\Leftrightarrow \mathrm{val}_\mathcal{I}(A) \leq \mathrm{val}_\mathcal{I}(B) \text{ and } \mathrm{val}_\mathcal{I}(A) \leq \mathrm{val}_\mathcal{I}(C) \text{ and} \\ &\quad\; (\mathrm{val}_\mathcal{I}(A) = \mathrm{val}_\mathcal{I}(B) \text{ or } \mathrm{val}_\mathcal{I}(A) = \mathrm{val}_\mathcal{I}(C)) \end{aligned}$$

Therefore $\mathcal{I}$ induces an DTOE-model $\mathcal{O}_\mathcal{I}$ satisfying the order clauses

$$\{A \leq B\}, \{A \leq C\}, \text{ and } \{A = B, A = C\}.$$

Conversely, every DTOE-model for this clause set induces an interpretation that evaluates $A \equiv_\triangle (B \wedge C)$ to 1. □

Theorem 28. *Any prenex formula* $Q_1 y_1 \ldots Q_n y_n P(y_1, \ldots, y_n)$ *of* $G_\infty^\triangle$ *is valid if and only if* $\mathrm{CF}^{\mathrm{d}}(\exists \overline{x} P^F(\overline{x}))$ *is* DTOE*-unsatisfiable.*

Proof. By Lemma 3 and Corollary 8 we have: $\models_{G_\infty^\triangle} Q_1 y_1 \ldots Q_n y_n P(y_1, \ldots, y_n)$ iff $\models_{G_\infty^\triangle} \exists \overline{x} P^F(\overline{x})$. By Lemma 22 we have: $\models_{G_\infty^\triangle} \exists \overline{x} P^F(\overline{x})$ iff $\models_{G_\infty^\triangle} \exists \overline{x} \mathrm{DEF}(P^F(\overline{x}))$. Since the conclusion as well as the conjuncts in the premise of $\mathrm{DEF}(P^F(\overline{x}))$ are prefixed by $\triangle$, those subformulas behave like in classical logic. Hence the validity problem can be dualized; i.e., $\exists \overline{x} \mathrm{DEF}(P^F(\overline{x}))$ is valid iff

$$\forall \overline{x} \neg \triangle p_P(\overline{x}) \wedge \bigwedge_{F \in \mathrm{nasf}(P)} \mathrm{df}(F)$$

is unsatisfiable. By Lemma 27 the latter is equivalent to the DTOE-unsatisfiability of $\mathrm{CF}^{\mathrm{d}}(\exists \overline{x} P^F(\overline{x}))$. □

Remark 29. By similar arguments Theorem 28 also holds for $\mathrm{CF}^{\mathrm{c}}(\exists \overline{x} P^F(\overline{x}))$.

6 Using an Ordered Chaining Calculus

In the previous sections, we have reduced the validity problem for prenex $G_\infty^\triangle$ to checking DTOE-unsatisfiability of certain sets of *order clauses*. Fortunately, efficient theorem proving for (various types of) order clauses has already received considerable attention in the literature; see [14,13] (and the references given there).

Some familiarity with basic notions from automated deduction, in particular the concept of a *most general unifier (mgu)* of two or more terms, is assumed in the following (see, e.g., [23].) We will identify a substitution σ with a set $\{x_1 \leftarrow t_1, \ldots, x_n \leftarrow t_n\}$ and define $codom(\sigma) = \{t_1, \ldots, t_n\}$.

We consider the following rules (cf. [13]) for order clauses:

Irreflexivity Resolution:

$$\frac{C \cup \{s < t\}}{C\sigma}$$

where σ is the mgu of s and t

(Factorized) Chaining:

$$\frac{C \cup \{u_1 \lhd_1 s_1, \ldots, u_m \lhd_m s_m\} \quad D \cup \{t_1 \lhd'_1 v_1, \ldots, t_n \lhd'_n v_n\}}{C\sigma \cup D\sigma \cup \{u_i\sigma \lhd_{i,j} v_j\sigma \mid 1 \le i \le m, 1 \le n\}}$$

where σ is the mgu of $s_1, \ldots, s_m, t_1, \ldots, t_n$ and $\lhd_{i,j}$ is $<$ if and only if either $\lhd_i$ is $<$ or $\lhd'_j$ is $<$. Moreover, $t_1\sigma$ occurs in $D\sigma$ only in inequalities $v \lhd t_1\sigma$.

These two rules constitute a refutationally complete inference system for the theory of all total orders in presence of set $\mathcal{E}q^{\mathrm{F}}$ of clauses

$$\{x_i < y_i, y_i < x_i \mid 1 \le i \le n\} \cup \{f(x_1, \ldots, x_n) \le f(y_1, \ldots, y_n)\}$$

where f ranges the set $\mathbf{F}$ of function symbols of the signature. Observe that, in translating a formula P from prenex $G_\infty^\triangle$ into a set of order clauses $\mathrm{CF^d}(P)$, we treat the predicate symbols of P as function symbols. Additional function symbols occur from Skolemization.

The inference system is not yet sufficiently restrictive for efficient proof search. We follow [13] and add conditions to the rules that refer to some complete reduction order $\succ$ (on the set of all terms). We write $s \not\preceq t$ if $\neg(s \succ t)$ and $s \neq t$; and "*t is basic in (clause) C*" if $t \lhd s \in C$ or $s \lhd t \in C$.

Maximality Condition for Irreflexivity Resolution: $s\sigma$ is a maximal term in $C\sigma$.
Maximality Condition for Chaining: (1) $u_i\sigma \not\preceq s_1\sigma$ for all $1 \leq i \leq n$, (2) $v_i\sigma \not\preceq t_1\sigma$ for all $1 \leq i \leq m$, (3) $u\sigma \not\preceq s_1\sigma$ for all terms u that are basic in C, and (4) $v\sigma \not\preceq t_1\sigma$ for all terms v that are basic in D.

For our purposes it is convenient to view the resulting inference system $\mathrm{MC}_\succ$ as a set operator.

Definition 30. *$\mathrm{MC}_\succ(\mathcal{S})$ is the set of all conclusions of Irreflexivity Resolution or Maximal Chaining where the premises are (variable renamed copies of) members of the set of clauses $\mathcal{S}$. Moreover, $\mathrm{MC}_\succ^0(\mathcal{S}) = \mathcal{S}$, $\mathrm{MC}_\succ^{i+1}(\mathcal{S}) = \mathrm{MC}_\succ(\mathrm{MC}_\succ^i(\mathcal{S})) \cup \mathrm{MC}_\succ^i(\mathcal{S})$, and $\mathrm{MC}_\succ^*(\mathcal{S}) = \bigcup_{i\geq 0} \mathrm{MC}_\succ^i(\mathcal{S})$.*

The set consisting of the three clauses $\{0 \leq x\}$, $\{x \leq 1\}$, and $\{0 < 1\}$, corresponding to the endpoint axioms, is called $\mathcal{E}p$. The set consisting of $\{y \leq x, d(x,y) < y\}$ and $\{y \leq x, x < d(x,y)\}$, corresponding to the usual density axiom, is called $\mathcal{D}o$.

The following completeness theorem follows directly from Theorem 2 of [13].

Theorem 31. *$\mathcal{S}$ has a dense total order with endpoints 0 and 1 as a model if and only if $\mathrm{MC}_\succ^*(\mathcal{S} \cup \mathcal{E}q^{\mathrm{F}} \cup \mathcal{E}p \cup \mathcal{D}o)$ does not contain the empty clause.*

Remark 32. Even more refined "chaining calculi" for handling orders have been defined by Bachmair and Ganzinger in [13,14]. However, $\mathrm{MC}_\succ$ turns out to be quite appropriate for our context. (In particular, since the problem of "variable chaining" does not occur for the sets of clauses considered here).

7 The Monadic Prenex Fragment

A formula is called *monadic* if all predicate symbols are monadic (unary) and no function symbols occur in it.

To support the claim that $\mathrm{MC}_\succ$ provides an efficient proof system for prenex $G_\infty^\triangle$, we conclude by investigating the special case of *monadic* formulas.

To appreciate the importance of this fragment, remember that monadic predicates are interpreted as fuzzy sets. We will show that $\mathrm{MC}_\succ$ allows to prevent the nesting of function symbols (beyond the level of the input set) in clauses derivable from chain-based clause normal forms of the Skolem form of a prenex and monadic formula.

To characterize the syntactic restrictions obeyed by clauses arising from translating prenex monadic formulas we need some additional notation.

From now on we assume that the set of function symbols $\mathbf{F}$ consists in the disjoint union $\mathbf{S} \cup \mathbf{P} \cup \{0, 1\} \cup \{d\}$, where $\mathbf{S}$ are the function symbols and constants arising from Skolemizing the original formula P, and $\mathbf{P}$ is the set of monadic predicate symbols occurring in P. We will distinguish the different types of function symbols syntactically by using lower case letters for symbols in $\mathbf{S}$ and upper case letters for symbols in $\mathbf{P}$. Moreover, we assume the set of variables $\mathcal{X}$ to be *stratified* in the following sense: $\mathcal{X}$ is the disjoint union $\biguplus_{1 \leq i \leq p} \mathcal{X}_i$, where each $\mathcal{X}_i$ is infinite and p is the maximal arity of function symbols in $\mathbf{F}$.

Definition 33. *We call a term* simple *if it is either a variable or a constant or of form* $f(x_1, \ldots, x_n)$ *where* $x_i \in \mathcal{X}_i$ *for* $1 \leq i \leq n$. *(We call terms of the latter type* stratified.*) A term is called* atom-like *if it is of form* $P(s)$*, where* P *is a monadic function symbol and* s *is a simple term.*

An inequality $t_1 \lhd t_2$ *is called* monadic *if* t_1, t_2 *are either simple or atom-like. A* clause *is called* monadic *if all its inequalities are monadic. Finally, a* set of clauses *is called* monadic *if all its clauses are monadic.*

Proposition 34. *Let* $\mathsf{Q}_1 y_1 \ldots \mathsf{Q}_n y_n P(y_1, \ldots, y_n)$ *be a monadic and prenex formula of* $\mathrm{G}^{\triangle}_{\infty}$. *Then* $\mathrm{CF}^{\mathrm{c}}(\exists \overline{x} P^F)$ *is monadic. Moreover,* $\mathcal{E}q^{\mathbf{F}}$, $\mathcal{E}p$, *and* $\mathcal{D}o$ *are monadic too, up to renaming of variables.*

To obtain the closure of the class of monadic sets of clauses with respect to $\mathrm{MC}_{\succ}$, we have to choose the reduction order $\succ$ appropriately. From now on we assume that $\succ$ fulfills all of the following, where $x \in \mathcal{X}$ and $P, Q \in \mathbf{P}$:

(a) $t \succ x$ if x is a proper subterm of t, and
(b) $t \succ P(x)$ if t is a simple term containing x as a proper subterm.
(c) $Q(t) \succ P(x)$ if t is simple term containing x as a proper subterm.

It is easy to check that these conditions are fulfilled if $\succ$ is a lexicographic path order based on a strict order $>_{\mathbf{F}}$ of the signature where $f >_{\mathbf{F}} p$ whenever $f \in \mathbf{S}$ and $p \in \mathbf{P}$. (See, e.g., [3].)

Lemma 35. *If* $\mathcal{S}$ *is monadic then* $\mathrm{MC}_{\succ}(\mathcal{S})$ *is monadic too.*

Proof. Consider *irreflexivity resolution*: i.e., $C\sigma$ where σ is the mgu of s and t in the monadic clause $C \cup \{s < t\}$.

(1) If *codom*(σ) contains only variables (or σ is the empty substitution) then the only condition on monadicity that is not already obviously fulfilled by $C\sigma$ is that that all terms of form $f(x_1, \ldots, x_n)$ occurring in $C\sigma$ are stratified. We have to check the following cases
   (1.1) s and t are variables: By the maximality condition, no term of form $f(x_1, \ldots, x_n)$ in C can contain s or t as a subterm. Therefore such terms remain unchanged and, in particular, stratified.
   (1.2) $s = f(x_1, \ldots, x_n)$ and $t = f(y_1, \ldots, y_n)$. Since $x_i \in \mathcal{X}_i$ and $y_i \in V_i$, stratification is preserved in $C\sigma$.
   (1.3) $s = P(f(x_1, \ldots, x_n))$ and $t = P(f(y_1, \ldots, y_n))$. Like case (1.2).

(1.4) $s = P(x)$ and $t = P(y)$; $\sigma = \{x \leftarrow y\}$ or $\sigma = \{y \leftarrow x\}$. By the maximality condition and conditions (b) and (c) no term of form $f(x_1, \ldots, x_n)$ in C can contain x or y as a subterm. Therefore such terms remain stratified.

(2) Otherwise, since $s < t$ is monadic, σ is of form $\{x \leftarrow r\}$ for some term r that is either simple or atom-like, but not a variable. Without loss of generality, we assume that x occurs in s (but not in t). Since r is not a variable, there are only the following two cases:

(2.1) $s = x$ and $t = r$: By the maximality condition and condition (i) for $\succ$, x cannot be a proper subterm of a term in C. I.e., x is basic in C, if it occurs in C at all. Therefore $C\sigma$ is monadic.

(2.2) $s = P(x)$ and $t = P(r)$ for some $P \in \mathbf{P}$: By the maximality condition and conditions (b) and (c) for $\succ$ we have: if x occurs in C, then x is basic in C or x occurs in an atom-like term of form $P(x)$ in C. In both cases $C\sigma$ is monadic.

The case for *chaining* is analogous. E.g., consider $m = n = 1$: $E = C\sigma \cup D\sigma \cup \{u\sigma \lhd^* v\sigma\}$, where σ is mgu of s and t in the monadic clauses $C \cup \{u \lhd s\}$ and $D \cup \{t \lhd v\}$. Again, if $codom(\sigma)$ consists of variables only then E is monadic, too, by the same arguments as in (1), above. Otherwise the same case distinction as for (2), above, and analogous arguments apply. □

Lemma 35 implies a bound on the *depth* of terms that occur in clauses derivable from monadic sets of clauses. This leaves open the question whether also the *length* of clauses (i.e., number of inequalities) can be bounded. However, this would contradict the following undecidability result. (We adapt a proof of Gabbay [19] for the monadic — but not prenex — fragment of G_∞.)

Theorem 36. *Validity of prenex monadic formulas of* $G_\infty^\triangle$ *is undecidable.*

Proof. In [25] it has been shown that the classical theory CE of two equivalence relations is undecidable. We faithfully interpret CE in the prenex monadic fragment of $G_\infty^\triangle$. In fact, already validity (and therefore also satisfiability) of a formula S of CE of form

$$Q_1 x_1 \ldots Q_n v_n (\bigwedge_j x_j \equiv y_j \supset \bigvee_k u_k \equiv v_k)$$

is undecidable, where each occurrence of $\equiv$ can be either $\equiv_1$ or $\equiv_2$. Let p_1 and p_2 be two monadic predicate symbols. We define $[x \equiv_i y]^* \stackrel{\text{def}}{=} \triangle(p_i(x) \leftrightarrow p_i(y))$, for $i = 1, 2$. Let S^* be the formula arising from S by replacing all subformulas $x \equiv_i y$ by $[x \equiv_i y]^*$.

We show that S has a CE-model $\mathcal{M} = (D; \equiv_1^{\mathcal{M}}, \equiv_2^{\mathcal{M}})$ if and only if $\text{val}_{\mathcal{I}}(S^*) = 1$ for some $G_\infty^\triangle$-interpretation $\mathcal{I}$. Without loss of generalization we will assume that the domain of $\mathcal{M}$ to be countable.

($\Rightarrow$) Note that each of two equivalence relations $\equiv_i^{\mathcal{M}}$ ($i = 1, 2$) of the CE-model $\mathcal{M}$ induces a partition of its domain $[0, 1]$ into equivalence classes $E_i^j = \{x \mid x \equiv_i^{\mathcal{M}} y_j\}$, where y_j is an element of the domain D of $\mathcal{M}$ and j is some index taken from a set J. Without loss of generality will assume that the index set J is the real unit interval $[0, 1]$. (An equivalence class may have many different indices.) We define $\mathcal{I} = (D, \text{val}_{\mathcal{I}})$ by setting (for $i = 1, 2$) $\text{val}_{\mathcal{I}}(p_i)(d) = j$ iff $d \in E_i^j$. By straightforward induction on the complexity of S it follows that $\text{val}_{\mathcal{I}}(S^*) = 1$ iff $\mathcal{M}$ a CE-model S.

($\Leftarrow$) Given a $G_\infty^\triangle$-interpretation $\mathcal{I} = (D, \mathrm{val}_\mathcal{I})$ for S^* we define the CE-model $\mathcal{M}$ for S by taking D as its domain and setting $x{\equiv_i}^\mathcal{M} y$ iff $\mathrm{val}_\mathcal{I}(p_i)(x) = \mathrm{val}_\mathcal{I}(p_i)(y)$ for $x, y \in D$, $i = 1, 2$. □

References

[1] A. Avron. Hypersequents, Logical Consequence and Intermediate Logics for Concurrency. *Annals of Mathematics and Artificial Intelligence* Vol. 4, 1991, 225–248.

[2] A. Avron. The Method of Hypersequents in Proof Theory of Propositional Non-Classical Logics. In *Logic: From Foundations to Applications. European Logic Colloquium, Keele, UK, July 20–29, 1993*. Oxford, Clarendon Press, 1996, 1–32.

[3] F. Baader, T. Nipkow. *Term Rewriting and All That*. Cambridge UP, 1998.

[4] M. Baaz. Infinite-valued Gödel logics with 0-1-projections and relativizations. In *Proceedings Gödel 96. Kurt Gödel's Legacy*. LNL 6, Springer, 23–33. 1996.

[5] M. Baaz, A. Ciabattoni, R. Zach. Quantified Propositional Gödel Logics. In *Proceedings LPAR 2000*. Eds. M. Parigot, A. Voronkov LNCS 1955 Springer, 2000, 240–256

[6] M. Baaz, U. Egly, A. Leitsch. Normal Form Transformations. *Handbook of Automated Reasoning 1* Eds: A. Robinson, A. Voronkov. Elsevier, 2001, 273–333.

[7] M. Baaz, C. Fermüller. Analytic Calculi for Projective Logics. *Automated Reasoning with Analytic Tableaux and Related Methods*, TABLEAUX'99, LNAI 1617, Springer, 1999, 36–50.

[8] M. Baaz, A. Leitsch, R. Zach. Incompleteness of an infinite-valued first-order Gödel Logic and of some temporal logic of programs. In: *Proceedings of Computer Science Logic CSL'95*. Berlin, 1996. Springer.

[9] M. Baaz, H. Veith. Quantifier Elimination in Fuzzy Logic. *Computer Science Logic, 12th International Workshop, CSL'98*, LNCS 1584, 1999, 399-414.

[10] M. Baaz, H. Veith. An Axiomatization of Quantified Propositional Gödel Logic Using the Takeuti-Titani Rule. Proc. Logic Colloquium 1998, LNML, Springer, to appear.

[11] M. Baaz, H. Veith. Interpolation in fuzzy logic. *Arch. Math. Logic*, 38 (1999), 461–489.

[12] M. Baaz, R. Zach. Hypersequents and the Proof Theory of Intuitionistic Fuzzy Logic. *Proc. CSL'2000*, 2000, 187–201.

[13] L. Bachmair, H. Ganzinger. Ordered Chaining for Total Orderings. *Proc. CADE'94*, Springer LNCS 814, 1994, 435–450.

[14] L. Bachmair, H. Ganzinger. Ordered Chaining Calculi for First-Order Theories of Transitive Relations. *J. ACM* 45(6) (1998), 1007-1049.

[15] A. Degtyarev, A. Voronkov. Decidability Problems for the Prenex Fragment of Intuitionistic Logic. In *Proceedings LICS'96*. IEEE Press, 503-509. 1996.

[16] M. Dummett. A propositional calculus with denumerable matrix. *J. Symbolic Logic*, 24(1959), 97–106.

[17] J.M. Dunn, R.K. Meyer. Algebraic completeness results for Dummett's *LC* and its extensions. *Z. Math. Logik Grundlagen Math.*, 17 (1971), 225–230.

[18] R. Dyckhoff. A Deterministic Terminating Sequent Calculus for Gödel-Dummett Logic. *Logic Journal of the IGPL*, 7(1999), 319-326.

[19] D.M. Gabbay. Decidability of some intuitionistic predicate theories. *J. of Symbolic Logic*, vol. 37, pp. 579-587. 1972.

[20] H. Ganzinger, V. Sofronie-Stokkermans. Chaining Techniques for Automated Theorem Proving in Many-Valued Logics. In: *Proceedings 30th IEEE Symposium on Multiple-Valued Logic*. IEEE Press, 337-344. 2000.

[21] P. Hájek. *Metamathematics of Fuzzy Logic*. Kluwer, 1998.

[22] A. Horn. Logic with truth values in a linearly ordered Heyting algebra. *J. Symbolic Logic*, 27 (1962), 159–170.

[23] A. Leitsch. *The Resolution Calculus*. Springer, 1997. Kluwer, 1998.

[24] D. Plaisted, S. Greenbaum. A Structure-Preserving Clause Form Translation. *J. Symbolic Computation* 2 (1986), 293–304.

[25] H. Rogers. Certain logical reduction and decision problems. *Annals of Mathematics*, vol. 64, pp. 264284. 1956.

[26] G. Takeuti, T. Titani. Intuitionistic fuzzy logic and intuitionistic fuzzy set theory. *J. Symbolic Logic*, 49 (1984), 851-866.

Unification in a Description Logic with Transitive Closure of Roles

Franz Baader[1] and Ralf Küsters[2]

[1] RWTH Aachen, Germany, baader@informatik.rwth-aachen.de
[2] CAU Kiel, Germany, kuesters@ti.informatik.uni-kiel.de

Abstract. Unification of concept descriptions was introduced by Baader and Narendran as a tool for detecting redundancies in knowledge bases. It was shown that unification in the small description logic $\mathcal{FL}_0$, which allows for conjunction, value restriction, and the top concept only, is already ExpTime-complete. The present paper shows that the complexity does not increase if one additionally allows for composition, union, and transitive closure of roles. It also shows that matching (which is polynomial in $\mathcal{FL}_0$) is PSpace-complete in the extended description logic. These results are proved via a reduction to linear equations over regular languages, which are then solved using automata. The obtained results are also of interest in formal language theory.

1 Introduction

Knowledge representation languages based on Description Logics (DL) can be used to represent the terminological knowledge of an application domain in a structured and formally well-understood way [10,4]. With the help of these languages, the important notions of the domain can be described by *concept descriptions*, i.e., expressions that are built from atomic concepts (unary predicates) and atomic roles (binary predicates) using the concept and role constructors provided by the DL language. Atomic concepts and concept descriptions represent sets of individuals, whereas roles and role descriptions represent binary relations between individuals.

Unification of concept descriptions was introduced by Baader and Narendran [8] as a new inference service for detecting and avoiding redundancies in DL knowledge bases. Unification considers concept patterns, i.e., concept descriptions with variables, and tries to make these descriptions equivalent by replacing the variables by appropriate concept descriptions. The technical results in [8] were concerned with unification in the small DL $\mathcal{FL}_0$, which allows for conjunction of concepts ($C \sqcap D$), value restriction ($\forall R.C$), and the top concept ($\top$). It is shown that unification of $\mathcal{FL}_0$-concept descriptions is equivalent to solving systems of linear equations over finite languages, and that this problem is ExpTime-complete.

In the present paper, we study unification in $\mathcal{FL}_{reg}$, the DL that extends $\mathcal{FL}_0$ by the role constructors identity role (ε), empty role ($\emptyset$), union ($R \cup S$),

R. Nieuwenhuis and A. Voronkov (Eds.): LPAR 2001, LNAI 2250, pp. 217–232, 2001.

composition ($R \circ S$), and reflexive-transitive closure (R^*).[1] Unification of $\mathcal{FL}_{reg}$-concept descriptions is again equivalent to solving systems of linear language equations, but the finite languages are now replaced by regular languages. The first contribution of the present paper is to show that deciding the solvability of such equations is, as in the finite case, ExpTime-complete. At first sight one might think that it is sufficient to show that the problem is in ExpTime, since ExpTime-hardness already holds for the "simpler" case of unification in $\mathcal{FL}_0$. However, unification in $\mathcal{FL}_{reg}$ is not a priori at least as hard as unification in $\mathcal{FL}_0$ since the set of potential solutions increases. Thus, an $\mathcal{FL}_0$-unification problem (which can also be viewed as an $\mathcal{FL}_{reg}$-unification problem) may be solvable in $\mathcal{FL}_{reg}$, but not in $\mathcal{FL}_0$. (We will see such an example later on.)

Our complexity results are by reduction to/from decision problems for tree-automata. Whereas for equations over finite languages automata on finite trees could be used, we now consider automata working on infinite trees. As a by-product of the reduction to tree automata, we also show that, if a system of linear equations has some (possibly irregular) solution, then it also has a regular one. That is, restricting solutions to substitutions that map variables to regular languages does not make a difference in terms of the solvability of an equation.

Equations over regular languages have already been considered by Leiss [12, 11]. However, he does not provide any decidability or complexity results for the case we are interested in. Closely related to the problem of solving linear language equations is the problem of solving set constraints [1], i.e., relations between sets of terms. Set constraints are usually more general than the kind of equations we are dealing with here. The case we consider here corresponds most closely to positive set constraints for terms over unary and nullary function symbols where only union of sets is allowed. For solvability of positive set constraints over (at least two) unary and (at least one) nullary function symbols, ExpTime-completeness is shown in [1]. However, this result does not directly imply the corresponding result for our case. On the one hand, for set constraints one considers equations with finite languages as coefficients, whereas we allow for regular languages as coefficients. It is, however, easy to see that regular coefficients can be expressed using set constraints. On the other hand, for set constraints one allows for arbitrary (possibly) infinite solutions, whereas we restrict the attention to regular solutions. Using the (new) result that the restriction to regular sets does not change the solvability of an equation, our exponential upper bound also follows from the complexity result in [1]. The hardness result in [1] does not directly carry over since even positive set constraints allow for more complex types of equations than the linear ones considered here.

Matching is a special case of unification where only one of the patterns contains variables. In [8] it was shown that matching in $\mathcal{FL}_0$ is polynomial, and in [7] this result was extended to the more expressive DL $\mathcal{ALN}$. We will show that matching in $\mathcal{FL}_{reg}$ is PSpace-complete.

In case a unification/matching problem is solvable, one is usually interested in obtaining an actual solution. In the context of matching in description logics,

[1] Transitive closure then corresponds to the expression $R \circ R^*$.

Table 1. Syntax and semantics of concept descriptions.

Syntax	Semantics	$\mathcal{FL}_0$	$\mathcal{FL}_{reg}$
$\top$	Δ^I	x	x
$C \sqcap D$	$C^I \cap D^I$	x	x
$\forall R.C$	$\{x \in \Delta^I \mid \forall y : (x,y) \in R^I \to y \in C^I\}$	x	x
ε	$\{(x,x) \mid x \in \Delta^I\}$		x
$\emptyset$	$\emptyset$		x
$R \circ S$	$\{(x,z) \mid \exists y : (x,y) \in R^I \wedge (y,z) \in S^I\}$		x
R^*	$\bigcup_{n \geq 0} (R^I)^n$		x

it has been argued [9,5] that not all solutions of a matching problem are of interest to a user. Therefore, one must look for solutions with certain desired properties; for instance, least solutions where all variables are substituted by concept descriptions that are as specific as possible turned out to be appropriate in some contexts [9,13]. For matching in $\mathcal{FL}_0$ and $\mathcal{FL}_{reg}$, solvable problems always have a least solution. For unification, we will show that this is only true for $\mathcal{FL}_{reg}$.

2 Unification in $\mathcal{FL}_{reg}$

Let us first introduce $\mathcal{FL}_0$- and $\mathcal{FL}_{reg}$-concept descriptions. Starting from the finite and disjoint sets N_C of concept names and N_R of role names, $\mathcal{FL}_0$-concept descriptions are built using the concept constructors conjunction ($C \sqcap D$), value restriction ($\forall r.C$), and the top concept ($\top$). $\mathcal{FL}_{reg}$ extends $\mathcal{FL}_0$ by additionally allowing for the role constructors identity role (ε), empty role ($\emptyset$), union ($R \cup S$), composition ($R \circ S$), and reflexive-transitive closure (R^*). As an example, consider the $\mathcal{FL}_{reg}$-concept description Woman $\sqcap \forall$child*.Woman, which represents the set of all women with only female offspring.

Role names will be denoted by lower case letters ($r, s, \ldots \in N_R$), and complex roles by upper case letters ($R, S, T \ldots$). Note that a complex role can be viewed as a regular expression over N_R where ε is taken as the empty word, role names as elements of the alphabet, the empty role as the empty language, union as union of languages, composition as concatenation, and reflexive-transitive closure as Kleene star. Therefore, we sometimes view a complex role R as a regular expression. In the following, we will abuse notation by identifying regular expressions with the languages they describe. In particular, if R and R' are regular expressions, then $R = R'$ will mean that the corresponding languages are equal.

As usual, the semantics of concept and role descriptions is defined in terms of an *interpretation* $\mathcal{I} = (\Delta^I, \cdot^I)$. The domain Δ^I of $\mathcal{I}$ is a non-empty set and the interpretation function $\cdot^I$ maps each concept name $A \in N_C$ to a set $A^I \subseteq \Delta^I$ and each role name $r \in N_R$ to a binary relation $r^I \subseteq \Delta^I \times \Delta^I$. The extension of $\cdot^I$ to arbitrary concept and role descriptions is defined inductively, as shown in the second column of Table 1. The interested reader may note that $\mathcal{FL}_{reg}$-concept descriptions can also be viewed as concepts defined by cyclic $\mathcal{FL}_0$-TBoxes interpreted with the greatest fixed-point semantics [2]. The concept description D *subsumes* the description C ($C \sqsubseteq D$) iff $C^I \subseteq D^I$ for all interpretations $\mathcal{I}$. Two concept descriptions C, D are *equivalent* ($C \equiv D$) iff they subsume each other.

In order to define unification of concept descriptions, we first have to introduce the notions concept patterns and substitutions operating on concept patters. To this purpose, we need a set of *concept variables* N_X (disjoint from $N_C \cup N_R$). $\mathcal{FL}_{reg}$*-concept patterns* are $\mathcal{FL}_{reg}$-concept descriptions defined over the set $N_C \cup N_X$ of concept names and the set N_R of role names. For example, given $A \in N_C$, $X \in N_X$, and $r \in N_R$, $\forall r.A \sqcap \forall r^*.X$ is an $\mathcal{FL}_{reg}$-concept pattern.

A *substitution* σ is a mapping from N_X into the set of all $\mathcal{FL}_{reg}$-concept descriptions. This mapping is extended from variables to concept patterns in the obvious way, i.e.,

- $\sigma(\top) := \top$ and $\sigma(A) := A$ for all $A \in N_C$,
- $\sigma(C \sqcap D) := \sigma(C) \sqcap \sigma(D)$ and $\sigma(\forall R.C) := \forall R.\sigma(C)$.

Definition 1. *An* $\mathcal{FL}_{reg}$-unification problem *is of the form* $C \equiv^? D$, *where* C, D *are* $\mathcal{FL}_{reg}$*-concept patterns. The substitution* σ *is a* unifier *of this problem iff* $\sigma(C) \equiv \sigma(D)$. *In this case, the unification problem is* solvable, *and* C *and* D *are called* unifiable.

For example, the substitution $\sigma = \{X \mapsto \forall r \circ r^*.A,\ Y \mapsto \forall r.A\}$ is a unifier of the unification problem

$$\forall s.\forall r.A \sqcap \forall r.A \sqcap \forall r.X \equiv^? X \sqcap \forall s.Y. \tag{1}$$

Note that this problem can also be viewed as an $\mathcal{FL}_0$-unification problem. However, in this case it does not have a solution since there are no $\mathcal{FL}_0$-concept descriptions that, when substituted for X and Y, make the two concept patterns equivalent.

For readers interested in unification theory, let us point out that (just as for $\mathcal{FL}_0$ [8]), unification in $\mathcal{FL}_{reg}$ can be viewed as unification modulo an appropriate equational theory, and that (like the theory corresponding to $\mathcal{FL}_0$) this theory is of unification type zero.

3 Reduction to Regular Language Equations

We now show how unification in $\mathcal{FL}_{reg}$ can be reduced to solving linear equations over regular languages built using the alphabet N_R of role names.

The equations we are interested in are built as follows. Let Σ be a finite alphabet. For languages $L, M \subseteq \Sigma^*$, their concatenation is defined by $LM := \{vw \mid v \in L, w \in M\}$. Let $X_1, \ldots, X_n$ be variables. Given regular languages $S_0, S_1, \ldots, S_n, T_0, T_1, \ldots, T_n$[2] over N_R, a *linear equation over regular languages*

[2] We assume that these languages are given by regular expressions or nondeterministic finite automata.

is of the form

$$S_0 \cup S_1X_1 \cup \cdots \cup S_nX_n = T_0 \cup T_1X_1 \cup \cdots \cup T_nX_n \tag{2}$$

A *(regular, finite) solution* θ of this equation is a substitution assigning to each variable a (regular, finite) language over Σ such that the equation holds. We are particularly interested in *regular* solutions since these can be turned into $\mathcal{FL}_{reg}$-concept descriptions.

A *system of regular language equations* is a finite set of regular language equations. A substitution θ solves such a system if it solves every equation in it simultaneously. A system of equations can easily (in linear time) be turned into a single equation with the same set of solutions by concatenating all constant languages in an equation with a role r (a new role for every equation), i.e., the languages S_i and T_i are replaced by $\{r\}S_i$ and $\{r\}T_i$. Then the different equations can be put together into a single equation without causing any interference (see [8] for details). Hence, for our complexity analysis we can focus on single equations.

To establish the reduction from unification in $\mathcal{FL}_{reg}$ to solvability of linear equations over regular languages, $\mathcal{FL}_{reg}$-concept patterns are written in the following normal form:

$$\bigsqcap_{A \in N_C} \forall R_A.A \sqcap \bigsqcap_{X \in N_X} \forall R_X.X,$$

where R_A and R_X are regular expressions over N_R. Every concept pattern can (in polynomial time) be turned into such a normal form by exhaustively applying the following equivalence preserving rule: $\forall R.C \sqcap \forall R'.C \longrightarrow \forall (R \cup R').C$, where R, R' are regular expressions over N_R and C is some $\mathcal{FL}_{reg}$-concept pattern. Correctness of our reduction from unification to solvability of linear equations depends on the following (easily provable [2,3]) characterization of equivalence:

Lemma 1. *Let C, D be $\mathcal{FL}_{reg}$-concept descriptions such that*

$$C \equiv \bigsqcap_{A \in N_C} \forall S_A.A \quad \text{and} \quad D \equiv \bigsqcap_{A \in N_C} \forall T_A.A.$$

Then $C \equiv D$ iff $S_A = T_A$ for all $A \in N_C$.

As an easy consequence, we obtain the following theorem, which shows that unification in $\mathcal{FL}_{reg}$ is equivalent via linear time reductions to solving regular language equations.

Theorem 1. *Let C, D be $\mathcal{FL}_{reg}$-concept patterns such that*

$$C \equiv \bigsqcap_{A \in N_C} \forall S_A.A \sqcap \bigsqcap_{X \in N_X} \forall S_X.X \quad \text{and} \quad D \equiv \bigsqcap_{A \in N_C} \forall T_A.A \sqcap \bigsqcap_{X \in N_X} \forall T_X.X.$$

Then C, D are unifiable iff, for all $A \in N_C$, the regular language equation $E_{C,D}(A)$ below has a solution:

$$S_A \cup \bigcup_{X \in N_X} S_X X_A = T_A \cup \bigcup_{X \in N_X} T_X X_A$$

Note that the language equations in this system do not share variables, and thus they can be solved separately. In the equation $E_{C,D}(A)$, the variable X_A is a new copy of $X \in N_X$. Different equations have different copies.

Continuing our example, from the unification problem (1) we obtain the following language equation (assuming $N_C = \{A\}$):

$$\{r, sr\} \cup \{r\}X_A = \{\varepsilon\}X_A \cup \{s\}Y_A$$

A solution of this equation is $X_A = rr^*$ and $Y_A = r$, which corresponds to the solution σ of (1).

4 The Decision Problem

The first theorem of this paper gives the exact complexity of solving systems of linear equations over regular languages.

Theorem 2. *Deciding (regular) solvability of (systems of) equations of the form (2) is an ExpTime-complete problem.*

As an immediate consequence, unification in $\mathcal{FL}_{reg}$ is ExpTime-complete as well.

The upper complexity bound. To prove that the problem can be solved in ExpTime, it suffices to concentrate on a single equation. Moreover, instead of (2) we consider equations where the variables occur in front of the coefficients. Such an equation can easily be obtained from (2) by considering the mirror images (or reverse) of the coefficient languages. That is, we go from a language $L \subseteq N_R^*$ to its mirror image $L^{mi} := \{r_m \cdots r_1 \mid r_1 \cdots r_m \in L\}$. The mirror equation of (2) is of the form

$$S_0^{mi} \cup X_1 S_1^{mi} \cup \cdots \cup X_n S_n^{mi} = T_0^{mi} \cup X_1 T_1^{mi} \cup \cdots \cup X_n T_n^{mi}. \quad (3)$$

Obviously, the mirror images of solutions of (3) are exactly the solutions of (2).

To test (3) for solvability, we build a looping tree-automaton $\mathcal{B}$, i.e., a Büchi tree-automaton where all states are final. Let us briefly introduce infinite trees and looping tree-automata (see [15] for details). Let Σ be a finite alphabet and, w.l.o.g., $N_R = \{1, \ldots, k\}$. A *Σ-labeled k-ary infinite tree* t is a mapping from N_R^* into Σ. (In particular, the nodes of t can be viewed as words over N_R.) In case Σ is a singleton, t is called *unlabeled*. A *looping tree-automaton* $\mathcal{A}$ is a tuple (Q, Σ, I, Δ) where Q is the finite set of states of $\mathcal{A}$, Σ is a finite alphabet, $I \subseteq Q$ is the set of initial states, and $\Delta \subseteq Q \times \Sigma \times Q^k$ is the transition relation. (Note that we do not define final states. Also, we will omit Σ in case it is a singleton.) A *run* r of $\mathcal{A}$ on the tree t is a Q-labeled k-ary tree such that $(r(u), t(u), r(u1), \ldots, r(uk)) \in \Delta$. It is called successful if $r(\varepsilon) \in I$. The tree language accepted by $\mathcal{A}$ is $L(\mathcal{A}) := \{t \mid \text{there exists a successful run of } \mathcal{A} \text{ on } t\}$.

Our looping tree-automaton $\mathcal{B}$ will work on the (unique) unlabeled k-ary infinite tree t (thus $L(\mathcal{B})$ will be the empty set or $\{t\}$). The idea underlying the construction is as follows. A Q-labeled k-ary infinite tree r can be used to describe sets of words by taking those words u for which the label $r(u)$ satisfies a certain property. In principle, a run of $\mathcal{B}$ on t represents i) a set of words over N_R obtained by instantiating the equation with one of its solutions (called *solution sets* in the following), and ii) the solution itself, i.e., the languages substituted for the variables. To achieve this, while working its way down t, in every step $\mathcal{B}$ guesses whether the current node (or more precisely the word it represents) a) belongs to the solution set, and b) to the language substituted for X_i ($i = 1, \ldots, n$). In addition, $\mathcal{B}$ checks whether the guesses made actually yield a solution.

Formally, $\mathcal{B} = (Q, I, \Delta)$ is defined as follows. (We provide a more detailed explanation after the definition.) Let $\mathcal{A}_{S,i} = (Q_{S,i}, N_R, q_{S,i}, \Delta_{S,i}, F_{S,i})$ and $\mathcal{A}_{T,i} = (Q_{T,i}, N_R, q_{T,i}, \Delta_{T,i}, F_{T,i})$ be (nondeterministic) finite automata accepting the languages S_i^{mi} and T_i^{mi} ($i = 0, \ldots, n$), respectively. We assume (w.l.o.g.) that the set of states of these automata are pairwise disjoint. Let $N := \{0, 1, \ldots, n\}$, Q_S (Q_T) be the union of the sets $Q_{S,i}$ ($Q_{T,i}$), $i = 0, \ldots, n$, and F_S (F_T) be the union of the sets $F_{S,i}$ ($F_{T,i}$).

1. $Q := 2^N \times 2^{Q_S} \times 2^{Q_T}$;
2. $I := \{(G, L, R) \mid G \subseteq N,\ L = \{q_{S,0}\} \cup \{q_{S,i} \mid i \in G\}$, and $R := \{q_{T,0}\} \cup \{q_{T,i} \mid i \in G\}$;
3. Δ consists of all tuples $((G_0, L_0, R_0), (G_1, L_1, R_1), \ldots, (G_k, L_k, R_k)) \in Q \times Q^k$ such that
   a) $0 \in G_0$ iff $L_0 \cap F_S \neq \emptyset$ iff $R_0 \cap F_T \neq \emptyset$;
   b) for all $i = 1, \ldots, k$,
   $L_i := \mathrm{suc}(L_0, i) \cup \{q_{S,j} \mid j \in G_i\}$ and $R_i := \mathrm{suc}(R_0, i) \cup \{q_{T,j} \mid j \in G_i\}$, where $\mathrm{suc}(L_0, i) := \{q \mid$ there exists q' and j with $q' \in L_0 \cap Q_{S,j}$ and $(q', i, q) \in \Delta_{S,j}\}$ and $\mathrm{suc}(R_0, i)$ is defined analogously.

Intuitively, $\mathcal{B}$ uses the first component of its states to guess whether a node (the word it represents) belongs to the solution set and/or to one of the variables X_i. That is, given a state (G, L, R), $0 \in G$ means that the current node belongs to the solution set and $i \in G$ means that the node belongs to X_i (more accurately, to the language substituted for X_i). The other two components are used to do the book-keeping necessary to check whether the guesses actually yield a solution. To understand their rôle, assume that r is a run of $\mathcal{B}$ on t. W.l.o.g. we consider the second component. If $r(u) = (G, L, R)$ and $j \in G$, for some $j \neq 0$, then u belongs to X_j, and thus uv belongs to $X_j S_j^{mi}$ for all $v \in S_j^{mi}$. Consequently, if $r(uv) = (G', L', R')$, then we must have $0 \in G'$. To enforce this, $q_{S,j}$ (the initial state of the automaton $\mathcal{A}_{S,j}$ accepting S_j^{mi}) is added to L. The transitions of $\mathcal{B}$ then simulate the transitions of $\mathcal{A}_{S,j}$ in the second component. Thus, in $r(uv)$ the set L' contains a final state of $\mathcal{A}_{S,j}$, and now (3a) implies that $0 \in G'$ must hold. Conversely, if $0 \in G'$, then L' must contain a final state of some of the automata $\mathcal{A}_{S,i}$ ($i = 0, \ldots, n$).

Given a successful run r of $\mathcal{B}$, it is now easy to prove that the substitution θ_r:

$$\theta_r(X_i) := \{u \mid r(u) = (G, L, R) \text{ and } i \in G\}$$

is a solution of (3). Conversely, it is not hard to show that a given solution of (3) induces a successful run of $\mathcal{B}$.

Lemma 2. *There is a one-to-one correspondence between solutions of (3) and successful runs of* $\mathcal{B}$.

The lemma implies that equation (3) has a solution iff $\mathcal{B}$ has a successful run (i.e., $L(\mathcal{B}) \neq \emptyset$). The size of the set of states of $\mathcal{B}$ is exponential in the size of equation (3), where the size of the regular sets S_i^{mi} and T_i^{mi} are measured by the size of nondeterministic finite automata accepting these sets. Since the emptiness problem for Büchi tree-automata (and thus looping tree-automata) can be solved in polynomial time in the size of the automaton [15] (and actually in linear time for looping automata), this yields the desired exponential time algorithm for deciding the solvability of equation (3). However, the existence of a solution does not a priori imply that there is also a regular one. Thus, we must still show that regular solvability can also be decided in ExpTime.

It is well-known [15] that a Büchi-automaton has a successful run iff it has a regular (or rational) run. It is easy to show that the solution corresponding to a regular run is a regular solution.

Proposition 1. *If (3) has a solution, then it also has a regular one.*

This proposition also follows from our results in Section 5.

The lower complexity bound. The hardness result can be shown similarly to the proof by Baader and Narendran [8] for systems of equations over finite languages. In their proof, the intersection emptiness problem for deterministic root-to-frontier automata on finite trees, which has been shown to be ExpTime-complete by Seidl [14], is reduced to the solvability of systems of equations over finite languages. The *intersection emptiness problem* is defined as follows: given a sequence $\mathcal{A}_1, \ldots, \mathcal{A}_n$ of deterministic root-to-frontier automata over the same ranked alphabet Σ, decide whether there exists a tree t accepted by $\mathcal{A}_1, \ldots, \mathcal{A}_n$.

Instead of deterministic root-to-frontier automata we will here use deterministic looping tree-automata: a looping tree-automaton is *deterministic* if it has one initial state and, for every state q and symbol f, there exists at most one transition of the form $(q, f, \ldots)$. We will show that Seidl's result easily carries over to these automata. However, we need to consider looping tree-automata over infinite trees labeled by elements of a *ranked* alphabet. That is, the number of successors of a node varies depending on the arity of the label attached to the node. Modifying the definition of looping tree-automata to work on these trees is straightforward.

Proposition 2. *The intersection emptiness problem for looping tree-automata over a ranked alphabet is ExpTime-hard.*

This can be shown by reducing the intersection emptiness problem for root-to-frontier automata to the intersection emptiness problem for looping tree-automata. The main idea is to turn every finite tree t into an infinite tree $\widehat{t}$ by adding a new symbol # (say of rank 1) to the alphabet, and extending the finite tree at every leaf by attaching the infinite tree labeled by # only. A given root-to-frontier automaton $\mathcal{A}$ can then easily be modified to a looping tree-automaton $\mathcal{B}$ such that every successful run of $\mathcal{A}$ on t corresponds to a successful run of $\mathcal{B}$ on $\widehat{t}$ and vice versa.

It remains to show how the intersection emptiness problem for looping tree-automata can be reduced to the solvability of systems of linear equations over regular languages. In the following, let Σ be a ranked alphabet. Seidl's result implies that it suffices to restrict the attention to symbols of rank 1 and 2.

We represent an infinite tree t over the ranked alphabet Σ by an infinite set $S(t)$ of words over $\Sigma \cup \{1, 2\}$. This set contains one element for every node of the tree. Given a node u, the corresponding word describes the path from this node to the root of the tree by listing the labels of the nodes v on this path together with the information whether v is the first or second successor of its parent node. To be more precise, if $t = f(t_1, t_2)$ is the tree whose root is labeled with f and has the two successor trees t_1 and t_2, then $S(t) := \{\varepsilon\} \cup \{u1f \mid u \in S(t_1)\} \cup \{u2f \mid u \in S(t_2)\}$. Accordingly, if $t = g(t')$, then $S(t) := \{\varepsilon\} \cup \{u1g \mid u \in S(t')\}$. For example, if f is binary, g is unary, and t is the infinite tree labeled with g only, then $S(f(t,t)) = \{\varepsilon\} \cup (1g)^*1f \cup (1g)^*2f$. Given a node u in t we denote the word representing u in $S(t)$ by $w^t(u)$. In the example, $w^{f(t,t)}(211) = 1g1g2f$.

Now, let $\mathcal{A} = (Q, \Sigma, q_0, \Delta)$ be a deterministic looping tree-automaton over the ranked alphabet Σ. We construct the following linear equation, where the variables $X_{(q,g)}$ range over (possibly infinite) sets of words over $\Sigma' := \Sigma \cup Q \cup \{1, 2\}$:

$$\bigcup_{(q,g)\in Suc} \{q\}X_{(q,g)} = \{q_0\} \cup \bigcup_{(q,g,q_1,\dots,q_k)\in\Delta} \{q_1 1g, \dots, q_k kg\}X_{(q,g)}, \tag{4}$$

where Suc denotes the set of tuples (q, g) for which there exist $q_1, \dots, q_k$ with $(q, g, q_1, \dots, q_k) \in \Delta$, and k denotes the rank of g.

We want to show that solutions of (4) induce accepting runs of $\mathcal{A}$ and vice versa. Assuming that (4) has the solution θ, let us try to construct a tree t and a successful run of $\mathcal{A}$ on t. Since q_0 occurs on the right-hand side of (4), it must also occur on the left-hand side. Thus, there must exist a symbol g such that $(q_0, g) \in Suc$ and $\varepsilon \in \theta(X_{(q_0,g)})$. Intuitively, this corresponds to setting $t(\varepsilon) := g$ and $r(\varepsilon) := q_0$. Now, since $\varepsilon \in \theta(X_{(q_0,g)})$, additional words occur on the right-hand side of (4). Indeed, since $(q_0, g) \in Suc$, there exist $q_1, \dots, q_k$ with $(q_0, g, q_1, \dots, q_k) \in \Delta$. Thus, the words $q_1 1g, \dots, q_k kg$ occur on the right-hand side. This corresponds to setting $r(1) := q_1, \dots, r(k) := q_k$. Let us look at $q_1 1g$. This word must also occur on the left-hand side of (4). Thus, there must exist a symbol f with $(q_1, f) \in Suc$ and $1g \in \theta(X_{(q_1,f)})$. This corresponds to setting $t(1) := f$. Now, since $1g \in \theta(X_{(q_1,f)})$, additional words occur on the right-hand side of (4), and one continues just as in the case $\varepsilon \in \theta(X_{(q_0,g)})$. This illustrates that, if (4) is solvable, then one can construct a tree t and an accepting run r of $\mathcal{A}$ on t. Moreover, it follows that $S(t) \subseteq V_\theta := \bigcup_{(q,g)\in Suc} \theta(X_{(q,g)})$.

Conversely, if $t \in L(\mathcal{A})$ and r is the (unique) accepting run of $\mathcal{A}$ on t, then we can use r to construct a solution θ of (4) such that $S(t) = V_\theta$:

$$\theta(X_{(q,g)}) := \{w^t(u) \mid t(u) = g \wedge r(u) = q\}.$$

Lemma 3. *If θ solves (4), then there exists $t \in L(\mathcal{A})$ with $S(t) \subseteq V_\theta$. Conversely, if $t \in L(\mathcal{A})$, then there exists a solution θ of (4) with $S(t) = V_\theta$.*

The inclusion in the first part of the lemma may be strict. In fact, by the second part, every tree in $L(\mathcal{A})$ yields a solution of (4). Since the solutions of such linear equations are closed under (argument-wise) union, there are solutions θ representing more than one accepted tree. Because of this fact, our reduction will depend on the following lemma.

Lemma 4. *Let θ be a solution of (4) and t a tree. If $S(t) \subseteq V_\theta$, then $t \in L(\mathcal{A})$.*

In contrast to the previous lemma, Lemma 4 holds only because the automaton $\mathcal{A}$ is assumed to be deterministic (see [6] for a proof).

We are now ready to reduce the intersection emptiness problem to solving a system of linear equations. Let $\mathcal{A}_1, \ldots, \mathcal{A}_n$ be deterministic looping-tree automata with pairwise disjoint sets of states. For every $\mathcal{A}_i$, we consider a system of equations E_i that consists of the equation of the form (4) induced by $\mathcal{A}_i$ together with the equation

$$X = \bigcup_{(q,g) \in Suc} X_{(q,g)}. \tag{5}$$

Now, let E be the union of the systems E_i $(i = 1, \ldots, n)$. Note that we use the same variable X for every equation E_i. Otherwise, the equations E_i do not share variables since the set of states of the automata $\mathcal{A}_i$ were assumed to be pairwise disjoint.

We need to show that E has a solution iff $L(\mathcal{A}_1) \cap \cdots \cap L(\mathcal{A}_n) \neq \emptyset$. If there exists $t \in L(\mathcal{A}_1) \cap \cdots \cap L(\mathcal{A}_n)$, then, according to Lemma 3, for every i there exists a solution θ_i of the equation corresponding to $\mathcal{A}_i$ satisfying $S(t) = V_{\theta_i}$. Let θ be the substitution defined by $\theta(X_{(q,g)}) := \theta_i(X_{(q,g)})$ if q is a state of $\mathcal{A}_i$, and $\theta(X) := S(t)$. Then θ solves the system E. Conversely, if θ is a solution of E, then it solves equation (4) for every automaton $\mathcal{A}_i$. In particular, by Lemma 3, there exists a tree $t_1 \in L(\mathcal{A}_1)$ such that $S(t_1) \subseteq V_\theta$. Since θ solves the equation corresponding to $\mathcal{A}_i$, Lemma 4 thus yields $t_1 \in L(\mathcal{A}_i)$ for every i. Thus, $t_1 \in L(\mathcal{A}_1) \cap \cdots \cap L(\mathcal{A}_n)$. This completes the proof of the lower complexity bound stated in Theorem 2.

5 Least Unifiers and Greatest Solutions

In case a unification problem is solvable, one is usually interested in obtaining an actual solution. Since a given unification problem may have infinitely many unifiers, one must decide which ones to prefer.[3] As mentioned in the introduction, least unifiers are of interest in some applications. The unifier σ is a *least unifier* of an $\mathcal{FL}_{reg}/\mathcal{FL}_0$ unification problem if it satisfies $\sigma(X) \sqsubseteq \sigma'(X)$ for all unifiers σ' and variables X occurring in the problem.

For $\mathcal{FL}_0$, least unifiers need not exist. For example, assume that $N_C = \{A\}$ and $N_R = \{r\}$. Then the (trivially solvable) unification problem $X \equiv^? X$ does not have a least unifier in $\mathcal{FL}_0$; however, σ with $\sigma(X) = \forall r^*.A$ is the least unifier of this problem in $\mathcal{FL}_{reg}$.

It is easy to see that the least unifier of a given $\mathcal{FL}_{reg}$ unification problem corresponds to the greatest regular solution of the corresponding formal language equations. The solution θ is a *greatest solution* of an equation of the form (2) (or (3)) iff it satisfies $\theta'(X) \subseteq \theta(X)$ for all solutions θ' and variables X occurring in the equation. Thus, we are interested in the existence and computability of greatest regular solutions of linear equations over regular languages.

The existence of a greatest solution of a solvable equation is obvious since the set of solutions is closed under union. In fact, if θ_j, $j \in J$, are solutions of (3), then so is θ with $\theta(X) := \bigcup_{j\in J} \theta_j(X)$ for all variables X occurring in the equation. Thus, the greatest solution can be obtained as the union over all solutions. However, this greatest solution can only be translated into a least unifier if it is regular. We will show that this is indeed always the case.

Theorem 3. *Every solvable equation of the form (3) has a greatest solution, and this solution is regular. This solution may grow exponentially in the size of (3), and it can be computed in exponential time.*

Assume that θ is the greatest solution of a solvable equation of the form (3). We first show that this solution is regular. Lemma 2 implies that there exists a corresponding run r_θ of the automaton $\mathcal{B}$ obtained from the equation (cf. Section 4). We proceed in three steps.

1. We restrict $\mathcal{B} = (Q, I, \Delta)$ to contain only so-called active states. The resulting automaton is called $\mathcal{B}' = (Q', I', \Delta')$.
2. Using $\mathcal{B}'$, we show that r_θ is regular, i.e., for every $q \in Q'$, the set $\{u \in N_R^* \mid r_\theta(u) = q\}$ is regular.
3. From r_θ, finite automata accepting $\theta(X_i)$ are derived.

A state q of $\mathcal{B}$ is called *active*, if $L(Q, \{q\}, \Delta) \neq \emptyset$, i.e., starting from q there exists a successful run of $\mathcal{B}$. Otherwise, q is called *passive*. The active states can be computed as follows. One first eliminates all states q for which there exist no transitions of the form $(q, \ldots)$. One also eliminates all transitions containing these states. This process is iterated until no more states are eliminated. It is easy to see that the remaining states are exactly the active ones. Obviously, this

[3] From the viewpoint of unification theory, we consider ground unifiers (i.e., substitutions whose images do not contain variables). Thus, it does not make sense to employ the usual instantiation pre-order on unifiers. Anyway, the equational theory corresponding to $\mathcal{FL}_{reg}$ is of unification type zero, and thus most general unifiers or even finite complete sets of unifiers need not exist.

procedure needs time polynomial in the size of $\mathcal{B}$. (There even exists a linear time algorithm for this task.) Let $\mathcal{B}' = (Q', I', \Delta')$ denote the automaton obtained from $\mathcal{B}$ by eliminating all passive states. (Note that $L(\mathcal{B}') = \emptyset$ iff $I' = \emptyset$.)

To show that r_θ is regular, we need the following partial ordering $\preceq$ on transitions of a state q. Let $\eta = (q, q_1, \ldots, q_k), \eta' = (q, q_1', \ldots, q_k') \in \Delta'$, $q_i = (G_i, L_i, R_i)$, and $q_i' = (G_i', L_i', R_i')$. Then, $\eta \preceq \eta'$ iff $G_i \setminus \{0\} \subseteq G_i' \setminus \{0\}$ for all $i = 1, \ldots, k$. Note that $\preceq$ is in fact antisymmetric: If $\eta \preceq \eta'$ and $\eta \preceq \eta'$, then $G_i \setminus \{0\} = G_i' \setminus \{0\}$ for all $i = 1, \ldots, k$. Since the sets L_i, R_i (L_i', R_i') are uniquely determined by G_i (G_i') and $0 \in G_i$ ($0 \in G_i'$) is determined by L_i, R_i (L_i', R_i'), this yields $\eta = \eta'$.

Now, let $u \in N_R^*$. We claim that the transition $\eta = (r_\theta(u), q_1, \ldots, q_k) \in \Delta'$, where $q_i = r_\theta(ui) =: (G_i, L_i, R_i)$, is the greatest transition among the transitions of $r_\theta(u)$ in $\mathcal{B}'$. Otherwise, there exists a transition $\eta' = (r_\theta(u), q_1', \ldots, q_k') \in \Delta'$, where $q_i' = (G_i', L_i', R_i')$, and $i \in \{1, \ldots, k\}$ such that $G_i' \setminus \{0\} \not\subseteq G_i \setminus \{0\}$, i.e., there exists $0 \neq j \in G_i' \setminus G_i$. We can construct a new run r' of $\mathcal{B}'$ that uses η' at node u instead of η. Since, by definition of $\mathcal{B}'$, the states q_i' in η' are all active, starting from these states there exist runs in $\mathcal{B}'$. Thus, a successful run r' using this transition at u really exists. This run corresponds to a solution of (3). However, in this solution ui belongs to X_j whereas this is not the case for the greatest solution, a contradiction. Thus, η must be the greatest transition.

As a consequence, if $\mathcal{B}'$ is in the same state at different nodes, then the same transition (namely, the greatest) is used by the run r_θ. From this, it easily follows that r_θ is regular: given $q \in Q'$, the following (deterministic) finite automaton $\mathcal{A}_q = (Q'', \{1, \ldots, k\}, q_I, \Delta'', \{q\})$ accepts the set $\{u \mid r_\theta(u) = q\}$:

- $Q'' := Q'$;
- $q_I := r_\theta(\varepsilon)$;
- $\Delta'' := \{(q, i, q_i) \mid (q, q_1, \ldots, q_k)$ is the greatest transition of q in Δ' and $i = 1, \ldots, k\}$.

If in $\mathcal{A}_q$ the set of final states is $\{(G, L, R) \in Q' \mid i \in G\}$ instead of $\{q\}$, then this automaton accepts the language substituted for X_i in the greatest solution. Thus, the greatest solution of (3) is regular. Finally, since $\mathcal{B}'$ and $\mathcal{A}_q$ can be computed in time exponential in the size of (3), the upper complexity bound for computing the greatest solution follows as well.

It remains to show that the size of the greatest solution may indeed grow exponentially. To this purpose, consider the equation

$$L_1\{1\} \cup \cdots \cup L_k\{k\} = L_1\{1\} \cup \cdots L_k\{k\} \cup X\{1, \ldots, k\}, \tag{6}$$

where the L_is are regular languages over N_R. Obviously, the greatest solution is the one that replaces X by $L_1 \cap \cdots \cap L_k$. From results shown in [16] it follows that the size of automata accepting this intersection may grow exponentially in the size of automata accepting $L_1, \ldots, L_k$.[4]

[4] Although these results have been shown for deterministic finite automata, they easily carry over to the nondeterministic case.

6 Matching in $\mathcal{FL}_{reg}$

Matching is the special case of unification where the pattern D on the right-hand side of the equation $C \equiv^? D$ does not contain variables. As an easy consequence of Theorem 1, matching in $\mathcal{FL}_{reg}$ can be reduced (in linear time) to solving linear equations over regular languages of the following form:

$$S_0 \cup S_1X_1 \cup \cdots \cup S_nX_n = T_0. \tag{7}$$

For $\mathcal{FL}_0$, one obtains the same kind of equations, but there $S_0, \ldots, S_n, T_0$ are finite languages, and one is interested in finite solvability. In [8] it was shown that matching in $\mathcal{FL}_0$ is polynomial, and in [7] this result was extended to the DL $\mathcal{ALN}$.

For $\mathcal{FL}_{reg}$, matching is at least PSpace-hard since equality of regular languages is a PSpace-complete problem if one assumes that the languages are given by regular expressions or nondeterministic finite automata. Thus, the equivalence problem in $\mathcal{FL}_{reg}$ is already PSpace-complete (this corresponds to the case $n = 0$ in equation (7)). We can show that matching is not harder than testing for equivalence.

Theorem 4. *Matching in $\mathcal{FL}_{reg}$ is a PSpace-complete problem.*

It remains to be shown that solvability of equations of the form (7) can be decided within polynomial space. Again, we consider the mirror equation

$$S_0^{mi} \cup X_1S_1^{mi} \cup \cdots \cup X_nS_n^{mi} = T_0^{mi} \tag{8}$$

in place of the original equation (7). The main idea underlying the proof of Theorem 4 is that such an equation has a solution iff a certain candidate solution solves the equation.

Lemma 5. *Let $L_i := \{w \mid \{w\}S_i^{mi} \subseteq T_0^{mi}\}$. Then equation (8) has a solution iff*

$$S_0^{mi} \cup L_1S_1^{mi} \cup \cdots \cup L_nS_n^{mi} = T_0^{mi}. \tag{9}$$

In this case, the L_is yield a greatest solution of (8).

The proof of this lemma is similar to the one for the case of finite languages given in [8]. It remains to be shown that the validity of identity (9) can be tested within polynomial space (in the size of nondeterministic finite automata for the languages $S_0^{mi}, \ldots, S_n^{mi}, T_0^{mi}$). By definition of the sets L_i, the inclusion from left-to-right holds iff $S_0^{mi} \subseteq T_0^{mi}$. Obviously, this can be tested in PSpace.

How to derive a PSpace-test for the inclusion in the other direction is not that obvious. Here, we sketch how the inclusion $T_0^{mi} \subseteq L_1S_1^{mi}$ can be tested (the extension to the union in identity (9) is then simple). First, we define an *exponentially large* automaton for $L_1S_1^{mi}$. However, the representation of each state of this automaton requires only polynomial space, and navigation in this automaton (i.e., determining initial states, final states, and state transitions) can also be realized within polynomial space. Thus, if we construct the automaton on-the-fly, we stay within PSpace.

An automaton $\mathcal{B}$ for $L_1 = \{w \mid \{w\}S_1^{mi} \subseteq T_0^{mi}\}$ can be obtained as follows. We construct the usual deterministic powerset automaton from the given nondeterministic automaton $\mathcal{A}$ for T_0^{mi}. The only difference is the definition of the final states. A state P of $\mathcal{B}$ (i.e., a subset of the set of states of $\mathcal{A}$) is a final state iff $S_1^{mi} \subseteq L_{\mathcal{A}}(P)$, where $L_{\mathcal{A}}(P)$ is the language accepted by $\mathcal{A}$ if P is taken as its set of initial states. It is easy to see that the automaton $\mathcal{B}$ obtained this way indeed accepts L_1, and that we can navigate in this automaton within PSpace. In particular, note that testing whether a state P of this automaton is a final state is a PSpace-complete problem.

The automaton $\mathcal{C}$ for $L_1 S_1^{mi}$ has as states tuples, where the first component is a state of $\mathcal{B}$ and the second component is a set of states of $\mathcal{A}_1$, the nondeterministic automaton for S_1^{mi}. Transitions in the first component are those of $\mathcal{B}$. In the second component, they are in principle the transitions of the powerset automaton corresponding to $\mathcal{A}_1$, with the following difference: if, on input r, the automaton $\mathcal{B}$ reaches a final state, then in the second component we extend the set reached with r in the powerset automaton of $\mathcal{A}_1$ by the initial states of $\mathcal{A}_1$. Final states of $\mathcal{C}$ are those whose second component contains a final state of $\mathcal{A}_1$. The initial state is (I, J), where I is the initial state of $\mathcal{B}$ and J is the set of initial states of $\mathcal{A}_1$ or empty, depending on whether I is a final state of $\mathcal{B}$ or not. Again, it is easy to see that navigation in $\mathcal{C}$ is possible within PSpace.

To decide whether $T_0^{mi} \subseteq L_1 S_1^{mi}$, we try to "guess" a counterexample (recall that PSpace = NPSpace). This is a word that is in T_0^{mi}, but not in $L_1 S_1^{mi}$. The length of a minimal such word can be bounded by the product of the size of $\mathcal{A}$ (the nondeterministic automaton for T_0^{mi}) and the size of $\mathcal{C}$ (the deterministic automaton for $L_1 S_1^{mi}$). We traverse $\mathcal{A}$ and $\mathcal{C}$ simultaneously, and have a counterexample if $\mathcal{A}$ is in a final state and $\mathcal{C}$ is not. The next letter and the successor state in $\mathcal{A}$ is guessed, and the successor state in $\mathcal{C}$ can be computed in PSpace. In addition, we use an exponential counter (requiring only polynomial space) that terminates the search if the (exponential) bound on the length of a minimal counterexample is reached.

7 Conclusion

We have shown that unification in $\mathcal{FL}_{reg}$ is equivalent via linear time reductions to solvability of linear equations over regular languages, and that these problems are ExpTime-complete. If we restrict the attention to matching problems (equations where one side does not contain variables), then the problem is PSpace-complete. In both cases, solvable problems (equations) have least (greatest) solutions, which may be exponential in the size of the problem (equation),[5] and which can be computed in exponential time. In addition to the application for description logics, we think that the results on solving linear equations over

[5] Note that equation (6) actually corresponds to a matching problem.

regular languages are also of interest in their own right (e.g., in formal language theory).

From the description logic point of view, one is of course also interested in unification in more expressive DLs, but this appears to be a hard problem. Recently, we have extended the decidability results to the DL obtained from $\mathcal{FL}_{reg}$ by adding inconsistency ($\bot$). Surprisingly, it is not clear how to handle the corresponding extension of $\mathcal{FL}_0$.

References

1. A. Aiken, D. Kozen, M. Vardi, and E. Wimmers. The Complexity of Set Constraints. In *Proc. 1993 Conf. Computer Science Logic (CSL'93)*, volume 832 of *LNCS*, pages 1–17. European Association Computer Science Logic, Springer, 1993.
2. F. Baader. Augmenting Concept Languages by Transitive Closure of Rules: An Alternativ to Terminological Cycles. In *Proc. of the 12th International Joint Conference on Artificial Intelligence (IJCAI'91)*, pages 446–451, 1991. Morgan Kaufmann Publishers.
3. F. Baader. Using Automata Theory for Characterizing the Semantics of Terminological Cycles. *Annals of Mathematics and Artificial Intelligence*, 18(2–4):175–219, 1996.
4. F. Baader and B. Hollunder. A Terminological Knowledge Representation System with Complete Inference Algorithms. In *Proc. of the First International Workshop on Processing Declarative Knowledge*, volume 572 of *LNCS*, pages 67–85, 1991. Springer–Verlag.
5. F. Baader and R. Küsters. Matching in Description Logics with Existential Restrictions. In *Proc. of the Seventh International Conference on Knowledge Representation and Reasoning (KR2000)*, pages 261–272, 2000. Morgan Kaufmann Publishers.
6. F. Baader and R. Küsters. Unification in a Description Logic with Transitive Closure of Roles. LTCS-Report 01-05, LuFG Theoretical Computer Science, RWTH Aachen, Germany, 2001. See http://www-lti.informatik.rwth-aachen.de/Forschung/Reports.html.
7. F. Baader, R. Küsters, A. Borgida, and D. McGuinness. Matching in Description Logics. *Journal of Logic and Computation*, 9(3):411–447, 1999.
8. F. Baader and P. Narendran. Unification of Concept Terms in Description Logics. In *Proc. of the 13th European Conference on Artificial Intelligence (ECAI-98)*, pages 331–335, 1998. John Wiley & Sons Ltd. An extended version has appeared in J. Symbolic Computation 31:277–305, 2001.
9. A. Borgida and D. L. McGuinness. Asking Queries about Frames. In *Proc. of the Fifth International Conference on Principles of Knowledge Representation and Reasoning (KR'96)*, pages 340–349, 1996. Morgan Kaufmann Publishers.
10. R. J. Brachman and J. G. Schmolze. An overview of the KL-ONE knowledge representation system. *Cognitive Science*, 9(2):171–216, 1985.
11. E. Leiss. Implicit language equations: Existence and uniqueness of solutions. *Theoretical Computer Science A*, 145:71–93, 1995.
12. E. Leiss. *Language Equations.* Springer-Verlag, 1999.
13. D.L. McGuinness. *Explaining Reasoning in Description Logics.* PhD thesis, Department of Computer Science, Rutgers University, October, 1996.

14. H. Seidl. Haskell overloading is DEXPTIME-complete. *Information Processing Letters*, 52(2), 1994.
15. W. Thomas. Automata on infinite objects. In J. van Leeuwen, editor, *Handbook of Theoretical Computer Science*, volume B, pages 133–191. Elsevier Science Publishers, Amsterdam, 1990.
16. S. Yu and Q. Zhuang. On the State Complexity of Intersection of Regular Languages. *ACM SIGACT News*, 22(3):52–54, 1991.

Intuitionistic Multiplicative Proof Nets as Models of Directed Acyclic Graph Descriptions

Guy Perrier

LORIA - Université Nancy 2
Campus Scientifique - B.P. 239 -
54506 Vandœuvre-les-Nancy Cedex - France
perrier@loria.fr

Abstract. Given an intuitionistic proof net of linear logic, we abstract an order between its atomic formulas. From this order, we represent intuitionistic multiplicative proof nets in the more compact form of models of directed acyclic graph descriptions. If we restrict the logical framework to the implicative fragment of intuitionistic linear logic, we show that proof nets reduce to models of tree descriptions.

1 Introduction

Resource sensitivity of linear logic entails a specific form of proof: *proof nets* [Gir87]. In the general framework of classical linear logic (CLL), these proof nets are not directed so that each extremity of a proof net can be viewed as either an input or an output; in other words, each formula that is attached to an extremity of a proof net can be considered either as an assumption (input) or as a conclusion (output) of the proof.
If we restrict ourselves to Intuitionistic Linear Logic (ILL), things freeze in a configuration where all formulas become *polarized*, one as the output and the others as the inputs. In particular, the assumptions of the proof are fixed once and for all and there is a unique conclusion which is also fixed once and for all, so that every proof net becomes directed from its assumptions to the conclusion. F. Lamarche has devised a correctness criterion for these proof nets which takes their specificity into account [Lam94]. This criterion is based on particular paths inside intuitionistic proof nets.
We restrict ourselves to the multiplicative fragment of ILL (IMLL) and we use these paths for designing a more abstract representation of proof net in the shape of *models of Directed Acyclic Graph (DAG) descriptions*. The paths which we call *dominance paths* induce a dominance order between the atomic formulas of each proof net which grounds this new representation of proof nets.
This view of proofs in the shape of models of DAG descriptions is not usual in the area of proof theory, it comes from the computational linguistics community. A major difficulty in the task of parsing sentences in natural language comes from the high degree of ambiguity they possess. If we use lexicalized grammars for parsing, all different syntactic uses of the same word are stored in a lexicon entry. If we represent syntactic structures with trees, every lexicon entry can contain more than hundred trees for a word. For solving this problem, recent works propose to replace the manipulation of completely specified

R. Nieuwenhuis and A. Voronkov (Eds.): LPAR 2001, LNAI 2250, pp. 233–248, 2001.

syntactic trees with the manipulation of set of properties representing under-specified syntactic trees [VS92,RVS94,RVSW95,Bla99]. The content of every lexical entry can be factorized in the shape of a *tree description*. Parsing a sentence consists first in gathering the tree descriptions given by the lexicon for all its words in a unique description. Then, the proper parsing process consists in searching for all syntactic trees that satisfy this description. Formally, tree descriptions are represented by classical logic first order formulas and the completely specified syntactic trees that satisfy these descriptions are represented by models of these formulas in the sense of model theory for classical logic [RVS94].
We propose to transpose this idea into the apparently very different framework of intuitionistic proof nets. When we want to prove an IMLL sequent, the forest of the syntactic trees of its formulas provides an initial proof frame which can be viewed as an under-specified proof net and represented in the shape of a DAG description. This description expresses the under-specified dominance order between the atomic formulas present in the sequent. Building a proof net from this sequent by linking atomic formulas in dual pairs by the means of axioms amounts to finding models of the initial description that completely specify the dominance order between atomic formulas.
The interest of such an approach is to simplify the notion of proof net by keeping what is essential while dropping unessential information. So there is a strict equivalence between provability of sequents and the existence of models for DAG descriptions but in these descriptions, formulas such as $(F_1 \otimes F_2) \multimap G$, $F_1 \multimap (F_2 \multimap G)$, $F_2 \multimap (F_1 \multimap G)$ are all represented in the same way.
We can take advantage of this simplification for theorem proving in ILL but also for linguistic applications, namely modelling the syntax of natural languages.

The full paper, with proofs, is available on *www.loria.fr/~perrier*. In both Sections 2 and 3, in a first stage, we recall the main results about intuitionistic proof nets, which can been already found in [Lam94]. Nevertheless, proofs of theorems are original, in particular that of the sequentialization theorem (Theorem 4). Then, in a second stage, we address what makes the originality of the paper: the reduction of theorem proving to the search for models of tree or DAG descriptions.

2 Intuitionistic Implicative Linear Logic (IILL)

2.1 IILL Proof Nets

In this subsection, we recall the definition of IILL proof nets and their characterization with Lamarche's criterion.
Let $\mathcal{A}$ be a set of atomic propositions. If A represents any element of $\mathcal{A}$, any IILL formula F is defined by the following grammar: $F ::= A \mid F \multimap F$.
The two-sided IILL sequent calculus handles sequents that are constituted of IILL formulas and that have exactly one formula in their succedent.
This calculus can be translated in the framework of the one-sided sequent calculus of CLL by means of polarities. Two functions $()^+$ and $()^-$ map IILL formulas to CLL formulas according to the following definition:

$$(A)^+ = A \qquad (A)^- = A^\perp$$
$$(F_1 \multimap F_2)^+ = (F_1)^- \wp (F_2)^+ \qquad (F_1 \multimap F_2)^- = (F_1)^+ \otimes (F_2)^-$$

CLL formulas that are positive or negative translations of IILL formulas are called IILL *polarized formulas*. Their syntax can be easily established independently from the IILL formulas which they represent.
IILL sequents $F_1, \ldots, F_n \vdash G$ are translated into CLL sequents $\vdash F_1^-, \ldots, F_n^-, G^+$. These sequents are called IILL *polarized sequents*.
The following proposition establishes the equivalence between the one-sided and the two-sided presentations of IILL.

Proposition 1.
An IILL sequent $F_1, \ldots, F_n \vdash G$ is provable iff the sequent $\vdash F_1^-, \ldots, F_n^-, G^+$ is provable in CLL.

In CLL, proving a sequent $\vdash F_1^-, \ldots, F_n^-, G^+$ amounts to building a proof net. This starts with the unfolding of the syntactic trees of the formulas $F_1^-, \ldots, F_n^-, G^+$. Since we are in a restricted fragment of CLL, these trees include only two kinds of links defined by Figure 1[1]. The forest of the syntactic trees of the formulas $F_1^-, \ldots, F_n^-, G^+$ constitutes

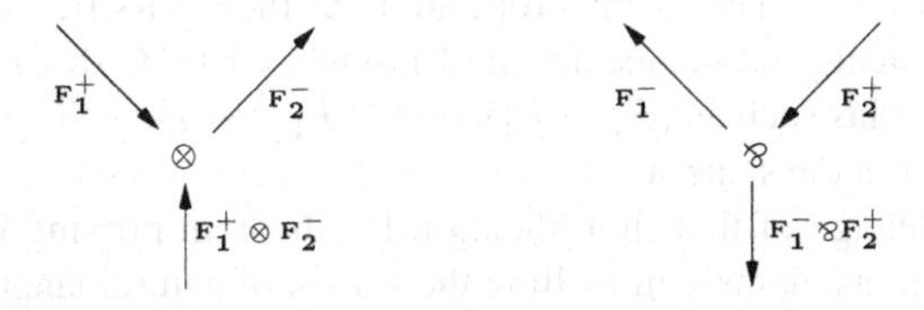

Fig. 1. Negative and positive heterogeneous links of IILL proof nets

an initial *proof frame*. Then, for proving the sequent, we have to connect each negative leaf with a positive leaf of the same type by means of a link which is called an *axiom link* in proof net theory. When all leaves are connected, the proof frame becomes a *proof structure*. The inputs of the proof structure represent the negative formulas $F_1^-, \ldots, F_n^-$ and its unique output represents G^+.
Of course, not all proof structures are proof nets. Among the variety of correctness criteria for proof nets, we have chosen that of Lamarche because it uses the specific properties of intuitionistic proof nets. This criterion uses particular paths in proof nets, which we call *dominance paths*. These paths presuppose an orientation of proof structures by the polarities of their formulas: positive formulas enter links for constituting bigger formulas and go out of the links which produce them and that is the contrary for negative formulas.

Definition 1. *In a proof structure, a* dominance path *is a path that includes no negative premises of positive nodes except possibly as its beginning.*
An occurrence of formula F_1 dominates *an occurrence of formula F_2 if there is a dominance path (possibly empty) from F_2 to F_1 in the proof structure.*

[1] Positive sub-formulas are represented by down arrows and negative sub-formulas by up arrows.

According to this definition and the syntax of proof structures, there is exactly one maximal dominance path that starts from a given formula. Either this path is infinite and includes one cycle or it ends at the output of the proof structure.

Definition 2. *A proof structure is a* proof net *if its output dominates any of its formula occurrences and if the positive premise of any positive link dominates the negative premise of the same link.*

In this definition, the first condition can be restricted to negative links and reformulated as follows: in a proof net, the positive premise of any negative link does not dominate the negative premise of the same link. In this way, the two conditions appear to be dual to each other. A corollary of the definition of a proof net is that the dominance relation is an order in a proof net.
The notion of proof net is justified by the following theorem.

Theorem 1. *An IILL sequent* $F_1, \ldots, F_n \vdash G$ *is provable iff there is a proof net of* $\vdash F_1^-, \ldots, F_n^-, G^+$.

Example 1. We consider the following IILL sequent:

$$a \multimap (b \multimap c),\ (d \multimap ((d \multimap b) \multimap c)) \multimap e \vdash a \multimap e$$

According to Proposition 1, the provability of this sequent in IILL amounts to the provability of the following sequent in CLL: $\vdash a \otimes (b \otimes c^\perp),\ (d^\perp \mathrm{O}\ ((d \otimes b^\perp) \mathrm{O} c)) \otimes e^\perp,$ $a^\perp \mathrm{O} e$. First, we construct the proof frame. By adding axiom links, we obtain the proof structure given by Figure 2 which is a proof net because it verifies Lamarche's criterion.

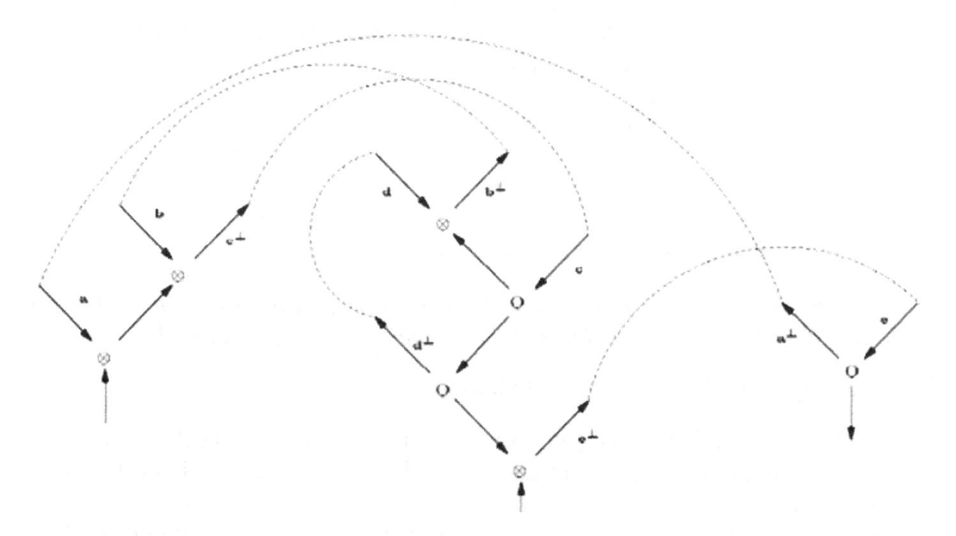

Fig. 2. Proof net of the sequent $\vdash a \otimes (b \otimes c^\perp),\ (d^\perp \mathrm{O}((d \otimes b^\perp) \mathrm{O} c)) \otimes e^\perp,\ a^\perp \mathrm{O} e$

2.2 Models of Tree Descriptions

From the notion of dominance paths in IILL proof nets, we abstract a more compact representation of IILL proofs which only takes atomic formulas into account. In a proof net, the dominance order between its atomic formulas is used to represent proof nets as models of *tree descriptions*. Even if this order is not sufficient to re-build the corresponding proof net, it is sufficient to verify its correctness.
Tree descriptions are abstract representation of IILL sequents in the shape of classical first order logic formulas which are defined from a set $\mathcal{N}$ of nodes. These descriptions are defined modulo a renaming of their nodes. If any node in $\mathcal{N}$ is denoted N, any *tree description* D is defined syntactically as follows:

$$D ::= N : A \mid N : A^{\perp} \mid N > N \mid N >^{*} N \mid D \wedge D$$

Relations $>$ and $>^{*}$ are respectively called *immediate dominance* and *dominance* relations.
Every IILL polarized formula F is translated into a tree description $Descr(F)$ according to the following definition.

Definition 3. *If F is an IILL polarized formula, then $Descr(F)$ is a tree description and $Root(Descr(F))$ is a node of $Descr(F)$ which are defined recursively in parallel as follows.*

1. *if $F = A$, then $Descr(F) = (N : A)$ and $Root(Descr(F)) = N$;*
2. *if $F = A^{\perp}$, then $Descr(F) = (N : A^{\perp})$ and $Root(Descr(F)) = N$;*
3. *if $F = (F_1^{-} \text{O} F_2^{+})$, then*

$$\begin{aligned} Descr(F) = {} & Descr(F_1^{-}) \wedge Descr(F_2^{+}) \wedge \\ & (Root(Descr(F_2^{+}) >^{*} Root(Descr(F_1^{-})) \text{ and} \\ Root(Descr(F)) = {} & Root(Descr(F_2^{+}); \end{aligned}$$

4. *if $F = (F_1^{+} \otimes F_2^{-})$, then*

$$\begin{aligned} Descr(F) = {} & Descr(F_1^{+}) \wedge Descr(F_2^{-}) \wedge \\ & (Root(Descr(F_2^{-}) > Root(Descr(F_1^{+})) \text{ and} \\ Root(Descr(F)) = {} & Root(Descr(F_2^{-}). \end{aligned}$$

Items 3 and 4 are bound by the condition that the nodes of the two descriptions that are composed together are disjoint, otherwise the common nodes are renamed.

The meaning of this translation is the following:

- if there exists a dominance path from a positive atomic formula A to a negative atomic formula $B^{\perp}$ in the syntactic tree of F, $B^{\perp}$ dominates A immediately in $Descr(F)$;
- if it is necessary to create a dominance path from a negative atomic formula $B^{\perp}$ to a positive atomic formula A in the syntactic tree of F for building a proof net from F, A dominates $B^{\perp}$ in $Descr(F)$.

Example 2.
Here is the tree description that represents the syntax of the formula $(d^{\perp}\text{O}((d \otimes b^{\perp})\text{O}c)) \otimes e^{\perp}$ already used in Example 1 : $(n_1 : d^{\perp}) \wedge (n_2 : d) \wedge (n_3 : b^{\perp}) \wedge (n_4 : c) \wedge (n_5 : e^{\perp}) \wedge (n_3 > n_2) \wedge (n_4 >^* n_3) \wedge (n_4 >^* n_1) \wedge (n_5 > n_4)$ This description can represented graphically[2] (see the middle tree on the diagram of Figure 3).

The map *Descr* is naturally extended from single polarized formulas to polarized sequents. The shape of the resulting descriptions is very specific and it can be characterized intrinsically by the following definition.

Definition 4. *An IILL tree description is a tree description such that:*

1. *if N is any node of the description, there is exactly one atomic formula of type $(N : A)$ or $(N : A^{\perp})$ in the description;*
2. *the reflexive and transitive closure of the union of dominance and immediate dominance relations is an order;*
3. *every node N_1 that immediately dominates a node N_2 is negative and N_2 is positive; moreover, N_1 is the only node that immediately dominates N_2;*
4. *every node N_1 that dominates a node N_2 is positive and N_2 is negative; moreover, N_1 is the only node that dominates N_2;*
5. *there exists exactly one positive node that is not immediately dominated and which is called the root of the description.*

The first condition expresses that every node of an IILL tree description has exactly one label which is a proposition and the other conditions express the treeness of such a description with constraints on polarities.
This definition delimits the set of IILL tree descriptions and its relationship with the set of IILL polarized sequents is clarified by the following theorem.

Theorem 2. *If Δ is any IILL polarized sequent, then $Descr(\Delta)$ is an IILL tree description. Conversely, if D is any IILL tree description, there exits an IILL polarized sequent Δ such that $Descr(\Delta) = D$.*

The previous proposition shows that the map *Descr* is surjective but it is not bijective because it erases unessential differences between logic formulas. For instance, $(F_1 \multimap (F_2 \multimap F_3))^+$ and $(F_2 \multimap (F_1 \multimap F_3))^+$ are translated into the same tree descriptions. If polarized sequents are translated into tree descriptions, proof nets are translated into specific models of such descriptions. Since descriptions are classical logic formulas, their models are models of these formulas in the sense of the model theory but they are constrained by additional conditions.

Definition 5. *A model of an IILL description D is a tree T together with an interpretation function I from the set $|D|$ of D nodes to the set $|T|$ of T nodes which respects the following conditions:*

1. *For every node N of $|T|$, $I^{-1}(N) = \{N_1, N_2\}$ and there exists two propositions $(N_1 : A)$ and $(N_2 : A^{\perp})$ in D.*

[2] Since node names do not matter, they do not appear on diagrams.

2. *For every relation* $N_1 > N_2$ *in* D, $I(N_1)$ *is the parent of* $I(N_2)$ *in* T.
3. *For every relation* $N_1 >^* N_2$ *in* D, $I(N_1)$ *is an ancestor of* $I(N_2)$ *or equal to* $I(N_2)$ *in* T.
4. *If* N_1 *is the parent of* N_2 *in* T, *there exists exactly one proposition* $(N_1' > N_2')$ *in* D *such that* $I(N_1') = N_1$ *and* $I(N_2') = N_2$.

Condition 1 guarantees the neutrality of models and Condition 4 guarantees their minimality. From the four conditions above, we can deduce that building a model of an IILL description amounts to plugging dual nodes of the description while respecting dominance and immediate dominance relations ; dominance relations are erased as soon as they are realized and the construction succeeds if all nodes are neutralized without creating cycles and if all dominance constraints are erased.
The notion of model is linked to the notion of provability by the following theorem.

Theorem 3. *An IILL sequent* $F_1, \ldots, F_n \vdash G$ *is provable iff there is model of the IILL tree description of the polarized sequent* $\vdash F_1^-, \ldots, F_n^-, G^+$.

Example 3. The sequent $\vdash\ a \otimes (b \otimes c^\perp),\ (d^\perp O((d \otimes b^\perp)Oc)) \otimes e^\perp,\ a^\perp Oe$ is translated into the tree description given by Figure 3. This description has a model[3] which

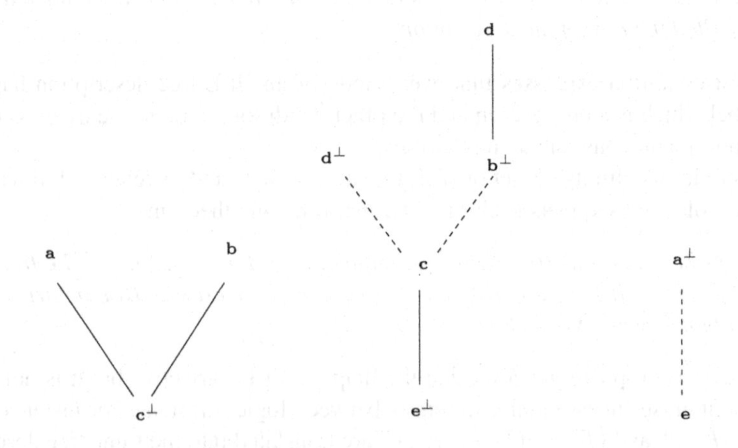

Fig. 3. Tree description of the sequent $\vdash\ a \otimes (b \otimes c^\perp),\ (d^\perp O((d \otimes b^\perp)Oc)) \otimes e^\perp,\ a^\perp Oe$

is presented in Figure 4. According to Theorem 3, this entails that the sequent $\vdash a \otimes (b \otimes c^\perp), (d^\perp O\ ((d \otimes b^\perp)Oc)) \otimes e^\perp,\ a^\perp Oe$ is provable in CLL

For completing the relationship between trees and IILL tree descriptions, we have to say how to go from any tree to an IILL tree description. This is the purpose of the following proposition.

[3] The nodes of the model are labelled with the pairs of formulas that come from the nodes of the description that they interpret.

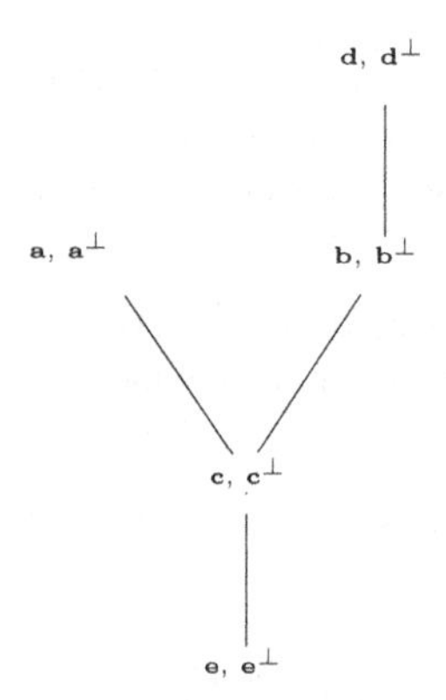

Fig. 4. Model of the tree description given in Figure 3

Proposition 2. *For any tree labelled with atomic formulas, there is a canonical way of building an IILL tree description which has this tree as model.*

3 Intuitionistic Multiplicative Linear Logic (IMLL)

3.1 IMLL Proof Nets

IMLL is an extension of IILL that results from adding a new logic connective, the tensor $\otimes$, to the linear implication. Now, if A represents any proposition, any IMLL formula F is defined by the grammar:

$$F \ ::= \ A \mid F \multimap F \mid F \otimes F$$

The two functions $()^+$ and $()^-$ are extended to tensorized formulas as follows:

$$(F_1 \otimes F_2)^+ = (F_1)^+ \otimes (F_2)^+ \qquad (F_1 \otimes F_2)^- = (F_1)^- \text{O} (F_2)^-$$

Proposition 1, which establishes the equivalence between the two-sided and the one-sided sequent calculi applies to IMLL. Proof frames are enriched with two kinds of links defined by Figure 5. The definition of dominance paths does not change but the

Fig. 5. Negative and positive homogeneous links of IMLL proof nets

presence of negative homogeneous links makes it possible for dominance paths to fork. As a consequence, the correctness criterion of proof nets must be made more precise.

Definition 6. *An IMLL proof structure is a* proof net *if its dominance relation is an ordering with the following properties: the output dominates any other formula occurrences and the positive premise of any positive link dominates the negative premise of the same link.*

The theorem that establishes the equivalence between provability in the sequent calculus and provability with proof nets has a proof which is more complicated than in IILL in its sequentialization part.

Theorem 4. *An IMLL sequent $F_1, \dots, F_n \vdash G$ is provable iff there is a proof net of $\vdash F_1^-, \dots, F_n^-, G^+$.*

Example 4. We consider the following IMLL sequent:

$$(((f \otimes g) \multimap a) \multimap (a \otimes b)) \multimap c,\ ((d \otimes g) \multimap c) \multimap e \vdash (d \multimap (b \otimes f)) \multimap e$$

The provability of this sequent in IMLL amounts to the provability of the following sequent in CLL:

$$\vdash\ (((f \otimes g) \otimes a^\perp) \mathrm{O} (a \otimes b)) \otimes c^\perp,\ ((d^\perp \mathrm{O} g^\perp) \mathrm{O} c) \otimes e^\perp,\ (d \otimes (b^\perp \mathrm{O} f^\perp)) \mathrm{O} e$$

By adding axiom links to the proof frame, we obtain the proof structure of Figure 6 which is a proof net because it verifies Lamarche's criterion.

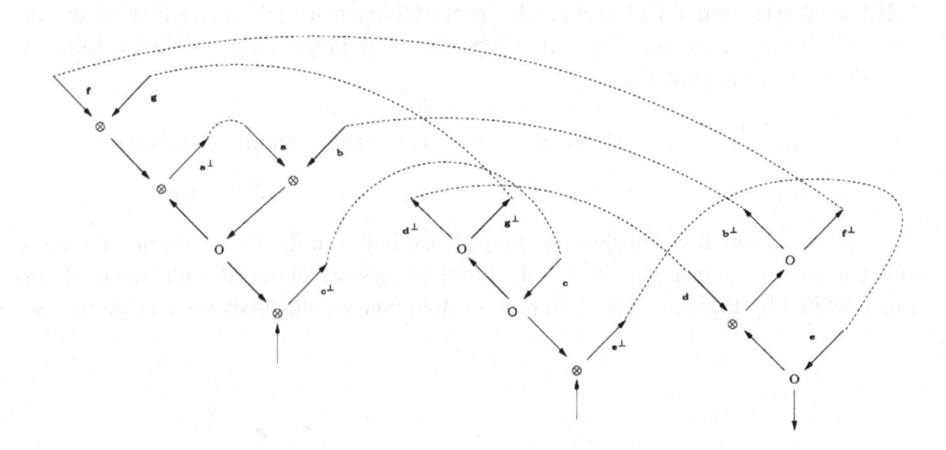

Fig. 6. Proof net of the sequent $\vdash\ (((f \otimes g) \otimes a^\perp) \mathrm{O} (a \otimes b)) \otimes c^\perp,\ ((d^\perp \mathrm{O}\, g^\perp) \mathrm{O} c) \otimes e^\perp,$ $(d \otimes (b^\perp \mathrm{O} f^\perp)) \mathrm{O} e$

3.2 Models of DAG Descriptions

If we try again to view proofs of sequents as models of descriptions, the main change that we have to do is to replace trees with DAGs.

First, we have to extend the syntax of descriptions with the use of classical disjunction so that a *DAG description* D is defined by the following grammar:

$$D ::= N : A \mid N : A^{\perp} \mid N > N \mid N >^{*} N \mid D \wedge D \mid D \vee D$$

The map $Descr$ that turns a polarized formula F into a DAG description $Descr(F)$ is more sophisticated. Now, $Root(Descr(F))$ is a set of nodes so that the definition of $Descr$ and $Root$ is the following:

Definition 7. *If F is an IMLL polarized formula, then $Descr(F)$ is a DAG description and $Root(Descr(F))$ is a set of nodes of $Descr(F)$ which are defined recursively in parallel as follows.*

1. *if $F = A$, then $Descr(F) = (N : A)$ and $Root(Descr(F)) = \{N\}$;*
2. *if $F = A^{\perp}$, then $Descr(F) = (N : A^{\perp})$ and $Root(Descr(F)) = \{N\}$;*
3. *if $F = (F_1^- \mathrm{O} F_2^+)$, then*

$$\begin{aligned} &Descr(F) = Descr(F_1^-) \wedge Descr(F_2^+) \wedge (\textstyle\bigwedge_{i=1}^{n} \bigvee_{j=1}^{m} (B_j >^{*} {A_i}^{\perp})) \text{ with} \\ &\quad Root(Descr(F_1^-)) = \{{A_1}^{\perp}, \ldots, {A_n}^{\perp}\} \text{ and} \\ &\quad Root(Descr(F_2^+)) = \{B_1, \ldots, B_m\}; \\ &Root(Descr(F)) = Root(Descr(F_2^+)). \end{aligned}$$

4. *if $F = (F_1^+ \otimes F_2^-)$, then*

$$\begin{aligned} &Descr(F) = Descr(F_1^+) \wedge Descr(F_2^-) \wedge (\textstyle\bigwedge_{i=1}^{n} \bigwedge_{j=1}^{m} (B_j^{\perp} > A_i)) \text{ with} \\ &\quad Root(Descr(F_1^+)) = \{A_1, \ldots, A_n\} \text{ and} \\ &\quad Root(Descr(F_2^-)) = \{B_1^{\perp}, \ldots, B_m^{\perp}\}; \\ &Root(Descr(F)) = Root(Descr(F_2^-)). \end{aligned}$$

5. *if $F = (F_1^+ \otimes F_2^+)$, then $Descr(F) = Descr(F_1^+) \wedge Descr(F_2^+)$;*
   $Root(Descr(F)) = Root(Descr(F_1^+) \cup Root(Descr(F_2^+)$;
6. *if $F = (F_1^- \mathrm{O} F_2^-)$, then $Descr(F) = Descr(F_1^-) \wedge Descr(F_2^-)$;*
   $Root(Descr(F)) = Root(Descr(F_1^-) \cup Root(Descr(F_2^-)$;

The four last items are bound by the condition that the nodes of the two descriptions that are composed together are disjoint, otherwise the common nodes are renamed.

In the same way as for IILL, the map *Descr* is extended to polarized sequents.

Example 5. Let us consider the following sequent again:
$\vdash (((f \otimes g) \otimes a^{\perp}) \mathrm{O} (a \otimes b)) \otimes c^{\perp}, ((d^{\perp} \mathrm{O} g^{\perp}) \mathrm{O} c) \otimes e^{\perp}, (d \otimes (b^{\perp} \mathrm{O} f^{\perp})) \mathrm{O} e$
It is translated into the DAG description which is represented graphically by the diagram of Figure 7. Disjunctions between dominance relations are represented by arcs of circle.

The shape of the DAG descriptions resulting from the translation of polarized sequents is more complicated in IMLL than in IILL. It needs the auxiliary definition of *parent set*.

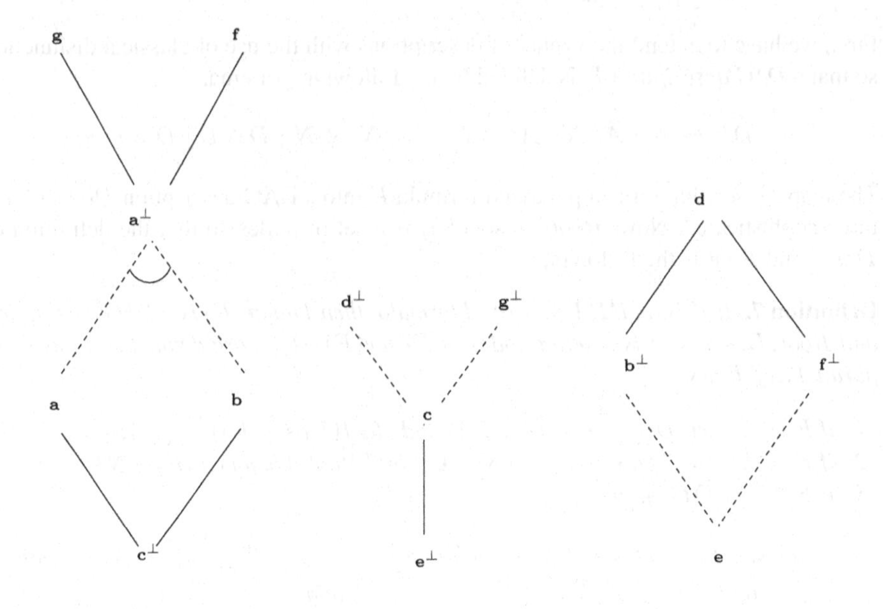

Fig. 7. DAG description of the sequent $\vdash\ (((f \otimes g)\otimes a^{\perp})\mathcal{O}(a \otimes b)) \otimes c^{\perp},\ ((d^{\perp}\mathcal{O}g^{\perp})\mathcal{O}c)\otimes e^{\perp},\ (d \otimes (b^{\perp}\mathcal{O}f^{\perp}))\mathcal{O}e$

Definition 8. *In a DAG description D, the parent set of a positive node N is the set of the nodes N_i such that $(N_i > N)$ belongs to D and the parent set of a negative node N' is the set of the nodes N_i such that $(N_i >^* N)$ belongs to D.*

With this notion, an IMLL DAG description is characterized intrinsically by the following definition.

Definition 9. *An IMLL DAG description is a DAG description that can be put in the shape $D_{Nodes} \wedge D_{DomIm} \wedge D_{Dom}$ with the following properties:*

1. *D_{Nodes} is a conjunction of propositions in the form $(N : L)$ such that N is an element of $\mathcal{N}$ and L is a positive or negative formula; every node of $\mathcal{N}$ is present one time at most in D_{Nodes};*
2. *D_{DomIm} is a conjunction of propositions in the form $(N_1 > N_2)$ such that N_1 and N_2 are present in D_{Nodes} with respectively a negative and a positive label;*
3. *D_{Dom} is a conjunction of disjunctions in the form $(N_1 >^* N) \vee \cdots \vee (N_p >^* N)$ such that $N_1, \ldots, N_p$ are present in D_{Nodes} with positive labels and N is present with a negative label;*
4. *the reflexive and transitive closure of the union of dominance and immediate dominance relations described by D_{DomIm} and D_{Dom} is an order;*
5. *two parent sets determined by D_{DomIm} or D_{Dom} either are disjoint or one is included in the other and the elements of any parent set are dominated and immediately dominated by the same nodes.*
6. *the set of positive nodes that are immediately dominated by no negative nodes is not empty.*

Condition 4 expresses acyclicity of DAGs. Condition 5 expresses structural constraints related to the relative positions of positive and negative links in a proof net. As we will see in the proof of Theorem 5, this condition is essential for recovering IMLL polarized sequents from DAG descriptions.

Theorem 5. *If Δ is any IMLL polarized sequent, then $Descr(\Delta)$ is an IMLL DAG description. Conversely, if D is any IMLL DAG description, there exits an IMLL polarized sequent Δ such that $Descr(\Delta) = D$.*

Now, we have established an equivalence between IMLL polarized sequents and IMLL descriptions and we have to establish a corresponding equivalence between proof nets and specific models of such descriptions. First, we must define the constraints that make the specificity of these models.

Definition 10. *A model of an IMLL DAG description D is a DAG G together with an interpretation function I from the set $|D|$ of D nodes to the set $|T|$ of G nodes which respects the following conditions:*

1. *For every node N of $|G|$, $I^{-1}(N) = \{N_1, N_2\}$ and there exists two propositions $(N_1 : A)$ and $(N_2 : A^{\perp})$ in D.*
2. *For every relation $N_1 > N_2$ in D, $I(N_1)$ is the parent of $I(N_2)$ in G.*
3. *In every disjunction $(N_1 >^* N) \vee \cdots \vee (N_p >^* N)$in D, there exists at least one proposition $(N_k >^* N)$ such that every path that starts from $I(N)$ in G goes through $I(N_k)$.*
4. *If N_1 is a parent of N_2 in G, there exists exactly one proposition $(N'_1 > N'_2)$ in D such that $I(N'_1) = N_1$ and $I(N'_2) = N_2$.*

What is new in this definition with respect to IILL is the interpretation of dominance relations. First, we have to interpret disjunctions and then, the interpretation of dominance is stronger than the existence of a path in a DAG: a node N_1 can be an ancestor of a node N_2 in a DAG but this relation is not an interpretation of a dominance relation if N_1 is an ancestor of a third node N_3 which is not comparable with N_2.

Theorem 6. *An IMLL sequent $F_1, \ldots, F_n \vdash G$ is provable iff there is an IMLL model of the tree description of the polarized sequent $\vdash F_1^-, \ldots, F_n^-, G^+$.*

Example 6. Let us take again the sequent
$\vdash (((f \otimes g) \otimes a^{\perp}) \mathrm{O} (a \otimes b)) \otimes c^{\perp},\ ((d^{\perp} \mathrm{O} g^{\perp}) \mathrm{O} c) \otimes e^{\perp},\ (d \otimes (b^{\perp} \mathrm{O} f^{\perp})) \mathrm{O} e$
Its description, given in Figure 7, has a model that is presented in Figure 8. Therefore, according to Theorem 6, the sequent is provable in CLL.

For completing the relationship between DAGs and IMLL DAG descriptions, we have to say how to go from any DAG to an IMLL DAG description. Unlike trees, we have to make a restriction that uses the notion of parent set which can be easily transposed from DAG descriptions to DAGs.

Proposition 3. *For any DAG labelled with atomic formulas, there is a canonical way of building an IMLL DAG description that has this DAG as model if it respects the following property: if two parent sets are not disjoint, one is included in the other.*

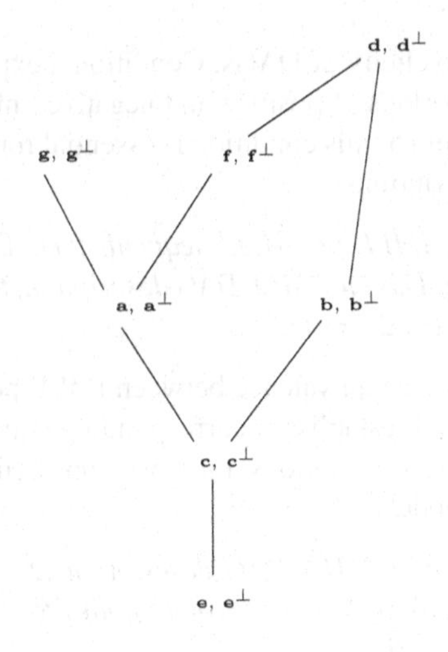

Fig. 8. Model of the DAG description given in Figure 7

4 Applications to Theorem Proving and Syntactic Analysis of Natural Languages

In this paper, we have shown that proof nets in the framework of IMLL reduce to specific models of DAG descriptions. Now, the question is what kinds of applications can find some interest in this new approach of proofs in linear logic. In the restricted space of this paper, we can merely give a flavour of possible applications.

4.1 Theorem Proving as a Constraint Satisfaction Problem

By reducing theorem proving to finding models of DAG descriptions, we obtain a formulation of this problem which is now monotone and can be treated as a constraint satisfaction problem:

- The variables of the problem are the nodes of the descriptions.
- There are two kinds of constraints on these variables: general constraints define the general shape of the models and specific constraints describe the particular sequents that have to be proved.
- Problems have solutions if all constraints are satisfiable.

For the moment, there exists no implementation of this approach but a sizeable amount of work has been done on the treatment of dominance constraints as finite set constraints [DT99], which can be easily re-used for IMLL tree or DAG descriptions. The idea behind this treatment is simple but very fruitful: every node of a tree or DAG description is associated with an integer; then, four or five finite set variables are associated with every node which represent a partition of the space with respect to the node that is considered (up, down, left, right, equal); then, dominance constraints are expressed in terms of relations between sets of integers (inclusion, disjunction,...).

4.2 Models of the Syntax of Natural Languages

Resource sensitivity of linear logic is used for modelling the syntax of natural languages in the approach of Categorial Grammars [Moo96,Ret96]. In this approach, grammars are lexicalized. The entries of lexicons are finite sets of logic formulas which represent syntactic types. Parsing a sentence $w_1.\dots.w_n$ consists first in selecting a type F_i from the lexicon for each word w_i of the sentence. Then the proper parsing process consists in proving the formula S, which represents the sentence type, from the hypotheses $F_1.\dots.F_n$.
The consequence of this approach is that syntactic structures are represented by proof nets. In these proof nets, axiom links represent syntactic dependencies between the constituents of a sentence.
Since IMLL does not bring significant advantages with respect to IILL from a linguistic point of view, most of time we use IILL as logical framework. In this framework, the interest of viewing proof nets as model of tree descriptions is to simplify the formalism in order to keep only the pieces of information that are linguistically pertinent: tree descriptions represent exactly under-specified syntactic trees such as grammarians know them.

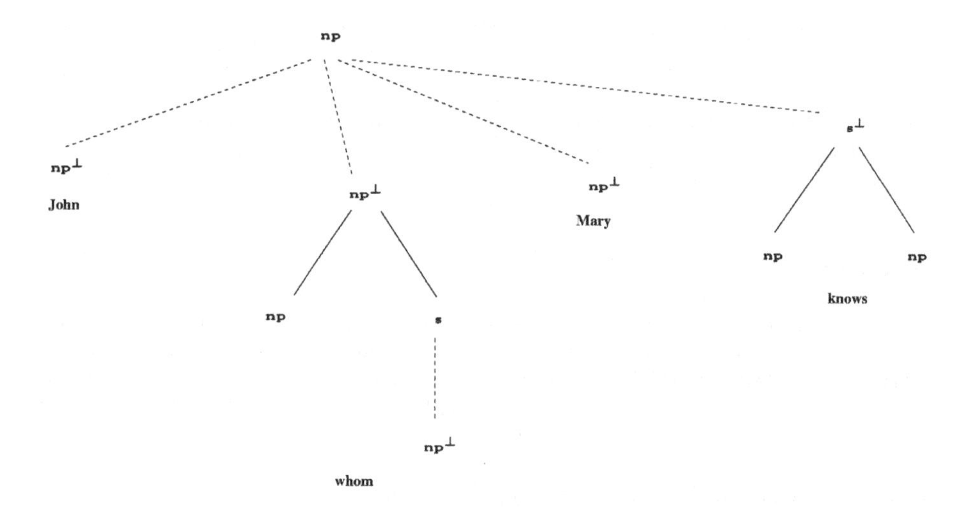

Fig. 9. Tree description representing the resources used for parsing *John whom Mary knows*

Example 7. In Figure 9, you find a very simple example of a tree description[4] representing the resources that are provided by a lexicon for parsing the noun phrase (np) *John whom Mary knows*. For sake of simplicity, we have dropped linguistic information and we have only kept the syntactic types of the words in the form of linear logic formulas. Our lexicon gives the following respective types for the words *John, whom, Mary* and *knows*: np, $np \multimap ((np \multimap s) \multimap np)$, np, $np \multimap (np \multimap s)$. Parsing the phase amounts

[4] As usually in linguistics, trees are oriented top-down.

to proving the IILL sequent: $np,\ np \multimap ((np \multimap s) \multimap np), np, np \multimap (np \multimap s) \vdash np$. Parsing succeeds because there is a model of the description [5] which is given in Figure 10 and which exactly represents the syntactic tree of the noun phrase *John whom Mary knows*.

This approach of the syntax of natural languages allows to put a bridge between two apparently opposite views: a proof theoretic view and a model theoretic view [PS01]. It also allows to design more flexible linguistic formalisms which take advantage of both resource sensitivity of Categorial Grammars and flexibility of tree descriptions [Per00].

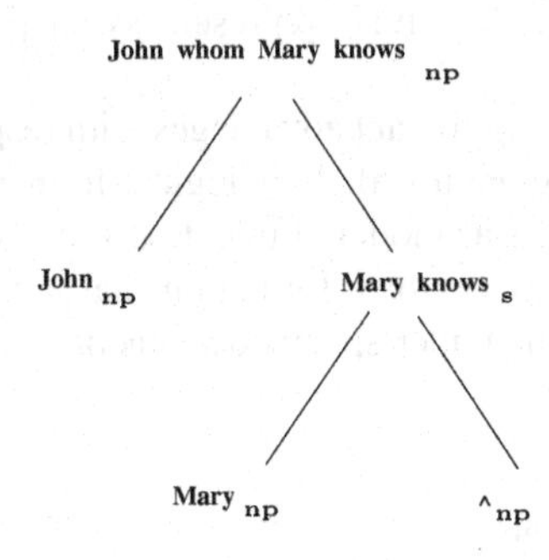

Fig. 10. Model of the tree description of Figure 9 representing the syntactic tree of *John whom Mary knows*

References

[Bla99] P. Blache. *"Contraintes et théories linguistiques : des Grammaires d'Unification aux Grammaires de Propriétés"*. Thèse d'habilitation, Université Paris 7, 1999.

[DT99] D. Duchier and S. Thater. Parsing with tree descriptions: a constraint based approach. In *Natural Language Understanding and Logic Programming NLULP'99,Dec 1999, Las Cruces, New Mexico*, 1999.

[Gir87] J.-Y. Girard. Linear logic. *Theoretical Computer Science*, 50(1):1–102, 1987.

[Lam94] F. Lamarche. Proof Nets for Intuitionistic Linear Logic I: Essential Nets. Preliminary report, Imperial College, April 1994. Available via the URL *http://hypatia.dcs.qmw.ac.uk/*.

[Moo96] M. Moortgart. Categorial Type Logics. In J. van Benthem and A. ter Meulen, editors, *Handbook of Logic and Language*, chapter 2. Elsevier, 1996.

[Per00] G. Perrier. Interaction grammars. In *CoLing '2000, Sarrebrücken*, 2000.

[PS01] G. K. Pullum and B. C. Scholz. On the Distinction between Model-Theoretic and Generative-Enumerative Syntactic Frameworks. In P. de Groote, G. Morrill, and C. Retoré, editors, *Logical Aspects of Computational Linguistics, LACL 2001, Le Croisic, France*, volume 2099 of *Lecture Notes in Computer Science*, pages 17–43. Springer Verlag, 2001.

[5] We have labelled the nodes of the tree with the phonological forms of the constituents and their syntactic types.

[Ret96] C. Retoré. Calcul de lambek et logique linéaire. *Traitement Automatique des Langues*, 37(2):39–70, 1996.

[RVS94] J. Rogers and K. Vijay-Shanker. Obtaining trees from their descriptions: an application to tree-adjoining grammars. *Computational Intelligence*, 10(4):401–421, 1994.

[RVSW95] O. Rambow, K. Vijay-Shanker, and D. Weir. D-tree grammars. In *33rd Annual Meeting of the Association for Computational Linguistics*, pages 151–158, 1995.

[VS92] K. Vijay-Shanker. Using description of trees in a tree adjoining grammar. *Computational Linguistics*, 18(4):481–517, 1992.

Coherence and Transitivity in Coercive Subtyping

Yong Luo and Zhaohui Luo*

Department of Computer Science,
University of Durham,
South Road, Durham, DH1 3LE , U.K.
{Yong.Luo, Zhaohui.Luo}@durham.ac.uk

Abstract. Coercive subtyping is a general approach to subtyping, inheritance and abbreviation in dependent type theories. A vital requirement for coercive subtyping is that of coherence – computational uniqueness of coercions between any two types. In this paper, we develop techniques useful in proving coherence and its related result on admissibility of transitivity and substitution. In particular, we consider suitable subtyping rules for Π-types and Σ-types and prove its coherence and the admissibility of substitution and transitivity rules at the type level in the coercive subtyping framework.

1 Introduction

Coercive subtyping, as studied in [Luo97,Luo99,SL01], represents a novel general approach to subtyping and inheritance in type theory. In particular, it provides a framework in which subtyping, inheritance, and abbreviation can be understood in dependent type theories where types are understood as consisting of canonical objects.

In this paper, we consider the issue of *coherence* in the framework of coercive subtyping; in particular, we develop techniques useful for proving coherence in coercive subtyping. The coherence conditions are the most basic requirement for the subtyping rules. In essence, it says that any two coercions between two types must be the same, which ensures the uniqueness of coercions (if any). Among other things, coherence is the basis for the whole coercive subtyping framework to be consistent and for it to be implemented in a correct way. A related important issue is that of admissibility of transitivity and substitution, which apart from its relationship with coherence, is essential for implementation of the theory.

We shall develop methods to prove coherence and the admissibility results. In particular, we consider suitable subtyping rules for Π and Σ-types as examples to demonstrate these proof techniques. Although some important meta-theoretic

* The first author thanks the support of the ORS Award and the Durham University studentship. This work by the second author is partly supported by the UK EPSRC grant GR/M75518 and the EU grant on the TYPES project.

R. Nieuwenhuis and A. Voronkov (Eds.): LPAR 2001, LNAI 2250, pp. 249–265, 2001.

results such as the conservativity result have been obtained for coercive subtyping, the current paper is the first attempt to prove coherence and admissibility results at the type level in the framework. The techniques developed here have wider and further applications.

In Section 2, we give an overview of coercive subtyping, presenting the formal framework and giving informal explanations of the coherence problem. In Section 3, a general strategy for proving coherence and the admissibility results is considered, and a formal definition of the so-called well-defined coercions is given as the basis for the proof techniques to be considered in the following sections. In Sections 4 and 5, we prove coherence and the admissibility of substitution and transitivity rules, respectively. Discussions are given in the concluding section (Section 6), where we discuss issues such as decidability and weak transitivity, the latter of which is important for the coercive subtyping framework and its applications.

2 Coercive Subtyping and the Coherence Problem

In this section, we give a brief introduction to coercive subtyping, explain the notion of coherence and its importance, and lay down the necessary formal details to be used in the following sections.

2.1 Coercive Subtyping

The basic idea of coercive subtyping, as studied in e.g., [Luo99], is that A is a subtype of B if there is a (unique) coercion c from A to B, and therefore, any object of type A may be regarded as object of type B via c, where c is a functional operation from A to B in the type theory.

A coercion plays the role of abbreviation. More precisely, if c is a coercion from K_0 to K, then a functional operation f with domain K can be applied to any object k_0 of K_0 and the application $f(k_0)$ is definitionally equal to $f(c(k_0))$. Intuitively, we can view f as a context which requires an object of K; then the argument k_0 in the context f stands for its image of the coercion, $c(k_0)$. Therefore, one can use $f(k_0)$ as an abbreviation of $f(c(k_0))$.

The above simple idea, when formulated in the logical framework, becomes very powerful. The second author and his colleagues have developed the framework of coercive subtyping that covers variety of subtyping relations including those represented by parameterised coercions and coercions between parameterised inductive types. See [Luo99,Bai99,CL01,LC98,CLP01] for details of some of these development and applications of coercive subtyping.

Some important meta-theoretic aspects of coercive subtyping have been studied. In particular, the results on conservativity and on transitivity elimination for subkinding have been proved in [JLS98,SL01]. The conservativity result says, intuitively, that every judgement that is derivable in the theory with coercive subtyping and that does not contain coercive applications is derivable in the original type theory. Furthermore, for every derivation in the theory with coercive subtyping, one can always insert coercions correctly to obtain a derivation in the original type theory. The main result of [SL01] is essentially that coherence of basic subtyping rules does imply conservativity. These results not only justify the adequacy of the theory from the proof-theoretic consideration, but also provide the proof-theoretic basis for implementation of coercive subtyping. (However, how to prove coherence and admissibility of transitivity at the type level has not been studied; this is the subject of this paper.)

Coercion mechanisms with certain restrictions have been implemented both in the proof development system Lego [LP92] and Coq [B+00], by Bailey [Bai99] and Saibi [Sai97], respectively. Callaghan of the Computer Assisted Reasoning Group at Durham has implemented Plastic [CL01], a proof assistant that supports logical framework and coercive subtyping with a mixture of simple coercions, parameterised coercions, coercion rules for parameterised inductive types, and dependent coercions [LS99].

A formal presentation. Here, before discussing further the problems of coherence and transitivity, we first give a formal presentation of the framework of coercive cubtyping, which is also the basis for our development in latter sections. We shall be brief in this paper (for details and more explanations, see [Luo99]).

Coercive subtyping is formally formulated as an extension of (type theories specified in) the logical framework LF [Luo94], whose rules are given in Appendix A. In LF, *Type* represents the conceptual universe of types and $(x : K)K'$ represents the dependent product with functional operations f as objects (e.g., abstraction $[x : K]k$) which can be applied to objects of kind K to form application $f(k)$. LF can be used to specify type theories, such as Martin-Löf's type theory [NPS90] and UTT [Luo94].

For example, Π-types, types of dependent functions, can be specified by introducing the constants for (1) formation: $\Pi(A, B)$ is a type for any type A and any family of types B, (2) introduction: $\lambda(A, B, f)$ is a function of type $\Pi(A, B)$ if f is a functional operation of kind $(x : A)B(x)$, and (3) elimination, from which we can define the application operator $app(A, B, F, a)$. Similarly, we can introduce Σ-types $\Sigma(A, B)$ with introduction operator to form $pair(A, B, a, b)$ and an elimination operator from which the projections $\pi_1(A, B, p)$ and $\pi_2(A, B, p)$ can be defined.

Notation. We shall use the following notations:

- We shall often omit the *El*-operator in LF to write A for $El(A)$ when no confusion may occur and may write $(K)K'$ for $(x : K)K'$ when x does not occur free in K'.
- We sometimes use $M[x]$ to indicate that variable x may occur free in M and subsequently write $M[N]$ for $[N/x]M$, when no confusion may occur.
- Functional composition: for $f : (K_1)K_2$ and $g : (y : K_2)K_3[y]$, define $g \circ f =_{\mathrm{df}} [x : K_1]g(f(x)) : (x : K_1)K_3[f(x)]$, where x does not occur free in f or g.
- Context equality: for $\Gamma \equiv x_1 : K_1, ..., x_n : K_n$ and $\Gamma' \equiv x_1 : K_1', ..., x_n : K_n'$, we shall write $\vdash \Gamma = \Gamma'$ for the sequence of judgements $\vdash K_1 = K_1'$, ..., $x_1 : K_1, ..., x_{n-1} : K_{n-1} \vdash K_n = K_n'$.

A system with coercive subtyping, T[$\mathcal{R}$], is an extension of any type theory T specified in LF by a set of basic subtyping rules $\mathcal{R}$. It can be presented in two stages: first we formulate the intermediate system T[$\mathcal{R}$]$_0$ with subtyping judgements of the form $\Gamma \vdash A <_c B{:}\,Type$, and then add the subkinding judgements of the form $\Gamma \vdash K <_c K'$ and rules concerning coercions between kinds.

T[$\mathcal{R}$]$_0$ is an extension of T (only) with the subtyping judgement form $\Gamma \vdash A <_c B{:}\,Type$ and the following rules:

- A set $\mathcal{R}$ of basic subtyping rules whose conclusions are subtyping judgements of the form $\Gamma \vdash A <_c B{:}\,Type$.
- The following congruence rule for subtyping judgements

$$(Cong)\quad \frac{\Gamma \vdash A <_c B{:}\,Type \qquad \Gamma \vdash A = A'{:}\,Type \quad \Gamma \vdash B = B'{:}\,Type \quad \Gamma \vdash c = c'{:}\,(A)B}{\Gamma \vdash A' <_{c'} B'{:}\,Type}$$

In the presentation of coercive subtyping in [Luo99], T[$\mathcal{R}$]$_0$ also has the following substitution and transitivity rules:

$$(Subst)\quad \frac{\Gamma, x : K, \Gamma' \vdash A <_c B{:}\,Type \quad \Gamma \vdash k{:}\,K}{\Gamma, [k/x]\Gamma' \vdash [k/x]A <_{[k/x]c} [k/x]B{:}\,Type}$$

$$(Trans)\quad \frac{\Gamma \vdash A <_c B{:}\,Type \quad \Gamma \vdash B <_{c'} C{:}\,Type}{\Gamma \vdash A <_{c' \circ c} C{:}\,Type}$$

Since we consider in this paper how to prove that the substitution and transitivity rules are admissible, we do not include them as basic rules.

Remark 1. We have the following remarks.

- T[$\mathcal{R}$]$_0$ is obviously a conservative extension of the original type theory T, since the subtyping judgements do not contribute to any derivation of a judgement of any other form.
- The set of basic coercion rules is supposed to be *coherent*; we shall give definition and discussions of this in the next subsection.

The system T[$\mathcal{R}$], the extension of T with coercive subtyping with respect to $\mathcal{R}$, is the system obtained from T[$\mathcal{R}$]$_0$ by adding the new subkinding judgement form $\Gamma \vdash K <_c K'$ and the rules in Appendix B. Note that the substitution rule and the transitivity rule for kinds (the last two rules in Appendix B) can be eliminated under the assumption that the set of basic subtyping rules $\mathcal{R}$ is coherent [SL01].

Notation. Since we are not much concerned with the subkinding judgements and are mainly concerned with the subtyping judgements, we shall simply write $\Gamma \vdash A <_c B$ for $\Gamma \vdash A <_c B{:}\,Type$, when there is no confusion may occur. Sometimes, we shall also write $\Gamma \vdash A = B$ for $\Gamma \vdash A = B{:}\,Type$.

2.2 Coherence of the Basic Subtyping Rules

The basic subtyping rules are the basis for the coercive subtyping system. Examples of such rules include

- simple coercion declarations such as those between basic inductive types: *Even* is a subtype of *Nat*;
- parameterised coercions representing (point-wise) subtyping (or subfamily relation) between two families of types indexed by objects of the same type; for example, each vector type $Vec(A, n)$ can be taken as a subtype of that of lists $List(A)$, parameterised by the index n, where the coercion would map the vector $< a_1, ..., a_n >$ to the list $[a_1, ..., a_n]$.
- coercions between parameterised inductive type: e.g., $\Sigma(A, B)$ is a subtype of $\Sigma(A', B')$ if A is a subtype of A' and B is a subfamily of B'.

The most basic requirement for such basic subtyping rules is that of coherence, given in the following definition, which essentially says that basic coercions between any two types must be unique.

Definition 1 (coherence condition). *We say that the basic subtyping rules are* coherent *if* $T[\mathcal{R}]_0$ *has the following* coherence properties*:*

1. *If* $\Gamma \vdash A <_c B : Type$, *then* $\Gamma \vdash A : Type$, $\Gamma \vdash B : Type$, *and* $\Gamma \vdash c : (A)B$.
2. $\Gamma \not\vdash A <_c A : Type$ *for any* Γ, A *and* c.
3. *If* $\Gamma \vdash A <_c B : Type$ *and* $\Gamma \vdash A <_{c'} B : Type$, *then* $\Gamma \vdash c = c' : (A)B$.

Remark 2. This is a weaker notion of coherence as compared with that given in [Luo99], since there the rules $(Subst)(Trans)$ are included in $T[\mathcal{R}]_0$. In general, when parameterised coercions and substitutions are present, coherence is undecidable. This is one of the reasons one needs to consider proofs of coherence in general.

Examples of basic coercion rules include those mentioned above, among which one can find the lifting operators between type universes, overloading coercions, etc. Also, for example, for parameterised Π-types and Σ-types, we can have their subtyping rules as given in Figure 1 and Figure 2. Note that these rules are suitable ones for which we can show that transitivity is admissible. If one chose inductively defined coercions, strong transitivity would not be admissible (see Section 6.2 for discussions.)

3 Well-Defined Coercions

As mentioned above, unless the coercions can be represented as a finite graph, coherence is in general undecidable, especially when we have parameterised coercions. So we need to consider how to prove coherence and the related admissibility results.

Domain rule

$$\frac{\Gamma \vdash A' <_c A \quad \Gamma \vdash B : (A)Type}{\Gamma \vdash \Pi(A,B) <_{d_1} \Pi(A', B \circ c)}$$

where $d_1 = [f : \Pi(A,B)]\lambda(A', B \circ c, app(A,B,f) \circ c)$.

Codomain rule

$$\frac{\Gamma \vdash B : (A)Type \quad \Gamma \vdash B' : (A)Type \quad \Gamma, x : A \vdash B(x) <_{e[x]} B'(x)}{\Gamma \vdash \Pi(A,B) <_{d_2} \Pi(A,B')}$$

where $d_2 = [f : \Pi(A,B)]\lambda(A, B', [x : A]e[x](app(A,B,f,x)))$.

Domain-Codomain rule

$$\frac{\begin{array}{c}\Gamma \vdash A' <_c A \quad \Gamma \vdash B : (A)Type \quad \Gamma \vdash B' : (A')Type \\ \Gamma, x : A' \vdash B(c(x)) <_{e[x]} B'(x)\end{array}}{\Gamma \vdash \Pi(A,B) <_{d_3} \Pi(A', B')}$$

where $d_3 = [f : \Pi(A,B)]\lambda(A', B', [x : A']e[x](app(A,B,f,c(x))))$.

Fig. 1. Basic subtyping rules for Π-types.

First Component rule

$$\frac{\Gamma \vdash A <_c A' \quad \Gamma \vdash B : (A')Type}{\Gamma \vdash \Sigma(A, B \circ c) <_{d_1} \Sigma(A', B)}$$

where $d_1 = [x : \Sigma(A, B \circ c)]pair(A', B, c(\pi_1(A, B \circ c, x)), \pi_2(A, B \circ c, x))$.

Second Component rule

$$\frac{\Gamma \vdash B : (A)Type \quad \Gamma \vdash B' : (A)Type \quad \Gamma, x : A \vdash B(x) <_{e[x]} B'(x)}{\Gamma \vdash \Sigma(A,B) <_{d_2} \Sigma(A,B')}$$

where $d_2 = [x : \Sigma(A,B)]pair(A, B', \pi_1(A,B,x), e[\pi_1(A,B,x)](\pi_2(A,B,x)))$.

First-Second Component rule

$$\frac{\begin{array}{c}\Gamma \vdash A <_c A' \quad \Gamma \vdash B : (A)Type \quad \Gamma \vdash B' : (A')Type \\ \Gamma, x : A \vdash B(x) <_{e[x]} B'(c(x))\end{array}}{\Gamma \vdash \Sigma(A,B) <_{d_3} \Sigma(A', B')}$$

where $d_3 = [x : \Sigma(A,B)]pair(A', B', c(\pi_1(A,B,x)), e[\pi_1(A,B,x)](\pi_2(A,B,x)))$.

Fig. 2. Basic subtyping rules for Σ-types.

A general strategy we adopt is to consider such proofs in a stepwise way. That is, if we know that some existing coercions (possibly generated by some existing rules) are coherent and have good admissibility properties, and we add some more subtyping rules, can we show that the newly extended system is still coherent and has good admissibility properties? This has led us to define the following concept of *well-defined coercions.* We shall then use subtyping rules for Π and Σ-types to demonstrate how coherence etc can be proved.

Definition 2 (Well-defined coercions). *If $\mathcal{C}$ is a set of subtyping judgements of the form $\Gamma \vdash M <_d M'\colon Type$ which satisfies the following conditions, we say that $\mathcal{C}$ is a* well-defined set of judgements for coercions, *or briefly called* well-defined coercions (WDC)*:*

1. *(Coherence)*
   a) $\Gamma \vdash A <_c B \in \mathcal{C}$ *implies* $\Gamma \vdash A : Type$, $\Gamma \vdash B : Type$ *and* $\Gamma \vdash c\colon (A)B$.
   b) $\Gamma \vdash A <_c A \notin \mathcal{C}$ *for any* Γ , A , *and* c.
   c) $\Gamma \vdash A <_{c_1} B \in \mathcal{C}$ *and* $\Gamma \vdash A <_{c_2} B \in \mathcal{C}$ *imply* $\Gamma \vdash c_1 = c_2\colon (A)B$.
2. *(Congruence)* $\Gamma \vdash A <_c B \in \mathcal{C}$, $\Gamma \vdash A = A'$, $\Gamma \vdash B = B'$ *and* $\Gamma \vdash c = c'\colon (A)B$ *imply* $\Gamma \vdash A' <_{c'} B' \in \mathcal{C}$.
3. *(Transitivity)* $\Gamma \vdash A <_{c_1} B \in \mathcal{C}$ *and* $\Gamma \vdash B <_{c_2} A' \in \mathcal{C}$ *imply* $\Gamma \vdash A <_{c_3} A' \in \mathcal{C}$ *for some* c_3 *such that* $\Gamma \vdash c_3 = c_2 \circ c_1\colon (A)A'$.
4. *(Substitution)* $\Gamma, x : K, \Gamma' \vdash A <_c B \in \mathcal{C}$ *implies for any* k *such that* $\Gamma \vdash k : K$, $\Gamma, [k/x]\Gamma' \vdash [k/x]A <_{c'} [k/x]B \in \mathcal{C}$ *for some* c' *such that* $\Gamma, [k/x]\Gamma' \vdash c' = [k/x]c\colon ([k/x]A)[k/x]B$.
5. *(Weakening)* $\Gamma \vdash A <_c B \in \mathcal{C}$, $\Gamma \subseteq \Gamma'$ *and* Γ' *is valid imply* $\Gamma' \vdash A <_c B \in \mathcal{C}$.

Remark 3. A WDC can be thought of as a set of coercions generated from some basic coercions, some basic subtyping rules, and the rules $(Cong)(Subst)(Trans)$ and that of weakening.

We have the following properties of WDCs.

Lemma 1.

1. *If* $\Gamma \vdash A <_{c_1} B \in \mathcal{C}$, $\Gamma \vdash B' <_{c_2} A' \in \mathcal{C}$ *and* $\Gamma \vdash B = B'$, *then* $\Gamma \vdash A <_{c_3} A' \in \mathcal{C}$ *for some* c_3 *and* $\Gamma \vdash c_3 = c_2 \circ c_1\colon (A)A'$.
2. *If* $\Gamma, x : K, \Gamma' \vdash A <_c B \in \mathcal{C}$, $\Gamma \vdash K = K'$, *then* $\Gamma, x : K', \Gamma' \vdash A <_c B \in \mathcal{C}$.
3. *If* $\Gamma \vdash A <_c B \in \mathcal{C}$, $\vdash \Gamma = \Gamma'$, *then* $\Gamma' \vdash A <_c B \in \mathcal{C}$.
4. *If* $\Gamma \vdash A <_c B \in \mathcal{C}$, $\Gamma' \vdash A' <_{c'} B' \in \mathcal{C}$, $\vdash \Gamma = \Gamma'$, $\Gamma \vdash A = A'$ *and* $\Gamma \vdash B = B'$, *then* $\Gamma \vdash c = c'\colon (A)B$.

In the following sections, we shall consider the system of coercive subtyping whose basic subtyping rules ($\mathcal{R}$) consist of the following rule, where $\mathcal{C}$ is a WDC:

$$(C) \qquad \frac{\Gamma \vdash A <_c B\colon Type \ \in \ \mathcal{C}}{\Gamma \vdash A <_c B\colon Type}$$

and the Π and Σ-subtyping rules in Figures 1 and 2. Furthermore, we assume that for any judgement $\Gamma \vdash A <_c B \in \mathcal{C}$, neither A nor B is computationally equal to a Π-type or a Σ-type. We denote the derivable subtyping judgements of this system by $\mathcal{C}_{\mathcal{M}}$. We also assume that the original type theory T has good properties, in particular the Church-Rosser property and the property of context replacement by equal kinds. In the following two sections, we shall show that $\mathcal{C}_{\mathcal{M}}$ is also a WDC.

Remark 4. The above system is equivalent to $\mathrm{T}[\mathcal{R}]_0$ where $\mathcal{R}$ consists of (C) and the Π/Σ subtyping rules.

4 Coherence

In this section, we give a proof of coherence of basic subtyping rules of Π-types and Σ-types.

Lemma 2. *If $\Gamma \vdash M_1 <_d M_2 \in \mathcal{C}_{\mathcal{M}}$, then one of the following holds:*

- $\Gamma \vdash M_1 <_d M_2 \in \mathcal{C}$;
- *Both M_1 and M_2 are computationally equal to Π-types; or*
- *Both M_1 and M_2 are computationally equal to Σ-types.*

Proof. By induction on derivations. If $\Gamma \vdash M_1 <_d M_2 \notin \mathcal{C}$, its derivation must end with a Π-subtyping rule, a Σ-subtyping rule, or the congruence rule. If it is one of the Π or Σ-subtyping rules, then we know both M_1 and M_2 are Π-types or Σ-types. If the last rule is the congruence rule ($Cong$),

$$\frac{\Gamma \vdash M_1' <_{d'} M_2' : Type \quad \Gamma \vdash M_1 = M_1' : Type \quad \Gamma \vdash M_2 = M_2' : Type \quad \Gamma \vdash d' = d : (M_1')M_2'}{\Gamma \vdash M_1 <_d M_2}$$

then by induction hypothesis, the lemma holds for $\Gamma \vdash M_1' <_{d'} M_2'$. If both M_1' and M_2' are computationally equal to Π-types or Σ-types, so are M_1 and M_2. If $\Gamma \vdash M_1' <_{d'} M_2' \in \mathcal{C}$, then $\Gamma \vdash M_1 <_d M_2 \in \mathcal{C}$ because $\mathcal{C}$ is a WDC, which is closed under congruence. □

Lemma 3.

1. *If $\Gamma \vdash \Pi(A,B) <_d \Pi(A',B') \in \mathcal{C}_{\mathcal{M}}$ then $\Gamma \vdash A = A'$ or $\Gamma \vdash A' <_c A \in \mathcal{C}_{\mathcal{M}}$ for some c.*
2. *If $\Gamma \vdash \Sigma(A,B) <_d \Sigma(A',B') \in \mathcal{C}_{\mathcal{M}}$ then $\Gamma \vdash A = A'$ or $\Gamma \vdash A <_c A' \in \mathcal{C}_{\mathcal{M}}$ for some c.*
3. *If $\Gamma \vdash \Pi(A,B) <_d \Pi(A',B') \in \mathcal{C}_{\mathcal{M}}$ and $\Gamma \vdash A = A'$ then $\Gamma, x : A \vdash B(x) <_{e[x]} B'(x) \in \mathcal{C}_{\mathcal{M}}$ for some e.*
4. *If $\Gamma \vdash \Sigma(A,B) <_d \Sigma(A',B') \in \mathcal{C}_{\mathcal{M}}$ and $\Gamma \vdash A = A'$ then $\Gamma, x : A \vdash B(x) <_{e[x]} B'(x) \in \mathcal{C}_{\mathcal{M}}$ for some e.*
5. *If $\Gamma \vdash \Pi(A,B) <_d \Pi(A',B') \in \mathcal{C}_{\mathcal{M}}$ and $\Gamma \vdash A' <_c A \in \mathcal{C}_{\mathcal{M}}$ then $\Gamma, x : A' \vdash B(c(x)) = B'(x)$ or $\Gamma, x : A' \vdash B(c(x)) <_{e[x]} B'(x) \in \mathcal{C}_{\mathcal{M}}$ for some e.*
6. *If $\Gamma \vdash \Sigma(A,B) <_d \Sigma(A',B') \in \mathcal{C}_{\mathcal{M}}$ and $\Gamma \vdash A <_c A' \in \mathcal{C}_{\mathcal{M}}$ then $\Gamma, x : A \vdash B(x) = B'(c(x))$ or $\Gamma, x : A \vdash B(x) <_{e[x]} B'(c(x)) \in \mathcal{C}_{\mathcal{M}}$ for some e.*

Proof. By induction on derivations. We only consider the first statement; the proofs of the others are similar. For the first, a derivation of the judgement $\Gamma \vdash \Pi(A,B) <_d \Pi(A',B')$ must be of the form

$$\begin{array}{c} \vdots \\ \dfrac{one\ of\ three\ \Pi - subtyping\ rules}{\Gamma \vdash \Pi(A_1,B_1) <_{d'} \Pi(A_2,B_2)} \\ \vdots \\ ...(Congruence\ rules)... \\ \vdots \\ \hline \Gamma \vdash \Pi(A,B) <_d \Pi(A',B') \end{array}$$

where $\Gamma \vdash \Pi(A_1, B_1) = \Pi(A, B){:}\, Type$, $\Gamma \vdash \Pi(A_2, B_2) = \Pi(A', B'){:}\, Type$, and $\Gamma \vdash d' = d{:}\,(C)C'$ for some C and C' computationally equal to $\Pi(A, B)$ and $\Pi(A', B')$, respectively. Hence, by the Church-Rosser theorem of the original type theory T and conservativity of $T[\mathcal{R}]_0$ over T, $\Gamma \vdash A_1 = A$, $\Gamma \vdash B_1 = B$, $\Gamma \vdash A_2 = A'$ and $\Gamma \vdash B_2 = B'$. So $\Gamma \vdash A = A'$ or $\Gamma \vdash A' <_c A$ by the congruence rule. □

Lemma 4. *If* $\Gamma \vdash M_1 <_c M_2 \in \mathcal{C}_\mathcal{M}$, *then* $\Gamma \nvdash M_1 = M_2$.

Theorem 1 (Coherence). *If* $\Gamma \vdash M_1 <_d M_2 \in \mathcal{C}_\mathcal{M}$, $\Gamma' \vdash M_1' <_{d'} M_2' \in \mathcal{C}_\mathcal{M}$, $\vdash \Gamma = \Gamma'$, $\Gamma \vdash M_1 = M_1'$, *and* $\Gamma \vdash M_2 = M_2'$ *then* $\Gamma \vdash d = d'{:}\,(M_1)M_2$.

Proof. By induction on derivations. By Lemma 2, we only have to consider the following cases.

- $\Gamma \vdash M_1 <_d M_2 \in \mathcal{C}$. Then, none of M_1 and M_2 is computationally equal to a Π-type or Σ-type. Therefore, nor is M_1' or M_2'. So, by Lemma 2, $\Gamma' \vdash M_1' <_{d'} M_2' \in \mathcal{C}$. Now, by Lemma 1(2), we have $\Gamma \vdash d = d'{:}\,(M_1)M_2$.
- Both M_1 and M_2 are computationally equal to Π-types. Then any derivation of $\Gamma \vdash M_1 <_d M_2$ contains a subderivation whose last rule is one of the Π-subtyping rules followed by congruence rules. We only consider the case the Π-subtyping rule concerned is the third rule in Figure 1; i.e., the derivation is of the form

$$\dfrac{\dfrac{\begin{matrix}\vdots & & \vdots\\ \Gamma \vdash A_2 <_c A_1 & & \Gamma, x : A_2 \vdash B_1(c(x)) <_{e[x]} B_2(x)\end{matrix}}{\Gamma \vdash \Pi(A_1, B_1) <_{d_1} \Pi(A_2, B_2)}}{\begin{matrix}\vdots\\ ...(Congruence\ rules)...\\ \vdots\\ \hline \Gamma \vdash M_1 <_d M_2\end{matrix}}$$

where $\Gamma \vdash \Pi(A_1, B_1) = M_1$, $\Gamma \vdash \Pi(A_2, B_2) = M_2$, and $\Gamma \vdash d_1 = d{:}\,(M_1)M_2$.
Now, it must be the case that any derivation of $\Gamma' \vdash M_1' <_{d'} M_2'$ must contain a subderivation whose last rule is also the same Π-subtyping rule as above, followed by applications of the congruence rule; i.e., it must be of the form

$$\dfrac{\dfrac{\begin{matrix}\vdots & & \vdots\\ \Gamma' \vdash A_2' <_{c'} A_1' & & \Gamma', x : A_2' \vdash B_1'(c'(x)) <_{e'[x]} B_2'(x)\end{matrix}}{\Gamma' \vdash \Pi(A_1', B_1') <_{d_1'} \Pi(A_2', B_2')}}{\begin{matrix}\vdots\\ ...(Congruence\ rules)...\\ \vdots\\ \hline \Gamma' \vdash M_1' <_{d'} M_2'\end{matrix}}$$

where $\Gamma' \vdash \Pi(A'_1, B'_1) = M'_1$, $\Gamma' \vdash \Pi(A'_2, B'_2) = M'_2$, and $\Gamma' \vdash d' = d'_1 : (M'_1)M'_2$. To see this is the case, by Lemma 3, we only have to show that

1. $\Gamma' \not\vdash A'_2 = A'_1$, and
2. $\Gamma', x : A'_2 \not\vdash B'_1(c'(x)) = B'_2(x)$.

For the first case, since $\Gamma \vdash M_1 = M'_1$ and $\Gamma \vdash M_2 = M'_2$, we have $\Gamma \vdash \Pi(A_1, B_1) = \Pi(A'_1, B'_1)$ and $\Gamma \vdash \Pi(A_2, B_2) = \Pi(A'_2, B'_2)$. Hence, by Church-Rosser theorem in T and conservativity of $\mathrm{T}[\mathcal{R}]_0$ over T, $\Gamma \vdash A_1 = A'_1$, $\Gamma \vdash B_1 = B'_1$, $\Gamma \vdash A_2 = A'_2$ and $\Gamma \vdash B_2 = B'_2$. As $\Gamma \vdash A_2 <_c A_1$, we have by Lemma 4, $\Gamma \not\vdash A_2 = A_1$. So $\Gamma' \not\vdash A'_2 = A'_1$.

For the second case, a similar argument suffices, except that we use the fact that, by the argument of the first case and induction hypothesis, $\Gamma \vdash c = c' : (A_2)A_1$.

Since the derivations must be of the above forms, by induction hypothesis, we have $\Gamma \vdash c = c' : (A_2)A_1$ and $\Gamma, x : A_2 \vdash e[x] = e'[x] : (B_1(c(x)))B_2(x)$. Hence $\Gamma \vdash d = d' : (M_1)M_2$.

- Both M_1 and M_2 are computationally equal to Σ-types. The proof of this case is similar to the above case. □

5 Admissibility of Substitution and Transitivity

In the presentation of coercive subtyping in [Luo99], substitution and transitivity are two of the basic rules in the theoretical framework. However, in an implementation of coercive subtyping, these rules are ignored simply because that they cannot be directly implemented. For this reason among others, proving admissibility of such rules (or their elimination) is always an important task for any subtyping systems.

In this paper, we do not take substitution and transitivity as basic rules, but we prove that they are both admissible when we extend a WDC by the Π and Σ-subtyping rules. In order to prove admissibility of transitivity, we also need to prove the theorem about weakening.

Theorem 2 (Substitution and weakening).

1. *(Substitution) If* $\Gamma, x : K, \Gamma' \vdash M_1 <_d M_2 \in \mathcal{C}_\mathcal{M}$ *and* $\Gamma \vdash k : K$*, then* $\Gamma, [k/x]\Gamma' \vdash [k/x]M_1 <_{d'} [k/x]M_2 \in \mathcal{C}_\mathcal{M}$ *for some* d' *such that* $\Gamma, [k/x]\Gamma' \vdash d' = [k/x]d : ([k/x]M_1)[k/x]M_2$.
2. *(Weakening) If* $\Gamma \vdash M_1 <_d M_2 \in \mathcal{C}_\mathcal{M}$, $\Gamma \subseteq \Gamma'$ *and* Γ' *is valid then* $\Gamma' \vdash M_1 <_d M_2 \in \mathcal{C}_\mathcal{M}$.

Proof. By induction on derivations and using Lemma 2. □

To prove the admissibility of transitivity, the usual measures (e.g., the size of types concerned) do not seem to work (or even to be definable), since types essentially involve computations. We use a measure developed by Chen in his PhD thesis [Che98], which only considers subtyping judgements in a derivation, defined as follows.

Definition 3 (depth). *Let D be a derivation of a subtyping judgement of the form $\Gamma \vdash A <_c B{:}Type$. Then*

1. *If the last rule of D is*

$$\frac{\Gamma \vdash A <_c B : Type \in \mathcal{C}}{\Gamma \vdash A <_c B{:}Type}$$

   then $depth(D) = 1$.
2. *If the last rule of D is*

$$\frac{S_1,\ ...,\ S_n,\ \ D_1,\ ...,\ D_m}{\Gamma \vdash A <_c B{:}Type}$$

   where $S_1,\ ...,\ S_n$ are derivations of subtyping judgements of the form $\Gamma' \vdash A' <_{c'} B'{:}Type$ and $D_1,\ ...,\ D_m$ are derivations of other forms of judgements, then $depth(D) = max\{depth(S_1), ..., depth(S_n)\} + 1$.

The following lemma shows that, from a derivation D of a subtyping judgement J one can always get a derivation D' of the judgement obtained from J by context replacement such that D and D' have the same depth.

Lemma 5.

1. *If $\vdash \Gamma = \Gamma'$, $\Gamma \vdash M_1 <_d M_2{:}Type \in \mathcal{C}_\mathcal{M}$, and D is a derivation of $\Gamma \vdash M_1 <_d M_2{:}Type$, then*
   a) *$\Gamma' \vdash M_1 <_d M_2{:}Type \in \mathcal{C}_\mathcal{M}$, and*
   b) *there is a derivation D' of $\Gamma' \vdash M_1 <_d M_2{:}Type$ such that $depth(D) = depth(D')$.*
2. *If $\Gamma, x : El(A), \Gamma' \vdash M_1 <_{c_1} M_2{:}Type \in \mathcal{C}_\mathcal{M}$, $\Gamma \vdash A' <_{c_2} A : Type \in \mathcal{C}_\mathcal{M}$, and D is a derivation of $\Gamma, x : El(A), \Gamma' \vdash M_1 <_{c_1} M_2{:}Type$, then*
   a) *$\Gamma, y : El(A'), [c_2(y)/x]\Gamma' \vdash [c_2(y)/x]M_1 <_{c_3} [c_2(y)/x]M_2{:}Type \in \mathcal{C}_\mathcal{M}$ for some c_3 such that $\Gamma, y : El(A'), [c_2(y)/x]\Gamma' \vdash c_3 = [c_2(y)/x]c_1 : ([c_2(y)/x]M_1)[c_2(y)/x]M_2$, and*
   b) *there is a derivation D' of $\Gamma, y : El(A'), [c_2(y)/x]\Gamma' \vdash [c_2(y)/x]M_1 <_{c_3} [c_2(y)/x]M_2{:}Type$ such that $depth(D) = depth(D')$.*

Proof. By induction on derivations. The key point is that, in the proofs briefly described below, the size of a derivation may change, but the depth of a derivation, which only counts the subtyping judgements, does not.

1. For (1), in the base case, we use Lemma 1(3), and in the step cases, the theorem of context replacement by equal kinds in T and conservativity of $T[\mathcal{R}]_0$ over T.
2. For (2), in the base case, we use the fact that, if $\Gamma, x : El(A), \Gamma' \vdash M_1 <_{c_1} M_2{:}Type \in \mathcal{C}$, then $\Gamma, y : El(A'), [c_2(y)/x]\Gamma' \vdash [c_2(y)/x]M_1 <_{c_3} [c_2(y)/x]M_2$:
   $Type \in \mathcal{C}$ for some c_3 such that $\Gamma, y : El(A'), [c_2(y)/x]\Gamma' \vdash c_3 = [c_2(y)/x]c_1 : ([c_2(y)/x]M_1)[c_2(y)/x]M_2$. In the step cases, use of induction hypothesis suffices. □

Now, we can prove the admissibility of transitivity.

Theorem 3 (Transitivity). *If $\Gamma \vdash M_1 <_{d_1} M_2 \in \mathcal{C}_{\mathcal{M}}$, $\Gamma \vdash M_2' <_{d_2} M_3 \in \mathcal{C}_{\mathcal{M}}$ and $\Gamma \vdash M_2 = M_2'$, then $\Gamma \vdash M_1 <_{d_3} M_3 \in \mathcal{C}_{\mathcal{M}}$ for some d_3 such that $\Gamma \vdash d_3 = d_2 \circ d_1 : (M_1)M_3$.*

Proof. By induction on $depth(D) + depth(D')$, where D and D' are derivations of $\Gamma \vdash M_1 <_{d_1} M_2$ and $\Gamma \vdash M_2' <_{d_2} M_3$, respectively. In the base case, we have that the judgements $\Gamma \vdash M_1 <_{d_1} M_2$ and $\Gamma \vdash M_2' <_{d_2} M_3$ are both in $\mathcal{C}$. By Lemma 1(1), we have $\Gamma \vdash M_1 <_{d_3} M_3 \in \mathcal{C}$ for some d_3 such that $\Gamma \vdash d_3 = d_2 \circ d_1 : (M_1)M_3$.

In the step case, if $\Gamma \vdash M_1 <_{d_1} M_2$ and $\Gamma \vdash M_2' <_{d_2} M_3$ are both in $\mathcal{C}$, then a similar argument as the base case suffices. Otherwise, we have that either $\Gamma \vdash M_1 <_{d_1} M_2$ or $\Gamma \vdash M_2' <_{d_2} M_3$ is not in $\mathcal{C}$. Therefore, by Lemma 2 and the assumption that $\Gamma \vdash M_2 = M_2'$, all of M_1, M_2, M_2' and M_3 are computationally equal to Π-types or Σ-types. We only consider the case that they are equal to Π-types. Suppose that the derivation D and D' be of the following forms (we only consider the only more difficult example among the combinations of Π-subtyping rules):

$$\cfrac{\cfrac{\cfrac{\begin{array}{cc} \vdots & \vdots \\ D_1 & D_2 \\ \vdots & \vdots \end{array}}{\Gamma \vdash A_2 <_{c_1} A_1 \quad \Gamma, x : A_2 \vdash B_1(c_1(x)) <_{e_1[x]} B_2(x)}}{\Gamma \vdash \Pi(A_1, B_1) <_{d_1'} \Pi(A_2, B_2)}}{\begin{array}{c} \vdots \\ ...(Congruence\ rules)... \\ \vdots \\ \hline \Gamma \vdash M_1 <_{d_1} M_2 \end{array}}$$

where $\Gamma \vdash \Pi(A_1, B_1) = M_1$, $\Gamma \vdash \Pi(A_2, B_2) = M_2$, $\Gamma \vdash d_1' = d_1 : (M_1)M_2$ and $d_1' = [f : \Pi(A_1, B_1)]\lambda(A_2, B_2, [x : A_2]e_1[x](app(A_1, B_1, f, c_1(x))))$, and

$$\cfrac{\cfrac{\cfrac{\begin{array}{cc} \vdots & \vdots \\ D_1' & D_2' \\ \vdots & \vdots \end{array}}{\Gamma \vdash A_3 <_{c_2} A_2' \quad \Gamma, x : A_3 \vdash B_2'(c_2(x)) <_{e_2[x]} B_3(x)}}{\Gamma \vdash \Pi(A_2', B_2') <_{d_2'} \Pi(A_3, B_3)}}{\begin{array}{c} \vdots \\ ...(Congruence\ rules)... \\ \vdots \\ \hline \Gamma \vdash M_2' <_{d_2} M_3 \end{array}}$$

where $\Gamma \vdash \Pi(A_2', B_2') = M_2'$, $\Gamma \vdash \Pi(A_3, B_3) = M_3$, $\Gamma \vdash d_2' = d_2 : (M_2')M_3$ and $d_2' = [f : \Pi(A_2', B_2')]\lambda(A_3, B_3, [x : A_3]e_2[x](app(A_2', B_2', f, c_2(x))))$. We obviously have $depth(D_1) < depth(D)$, $depth(D_2) < depth(D)$, $depth(D_1') < depth(D')$, and $depth(D_2') < depth(D')$.

Now, since $\Gamma \vdash M_2 = M_2'$, we have by Church-Rosser theorem of T and conservativity of $\mathrm{T}[\mathcal{R}]_0$ over T, $\Gamma \vdash A_2 = A_2'$ and $\Gamma \vdash B_2 = B_2' : (A_2)Type$. From the former, $\Gamma \vdash A_3 <_{c_2} A_2$ by the congruence rule. By Lemma 5(2), $\Gamma, x : A_3 \vdash B_1(c_1(c_2(x))) <_{e_3[x]} B_2(c_2(x))$ for some e_3 such that $\Gamma, x : A_3 \vdash e_3[x] = e_1[c_2(x)]$ and there is a derivation D_3 of the judgement $\Gamma, x : A_3 \vdash B_1(c_1(c_2(x))) <_{e_3[x]} B_2(c_2(x))$ and $depth(D_3) = depth(D_2) < depth(D)$.

Now, we have

$$depth(D_1) + depth(D_1') < depth(D) + depth(D')$$

$$depth(D_3) + depth(D_2') < depth(D) + depth(D')$$

By induction hypothesis, there is c_3 such that $\Gamma \vdash A_3 <_{c_3} A_1 \in \mathcal{C}_{\mathcal{M}}$ and $\Gamma \vdash c_3 = c_1 \circ c_2 : (A_3)A_1$. And because $\Gamma, x : A_3 \vdash B_2(c_2(x)) = B_2'(c_2(x))$ (as we have $\Gamma \vdash B_2 = B_2' : (A_2)Type$), by induction hypothesis, there is e_4 such that

$$\Gamma, x : A_3 \vdash B_1(c_1(c_2(x))) <_{e_4[x]} B_3(x) \in \mathcal{C}_{\mathcal{M}}$$

$$\Gamma, x : A_3 \vdash e_4[x] = e_2[x] \circ e_3[x] : (B_1(c_1(c_2(x))))B_3(x).$$

Hence $\Gamma, x : A_3 \vdash e_4[x] = e_2[x] \circ e_1[c_2(x)] : (B_1(c_1(c_2(x))))B_3(x)$. So by the Domain-Codomain rule (the third rule in Figure 1), $\Gamma \vdash \Pi(A_1, B_1) <_{d_3} \Pi(A_3, B_3) \in \mathcal{C}_{\mathcal{M}}$, where

$$d_3 =_{df} [f : \Pi(A_1, B_1)]\lambda(A_3, B_3, [x : A_2]e_4[x](app(A_1, B_1, f, c_3(x))))$$

and we have $d_3 = d_2 \circ d_1$. Finally, by the congruence rule, we have $\Gamma \vdash M_1 <_{d_3} M_3 \in \mathcal{C}_{\mathcal{M}}$. □

Corollary 1. *$\mathcal{C}_{\mathcal{M}}$ is a WDC.*

Proof. By Lemma 4 and Theorems 1, 2, and 3. □

6 Discussions

In this section, we briefly discuss several issues of interest such as those concerning decidability and transitivity, and related work.

6.1 Decidability

Once we have proven coherence and admissibility of substitution and transitivity (as we have done for Π and Σ-subtyping rules), we can be sure that coercion searching is decidable for $\mathcal{C}_{\mathcal{M}}$ if it is decidable for $\mathcal{C}$; in other words, it is decidable whether $\Gamma \vdash A <_c B : Type$ is derivable. One can give a sound and complete algorithm to do this. We omit the details here. This is of course important in implementations.

6.2 Weak Transitivity

The transitivity rule $(Trans)$ states that $c' \circ c$ is a coercion from A to C if c and c' are coercions from A to B and from B to C, respectively. In fact, this transitivity rule is very strong. For instance, if we introduce subtyping rule for lists:

$$\frac{\Gamma \vdash A <_c B : Type}{\Gamma \vdash List(A) <_d List(B) : Type}$$

where d is defined inductively such that $d(nil(A)) = nil(B)$ and $d(cons(A, a, l)) = cons(B, c(a), d(l))$, then the rule $(Trans)$ fails to be admissible.

A weaker version is

$$(WTrans) \qquad \frac{\Gamma \vdash A < B \quad \Gamma \vdash B < C}{\Gamma \vdash A < C}$$

where the judgement $\Gamma \vdash A < B$ means that '$\Gamma \vdash A <_c B$ for some c'. In fact, this weaker version of transitivity seems to be better suited to the wider applications. Furthermore, if the type theory T has a propositional equality $=_A$ (e.g., Leibniz's equality or Martin-Löf's equality type), we can prove that

- If $\Gamma \vdash A <_c B$, $\Gamma \vdash B <_d C$, and $\Gamma \vdash A <_e C$, then e is extensionally equal to $d \circ c$ in the sense that the proposition $\forall x : A.e(x) =_C d(c(x))$ is provable in the type theory.

The admissibility of weak transitivity and the above extensional justification will be discussed in a forthcoming paper [LLS01]. And the admissibility of $(Trans)$ rule and $(WTrans)$ rule in extensional type theory needs futhur study.

6.3 Related Work

Besides those mentioned above, the related work includes previous meta-theoretic studies about coercive subtyping. One of the future tasks to be done is to consider how the conservativity result and related work at the kind level [SL01] can be related to the current development and hence to obtain an overall better understanding of the framework. We should mention again Chen's work [Che98], in particular his development of the depth measure, which seems to be very useful in proving admissibility of transitivity.

Acknowledgements. We would like to thank Jianming Pang and Sergei Soloviev for their helpful comments and corrections on an earlier draft of this paper, and the members of the Computer-Assisted Reasoning Group at Durham for discussions of the issues concerned. Thanks also go to the LPAR'01 referees who made helpful comments on the paper.

References

[B+00] B. Barras et al. *The Coq Proof Assistant Reference Manual (Version 6.3.1)*. INRIA-Rocquencourt, 2000.

[Bai99] A. Bailey. *The Machine-checked Literate Formalisation of Algebra in Type Theory.* PhD thesis, University of Manchester, 1999.

[Che98] G. Chen. *Subtyping, Type Conversion and Transitivity Elimination.* PhD thesis, University of Paris VII, 1998.

[CL01] P. Callaghan and Z. Luo. An implementation of LF with coercive subtyping and universes. *Journal of Automated Reasoning*, 27(1):3–27, 2001.

[CLP01] P. C. Callaghan, Z. Luo, and J. Pang. Object languages in a type-theoretic meta-framework. *Workshop of Proof Transformation and Presentation and Proof Complexities (PTP'01)*, 2001.

[JLS98] A. Jones, Z. Luo, and S. Soloviev. Some proof-theoretic and algorithmic aspects of coercive subtyping. *Types for proofs and programs (eds, E. Gimenez and C. Paulin-Mohring), Proc. of the Inter. Conf. TYPES'96, LNCS 1512*, 1998.

[LC98] Z. Luo and P. Callaghan. Coercive subtyping and lexical semantics (extended abstract). *LACL'98*, 1998.

[LLS01] Y. Luo, Z. Luo, and S. Soloviev. Weak transitivity in coercive subtyping. In preparation, 2001.

[LP92] Z. Luo and R. Pollack. LEGO Proof Development System: User's Manual. LFCS Report ECS-LFCS-92-211, Department of Computer Science, University of Edinburgh, 1992.

[LS99] Z. Luo and S. Soloviev. Dependent coercions. *The 8th Inter. Conf. on Category Theory and Computer Science (CTCS'99), Edinburgh, Scotland. Electronic Notes in Theoretical Computer Science*, 29, 1999.

[Luo94] Z. Luo. *Computation and Reasoning: A Type Theory for Computer Science.* Oxford University Press, 1994.

[Luo97] Z. Luo. Coercive subtyping in type theory. *Proc. of CSL'96, the 1996 Annual Conference of the European Association for Computer Science Logic, Utrecht. LNCS 1258*, 1997.

[Luo99] Z. Luo. Coercive subtyping. *Journal of Logic and Computation*, 9(1):105–130, 1999.

[NPS90] B. Nordström, K. Petersson, and J. Smith. *Programming in Martin-Löf's Type Theory: An Introduction.* Oxford University Press, 1990.

[Sai97] A. Saibi. Typing algorithm in type theory with inheritance. *Proc of POPL'97*, 1997.

[SL01] S. Soloviev and Z. Luo. Coercion completion and conservativity in coercive subtyping. To be published in Annals of Pure and Applied Logic, 2001.

Appendix A

The following gives the rules of the logical framework LF.

Contexts and assumptions

$$\frac{}{\langle\rangle\ valid} \qquad \frac{\Gamma \vdash K\ kind \quad x \notin FV(\Gamma)}{\Gamma, x : K\ valid} \qquad \frac{\Gamma, x : K, \Gamma'\ valid}{\Gamma, x : K, \Gamma' \vdash x : K}$$

Equality rules

$$\frac{\Gamma \vdash K\ kind}{\Gamma \vdash K = K} \quad \frac{\Gamma \vdash K = K'}{\Gamma \vdash K' = K} \quad \frac{\Gamma \vdash K = K' \quad \Gamma \vdash K' = K''}{\Gamma \vdash K = K''}$$

$$\frac{\Gamma \vdash k{:}\, K}{\Gamma \vdash k = k{:}\, K} \quad \frac{\Gamma \vdash k = k'{:}\, K}{\Gamma \vdash k' = k{:}\, K} \quad \frac{\Gamma \vdash k = k'{:}\, K \quad \Gamma \vdash k' = k''{:}\, K}{\Gamma \vdash k = k''{:}\, K}$$

$$\frac{\Gamma \vdash k{:}\, K \quad \Gamma \vdash K = K'}{\Gamma \vdash k{:}\, K'} \quad \frac{\Gamma \vdash k = k'{:}\, K \quad \Gamma \vdash K = K'}{\Gamma \vdash k = k'{:}\, K'}$$

Substitution rules

$$\frac{\Gamma, x : K, \Gamma'\ valid \quad \Gamma \vdash k{:}\, K}{\Gamma, [k/x]\Gamma'\ valid}$$

$$\frac{\Gamma, x : K, \Gamma' \vdash K'\ kind \quad \Gamma \vdash k{:}\, K}{\Gamma, [k/x]\Gamma' \vdash [k/x]K'\ kind} \quad \frac{\Gamma, x : K, \Gamma' \vdash K'\ kind \quad \Gamma \vdash k = k'{:}\, K}{\Gamma, [k/x]\Gamma' \vdash [k/x]K' = [k'/x]K'}$$

$$\frac{\Gamma, x : K, \Gamma' \vdash k'{:}\, K' \quad \Gamma \vdash k{:}\, K}{\Gamma, [k/x]\Gamma' \vdash [k/x]k'{:}\, [k/x]K'} \quad \frac{\Gamma, x : K, \Gamma' \vdash k'{:}\, K' \quad \Gamma \vdash k_1 = k_2{:}\, K}{\Gamma, [k_1/x]\Gamma' \vdash [k_1/x]k' = [k_2/x]k'{:}\, [k_1/x]K'}$$

$$\frac{\Gamma, x : K, \Gamma' \vdash K' = K'' \quad \Gamma \vdash k{:}\, K}{\Gamma, [k/x]\Gamma' \vdash [k/x]K' = [k/x]K''} \quad \frac{\Gamma, x : K, \Gamma' \vdash k' = k''{:}\, K' \quad \Gamma \vdash k{:}\, K}{\Gamma, [k/x]\Gamma' \vdash [k/x]k' = [k/x]k''{:}\, [k/x]K'}$$

The kind Type

$$\frac{\Gamma\ valid}{\Gamma \vdash Type\ kind} \quad \frac{\Gamma \vdash A{:}\, Type}{\Gamma \vdash El(A)\ kind} \quad \frac{\Gamma \vdash A = B{:}\, Type}{\Gamma \vdash El(A) = El(B)}$$

Dependent product kinds

$$\frac{\Gamma \vdash K\ kind \quad \Gamma, x : K \vdash K'\ kind}{\Gamma \vdash (x : K)K'\ kind} \quad \frac{\Gamma \vdash K_1 = K_2 \quad \Gamma, x : K_1 \vdash K_1' = K_2'}{\Gamma \vdash (x : K_1)K_1' = (x : K_2)K_2'}$$

$$\frac{\Gamma, x : K \vdash k{:}\, K'}{\Gamma \vdash [x : K]k{:}\, (x : K)K'} \quad \frac{\Gamma \vdash K_1 = K_2 \quad \Gamma, x : K_1 \vdash k_1 = k_2{:}\, K}{\Gamma \vdash [x : K_1]k_1 = [x : K_2]k_2{:}\, (x : K_1)K}$$

$$\frac{\Gamma \vdash f{:}\, (x : K)K' \quad \Gamma \vdash k{:}\, K}{\Gamma \vdash f(k){:}\, [k/x]K'} \quad \frac{\Gamma \vdash f = f'{:}\, (x : K)K' \quad \Gamma \vdash k_1 = k_2{:}\, K}{\Gamma \vdash f(k_1) = f'(k_2){:}\, [k_1/x]K'}$$

$$\frac{\Gamma, x : K \vdash k'{:}\, K' \quad \Gamma \vdash k{:}\, K}{\Gamma \vdash ([x : K]k')(k) = [k/x]k'{:}\, [k/x]K'} \quad \frac{\Gamma \vdash f{:}\, (x : K)K' \quad x \notin FV(f)}{\Gamma \vdash [x : K]f(x) = f{:}\, (x : K)K'}$$

Appendix B

The following are the inference rules for the coercive subkinding extension $T[\mathcal{R}]$ (not including the rules for subtyping).

New rules for application

$$\frac{\Gamma \vdash f{:}\, (x : K)K' \quad \Gamma \vdash k_0{:}\, K_0 \quad \Gamma \vdash K_0 <_c K}{\Gamma \vdash f(k_0){:}\, [c(k_0)/x]K'}$$

$$\frac{\Gamma \vdash f = f'{:}\, (x : K)K' \quad \Gamma \vdash k_0 = k_0'{:}\, K_0 \quad \Gamma \vdash K_0 <_c K}{\Gamma \vdash f(k_0) = f'(k_0'){:}\, [c(k_0)/x]K'}$$

Coercive definition rule

$$\frac{\Gamma \vdash f:(x:K)K' \quad \Gamma \vdash k_0:K_0 \quad \Gamma \vdash K_0 <_c K}{\Gamma \vdash f(k_0) = f(c(k_0)):[c(k_0)/x]K'}$$

Basic subkinding rule

$$\frac{\Gamma \vdash A <_c B: Type}{\Gamma \vdash El(A) <_c El(B)}$$

Subkinding for dependent product kinds

$$\frac{\Gamma \vdash K_1' = K_1 \quad \Gamma, x:K_1' \vdash K_2 <_c K_2' \quad \Gamma, x:K_1 \vdash K_2\ kind}{\Gamma \vdash (x:K_1)K_2 <_{[f:(x:K_1)K_2][x:K_1']c(f(x))} (x:K_1')K_2'}$$

$$\frac{\Gamma \vdash K_1' <_c K_1 \quad \Gamma, x:K_1' \vdash [c(x)/x]K_2 = K_2' \quad \Gamma, x:K_1 \vdash K_2\ kind}{\Gamma \vdash (x:K_1)K_2 <_{[f:(x:K_1)K_2][x:K_1']f(c(x))} (x:K_1')K_2'}$$

$$\frac{\Gamma \vdash K_1' <_{c_1} K_1 \quad \Gamma, x:K_1' \vdash [c_1(x)/x]K_2 <_{c_2} K_2' \quad \Gamma, x:K_1 \vdash K_2\ kind}{\Gamma \vdash (x:K_1)K_2 <_{[f:(x:K_1)K_2][x:K_1']c_2(f(c_1(x)))} (x:K_1')K_2'}$$

Congruence rule for subkinding

$$\frac{\Gamma \vdash K_1 <_c K_2 \quad \Gamma \vdash K_1 = K_1' \quad \Gamma \vdash K_2 = K_2' \quad \Gamma \vdash c = c':(K_1)K_2}{\Gamma \vdash K_1' <_{c'} K_2'}$$

Transitivity and substitution rules for subkinding

$$\frac{\Gamma \vdash K <_c K' \quad \Gamma \vdash K' <_{c'} K''}{\Gamma \vdash K <_{c' \circ c} K''} \qquad \frac{\Gamma, x:K, \Gamma' \vdash K_1 <_c K_2 \quad \Gamma \vdash k:K}{\Gamma, [k/x]\Gamma' \vdash [k/x]K_1 <_{[k/x]c} [k/x]K_2}$$

A Type-Theoretic Approach to Induction with Higher-Order Encodings

Carsten Schürmann

Yale University
carsten@cs.yale.edu

Abstract. Reasoning by induction is common practice in computer science and mathematics. In formal logic, however, standard induction principles exist only for a certain class of inductively defined structures that satisfy the positivity condition. This is a major restriction considering that many structures in programming languages and logics are best expressed using higher-order representation techniques that violate exactly this condition. In this paper we develop induction principles for higher-order encodings in the setting of first-order intuitionistic logic. They differ from standard induction principles in that they rely on the concept of worlds [Sch01] which admits reasoning about open terms in regularly formed contexts. The soundness of these induction principles follows from external termination and coverage considerations about a realizability interpretation of proofs.

1 Introduction

Reasoning by induction is common practice in computer science and mathematics, it is well understood, and it is admissible when reasoning about objects whose types are inductively defined. But standard induction principles only exist for those types whose constructors satisfy the so called positivity condition [PM93, SH93]. This condition requires that the type that is being defined does not occur in a negative position in any of its constructor types. Types that violate this condition are not inductive and therefore excluded from inductive reasoning.

Many concepts however that are prevalent in programming languages, logics, and type theory such as for example operational semantics, compilers, transformations, logics, and proof systems, have elegant, dependently typed, higher-order encodings (see [Pfe99] for an overview) but violate this positivity condition. These encodings are therefore not inductive in the standard sense, which hampers their use in programming and renders them inappropriate for modeling in automated proof assistants based on standard induction principles, such as, for example, Coq [DFH$^+$93] or Isabelle/HOL [Pau94].

In previous years, this problem has been actively worked on, and much progress has been made [DPS97,Hof99,GP99,HMS01] with a variety of ideas inspired from modal logic, category theory, FM set theory, and the π-calculus. In this paper we propose a type theoretic solution to this problem. Specifically, we

R. Nieuwenhuis and A. Voronkov (Eds.): LPAR 2001, LNAI 2250, pp. 266–281, 2001.

define an induction principle for any higher-order encoding in the logical framework LF. Our technique is based on the observation that standard induction principles leverage off on the existence of canonical (β-normal η-long) forms. For example, in totally freely generated term algebras, canonical forms of first-order encodings are guaranteed to exist if only closed objects are being considered.

Canonical forms also exists in the higher-order setting and they are inductively defined. This makes them great candidates for inductive reasoning, however they have one serious problem. Canonical forms are in general open, i.e. they may contain free parameters, which is common to all higher-order encodings. If we include these parameters in the inductive reasoning process we obtain the sound induction principle described in this paper that is based on the idea of distinguishing cases of canonical forms. It is expressive enough to reason about properties of logics, operational semantics, and abstract machines. The underlying assumption is called the *regular world assumption* [Sch01] which allows quantifiers to range over open objects whose free variables are declared in a *regularly* formed (and hence subject to reasoning) context. Those regular contexts are characterized by so called *worlds* whose structure may be freely chosen, but must be fixed ahead of time [Sch00].

The main contribution of this paper is an induction principle for higher-order encodings that extends first-order intuitionistic logic. Its quantifiers range over objects which live in the dependent type theory LF [HHP93] for which canonical forms are known to exist. A prototype theorem prover for this logic has been implemented in the Twelf system [PS99].

This paper is organized as follows. In Section 2 we revisit standard induction principles for first-order encodings and give in Section 3 a brief overview over higher-order encodings. In Section 4 we then motivate and define our induction principle. In Section 5 we argue for the soundness of the design before we discuss related work in Section 6. We comment on the implementation and assess results and future work in Section 7.

2 Standard Induction Principles

One of the most intuitive forms of an induction principle is the one for natural numbers. But first, how shall we represent natural numbers? In this paper we represent all data structures uniformly in a logical framework. The logical framework of choice is LF [HHP93], but for now, the reader is invited to think of it as the simply typed λ-calculus. The representation of natural numbers leads to the following signature Σ of constant declarations:

$$\begin{aligned} \Sigma = \mathsf{nat} &: \mathsf{type}, \\ \mathsf{z} &: \mathsf{nat}, \\ \mathsf{s} &: \mathsf{nat} \rightarrow \mathsf{nat}. \end{aligned}$$

The '$\rightarrow$' type constructor denotes the function space of the logical framework.

Standard induction principles, which are commonly used in proof assistants and automated theorem proving systems, require that the respective datatypes

$$\frac{}{\Psi \Vdash_\Sigma \top}\,\mathsf{\top I} \qquad \frac{\Psi, x : A \Vdash_\Sigma \mathcal{P}(x)}{\Psi \Vdash_\Sigma \forall x : A.\mathcal{P}(x)}\,\forall\mathsf{I}^x \qquad \frac{\Psi \Vdash_\Sigma \forall x : A.\mathcal{P}(x) \qquad \overline{\Psi} \vdash_\Sigma M \Uparrow A}{\Psi \Vdash_\Sigma \mathcal{P}(M)}\,\forall\mathsf{E}$$

$$\frac{\overline{\Psi} \vdash_\Sigma M \Uparrow A \quad \Psi \Vdash_\Sigma \mathcal{P}(M)}{\Psi \Vdash_\Sigma \exists x : A.\mathcal{P}(x)}\,\exists\mathsf{I} \qquad \frac{\Psi \Vdash_\Sigma \exists x : A.\mathcal{P}(x) \qquad \Psi, x : A, \mathbf{x} \in \mathcal{P}(x) \Vdash_\Sigma \mathcal{P}'}{\Psi \Vdash_\Sigma \mathcal{P}'}\,\exists\mathsf{E}^{x,\mathbf{x}}$$

Fig. 1. Intuitionistic first-order logic $\mathcal{IL}$.

are inductive. They satisfy the "positivity condition" [PM93] which requires that the type of each constructor contains only positive occurrences of the type that is defined. Because z and s satisfy this condition, nat is inductive and a standard induction principle exists. This principle can be safely added to a logic, such as, for example, first-order intuitionistic logic $\mathcal{IL}$ whose first-order fragment is depicted in Figure 1.

$$\begin{array}{ll} \text{Formulas: } & \mathcal{P} ::= \top \mid \forall x : A.\mathcal{P} \mid \exists x : A.\mathcal{P} \\ \text{Context: } & \Psi ::= \cdot \mid \Psi, x : A \mid \Psi, \mathbf{x} \in \mathcal{P} \end{array}$$

We write $\Psi \Vdash_\Sigma \mathcal{P}$ for the logical entailment relation, where we use the symbol $\Vdash$ in order to distinguish it cleanly from the symbol $\vdash$ used by the logical framework. Ψ makes the list of term parameters $x : A$ (introduced by $\forall\mathsf{I}$ and $\exists\mathsf{E}$) and logical assumptions $\mathbf{x} \in \mathcal{P}$ (introduced by $\exists\mathsf{E}$) explicit. Objects that are substituted for parameters must be valid in the logical framework, which is indicated by the left premiss of $\forall\mathsf{E}$ and $\exists\mathsf{I}$. We write $\overline{\Psi}$ for the result of mapping a meta level context down to the logical framework level (by removing all declarations of the form $\mathbf{x} \in \mathcal{P}$). The induction principle for natural numbers is standard

$$\frac{\Psi \Vdash_\Sigma \mathcal{P}(\mathsf{z}) \qquad \Psi, n' : \mathsf{nat}, \mathbf{x} \in \mathcal{P}(n') \Vdash_\Sigma \mathcal{P}(\mathsf{s}\, n')}{\Psi, n : \mathsf{nat} \Vdash_\Sigma \mathcal{P}(n)}\,\mathsf{ind\_nat}^{n',\mathbf{x}}.$$

$\mathcal{P}(n)$ or $\Psi(n)$ indicate that n can occur freely in $\mathcal{P}$ or Ψ, respectively. $\mathsf{ind\_nat}$, $\forall\mathsf{I}$, and $\exists\mathsf{E}$ discharge assumptions that are listed with the rule name.

The logical framework LF [HHP93] extends the simply typed λ-calculus by dependent types. We write $\Gamma \vdash_\Sigma M : A$ for the LF typing judgment where Γ is the standard LF context, M is an object and A its type. Every object in LF has a canonical (β-normal η-long) form for which we write $\Gamma \vdash_\Sigma M \Uparrow A$. LF's formulation is standard and we take $\beta\eta$-conversion as the notion of definitional equality [HHP93,Coq91]. An induction principle for natural numbers in the LF setting is slightly more complicated then the one above, because dependencies among the declarations in Ψ must be respected.

$$\frac{\begin{array}{l}\Psi_1, \Psi_2(\mathsf{z}) \Vdash_\Sigma \mathcal{P}(\mathsf{z}) \\ \Psi_1, n' : \mathsf{nat}, \mathbf{x} \in \mathcal{P}(n'), \Psi_2(\mathsf{s}\, n') \Vdash_\Sigma \mathcal{P}(\mathsf{s}\, n')\end{array}}{\Psi_1, n : \mathsf{nat}, \Psi_2(n) \Vdash_\Sigma \mathcal{P}(n)}\,\mathsf{ind\_nat}^{n',\mathbf{x}}. \tag{1}$$

$$\frac{}{\Delta, G \vdash^{ND} G} \qquad \frac{\Delta, G_1 \vdash^{ND} G_2}{\Delta \vdash^{ND} G_1 \supset G_2} \supset \mathsf{I} \qquad \frac{\Delta \vdash^{ND} G_1 \supset G_2 \quad \Delta \vdash^{ND} G_1}{\Delta \vdash^{ND} G_2} \supset \mathsf{E}$$

Fig. 2. Natural deduction calculus

3 Higher-Order Encodings

Our approach to induction principles scales to arbitrary higher-order representations. In fact it scales to any deductive system that can be represented in LF. Our running example is the natural deduction calculus [Gen35], which is depicted in Figure 2. The judgment is hypothetical, and its encoding uses binding constructs to represent the hypotheses from Δ.

$$\textit{Hypotheses: } \Delta ::= \cdot \mid \Delta, G \tag{2}$$

Although we restrict this presentation to the implicational fragment of the natural deduction calculus, all technology developed in this paper scales to full first-order logic. Formulas $G_1 \supset G_2$ are represented in LF as $\ulcorner G_1 \urcorner \supset \ulcorner G_2 \urcorner$ where $\ulcorner \cdot \urcorner$ denotes the standard representation function. We write $\llcorner \cdot \lrcorner$ for its inverse whose existence we can assume. Consult [HHP93] for an in depth coverage of this example.

Example 1 (Natural Deduction Calculus).

$$\begin{aligned} \Sigma = \mathsf{o} \; & : \text{type}, \\ \supset \; & : \mathsf{o} \to (\mathsf{o} \to \mathsf{o}), \\ \mathsf{nd} \; & : \mathsf{o} \to \text{type}, \\ \mathsf{impI} \; & : (\mathsf{nd}\; G_1 \to \mathsf{nd}\; G_2) \to \mathsf{nd}\; (G_1 \supset G_2), \\ \mathsf{impE} \; & : \mathsf{nd}\; (G_1 \supset G_2) \to \mathsf{nd}\; G_1 \to \mathsf{nd}\; G_2. \end{aligned}$$

Following standard practice [Pfe91], we omit in this presentation all implicit Π-abstractions from types.

When working with complex encodings such as the one of a proof calculus, the first question that should come to mind is if the representation is *adequate*, i.e. if natural deduction derivations are in one to one correspondence with canonical LF objects of appropriate type. Adequacy is proven by induction. In the case of natural deductions however, special care must be taken in formulating the induction hypothesis of the adequacy theorem. Hypothetical judgments are encoded as higher-order functions and consequently already the formulation of the theorem must establish the connection between free variables (or parameters) in an LF encoding and valid hypotheses in the natural deduction calculus.

Therefore adequacy is a property of open objects, and not just of closed objects as in the case of natural numbers. Here is a first attempt to formulate the adequacy property: For any canonical LF object $\Gamma \vdash_\Sigma M \Uparrow \mathsf{nd}\, \ulcorner G \urcorner$ there exists a *unique* derivation $\mathcal{D}$ of judgment $\Delta \vdash^{ND} G$ (written as $\mathcal{D} :: \Delta \vdash^{ND} G$), such that $M = \ulcorner \mathcal{D} \urcorner$ and $\Gamma = \ulcorner \Delta \urcorner$ — and vice versa.

Also for hypothetical judgments, which are represented as open objects, $\ulcorner \cdot \urcorner$ must be a bijection. Clearly, Δ can be mapped directly to Γ, but the reverse does not hold in general. Not every Γ corresponds to a Δ as $\Gamma = u_1 : \ulcorner G_1 \urcorner, \ldots, u_n : \ulcorner G_n \urcorner, A : \mathsf{o}$ shows. Consequently, in the interest of adequacy, we must restrict the set of Γ's to those that are structurally constructed the same way Δ is.

In fact, without loss of generality, we can always assume that Δ is a regularly formed list, and we propose a formal way of characterizing valid contexts (which we call *regular* for this reason). We write $\Gamma \in \mathcal{L}(\Phi)$ if Γ is an instance of *world* Φ, the "type of all valid contexts". With $\mathcal{L}(\Phi)$ we refer to the set of all regular contexts generated by world Φ.

$$\text{Worlds: } \Phi ::= L : \text{some } \Gamma_1 \text{ block } \Gamma_2 \mid \Phi + \Phi \mid \Phi^*$$

In our example, $\Gamma \in \mathcal{L}((L : \text{some } G : \mathsf{o} \text{ block } u : \mathsf{nd}\ G)^*)$. $\mathcal{L}(\Phi)$ is defined in Figure 3. Intuitively, worlds are regular expressions with "L : some Γ_1 block Γ_2" as terminals, where $+$ describes alternatives, and * repetition. The terminal "L : some Γ_1 block Γ_2" satisfies the invariant that Γ_1, Γ_2 form a valid context. L is used to label blocks of declarations of a context,which allows us to distinguish different blocks from each other. In context Γ_0, the set of regular contexts $\mathcal{L}(L : \text{some } \Gamma_1 \text{ block } \Gamma_2)$ consists of all α-variants of the block Γ_2 where its free variables declared in Γ_1 have been instantiated by objects (summarized as substitution σ) valid in Γ_0. We write $[\sigma]\Gamma_2$ for a context under a substitution. That σ is valid is enforced by the first premiss $\Gamma_0 \vdash \sigma : \Gamma_1$ of the "block"-rule whose definition we omit. The second premiss of the same rule is the standard α-conversion congruence $\Gamma_0 \vdash \Gamma_1 \equiv_\alpha \Gamma_2$ which permits tacit variable renaming on regular contexts. Consequently, without loss of generality all contexts in $\mathcal{L}(\Phi)$ are valid.

Worlds are the "types of valid contexts" which can also be interpreted as grammars that generate Δ, written as $\Delta \in \mathcal{L}(\llcorner \Phi \lrcorner)$. As example, compare the world $\Phi = (L : \text{some } G : \mathsf{o} \text{ block } u : \mathsf{nd}\ G)^*$ with (2).

Theorem 1 (Adequacy for worlds). *Let Φ be a world, and $\ulcorner \cdot \urcorner$ an adequate representation function for all types that occur in Φ. $\ulcorner \cdot \urcorner$ extends to a bijection between LF contexts Γ that satisfy $\cdot \vdash \Gamma \in \mathcal{L}(\Phi)$ and Δ that satisfy $\Delta \in \mathcal{L}(\llcorner \Phi \lrcorner)$.*

Theorem 2 (Adequacy of nd). *Let $\Phi = (L : \text{some } G : \mathsf{o} \text{ block } u : \mathsf{nd}\ G)^*$ and $\cdot \vdash \Gamma \in \mathcal{L}(\Phi)$. We have $\Gamma \vdash M \Uparrow \mathsf{nd}\ \ulcorner G \urcorner$ iff $M = \ulcorner \mathcal{D} \urcorner$ and $\mathcal{D} :: \llcorner \Gamma \lrcorner \vdash G$.*

Proof. By structural induction on the derivation of $\Gamma \vdash M \Uparrow \mathsf{nd}\ \ulcorner G \urcorner$ in one direction and $\mathcal{D}$ in the other.

This answers the first question. Natural deduction derivations can be adequately represented in LF. But are these representations inductive in the sense that they possess standard induction principles? Following standard definitions, they are not, because impl's type refers to nd in a negative position. However, every term in LF has a canonical form in a given world, and canonical forms are inductively defined, and therefore nd is still inductive as we elaborate on next.

$$\frac{\Gamma_0 \vdash \sigma : \Gamma_1 \qquad \Gamma_0 \vdash \Gamma \equiv_\alpha [\sigma]\Gamma_2}{\Gamma_0 \vdash \Gamma \in \mathcal{L}(L : \text{some } \Gamma_1 \text{ block } \Gamma_2)}\text{block}$$

$$\frac{}{\Gamma_0 \vdash \cdot \in \mathcal{L}(\Phi^*)}\text{empty} \qquad \frac{\Gamma_0 \vdash \Gamma_1 \in \mathcal{L}(\Phi) \qquad \Gamma_0, \Gamma_1 \vdash \Gamma_2 \in \mathcal{L}(\Phi^*)}{\Gamma_0 \vdash \Gamma_1, \Gamma_2 \in \mathcal{L}(\Phi^*)}\text{unfold}$$

$$\frac{\Gamma_0 \vdash \Gamma \in \mathcal{L}(\Phi_1)}{\Gamma_0 \vdash \Gamma \in \mathcal{L}(\Phi_1 + \Phi_2)}\text{left} \qquad \frac{\Gamma_0 \vdash \Gamma \in \mathcal{L}(\Phi_2)}{\Gamma_0 \vdash \Gamma \in \mathcal{L}(\Phi_1 + \Phi_2)}\text{right}$$

Fig. 3. Set of regular contexts generated by world Φ.

4 Higher-Order Induction Principles

Proofs by induction are common in computer science. However, not every type that can be defined inductively possesses an appropriate induction principle. Natural numbers do, lists do, trees do, essentially any data type that is defined satisfying the positivity condition [PM93] does. Higher-order representations however do not.

Recall that higher-order abstract syntax is characterized by using meta-level variables to encode object-level variables, and meta-level binders to encode object-level binders. $\supset$ I introduces a new assumption, for example, which is captured by the functional argument to impl. Therefore, by design, higher-order representations may not satisfy the positivity condition. Consequently, induction on higher-order representations is fundamentally problematic.

This observation could lead one to believe that induction principles for higher-order encodings do not exist. Against this intuition speaks the observation that every LF object — functional or non-functional — has an inductively defined canonical (β-normal η-long) form. How to exploit this property to derive an induction principle for higher-order encodings is the main contribution of this paper. We demonstrate our solution by an induction principle for natural deduction derivations which is used in the proof of the following property: Every natural deduction derivation can be translated into a sequent derivation.

The sequent calculus [Gen35] defining judgment $\Delta \Longrightarrow G$ is depicted in Figure 4 is defined for the same fragment as the natural deduction calculus from Figure 2. For this example it is not so important what the sequent calculus actually is, but it is important how it is represented in LF [Pfe95].

Example 2 (Sequent deductions). Extends Σ from Example 1.

$$\begin{aligned}
\Sigma = \ldots, \mathsf{hyp} &: \mathsf{o} \to \mathsf{type}, \\
\mathsf{conc} &: \mathsf{o} \to \mathsf{type}, \\
\mathsf{init} &: \mathsf{hyp}\ G \to \mathsf{conc}\ G, \\
\mathsf{impR} &: (\mathsf{hyp}\ G_1 \to \mathsf{conc}\ G_2) \to \mathsf{conc}\ (G_1 \supset G_2), \\
\mathsf{impL} &: \mathsf{conc}\ G_1 \to (\mathsf{hyp}\ G_2 \to \mathsf{conc}\ G_3) \to (\mathsf{hyp}\ (G_1 \supset G_2) \to \mathsf{conc}\ G_3), \\
\mathsf{cut} &: \mathsf{conc}\ G_1 \to (\mathsf{hyp}\ G_1 \to \mathsf{conc}\ G_2) \to \mathsf{conc}\ G_2.
\end{aligned}$$

$$\frac{}{\Gamma, G \Longrightarrow G}\text{init} \qquad \frac{\Gamma \Longrightarrow G_1 \qquad \Gamma, G_1 \Longrightarrow G_2}{\Gamma \Longrightarrow G_2}\text{cut} \qquad \frac{\Gamma, G_1 \Longrightarrow G_2}{\Gamma \Longrightarrow G_1 \supset G_2}{\supset}\text{R}$$

$$\frac{\Gamma, G_1 \supset G_2 \Longrightarrow G_1 \qquad \Gamma, G_1 \supset G_2, G_2 \Longrightarrow G_3}{\Gamma, G_1 \supset G_2 \Longrightarrow G_3}{\supset}\text{L}$$

Fig. 4. Sequent calculus

Sequents $\Delta \Longrightarrow G$ are encoded by two separate type families. Hypotheses in Δ are encoded using hyp as LF contexts and G as an object of type conc $\ulcorner G \urcorner$. The representation of the inference rules is straightforward, well understood, and adequacy can be established in the world $\Phi = (L : \text{some } G : \mathsf{o} \text{ block } h : \mathsf{hyp}\ G)^*$.

We begin now with the presentation of the central example of this paper: What is a formal proof of the following statement?

$$\forall G : \mathsf{o}.\forall D : \mathsf{nd}\ G.\exists Q : \mathsf{conc}\ G.\top \tag{3}$$

Informally, the proof of this theorem proceeds by structural induction on $\llcorner D \lrcorner :: \llcorner \mathsf{nd}\ G \lrcorner$ — it is a hypothetical proof because appeals of the induction hypothesis to the premiss of impl introduces a new nd-hypothesis. But there is a problem here! The adequacy result for natural deductions and for sequent derivations differ in what kind of declarations are permitted. For one it is $u : \mathsf{nd}\ \ulcorner G \urcorner$ and for the other $h : \mathsf{hyp}\ \ulcorner G \urcorner$. The solution involves merging both worlds into one, namely $\Phi = (L : \text{some } G : \mathsf{o} \text{ block } u : \mathsf{nd}\ G, h : \mathsf{hyp}\ G)^*$, and reproving the adequacy results for natural deduction and sequent encodings. Those proofs rely on the following two strengthen properties.

Lemma 1 (Strengthening natural deductions). *If h does not occur free in Γ' and $\Gamma, h : \mathsf{hyp}\ G_1, \Gamma' \vdash_\Sigma M \Uparrow \mathsf{nd}\ G_2$ then $\Gamma, \Gamma' \vdash_\Sigma M \Uparrow \mathsf{nd}\ G_2$.*

Lemma 2 (Strengthening sequent derivations). *If u does not occur free in Γ' and $\Gamma, u : \mathsf{nd}\ G_1, \Gamma' \vdash_\Sigma M \Uparrow \mathsf{conc}\ G_2$ then $\Gamma, \Gamma' \vdash_\Sigma M \Uparrow \mathsf{conc}\ G_2$.*

Theorem 3 (Adequacy for nd and hyp/conc). *Let $\cdot \vdash \Gamma \in \mathcal{L}(\Phi)$.*

1. *$\Gamma \vdash M \Uparrow \mathsf{nd}\ \ulcorner G \urcorner$ iff $M = \ulcorner \mathcal{D} \urcorner$ and $\mathcal{D} :: \llcorner \Gamma \lrcorner \vdash G$.*
2. *$\Gamma \vdash M \Uparrow \mathsf{conc}\ \ulcorner G \urcorner$ iff $M = \ulcorner \mathcal{D} \urcorner$ and $\mathcal{D} :: \llcorner \Gamma \lrcorner \Longrightarrow G$.*

Proof. By structural induction on the derivation of $\Gamma \vdash M \Uparrow \mathsf{nd}\ \ulcorner G \urcorner$, $\Gamma \vdash M \Uparrow \mathsf{conc}\ \ulcorner G \urcorner$ in one direction and $\mathcal{D}$ in the other, respectively, using Lemma 1 and Lemma 2.

As this example shows, worlds are as important for proving the adequacy of encodings as the signatures themselves. With this in mind, let us return to the definition of intuitionistic first-order logic presented in Figure 1 and index the judgment by $\Sigma;\Phi$ instead of just Σ. Endowing the logic with worlds has consequences on the definition of the context Ψ which we address below.

Contexts Ψ capture all assumptions that are valid in a respective state of a proof. $\mathbf{x} \in \mathcal{P}$, for example, assumes that $\mathcal{P}$ holds. Without worlds $x : A$ stands for the assumption that there exists a *closed* LF object of type A. But in the presence of worlds this setting may be generalized; we let $x : A$ stand for the assumption that there exists an *open* object that is valid in some context $\Gamma \in \mathcal{L}(\Phi)$. But how can we express assumptions about the form of Γ, such as that Γ contains certain parameters?

The answer to this question has already been proposed in [Sch00,Sch01]. A new concept of *block variables* ρ^L is required, that ranges over valid parameter blocks in accordance with the world Φ (written as $\rho^L : \Phi$). Block variables are of the form $\rho ::= \cdot \mid \rho, \underline{x} : A$. Each block variable follows the structure Γ_2 in "L : some Γ_1 block Γ_2" and is labeled with the appropriate label L. They capture assumptions about the context valid in a respective state of a proof.

$$\Psi ::= \cdot \mid \Psi, x : A \mid \Psi, [\rho]^L \mid \Psi, \mathbf{x} \in \mathcal{P}$$

Still, $\overline{\Psi}$ stands for the LF-context obtained from Ψ by removing all declarations of the form $\mathbf{x} \in \mathcal{P}$, and flattening out the individual declarations in $[\rho]^L$.

Example 3. Let $\Phi = (L : \text{some } G : \mathsf{o} \text{ block } \underline{u} : \mathsf{nd}\ G, \underline{h} : \mathsf{hyp}\ G)^*$ then $\Psi = G : \mathsf{o}, [\underline{u} : \mathsf{nd}\ G, \underline{h} : \mathsf{hyp}\ G]^L$ is a valid context.

What will happen if the induction hypothesis (3) is applied to the premiss of the impl rule $D : \mathsf{nd}\ \ulcorner G_1 \urcorner \to \mathsf{nd}\ \ulcorner G_2 \urcorner$? Informally one would assume G_1 and then apply the induction hypothesis to $\llcorner D \lrcorner$ which guarantees that there exists a sequent derivation of G_2. Formally, one first assumes $\underline{u} : \mathsf{nd}\ \ulcorner G_1 \urcorner$ and $\underline{h} : \mathsf{hyp}\ \ulcorner G_1 \urcorner$ (to be conform with Φ) followed by an appeal to the induction hypothesis to $\ulcorner G_2 \urcorner$ and $(D\ \underline{u}) : \mathsf{nd}\ \ulcorner G_2 \urcorner$. By Lemma 2 and a process called abstraction defined below we conclude

$$\Psi \Vdash_{\Sigma;\Phi} \exists x : \mathsf{hyp}\ G_1 \to \mathsf{conc}\ G_2.\top. \tag{4}$$

For the general case, dependency relations pose an answer on how to strengthen in a logical framework [Vir99]. We say that one type is dependent on another if objects of the former are build in terms of objects of the latter. For example, '$\mathsf{conc}\ G_2$' is dependent on '$\mathsf{hyp}\ G_1$' by rule init, but not '$\mathsf{nd}\ G_1$' by Lemma 2. Formally we write '$\mathsf{hyp}\ G_1 \prec \mathsf{conc}\ G_2$', but '$\mathsf{nd}\ G_1 \not\prec \mathsf{conc}\ G_2$'.

The process of incorporating assumptions of the form $x : A$ in a type or formula is called *abstraction.* Intuitively, it turns derivations of hypothetical judgments into functions while applying the a priori proven strengthening results as stringently as possible. In the example above, we write '$\nu(\underline{u} : \mathsf{nd}\ G_1, \underline{h} : \mathsf{hyp}\ G_1).\exists x : \mathsf{conc}\ G_2.\top$' for $\exists x : \mathsf{hyp}\ G_1 \to \mathsf{conc}\ G_2.\top$ for the abstracted formula, and '$\nu(\underline{u} : \mathsf{nd}\ G_1, \underline{h} : \mathsf{hyp}\ G_1).\mathsf{conc}\ G_2$' for the abstracted LF type.

Definition 1 (Abstraction).

1. *Type-level abstraction:*

$$\nu\rho.\, A_2 = \begin{cases} A_2 & \text{if } \rho = \cdot \\ \nu\rho'.\, A_2 & \text{if } \rho = x : A_1, \rho' \text{ and } A_1 \not\prec A_2 \\ \Pi x : A_1.\, (\nu\rho'.\, A_2) & \text{if } \rho = x : A_1, \rho' \text{ and } A_1 \prec A_2 \end{cases}$$

2. *Object-level abstraction: Let M be well-typed of type A_2*

$$\nu\rho.\, M = \begin{cases} M & \text{if } \rho = \cdot \\ \nu\rho'.\, M & \text{if } \rho = x : A_1, \rho' \text{ and } A_1 \not\prec A_2 \\ \lambda x : A_1.\, (\nu\rho'.\, M) & \text{if } \rho = x : A_1, \rho' \text{ and } A_1 \prec A_2 \end{cases}$$

3. *Object-level application: Let M be well-typed of type $\nu\rho.\, A_2$*

$$M\ \rho = \begin{cases} M & \text{if } \rho = \cdot \\ M\ \rho' & \text{if } \rho = x : A_1, \rho' \text{ and } A_1 \not\prec A_2 \\ (M\ x)\ \rho' & \text{if } \rho = x : A_1, \rho' \text{ and } A_1 \prec A_2 \end{cases}$$

4. *Meta-level abstraction: Let F be a well-formed formula*

$$\nu\rho.\, \mathcal{P} = \begin{cases} \top & \text{if } \mathcal{P} = \top \\ \forall x : (\nu\rho.\, A).\nu\rho.\, \mathcal{P}'(x\ \rho) & \text{if } \mathcal{P} = \forall x : A.\mathcal{P}'(x) \\ \exists x : (\nu\rho.\, A).\nu\rho.\, \mathcal{P}'(x\ \rho) & \text{if } \mathcal{P} = \exists x : A.\mathcal{P}'(x) \end{cases}$$

Lemma 3 (Soundness of Abstraction).

1. *If $\Gamma, \rho \vdash A : type$ then $\Gamma \vdash \nu\rho.\, A : type$*
2. *If $\Gamma, \rho \vdash M : A$ then $\Gamma \vdash \nu\rho.\, M : \nu\rho.\, A$*
3. *If $\Gamma \vdash M : \nu\rho.\, A$ then $\Gamma \vdash M\ \rho : A$*

With all this machinery in place, we can give a specialized induction principle for the higher-order type of natural deductions nd.

Definition 2 (Specialized induction principle for type family 'nd'). *This induction principle is designed for the world*

$$\Phi = (L : \text{some } G : \mathsf{o} \text{ block } \underline{u} : \mathsf{nd}\ G, \underline{h} : \mathsf{hyp}\ G)^*$$

Let $\mathcal{P}$ be the property to be proven. ind_nd *is the induction principle for* nd.

$$\dfrac{\begin{array}{l} \Psi_1, G : \mathsf{o}, [\underline{u} : \mathsf{nd}\ G, \underline{h} : \mathsf{hyp}\ G]^L, \Psi_2(G, \underline{u}) \\ \quad \Vdash_{\Sigma;\Phi} \mathcal{P}(G, \underline{u}) \\ \Psi_1, G_1 : \mathsf{o}, G_2 : \mathsf{o}, D' : \mathsf{nd}\ G_1 \to \mathsf{nd}\ G_2, \\ \quad \mathbf{x} \in \nu(\underline{u} : \mathsf{nd}\ G_1, \underline{h} : \mathsf{hyp}\ G_1).\mathcal{P}(G_2, D'\ \underline{u}), \Psi_2(G_1 \supset G_2, \mathsf{impl}\ D') \\ \quad \Vdash_{\Sigma;\Phi} \mathcal{P}(G_1 \supset G_2, \mathsf{impl}\ D') \\ \Psi_1, G_1 : \mathsf{o}, G_2 : \mathsf{o}, D_1 : \mathsf{nd}\ (G_2 \supset G_1), D_2 : \mathsf{nd}\ G_2, \\ \quad \mathbf{x}_1 \in \mathcal{P}(G_2 \supset G_1, D_1), \mathbf{x}_2 \in \mathcal{P}(G_2, D_2), \Psi_2(G_1, \mathsf{impE}\ D_1\ D_2) \\ \quad \Vdash_{\Sigma;\Phi} \mathcal{P}(G_1, \mathsf{impE}\ D_1\ D_2) \end{array}}{\Psi_1, G : \mathsf{o}, D : \mathsf{nd}\ G, \Psi_2(G, D) \Vdash_{\Sigma;\Phi} \mathcal{P}(G, D)}\ \mathsf{ind\_nd}$$

The first premiss enforces that $\mathcal{P}$ holds for an arbitrary but fixed parameter block $[\underline{u} : \mathsf{nd}\ G, \underline{h} : \mathsf{hyp}\ G]^L \in \Gamma$. The second premiss guarantees that $\mathcal{P}$ holds for any derivation ending in $(\mathsf{impI}\ D')$, and the third that $\mathcal{P}$ holds for any derivation ending in $(\mathsf{impE}\ D_1\ D_2)$.

The soundness of this induction principle follows from considerations presented in Section 5. With this induction principle formula (3) is directly, elegantly, and formally provable.

Proof.

$\mathcal{P}_1 :: G : \mathsf{o}, [\underline{u} : \mathsf{nd}\ G, \underline{h} : \mathsf{hyp}\ G]^L \vdash \mathsf{init}\ \underline{h} : \mathsf{conc}\ G$ in LF
$\mathcal{P}_2 :: G : \mathsf{o}, [\underline{u} : \mathsf{nd}\ G, \underline{h} : \mathsf{hyp}\ G]^L \Vdash_{\Sigma;\Phi} \exists Q : \mathsf{conc}\ G.\top$ by $\exists\mathsf{I}$ on $\mathcal{P}_1$ and $\top\mathsf{I}$

Let $\Psi_2 = G_1 : \mathsf{o}, G_2 : \mathsf{o}, D' : \mathsf{nd}\ G_1 \to \mathsf{nd}\ G_2, \mathbf{x} \in \exists Q_1 : \mathsf{hyp}\ G_1 \to \mathsf{conc}\ G_2.\top$.
$\mathcal{Q}_1 :: \Psi_2 \Vdash_{\Sigma;\Phi} \exists Q_1 : \mathsf{hyp}\ G_1 \to \mathsf{conc}\ G_2.\top$ by assumption
$\mathcal{Q}_2 :: \Psi_2, Q' : \mathsf{hyp}\ G_1 \to \mathsf{conc}\ G_2 \vdash \mathsf{impR}\ Q' : \mathsf{conc}\ (G_1 \supset G_2)$ in LF
$\mathcal{Q}_3 :: \Psi_2, Q' : \mathsf{hyp}\ G_1 \to \mathsf{conc}\ G_2 \Vdash_{\Sigma;\Phi} \exists Q : \mathsf{conc}\ (G_1 \supset G_2).\top$ by $\exists\mathsf{I}$ on $\mathcal{Q}_2$ and $\top\mathsf{I}$
$\mathcal{Q}_4 :: \Psi_2 \Vdash_{\Sigma;\Phi} \exists Q : \mathsf{conc}\ (G_1 \supset G_2).\top$ by $\exists\mathsf{E}$ on $\mathcal{Q}_1$ and $\mathcal{Q}_3$

Let $\Psi_3 = G_1 : \mathsf{o}, G_2 : \mathsf{o}, D_1 : \mathsf{nd}\ (G_1 \supset G_2), D_2 : \mathsf{nd}\ G_2,$
$\mathbf{x}_1 : \exists Q_1 : \mathsf{conc}\ (G_2 \supset G_1).\top, \mathbf{x}_2 : \exists Q_2 : \mathsf{conc}\ G_2.\top$.
and $\Psi_3' = \Psi_3, Q_1 : \mathsf{conc}\ (G_2 \supset G_1), Q_2 : \mathsf{conc}\ G_2$
$\mathcal{R}_1 :: \Psi_3 \vdash \exists Q_1 : \mathsf{conc}\ (G_2 \supset G_1).\top$ by assumption
$\mathcal{R}_2 :: \Psi_3, Q_1 : \mathsf{conc}\ (G_2 \supset G_1) \vdash \exists Q_2 : \mathsf{conc}\ G_2.\top$ by assumption
$\mathcal{R}_3 :: \Psi_3', h : \mathsf{hyp}(G_2 \supset G_1) \vdash \mathsf{impL}\ Q_2\ \mathsf{init}\ h : \mathsf{conc}\ G_1$ in LF
$\mathcal{R}_4 :: \Psi_3' \vdash \mathsf{impL}\ Q_2\ \mathsf{init} : \mathsf{hyp}(G_2 \supset G_1) \to \mathsf{conc}\ G_1$ in LF using $\mathcal{R}_3$
$\mathcal{R}_5 :: \Psi_3' \vdash \mathsf{cut}\ Q_1(\mathsf{impL}\ Q_2\ \mathsf{init}) : \mathsf{conc}\ G_1$ in LF using $\mathcal{R}_4$
$\mathcal{R}_6 :: \Psi_3' \Vdash_{\Sigma;\Phi} \exists Q : \mathsf{conc}\ G_1.\top$ by $\exists\mathsf{I}$ on $\mathcal{R}_5$ and $\top\mathsf{I}$
$\mathcal{R}_7 :: \Psi_3, Q_1 : \mathsf{conc}\ (G_2 \supset G_1) \Vdash_{\Sigma;\Phi} \exists Q : \mathsf{conc}\ G_1.\top$ by $\exists\mathsf{E}$ on $\mathcal{R}_2$ and $\mathcal{R}_6$
$\mathcal{R}_8 :: \Psi_3 \Vdash_{\Sigma;\Phi} \exists Q : \mathsf{conc}\ G_1.\top$ by $\exists\mathsf{E}$ on $\mathcal{R}_1$ and $\mathcal{R}_7$

$\mathcal{D}_1 :: G : \mathsf{o}, D : \mathsf{nd}\ G \Vdash_{\Sigma;\Phi} \exists Q : \mathsf{conc}\ G.\top$ by ind_nd on $\mathcal{P}_2$, $\mathcal{Q}_4$ and $\mathcal{R}_8$
$\mathcal{D}_2 :: G : \mathsf{o} \Vdash_{\Sigma;\Phi} \forall D : \mathsf{nd}\ G.\exists Q : \mathsf{conc}\ G.\top$ by $\forall\mathsf{I}$ on $\mathcal{D}_1$
$\mathcal{D}_3 :: \cdot \Vdash_{\Sigma;\Phi} \forall G : \mathsf{o}.\forall D : \mathsf{nd}\ G.\exists Q : \mathsf{conc}\ G.\top$ by $\forall\mathsf{I}$ on $\mathcal{D}_2$

We begin now with the presentation of the general form of the induction principle that works for all higher-order encodings in LF. This principle ends in a conclusion of the form $\Psi \Vdash_{\Sigma;\Phi} \mathcal{P}$. The challenge in designing this principle is (a) we need to pick one or more declarations in Ψ as case subjects (b) we cannot rely on patterns to be linear (in the sense of linear pattern as in pattern-matching), and (c) case subjects might be instantiated by parameters from an LF context. All three points are illustrated by the principle ind_nd: It shows that (a) we distinguish cases over G, and D simultaneously, (b) G occurs by itself and as an index to D, and (c) D might be instantiated by an $\underline{u} : \mathsf{nd}\ G \in \Gamma \in \mathcal{L}(\Phi)$.

Our solution employs substitutions as patterns, i.e. patterns in the sense of pattern matching. A pattern is a pair of a context which gathers all free variables that occur in the pattern, and a substitution σ that is defined as follows:

$$\sigma ::= \cdot \mid \sigma, M/x \mid \sigma, \rho'/\rho \mid \sigma, \mathbf{x}'/\mathbf{x}$$

$$\frac{}{\Psi' \Vdash_{\Sigma;\Phi} \cdot : \Psi}\text{sub-empty} \qquad \frac{\Psi' \Vdash_{\Sigma;\Phi} \sigma : \Psi \qquad \overline{\Psi} \vdash_{\Sigma} M : [\sigma]A}{\Psi' \Vdash_{\Sigma;\Phi} \sigma, M/x : \Psi, x : A}\text{sub-lf}$$

$$\frac{\Psi' \Vdash_{\Sigma;\Phi} \sigma : \Psi \qquad [\rho']^L \in \Psi' \qquad \overline{\Psi'} \vdash \rho' \equiv_\alpha [\sigma]\rho}{\Psi' \Vdash_{\Sigma;\Phi} \sigma, \rho'/\rho : \Psi, [\rho]^L}\text{sub-block}$$

$$\frac{\Psi' \Vdash_{\Sigma;\Phi} \sigma : \Psi \qquad \Psi'(\mathbf{x}') = [\sigma]\mathcal{P}}{\Psi' \Vdash_{\Sigma;\Phi} \sigma, \mathbf{x}'/\mathbf{x} : \Psi, \mathbf{x} \in \mathcal{P}}\text{sub-meta}$$

Fig. 5. Well-defined substitutions

The domain of σ is always Ψ. Example ind_nd used three patterns $(\Psi_i; \sigma_i)$:

$$\begin{aligned}
\Psi_1 &= G : \mathsf{o}, [\underline{u} : \mathsf{nd}\ G, \underline{h} : \mathsf{hyp}\ G]^L \\
\sigma_1 &= G/G, \underline{u}/D \\
\Psi_2 &= G_1 : \mathsf{o}, G_2 : \mathsf{o}, D' : \mathsf{nd}\ G_1 \to \mathsf{nd}\ G_2, \mathbf{x}_1 \in \exists x : \mathsf{hyp}\ G_1 \to \mathsf{conc}\ G_2.\top \\
\sigma_2 &= G_1 \supset G_2/G, \mathsf{impl}\ D'/D \\
\Psi_3 &= G_1 : \mathsf{o}, G_2 : \mathsf{o}, D_1 : \mathsf{nd}\ (G_2 \supset G_1), D_2 : \mathsf{nd}\ G_2, \\
&\quad\ \mathbf{x}_1 \in \exists x : \mathsf{conc}\ (G_2 \supset G_1).\top, \mathbf{x}_2 \in \exists x : \mathsf{conc}\ G_2.\top \\
\sigma_3 &= G_1/G, \mathsf{impE}\ D_1\ D_2/D
\end{aligned}$$

We write $\Psi_i \Vdash_{\Sigma;\Phi} \sigma_i : \Psi$ for well-defined substitutions which are defined in Figure 5. Not every pair $(\Psi'; \sigma)$ however is a valid pattern. Intuitively, all free variables in σ should be instantiated when matching against an instantiation of Ψ'. This requirement excludes Ψ''s that are too large containing unnecessary declarations. It also excludes patterns that contain variables that may not be instantiated by matching. These are variables that occur in flex/flex positions during matching, i.e. variables that do not occur in strict positions in the pattern. Therefore, we restrict arbitrary context/substitutions pairs to patterns. Third when new hypotheses $\mathbf{x} \in \mathcal{P}$ are introduced, we must carefully ensure that they are "smaller" than the property to be proven.

Definition 3 (Patterns). *$(\Psi'; \sigma)$ is a pattern for $(\Psi; \mathcal{P})$ iff $\Psi' \Vdash_{\Sigma;\Phi} \sigma : \Psi$ and there exists a well-founded ordering on substitutions $\prec$, s.t. Ψ' is* safe. *Ψ' is an safe context iff*

1. *$\Psi' = \cdot$.*
2. *$\Psi' = \Psi'', x : A$ and Ψ'' is safe and x occurs in a strict position in σ.*
3. *$\Psi' = \Psi'', [\rho]^L$ and Ψ'' is safe and $\underline{u} \in \rho$ occurs in a strict position in σ.*
4. *$\Psi' = \Psi'', [\rho]^L$ and Ψ'' is safe and ρ occurs in a strict position in σ.*
5. *$\Psi' = \Psi'', \mathbf{x} \in \mathcal{P}'$ and Ψ'' is safe and $\mathbf{x}$ occurs in a strict position in σ.*
6. *$\Psi' = \Psi'', \mathbf{x} \in \mathcal{P}'$ and Ψ'' is safe and $\mathcal{P}' = \nu\rho_1. \dots \nu\rho_n. [\sigma']\mathcal{P}$ and $\sigma' \prec \sigma$ for some block variables $\rho_1^{L_1}, \dots, \rho_n^{L_n} \in \Phi$*

Properties 1. through 5. guarantee that each variable declared in Ψ' will be instantiated once σ is matched against an instantation of Ψ. 6. enforces the well-foundedness of the principle.

Finally, we can address the question when an induction principle covers all cases. Because LF possesses canonical forms, any object of given type has only finitely many head constructors (buried under finitely many abstractions). Let Φ be a world, $\Gamma \in \mathcal{L}(\Phi)$, and $\Psi \Vdash_{\Sigma;\Phi} \mathcal{P}$ the conclusion of the induction principle. Furthermore, let $\{(\Psi_1; \sigma_1) \dots (\Psi_n; \sigma_n)\}$ a set of patterns. The induction principle is valid only if for any possible instantiation of declarations in Ψ one pattern exists that matches it.

Definition 4 (Cover). *A set of patterns* $\{(\Psi_1; \sigma_1) \dots (\Psi_n; \sigma_n)\}$ *for* $(\Psi; \mathcal{P})$ *is a* cover *for a world* Φ *if for any* $\Gamma \in \mathcal{L}(\Phi)$ *and* η *with satisfies* $\Gamma \vdash \eta : \Psi$ *there exists* $1 \le i \le n$ *and an* η' *for which* $\Gamma \vdash \eta' : \Psi^i$*, s.t.*

$$\eta = \sigma_i \circ \eta'$$

Definition 5 (Induction principle for higher-order LF encodings). *Let* $\{(\Psi_1; \sigma_1) \dots (\Psi_n; \sigma_n)\}$ *a set of patterns for* $(\Psi; \mathcal{P})$ *that form a* cover *for the world* Φ*. Then we define the induction principle for higher-order encodings as follows.*

$$\frac{\Psi_1 \Vdash_{\Sigma;\Phi} \mathcal{P}[\sigma_1] \qquad \dots \qquad \Psi_n \Vdash_{\Sigma;\Phi} \mathcal{P}[\sigma_n]}{\Psi \Vdash_{\Sigma;\Phi} \mathcal{P}}\ \mathsf{ind}$$

In the interest of space, we omit the two syntactical criteria for termination and coverage [Sch00].

5 Meta-theory

The fragment of $\mathcal{IL}$ that is defined in Figure 1 and used throughout this paper is closely connected to the λ-calculus through a realizability interpretation similar to the Curry-Howard isomorphism. Every rule in $\mathcal{IL}$ can be endowed with a proof term, that corresponds to a total function. Formulas correspond to types. The calculus of recursive functions for higher-order encodings [Sch01] forms the type-theoretic foundation of this realizer calculus. In this section we show, that $\mathcal{IL}$ endowed with rule ind (written as $\mathcal{IL}^{\mathsf{ind}}$) is a sound extension of $\mathcal{IL}$.

The induction principle ind is compatible with this view of provability, and it extends the realizability interpretation from above in a natural and straightforward way. Concretely, it allows realizers to be defined by case analysis and recursion. In addition, $\mathcal{IL}^{\mathsf{ind}}$'s derivations still correspond to proof terms, because ind satisfies Definition 4 which means that the functions corresponding to derivations are guaranteed to cover all cases at all times, and since ind also satisfies Condition 6. of Definition 3, recursion is always terminating.

We show that $\mathcal{IL}^{\mathsf{ind}}$ is sound by extending the realizability interpretation of $\mathcal{IL}$. First we show the admissibility of the ind rule in Lemma 4 which we generalize to a proof that any derivation in $\mathcal{IL}^{\mathsf{ind}}$ corresponds to a realizer in Theorem 4.

Lemma 4 (Admissibility of $\mathcal{IL}^{\mathsf{ind}}$). *Let $\Psi \overset{\mathcal{D}}{\Vdash}_{\Sigma;\Phi} \mathcal{P}$ be a derivation in $\mathcal{IL}^{\mathsf{ind}}$ with* ind *being the last applied rule whose premisses $\mathcal{D}_1 \dots \mathcal{D}_n$ have corresponding realizers. Let $\Gamma \in \mathcal{L}(\Phi)$. Then, for all substitutions (environments) η, $\Gamma \Vdash_{\Sigma;\Phi} \eta : \Psi$, there exists a total function f (of type $\mathcal{P}$) that realizes $\mathcal{D}$.*

Proof. Let $\mathcal{D}$ be the following derivation in $\mathcal{IL}^{\mathsf{ind}}$.

$$\frac{\begin{array}{c}\mathcal{D}_1\\ \Psi_1 \Vdash_{\Sigma;\Phi} \mathcal{P}[\sigma_1]\end{array} \quad \dots \quad \begin{array}{c}\mathcal{D}_n\\ \Psi_n \Vdash_{\Sigma;\Phi} \mathcal{P}[\sigma_n]\end{array}}{\Psi \Vdash_{\Sigma;\Phi} \mathcal{P}}\,\mathsf{ind}$$

For any instantiation of Ψ, there exists a pattern $(\Psi_i; \sigma_i)$ that matches it, by Definition 4. This matching operation instantiates all declarations in Ψ (by Properties 1. to 5. in Definition 3) that occur strictly in σ_i by LF objects (for $x : A$), parameters from the LF contexts (for the $[\rho]^L$), and values computed by the realizers (for $\mathbf{x} \in \mathcal{P}$). Variable $\mathbf{x}$ declared in Ψ that do not occur strictly have to be computed recursively an operation that terminates by Property 6. in Definition 3. Once fully applied, the realizer that corresponds to $\mathcal{D}_i$ computes the desired result.

Theorem 4 (Soundness of $\mathcal{IL}^{\mathsf{ind}}$). *Let $\Psi \overset{\mathcal{D}}{\Vdash}_{\Sigma;\Phi} \mathcal{P}$ be a derivation in $\mathcal{IL}^{\mathsf{ind}}$ and Γ be a valid world. Then, for all substitutions (environments) η, $\Gamma \Vdash_{\Sigma;\Phi} \eta : \Psi$, there exists a total function f of type $\mathcal{P}$ that realizes $\mathcal{D}$.*

Proof. By induction on $\mathcal{D}$ using Lemma 4 and the Curry-Howard isomorphism.

6 Related Work

In earlier work we have used modal logic to add induction and primitive recursion principles to the simply typed λ-calculus while preserving higher-order encodings [DPS97,Hof99]. The calculus differs from this work in that it defines only one language suitable for representation and reasoning simultaneously. In its original formulation, the calculus was lacking dependent types, parts of which were added in [Lel98]. Others have followed a categorical approach. Hofmann [Hof99], for example, suggests a number of different induction and reasoning principles for higher-order abstract syntax and he proved all adequate using a category-theoretic method. Earlier, [DH94] has proposed techniques to reformulate natural higher-order as first-order encodings using auxiliary types reducing hereby the problem of induction for higher-order to standard induction. With this approach, however, the user remains responsible for proving substitution lemmas.

One advantage of using a logical framework such as LF is that the choice of variable names can be left to the logical framework. The same goal is pursued by [GM96,GP99] by exploiting permutation properties among variable names. Their work has been implemented in FreshML [PG00] and is therefore related to the realizer calculus underlying this work [Sch01]. FreshML supports higher-order abstract syntax as well but it does not support dependent types.

Honsell et al. [HMS01] use higher-order representation techniques to formalize concepts from process algebras. They have combined higher-order encodings with coinduction principles and implemented their design in Coq [DFH+93].

Reasoning by induction is also supported by the calculus of partial inductive definitions [Hal87] and definitional reflection [SH93], however, both designs require induction subjects to be closed.

7 Conclusion

Higher-order encodings supported by logical frameworks such as LF bring many advantages in terms of elegance, efficiency, and maintenance, especially when representing complex systems, such as derivation systems, logics, type systems, operational semantics and others. They bring, however, at least one disadvantage: it is not easy to reason about them. In this paper we have developed a general induction principle for higher-order encodings and added it to first-order intuitionistic logic. The soundness of the design follows from a type theoretic argument by restricting LF contexts to be regularly formed.

We have implemented a prototype version of a theorem prover that uses worlds and the ind-rule in Twelf [PS99]. Twelf has successfully proven, for example, the equivalence of Hilbert's calculus, natural deduction calculus, and the sequent calculus. Other experiments include the proof of the Church-Rosser theorem for the untyped and the simply-typed λ-calculus, and cut-elimination results for various propositional and first-order sequent calculi.

Our proposal provides one possible solution for the tension between reasoning by induction and higher-order encodings. It is applicable to the untyped, simply typed, and dependently typed setting. In addition, it does not interfere with any properties of the underlying logical framework, such as properties that are associated with contexts or variables.

References

[Coq91] Thierry Coquand. An algorithm for testing conversion in type theory. In Gérard Huet and Gordon Plotkin, editors, *Logical Frameworks*, pages 255–279. Cambridge University Press, 1991.

[DFH+93] Gilles Dowek, Amy Felty, Hugo Herbelin, Gérard Huet, Chet Murthy, Catherine Parent, Christine Paulin-Mohring, and Benjamin Werner. The Coq proof assistant user's guide. Rapport Techniques 154, INRIA, Rocquencourt, France, 1993. Version 5.8.

[DH94] Joëlle Despeyroux and André Hirschowitz. Higher-order abstract syntax with induction in Coq. In Frank Pfenning, editor, *Proceedings of the 5th International Conference on Logic Programming and Automated Reasoning*, pages 159–173, Kiev, Ukraine, July 1994. Springer-Verlag LNAI 822.

[DPS97] Joëlle Despeyroux, Frank Pfenning, and Carsten Schürmann. Primitive recursion for higher-order abstract syntax. In R. Hindley, editor, *Proceedings of the Third International Conference on Typed Lambda Calculus and Applications (TLCA'97)*, pages 147–163, Nancy, France, April 1997. Springer-Verlag LNCS 1210.

[Gen35] Gerhard Gentzen. Untersuchungen über das logische Schließen. *Mathematische Zeitschrift*, 39:176–210, 405–431, 1935.

[GM96] Andrew D. Gordon and Tom Melham. Five axioms of alpha-conversion. In J. von Wright, J. Grundy, and J. Harrison, editors, *Proceedings of the 9th International Conference on Theorem Proving in Higher Order Logics (TPHOLs'96)*, pages 173–191, Turku, Finland, August 1996. Springer-Verlag LNCS 1125.

[GP99] Murdoch Gabbay and Andrew Pitts. A new approach to abstract syntax involving binders. In G. Longo, editor, *Proceedings of the 14th Annual Symposium on Logic in Computer Science (LICS'99)*, pages 214–224, Trento, Italy, July 1999. IEEE Computer Society Press.

[Hal87] Lars Hallnäs. A note on the logic of a logic program. In *Proceedings of the Workshop on Programming Logic*. University of Göteborg and Chalmers University of Technology, Report PMG-R37, 1987.

[HHP93] Robert Harper, Furio Honsell, and Gordon Plotkin. A framework for defining logics. *Journal of the Association for Computing Machinery*, 40(1):143–184, January 1993.

[HMS01] Furio Honsell, Marino Miculan, and Ivan Scagnetto. π-calculus in (Co)inductive type theory. *Theoretical Computer Science*, 253(2):239–285, 2001.

[Hof99] Martin Hofmann. Semantical analysis for higher-order abstract syntax. In G. Longo, editor, *Proceedings of the 14th Annual Symposium on Logic in Computer Science (LICS'99)*, pages 204–213, Trento, Italy, July 1999. IEEE Computer Society Press.

[Lel98] Pierre Leleu. *Induction et Syntaxe Abstraite d'Ordre Supérieur dans les Théories Typées*. PhD thesis, Ecole Nationale des Ponts et Chaussees, Marne-la-Vallee, France, December 1998.

[Pau94] Lawrence C. Paulson. *Isabelle: A Generic Theorem Prover*. Springer-Verlag LNCS 828, 1994.

[Pfe91] Frank Pfenning. Logic programming in the LF logical framework. In Gérard Huet and Gordon Plotkin, editors, *Logical Frameworks*, pages 149–181. Cambridge University Press, 1991.

[Pfe95] Frank Pfenning. Structural cut elimination. In D. Kozen, editor, *Proceedings of the Tenth Annual Symposium on Logic in Computer Science*, pages 156–166, San Diego, California, June 1995. IEEE Computer Society Press.

[Pfe99] Frank Pfenning. Logical frameworks. In Alan Robinson and Andrei Voronkov, editors, *Handbook of Automated Reasoning*, volume II. Elsevier Science Publishers, 1999.

[PG00] A. M. Pitts and M. J. Gabbay. A metalanguage for programming with bound names modulo renaming. In R. Backhouse and J. N. Oliveira, editors, *Mathematics of Program Construction, MPC2000, Proceedings, Ponte de Lima, Portugal, July 2000*, volume 1837 of *Lecture Notes in Computer Science*, pages 230–255. Springer-Verlag, Heidelberg, 2000.

[PM93] Christine Paulin-Mohring. Inductive definitions in the system Coq: Rules and properties. In M. Bezem and J.F. Groote, editors, *Proceedings of the International Conference on Typed Lambda Calculi and Applications*, pages 328–345, Utrecht, The Netherlands, March 1993. Springer-Verlag LNCS 664.

[PS99] Frank Pfenning and Carsten Schürmann. System description: Twelf — a meta-logical framework for deductive systems. In H. Ganzinger, editor, *Proceedings of the 16th International Conference on Automated Deduction (CADE-16)*, pages 202–206, Trento, Italy, July 1999. Springer-Verlag LNAI 1632.

[Sch00] Carsten Schürmann. *Automating the Meta-Theory of Deductive Systems.* PhD thesis, Carnegie Mellon University, 2000. CMU-CS-00-146.

[Sch01] Carsten Schürmann. Recursion for higher-order encodings. In Laurent Fribourg, editor, *Proceedings of the Conference on Computer Science Logic (CSL 2001)*, pages 585–599, Paris, France, August 2001. Springer-Verlag LNCS 2142.

[SH93] Peter Schroeder-Heister. Rules of definitional reflection. In M. Vardi, editor, *Proceedings of the Eighth Annual IEEE Symposium on Logic in Computer Science*, pages 222–232, Montreal, Canada, June 1993.

[Vir99] Roberto Virga. *Higher-Order Rewriting with Dependent Types.* PhD thesis, Carnegie Mellon University, 1999. CMU-CS-99-167.

Analysis of Polymorphically Typed Logic Programs Using ACI-Unification

Jan-Georg Smaus

Universität Freiburg, Germany, smaus@informatik.uni-freiburg.de

Abstract. Analysis of (partial) groundness is an important application of abstract interpretation. There are several proposals for improving the precision of such an analysis by exploiting type information, including our own work [15], where we had shown how the information present in the type declarations of a program can be used to characterise the degree of instantiation of a term in a precise but finite way. This approach worked for *polymorphically* typed logic programs. Here, we recast this approach following [5,11]. To formalise which properties of terms we want to characterise, we use *labelling functions*, which are functions that extract subterms from a term along certain paths. An *abstract term* collects the results of all labelling functions of a term. For the analysis, programs are executed on abstract terms instead of the concrete ones, and usual unification is replaced by unification modulo an equality theory which includes the well-known ACI-theory. Thus we generalise [5,11] w.r.t. the type systems considered and relate those two works.

1 Introduction

Analysing logic programs for (partial) groundness is important e.g. in compiler optimisations. Analysis is usually based on abstract interpretation [6].

It is known that abstract interpretation can be used to derive type information, and conversely, that type information can improve the precision of an analysis. E.g., being able to say that [1, X] is a list skeleton with possibly uninstantiated elements is more precise than only being able to distinguish a ground from a non-ground term. Underlying most works is a *descriptive* view of types: types are not part of the programming language, but introduced to analyse an arbitrary, say Prolog, program. In such works, there is no sharp line between *type* and *mode* (groundness, instantiation) analysis: saying that a term is a list is at the same time a statement about its type and about its degree of instantiation.

We adopt a *prescriptive* view of types. We analyse programs in typed languages, e.g. Gödel [9], HAL [7], Mercury [16]. Therefore the types need not be analysed since they are given by declarations or inference. Also, unlike [5], we need not consider "ill-typed" terms such as [1|2], since these can never occur.

This paper is a synthesis of two other works taking the prescriptive view [11, 15] and [5]. The generalisation w.r.t. [5,11] concerns *polymorphism*, which is disregarded in [11] and considered in [5] only in a restricted form. We recast [15] using some aspects of their formalisms. In particular, the notions of *grammar*

R. Nieuwenhuis and A. Voronkov (Eds.): LPAR 2001, LNAI 2250, pp. 282–298, 2001.

and *variables labelling non-terminals* [11] should improve the understanding of what properties of terms our analysis captures, whereas ACI-unification [5] may provide the basis for an implementation using well-studied algorithms.

In the intuitive explanations that follow, we refer to a set of possible characterisations of the instantiation of a term as *abstract domain*.

The standard example to explain the benefits of a typed analysis is the APPEND program. E.g., given the query append([A], [B], C), a typed analysis infers that any answer substitution binds C to a list. However, we need a more complex example to explain the advance of this paper over previous works.

A *table* contains a collection of nodes, each of which has a key of type string[1], and a value of arbitrary type. For any type τ, table(τ) is the type of tables whose values have type τ. Tables can be implemented as AVL-tree [8]: a non-leaf node has a *key* argument, a *value* argument, arguments for the left and right subtrees, and an argument representing balancing information. For a term of type table(τ), our abstract domain characterises the instantiation of all key arguments, all value arguments, and all the "balancing" arguments.

The characterisation of the instantiation of the value arguments depends on τ. Hence, our analysis supports parametric polymorphism. In devising an analysis for polymorphically typed programs, there are two desirable properties: the construction of an abstract domain for table(τ) should be truly parametric in τ, and the abstract domains should be finite for a given program and query.

Being truly parametric means, e.g., that the abstract domain for table(str) relates to str exactly as the abstract domain for table(int) relates to int[1].

In [11], types have been formalised as *regular tree grammars*. Each type is identified with a non-terminal, and it is assumed that there are only finitely many types, which is crucial for the termination of an analysis. In the presence of polymorphism, finiteness is problematic, since there are infinitely many types, e.g. list(int), list(list(int)), ... Nevertheless, under certain conditions, it can be ensured that for a given program, there are only finitely many types. This is in contrast to imposing an ad-hoc bound on the depth of types [5].

This paper is organised as follows. The next section provides some preliminaries. In Sec. 3, following [11], we show how the type of a term allows to characterise its degree of instantiation. In Sec. 4, following [5], we define abstract terms based on the ACI1 equality theory. In Sec. 5, we formalise how abstract terms capture the degree of instantiation of concrete terms, thereby linking [11] and [5]. Section 6 defines an abstraction of programs, and relates the semantics of a concrete program and its abstraction. Section 7 makes some comments on a possible future implementation, and Sec. 8 discusses our results.

A long version of this paper containing all proofs can be found in [14].

2 Preliminaries

We assume familiarity with the basic notions of logic programming [12]. We use a type system for logic programs with parametric polymorphism [7,9,16].

[1] We abbreviate string by str and integer by int.

Let $\mathcal{K}$ be a finite set of (type) **constructors**, each $c \in \mathcal{K}$ with an arity $n \geq 0$ associated (by writing c/n), and $\mathcal{U}$ be a set of **parameters**. The set of types is the term structure $\mathcal{T}(\mathcal{K},\mathcal{U})$. A **type substitution** is an idempotent mapping from parameters to types which is the identity almost everywhere. We define the order $\prec$ on types as the order induced by some (e.g. lexicographical) order on constructor and parameter symbols, where parameter symbols come before constructor symbols. The set of parameters in a syntactic object o is denoted by $pars(o)$. Parameters are denoted by u, v, in concrete examples by $\mathtt{U}, \mathtt{V}$. A tuple of *distinct* parameters ordered w.r.t. $\prec$ is denoted by $\bar{u}, \bar{v}$. A **flat type** is a type of the form $c(\bar{u})$, where $c \in \mathcal{K}$.

Let $\mathcal{V}$ be a denumerable set of **variables**. The set of variables in a syntactic object o is denoted by $vars(o)$. Variables are denoted by x, y, in concrete examples by $\mathtt{X}, \mathtt{Y}$. A tuple of *distinct* variables is denoted by $\bar{x}, \bar{y}$.

A **variable typing** is a mapping from a finite subset of $\mathcal{V}$ to $\mathcal{T}(\mathcal{K},\mathcal{U})$, written as $\{x_1 : \tau_1, \ldots, x_n : \tau_n\}$.

Let $\mathcal{F}$ (resp. $\mathcal{P}$) be a finite set of **function** (resp. **predicate**) symbols, each with an arity and a **declared type** associated, such that: for each $f/n \in \mathcal{F}$, the declared type has the form $(\tau_1, \ldots, \tau_n, \tau)$, where $(\tau_1, \ldots, \tau_n, \tau) \in \mathcal{T}(\mathcal{K},\mathcal{U})^{n+1}$ and $pars(\tau_1, \ldots, \tau_n) \subseteq pars(\tau)$; for each $p/n \in \mathcal{P}$, the declared type has the form $(\tau_1, \ldots, \tau_n)$, where $(\tau_1, \ldots, \tau_n) \in \mathcal{T}(\mathcal{K},\mathcal{U})^n$. We indicate the declared types by writing $f_{\tau_1 \ldots \tau_n \to \tau}$ and $p_{\tau_1 \ldots \tau_n}$.

Throughout, we assume $\mathcal{K}$, $\mathcal{F}$, and $\mathcal{P}$ arbitrary but fixed. Terms are defined by the following inference rules, which allow to infer judgements of the form $t : \tau$, read "t is of type τ".

$$\{x : \tau, \ldots\} \vdash x : \tau \qquad \frac{\Gamma \vdash t_1 : \tau_1 \Theta \ \cdots \ \Gamma \vdash t_n : \tau_n \Theta}{\Gamma \vdash f_{\tau_1 \ldots \tau_n \to \tau}(t_1, \ldots, t_n) : \tau\Theta} \ (\Theta \text{ is a type substitution})$$

There are similar rules for defining atoms, clauses etc. [14]. All objects are defined relative to a variable typing Γ. Any objects we will encounter while analysing a typed program will be correctly typed according to those rules [13].

The set of atoms is denoted by $\mathcal{B}$, and elements of $2^{\mathcal{B}}$ are called **interpretations**. We denote by $\langle C_1, \ldots, C_n \rangle \ll_o I$ that $C_1, \ldots, C_n$ are elements of I renamed apart from o and from each other. Like [5], our analysis is independent from any particular concrete semantics. Examples will be given using the s-semantics, i.e. the semantics based on the non-ground T_P-operator:

$$T_P(I) := \{H\theta \mid C = H \leftarrow B_1, \ldots, B_n \in P, \langle A_1, \ldots, A_n \rangle \ll_C I,$$
$$\theta = MGU(\langle B_1, \ldots, B_n \rangle, \langle A_1, \ldots, A_n \rangle)\}.$$

We denote by $[\![P]\!]_s$ the least fixpoint of T_P. We denote by $t_1 \leq t_2$ that t_1 is an instance if t_2. The domain of a substitution θ is denoted as $dom(\theta)$.

3 The Structure of Terms and Types

We show how the type of a term allows to characterise its structure. We alternate between recalling the formalism of [11] and adapting it to polymorphism.

3.1 Regular Types as Presented in [11]

Definition 3.1. A **regular tree grammar** is a tuple $\langle S, W, \Sigma, \Delta \rangle$, where W is a finite set of **non-terminals**, $S \in W$ is a **starting** non-terminal, Δ is a set of **productions** of the form $X \to f(Y_1, \dots, Y_n)$ s.t. $X, Y_1, \dots, Y_n \in W$ and $f/n \in \Sigma$. A regular tree grammar is **deterministic** if for any non-terminal X and any two productions $X \to f(Y_1, \dots, Y_n)$ and $X \to g(Z_1, \dots, Z_m)$, $f/n \neq g/m$.

Regular grammars define the class of languages called *regular types.*

Example 3.2. The grammar $L \to \mathtt{nil}|\mathtt{cons}(E, L)$, $E \to \mathtt{a}|\mathtt{b}$ defines the language of ground lists of a's and b's.

Using an analogy to tree automata [11], we represent derivations of a grammar $\mathcal{G}$ as transitions $N(f(t_1, \dots, t_n)) \to f(N_1(t_1), \dots, N_n(t_n))$, where $N \to f(N_1, \dots, N_n)$ is a production of $\mathcal{G}$ ($n \geq 0$). We say that $\mathcal{G} = \langle S, W, \Sigma, \Delta \rangle$ **accepts** a term t if $S(t) \to^* t$. We are also interested in segments of a single path in a derivation tree starting from root S and reaching a non-terminal N with a subterm t' of t, i.e., in derivations $S(t) \to^* s[N(t')]$, where $s[N(t')]$ means that s has $N(t')$ as a subterm. Abusing notation, we write $S(t) \to^* N(t')$ in this case.

Example 3.3. Given the grammar in Ex. 3.2, we have

$$L(\mathtt{cons}(\mathtt{a}, \mathtt{nil})) \to \mathtt{cons}(E(\mathtt{a}), L(\mathtt{nil})) \to \mathtt{cons}(\mathtt{a}, L(\mathtt{nil})) \to \mathtt{cons}(\mathtt{a}, \mathtt{nil}).$$

We also write $L(\mathtt{cons}(\mathtt{a}, \mathtt{nil})) \to^* E(\mathtt{a})$ and $L(\mathtt{cons}(\mathtt{a}, \mathtt{nil})) \to^* L(\mathtt{nil})$. The notation can also be applied to non-ground terms, e.g. $L(\mathtt{cons}(\mathtt{X}, \mathtt{Y})) \to^* L(\mathtt{Y})$.

It is also convenient to depict a grammar as a *type graph* [10]. We define a type graph for $\mathcal{G} = \langle S, W, \Sigma, \Delta \rangle$ as a directed graph whose nodes are labelled by non-terminals, and there is an edge from N to N' iff there is a production $N \to f(\dots, N', \dots)$ in Δ. We call the node labelled S the **starting node**. Figure 1 shows the type graph for Ex. 3.2.

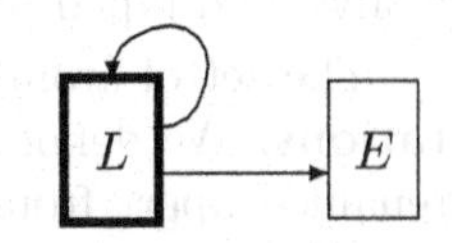

Fig. 1: Type graph

3.2 Regular Types and Polymorphism

Without polymorphism, type declarations can be easily translated into grammar rules. $\mathcal{K}$ is a *finite* set of type constants, so we can identify each type with a non-terminal, and each $f_{\tau_1 \dots \tau_n \to \tau} \in \mathcal{F}$ is translated into a production $\tau \to f(\tau_1, \dots, \tau_n)$. So each τ corresponds to a grammar with starting non-terminal τ.

We now give a pseudo-definition of a grammar corresponding to a polymorphic type — "pseudo" because the set of non-terminals may be infinite.

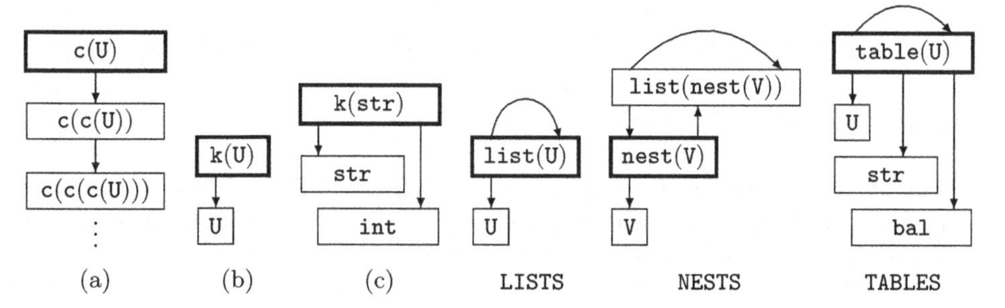

Fig. 2. Some type graphs, with starting node highlighted

Definition 3.4. Consider a typed language given by $\mathcal{K}, \mathcal{F}$ and a type ϕ. The **grammar corresponding to** ϕ, denoted $\mathcal{G}(\phi)$, is the grammar $\langle `\phi', W, \mathcal{F}, \Delta \rangle$, where W is inductively defined as follows:

- $`\phi' \in W$,
- $f_{\tau_1 \ldots \tau_n \to \tau} \in \mathcal{F}$ and $`\tau\Theta' \in W$ for some type substitution $\Theta$ implies $`\tau_1\Theta', \ldots, `\tau_n\Theta' \in W$,

and $\Delta = \{`\tau\Theta' \to f_{\tau_1 \ldots \tau_n \to \tau}(`\tau_1\Theta', \ldots, `\tau_n\Theta') \mid `\tau\Theta' \in W\}$.

The ' ' indicate that w.r.t the grammar, types are just non-terminal symbols. Type graphs are defined as before. Figure 2 shows some type graphs.

It is also useful to have names and a notation for the relations holding between the types in a type graph.

Definition 3.5. A type σ is a **direct subterm type of** ϕ (denoted as $\sigma \lhd \phi$) if there is $f_{\tau_1 \ldots \tau_n \to \tau} \in \mathcal{F}$ and a type substitution Θ such that $\tau\Theta = \phi$ and $\tau_i\Theta = \sigma$ for some $i \in \{1, \ldots, n\}$. The transitive, reflexive closure of $\lhd$ is denoted as $\lhd^*$. If $\sigma \lhd^* \phi$, then σ is a **subterm type of** ϕ.

We had defined these relations previously [15]. In [2], subterm types are called *constituents*.

We now discuss two problems related to the generalisation to polymorphism. They have been mentioned previously [15] and are illustrated here with examples.

Example 3.6. Whenever we give a particular typed language, $\mathcal{K}$ is given implicitly as the set of all type constructors occurring in the type subscripts in $\mathcal{F}$.

One would hope that even if a type language contains an infinite set of types, the type graph taking a fixed type as starting node should be finite. However, consider $\mathcal{F} = \{\mathtt{f}_{\mathtt{c(c(U))} \to \mathtt{c(U)}}\}$. The type graph of $\mathtt{c(U)}$ is infinite (see Fig. 2 (a)).

To ensure finiteness, we impose the following condition on $\mathcal{K}, \mathcal{F}$.

Reflexive Condition: For all $c \in \mathcal{K}$ and types $\sigma = c(\bar{\sigma}), \tau = c(\bar{\tau})$, if $\sigma \lhd^* \tau$, then σ is a sub"term" (in the syntactic sense) of τ.

This condition is violated by Ex. 3.6 since $\mathtt{c(c(U))} \lhd \mathtt{c(U)}$. With this condition in place, Def. 3.4 becomes a real definition rather than a pseudo-definition.

The second problem is to make the grammars (or equivalently, type graphs) truly parametric. This will be crucial to make the abstract domains truly parametric, as mentioned in the introduction.

Example 3.7. Consider $\mathcal{F} = \{\mathtt{f}_{\mathtt{U}\to\mathtt{k(U)}}, \mathtt{g}_{\mathtt{int}\to\mathtt{k(str)}}\}$. Figure 2 shows the type graphs for k(U) and k(str). It would clearly be wrong to say that "k(U) relates to U in the same way as k(str) relates to str".

To rule out this anomaly, we impose the following condition on $\mathcal{K}, \mathcal{F}$.

Flat Range Condition: For all $f_{\tau_1\ldots\tau_n\to\tau} \in \mathcal{F}$, τ is a flat type.

In Mercury (and in ML and Haskell), this condition is enforced by the syntax. In the recent work of [2], we also find similar conditions. So from now on, we assume that any typed language meets these two conditions.

3.3 Labelling as Presented in [11]

Labellings can be used to characterise the degree of instantiation of a term taking its type into account, i.e., analyse a term on a *per-role* basis [11].

Definition 3.8. A variable x in a term t **labels** a non-terminal N of a grammar $\mathcal{G}$ if $S(t) \to^* N(x)$, where S is the starting non-terminal of $\mathcal{G}$.

We denote by $\zeta(S, N, t)$ the function which returns the set of variables x such that $S(t) \to^* N(x)$ (one could also write $\zeta(\mathcal{G}, N, t)$ [11]).

Example 3.9. The grammar $LL \to \mathtt{nil}|\mathtt{cons}(L, LL)$, $L \to \mathtt{nil}|\mathtt{cons}(E, L)$, $E \to \mathtt{a}|\mathtt{b}$ accepts ground lists of lists of a's and b's. We use the usual list notation. The type graph of LL is shown in Fig. 3. We are interested in the labelling of all non-terminals reachable from LL. Let $t = [[\mathtt{a}], [\mathtt{b}]]$. Then $\zeta(LL, E, t) = \zeta(LL, L, t) = \zeta(LL, LL, t) = \emptyset$. Now let $t = [[\mathtt{a}], [\mathtt{X}]]$. Then $\zeta(LL, E, t) = \{\mathtt{X}\}$ and $\zeta(LL, L, t) = \zeta(LL, LL, t) = \emptyset$. Now let $t = [[\mathtt{a}], \mathtt{X}]$. Then $\zeta(LL, E, t) = \emptyset$, $\zeta(LL, L, t) = \{\mathtt{X}\}$ and $\zeta(LL, LL, t) = \emptyset$.

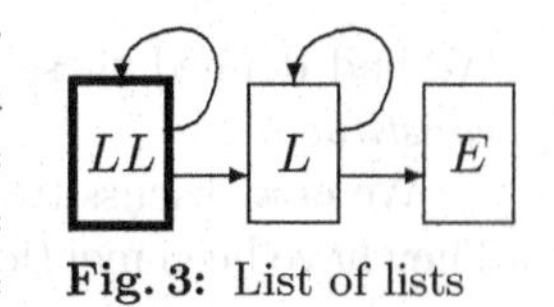

Fig. 3: List of lists

Ultimately, one is interested in whether a labelling function returns variables at all and not in their names. Nevertheless, it fits into the formalisms of [5,11] and this paper to define labelling functions the way we do. We also refer to Sec. 8.

3.4 Labelling and Polymorphism

In the presence of polymorphism, type graphs can become arbitrarily big. Also, it would be desirable to describe the labellings for say list(int), list(list(int)), ... in a uniform way. This motivates defining a hierarchy in the type graph [15].

Definition 3.10. A type σ is a **recursive type of** ϕ (denoted as $\sigma \bowtie \phi$) if $\sigma \lhd^* \phi$ and $\phi \lhd^* \sigma$. We write $\bowtie(\phi)$ for the tuple of recursive types of ϕ other than ϕ itself, ordered by $\prec$ (see Sec. 2).

A type σ is a **non-recursive subterm type (NRS) of** ϕ (denoted as $\sigma \lll \phi$) if $\phi \not\lhd^* \sigma$ and there is a type τ such that $\sigma \lhd \tau$ and $\tau \bowtie \phi$. We write $\lll(\phi)$ for the tuple of NRSs of ϕ, ordered by $\prec$.

Consider the type graph for ϕ. The recursive types of ϕ are the types in the strongly connected component (SCC) containing ϕ. The NRSs of ϕ are the types σ such that there is an edge from the SCC containing ϕ to σ.

Example 3.11. Consider Fig. 2. Let $\mathcal{F}_{\text{LISTS}} = \{\mathtt{nil}_{\rightarrow\mathtt{list(U)}}, \mathtt{cons}_{\mathtt{U},\mathtt{list(U)}\rightarrow\mathtt{list(U)}}\}$. We have $\mathtt{list(U)} \bowtie \mathtt{list(U)}$ and $\mathtt{U} \lll \mathtt{list(U)}$.

Let $\mathcal{F}_{\text{NESTS}} = \mathcal{F}_{\text{LISTS}} \cup \{\mathtt{e}_{\mathtt{V}\rightarrow\mathtt{nest(V)}}, \mathtt{n}_{\mathtt{list(nest(V))}\rightarrow\mathtt{nest(V)}}\}$. NESTS implements *rose trees*, i.e., trees where the number of children of each node is arbitrary. Then $\mathtt{list(nest(V))} \bowtie \mathtt{nest(V)}$ and $\mathtt{nest(V)} \bowtie \mathtt{nest(V)}$ and $\mathtt{V} \lll \mathtt{nest(V)}$.

Suppose $\mathcal{F}_{\text{STRINGS}}$ contains all strings. Let $\mathcal{F}_{\text{TABLES}} = \mathcal{F}_{\text{STRINGS}} \cup$

$$\{\mathtt{lh}_{\rightarrow\mathtt{bal}}, \mathtt{rh}_{\rightarrow\mathtt{bal}}, \mathtt{eq}_{\rightarrow\mathtt{bal}}, \mathtt{null}_{\rightarrow\mathtt{table(U)}}, \mathtt{node}_{\mathtt{table(U)},\mathtt{str},\mathtt{U},\mathtt{bal},\mathtt{table(U)}\rightarrow\mathtt{table(U)}}\}.$$

Then $\mathtt{table(U)} \bowtie \mathtt{table(U)}$ and $\lll(\mathtt{table(U)}) = \langle \mathtt{U}, \mathtt{bal}, \mathtt{str} \rangle$.

An NRS of a flat type is often just a parameter of that type, as in $\mathtt{U} \lll \mathtt{list(U)}$. However, this is not always the case, as witnessed by $\mathtt{str} \lll \mathtt{table(U)}$.

Instead of looking at the labellings of *all* non-terminals reachable from some ϕ [11], we look only at $\lll(\phi)$ and $\bowtie(\phi)$. This is crucial for polymorphism, since we cannot predict for all instances of ϕ which non-terminals are reachable from it. But the point can be explained even for a monomorphic example, so consider Fig. 3. We have $LL \bowtie LL$ and $L \lll LL$. In the approach of [11], we may be interested in $\zeta(LL, E, t)$ for some term t, so in the labellings of E. In our approach, the domain construction for LL depends on E only indirectly, via the abstract domain for L.

The key to a "parametric" abstract domain construction is to focus on type constructors, or equivalently, on flat types $c(\bar{u})$. E.g., we should focus on $\mathtt{list(U)}$ and not $\mathtt{list(int)}$. This is not surprising but has two non-obvious consequences.

First, the relation $\lll$ is not stable under instantiation. Compare LISTS with NESTS. We have $\mathtt{U} \lll \mathtt{list(U)}$, but $\mathtt{nest(V)} \bowtie \mathtt{list(nest(V))}$. The abstract domain for $\mathtt{list(nest(V))}$ however, being derived from the abstract domain for $\mathtt{list(U)}$, must relate to $\mathtt{nest(V)}$ as if $\mathtt{nest(V)}$ was an NRS of $\mathtt{list(nest(V))}$.

We illustrate the second consequence with TABLES. The type $\mathtt{table(U)}$ has three NRSs. However, $\mathtt{table(string)}$ has only two NRSs, as $\mathtt{U}$ becomes instantiated to $\mathtt{string}$. The domain for $\mathtt{table}(\tau)$ will always be based on assuming *three* NRSs, even if by coincidence $\tau = \mathtt{string}$.

We now define a function $\mathcal{Z}$ in analogy to ζ, but also collecting non-variable terms. In [11], a grammar could effectively be identified with its starting non-terminal. In what follows, we will always assume a grammar $\mathcal{G}(\phi)$ where ϕ is flat (Def. 3.4). However, it is also useful to consider productions of that grammar starting from some other non-terminal. Therefore $\mathcal{Z}$ has *four* arguments, the additional first one specifying the grammar and the second the starting symbol. In [15], we had defined similar functions.

Definition 3.12. Let ϕ be a flat type, τ be a type such that $\tau \bowtie \phi$, and σ a type such that either $\sigma \bowtie \phi$ or $\sigma \lll \phi$. We denote by $\mathcal{Z}(\phi, \tau, \sigma, t)$ the function returning the set of all terms s such that 'τ'$(t) \to^*$ 'σ'(s) in the grammar $\mathcal{G}(\phi)$. The function $\mathcal{Z}$ is lifted to sets (in the fourth argument) in the obvious way.

Example 3.13. Let $\mathcal{F} = \mathcal{F}_{\mathtt{LISTS}} \cup \{\mathtt{a_{char}}, \mathtt{b_{char}}\}$. We have

$$\mathcal{Z}(\mathtt{list(U)}, \mathtt{list(U)}, \mathtt{list(U)}, [[\mathtt{a}], [\mathtt{X}]]) = \{[[\mathtt{a}], [\mathtt{X}]], [[\mathtt{X}]], []\}$$
$$\mathcal{Z}(\mathtt{list(U)}, \mathtt{list(U)}, \mathtt{U}, [[\mathtt{a}], [\mathtt{X}]]) = \{[\mathtt{a}], [\mathtt{X}]\}$$

$$\mathcal{Z}(\mathtt{list(U)}, \mathtt{list(U)}, \mathtt{list(U)}, [[\mathtt{a}]|\mathtt{X}]) = \{[[\mathtt{a}]|\mathtt{X}], \mathtt{X}\}.$$

Unlike ζ (Ex. 3.9), $\mathcal{Z}$ cannot extract from $[[\mathtt{a}], [\mathtt{X}]]$ the subterm X directly.

Now consider NESTS augmented with the integers $0_{\mathtt{int}}, 1_{\mathtt{int}}, \ldots$. We have

$$\mathcal{Z}(\mathtt{nest(V)}, \mathtt{list(nest(V))}, \mathtt{nest(V)}, [\mathtt{n}([\mathtt{e}(7)])]) = \{\mathtt{n}([\mathtt{e}(7)]), \mathtt{e}(7)\} \quad (1)$$
$$\mathcal{Z}(\mathtt{nest(V)}, \mathtt{list(nest(V))}, \mathtt{list(nest(V))}, [\mathtt{n}([\mathtt{e}(7)])]) = \{[\mathtt{n}([\mathtt{e}(7)])], [\mathtt{e}(7)], []\}$$
$$\mathcal{Z}(\mathtt{nest(V)}, \mathtt{list(nest(V))}, \mathtt{V}, [\mathtt{n}([\mathtt{e}(7)])]) = \{7\} \quad (3)$$

$$\mathcal{Z}(\mathtt{list(U)}, \mathtt{list(U)}, \mathtt{list(U)}, [\mathtt{n}([\mathtt{e}(7)])]) = \{[\mathtt{n}([\mathtt{e}(7)])], []\} \quad (4)$$
$$\mathcal{Z}(\mathtt{list(U)}, \mathtt{list(U)}, \mathtt{U}, [\mathtt{n}([\mathtt{e}(7)])]) = \{\mathtt{n}([\mathtt{e}(7)])\} \quad (5)$$

Note the difference between the labellings for $[\mathtt{n}([\mathtt{e}(7)])]$ depending on whether we use the grammar for nest(V) (1 – 3), or the grammar for list(U) (4, 5). E.g., in (5), we extract the only element from a list; coincidentally, this element is a nest. In (1), we extract all nests from a list of nests, thus including e(7).

4 Abstract Terms

We define an abstraction of terms based on Def. 3.10, thereby generalising [5]. The *abstract term* $\alpha(t)$ describes the instantiation degree of t by collecting t's variables in a structure: roughly, by grouping subterms of the same type together.

We first introduce *set logic programs* [11]. Consider a set of variables $\mathcal{V}$ and a set of functions $\mathcal{F}^{\oplus} = \{\emptyset, \oplus\}$, where $\emptyset/0$ represents the empty set and $\oplus/2$ is a set constructor. *Set expressions* are elements of the term algebra $\mathcal{T}(\mathcal{F}^{\oplus}, \mathcal{V})$ modulo the ACI1 equality theory, consisting of:

$$\begin{array}{llll} (x \oplus y) \oplus z = x \oplus (y \oplus z) & \text{(associativity)} & x \oplus x = x & \text{(idempotence)} \\ x \oplus y = y \oplus x & \text{(commutativity)} & x \oplus \emptyset = x & \text{(unity)} \end{array} \quad (6)$$

In addition to $\emptyset$ and $\oplus$, we introduce a function symbol $c^{\mathcal{A}}$ for each $c \in \mathcal{K}$. The arity of $c^{\mathcal{A}}$ is given by the sum of cardinalities of $\lll(c(\bar{u}))$ and $\bowtie(c(\bar{u}))$.

Definition 4.1. We define

$$\mathcal{F}^{\mathcal{A}} := \mathcal{F}^{\oplus} \cup \{c^{\mathcal{A}}/m \mid c \in \mathcal{K},\ m = \#(\lll(c(\bar{u}))) + \#(\bowtie(c(\bar{u})))\}.$$

Now let $\tau = c(\bar{u})$, $\lll(\tau) = \langle \rho_1, \dots, \rho_{m'} \rangle$, and $\bowtie(\tau) = \langle \rho_{m'+1}, \dots, \rho_m \rangle$. For a term $t = f_{\tau_1 \dots \tau_n \to \tau}(t_1, \dots, t_n)$, we define

$$\alpha(t) = c^{\mathcal{A}} \left(\bigoplus_{\tau_i = \rho_1} \alpha(t_i), \dots, \bigoplus_{\tau_i = \rho_m} \alpha(t_i) \right) \oplus \bigoplus_{\tau_i = \tau} \alpha(t_i).$$

For a variable x we define $\alpha(x) = x$.

In [4], the abstraction function is denoted *type*, and it is a special case of the above definition for $\#(\lll(c(\bar{u}))) = 1$ and $\#(\bowtie(c(\bar{u}))) = 0$. The information we extract from the type declarations is formalised there by two functions α and π. Since their typing is descriptive, those have to be provided by the user.

Example 4.2. Consider again Ex. 3.13.

$$\begin{aligned}
\alpha(7) &= \mathtt{int}^{\mathcal{A}} \\
\alpha([7]) &= \mathtt{list}^{\mathcal{A}}(\alpha(7)) \oplus \alpha(\mathtt{nil}) = \mathtt{list}^{\mathcal{A}}(\mathtt{int}^{\mathcal{A}}) \oplus \mathtt{list}^{\mathcal{A}}(\emptyset) \\
\alpha(\mathtt{e}(7)) &= \mathtt{nest}^{\mathcal{A}}(\alpha(7), \emptyset) \qquad\qquad = \mathtt{nest}^{\mathcal{A}}(\mathtt{int}^{\mathcal{A}}, \emptyset) \\
\alpha(\mathtt{n}([\mathtt{e}(7)])) &= \mathtt{nest}^{\mathcal{A}}(\emptyset, \alpha([\mathtt{e}(7)])) \qquad = \mathtt{nest}^{\mathcal{A}}(\emptyset, \mathtt{list}^{\mathcal{A}}(\mathtt{nest}^{\mathcal{A}}(\mathtt{int}^{\mathcal{A}}, \emptyset))).
\end{aligned}$$

Note how it comes into play (e.g., in the abstraction of `nil`) that the empty $\oplus$-sequence is defined as $\emptyset$. In [5], unlike in [4], there is no $\emptyset$. The list `nil` is abstracted as `nil`, and as a consequence, the list [7] is abstracted as $\mathtt{list(int)} \oplus \mathtt{nil}$. We believe that an object $\mathtt{list(int)} \oplus \mathtt{nil}$ mixes types (abstract terms) and concrete terms in an undesirable way.

Here, whenever an expression $c^{\mathcal{A}}(\dots) \oplus c'^{\mathcal{A}}(\dots)$ occurs, then $c = c'$. This explains why in Def. 4.1, the abstraction of those t_i such that $\tau_i \bowtie \tau$ but $\tau_i \neq \tau$ is included in reserved argument positions of $c^{\mathcal{A}}(\dots)$, whereas the abstraction of those t_i such that $\tau_i = \tau$ is directly conjoined (using $\oplus$) with $c^{\mathcal{A}}(\dots)$.

As defined, $\alpha(t)$ is no smaller than t. But one would expect that $\mathtt{list}^{\mathcal{A}}(\mathtt{int}^{\mathcal{A}}) \oplus \mathtt{list}^{\mathcal{A}}(\emptyset)$ can be simplified to $\mathtt{list}^{\mathcal{A}}(\mathtt{int}^{\mathcal{A}})$. Maybe less obvious, one might expect that $\mathtt{nest}^{\mathcal{A}}(\emptyset, \mathtt{list}^{\mathcal{A}}(\mathtt{nest}^{\mathcal{A}}(\mathtt{int}^{\mathcal{A}}, \emptyset)))$ can be simplified to $\mathtt{nest}^{\mathcal{A}}(\mathtt{int}^{\mathcal{A}}, \emptyset)$. To this end, we now define further axioms.

Definition 4.3. For each $c^{\mathcal{A}}/m \in \mathcal{F}^{\mathcal{A}}$, the **distributivity axiom** is:

$$c^{\mathcal{A}}(x_1, \dots, x_m) \oplus c^{\mathcal{A}}(y_1, \dots, y_m) = c^{\mathcal{A}}(x_1 \oplus y_1, \dots, x_m \oplus y_m) \tag{7}$$

Moreover, consider a flat type $\phi = d(\bar{v})$ such that $\lll(\phi) = \langle \sigma_1, \dots, \sigma_{l'} \rangle$, $\bowtie(\phi) = \langle \sigma_{l'+1}, \dots, \sigma_l \rangle$. For each $j \in \{l'+1, \dots, l\}$, we have $\sigma_j = \tau\Theta$ for some flat type $\tau = c(\bar{u})$ and some Θ. Suppose $\lll(\tau) = \langle \rho_1, \dots, \rho_{m'} \rangle$, $\bowtie(\tau) = \langle \rho_{m'+1}, \dots, \rho_m \rangle$,

We define the **extraction axiom** for ϕ and σ_j as follows:

$$d^{\mathcal{A}}(x_1,\ldots,x_{j-1},c^{\mathcal{A}}(y_1,\ldots,y_m)\oplus x_j,x_{j+1},\ldots,x_l) =$$

$$d^{\mathcal{A}}\left(x_1 \oplus \bigoplus_{\rho_k\Theta=\sigma_1} y_k,\ \ldots,\ x_{j-1} \oplus \bigoplus_{\rho_k\Theta=\sigma_{j-1}} y_k,\ x_j,\ x_{j+1} \oplus \bigoplus_{\rho_k\Theta=\sigma_{j+1}} y_k,\ \ldots,\ x_m \oplus \bigoplus_{\rho_k\Theta=\sigma_l} y_k\right) \oplus \bigoplus_{\rho_k\Theta=\phi} y_k .$$

Let **ACI1DE** be the theory given by the axioms in (6) and the distributivity and extraction axioms. We abbreviate ACI1DE by **AC+** and denote equality modulo AC+ by $=_{\mathrm{AC+}}$.

Example 4.4. Consider `LISTS` and `NESTS`. The extraction axiom for `nest(V)` and `list(nest(V))` is $\mathtt{nest}^{\mathcal{A}}(x_1,\mathtt{list}^{\mathcal{A}}(y)\oplus x_2) = \mathtt{nest}^{\mathcal{A}}(x_1,x_2)\oplus y$. We have

$$\mathtt{list}^{\mathcal{A}}(\mathtt{int}^{\mathcal{A}}) \oplus \mathtt{list}^{\mathcal{A}}(\emptyset) =_{\mathrm{AC+}} \mathtt{list}^{\mathcal{A}}(\mathtt{int}^{\mathcal{A}} \oplus \emptyset) =_{\mathrm{AC+}} \mathtt{list}^{\mathcal{A}}(\mathtt{int}^{\mathcal{A}})$$

$$\mathtt{nest}^{\mathcal{A}}(\emptyset,\mathtt{list}^{\mathcal{A}}(\mathtt{nest}^{\mathcal{A}}(\mathtt{int}^{\mathcal{A}},\emptyset))) =_{\mathrm{AC+}} \mathtt{nest}^{\mathcal{A}}(\emptyset,\emptyset) \oplus \mathtt{nest}^{\mathcal{A}}(\mathtt{int}^{\mathcal{A}},\emptyset) =_{\mathrm{AC+}} \mathtt{nest}^{\mathcal{A}}(\mathtt{int}^{\mathcal{A}},\emptyset).$$

The last line says, intuitively: a nest containing a list containing a nest containing a (ground) integer is actually just a nest containing a (ground) integer.

We can now define abstract terms that are simplified as much as possible. We denote a variable sequence $x_1 \oplus \cdots \oplus x_n$ as $x^{\oplus}$ (this is $\emptyset$ if $n = 0$). The following definition is by a structural induction that is well-founded by [15, Lemma 4.3].

Definition 4.5. For a parameter, a **normal abstract term** has the form $x^{\oplus}$.

Now let $\tau = c(\bar{u})$ be a flat type such that $\lll(\tau) = \langle \rho_1,\ldots,\rho_{m'}\rangle$ and $\bowtie(\tau) = \langle \rho_{m'+1},\ldots,\rho_m\rangle$, and Θ be any type substitution. A **normal abstract term for** $\tau\Theta$ is $\emptyset$ or of the form $c^{\mathcal{A}}(a_1 \oplus x_1^{\oplus},\ldots,a_{m'} \oplus x_{m'}^{\oplus}, x_{m'+1}^{\oplus},\ldots,x_m^{\oplus}) \oplus x^{\oplus}$, where for each $i \in \{1,\ldots,m'\}$, a_i is a normal abstract term for $\rho_i\Theta$.

Theorem 4.6. For any t with $\_ \vdash t : \phi$, $\alpha(t)$ has a representative which is a normal abstract term for ϕ. The representative is unique up to the order of variables in $\oplus$-sequences.

Example 4.4 shows the conversion of two abstract terms to their normal forms.

5 Relating the Abstraction and the Labels

The following theorem relates the abstraction of a term to the labellings (Sec. 3), thus linking [5] with [11]. Note how α is lifted to sets: $\alpha(S) := \bigoplus_{t\in S} \alpha(t)$.

Theorem 5.1. Let $\tau = c(\bar{u})$ be a flat type such that $\lll(\tau) = \langle \rho_1, \ldots, \rho_{m'} \rangle$ and $\bowtie(\tau) = \langle \rho_{m'+1}, \ldots, \rho_m \rangle$. For any term $t = f_{\tau_1 \ldots \tau_n \to \tau}(\ldots)$, we have $\alpha(t) =_{\mathrm{AC+}}$

$$c^{\mathcal{A}}\big(\alpha(\mathcal{Z}(\tau, \tau, \rho_1, t)), \ldots, \alpha(\mathcal{Z}(\tau, \tau, \rho_{m'}, t)),\\ \alpha(\mathcal{Z}(\tau, \tau, \rho_{m'+1}, t)) \cap \mathcal{V}, \ldots, \alpha(\mathcal{Z}(\tau, \tau, \rho_m, t)) \cap \mathcal{V}\big) \oplus (\mathcal{Z}(\tau, \tau, \tau, t) \cap \mathcal{V}).$$

Example 5.2. Consider `LISTS`. We have

$$\begin{aligned} \alpha([[\mathtt{X}], [7]]) = \quad & \mathtt{list}^{\mathcal{A}}(\alpha(\mathcal{Z}(\mathtt{list(U)}, \mathtt{list(U)}, \mathtt{U}, [[\mathtt{X}], [7]]))) \\ & \oplus \mathcal{Z}(\mathtt{list(U)}, \mathtt{list(U)}, \mathtt{list(U)}, [[\mathtt{X}], [7]]) \cap \mathcal{V}) \\ = \quad & \mathtt{list}^{\mathcal{A}}(\alpha(\{[\mathtt{X}], [7]\})) \oplus (\{[[\mathtt{X}], [7]], [[7]], []\} \cap \mathcal{V}) \\ = \quad & \mathtt{list}^{\mathcal{A}}(\mathtt{list}^{\mathcal{A}}(\mathtt{X} \oplus \mathtt{int}^{\mathcal{A}})) \oplus \emptyset \\ =_{\mathrm{AC+}} & \mathtt{list}^{\mathcal{A}}(\mathtt{list}^{\mathcal{A}}(\mathtt{X} \oplus \mathtt{int}^{\mathcal{A}})). \end{aligned}$$

The theorem tells us how to read the abstract term. First, the absence of variable on the highest level (i.e. $\alpha([[\mathtt{X}], [7]])$ is not of the form $x \oplus \ldots$) means that $\mathcal{Z}(\mathtt{list(U)}, \mathtt{list(U)}, \mathtt{list(U)}, [[\mathtt{X}], [7]])$ contains no variables, or, to refer to Ex. 3.9, $\zeta(LL, LL, [[\mathtt{X}], [7]])$ is empty. Likewise, the theorem states that the argument of the outermost $\mathtt{list}^{\mathcal{A}}$ contains the abstraction of all subterms of $[[\mathtt{X}], [7]]$ returned by $\mathcal{Z}(\mathtt{list(U)}, \mathtt{list(U)}, \mathtt{U}, [[\mathtt{X}], [7]])$, and again in terms of [11], the absence of variables at this level tells us that $\zeta(LL, L, [[\mathtt{X}], [7]])$ is empty.

6 The Analysis

We show how an entire program is abstracted and how the abstract and concrete program are related semantically. We also show that the abstract semantics is finitely computable. Our analysis is an application of abstract interpretation [6].

6.1 Abstract Substitutions and Abstract Unification

Substitutions for abstract terms are defined as expected, their range containing abstract terms. The instantiation order $\leq_{\mathrm{AC+}}$ is defined as: $a \leq_{\mathrm{AC+}} b$ if $b\theta^{\mathcal{A}} =_{\mathrm{AC+}} a$ for some $\theta^{\mathcal{A}}$. It is lifted to substitutions. We write $a \approx b$ for $a \leq_{\mathrm{AC+}} b \ \wedge\ b \leq_{\mathrm{AC+}} a$. One should not confuse $\approx$ with $=_{\mathrm{AC+}}$! An **abstract atom** is an atom using abstract terms. The set of abstract atoms is denoted as $\mathcal{B}^{\mathcal{A}}$. For sets of abstract atoms $I_1^{\mathcal{A}}$ and $I_2^{\mathcal{A}}$, we define

$$I_1^{\mathcal{A}} \leq_{\mathrm{AC+}} I_2^{\mathcal{A}} \Leftrightarrow \forall A_1^{\mathcal{A}} \in I_1^{\mathcal{A}} \quad \exists A_2^{\mathcal{A}} \in I_2^{\mathcal{A}} \,.\, A_1^{\mathcal{A}} \leq_{\mathrm{AC+}} A_2^{\mathcal{A}},$$

and $I_1^{\mathcal{A}} \approx I_2^{\mathcal{A}}$ if $I_1^{\mathcal{A}} \leq_{\mathrm{AC+}} I_2^{\mathcal{A}}$ and $I_2^{\mathcal{A}} \leq_{\mathrm{AC+}} I_1^{\mathcal{A}}$. The elements of $[2^{\mathcal{B}^{\mathcal{A}}}]_{\approx}$ are called **abstract interpretations**. Abusing notation, we denote $[2^{\mathcal{B}^{\mathcal{A}}}]_{\approx}$ by $2^{\mathcal{B}^{\mathcal{A}}}$.

Definition 6.1. An abstract term a **describes** a concrete term t, denoted $a \propto t$, if $\alpha(t) \leq_{\mathrm{AC+}} a$ (and likewise for atoms).

For an interpretation I and an abstract interpretation $I^{\mathcal{A}}$, we define $I^{\mathcal{A}} \propto I$ if $\alpha(I) \leq_{\mathrm{AC+}} I^{\mathcal{A}}$. We now relate abstraction and application of a substitution.

Lemma 6.2. [5, Lemma 4.1] Let t be a term an θ a substitution. Then $\alpha(t\theta) =_{\mathrm{AC+}} \alpha(t)\{x/\alpha(x\theta) \mid x \in dom(\theta)\}$.

Example 6.3. We have $\alpha([\mathtt{X}|\mathtt{Y}]\,\{\mathtt{X}/7, \mathtt{Y}/\mathtt{nil}\}) = \alpha([7]) = \mathtt{list}^{\mathcal{A}}(\mathtt{int}^{\mathcal{A}}) =_{\mathrm{AC+}} \mathtt{list}^{\mathcal{A}}(\mathtt{int}^{\mathcal{A}}) \oplus \mathtt{list}^{\mathcal{A}}(\emptyset) = (\mathtt{list}^{\mathcal{A}}(\mathtt{X}) \oplus \mathtt{Y})\,\{\mathtt{X}/\mathtt{int}^{\mathcal{A}}, \mathtt{Y}/\mathtt{list}^{\mathcal{A}}(\emptyset)\} = \alpha([\mathtt{X}|\mathtt{Y}])\,\{\mathtt{X}/\alpha(7), \mathtt{Y}/\alpha(\mathtt{nil})\}$.

The following theorem is a straightforward consequence.

Theorem 6.4. [5, Thm. 4.2] Let t_1, t_2 be terms. If $t_1 \leq t_2$ then $\alpha(t_1) \leq_{\mathrm{AC+}} \alpha(t_2)$ (and likewise for atoms).

Definition 6.5. We denote by $cU_{\mathrm{AC+}}(o_1, o_2)$ a complete set of AC+-unifiers of syntactic objects o_1, o_2, i.e., a set of abstract substitutions such that for each $\theta^{\mathcal{A}} \in cU_{\mathrm{AC+}}(o_1, o_2)$, we have $o_1\theta^{\mathcal{A}} =_{\mathrm{AC+}} o_2\theta^{\mathcal{A}}$, and moreover, for any $\tilde{\theta}^{\mathcal{A}}$ such that $o_1\tilde{\theta}^{\mathcal{A}} =_{\mathrm{AC+}} o_2\tilde{\theta}^{\mathcal{A}}$, we have $\tilde{\theta}^{\mathcal{A}} \leq_{\mathrm{AC+}} \theta^{\mathcal{A}}$ for some $\theta^{\mathcal{A}} \in cU_{\mathrm{AC+}}(o_1, o_2)$.

AC+-unification of abstract terms is a correct abstract unification.

Theorem 6.6. [5, Thm. 4.4] Let A_1, A_2 be atoms that are unifiable with MGU θ, and $A_1^{\mathcal{A}}, A_2^{\mathcal{A}}$ be abstract atoms such that $A_1^{\mathcal{A}} \propto A_1$ and $A_2^{\mathcal{A}} \propto A_2$. Then there exists a unifier $\theta^{\mathcal{A}} \in cU_{\mathrm{AC+}}(A_1^{\mathcal{A}}, A_2^{\mathcal{A}})$ such that $A_1^{\mathcal{A}}\theta^{\mathcal{A}} \propto A_1\theta$.

We also have that AC+-unification is optimal in the sense of [5, Thm. 4.6].

6.2 Abstraction of Programs

A program is abstracted by replacing each term with its abstraction. Thus α is lifted in the obvious way to atoms, clauses, programs and queries. The semantics of the abstract program is defined by an AC+-enhanced T_P-operator. Formally

$$T_P^{\mathcal{A}}(I^{\mathcal{A}}) = \{\alpha(H)\theta^{\mathcal{A}} \mid C = H \leftarrow B_1, \dots, B_n \in P, \langle A_1^{\mathcal{A}}, \dots, A_n^{\mathcal{A}}\rangle \ll_C I^{\mathcal{A}}, \theta^{\mathcal{A}} \in cU_{\mathrm{AC+}}(\langle \alpha(B_1), \dots, \alpha(B_n)\rangle, \langle A_1^{\mathcal{A}}, \dots, A_n^{\mathcal{A}}\rangle)\}.$$

Note that unlike for the usual T_P-operator, we have to consider a *set* of unifiers. We denote by $[\![P^{\mathcal{A}}]\!]_{\mathrm{AC+}}$ the least fixpoint of $T_P^{\mathcal{A}}$, which exists [5, Cor. 5.2]. The next theorem says that the abstract semantics describes the concrete semantics. It is proven as in [5], by induction on applications of T_P and $T_P^{\mathcal{A}}$ using Thm. 6.6.

Theorem 6.7. [5, Thm. 5.4] Let P be a program. Then $[\![\alpha(P)]\!]_{\mathrm{AC+}} \propto [\![P]\!]_s$.

In the technicalities of this section, it may not have become clear in what sense our analysis is polymorphic. In any interesting example, the polymorphism is apparent in multiple occurrences of the same variable in an atom in the abstract semantics. These multiple occurrences indicate that the degree of instantiation is propagated by the program in a certain way. E.g., taking as P the usual `APPEND` program, we obtain $[\![\alpha(P)]\!]_{\mathrm{AC+}} = \{\mathtt{append}(\mathtt{list}^{\mathcal{A}}(\mathtt{X}), \mathtt{Y}, \mathtt{list}^{\mathcal{A}}(\mathtt{X}) \oplus \mathtt{Y})\}$. This atom represents the dependency between the degrees of instantiation of the different arguments of append, for any answer to a call to append. This information is polymorphic and can be combined with a more specialised analysis for a particular call to append. This call will have a particular degree of instantiation and a particular type. Take a call described by $\mathtt{append}(\mathtt{list}^{\mathcal{A}}(\mathtt{int}^{\mathcal{A}}), \mathtt{list}^{\mathcal{A}}(\mathtt{int}^{\mathcal{A}}), \mathtt{Z})$, i.e., the first two arguments are ground integer lists. Then AC+-unification of $\mathtt{append}(\mathtt{list}^{\mathcal{A}}(\mathtt{int}^{\mathcal{A}}), \mathtt{list}^{\mathcal{A}}(\mathtt{int}^{\mathcal{A}}), \mathtt{Z})$ and $\mathtt{append}(\mathtt{list}^{\mathcal{A}}(\mathtt{X}), \mathtt{Y}, \mathtt{list}^{\mathcal{A}}(\mathtt{X}) \oplus \mathtt{Y})$ yields $\mathtt{append}(\mathtt{list}^{\mathcal{A}}(\mathtt{int}^{\mathcal{A}}), \mathtt{list}^{\mathcal{A}}(\mathtt{int}^{\mathcal{A}}), \mathtt{list}^{\mathcal{A}}(\mathtt{int}^{\mathcal{A}}))$. In contrast to [5], we should not read this as: we have inferred the type of the third argument. Rather, we have inferred its degree of instantiation.

In [5] we find a result that the abstract semantics of a program is finite provided that the type abstraction is monomorphic. The result does not hold anymore for polymorphic type abstractions, and the authors give the program $\{\mathtt{p(0).},\ \mathtt{p([X])} \leftarrow \mathtt{p(X).}\}$ as an example. As a solution, the authors propose a *depth-k abstraction*, i.e., some ad-hoc bound on the depth of types.

In a prescriptive approach to typing, the above program is forbidden as it violates the *head condition* [13]. This condition says that the arguments in a head must be of the declared type of the predicate, rather than of a proper instance of that type. The second clause alone already violates it: whatever the declared type τ of p, the term [X] has type $\mathtt{list}(\tau)$. Disregarding such programs, we have:

Theorem 6.8. Let P be a typed program. Then $[\![\alpha(P)]\!]_{\mathrm{AC+}}$ is finite.

As it stands, the theorem depends critically on the fact that we assume a *bottom-up* semantics. For lack of space, we refer to [14].

Along the lines of [4,5], we could make further statements about the semantics, e.g. about call and answer patterns or optimality of the abstract semantics.

7 Towards an Implementation

So far, we have not implemented the analysis proposed in this paper. As far as computing the semantics of the abstract program is concerned, the only difference w.r.t. [4,5] is that instead of ACI or ACI1 we have the equality theory AC+. The unification problems for ACI and ACI1 are NP-complete. Studying AC+ is a topic for future work. While the extraction axioms seem somewhat non-standard [1], one would hope that they do not actually enter the algorithm provided one unifies two *normal* abstract terms.

There is an implementation of the analysis we proposed in [15]. In fact, this paper relates to [15] as [4,5] relates to [3]. This is interesting because the authors mention that an implementation using ACI-unification turned out to be much faster than the implementation in [3]. In particular, abstract unification is not as bad in practice as it seems by the theoretical result that it is NP-complete.

To compute the abstraction of a program, in [3,5], the user must provide information about the particular type language used in a program (see paragraph after Def. 4.1), whereas we extract this information from the declared types. We had demonstrated [15] that analysing the type declarations (computing the NRSs and recursive types) is viable even for some contrived, complex type declarations.

To give at least one example of the advance of our analysis over [5], we use `table(int)`. Suppose there is a predicate `insert/4` whose arguments represent: a table t, a key k, a value v, and a table obtained from t by inserting the node whose key is k and whose value is v. From the abstract semantics of the program, it is possible to read that a query whose abstraction is

$$\mathtt{insert}(\mathtt{table}^{\mathcal{A}}(\mathtt{int}^{\mathcal{A}}, \mathtt{bal}^{\mathcal{A}}, \mathtt{str}^{\mathcal{A}}), \mathtt{str}^{\mathcal{A}}, \mathtt{X}, \mathtt{T}),$$

i.e., a query to insert an *uninstantiated* value into a ground table, yields an answer whose abstraction is

$$\mathtt{insert}(\mathtt{table}^{\mathcal{A}}(\mathtt{int}^{\mathcal{A}}, \mathtt{bal}^{\mathcal{A}}, \mathtt{str}^{\mathcal{A}}), \mathtt{str}^{\mathcal{A}}, \mathtt{X}, \mathtt{table}^{\mathcal{A}}(\mathtt{int}^{\mathcal{A}} \oplus \mathtt{X}, \mathtt{bal}^{\mathcal{A}}, \mathtt{str}^{\mathcal{A}})),$$

i.e., the result is a table whose values may be uninstantiated.

8 Discussion

We have proposed a formalism for deriving abstract domains from the type declarations of a typed program. Effectively, we have recast our previous work [15] using the formalisms of [5,11]. We argue briefly why abstract interpretation using a unification theory such as ACI is elegant. The main reason is that the abstraction of a program turns out to be so simple (Subsec. 6.2). The operations on abstract terms that ensure that the abstract semantics is always finite are all encoded into the equality axioms. It is intriguing that the abstraction of program variables as themselves does not imply infinity of the abstract semantics.

We now compare this paper with [5,11,15] under several aspects. The contribution of this paper is entirely defined by the advance it makes w.r.t. [5,11,15]. Concerning the relationship with other works, we refer to the discussions found there. However, we mention one recent work [2], which also claims to provide a generalisation of [11] to polymorphism, but it does not involve ACI-unification. Unfortunately, [2] contains no comparison with [5]. Such a comparison would also clarify the differences between [2] and our approach. One difference is that in [2], each clause is analysed separately for each type occurring in it. This can lead to a loss of precision since certain dependencies between the different types used in the clause may be lost. This cannot happen in our approach and [5].

The type system. Put in our terminology, [5] makes the following assumptions: types are either monomorphic or unary, and the only subterm types of a type $c(u)$ are $c(u)$ and u. This is the simplest thinkable scenario of proper polymorphism: only lists and trees are covered, our `TABLES` and `NESTS` examples are not. In contrast, [11] assumes regular types without polymorphism. Thus there are only finitely many, but possibly very complex, types. So the type systems of [5,11] are not formally comparable, but our type system is a generalisation of both.

Descriptive vs. prescriptive types. According to the authors' claims, [5] takes a descriptive view of typing, whereas [11] takes a prescriptive view.

Since the typing approach of [5] is descriptive, it is reasonable that they must consider "ill-typed" terms such as [1|2]. In this paper, all terms are "well-typed".

In [11], a unique grammar (type) is associated with each program variable. A unification constraint in a program gives rise to operations such as computing the intersection of two types. In our opinion, such operations introduce an aspect of type *inference* into their formalism contradicting a *prescriptive* view of typing.

Labellings. Labellings are used to formalise which aspects of the structure of a term we capture. In [5], they are absent, although they might have been useful. In [15], there are similar functions called *extractors* and *termination functions.*

Unlike ζ [11], our $\mathcal{Z}$ also collects non-variable terms. This generalisation allows us to describe the relation between a term and its abstraction (see Sec. 5).

The function ζ has three arguments: a grammar (which however can be identified with its starting non-terminal), a non-terminal to be labelled, and a labelling term. Our labelling function $\mathcal{Z}$ has *four* arguments. We found it useful to have as first argument a *flat* type (e.g. `nest(V)`) which gives us a certain grammar, but also allow for productions of that grammar starting from some other non-terminal (e.g. `list(nest(V))`). The difference between our labelling function and that of [11] is due to polymorphism. In a monomorphic setting, one would define the grammar for, say, "list of nest of integer" in an ad-hoc way, and then having two arguments to characterise the grammar would be unnecessary.

Abstract terms. In [11], the abstraction of terms is not made explicit, but effectively, given a program variable x, its abstraction is the (somehow ordered) tuple of non-terminals of the grammar of x. Non-terminals are thought of as *abstract variables.* Our abstraction of terms, denoted α, is designed in such a way that the abstraction *type* in [5] is essentially a special case of it. The reason for having explicit abstract terms is related to polymorphism. They allow an encoding of the instantiation information present in a program which can then be combined with calls for particular polymorphic instances (see the example after Thm. 6.7).

Type hierarchies. Given a function $f_{\dots\to c(u)}$, the abstraction *type* in [5] distinguishes between the argument positions of declared type u and the "recursive" argument positions. Our concepts of *non-recursive subterm type* and *recursive type* generalise this idea. An NRS of a flat type is not necessarily a parameter, and τ can have other recursive types than τ itself. In contrast, in [11], all non-terminals (types) reachable from the starting node of a grammar are treated in the same way. This is viable since the size of the grammars is fixed beforehand.

Equality theory. The equality theory in [11] is ACI1. Distributivity is not applicable. In [5], the equality theory is ACI, so there is no neutral element and no distributivity. This is in contrast to [4] where the equality theory is ACI1 plus distributivity. We believe that regardless of concerns of implementation, a neutral element and the distributivity axioms should be present at least conceptually. Our extraction axioms are not applicable to [4,5].

Types = abstract terms? In [5], there is no distinction between a type constructor c (resp. type) and the function $c^{\mathcal{A}}$ (resp. abstract term). Also, the equivalent of our α is called *type abstraction* and denoted by *type*. However, this identification only works because the assumptions about the type system are so restrictive.

Precision. In [11], the precision of an analysis depends on how the types (grammars) are defined. E.g., one could formalise the type "list of integer" in such a way that one can characterise that every 5th element of a list is ground. For lists and trees, the precision of [5] is the same as in our approach. More complex types cannot be handled by [5]. Also, there is no essential difference w.r.t. precision between this work and [15]. Underlying any analysis is a decision on what is a "reasonable" degree of precision. Here we decided that subterms of the same type belong together since they are likely to serve a similar purpose. Note that writing programs as polymorphically as possible helps improve precision. E.g., if one defines the type of pairs as `pair(U,V)`, the two components will be distinguished; if one defines the monomorphic type of integer pairs, they will not be.

Thus we have generalised [5,11] by considering a type system which corresponds to the type system of existing typed programming languages. We have given several examples in Sec. 3 showing that such a generalisation is non-trivial. In particular, there are two requirements: the construction of an abstract domain for a polymorphic type should be truly parametric, and the abstract domains should be finite for a given program and query. The biggest problem on a technical level is the fact that the SCCs of a type graph are not stable under instantiation.

As future work, the analysis in this paper should be implemented, which requires first some studies about the equality theory AC+ and unification algorithms for it. Moreover, we expect that the domains we propose here are also useful for *sharing* analysis, as this has been shown in [11].

Acknowledgements. I want to thank the anonymous referees for their helpful comments. This research was mostly carried out while I was an ERCIM fellow at CWI Amsterdam.

References

1. F. Baader and K. U. Schulz. Unification theory. In W. Bibel and P. H. Schmidt, editors, *Automated Deduction – A Basis for Applications, Vol. I: Foundations – Calculi and Methods*, volume 8 of *Applied Logic Series*, pages 225–263. Kluwer Academic Publishers, Dordrecht, NL, 1998.
2. M. Bruynooghe, W. Vanhoof, and M. Codish. *POS*($\mathcal{T}$): Analyzing dependencies in typed logic programs. In D. Bjørner, M. Broy, and A. Zamulin, editors, *Pre-proceedings of the Andrei Ershov Fourth International Conference*, pages 212–218. Final version to appear in LNCS series of Springer-Verlag, 2001.
3. M. Codish and B. Demoen. Deriving polymorphic type dependencies for logic programs using multiple incarnations of *Prop*. In B. Le Charlier, editor, *Proceedings of the 1st Static Analysis Symposium*, volume 864 of *LNCS*, pages 281–296. Springer-Verlag, 1994.

4. M. Codish and V. Lagoon. Type dependencies for logic programs using ACI-unification. In *Proceedings of the Israeli Symposium on Theory of Computing and Systems*, pages 136–145. IEEE Press, 1996.
5. M. Codish and V. Lagoon. Type dependencies for logic programs using ACI-unification. *Theoretical Computer Science*, 238(1–2):131–159, 2000.
6. P. Cousot and R. Cousot. Abstract interpretation: A unified lattice model for static analysis of programs by construction or approximation of fixpoints. In *Proceedings of the 4th Symposium on Principles of Programming Languages*, pages 238–252. ACM Press, 1977.
7. B. Demoen, M. García de la Banda, W. Harvey, K. Marriott, and P. Stuckey. An overview of HAL. In J. Jaffar, editor, *Proceedings of Principles and Practice of Constraint Programming*, volume 1713 of *LNCS*, pages 174–188. Springer-Verlag, 1999.
8. M. van Emden. AVL tree insertion: A benchmark program biased towards Prolog. *Logic Programming Newsletter 2*, 1981.
9. P. M. Hill and J. W. Lloyd. *The Gödel Programming Language.* MIT Press, 1994.
10. G. Janssens and M. Bruynooghe. Deriving descriptions of possible values of program variables by means of abstract interpretation. *Journal of Logic Programming*, 13(2 & 3):205–258, 1992. First author name erroneously spelt "Janssen".
11. V. Lagoon and P. J. Stuckey. A framework for analysis of typed logic programs. In H. Kuchen and K. Ueda, editors, *Proceedings of the 5th International Symposium on Functional and Logic Programming*, volume 2024 of *LNCS*, pages 296–310. Springer-Verlag, 2001.
12. J. W. Lloyd. *Foundations of Logic Programming.* Springer-Verlag, 1987.
13. F. Pfenning, editor. *Types in Logic Programming*, chapter 1, pages 1–61. MIT Press, 1992.
14. J.-G. Smaus. Analysis of polymorphically typed logic programs using ACI-unification. Available via CoRR: `http://arXiv.org/archive/cs/intro.html`, 2001.
15. J.-G. Smaus, P. M. Hill, and A. M. King. Mode analysis domains for typed logic programs. In A. Bossi, editor, *Proceedings of the 9th International Workshop on Logic-based Program Synthesis and Transformation*, volume 1817 of *LNCS*, pages 83–102, 2000. Long version appeared as Report 2000.06, University of Leeds.
16. Z. Somogyi, F. Henderson, and T. Conway. The execution algorithm of Mercury, an efficient purely declarative logic programming language. *Journal of Logic Programming*, 29(1–3):17–64, 1996.

Model Generation with Boolean Constraints

Miyuki Koshimura, Hiroshi Fujita, and Ryuzo Hasegawa

Graduate School of Information Science and Electrical Engineering,
Kyushu University, 6-1 Kasuga-Kouen, Kasuga, Fukuoka 816-8580, Japan
{koshi, fujita, hasegawa}@ar.is.kyushu-u.ac.jp

Abstract. We present a simple method for eliminating redundant searches in model generation. The method employs *Boolean Constraints* which are conjunctions of ground instances of clauses having participated in proofs. Boolean Constraints work as sets of lemmas with which duplicate subproofs and irrelevant model extensions can be eliminated. The method has been tentatively implemented on a constraint logic programming system. We evaluated effects of the method by proving some typical problems taken from the CASC-JS system competition.

1 Introduction

The model generation procedure tries to construct Herbrand models for a given clause set and determines its satisfiability. It maintains a set M of ground atoms called a model candidate, finds violated clauses that are not satisfied under M, then extends M to satisfy them, and repeats this process until a model is found or all model candidates are rejected.

There are two types of redundancy in model generation: One is that the same subproof tree may be generated at several descendant nodes after a case-splitting occurs. Another is caused by unnecessary model candidate extensions with irrelevant clauses. We embedded both folding-up [5] and proof condensation [8] into model generation for eliminating these redundancies by analyzing dependency in a proof [4]. The embedded function examines the structure of proof in order to append a solved subproof-tree to an open branch. Nogood recording [9] is a similar approach in the constraint satisfaction framework.

This paper presents yet another method to eliminate the redundancies on the basis of semantical information. If the current model candidate conflicts with a set of instances of clauses that have participated in model generation so far, we can reject the model candidate without further exploration. We call the set a *Boolean Constraint*. It is worth noting that the Boolean Constraint consists of only ground instances of clauses and all atoms in model candidates are ground. Therefore, a conflict test is essentially propositional theorem proving.

In this work, we utilize a constraint solver [11] on Boolean expressions for the test, though we could utilize model generation itself or other proving methods in principle. The main reason for utilizing the constraint solver is that it can compute a simple (canonical) form of the Boolean Constraint which is incrementally updated as the proof progresses. Since the constraint solver reduces the Boolean Constraint as simple as possible, it can detect the conflict efficiently.

R. Nieuwenhuis and A. Voronkov (Eds.): LPAR 2001, LNAI 2250, pp. 299–308, 2001.

2 Model Generation

Throughout this paper, a *clause* $\neg A_1 \vee \ldots \vee \neg A_n \vee B_1 \vee \ldots \vee B_m$ is represented in implicational form: $A_1 \wedge \ldots \wedge A_n \rightarrow B_1 \vee \ldots \vee B_m$, where A_i $(1 \leq i \leq n)$ and B_j $(1 \leq j \leq m)$ are atoms; the left hand side of "$\rightarrow$" is said to be the *antecedent*; and the right hand side of "$\rightarrow$" the *consequent*.

A clause is said to be *positive* if its antecedent is $\top$ $(n = 0)$, and *negative* if its consequent is $\bot$ $(m = 0)$; otherwise it is *mixed* $(n \neq 0, m \neq 0)$. A clause is said to be *violated* under a set M of ground atoms if the following condition holds with some ground substitution σ: $\forall i(1 \leq i \leq n)A_i\sigma \in M \wedge \forall j(1 \leq j \leq m)B_j\sigma \notin M$.

A model generation proof procedure is sketched in Fig.1. Given a set S of clauses, MG tries to construct a model by extending the current model candidate M so as to satisfy violated clauses under M (model extension). When a negative clause is violated under M, MG rejects M because there is no way of extending M (model rejection). If no clause is violated under M, we conclude M is a model of S, that is, S is satisfiable (model finding).

procedure $MGTP(S) : Res$;
/* Input(S):Clause set, Output(Res):satisfiability of S */
return($MG(\emptyset)$);

procedure $MG(M) : Res$; /* Input(M): Model candidate*/

1. (Model rejection) If a negative clause $A_1 \wedge \ldots \wedge A_n \rightarrow \bot \in S$ is violated under M with a ground substitution σ, **return** *unsatisfiable*;
2. (Model extension) If a positive or mixed clause $A_1 \wedge \ldots \wedge A_n \rightarrow B_1 \vee \ldots \vee B_m \in S$ is violated under M with a ground substitution σ,
   for $(i = 1; i \leq m; i++)$ {
   if $(MG(M \cup \{B_i\sigma\}) = satisfiable)$ **return** *satisfiable*;
   }
   return *unsatisfiable*;
3. (Model finding) If neither 1 nor 2 is applicable, **return** $satisfiable$;

Fig. 1. Model generation procedure

Consider the following set of clauses $S1$:

$C1: \top \rightarrow p(a) \vee p(c)$ $\quad$ $C2: p(a) \rightarrow q(b)$
$C3: p(X) \wedge q(Y) \rightarrow r(X,Y) \vee r(X,X) \vee r(Y,X)$
$C4: p(X) \wedge q(Y) \rightarrow r(s(X),Y) \vee r(X,X) \vee r(Y,X)$
$C5: p(X) \wedge r(s(X),Y) \rightarrow r(Y,s(X))$
$C6: r(s(X),Y) \wedge r(Y,s(X)) \rightarrow r(X,X)$
$C7: r(X,X) \rightarrow r(s(X),X) \vee r(X,s(X))$
$C8: p(X) \wedge q(Y) \wedge r(Y,X) \rightarrow r(X,X)$ $\quad$ $C9: r(s(X),X) \rightarrow \bot$
$C10: r(X,s(X)) \rightarrow \bot$ $\quad$ $C11: p(c) \rightarrow \bot$

Fig.2(a) shows a proof-tree for $S1$. The inner nodes of a proof-tree except the root node are labeled with atoms used for model extension. A branch or a path from the root to a node corresponds to a model candidate. A leaf labeled with $\perp$ indicates that the corresponding model candidate has been rejected. $S1$ is unsatisfiable because all leaves of its proof-tree are labeled with $\perp$.

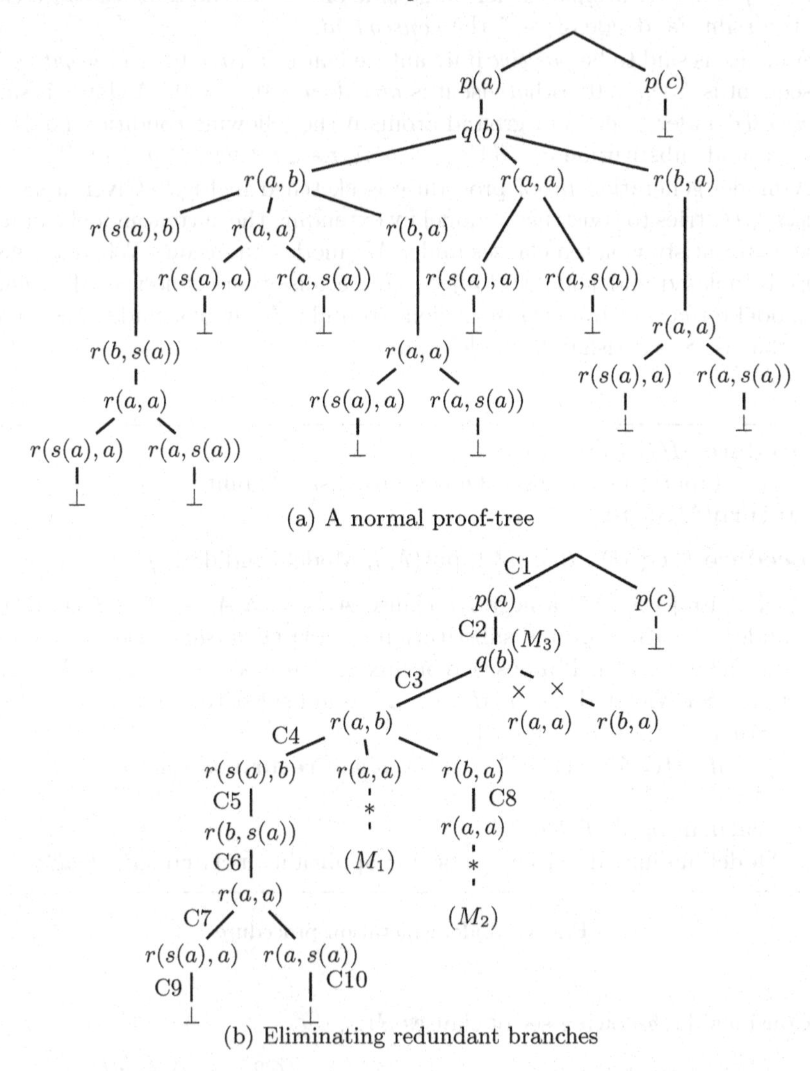

Fig. 2. Proof-trees of $S1$

The procedure MG in the above figure can be proved sound and complete in the sense that MG examines only models containing the model candidate M [7].

Theorem 1. *Let S be a set of clauses and M be a set of ground atoms. Then $MG(M)$ return unsatisfiable if and only if there is no model containing M.*

Let BC be a set of ground instances of clauses in S that have been used for model rejection and extension. If $BC \cup M$ is unsatisfiable, $S \cup M$ is unsatisfiable. In this case, according to Theorem 1, we can reject M without further proving. This rejection mechanism can reduce search spaces by orders of magnitude. Fig.3 shows a model generation procedure in which the rejection mechanism is embedded. The framed parts are embedded ones. We call the procedure *model generation with Boolean Constraints* because BC is essentially the conjunction of propositional clauses and can be treated as a Boolean expression.

procedure $MGTP(S) : Res$;
  [$BC := \emptyset$; (1)]
  return($MG(\emptyset)$);

procedure $MG(M) : Res$;

1. (Model rejection by BC)
   [If ($BC \cup M$ is unsatisfiable) **return** *unsatisfiable*; (2)]
2. (Model rejection by negative clauses) If a negative clause $(A_1 \wedge \ldots \wedge A_n \rightarrow \bot) \in S$ is violated under M with a ground substitution σ,
   [$BC := BC \cup \{A_1\sigma \wedge \ldots \wedge A_n\sigma \rightarrow \bot\}$; (3)]
   return *unsatisfiable.*
3. (Model extension) If a positive or mixed clause $(A_1 \wedge \ldots \wedge A_n \rightarrow B_1 \vee \ldots \vee B_m) \in S$ is violated under M with a ground substitution σ,
   [$BC := BC \cup \{A_1\sigma \wedge \ldots \wedge A_n\sigma \rightarrow B_1\sigma \vee \ldots \vee B_m\sigma\}$; (4)]
   for $(i = 1; i \leq m; i++)$ {
     if $(MG(M \cup \{B_i\sigma\}) = satisfiable)$ **return** *satisfiable*
     [**elseif** ($BC \cup M$ is unsatisfiable) **return** *unsatisfiable* (5)]
   }
   return *unsatisfiable*;
4. (Model finding) If neither rule is applicable, **return** $satisfiable$;

Fig. 3. Model generation with Boolean Constraint

Initially, the set BC is set to the empty set ((1)). BC is updated whenever ground instances of clauses are used for model extension or model rejection ((3),(4)). BC is used for model rejection prior to performing normal model rejection and extension ((2)). This rejection works as folding-up to eliminate duplicates subproofs. BC is also used for model rejection testing whenever each extension $MG(M \cup \{B_i\sigma\})$ is finished ((5)). This rejection test works as proof condensation to avoid unnecessary model extensions.

Fig.2(b) shows a proof tree for $S1$ obtained by model generation with Boolean Constraints. The mark $*$ indicates a branch pruned by operation (2), while the mark $\times$ indicates that by operation (5).

BC becomes $BC_1 = \{C1, C2, C3\sigma_1, C4\sigma_1, C5\sigma_1, C6\sigma_1, C7\sigma_2, C9\sigma_2, C10\sigma_2\}$ after the second branch from the left has been rejected where $\sigma_1 = \{X \leftarrow a, Y \leftarrow b\}$ and $\sigma_2 = \{X \leftarrow a\}$. Then, the next model candidate M_1 to be solved is $\{p(a), q(b), r(a,b), r(a,a)\}$. However, since $BC_1 \cup M_1$ is unsatisfiable, M_1 is rejected. After the model extension under $r(b,a)$ with clause $C8\sigma_2$ has been performed, BC becomes $BC_2 = BC_1 \cup \{C8\sigma_2\}$. The corresponding model candidate M_2 is $\{p(a), q(b), r(a,b), r(b,a), r(a,a)\}$. In this case, $BC_2 \cup M_2$ is unsatisfiable as well, so that M_2 is rejected.

On the other hand, $BC_2 \cup \{p(a), q(b)\}$, that is, $BC_2 \cup M_3$ is unsatisfiable. Therefore, the exploration of $r(a,a)$ and $r(b,a)$ below $q(b)$ can be eliminated. Thus, we obtain a proof-tree which has 12 inner nodes while the normal proof-tree shown in (a) has 23 inner nodes.

3 Implementation and Modifications

The method is implemented on top of a constraint logic programming system B-Prolog [11] which supports constraint solvers over trees, Boolean, finite-domains and sets. We manipulate a set BC of ground instances of clauses through the constraint solver. Thus, BC is maintained within the constraint solver. When updating BC (Fig.3(3)(4)), we tell $(\neg A_1\sigma \vee \ldots \vee \neg A_n\sigma) = TRUE$ or $(\neg A_1\sigma \vee \ldots \vee \neg A_n\sigma \vee B_1\sigma \vee \ldots \vee B_m\sigma) = TRUE$ to the constraint solver. On the other hand, when testing whether a conflict occurs (Fig.3(2)(5)), we ask the constraint solver "Is $A = TRUE$ possible for all $A \in M$?" If they become all $TRUE$, $BC \cup M$ is satisfiable, otherwise, it is unsatisfiable.

We give two modifications of the method, in order to reduce a heavy load on the conflict test (Fig.3(2)(5)) which is essentially propositional theorem proving. One ignores some ground instances of clauses which participate in model extensions so as to reduce the number of elements in BC. Another reduces the number of the conflict tests.

The first one is realized by delaying the operation (4) in Fig.3 as shown in Fig.4. A clause $A_1\sigma \wedge \ldots \wedge A_n\sigma \rightarrow B_1\sigma \vee \ldots \vee B_m\sigma$ is not added to BC when $\exists i(1 \le i \le m)(MG(M \cup \{B_i\sigma\}) = \mathit{satisfiable})$ or $BC \cup M$ becomes unsatisfiable at the operation (5). In other words, we add the clause to BC only when it contributes to deriving *unsatisfiable.*

The second one is realized by delaying the operation (2) until performing model extensions with non-Horn clauses as shown in Fig.5.

4 Experimental Results

This section compares five versions:

(1) Model generation without boolean constrains as shown in Fig.1.

```
for (i = 1; i ≤ m; i++) {
    if (MG(M ∪ {B_iσ}) = satisfiable) return satisfiable
    elseif (BC ∪ M is unsatisfiable) return unsatisfiable   (5)
}
BC := BC ∪ {A_1σ ∧ ... ∧ A_nσ → B_1σ ∨ ... ∨ B_mσ};   (4)
return unsatisfiable;
```

Fig. 4. Delaying BC updating in model extension

(Model extension) If a positive or mixed clause $(A_1 \wedge \ldots \wedge A_n \rightarrow B_1 \vee \ldots \vee B_m) \in S$ is violated under M with a ground substitution σ,

if ($m > 1$ and $BC \cup M$ is unsatisfiable) **return** *unsatisfiable*; (2)

...

Fig. 5. Delaying model rejection by BC

(2) Model generation with boolean constrains as shown in Fig.3.
(3) Model generation with boolean constrains modified as shown in Fig.4.
(4) Model generation with boolean constrains modified as shown in Fig.5.
(5) Model generation with boolean constrains modified as shown in Fig.4 and Fig.5.

We select problems in the EPR division of CASC-JC system competition 2001 [1] as benchmarks. The EPR division collects non-propositional theorems and non-theorems with a finite Herbrand Universe. The EPR division consists of the EPT category (unsatisfiable clauses) and the EPS category (satisfiable clauses). The model generation procedure seems to be suitable for the EPR division because it can generate only finite Herbrand models in practice.

Table 1 and 2 show the proving performance of the five versions. The problems were run on a SUN Ultra 60 (450MHz, 1GB, Solaris2.7) workstation with a time limit of 5 minutes and a space limit of 240MB. There are 16 EPT[1] and 7 EPS[2] problems which all versions fail in solving. These problems are not listed in the tables.

The version (5) outperforms other versions for both EPT and EPS categories according to the number of problems solved and average runtimes over solutions found. This shows that the combination of two modifications has a great effect

[1] GRP125-2.005, GRP127-2.006, GRP128-2.006, PUZ010-1, PUZ017-1, PUZ037-3*, SYN436-1, SYN439-1, SYN440-1, SYN447-1, SYN457-1, SYN460-1, SYN466-1, SYN467-1, SYN472-1, SYN482-1 (* Horn problem)

[2] GRP123-2.005, GRP124-7.005, SYN423-1, SYN428-1, SYN437-1, SYN438-1, SYN544-1

Table 1. Experimental results for EPR division

Problems solved in EPT category (25 problems)

	(1)	(2)	(3)	(4)	(5)
GRP128-3.	T.O.	T.O.	T.O.	T.O.	266.50
005	-	-	-	-	15456(637)
	-	-	-	-	4825+5544
GRP129-3.	M.O.	T.O.	23.19	T.O.	10.24
004	-	-	2718(234)	-	2868(276)
	-	-	543+977	-	501+977
GRP129-4.	M.O.	T.O.	5.99	16.29	4.24
004	-	-	2136(18)	1584(37)	2393(63)
	-	-	302+1290	280+791	257+1290
LAT005-1*	1.84	6.14	23.90	2.06	2.00
	248(1)	249(1)	249(1)	249(1)	249(1)
	-	0+0	0+0	0+0	0+0
LAT005-2*	1.54	5.29	20.91	1.73	1.68
	248(1)	249(1)	249(1)	249(1)	249(1)
	-	0+0	0+0	0+0	0+0
PUZ018-1	T.O.	48.86	18.61	2.48	1.95
	-	437(72)	454(80)	435(71)	456(80)
	-	7+210	8+206	8+209	8+206
PUZ036-1.	1.01	7.26	T.O.	3.19	2.32
005*	1396(1)	1397(1)	-	1397(1)	1397(1)
	-	0+0	-	0+0	0+0
PUZ037-1*	0.01	0.02	0.03	0.02	0.02
	13(1)	14(1)	14(1)	14(1)	14(1)
	-	0+0	0+0	0+0	0+0
PUZ037-2*	31.33	63.69	T.O.	54.78	T.O
	2736(1)	2737(1)	-	2737(1)	-
	-	0+0	-	0+0	-
Solved	5	6	6	7	8
Av. Time (secs)	7.15	21.88	15.44	11.51	36.12

Problems solved in EPS category (25 problems)

	(1)	(2)	(3)	(4)	(5)
GRP126-2.	M.O.	T.O.	78.20	T.O.	32.89
005	-	-	9389(405)	-	10204(533)
	-	-	2707+3133	-	2579+3133
GRP126-3.	M.O.	T.O.	88.65	T.O.	33.62
005	-	-	8790(345)	-	9695(470)
	-	-	2458+3067	-	2333+3067
GRP127-3.	M.O.	T.O.	196.59	T.O.	86.11
005	-	-	8914(742)	-	9126(793)
	-	-	2285+3112	-	2234+3112
GRP128-1.	M.O.	T.O.	4.80	T.O.	2.49
004	-	-	1891(60)	-	1996(94)
	-	-	316+777	-	282+777
GRP129-3.	T.O.	T.O.	95.38	T.O.	50.13
005	-	-	12698(197)	-	13286(371)
	-	-	3932+5109	-	3758+5109

(continues)

Table 2. Experimental results for EPR division (continued)

EPS	(1)	(2)	(3)	(4)	(5)
GRP130-3. 004	M.O. - -	154.43 1838(112) 235+627	8.40 1967(117) 262+677	12.80 1826(119) 213+606	3.83 2054(134) 245+677
GRP130-4. 004	M.O. - -	40.38 716(18) 48+439	2.14 766(18) 57+470	2.05 549(19) 36+313	1.26 815(28) 47+470
GRP133-2. 004	M.O. - -	T.O. - -	8.92 2432(214) 440+718	43.66 2117(177) 404+617	4.10 2501(235) 419+718
NLP005-1	0.20 66(1) -	0.24 66(1) 0+0	0.29 66(1) 0+0	0.17 66(1) 0+0	0.18 66(1) 0+0
NLP006-1	1.22 375(12) -	0.41 113(2) 10+0	0.41 113(2) 10+0	1.44 386(12) 0+0	1.35 386(12) 0+0
NLP008-1	0.17 67(1) -	0.24 67(1) 0+0	0.26 67(1) 0+0	0.18 67(1) 0+0	0.18 67(1) 0+0
NLP012-1	0.17 66(1) -	0.23 66(1) 0+0	0.25 66(1) 0+0	0.20 66(1) 0+0	0.18 66(1) 0+0
NLP013-1	0.18 66(1) -	0.23 66(1) 0+0	0.26 66(1) 0+0	0.19 66(1) 0+0	0.17 66(1) 0+0
PUZ018-2	T.O. - -	132.82 764(167) 7+210	40.68 778(174) 7+207	4.88 773(167) 7+210	3.17 787(174) 7+207
SYN307-1	0.00 5(1) -	0.01 5(1) 0+0	0.00 5(1) 0+0	0.01 5(1) 0+0	0.01 5(1) 0+0
SYN434-1	M.O. - -	T.O. - -	185.30 506(112) 11+41	13.33 492(104) 13+42	13.33 509(112) 11+41
SYN446-1	M.O. - -	T.O. - -	113.26 1204(256) 116+158	180.57 1091(183) 107+153	28.59 1314(256) 116+158
SYN463-1	M.O. - -	T.O. - -	58.13 1503(318) 132+218	19.06 1193(189) 97+211	12.38 1643(318) 132+218
Solved	6	9	18	13	18
Av. Time (secs)	0.32	36.55	49.00	21.43	15.22

top: cpu times in seconds * Horn problem
middle: No. of nodes in proof trees
(No. of branches in proof trees)
bottom: No. of branches pruned by operation (2)+
No. of model extensions eliminated by operation (5)
T.O.: Time out (> 300 secs) M.O.: Memory overflow (> 240MB)

on pruning search space. The number of problems solved has increased by 3 to 8 for EPT and by 12 to 18 for EPS.

One exception is statistics for PUZ037-2[3] which the version (5) (and (3)) can not solve because of time limit while other versions including (1) can solve it. The reason for the exception is that the tail recursion elimination [10] is not applicable to the current implementations of the versions (5) and (3). Therefore thousands of stack frames need to be allocated for solving PUZ037-2. These allocations are space and time consuming[4].

Delaying BC updating (in versions (3) and (5)) enlarges search space (numbers of nodes of proof trees in this experiment) a little but reduces cpu time in many cases. For example, compare (2) and (3), or (4) and (5) of PUZ018-1 or GRP130-3.004 in the tables. Delaying BC updating also delays to detect the conflict, and then enlarge proof trees. However, it reduces the number of elements in BC so as to decrease the number of distinct atoms in BC. Thus, it decrease the complexity of the conflict test.

There are few cases in which the version (2), (3), (4), or (5) exhausts memories, though the size of BC becomes exponential large in the worst case. This space efficiency is due to the implementation technology of B-Prolog which maintains BC as a canonical form.

Compared to 8 systems which attend the EPR division of the competition, the version (5) scores rank 7 of 8 for EPT and rank 3 of 8 for EPS. Experimental results show that the presented method seems to prefer satisfiable problems to unsatisfiable ones. The reason for this is that proving unsatisfiability corresponds with an exhaustive search while proving satisfiability corresponds with a single solution search from searching models point of view.

Compared with model generation with folding-up and proof condensation (MGFP), many problems solved are overlapped in EPR division. The following problems show the difference. GRP128-3.005 is solved by the version (5) while it is not solved by MGFP. On the other hand, experimental results for PUZ037-2, SYN482-1, and SYN438-1 show the reverse. Model generation with Boolean Constraints includes MGFP as a special case, that is, any branches pruned by the latter are also pruned by the former, but the reverse does not hold. This experimental results suggest that boolean constraints require more space or time than MGFP does in some cases.

5 Future Work

Generating minimal Herbrand models of clausal theories is useful in several areas of computer science. Bry and Yahya presented a sound and complete procedure for generating minimal models [2]. The procedure rejects nonminimal models

[3] This is a Horn problem. That is, no case-splitting occurs in model generation. The method described in this paper has no effect on Horn problems. Therefore, it is not necessary for the versions (2), (3), (4), and (5) to solve Horn problems in practice.

[4] Actually, applying the version (5) on PUZ037-2 causes "Stack Overflow" within two hours.

by means of complement splitting and constrained search. Using boolean constraints replaces the constrained search and has pruning effect stronger than that of factorization [5] for model generation. We will implement minimal model generation with boolean constraints.

In the current implementation, the most time consuming task is the conflict test (Fig.3 (2)(5)). The cost of this task may be reduced by using Binary Decision Diagrams (BDDs). We are considering two approaches using BDD: One is to replace the constraint solver with BDD. Another is to use a BDD for representing a proof tree of model generation [3].

In the latter, all model candidates are simultaneously represented as the paths ending with a truth node in a BDD. With this representation, model candidates conflicting with the Boolean Constraint are automatically eliminated by standard BDD functions. Thus, the conflict test can be ignored. However, an implementation of the latter approach is more difficult than that of the former because BDD may create more model candidates than the model generation procedure, and it would be necessary to select a minimal one for efficiency. We are now developing a prototype for the former.

References

1. The CADE ATP System Competition. `http://www.cs.miami.edu/ tptp/CASC/JC/`, June 2001.
2. F. Bry and A. Yahya. Minimal Model Generation with Positive Unit Hyper-Resolution Tableaux. In Miglioli et al. [6], pages 143–159.
3. R. Hähnle. BDDs for Representation of Model Candidates in MGTP. a private talk at Kyushu University, September 1998.
4. M. Koshimura and R. Hasegawa. Proof Simplification for Model Generation and Its Applications. In M. Parigot and A. Voronkov, editors, *Proceedings of 7th International Conference, LPAR2000*, volume 1955 of *Lecture Notes in Artificial Intelligence*, pages 96–113. Springer, November 2000.
5. R. Letz, K. Mayr, and C. Goller. Controlled Integration of the Cut Rule into Connection Tableau Calculi. *Journal of Automated Reasoning*, 13:297–337, 1994.
6. P. Miglioli, U. Moscato, D. Mundici, and M. Ornaghi, editors. *5th International Workshop, TABLEAUX'96*, volume 1071 of *Lecture Notes in Artificial Intelligence.* Springer, May 1996.
7. I. Niemelä. A Tableau Calculus for Minimal Model Reasoning. In Miglioli et al. [6], pages 278–294.
8. F. Oppacher and E. Suen. HARP: A Tableau-Based Theorem Prover. *Journal of Automated Reasoning*, 4:69–100, 1988.
9. T. Schiex and G. Verfaillie. Nogood Recording for Static and Dynamic Constraint Satisfaction Problems. *International Journal of Artificial Intelligence Tools*, 3(2):187–207, 1994.
10. N.-F. Zhou. Parameter Passing and Control Stack Management in Prolog Implementation Revisited. *ACM Transactions on Programming Languages and Systems*, 18(6):752–779, November 1996.
11. N.-F. Zhou. *B-Prolog User's Manual (Version 5.0)*, 2000. http://www.probp.com.

First-Order Atom Definitions Extended

Bijan Afshordel, Thomas Hillenbrand, and Christoph Weidenbach

Max-Planck-Institut für Informatik
Stuhlsatzenhausweg 85
D-66123 Saarbrücken
{afshorde,hillen,weidenb}@mpi-sb.mpg.de

Abstract. We extend the notion of atom definitions in first-order formulae by guards. These are conditions restricting the atom definition in a form that frequently occurs in many application areas of automated theorem proving. We give a sufficient and complete criterion for a formula to contain such a definition and provide an effective algorithm to actually retrieve the definition in an applicable form. An implementation within our prover SPASS leads to significant performance improvements in application areas where atom definitions are present.

1 Introduction

The question of when to expand and when to contract a definition is mentioned by Larry Wos as the 30th of his 33 basic research problems [6] in automated theorem proving, commented that "wise use of both definition expansion and definition contraction could sharply increase the effectiveness of various procedures that manipulate large amounts of knowledge".

As a supposition to the problem in the context of automated reasoning, techniques have to be developed to actually detect, expand and contract definitions. This paper is a contribution to the automatic detection and expansion of (atom) definitions that generalizes existing work in that a definition may be restricted by a so-called guard formula.

The conventional notion of atom definitions is logical equivalence of atom instances and replacement formulae, i.e. an expression

$$\forall x_1, \ldots, x_m \, (P(t_1, \ldots, t_n) \equiv \psi).$$

However, when we were working with our formula translator, practice revealed that this notion is too weak to successfully deal with important application domains such as set theory or software verification/analysis where typically such an equivalence holds under certain guarding conditions only.[1] In this paper we therefore work out the notion of an atom definition extended by a guard as in

$$\forall x_1, \ldots, x_m \, (\phi \supset (P(t_1, \ldots, t_n) \equiv \psi)).$$

Now in order to apply such a definition, the subformula ϕ, the so-called guard, must be valid in the context of the atom to be replaced. For this subproof, we

[1] For example, in the software context, type information already builds guard formulae.

R. Nieuwenhuis and A. Voronkov (Eds.): LPAR 2001, LNAI 2250, pp. 309–319, 2001.

employ the very same techniques that already showed to be useful in the context of optimized Skolemization [2]. Furthermore, a formula may not always contain an atom definition in the nice form presented above. For this case we give a syntactic criterion for a formula to contain an atom definition and provide an effective algorithm to actually retrieve the definition in the above applicable form. We show that the algorithm is correct and complete with respect to the syntactic criterion. A similar procedure is used to derive the application context.

A typical example for an atom definition with guard in the set theory domain is the definition of function composition: If f_{AB}, read as a triple, denotes a function from the set A into the set B, and g_{BC} from B to C, then composition can be defined in a point-wise fashion as follows:

$$\begin{array}{l} \forall f_{AB}, g_{BC}, x, z \\ \quad (x \in A \land z \in C) \supset \\ \qquad [g_{BC} \circ f_{AB}(x) = z \equiv \exists y\, (y \in B \land f_{AB}(x) = y \land g_{BC}(y) = z)]. \end{array}$$

Here $(x \in A \land z \in C)$ is the guard that has to be checked before the atom definition of $g_{BC} \circ f_{AB}(x) = z$ can be applied.

In the context of clause-based automated theorem proving, the detection and expansion of atom definitions is a preprocessing step of the clause normal form (CNF) translation procedure. It is build into the SPASS transformation process that is organized in three stages: *formula renaming*, *optimized Skolemization* and *simplification*. In the first stage, subformulae are replaced with new predicates and the definitions thereof added, provided the replacement eventually leads to fewer clauses. This step is closely related to the automatic detection and contraction of definitions. In the optimized Skolemization stage existential quantifiers are removed in exchange for carefully introduced new functions. In the last stage domain specific simplification techniques, e.g. based on the domain size, are applied along with more general techniques like equality simplifications and expansion of (atom) definitions. This expansion step can be considered as symmetrical to formula renaming.

Thus by adding the techniques described in this paper to SPASS, we complete the picture of techniques in the CNF transformation process. Altogether we can now provide a framework within which appropriate instantiation strategies can be developed and tested.

An experimental evaluation gives strong evidence that our approach is promising. It was performed in the SET (set theory) application area of the TPTP [4], feeding the resulting clausal specifications into the SPASS theorem prover. This way we could solve about 60 extra problems that make up almost 20% of the overall first-order SET problems in the TPTP. For many of these newly solved proof tasks, no previous fully automated proof attempt with any other prover had been reported.

Now the paper is organized as follows: Section 2 introduces the relevant notions and notations. In Section 3 we develop the notion of an atom definition and show under which conditions the expansion of atom definitions preserves equivalence/satisfiability. As atom definitions do not always have the desired shape required in Section 3 the shape has often first to be extracted from a given formula. Section 4 provides a syntactic criterion for the existence of an atom definition and an effective correct and complete algorithm to actually compute the desired shape. Section 5 demonstrates that the theory is successfully implemented in SPASS. We end the paper with a short summary and a discussion of related work, Section 6.

2 Preliminaries

We rely on the terminology described in [2]. Therefore, we only repeat the more sophisticated concepts and some notation.

We recursively construct *formulae* over atoms, the logical constants $\top$ (truth), $\bot$ (falsity) and the operators $\supset$ (implication), $\equiv$ (equivalence), $\wedge$ (conjunction), $\vee$ (disjunction), $\neg$ (negation) and the quantifiers $\forall$ (universal), $\exists$ (existential) as usual. We sometimes omit parentheses to ease readability; especially, highest priority is given to quantification, negation, equivalence, implication, in descending order.

For the sequence $x_1, \ldots, x_n$ $(t_1, \ldots, t_n)$ we use the abbreviation $\overline{x_n}$ $(\overline{t_n})$. For convenience, we often write $\forall x_1, \ldots, x_n\, \phi$ or $\forall \overline{x_n}$ instead of $\forall x_1 \ldots \forall x_n\, \phi$ and analogously for the existential quantifier. If $Q_1, \ldots, Q_n$ denotes a sequence of quantifier symbols, then $\overline{Q_n x_n}$ is short for $Q_1 x_1 \ldots Q_n x_n$. To simplify the discussion we always assume that in a formula any variable is bound by at most one quantifier.

An *interpretation* is a triple $\mathcal{M} = \langle \mathcal{D}, \mathcal{I}, \nu \rangle$ where $\mathcal{D}$ is a non-empty set, namely the domain of discourse, $\mathcal{I}$ associates n-ary predicate symbols and function symbols with n-place relations and functions respectively. We use $\mathcal{M}[x/a]$ as a short form for $\langle \mathcal{D}, \mathcal{I}, \nu[x/a] \rangle$ provided $\mathcal{M} = \langle \mathcal{D}, \mathcal{I}, \nu \rangle$. The *satisfies* relation $\models$ is defined as usual.

For the purpose of this paper, we extend substitutions to formulae as follows: $P(t_1, \ldots, t_n)\sigma = P(t_1\sigma, \ldots, t_n\sigma)$, $(\neg\phi)\sigma = \neg(\phi\sigma)$, $(\phi_1 \circ \phi_2)\sigma = \phi_1\sigma \circ \phi_2\sigma$ where $\circ \in \{\supset, \equiv, \wedge, \vee\}$, $(\forall x\, \phi)\sigma = \forall x\sigma\, \phi\sigma$ if $x\sigma$ is a variable and $\forall x\, \phi$ otherwise, $(\exists x\, \phi)\sigma = \exists x\sigma\, \phi\sigma$ if $x\sigma$ is a variable and $\exists x\, \phi$ otherwise. In general, the extension of substitutions to formulae is problematic, because it might accidentally turn free variables into bound variables. However, we shall only make use of this definition in very restricted contexts where the desired semantics is preserved by the application of the substitution.

A *position* is a word over the natural numbers. The set $pos(\phi)$ of positions of a given formula ϕ is defined as follows: (i) the empty word $\epsilon \in pos(\phi)$ (ii) $i.\pi \in pos(\phi)$ if $\phi = \phi_1 \circ \phi_2$ and $\pi \in pos(\phi_i)$, $i \in \{1, 2\}$ where $\circ \in \{\supset, \equiv, \wedge, \vee\}$ and (iii) $1.\pi \in pos(\phi)$ if $\phi = \neg\psi$ or $\phi = \forall x\, \psi$ or $\phi = \exists x\, \psi$ and $\pi \in pos(\psi)$. Now, if $\pi \in pos(\phi)$ we define $\phi|_\epsilon = \phi$ and $\phi|_{i.\tau} = \phi_i|_\tau$ where $\phi = \phi_1 \circ \phi_2$, $\circ \in \{\supset, \equiv, \wedge, \vee\}$ and define $\phi|_{1.\tau} = \psi|_\tau$ if $\phi = \neg\psi$ or $\phi = \forall x\, \psi$ or $\phi = \exists x\, \psi$. We write $\psi[\phi]_\pi$ for $\psi|_\pi = \phi$. With $\psi[\pi/\phi]$, where $\pi \in pos(\psi)$, we denote the formula obtained by replacing $\psi|_\pi$ with ϕ at position π in ψ. The *length* of a position π is defined by $|\epsilon| = 0$ and $|i.\tau| = 1 + |\tau|$. Let $\leq$ denote the usual prefix ordering on positions:

$\pi \leq \tau$ iff there exists a position ι with $\pi.\iota = \tau$, and $\pi < \tau$ iff $\pi \leq \tau$ and not $\tau \leq \pi$.

The polarity of a formula occurring at position π in a formula ψ is denoted by $pol(\psi, \pi)$ and is defined in the usual way: $pol(\psi, \epsilon) = 1$; $pol(\psi, \pi.i) = pol(\psi, \pi)$ if $\psi|_\pi$ is a conjunction, disjunction, formula starting with a quantifier or an implication with $i = 2$; $pol(\psi, \pi.i) = -pol(\psi, \pi)$ if $\psi|_\pi$ is a formula starting with a negation symbol or an implication with $i = 1$ and, finally, $pol(\psi, \pi.i) = 0$ if $\psi|_\pi$ is an equivalence.

The set of *free*, *bound* and *all* variables of a formula ϕ (term t) is defined in the usual way and denoted by the functions *free*(), *bound*() and *vars*(), respectively.

3 Atom Definitions and Their Application

In this section we develop the notion of an atom definition and its expansion inside some other sentence. We give necessary conditions for an expansion to preserve satisfiability or even equivalence.

Definition 1 (Atom definition).
An *atom definition for a predicate* P is a sentence of the form

$$\forall x_1, \ldots, x_m \, (\varphi \supset P(t_1, \ldots, t_n) \equiv \psi)$$

where $free(P(t_1, \ldots, t_n)) = \{x_1, \ldots, x_m\}$. The formula φ is called the *guard formula* of the atom definition and ψ its *expansion formula*. We also say that $\forall x_1, \ldots, x_m \, (\varphi \supset P(t_1, \ldots, t_n) \equiv \psi)$ is an atom definition for P at position $1^m.2$.

Note that we consider the above definition with respect to the symmetry of $\equiv$. We do not restrict the shape of the expansion term. For example, the defined predicate P may occur in the expansion formula, since practice has shown that even the replacement of the atom by such an expansion formula can be of great benefit. As only sentences are considered, the condition $free(P(t_1, \ldots, t_n)) = \{x_1, \ldots, x_m\}$ already implies that $free(\psi), free(\varphi) \subseteq free(P(t_1, \ldots, t_n))$ which makes sense, because eventually we want to apply the atom definition to an atom $P(s_1, \ldots, s_n)$ occurring in some sentence ϕ_2 without creating free variables.

We want to replace the atom $P(s_1, \ldots, s_n)$ in ϕ_2 by the expansion formula of the definition. In order to do this we first have to find a matcher σ with $P(t_1, \ldots, t_n)\sigma = P(s_1, \ldots, s_n)$. Second, we have to check the validity of the guard in the context of $P(s_1, \ldots, s_n)$. In order to make this more precise, let us assume without loss of generality that $\phi_2 = Qz_{i_1} \ldots Qz_{i_j}(\varphi' \supset \phi[P(s_1, \ldots, s_n)]_\pi)$ where φ' is the already mentioned context of $P(s_1, \ldots, s_n)$. Note that if $j = 0$ and $\varphi' = \top$ the sentence represents the case where no context is explicitly available. So we can further assume that $\{z_{i_1}, \ldots, z_{i_j}\} \subseteq vars(P(s_1, \ldots, s_n))$. Then proving the validity of the guard amounts to showing $\models \forall z_1, \ldots, z_k(\varphi' \supset \varphi\sigma)$, where $\{z_1, \ldots, z_k\} = vars(P(s_1, \ldots, s_n))$. The theorem below states that in fact if all conditions we discussed so far are fulfilled, the replacement of the atom by the expansion formula preserves equivalence.

Theorem 2. Let $\phi_1 = \forall x_1, \ldots, x_m (\varphi \supset P(t_1, \ldots, t_n) \equiv \psi)$ be an atom definition, let $\phi_2 = Qz_{i_1} \ldots Qz_{i_j} (\varphi' \supset \phi[P(s_1, \ldots, s_n)]_\pi)$ be a sentence to which we want to apply the atom definition, let both sentences have no variable symbols in common and let σ be a substitution with $P(t_1, \ldots, t_n)\sigma = P(s_1, \ldots, s_n)$. Furthermore we assume $\models \forall z_1, \ldots, z_k(\varphi' \supset \varphi\sigma)$ where $\{z_{i_1}, \ldots, z_{i_j}\} \subseteq \{z_1, \ldots, z_k\} = vars(P(s_1, \ldots, s_n))$. Then

$$\mathcal{M} \models \phi_1 \wedge \phi_2 \quad \text{iff} \quad \mathcal{M} \models \phi_1 \wedge \phi_2[1^j.2.\pi/\psi\sigma]$$

Proof. Note that $free(\varphi') \subseteq \{z_{i_1}, \ldots, z_{i_j}\}$ as well as $free(\varphi\sigma) \subseteq \{z_1, \ldots, z_k\}$ and $free(\psi\sigma) \subseteq \{z_1, \ldots, z_k\}$, because both ϕ_1 and ϕ_2 are sentences. We only show the left-to-right part of the theorem, the other part is a simple syntactic variant of this one. So let us assume $\mathcal{M} \models \phi_1 \wedge \phi_2$ and we must show $\mathcal{M} \models \phi_2[1^j.2.\pi/\psi\sigma]$, in more detail $\mathcal{M} \models Qz_{i_1} \ldots Qz_{i_j}(\varphi' \supset \phi[\pi/\psi\sigma])$. Let us assume that $\mathcal{M}[z_{i_1}/a_1, \ldots, z_{i_j}/a_j] \models \varphi'$ for some arbitrary $a_1, \ldots, a_j$, for otherwise we are already done. Now let $\{z_{h_1}, \ldots, z_{h_l}\} = \{z_1, \ldots, z_k\} \setminus \{z_{i_1}, \ldots, z_{i_j}\}$. Then for arbitrary $a_{j+1}, \ldots, a_k$ we know that $\mathcal{M}[z_{i_1}/a_1, \ldots, z_{i_j}/a_j][z_{h_1}/a_{j+1}, \ldots, z_{h_l}/a_k] \models P(s_1, \ldots, s_n) \equiv \psi\sigma$, because $P(t_1, \ldots, t_n)\sigma = P(s_1, \ldots, s_n)$, $\models \forall z_1, \ldots, z_k(\varphi' \supset \varphi\sigma)$, $\mathcal{M} \models \phi_1$ and ϕ_1, ϕ_2 have no variables in common. Finally, by an inductive argument on the length of π we conclude $\mathcal{M}[z_{i_1}/a_1, \ldots, z_{i_j}/a_j] \models \phi[\pi/\psi'\sigma]$. □

There are several aspects that can be further discussed here. First, a formula representing an atom definition needs not be of the shape introduced in Definition 1. Furthermore, the context in the application formula may not be syntactically available in the form required by Theorem 2. A possible answer to both questions is contained in Section 4, where techniques are discussed that actually extract atom definitions. The very same techniques can also be applied to retrieve potential contexts of an atom to be replaced in a formula.

Second, the validity of the guard formula $\models \forall z_1, \ldots, z_k(\varphi' \supset \varphi\sigma)$ is undecidable in general. We already explored this kind of problem when we introduced optimized Skolemization [2]. In practice, the answer is to apply an inference procedure for this proof attempt that is guaranteed to terminate but still valuable. In SPASS we employ an implementation of depth-bounded unit resolution for this purpose [5].

Third, if the predicate P does not occur in the expansion formula ψ and if all occurrences of P in other formulae can be replaced, then the atom definition can be deleted, preserving satisfiability. Of course, this does only apply to predicates that are freely interpreted. For example, equality cannot be eliminated this way.[2]

4 Contained Atom Definitions

Atom definitions considered so far have been required to be presented in the syntactical form of a universally quantified conditional equivalence. In order to increase the number of situations where our concept is applicable, we now

[2] Except all equality axioms are explicitly added before the expansion is started.

develop a notion of atom definitions being contained in other formulae such that the superformulae can, preserving equivalence, effectively be transformed into the syntactical form of Definition 1. This may be looked upon as extracting definitions from formulae. We start with the following technical term:

Definition 3 (Contain disjunctively). Let ϕ be a formula containing a subformula φ at a position π. If for all $\nu \in pos(\phi)$ with $\nu < \pi$, $\phi|_\nu$ is
(i) a disjunction or implication with $pol(\phi, \nu) = 1$, or
(ii) a conjunction with $pol(\phi, \nu) = -1$, or
(iii) a quantification or a negation,
then we say that *ϕ contains φ disjunctively at π*.

The essence of this notion is that, the three conditions being fulfilled, the formula ϕ can effectively be transformed into an equivalent one of the form $\overline{Q_k x_k}(\psi \vee \varphi)$ or $\overline{Q_k x_k}(\psi \vee \neg\varphi)$, depending on the polarity $pol(\phi, \pi)$. This will be useful within our extraction algorithm; but to result in atom definitions, further conditions are necessary.

Definition 4 (Contain atom definition). Let ϕ be a formula with a subformula $P(t_1, \ldots, t_n) \equiv \psi$ or $\psi \equiv P(t_1, \ldots, t_n)$ at position π. Then ϕ is said to *contain an atom definition for the predicate P at π* if
(i) ϕ contains disjunctively the subformula $\phi|_\pi$ with $pol(\phi, \pi) = 1$,
(ii) each free variable in $P(t_1, \ldots, t_n)$ is bound by a universal quantifier with polarity 1 or by an existential quantifier with polarity -1,
(iii) $free(\psi) \subseteq free(P(t_1, \ldots, t_n))$ and
(iv) for all positions ξ, ν with $\xi < \nu \leq \pi$ we have: if $\phi|_\nu$ is a quantification binding a free variable in $P(t_1, \ldots, t_n)$, and $\phi|_\xi$ is a quantification, then the latter also binds a free variable in $P(t_1, \ldots, t_n)$.

Now the algorithm to extract atom definitions needs to be formulated. It will be specified as stratified application of extraction rules that perform a transformation of formulae. The rules are organized in three groups.

Definition 5 (Extraction rules). The list in Table 1 contains the *extraction rules* as set of transformations on formulae and positions. Note that for each of the rules in groups *(R2)* and *(R3)*, due to the symmetry of the operators $\vee$ and $\equiv$, copies with corresponding permutations of left-hand sides have been omitted to ease readability.

The application of extraction rules preserves a number of important properties that are listed in the subsequent lemma. The proof is simply by inspection of the transformations.

Lemma 6. Consider an extraction step $(\phi, \pi) \rightarrow (\phi', \pi')$.
(i) Then ϕ is logically equivalent to ϕ'.
(ii) The polarities $pol(\phi, \pi)$ and $pol(\phi', \pi')$ are the same.
(iii) If ϕ contains $\phi|_\pi$ disjunctively at π, then so does ϕ' with $\phi'|_{\pi'}$ at π'.
(iv) If ϕ contains an atom definition for a predicate P at π, so does ϕ' at π'.

Table 1. Extraction Rules

(R1)	$(\phi[\varphi_1 \supset \varphi_2]_\xi, \xi.n.\iota)$	$\rightarrow (\phi[\xi/\neg\varphi_1 \vee \varphi_2], \xi.\iota'.n.\iota)$
	where $\iota' = 1$ if $n = 1$ and else $\iota' = \epsilon$	
	$(\phi[\neg\neg\varphi]_\xi, \xi.1.1.\iota)$	$\rightarrow (\phi[\xi/\varphi], \xi.\iota)$
	$(\phi[\neg\exists x\, \varphi]_\xi, \xi)$	$\rightarrow (\phi[\xi/\forall x\, \neg\varphi], \xi)$
	$(\phi[\neg\forall x\, \varphi]_\xi, \xi)$	$\rightarrow (\phi[\xi/\exists x\, \neg\varphi], \xi)$
	$(\phi[\neg(\varphi_1 \vee \varphi_2)]_\xi, \xi.1.n.\iota)$	$\rightarrow (\phi[\xi/\neg\varphi_1 \wedge \neg\varphi_2], \xi.n.1.\iota)$
	$(\phi[\neg(\varphi_1 \wedge \varphi_2)]_\xi, \xi.1.n.\iota)$	$\rightarrow (\phi[\xi/\neg\varphi_1 \vee \neg\varphi_2], \xi.n.1.\iota)$
(R2)	$(\phi[\varphi_1 \vee (\varphi_2 \vee P(\overline{t_n}) \equiv \psi)]_\xi, \xi.2.2)$	$\rightarrow (\phi[\xi/(\varphi_1 \vee \varphi_2) \vee P(\overline{t_n}) \equiv \psi], \xi.2)$
	$(\phi[\exists x\, (\varphi \vee P(\overline{t_n}) \equiv \psi)]_\xi, \xi.1.2)$	$\rightarrow (\phi[\xi/\exists x\, \varphi \vee P(\overline{t_n}) \equiv \psi], \xi.2)$
	if $x \notin \mathit{free}(P(\overline{t_n}))$	
	$(\phi[\forall x\, (\varphi \vee P(\overline{t_n}) \equiv \psi)]_\xi, \xi.1.2)$	$\rightarrow (\phi[\xi/\forall x\, \varphi \vee P(\overline{t_n}) \equiv \psi], \xi.2)$
	if $x \notin \mathit{free}(P(\overline{t_n}))$	
	$(\phi[\varphi_1 \vee \forall x\, \varphi_2]_\xi, \xi.2.1.\iota)$	$\rightarrow (\phi[\xi/\forall x\, (\varphi_1 \vee \varphi_2)], \xi.1.2.\iota)$
	if $\varphi_2\|_\iota$ is $P(\overline{t_n}) \equiv \psi$ or $\psi \equiv P(\overline{t_n})$ and $x \in \mathit{free}(P(\overline{t_n}))$	
(R3)	$(\phi[\varphi \vee P(\overline{t_n}) \equiv \psi]_\xi, \xi.2)$	$\rightarrow (\phi[\xi/\neg\varphi \supset P(\overline{t_n}) \equiv \psi], \xi.2)$

The algorithm is now composed of successive exhaustive application of each group of transformation rules.

Definition 7 (Extraction algorithm for atom definitions). Given a formula ϕ and a position π in ϕ, the *extraction algorithm* consists of the following stages of successive extraction steps that start from (ϕ, π):
Stage 1: Apply *(R1)* exhaustively.
Stage 2: Apply *(R2)* exhaustively.
Stage 3: Apply *(R3)* if possible.

We now prove that this algorithm is terminating, equivalence preserving, correct and complete with respect to Definition 4.

Theorem 8. The extraction algorithm terminates for any input (ϕ, π) with π a position in the formula ϕ. Furthermore, let (ϕ', π') be the output of the algorithm for input (ϕ, π). Then ϕ and ϕ' are equivalent; and ϕ' is an atom definition for P at π' if and only if ϕ contains an atom definition for P at π.

Proof. (Termination) Within the first stage, termination can already be established if the transformation rules are considered as a rewrite system, interpreting formulae as terms and embedding the system into a recursive path ordering with appropriate precedence. The rules in the second stage either decrease the length of the position, or that length remains unchanged, but the length of a position of a quantifier for one of the finitely many free variables in the subformula at hand is decreased. Finally, the rule in the third stage is applied no more than once.

(Equivalence preservation.) This follows immediately from Lemma 6.

(Correctness.) One has to show that if the algorithm outputs (ϕ', π') where ϕ' is an atom definition for a predicate P at π', then the input ϕ contains an atom definition for P at π. In fact, the formula ϕ' of course contains an atom definition for P at π'; and one easily shows by inspection of the extraction rules that, if the resulting formula of a transition contains a definition, then the original formula did as well.

(Completeness.) Assume the algorithm starts with a formula ϕ as input which contains an atom definition for P at π. By Lemma 6, the output formula ϕ' contains such a definition at π'. We have to show that ϕ' even adheres to the syntactically stricter form of an atom definition. Let (ϕ_2, π') denote the result of the Stages 1 and 2, i.e. before (possible) single application of the rule of the last stage.

What are the operators that may appear on the path from the root position of the formula ϕ_2 to the position π'? First of all, due to the positive polarity $pol(\phi_2, \pi')$, no equivalence is possible there. Second, because of the exhaustive application of rules in Stage 1, $\phi_2|_\xi$ cannot be an implication for any position ξ above π'. Third, since negations have uniformly been moved downwards, they could only appear immediately above the position π'. Due to the elimination of double negations, their number is 0 or 1, the latter being impossible since $pol(\phi_2, \pi') = 1$. Finally, if there were a conjunction, then because of its negative polarity there should be a negation above it, but there is actually none. So $\phi_2|_\xi$ is a disjunction or a quantification for all $\xi < \pi'$.

Let us now have a look at a quantification $\phi_2|_\xi$ at a position ξ above π'. Because of Stage 2 it must bind a variable in $\phi_2|_{\pi'}$. Since there are no more negations, its polarity is positive, hence it can only be a universal one. In fact, since every free variable in the equivalence $\phi_2|_{\pi'}$ is bound, there is one quantification for each free variable thereof. These quantifications do not appear within disjunctions, i.e. they form some prenex, whereas the underlying disjunction must contain the equivalence $\phi_2|_{\pi'}$ as right top-level disjunct. So ϕ_2 is a formula of the form $\overline{\forall x_k}\,(\varphi' \vee P(\overline{t_n}) \equiv \psi)$. Finally Stage 3 transforms ϕ_2 into $\phi' = \overline{\forall x_k}\,(\varphi \supset P(\overline{t_n}) \equiv \psi)$ where $\varphi = \neg\varphi'$, which indeed is an atom definition for P. □

The notions developed so far can straightforwardly be extended to cover also *conjunctive occurrence* of subformulae, and thereby to handle atom definitions contained in a conjunctive fashion.

Finally, note that the extraction algorithm presented here is in principle also applicable to transform the contexts in which an atom definition is to be applied. One starts with the corresponding notion of a formula containing an atom occurrence and modifies Stage 2 such that it works on occurrences instead of equivalences.

5 Experiments

Several problem domains are naturally formalized using atom definitions, like software verification/analysis or set theory. We concentrate on the latter, because the examples presented below are widely available through the TPTP [4]. The current version of the TPTP at this writing is 2.4.1.

The previous chapter leaves open any aspects of an actual implementation of the theory. We found the following settings to be useful: (i) all found atom definitions are only applied to the conjecture formula, (ii) for the proof of the guard formula, we use SPASS itself restricted to depth-bounded unit resolution [5], (iii) the number of atom definition applications is limited to at most 10 applications,[3] (iv) all atom definitions are kept, even if the defined predicate could be completely eliminated through expansions. These features are available in SPASS Version 2.0 that is available from the SPASS homepage: `http://spass.mpi-sb.mpg.de/`.

The hardware used for the test are old-fashioned PCs (333MHz Pentium II) running SUN OS 5.6, so the results should be easily reproducible on any current hardware. The examples shown in Table 2 are all examples that SPASS could not solve without detecting and expanding atom definitions in the way described before. These examples make up about 20% of all first-order SET examples in the TPTP. The table shows the TPTP problem name together with the time in seconds needed for SPASS to prove the problem. All numbers are upwards rounded to seconds. Summing it up, with the techniques described in this paper, SPASS can solve in a few seconds many problems that without them could not be done at all within any reasonable time limit. For many of these examples, SPASS was the first automatic prover to report a successful proof attempt to the TPTP; so we encourage the reader to test these examples using his/her favorite theorem proving system.

In general, it is pretty clear that changes to any parameter chosen for this experiment have influence on the success or non-success of a particular proof attempt. It is well known from proof attempts in mathematics that there are problems where the expansion of definitions in the conjecture is the key to a successful proof and that there are problems where just the opposite is the case.

Nevertheless, we made some additional runs on the TPTP SET first-order problems that may give a feeling for the influence the parameters have on SPASS's success. If we change the number of atom definition applications from 10 to 5, then we loose 15 out of the above 60 problems. If we change it from 10 to 15, then we loose 2 problems. However, beside the above 60 problems, both parameter settings can prove further problems. For all experiments we made on the TPTP SET domain, the time needed by SPASS to actually extract the atom definition, the context of the atom to be replaced and to prove the guard formula could be neglected.

If we compare SPASS with and without expansion of atom definitions on all SET first-order examples of the TPTP except the above 60 problems, the

[3] We will discuss this "magic number"at the end of the section.

Table 2. SET Experiments

Problem	time	Problem	time	Problem	time	Problem	time	Problem	time
SET010+3	1	SET011+3	1	SET012+4	1	SET013+4	1	SET016+4	1
SET066+1	2	SET069+1	192	SET071+1	1	SET143+3	1	SET143+4	1
SET144+3	1	SET155+4	2	SET156+4	5	SET159+3	1	SET159+4	1
SET169+3	1	SET169+4	1	SET171+3	1	SET171+4	1	SET173+3	1
SET175+3	1	SET351+4	1	SET352+4	1	SET358+4	21	SET593+3	1
SET595+3	1	SET606+3	1	SET607+3	1	SET608+3	1	SET609+3	1
SET610+3	1	SET611+3	1	SET612+3	1	SET613+3	1	SET614+3	1
SET615+3	1	SET624+3	101	SET634+3	1	SET690+4	15	SET692+4	1
SET693+4	1	SET694+4	1	SET695+4	1	SET696+4	1	SET698+4	71
SET699+4	1	SET700+4	1	SET701+4	1	SET702+4	1	SET703+4	1
SET706+4	5	SET720+4	31	SET722+4	18	SET731+4	2	SET734+4	18
SET751+4	3	SET753+4	4	SET754+4	4	SET755+4	3	SET763+4	2

expansion version looses 5 problems compared to the version without expansion of atom definitions. However, it also wins several new problems beside the above 60 problems. We didn't include these problems into the above 60 ones, because they can also be solved with SPASS without expansion of atom definitions, but other parameter variations.

6 Summary and Related Work

We have extended the notion of atom definitions in first-order logic by guards and presented conditions under which atom definitions can be expanded within formulae. Furthermore, we gave an effective algorithm to retrieve such definitions from equivalences within complex formulae. We presented a syntactic criterion for a formula to contain a definition and showed that our algorithm is correct and complete with respect to the criterion. To the best of our knowledge, there is no previous work in the context of automated theorem proving that relates to these results on atom definitions with guards on the formula level.

The theory is implemented within the CNF translation module of SPASS. Feeding its outcome into SPASS, we have performed an experimental evaluation showing that the prover can benefit tremendously in application domains where atom definitions with guards are frequent. Our approach being that successful already, future work will focus on the question of expanding atom definitions with guard dynamically also in the theorem proving process itself.

On the clause level, there exist contributions how definitions can be detected and utilized. Plaisted and Zhu [3] presented an approach how to detect definitions on the clause level and to turn them into replacement rules. These rules are then employed to simulate the expansion of atom definitions on the clause level. Despite from the fact that the detection of guards on the clause level is not straightforward, applying this work to atom definitions with guards means that the guards are checked after expansion.

More recently, Degtyarev and Voronkov [1] introduced stratified resolution, a sound and complete resolution calculus that can in particular be used to restrict resolution on clauses resulting from atom definitions such that only expansion steps are preformed.

Acknowledgments. We thank Andrei Voronkov for many discussions and a number of valuable comments.

References

1. A. Degtyarev and A. Voronkov. Stratified resolution. In D. McAllester, editor, *17th International Conference on Automated Deduction (CADE-17)*, volume 1831, pages 365–384, Pittsburgh, 2000.
2. Andreas Nonnengart, Georg Rock, and Christoph Weidenbach. On generating small clause normal forms. In Claude Kirchner and Hélène Kirchner, editors, *15th International Conference on Automated Deduction, CADE-15*, volume 1421 of *LNAI*, pages 397–411. Springer, 1998.
3. David A. Plaisted and Yunshan Zhu. Replacement rules with definition detection. In Ricardo Caferra and Gernot Salzer, editors, *Automated Deduction in Classical and Non-Classical Logics*, volume 1761 of *LNAI*, pages 80–94. Springer, 1998.
4. Geoff Sutcliffe, Christian B. Suttner, and Theodor Yemenis. The TPTP problem library. In Alan Bundy, editor, *Twelfth International Conference on Automated Deduction, CADE-12*, volume 814 of *LNAI*, pages 252–266, Nancy, France, June 1994. Springer.
5. Christoph Weidenbach. Combining Superposition, Sorts and Splitting. In Alan Robinson and Andrei Voronkov, editors, *Handbook of Automated Reasoning*, chapter 27, pages 1965–2013. Elsevier Science Publishers B.V., 2001.
6. Larry Wos. *Automated Reasoning, 33 Basic Research Problems.* Prentice Hall, 1988.

Automated Proof Support for Interval Logics

Thomas Marthedal Rasmussen

Informatics and Mathematical Modeling,
Technical University of Denmark, Building 321,
DK-2800 Kgs. Lyngby, Denmark
tmr@imm.dtu.dk

Abstract. We outline the background and motivation for the use of interval logics and consider some initial attempts toward proof support and automation. The main focus, though, is on recent work on these subjects. We compare different proof theoretical formalisms, in particular a "classical" versus a "labelled" one. We discuss encodings of these in the generic proof assistant Isabelle and consider some examples which show that in some cases the labelled formalism gives an order of magnitude improvement in proof length compared to a classical approach.

1 Introduction

Interval logic was introduced in computer science in the beginning of the 1980's and various work was carried out during the 1980's. With the introduction of Duration Calculus (DC) in the beginning of the 1990's, renewed interest in interval logics flourished. During the 1990's a lot of work on interval logics has been carried out (including work on more DC specific parts as such).

The purpose of this paper is to discuss initiatives toward automated proof support for interval logics. We consider some initial attempts but the main focus is on recent work on these subjects. We compare different proof theoretical formalisms, in particular a "classical" versus a "labelled" one. We discuss encodings of these in the generic proof assistant Isabelle and consider some examples which show that in some cases the labelled formalism gives an order of magnitude improvement in proof length compared to a classical approach.

The results of the paper go beyond the interval logic world, in that they can be seen as supporting the program of Gabbay [4] on using labelled formalisms for non-classical logics.

The rest of the paper is organized as follows: In the following section, Section 2, we give a brief outline of the development of interval logics used in computer science during the past 20 years. In Section 3 we become more technical, and consider syntax and semantics of the interval logics we are particularly interested in here. Section 4 more specifically starts to address the proof theory by considering different attempts to define (in a "classical" way) a sequent calculus for certain interval logics. Then, in Section 5, we turn to a fundamentally different proof theoretic formalism, namely that of Labelled Natural Deduction. We give examples convincingly conveying the benefits of this formalism and discuss

R. Nieuwenhuis and A. Voronkov (Eds.): LPAR 2001, LNAI 2250, pp. 320–329, 2001.

how an implementation in Isabelle can act as a framework for a certain class of interval logics. Finally, in Section 6, we discuss the results obtained.

2 Background

It is generally acknowledged that Pnueli [13] was the first to introduce temporal logic in computer science. In this (original kind of) temporal logic one can make qualitative reasoning over sequences of discrete time points. The use of these temporal logics is widespread today, e.g., within the model checking community.

But even though such temporal logics have turned out the most popular, variations over the theme have also been thoroughly considered, among these the topic of this paper: Interval (Temporal) Logics. In these logics, one reasons on the relationships of temporal intervals (which are most often represented as a pair of a beginning point and an end point). These can be based on either a discrete or a dense time domain. It is possible to express properties such as "if property ϕ holds on this interval then property ψ must hold on all subintervals" or "property φ must hold on some interval eventually".

One of the first uses of such a formalism was the work of [5,10] where timing aspects of hardware components were modeled. There has been a lot of work since, on many different aspects of interval logics, e.g., [9,6,21,11,14].

In the ProCoS project [1] in the end of the 1980's and the beginning of the 1990's it was realized that a convenient formalism for specifying and reasoning on accumulated durations of Boolean valued functions over time periods were required for expressing certain properties of real-time systems. This lead to the development of Duration Calculus (DC) [25] which is an extension of the interval logic ITL [10] with term-level notions for accumulated durations. The introduction of DC initiated much work on aspects of DC as well as, importantly, interval logics proper. As DC was introduced, the underlying version of ITL had not been thoroughly investigated; no complete axiomatization existed. This was not given until 1995 [3]. Together with a relative completeness result for DC and (un)decidability results this lead to [7] which is the most comprehensive reference for the logical foundations of DC.

Soon it became apparent that the original ITL had some limitations which made it difficult to specify (unbounded) liveness properties. An initial attempt to overcome this was [19]. Later, Neighbourhood Logic (NL) [24] was introduced on a more firm theoretical basis. Fairly recently, Signed Interval Logic (SIL) [16] was proposed, with the introduction of the notion of a direction of an interval. SIL has (as ITL) only one interval modality but SIL is (contrary to ITL) capable of specifying liveness properties. Other interval logics capable of this (such as NL) have more than one interval modality.

Not long time after the introduction of DC it was realized that some kind of proof support was needed for interval logics to be more widely applicable, in particular for the conduction of larger case-studies. Initial work in this directions was a semantic encoding in PVS in '94, giving PVS/DC [18]. As mentioned above, at that time no complete axiomatization for ITL existed. Later, based on the complete axiomatization, an encoding of ITL and DC in Isabelle was carried out, giving Isabelle/DC [8]. This latter work was somewhat ad hoc as the emphasis mainly was on getting the system "up and running" such as to be able to conduct case studies.

Only recently, [17,15], have the proof theoretical foundations necessary for automated proof support been more closely investigated. In Sections 4 and 5 we will discuss how these formalisms work from a more applied viewpoint, by considering different examples of reasoning.

3 Interval Logic

In this section we become more technical and consider syntax and semantics of the interval logics we are particularly interested in, namely ITL [3] and SIL [16].

The syntax of ITL and SIL is basically the same, namely that of First Order Logic (FOL) with equality, with the addition of formulas built from the binary interval modality *chop*: $\frown$. We let $x, y, z, \ldots$ denote variables, $s, t, u, \ldots$ denote terms and $\phi, \psi, \varphi, \ldots$ denote formulas. Hence, syntactically, we have formulas of the form $\phi \frown \psi$ beside the usual FOL formulas. Furthermore, both ITL and SIL include a special nullary function symbol ℓ which gives the *length* of an interval. This is the most distinguished feature of the interval logics we consider here compared to other kinds of interval logics.

Semantically, formulas of ITL are interpreted with respect to a given interval, which is represented by a pair $[i, j]$ (where $i \leq j$) of elements from an ordered temporal domain of time points. The meaning of the usual operators of FOL is independent of this interval whereas the meaning of $\frown$ is not; the semantics of $\frown$ is indicated in Fig. 1. We will refer to k of Fig. 1 as the chopping point of $\frown$. The chopping point will always lie inside the current interval on which we interpret a given formula. In general, modalities with this property are called contracting. With contracting modalities it is only possible to specify safety properties of a system. This is because once we have chosen the interval we want to observe we are restricted to specifying properties of this interval and its subintervals.

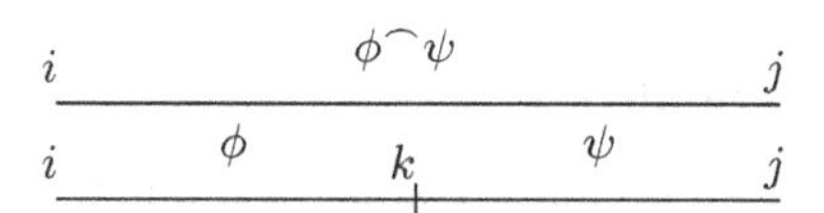

Fig. 1. $\phi \frown \psi$ holds on $[i, j]$ iff there is $k \in [i, j]$ such that ϕ holds on $[i, k]$ and ψ on $[k, j]$

To specify (unbounded) liveness properties, we need to reach intervals outside the current interval. In general, modalities which can do this are called expanding. NL is an example of an interval logic with expanding modalities.

SIL is a generalization of ITL with the introduction of the notion of a direction (which can be either forward or backward) of an interval. An interval with a direction is represented in SIL by a *signed interval* (i, j). Both the pair (i, j) and the pair (j, i) represent the same interval but (j, i) has opposite direction of (i,j). In SIL, ℓ now gives the signed length of an interval. Intuitively, the absolute value of ℓ gives the length of the interval and the sign of ℓ determines the direction. Because of the directions of intervals, the meaning of $\frown$ in SIL is altered: See Fig. 2. In the figure the direction of an interval is marked with a small arrowhead in either end of the interval. The chopping point can now lie anywhere and not just inside the current interval. This means that $\frown$ of SIL has become an expanding modality, hence SIL can specify liveness properties.

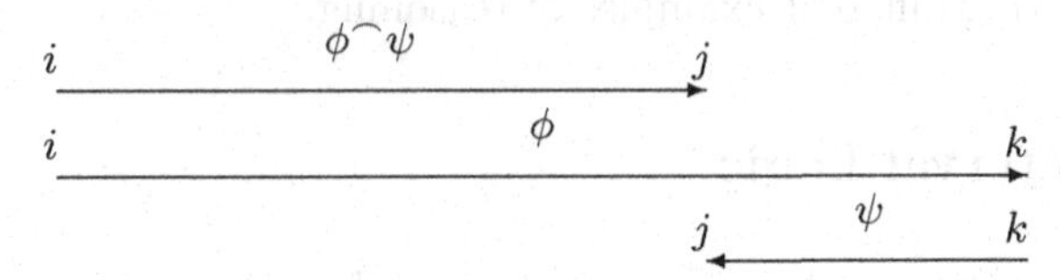

Fig. 2. $\phi\frown\psi$ holds on (i,j) iff there is k such that ϕ holds on (i,k) and ψ on (k,j)

ITL and SIL are modal logics. Formally, the semantics sketched above is given in terms of Kripke structures where the possible worlds are intervals. If we let $\mathfrak{M}$ be a first order Kripke model, the formal semantics of, e.g., $\wedge$ can be given as

$$\mathfrak{M},(i,j) \models \alpha \wedge \beta \quad \text{iff} \quad \mathfrak{M},(i,j) \models \alpha \text{ and } \mathfrak{M},(i,j) \models \beta \ .$$

Thus, the semantics of $\wedge$ is independent of the interval (i,j). Similarly for the other Boolean connectives. In the case of $\frown$ of SIL we have

$$\mathfrak{M},(i,j) \models \alpha\frown\beta \quad \text{iff} \quad \mathfrak{M},(i,k) \models \alpha \text{ and } \mathfrak{M},(k,j) \models \beta \text{ for some } k \ .$$

In the case of $\frown$ of ITL the semantics is the same except that k is restricted by $i \leq k \leq j$. The semantics of ℓ is given by a certain measure which of course is dependent on the given interval.

For fully formal treatments of the semantics of ITL and SIL we refer to [3] and [16], respectively. There, soundness and completeness results with respect to Hilbert-style proof systems are also proved.

3.1 The Converse Modality I

We will end this section by giving a simple example of what can be expressed in SIL (at the same time showing something that cannot be expressed in ITL). The example is concerned with properties of a (definable) unary modality $^{-1}$, which "reverses" the direction of an interval:

$$\phi^{-1} \ \widehat{=} \ (\exists x)(\,(\ell = x) \wedge (\,(\ell = 0) \wedge (\ell = x)\frown\phi\,)\frown\text{true}\,) \ .$$

One can straightforwardly semantically show that ϕ^{-1} holds on an interval (i,j) iff ϕ holds on the interval (j,i). We would like to show the following properties of $^{-1}$:

$$1)\ \ (\phi^{-1})^{-1} \leftrightarrow \phi\,, \qquad 2)\ \ (\phi\frown\psi)^{-1} \leftrightarrow (\psi^{-1}\frown\phi^{-1}) \ .$$

It is quite easy to informally convince oneself of the correctness of 1) and 2) by drawing signed intervals (in the style of Fig. 2) and see how they fit together. In later sections we will see how these properties can be proven formally and more or less automatically.

Note how $^{-1}$ and the properties 1) and 2) are related to classical (binary) relational algebra [20]. This connection (and others) is further discussed in [16].

4 Sequent Calculus

In this section we consider some initiatives toward automated proof support for interval logics which have in common that they are all based on a sequent calculus formulation.

In PVS/DC [18] various inference rules for ITL and DC are formulated in a sequent style. As mentioned in Section 2, this work is not based on a complete axiomatization and the rules are hence quite ad hoc. We will therefore not say more about this here.

The first attempt at (automated) proof support for ITL/DC with a complete axiomatic basis is that of [8]. There, ITL and DC are encoded on top of a FOL sequent calculus LK in Isabelle [12]. The result, Isabelle/DC, does not take much advantage of the sequent formalism: In essence, the axioms of the Hilbert system are added directly as axioms to LK, thus giving a mix of a Hilbert and a sequent system. As a consequence, not much automation is achieved.

In [17] a sequent calculus proof system for SIL is considered. Here an attempt is made to take advantage of the sequent calculus formalism as such and not just add axioms. This results in rules such as

$$\frac{\Gamma, \phi^\frown\varphi \vdash \Delta \quad \Gamma, \psi^\frown\varphi \vdash \Delta}{\Gamma, (\phi \vee \psi)^\frown\varphi \vdash \Delta}$$

which mimics the left-introduction rule for $\vee$ known from propositional logic but here "under the chop". There are more rules in the same style, resulting in a complete system. It is not a "proper" sequent calculus system though, in that, $^\frown$ does not appear in exactly one left and one right introduction rule. This aspect, and other important sequent calculus properties, is further discussed in [17]. By these measures it is not likely that a proper system exists at all; this also seems to be the case for most modal logics in general [2]. Despite this negative indication, it is seen how far the formalism can be "pushed": The main theoretical result of [17] is a "decidability modulo cut" result which entails that if one ignores the cut rule (which is necessary for completeness) provability is decidable (SIL is provably undecidable in general). Finally, [17] sketches how this sequent calculus system for SIL has been encoded in Isabelle, giving Isabelle/SIL.

4.1 The Converse Modality II

As an example of reasoning in Isabelle/SIL we consider mechanically proving 1) and 2) (cf. Section 3.1).

This required proving a substantial amount of initial results including many derived rules concerning the interplay between $\frown$ and the Boolean operators as well as the special ℓ symbol. Many of these were added to Isabelle's Classical Reasoner which encapsulates several search tacticals adopting various strategies. A lot of rewrite rules suitable for Isabelle's Simplifier were proved too.[1]

Based on this initial development, the proof of 1) and 2) took up approximately 200 lines of the proof script. The proof is not very straightforward and took some ingenuity to complete. We will in the following section see how this can be done much better.

5 Labelled Natural Deduction

In this section we consider Labelled Natural Deduction (LND) systems for interval logics. This proof theoretical framework is fundamentally different from the classical approaches: The intervals, which so far only have appeared in the semantics, are made part of the syntax and thereby an important part of the proof system. This approach is inspired by the work on Labelled Modal Logic [22] which in turn was carried out in response to Gabbay's program on Labelled Deductive Systems [4].

The most important consequence of the LND formalism is that it is possible to have a "proper" natural deduction system with exactly one I-(ntroduction) and one E-(limination) rule for each connective — including the modalities. In the case of $\frown$ of SIL we have the following rules:

$$\frac{(i,k):\phi \quad (k,j):\psi}{(i,j):\phi\frown\psi}\frown I \qquad \frac{(i,j):\phi\frown\psi \qquad \begin{matrix}[(i,k):\phi]\;[(k,j):\psi]\\ \vdots\\ (m,n):\varphi\end{matrix}}{(m,n):\varphi}\frown E$$

In [15] a sound and complete LND system for SIL is given. The main theoretical result is a normalization result which implies that normal derivations satisfy a subformula property. How an encoding of this labelled formalism could be done in Isabelle (giving Isabelle/LSIL) is indicated and the advantages are postulated.

5.1 The Converse Modality III

In this section we revisit the example concerning the converse modality $^{-1}$. As in Section 4.1 we want to mechanically prove the properties 1) and 2) but this time we use a version of Isabelle/LSIL which turns out much more convenient. Below we give (essentially) the whole proof script for the proofs of 1) and 2). (Note how `conv(P)` is used as concrete syntax for ϕ^{-1} and `len` is used for ℓ.)

[1] We refer to [12] for details on Isabelle specific aspects in general.

```
val [prem] =
Goal "(<i,j>:EX x. len=x ==> <i,j>:P) ==> <i,j>:P";
by (fast_tac (claset() addIs [prem,exICF]) 1);
qed "len_ex";

Goalw [conv_def] "<i,j>:P ==> <j,i>:conv(P)";
br len_ex 1;
by (fast_tac (claset() addEs [exE] addIs [exIRI]) 1);
qed "convI";

Goalw [conv_def] "<i,j>:conv(P) ==> <j,i>:P";
by (slow_tac (claset() addEs [exE,uniq1,zeroE2rev]) 1);
qed "convE";

Goal "<i,j>:conv(conv(P)) <-> P";
by (fast_tac (claset() addIs [convI] addDs [convE]) 1);
qed "conv_conv";

Goal "<i,j>:conv(P Q) <-> conv(Q) conv(P)";
by (fast_tac (claset() addIs [convI] addDs [convE]) 1);
qed "conv_chop";
```

As part of the proof we derive I- and E-rules for the $^{-1}$ modality. These rules, and subsequently 1) and 2), can be proven using `fast_tac` and `slow_tac` which are tactics (provided by Isabelle's Classical Reasoner) performing depth-first search, using I- and E-rules for the usual Boolean connectives and chop (encapsulated in `claset()`).[2] Besides this, I-/E-rules for the existential quantifier (`exE`,`exIRI`,`exICF`) are added where needed. Furthermore, two simple rules expressing uniqueness constraints on intervals (`uniq1`,`zeroE2rev`) are utilized. We will for space reasons not go into further explanation of details of the above proof script. The important thing to note is that the proof script only takes up roughly 20 lines. Hence, we have achieved an order of magnitude improvement in proof length compared to the Isabelle/SIL proof. We have here not taken into account that the initial development necessary for the above proof is shorter than the corresponding in Isabelle/SIL too.

5.2 Isabelle/LSIL as a General Framework

Above we have discussed the LND system for SIL together with an example in Isabelle/LSIL. What if we do not need/want the expressive power of signed intervals but prefer the standard intervals of ITL? Semantically, ITL can be regarded as a restriction of SIL as only a subset of the signed intervals are allowed: The intervals where the end point is greater than the beginning point (i.e., all forward intervals). This intuition motivates the following LND rules for $\frown$ in ITL.

[2] Contrary to `fast_tac`, `slow_tac` backtracks over proof by assumption.

$$\frac{(i,k):\phi \quad (k,j):\psi \quad i \sqsubseteq k \quad k \sqsubseteq j}{(i,j):\phi\frown\psi} \frown I \qquad \frac{(i,j):\phi\frown\psi \qquad \begin{array}{c}[(k,j):\psi]\ [k \sqsubseteq j] \\ [(i,k):\phi]\ [i \sqsubseteq k] \\ \vdots \\ (m,n):\varphi\end{array}}{(m,n):\varphi} \frown E$$

Loosely speaking, by restricting the other rules of SIL in a similar way we will arrive at an LND system for ITL. The relation $\sqsubseteq$ defines an ordering over the temporal domain and to reason with $\sqsubseteq$ judgments we add rules defining its properties (such as transitivity).

One could now make an ITL encoding in Isabelle in parallel to the SIL encoding. This encoding would actually be a little more complicated as one would have to take care of the $\sqsubseteq$ judgments as well. But a little thought shows that it is possible to encode ITL directly in Isabelle/LSIL. This owes to the following observations:

1. $i \sqsubseteq j$ is semantically equivalent to $(i,j) : \mathit{fwd}$ (we use *fwd* as an abbreviation for $\ell \geq 0$). By exploiting this we do not have to introduce a new judgment.
2. By defining a special contracting chop modality as $\phi \sqcap\!| \psi \ \widehat{=}\ (\phi \wedge \mathit{fwd})\frown(\psi \wedge \mathit{fwd})$ we get the intended semantics of chop of ITL within SIL.
3. We can derive an I- and an E-rule for $\sqcap\!|$ within the SIL system. In Isabelle/LSIL the result looks like follows:

```
itlchopI "[| <i,k>:P; <k,j>:Q; <i,k>:fwd; <k,j>:fwd |]
          ==> <i,j>:P| |Q";

itlchopE "[| <i,j>:P| |Q; <i,j>:fwd;
             !!k. [| <i,k>:P; <k,j>:Q; <i,k>:fwd; <k,j>:fwd |]
             ==> <l,m>:R |] ==> <l,m>:R";
```

In conclusion, we can say that if we from the start assume $(i,j) : \mathit{fwd}$ and thereafter use the above I-/E-rules, we have a sound framework for reasoning within ITL with minimal effort and we have most of the "infrastructure" of Isabelle/LSIL at our disposal. It is fairly straightforward to formally justify this.

Note that the above sketched idea can be taken a step further: We can also encode, e.g., NL in Isabelle/LSIL. Thus, we still only consider forward intervals but we do include liveness. We can derive I- and E-rules for the two expanding modalities of NL and then reason within this framework; again, most of the "infrastructure" of Isabelle/LSIL comes for free.

An Example. We will here consider an example which is based on an encoding of ITL in Isabelle/LSIL as sketched above. Furthermore, DC has been encoded on top of this ITL encoding.

The example is the classical Gas Burner example [25]; the motivating example for the introduction of Duration Calculus. This small case-study is mainly focused on illustrating the DC extension of ITL. Thus, it is reasoning on the term-level which is (primarily) exercised.

The example is concerned with proving an implementation correct with respect to a specification. The proof script in Isabelle/LSIL takes up more than 400 lines. This is not too impressive as we are using the labelled formalism. There are both intrinsic and more practical explanations for this somewhat disappointing result: Reasoning on the term level means reasoning on the same interval. Clearly, the labelled formalism is only advantageous when relating intervals; thus, in the term level case we do not gain compared to a classical approach. There is not much to do about that. What can be done something about is the amount of automation for term level reasoning. This in particular is the case for arithmetic reasoning on integers, including representation of integers. A lot could here be learned from the quite elaborate theories and tools (in particular the use of the Simplifier) in Isabelle/HOL [12]. Another possibility is the use of external decision procedures (such as SVC). The problem here is to make a convenient interface. An initial attempt toward this is made in [8].

6 Discussion

We have in this paper seen how much the choice of formalism for reasoning in a certain logic means for the amount of work needed to conduct proofs. We in particular saw how much we gained when going from a "classical" (Isabelle/SIL) to a "labelled" formalism (Isabelle/LSIL) in the case of proving properties 1) and 2) concerning the $^{-1}$ modality. But the gain is not only apparent in such somewhat academic examples. Also in more interesting examples are the benefits clear: This is, e.g., the case for an example conducted using Isabelle/LSIL concerning properties of a simple oscillator. Here various modalities are derived for expressing certain liveness properties. Because of the nice structure of the LND system many parts of the proof can be automated in the style of 1) and 2). Even if a lot of automation is not possible in other parts of the proof it is still intuitively easier to reason as the proofs are closer to informal "pen and paper" reasoning because the intervals in the logic can be visualized as intervals in the style of Fig. 2. (This aspect is further discussed in [15].) The parts which are hard to automate can be identified as concerning an amount of term level reasoning. The same lesson was learned in recent work by Henrik Pilegård on formalizing and proving some simple properties of the Deadline Driven Scheduler (DDS) in Isabelle/LSIL. This work was inspired by an earlier formalization of the DDS in DC where proofs were done by hand [23].

In conclusion, we can say that reasoning on the formula level, where intervals are related, have been greatly improved by using the labelled framework. In "real-life" examples we also have to do parts of the reasoning on the term level. For this, work still has to be done on improving the tools and some directions for this were mentioned in connection with the Gas Burner example of the above section.

Finally, it is important to realize that the results of this paper have implications outside the realm of interval logics as they support the program of Gabbay [4] on using labelled formalisms for non-classical logics.

References

1. D. Bjørner et al. A ProCoS Project Description: ESPRIT BRA 3104. *Bulletin of the EATCS, G. Rozenberg (Ed.)*, (39):60–73, 1989.
2. R.A. Bull and K. Segerberg. Basic Modal Logic. In D.M. Gabbay and F. Guenthner, editors, *Handbook of Philosophical Logic*, volume II, pages 1–88. Reidel, 1984.
3. B. Dutertre. Complete Proof Systems for First Order Interval Temporal Logic. In *LICS'95*, pages 36–43. IEEE, 1995.
4. D.M. Gabbay. *Labelled Deductive Systems*, volume I. Oxford, 1996.
5. J.Y. Halpern, B. Moszkowski, and Z. Manna. A Hardware Semantics based on Temporal Intervals. In *ICALP'83*, volume 154 of *LNCS*, pages 278–291. Springer, 1983.
6. J.Y. Halpern and Y. Shoham. A Propositional Modal Logic of Time Intervals. *Journal of the ACM*, 38(4):935–962, 1991.
7. M.R. Hansen and Zhou Chaochen. Duration Calculus: Logical Foundations. *Formal Aspects of Computing*, 9(3):283–330, 1997.
8. S.T. Heilmann. *Proof Support for Duration Calculus*. PhD thesis, Dept. of Information Technology, Technical University of Denmark, January 1999.
9. H.R. Lewis. A Logic of Concrete Time Intervals. In *LICS'90*, pages 380–389. IEEE, 1990.
10. B. Moszkowski. A Temporal Logic for Multilevel Reasoning about Hardware. *IEEE Computer*, 18(2):10–19, 1985.
11. B. Moszkowski. Compositional Reasoning about Projected and Infinite Time. In *Engineering of Complex Computer Systems*, pages 238–245. IEEE, 1995.
12. L.C. Paulson. *Isabelle, A Generic Theorem Prover*, volume 828 of *LNCS*. Springer, 1994.
13. A. Pnueli. Temporal Logic of Programs. In *LICS'77*, pages 46–57. IEEE, 1977.
14. Y.S. Ramakrishna, P.M. Melliar-Smith, L.E. Moser, L.K. Dillon, and G. Kutty. Interval logics and their decision procedures. Part I: An interval logic. *Theoretical Computer Science*, 166(1–2):1–47, 1996.
15. T.M. Rasmussen. Labelled Natural Deduction for Interval Logics. In *CSL'01*, volume 2142 of *LNCS*, pages 308–323. Springer, 2001.
16. T.M. Rasmussen. Signed Interval Logic. In *CSL'99*, volume 1683 of *LNCS*, pages 157–171. Springer, 1999.
17. T.M. Rasmussen. A Sequent Calculus for Signed Interval Logic. Technical Report IMM-TR-2001-06, IMM, Technical University of Denmark, 2001.
18. J.U. Skakkebæk. *A Verification Assistant for a Real-Time Logic*. PhD thesis, Dept. of Computer Science, Technical University of Denmark, November 1994.
19. J.U. Skakkebæk. Liveness and Fairness in Duration Calculus. In *CONCUR'94*, volume 836 of *LNCS*, pages 283–298. Springer, 1994.
20. A. Tarski. On the Calculus of Relations. *Journal of Symbolic Logic*, 6(3):73–89, 1941.
21. Y. Venema. A Modal Logic for Chopping Intervals. *Journal of Logic and Computation*, 1(4):453–476, 1991.
22. L. Viganò. *Labelled Non-Classical Logics*. Kluwer, 2000.
23. Zheng Yuhua and Zhou Chaochen. A Formal Proof of the Deadline Driven Scheduler. In *FTRTFT'94*, volume 863 of *LNCS*, pages 756–775. Springer, 1994.
24. Zhou Chaochen and M.R. Hansen. An Adequate First Order Interval Logic. In *COMPOS'97*, volume 1536 of *LNCS*, pages 584–608. Springer, 1998.
25. Zhou Chaochen, C.A.R. Hoare, and A.P. Ravn. A Calculus of Durations. *Information Processing Letters*, 40(5):269–276, 1991.

The Functions Provable by First Order Abstraction

Daniel Leivant*

Computer Science Department
Indiana University
Bloomington, IN 47405.
leivant@cs.indiana.edu

Abstract. Function provability in higher-order logic is a versatile and powerful framework for conceptual classification as well as verification and derivation of declarative programs. Here we show that the functions provable in second-order logic with first-order set-abstraction are precisely the elementary functions. This holds regardless of whether the logic is classical, intuitionistic, or minimal.
The notion of provability here is not purely logical, as it incorporates a trivial theory of data, with axioms stating that each data object has a detectable main constructor which can be destructed. We show that this is necessary, by proving that without such rudimentary axioms the provable functions are merely the functions broadly-represented in the simply typed lambda calculus, a collection that does not even include integer subtraction.

1 Introduction

Proof Theory provides a classification of computable functions by the strength of formal theories used in proving their convergence for all input. For instance, Gödel showed that the provably total functions of first-order (Peano) arithmetic are precisely the functions definable by primitive recursion in finite types [10], and Parsons showed that if induction is restricted to Σ_1^0-formulas[1] then exactly the primitive recursive functions are probably recursive [24]. Sam Buss continued this line of research, and showed how further restrictions lead to formalisms whose provably total functions are exactly major computational complexity classes, such as poly-time and poly-space [6]. These results are of proof theoretic rather than computational interest, because the formalisms considered incorporate explicit restrictions on resources, akin to Cobham's characterization of poly-time in terms of initial functions that capture poly-time size growth plus a non-size-increasing recursion schema [7].

* Research supported by NSF grant CS-0105651

[1] These are just the existential formulas if the formalism admits defining equations for all elementary functions; for Peano's Arithmetic one must discount the use of bounded quantifiers.

R. Nieuwenhuis and A. Voronkov (Eds.): LPAR 2001, LNAI 2250, pp. 330–346, 2001.

One would wish to develop proof theoretic methodologies that capture complexity classes by limiting conceptual abstraction rather than resources. One such line of research has explored first-order theories whose provably-total functions form certain complexity classes [19,3,22]. The main ingredient there is a calibration of induction, not in terms of bounding size of values, but in terms of formula complexity, data ramification, and control and information flow in the proofs.

An alternative paradigm, set forth in [16], is based on the second-order definability of inductive data types, such as the natural numbers and strings over a finite alphabet. For instance, if $N[x]$ is the formula that states that every set containing zero and closed under the successor function **s** contains x, then N defines, in every structure, the set of numeral-denotations. Consequently, second-order theories of data, such as second order Peano Arithmetic, are easily interpretable in pure second-order logic [26]. Moreover, the canonical proof system for second-order logic, summarized in Table 1, although not semantically complete, has the same proof theoretic power as second-order arithmetic.

Since second-order logic is far more powerful than first-order arithmetic, one might expect that it is a less propitious setting than first-order theories for characterizing feasible complexity classes and reasoning about them. In fact, the opposite is the case. The key parameter for calibrating the power of second-order logics is the scope of permissible set-definitions, often referred to as the *Comprehension Principle* or *Set-existence* Principle, and expressed by the following axiom schema.

$$\exists R\, \forall x_1 \ldots x_k\; R(\boldsymbol{x}) \leftrightarrow \psi$$

Here $k \geqslant 0$, R is a k-ary relational variable, and φ is a formula in which R does not occur free:[2] In natural deduction formalisms the Comprehension Principle can be conveyed instead by the rule for second-order $\forall$-elimination (or $\forall$R for sequential formalisms):[3]

$$\frac{\forall R\, \varphi[R]}{\varphi[\lambda \boldsymbol{x} \psi]}$$

We can now consider variants of second-order logic where the Comprehension Principle is restricted to formulas ψ of certain form. For example, restricting set-existence to first-order formulas ψ conveys the conviction that only sets defined by first-order properties are sufficiently well-formed to allow quantification over them.[4] This is a particularly natural restriction, because allowing ψ itself to contain a relational quantifier is conceptually circular: the admitted relations ψ are then defined in terms of quantification over all admitted relations.

It would seem natural to conjecture that restricting Comprehension to first-order formulas yields a formalism closely related to first-order arithmetic. Not

[2] ψ may refer to variables other than $x_1 \ldots x_k$, and need not refer to of the latter.

[3] Here $\varphi[\lambda \boldsymbol{x} \psi]$ stands for the result of replacing every subformula $R(\mathbf{t}_1 \ldots \mathbf{t}_k)$ of φ by $\{\mathbf{t}/\boldsymbol{x}\}\varphi$, i.e. the result of simultaneously substituting in φ the terms $\mathbf{t}_1 \ldots \mathbf{t}_k$ for the variables $x_1 \ldots x_k$, respectively.

[4] In model theoretic terms this corresponds to Henkin models that are closed under first-order definability; see e.g. [17] for an exposition.

Table 1. Second-order natural deduction: core formalism $\mathbf{L}_2$

$$\frac{\varphi_0 \quad \varphi_1}{\varphi_0 \wedge \varphi_1} \qquad \frac{\varphi_0 \wedge \varphi_1}{\varphi_i}$$

$$\frac{\begin{array}{c}[\ell]\,\varphi\\ \cdots\\ \varphi\end{array}}{\varphi \to \psi}\,\ell \qquad \frac{\varphi \to \psi \quad \varphi}{\psi}$$

ℓ a reserved label

$$\frac{\varphi[z]}{\forall x\, \varphi[x]} \qquad \frac{\forall x\, \varphi[x]}{\varphi[\mathbf{t}]}$$

no z in open assumptions

$$\frac{\varphi[Q]}{\forall R\, \varphi[R]} \qquad \frac{\forall R\, \varphi[R]}{\varphi[\lambda \boldsymbol{x} \psi]}$$

no Q in open assumptions

$\mathbf{L}_2(\mathcal{C})$ is $\mathbf{L}_2$ with $\psi \in \mathcal{C}$ in relational $\forall$-elimination.
The intuitionistic variant $\mathbf{L}_2^I$ of $\mathbf{L}_2$ has the additional inference rule

$$\frac{\bot}{\varphi}$$

The classical variant $\mathbf{L}_2^C$ of $\mathbf{L}_2$ has the additional inference rule

$$\frac{\begin{array}{c}[\ell]\,\varphi \to \bot\\ \cdots\\ \bot\end{array}}{\varphi}\,\ell$$

so. The interpretation of second-order arithmetic in second-order logic is possible because induction over $\mathbb{N}$ is provable: if $N[x]$ is the definition above of $\mathbb{N}$, then from $N[x]$ one obtains, by Comprehension, particular instances for its set quantifier, namely: that if ψ is a property that holds for $\mathbf{0}$ and is closed under successor, then ψ holds for x. In addition, the interpretation relies on a relativization of first-order quantifiers to the formula N. Thus, to obtain induction for a first-order formula ψ_0 of first-order arithmetic, we would need Comprehension for the formula ψ obtained by relativizing all quantifiers in ψ_0 to N. But since N is not first-order, neither is ψ ! Indeed, the Set Existence principle that corresponds to first-order arithmetic is analyzed in [15,21], and is far stronger than Set Existence for first-order formulas.

What is, then, the computational complexity corresponding to first-order set existence? We show in this paper that it is precisely the Kalmar elementary functions, i.e. the functions computable in resources (time and space) of order $E_k(n)$, where $E_0(x) =_{\text{df}} x$, and $E_{k+1}(x) =_{\text{df}} 2^{E_k(x)}$. Setting aside for the moment the exact formulation of this correspondence, this result is not altogether unexpected. In a certain precise sense, second-order logic with first-order set existence is an expressive variant of first-order logic. However, the combinatorics of first-order derivations is fundamentally the same as that of propositional logic [28], and normalization for order-bounded fragments of propositional logic is elementary.

Our proof that every function provable using first-order set existence is elementary indeed follows the outline above. More delicate is the proof of the converse. In the first place, one needs to craft a notion of function provability within second-order logic which is appropriate for weak set existence principles. A methodology for reasoning about computations in higher order logics is laid out in [16]. Rather than using syntax coding, as in traditional reasoning about computation within Peano Arithmetic and similar first-order theories (see e.g. [12,13]), it integrates programs into the logical formalism. However, this approach has to be refined when set existence is restricted all the way to first-order formulas, because certain basic properties of data that are trivially provable using slightly stronger set existence, are no longer available at this level. Indeed, we shall show (Theorem 9) that too simple a notion of function provability does not even yield a reasonable computational complexity class.

In recent years a number of approaches have established machine independent characterizations of the class of elementary functions (see e.g. [11,1,18,8,22]). However, the interest of the present results lies in their being a component of a broad and promising methodology, more than in merely offering yet another link between logic and the Kalmar-elementary functions. Set-existence principles in analysis have been known for almost two decades to provide a methodology for classifying the proof theoretic strength of various theorems of mathematical analysis; this is the Reverse Mathematics project that has been initiated and developed primarily by Harvey Friedman and Stephen Simpson [27]. However, in that project the *basic* theory is primitive recursive arithmetic, thus divorcing the it from connections to computational complexity and feasible mathematics. In contradistinction, our focus on set-existence principles in second-order *logic* offers new vistas while preserving the old ones. By the interpretation of second-order arithmetic in second-order logic (see e.g. [26]), sufficiently powerful set-existence span all the proof theoretic power of second-order arithmetic. However, we are in a position to consider very weak comprehension principles, which correspond to feasible complexity classes, as shown in [16].

More importantly perhaps, the formalisms presented here are promising as a conceptually transparent and practically flexible formalization of Kalmar-elementary mathematics. The method is generic to all inductive data types[5], it is axiomatically lean and unobtrusive, and it incorporates equational computing directly and seamlessly. Moreover, the relation to Kalmar-elementary resources is transparent: one can develop virtually all Mathematical Analysis in second-order logic, and proceed to identify the Kalmar-elementary portions as an afterthought, by inspecting the formulas for which set-existence is used.

[5] Indeed, it is generic for the broader notion of inductive data-system, see [20].

2 Provable Programs of Higher-Order Logics

2.1 Second-Order Delineation of Data

We refer to symbolic data in the guise of inductively generated word algebras. We focus on the most fundamental form of symbolic data, the set $\mathbb{W} =_{\text{df}} \{a, b\}^*$ of words over a two letter alphabet. Our treatment can be extended trivially to other inductive data types and data-systems (see [20]). We identify $\mathbb{W}$ with the algebra generated from three constructors, the 0-ary ε (the empty string) and unary **a** and **b**, so e.g. aab is identified with **aab**ε. We write V_0 for the vocabulary consisting of these three constructors. We dub the closed V_0-terms the *base-terms.*

Consider second-order logic, obtained by augmenting the syntax of first-order formulas with variables ranging over relations, and quantification over such variables. It is well-known that inductively generated algebras are second-order definable. For instance, the natural numbers are second-order definable in the sense that in every structure the elements satisfying the following predicate N are precisely the denotations of the numerals $\mathbf{0}, \mathbf{s}(\mathbf{0})....$

$$N[x] \quad \equiv_{\text{df}} \quad \forall Q \; (\; \text{Cl}_N[Q] \; \rightarrow \; Q(x) \;).$$

where

$$\text{Cl}_N[Q] \quad \equiv_{\text{df}} \quad Q(\mathbf{0}) \wedge \forall u(Q(u) \rightarrow Q(\mathbf{s}(u))).$$

Similarly, in every structure for a vocabulary containing V_0 the elements satisfying the following formulas $W[x]$ are precisely the denotations of the base terms:

$$W[x] \quad \equiv_{\text{df}} \; \forall Q \; (\; \text{Cl}_W[Q] \; \rightarrow \; Q(x) \;),$$

where

$$\text{Cl}_W[Q] \; \equiv_{\text{df}} \quad Q(\varepsilon) \wedge \forall u(Q(u) \rightarrow Q(\mathbf{a}(u))) \wedge \forall u(Q(u) \rightarrow Q(\mathbf{b}(u))).$$

2.2 Equational Programs

As in earlier works, we consider a functional/equational computation model, in the style of Herbrand-Gödel, familiar from the extensive literature on algebraic semantics of programs. This rudimentary model is particularly suited for integration into logic, since its syntax is contained in the syntax of equational logic.

We posit a stock of fresh function identifiers dubbed the *program-functions.* Each program-function is assigned some arity $\geqslant 0$.[6] Consider *terms* generated by

[6] Insisting on positive arities makes no difference, because each constant **c** can be simulated by **f**(**c**) for a fresh function identifier **f** and a 0-ary constructor **c**.

arity-correct application from the constructors, free variables, and the function-identifiers.[7] A *program-body* over $\mathbb{W}$ is a finite set of equations between terms. A *program* is a pair $(P, \mathbf{f})$ of a program-body P and a program-function $\mathbf{f}$, called the program's *principal identifier*. We refer to P itself as the program, where in no danger of confusion. We write V_P for the vocabulary of P, i.e. the set consisting of the constructors and the program-functions of P.

Given a program P, we write $P \vdash^{=} E$ if E is a V_P-equation derivable from P in equational logic. That is,[8]

1. $P \vdash^{=} E$ for every $E \in P$;
2. $P \vdash^{=} t{=}t$ for every V_P-term t;
3. If $P \vdash^{=} E$ then $P \vdash^{=} \{t/u\}E$ for every V_P-term t and variable u;
4. If $P \vdash^{=} \{\mathbf{t}/u\}E$ and $P \vdash^{=} \mathbf{t}{=}\mathbf{t}'$, then $P \vdash^{=} \{\mathbf{t}'/u\}E$.

We say that P is *coherent* if $P \not\vdash^{=} \mathbf{t}{=}'$ for distinct base-terms $\mathbf{t}, \mathbf{t}' \in \mathbb{W}$.

Each program-function $\mathbf{g}$ of arity r induces on $\mathbb{W}$ the relation

$$\mathbf{g}^P =_{\text{df}} \{(w_1 \dots w_r, v) \in \mathbb{W}^{r+1} \mid P \vdash^{=} \mathbf{g}(w_1 \dots w_r){=}v\}.$$

If P is coherent, then each $\mathbf{g}^P$ is univalent, i.e. (the graph of) a partial function. The function *computed* by $(P, \mathbf{f})$ is then the partial function $\mathbf{f}^P$ over $\mathbb{W}$. For examples of programs see [20].

2.3 Simulating Turing Machines

Let M be a deterministic TM over the alphabet $\{0,1\}$, with states $q_1 \dots q_m$. Assume, w.l.o.g., that M never writes a blank nor moves the head past the first blank. Then each tape-configuration of M can be represented by two words in $\{0,1\}$: the configuration's *left-word* representing the portion of tape preceding the reading head, and the *right-word*, representing the non-blank portion of the tape from the head and on (using ε in case the head reads the first blank). If we code each state s_i by some word $\#q_i = \{a,b\}^*$, then a configuration of M with state s is represented by $\#q$, the left-word, and the right-word.

Let S, L and R be the binary functions over $\mathbb{W}$ defined by

$$\left.\begin{array}{l} S(w,t) = \text{the code of the state of } M \\ L(w,t) = \text{the left-word} \\ R(w,t) = \text{the right-word} \end{array}\right\} \text{after } |t| \text{ steps of } M\text{'s run on input } w.$$

LEMMA 1 *Let M, S, L, R be as above. There is a coherent program $(P, \mathbf{R})$ that computes the function R associated with M.*

[7] An alternative approach is to have each variable assigned a sort and each program-function a first-order type over the sorts, and to require that terms be correctly sorted. The two approach are identical in the case of a single sort, and they differ in inessential ways for the general case. The present approach is more in keeping with a semantic, "Curry-style," type system.

[8] We write $\{t/x\}$ for the operation of substituting t for x in the argument.

Proof. P contains the defining equations for the destructor and case functions, as well as the following equations for the program-functions **S**, **L** and **R**, that convey the operational semantics of the functions S, L and R, respectively. $S(w,\varepsilon)$ is defined as the code of the initial state, $L(w,\varepsilon) = \varepsilon$, and $R(w,\varepsilon) = w$. The values of $S(w,\mathbf{c}t)$, $L(w,\mathbf{c}t)$, and $R(w,\mathbf{c}t)$ (where $\mathbf{c} = \mathbf{a}, \mathbf{b}$) are defined in terms of $S(w,t)$, $L(w,t)$, and $R(w,t)$ according to the transition rules of M, using the constructors and the destructor and case functions.

To see that P is coherent, consider the structure $\mathcal{W}$ for the vocabulary V_P, obtained by expanding the free algebra $\mathbb{W}$ with the intended interpretations of the destructor and case functions, and the interpretation of **S**, **L** and **R** as S, L and R. Since M is a deterministic TM, these interpretations are functions, and so $\mathcal{W}$ is a model of P. Since every equation derivable from P is true in $\mathcal{W}$, no equation between distinct base-terms can be derived from P. ⊣

2.4 Models for Programs

We model equational programs in the vein of universal algebra and the algebraic semantics of programs (see e.g. [23,30,25]). The main concepts go back to Birkhoff's classical development of equational theories and quotient relations over free algebras [4].

Given a program P over $\mathbb{W}$, let us write P also for the conjunction of the universal closures of all equations in P. There is no danger of ambiguity, since this convention will apply uniformly to occurrences of P as a logical formula. Our canonical model of P, denoted $\mathcal{M}(P)$, has as universe the quotient algebra $\mathbb{W}/(\approx_P)$, where $\mathbb{W}(P)$ is the free algebra generated from the constructors and $\mathbf{t} \approx_P \mathbf{t}'$ iff $P \vdash^{=} \mathbf{t}{=}\mathbf{t}'$. Since $\approx_P$ is an equivalence relation (indeed a congruence relation), we write $[\mathbf{t}]_\approx$ (or simply $[\mathbf{t}]$) for the equivalence class of a term $\mathbf{t}$. The identifiers of V_P are interpreted in $\mathcal{M}(P)$ in the obvious way; e.g. if $\mathbf{f}$ is unary then $[\![\mathbf{f}]\!][\mathbf{t}] = [\mathbf{ft}]$. In particular, for $n \in \mathbb{N}$ we have $[\![\bar{n}]\!] = [\bar{n}]_\approx$, as can be seen by induction on n.

If σ is a substitution of closed V_P-terms for variables,[9] then we write $[\sigma]$ for the environment over $\mathcal{M}(P)$ defined by $[\sigma]x = [\sigma x]_\approx$.[10] By induction on terms, we can verify that $[\sigma]t = [\sigma t]_\approx$, for all V_P-terms t.

LEMMA 2 *For every program P, $\mathcal{M}(P) \models P$, that is, all equations in P are valid in the structure $\mathcal{M}(P)$.*[11] ⊣

2.5 A Logical Rendition of Program Convergence

For an r-ary function identifier $\mathbf{f}$ let

$$Tot(\mathbf{f}) \;\equiv_{\mathrm{df}}\; \forall x_1 \ldots x_r.\, (\, W[x_1] \wedge \cdots \wedge W[x_r] \;\rightarrow\; W[\mathbf{f}(\boldsymbol{x})]\,)$$

[9] I.e. there is a finite set X of variables such that σx is a closed term for $x \in X$, $\sigma x = x$ otherwise.

[10] As usual, an *environment* is a mapping from the formal variables to structure elements.

[11] For a proof see [20].

PROPOSITION **3** *Let* $(P, \mathbf{f})$ *be a coherent program, computing a partial function* f *over* $\mathbb{W}$*. The following conditions are equivalent:*

1. f *is total.*
2. *Tot*($\mathbf{f}$) *is true in every model of* P*.*
3. *Tot*($\mathbf{f}$) *is true in the canonical model* $\mathcal{M}(P)$*.*

Proof. Without loss of generality, let f be unary.

(1) $\Rightarrow$ (2): Suppose $\mathcal{W}$ is a model of P, and assume $W[a]$ where a is an element of $\mathcal{W}$. Then a is a denotation of a base-term $\mathbf{t}$. Since f is total, there is a complete P-computation terminating with $\mathbf{f}(\mathbf{t})\mathbf{=}\mathbf{t}'$ for some base-term $\mathbf{t}'$. Since $\mathcal{W}$ is a model of P, and all computation steps are valid inferences from P (in equational logic), we obtain $\mathcal{W} \models \mathbf{f}(\mathbf{t})\mathbf{=}\mathbf{t}'$. On the other hand, since $\mathbf{t}'$ is a base-term, $\mathcal{W} \models W[\mathbf{t}']$. Put together, we obtain $\mathcal{W} \models A[\mathbf{f}(\mathbf{t})]$, i.e. Thus $\mathcal{W} \models Tot(\mathbf{f}_i)$.

Clearly (2) implies (3), since $\mathcal{M}(P)$ is a model of P.

Finally, to see that (3) implies (1) suppose that $\mathcal{M}(P) \models Tot(\mathbf{f})$. Then, for every base-term $\mathbf{t}$ there is a base-term $\mathbf{t}'$ for which $\mathcal{M}(P) \models \mathbf{f}(\mathbf{t})\mathbf{=}\mathbf{t}'$. By the definition of $\mathcal{M}(P)$, this means that the equation $\mathbf{f}(\mathbf{t})\mathbf{=}\mathbf{t}'$ is derived from P. Thus $\mathbf{f}^P$ is total. ⊣

2.6 Function Pure-Provability

Proposition 3 motivates the following definition.

DEFINITION **4** *Let* $\mathbf{T}$ *be a higher-order deductive system over a vocabulary containing the vocabulary* V_P *of* P*. We say that a coherent program* $(P, \mathbf{f})$ *is* purely provable *in* $\mathbf{T}$ *if* $Tot[\mathbf{f}]$ *is derivable in* $\mathbf{T}$ *from* P*. In that case we also say that the function* f *computed is* purely provable.

The deductive systems considered here can be purely logical, e.g. the natural deduction formalism laid out in Table 1 above.

The following proposition illustrates the concept of function provability in second-order logic.

PROPOSITION **5** *All primitive recursive functions (over* $\mathbb{N}$*) are purely provable in second-order logic.*

Proof. The initial functions are purely-provable trivially, and the purely-provable functions are obviously closed under composition. To see that the purely-provable functions are also closed under primitive recursion, let f be defined by

$$f(\mathbf{0}, \boldsymbol{x}) = g_0(\boldsymbol{x})$$
$$f(\mathbf{s}n, \boldsymbol{x}) = g_s(f(n, \boldsymbol{x}), n, \boldsymbol{x})$$

where g_0 and g_s are provable. Reasoning within second-order logic, assume that n and $\boldsymbol{x}$ satisfy $\mathbf{N}$. From $\mathbf{N}[n] \equiv \forall Q \ \mathrm{Cl}_N[Q] \rightarrow Q(n)$ we conclude, by instantiating Q to the unary relation $\psi[y] \ \equiv_{\mathrm{df}} \ \mathbf{N}[f(y, \boldsymbol{x})] \wedge \mathbf{N}[y]$,

$$\mathrm{Cl}_N[\psi] \rightarrow \psi[n].$$

Given that $\boldsymbol{x}$ satisfy $\mathbf{N}$, and that g_0 and g_s are purely-provable, it is easy to conclude $\mathrm{Cl}_N[\psi]$, and so $\psi[n]$, which concludes the proof. ⊣

In fact, we have the following result, which is implicit already in [9].

THEOREM **6** *The functions purely-provable in second-order logic are precisely the provably recursive functions of second-order arithmetic.*

More generally, for each $k \geqslant 2$, the functions purely-provable in k-order logic are precisely the provably recursive functions of k-order arithmetic. ⊣

The proof of Theorem 6 is based on an interpretation of k-order arithmetic in k-order logic. The crucial aspect of that interpretation is the relativization of quantifiers to the predicate N above. The schema of Induction,

$$\mathrm{Cl}_N[\lambda x \varphi] \rightarrow \forall x \ N[x] \rightarrow \varphi$$

is then provable, by instantiating the relational quantifier in N to $\lambda x.\varphi$. As mentioned in the Introduction above, this translation maps formulas of first-order arithmetic to formulas in which quantifiers are relativized to N, i.e. to second-order formulas. Indeed, $\mathbf{L}_2(FO)$, where FO is the class of first-order formulas, in already much weaker than first-order arithmetic.

We thus have a methodology for correlating complexity classes with natural proof formalism, without explicit use of resource bounds. As the class $\mathcal{C}$ of formulas is shrinking, the functions provable in $\mathbf{L}_2(\mathcal{C})$ are computationally more manageable, leading to a spectrum of purely logical proof theoretic characterizations of major complexity classes. Indeed, we showed in [16] that $\mathbf{L}_2(Pos)$, where Pos is the class of positive formulas, i.e. without implication or negation, is closely related to poly-time. More precisely, for a notion of function provability different from the ones used here, the "provable"-functions of $\mathbf{L}_2(Pos)$ are precisely the poly-time functions. The notion of function provability we develop here is far preferable to that of [16]. We shall prove elsewhere that the functions provable in $\mathbf{L}_2(Pos)$, according to our new definition, are also precisely the functions in poly-time.

3 The Purely-Provable Functions of First-Order Set Existence

3.1 Some Examples of Purely-Provable Functions

It is of interest to note from the outset that the proof of Proposition 5 uses set existence for a second-order formula, so it does not establish the pure-provability in $\mathbf{L}_2(FO)$ of all primitive recursive functions (which indeed does not hold). However, we can easily show the pure-provability in $\mathbf{L}_2(FO)$ of some basic numeric functions, such as addition, multiplication, and exponentiation. Our programs for addition and multiplication are simply the defining equations for these functions:

$$\begin{array}{ll} +(x)(\mathbf{0}) = x & *(x)(\mathbf{0}) = \mathbf{0} \\ +(x)(\mathbf{s}y) = \mathbf{s}(+(x)(y)) & *(x)(\mathbf{s}y) = +(*(x)(y))(x) \end{array}$$

A program for an exponential-growth function that lends itself to a short proof is $\mathbf{e}(0, y) = \mathbf{s}y$, $\mathbf{e}(\mathbf{s}x, y) = \mathbf{e}(x, \mathbf{e}(x, y))$. This defines the function $e(x, y) = 2^x + y$.

To prove the addition function in $\mathbf{L}_2(FO)$ assume $N[x]$ and $N[y]$. Towards proving $N[+(x)(y)]$ assume $\mathrm{Cl}_N[Q]$. By $N[x]$, the latter implies $Q(x)$. Instantiating the universal set quantifier of $N[y]$ to the (first-order!) predicate $\psi_+[z] \equiv_{\mathrm{df}} \lambda z.Q(+(x)(z))$ we have $\mathrm{Cl}_N[\psi_+] \to \psi_+[y]$. From $Q(x)$ and the program for $+$ we obtain $\psi_+[\mathbf{0}]$. From the program and $\mathrm{Cl}_N(Q)$, and using equational rules, we obtain $\psi_+[z] \to \psi_+[\mathbf{s}(z)]$. Thus we conclude $\mathrm{Cl}_N[\psi_+]$, and so $\psi_+[y]$. We have shown $\mathrm{Cl}_N[Q] \to Q(+(x)(y))$ for arbitrary Q, i.e. $N[+(x)(y)]$ has been proved from $N[x]$ and $N[y]$.

To prove the multiplication function in $\mathbf{L}_2(FO)$ assume $N[x]$ and $N[y]$. Towards proving $N[*(x)(y)]$ assume $\mathrm{Cl}_N[Q]$. Instantiating the universal set quantifier of $N[y]$ to the (first-order!) predicate $\psi_*[z] \equiv_{\mathrm{df}} \lambda z.Q(*(x)(z))$ we obtain $\mathrm{Cl}_N[\psi_*] \to \psi_*[y]$. From $Q(\mathbf{0})$ and the program for $*$ we get $\psi[\mathbf{0}]$. Now, towards proving $\psi_*[z] \to \psi_*[\mathbf{s}z]$ assume $Q(*(x)(z))$. Since $N[x]$ is given we obtain from this, as in the proof above for addition, that $Q(+(*(x)(z))(x))$, which by an equational rule and the program implies $Q(*(x)(s\mathbf{s}z))$, i.e. $\psi_*[\mathbf{s}z]$. We thus conclude $\mathrm{Cl}_N[\psi_*]$, and so $\psi_*[y]$. We have proved $\mathrm{Cl}_N[Q] \to Q(*(x)(y))$ for an arbitrary Q, given $N[x]$ and $N[y]$.

Finally, to prove the function e in $\mathbf{L}_2(FO)$ assume $N[x]$ and $N[y]$. Towards proving $N[e(x)(y)]$ assume $\mathrm{Cl}_N[Q]$. Instantiating the universal set quantifier of $N[x]$ to the predicate $\psi_e[z] \equiv_{\mathrm{df}} \lambda z. (\forall u. Q(u) \to Q(\mathbf{e}(z)(u)))$ we obtain $\mathrm{Cl}_N[\psi_e] \to \psi_e[y]$. Since Q is closed under successor, and $\mathbf{e}(\mathbf{0})(u) = \mathbf{s}u$, we have $\psi_e[\mathbf{0}]$. Towards proving $\psi_e[z] \to \psi_e[\mathbf{s}z]$ assume $\psi_e[z]$, i.e. $\forall u. Q(u) \to Q(\mathbf{e}(z)(u))$. Towards proving $\psi_e[\mathbf{s}z]$ assume $Q(v)$. From this we get $Q(\mathbf{e}(z)(v))$. Using $\psi_e[z]$ again, this time with u instantiated to $\mathbf{e}(z)(v)$, yields $Q(\mathbf{e}(z)(\mathbf{e}(z)(v))$. By the program and equational rules we get from the latter $Q(\mathbf{e}(\mathbf{s}z)(v))$. We have thus proved $\forall v. Q(v) \to Q(\mathbf{e}(z)(v))$, and so $\mathrm{Cl}_N[\psi_e]$. Therefore $\psi_e[x]$. Instantiating u in the latter to y yields $Q(y) \to Q(\mathbf{e}(x)(y)))$. But we have $N[y]$ and $\mathrm{Cl}_N[Q]$, from which we get $Q(y)$. Thus we proved $Q(\mathbf{e}(x)(y)))$ from $\mathrm{Cl}_N[Q]$, for an arbitrary Q. Hence $N[\mathbf{e}(x)(y))]$ has been proved from the assumptions $N[x]$ and $N[y]$.

Since the purely-provable functions are trivially closed under composition, the pure-provability of the function e immediately yields

LEMMA 7 *Every elementary function is majorized by a function purely-provable in $\mathbf{L}_2(FO)$.*

3.2 Classical vs. Constructive Function Provability

It is well-known that the functions provably recursive in classical theories, such as first and second-order arithmetic, are already provable in their intuitionistic counterparts. Analogous results hold for function provability and pure-provability.

THEOREM 8 *Let $\mathcal{C}$ be a class of first-order formulas, with the following closure property: if φ' arises from $\varphi \in \mathcal{C}$ by double-negating all atomic, disjunctive, and existential subformulas, then $\varphi' \in \mathcal{C}$. If $(P, \mathbf{f})$ is a program purely-provable in the classical variant $\mathbf{L}_2^C(\mathcal{C})$ (see Table 1), then it is purely-provable in $\mathbf{L}_2(\mathcal{C})$.*

Proof sketch. Suppose $P, \vdash W[x] \to W[\mathbf{f}(x)]$ in $\mathbf{L}_2^C(\mathcal{C})$. By standard proof theoretic analysis, there is a classical deduction of $\mathrm{Cl}_W[R] \to R(\mathbf{f}(x))$ from P and formulas $\mathrm{Cl}_W[\varphi_i] \to \varphi_i[x]$, where φ_i are in $\mathcal{C}$. By standard translations (see e.g. SchwichTroel sec 2.3), there is a deduction in minimal first-order logic of $\mathrm{Cl}_W[\neg\neg R] \to \neg\neg R(\mathbf{f}(x))$ from P and $\mathrm{Cl}_W[\varphi_i'] \to \varphi_i'[x]$.

But $\mathrm{Cl}_W[R]$ implies, in minimal first-order logic, $\mathrm{Cl}_W[\neg\neg R]$, and $\varphi_i' \in \mathcal{C}$ by assumption; so $\neg\neg R(\mathbf{f}(x))$, i.e. $(R(\mathbf{f}(x)) \to \bot) \to \bot$, is derived from $P, W[x]$ and $\mathrm{Cl}_W[R]$ in $\mathbf{L}_2(\mathcal{C})$. Since there is no rule for $\bot$ in $\mathbf{L}_2$, it can be replaced in the proof by $R(\mathbf{f}(x))$, yielding a proof of $\mathrm{Cl}_W[R] \to R(\mathbf{f}(x))$ from P and $W[x]$. Universally closing with respect to R, we obtain the provability of $(P, \mathbf{f})$ in $\mathbf{L}_2(\mathcal{C})$. ⊣

3.3 Pure-Provability and λ-Representability

We write **1λ** for the (Church-style) simply typed lambda calculus, based on abstraction and application only. The types here are generated from a base type o by the arrow construction $\to$. We omit some parentheses by associating arrow to the right, and write $\tau_1, \ldots, \tau_r \to \sigma$ for $\tau_1 \to \cdots \to \tau_r \to \sigma$. Each variable comes with an assigned type. Terms are formed using λ-abstraction and application. We optionally superscript terms to indicate their type. Thus we have $(\lambda x^\sigma . E^\tau)^{\sigma \to \tau}$, and $(E^{\sigma \to \tau} F^\sigma)^\tau$. We write $=_\beta$ for term β-equality.

Base terms of $\mathbb{N}$ and $\mathbb{W}$ can be usefully represented in **1λ** by abstracting with respect to the constructors. E.g. the numeral for 2, **ss0**, is represented by $\lambda s^{o \to o} z . ssz$, i.e. the Church numeral for 2. We denote the Church-numeral for $n \in \mathbb{N}$ by $n^{[o]}$. The type of the Church-numerals is thus $\nu \equiv \nu[o] =_{\mathrm{df}} (o \to o) \to o \to o$.

The λ-representation of $\mathbb{W}$ is similar: the word $w = \mathbf{abb}\varepsilon$ is represented by $\lambda ao \to ob_1^{o \to o} e^o . abbe$, for which we write $w^{[o]}$ (this construction is due to [5]). That is, $w^{[o]}$ is obtained from w by treating the identifiers $\mathbf{a}, \mathbf{b}$ and $\mathbf{e}$ as variables of the corresponding types, and then λ-abstracting with respect to these variables. The type of these word-terms is thus $\omega \equiv \omega[o] =_{\mathrm{df}} (o \to o) \to (o \to o) \to o \to o$.

The constructions above can be restated using any given type τ in place of the base type o. We obtain then a λ-representations $n^{[\tau]}$ for $n \in \mathbb{N}$, of type $\nu[\omega]$, and a λ-representation $w^{[\tau]}$ for $w \in \mathbb{W}$, of type $\omega[\tau]$.

A λ-term $F^{\nu \to \nu}$ is said to *Church-represent* a function $f : \mathbb{N} \to \mathbb{N}$ if for all $n \in \mathbb{N}$, $Fn^{[o]} =_{\beta} (fn)^{[o]}$. We then say that f is representable in $\mathbf{1\lambda}$. The definition of Church-representability is similar for functions of higher arity, and for functions over $\mathbb{W}$.

Let $\tau_1 \ldots \tau_r$ be types, and let $\nu_i =_{\mathrm{df}} \nu[\tau_i]$. A λ-term $F^{\nu_1 \ldots \nu_r \to \nu}$ is said to *broadly-represent* a function $f : \mathbb{N}^r \to \mathbb{N}$ if

$$Fn_1^{[\nu_1]} \cdots n_r^{[\nu_r]} =_{\beta} (fn_1 \cdots n_r)^{[\nu]}$$

(Relaxing the definition to allow the output to have type $\nu[\sigma]$ for some σ other than o makes no difference.) We say that a function $g : \mathbb{N}^r \to \mathbb{N}$ is *broadly-represented* in $\mathbf{1\lambda}$ if it is definable by diagonalization (i.e. identifying inputs) from a broadly-representable function. The definition for functions over $\mathbb{W}$ is similar.

By [29] we know that the predecessor function is not Church-representable in $\mathbf{1\lambda}$, from which it follows that subtraction is not broadly-representable.

THEOREM **9** *If a function over* $\mathbb{W}$ *is purely-provable in* $\mathbf{L}_2(FO)$ *then it is broadly-representable in the simply typed* λ*-calculus* $\mathbf{1\lambda}$.

Note that, by Lemma 8, it does not matter whether $\mathbf{L}_2(FO)$ is based on classical, intuitionistic, or minimal logic.

Proof Outline. By a deduction-normalization argument it follows that if a program $(P, \mathbf{f})$ is purely-provable in $\mathbf{L}_2(FO)$, with $\mathbf{f}$ unary say, then $Q(\mathbf{f}(x))$ is provable in first-order logic from $\mathrm{Cl}[Q]$ and formulas of the form $\mathrm{Cl}[\varphi_i] \to \varphi_i[x]$, where φ_i are all first-order. This first-order proof maps, under the Curry-Howard morphism defined in [20] (which disregards quantifiers and equality), to a term of $\mathbf{1\lambda}$ that broadly-represents the function computed by P. ⊣

In fact, we also have the converse:[12]

THEOREM **10** *All functions broadly-represented in* $\mathbf{1\lambda}$ *are purely-provable in* $\mathbf{L}_2(FO)$.

Proof Outline. We generalize the notion of function representation to functionals of all types, with, in addition, a distinction between weak representation of data (over type o) and a spectrum of strong representations (over types such as $\nu[\tau]$ and $\omega[\tau]$). This construction is best captured by a notion of tiered functions, as defined in [14].[13] One proves then that the tiered functionals represented in $\mathbf{1\lambda}$

[12] We take the liberty of giving a greatly condensed proof-outline here, since this observation and proof, albeit of independent interest, have no bearing on our main results.

[13] Tiered functions underly the characterization of poly-time in [16] and the elementary functions in [18]. A variant was used by Bellantoni and Cook to also characterize poly-time [2].

are precisely the functionals defined by tiered parametrized-iteration in higher type.[14]

One then generalizes the notion of pure-provability to functionals of all finite types, as follows. The language of $\mathbf{L}_2$ is extended to allow variables for functions of all finite type, but with no comprehension principle for these. The notion of equational program is also generalized to all finite types. The definition of function provability is generalized to all types as follows. Define $Tot^o[x] =_{\mathrm{df}} N[x]$, and $Tot^{\sigma\to\tau}[F^{\sigma\to\tau}] =_{\mathrm{df}} \forall f^\sigma\ Tot^\sigma[f] \to Tot^\tau[Ff]$. A program $(P, \mathbf{F})$, for a functional F of type τ, is said to be purely-provable if $Tot^\tau[\mathbf{F}]$ is provable from P.

Finally, one shows that every functional defined by tiered monotonic recurrence is provable. Restricted to first-order types, this is the sought result. ⊣

4 Function Provability

4.1 Proving Functions over Rudimentary Data-Axioms

Theorem 9 shows that the notion of pure-provability, which is natural and satisfactory for sufficiently powerful logics, is not appropriate when the logic is weak. This can be explained by the fact that data objects are used in computing in two orthogonal ways: as structured storage of bits of information, and as template that drive iterative constructs. The first aspect is examplified by data-storage devices, whose memory architecture may in fact be non-sequential (e.g. hypercubes). Essential to this role is the ability to (1) recognize the data visited; and (2) navigate efficiently within the store, e.g. move forward and backward within a linear memory structure (such as strings). When data is represented as a free term algebra, data recognition means simply the detection of the main constructor of a term, and backward navigation is conveyed by the presence of destructor functions.

In contrast, the use of data as templates for iteration and recursion is umbilically tied to the inductive construction of data, on which the the second order definition of data is based. Data detection and backward navigation can be recovered, as illustrated by Theorem 6, but at a cost, both logical and computational, that is no longer available in weak formalisms.

In [16] we addressed this issue by considering an asymmetric statement of program provability, where the characterization of the input as correct data is formally stronger than the characterization of the output as correct data. Here we consider instead the inclusion of rudimentary properties of data detection as axioms, resulting in a simpler, cleaner, and more useful notions and theorems.

To focus on the essentials, we continue to refer to the algebra $\mathbb{W}$ of words, generated from the 0-ary constructor (i.e. constant) ε and the unary constructore

[14] *Parameterized iteration,* also referred to as *monotonic recurrence,* disallows reference to previous values of the recurrence argument, allowing a definition $f(\mathbf{s}n, \boldsymbol{x}) = g(f(n, \boldsymbol{x}), \boldsymbol{x})$, but not is $f(\mathbf{s}n, \boldsymbol{x}) = g(f(n, \boldsymbol{x}), n, \boldsymbol{x})$.

a and **b**. We rephrase the second order definition of data to address the issue of navigation directly, and define

$$W'[x] \quad \equiv_{\rm df} \; \forall Q \; (\; \mathrm{Cl}'_W[Q] \;\rightarrow\; Q(x)\;),$$

where

$$\mathrm{Cl}'_W[Q] \;\; \equiv_{\rm df} \;\; Q(\varepsilon) \wedge \forall u (Q(u) \leftrightarrow Q(\mathbf{a}(u))) \wedge \forall u (Q(u) \leftrightarrow Q(\mathbf{b}(u))).$$

We redefine the rendition of function totality accordingly: For an r-ary function identifier **f** let

$$Tot'(\mathbf{f}) \;\; \equiv_{\rm df} \;\; \forall x_1 \ldots x_r. \, (\, W'[x_1] \wedge \cdots \wedge W'[x_r] \;\rightarrow\; W'[\mathbf{f}(\mathbf{x})]\,)$$

The *Rudimentary Theory* for $\mathbb{W}$, $\mathbf{RT}(\mathbb{W})$, has as vocabulary the constructors of $\mathbb{W}$ and a unary predicate identifier $\mathbf{W}_0$, intended to range over $\mathbb{W}$.[15] The axioms are:

- $\mathbf{W}_0(\varepsilon)$
- $\forall x \, \mathbf{W}_0(x) \leftrightarrow \mathbf{W}_0(\mathbf{a}x), \quad \forall x \, \mathbf{W}_0(x) \leftrightarrow \mathbf{W}_0(\mathbf{b}x),$
- Det $\;\equiv_{\rm df}\;\; \forall x \; (\, \mathbf{W}_0(x) \rightarrow \; (\, x{=}\varepsilon \;\vee\; \exists y \; x{=}\mathbf{a}(y) \;\vee\; \exists y \; x{=}\mathbf{b}(y)\,)\,)$

DEFINITION **11** *Let $(P, \mathbf{f})$ be a coherent program over $\mathbb{W}$. Let* **T** *be a higher-order deductive system over a vocabulary containing the vocabulary V_P. We say that P is* provable *in* **T** *if* Tot$'(\mathbf{f})$ *is derivable in* **T** *from* $\mathbf{RT}(\mathbb{W})$. *In that case we also say that the function f computed by $(P, \mathbf{f})$ is* provable *in* **T**.

The proof of Theorem 8 applies verbatim to function provability, yielding

THEOREM **12** *Let $\mathcal{C}$ be a class of first-order formulas, with the following closure property: if φ' arises from $\varphi \in \mathcal{C}$ by double-negating all atomic, disjunctive, and existential subformulas, then $\varphi' \in \mathcal{C}$. If $(P, \mathbf{f})$ is a program provable in $\mathbf{L}_2^{\mathcal{C}}(\mathcal{C})$, then it is provable in $\mathbf{L}_2(\mathcal{C})$.* ⊣

THEOREM **13** *A function over $\mathbb{W}$ is provable in $\mathbf{L}_2(FO)$ (based on classical, intuistionsic, or minimal logic) iff it is elementary (in the sense of Kalmar).*

This follows from Propositions 14 and 15 below.

[15] We use the subscript to disambiguate this primitive identifier from the defined predicate W.

4.2 Function Provability Implies Elementary Complexity

PROPOSITION **14** *If a function over $\mathbb{W}$ is provable in $\mathbf{L}_2(FO)$ then it is elementary.*

Proof Outline. As in the proof of Theorem 9, if a program $(P, \mathbf{f})$ over $\mathbb{W}$ is provable in $\mathbf{L}_2(FO)$, with $\mathbf{f}$ unary say, then there is a normal first-order deduction $\mathcal{D}[x]$, deriving $Q(\mathbf{f}(x))$ from the axioms of $\mathbf{RT}(\mathbb{W})$, $\mathrm{Cl}'_W[Q]$, and formulas of the form $\mathrm{Cl}'_W[\varphi_i] \rightarrow \varphi_i[x]$, where φ_i are all first-order.

Given an input $w \in \mathbb{W}$, the deduction $\mathcal{D}[w]$ can be combined with the deductions of $\mathrm{Cl}'_W[\varphi_i] \rightarrow \varphi_i[w]$, to form a deduction $\mathcal{D}_{fw}$, that derives $Q(\mathbf{f}(w))$ from $\mathbf{RT}(\mathbb{W})$ and $\mathrm{Cl}'_W[Q]$. Since the size of detours (cut-formulas) in $\mathcal{D}_{fw}$ is bounded independently of w, $\mathcal{D}_{fw}$ can be normalized, in time elementary in the size of w, yielding a closed and normal derivation $\mathcal{D}^n_{fw}$. Since the latter is closed and normal (whence also satisfies the subformula property), the axioms $\mathbf{RT}(\mathbb{W})$ are not used, and the proof consists of equations and implication eliminations corresponding to the biconditionals in $\mathrm{Cl}'_W[Q]$. The value fw can be read-off trivially from that derivation. ⊣

4.3 Elementary Functions Are Provable in $\mathbf{L}_2(FO)$

PROPOSITION **15** *Every elementary function is provable in $\mathbf{L}_2(FO)$.*

Proof Outline. Let $f : \mathbb{W} \rightarrow \mathbb{W}$ be Turing-computable in elementary time. By the proof of Proposition 1, there is an equational program $(P, \mathbf{R})$ referring to program-functions $\mathbf{R}$, $\mathbf{L}$ and $\mathbf{S}$, and such that $f(x) = R(t, x)$ for all t exceeding some $T(x)$, where T is elementary, and R is the function computed by $(P, \mathbf{R})$. By Proposition 7 we may assume that T in (purely-) provable in $\mathbf{L}_2(FO)$; in particular, $f(x) = R(T(x), x)$.

It therefore suffices to show that the function $R(t, x)$, i.e. the program $(P, \mathbf{R})$, is provable. Assume $W'[t]$ and $W'[x]$. Towards proving $W'[\mathbf{R}(t, x)]$ assume $\mathrm{Cl}'_W[Q]$. Instantiating the relational quantifier in $W'[t]$ to

$$\psi[z] \ \equiv_{\mathrm{df}} \ Q(\mathbf{R}(z, x)) \wedge Q(\mathbf{L}(z, x)) \wedge \mathbf{W}_0(\mathbf{R}(z, x)) \wedge \mathbf{W}_0(\mathbf{L}(z, x)),$$

we have $\mathrm{Cl}'_W[\psi] \rightarrow \psi[t]$.

We show $\mathrm{Cl}'_W[\psi]$. From $W'[x]$ and $\mathrm{Cl}'_W[Q]$ we have $Q(x)$, from which $\psi[\varepsilon]$ follows. Using $\mathrm{Cl}'_W[Q]$ and all axioms of $\mathbf{RT}(\mathbb{W})$, we obtain $\psi[w] \leftrightarrow \psi[\mathbf{a}w]$ and $\psi[w] \leftrightarrow \psi[\mathbf{b}w]$. We thus have $\mathrm{Cl}'_W[\psi]$, and therefore $\psi[t]$. In particular, $Q(\mathbf{R}(t, x))$. Since Q is arbitrary, we conclude $W'[\mathbf{R}(t, x)]$, concluding the proof. ⊣

References

1. Arnold Beckmann and Andreas Weiermann. Characterizing the elementary recursive functions by a fragment of Gödel's T. *Archive for Mathematical Logic*, 39:475–491, 2000.
2. Stephen Bellantoni and Stephen Cook. A new recursion-theoretic characterization of the poly-time functions, 1992. To appear in *Computational Complexity*.
3. Stephen Bellantoni and Martin Hofmann. A new feasible arithmetic. *Journal for Symbolic Logic*, 2001.
4. Garrett Birkhoff. On the structure of abstract algebras. *Proc. Cambridge Phil. Soc.*, 31:433–454, 1935.
5. Corrado Böhm and Allessandro Berarducci. Automatic synthesis of typed λ-programs on term algebras. *Theoretical Computer Science*, 39:135–154, 1985.
6. Samuel Buss. *Bounded Arithmetic*. Bibliopolis, Naples, 1986.
7. A. Cobham. The intrinsic computational difficulty of functions. In Y. Bar-Hillel, editor, *Proceedings of the International Conference on Logic, Methodology, and Philosophy of Science*, pages 24–30. North-Holland, Amsterdam, 1962.
8. Vicent Danos and Jean-Baptiste Joinet. Linear logic and elementary time. *Information and Computation*, to appear.
9. Jean-Yves Girard. Une extension de l'interprétation de Gödel à l'anal yse, et son application a l'élimination des coupures dans l'analyse et la théorie des types. In J.E. Fenstad, editor, *Proceedings of the Second Scandinavian Logic Symposium*, pages 63–92, Amsterdam, 1971. North-Holland.
10. Kurt Gödel. Über eine bisher noch nicht benutzte erweiterung des finiten standpunktes. *Dialectica*, 12:280–287, 1958.
11. Herman Ruge Jervell and Wenhui Zhang. Cut formulas for kalmar elementary functions. Technical Report issn: 1103-467x, Institut Mittag-Leffler, June 2001.
12. Stephen C. Kleene. *Introduction to Metamathematics*. Wolters-Noordhof, Groningen, 1952.
13. Stephen C. Kleene. *Formalized Recursive Functions and Formalized Realizability*, volume 89 of *Memoirs of the AMS*. American Mathematical Society, Providence, 1969.
14. Daniel Leivant. Subrecursion and lambda representation over free algebras. In Samuel Buss and Philip Scott, editors, *Feasible Mathematics*, Perspectives in Computer Science, pages 281–291. Birkhauser-Boston, New York, 1990.
15. Daniel Leivant. Semantic characterization of number theories. In Y. Moschovakis, editor, *Logic from Computer Science*, pages 295–318. Springer-Verlag, New York, 1991.
16. Daniel Leivant. A foundational delineation of poly-time. *Information and Computation*, 110:391–420, 1994. (Special issue of selected papers from LICS'91, edited by G. Kahn). Preminary report: A foundational delineation of computational feasibility, in Proceedings of the Sixth IEEE Conference on Logic in Computer Science, IEEE Computer Society Press, 1991.
17. Daniel Leivant. Higher-order logic. In D.M. Gabbay, C.J. Hogger, J.A. Robinson, and J. Siekmann, editors, *Handbook of Logic in Artificial Intelligence and Logic Programming, Volume 2: Deduction Methodologies*, pages 230–321. Oxford University Press, Oxford, 1994.
18. Daniel Leivant. Predicative recurrence in finite type. In A. Nerode and Yu.V. Matiyasevich, editors, *Logical Foundations of Computer Science (Third International Symposium)*, LNCS, pages 227–239, Berlin, 1994. Springer-Verlag.

19. Daniel Leivant. Intrinsic theories and computational complexity. In D. Leivant, editor, *Logic and Computational Complexity*, LNCS, pages 177–194, Berlin, 1995. Springer-Verlag.
20. Daniel Leivant. Intrinsic reasoning about functional programs I: First order theories. *Annals of Pure and Applied Logic*, 2001.
21. Daniel Leivant. Peano's lambda calculus: The functional abstraction implicit in arithmetic. In C. Anthony Anderson and Mikhail Zeleny, editors, *Church Memorial Volume: Logic, Language, and Computation.* Kluwer Academic Publishing, Dordrecht, 2001.
22. Daniel Leivant. Termination proofs and complexity certification. In N. Kobayasi and B. Pierce, editors, *Proceedings of TACS'01*, LNCS, Berlin, 2001. Springer-Verlag.
23. K. Meinke and J.V. Tucker. Universal algebra. In D.M. Gabbay S. Abramsky and T.S.E. Maibaum, editors, *Handbook of Logic in Computer Science*, pages 189–411. Oxford University Press, Oxford, 1992.
24. Charles Parsons. On a number-theoretic choice schema and its relation to induction. In A. Kino, J. Myhill, and R. Vesley, editors, *Intuitionism and Proof Theory*, pages 459–473. North-Holland, Amsterdam, 1977.
25. B. Plotkin. *Universal Algebra, ALgebraic Logic, and Databases.* Kluwer, Dordrecht, 1994.
26. D. Prawitz. *Natural Deduction.* Almqvist and Wiksell, Uppsala, 1965.
27. Stephen Simpson. *Subsystems of Second-Order Arithmetic.* Springer-Verlag, Berlin, 1999.
28. Richard Statman. *Structural complexity of proofs.* PhD thesis, Stanford University, 1974. PhD Thesis.
29. Richard Statman. The typed λ-calculus is not elementary recursive. *Theoretical Computer Science*, 9:73–81, 1979.
30. W. Wechler. *Universal Algebra for Computer Scientists.* Springer-Verlag, Berlin, 1992.

A Local System for Classical Logic

Kai Brünnler[1] and Alwen Fernanto Tiu[1,2]
kai.bruennler@inf.tu-dresden.de and tiu@cse.psu.edu

[1] Technische Universität Dresden, Fakultät Informatik, D - 01062 Dresden, Germany
[2] The Pennsylvania State University, Department of Computer Science and Engineering, University Park, PA 16802 USA

Abstract. The *calculus of structures* is a framework for specifying logical systems, which is similar to the one-sided sequent calculus but more general. We present a system of inference rules for propositional classical logic in this new framework and prove cut elimination for it. The system enjoys a decomposition theorem for derivations that is not available in the sequent calculus. The main novelty of our system is that all the rules are *local*: contraction, in particular, is reduced to atomic form. This should be interesting for distributed proof-search and also for complexity theory, since the computational cost of applying each rule is bounded.

1 Introduction

When implementing inference systems, in a distributed fashion especially, the need to copy formulae of unbounded size is generally considered problematic. In the sequent calculus, it is caused by the contraction rule, e.g. in Gentzen's LK [2]:

$$\frac{\Gamma \vdash \Phi, A, A}{\Gamma \vdash \Phi, A} \quad .$$

Here, going from bottom to top in constructing a proof, a formula A of unbounded size is duplicated. Whatever mechanism performs this duplication, it has to inspect all of A, so it has to have a *global* view on A. While this can be taken for granted on a single processor system, it is harder to achieve on a distributed system, where each processor has a limited amount of local memory. The formula A could be spread over a number of processors. In that case, no single processor has a global view on A.

Let us call *local* those inference rules that do not require such a global view on formulae of unbounded size, and *non-local* those rules that do. Besides contraction, another example of clearly non-local behaviour is provided by the promotion rule in the sequent calculus for linear logic [3]. To remove an exclamation mark from one formula, it has to check whether all formulae in the context are prefixed with a question mark. The number of formulae to check is unbounded:

$$\frac{\vdash A, ?B_1, \ldots, ?B_n}{\vdash !A, ?B_1, \ldots, ?B_n} \quad .$$

R. Nieuwenhuis and A. Voronkov (Eds.): LPAR 2001, LNAI 2250, pp. 347–361, 2001.

While there are methods to solve these problems in the implementation, an interesting question is whether it is possible to solve them proof-theoretically, i.e. by avoiding non-local rules altogether. This question is answered positively in this paper for the case of classical propositional logic. The predicative case is work in progress and is sketched in the conclusion.

Locality is achieved by reducing the problematic rules to their atomic forms. This is not entirely new: there are sequent systems for classical logic in which the identity axiom is reduced to its atomic form, i.e.

$$\overline{A \vdash A} \qquad \text{is admissible for} \qquad \overline{a \vdash a} \quad ,$$

where a is an atom. However, we do not know of any sequent system in which contraction and weakening are admissible for their atomic forms. In fact, we believe that such a system does not exist. To achieve our goal, we depart from the sequent calculus and employ the recently conceived *calculus of structures* [5]. In contrast to the sequent calculus, it does not rely on the notion of main connective and permits the application of rules anywhere *deep* inside a formula, exploiting the fact that implication is closed under disjunction and conjunction. This ability is crucial for the rules of our system. The calculus of structures has already successfully been employed in [7] to solve the problem of the non-local behaviour of the promotion rule.

This paper is structured as follows: first, we introduce basic notions of the calculus of structures. Then we present our system, named SKS, and argue that its rules are local. We prove that it is equivalent to the Gentzen-Schütte formulation of classical logic, prove cut elimination and state two decomposition theorems for derivations. In the end, some open problems are identified.

2 Structures and Derivations

Definition 2.1. There are infinitely many *literals*. Literals, positive or negative, are denoted by a, b, ... There are two special literals, *true* and *false*, denoted t and f. The *structures* of the language KS are generated by

$$S ::= a \mid [\underbrace{S, \ldots, S}_{>0}] \mid (\underbrace{S, \ldots, S}_{>0}) \mid \bar{S} \quad ,$$

where $[S_1, \ldots, S_h]$ is a *disjunction* and $(S_1, \ldots, S_h)$ is a *conjunction*. $\bar{S}$ is the *negation* of the structure S. Structures are denoted by S, P, Q, R, T, U, V and W. Structures with a hole that does not appear in the scope of a negation are denoted by $S\{\ \}$. The structure R is a *substructure* of $S\{R\}$, and $S\{\ \}$ is its *context*. We simplify the indication of context in cases where structural parentheses fill the hole exactly: for example, $S[R, T]$ stands for $S\{[R, T]\}$. Structures are considered to be syntactically equivalent modulo the relation $=$, which is the smallest congruence relation induced by the equations shown in Fig. 1, where $\boldsymbol{R}$ and $\boldsymbol{T}$ stand for finite, non-empty sequences of structures.

Associativity

$$[\boldsymbol{R},[\boldsymbol{T}]] = [\boldsymbol{R},\boldsymbol{T}]$$
$$(\boldsymbol{R},(\boldsymbol{T})) = (\boldsymbol{R},\boldsymbol{T})$$

Commutativity

$$[\boldsymbol{R},\boldsymbol{T}] = [\boldsymbol{T},\boldsymbol{R}]$$
$$(\boldsymbol{R},\boldsymbol{T}) = (\boldsymbol{T},\boldsymbol{R})$$

Singleton

$$[R] = R = (R)$$

Constants

$$[\mathsf{f},\boldsymbol{R}] = [\boldsymbol{R}]$$
$$(\mathsf{t},\boldsymbol{R}) = (\boldsymbol{R})$$

Negation

$$\bar{\mathsf{t}} = \mathsf{f}$$
$$\bar{\mathsf{f}} = \mathsf{t}$$
$$\overline{[R_1,\dots,R_h]} = (\bar{R}_1,\dots,\bar{R}_h)$$
$$\overline{(R_1,\dots,R_h)} = [\bar{R}_1,\dots,\bar{R}_h]$$
$$\bar{\bar{R}} = R$$

Fig. 1. Syntactic equivalence on structures

Structures are somewhere between formulae and sequents. They share with formulae their tree-like shape and with sequents the built-in, decidable equivalence modulo associativity and commutativity. Structures have a normal form, unique modulo commutativity, where negation only occurs in the form of negative literals and all constants that can be removed are removed. In all inductive arguments to come, structures are considered to be in normal form.

Definition 2.2. An *inference rule* is a scheme of the kind

$$\rho\,\frac{S\{T\}}{S\{R\}} \quad ,$$

where ρ is the *name* of the rule, $S\{T\}$ is its *premise* and $S\{R\}$ is its *conclusion*. The context $S\{\ \}$ may be empty. In an instance of ρ, the structure taking the place of R is called *redex* and the structure taking the place of T is called *contractum*. A (*formal*) *system* $\mathscr{S}$ is a set of inference rules.

Definition 2.3. A *derivation* Δ in a certain formal system is a finite chain of instances of inference rules in the system:

$$\begin{array}{l} \pi' \,\dfrac{T}{V} \\ \pi \,\dfrac{}{\vdots} \\ \rho' \,\dfrac{}{U} \\ \rho \,\dfrac{}{R} \end{array} \quad .$$

A derivation can consist of just one structure. The topmost structure in a derivation is called the *premise* of the derivation, and the structure at the bottom is called its *conclusion*. A derivation Δ whose premise is T, whose conclusion is R, and whose inference rules are in $\mathscr{S}$ will be indicated with $\begin{array}{c} T \\ \Delta \| \mathscr{S} \\ R \end{array}$. A *proof* Π in the calculus of structures is a derivation whose premise is t. It will be denoted by $\begin{array}{c} \Pi \| \mathscr{S} \\ R \end{array}$. A rule ρ is *strongly admissible* for a system $\mathscr{S}$ if $\rho \notin \mathscr{S}$ and for every instance of $\rho \frac{T}{R}$ there is a derivation $\begin{array}{c} T \\ \Delta \| \mathscr{S} \\ R \end{array}$. A rule ρ *permutes over* a rule π (or π *permutes under* ρ) if for every derivation $\pi \frac{T}{\rho \frac{U}{R}}$ there is a derivation $\rho \frac{T}{\pi \frac{V}{R}}$ for some structure V.

3 System SKS

System SKS is shown in Fig. 2. The first S stands for "symmetric" or "self-dual", meaning that for each rule its dual (or contrapositive) is also in the system. The K stands for "klassisch" as in Gentzen's LK and the last S means that it is a system on structures.

The rules $\mathsf{ai}\!\downarrow, \mathsf{s}, \mathsf{m}, \mathsf{aw}\!\downarrow, \mathsf{ac}\!\downarrow$ are called respectively *atomic identity*, *switch*, *medial*, *atomic weakening* and *atomic contraction*. Their dual rules carry the same name prefixed with a "co-", so e.g. $\mathsf{aw}\!\uparrow$ is called *atomic co-weakening*. The rule $\mathsf{ai}\!\uparrow$ is special, it is called *atomic cut*. Rules $\mathsf{ai}\!\downarrow, \mathsf{aw}\!\downarrow, \mathsf{ac}\!\downarrow$ are called *down-rules* and their duals are called *up-rules*.

Note that no rule requires the duplication or the comparison of structures of unbounded size. The atomic rules only need to duplicate or compare literals. The two rules that involve structures of unbounded size are m and s. Since they do not duplicate or compare the structures held by R, T, U and V, there is no need to inspect those structures at all. Consider structures represented as trees in the obvious way. Then the switch rule can be implemented by changing the marking of two nodes and exchanging two pointers (similarly for medial):

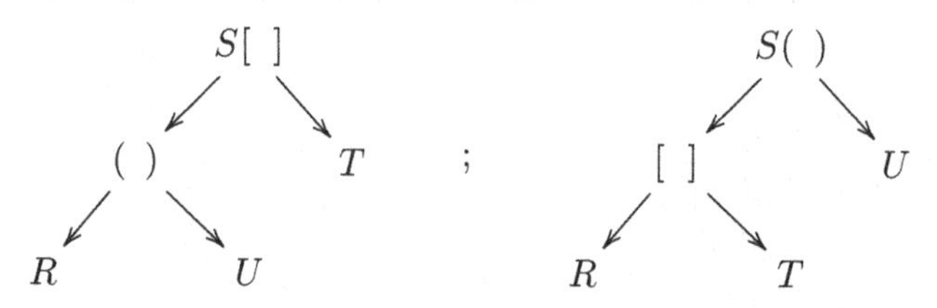

In the sequent calculus, a logical rule gives meaning to the main connective of a formula by saying that the formula is provable if certain immediate subformulae are provable. During a proof-search, formulae successively get decomposed, with their main connectives disappearing.

$$\mathsf{ai}\!\downarrow \frac{S\{\mathsf{t}\}}{S[a,\bar{a}]} \qquad \mathsf{ai}\!\uparrow \frac{S(a,\bar{a})}{S\{\mathsf{f}\}}$$

$$\mathsf{s}\,\frac{S([R,U],T)}{S[(R,T),U]}$$

$$\mathsf{m}\,\frac{S[(R,U),(T,V)]}{S([R,T],[U,V])}$$

$$\mathsf{aw}\!\downarrow \frac{S\{\mathsf{f}\}}{S\{a\}} \qquad \mathsf{aw}\!\uparrow \frac{S\{a\}}{S\{\mathsf{t}\}}$$

$$\mathsf{ac}\!\downarrow \frac{S[a,a]}{S\{a\}} \qquad \mathsf{ac}\!\uparrow \frac{S\{a\}}{S(a,a)}$$

Fig. 2. System SKS

The rules switch and medial of system SKS do not fit into this scheme. Not only are they applicable deep inside a formula (or structure, for that matter), there also is no main connective that is removed. While there is a connection between the switch rule and the R∧ rule in the sequent calculus (cf. the proof of Theorem 4.2), the medial rule bears no resemblance of any sequent calculus rule. Its premise is a disjunction and its conclusion a conjunction. This is impossible in the sequent calculus, where the conclusion of a rule is always a disjunction (a sequent) and the premise of a rule is either also a disjunction (for single premise rules) or a conjunction (for two premise rules, since the two premises are logically in a conjunction).

Remark 3.1. When talking about derivations, taking the dual means turning them upside-down, thereby exchanging premise and conclusion, and replacing each connective and constant by its De Morgan dual. For example

$$\mathsf{s}\,\frac{\mathsf{s}\,\dfrac{\mathsf{ai}\!\downarrow\dfrac{\mathsf{ai}\!\downarrow\dfrac{\mathsf{t}}{[b,\bar{b}]}}{([a,\bar{a}],[b,\bar{b}])}}{[b,([a,\bar{a}],\bar{b})]}}{[a,b,(\bar{a},\bar{b})]} \quad \text{is dual to} \quad \mathsf{ai}\!\uparrow\frac{\mathsf{ai}\!\uparrow\dfrac{\mathsf{s}\,\dfrac{\mathsf{s}\,\dfrac{(a,b,[\bar{a},\bar{b}])}{(b,[(a,\bar{a}),\bar{b}])}}{[(a,\bar{a}),(b,\bar{b})]}}{(b,\bar{b})}}{\mathsf{f}} \quad .$$

While atomic rules are good e.g. from the point of view of mechanized proof-search, they are cumbersome for a user of the system. Of course, it should be possible to contract and weaken on arbitrarily large formulas, just as it should

$$\mathsf{i}{\downarrow}\,\frac{S\{\mathsf{t}\}}{S[R,\bar{R}]} \qquad \mathsf{i}{\uparrow}\,\frac{S(R,\bar{R})}{S\{\mathsf{f}\}}$$

$$\mathsf{w}{\downarrow}\,\frac{S\{\mathsf{f}\}}{S\{R\}} \qquad \mathsf{w}{\uparrow}\,\frac{S\{R\}}{S\{\mathsf{t}\}}$$

$$\mathsf{c}{\downarrow}\,\frac{S[R,R]}{S\{R\}} \qquad \mathsf{c}{\uparrow}\,\frac{S\{R\}}{S(R,R)}$$

Fig. 3. General identity, weakening, contraction and their duals

be possible to introduce arbitrarily large lemmas through the cut rule. Figure 3 shows the general, i.e. non-atomic, versions of the atomic rules in SKS. The following theorem shows that they can be used.

Theorem 3.2. General identity, weakening, contraction and their duals, i.e. the rules $\{\mathsf{i}{\downarrow},\mathsf{i}{\uparrow},\mathsf{w}{\downarrow},\mathsf{w}{\uparrow},\mathsf{c}{\downarrow},\mathsf{c}{\uparrow}\}$ are strongly admissible for system SKS. In particular, the rules $\mathsf{i}{\downarrow}$, $\mathsf{w}{\downarrow}$ and $\mathsf{c}{\downarrow}$ are strongly admissible for $\{\mathsf{ai}{\downarrow},\mathsf{s}\}$, $\{\mathsf{aw}{\downarrow},\mathsf{ac}{\uparrow}\}$ and $\{\mathsf{ac}{\downarrow},\mathsf{m}\}$, respectively. Dually, the rules $\mathsf{i}{\uparrow}$, $\mathsf{w}{\uparrow}$ $\mathsf{c}{\uparrow}$ are strongly admissible for $\{\mathsf{ai}{\uparrow},\mathsf{s}\}$, $\{\mathsf{aw}{\uparrow},\mathsf{ac}{\downarrow}\}$ and $\{\mathsf{ac}{\uparrow},\mathsf{m}\}$, respectively.

Proof. We will show strong admissibility of the rules $\{\mathsf{i}{\downarrow},\mathsf{w}{\downarrow},\mathsf{c}{\downarrow}\}$ for the respective subsystems of SKS. The proof of strong admissibility of their co-rules is dual.

Given an instance of one of the following rules:

$$\mathsf{i}{\downarrow}\,\frac{S\{\mathsf{t}\}}{S[R,\bar{R}]}\;,\qquad \mathsf{w}{\downarrow}\,\frac{S\{\mathsf{f}\}}{S\{R\}}\;,\qquad \mathsf{c}{\downarrow}\,\frac{S[R,R]}{S\{R\}}\;,$$

construct a new derivation by structural induction on R:

1. R is a literal: Then the instance of the general rule is also an instance of its atomic form.
2. $R=[P,Q]$, where $P\neq\mathsf{f}\neq Q$: Note that $[\mathsf{f},\mathsf{f}]=\mathsf{f}$. Apply the induction hypothesis respectively on

$$\mathsf{s}\,\frac{\mathsf{s}\,\dfrac{\mathsf{i}{\downarrow}\,\dfrac{\mathsf{i}{\downarrow}\,\dfrac{S\{\mathsf{t}\}}{S[Q,\bar{Q}]}}{S([P,\bar{P}],[Q,\bar{Q}])}}{S[Q,([P,\bar{P}],\bar{Q})]}}{S[P,Q,(\bar{P},\bar{Q})]}\;,\qquad \mathsf{w}{\downarrow}\,\frac{\mathsf{w}{\downarrow}\,\dfrac{S\{\mathsf{f}\}}{S[\mathsf{f},Q]}}{S[P,Q]}\;,\qquad \mathsf{c}{\downarrow}\,\frac{\mathsf{c}{\downarrow}\,\dfrac{S[P,P,Q,Q]}{S[P,P,Q]}}{S[P,Q]}\;.$$

3. $R = (P, Q)$, where $P \neq \mathsf{t} \neq Q$: Apply the induction hypothesis respectively on

$$\mathsf{s}\frac{\mathsf{s}\frac{\mathsf{i}\!\downarrow\frac{\mathsf{i}\!\downarrow\frac{S\{\mathsf{t}\}}{S[Q,\bar{Q}]}}{S([P,\bar{P}],[Q,\bar{Q}])}}{S[\bar{Q},([P,\bar{P}],Q)]}}{S[\bar{P},\bar{Q},(P,Q)]} \quad , \quad \mathsf{w}\!\downarrow\frac{\mathsf{w}\!\downarrow\frac{\mathsf{ac}\!\uparrow\frac{S\{\mathsf{f}\}}{S(\mathsf{f},\mathsf{f})}}{S(\mathsf{f},Q)}}{S(P,Q)} \quad , \quad \mathsf{c}\!\downarrow\frac{\mathsf{c}\!\downarrow\frac{\mathsf{m}\frac{S[(P,Q),(P,Q)]}{S([P,P],[Q,Q])}}{S([P,P],Q)}}{S(P,Q)} \quad .$$

□

Example 3.3. Here are two proofs, one using the general rules, the other one in SKS, i.e. without using the general rules:

$$\mathsf{w}\!\downarrow\frac{\mathsf{c}\!\uparrow\frac{\mathsf{i}\!\downarrow\frac{\mathsf{t}}{[[\bar{a},\bar{b}],(a,b)]}}{[([\bar{a},\bar{b}],[\bar{a},\bar{b}]),(a,b)]}}{[([\bar{a},\bar{b},c,d],[\bar{a},\bar{b}]),(a,b)]} \quad \text{and} \quad \mathsf{aw}\!\downarrow\frac{\mathsf{aw}\!\downarrow\frac{\mathsf{m}\frac{\mathsf{ac}\!\uparrow\frac{\mathsf{ac}\!\uparrow\frac{\mathsf{s}\frac{\mathsf{ai}\!\downarrow\frac{\mathsf{ai}\!\downarrow\frac{\mathsf{t}}{[\bar{b},b]}}{[\bar{b},([\bar{a},a],b)]}}{[\bar{a},\bar{b},(a,b)]}}{[\bar{a},(\bar{b},\bar{b}),(a,b)]}}{[(\bar{a},\bar{a}),(\bar{b},\bar{b}),(a,b)]}}{[([\bar{a},\bar{b}],[\bar{a},\bar{b}]),(a,b)]}}{[([\bar{a},\bar{b},c],[\bar{a},\bar{b}]),(a,b)]}}{[([\bar{a},\bar{b},c,d],[\bar{a},\bar{b}]),(a,b)]} \quad .$$

4 Equivalence to Classical Logic

In this section we will see translations between system SKS and system GS1p, a Gentzen-Schütte formulation of classical logic [8]. Derivations in GS1p are translated to derivations in SKS (without introducing cuts), and proofs in SKS are translated to proofs in GS1p (possibly introducing cuts). Cut elimination for SKS is a consequence of these translations and cut elimination in GS1p.

System GS1p is shown in Figure 4. Its formulae are denoted by A and B. They contain negation only on atoms. Sequents are denoted by Σ or by $\vdash A_1, \dots, A_h$, where $h \geq 0$. Multisets of formulae are denoted by Φ and Ψ. Derivations are denoted by Δ or $\begin{matrix}\Sigma_1 \cdots \Sigma_h \\ \bigtriangledown \Delta \\ \Sigma\end{matrix}$, where $h \geq 0$, the sequents $\Sigma_1, \dots, \Sigma_h$ are the premises and Σ is the conclusion. Proofs are denoted by Π.

$$\mathsf{i}\!\downarrow \frac{S\{\mathsf{t}\}}{S[R,\bar{R}]} \qquad \mathsf{i}\!\uparrow \frac{S(R,\bar{R})}{S\{\mathsf{f}\}}$$

$$\mathsf{w}\!\downarrow \frac{S\{\mathsf{f}\}}{S\{R\}} \qquad \mathsf{w}\!\uparrow \frac{S\{R\}}{S\{\mathsf{t}\}}$$

$$\mathsf{c}\!\downarrow \frac{S[R,R]}{S\{R\}} \qquad \mathsf{c}\!\uparrow \frac{S\{R\}}{S(R,R)}$$

Fig. 3. General identity, weakening, contraction and their duals

be possible to introduce arbitrarily large lemmas through the cut rule. Figure 3 shows the general, i.e. non-atomic, versions of the atomic rules in SKS. The following theorem shows that they can be used.

Theorem 3.2. General identity, weakening, contraction and their duals, i.e. the rules $\{\mathsf{i}\!\downarrow, \mathsf{i}\!\uparrow, \mathsf{w}\!\downarrow, \mathsf{w}\!\uparrow, \mathsf{c}\!\downarrow, \mathsf{c}\!\uparrow\}$ are strongly admissible for system SKS. In particular, the rules $\mathsf{i}\!\downarrow$, $\mathsf{w}\!\downarrow$ and $\mathsf{c}\!\downarrow$ are strongly admissible for $\{\mathsf{ai}\!\downarrow, \mathsf{s}\}$, $\{\mathsf{aw}\!\downarrow, \mathsf{ac}\!\uparrow\}$ and $\{\mathsf{ac}\!\downarrow, \mathsf{m}\}$, respectively. Dually, the rules $\mathsf{i}\!\uparrow$, $\mathsf{w}\!\uparrow$ $\mathsf{c}\!\uparrow$ are strongly admissible for $\{\mathsf{ai}\!\uparrow, \mathsf{s}\}$, $\{\mathsf{aw}\!\uparrow, \mathsf{ac}\!\downarrow\}$ and $\{\mathsf{ac}\!\uparrow, \mathsf{m}\}$, respectively.

Proof. We will show strong admissibility of the rules $\{\mathsf{i}\!\downarrow, \mathsf{w}\!\downarrow, \mathsf{c}\!\downarrow\}$ for the respective subsystems of SKS. The proof of strong admissibility of their co-rules is dual.

Given an instance of one of the following rules:

$$\mathsf{i}\!\downarrow \frac{S\{\mathsf{t}\}}{S[R,\bar{R}]} \;,\qquad \mathsf{w}\!\downarrow \frac{S\{\mathsf{f}\}}{S\{R\}} \;,\qquad \mathsf{c}\!\downarrow \frac{S[R,R]}{S\{R\}} \;,$$

construct a new derivation by structural induction on R:

1. R is a literal: Then the instance of the general rule is also an instance of its atomic form.
2. $R = [P,Q]$, where $P \neq \mathsf{f} \neq Q$: Note that $[\mathsf{f},\mathsf{f}] = \mathsf{f}$. Apply the induction hypothesis respectively on

$$\mathsf{s}\frac{\mathsf{s}\dfrac{\mathsf{i}\!\downarrow\dfrac{\mathsf{i}\!\downarrow\dfrac{S\{\mathsf{t}\}}{S[Q,\bar{Q}]}}{S([P,\bar{P}],[Q,\bar{Q}])}}{S[Q,([P,\bar{P}],\bar{Q})]}}{S[P,Q,(\bar{P},\bar{Q})]} \;,\qquad \mathsf{w}\!\downarrow\frac{\mathsf{w}\!\downarrow\dfrac{S\{\mathsf{f}\}}{S[\mathsf{f},Q]}}{S[P,Q]} \;,\qquad \mathsf{c}\!\downarrow\frac{\mathsf{c}\!\downarrow\dfrac{S[P,P,Q,Q]}{S[P,P,Q]}}{S[P,Q]} \;.$$

following derivations:

$$\begin{array}{c}(\underline{\Sigma'_1}_{\mathsf{s}},\dots,\underline{\Sigma'_k}_{\mathsf{s}})\\ \Delta_1 \Big\| \mathsf{SKS}\\ [\underline{\Phi}_{\mathsf{s}},\underline{A}_{\mathsf{s}}]\end{array} \quad\text{and}\quad \begin{array}{c}(\underline{\Sigma''_1}_{\mathsf{s}},\dots,\underline{\Sigma''_l}_{\mathsf{s}})\\ \Delta_2 \Big\| \mathsf{SKS}\\ [\underline{\Phi}_{\mathsf{s}},\underline{B}_{\mathsf{s}}]\end{array} \quad\Rightarrow\quad \begin{array}{c}(\underline{\Sigma'_1}_{\mathsf{s}},\dots,\underline{\Sigma'_k}_{\mathsf{s}},\underline{\Sigma''_1}_{\mathsf{s}},\dots,\underline{\Sigma''_l}_{\mathsf{s}})\\ \Delta_1;\Delta_2 \Big\| \mathsf{SKS}\\ \mathsf{c}\!\downarrow \dfrac{\mathsf{s};\mathsf{s}\,\dfrac{([\underline{\Phi}_{\mathsf{s}},\underline{A}_{\mathsf{s}}],[\underline{\Phi}_{\mathsf{s}},\underline{B}_{\mathsf{s}}])}{[\underline{\Phi}_{\mathsf{s}},\underline{\Phi}_{\mathsf{s}},(\underline{A}_{\mathsf{s}},\underline{B}_{\mathsf{s}})]}}{[\underline{\Phi}_{\mathsf{s}},(\underline{A}_{\mathsf{s}},\underline{B}_{\mathsf{s}})]}\end{array}\quad .$$

□

Corollary 4.3. If $\vdash A$ is provable in GS1p then $\vdash \underline{A}_{\mathsf{s}}$ is provable in SKS.

Theorem 4.4. If P is provable in SKS then $\vdash \underline{P}_{\mathsf{K}}$ is provable in GS1p.

Proof. Let $P = S\{R\}$ and $\begin{array}{c}\Pi \Big\| \mathsf{SKS}\\ \rho\,\dfrac{S\{T\}}{S\{R\}}\end{array}$ be its proof in SKS. The proof of this theorem is based on a known property of GS1p, that is, if $\vdash \underline{R}_{\mathsf{K}},\overline{\underline{T}}_{\mathsf{K}}$ is provable then so is $\vdash \underline{S\{R\}}_{\mathsf{K}},\overline{\underline{S\{T\}}}_{\mathsf{K}}$.

Base Cases

If $\Pi = \mathsf{t}$ then take $\mathsf{RC}\,\dfrac{\mathsf{RV_L};\mathsf{RV_R}\,\dfrac{\mathsf{Ax}\,\dfrac{}{\vdash a^\bullet,\bar a^\bullet}}{\vdash a^\bullet\vee\bar a^\bullet, a^\bullet\vee\bar a^\bullet}}{a^\bullet\vee\bar a^\bullet}$, otherwise, if $\Pi = \mathsf{ai}\!\downarrow\dfrac{\mathsf{t}}{[a,\bar a]}$ then take the same derivation, but with $a^\bullet$ replaced by a.

Inductive Cases

We assume that $\underline{S\{T\}}_{\mathsf{K}}$ is provable in GS1p. By using the cut rule, we get $\mathsf{Cut}\,\dfrac{\vdash \underline{S\{T\}}_{\mathsf{K}} \quad \vdash \underline{S\{R\}}_{\mathsf{K}},\overline{\underline{S\{T\}}}_{\mathsf{K}}}{\vdash \underline{S\{R\}}_{\mathsf{K}}}$. It is enough to show that $\vdash \underline{R}_{\mathsf{K}},\overline{\underline{T}}_{\mathsf{K}}$ is provable.

We show the case for $\rho = \mathsf{s}\,\dfrac{S([U,V],W)}{S[(U,W),V]}$. The property holds for the rest of the rules of SKS as well, as can easily be verified.

$$\mathsf{RC}^2\,\dfrac{\mathsf{RV_L}^2;\mathsf{RV_R}^2\,\dfrac{\mathsf{R}\wedge\,\dfrac{\mathsf{R}\wedge\,\dfrac{\mathsf{RW}^2\,\dfrac{\mathsf{Ax}\,\dfrac{}{\vdash \underline{U}_{\mathsf{K}},\overline{\underline{U}}_{\mathsf{K}}}}{\vdash \underline{U}_{\mathsf{K}},\overline{\underline{U}}_{\mathsf{K}},\underline{V}_{\mathsf{K}},\overline{\underline{W}}_{\mathsf{K}}} \quad \mathsf{RW}^2\,\dfrac{\mathsf{Ax}\,\dfrac{}{\vdash \underline{V}_{\mathsf{K}},\overline{\underline{V}}_{\mathsf{K}}}}{\vdash \underline{V}_{\mathsf{K}},\overline{\underline{V}}_{\mathsf{K}},\underline{U}_{\mathsf{K}},\overline{\underline{W}}_{\mathsf{K}}}}{\vdash \underline{U}_{\mathsf{K}},\underline{V}_{\mathsf{K}},\overline{\underline{U}}_{\mathsf{K}}\wedge\overline{\underline{V}}_{\mathsf{K}},\overline{\underline{W}}_{\mathsf{K}}} \quad \mathsf{RW}^2\,\dfrac{\mathsf{Ax}\,\dfrac{}{\vdash \underline{W}_{\mathsf{K}},\overline{\underline{W}}_{\mathsf{K}}}}{\vdash \underline{W}_{\mathsf{K}},\overline{\underline{W}}_{\mathsf{K}},\underline{V}_{\mathsf{K}},\overline{\underline{U}}_{\mathsf{K}}\wedge\overline{\underline{V}}_{\mathsf{K}}}}{\vdash \underline{U}_{\mathsf{K}}\wedge\underline{W}_{\mathsf{K}},\underline{V}_{\mathsf{K}},\overline{\underline{U}}_{\mathsf{K}}\wedge\overline{\underline{V}}_{\mathsf{K}},\overline{\underline{W}}_{\mathsf{K}}}}{\vdash (\underline{U}_{\mathsf{K}}\wedge\underline{W}_{\mathsf{K}})\vee\underline{V}_{\mathsf{K}},(\overline{\underline{U}}_{\mathsf{K}}\wedge\overline{\underline{V}}_{\mathsf{K}})\vee\overline{\underline{W}}_{\mathsf{K}},(\underline{U}_{\mathsf{K}}\wedge\underline{W}_{\mathsf{K}})\vee\underline{V}_{\mathsf{K}},(\overline{\underline{U}}_{\mathsf{K}}\wedge\overline{\underline{V}}_{\mathsf{K}})\vee\overline{\underline{W}}_{\mathsf{K}}}}{\vdash (\underline{U}_{\mathsf{K}}\wedge\underline{W}_{\mathsf{K}})\vee\underline{V}_{\mathsf{K}},(\overline{\underline{U}}_{\mathsf{K}}\wedge\overline{\underline{V}}_{\mathsf{K}})\vee\overline{\underline{W}}_{\mathsf{K}}}$$

The rule ρ^n denotes n applications of ρ. □

Cut elimination for SKS can be obtained by using the above translations: Given a proof Π in SKS, we can transform it to a proof Π' in GS1p and eliminate all the cuts there. The resulting cut-free proof in GS1p can then be translated back to a proof Π'' in SKS. The complete case analysis of the proof of Theorem 4.2 shows that this transformation does not produce new cuts, and hence Π'' is a cut-free proof in SKS.

5 Cut Elimination and Decomposition

There is a very natural way of proving cut elimination for system SKS by using semantics, using the idea employed in [8] for the system G3. The proof actually gives us something more than just cut elimination, it eliminates all up-rules and also yields a decomposition of proofs into separate phases.

Theorem 5.1 (Cut Elimination, semantically).

For every proof $\begin{array}{c}\Vert \mathsf{SKS}\\ S\end{array}$ there is a proof $\begin{array}{c}\Vert \{\mathsf{ai}\!\downarrow\}\\ S''\\ \Vert \{\mathsf{aw}\!\downarrow\}\\ S'\\ \Vert \{\mathsf{s},\mathsf{ac}\!\downarrow,\mathsf{m}\}\\ S\end{array}$.

Proof. Consider the rule *distribute*

$$\mathsf{d}\!\downarrow \frac{S([R,T],[R,U])}{S[R,(T,U)]},$$

which can be realized by a contraction and two switches:

$$\mathsf{c}\!\downarrow \frac{\mathsf{s}\frac{\mathsf{s}\frac{S([R,T],[R,U])}{S[R,([R,T],U)]}}{S[R,R,(T,U)]}}{S[R,(T,U)]}$$

and thus by Theorem 3.2 is strongly admissible for $\{\mathsf{s}, \mathsf{ac}\!\downarrow, \mathsf{m}\}$. Build a derivation $\begin{array}{c}S'\\ \Vert \{\mathsf{d}\!\downarrow\}\\ S\end{array}$, by going upwards from S applying $\mathsf{d}\!\downarrow$ as many times as possible. Then S' will be in conjunctive normal form, i.e.

$$S' = ([a_{11}, a_{12}, \ldots], [a_{21}, a_{22}, \ldots], \ldots, [a_{n1}, a_{n2}, \ldots]) \quad .$$

S is valid because there is a proof of it. The rule $\mathsf{d}\!\downarrow$ is invertible, so S' is also valid. A conjunction is valid only if all its immediate substructures are valid. Those are disjunctions of atoms. A disjunction of atoms is valid only if it contains an atom a together with its negation $\bar{a}$. Thus, more specifically, S' is of the form

$$S' = ([b_1, \bar{b}_1, a_{11}, a_{12}, \ldots], [b_2, \bar{b}_2, a_{21}, a_{22}, \ldots], \ldots, [b_n, \bar{b}_n, a_{n1}, a_{n2}, \ldots]) \quad .$$

Let $S'' = ([b_1, \bar{b}_1], [b_2, \bar{b}_2], \ldots, [b_n, \bar{b}_n])$.

Obviously, there is a derivation $\begin{array}{c} S'' \\ \Vert\{\mathsf{aw}\downarrow\} \\ S' \end{array}$ and a proof $\begin{array}{c} \overline{\Vert}\{\mathsf{ai}\downarrow\} \\ S'' \end{array}$. □

Let us call system KS the rules shown in Fig. 5. We know that for proof-search in SKS system KS is sufficient:

Corollary 5.2. For every proof $\begin{array}{c} \overline{\Vert}\mathsf{SKS} \\ S \end{array}$ there is a proof $\begin{array}{c} \overline{\Vert}\mathsf{KS} \\ S \end{array}$.

As a result of cut elimination, sequent systems fulfill the subformula property. Our case is different, because our rules do not split the derivation according to the main connective of the active formula. However, system KS satisfies the main consequence of the subformula property: no new atoms have to be introduced in proof-search, i.e. the branching of the search tree is finite.

$$\mathsf{ai}\downarrow \frac{S\{\mathsf{t}\}}{S[a, \bar{a}]} \qquad \mathsf{aw}\downarrow \frac{S\{\mathsf{f}\}}{S\{a\}} \qquad \mathsf{ac}\downarrow \frac{S[a, a]}{S\{a\}}$$

$$\mathsf{s} \frac{S([R, T], U)}{S[(R, U), T]} \qquad \mathsf{m} \frac{S[(R, T), (U, V)]}{S([R, U], [T, V])}$$

Fig. 5. System KS

Given that in system SKS the identity is a rule, not an axiom as in the sequent calculus, a natural question to ask is whether the applications of the identity rule can be restricted to the top of a derivation. For proofs, this question is already answered positively by Theorem 5.1. It turns out that it is also true for derivations. Because of the duality between ai↓ and ai↑ we can also push the cuts to the bottom of a derivation. While this can be obtained in the sequent calculus (using cut elimination), it can not be done with a simple permutation argument.

We first reduce atomic identity and cut to *shallow* atomic identity and cut, the following rules:

$$\mathsf{ai_s}\downarrow \frac{S}{(S, [a, \bar{a}])} \quad \text{and} \quad \mathsf{ai_s}\uparrow \frac{[S, (a, \bar{a})]}{S} \quad .$$

Lemma 5.3. The rule $\mathsf{ai}{\downarrow}$ is strongly admissible for $\{\mathsf{ai_s}{\downarrow}, \mathsf{s}\}$. Dually, the rule $\mathsf{ai}{\uparrow}$ is strongly admissible for $\{\mathsf{ai_s}{\uparrow}, \mathsf{s}\}$.

Proof. By an easy structural induction on the context $S\{\ \}$. Details are in [1]. □

Theorem 5.4 (Decomposition: separation of identity and cut).

For every derivation $\begin{array}{c} T \\ \| \mathsf{SKS} \\ R \end{array}$ there is a derivation $\begin{array}{c} T \\ \| \{\mathsf{ai}{\downarrow}\} \\ V \\ \| \mathsf{SKS} \setminus \{\mathsf{ai}{\downarrow}, \mathsf{ai}{\uparrow}\} \\ U \\ \| \{\mathsf{ai}{\uparrow}\} \\ R \end{array}$.

Proof. By Lemma 5.3 we can reduce atomic identities to shallow atomic identities and the same for the cuts. It is easy to check that the rule $\mathsf{ai_s}{\downarrow}$ permutes over every rule in SKS and the rule $\mathsf{ai_s}{\uparrow}$ permutes under every rule in SKS. Instances of $\mathsf{ai_s}{\downarrow}$ and $\mathsf{ai_s}{\uparrow}$ are instances of $\mathsf{ai}{\downarrow}$ and $\mathsf{ai}{\uparrow}$, respectively. □

Contraction allows the repeated use of a statement in a proof by allowing to copy it at will. It should be possible to copy everything needed in the beginning, and then go on with the proof without ever having to copy again. This intuition is made precise by the following theorem and holds for system SKS. We do not know of such a result for the sequent calculus. There are sequent systems for classical propositional logic that do not have an explicit contraction rule, however, they treat the context additively, so contraction is "built-in" and used throughout the proof.

Theorem 5.5 (Decomposition: separation of atomic contraction).

For every derivation $\begin{array}{c} T \\ \| \mathsf{SKS} \\ R \end{array}$ there is a derivation $\begin{array}{c} T \\ \| \{\mathsf{ac}{\uparrow}\} \\ V \\ \| \mathsf{SKS} \setminus \{\mathsf{ac}{\downarrow}, \mathsf{ac}{\uparrow}\} \\ U \\ \| \{\mathsf{ac}{\downarrow}\} \\ R \end{array}$.

Proof. The obstacles to permuting up the instances of $\mathsf{ac}{\uparrow}$ and down those of $\mathsf{ac}{\downarrow}$ are identity and cut, respectively. The solution is to turn the derivation into a proof, eliminate the cuts, turn the proof into a derivation again (using one cut), and then permuting up or down the contractions. The proof can be found in [1]. □

6 Conclusions and Open Problems

We have presented SKS, a system of inference rules for classical logic in the calculus of structures. Its main novelty is that all rules are local and their computational cost can thus be bounded. To achieve this, the greater expressivity of the calculus of structures wrt. the sequent calculus was used, in particular its ability of making deep inferences. We proved cut elimination for system SKS which makes it suitable for proof-search. Actually, a subset KS of inference rules is already complete. We have also shown properties of our system that seem not to hold for any sequent presentation of classical logic, that is, strong admissibility of cut, weakening and contraction for their atomic forms and the decomposition theorems for derivations.

The main open problem is a more powerful decomposition theorem. To that end, let us call *core* those rules in the system that are necessary for decomposing the general cut into atomic cuts. In SKS, the core consists of one single rule: the switch. Can we separate out, i.e. push above the identities or below the cuts, anything that is not core?

Conjecture 6.1. For every derivation $\begin{array}{c} T \\ \| \mathsf{SKS} \\ R \end{array}$ there is a derivation $\begin{array}{c} T \\ \| \textit{non-core} \\ U_4 \\ \| \{\mathsf{ai}\!\downarrow\} \\ U_3 \\ \| \textit{core} \\ U_2 \\ \| \{\mathsf{ai}\!\uparrow\} \\ U_1 \\ \| \textit{non-core} \\ R \end{array}$.

This conjecture has been proved for two other systems in the calculus of structures [6] and this led to cut elimination. In these cut elimination proofs, atomic cuts are seen as instances of a super atomic cut, which is then pushed up all the way through the proof until it hits an identity that makes it disappear. In system SKS, such a super atomic cut cannot be pushed up over the rules ac↓ and m. Cut elimination would be much easier to prove syntactically could we rely on Conjecture 6.1. Then all the problematic rules that could stand in the way of the cut are either below all the cuts already or at the top of the proof and thus trivial, since their premise is t. Cut elimination is thus an easy consequence of such a decomposition theorem. Note that the proof of Theorem 5.5 falls short of simplifying a syntactical proof of cut elimination not only because instances of the rule m remain above the cuts, but also because it *uses* cut elimination.

Modularity We have proved cut elimination for system SKS, but we have no syntactic proof inside the calculus of structures, i.e. without detour through the sequent calculus and without resorting to semantics. We are interested in such a proof because it can be *modular*, contrary to cut elimination proofs in the sequent calculus, cf. Girard [4] p.15. This modularity stems from the fact that due to atomicity of the cut, cut elimination in the calculus of structures is not a nested induction taking into account the cut rank; instead it is based on a number of lemmas about permutability of rules wrt. one another (for a rather general notion of permutability). Those lemmas of course are not affected when new rules are added to the system.

Predicative logic We are currently investigating the following extension of system SKS to predicative logic: adding quantifiers to the language in the obvious way, adding the corresponding De Morgan laws and the equation

$$\forall x R = \exists x R = R \qquad \text{if } x \text{ is not free in } R,$$

and adding the rules from Fig. 6. Very roughly, rules $\{u\downarrow, u\uparrow\}$ correspond to the R∀ rule in GS1 while rules $\{n\downarrow, n\uparrow\}$ correspond to R∃. The rules $\{ce\downarrow, ce\uparrow, ca\downarrow, ca\uparrow\}$ are just needed to reduce contraction to its atomic form. For proofs, the up-rules $\{n\uparrow, u\uparrow, ce\uparrow, ca\uparrow\}$ are admissible. A nice common feature of all these rules is that their premise implies their conclusion (literally, without any added quantification). This is not true of any sequent calculus presentation known to us because of the R∀ rule.

We do not claim that this system is local. In the rule $n\downarrow$ a term t of unbounded size is copied into an unbounded number of occurrences of x in R. Maybe unification could be incorporated into the system to deal with this in a local manner, but we have not explored this option. The question is whether this can be done without losing the good properties, cut elimination especially.

$$u\downarrow \frac{S\{\forall x[R,T]\}}{S[\forall xR, \exists xT]} \qquad u\uparrow \frac{S(\exists xR, \forall xT)}{S\{\exists x(R,T)\}} \qquad n\downarrow \frac{S\{R[x \leftarrow t]\}}{S\{\exists xR\}} \qquad n\uparrow \frac{S\{\forall xR\}}{S\{R[x \leftarrow t]\}}$$

$$ce\downarrow \frac{S[\exists xR, \exists xT]}{S\{\exists x[R,T]\}} \qquad ce\uparrow \frac{S\{\forall x(R,T)\}}{S(\forall xR, \forall xT)} \qquad ca\downarrow \frac{S[\forall xR, \forall xT]}{S\{\forall x[R,T]\}} \qquad ca\uparrow \frac{S\{\exists x(R,T)\}}{S(\exists xR, \exists xT)}$$

Fig. 6. Extension to predicative logic

Semantics for derivations Structures are in a one-to-one correspondence with *traces* [5] that are graphs with colored edges satisfying certain simple properties. The atom occurrences of a structure are the nodes of its trace and the colors of the edges are determined by the logical relation between the atom occurrences. In [5] it is shown that the switch rule can be characterized in terms of conditions on traces. Those conditions can be checked locally in the sense that they involve at most four atoms at a time.

The question is whether the rule m can be characterized in the same way. This would be a step towards a distributed system in which proof-search is driven by pairs of complementary atoms, comparable in spirit to the connection method [9]. At present, however, this question is entirely open.

Hopefully, trace semantics can help in understanding derivations. Given the existence of a derivation in a subset of SKS from a known S to an unknown T, what is the relation between (the traces of) S and T? What can be inferred about T, i.e. what graph-theoretic properties on traces are preserved by the inference rules? By classical semantics we know that all of them preserve truth (successful valuations). The problem is that this does not tell us much about T, in particular it tells us nothing about atom occurrences, their number, and their logical relations. A better understanding of this would also help in finding a decomposition theorem as sketched in Conjecture 6.1.

Acknowledgments

This work has been accomplished while the first author was supported by the DFG Graduiertenkolleg 334. We would like to thank the members of the proof theory group at Dresden for providing an inspiring environment, especially Alessio Guglielmi, who introduced us to proof theory. He discovered the rules for predicative logic $\{\mathsf{u}\downarrow, \mathsf{u}\uparrow, \mathsf{n}\downarrow, \mathsf{n}\uparrow\}$ and helped us with this paper in numerous ways. Steffen Hölldobler and Lutz Straßburger carefully read preliminary versions of this paper and made helpful suggestions. We are grateful to Bernhard Ganter for noting the similarity between the medial law studied in algebra and our rule m, giving it its current name.

References

1. Kai Brünnler and Alwen Fernanto Tiu. A local system for classical logic. Technical Report WV-2001-02, Dresden University of Technology, 2001. On the web at: http://www.wv.inf.tu-dresden.de/~kai/LocalClassicalLogic.ps.gz.
2. Gerhard Gentzen. Investigations into logical deduction. In M. E. Szabo, editor, *The Collected Papers of Gerhard Gentzen*, pages 68–131. North-Holland, Amsterdam, 1969.
3. Jean-Yves Girard. Linear logic. *Theoretical Computer Science*, 50:1–102, 1987.
4. Jean-Yves Girard. *Proof Theory and Logical Complexity, Volume I*, volume 1 of *Studies in Proof Theory*. Bibliopolis, Napoli, 1987. Distributed by Elsevier.
5. Alessio Guglielmi. A calculus of order and interaction. Technical Report WV-99-04, Dresden University of Technology, 1999. Available on the web at http://www.wv.inf.tu-dresden.de/~guglielm/Research/Gug/Gug.pdf.
6. Alessio Guglielmi and Lutz Straßburger. Non-commutativity and MELL in the calculus of structures. Technical Report WV-01-04, Dresden University of Technology, 2001. Accepted by the Annual Conference of the European Association for Computer Science Logic, CSL'01.
7. Lutz Straßburger. MELL in the calculus of structures. Technical Report WV-2001-03, Dresden University of Technology, 2001. On the web at: http://www.ki.inf.tu-dresden.de/~lutz/els.pdf.
8. Anne Sjerp Troelstra and Helmut Schwichtenberg. *Basic Proof Theory*. Cambridge University Press, 1996.
9. W. Bibel. On matrices with connections. *Journal of the Association for Computing Machinery*, 28(4):633–645, 1981.

Partial Implicit Unfolding in the Davis-Putnam Procedure for Quantified Boolean Formulae

Jussi Rintanen

Albert-Ludwigs-Universität Freiburg, Institut für Informatik
Georges-Köhler-Allee, 79110 Freiburg im Breisgau
Germany

Abstract. Quantified Boolean formulae offer a means of representing many propositional formula exponentially more compactly than propositional logic. Recent work on automating reasoning with QBF has concentrated on extending the Davis-Putnam procedure to handle QBF. Although the resulting procedures make it possible to evaluate QBF that could not be efficiently reduced to propositional logic (requiring worst-case exponential space), its efficiency often lags much behind the reductive approach when the reduction is possible. We attribute this inefficiency to the fact that many of the unit resolution steps possible in the reduced (propositional logic) formula are not performed in the corresponding QBF. To combine the conciseness of the QBF representation and the stronger inferences available in the unquantified representation, we introduce a stronger propagation algorithm for QBF which could be seen as partially unfolding the universal quantification. The algorithm runs in worst-case exponential time, like the reduction of QBF to propositional logic, but needs only polynomial space. By restricting the algorithm the exponential behavior can be avoided while still preserving many of the useful inferences.

1 Introduction

Quantified Boolean formulae are a generalization of the satisfiability problem of the propositional logic that allows a more concise representation of many classes of formulae. The additional conciseness lifts the complexity of evaluating QBF to PSPACE-complete, which is in strong contrast to the NP-completeness of propositional satisfiability. However, the connection between the two problems is close, and not surprisingly some of the recent procedures for evaluating QBF [3,20] are extensions of the Davis-Putnam procedure [4]. An alternative solution technique is to reduce a QBF to an unquantified propositional formula, and to test its truth by a conventional satisfiability algorithm. The drawback of this reductive approach is that the size of the propositional formula is worst-case exponential in the size of the QBF, which usually makes it impractical for all but the simplest QBF.

A problem with the extensions of the Davis-Putnam procedure to QBF is that many of the unit resolution steps that would be possible with the reduced

R. Nieuwenhuis and A. Voronkov (Eds.): LPAR 2001, LNAI 2250, pp. 362–376, 2001.

formula do not take place. For restricted types of QBF, when the number of quantifier alternations is small, this problem has been partially overcome [20].

In this paper we attempt to provide a more general solution to this problem. The solution departs from earlier work on evaluating QBF in that the binary search algorithm is combined with a propagation algorithm that runs in *exponential time* in the size of the QBF. In general, algorithms for intractable problems have a restricted number of sources of non-polynomial behavior, and it is not a priori clear that using an exponential time subprocedure is sensible. Therefore, we present techniques for avoiding the exponentiality of the propagation algorithm to make the algorithm more practical. Our hypothesis is that the exponential reduction in problem size, due to the use of QBF instead of an equivalent unquantified formula, justifies a more expensive propagation algorithm. We also believe that in some cases even an exponential time propagation algorithm could be justified. The algorithm can be viewed as a conventional unit propagation algorithm for a QBF representation of unquantified clause sets.

The structure of the paper is as follows. In Sect. 4 we discuss the computational problem in detail by giving practically motivated examples of QBF that are very difficult for the current QBF algorithms. In Sect. 5 we outline the propagation algorithm, and in Sect. 6 we propose improvements and give a restricted variant of the algorithm that runs in polynomial time. Sect. 7 gives a preliminary experimental analysis of the algorithm, and Sect. 8 discusses related work.

2 Preliminaries

Quantified Boolean formulae are of the form $q_1 x_1 \cdots q_n x_n \phi$ where ϕ is a propositional formula and the prefix consists of universal $\forall$ and existential $\exists$ quantifiers q_i and the propositional variables x_i occurring in ϕ. Define $\phi[\psi/x]$ as the formula obtained from ϕ by replacing occurrences[1] of the propositional variable x by the formula ψ. The truth of formulae is defined recursively as follows. The truth of a formula that does not contain variables, that is, that consists of connectives and the constants true $\top$ and false $\bot$, is defined by the truth-tables for the connectives. A formula $\exists x \phi$ is true if and only if $\phi[\top/x]$ or $\phi[\bot/x]$ is true. A formula $\forall x \phi$ is true if and only if $\phi[\top/x]$ and $\phi[\bot/x]$ are true. Examples of true formulae are $\forall x \exists y (x \leftrightarrow y)$ and $\exists x \exists y (x \wedge y)$. The formulae $\exists x \forall y (x \leftrightarrow y)$ and $\forall x \forall y (x \vee y)$ are false. Changing the order of two consecutive variables quantified by the same quantifier does not affect the truth-value of the formula. It is often useful to ignore the ordering of consecutive variables and view each quantifier as quantifying a set of formulae, for example $\exists x_1 x_2 \forall y_1 y_2 \phi$.

3 The Extension of the Davis-Putnam Procedure to QBF

We have designed and implemented an algorithm that determines the truth-value of quantified Boolean formulae [20]. The Davis-Putnam procedure [4] is a

[1] We assume that nested quantifiers do not quantify the same variable.

special case of the algorithm. The main differences are that instead of only or-nodes, the search tree for quantified Boolean formulae contains also and-nodes that correspond to universally quantified variables, and that the order of the variables in the prefix constrains the order in which the variables generate a search tree. The algorithm takes as input formulae in which all quantifiers are in front of the formulae and the body is in conjunctive normal form.

The main procedure of the algorithm sketched in Fig. 1 takes three parameters.[2] The variable e is true if the first quantifier in the prefix of the formula is $\exists$. The sequence $\langle V_1, \ldots, V_n \rangle$ represents the prefix. For example, if the prefix is $\exists x_1 \exists x_2 \forall x_3 \exists x_4$, then $V_1 = \{x_1, x_2\}, V_2 = \{x_3\}$ and $V_3 = \{x_4\}$. The set C consists of clauses $\{l_1, \ldots, l_n\}$ where $n \geq 0$ and l_i are literals. The empty clause $\emptyset$ is false.

PROCEDURE decide($e, \langle V_1, V_2, \ldots, V_n \rangle, C$)
BEGIN
  $C :=$ unit(C);
  IF $\emptyset \in C$ *THEN RETURN* false;
  IF $n = 0$ *THEN RETURN* true;
  remove from V_1 all variables occurring in a unit clause in C;
  IF $V_1 = \emptyset$ *THEN*
    RETURN decide(not $e, \langle V_2, \ldots, V_n \rangle, C$);
  $x :=$ a member of V_1;
  $V_1 := V_1 \backslash \{x\}$;
  IF e *THEN*
    IF decide($e, \langle V_1, \ldots, V_n \rangle, C \cup \{\{x\}\}$)
    THEN RETURN true;
  ELSE
    IF not decide($e, \langle V_1, \ldots, V_n \rangle, C \cup \{\{x\}\}$)
    THEN RETURN false;
  RETURN decide($e, \langle V_1, \ldots, V_n \rangle, C \cup \{\{\neg x\}\}$)
END

Fig. 1. The extension of the Davis-Putnam procedure to QBF

The subprocedure *unit* performs simplification by unit resolution and unit subsumption; unit(S) is defined as the fixpoint of F under a set S of clauses.

$$\begin{aligned} F(C) = & \{c \backslash \{l\} | c \in C, \{\bar{l}\} \in C, l \in c\} \\ & \cup \{c \in C | l \notin c \text{ and } \bar{l} \notin c \text{ for all } \{l\} \in C\} \\ & \cup \{\{l\} \in C\} \end{aligned}$$

[2] The algorithm is simplified because we just want to indicate what the main differences to the Davis-Putnam procedure are. For example, we do not require that the variable x does not have a truth-value when it is branched on.

4 Motivating Examples

First we give simple examples illustrating which unit propagations are not performed by the Davis-Putnam QBF procedure of Section 3, and then we show a practical example of a class of formulae that are equivalent to exponentially bigger propositional formulae, and for which the lack of unit propagations makes even small formulae very difficult.

Example 1. Consider the QBF $\exists x \forall y \exists z (y \rightarrow z, z \rightarrow x)$. By considering the case when the universally quantified variable y gets the value true, one sees that also x has to be true. That this kind of reasoning may speed up evaluation of QBF considerably is shown by Rintanen [20].

The above line of reasoning often allows inferring some of the truth-values of the outermost variables in the Davis-Putnam QBF procedure. For QBF with prefix $\exists\forall\exists$, considering all valuations of the universal variables allows performing all the desired unit propagation steps.[3] However, when the prefix contains more than one block of universal variables, this is not the case.

Example 2. Consider the QBF $\exists a \forall b \exists x_1 x_2 \forall y \exists z_1 z_2 ((y \rightarrow z_1) \wedge (z_1 \rightarrow x_1) \wedge ((\neg y \wedge x_1) \rightarrow z_2) \wedge (z_2 \rightarrow x_2) \wedge ((x_1 \wedge x_2 \wedge b) \rightarrow a))$. Unlike in Example 1 where (repeatedly) choosing truth-values for all universal variables and then performing unit propagation yielded all desired values for the outermost variables, in this example the same strategy does not suffice. The problem is that two valuations, respectively assigning $b = \top, y = \top$ and $b = \top, y = \bot$, are needed, and neither of these alone allows inferring a. First one uses the first assignment and infers x_1, exchanges $y = \top$ to $y = \bot$, and only then can one infer a with x_2. After using the first assignment, one in general cannot preserve the values obtained for x_1 and x_2, because these could depend on the choice $b = \top$, to which we have not committed to.

The propagation pattern present in Example 2 could be made still more intricate. In $\exists T \forall U \exists X \forall Y \Phi$ we could be forced to repeatedly alternate between valuations v_1 and v_2 of the universal variables Y in order to infer more and more values for the existential variables X, keeping part of the valuation (for the outermost universal variables U) fixed. The second example shows that the hierarchical propagation structure could be vital for solving naturally occurring QBF.

Example 3. Consider the following formula that represents the existence of transition sequences of length 2^n between two states [21].

$$\exists S S' (\text{reach}_n(S, S') \wedge I \wedge G) \tag{1}$$

Here I and G are the formulae describing the initial and goal states respectively expressed in terms of variables from sets S and S'. Here $\text{reach}_i(S, S')$ means that

[3] Of course, performing this computation that is exponential in the number of universal variables may in practise be too expensive to be useful.

a state represented in terms of variables from S' can be reached with 2^i steps from a state represented in terms of variables from S. It is recursively defined as follows.

$$\begin{aligned}\text{reach}_0(S,S') &\stackrel{\text{def}}{\equiv} R(S,S')\\ \text{reach}_{i+1}(S,S') &\stackrel{\text{def}}{\equiv} \exists T\forall c\exists T_1\exists T_2(\text{reach}_i(T_1,T_2)\\ &\quad\wedge(c\rightarrow(T_1=S\wedge T_2=T))\\ &\quad\wedge(\neg c\rightarrow(T_1=T\wedge T_2=S')))\end{aligned}$$

Here R is the one-step transition relation on two sets of variables that respectively represent the state variables for the predecessor and the successor states. The sets T and S consist of propositional variables, and $S=T$ for $S=\{s_1,\ldots,s_n\}$ and $T=\{t_1,\ldots,t_n\}$ means $(s_1\leftrightarrow t_1)\wedge\cdots\wedge(s_n\leftrightarrow t_n)$. The idea of the definition of $\text{reach}_{i+1}(S,S')$ is that the variables T describe a state halfway between S and S', and the two values for the variable c correspond to two reachability tests, one between S and T, and the other between T and S'. This is very close to the PSPACE membership proof of s-t reachability of graphs represented in terms of state variables [15,14,2].

If we eliminate all universal variables from Formula 1, we see that it is essentially a concise $O(\log t)$ space ($t=2^n$) representation of

$$I_0\wedge R(S_0,S_1)\wedge R(S_1,S_2)\wedge\cdots\wedge R(S_{t-1},S_t)\wedge G_t \tag{2}$$

with only one occurrence of the transition relation R. Now, there are many instances of Formula 2 (especially if the estimated transition sequence length 2^i is "low") in which unit propagation immediately yields many state variable values [9,18]. However, for the corresponding Formula 1 none of this takes place. The Davis-Putnam QBF procedure performs an exhaustive search through the valuations of all the variables but the innermost ones. This makes even small reachability problems (a couple of dozen state variables and transition sequence length 4) practically unsolvable on the Davis-Putnam QBF procedure, while the corresponding Formula 2 would be solved immediately by any reasonable satisfiability algorithm.

Example 4. When the transition relation R is the implication $s_0\rightarrow s_1$, we obtain the following formula for reachability of length 4.

$$\begin{aligned}&\exists ab\\ &\exists x_1\forall c_1\exists s_1\exists t_1\\ &\exists x_2\forall c_2\exists s_2\exists t_2\ (a\wedge\\ &\qquad c_1\rightarrow((a\leftrightarrow s_1)\wedge(x_1\leftrightarrow t_1))\wedge\\ &\qquad \neg c_1\rightarrow((x_1\leftrightarrow s_1)\wedge(b\leftrightarrow t_1))\wedge\\ &\qquad c_2\rightarrow((s_1\leftrightarrow s_2)\wedge(x_2\leftrightarrow t_2))\wedge\\ &\qquad \neg c_2\rightarrow((x_2\leftrightarrow s_2)\wedge(t_1\leftrightarrow t_2))\wedge\\ &\qquad (s_2\rightarrow t_2))\end{aligned}$$

This formula is equivalent to (with respect to a and b)

$$a\wedge(a\rightarrow s_1)\wedge(s_1\rightarrow s_2)\wedge(s_2\rightarrow s_3)\wedge(s_3\rightarrow b),$$

and by unit resolution one can directly infer that b has to be true.

5 The New Unit Propagation Algorithm

Let u be the first universal variable in the prefix of a QBF Φ, and let $x_1, \ldots, x_n$ be the existential variables in the prefix *after* u. Then u can be eliminated from Φ by producing the QBF $\Phi_u = \Phi[x'_1/x_1, \ldots, x'_n/x_n, \top/u] \wedge \Phi[\bot/u]$. If $u_1, \ldots, u_m$ are the universal variables in Φ, then Φ is true if and only if $\Phi_{u_1,\ldots,u_m}$ is true. This latter formula is the one obtained by eliminating the universal variables from Φ in the given order that agrees with their order in the prefix. Now $\Phi_{u_1,\ldots,u_m}$ contains existential variables only, and it – when ignoring the quantifiers – can be viewed as a normal satisfiability problem in the propositional logic. Because $\Phi_{u_1,\ldots,u_m}$ can have a size exponential in the size of Φ, this reduction is usually not a practical way of evaluating QBF.

The algorithm we propose could be viewed as partially unfolding the QBF: at any point of time only one of the 2^m conjuncts of $\Phi_{u_1,\ldots,u_m}$ is produced, call it χ, which corresponds to a single valuation of all the universal variables. Such formulae χ typically share (existential) variables, because existential variables get renamed in the reduction only when they follow a universal variable in the prefix. We would like to perform unit resolution on these formulae χ so that truth-values obtained for shared variables would be propagated also to other formulae χ' obtained by partially unfolding Φ.

This idea leads to the hierarchical propagation algorithm in Fig. 2 that does not explicitly produce the formulae $\Phi_{u_1,\ldots,u_m}$. It takes the following parameters.

- $Q = \langle V_1, \ldots, V_n \rangle$ is a sequence of sets of variables that represents the quantifiers of the QBF, where V_{2i+1} for $i \geq 0$ are universally quantified and V_{2i} for $i \geq 1$ are existentially quantified, and
- C is the body of the formula (a set of clauses).

```
PROCEDURE propagate(⟨V1, V2, V3, ..., Vn⟩, C)
IF n = 0 THEN RETURN unit(C);
again:
FOR EACH valuation v of V1 DO
  C' := propagate(⟨V3, ..., Vn⟩, C ∪ v);
  IF {p} ∈ C'\C or {¬p} ∈ C'\C for some p ∈ P
                        where P = V\(V1 ∪ ··· ∪ Vn)
  THEN
    BEGIN
      C := C ∪ (C' ∩ ({{p}|p ∈ P} ∪ {{¬p}|p ∈ P}));
      GOTO again;
    END
END
RETURN C;
```

Fig. 2. The hierarchical unit propagation algorithm

Valuations v of V_1 above are sets of unit clauses with exactly one occurrence of every variable in V_1. The set V consists of all variables occurring in the

QBF. The existential variables V_{2i} in the prefix Q are used by the propagation algorithm only as far as conventional unit propagation produces them.

The algorithm runs in exponential time on the size of the QBF because the number of valuations may be exponential. However, it needs only polynomial space. This is because at any given point of time only one valuation of the universal variables and the values inferred for the existential variables need to be stored explicitly.

6 Improvements

The algorithm can be improved by taking into account properties of the body C of the formula, and by preventing the worst-case exponential running time. First, we give stricter conditions on the selection of valuations v based on the possibilities of performing unit resolution steps. This often leads to a big reduction in the runtime but does not eliminate the exponential time worst-case behavior. Second, in Sect. 6.1 we consider further restrictions that lead to a polynomial runtime.

Example 5. Consider a clause set C in which only the clause $u_1 \vee u_2 \vee x$ contains less than two existential variables, namely the variable x. The only possibility of performing unit resolution is to assign both u_1 and u_2 false.

Therefore, only such values should be assigned to the universal values that contribute to producing a unit clause. It would be possible to take the usefulness criterion further. The new unit clause that is obtained should have a complementary occurrence in a clause with less than 3 literals: otherwise the unit clause would be the only one that is produced, and therefore often not very useful.

6.1 Restrictions Leading to Polynomial Runtime

Producing unit clauses from two clauses $u \vee \phi_1$ and $\neg u \vee \phi_2$ is complementary. This is the reason why the worst-case runtime of the algorithm is exponential: otherwise it would suffice to choose one valuation for the universal variables so that all possible unit clauses are produced.

Example 6. Consider a clause set that includes the clauses $(u_1 \vee x_1), (\neg u_1 \vee x_1'), (u_2 \vee x_2), (\neg u_2 \vee x_2'), \cdots, (u_n \vee x_n), (\neg u_n \vee x_n')$. One can obtain 2^n different sets of unit clauses by assigning 2^n different combinations of truth-values to the universal variables $u_1, \ldots, u_n$.

The exponential behavior of the propagation algorithm can be avoided by refraining from trying out all valuations of the universal variables. A reasonable strategy would be to try only enough valuations so that each unit clause (but not necessarily every combination of unit clauses) is obtained once. Of course, this restriction means that correspondence between the unit resolution steps available in the unquantified propositional formula and in the corresponding QBF is lost.

Depending on the QBF in question, this could be a big loss or not. For the $O(\log n)$ QBF encoding of the s-t reachability problem one may be forced to try out an exponential number of combinations of unit clauses to obtain all inference steps.

7 An Implementation of the Algorithm

We have implemented the propagation algorithm as a variant of the QBF solver described by us earlier [20]. The new propagation algorithm replaces the less general inversion and sampling techniques. The solver heavily uses a general form of the failed literal rule for reducing the size of the search tree: see Li and Anbulagan's work on the sat00 implementation of the Davis-Putnam procedure [12]. From the other techniques described by Rintanen [20] only the splitting of the clause set to disjoint subsets with no shared variables is used.

The new propagation algorithm is used at every node of the search tree, just like the standard unit propagation algorithm. The implementation consists of two mutually recursive subprocedures, the first traversing through all the valuations of a block of universal quantifiers, and the second keeping track of the existential variables that have been inferred. The polynomial time behavior described in Sect. 6.1 is achieved by labeling every clause that has been made a unit clause, and refraining from trying a truth-value (true or false) for a universal variable if it would not help producing a unit clause that has not already been labeled. This way the number of valuations tried is at most as high as the number of clauses with one existential literal and one or more universal literals.

7.1 Structured Formulae

We evaluated the algorithm on problems from AI planning that are encoded like Example 3. They solve a small blocks' world problem with 4 blocks, the Towers of Hanoi with 3 disks, and the well-known bw-large.a and bw-large.b blocks world problems. We list the runtimes on our implementations of the basic Davis-Putnam QBF procedure, with the inversion/sampling techniques from [20], and with the new propagation algorithm, in Table 1. The runs were on a 360MHz Sun Sparc. We terminated each run that lasted for more than one hour. Even the best runtimes presented here are worse than the runtimes of conventional satisfiability algorithms on the reduced formulae. A bigger set of test runs is reported in Table 2. These QBF include ones representing planning under incomplete information [19], some randomly generated problems, and the encoding of long chains of implications as in Example 4. On some of the problems the stronger propagation algorithms slow down QBF evaluation because only very few or no new literals can be inferred, and running the algorithms is relatively expensive.

7.2 Random Formulae

Contrary to what was reported by us earlier for the less general unfolding techniques [20], our implementation of the new propagation algorithm improves the

Table 1. Runtimes of the QBF algorithm on QBF from AI planning. The last QBF for each problem is true, the preceding ones are false.

					runtime in seconds		
problem	path length	prefix	vars	clauses	DP/QBF	DP+inversion	DP+new alg.
BLOCKS4	2	∃∀∃	149	1183	> 3600	0.03	0.04
BLOCKS4	4	∃∀∃∀∃	210	1505	> 3600	1527.55	3.20
BLOCKS4	8	∃∀∃∀∃∀∃	271	1827	> 3600	> 3600	4.22
HANOI3	2	∃∀∃	709	16599	> 3600	0.56	0.54
HANOI3	4	∃∀∃∀∃	962	17553	> 3600	> 3600	23.08
HANOI3	8	∃∀∃∀∃∀∃	1215	18507	> 3600	> 3600	> 3600
bw-large.a	2	∃∀∃	1099	62916	> 3600	0.89	1.13
bw-large.a	4	∃∀∃∀∃	1370	65688	> 3600	> 3600	256.75
bw-large.b	2	∃∀∃	1871	178890	> 3600	1.74	2.38
bw-large.b	4	∃∀∃∀∃	2268	183741	> 3600	> 3600	15.65
bw-large.b	8	∃∀∃∀∃∀∃	2665	188592	> 3600	> 3600	> 3600

Davis-Putnam QBF procedure runtimes on difficult randomly generated problems substantially. This is because of the stricter and more goal-directed criteria for selecting truth-values for universal variables.

Tables 3 and 4 show the runtimes of our QBF solver on random QBF (model A of Gent and Walsh [6]) respectively without and with the new propagation algorithm. The times reported are runtimes (in milliseconds) of 150 variable ∃∀∃ formulae with varying numbers of universal variables and clauses/variables ratios. The runtimes are averages on 1000 formulae. The percentage of universal variables (rows in the tables) varies from 0 to 53.3, and the number of existential variables before and after the universal variables is the same. The clauses/variables ratio varies from 1 to 4 (the columns in the tables.) The propagation algorithm produced each unit clause at least once, but did not produce all combinations of unit clauses. The ratios of the runtimes with and without the new propagation algorithm are shown in Table 5. In the phase transition region on the most difficult QBF (see [20]) the new propagation algorithm speeds up the evaluation by a factor of ten. On easier formulae, especially those containing a high number of universal variables, the algorithm slows down the evaluation, up to a factor of five. On bigger formulae and with more quantifiers the speed-ups are much bigger.

8 Related Work

Early work on quantified Boolean formulae include the polynomial time algorithm by Aspvall et al. [1] for quantified 2-literal clauses, and the polynomial time decision algorithm for quantified Horn clauses by Kleine Büning et al. [10]. Kleine Büning et al. also define a resolution rule for QBF.

Cadoli et al. [3] extended the Davis-Putnam procedure to handle quantified Boolean formulae. Their algorithm is similar to the one in Sect. 3, first defined in [20], but is based on two mutually recursive procedures that respectively

Table 2. Comparison of the runtimes of the basic Davis-Putnam QBF procedure, the same with the new propagation algorithm restricted to polynomial runtime, and the unrestricted new propagation algorithm, on a number of QBF.

	basic DP/QBF		new algo. $O(p(n))$		new algo. $O(2^n)$	
problem	runtime	tree size	runtime	tree size	runtime	tree size
BLOCKS3i.4.4.qcnf	> 10 min.	-	0.20	0	0.17	0
BLOCKS3i.5.3.qcnf	> 10 min.	-	94.10	378	101.80	378
BLOCKS3i.5.4.qcnf	> 10 min.	-	9.19	50	9.80	50
BLOCKS3ii.4.3.qcnf	18.53	1015	0.15	0	0.11	0
BLOCKS3ii.5.2.qcnf	345.98	10021	0.19	0	0.18	0
BLOCKS3ii.5.3.qcnf	> 10 min.	-	1.49	29	1.44	29
BLOCKS3iii.4.qcnf	20.35	1728	0.05	0	0.03	0
BLOCKS3iii.5.qcnf	> 10 min.	-	0.73	26	0.70	26
BLOCKS4i.6.4.qcnf	> 10 min.	-	8.96	0	9.00	0
BLOCKS4i.7.3.qcnf	> 10 min.	-	> 10 min.	-	> 10 min.	-
BLOCKS4i.7.4.qcnf	> 10 min.	-	> 10 min.	-	> 10 min.	-
BLOCKS4ii.6.3.qcnf	> 10 min.	-	8.78	0	8.85	0
BLOCKS4ii.7.2.qcnf	> 10 min.	-	15.21	0	15.12	0
BLOCKS4ii.7.3.qcnf	> 10 min.	-	453.03	190	455.85	190
BLOCKS4iii.6.qcnf	> 10 min.	-	4.39	0	4.45	0
BLOCKS4iii.7.qcnf	> 10 min.	-	230.21	178	218.21	178
CHAIN12v.13.qcnf	0.25	36	0.43	12	73.67	12
CHAIN13v.14.qcnf	0.31	39	0.55	13	182.61	13
CHAIN14v.15.qcnf	0.38	42	0.74	14	449.17	14
CHAIN15v.16.qcnf	0.52	45	0.92	15	> 10 min.	-
CHAIN16v.17.qcnf	0.64	48	1.13	16	> 10 min.	-
CHAIN17v.18.qcnf	0.74	51	1.43	17	> 10 min.	-
CHAIN18v.19.qcnf	0.91	54	1.74	18	> 10 min.	-
CHAIN19v.20.qcnf	1.07	57	2.15	19	> 10 min.	-
CHAIN20v.21.qcnf	1.23	60	2.68	20	> 10 min.	-
CHAIN21v.22.qcnf	0.51	63	2.12	21	> 10 min.	-
CHAIN22v.23.qcnf	0.71	66	2.57	22	> 10 min.	-
CHAIN23v.24.qcnf	1.05	69	3.18	23	> 10 min.	-
TOILET10.1.iv.19.qcnf	> 10 min.	-	> 10 min.	-	> 10 min.	-
TOILET10.1.iv.20.qcnf	1.54	19	5.84	18	5.83	18
TOILET16.1.iv.31.qcnf	> 10 min.	-	> 10 min.	-	> 10 min.	-
TOILET16.1.iv.32.qcnf	10.83	31	61.51	30	62.22	30
TOILET2.1.iv.3.qcnf	0.01	3	0.01	0	0.01	0
TOILET2.1.iv.4.qcnf	0.00	3	0.00	2	0.03	2
TOILET6.1.iv.11.qcnf	554.59	111102	46.63	1658	46.52	1658
TOILET6.1.iv.12.qcnf	0.20	11	0.51	10	0.53	10
TOILET7.1.iv.13.qcnf	> 10 min.	-	659.26	17851	> 10 min.	-
TOILET7.1.iv.14.qcnf	0.42	13	1.58	12	1.61	12
R3CNF_150_3_15_2.50_0.T.qcnf	0.82	549	0.05	5	0.05	5
R3CNF_150_3_15_2.50_1.F.qcnf	5.75	3388	0.59	24	0.67	24
R3CNF_150_3_15_2.50_2.T.qcnf	1.54	859	0.13	9	0.15	9
R3CNF_150_3_15_2.50_3.T.qcnf	0.38	300	0.06	6	0.09	6
R3CNF_150_3_15_2.50_4.T.qcnf	2.26	1394	0.32	17	0.34	17
R3CNF_150_3_15_2.50_5.T.qcnf	0.69	522	0.18	9	0.23	11
R3CNF_150_3_15_2.50_6.F.qcnf	14.59	11165	0.92	31	1.14	22
R3CNF_150_3_15_2.50_7.F.qcnf	11.79	7460	1.58	51	1.96	41
R3CNF_150_3_15_2.50_8.F.qcnf	19.34	9865	0.87	34	0.88	33
R3CNF_150_3_15_2.50_9.T.qcnf	0.66	423	0.11	7	0.11	7
impl02.qcnf	0.01	11	0.01	1	0.00	0
impl04.qcnf	0.02	91	0.02	14	0.01	0
impl06.qcnf	0.12	563	0.09	117	0.01	0
impl08.qcnf	0.90	3249	0.96	713	0.05	0
impl10.qcnf	5.62	18435	13.21	4097	0.27	0
impl12.qcnf	25.92	104193	19.59	23223	1.32	0
impl14.qcnf	112.71	588383	118.66	131225	7.21	0
impl16.qcnf	595.66	3322021	650.82	740999	33.72	0
impl18.qcnf	> 10 min.	-	> 10 min.	-	126.96	0
impl20.qcnf	> 10 min.	-	> 10 min.	-	579.23	0

Table 3. Runtimes the basic QBF solver on 150 variable ∃∀∃ QBF. The columns correspond to an increasing clauses-to-variables ratio, and the rows correspond to an increasing percentage of universal variables.

	1.00	1.50	2.00	2.50	3.00	3.50	4.00
0.0%	5.14	8.80	18.62	27.11	34.16	51.22	313.54
5.3%	5.19	9.43	152.52	1874.86	5679.83	4225.16	988.06
10.7%	5.29	10.97	847.85	6815.47	3922.47	1141.70	450.39
16.0%	5.60	16.67	1369.13	1985.74	869.00	402.73	232.92
21.3%	5.60	28.63	491.05	438.56	281.99	207.00	134.24
26.7%	5.84	43.45	149.33	140.81	120.16	98.20	86.07
32.0%	6.27	39.42	63.22	64.31	65.86	60.30	59.77
37.3%	7.09	23.06	33.59	36.49	40.14	43.78	47.44
42.7%	8.07	15.91	21.08	26.02	30.12	32.94	37.32
48.0%	8.70	15.52	20.65	21.10	25.49	27.60	29.01
53.3%	6.98	9.68	12.56	15.54	18.98	21.61	25.08

Table 4. Runtimes on 150 variable QBF with the new propagation algorithm

	1.00	1.50	2.00	2.50	3.00	3.50	4.00
0.0%	5.20	9.06	19.20	28.35	36.26	54.76	392.60
5.3%	5.82	12.00	80.59	107.53	369.88	439.06	153.00
10.7%	5.97	14.26	80.64	382.74	240.94	122.04	84.91
16.0%	6.00	19.93	195.35	228.58	131.70	126.41	85.20
21.3%	6.86	34.37	181.10	173.56	140.23	95.50	88.40
26.7%	7.19	56.05	164.50	160.94	117.94	100.16	87.78
32.0%	7.87	74.94	199.48	141.58	106.85	97.14	96.59
37.3%	10.03	84.98	155.40	119.27	97.54	94.36	101.35
42.7%	12.81	75.78	109.68	94.22	84.99	88.74	118.92
48.0%	17.88	67.29	84.90	73.21	78.43	88.52	106.42
53.3%	14.18	39.02	51.43	62.12	67.55	82.78	100.19

Table 5. The ratio between the runtimes in Tables 4 and 3

	1.00	1.50	2.00	2.50	3.00	3.50	4.00
0.0%	1.011	1.029	1.031	1.045	1.061	1.069	1.252
5.3%	1.121	1.272	0.528	0.057	0.065	0.103	0.154
10.7%	1.128	1.299	0.095	0.056	0.061	0.106	0.188
16.0%	1.071	1.195	0.142	0.115	0.151	0.313	0.365
21.3%	1.225	1.200	0.368	0.395	0.497	0.461	0.658
26.7%	1.231	1.289	1.101	1.142	0.981	1.019	1.019
32.0%	1.255	1.901	3.155	2.201	1.622	1.610	1.616
37.3%	1.414	3.685	4.626	3.268	2.429	2.155	2.136
42.7%	1.587	4.763	5.203	3.621	2.821	2.693	3.186
48.0%	2.055	4.335	4.111	3.469	3.076	3.207	3.668
53.3%	2.031	4.030	4.094	3.997	3.559	3.830	3.994

handle the existential and the universal variables. Cadoli et al. also give a pure literal rule for universal variables, and propose a test that detects the truth of a QBF by performing a satisfiability test of the QBF with the universal variables ignored. Giunchiglia et al. [8] generalize backjumping [17] to QBF so that also universal variables can be jumped over. Backjumping speeds up the evaluation of some classes of randomly generated QBF substantially. Also Letz [11] discusses backjumping, as well as other QBF extensions of techniques that have been used in implementations of the Davis-Putnam procedure. The techniques discussed by Cadoli et al., Giunchiglia et al. and Letz in general improve the runtimes, backjumping on certain randomly generated problems substantially, but on the kind of structured problems discussed in Sect. 7.1 the implementations of all these algorithms have the same extremely high runtimes as our implementation without the stronger propagation algorithm.

Plaisted et al. [16] have presented a decision procedure for QBF that is not based on the Davis-Putnam procedure. The procedure recursively eliminates variables from a formula by repeatedly replacing a subformulae by another that allows same valuations for the variables that occur also outside the subformula but does not contain the variables that occur only in the original subformula. No comparison of the algorithm to other algorithms for evaluating QBF has been carried out, because only an implementation of the algorithm for the unquantified propositional case exists.

Work directly related to the new propagation algorithm has been presented earlier by us and other authors. A restricted form of partial unfolding was first considered by Rintanen [20]. The technique presented there is capable of obtaining all unit resolution steps only when there is one group of universal variables; that is, when the prefix is $\exists\forall\exists$. The technique is applicable to longer prefixes, but in those cases it is incomplete. A variant of the technique was presented by Feldmann et al. [5], but experiments by Giunchiglia et al. [8] suggest that it is not a proper improvement over Rintanen's original proposal.

The unit resolution problem is not restricted to the Davis-Putnam QBF procedure: it is also present in algorithms for other problems, most notably in algorithms for stochastic satisfiability [13]. The propagation algorithm could be also applied in algorithms for QBF that are not in CNF. In this context an important question is detecting – from the non-clausal formula – the possibilities of performing inference steps corresponding to unit resolution. Once this question is answered, application of the propagation algorithm with its improvements is straightforward.

The new propagation algorithm for QBF could be contrasted to the work by Ginsberg and Parkes [7] which generalizes the Davis-Putnam procedure to schematically represented propositional formulae. Ginsberg and Parkes consider quantification over constant symbols, and restrict to universal quantification. Both algorithms process conventional propositional formulae that are represented compactly (exponential size reduction), and an intractable subproblem emerges because of the exponential reduction in problem size. In Ginsberg and Parkes' algorithm clauses and propositional variables are represented schematically, for example $p(a, b)$ where a and b are members of a fixed set of constants, and the computational problem to be solved is to find out – given a partial valuation and a set of schematically represented clauses – whether there are unit clauses with the literal $p(a, b)$ or $\neg p(a, b)$. Note that Ginsberg and Parkes represent only the clause set implicitly; all of the parametric propositional variables are represented explicitly. In the QBF case, the clauses and existential variables are parameterized by the universal variables that occur in the prefix before the relevant existential variables. Our algorithm performs unit resolution with the implicitly represented unquantified clause set. We do not represent the parameterized variables explicitly (there is an exponential number of them), and only infer truth-values for the current outermost existential variables.

9 Conclusions

We have presented a propagation algorithm for QBF that takes advantage of the possibility of partially unfolding the QBF, that is, making explicit part of the propositional formula that would be obtained by eliminating the universal variables from the QBF. The algorithm tries to infer truth-values for the outermost existential variables in the QBF, thereby reducing the need for exhaustive case-analysis on those variables. The algorithm may need exponential time because the fully unfolded propositional formula can have a size exponential in the size of the QBF. We discussed improvements to the algorithm and restrictions that make the algorithm run in polynomial time.

We investigated the behavior of the algorithm on a narrow class of formulae that was part of the initial motivation for studying the problem, and on these formulae the algorithm is a differentiating factor between practically unsolvable and easily solvable QBFs. Whether the algorithm is useful on more general classes of QBF remains to be seen. To investigate the topic further we would need QBF with three or more alternations of quantifiers in the prefix. For QBF with prefix $\exists\forall\exists$ the algorithm works like a technique earlier proposed by us [20]. We believe that on many QBF with a longer prefix the hierarchical propagation algorithm substantially reduces the need for exhaustive search. However, the overhead of the algorithm is relatively high, and when the reduction in search space does not take place, the propagation algorithm slows down QBF evaluation.

There are some areas in QBF implementations that potentially benefit from observing the presence of the new propagation algorithm. For example, branching heuristics should prefer variables that increase the number of clauses that contain only one existential variable (and possibly some universal variables.) The branching heuristics of our current implementation just count the number of new one and two literal clauses. However, for most of the QBF obtained by translation from the planning problems discussed in this paper, this would not appear to make a difference, because there are few clauses that contain universal variables and more than one existential variable.

The ideas behind the paper point to possible improvements to the Davis-Putnam QBF procedure. A general problem with the procedure is that branching variables have to be selected from the variables quantified by the outermost quantifier, and therefore the choice of the variables is much less flexible than in the unquantified case. The problem is that – at a given state of the search process – none of the values chosen for the outermost variables might immediately constrain the values of the remaining variables, which leads to blind and exhaustive search. The idea of viewing the QBF as explicitly standing for an unquantified propositional formulae suggests that branching variables could be inner variables when they are viewed as being parameterized by the values of the preceding universal variables. It could be the case that assigning a truth-value to some of the inner variables could constrain the other variables considerably, which would reduce the search space. However, because the number of parametric variables can be exponential in the number of variables in the QBF, it is not clear how and why this would lead to more efficient evaluation of QBF.

References

[1] Bengt Aspvall, Michael F. Plass, and Robert Endre Tarjan. A linear time algorithm for testing the truth of certain quantified Boolean formulas. *Information Processing Letters*, 8(3):121–123, 1979. Erratum in 14(4):195, June 1982.

[2] Tom Bylander. The computational complexity of propositional STRIPS planning. *Artificial Intelligence*, 69(1-2):165–204, 1994.

[3] M. Cadoli, A. Giovanardi, and M. Schaerf. An algorithm to evaluate quantified Boolean formulae. In *Proceedings of the Fifteenth National Conference on Artificial Intelligence (AAAI-98) and the Tenth Conference on Innovative Applications of Artificial Intelligence (IAAI-98)*, pages 262–267. AAAI Press, July 1998.

[4] M. Davis, G. Logemann, and D. Loveland. A machine program for theorem proving. *Communications of the ACM*, 5:394–397, 1962.

[5] Rainer Feldmann, Burkhard Monien, and Stefan Schamberger. A distributed algorithm to evaluate quantified Boolean formulae. In *Proceedings of the Seventeenth National Conference on Artificial Intelligence (AAAI-2000) and the Twelfth Conference on Innovative Applications of Artificial Intelligence (IAAI-2000)*, pages 285–290. AAAI Press, 2000.

[6] Ian Gent and Toby Walsh. Beyond NP: the QSAT phase transition. In *Proceedings of the Sixteenth National Conference on Artificial Intelligence (AAAI-99) and the Eleventh Conference on Innovative Applications of Artificial Intelligence (IAAI-99)*, pages 648–653. AAAI Press / The MIT Press, 1999.

[7] Matthew L. Ginsberg and Andrew J. Parkes. Satisfiability algorithms and finite quantification. In Anthony G. Cohn, Fausto Giunchiglia, and Bart Selman, editors, *Principles of Knowledge Representation and Reasoning: Proceedings of the Seventh International Conference (KR2000)*, pages 690–701. Morgan Kaufmann Publishers, 2000.

[8] Enrico Giunchiglia, Massimo Narizzano, and Armando Tacchella. An analysis of backjumping and trivial truth in quantified Boolean formulas satisfiability. In F. Esposito, editor, *AI*AI 2001: Advances in Artificial Intelligence. 7th Congress of the Italian Association for Artificial Intelligence, Proceedings*, number 2175 in Lecture Notes in Computer Science, pages 111–122. Springer-Verlag, 2001.

[9] Henry Kautz and Bart Selman. Pushing the envelope: planning, propositional logic, and stochastic search. In *Proceedings of the Thirteenth National Conference on Artificial Intelligence and the Eighth Innovative Applications of Artificial Intelligence Conference*, pages 1194–1201, Menlo Park, California, August 1996. AAAI Press.
[10] Hans Kleine Büning, Marek Karpinski, and Andreas Flögel. Resolution for quantified Boolean formulas. *Information and Computation*, 117:12–18, 1995.
[11] Reinhold Letz. Advances in decision procedures for quantified Boolean formulas. working notes of the IJCAR 2001 workshop on Theory and Applications of Quantified Boolean Formulas, 2001.
[12] Chu Min Li and Anbulagan. Heuristics based on unit propagation for satisfiability problems. In *Proceedings of the 15th International Joint Conference on Artificial Intelligence*, pages 366–371, Nagoya, Japan, August 1997.
[13] Michael L. Littman. Initial experiments in stochastic satisfiability. In *Proceedings of the Sixteenth National Conference on Artificial Intelligence (AAAI-99) and the Eleventh Conference on Innovative Applications of Artificial Intelligence (IAAI-99)*, pages 667–672. AAAI Press / The MIT Press, 1999.
[14] Antonio Lozano and José L. Balcázar. The complexity of graph problems for succinctly represented graphs. In Manfred Nagl, editor, *Graph-Theoretic Concepts in Computer Science, 15th International Workshop, WG'89*, number 411 in Lecture Notes in Computer Science, pages 277–286, Castle Rolduc, The Netherlands, 1990. Springer-Verlag.
[15] Christos H. Papadimitriou and Mihalis Yannakakis. A note on succinct representations of graphs. *Information and Control*, 71:181–185, 1986.
[16] David A. Plaisted, Armin Biere, and Yunshan Zhu. A satisfiability procedure for quantified Boolean formulae, 2001. unpublished.
[17] Patrick Prosser. Hybrid algorithms for the constraint satisfaction problem. *Computational Intelligence*, 9(3):268–299, 1993.
[18] Jussi Rintanen. A planning algorithm not based on directional search. In A. G. Cohn, L. K. Schubert, and S. C. Shapiro, editors, *Principles of Knowledge Representation and Reasoning: Proceedings of the Sixth International Conference (KR '98)*, pages 617–624. Morgan Kaufmann Publishers, June 1998.
[19] Jussi Rintanen. Constructing conditional plans by a theorem-prover. *Journal of Artificial Intelligence Research*, 10:323–352, 1999.
[20] Jussi Rintanen. Improvements to the evaluation of quantified Boolean formulae. In Thomas Dean, editor, *Proceedings of the 16th International Joint Conference on Artificial Intelligence*, pages 1192–1197. Morgan Kaufmann Publishers, August 1999.
[21] Roberto Sebastiani. Personal communication, Breckenridge, Colorado, April 2000.

Permutation Problems and Channelling Constraints

Toby Walsh

University of York, York, England. tw@cs.york.ac.uk

Abstract. When writing a constraint program, we have to decide what to make the decision variable, and how to represent the constraints on these variables. In many cases, there is considerable choice for the decision variables. For example, with permutation problems, we can choose between a primal and a dual representation. In the dual representation, dual variables stand for the primal values, whilst dual values stand for the primal variables. By means of channelling constraints, a combined model can have both primal and dual variables. In this paper, we perform an extensive theoretical and empirical study of these different models. Our results will aid constraint programmers to choose a model for a permutation problem. They also illustrate a general methodology for comparing different constraint models.

1 Introduction

Constraint programming is a highly successful technology for solving a wide variety of combinatorial problems like resource allocation, transportation, and scheduling. A constraint program consists of a set of decision variables, each with an associated domain of values, and a set of constraints defining allowed values for subsets of these variables. The efficiency of a constraint program depends on a good choice for the decision variables, and a careful modelling of the constraints on these variables. Unfortunately, there is often considerable choice as to what to make the variables, and what to make the values. For example, in an exam timetabling problem, the variables could be the exams, and the values could be the times. Alternatively, the variables could be the times, and the values could be the exams. This choice is especially difficult in permutation problems. In a permutation problem, we have as many values as variables, and each variable takes an unique value. We can therefore easily exchange variables for values. Many assignment, scheduling and routing problems are permutation problems. For example, sports tournament scheduling can be modeled as finding a permutation of the games to fit into the time slots, or a permutation of the time slots to fit into the games. The aim of this paper is to compare such different models both theoretically and empirically.

2 Formal Background

A *constraint satisfaction problem* (CSP) is a set of variables, each with a finite domain of values, and a set of constraints. A (binary) constraint is a (binary) relation defining the allowed values for a (binary) subset of variables. A solution is an assignment of values to variables consistent with all constraints. Many lesser levels of consistency have been

R. Nieuwenhuis and A. Voronkov (Eds.): LPAR 2001, LNAI 2250, pp. 377–391, 2001.

defined (see [DB97]). A problem is (i, j)-*consistent* iff it has non-empty domains and any consistent instantiation of i variables can be consistently extended to j additional variables. A problem is *arc-consistent* (AC) iff it is $(1, 1)$-consistent. A problem is *path-consistent* (PC) iff it is $(2, 1)$-consistent. A problem is *strong path-consistent* (ACPC) iff it is AC and PC. A problem is *path inverse consistent* (PIC) iff it is $(1, 2)$-consistent. A problem is *restricted path-consistent* (RPC) iff it is AC and if a value assigned to a variable is consistent with just one value for an adjoining variable then for any other variable there is a compatible value. A problem is *singleton arc-consistent* (SAC) iff it has non-empty domains and for any instantiation of a variable, the resulting subproblem can be made AC. A CSP with binary or non-binary constraints is *generalized arc-consistent* (GAC) iff for any value for a variable in a constraint, there exist compatible values for all the other variables in the constraint. For ordered domains, a problem is *bounds consistent* (BC) iff it has non-empty domains and the minimum and maximum values for any variable in a constraint can be consistently extended.

Backtracking algorithms are often used to find solutions to CSPs. Such algorithms try to extend partial assignments, enforcing a local consistency after each extension and backtracking when this local consistency no longer holds. For example, the *forward checking* algorithm (FC) maintains a restricted form of AC that ensures that the most recently instantiated variable and any uninstantiated variables are AC. FC has been generalized to non-binary constraints [BMFL99]. nFC0 makes every k-ary constraint with $k-1$ variables instantiated AC. nFC1 applies (one pass of) AC to each constraint or constraint projection involving the current and exactly one future variable. nFC2 applies (one pass of) GAC to each constraint involving the current and at least one future variable. Three other generalizations of FC to non-binary constraints, nFC3 to nFC5 degenerate to nFC2 on the single non-binary constraint describing a permutation, so are not considered here. Finally, the *maintaining arc-consistency* algorithm (MAC) maintains AC during search, whilst MGAC maintains GAC.

3 Permutation Problems

A *permutation problem* is a constraint satisfaction problem with the same number of variables as values, in which each variable takes an unique value. We also consider *multiple permutation problems* in which the variables divide into a number of (possibly overlapping) sets, each of which is a permutation problem. Smith has proposed a number of different models for permutation problems [Smi00]. The *primal* not-equals model has not-equals constraints between the variables in each permutation. The *primal* all-different model has an all-different constraint between the variables in each permutation. In a *dual* model, we swop variables for values. *Primal and dual* models have primal and dual variables, and *channelling constraints* linking them of the form: $x_i = j$ iff $d_j = i$ where x_i is a primal variable and d_j is a dual variable. Primal and dual models can also have not-equals and all-different constraints on the primal and/or dual variables. There will, of course, typically be other constraints which depend on the nature of the permutation problem. In what follows, we do not consider directly the contribution of such additional constraints to pruning. However, the ease with which we can specify and reason with these additional constraints may have a large impact on our choice of the primal, dual or primal and dual models. We will use the following subscripts: "$\neq$" for the primal not-equals constraints, "c" for channelling constraints, "$\neq c$" for the primal not-equals and channelling constraints, "$\neq c \neq$" for the primal not-equals, dual not-equals and channelling constraints, "$\forall$" for the primal all-different constraint, "$\forall c$" for the primal all-different and channelling constraints, and "$\forall c \forall$" for the primal all-different, dual all-different and channelling constraints. Thus $\text{SAC}_{\neq c}$ is SAC applied to the primal not-equals and channelling constraints.

4 Constraint Tightness

To compare how different models of permutation problems prune the search tree, we define a new measure of constraint tightness. Our definition assumes constraints are defined over the same variables and values or, as in the case of primal and dual models, variables and values which are bijectively related. An interesting extension would be to compare two sets of constraints up to permutation of their variables and values. Our definition of constraint tightness is strongly influenced by the way local consistency properties are compared in [DB97]. Indeed, the definition is parameterized by a local consistency property since, as we show later, the amount of pruning provided by a set of constraints depends upon the level of local consistency being enforced. This measure of constraint tightness would also be useful in a number of other applications (e.g. reasoning about the value of implied constraints).

We say that a set of constraints A is *at least as tight as* a set B with respect to Φ-consistency (written $\Phi_A \leadsto \Phi_B$) iff, given any domains for their variables, if A is Φ-consistent then B is also Φ-consistent. By considering all possible domains for the variables, this ordering measures the potential for domains to be pruned during search as variables are instantiated and domains pruned (possibly by other constraints in the problem). We say that a set of constraints A is *tighter* than a set B wrt Φ-consistency (written $\Phi_A \rightarrow \Phi_B$) iff $\Phi_A \leadsto \Phi_B$ but not $\Phi_B \leadsto \Phi_A$, A is *incomparable* to B wrt Φ-consistency (written $\Phi_A \otimes \Phi_B$) iff neither $\Phi_A \leadsto \Phi_B$ nor $\Phi_B \leadsto \Phi_A$, and A is *equivalent* to B wrt Φ-consistency (written $\Phi_A \leftrightarrow \Phi_B$) iff both $\Phi_A \leadsto \Phi_B$ and $\Phi_B \leadsto \Phi_A$. We can easily generalize these definitions to compare Φ-consistency on A with Θ-consistency on B. This definition of constraint tightness has some nice monotonicity and fixed-point properties which we will use extensively throughout this paper.

Theorem 1 (monotonicity and fixed-point).

1. $AC_{A \cup B} \leadsto AC_A \leadsto AC_{A \cap B}$
2. $AC_A \rightarrow AC_B$ *implies* $AC_{A \cup B} \leftrightarrow AC_A$

Similar monotonicity and fixed-point results hold for BC, RPC, PIC, SAC, ACPC, and GAC. We also extend these definitions to compare constraint tightness wrt search algorithms like MAC that maintain some local consistency. For example, we say that A is *at least as tight as* B wrt algorithm X (written $X_A \leadsto X_B$) iff, given any fixed variable and value ordering and any domains for their variables, X visits no more nodes on A than on B, whilst A is *tighter* than B wrt algorithm X (written $X_A \rightarrow X_B$) iff $X_A \leadsto X_B$ but not $X_B \leadsto X_A$.

5 Theoretical Comparison

5.1 Arc-Consistency

We first prove that, with respect to AC, channelling constraints are tighter than the primal not-equals constraints, but less tight than the primal all-different constraint.

Theorem 2. *On a permutation problem:*

$$
\begin{array}{l}
GAC_{\forall c \forall} \\
\quad \updownarrow \\
GAC_{\forall} \rightarrow AC_{\neq c \neq} \leftrightarrow AC_{\neq c} \leftrightarrow AC_{c} \rightarrow AC_{\neq} \\
\quad \updownarrow \\
GAC_{\forall c}
\end{array}
$$

Proof. In this and following proofs, we just prove the most important results. Others follow quickly, often using transitivity, monotonicity and the fixed-point theorems.

To show $\text{GAC}_{\forall} \rightarrow \text{AC}_c$, consider a permutation problem whose primal all-different constraint is GAC. Suppose the channelling constraint between x_i and d_j was not AC. Then either x_i is set to j and d_j has i eliminated from its domain, or d_j is set to i and x_i has j eliminated from its domain. But neither of these two cases is possible by the construction of the primal and dual model. Hence the channelling constraints are all AC. To show strictness, consider a 5 variable permutation problem in which $x_1 = x_2 = x_3 = \{1, 2\}$ and $x_4 = x_5 = \{3, 4, 5\}$. This is AC_c but not $\text{GAC}_{\forall}$.

To show $\text{AC}_c \rightarrow \text{AC}_{\neq}$, suppose that the channelling constraints are AC. Consider a not-equals constraint, $x_i \neq x_j$ $(i \neq j)$ that is not AC. Now, x_i and x_j must have the same singleton domain, $\{k\}$. Consider the channelling constraint between x_i and d_k. The only AC value for d_k is i. Similarly, the only AC value for d_k in the channelling constraint between x_j and d_k is j. But $i \neq j$. Hence, d_k has no AC values. This is a contradiction as the channelling constraints are AC. Hence all not-equals constraints are AC. To show strictness, consider a 3 variable permutation problem with $x_1 = x_2 = \{1, 2\}$ and $x_3 = \{1, 2, 3\}$. This is $\text{AC}_{\neq}$ but is not AC_c.

To show $\text{AC}_{\neq c \neq} \leftrightarrow \text{AC}_c$, by monotonicity, $\text{AC}_{\neq c \neq} \rightsquigarrow \text{AC}_c$. To show the reverse, consider a permutation problem which is AC_c but not $\text{AC}_{\neq c \neq}$. Then there exists at least one not-equals constraints that is not AC. Without loss of generality, let this be on two dual variables (a symmetric argument can be made for two primal variables). So both the associated (dual) variables, call them d_i and d_j must have the same unitary domain, say $\{k\}$. Hence, the domain of the primal variable x_k includes i and j. Consider the channelling constraint between x_k and d_i. Now this is not AC as the value $x_k = j$ has no support. This is a contradiction.

To show $\text{GAC}_{\forall c \forall} \leftrightarrow \text{GAC}_{\forall}$, consider a permutation problem that is $\text{GAC}_{\forall}$. For every possible assignment of a value to a variable, there exist a consistent extension to the other variables, $x_1 = d_{x_1}, \ldots x_n = d_{x_n}$ with $x_i \neq x_j$ for all $i \neq j$. As this is a permutation, this corresponds to the assignment of unique variables to values. Hence, the corresponding dual all-different constraint is GAC. Finally, the channelling constraints are trivially AC. □

5.2 Maintaining Arc-Consistency

These results can be lifted to algorithms that maintain (generalized) arc-consistency during search. Indeed, the gaps between the primal all-different and the channelling constraints, and between the channelling constraints and the primal not-equals constraints can be exponentially large[1]. We write $X_A \Rightarrow X_B$ iff $X_A \rightarrow X_B$ and there is a problem on which algorithm X visits exponentially fewer branches with A than B. Note that $\text{GAC}_\forall$ and AC are both polynomial to enforce so an exponential reduction in branches translates to an exponential reduction in runtime.

Theorem 3. *On a permutation problem:*

$$MGAC_\forall \Rightarrow MAC_{\neq c \neq} \leftrightarrow MAC_{\neq c} \leftrightarrow MAC_c \Rightarrow MAC_{\neq}$$

Proof. We give proofs for the most important identities. Other results follow immediately from the last theorem. To show $\text{GMAC}_\forall \Rightarrow \text{MAC}_c$, consider a $n+3$ variable permutation problem with $x_i = \{1,\ldots,n\}$ for $i \leq n+1$ and $x_{n+2} = x_{n+3} = \{n+1, n+2, n+3\}$. Then, given a lexicographical variable ordering, $\text{GMAC}_\forall$ immediately fails, whilst MAC_c takes $n!$ branches. To show $\text{MAC}_c \Rightarrow \text{MAC}_{\neq}$, consider a $n+2$ variable permutation problem with $x_1 = \{1,2\}$, and $x_i = \{3,\ldots,n+2\}$ for $i \geq 2$. Then, given a lexicographical variable ordering, MAC_c takes 2 branches to show insolubility, whist $\text{MAC}_{\neq}$ takes $2.(n-1)!$ branches. □

5.3 Forward Checking

Maintaining (generalized) arc-consistency on large permutation problems can be expensive. We may therefore decide to use a cheaper local consistency property like that maintained by forward checking. For example, the Choco finite-domain toolkit in Claire uses just nFC0 on all-different constraints. The channelling constraint remain tighter than the primal not-equals constraints wrt FC.

Theorem 4. *On a permutation problem:*

$$\begin{array}{l} nFC2_\forall \rightarrow FC_{\neq c \neq} \leftrightarrow FC_{\neq c} \leftrightarrow FC_c \rightarrow FC_{\neq} \rightarrow nFC0_\forall \\ \qquad\qquad\qquad\qquad\qquad\qquad\quad \uparrow \\ \qquad\qquad\qquad\qquad\quad nFC2_\forall \rightarrow nFC1_\forall \end{array}$$

Proof. [GSW00] proves $\text{FC}_{\neq}$ implies $\text{nFC0}_\forall$. To show strictness on permutation problems (as opposed to the more general class of decomposable constraints studied in [GSW00]), consider a 5 variable permutation problem with $x_1 = x_2 = x_3 = x_4 = \{1,2,3\}$ and $x_5 = \{4,5\}$. FC shows the problem is unsatisfiable in at most 12 branches. nFC0 by comparison takes at least 18 branches.

To show $\text{FC}_c \rightarrow \text{FC}_{\neq}$, consider assigning the value j to the primal variable x_i. $\text{FC}_{\neq}$ removes j from the domain of all other primal variables. FC_c instantiates the dual variable d_j with the value i, and then removes i from the domain of all other primal

[1] Note that not all difference in constraint tightness result in exponentially reductions in search (e.g. [Che00] identifies some differences which are only polynomial).

variables. Hence, FC_c prunes all the values that $FC_{\neq}$ does. To show strictness, consider a 4 variable permutation problem with $x_1 = \{1,2\}$ and $x_2 = x_3 = x_4 = \{3,4\}$. Given a lexicographical variable and numerical value ordering, $FC_{\neq}$ shows the problem is unsatisfiable in 4 branches. FC_c by comparison takes just 2 branches.

[GSW00] proves $nFC1_{\forall}$ implies $FC_{\neq}$. To show the reverse, consider assigning the value j to the primal variable x_i. $FC_{\neq}$ removes j from the domain of all primal variables except x_i. However, $nFC1_{\forall}$ also removes j from the domain of all primal variables except x_i since each occurs in a binary not-equals constraint with x_i obtained by projecting out the all-different constraint. Hence, $nFC1_{\forall} \leftrightarrow FC_{\neq}$.

To show $nFC2_{\forall} \rightarrow FC_{\neq c \neq}$, consider instantiating the primal variable x_i with the value j. $FC_{\neq c \neq}$ removes j from the domain of all primal variables except x_i, i from the domain of all dual variables except d_j, instantiate d_j with the value i, and then remove i from the domain of all dual variables except d_j. $nFC2_{\forall}$ also removes j from the domain of all primal variables except x_i. The only possible difference is if one of the other dual variables, say d_l has a domain wipeout. If this happens, x_i has one value in its domain, l that is in the domain of no other primal variable. Enforcing GAC immediately detects that x_i cannot take the value j, and must instead take the value k. Hence $nFC2_{\forall}$ has a domain wipeout whenever $FC_{\neq c \neq}$ does. To show strictness, consider a 7 variable permutation problem with $x_1 = x_2 = x_3 = x_4 = \{1,2,3\}$ and $x_5 = x_6 = x_7 = \{4,5,6,7\}$ $FC_{\neq c \neq}$ takes at least 6 branches to show the problem is unsatisfiable. $nFC2_{\forall}$ by comparison takes no more than 4 branches.

[BMFL99] proves $nFC2_{\forall}$ implies $nFC1_{\forall}$. To show strictness on permutation problems, consider a 5 variable permutation problem with $x_1 = x_2 = x_3 = x_4 = \{1,2,3\}$ and $x_5 = \{4,5\}$. nFC1 shows the problem is unsatisfiable in at least 6 branches. nFC2 by comparison takes no more than 3 branches. □

5.4 Bounds Consistency

Another common method to reduce costs is to enforce just bounds consistency. For example, [RR00] use bounds consistency to prune a global constraint involving a sum of variables and a set of inequalities. As a second example, some of the experiments on permutation problems in [Smi00] used bounds consistency on certain of the constraints. With bounds consistency on permutation problems, we obtain a very similar ordering of the models as with AC.

Theorem 5. *On a permutation problem:*

$$\begin{array}{ccccccccc} BC_{\forall} & \rightarrow & BC_{\neq c \neq} & \leftrightarrow & BC_{\neq c} & \leftrightarrow & BC_c & \rightarrow BC_{\neq} & \leftarrow AC_{\neq} \\ & & & & & & \updownarrow & & \\ & & & & & & AC_{\neq} & & \end{array}$$

Proof. To show $BC_c \rightarrow BC_{\neq}$, consider a permutation problem which is BC_c but one of the primal not-equals constraints is not BC. Then, it would involve two variables, x_i and x_j both with identical interval domains, $[k,k]$. Enforcing BC on the channelling constraint between x_i and d_k would reduce d_k to the domain $[i,i]$. Enforcing BC on the channelling constraint between x_j and d_k would then cause a domain wipeout. But this contradicts the channelling constraints being BC. Hence, all the primal not-equals constraints must be BC. To show strictness. consider a 3 variable permutation problem with $x_1 = x_2 = [1, 2]$ and $x_3 = [1, 3]$. This is BC$_{\neq}$ but not BC$_c$.

To show BC$_\forall \rightarrow$ BC$_{\neq c \neq}$, consider a permutation probem which is BC$_\forall$. Suppose we assign a boundary value j to a primal variable, x_i (or equivalently, a boundary value i to a dual variable, d_j). As the all-different constraint is BC, this can be extended to all the other primal variables using each of the values once. This gives us a consistent assignment for any other primal or dual variable. Hence, it is BC$_{\neq c \neq}$. To show strictness, consider a 5 variable permutation problem with $x_1 = x_2 = x_3 = [1, 2]$ and $x_4 = x_5 = [3, 5]$. This is BC$_{\neq c \neq}$ but not BC$_\forall$.

To show BC$_c \rightarrow$ AC$_{\neq}$, consider a permutation problem which is BC$_c$ but not AC$_{\neq}$. Then they must be one constraint, $x_i \neq x_j$ with x_i and x_j having the same singleton domain, $\{k\}$. But, if this is the case, enforcing BC on the channelling constraint between x_i and d_k and between x_j and d_k would prove that the problem is unsatisfiable. Hence, it is AC$_{\neq}$. To show strictness, consider a 3 variable permutation problem with $x_1 = x_2 = [1, 2]$ and $x_3 = [1, 3]$. This is AC$_{\neq}$ but not BC$_c$. □

5.5 Restricted Path Consistency

Debruyne and Bessière have shown that RPC is a promising filtering technique above AC [DB97]. It prunes many of the PIC values at little extra cost to AC. Surprisingly, channelling constraints are incomparable to the primal not-equals constraints wrt RPC. Channelling constraints can increase the amount of propagation (for example, when a dual variable has only one value left in its domain). However, RPC is hindered by the bipartite constraint graph between primal and dual variables. Additional not-equals constraints on primal and/or dual variables can therefore help propagation.

Theorem 6. *On a permutation problem;*

$$GAC_\forall \rightarrow RPC_{\neq c \neq} \rightarrow RPC_{\neq c} \rightarrow RPC_c \otimes RPC_{\neq} \otimes AC_c$$

Proof. To show RPC$_c \otimes$ RPC$_{\neq}$, consider a 4 variable permutation problem with $x_1 = x_2 = x_3 = \{1, 2, 3\}$ and $x_4 = \{1, 2, 3, 4\}$. This is RPC$_{\neq}$ but not RPC$_c$. For the reverse direction, consider a 5 variable permutation problem with $x_1 = x_2 = x_3 = \{1, 2\}$ and $x_4 = x_5 = \{3, 4, 5\}$. This is RPC$_c$ but not RPC$_{\neq}$.

To show RPC$_{\neq c} \rightarrow$ RPC$_c$, consider again the last example. This is RPC$_c$ but not RPC$_{\neq c}$.

To show RPC$_{\neq c \neq} \rightarrow$ RPC$_{\neq c}$, consider a 6 variable permutation problem with $x_1 = x_2 = \{1, 2, 3, 4, 5, 6\}$ and $x_3 = x_4 = x_5 = x_6 = \{4, 5, 6\}$. This is RPC$_{\neq c}$ but not RPC$_{\neq c \neq}$.

To show GAC$_\forall \rightarrow$ RPC$_{\neq c \neq}$, consider a permutation problem which is GAC$_\forall$. Suppose we assign a value j to a primal variable, x_i (or equivalently, a value i to a dual variable, d_j). As the all-different constraint is GAC, this can be extended to all the other primal variables using up all the other values. This gives us a consistent assignment for any two other primal or dual variables. Hence, the problem is PIC$_{\neq c \neq}$ and thus RPC$_{\neq c \neq}$. To show strictness, consider a 7 variable permutation problem with

$x_1 = x_2 = x_3 = x_4 = \{1, 2, 3\}$ and $x_5 = x_6 = x_7 = \{4, 5, 6, 7\}$. This is $\text{RPC}_{\neq c \neq}$ but not $\text{GAC}_{\forall}$.

To show $\text{AC}_c \otimes \text{RPC}_{\neq}$, consider a 4 variable permutation problem with $x_1 = x_2 = x_3 = \{1, 2, 3\}$ and $x_4 = \{1, 2, 3, 4\}$. This is $\text{RPC}_{\neq}$ but not AC_c. For the reverse direction, consider a 5 variable permutation problem with $x_1 = x_2 = x_3 = \{1, 2\}$ and $x_4 = x_5 = \{3, 4, 5\}$. This is AC_c but not $\text{RPC}_{\neq}$. □

5.6 Path Inverse Consistency

The incomparability of channelling constraints and primal not-equals constraints remains when we move up the local consistency hierarchy from RPC to PIC.

Theorem 7. *On a permutation problem:*

$GAC_{\forall} \rightarrow PIC_{\neq c \neq} \rightarrow PIC_{\neq c} \rightarrow PIC_c \otimes PIC_{\neq} \otimes AC_c$

Proof. To show $\text{PIC}_c \otimes \text{PIC}_{\neq}$, consider a 4 variable permutation problem with $x_1 = x_2 = x_3 = \{1, 2, 3\}$ and $x_4 = \{1, 2, 3, 4\}$. This is $\text{PIC}_{\neq}$ but not PIC_c. Enforcing PIC on the channelling constraints reduces x_4 to the singleton domain $\{4\}$. For the reverse direction, consider a 5 variable permutation problem with $x_1 = x_2 = x_3 = \{1, 2\}$ and $x_4 = x_5 = \{3, 4, 5\}$. This is PIC_c but not $\text{PIC}_{\neq}$.

To show $\text{PIC}_{\neq c} \rightarrow \text{PIC}_c$, consider a 5 variable permutation problem with $x_1 = x_2 = x_3 = \{1, 2\}$ and $x_4 = x_5 = \{3, 4, 5\}$. This is PIC_c but not $\text{PIC}_{\neq c}$.

To show $\text{PIC}_{\neq c \neq} \rightarrow \text{PIC}_{\neq c}$, consider a 6 variable permutation problem with $x_1 = x_2 = \{1, 2, 3, 4, 5, 6\}$ and $x_3 = x_4 = x_5 = x_6 = \{4, 5, 6\}$. This is $\text{PIC}_{\neq c}$ but not $\text{PIC}_{\neq c \neq}$.

To show $\text{GAC}_{\forall} \rightarrow \text{PIC}_{\neq c \neq}$, consider a permutation problem in which the all-different constraint is GAC. Suppose we assign a value j to a primal variable, x_i (or equivalently, a value i to a dual variable, d_j). As the all-different constraint is GAC, this can be extended to all the other primal variables using up all the other values. This gives us a consistent assignment for any two other primal or dual variables. Hence, the not-equals and channelling constraints are PIC. To show strictness, consider a 7 variable permutation problem with $x_1 = x_2 = x_3 = x_4 = \{1, 2, 3\}$ and $x_5 = x_6 = x_7 = \{4, 5, 6, 7\}$. This is $\text{PIC}_{\neq c \neq}$ but not $\text{GAC}_{\forall}$.

To show $\text{PIC}_{\neq} \otimes \text{AC}_c$, consider a 4 variable permutation problem with $x_1 = x_2 = x_3 = \{1, 2, 3\}$ and $x_4 = \{1, 2, 3, 4\}$. This is $\text{PIC}_{\neq}$ but not AC_c. Enforcing AC on the channelling constraints reduces x_4 to the singleton domain $\{4\}$. For the reverse direction, consider a 5 variable permutation problem with $x_1 = x_2 = x_3 = \{1, 2\}$ and $x_4 = x_5 = \{3, 4, 5\}$. This is AC_c but not $\text{PIC}_{\neq}$. □

5.7 Singleton Arc-Consistency

Debruyne and Bessière also showed that SAC is a promising filtering technique above both AC, RPC and PIC, pruning many values for its CPU time [DB97]. Prosser et al. reported promising experimental results with SAC on quasigroup problems, a multiple permutation problem [PSW00]. Interestingly, as with AC (but unlike RPC and PIC which lie between AC and SAC), channelling constraints are tighter than the primal not-equals constraints wrt SAC.

Theorem 8. *On a permutation problem:*

$$GAC_{\forall} \rightarrow SAC_{\neq c\neq} \leftrightarrow SAC_{\neq c} \leftrightarrow SAC_c \rightarrow SAC_{\neq} \otimes AC_c$$

Proof. To show $SAC_c \rightarrow SAC_{\neq}$, consider a permutation problem that is SAC_c and any instantiation for a primal variable x_i. Suppose that the primal not-equals model of the resulting problem cannot be made AC. Then there must exist two other primal variables, say x_j and x_k which have at most one other value. Consider the dual variable associated with this value. Then under this instantiation of the primal variable x_i, enforcing AC on the channelling constraint between the primal variable x_i and the dual variable, and between the dual variable and x_j and x_k results in a domain wipeout on the dual variable. Hence the problem is not SAC_c. This is a contradiction. The primal not-equals model can therefore be made AC following the instantiation of x_i. That is, the problem is $SAC_{\neq}$. To show strictness, consider a 5 variable permutation problem with domain $x_1 = x_2 = x_3 = x_4 = \{0, 1, 2\}$ and $x_5 = \{3, 4\}$. This is $SAC_{\neq}$ but not SAC_c.

To show $GAC_{\forall} \rightarrow SAC_c$, consider a permutation problem that is $GAC_{\forall}$. Consider any instantiation for a primal variable. This can be consistently extended to all variables in the primal model. But this means that it can be consistently extended to all variables in the primal and dual model, satisfying any (combination of) permutation or channelling constraints. As the channelling constraints are satisfiable, they can be made AC. Consider any instantiation for a dual variable. By a similar argument, taking the appropriate instantiation for the associated primal variable, the resulting problem can be made AC. Hence, given any instantiation for a primal or dual variable, the channelling constraints can be made AC. That is, the problem is SAC_c, To show strictness, consider a 7 variable permutation problem with $x_1 = x_2 = x_3 = x_4 = \{0, 1, 2\}$ and $x_5 = x_6 = x_7 = \{3, 4, 5, 6\}$. This SAC_c but is not $GAC_{\forall}$.

To show $SAC_{\neq} \otimes AC_c$, consider a four variable permutation problem in which x_1 to x_3 have the $\{1, 2, 3\}$ and x_4 has the domain $\{0, 1, 2, 3\}$. This is $SAC_{\neq}$ but not AC_c. For the reverse, consider a 4 variable permutation problem with $x_1 = x_2 = \{0, 1\}$ and $x_3 = x_4 = \{0, 2, 3\}$. This is AC_c but not $SAC_{\neq}$. □

5.8 Strong Path-Consistency

Adding primal or dual not-equals constraints to channelling constraints does not help AC or SAC. The following result shows that their addition does not help higher levels of local consistency like strong path-consistency (ACPC).

Theorem 9. *On a permutation problem:*

$$GAC_{\forall} \otimes ACPC_{\neq c\neq} \leftrightarrow ACPC_{\neq c} \leftrightarrow ACPC_c \rightarrow ACPC_{\neq} \otimes AC_c$$

Proof. To show $ACPC_c \rightarrow ACPC_{\neq}$, consider some channelling constraints that are ACPC. Now $AC_c \rightarrow AC_{\neq}$, so we just need to show $PC_c \rightarrow PC_{\neq}$. Consider a consistent pair of values, l and m for a pair of primal variables, x_i and x_j. Take any third primal variable, x_k. As the constraint between d_l, d_m and x_k is PC, we can find a value for x_k consistent with the channelling constraints. But this also satisfies the not-equals constraint between primal variables. Hence, the problem is $PC_{\neq}$. To show strictness, consider a 4 variable permutation problem with $x_1 = x_2 = x_3 = x_4 = \{1, 2, 3\}$. This is ACPC$_{\neq}$ but not ACPC$_c$.

To show ACPC$_{\neq c \neq}$ $\leftrightarrow$ ACPC$_{\neq c}$ $\leftrightarrow$ ACPC$_c$, we recall that AC$_{\neq c}$ $\leftrightarrow$ AC$_{\neq c}$ $\leftrightarrow$ AC$_c$. Hence we need just show that PC$_{\neq c}$ $\leftrightarrow$ PC$_{\neq c}$ $\leftrightarrow$ PC$_c$. Consider a permutation problem. Enforcing PC on the channelling constraints alone infers both the primal and the dual not-equals constraints. Hence, PC$_{\neq c}$ $\leftrightarrow$ PC$_{\neq c}$ $\leftrightarrow$ PC$_c$.

To show GAC$_\forall$ $\otimes$ ACPC$_{\neq c \neq}$, consider a 6 variable permutation problem with $x_1 = x_2 = x_3 = x_4 = \{1, 2, 3\}$, and $x_5 = x_6 = \{4, 5, 6\}$. This is ACPC$_{\neq c \neq}$ but not GAC$_\forall$. For the reverse direction, consider a 3 variable permutation problem with the additional binary constraint $even(x_1 + x_3)$. Enforcing GAC$_\forall$. prunes the to $x_1 = x_3 = \{1, 3\}$, and $x_2 = \{2\}$. However, these domains are not ACPC$_{\neq c \neq}$. Enforcing ACPC tightens the constraint between x_1 and x_3 from not-equals to $x_1 = 1, x_3 = 3$ or $x_1 = 3, x_3 = 1$.

To show ACPC$_{\neq}$ $\otimes$ AC$_c$, consider a 5 variable permutation problem with $x_1 = x_2 = x_3 = \{1, 2\}$, and $x_4 = x_5 = \{3, 4, 5\}$. This is AC$_c$ but not ACPC$_{\neq}$. For the reverse direction, consider again the 4 variable permutation problem with $x_1 = x_2 = x_3 = x_4 = \{1, 2, 3\}$. This is ACPC$_{\neq}$ but not AC$_c$. □

5.9 Multiple Permutation Problems

These results extend to multiple permutation problems under a simple restriction that the problem is *triangle preserving* [SW99] (that is, any triple of variables which are all-different must occur together in at least one permutation). For example, all-diff(x_1, x_2, x_4), all-diff(x_1, x_3, x_5), and all-diff(x_2, x_3, x_6) are not triangle preserving as x_1, x_2 and x_3 are all-different but are not in the same permutation. The following theorem collects together and generalizes many of the previous results.

Theorem 10. *On a multiple permutation problem:*

$$
\begin{array}{lllllllllll}
GAC_\forall \otimes & ACPC_{\neq c \neq} & \leftrightarrow & ACPC_{\neq c} & \leftrightarrow & ACPC_c & \rightarrow & ACPC_{\neq} & \otimes & AC_c \\
 & \downarrow & & \downarrow & & \downarrow & & \downarrow & & \\
GAC_\forall \rightarrow & SAC_{\neq c \neq} & \leftrightarrow & SAC_{\neq c} & \leftrightarrow & SAC_c & \rightarrow & SAC_{\neq} & \otimes & AC_c \\
 & \downarrow & & \downarrow & & \downarrow & & \downarrow & & \\
GAC_\forall \rightarrow & PIC_{\neq c \neq} & \rightarrow & PIC_{\neq c} & \rightarrow & PIC_c & \otimes & PIC_{\neq} & \otimes & AC_c \\
 & \downarrow & & \downarrow & & \downarrow & & \downarrow & & \\
GAC_\forall \rightarrow & RPC_{\neq c \neq} & \rightarrow & RPC_{\neq c} & \rightarrow & RPC_c & \otimes & RPC_{\neq} & \otimes & AC_c \\
 & \downarrow & & \downarrow & & \downarrow & & \downarrow & & \\
GAC_\forall \rightarrow & AC_{\neq c \neq} & \leftrightarrow & AC_{\neq c} & \leftrightarrow & AC_c & \rightarrow & AC_{\neq} & \leftarrow & BC_c \\
\downarrow & \downarrow & & \downarrow & & \downarrow & & \downarrow & & \\
BC_\forall \rightarrow & BC_{\neq c \neq} & \leftrightarrow & BC_{\neq c} & \leftrightarrow & BC_c & \rightarrow & BC_{\neq} & &
\end{array}
$$

Proof. The proofs lift in a straight forward manner from the single permutation case. Local consistencies like ACPC, SAC, PIC and RPC consider triples of variables. If these are linked together, we use the fact that the probem is triangle preserving and a permutation is therefore defined over them. If these are not linked together, we can decompose the argument into AC on pairs of variables. Without triangle preservation, GAC$_\forall$, may only achieve as high a level of consistency as AC$_{\neq}$. For example, consider again the non-triangle preserving constraints in the last paragraph. If $x_1 = x_2 = x_3 = \{1,2\}$ and $x_4 = x_5 = x_6 = \{1,2,3\}$ then the problem is GAC$_\forall$, but it is not RPC$_{\neq}$, and hence neither PIC$_{\neq}$, SAC$_{\neq}$ nor ACPC$_{\neq}$. □

6 SAT Models

Another solution strategy is to encode permutation problems into SAT and use a fast Davis-Putnam (DP) or local search procedure. For example, [BM00] report promising results for propositional encodings of round robin problems, which include permutation constraints. We consider just "direct" encodings into SAT (see [Wal00] for more details). We have a Boolean variable X_{ij} which is *true* iff the primal variable x_i takes the value j. In the primal SAT model, there are n clauses to ensure that each primal variable takes at least one value, $O(n^3)$ clauses to ensure that no primal variable gets two values, and $O(n^3)$ clauses to ensure that no two primal variables take the same value. Interestingly the channelling SAT model has the same number of Boolean variables as the primal SAT model (as we can use X_{ij} to represent both the jth value of the primal variable x_i *and* the ith value for the dual variable d_j), and just n additional clauses to ensure each dual variable takes a value. The $O(n^3)$ clauses to ensure that no dual variable gets two values are equivalent to the clauses that ensure no two primal variables get the same value. The following result show that MAC is tighter than DP, and DP is equivalent to FC on these different models.

Theorem 11. *On a permutation problem:*

$$\begin{array}{ccccccccc}
MGAC_\forall & \rightarrow & MAC_{\neq c \neq} & \leftrightarrow & MAC_{\neq c} & \leftrightarrow & MAC_c & \rightarrow & MAC_{\neq} \\
 & & \downarrow & & \downarrow & & \downarrow & & \downarrow \\
MGAC_\forall & \rightarrow & DP_{\neq c \neq} & \leftrightarrow & DP_{\neq c} & \leftrightarrow & DP_c & \rightarrow & DP_{\neq} \\
 & & \updownarrow & & \updownarrow & & \updownarrow & & \updownarrow \\
MGAC_\forall & \rightarrow & FC_{\neq c \neq} & \leftrightarrow & FC_{\neq c} & \leftrightarrow & FC_c & \rightarrow & FC_{\neq}
\end{array}$$

Proof. DP$_{\neq} \leftrightarrow$ FC$_{\neq}$ is a special case of Theorem 14 in [Wal00], whilst MAC$_{\neq} \rightarrow$ FC$_{\neq}$ is a special case of Theorem 15. To show DP$_c \leftrightarrow$ FC$_c$ suppose unit propagation sets a literal l. There are four cases. In the first case, a clause of the form $X_{i1} \vee \ldots \vee X_{in}$ has been reduced to an unit. That is, we have one value left for a primal variable. A fail first heuristic in FC picks this last value to instantiate. In the second case, a clause of the form $\neg X_{ij} \vee \neg X_{ik}$ for $j \neq k$ has been reduced to an unit. This ensures that no primal variable gets two values. The FC algorithm trivially never tries two simultaneous values for a primal variable. In the third case, a clause of the form $\neg X_{ij} \vee \neg X_{kj}$ for $i \neq k$ has been reduced to an unit. This ensures that no dual variable gets two values. Again, the FC algorithm trivially never tries two simultaneous values for a dual variable. In the fourth case, $X_{1j} \vee \ldots \vee X_{nj}$ has been reduced to an unit. That is, we have one value left for a dual variable. A fail first heuristic in FC picks this last value to instantiate. Hence, given a suitable branching heuristic, the FC algorithm tracks the DP algorithm. To show the reverse, suppose forward checking removes a value. There are two cases. In the first case, the value i is removed from a dual variable d_j due to some channelling constraint. This means that there is a primal variable x_k which has been set to some value $l \neq j$.

Unit propagation on $\neg X_{kl} \vee \neg X_{kj}$ sets X_{kj} to false, and then on $\neg X_{ij} \vee \neg X_{kj}$ sets X_{ij} to false as required. In the second case, the value i is removed from a dual variable d_j, again due to a channelling constraint. The proof is now dual to the first case.

To show $\text{MAC}_c \rightarrow \text{DP}_c$, we use the fact that MAC dominates FC and $\text{FC}_c \leftrightarrow \text{DP}_c$. To show strictness, consider a 3 variable permutation problem with additional binary constraints that rule out the same value for all 3 primal variables. Enforcing AC on the channelling constraints causes a domain wipeout on the dual variable associated with this value. As there are no unit clauses, DP does not immediately solve the problem.

To show $\text{DP}_c \rightarrow \text{DP}_{\neq}$, we note that the channelling SAT model contains more clauses. To show strictness, consider a four variable permutation problem with three additional binary constraints that if $x_1 = 1$ then $x_2 = 2$, $x_3 = 2$ and $x_4 = 2$ are all ruled out. Consider branching on $x_1 = 1$. Unit propagation on both models sets X_{12}, X_{22}, X_{32}, X_{42}, X_{21}, X_{31} and X_{41} to false. On the channelling SAT model, unit propagation against the clause $X_{12} \vee X_{22} \vee X_{32} \vee X_{42}$ then generates an empty clause. By comparison, unit propagation on the primal SAT model does no more work. □

7 Asymptotic Comparison

The previous results tell us nothing about the relative cost of achieving these local consistencies. Asymptotic analysis adds detail to the results. Regin's algorithm achieves $\text{GAC}_{\forall}$ in $O(n^4)$ [Ré94]. AC on binary constraints can be achieved in $O(ed^2)$ where e is the number of constraints and d is their domain size. As there are $O(n^2)$ channelling constraints, AC_c naively takes $O(n^4)$ time. However, by taking advantage of the functional nature of channelling constraints, we can reduce this to $O(n^3)$ using the AC-5 algorithm of [HDT92]. $\text{AC}_{\neq}$ also naively takes $O(n^4)$ time as there are $O(n^2)$ binary not-equals constraints. However, we can take advantage of the special nature of a binary not-equals constraint to reduce this to $O(n^2)$ as each not-equals constraint needs to be made AC just once. Asymptotic analysis thus offers no great surprises: we proved that $\text{GAC}_{\forall} \rightarrow \text{AC}_c \rightarrow \text{AC}_{\neq}$ and this is reflected in their $O(n^4)$, $O(n^3)$, $O(n^2)$ respective costs. Thus, $\text{GAC}_{\forall}$ achieves the greatest pruning but at the greatest cost. We need to run experiments to see if this cost is worth the additional pruning.

8 Experimental Comparison

On Langford's problem, a permutation problem from CSPLib, Smith found that MAC on the channelling and other problem constraints is often the most competitive model for finding all solutions [Smi00]. MAC_c (which takes $O(n^3)$ time at each node in the search tree if carefully implemented) explores a similar number of branches to the more powerful $\text{MGAC}_{\forall}$ (which takes $O(n^4)$ time at each node in the search tree). This suggests that MAC_c may offer a good tradeoff between the amount of constraint propagation and the amount of search required. For finding single solutions, Smith's results are somewhat confused by the heuristic accuracy. She predicts that these results will transfer over to other permutation problems. To confirm this, we ran experiments in three other domains, each of which is combinatorially challenging.

8.1 All-Interval Series

Hoos has proposed the all-interval series problem from musical composition as a benchmark for CSPLib. The $ais(n)$ problem is to find a permutation of the numbers 1 to n, such that the differences between adjacent numbers form a permutation from 1 to $n-1$. Computing all solutions is a difficult combinatorial problem. As on Langford's problem [Smi00], MAC_c visits only a few more branches than $MGAC_\forall$. Efficiently implemented, MAC_c is therefore the quickest solution method.

Table 1. Branches to compute all solutions to $ais(n)$.

n	$MAC_{\neq}$	MAC_c	$MGAC_\forall$
6	135	34	34
7	569	153	152
8	2608	627	626
9	12137	2493	2482
10	60588	10552	10476
11	318961	47548	47052

8.2 Circular Golomb Rulers

A perfect circular Golomb ruler consists of n marks arranged on the circumference of a circle of length $n(n-1)$ such that the distances between any pair of marks, in either direction along the circumference, form a permutation. Computing all solutions is again a difficult combinatorial problem. Table 2 shows that $MGAC_\forall$ is very competitive with MAC_c. Indeed, $MGAC_\forall$ has the smallest runtimes. We conjecture that this is due to circular Golomb rulers being more constrained than all-interval series.

Table 2. Branches to compute all order n perfect circular Golomb rulers.

n	$MAC_{\neq}$	MAC_c	$MGAC_\forall$
6	202	93	53
7	1658	667	356
8	15773	5148	2499
9	166424	43261	19901

8.3 Quasigroups

Achlioptas et al have proposed completing a partial filled quasigroup as a benchmark for SAT and CSP algorithms [AGKS00]. This can be modeled as a multiple permutation problem with $2n$ intersecting permutation constraints. A complexity peak is observed when approximately 40% of the quasigroup is replaced by "holes". Table 3 shows the increase in problem difficulty with n. Median behavior for MAC_c is competitive with $MGAC_\forall$. However, mean performance is not due to a few expensive outliers. A randomization and restart strategy reduces the size of this heavy-tailed distribution.

Table 3. Branches to complete 100 order n quasigroup problems with 40% holes.

	median			mean		
n	$MAC_{\neq}$	MAC_c	$MGAC_{\forall}$	$MAC_{\neq}$	MAC_c	$MGAC_{\forall}$
5	1	1	1	1	1	1
10	1	1	1	1.03	1.00	1.01
15	3	1	1	7.17	1.17	1.10
20	23313	7	4	312554	21.76	12.49
25	-	249	53	-	8782.4	579.7
30	-	5812	398	-	2371418	19375

9 Related Work

Chen et al. studied modeling and solving the n-queens problem, and a nurse rostering problem using channelling constraints [CCLW99]. They show that channelling constraints increase the amount of constraint propagation. They conjecture that the overheads associated with channelling constraints will pay off on problems which require large amounts of search, or lead to thrashing behavior. They also show that channelling constraints open the door to interesting value ordering heuristics.

As mentioned before, Smith studied a number of different models for Langford's problem, a permutation problem in CSPLib [Smi00]. Smith argues that channelling constraints make primal not-equals constraints redundant. She also observes that MAC on the model of Langford's problem using channelling constraints explores more branches than MGAC on the model using a primal all-different constraint, and the same number of branches as MAC on the model using channelling and primal not-equals constraints. We prove these results hold in general for (multiple) permutation problems and that the gap can be exponential. However, we also show that they do not extend to algorithms that maintain certain other levels of local consistency like restricted path-consistency. Smith also shows the benefits of being able to branch on dual variables.

10 Conclusions

We have performed an extensive study of a number of different models of permutation problems. To compare models, we defined a measure of constraint tightness parameterized by the level of local consistency being enforced. We used this to prove that, with respect to arc-consistency, a single primal all-different constraint is tighter than channelling constraints, but that channelling constraints are tighter than primal not-equals constraints. Both these gaps can lead to an exponential reduction in search cost. For lower levels of local consistency (e.g. that maintained by forward checking), channelling constraints remain tighter than primal not-equals constraints. However, for certain higher levels of local consistency like path inverse consistency, channelling constraints are incomparable to primal not-equals constraints.

Experimental results on three different and challenging permutation problems confirmed that MAC on channelling constraints outperformed MAC on primal not-equals constraints, and could be competitive with maintaining GAC on a primal all-different constraint. However, on more constrained problems, the additional constraint propagation provided by maintaining GAC on the primal all-different constraint was beneficial. We believe that these results will aid users of constraints to choose a model for a permutation problem, and a local consistency property to enforce on it. They also illustrate a methodology, as well as a measure of constraint tightness, that can be used to compare different constraint models in other problem domains.

Acknowledgements. The author is an EPSRC advanced research fellow. He thanks the other members of the APES research group, especially Barbara Smith for helpful discussions, and Carla Gomes and her colleagues for providing code to generate quasigroups with holes.

References

[AGKS00] Dimitris Achlioptas, Carla P. Gomes, Henry A. Kautz, and Bart Selman. Generating satisfiable problems instances. In *Proc. of 17th National Conference on Artificial Intelligence*, pages 256–261. 2000.

[BM00] R. Bejar and F. Manya. Solving the round robin problem using propositional logic. In *Proc. of 17th National Conference on Artificial Intelligence*, pages 262–266. 2000.

[BMFL99] C. Bessière, P. Meseguer, E.C. Freuder, and J. Larrosa. On forward checking for non-binary constraint satisfaction. In *Proc. of 5th Int. Conf. on Principles and Practice of Constraint Programming (CP99)*, pages 88–102. 1999.

[CCLW99] B.M.W. Cheng, K.M.F. Choi, J.H.M. Lee, and J.C.K. Wu. Increasing constraint propagation by redundant modeling: an experience report. *Constraints*, 4:167–192, 1999.

[Che00] Xinguang Chen. *A Theoretical Comparison of Selected CSP Solving and Modelling Techniques*. PhD thesis, Dept. of Computing Science, University of Alberta, 2000.

[DB97] R. Debruyne and C. Bessière. Some practicable filtering techniques for the constraint satisfaction problem. In *Proc. of the 15th IJCAI*, pages 412–417. 1997.

[GSW00] I.P. Gent, K. Stergiou, and T. Walsh. Decomposable constraints. *Artificial Intelligence*, 123(1-2):133–156, 2000.

[HDT92] P. Van Hentenryck, Y. Deville, and C. Teng. A Generic Arc Consistency Algorithm and its Specializations. *Artificial Intelligence*, 57:291–321, 1992.

[PSW00] P. Prosser, K. Stergiou, and T. Walsh. Singelton consistencies. In *Proc of 6th Int. Conf. on Principles and Practices of Constraint Programming (CP-2000)*, pages 353–368. 2000.

[Ŕ94] J.C. Régin. A filtering algorithm for constraints of difference in CSPs. In *Proc. of the 12th National Conference on AI*, pages 362–367. 1994.

[RR00] J.C. Régin and M. Rueher. A global constraint combining a sum constraint and difference constraints. In *Proc. of 6th Int. Conf. on Principles and Practice of Constraint Programming (CP2000)*, pages 384–395. 2000.

[Smi00] B.M. Smith. Modelling a Permutation Problem. In *Proc. of ECAI'2000 Workshop on Modelling and Solving Problems with Constraints*, 2000.

[SW99] K. Stergiou and T. Walsh. The difference all-difference makes. In *Proceedings of 16th IJCAI*. 1999.

[Wal00] T. Walsh. SAT v CSP. In *Proc. of 6th Int. Conf. on Principles and Practices of Constraint Programming (CP-2000)*, pages 441–456. 2000.

Simplifying Binary Propositional Theories into Connected Components Twice as Fast

Alvaro del Val

E.T.S. Informática
Universidad Autónoma de Madrid
delval@ii.uam.es
http://www.ii.uam.es/ delval

Abstract. Binary propositional theories, composed of clauses with at most two literals, are one of the most interesting tractable subclasses of the satisfiability problem. We present two hybrid simplification algorithms for binary theories, which combine the unit-resolution-based 2SAT algorithm BinSat [9] with refined versions of the classical strongly connected components (SCC) algorithm of [1]. We show empirically that the algorithms are considerably faster than other SCC-based algorithms, and have greater simplifying power, as they combine detection of entailed literals with identification of SCCs, i.e. sets of equivalent literals. By developing faster simplification algorithms we hope to contribute to attempts to integrate simplification of binary theories within the search phase of general SAT solvers.

1 Introduction

Binary propositional theories, composed of clauses with at most two literals, are one of the most interesting tractable subclasses of the well-known satisfiability problem. In addition to quick decision of satisfiability, binary theories also offer opportunities for efficient simplification, in particular through the derivation of *entailed literals* and of sets of *equivalent literals*, which can be eliminated.

The goal of this paper is to reduce the overhead of binary clause reasoning so that it results (hopefully) in affordable per-node costs when used within the search phase of a DPLL-style general SAT solver [7,11]. While solving pure binary problems is by itself not that interesting, simplifying the binary subset of a general propositional theory has a lot of potential in helping to solve general SAT problems. Indeed, binary clause reasoning has demonstrated substantial pruning power when used on the binary subsets of the theories associated to each node in the backtracking search tree of such solvers [12,4,18], or even only at the root of this tree, i.e. as preprocessing [2,3].

But the additional simplifying power of binary clause reasoning is not without cost, and this cost cannot always be justified. Hence our goal to reduce the overhead. The lack of a measurable impact in overall efficiency probably explains the relative scarcity of literature on integrating binary simplification methods

R. Nieuwenhuis and A. Voronkov (Eds.): LPAR 2001, LNAI 2250, pp. 392–406, 2001.

into general SAT solvers. Most telling, and probably still valid, is the story beyond one of the earliest attempts known to us toward integrating binary clause reasoning into general solvers. In the 1993 SAT competition held in Paderborn [4], the second-rated solver was identical to the top-rated solver except for the addition of significant amounts of binary clause reasoning. The second solver eliminated equivalent literals, as found by the classical strongly connected components (SCCs) algorithm for 2SAT presented by Aspvall et al. in [1], and derived unit clauses entailed by the binary subset of a theory at each search node. Unfortunately, *the second solver was significantly slower, even though it expanded a significantly smaller search tree.* Though there's been other quite interesting approaches to incorporating binary reasoning, perhaps most competitively the solver `2cl` by van Gelder [18], we can record the fact that this kind of reasoning has not really made it into current general SAT solvers, except as a preprocessing stage or in ad hoc ways. For example, Brafman recently reports [3] abandoning an attempt to integrate his successful preprocessing 2SAT-based simplifier within search, again after noticing a very high overhead.

1.1 Contributions

We present two new simplification methods for binary theories which reduce the overhead, and thus have better potential for successful integration within search. Both algorithms, to which we will refere generically as BinSatSCC, are hybrids between the unit-resolution-based algorithm BinSat recently proposed by del Val [9], and the classical SCC-based 2SAT algorithm introduced by Aspvall et al. in [1], which we will call APT-SCC. Both versions of BinSatSCC augment BinSat's depth-first unit resolution with the ability to detect SCCs, differing only in the underlying SCC algorithm. BinSatSCC-1 uses a variant of the SCC algorithm of [17], and is closely related to the algorithm HyperCC of [16]. BinSatSCC-2, in turn, is based on the SCC algorithm described in [5], using BinSat to dynamically restrict the implication graph of a binary theory to the nodes appearing in the model generated by BinSat, and thus to half the nodes of the graph searched by other SCC algorithms. Both BinSatSCC algorithms yield: (a) much faster detection of unsatisfiability than with APT-SCC; (b) identification of a significant subset of the entailed literals, which is out of the scope of APT-SCC; (c) faster identification of sets of equivalent literals than with APT-SCC.

Our general conclusion is unequivocally positive: *BinSatSCC achieves strictly more simplification than APT-SCC in significantly less time.* The greater simplifying power derives from (b) and (c), where BinSat only achieves (b) and APT-SCC only achieves (c). As for efficiency, we show empirically that BinSatSCC algorithms provide a speed up by a factor of at least close to 2 with respect to APT-SCC on all problems, and even more on unsatisfiable ones. Compared to BinSat, we must again distinguish between satisfiable and unsatisfiable problems. On satisfiable problems, both versions of BinSatSCC are less efficient than BinSat (it could not be otherwise, as both algorithms augment BinSat), in return for greater simplifying power; and BinSatSCC-1 is clearly the fastest version. On unsatisfiable problems, on the other hand, BinSatSCC-2 is exactly as efficient as BinSat, whereas BinSatSCC-1 incurs a relatively significant overhead. There is thus no clear winner, but since unsatisfiable problems are usually easier, the balance seems to lean towards BinSatSCC-1.

1.2 Structure of the Paper

The structure of this paper is as follows. Section 2 introduces the implication graph of binary theories, the main data-structure used by all algorithms studied in this paper. Sections 3 and 4 review the building blocks of our new algorithms, respectively SCC-based algorithms and BinSat. Section 5 presents the BinSatSCC algorithms and prove their correctness. Section 6 provides experimental data which confirm the claims made in this paper, in particular the advantages of BinSatSCC over APT-SCC in efficiency and simplifying power.

2 Searching the Implication Graph

We begin with some formal preliminaries, in particular in connection with the "implication graph" of binary theories, which is searched by all algorithms in this paper. We assume familiarity with the standard literature on propositional reasoning, specially with clausal theories. We use lower case letters for literals (e.g. $a, \bar{b}, x, y$, where $\bar{b}$ is b negated), and treat clauses as sets, though we write them as sequences (e.g. $a\bar{b}c$ is the disjunction of these three literals).

Definition 1 (Aspvall et al. [1]). *The* implication graph $G(S)$ *for a set of binary clauses S contains one node for each literal of S, and directed edges $x \longrightarrow y$ whenever the clause $\bar{x}y$ is in S.*

An edge $x \longrightarrow y$ graphically represents an implication from x to y in S, where each clause provides two such implications. Paths in $G(S)$ also correspond to logical implication, by the transitivity of the latter.

For completeness, let us also define here:

Definition 2. *The* transposed implication graph $G_T(S)$ *is defined by inverting the direction of all edges in $G(S)$.*

Definition 3. *A strongly connected component (SCC) of a graph G is a maximal subset C of nodes of G such that for every $u, v \in C$, there are paths in G from u to v and from v to u.*

Clearly, if two literals belong to a SCC of $G(S)$, then S entails that they are equivalent, because of the correspondence between paths and implications.

Example 1. Consider the theory $S = \{\bar{a}b, \bar{b}c, \bar{c}\bar{b}, \bar{c}d, \bar{d}e, \bar{e}c\}$. Its implication graph is shown in Figure 1.a. We can see, for example, that there is a path from b to $\bar{b}$, indicating the chain of implications $b \longrightarrow c \longrightarrow \bar{b}$, from which $\bar{b}$, and then $\bar{a}$, can be derived as unit clauses entailed by S. We can also see that there is

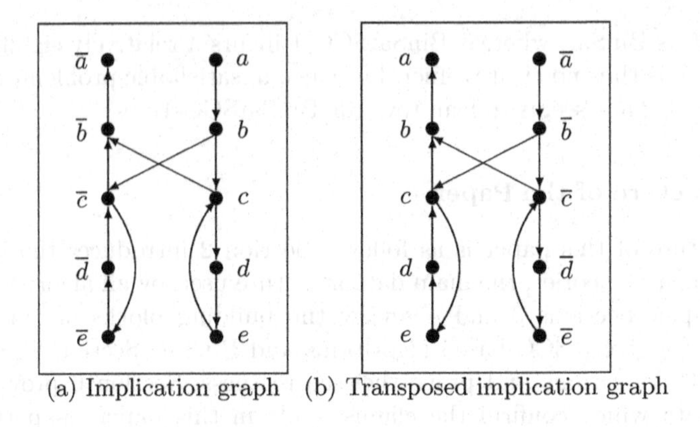

(a) Implication graph (b) Transposed implication graph

Fig. 1. Graphs for Example 1.

a cycle, $c \to d \to e \to c$, which constitutes one SCC of $G(S)$. Thus, S entails that all the literals in the cycle are equivalent, so all occurrences of, say, d and e can be replaced by c, and the clauses linking variables from the SCC eliminated. If this simplification is performed during expansion of a backtrack-like search tree, it directly prunes the exponential growing factor of this tree, by decreasing the number of variables. In this particular example, we began with a five variable problem which contained no unit clauses and we ended up with a single unassigned variable, namely c.

The implication graph presents a large degree of symmetry as a result of its "redundant" representation of each binary clause by two edges in the graph. This has some interesting properties. For every edge $x \to y$, there's an edge $\overline{y} \to \overline{x}$, a notion of "contraposition" which can also be generalized to paths. For every (consistent) SCC, furthermore, there's a *complementary* SCC with the sign of all literals changed (in the example, the cycle $\overline{c} \to \overline{d} \to \overline{e} \to \overline{c}$). Finally, symmetry also shows up in the the transposed graph $G_T(S)$, which, as can be seen in Figure 1.b, can be obtained by simply swapping each pair of complementary literals in $G(S)$, i.e. by negating the label associated to each node.

All the algorithms discussed in this paper can be entirely cast as depth first search of the implication graph. It is worth noting that $G(S)$ is at least implicitly built by any DPLL solver, which must index its binary clauses somehow. In the implementations tested, we used the data-structures of `compact` [6], which include an explicit representation of $G(S)$ in the form of adjacency lists for each literal. At any rate, any data structure that supports efficient unit resolution on binary clauses can be used to represent $G(S)$ and search it. Thus, the studied algorithms represent no data-structure overhead for standard DPLL solvers.

3 SCC Algorithms

We begin our review of the building blocks of BinSatSCC by SCC algorithms. As said, such algorithms are based on depth first search (DFS) of $G(S)$, so let's fix some terminology about DFS for later reference. Following a classic algorithm book [5], DFS has a top level loop which iterates over all nodes of a graph, calling a subroutine DFS-Visit for each undiscovered node. DFS-visit, in turn, simply marks the node as discovered, and iterates over its adjacency list, recursively calling DFS-visit on each as yet undiscovered node in the list. When finished with an adjacency list, DFS-visit terminates, possibly associating a "finishing time" to the node whose visit is concluding.

APT-SCC searches for SCCs of $G(S)$, determining S unsatisfiable just in case it finds a SCC with complementary literals. If no such SCC is found, APT-SCC can output the SCCs for simplification of the theory. We consider in fact two different SCC algorithms for APT-SCC. SCC-1, as we will call it, is the classical SCC algorithm by Tarjan [17]. It obtains SCCs with *one* DFS over $G(S)$, by keeping track of earliest "back edges" (leading to an ancestor node) found along the search. SCC-2 is an alternative algorithm described in e.g. [5], which requires *two* depth first searches. The goal of the first DFS, over $G(S)$, is only to sort the nodes (literals) by reverse ordering of finishing time. This can be achieved quite simply by pushing nodes into a stack as they are finished, so that the latest finished node is on top of the stack at the end. The second DFS is over the transposed graph $G_T(S)$, processing nodes in the top loop in the ordering returned by the first search. Each of the trees in the depth first forest generated by the second DFS is a SCC of $G(S)$.[1]

Accordingly, we have two algorithms, APT-SCC-1 and APT-SCC-2. We note that APT-SCC-1 is the original APT-SCC as proposed in [1], whereas APT-SCC-2 is a previously unreported variation, which happens to yield quite interesting conclusions. In particular, APT-SCC-2 benefits from the fact that the transposed graph is already implicit in $G(S)$, and thus needs not be computed explicitly. This is illustrated in Figure 1.b. Specifically, the adjacency list of a literal x in $G_T(S)$ can be obtained by inverting the sign of all literals in the adjacency list of the (also negated) literal $\overline{x}$ in the original graph $G(S)$. For $x \rightarrow y$ is an edge in in the transposed graph $G_T(S)$ iff $y \rightarrow x$ is an edge in the original $G(S)$, iff $\overline{y}x \in S$, iff $\overline{x} \rightarrow \overline{y}$ is an edge of $G(S)$.

4 BinSat

The algorithm BinSat proposed by del Val in [9] does a single depth first search of the graph, following "unit resolution paths" across $G(S)$. The algorithm appears in Figure 2, taken from [9]. Further description of BinSat can be found there, though we provide below some explanation to understand the pseudocode.

[1] Note that the numbers in SCC-1 and SCC-2 can be used to denote historical precedence, but also as mnemonic for the number of DFSs done by each algorithm.

Procedure TempPropUnit(x)
/* *Input: A literal x to be tentatively assigned.* */

if $tempval(x) = false$ /* temporary conflict, $S \models \overline{x} \rightarrow x$ */
then set $S := PropUnit(S \cup \{x\})$ and **return**;
$tempval(x) := true$; $tempval(\overline{x}) := false$;
foreach $y\overline{x} \in S$ **do:**
  if ($\Box \in S$ **or** $permval(x) \neq NIL$) **then return**;
  if ($permval(y) = NIL$ **and** $tempval(y) \neq true$) **then** TempPropUnit(y);

Procedure BinSat(S)
/* *Input: A binary clausal theory S* */

foreach literal x of S **do:**
  $tempval(x) := permval(x) := NIL$;
$S := PropUnit(S)$;
while ($\Box \notin S$ **and** there exists a literal x s.t. $permval(x) = tempval(x) = NIL$) **do:**
  TempPropUnit(x);
If $\Box \in S$
then return Unsatisfiable;
else return GetModel();

Fig. 2. BinSat algorithm for 2-SAT [9]. See text for explanations. GetModel() returns, for each variable, its *permval* if non-null, and otherwise its *tempval*.

BinSat keeps track of tentative assignments *tempval*, and permanent assignments *permval* for each literal (in practice, for each variable, but this would obscure the pseudocode). The former are assigned as a result of tentatively assuming a literal and propagating its consequences by depth-first unit resolution, using the subroutine TempPropUnit; the latter denote forced (entailed) literals, and are set by a subroutine PropUnit, which (unlike TempPropUnit) stands for any implementation of unit resolution. We only assume that the assignments forced by PropUnit are recorded as permanent values by setting *permval*'s, and that it generates the empty clause, denoted $\Box$ in the pseudocode, when it reaches a global contradiction.[2]

BinSat shares the structure of DFS. TempPropUnit corresponds to DFS-Visit, recursively calling itself for each undiscovered member of the "adjacency list". It takes charge of propagating tentative assignments in depth first fashion,

[2] Figure 2 differs from the original in [9] in explicit tests for null *permval*'s, so that no processing of forced variables takes place after they are set by PropUnit. These tests were unnecessary in [9] because of an explicit assumption (which is lifted here) that PropUnit effectively deleted subsumed clauses.

with *tempval*'s being used as "discovered" marks. It differs from DFS-Visit only in its ability to detect entailed literals, triggering a call to PropUnit which propagates permanent assignments. The top level loop of BinSat is also identical to DFS, except that it only iterates over half the nodes of $G(S)$, as it only tries each variable with one sign. The same applies to TempPropUnit, if we disregard variables which are assigned by PropUnit. These are the only ones visited by TempPropUnit with both signs; once they are assigned, we can treat them as if they no longer existed in the graph.

Example 2 (continued). A sample run of BinSat on Example 1 could start by calling TempPropUnit(a). This would result in traversing the path $a \rightarrow b \rightarrow c \rightarrow \overline{b}$ in $G(S)$ (see Figure 1), causing a subsequent call to $PropUnit(\overline{b})$ which would conclude $\overline{b}$ and $\overline{a}$ as entailed literals. As shown in [9], the DFS approach of TempPropUnit guarantees that such path is detected when TempPropUnit($\overline{b}$) is called after $tempval(b)$ was already set to true. At any rate, search by TempPropUnit continues from c along the path $c \rightarrow d \rightarrow e$. After exhausting the adjacency lists for these literals, we are back into the TempPropUnit($\overline{b}$) call, which terminates immediately as b is now permanently valued; back into TempPropUnit(a), same thing happens, returning control to BinSat. Since all variables have a tentative or permanent (forced) value, BinSat terminates, returning the model $M = \{\overline{a}, \overline{b}, c, d, e\}$, where c, d and e are the "tentatively assigned" literals of M (whose assignment does not lead to contradiction by unit resolution), and $\overline{a}$ and $\overline{b}$ are the entailed literals.

5 BinSatSCC Algorithms

We now present the new algorithms, which detect both (a subset of) entailed literals and the sets of equivalent literals provided by SCCs. As said, both operate over $G(S)$, and use BinSat, either implicitly or explicitly, as depth-first search of $G(S)$. As in BinSat, in a real implementation all information associated to literals in the pseudocode would actually be associated to variables.[3]

BinSatSCC-1, described in Figure 3, uses a variant of Tarjan's SCC-1 algorithm presented in [15]. BinSatSCC-1 and its auxiliary routine TempPropUnit-SCC are augmented versions of BinSat and TempPropUnit, respectively. The additions are pretty straightforward, given [15]. We associate to each variable x a discovery time $discovered(x)$ when its visit begins, and we keep track through $lowlink(x)$ of the discovery time of the earliest ancestor of x in the DFS tree which is reachable from x. If the visit of x reaches some of its ancestors, then at the end of the visit $discovered(x) \neq lowlink(x)$, and x is added to a stack of literals whose SCC has not yet been identified. Otherwise, $discovered(x) = lowlink(x)$ at the end of the visit, and x is the root of a SCC

[3] This follows from properties of BinSat, which guarantee that if a variable is visited with both signs then it acquires a permanent value, and hence becomes irrelevant for SCC computation. In contrast, APT-SCC algorithms must keep information for both signs of a variable.

Procedure TempPropUnit-SCC(x)

```
if tempval(x) = false /* temporary conflict, S ⊨ x̄ → x */
then set S := PropUnit(S ∪ {x}) and return;
tempval(x) := true; tempval(x̄) := false;
time := time + 1;
discovered(x) := lowlink(x) := time;
foreach yx̄ ∈ S do:
   if (□ ∈ S or permval(x) ≠ NIL) then return;
   if permval(y) = NIL
   then if tempval(y) ≠ true /* if literal y not visited yet (with same sign) */
          then TempPropUnit-SCC(y);
               lowlink(x) := min(lowlink(x),lowlink(y));
        elseif not done(y)
        then lowlink(x) := min(lowlink(x),discovered(y));
if permval(x) = NIL
then if lowlink(x) ≠ discovered(x)
     then push(x,stack);
     else /* x is root of SCC */
        done(x) := true;
        make the set currentSCC empty
        while (stack ≠ ∅ and discovered(top(stack)) > discovered(x))
               z = pop(stack);
               done(z) := true;
               if (permval(z) = NIL) then push(z,currentSCC);
        output currentSCC ∪{x};
```

Procedure BinSatSCC-1(S)

```
time := 0; stack := ∅;
foreach literal x of S do:
   tempval(x) := permval(x) := NIL;
   done(x) := false;
S := PropUnit(S);
while (□ ∉ S and there exists a literal x s.t. permval(x) = tempval(x) = NIL) do:
   TempPropUnit-SCC(x);
if □ ∈ S
then return Unsatisfiable;
else return GetModel();
```

Fig. 3. Algorithm BinSatSCC-1. The framed code corresponds to the original TempPropUnit, so that the additions can be seen clearly.

whose other members are all literals in the stack discovered later than x. All of them are then popped and outputted as a SCC, all of whose members are marked as *done*.

Example 3 (continued). We illustrate a possible run of BinSatSCC on Example 1. The structure of the DFS is identical to that of BinSat, so that reaching $\bar{b}$ makes a and b permanently valued false. The visit to c (originating from b) reaches d and then e, at which point the edge $e \rightarrow c$ is found. This causes the update of *lowlink*(e), and thus e is pushed to the stack, and then similarly for d. After finishing d, c is found to be the root of a SCC which also contains all literals in the stack discovered after c (i.e. d and e).

BinSatSCC-1 can be seen as a simplified (and correct) version of the HyperCC algorithm introduced by Pretolani in [16]. The main differences are: a) we use the simpler implication graph instead of Pretolani's hypergraph representation, thus requiring basically no additional data structures beyond those used by standard DPLL SAT solvers; b) our formulation is in term of unit resolution, which we believe is easier to understand and makes the relationship with standard SAT solvers more transparent; c) BinSatSCC-1 uses a slightly more efficient version of Tarjan's SCC-1 algorithm, which reduces the number of stack operations[4]; d) finally, we fix a bug in Pretolani's algorithm, by which literals which become permanently valued *during* their own visit (and thus after being pushed onto the stack in Tarjan's algorithm, see previous footnote) will be incorrectly reported as members of the next generated (unvalued) SCC.

BinSatSCC-2, our second algorithm, can be described as a modified SCC-2 algorithm over a restricted implication graph, where this restriction is obtained by using BinSat as first DFS of the SCC-2 algorithm. Pseudocode is provided in Figure 4. The first step of BinSatSCC-2 is to call BinSat. This call ensures fast detection of unsatisfiable theories, and will detect a portion of entailed literals, for satisfiable ones (just as BinSatSCC-1). For the latter, the model obtained by BinSat is used to dynamically restrict $G(S)$ to nodes (literals) satisfied in the model (and which are not known to be entailed); it also provides an ordering of those nodes for a second DFS on the restricted (transposed) graph. This second DFS is performed by BinSatSCC in the loop after the call to BinSat, with the procedure FindSCC corresponding to DFS-Visit over the restricted transposed graph. FindSCC keeps its own *discovered* mark for each literal to do the DFS, working on the transposed graph by examining adjacency lists of $G(S)$ as described earlier. Note that it implicitly eliminates from the graph forced variables, by ignoring variables whose *permval* is set; and unforced literals not in the model, by requiring a true *tempval* to visit a node.

[4] Specifically, while Tarjan's algorithm adds each literal to the stack when its visit begins, [15] version only pushes them onto the stack when the visit finishes, and only if they are not the root of a SCC. As a byproduct, "trivial" singleton SCCs are never added to the stack, nor literals which become permanently valued *during* their visit. Obviously, this can be beneficial if there are many literals of either kind. Note however that a SCC may become permanently valued *true after* being finished.

```
Procedure FindSCC(literal x)

discovered(x) := true;
push(x,currentSCC);
foreach yx ∈ S  /* working on transposed graph, visit each ȳ s.t. y ∈ Adj(x̄, G(S)) */
   if (permval(ȳ) = NIL and            /* if ȳ unforced/unvalued, and... */
       tempval(ȳ) = true and           /* ...ȳ visited by BinSat, and... */
       discovered(ȳ) = false)          /* ...ȳ not yet visited in second DFS */
   then FindSCC(ȳ)                     /* Note sign inversions throughout */
```

```
Procedure BinSatSCC-2(S)

if (BinSat(S) = Unsatisfiable) then return Unsatisfiable;
foreach literal x, discovered(x) := false;
foreach literal x visited by BinSat, /* i.e. with tempval(x) = true */
      in reverse order of finishing time, do:
   if (permval(x) = NIL and discovered(x) = false)
   then make the set currentSCC empty;
         FindSCC(x);
         output currentSCC;
```

Fig. 4. Algorithm BinSatSCC-2.

Example 4 (continued). BinSatSCC-2 on Example 1 could proceed as follows. First, the call to BinSat can proceed as in Example 2. The ordering for the second search, which will ignore the entailed literals $\overline{a}$ and $\overline{b}$, is c, d, e. Search on the transposed graph traverses backwards the $c \leftarrow e \leftarrow d$ path of $G(S)$, outputting the SCC with these three literals, and then terminates since all remaining literals in the model are visited. Note that BinSatSCC traverses fewer edges in total than APT-SCC-2 in its first search.

Thus, if we ignore the derivation of entailed literals by BinSat (which is itself a source of significant simplification), BinSatSCC-2 can be described as APT-SCC-2 on the restricted graph, which, note, has at most *half* as many nodes as $G(S)$. For whatever is worth, we remark that this a "semantic" restriction of $G(S)$, as is determined by a model, and that it is "dynamically generated" during search, i.e. it is not known in advance before calling BinSat.

Theorem 1. *BinSatSCC-1 and BinSatSCC-2 correctly decide the satisfiability of any binary propositional theory S, and correctly identify a subset of the literals entailed by S. If S is satisfiable, both algorithms correctly output a set of SCCs (sets of equivalent literals) which includes all variables without permanent value. The algorithm runs in time linear in the number of clauses.*

Proof. For both algorithms, complexity follows from the complexity of BinSat and depth first search. Correct decision of satisfiability and detection of entailed literals also follows from correctness of BinSat [9]. Assume therefore in what follows that S is satisfiable, to prove correct SCC detection.

The correctness of BinSatSCC-1 follows from the correctness of the version of SCC-1 we use, since the SCC aspects of TemPropUnitSCC simply ignore literals with permanent value (in particular, no such literal will be added to currentSCC).

For BinSatSCC-2, assume that all literals discovered by BinSat to be entailed by S have been simplified away from S (as said in the text, the algorithm ensures this in practice by ignoring variables with permanent, forced values). Thus we assume that all literals in S are only tentatively valued (with *tempval*) by BinSat.

As already pointed out, BinSat's control flow is the same as depth first search of $G(S)$. In the top level loop it imposes the restriction that no variable is visited with both signs, then it interrupts the search before completion (with respect to $G(S)$) when every variable is visited with exactly one sign. Let us now suppose that we take this initial DFS by BinSat (over the possibly simplified $G(S)$, thus ignoring forced literals) as part of the initial DFS by APT-SCC-2, and let's hypothetically proceed with a run of APT-SCC-2 on $G(S)$. We'll claim that the main loop of BinSatSCC-2 will obtain exactly the same SCCs as would be obtained by APT-SCC-2 when processing, in its second, transposed DFS, the literals visited by BinSat. Since these SCCs include every non-forced variable, the conclusion of the theorem follows from correctness of SCC-2.

Let VISITED be the set of tentative literals assigned true by BinSat. Ignoring again forced values, continuing the first DFS by APT-SCC-2 would visit the literals, call them UNVISITED, that were not visited by BinSat (which are the complements of the literals in VISITED). Then APT-SCC-2 would start a second DFS, now on $G_T(S)$, in reverse order of finishing times. Clearly, this means processing, at top level, all literals in UNVISITED before any one in VISITED (as the former were finished later in the first search). We claim that this processing does not discover any VISITED literal. For suppose $x \in$ UNVISITED is visited at top level by the second DFS of APT-SCC-2, and let y be any descendant of x in this search. This implies that there is a "backwards" path $x \leftarrow \ldots \leftarrow y$ in $G(S)$. It follows that $y \notin$ VISITED, since otherwise x should have been reached during or before the visit of y by *BinSat*, in contradiction with $x \in$ UNVISITED.

We conclude that the transposed search over all literals in UNVISITED reaches no literal in VISITED. It follows that, when APT-SCC-2 concludes processing the UNVISITED literals in its transposed search, all the VISITED literals remain to be visited by the transposed search, and all UNVISITED literals are already discovered. BinSatSCC in effect treats all literals in UNVISITED as if they had already been discovered in the second search (by the simple device of ignoring literals not discovered in the first search by BinSat, i.e. whose *tempval* is not true); and when BinSatSCC begins its loop, no VISITED literal is marked as discovered, just as would happen with APT-SCC-2 when reaching that stage of its transposed search. Thus, BinSatSCC will do exactly the same processing of the VISITED literals as APT-SCC-2 would do, and in particular it will generate the same SCCs as APT-SCC-2 processing the VISITED literals. But the VISITED literals include all (unforced) variables with one sign, hence it will include every variable in some SCC in this phase. And this is all we need. □

6 Experimental Study

In this section, we present extracts from a substantial experimental study on binary clause reasoning algorithms. All algorithms were implemented using data-structures similar to `compact` [6], a polynomial simplifier for propositional clausal theories. In particular, `compact` uses, for each literal x, a list of literals y such that $\overline{x}y$ is a clause of the input theory. It is easy to see that this is a quite explicit representation of $G(S)$, though `compact` uses it to do unit resolution much as most SAT solvers. BinSat in fact uses the implementation of unit resolution of `compact`, while APT-SCC-1 and APT-SCC-2 use this representation of $G(S)$ to do their depth first visit(s). This common implementation makes the comparisons more meaningful.

The implementations were as efficient as we could make them. One particular optimization which is worth mentioning is that neither APT-SCC algorithm generates complementary SCCs. For APT-SCC-1, this is achieved by visiting each variable with only one sign in the top level loop of DFS; the rationale is that after finishing a top level visit of x we have already generated its SCC, so there is no point in trying $\overline{x}$. For APT-SCC-2, this is achieved by making its second search ignore, at the top level, variables already assigned to some SCC, with the same rationale.[5] While these optimizations may appear obvious, they are not always implemented (e.g. [3]); we ourselves didn't optimize APT-SCC-1 until late in the process, which initially led us to wrongly conclude that APT-SCC-2 was clearly superior to APT-SCC-1 on satisfiable problems. At any rate, these optimizations considerably reduce the difference in cost of both algorithms with respect to BinSatSCC.

We used various random and non-random problem generators. First, we generated random problems according to the fixed probability model of [14][6]. We found a very sharp phase transition, so sharp that it seriously limited the range of interesting tests; a ratio between 0.9 and 1.1 clauses per variable was the only one likely to yield problems which were not trivially under or over constrained. We run tests on instances with 20,000, 60,000 and 100,000 variables, and also considered theories forced to be satisfiable. In the tables below, they are denoted `R-numvars-numclauses`, with qualifiers "forced" for instances forced satisfiable, and "sat" and "unsat" for unforced instances, with the obvious meaning. Second, we considered *chains* of binary theories, each on some subset of the vocabulary, linked in sequence by a couple of clauses with literals from precedent and subsequent cluster (these chains are introduced in [8]). They are denoted by `CH-numvars-numclauses-numtheories`, where numvar and numclauses are the numbers for each cluster (theory) in the chain. This gave raise to a much more interesting range of behaviors, and a less sharp transition, with respect to the

[5] As can be gathered from the proof of correctness of BinSatSCC-2, we could further improve APT-SCC-2 by restricting its *first* DFS just as with APT-SCC-1. However, we feel that the resulting algorithm is more like "BinSatSCC-2 without detection of entailed literals" than "optimized APT-SCC-2," so we see little point in testing it.

[6] We used a variant of Van Gelder's generator `cnfgen`, available at Dimacs, ftp://dimacs.rutgers.edu/pub/challenge/satisfiability/

number of clusters (whereas increasing the clause/variable ratio per cluster yields very easy unsatisfiable problems). Instance size ranges from clusters of 50 to 250 variables, from 100 to 2000 clusters. Finally, we considered "variable chains", the worst case instances described in Example 1 of [9], where each variable implies the next one, but the last variable in the chain is entailed false. These are denoted as `VC-numvars`. All data points include at least 20 instances, and were collected on a Pentium II 400MHz with 128MB of RAM, running Linux.

Table 1. Average CPU time normalized for BinSat = 1. The numbers in parenthesis are average CPU time for BinSat, in milliseconds.

Problem	**APT-SCC** ver. 1	**APT-SCC** ver. 2	**BinSatSCC** ver. 1	**BinSatSCC** ver. 2	**BinSat**
R-100000-100000 sat	3.12	2.97	1.51	2.16	1 (67)
R-100000-100000 forced	3.11	3.04	1.50	2.20	1 (64)
R-100000-140000 forced	3.43	3.09	1.55	2.28	1 (74)
R-100000-200000 forced	3.28	2.72	1.45	1.92	1 (102)
R-100000-120000 unsat	41.14	76.70	3.78	1.01	1 (2)
R-100000-140000 unsat	78.06	91.00	3.97	1.04	1 (2)
R-100000-200000 unsat	188.91	139.64	4.91	1.02	1 (1)
CH-100-60-1000 sat	2.30	2.87	1.30	2.09	1 (45)
CH-100-100-1000 forced	2.55	3.00	1.29	2.14	1 (50)
CH-100-140-1000 forced	2.71	2.98	1.28	2.10	1 (56)
CH-150-90-1000 sat	2.24	2.70	1.30	1.94	1 (73)
CH-150-90-2000 forced	2.23	2.68	1.28	1.94	1 (145)
CH-200-120-1000 sat	2.23	2.70	1.29	1.93	1 (97)
CH-100-60-1000 unsat	2.90	8.58	1.60	1.06	1 (12)
CH-150-90-1000 unsat	2.39	4.01	1.36	1.03	1 (36)
CH-150-90-2000 unsat	2.75	6.16	1.49	1.05	1 (53)
VC-50000 sat	1.57	1.55	1.06	1	1 (77)
VC-50000 unsat	2.90	2.97	1.08	1	1 (39)

Table 1 provides normalized average CPU time for all the algorithms considered in this paper, on a number of typical problem sets. The data shows, first, that there are clear differences in performance between APT-SCC-1 and APT-SCC-2, but neither dominates. Second, BinSatSCC algorithms are much faster than APT-SCC algorithms, often by a factor of 2 or more. BinSatSCC-1 clearly dominates on satisfiable problems, but may incur a significant overhead with respect to BinSatSCC-2 on unsatisfiable ones, where the latter behaves exactly as BinSat. Finally, of course, BinSat is faster than BinSatSCC.

Table 2 compares the algorithms in terms of their simplifying power, measured by the number of literals that can be eliminated by each algorithm. We count the entailed literals and all but one literal from each SCC. Obviously, both versions of APT-SCC yield the same result here, and the same applies to BinSatSCC. We consider satisfiable instances only, since otherwise simplification is useless. We can see that, as expected, BinSatSCC can simplify theories much more than either BinSat or APT-SCC alone. (Note that the value for BinSatSCC is not the sum of the other two values because APT-SCC sometimes finds SCCs which in fact are entailed). We also found that BinSat typically finds 25–50% of the total entailed literals, which is good but leaves significant room for improvement.

Table 2. Average number of eliminated literals, normalized for BinSat = 1. The numbers in parenthesis are the actual average number of eliminated literals for BinSat.

Problem	APT-SCC	BinSatSCC	BinSat
R-100000-100000 sat	0.08	1.06	1 (671)
R-100000-100000 forced	0.33	1.33	1 (1)
R-100000-200000 forced	1.13	1.68	1 (18146)
CH-100-140-1000 forced	0.75	1.61	1 (4028)
CH-150-90-1000 sat	0.95	1.93	1 (267)
CH-150-90-1000 forced	1.22	2.20	1 (134)
CH-150-90-2000 forced	1.29	2.27	1 (229)
CH-200-120-1000 sat	0.91	1.89	1 (292)
VC-50000 sat	0	1	1 (49999)

Though it's out of the scope of this paper, we remark that on all these problems, the original unit resolution algorithm of Even et al. [10] is generally around 20–40% slower than BinSat (and that only after careful tuning), and thus better than either APT-SCC algorithm on most problem classes; but it can also be orders of magnitude worse, for example in the VC examples. It also detects fewer entailed literals than BinSat, roughly around 50-70%.

One final methodological point. Our conclusions are supported by controlled experiments of the studied algorithms for binary simplification on *purely binary theories*, even though our stated goal is helping to solve *general* SAT problems. Because of their consistency and regularity, we do expect our conclusions on performance rankings for various binary clause algorithms to carry over to the general case. Furthermore, we believe this is the right methodological choice, as opposed to testing the various algorithms within a general solver first off. The latter choice would raise more questions as to the generality of its findings, as trying to add binary simplification to a general SAT solver introduces too many uncontrolled variables in the experiments which may affect our ability to estimate accurately the benefit/cost ratio of binary clause reasoning in isolation from other factors such as its interaction with heuristics, backjumping, and learning.

7 Conclusion

We presented new hybrid algorithms for simplification of binary propositional theories, which combine the more advanced unit resolution algorithm for 2SAT with more efficient identification of sets of mutually equivalent literals (SCCs) than previous algorithms. We also demonstrated empirically the advantages of the new algorithms. BinSatSCC is a step forward toward efficient binary clause reasoning with less overhead, so that its pruning power can be used during search in general SAT problems.

References

[1] B. Aspvall, M. F. Plass, and R. E. Tarjan. A linear-time algorithm for testing the truth of certain quantified Boolean formulas. *Information Processing Letters*, 8(3):121–123, 1979.
[2] R. I. Brafman. Reachability, relevance, resolution, and the planning as satisfiability approach. In *IJCAI'99, Proc. 16th International Joint Conference on Artificial Intelligence*, pages 2010–2016, 1999.
[3] R. I. Brafman. A simplifier for propositional formulas with many binary clauses. In *IJCAI'01, Proc. 17th International Joint Conference on Artificial Intelligence*, 2001.
[4] M. Buro and H. Kleine Büning. Report on a sat competition. *Bulletin of the European Association for Theoretical Computer Science*, 49:143–151, 1993.
[5] T. H. Cormen, C. E. Leiserson, and R. L. Rivest. *Introduction to Algorithms.* The MIT Press, 1991.
[6] J. Crawford. Compact. Available from http://www.cirl.uoregon.edu/~crawford, 1996.
[7] M. Davis, G. Logemann, and D. Loveland. A machine program for theorem proving. *Communications of the ACM*, 5:394–397, 1962.
[8] R. Dechter and I. Rish. Directional resolution: The Davis-Putnam procedure, revisited. In *KR'94, Proc. 4th International Conference on Principles of Knowledge Representation and Reasoning*, pages 134–145. Morgan Kaufmann, 1994.
[9] A. del Val. On 2-SAT and Renamable Horn. In *AAAI'2000, Proc. 17th (U.S.) National Conference on Artificial Intelligence*, pages 279–284. AAAI Press/MIT Press, 2000.
[10] S. Even, A. Itai, and A. Shamir. On the complexity of timetable and multicommodity flow problems. *SIAM Journal of Computing*, 5(4):691–703, 1976.
[11] I. Gent and T. Walsh. The search for satisfaction. Technical report, APES Research Group, 1999.
[12] T. Larrabee. Test pattern generation using boolean satisfiability. *IEEE Transactions on Computer-Aided Design*, pages 4–15, 1992.
[13] Chu Min Li and Abulagan. Heuristics based on unit propagation for satisfiability problems. In *IJCAI'97, Proc. 15th International Joint Conference on Artificial Intelligence*, 1997.
[14] D. G. Mitchell, B. Selman, and H. J. Levesque. Hard and easy distributions of sat problems. In *AAAI'92, Proc. 10th (U.S.) National Conference on Artificial Intelligence*, pages 459–465, 1992.
[15] E. Nuutila and E. Soisalon-Soininen. On finding the strongly connected components in a directed graph. *Information Processing Letters*, 49:9–14, 1993.
[16] D. Pretolani. *Satisfiability and Hypergraphs.* PhD thesis, Università di Pisa, 1993.
[17] R. E. Tarjan. Depth first search and linear graph algorithms. *SIAM Journal of Computing*, 1:146–160, 1972.
[18] A. van Gelder and Y.K. Tsuji. Satisfiability testing with more reasoning and less guessing. In D.S. Johnson and M. Trick, editors, *Cliques, Coloring and Satisfiability: Second DIMACS Implementation Challenge.* American Mathematical Society, 1996.

Reasoning about Evolving Nonmonotonic Knowledge Bases*

Thomas Eiter, Michael Fink, Giuliana Sabbatini, and Hans Tompits

Institut für Informationssysteme, Technische Universität Wien
Favoritenstraße 9-11, A-1040 Vienna, Austria
{eiter,michael,giuliana,tompits}@kr.tuwien.ac.at

Abstract. Recently, several approaches to updating knowledge bases modeled as extended logic programs (ELPs) have been introduced, ranging from basic methods to incorporate (sequences of) sets of rules into a logic program, to more elaborate methods which use an update policy for specifying how updates must be incorporated. In this paper, we introduce a framework for reasoning about evolving knowledge bases, which are represented as ELPs and maintained by an update policy. We describe a formal model which captures various update approaches, and define a logical language for expressing properties of evolving knowledge bases. We further investigate the semantical properties of knowledge states with respect to reasoning. In particular, we describe finitary characterizations of the evolution, and derive complexity results for our framework.

1 Introduction

Updating knowledge bases is an important issue in the area of data and knowledge representation. While this issue has been studied extensively in the context of classical knowledge bases [18,11], attention to it in the area of nonmonotonic knowledge bases, in particular in logic programming, is more recent. Various approaches to evaluating logic programs in the light of new information have been presented, cf. [1]. The proposals range from basic methods to incorporate an update U, given by a set of rules, or a sequence $U_1, \ldots, U_n$ of such updates into a (nonmonotonic) logic program P [1,21,13, 6], to more general methods which use an *update policy* to specify, by means of update actions, how the updates $U_1, \ldots, U_n$ should be incorporated into the current state of knowledge [17,2,8]. Using these approaches, queries to the knowledge base, like "is a fact f true in P after updates $U_1, \ldots, U_n$?", can then be evaluated.

Notably, the formulation of such queries is treated on an *ad-hoc basis*, and more involved queries such as "is a fact f true in P after updates $U_1, \ldots, U_n$ and possibly further updates?" are not considered. More generally, reasoning about an evolving knowledge base KB, maintained using an update policy, is not formally addressed. However, it is desirable to know about properties of the contents of the evolving knowledge base, which also can be made part of a specification for an update policy. For example, it may be important to know that a fact a is always true in KB, or that a fact b is never true in

* This work was supported by the Austrian Science Fund (FWF) under grants P13871-INF and N Z29-INF.

R. Nieuwenhuis and A. Voronkov (Eds.): LPAR 2001, LNAI 2250, pp. 407–421, 2001.

KB. Analogous issues, called *maintenance* and *avoidance*, have been recently studied in the agent community [20]. Other properties may involve temporal relationships such as if $message\_to(tom)$ is true in KB at some point, meaning that a message should be sent to Tom, then $sent\_message\_to(tom)$ will become true in the evolving KB at some point, representing that a message to Tom was sent.

In this paper, we aim at a framework for expressing reasoning problems over evolving knowledge bases, which are modeled as extended logic programs [12] and possibly maintained by an update policy as described above. In particular, we are interested in a logical language for expressing properties of the evolving knowledge base, whose sentences can be evaluated using a clear-cut formal semantics. The framework should, on the one hand, be general enough to capture different approaches to incorporating updates $U_1, \ldots, U_n$ into a logic program P and, on the other hand, pay attention to the specific nature of the problem. Furthermore, it should be possible to evaluate a formula, which specifies a desired evolution behavior, across different realizations of update policies based on different grounds.

The main contributions of this paper are summarized as follows.

(1) We introduce a formal model in which various approaches for updating extended logic programs can be expressed (Section 3). In particular, we introduce the concept of an *evolution frame*, which is a structure $EF = \langle \mathcal{A}, \mathcal{EC}, \mathcal{AC}, \Pi, \rho, Bel \rangle$ whose components serve to describe the evolution of knowledge states. Informally, a *knowledge state* $s = \langle KB; E_1, \ldots, E_n \rangle$ consists of an initial knowledge base KB, given by an extended logic program over an alphabet $\mathcal{A}$, and a sequence $E_1, \ldots, E_n$ of *events*, which are sets of rules E_i, drawn from a class of possible events $\mathcal{EC}$, that are communicated to an agent maintaining the knowledge base. The agent reacts on an event by adapting its belief set through the update policy Π, which singles out update actions $A \subseteq \mathcal{AC}$ from a set of possible update actions $\mathcal{AC}$ for application. These update actions are executed, at a physical level, by compilation, using a function ρ into a single logic program P, or, more generally, into a sequence $(P_1, \ldots, P_n)$ of logic programs, denoted $comp_{EF}(s)$. The semantics of the knowledge state s, its *belief set*, $Bel(s)$, is given by the belief set of the compiled knowledge state, and is obtained by applying a belief operator $Bel(\cdot)$ for (sequences of) logic programs to $comp_{EF}(s)$. Suitable choices of EF allow one to model different settings of logic program updates, such as [1,17,13,6].

(2) We define the syntax and, based on evolution frames, the semantics of a logical language for reasoning about evolving knowledge bases (Section 4), which employs linear and branching-time operators familiar from Computational Tree Logic (CTL) [9]. Using this language, properties of an evolving knowledge base can be formally stated and evaluated in a systematic fashion, rather than ad hoc. For example, the above maintenance and avoidance problems can be expressed by formulas $\mathsf{AG}\, a$ and $\mathsf{AG}\neg b$, respectively.

(3) We investigate semantical properties of knowledge states for reasoning (Section 5). In particular, since in principle a knowledge base may evolve forever, we are concerned with finitary characterizations of evolution. To this end, we introduce various notions of equivalence between knowledge states, and show several filtration results.

(4) We derive complexity results for reasoning (Section 6). Namely, given an evolution frame EF, a knowledge state s, and a formula φ, does $EF, s \models \varphi$ hold? While this problem is undecidable in general, we single out meaningful conditions under which the

problem has 2-EXPSPACE, EXPSPACE, and PSPACE complexity, respectively, and apply this to the EPI framework under the answer set semantics [8], showing that its propositional fragment has PSPACE-complexity. We also consider the complexity of sequences of extended logic programs (ELPs). We show that deciding whether two sequences $\boldsymbol{P} = (P_1, \ldots, P_n)$ and $\boldsymbol{Q} = (Q_1, \ldots, Q_m)$ of propositional ELPs are strongly equivalent under update answer set semantics, i.e., for every sequence $\boldsymbol{R} = (R_1, \ldots, R_k)$, $k \geq 0$, the concatenated sequences $\boldsymbol{P}+\boldsymbol{R}$ and $\boldsymbol{Q}+\boldsymbol{R}$ have the same belief sets, is coNP-complete. This is not immediate, since potentially infinitely many $\boldsymbol{P}+\boldsymbol{R}$ and $\boldsymbol{Q}+\boldsymbol{R}$ need to be checked.

By expressing various approaches in our framework, we obtain a formal semantics for reasoning problems in them. Furthermore, results about properties of these approaches (e.g., complexity results) may be concluded from the formalism by this embedding, as we illustrate for the EPI framework.

2 Preliminaries

We consider knowledge bases represented as *extended logic programs* (ELPs) [12], which are finite sets of rules built over a first-order alphabet $\mathcal{A}$ using default negation not and strong negation $\neg$. A rule has the form

$$r: \quad L_0 \leftarrow L_1, \ldots, L_m, not\, L_{m+1}, \ldots, not\, L_n, \tag{1}$$

where each L_i is a literal of form A or $\neg A$, where A is an atom over $\mathcal{A}$. The set of all rules is denoted by $\mathcal{L}_\mathcal{A}$. We call L_0 the *head* of r (denoted by $H(r)$), and the set $\{L_1, \ldots, L_m, not\, L_{m+1}, \ldots, not\, L_n\}$ the *body* of r (denoted by $B(r)$). We allow the case where L_0 is absent from r; such a rule r is called a *constraint*. If $B(r) = \emptyset$, then r is called *fact*. We often write L_0 for a fact $r = L_0 \leftarrow$. Further extensions, e.g., not in the rule head [1], might be added to fit other frameworks.

An *update program*, $\boldsymbol{P}$, is a sequence $(P_1, \ldots, P_n)$ of ELPs ($n \geq 1$), representing the evolution of program P_1 in the light of new rules $P_2, \ldots, P_n$. The semantics of update programs can abstractly be described as a mapping $Bel(\cdot)$, which associates with every sequence $\boldsymbol{P}$ a set $Bel(\boldsymbol{P}) \subseteq \mathcal{L}_\mathcal{A}$ of rules, intuitively viewed as the consequences of $\boldsymbol{P}$. $Bel(\cdot)$ may be instantiated in terms of various proposals for update semantics, like, e.g., the approaches described in [1,21,13,6,17].

For a concrete example, we consider the answer set semantics for propositional update programs introduced in [6,7], which defines answer sets of $\boldsymbol{P} = (P_1, \ldots, P_n)$ in terms of answers sets of a single ELP P as follows. An *interpretation*, S, is a set of classical literals containing no opposite literals A and $\neg A$. The *rejection set*, $Rej(S, \boldsymbol{P})$, of $\boldsymbol{P}$ with respect to an interpretation S is $Rej(S, \boldsymbol{P}) = \bigcup_{i=1}^{n} Rej_i(S, \boldsymbol{P})$, where $Rej_n(S, \boldsymbol{P}) = \emptyset$, and, for $n > i \geq 1$, $Rej_i(S, \boldsymbol{P})$ contains every rule $r \in P_i$ such that $H(r') = \neg H(r)$ and $S \models B(r) \cup B(r')$, for some $r' \in P_j \setminus Rej_j(S, \boldsymbol{P})$ with $j > i$. That is, $Rej(S, \boldsymbol{P})$ contains the rules in $\boldsymbol{P}$ which are rejected by unrejected rules from later updates. Then, an interpretation S is an *answer set* of $\boldsymbol{P} = (P_1, \ldots, P_n)$ iff S is a consistent answer set [12] of the program $P = \bigcup_i P_i \setminus Rej(S, \boldsymbol{P})$. The set of all answer sets of $\boldsymbol{P}$ is denoted by $\mathcal{AS}(\boldsymbol{P})$. This definition properly generalizes consistent answer sets from single ELPs to sequences of ELPs. Update answer sets for arbitrary (non-ground) update programs $\boldsymbol{P}$ are defined in terms of their ground instances similar to the case of answer sets for ELPs [12].

Example 1. Let $P_0 = \{b \leftarrow not\, a,\ a \leftarrow\}$, $P_1 = \{\neg a \leftarrow,\ c \leftarrow\}$, and $P_2 = \{\neg c \leftarrow\}$. Then, P_0 has the single answer set $S_0 = \{a\}$ with $Rej(S_0, P_0) = \emptyset$; (P_0, P_1) has as answer set $S_1 = \{\neg a, c, b\}$ with $Rej(S_1, (P_0, P_1)) = \{a \leftarrow\}$; and (P_0, P_1, P_2) has the unique answer set $S_2 = \{\neg a, \neg c, b\}$ with $Rej(S_2, (P_0, P_1, P_2)) = \{c \leftarrow, a \leftarrow\}$.

The belief operator $Bel_E(\cdot)$ in the framework of [6] is given by $Bel_E(\boldsymbol{P}) = \{r \in \mathcal{L}_\mathcal{A} \mid S \models r$ for all $S \in \mathcal{AS}(\boldsymbol{P})\}$, where $S \models r$ means that for each ground instance r' of r, either $H(r') \in S$, or $L \notin S$ for some $L \in B(r')$, or $L \in S$ for some $not\, L \in B(r')$.

3 Knowledge-Base Evolution

We start with the basic formal notions of an *event* and of the *knowledge state* of an agent maintaining a knowledge base.

Definition 1. *Let $\mathcal{A}$ be some alphabet. An* event class over $\mathcal{A}$ (*or simply* event class, *if no ambiguity arises*) *is a collection $\mathcal{EC} \subseteq 2^{\mathcal{L}_\mathcal{A}}$ of finite sets of rules. The members $E \in \mathcal{EC}$ are called* events.

Informally, $\mathcal{EC}$ describes the possible events (i.e., sets of communicated rules) an agent may experience. In the most general case, an event is an arbitrary ELP; in a simpler setting, an event may just be a set facts. In a deductive database setting, the latter case corresponds to an extensional database undergoing change while the intensional part of the database remains fixed.

Definition 2. *Let $\mathcal{EC}$ be an event class over some alphabet $\mathcal{A}$. A* knowledge state over $\mathcal{EC}$ (*simply, a* knowledge state) *is a tuple $s = \langle KB; E_1, \ldots, E_n\rangle$, where $KB \subseteq \mathcal{L}_\mathcal{A}$ is an ELP* (*called* initial knowledge base) *and each E_i $(1 \leq i \leq n)$ is an event from $\mathcal{EC}$. The* length of s, *denoted $|s|$, is n.*

Intuitively, $s = \langle KB; E_1, \ldots, E_n\rangle$ captures the agent's knowledge, starting from its initial knowledge base. When a new event E_{n+1} occurs, the current knowledge state s changes to $s' = \langle KB; E_1, \ldots, E_n, E_{n+1}\rangle$, and the agent is required to adapt its belief set in accordance with the new event by obeying its given update policy.

The "universe" in which the evolution of an agent's knowledge base takes place is given by the following concept:

Definition 3. *An* evolution frame *is a tuple $EF = \langle \mathcal{A}, \mathcal{EC}, \mathcal{AC}, \Pi, \rho, Bel\rangle$, where*

- *$\mathcal{A}$ is a finite (first-order) alphabet;*
- *$\mathcal{EC}$ is an event class over $\mathcal{A}$;*
- *$\mathcal{AC}$ is a set of* update commands (*or* actions)*;*
- *Π is an* update policy, *which is a function mapping every knowledge state s over $\mathcal{EC}$ and an event $E \in \mathcal{EC}$ into a set $\Pi(s, E) \subseteq \mathcal{AC}$ of update commands;*

- ρ *is a mapping, called* realization assignment, *which assigns to each knowledge state* s *over* $\mathcal{EC}$ *and each set* $A \subseteq \mathcal{AC}$ *of update commands a sequence* $\rho(s, A) = (P_0, \ldots, P_n)$ *of ELPs* $P_i \subseteq \mathcal{L}_\mathcal{A}$ $(1 \leq i \leq n)$*; and*
- *Bel is a belief operator for sequences of ELPs.*

The set of all knowledge states determined by EF is denoted by $\mathcal{S}_{EF}$.

The components of an evolution frame allow us to model various update approaches, as we discuss later on.

We already mentioned above that different event classes $\mathcal{EC}$ might be conceived. Simple, elementary update commands are $insert(r)$ and $delete(r)$, which add and remove a rule to a logic program, respectively, without a sophisticated semantics handling potential inconsistencies (which may be delegated to the underlying update semantics). More involved update commands have been proposed in the literature (cf., e.g., [2,8]). However, several update frameworks can be modeled using these simple commands.

Update policies Π allow for specifying sensible and flexible ways to react upon incoming events. A very simple policy is $\Pi_{ins}(s, E) = \{insert(r) \mid r \in E\}$; it models an agent which incorporates the new information unconditionally. More sophisticated policies may define exceptions for the incorporation of rules from events, or the insertion of rules may be conditioned on the belief in other rules.

While Π determines *what* to do, the realization assignment ρ states *how* this should be done. Informally, $\rho(s, A)$ "executes" actions A on the knowledge state s by producing a logic program P or, more generally, a sequence $\boldsymbol{P}$ of logic programs. We can use ρ to "compile" a knowledge state s into a (sequence of) logic programs, by determining the set of actions A from the last event in s. We introduce the following notation.

For any knowledge state $s = \langle KB; E_1, \ldots, E_n\rangle$ over $\mathcal{EC}$, denote by $\pi_i(s) = \langle KB; E_1, \ldots, E_i\rangle$ its projection to the first i events, for $0 \leq i \leq n$. We call $\pi_i(s)$ a *previous knowledge state* (or simply an *ancestor*) of s if $i < n$. Dually, each knowledge state s' over $\mathcal{EC}$ is *a future knowledge state* (or simply a *descendant*) of s if s is previous to s'. Furthermore, $\pi_{n-1}(s)$ is the *predecessor* of s, and s' is a *successor* of s if s is predecessor of s'. Finally, for events $E'_1, \ldots, E'_m$, we write $s + E'_1, \ldots, E'_m$ to denote the concatenated knowledge state $\langle KB; E_1, \ldots, E_n, E'_1, \ldots, E'_m\rangle$ (a similar notation applies to the concatenation of sequences of logic programs).

Definition 4. *Let* $EF = \langle \mathcal{A}, \mathcal{EC}, \mathcal{AC}, \Pi, \rho, Bel\rangle$ *be an evolution frame. For any knowledge state* $s = \langle KB; E_1, \ldots, E_n\rangle$ *over* $\mathcal{EC}$*, the* compilation associated with s *is*

$$comp_{EF}(s) = \begin{cases} \rho(s, \emptyset) & \textit{if } |s| = 0, \textit{ i.e., } s = \langle KB\rangle; \\ \rho(\pi_{n-1}(s), \Pi(\pi_{n-1}(s), E_n)) & \textit{otherwise.} \end{cases}$$

This definition of compilation is fairly general. It first computes the actions for the latest event E_n, and then requires that these actions are executed on the predecessor state. Observe that, in view of $comp_{EF}(s)$, we could equally well model update policies as unary functions $\hat{\Pi}(\cdot)$ such that $\hat{\Pi}(s) = \Pi(\pi_{n-1}(s), E_n)$. However, we chose binary update policies to stress the importance of the last event in s.

An important class of compilations are those in which $comp(s')$ for a future knowledge state s' results by appending some further elements to the sequence $comp(s)$ of logic programs for the current knowledge state s. This motivates the following notion:

Definition 5. *Given an evolution frame* $EF = \langle \mathcal{A}, \mathcal{EC}, \mathcal{AC}, \Pi, \rho, Bel \rangle$, $comp_{EF}(\cdot)$ *is* incremental *iff, for each* $s = \langle KB; E_1, \ldots, E_n \rangle$, $comp_{EF}(s) = (P_0, \ldots, P_n)$ *such that* $\rho(\langle KB \rangle, \emptyset) = P_0$ *and* $\rho(\pi_{i-1}(s), \Pi(\pi_{i-1}(s), E_i)) = (P_0, \ldots, P_i)$ *for* $1 \leq i \leq n$.

This amounts to the expected meaning:

Proposition 1. *The mapping* $comp_{EF}(\cdot)$ *is incremental iff, for each knowledge state* s, $comp_{EF}(s) = Q$ *if* $|s| = 0$, *and* $comp_{EF}(s) = comp_{EF}(\pi_{|s|-1}(s)) + Q$ *otherwise, where* Q *is a logic program and "+" is the concatenation of sequences.*

A simple, incremental compilation results for $\mathcal{AC}_{ins} = \{insert(r) \mid r \in \mathcal{L}_{\mathcal{A}}\}$, $\Pi = \Pi_{ins}$ as defined above, and ρ_{ins} such that $comp_{EF}(\langle KB \rangle) = KB$ and $comp_{EF}(s) = comp_{EF}(\pi_{|s|-1}(s)) + (\{r \mid insert(r) \in A\})$. Note that $comp_{EF}(\langle KB; E_1, \ldots, E_n \rangle)$ is in this setting just the sequence $(KB, E_1, \ldots, E_n)$.

While incremental compilations are natural, we stress that others are of course also relevant. In particular, the compilation might perform optimizations (cf. Section 5.2), or output only an ordinary logic program.

Finally, the belief set emerging from a knowledge state is as follows:

Definition 6. *Let* $EF = \langle \mathcal{A}, \mathcal{EC}, \mathcal{AC}, \Pi, \rho, Bel \rangle$ *be an evolution frame and* s *a knowledge state. The belief set of* s, *denoted* $Bel(s)$, *is given by* $Bel(comp_{EF}(s))$.

Remarks. Our definition of an update policy and of a realization assignment, which effectively lead to the notion of a compilation, is quite general. We may stipulate additional postulates upon them, like the incrementability property or an iterativity property (which me omit here), and similar on $Bel(\cdot)$.

Our definition does not capture nondeterministic update policies, where $\Pi(s, E)$ may return one out of several possible sets of update actions. Accordingly, the notion of a knowledge state can be extended by taking previous actions into account, i.e., a knowledge state s is then of the form $\langle KB, (E_1, A_1), \ldots, (E_n, A_n) \rangle$, where each E_i is an event, and A_i is the set of update commands executed at step i. In practice, we may assume a suitable *selection function* σ, which chooses one of the possible outcomes of $\Pi(s, E)$, and we are back to a deterministic update policy Π_σ. If the selection function σ is unknown, we may consider all evolution frames EF_σ arising for each σ.

Example 2. Consider a rather simple mailing agent, which has the following initial knowledge base KB, whose rules are instantiated over suitable variable domains:

$$
\begin{array}{lrl}
r_1: & type(M, private) & \leftarrow from(M, tom); \\
r_2: & type(M, business) & \leftarrow subject(M, project); \\
r_3: & type(M, other) & \leftarrow not\ type(M, private), not\ type(M, business), msg(M); \\
r_4: & trash(M) & \leftarrow remove(M), not\ save(M); \\
r_5: & remove(M) & \leftarrow date(M, T), today(T'), not\ save(M), T' > (T + 30); \\
r_6: & found(M) & \leftarrow search(T), type(M, T), not\ trash(M); \\
r_7: & success & \leftarrow found(M); \\
r_8: & failure & \leftarrow search(T), not\ success.
\end{array}
$$

The knowledge base contains rules about classifying message types (r_1–r_3), trash and removal of mails (r_4, r_5), and further rules (r_6–r_8) to determine success or failure of a search for messages of a particular type. An event E might consist in this setting of one or more of the following items:

- at most one fact $today(d)$, for some date d;
- a fact $empty\_trash$, which causes messages in the trash to be eliminated;
- facts $save(m)$ or $remove(m)$, for mail identifiers m;
- at most one fact $search(t)$, for some mail type $t \in \{other, business, private\}$;
- zero or more sets of facts $from(m, n)$, $subject(m, s)$, or $date(m, d)$ for mail identifier m, name n, subject s, and date d.

The update policy Π may be as follows:

$$\begin{aligned}\Pi(s, E) = {} & \{insert(R) \mid R \in E\} \cup \{insert(msg(M)) \mid from(M, N) \in E\} \\ & \cup \{delete(today(D)) \mid today(D') \in E, today(D) \in Bel(s)\} \\ & \cup \{delete(\alpha) \mid \alpha \in \{trash(M), msg(M), type(M, T)\}, \\ & \qquad empty\_trash \in E, trash(M) \in Bel(s)\} \\ & \cup \{delete(\alpha) \mid \alpha \in \{from(M, N), subject(M, S), date(M, D)\}, \\ & \qquad save(M) \notin Bel(s), msg(M) \in Bel(s), remove(M) \in E\} \\ & \cup \{delete(\alpha) \mid \alpha \in Bel(s) \cap \{search(T), found(T), success, \\ & \qquad failure, empty\_trash\}\}\end{aligned}$$

This update policy (which does not respect possible conflicts of *save* and *remove*), intuitively adds all incoming information, plus a fact $msg(M)$ for each incoming mail to the knowledge base. The current date is maintained by deleting the old date. As well, all old information from a previous event, relative to a search or to the trash, is removed. If an event contains $empty\_trash$, then all messages in the trash are eliminated.

Capturing frameworks for knowledge evolution. Finally, we briefly discuss how existing frameworks for updating nonmonotonic knowledge bases can be captured in terms of evolution frames. This is possible at two different levels:

(1) At an "immediate update" level, frameworks for updating logic programs can be considered, where each event is an *update program*, and the update policy is the (implicit) way in which update programs and the current knowledge are combined, depending on the semantics of updates of each approach. For example, the formalisms of update programs [6,7], dynamic logic programming [1], revision programming [16,17], abductive theory updates [13], and updates through prioritized logic programs (PLPs) [21] fall into this category.

(2) At a higher level, frameworks can be considered which allow for specifying an explicit *update policy* in some specification language, and which offer a greater flexibility in the handling of updates. Examples of such frameworks are EPI [8], LUPS [2], and, while not directly given in these terms, $\mathcal{PDL}$ [14].

For illustration, we consider update programs [6] and the EPI framework for update policies. Update programs are captured by the following evolution frame:

$$EF_{\triangleleft} = \langle \mathcal{A}, \mathcal{EC}_{\mathcal{A}}, \mathcal{AC}_{ins}, \Pi_{ins}, \rho_{ins}, Bel_E \rangle,$$

where $\mathcal{EC}_{\mathcal{A}}$ is the collection of all ELPs over $\mathcal{A}$, and Bel_E is the belief operator defined in Section 2. The EPI framework corresponds to the evolution frame

$$EF_{\mathsf{EPI}} = \langle \mathcal{A}, \mathcal{EC}, \mathcal{AC}_{\mathsf{EPI}}, \Pi_{\mathsf{EPI}}, \rho_{\mathsf{EPI}}, Bel_E \rangle,$$

where

- $\mathcal{AC}_{\mathsf{EPI}} = \{\mathbf{assert}(r), \mathbf{retract}(r), \mathbf{always}(r), \mathbf{cancel}(r),$
  $\mathbf{assert\_event}(r), \mathbf{retract\_event}(r), \mathbf{always\_event}(r) \mid r \in \mathcal{L_A}\}$
  and the commands have the meaning as in [8];
- Π_{EPI} is defined by any set of update statements in the language EPI, which are evaluated through a logic program as defined in [8];
- ρ_{EPI} realizes the translation $tr(KB; U_1, \ldots, U_n)$ from [8], which compiles the initial knowledge base KB and the sets of update commands $U_1, \ldots, U_n$, in response to the events $E_1, \ldots, E_n$ in $s = \langle KB, E_1, \ldots, E_n \rangle$, into a sequence $(P_0, \ldots, P_n)$ of ELPs. The resulting compilation $comp_{\mathsf{EPI}}$ is incremental.

Furthermore, the following formalisms can be expressed in a similar fashion: dynamic logic programming [1] (by allowing *not* in rule heads), LUPS [2], abductive theory updates [13], and program updates by means of PLPs [21]. Thus, several well-known approaches to updating logic programs can be modeled by evolution frames.

4 Reasoning about Knowledge-Base Evolution

We now introduce our logical language for expressing properties of evolving knowledge bases. The primitive logical operators of the language are: (i) the Boolean connectives $\wedge$ ("and") and $\neg$ ("not"); (ii) the evolution quantifiers A ("for all futures") and E ("for some future"); and (iii) the linear temporal operators X ("next time") and U ("until").

Atomic formulas are identified with rules in $\mathcal{L_A}$; composite formulas are either *state formulas* or *evolution formulas*, defined as follows:

1. Each atomic formula is a state formula.
2. If φ, ψ are state formulas, then $\varphi \wedge \psi$ and $\neg\varphi$ are state formulas.
3. If φ is an evolution formula, then $\mathsf{E}\varphi$ and $\mathsf{A}\varphi$ are state formulas.
4. If φ, ψ are state formulas, then $\mathsf{X}\varphi$ and $\varphi\mathsf{U}\psi$ are evolution formulas.

Further Boolean connectives $\vee$ ("or"), $\supset$ ("implies"), and $\equiv$ ("equivalence") are defined in the usual manner. As well, we use $\mathsf{F}\varphi = \top\mathsf{U}\varphi$ ("finally ϕ"), where $\top$ stands for any tautology, $\mathsf{AG}\varphi = \neg\mathsf{EF}\neg\phi$, and $\mathsf{EG}\phi = \neg\mathsf{AF}\phi$ ("globally ϕ").

Next, we define the semantics of such formulas with respect to a given evolution frame $EF = \langle \mathcal{A}, \mathcal{EC}, \mathcal{AC}, \Pi, \rho, Bel \rangle$. To this end, we introduce the following notation:

A sequence $p = (s_i)_{i \geq 0}$ of knowledge states over $\mathcal{EC}$ is called a *path* iff each s_i $(i > 0)$ is a successor of s_{i-1}. We denote by p_i the state at position i in p, i.e., $p_i = s_i$.

Definition 7. *Let $EF = \langle \mathcal{A}, \mathcal{EC}, \mathcal{AC}, \Pi, \rho, Bel \rangle$ be an evolution frame, s a knowledge state over $\mathcal{EC}$, and p a path. The relation $\models$ is recursively defined as follows:*

1. *$EF, s \models r$ iff $r \in Bel(s)$, for any atomic formula r;*
2. *$EF, s \models \varphi_1 \wedge \varphi_2$ iff $EF, s \models \varphi_1$ and $EF, s \models \varphi_2$;*
3. *$EF, s \models \neg\varphi$ iff $EF, s \not\models \varphi$;*
4. *$EF, s \models \mathsf{E}\varphi$ iff $EF, p' \models \varphi$, for some path p' starting at s;*
5. *$EF, s \models \mathsf{A}\varphi$ iff $EF, p' \models \varphi$, for each path p' starting at s;*
6. *$EF, p \models \mathsf{X}\varphi$ iff $EF, p_1 \models \varphi$;*
7. *$EF, p \models \varphi_1\mathsf{U}\varphi_2$ iff $EF, p_i \models \varphi_2$ for some $i \geq 0$ and $EF, p_j \models \varphi_1$ for all $j < i$.*

If $EF, s \models \varphi$ holds, then knowledge state s is said to *satisfy* formula φ *in the evolution frame EF* (or φ is a *consequence of s in the evolution frame EF*).

Notice that any evolution frame EF induces an infinite transition graph which amounts to a standard Kripke structure $K_{EF} = \langle S, R, L \rangle$, where $S = \mathcal{S}_{EF}$ is the set of knowledge states, R is the successor relation between knowledge states, and L labels each state s with $Bel(S)$, such that s satisfies φ in EF iff $K_{EF}, s \models \varphi$ (where $\models$ is defined in the usual way).

Example 3. In order to see whether the mailing agent in Example 2 works properly, we may consider the following properties. For convenience, we allow in formulas non-ground rules as atoms, which stand for the conjunction of all ground instances which is assumed to be finite. Recall that we identify facts with literals.

1. There can never be two current dates:

$$\mathsf{AG}((today(D) \wedge today(D')) \supset D = D'). \tag{2}$$

2. The type of a message cannot change:

$$\mathsf{AG}(type(M,T) \supset \neg\mathsf{EF}(type(M,T') \wedge T \neq T')). \tag{3}$$

3. A message is not trashed until it is either deleted or saved:

$$\mathsf{AG}(msg(m) \supset \mathsf{AG}(\neg trash(m)\mathsf{U}(delete(m) \vee save(m)))). \tag{4}$$

While the initial KB satisfies formulas (2) and (4) in the respective EPI evolution frame EF_{EPI}, it is easily seen that it does not satisfy formula (3).

5 Knowledge-State Equivalence

While syntactically different, it may happen that knowledge states s and s' are semantically equivalent in an evolution frame, i.e., s and s' may have the same set of consequences for the current and all future events. We now consider how such equivalences can be exploited to filtrate a given evolution frame EF such that, under suitable conditions, we can decide $EF, s \models \varphi$ in a finite structure extracted from the associated Kripke structure K_{EF}. We start with the following notions of equivalence.

Definition 8. *Let $EF = \langle \mathcal{A}, \mathcal{EC}, \mathcal{AC}, \Pi, \rho, Bel \rangle$ be an evolution frame and $k \geq 0$ some integer. Furthermore, let s, s' be knowledge states over $\mathcal{EC}$. Then,*

1. *s and s' are* k-equivalent *in EF, denoted $s \equiv^k_{EF} s'$, if $Bel(s + E_1, \ldots, E_{k'}) = Bel(s' + E_1, \ldots, E_{k'})$, for all events $E_1, \ldots, E_{k'}$ from $\mathcal{EC}$ and all $k' \leq k$;*
2. *s and s' are* strongly equivalent *in EF, denoted $s \equiv_{EF} s'$, iff $s \equiv^k_{EF} s'$ for every $k \geq 0$.*

We call 0-equivalent states also *weakly equivalent*. The following result is obvious.

Theorem 1. *Let $EF = \langle \mathcal{A}, \mathcal{EC}, \mathcal{AC}, \Pi, \rho, Bel \rangle$ be an evolution frame and s, s' knowledge states over $\mathcal{EC}$. Then,*

1. *$s \equiv_{EF} s'$ implies that $EF, s \models \varphi$ is equivalent to $EF, s' \models \varphi$, for any formula φ;*
2. *$s \equiv_{EF}^{k} s'$ implies that $EF, s \models \varphi$ is equivalent to $EF, s' \models \varphi$, for any formula φ in which* U *does not occur and the nesting depth w.r.t.* E *and* A *is at most k.*

Due to Part 1 of Theorem 1, strong equivalence can be used to filtrate an evolution frame EF in the following way. For an equivalence relation E over some set X, and any $x \in X$, let $[x]_E = \{y \mid \langle x, y\rangle \in E\}$ be the equivalence class of x and let $X/E = \{[x]_E \mid x \in X\}$ be the set of all equivalence classes. Furthermore, E is said to have a *finite index* (*with respect to* X) iff X/E is finite. Then, any equivalence relation E over some set $S \subseteq S_{EF}$ of knowledge states of EF compatible with $\equiv_{EF}$ (i.e., such that $s\, E\, s'$ implies $s \equiv_{EF} s'$, for all $s, s' \in S$) induces a Kripke structure $K_{EF}^{E,S} = \langle S/E, R_E, L_E\rangle$, where $[s]_E\, R_E\, [s']_E$ iff $s\, R\, s'$ and $L_E([s]_E) = L(s)$, which is bisimilar to the Kripke structure K_{EF} restricted to the knowledge states in S. Thus, for every knowledge state s and formula φ, it holds that $EF, s \models \phi$ iff $K_{EF}^{E,S}, [s]_E \models \phi$, for any $S \subseteq S_{EF}$ such that S contains all descendants of s.

In the following, we consider two cases in which S/E has finite index.

5.1 Local Belief Operators

In the first case, we consider $\equiv_{EF}$ itself as a relation compatible with strong equivalence. We obtain a finite index if, intuitively, the belief set $Bel(s)$ associated with s evolves differently only in a bounded context. We have the following result.

Theorem 2. *Let $EF = \langle \mathcal{A}, \mathcal{EC}, \mathcal{AC}, \Pi, \rho, Bel\rangle$ be an evolution frame such that $\mathcal{EC}$ is finite, and let $S \subseteq S_{EF}$ be some set of knowledge states over $\mathcal{EC}$. Then, the following two conditions are equivalent:*

(a) *$\equiv_{EF}$ has a finite index with respect to S.*
(b) *$\equiv_{EF}^{0}$ has a finite index with respect to S and there is some $k \geq 0$ such that $s \equiv_{EF}^{k} s'$ implies $s \equiv_{EF} s'$, for all $s, s' \in S$.*

Moreover, in case (a)*, there is some $k \geq 0$ such that $|S/\equiv_{EF}| < d^{|\mathcal{EC}|^k}$, where $d = |S/\equiv_{EF}^{0}|$.*

The condition that $\equiv_{EF}^{0}$ has a finite index, i.e., such that only finitely many knowledge states s have different belief sets, is, e.g., satisfied by common belief operators if every s is compiled to a sequence $comp_{EF}(s)$ of ELPs over a finite set of function-free atoms (in particular, if $\mathcal{A}$ is a finite propositional alphabet).

By taking natural properties of $Bel(\cdot)$ and $comp_{EF}(\cdot)$ into account, we can derive an alternative version of Theorem 2. To this end, we introduce the following notation.

Given a belief operator $Bel(\cdot)$, we call update programs $\boldsymbol{P}$ and $\boldsymbol{P}'$ *k-equivalent*, if $Bel(\boldsymbol{P} + (Q_1, \ldots, Q_k)) = Bel(\boldsymbol{P}' + (Q_1, \ldots, Q_k))$, for every ELPs $Q_1, \ldots, Q_i$ $(0 \leq i \leq k)$. Likewise, $\boldsymbol{P}$ and $\boldsymbol{P}'$ are *strongly equivalent*, if they are k-equivalent for all $k \geq 0$. We say that $Bel(\cdot)$ is *k-local*, if k-equivalence of $\boldsymbol{P}$ and $\boldsymbol{P}'$ implies strong equivalence of $\boldsymbol{P}$ and $\boldsymbol{P}'$, for any update programs $\boldsymbol{P}$ and $\boldsymbol{P}'$. Furthermore, $Bel(\cdot)$ is *local*, if $Bel(\cdot)$ is k-local for some $k \geq 0$. We obtain the following result:

Theorem 3. *Let $EF = \langle \mathcal{A}, \mathcal{EC}, \mathcal{AC}, \Pi, \rho, Bel \rangle$ be an evolution frame such that $\mathcal{EC}$ is finite and $\equiv^0_{EF}$ has a finite index with respect to $S \subseteq S_{EF}$. If $Bel(\cdot)$ is local and $comp_{EF}(\cdot)$ is incremental, then $\equiv_{EF}$ has a finite index with respect to S.*

As an application of this result, we show that certain EPI evolution frames have a finite index. Recall that $Bel_E(\cdot)$ is the belief operator of the answer set semantics of update programs [7], as described in Section 2. We can show the following result:

Theorem 4. *Bel_E is local. In particular, 1-equivalence of update programs $\boldsymbol{P}$ and $\boldsymbol{P}'$ implies k-equivalence of $\boldsymbol{P}$ and $\boldsymbol{P}'$, for all $k \geq 1$.*

The proof is by induction and appeals to the rejection mechanism of the semantics. Furthermore, in any EPI evolution frame $EF = \langle \mathcal{A}, \mathcal{EC}, \mathcal{AC}_{\mathsf{EPI}}, \Pi_{\mathsf{EPI}}, \rho_{\mathsf{EPI}}, Bel_E \rangle$, the update policy Π_{EPI} is, informally, given by a logic program such that Π_{EPI} returns a set of update actions from a finite set A_0 of update actions, which are compiled to rules from a finite set R_0 of rules, provided $\mathcal{EC}$ is finite. Consequently, $\equiv^0_{EF}$ has finite index with respect to any set S of knowledge states s which coincide on $\pi_0(s)$, i.e. the initial knowledge base KB. Furthermore, $comp_{\mathsf{EPI}}(\cdot)$ is incremental. Thus, we obtain:

Corollary 1. *Let $EF = \langle \mathcal{A}, \mathcal{EC}, \mathcal{AC}_{\mathsf{EPI}}, \Pi_{\mathsf{EPI}}, \rho_{\mathsf{EPI}}, Bel_E \rangle$ be an EPI evolution frame such that $\mathcal{EC}$ is finite, and let $S \subseteq S_{EF}$ be a set of knowledge states such that $\{\pi_0(s) \mid s \in S\}$ is finite. Then, $\equiv_{EF}$ has a finite index with respect to S. Moreover, $|S/\equiv_{EF}| \leq d^{|\mathcal{EC}|}$, where $d = |S/\equiv^0_{EF}|$.*

5.2 Contracting Belief Operators

Next, we discuss a refinement of strong equivalence, called *canonical equivalence*, which also yields a finite index, providing the evolution frame possesses, in some sense, only a "bounded history". In contradistinction to the previous case, canonical equivalence uses semantical properties which allow for a syntactic simplification of update programs. We need the following notions.

Definition 9. *Let $Bel(\cdot)$ be a belief operator. Then, $Bel(\cdot)$ is called* contracting *iff the following conditions hold: (i) $Bel(\boldsymbol{P} + \emptyset + \boldsymbol{P}') = Bel(\boldsymbol{P} + \boldsymbol{P}')$, for all update programs $\boldsymbol{P}$ and $\boldsymbol{P}'$; and (ii) $Bel(\boldsymbol{P}) = Bel(P_0, \ldots, P_{i-1}, P_i \setminus \{r\}, P_{i+1}, \ldots, P_n)$, for any sequence $\boldsymbol{P} = (P_0, \ldots, P_n)$ and any rule $r \in P_i \cap P_j$ such that $i < j$. An evolution frame $EF = \langle \mathcal{A}, \mathcal{EC}, \mathcal{AC}, \Pi, \rho, Bel \rangle$ is contracting iff $Bel(\cdot)$ is contracting.*

Examples of contracting belief operators are $Bel_E(\cdot)$ and the analogous operator from [1]. By repeatedly removing duplicate rules r and empty programs P_i from any sequence $\boldsymbol{P} = (P_0, \ldots, P_n)$ of ELPs, we eventually obtain a non-reducible sequence $\boldsymbol{P}^* = (P^*_1, \ldots, P^*_m)$, which is called the *canonical form* of $\boldsymbol{P}$. Observe that $m \leq n$ always holds, and that $\boldsymbol{P}^*$ is uniquely determined, i.e., the reduction process is Church-Rosser. We get the following property:

Theorem 5. *For any contracting belief operator $Bel(\cdot)$ and any update sequence $\boldsymbol{P}$, we have that $\boldsymbol{P}$ and $\boldsymbol{P}^*$ are strongly equivalent.*

Let us call knowledge states s and s' in an evolution frame EF *canonically equivalent*, denoted $s \equiv_{EF}^{can} s'$, iff they are strongly equivalent in the canonized evolution frame EF^*, which results from EF by replacing $comp_{EF}(s)$ with its canonical form $comp_{EF}(s)^*$ (i.e., $comp_{EF^*}(s) = comp_{EF}(s)^*$). We note the following property.

Theorem 6. *Let EF be a contracting evolution frame. Then, $EF, s \models \varphi$ iff $EF^*, s \models \varphi$, for any knowledge state s and any formula φ. Furthermore, $\equiv_{EF}^{can}$ is compatible with $\equiv_{EF}$ for any $S \subseteq \mathcal{S}_{EF}$, i.e., $s \equiv_{EF}^{can} s'$ implies $s \equiv_{EF} s'$, for every $s, s' \in S$.*

As a result, we may use $\equiv_{EF}^{can}$ for filtration of EF, based on the following concept.

Definition 10. *Let $EF = \langle \mathcal{A}, \mathcal{EC}, \mathcal{AC}, \Pi, \rho, Bel \rangle$ be an evolution frame and $c \geq 0$ an integer. We say that EF is c-*bounded *iff there are functions α, f, and g such that*

1. *α is a function mapping knowledge states into sets of events such that, for each $s = \langle KB; E_1, \ldots, E_n \rangle$, $\alpha(s) = \langle E_{n-c'+1}, \ldots, E_n \rangle$, where $c' = \min(n, c)$; and*
2. *$\Pi(s, E) = f(Bel(s), \alpha(s), E)$ and $\rho(s, A) = g(Bel(s), \alpha(s), A)$, for each knowledge state $s \in \mathcal{S}_{EF}$, each event $E \in \mathcal{EC}$, and each $A \subseteq \mathcal{AC}$.*

This means that, in a c-bounded evolution frame, the compilation $comp_{EF}(s)$ depends only on the belief set of the predecessor s' of s and the latest c events in s.

Theorem 7. *Let $EF = \langle \mathcal{A}, \mathcal{EC}, \mathcal{AC}, \Pi, \rho, Bel \rangle$ be an evolution frame where $\mathcal{EC}$ is finite, and let $S \subseteq \mathcal{S}_{EF}$. If (i) EF is contracting, (ii) there is some finite set $R_0 \subseteq \mathcal{L}_{\mathcal{A}}$ such that $comp_{EF}(s) \subseteq R_0$, for any $s \in S$, and (iii) EF is c-bounded, for some $c \geq 0$, then $\equiv_{EF}^{can}$ has a finite index with respect to S.*

6 Complexity

In this section, we study the computational complexity of the following reasoning task:

TEMPEVO: Given an evolution frame $EF = \langle \mathcal{A}, \mathcal{EC}, \mathcal{AC}, \Pi, \rho, Bel \rangle$, a knowledge state s over $\mathcal{EC}$, and some formula φ, does $EF, s \models \varphi$ hold?

In order to obtain decidability results, we assume that the constituents of the evolution frame EF in TEMPEVO are all computable. More specifically, we assume that (i) $\mathcal{EC}$, $\mathcal{AC}$, and Bel are given as computable functions deciding $E \in \mathcal{EC}$, $a \in \mathcal{AC}$, and $r \in Bel(\boldsymbol{P})$, and (ii) Π and ρ are given as computable functions. Nonetheless, even under these stipulations, it is easy to see that TEMPEVO is undecidable.

The results of Section 5 provide a basis for characterizing some decidable cases. We consider here the following class of propositional evolution frames $EF = \langle \mathcal{A}, \mathcal{EC}, \mathcal{AC}, \Pi, \rho, Bel \rangle$ (i.e., $\mathcal{A}$ is propositional). Call EF *regular*, if the following applies:

1. the membership tests $E \in \mathcal{EC}$ and $r \in Bel(\boldsymbol{P})$, as well as Π and ρ are computable in polynomial space (the latter with polynomial size output); e.g., the functions may be computable in the polynomial hierarchy;
2. rules in compilations $comp_{EF}(s)$ and events E have size polynomial in the representation size of EF, denoted by $\|EF\|$ (i.e., repetition of the same literal in a rule is bounded), and events have size at most polynomial in $\|EF\|$;

3. $Bel(\cdot)$ is model based, i.e., $Bel(\boldsymbol{P})$ is determined by a set of k-valued models, where k is small (typically, $k \leq 3$ as for $Bel_E(\cdot)$).

The conditions 1 and 3 apply to the approaches in [1,6,8,16,17,13,21], and condition 2 is reasonable to impose; note that none of these semantics is sensible to repetitions of literals in rule bodies.

Theorem 8. *Deciding $EF, s \models \varphi$, given a regular propositional evolution frame $EF = \langle \mathcal{A}, \mathcal{EC}, \mathcal{AC}, \Pi, \rho, Bel \rangle$, a knowledge state s, and a formula φ is*

1. 2-EXPSPACE-*complete, if $Bel(\cdot)$ is k-local for some k which is polynomial in $\|EF\|$, and $comp_{EF}(\cdot)$ is incremental;*
2. EXPSPACE-*complete, if EF is contracting and c-bounded, where c is polynomial in $\|EF\|$; and*
3. PSPACE-*complete, if EF is as in 2 and, moreover, all rules in the compilations $comp_{EF}(s')$ of successors s' of s are from a set R_0 of size polynomial in $\|EF\|$.*

For the upper bounds of these results, we note that in the case where φ has form $\mathsf{E}\psi$, only finite paths of length at most $|S/\equiv_{EF}|$ must be considered for satisfying ψ, where S is the set of all future knowledge states of s. Part 1 of the theorem can then be shown by Theorem 3 using the estimation given in Theorem 2. Concerning Part 2, there are $\mathcal{O}(2^{l^{|\mathcal{A}|}+\|EF\|^m}) = \mathcal{O}(2^{2^{m'\|EF\|}})$ many knowledge states s that are not strongly equivalent, for some constants l, m and m'; each $Bel(s)$ can be represented, using canonical update programs, together with the last c events, in single exponential space. Furthermore, the representation of every successor state is computable in polynomial space in the input size. Hence, overall exponential space is sufficient. Finally, the additional condition in Part 3 of the theorem guarantees PSPACE complexity. The lower bounds can be shown by encoding Turing machine computations into particular evolution frames.

Part 3 of Theorem 8 implies that the propositional EPI framework has also PSPACE complexity. While here, in general, $Bel(s)$ depends on all events in s, it is possible to restrict $\mathcal{AC}_{\mathsf{EPI}}$ to the commands **assert** and **retract**, by efficient coding techniques which store relevant history information in $Bel(s)$, such that the compilation in $comp_{\mathsf{EPI}}(s)$ depends only on $Bel(\pi_{n-1}(s))$ and the last event E_n in s. Furthermore, the policy Π_{EPI} is sensible only to polynomially many rules in events, and $comp_{\mathsf{EPI}}(s)$ contains only rules from a fixed set R_0 of rules, whose size is polynomial in the representation size of EF. Thus, we get the following corollary.

Corollary 2. *Let $EF = \langle \mathcal{A}, \mathcal{EC}, \mathcal{AC}_{\mathsf{EPI}}, \Pi_{\mathsf{EPI}}, \rho_{\mathsf{EPI}}, Bel_E \rangle$ be a propositional* EPI *evolution frame, let s be a knowledge state, and let φ be a formula. Then, deciding $EF, s \models \varphi$ is in* PSPACE.

On the other hand, computations of a PSPACE Turing machine can be easily encoded in a propositional EPI evolution frame using a single event which models the clock. Thus, Corollary 2 has a matching lower bound.

We conclude our complexity analysis with results concerning weak, strong, and k-equivalence of two propositional update programs, respectively.

Theorem 9. *Deciding whether two given propositional update programs **P** and **Q** are weakly equivalent, i.e., satisfying $Bel_E(\boldsymbol{P}) = Bel_E(\boldsymbol{Q})$, is* coNP-*complete.*

Intuitively, the upper bound follows from the property that, for any propositional update programs $\boldsymbol{P}$ and $\boldsymbol{Q}$, $Bel(\boldsymbol{P}) = Bel(\boldsymbol{Q})$ is equivalent to $\mathcal{AS}(\boldsymbol{P}) = \mathcal{AS}(\boldsymbol{Q})$. The matching lower bound follows easily from the coNP-completeness of deciding whether an ELP has no answer set (cf. [5]).

For deciding 1-equivalence, the following lemma is useful:

Lemma 1. *Let $\boldsymbol{P}$ and $\boldsymbol{Q}$ be propositional update programs. Then, $\boldsymbol{P}$ and $\boldsymbol{Q}$ are not 1-equivalent under Bel_E iff there is an ELP P and a set S such that (i) $S \in \mathcal{AS}(\boldsymbol{P} + P)$ but $S \notin \mathcal{AS}(\boldsymbol{Q} + P)$, or vice versa, (ii) $|S|$ is at most the number of atoms in $\boldsymbol{P} + \boldsymbol{Q}$ plus 1, and (iii) $|P| \leq |S| + 1$. Furthermore, P has polynomial size in the size of $\boldsymbol{P}$ and $\boldsymbol{Q}$.*

Intuitively, this holds since any answer set S of $\boldsymbol{P} + P$ can be generated by at most $|S|$ many rules. Furthermore, if S is not an answer set of $\boldsymbol{Q} + P$, by unfolding rules in P we may disregard for an S all but at most one atom which does not occur in $\boldsymbol{P}$ or $\boldsymbol{Q}$. To generate a violation of S in $\boldsymbol{Q} + P$, an extra rule might be needed; this means that a P with $|P| \leq |S| + 1$ is sufficient.

Theorem 10. *Deciding strong equivalence (or k-equivalence, for any fixed $k \geq 0$) of two given propositional update programs $\boldsymbol{P}$ and $\boldsymbol{Q}$ is* coNP*-complete.*

Proof. (Sketch) For $k = 0$, the result is given by Theorem 9. For $k \geq 1$, the membership part follows from Lemma 1, in virtue of Theorem 4. Hardness can be shown by constructing, given a propositional DNF ϕ, suitable programs P and Q in polynomial time such that ϕ is valid in classical logic iff $\boldsymbol{P} = (P)$ and $\boldsymbol{Q} = (Q)$ are 1-equivalent. □

Note that Theorems 9, 10 and Lemma 1 make no finiteness assumption on the alphabet $\mathcal{A}$. They also hold for ground update programs $\boldsymbol{P}$ and $\boldsymbol{Q}$ in a first-order alphabet, where P in Lemma 1 is ground.

7 Discussion and Conclusion

We presented a general framework for reasoning about evolving logic programs, which can be applied to several approaches for updating logic programs in the literature. Since the semantics of evolution frames can be captured by Kripke structures, it is suggestive to transform reasoning problems on them into model checking problems [4]. However, in current model checking systems, state transitions must be stated in a polynomial-time language, and descriptions of these Kripke structures would require exponential space also for evolution frames with PSPACE complexity (e.g., EPI evolution frames). Thus, extensions of model checking systems would be needed for fruitful usability.

Lobo et al. introduced the $\mathcal{PDL}$ [14] language for policies, which contain event-condition-action rules and serve for modeling reactive behavior on observations from an environment. While similar in spirit, their model is different, and [14] focuses on detecting action conflicts (which, in our framework, is not an issue). In [15], reasoning tasks are considered which center around actions. Further related research is on planning, where certain reachability problems are PSPACE-complete (cf. [3]). Similar results were obtained in [20] for related agent design problems. However, in all these works, the problems considered are ad hoc, and no reasoning language is considered.

Fagin et al.'s [10] important work on knowledge in multi-agent systems addresses evolving knowledge, but mainly at an axiomatic level. Wooldridge's [19] logic for reasoning about multi-agent systems embeds CTL* and has belief, desire and intention modalities. The underlying model is very broad, and aims at agent communication and cooperation. It remains to see how our particular framework fits into these approaches.

Our ongoing work addresses these and further issues. Further meaningful properties of evolution frames would be interesting; e.g., iterativity of the compilation $comp_{EF}$, i.e., the events are incorporated one at a time, or properties of the belief operator Bel. Other issues are algorithms and fragments of lower (especially, polynomial) complexity.

References

1. J. Alferes, J. Leite, L. Pereira, H. Przymusinska, and T. Przymusinski. Dynamic Updates of Non-Monotonic Knowledge Bases. *J. Logic Programming*, 45(1–3):43–70, 2000.
2. J. Alferes, L. Pereira, H. Przymusinska, and T. Przymusinski. LUPS - A Language for Updating Logic Programs. In *Proc. LPNMR'99*, LNAI 1730, pp. 162–176. Springer, 1999.
3. C. Baral, V. Kreinovich, and R. Trejo. Computational Complexity of Planning and Approximate Planning in the Presence of Incompleteness. *AIJ*, 122(1–2):241–267, 2000.
4. E. Clarke, O. Grumberg, and D. Peled. *Model Checking*. MIT Press, 1999.
5. E. Dantsin, T. Eiter, G. Gottlob, and A. Voronkov. Complexity and Expressive Power of Logic Programming. In *Proc. 12th IEEE International Conference on Computational Complexity (CCC '97)*, pp. 82–101, 1997. Full paper *ACM Computing Surveys*, to appear.
6. T. Eiter, M. Fink, G. Sabbatini, and H. Tompits. Considerations on Updates of Logic Programs. In *Proc. JELIA 2000*, LNAI 1919, pp. 2–20. Springer, 2000.
7. T. Eiter, M. Fink, G. Sabbatini, and H. Tompits. On Properties of Update Sequences Based on Causal Rejection. *Theory and Practice of Logic Programming*, to appear.
8. T. Eiter, M. Fink, G. Sabbatini, and H. Tompits. A Framework for Declarative Update Specifications in Logic Programs. In *Proc. IJCAI'01*, pp. 649–654.
9. E. Emerson. Temporal and Modal Logics, Vol. B. In J. van Leeuwen, editor, *Handbook of Theoretical Computer Science*. Elsevier, 1990.
10. R. Fagin, J. Halpern, Y. Moses, and M. Vardi. *Reasoning about Knowledge*. MIT, 1995.
11. D. Gabbay and P. Smets, editors. *Handbook on Defeasible Reasoning and Uncertainty Management Systems, Vol. III*. Kluwer Academic, 1998.
12. M. Gelfond and V. Lifschitz. Classical Negation in Logic Programs and Disjunctive Databases. *New Generation Computing*, 9:365–385, 1991.
13. K. Inoue and C. Sakama. Updating Extended Logic Programs through Abduction. In *Proc. LPNMR'99*, LNAI 1730, pp. 147–161. Springer, 1999.
14. J. Lobo, R. Bhatia, and S. Naqvi. A Policy Description Language. In *Proc. AAAI/IAAI'99*, pp. 291–298. AAAI Press / MIT Press, 1999.
15. J. Lobo and T. Son. Reasoning about Policies Using Logic Programs. In *Proc. AAAI 2001 Spring Symposium on Answer Set Programming*, pp. 210–216, 2001.
16. V. Marek and M. Truszczyński. Revision Specifications by Means of Programs. In *Proc. JELIA'94*, LNAI 838, pp. 122–136. Springer, 1994.
17. V. Marek and M. Truszczyński. Revision Programming. *TCS*, 190(2):241–277, 1998.
18. M. Winslett. *Updating Logical Databases*. Cambridge University Press, 1990.
19. M. Wooldridge. *Reasoning about Rational Agents*. MIT Press, 2000.
20. M. Wooldridge. The Computational Complexity of Agent Design Problem. In *Proc. International Conference on Multi-Agent Systems (ICMAS) 2000*. IEEE Press, 2000.
21. Y. Zhang and N. Foo. Updating Logic Programs. In *Proc. ECAI'98*, pp. 403–407. 1998.

Efficient Computation of the Well-Founded Model Using Update Propagation

Andreas Behrend

University of Bonn, Institute of Computer Science III,
Römerstr. 164, D-53117 Bonn, Germany
behrend@cs.uni-bonn.de

Abstract. In this paper we present a bottom-up algorithm for computing the well-founded model of general normal logic programs by means of range-restricted *Datalog*$^{\neg}$ rules automatically generated from the source program. The drawback of repeated computation of facts from which Van Gelder's alternating fixpoint procedure is suffering is avoided by using update propagation rules, generalizing the differential fixpoint computation well-known for stratifiable deductive databases.

1 Introduction

In the field of deductive databases, a considerable amount of research has been devoted to the efficient bottom-up evaluation of queries against the intensional part of a database (e.g. magic sets [3], counting [4], Alexander method [14]). Another branch of research has been dealing with the problem of efficient computation of induced changes by means of update propagation (e.g. [1,9,12, 13]). These results are particularly relevant for systems which will implement the new SQL99 standard and hence will allow the definition of recursive views. The intuitive semantics of function-free deductive rules without or with at least stratifiable negation is well understood by now. However, when unstratifiable negation is considered, the intended meaning becomes less clear and several proposals for a suitable semantics based on model theory have been made. The most established of these are the stable model semantics and the well-founded semantics, the latter one being preferred by many authors because of its unique model [17]. The reason for dealing with this general class of deductive databases is twofold: On the one hand, it is known from [11] that unstratifiable rules are strictly more expressive than stratifiable ones and that there are interesting queries not expressible by stratifiable databases. On the other hand, unstratifiable databases may result when applying rewriting techniques such as magic sets to stratifiable databases. Thus, efficient techniques for handling unstratifiable rules are of interest in the context of SQL, too, where user rules have to be stratified.

Bottom-up approaches to the computation of well-founded models based on the alternating fixpoint operator introduced by Van Gelder [16] have been proposed

R. Nieuwenhuis and A. Voronkov (Eds.): LPAR 2001, LNAI 2250, pp. 422–437, 2001.

in [10,15], while in [5,6] the computation is based on the residual program suggested by [7,8]. Despite of the advantages of the residual program approach, its notion of conditional facts is hard to implement in a database context. We will therefore concentrate on the efficient implementation of the alternating fixpoint procedure and on its well-known drawback of repeated computations. In our approach, such recomputation is avoided by using update propagation rules leading to an incremental algorithm extending the differential evaluation techniques for stratifiable databases [2]. In addition, we will provide a solution to stratification problems that arise when the magic set method is used in combination with update propagation rules.

2 Basic Concepts

We consider a first order language with a universe of constants $U = \{a, b, c, \dots\}$, a set of variables $\{X, Y, Z, \dots\}$ and a set of predicate symbols $\{p, q, r \dots\}$. A *term* is a variable or a constant (i.e., we restrict ourselves to function-free terms). Let p be an n-ary predicate symbol and t_i ($i = 1, \dots, n$ and $n \geq 0$) terms then $p(t_1, \dots, t_n)$ (or simply $p(\vec{t}\,)$) is denoted *atom*. An atom is *ground* if every t_i is a constant. If A is an atom, we use $pred(A)$ to refer to the predicate symbol of A. A *fact* is a clause of the form $p(t_1, \dots, t_n) \leftarrow true$ where $p(t_1, \dots, t_n)$ is a ground atom. A *literal* is either an atom or a negated atom. A *deductive rule* is a clause of the form

$$p(t_1, \dots, t_n) \leftarrow L_1 \wedge \dots \wedge L_m \text{ with } n \geq 0 \text{ and } m \geq 1,$$

where $p(t_1, \dots, t_n)$ is an atom denoting the rule's head, and $L_1, \dots, L_m$ are literals representing the rule's body. We assume all deductive rules to be *safe* (allowed or range-restricted, respectively); that is, all variables occurring in the head or in any negated literal of a rule must be present in some positive literal in this rule's body as well. This ensures that all negated literals can be fully instantiated before they are evaluated according to the negation as failure principle. If A is the head of a given deductive rule R, we use $pred(R)$ to refer to the predicate symbol of A.

Definition 1 (Deductive Database). *A deductive database $\mathcal{D}$ is a tuple $\langle \mathcal{F}, \mathcal{R} \rangle$ where $\mathcal{F}$ is a finite set of facts and $\mathcal{R}$ a finite set of deductive rules such that $pred(\mathcal{F}) \cap pred(\mathcal{R}) = \emptyset$. Within a deductive database $\mathcal{D} = \langle \mathcal{F}, \mathcal{R} \rangle$, a predicate symbol p is called derived (view predicate), if $p \in pred(\mathcal{R})$. The predicate p is called extensional (or base predicate), if $p \in pred(\mathcal{F})$.*

Stratifiable deductive rules do not allow recursion through negative predicate occurrences. A stratification partitions a given rule set such that all positive derivations of relations can be determined before a negative literal with respect to one of those relations is evaluated. Given a deductive database $\mathcal{D}$, the Herbrand base $\mathcal{H}_\mathcal{D}$ of $\mathcal{D}$ is the set of all ground atoms that can be constructed from the predicate symbols and constants occurring in $\mathcal{D}$. Based on these notions we will now define the semantics of a deductive database. First, we present the immediate consequence operator introduced by van Emden and Kowalski that will serve as the basic operator for determining the semantics of different classes of deductive databases.

Definition 2 (Immediate Consequence Operator). *Let $\mathcal{D} = \langle \mathcal{F}, \mathcal{R} \rangle$ be a deductive database. The immediate consequence operator $T_{\mathcal{R}}$ is a mapping on sets of ground atoms and is defined for $\mathcal{I} \subseteq \mathcal{H}_{\mathcal{D}}$ as follows:*

$$\begin{aligned} T_{\mathcal{R}}(\mathcal{I}) = \{A \mid\ & A \in \mathcal{I} \text{ or there exists a rule } A \leftarrow L_1 \wedge \ldots \wedge L_n \in [[\mathcal{R}]] \\ & \text{such that } L_i \in \mathcal{I} \text{ for all positive literals } L_i \\ & \text{and } L \notin \mathcal{I} \text{ for all negative literals } L_j \equiv \neg L\} \end{aligned}$$

where $[[\mathcal{R}]]$ denotes the set of all ground instances of rules in $\mathcal{R}$.

As the immediate consequence operator $T_{\mathcal{R}}$ is monotonic for semi-positive databases, i.e., databases in which negative literals reference base relations only, its least fixpoint exists and coincides with the least Herbrand model $\mathcal{S}_{\mathcal{D}}$ of $\mathcal{D}$, i.e., $\mathcal{S}_{\mathcal{D}} = \text{lfp}\ (T_{\mathcal{R}}, \mathcal{F})$, where lfp $(T_{\mathcal{R}}, \mathcal{F})$ denotes the least fixpoint of operator $T_{\mathcal{R}}$ containing $\mathcal{F}$.

For stratifiable databases, however, the semantics is defined as the iterated fixpoint model $\mathcal{M}_{\mathcal{D}}$ which can be constructed as follows: Let $\mathcal{D} = \langle \mathcal{F}, \mathcal{R} \rangle$ be a stratifiable database and λ a stratification on $\mathcal{D}$. The partition $\mathcal{R}_1 \uplus \ldots \uplus \mathcal{R}_n$ [1] of $\mathcal{R}$ defined by λ induces a sequence of least Herbrand models $M_1, \ldots M_n$:

$$M_1 := \text{lfp}\ (T_{\mathcal{R}_1}, \mathcal{F}),\ M_2 := \text{lfp}\ (T_{\mathcal{R}_2}, M_1),\ \ldots\ ,\ M_n := \text{lfp}\ (T_{\mathcal{R}_n}, M_{n-1}) =: \mathcal{M}_{\mathcal{D}}.$$

For illustrating the notations introduced above consider the following example of a stratifiable deductive database $\mathcal{D} = \langle \mathcal{F}, \mathcal{R} \rangle$:

$$\begin{array}{llll} \underline{\mathcal{R}}: & h(X,Y) \leftarrow p(X,Y) \wedge \neg p(Y,X) & \underline{\mathcal{F}}: & b(1,2) \\ & p(X,Y) \leftarrow b(X,Y) & & b(2,1) \\ & p(X,Y) \leftarrow b(X,Z) \wedge p(Z,Y) & & b(2,3) \end{array}$$

Relation p represents the transitive closure of relation b while relation h selects all $p(X,Y)$-facts where Y is reachable from X but not vice versa. A stratification postpones the evaluation of h until all p tuples have been derived and the iterated fixpoint model is given by $\mathcal{M}_{\mathcal{D}} = \mathcal{F} \cup \{p(1,1), p(1,2), p(1,3), p(2,1), p(2,2), p(2,3), h(1,3), h(2,3)\}$. Note that the iterated fixpoint model is a generalization of the least Herbrand model for semi-positive databases. In chapter 4 we recall the well-founded semantics for possibly unstratifiable rule sets which represents again a generalization subsuming stratifiable and semi-positive databases.

3 Update Propagation

The aim of update propagation is the computation of implicit changes of derived relations resulting from explicitly performed updates of the extensional

[1] The symbol $\uplus$ denotes the union of disjoint sets.

fact base. As in most cases an update will affect only a small portion of the database, it is rarely reasonable to compute the induced changes by comparing the entire old and new database states. Instead, the implicit modifications should be iteratively computed by propagating the individual updates through the possibly affected rules and computing their consequences. Update propagation has been mainly studied in order to provide methods for incremental view maintenance and integrity checking in stratifiable databases.

During the last decade, many update propagation methods have been proposed, e.g., [1,9,12,13]. In the following, however, we will focus on a propagation method which uses the deductive rules given in a database schema to derive *deductive propagation rules* for computing induced updates as proposed in [9]. In the following we will use the notions `old` and `new` database state to refer to the database state before and after an update has been performed. In addition, we use the superscripts "+" and "−" in relation names in order to represent (propagated) insertions and deletions respectively. For a positive literal $A \equiv r(t_1, \ldots, t_n)$ we define $A^+ := r^+(t_1, \ldots, t_n)$ and $A^- := r^-(t_1, \ldots, t_n)$. For a negative literal $L \equiv \neg A$, we use $L^+ := A^-$ and $L^- := A^+$. Since an induced insertion or induced deletion can be simply represented by the difference between the two consecutive database states, the propagation rules for a given rule $A \leftarrow L_1 \wedge \ldots \wedge L_n$ may look as follows:

$$A^+ \leftarrow L_i^+ \wedge \text{new}(L_1 \wedge \ldots \wedge \; L_{i-1} \wedge \; L_{i+1} \wedge \ldots \wedge \; L_n) \wedge \text{old}\neg A$$
$$A^- \leftarrow L_i^- \wedge \text{old}(L_1 \wedge \ldots \wedge \; L_{i-1} \wedge \; L_{i+1} \wedge \ldots \wedge \; L_n) \wedge \text{new}\neg A.$$

The propagation rules basically perform a comparison of the `old` and `new` database states while providing a focus on individual updates by L_i^ν with $\nu \in \{+,-\}$. Each propagation rule body may be divided into two further parts:

1. The *derivability test* ({`new` | `old`}$(L_1 \wedge \ldots L_n)$) is performed in order to determine whether A is derivable in the new or old state, respectively.
2. The *effectiveness test* ({`new` | `old`}$(\neg A)$) checks whether the fact obtained by the derivability test is not derivable in the opposite state.

Propagation rules reference both, the `old` and the `new` database state. The idea is to introduce so called *transition rules* that simulate the other state from a given one. A major advantage of such state simulation is that the underlying system need not provide a mechanism allowing deduction on two different database states. Although both directions are possible, we will concentrate on a somehow pessimistic approach, the simulation of the `new` state while the `old` one is actually given. In principle, there are two kinds of rules to be considered:

1. The *naive transition rules* of a derived relation infer its new state from the new states of the underlying relations. Thus, for a rule $A \leftarrow L_1 \wedge \ldots \wedge L_n$ a transition rule of the following form has to be considered:

   $$\text{new } A \leftarrow \text{new}(L_1 \wedge \ldots \wedge L_n).$$

2. The *incremental transition rules* explicitly refer to the computed changes such that for every relation two rules of the following form are used:

$$\text{new } A \leftarrow \text{old } A \wedge \neg A^-$$
$$\text{new } A \leftarrow A^+.$$

As transition rules for base relations must explicitly refer to the given update, incremental rules are used in this case. It seems obvious to use incremental transition rules for derived relations also as they provide a much better focus on the induced updates. However, doing so may cause stratification problems when propagation and transition rules are considered together [12]. [9] proposes an approach which combines incremental and naive transition rules for derived relations in such a way that the resulting set of rules is still stratifiable.

As an example, consider again the deductive database $\mathcal{D}$ from chapter 2. The update propagation rules for p with respect to insertions into b are as follows:

propagation rules	**transition rules**
$p^+(X,Y) \leftarrow b^+(X,Y) \wedge \neg p(X,Y)$	$p^{new}(X,Y) \leftarrow b^{new}(X,Y)$
$p^+(X,Y) \leftarrow b^+(X,Z) \wedge p^{new}(Z,Y) \wedge \neg p(X,Y)$	$p^{new}(X,Y) \leftarrow b^{new}(X,Z) \wedge p^{new}(Z,Y)$
$p^+(X,Y) \leftarrow p^+(Z,Y) \wedge b^{new}(X,Y) \wedge \neg p(X,Y)$	$b^{new}(X,Y) \leftarrow b^+(X,Y)$
$h^+(X,Y) \leftarrow p^-(Y,X) \wedge p^{new}(X,Y) \wedge \neg h(X,Y)$	$b^{new}(X,Y) \leftarrow b(X,Y) \wedge \neg b^-(X,Y)$
$h^+(X,Y) \leftarrow p^+(X,Y) \wedge \neg p^{new}(Y,X) \wedge \neg h(X,Y)$	

Note that these rules can be determined at schema definition time and don't have to be recompiled whenever a new transaction is applied. Since we work on the old database state, the old-annotations are omitted in the effectiveness test. Given the following changes of base relations $\{b^+(3,1), b^+(3,4)\}$, the corresponding induced updates computed by the propagation rules are $\{p^+(1,4), p^+(2,4), p^+(3,1), p^+(3,2), p^+(3,3), p^+(3,4)\} \cup \{h^-(1,3), h^-(2,3)\} \cup \{h^+(1,4), h^+(2,4), h^+(3,4)\}$. The effectiveness test makes sure that only true updates are computed by the propagation rules; that is, only facts are derived which were not derivable in the old database state. Although the application of propagation rules indeed restricts the computation of induced updates, the transition rules of this example require the entire new state of relation b and p to be derived. In order to avoid this drawback, in [9] the evaluation of transition rules is already restricted by using the magic set method. As this plays an important role for our approach as well, we will discuss and develop this idea further in the subsequent sections.

4 Alternating Fixpoint Computation

For unstratifiable rule sets, it is no more sufficient to consider positive and negative conclusions only, as we did in the previous chapters. Instead, a three-valued semantics ought to be used that allows the specification of undefined facts, too.

The implicit state of $\mathcal{D}$ may then be defined as the well-founded model

$$\widetilde{\mathcal{S}}_{\mathcal{D}} := \mathcal{I}^+ \uplus \neg \cdot \mathcal{I}^-,$$

where $\mathcal{I}^+, \mathcal{I}^- \subseteq \mathcal{H}_{\mathcal{D}}$ are sets of ground atoms and $\neg \cdot \mathcal{I}^-$ consists of all negations of atoms in $\mathcal{I}^-$. The set $\mathcal{I}^+$ represents the true portion of the well-founded model while $\neg \cdot \mathcal{I}^-$ comprises all true negative conclusions. The set of undefined atoms is implicitly given by $\mathcal{H}_{\mathcal{D}} \setminus (\mathcal{I}^+ \uplus \mathcal{I}^-)$. The exact definition of $\mathcal{I}^+$ and $\mathcal{I}^-$ can be found in [17]. For databases having a total well-founded model, as guaranteed for stratifiable ones, the set of undefined atoms is empty, and hence the set of false atoms can be derived from the set of true ones, i.e.,

$$\mathcal{I}^- = \neg \cdot \overline{\mathcal{I}^+},$$

where $\overline{\mathcal{I}^+}$ denotes the complement of $\mathcal{I}^+$ with respect to the Herbrand base, i.e., $\mathcal{I}^- = \mathcal{H}_{\mathcal{D}} \setminus \mathcal{I}^+$. For simplicity we will omit the set of negative conclusions in the following for databases with a total well-founded model. For the general case, however, it is necessary to determine at least two sets of the well-founded model. We will now present the alternating fixpoint computation proposed by Van Gelder for determining the well-founded model of unstratifiable databases. The basic idea of alternating fixpoint computation [16] is to repeatedly compute fixpoints of the given database, each time evaluating negative literals with respect to the complement of the previously obtained fixpoint. Assuming a fixed semantics for negative literals, even unstratifiable databases are reduced to semi-positive ones, such that traditional two-valued fixpoint semantics is applicable. The subsequently performed fixpoint computations alternately yield underestimates and overestimates of the set of actually true negative conclusions. The composition, however, of two such fixpoint computations is monotonic. Starting from an empty set of negative literals, the set of negative conclusions is constructed monotonically. In order to work on negative conclusions, a new consequence operator $T_{\mathcal{D},\mathcal{N}}$ is used that gives the set of all positive conclusions derivable from $\mathcal{D}$ and from the fixed set of negative literals $\mathcal{N}$. During an application of $T_{\mathcal{D},\mathcal{N}}$, a negative literal $\neg A$ is considered true if $\neg \cdot A$ is present in $\mathcal{N}$. In the following we describe the course of computing the alternating fixpoint by means of an example. Consider the following unstratifiable deductive database $\mathcal{D} = \langle \mathcal{R}, \mathcal{F} \rangle$ consisting of the rule

```
e(X) ← succ(X,Y) ∧ ¬e(Y)
```

and the facts

```
succ(0,1),succ(1,2),succ(2,3),succ(3,4),succ(4,5).
```

The deductive rule defines the even numbers between 0 and 5. At the beginning of the alternating fixpoint computation we assume all negative literals to be false, i.e., $\mathcal{N} = \emptyset$. Thus, the first fixpoint coincides with the given fact base:

$$\text{lfp}\ (T_{\mathcal{D},\emptyset}, \mathcal{F}) = \mathcal{F} \qquad (=DT^1)$$

The subsequent applications produce the following sequence where N_0 is the set of negative succ/2 literals:

$$\begin{array}{lll}
\mathrm{lfp}(T_{\mathcal{D},N_0\cup\neg\cdot\{e(0),e(1),e(2),e(3),e(4),e(5)\}},\mathcal{F}) & = \mathcal{F}\cup\{e(0),\ \ldots,e(3),e(4)\} & (=NDF^1)\\
\mathrm{lfp}(T_{\mathcal{D},N_0\cup\neg\cdot\{e(5)\}},\mathcal{F}) & = \mathcal{F}\cup\{e(4)\} & (=DT^2)\\
\mathrm{lfp}(T_{\mathcal{D},N_0\cup\neg\cdot\{e(0),e(1),e(2),e(3),e(5)\}},\mathcal{F}) & = \mathcal{F}\cup\{e(0),e(1),e(2),e(4)\} & (=NDF^2)\\
\mathrm{lfp}(T_{\mathcal{D},N_0\cup\neg\cdot\{e(3),e(5)\}},\mathcal{F}) & = \mathcal{F}\cup\{e(2),e(4)\} & (=DT^3)\\
\mathrm{lfp}(T_{\mathcal{D},N_0\cup\neg\cdot\{e(0),e(1),e(3),e(5)\}},\mathcal{F}) & = \mathcal{F}\cup\{e(0),e(2),e(4)\} & (=NDF^3)\\
\mathrm{lfp}(T_{\mathcal{D},N_0\cup\neg\cdot\{e(1),e(3),e(5)\}},\mathcal{F}) & = \mathcal{F}\cup\{e(0),e(2),e(4)\} & (=DT^4)\\
\mathrm{lfp}(T_{\mathcal{D},N_0\cup\neg\cdot\{e(1),e(3),e(5)\}},\mathcal{F}) & = \mathcal{F}\cup\{e(0),e(2),e(4)\} & (=NDF^4)\\
\mathrm{lfp}(T_{\mathcal{D},N_0\cup\neg\cdot\{e(1),e(3),e(5)\}},\mathcal{F}) & = \mathcal{F}\cup\{e(0),e(2),e(4)\} & (=DT^5)
\end{array}$$

The calculation alternates between the computation of subsets of definitely true facts (DT^i) and the computation of supersets of not definitely false facts (NDF^i) using subsets of definitely false and supersets of not definitely true facts in $\mathcal{N}$, respectively. The composition of two steps is monotonic, i.e., the set of true facts as well as the set of definitely false facts is monotonically increasing. A fixpoint has been reached when the set of definitely false facts does not change any more. In the example the well-founded model is then given by

$$\widetilde{\mathcal{S}}_{\mathcal{D}} = DT^5 \uplus \neg\cdot\overline{NDF^4}$$

with the set of true conclusions $DT^5{=}\mathcal{F}\cup\{e(0),e(2),e(4)\}$, the set of true negative conclusions $\neg\cdot\overline{NDF^4}{=}\{\neg e(1),\neg e(3),\neg e(5),\neg succ(1,1),\ldots\}$ and the empty set of undefined facts.

This approach to constructing the well-founded model is not particularly well-suited for being directly implemented, as it works on negative conclusions. From a practical point of view, it would be preferable to deal with positive facts, since they can be more easily represented in and retrieved from a database. Such a reformulation of the alternating fixpoint procedure has been presented in [10] where the sets of not definitely false facts are explicitly stored and only their complement is used to refer to true negative conclusions implicitly. This has led to the so-called *doubled program approach* for computing the well-founded model. The idea is to introduce for each unstratifiable derived relation referencing definitely true facts a second relation for not definitely false facts. In order to work on these relations the entire database is doubled and in each half the deductive rules are rewritten such that negative literals reference relations of the other half. This way, one half is employed for computing definitely true facts, and the other one for determining not definitely false facts. However, rules from the two halves are never applied together. For our previous sample database this leads to

```
dt_e(X)  ← succ(X,Y) ∧ ¬ndf_e(Y)

ndf_e(X) ← succ(X,Y) ∧ ¬dt_e(Y).
```

It is not necessary to double base relations [2] because they are known to have

[2] It is even not necessary to double relations not relying on unstratified negation but this optimization is orthogonal to the following ideas and is left out for simplicity.

a total well-founded model. Therefore, the transformation leaves base relation succ/2 in its original form. Note that both parts of the doubled database are semi-positive if considered separately. In the following we will call this transformation *doubled-program rewriting* [10].

Definition 3 (Doubled-Program Rewriting). *Let $\mathcal{D} = \langle \mathcal{F}, \mathcal{R} \rangle$ be a deductive database and $G_\mathcal{D}$ the corresponding predicate dependency graph. The injective mapping* **dt** *assigns to each literal L with $pred(L) \in pred(\mathcal{R})$ its definitely true form such that*

- $dt(L) := dt\_p(t_1, \ldots, t_n)$ *if* $L \equiv p(t_1, \ldots, t_n)$ *is a positive derived literal*
- $dt(L) := \neg ndf\_p(t_1, \ldots, t_n)$ *if* $L \equiv \neg p(t_1, \ldots, t_n)$ *is a negative literal.*

The injective mapping **ndf** *assigns to each literal L its not definitely false form such that*

- $ndf(L) := ndf\_p(t_1, \ldots, t_n)$ *if* $L \equiv p(t_1, \ldots, t_n)$ *is a positive derived literal*
- $ndf(L) := \neg dt\_p(t_1, \ldots, t_n)$ *if* $L \equiv \neg p(t_1, \ldots, t_n)$ *is a negative literal.*

Both mappings may also be applied to conjunctions and sets of literals, i.e.,

$$
\begin{aligned}
dt(L_1 \wedge \ldots \wedge L_n) &:= \bigwedge_{1 \le i \le n} dt(L_i), & dt(\{L_1, \ldots, L_n\}) &:= \bigcup_{1 \le i \le n} dt(L_i) \\
ndf(L_1 \wedge \ldots \wedge L_n) &:= \bigwedge_{1 \le i \le n} ndf(L_i), & ndf(\{L_1, \ldots, L_n\}) &:= \bigcup_{1 \le i \le n} ndf(L_i).
\end{aligned}
$$

The doubled-program rewriting of $\mathcal{R}$ is the set of rules $\mathcal{R}^{wf} := \mathcal{R}^{dt} \uplus \mathcal{R}^{ndf}$ where $\mathcal{R}^{dt}$ and $\mathcal{R}^{ndf}$ are stratifiable rule sets defined as follows:

$$
\begin{aligned}
\mathcal{R}^{dt} &:= \{dt(A) \leftarrow dt(W) \mid A \leftarrow W \in \mathcal{R}\} \\
\mathcal{R}^{ndf} &:= \{ndf(A) \leftarrow ndf(W) \mid A \leftarrow W \in \mathcal{R}\}.
\end{aligned}
$$

In order to get access to definitely true and not definitely false facts separately after a fixpoint computation has been applied, we introduce the notion dt- and ndf-restriction. This is because the fact base contains both, and hence each fixpoint may include facts belonging to the other half of the database.

Definition 4 (dt- and ndf-Restriction). *Let $\mathcal{D} = \langle \mathcal{F}, \mathcal{R} \rangle$ be a deductive database, $\mathcal{D}^{wf} = \langle \mathcal{F}, \mathcal{R}^{wf} \rangle$ the deductive database derived from $\mathcal{D}$ by applying the doubled-program rewriting to $\mathcal{R}$ and $\mathcal{H}_{\mathcal{D}^{wf}}$ the Herbrand base of $\mathcal{D}^{wf}$. For a set of ground atoms $I \subseteq \mathcal{H}_{\mathcal{D}^{wf}}$ we define:*

$$
\begin{aligned}
I|_{dt} &:= \{\ dt(A) \mid A \in \mathcal{H}_\mathcal{D} \setminus \mathcal{F} \text{ and } dt(A) \in I\} \\
I|_{ndf} &:= \{\ ndf(A) \mid A \in \mathcal{H}_\mathcal{D} \setminus \mathcal{F} \text{ and } ndf(A) \in I\}.
\end{aligned}
$$

The algorithm for computing the alternating fixpoint model, called AFP materialization in [9], is given in Alg. 1. Note that because of the doubled-program rewriting the inner fixpoint computations may use the simpler immediate consequence operator again. In the following sections, this algorithm will serve as the starting point for developing techniques that will improve its performance.

Algorithm 1 AFP materialization

$i := 0;$
$\mathbb{DT}^0 := \emptyset;$
repeat
  $i := i + 1;$
  $\mathbb{NDF}^i := \text{lfp}\ (T_{\mathcal{R}^{\mathsf{ndf}}}, \mathbb{DT}^{i-1} \cup \mathsf{ndf}(\mathbb{DT}^{i-1}) \cup \mathcal{F})|_{\mathsf{ndf}};$
  $\mathbb{DT}^i := \text{lfp}\ (T_{\mathcal{R}^{\mathsf{dt}}}, \mathbb{DT}^{i-1} \cup \mathbb{NDF}^i \cup \mathcal{F})|_{\mathsf{dt}};$
until $\mathbb{DT}^i = \mathbb{DT}^{i-1};$
$\mathbb{DT} := \mathbb{DT}^i \cup \mathcal{F};$
$\mathbb{NDF} := \mathbb{NDF}^i \cup \mathcal{F};$

The scheme in Alg. 1 defines alternating fixpoint computation as follows: At the beginning, $\mathbb{DT}^0$ is initialized with the empty set. Afterwards, in each round of the iteration phase, not definitely false facts are computed and then definitely true facts, each time employing the previously obtained fixpoint for evaluating negative literals. The iteration terminates if the set of definitely true facts does not change any more. The well-founded model $\widetilde{\mathcal{S}}_{\mathcal{D}}$ is then represented by $\text{dt}^{-1}(\mathbb{DT}) \uplus \neg \cdot \overline{\text{ndf}^{-1}(\mathbb{NDF})}$.

5 AFP Materialization Using Update Propagation

Several optimizations have been proposed for the scheme in Alg. 1 (e.g. in [10] and in [9]) including layering of rule sets and further rule set restrictions for stratifiable and semi-positive rules. However, the problem of repeated computations of facts remained. Consider again our previous example and the corresponding results when applying the scheme in Alg. 1. Starting from $\mathbb{DT}^0 = \emptyset$ we obtain:

$$
\begin{aligned}
\mathbb{NDF}^1 &= \{ndf\_e(0), ndf\_e(1), ndf\_e(2), ndf\_e(3), ndf\_e(4)\} \\
\mathbb{DT}^1 &= \{dt\_e(4)\} \\
\mathbb{NDF}^2 &= \{ndf\_e(0), ndf\_e(1), ndf\_e(2), ndf\_e(4)\} \\
\mathbb{DT}^2 &= \{dt\_e(2), dt\_e(4)\} \\
\mathbb{NDF}^3 &= \{ndf\_e(0), ndf\_e(2), ndf\_e(4)\} \\
\mathbb{DT}^3 &= \{dt\_e(0), dt\_e(2), dt\_e(4)\} \\
\mathbb{NDF}^4 &= \{ndf\_e(0), ndf\_e(2), ndf\_e(4)\} \\
\mathbb{DT}^4 &= \{dt\_e(0), dt\_e(2), dt\_e(4)\}
\end{aligned}
$$

In each phase many facts of the previous iteration round are repeatedly computed, e.g. all definitely true facts of previous iterations are repeated. The changes to the sets of definitely true and not definitely false facts, however, are caused only by the changes of the other set computed before respectively. Since $\mathbb{DT}$-facts as well as $\mathbb{NDF}$-facts represent base facts for the other half, it seems to be useful to compute the changes of the $\mathbb{DT}$-facts and $\mathbb{NDF}$-facts only. This can be achieved by means of update propagation rules for true updates that explicitly refer to the given changes of the base facts. Since the set of $\mathbb{DT}$-facts monotonically increases, it is sufficient to consider propagation rules for induced insertions only, whereas for the monotonically decreasing set of $\mathbb{NDF}$-facts, propagation rules for induced deletions have to be considered only. As stated before, for computing true updates, references to both the old as well as the new state are necessary. As proposed in chapter 3, we define now propagation and transition rules assuming that the old state is present and the new one is simulated, generally. For the algorithms to come, however, it turned out to be quite useful to consider certain combinations of states in order to get a smaller set of propagation rules. Therefore, in the following we assume the old $\mathbb{DT}$-, the new $\mathbb{NDF}$- and $\mathbb{NDF}^-$-facts to be present when propagation rules for computing insertions for $\mathbb{DT}$-facts are considered whereas the old $\mathbb{DT}$-, the old $\mathbb{NDF}$- and $\mathbb{DT}^+$-facts are present when propagation rules for deletions from the $\mathbb{NDF}$ set are evaluated.

Definition 5 ($\mathcal{R}^{dt}_{\Delta}$ Propagation Rules). *Let $\mathcal{R}^{dt}$ be a stratifiable deductive rule set. The* $\mathbf{new}_{dt}$*-mapping assigns to each literal L with $pred(L) \in pred(\mathcal{R}^{dt})$ its new dt state relation such that*

- $new_{dt}(L) := dt\_p^{new}(\vec{x})$, *if* $L \equiv dt\_p(\vec{x})$ *is a positive derived literal*
- $new_{dt}(L) := \neg ndf\_p(\vec{x})$, *if* $L \equiv \neg ndf\_p(\vec{x})$ *is a negative literal.*

The mapping may also be applied to conjunctions of literals. The set of propagation rules for true updates with respect to $\mathcal{R}^{dt}$ is denoted $\mathcal{R}^{dt}_{\Delta}$ and is defined as follows: For each rule $A \leftarrow L_1 \wedge \ldots \wedge L_n \in \mathcal{R}^{dt}$ with $A \equiv dt\_p(\vec{x})$ and each negative body literal $L_i \equiv \neg ndf\_q(\vec{y})$ a propagation rule of the form

$$dt\_p^+(\vec{x}) \leftarrow ndf\_q^-(\vec{y}) \wedge new_{dt}(L_1 \wedge \ldots \wedge L_{i-1} \wedge L_{i+1} \wedge \ldots \wedge L_n) \wedge \neg A$$

is in $\mathcal{R}^{dt}_{\Delta}$, whereas for each positive derived body literal $L_j \equiv dt\_r(\vec{z})$ a propagation rule of the form

$$dt\_p^+(\vec{x}) \leftarrow dt\_r^+(\vec{z}) \wedge new_{dt}(L_1 \wedge \ldots \wedge L_{j-1} \wedge L_{j+1} \wedge \ldots \wedge L_n) \wedge \neg A$$

is in $\mathcal{R}^{dt}_{\Delta}$. No other rules are in $\mathcal{R}^{dt}_{\Delta}$.

Simulating the new state as in our approach requires the definition of transition rules for $\mathbb{DT}$-facts that are positively referenced in a rule's body in $\mathcal{R}^{dt}_{\Delta}$. Since we know that the new state of $\mathbb{DT}$-facts is simply the union of computed insertions and (old) facts already stored in the database, i.e.,

$$dt\_p^{new}(\vec{x}) \leftarrow dt\_p(\vec{x}) \qquad dt\_p^{new}(\vec{x}) \leftarrow dt\_p^+(\vec{x}),$$

we will fold the transition rules into the rules in $\mathcal{R}^{dt}_{\Delta}$ and denote the resulting rule set by $\mathcal{R}^{dt}_{\Delta^f}$. For the propagation and transition rules of the $\mathbb{NDF}$-facts we will now define the sets $\mathcal{R}^{ndf}_{\Delta}$ and $\mathcal{R}^{ndf}_{new}$, respectively.

Definition 6 ($\mathcal{R}^{ndf}_{\Delta}$ Propagation Rules). *Let $\mathcal{R}^{ndf}$ be a stratifiable deductive rule set. The set of propagation rules for true updates with respect to $\mathcal{R}^{ndf}$ is defined as follows: For each rule $A \leftarrow L_1 \wedge \ldots \wedge L_n \in \mathcal{R}^{ndf}$ with $A \equiv ndf\_p(\vec{x})$*

Algorithm 2 AFP materialization using update propagation rules

$i := 0;$
$\mathbb{DT} := \mathcal{F};$
$\mathbb{NDF} := \text{lfp}\ (T_{\mathcal{R}^{\mathsf{ndf}}}, \mathbb{DT})|_{\mathsf{ndf}};$
$\Delta^+\mathbb{DT}^0 := + \cdot \text{lfp}\ (T_{\mathcal{R}^{\mathsf{dt}}}, \mathbb{DT} \cup \mathbb{NDF})|_{\mathsf{dt}};$
repeat
  $i := i + 1;$
  $\Delta^-\mathbb{NDF}^i := \mathcal{M}_{\langle \mathbb{NDF} \cup \mathbb{DT} \cup \Delta^+\mathbb{DT}^{i-1}, \mathcal{R}^{\mathsf{ndf}}_{\Delta} \cup \mathcal{R}^{\mathsf{ndf}}_{\mathsf{new}^f} \rangle}|_{\mathsf{ndf}};$
  $\mathbb{DT} := \mathbb{DT} \cup \text{tf}(\Delta^+\mathbb{DT}^{i-1});$
  $\mathbb{NDF} := \mathbb{NDF} \setminus \text{tf}(\Delta^-\mathbb{NDF}^i);$
  $\Delta^+\mathbb{DT}^i := \text{lfp}\ (T_{\mathcal{R}^{\mathsf{dt}}_{\Delta^f}}, \mathbb{NDF} \cup \mathbb{DT} \cup \Delta^-\mathbb{NDF}^{i-1})|_{\mathsf{dt}};$
until $\Delta^+\mathbb{DT}^i = \emptyset;$

and each negative body literal $L_i \equiv dt\_q(\vec{y})$ a propagation rule of the form

$$ndf\_p^-(\vec{x}) \leftarrow dt\_q^+(\vec{y}) \wedge L_1 \wedge \ldots \wedge L_{i-1} \wedge L_{i+1} \wedge \ldots \wedge L_n \wedge \neg ndf\_p^{new}(\vec{x})$$

is in $\mathcal{R}^{ndf}_{\Delta}$, whereas for each positive derived body literal $L_j \equiv ndf\_r(\vec{z})$ a propagation rule of the form

$$ndf\_p^-(\vec{x}) \leftarrow ndf\_r^-(\vec{z}) \wedge L_1 \wedge \ldots \wedge L_{j-1} \wedge L_{j+1} \wedge \ldots \wedge L_n \wedge \neg ndf\_p^{new}(\vec{x})$$

is in $\mathcal{R}^{ndf}_{\Delta}$. No other rules are in $\mathcal{R}^{ndf}_{\Delta}$.

Simulating the new state as proposed in the previous section, we have then to consider transition rules for the $\mathcal{R}^{\mathsf{ndf}}_{\Delta}$ rules, while for $\mathcal{R}^{\mathsf{dt}}_{\Delta^f}$ the effectiveness test can be performed simply over the current database state.

Definition 7 ($\mathcal{R}^{ndf}_{new}$ Transition Rules). *Let $\mathcal{R}^{ndf}$ be a stratifiable deductive rule set. The* **new**$_{ndf}$*-mapping assigns to each literal L with $pred(L) \in pred(\mathcal{R}^{ndf})$ its new ndf state relation such that*

- *$new_{ndf}(L) := ndf\_p^{new}(\vec{x})$, if $L \equiv ndf\_p(\vec{x})$ is a positive derived literal*
- *$new_{ndf}(L) := \neg dt\_p^{new}(\vec{x})$, if $L \equiv \neg dt\_p(\vec{x})$ is a negative literal.*

The mapping may also be applied to conjunctions of literals. The set of transition rules $\mathcal{R}^{ndf}_{new}$ with respect to $\mathcal{R}^{ndf}_{\Delta}$ is defined as follows: For each rule $A \leftarrow L_1 \wedge \ldots \wedge L_n \in \mathcal{R}^{ndf}$ a transition rule of the form

$$new_{ndf}(A) \leftarrow new_{ndf}(L_1, \ldots L_n)$$

is in $\mathcal{R}^{ndf}_{new}$ while for each negative literal $L_j \equiv \neg dt\_p(\vec{x})$ two transition rules

$$dt\_p^{new}(\vec{x}) \leftarrow dt\_p(\vec{x}) \qquad dt\_p^{new}(\vec{x}) \leftarrow dt\_p^+(\vec{x})$$

are in $\mathcal{R}^{ndf}_{new}$.

Similar to the previous case, we will fold the transition rules for $\mathbb{DT}$-facts into the transition rules for $\mathbb{NDF}$-facts in $\mathcal{R}^{ndf}_{new}$ and denote the resulting rule set as $\mathcal{R}^{ndf}_{new^f}$.

Before integrating propagation rules into the AFP materialization scheme, we still have to introduce two more notions that allow to transform literals to their dynamic form and vice versa. For a ground atom $A \equiv p^{\nu}(t_1, \ldots, t_n)$ with $\nu \in \{+,-\}$ the **tf**-mapping is defined as $tf(A) := \{p(t_1, \ldots, t_n)\}$ while for $\nu = new$ the empty set is returned. The mapping may also be applied to a set of ground atoms. For a ground atom $A \equiv p(t_1, \ldots, t_n)$ we will use $+ \cdot A$ to refer to $p^{+}(t_1, \ldots, t_n)$. This concatenation may also be applied to a set of ground atoms and is simply used to transform the initial $\mathbb{DT}$-facts into their dynamic form. The modified algorithm for computing the alternating fixpoint model based on calculating updates is presented in Alg. 2. The essential difference to the AFP materialization procedure is that the algorithm starts with sets of $\mathbb{DT}$- and $\mathbb{NDF}$-facts which will be updated only by new $\mathbb{DT}$-facts to be added and $\mathbb{NDF}$-facts to be removed within each iteration round until no more new $\mathbb{DT}$-facts can be derived. The expensive evaluation of rules with respect to the underlying database is restricted to the calculation of the smaller set of induced updates. Consider once again our previous example when using the scheme in Alg. 2. First, we determine the update propagation rules for the sets $\mathcal{R}^{\mathsf{dt}}$ and $\mathcal{R}^{\mathsf{ndf}}$:

$$\underline{\mathcal{R}^{\mathsf{dt}}_{\Delta^f}:} \quad dt\_e^{+}(X) \leftarrow ndf\_e^{-}(Y) \wedge succ(X,Y) \wedge \neg dt\_e(X)$$

$$\underline{\mathcal{R}^{\mathsf{ndf}}_{\Delta}:} \quad ndf\_e^{-}(X) \leftarrow dt\_e^{+}(Y) \wedge succ(X,Y) \wedge \neg ndf\_e^{new}(X).$$

The transition rules for ndf_e^{new} are

$$\begin{array}{ll} \underline{\mathcal{R}^{\mathsf{ndf}}_{new^f}:} & ndf\_e^{new}(X) \leftarrow succ(X,Y) \wedge \neg dt\_e(Y) \\ & ndf\_e^{new}(X) \leftarrow succ(X,Y) \wedge \neg dt\_e^{+}(Y). \end{array}$$

At the beginning, the set of $\mathbb{DT}$-facts is initialized with the set of base facts and the resulting $\mathbb{NDF}$-facts are determined. From this set, the first new $\mathbb{DT}$-facts can be calculated yielding $\Delta^{+}\mathbb{DT}^{0} = \{dt\_e^{+}(4)\}$. In the following loop, $\Delta^{-}\mathbb{NDF}^{i}$ and $\Delta^{+}\mathbb{DT}^{i}$ are computed and the corresponding $\mathbb{NDF}$- and $\mathbb{DT}$-set is updated:

$$\begin{array}{ll} \Delta^{-}\mathbb{NDF}^{1} & = \{ndf\_e^{-}(3), ndf\_e^{new}(0), ndf\_e^{new}(1), ndf\_e^{new}(2), ndf\_e^{new}(4)\} \\ \Delta^{+}\mathbb{DT}^{1} & = \{dt\_e^{+}(2)\} \\ \Delta^{-}\mathbb{NDF}^{2} & = \{ndf\_e^{-}(1), ndf\_e^{new}(0), ndf\_e^{new}(2), ndf\_e^{new}(4)\} \\ \Delta^{+}\mathbb{DT}^{2} & = \{dt\_e^{+}(0)\} \\ \Delta^{-}\mathbb{NDF}^{3} & = \{ndf\_e^{new}(0), ndf\_e^{new}(2), ndf\_e^{new}(4)\} \\ \Delta^{+}\mathbb{DT}^{3} & = \emptyset \end{array}$$

Note that using the rule set $\mathcal{R}^{\mathrm{ndf}}_{\Delta} \cup \mathcal{R}^{\mathrm{ndf}}_{new^f}$ it is necessary to determine the iterated fixpoint model $\mathcal{M}_{\mathcal{D}}$ for evaluating $\Delta^{-}\mathbb{NDF}^{i}$. Although Alg. 2 already provides a focus on the changes of $\mathbb{DT}$- and $\mathbb{NDF}$-sets, the iterated fixpoint still includes the complete `new` state simulation of ndf relations derived by their corresponding transition rules. The reason for this redundancy is that the materialization of side literals within the derivability- and effectiveness test is not restricted to the facts that are relevant for the particular propagated update. Hence, even the usage of incremental transition rules offers no advantage over the naive ones.

The idea adopted from [9] is to use the magic set method in order to focus on the relevant part of derivability- and effectiveness test only. The application of magic sets with respect to a stratifiable rule set, however, may introduce unstratifiable cycles within these rules and thus for their evaluation the alternating fixpoint would be necessary. To avoid this twist, we propose a different consequence operator $\widetilde{T}$ in order to get rid of the concept of stratification at all.
We will now introduce the new rule sets for $\mathcal{R}^{\mathrm{ndf}}_{\Delta}$ and $\mathcal{R}^{\mathrm{ndf}}_{new^f}$ after applying magic set by means of our example. For each rule in $\mathcal{R}^{\mathrm{ndf}}_{\Delta}$ we apply the magic set rewriting with respect to the abstract (propagation) queries represented by $ndf\_p^-(\vec{x})$ atoms with $ndf\_p^- \in pred(\mathcal{R}^{\mathrm{ndf}}_{\Delta})$. In the example this would lead to

$$\underline{\mathcal{R}^{\Delta ndf}:}\quad ndf\_e^-(X) \leftarrow dt\_e^+(Y) \wedge succ(X,Y) \wedge \neg ndf\_e^{new}_b(X)$$

$$\underline{\mathcal{R}^{\Delta ndf}_{ms}:}\quad ms\_ndf\_e^{new}_b(X) \leftarrow dt\_e^+(Y) \wedge succ(X,Y)$$

where the rule set $\mathcal{R}^{\Delta ndf}$ consists of all transformed propagation rules and the rule set $\mathcal{R}^{\Delta ndf}_{ms}$ contains all corresponding sub-query rules. For each rule in $\mathcal{R}^{\mathrm{ndf}}_{new^f}$, we apply the magic set rewriting with respect to all sub-queries defined in $\mathcal{R}^{\Delta ndf}_{ms}$ leading to rule set $\mathcal{R}^{new}_{ms}$. In the example this set is given by

$$\begin{aligned}\underline{\mathcal{R}^{new}_{ms}:}\quad & ndf\_e^{new}_b(X) \leftarrow ms\_ndf\_e^{new}_b(X) \wedge succ(X,Y) \wedge \neg dt\_e(Y)\\ & ndf\_e^{new}_b(X) \leftarrow ms\_ndf\_e^{new}_b(X) \wedge succ(X,Y) \wedge \neg dt\_e^+(Y).\end{aligned}$$

As mentioned above, combining these three sets would lead to an unstratifiable rule set. This unstratifiability is solely caused by the effectiveness test in $\mathcal{R}^{\Delta ndf}$ which negatively refers to new state literals in $\mathcal{R}^{new}_{ms}$. We will therefore consider the transformed propagation rules $\mathcal{R}^{\Delta ndf}$ and the transformed transition rules

$$\mathcal{R}^{\mathsf{newndf}}_{\mathsf{ms}} := \mathcal{R}^{\Delta ndf}_{ms} \uplus \mathcal{R}^{new}_{ms}$$

separately (getting two stratifiable rule sets) and introduce a new sequential consequence operator $\widetilde{T}$ for their evaluation.

Definition 8 (Sequential Consequence Operator). *Let $\mathcal{D} = \langle \mathcal{F}, \mathcal{R} \rangle$ be a deductive database, $\mathcal{R}_1 \uplus \mathcal{R}_2$ a partition of $\mathcal{R}$ and $\mathcal{I} \subseteq \mathcal{H}_{\mathcal{D}}$ a set of ground atoms. The sequential consequence operator is defined as*

$$\widetilde{T}_{\langle \mathcal{R}_1, \mathcal{R}_2 \rangle}(\mathcal{I}) := T_{\mathcal{R}_2}(\mathit{lfp}\ (T_{\mathcal{R}_1}, \mathcal{I})).$$

The basic property of $\widetilde{T}_{\langle \mathcal{R}_1, \mathcal{R}_2 \rangle}$ is that before R_2 is applied once, the rule set R_1 is evaluated until no more derivations can be made. Using $\mathcal{R}^{\mathsf{newndf}}_{\mathsf{ms}}$ and $\mathcal{R}^{\Delta ndf}$ as first and second rule set, the operator makes sure that all necessary new state facts are derived before a propagation rule using these facts within its derivability and effectiveness test is evaluated. As the sequential consequence operator is monotonic for the stratifiable rule sets $\mathcal{R}^{\mathsf{newndf}}_{\mathsf{ms}}$ and $\mathcal{R}^{\Delta ndf}$, its least fixpoint exists and coincides with the total well-founded model $\widetilde{S}_{\mathcal{D}}$ of $D = \langle \mathcal{F}, \mathcal{R}^{\mathsf{newndf}}_{\mathsf{ms}} \uplus \mathcal{R}^{\Delta ndf} \rangle$:

$$\widetilde{S}_{\langle \mathcal{F}, \mathcal{R}^{\mathsf{newndf}}_{\mathsf{ms}} \uplus \mathcal{R}^{\Delta ndf} \rangle} = \mathrm{lfp}\ (\widetilde{T}_{\langle \mathcal{R}^{\mathsf{newndf}}_{\mathsf{ms}}, \mathcal{R}^{\Delta ndf} \rangle}, \mathcal{F}).$$

Algorithm 3 AFP materialization using magic update propagation rules

$i := 0;$
$\mathbb{DT} := \mathcal{F};$
$\mathbb{NDF} := \text{lfp}\ (T_{\mathcal{R}^{\mathsf{ndf}}}, \mathbb{DT})|_{\mathsf{ndf}};$
$\Delta^{+}\mathbb{DT}^{0} := + \cdot \text{lfp}\ (T_{\mathcal{R}^{\mathsf{dt}}}, \mathbb{DT} \cup \mathbb{NDF})|_{\mathsf{dt}};$
repeat
$i := i + 1;$
$\Delta^{-}\mathbb{NDF}^{i} := \text{lfp}\ (\widetilde{T}_{\langle \mathcal{R}^{\mathsf{newndf}}_{\mathsf{ms}}, \mathcal{R}^{\Delta \mathsf{ndf}} \rangle}, \mathbb{NDF} \cup \mathbb{DT} \cup \Delta^{+}\mathbb{DT}^{i-1})|_{\mathsf{ndf}};$
$\mathbb{DT} := \mathbb{DT} \cup \text{tf}(\Delta^{+}\mathbb{DT}^{i-1});$
$\mathbb{NDF} := \mathbb{NDF} \setminus \text{tf}(\Delta^{-}\mathbb{NDF}^{i});$
$\Delta^{+}\mathbb{DT}^{i} := \text{lfp}\ (\widetilde{T}_{\langle \emptyset, \mathcal{R}^{\Delta \mathsf{dt}} \rangle}, \mathbb{NDF} \cup \mathbb{DT} \cup \Delta^{-}\mathbb{NDF}^{i-1})|_{\mathsf{dt}};$
until $\Delta^{+}\mathbb{DT}^{i} = \emptyset;$

The least fixpoint of $\widetilde{T}$ with respect to the rule sets $\mathcal{R}^{\mathsf{newndf}}_{\mathsf{ms}}$ and $\mathcal{R}^{\Delta ndf}$ corresponds to the fixpoint of the following sequence:

$$\begin{aligned}
\mathcal{F}_1 &:= \text{lfp}\ (T_{\mathcal{R}^{\mathsf{newndf}}_{\mathsf{ms}}}, \mathcal{F}) \\
\mathcal{F}_2 &:= T_{\mathcal{R}^{\Delta ndf}}(\mathcal{F}_1) \\
\mathcal{F}_3 &:= \text{lfp}\ (T_{\mathcal{R}^{\mathsf{newndf}}_{\mathsf{ms}}}, \mathcal{F}_2) \\
\mathcal{F}_4 &:= T_{\mathcal{R}^{\Delta ndf}}(\mathcal{F}_3) \\
&\vdots \\
\mathcal{F}_i &= T_{\mathcal{R}^{\Delta ndf}}(\mathcal{F}_{i-1})
\end{aligned}$$

As the transition rules in $\mathcal{R}^{ndf}_{new^f}$ contain negative literals referencing base relations only, i.e., $\mathbb{DT}$ and $\mathbb{DT}^{+}$ relations, the semantics of $\mathcal{R}^{\mathsf{newndf}}_{\mathsf{ms}}$ can be determined by applying the simple immediate consequence operator. The application of $\widetilde{T}_{\langle \mathcal{R}^{\mathsf{newndf}}_{\mathsf{ms}}, \mathcal{R}^{\Delta ndf} \rangle}$ then alternates between the determination of induced deletions from $\mathbb{NDF}$ after proving their effectiveness within the inner fixpoint calculation. Starting from the set of base facts, the effectiveness of all induced updates to be derived is tested one iteration round before in the inner fixpoint computation such that the operator never evaluates negative literals too early. The scheme in Alg. 3 defines how to compute the well-founded model using magic set transformed update propagation rules.

The overall evaluation scheme remained as in Alg. 2. The basic difference can be found in the $\Delta^{-}\mathbb{NDF}^{i}$-sets, as only relevant new state facts are computed:

$$\begin{aligned}
\mathbb{DT} &= \mathcal{F} \\
\mathbb{NDF} &= \{ndf_e(0), ndf_e(1), ndf_e(2), ndf_e(3), ndf_e(4)\}
\end{aligned}$$

$$\begin{aligned}
\Delta^{+}\mathbb{DT}^{0} &= \{dt_e^{+}(4)\} \\
\Delta^{-}\mathbb{NDF}^{1} &= \{ndf_e^{-}(3), ms_ndf_e^{new}(3)\} \\
\Delta^{+}\mathbb{DT}^{1} &= \{dt_e^{+}(2)\} \\
\Delta^{-}\mathbb{NDF}^{2} &= \{ndf_e^{-}(1), ms_ndf_e^{new}(1)\}
\end{aligned}$$

$$\Delta^+\mathbb{DT}^2 \;= \{dt\_e^+(0)\}$$
$$\Delta^-\mathbb{NDF}^3 = \Delta^+\mathbb{DT}^3 = \emptyset$$

In each phase, only those facts are computed that lead to changes in the corresponding $\mathbb{DT}$- and $\mathbb{NDF}$-set avoiding full materialization of new state relations.

6 Conclusion

In this paper, we have presented a new efficient bottom-up evaluation procedure for computing well-founded models of function-free rules in the context of deductive databases. This procedure provides a practical method for handling normal logic programs that involve unstratified negation in a manner that may be mixed with other approaches such as layering, sips and further rule set restrictions [9]. Based on the doubled program approach [10] we use update propagation rules in order to restrict computation to changes of definitely true and not definitely false facts. Because of the specific context, we are able to solve stratification problems which arise if the magic set transformation is used in combination with propagation rules by introducing a new consequence operator. Although the technique of combining magic sets with update propagation rules as proposed in [9] needs to be further investigated we showed its useful application in our context already. Our approach is closely related to the work in [6] for optimizing the residual program evaluation. Despite of the additional sub-query and transitional facts needed in our approach our transformation based method is easy to implement providing similar enhancements as [6].

References

1. Ceri S., Widom J.: *Deriving Incremental Production Rules for Deductive Data.* Information Systems 19(6): 467-490 (1994).
2. Balbin I., Ramamohanarao K.: *A Generalization of the Differential Approach to Recursive Query Evaluation.* JLP 4(3): 259-262 (1987).
3. Bancilhon F., Ramakrishnan R.: *An Amateur's Introduction to Recursive Query Processing Strategies.* SIGMOD Conference 1986: 16-52.
4. Beeri C., Ramakrishnan R.: *On the Power of Magic.* JLP 10(1-4): 255-299 (1991).
5. Brass S., Dix J.: *Characterizations of the Stable Semantics by Partial Evaluation.* LPNMR 1995: 85-98.
6. Brass S., Zukowski U., Freitag B.: *Transformation-Based Bottom-Up Computation of the Well-Founded Model.* NMELP 1996 (LNCS 1216): 171-201.
7. Bry F.: *Logic Programming as Constructivism: A Formalization and its Application to Databases.* PODS 1989: 34-50.
8. Dung P. M., Kanchanasut K.: *A Fixpoint Approach to Declarative Semantics of Logic Programs.* NACLP 1989: 604-625.
9. Griefahn, U.: *Reactive Model Computation - A Uniform Approach to the Implementation of Deductive Databases.* Dissertation, University of Bonn, 1997, http://www.cs.uni-bonn.de/~idb/publications/diss_griefahn.ps.gz

10. Kemp D., Srivastava D., Stuckey P.: *Bottom-Up Evaluation and Query Optimization of Well-Founded Models.* Theoretical Computer Science 146(1 & 2): 145-184 (1995).
11. Kolaitis P.: *The Expressive Power of Stratified Programs.* Information and Computation 90(1): 50-66 (1991).
12. Manthey R.: *Reflections on Some Fundamental Issues of Rule-based Incremental Update Propagation.* DAISD 1994: 255-276.
13. Olivé A.: *Integrity Constraints Checking In Deductive Databases.* VLDB 1991: 513-523.
14. Rohmer J., Lescoeur R., Kerisit J.-M.: *The Alexander Method - A Technique for The Processing of Recursive Axioms in Deductive Databases.* New Generation Computing 4(3): 273-285 (1986).
15. Subrahmanian V. S., Nau D. S., Vago C.: *WFS + Branch and Bound = Stable Models.* TKDE 7(3): 362-377 (1995).
16. Van Gelder A.: *The Alternating Fixpoint of Logic Programs with Negation.* JCSS 47(1): 185-221 (1993).
17. Van Gelder A., Ross K., Schlipf J.: *The Well-Founded Semantics for General Logic Programs.* JACM 38(3): 620-650 (1991).

Indexed Categories and Bottom-Up Semantics of Logic Programs

Gianluca Amato[1] and James Lipton[2]

[1] Dipartimento di Matematica e Informatica, Università di Udine
via delle Scienze 206, Udine, Italy
amato@dimi.uniud.it
[2] Mathematics Department, Wesleyan University
265 Church St., Middletown (CT), USA
lipton@wesleyan.edu

Abstract. We propose a categorical framework which formalizes and extends the syntax, operational semantics and declarative model theory of a broad range of logic programming languages. A program is interpreted in an indexed category in such a way that the base category contains all the possible states which can occur during the execution of the program (such as global constraints or type information), while each fiber encodes the logic at each state.
We define appropriate notions of categorical resolution and models, and we prove the related correctness and completeness properties.

1 Introduction

One of the greatest benefits of logic programming is that it is based upon the notion of *executable specifications.* The text of a logic program is endowed with both an operational (algorithmic) interpretation and an independent mathematical meaning which agree each other in several ways.

An operational interpretation is needed if we wish to specify programs which can be executed with some degree of efficiency, while a clear mathematical (declarative) meaning simplifies the work of the programmer, who can –to some extent– focus on "what to do" instead of "how". The problem is that operational expressiveness (i.e. the capability of directing the flow of execution of a program) tends to obscure declarative meaning. Research in logic programming strives to find a good balance between these opposite needs.

Horn logic programming was one of the first attempts in this area and surely the most famous. However it has limitations when it comes to real programming tasks. Its forms of control flow are too primitive: there are simple problems (such as computing the reflexive closure of a relation) which cannot be coded in the obvious way since the programs so obtained do not terminate. The expressive power of its logic is too weak, both for programming in the small and in the large: it lacks any mathematically precise notion of module, program composition, typing. Moreover, if we want to work with some data structure, we need to

R. Nieuwenhuis and A. Voronkov (Eds.): LPAR 2001, LNAI 2250, pp. 438–454, 2001.

manually code the behavior and constraints of such a structure in the Horn logic, often obscuring the intended meaning of the code.

For these reasons, various extensions have been proposed to the original framework of Horn clause, often borrowing ideas from other paradigms. Some noteworthy extensions are the use of algebraic operators for modularization [7], the use of more powerful extensions to the logic [21], control operators like the "cut" of PROLOG and abstract data types [20]. The effect has been to expand the boundaries of the field and the notion itself of declarative content of a program. We lack criteria for good language design and models to evaluate the new features, or to formalize the very notion of declarative programming.

Moreover, semantic methods for Horn logic programming are increasingly similar in spirit to those for functional and imperative programming, under the stimulus of techniques such as abstract interpretation [12,8]. This suggests looking for a sufficiently flexible new logic programming foundation using a framework in which all these paradigms can be well understood. Categorical logic seems an excellent candidate for such an undertaking.

Categorical approaches to logic programming go back to the treatment of unification given by Rydeheard and Burstall in [23]. Building on this work, in [3] the syntax of Horn clause logic is formalized using categorical tools and a topos-theoretic semantics. In [10], following some basic ideas already developed in [11], a categorical analysis of logic program transitions and models is given using indexed monoidal categories. The framework that we propose here builds on some of the ideas in that paper, which have proved seminal, but which fall short of formulating the kind of general blueprint we seek for declarative programming.

The approaches just cited focus on the operational or model theoretic side of logic programming, but lack any bottom-up denotational semantics like the T_P operator of van Emden and Kowalski [25]. For us, the immediate consequence operator seems to be a cornerstone of logic programming, since it appears, in one form or another, across several semantic treatments of logic programs [4]. Most of the studies in the semantics of logic programming are heavily based on the existence of some fixpoint construction: treatments of compositionality of semantics [8], modularity [6], static analysis [12], and debugging [9]. For this reason, it seems to us that further investigation of a categorical framework which includes a form of bottom-up semantics is advisable.

The first step in this direction was taken in [13], which uses categorical syntax over finite τ-categories [15]. It is the starting point for introducing both a notion of categorical SLD derivation and a denotational semantics which resembles the correct answer semantics for Horn logic programs. This semantics can be computed with a fixpoint construction and it can be shown to agree with a more general notion of categorical derivation.

1.1 The New Approach

Our framework starts from the work in [13] and [14]. However, we redefine the fundamental categorical structures with the hope of generalizing the methods in three main directions:

- in the ability to treat other kinds of semantics other than the "correct answers" one. The concept of interpretation must be far broader than that of [13], allowing for semantic domains different from $Set^{\mathbb{C}^o}$;
- in the ability to treat programs with constraints between goals. This means that we must provide a new bottom-up operator which works for a generic syntactic category and not only with $\mathbb{C}[X_1, \ldots, X_n]$;
- in the adaptability to different logic languages. In particular, we would like to treat languages such as CLP or add some control operators to the pure logic programming.

To pursue these goals, we move to a more general categorical interpretation of logic. Instead of taking goals to be monics in the category $\mathbb{C}$, we use an indexed category over $\mathbb{C}$. An object in the fiber $\sigma \in \mathrm{Obj}(\mathbb{C})$ will be the categorical counterpart of a goal of sort σ. It is the standard indexed/fibrational categorical interpretation of full first order logic, as can be found in, e.g. [24,16].

To simplify the presentation, we begin without any kind of monoidal structure in the fibers. These means we are not able to handle conjunction in goals externally and compositionally: we are restricted to so-called binary clauses. However, adding monoidal structures is quite straightforward, and it has been done in [1].

1.2 Notation

We will assume the reader is familiar with the basic concepts of logic programming [2] and category theory [5]. Here, we only give some brief definitions and notation. Basic categorical background for logic programming can be found in e.g. [14,18]

Given a category $\mathbb{C}$, we denote by $\mathrm{Obj}(\mathbb{C})$ and $\mathrm{Mor}(\mathbb{C})$ the corresponding classes of objects and morphisms (arrows). With id_A we denote the identity arrow for the object A, while 1 is the terminator, $\times$ the product and $\vee$ denotes coproducts. We use $\vee$ as a functor, applying it to objects and arrows as well. Given $f : A \longrightarrow B$ and $g : B \longrightarrow C$, we write $f\, ;\, g$ for their composition. With $\mathrm{Hom}_{\mathbb{C}}(A, B)$ we denote the class of morphisms from A to B in $\mathbb{C}$. We omit the index $\mathbb{C}$ when it is clear from the context. Given a functor $F : \mathbb{C} \longrightarrow \mathbb{C}$, a fixpoint for F is a pair (σ, t) such that $t : F\sigma \longrightarrow \sigma$ is an isomorphism.

We denote sequences by writing one after the other its elements. We use λ to denote an empty sequence and $\cdot$ as the juxtaposition operator.

A (strict) indexed category over $\mathbb{C}$ is a functor $\mathcal{P} : \mathbb{C}^o \longrightarrow \mathsf{Cat}$, where $\mathbb{C}^o$ is the opposite category of $\mathbb{C}$ and Cat is the category of all small categories. We refer to objects and arrows in $\mathbb{C}^o$ with the same symbols of their counterparts in $\mathbb{C}$. Given $\sigma \in \mathrm{Obj}(C^o)$, the category $\mathcal{P}\sigma$ is the *fiber* of $\mathcal{P}$ over σ. An indexed functor from $\mathcal{P} : \mathbb{C}^o \longrightarrow \mathsf{Cat}$ to $\mathcal{Q} : \mathbb{D}^o \longrightarrow \mathsf{Cat}$ is a pair (F, τ) such that $F : \mathbb{C} \longrightarrow \mathbb{D}$ is the *change of base* functor and $\tau : \mathcal{P} \longrightarrow F^o\, ;\, \mathcal{Q}$ is a natural transformation. An indexed natural transformation $\eta : (F, \tau) \longrightarrow (F', \tau') : \mathcal{P} \longrightarrow \mathcal{Q}$ is given by a pair (ξ, δ) such that $\xi : F \longrightarrow F'$ is a natural transformation and δ is a $\mathbb{C}$-indexed family of natural transformations

$$\delta_\sigma : \tau_\sigma \longrightarrow \tau'_\sigma; \mathcal{Q}(\xi_\sigma) \tag{1}$$

subject to some coherence conditions. A detailed treatment of indexed categories and fibrations can be found in [16].

2 Syntax

In the following, we introduce several kinds of indexed categories called doctrines [19]. We abuse terminology, since a doctrine is generally understood to be an indexed category where reindexing functors have left adjoints, and this property does not always holds for our doctrines. We have chosen this terminology to emphasize the relation between indexed categories used for the syntax and the semantics (which are actually Lawvere doctrines).

Definition 1 (Logic programming doctrine). *An* LP doctrine *(logic programming doctrine) is an indexed category $\mathcal{P}$ over a base category $\mathbb{C}$. For each $\sigma \in \mathrm{Obj}(\mathbb{C})$, objects and arrows in $\mathcal{P}\sigma$ are called* goals *and* proofs *(of sort σ) respectively. Given a goal $\mathbf{G}$ of sort σ and $f : \rho \to \sigma$ in $\mathbb{C}$, $\mathcal{P}f(\mathbf{G})$ is an* instance *of $\mathbf{G}$. We also denote it by $f^\sharp\mathbf{G}$ or $\mathbf{G}(f)$.*

We write $\mathbf{G} : \sigma$ and $f : \sigma$ as a short form for $\mathbf{G} \in \mathrm{Obj}(\mathcal{P}\sigma)$ and $f \in \mathrm{Mor}(\mathcal{P}\sigma)$. Given an LP doctrine $\mathcal{P}$, a clause (of sort σ) is a name cl, with an associated pair $(\mathbf{Tl}, \mathbf{Hd})$ of goals of sort σ, that we write as $\mathbf{Hd} \xleftarrow{cl} \mathbf{Tl}$.

Definition 2 (Logic program). *A* logic program *is a pair $(P, \mathcal{P})$ where $\mathcal{P}$ is an LP doctrine and P a set of clauses. We often say that P is a program over $\mathcal{P}$.*

It is possible to see a logic program as an indexed category P over $\mathrm{Obj}(\mathbb{C})$ such that $P\sigma$ is the category of goals of sort σ with arrows given by clauses of sort σ.

The idea underlying the framework is that the base category represents the world of all possible states to which program execution can lead. At each state, the corresponding fiber represents an underlying theory: a set of deductions which can always be performed, independently of the actual program. A clause is a new deduction, which we want to consider, freely adjoined to the proofs in the fibers.

The advantage of using categories is that we do not need to restrict our interest to syntactical terms and goals. We can choose any base category we desire and build binary logic programs over terms which are interpreted already at the syntactic level in the base.

Example 3 (Binary logic programs). Assume $\mathbb{C}$ is a finite product category. We can think of $\mathbb{C}$ as a not necessarily free model of an appropriate many-sorted signature. We can build a syntactic doctrine for binary logic programs where terms are arrows in this category. We need to fix a signature Π for predicates over $\mathbb{C}$, i.e. a set of predicate symbols with associated sort among $\mathrm{Obj}(\mathbb{C})$. We write $p : \sigma$ when p is a predicate symbol of sort σ. Then, we define an indexed category $\mathcal{P}_\Pi$ over $\mathbb{C}$:

- $\mathcal{P}_\Pi(\sigma)$ is the discrete category whose objects are pairs $\langle p, f\rangle$ such that $p : \rho$ in Π and $f : \sigma \longrightarrow \rho$ is an arrow in $\mathbb{C}$. To ease notation, we write $p(f)$ instead of $\langle p, f\rangle$;
- $\mathcal{P}_\Pi(f)$, where $f : \rho \longrightarrow \sigma$, is the functor mapping $p(t) \in \mathrm{Obj}(\mathcal{P}_\Pi(\sigma))$ to $p(f\,; t)$.

The interesting point here is that terms are treated semantically. For example, assume $\mathbb{C}$ is the full subcategory of *Set* whose objects are the sets $\mathbb{N}^i$ for every natural i and $p : \mathbb{N}$ is a predicate symbol. If succ and fact are the functions for the successor and factorial of a natural number, then $(\mathsf{succ}\,;\mathsf{succ}\,;\mathsf{succ})^\sharp(p(3)) = \mathsf{fact}^\sharp(p(3)) = p(6)$.

In the previous example, the fibers of the syntactic doctrine were discrete categories freely generated by a set of predicate symbols. When we define the concept of model for a program, below, it will be clear we are not imposing any constraints on the meaning of predicates. In general, we can use more complex categories for fibers.

Example 4 (Symmetric closure of predicates). In the hypotheses of Example 3, assume we have two predicate symbols p and $symp$ of sort $\rho \times \rho$, and we want to encode in the syntactic doctrine the property that $symp$ contains the symmetric closure of p. Then, we freely adjoin to $\mathcal{P}_\Pi$ the following two arrows in the fiber $\rho \times \rho$:

$$r_1 : p \longrightarrow symp \ ,$$
$$r_2 : p \longrightarrow symp(\langle \pi_2, \pi_1\rangle) \ ,$$

where π_1 and π_2 are the obvious cartesian projections. We call $\mathcal{P}_\Pi^{symp}$ the new LP doctrine we obtain. The intuitive meaning of the adjoined arrows is evident.

3 Models

A key goal of our treatment is to consider extensions to definite logic programs without losing the declarative point of view, namely by defining a corresponding straightforward extension of the notion of model for a program.

Functors (F, τ) of LP doctrines will be called *interpretations*. For every goal or proof x in the fiber σ, we write $\tau_\sigma(x)$ as $[\![x]\!]_\sigma$. We also use $[\![x]\!]$ when the fiber of x is clear from the context.

Definition 5 (Models). *Given a program P over the doctrine $\mathcal{P}$, a* model *of P is a pair $([\![\text{-}]\!], \iota)$ where $[\![\text{-}]\!] : \mathcal{P} \longrightarrow \mathcal{Q}$ is an interpretation and ι is a function which maps a clause $\mathbf{Hd} \xleftarrow{cl} \mathbf{Tl} \in P$ to an arrow $[\![\mathbf{Hd}]\!] \xleftarrow{\iota(cl)} [\![\mathbf{Tl}]\!]$.*

In the following, a model $M = (\llbracket \_ \rrbracket, \iota)$ will be used as an alias for its constituent parts. Hence, $M(cl)$ will denote $\iota(cl)$ and $M_\sigma(\mathbf{G})$ will denote $\llbracket \mathbf{G} \rrbracket_\sigma$. The composition of M with an interpretation N is given as the model $(\llbracket \_ \rrbracket ; N, \iota ; N)$.

Example 6 (Ground answers for binary logic programs). Consider the LP doctrine $\mathcal{P}_\Pi$ defined in Example 3 and the indexed category $\mathcal{Q}$ over $\mathbb{C}$ such that

- for each $\sigma \in \mathrm{Obj}(\mathbb{C})$, $\mathcal{Q}(\sigma) = \wp(\mathrm{Hom}_\mathbb{C}(1, \sigma))$, which is an ordered set viewed as a category;
- for each $f \in \mathrm{Hom}_\mathbb{C}(\sigma, \rho)$, $\mathcal{Q}(f)(X) = \{r \in \mathrm{Hom}_\mathbb{C}(1, \sigma) \mid r ; f \in X\}$.

An interpretation $\llbracket \_ \rrbracket$ maps an atomic goal of sort σ to a set of arrows from the terminal object of $\mathbb{C}$ to σ. These arrows are indeed the categorical counterpart of ground terms.

Two significant models are given by the interpretations which map every goal $\mathbf{G}$ of sort σ to $\mathrm{Hom}(1, \sigma)$ or to $\emptyset$. Clauses and arrows are obviously mapped to identities. If we see $\mathrm{Hom}(1, \sigma)$ as the true value and $\emptyset$ as false, they correspond to the interpretations where everything is true or everything is false.

When the syntactic doctrine is discrete, as in the previous example, an interpretation from $\mathcal{P}$ to $\mathcal{Q}$ can map every object in $\mathcal{P}$ to every object in $\mathcal{Q}$, provided this mapping is well-behaved w.r.t. reindexing. However, in the general case, other restrictions are imposed.

Example 7. Assume the hypotheses of Example 4. Consider the LP doctrine $\mathcal{Q}$ as defined in Example 6. An interpretation $\llbracket \_ \rrbracket$ from $\mathcal{P}_\Pi^{symp}$ to $\mathcal{Q}$ is forced to map the arrows r_1 and r_2 to arrows in $\mathcal{Q}$. This means that $\llbracket symp \rrbracket \supseteq \llbracket p \rrbracket$ and $\llbracket symp \rrbracket \supseteq \llbracket p(\langle \pi_2, \pi_1 \rangle) \rrbracket$, i.e. $\llbracket symp \rrbracket \supseteq \llbracket p \rrbracket ; \langle \pi_2, \pi_1 \rangle$. In other words, the interpretation of *symp* must contain both the interpretation of p and its symmetric counterpart.

One of the way to obtain a model of a program P over $\mathcal{P}$ is *freely adjoining* the clauses of P to the fibers of $\mathcal{P}$. We obtain a *free model* of P over $\mathcal{P}$.

Definition 8 (Free model). *A model M of $(P, \mathcal{P})$ is said to be* free *when, for each model M' of $(P, \mathcal{P})$, there exists an unique interpretation N such that $M' = M ; N$.*

It is easy to prove that, if M and M' are both free models for a program $(P, \mathcal{P})$ in two different logic doctrines $\mathcal{Q}$ and $\mathcal{R}$, then $\mathcal{Q}$ and $\mathcal{R}$ are isomorphic.

4 Operational Semantics

Our logic programs also have a quite straightforward operational interpretation. Given a goal $\mathbf{G}$ of sort σ in a program $(P, \mathcal{P})$, we want to reduce $\mathbf{G}$ using both arrows in the fibers of $\mathcal{P}$ and clauses. This means that, if $x : \mathbf{G} \leftarrow \mathbf{Tl}$ is a clause or a proof in $\mathcal{P}$, we want to perform a reduction step from $\mathbf{G}$ to $\mathbf{Tl}$.

In this way, the only rewritings we can immediately apply to $\mathbf{G}$ are given by rules (proofs or clauses) of sort σ. It is possible to rewrite using a clause *cl* of another sort ρ only if we find a common "ancestor" α of σ and ρ, i.e. a span

in the base category such that $\mathbf{G}$ and the head of *cl* become equal once they are reindexed to the fiber α.

Definition 9 (Unifier). *Given two goals* $\mathbf{G}_1 : \sigma_1$ *and* $\mathbf{G}_2 : \sigma_2$ *in an LP doctrine* $\mathcal{P}$, *an* unifier *for them is a span* $\langle t_1, t_2 \rangle$ *of arrows of the base category such that* $t_1 : \alpha \longrightarrow \sigma_1$, $t_2 : \alpha \longrightarrow \sigma_2$ *and* $t_1{}^\sharp \mathbf{G}_1 = t_2{}^\sharp \mathbf{G}_2$

Unifiers for a pair of goals form a category $\mathit{Unif}_{\mathbf{G}_1,\mathbf{G}_2}$ where arrows from $\langle t_1, t_2 \rangle$ to $\langle r_1, r_2 \rangle$ are given by the common notion of arrow between spans, i.e. a morphism $f : \mathsf{dom}(t_1) \longrightarrow \mathsf{dom}(r_1)$ such that $f; r_1 = t_1$ and $f; r_2 = t_2$.

Definition 10 (MGU). *A* most general unifier *(MGU) for goals* $\mathbf{G}_1 : \sigma_1$ *and* $\mathbf{G}_2 : \sigma_2$ *in an LP doctrine* $\mathcal{P}$ *is a maximal element of* $\mathit{Unif}_{\mathbf{G}_1,\mathbf{G}_2}$.

Example 11 (Standard mgu). Consider the indexed category $\mathcal{P}_\Pi$ as in Example 3. Given goals $p_1(t_1) : \sigma_1$ and $p_2(t_2) : \sigma_2$, an unifier is a pair of arrows $r_1 : \alpha \longrightarrow \sigma_1$ and $r_2 : \alpha \longrightarrow \sigma_2$ such that the following diagram commute:

$$\begin{array}{ccc} \alpha & \xrightarrow{r_1} & \sigma_1 \\ {\scriptstyle r_2}\downarrow & & \downarrow{\scriptstyle t_1} \\ \sigma_2 & \xrightarrow[t_2]{} & \rho \end{array} \tag{3}$$

This is exactly the definition of unifier for renamed apart terms t_1 and t_2 given in [3], which corresponds to unifiers in the standard syntactic sense. Moreover, the span $\langle r_1, r_2 \rangle$ is maximal when (3) is a pullback diagram, i.e. a most general unifier.

Note that in the standard syntactic categories with freely adjoined predicates there is no unifier between goals $p_1(t_1)$ and $p_2(t_2)$ if $p_1 \neq p_2$. However, this does not hold in our more general setting. Actually, in a completely general doctrine, we have a notion of logic program and execution without any notion of predicate symbol at all.

In the same way, it is possible to reduce a goal $\mathbf{G} : \sigma$ with a proof $f : \mathbf{Hd} \leftarrow \mathbf{Tl}$ in the fiber ρ iff there exists an arrow $r : \rho \longrightarrow \sigma$ such that $r^\sharp \mathbf{G} = \mathbf{Hd}$. We call a pair $\langle r, f \rangle$ with such properties a *reduction pair*. Reduction pairs form a category such that $t \in \mathrm{Mor}(\mathbb{C})$ is an arrow from $\langle r_1, f_1 \rangle$ to $\langle r_2, f_2 \rangle$ if $r_1 = t; r_2$ and $t^\sharp f_2 = f_1$. A *most general* reduction pair is a maximal reduction pair. Note that most general unifiers or reduction pairs do not necessarily exist. This is not a big problem since all the theory we develop works the same.

Following these ideas, it is possible to define a categorical form of SLD derivation.

Definition 12 (Categorical derivation). *Given a program* $(P, \mathcal{P})$*, we define a labeled transition system* $(\biguplus_{\sigma \in \mathsf{Obj}(\mathbb{C})} \mathsf{Obj}(\mathcal{P}\sigma), \leadsto)$ *with goals as objects, according to the following rules:*

backchain-clause $\mathbf{G} \overset{\langle r,t,cl \rangle}{\leadsto} t^\sharp \mathbf{Tl}$ *if cl is a clause* $\mathbf{Hd} \overset{cl}{\longleftarrow} \mathbf{Tl}$ *and $\langle r, t\rangle$ is an unifier for* $\mathbf{G}$ *and* $\mathbf{Hd}$ *(i.e.* $r^\sharp \mathbf{G} = t^\sharp \mathbf{Hd}$*);*

backchain-arrow $\mathbf{G} \overset{\langle r,f \rangle}{\leadsto} \mathbf{Tl}$ *if* $\mathbf{G}$ *is a goal in the fiber σ, $f : \mathbf{Hd} \leftarrow \mathbf{Tl}$ is a proof in the fiber ρ and $\langle r, f\rangle$ is a reduction pair for* $\mathbf{G}$*.*

A categorical derivation *is a (possibly empty) derivation in this transition system.*

If we restrict SLD-steps to the use of most general unifiers and most general reduction pairs, we have a new transition system $(\biguplus_{\sigma \in \mathsf{Obj}(\mathbb{C})} \mathsf{Obj}(\mathcal{P}\sigma), \leadsto_g)$ and a corresponding notion of *most general* (m.g.) categorical derivation. In the following, when not otherwise stated, everything we say about derivations can be applied to m.g. ones.

If there are goals $\mathbf{G}_0, \ldots, \mathbf{G}_i$ and labels $l_0, \ldots, l_{i-1}$ with $i \geq 0$ such that

$$\mathbf{G}_0 \overset{l_0}{\leadsto} \mathbf{G}_1 \cdots \mathbf{G}_{i-1} \overset{l_{i-1}}{\leadsto} \mathbf{G}_i \tag{4}$$

we write $\mathbf{G}_0 \overset{d}{\leadsto}^* \mathbf{G}_i$ where $d = l_0 \cdots l_{i-1}$ is the string obtained by concatenating all the labels. Note that $d \neq \lambda$ uniquely induces the corresponding sequence of goals. We will write $\epsilon_{\mathbf{G}}$ for the empty derivation starting from goal $\mathbf{G}$.

Given a derivation d, we call *answer* of d (and we write $\mathsf{answer}(d)$) the arrow in $\mathbb{C}$ defined by induction on the length of d as follows

$$\begin{aligned}
&\mathsf{answer}(\epsilon_{\mathbf{G}}) = id_\sigma && \text{if } \mathbf{G} : \sigma \\
&\mathsf{answer}(\langle r, f\rangle \cdot d) = \mathsf{answer}(d)\,;r \\
&\mathsf{answer}(\langle r, t, a\rangle \cdot d) = \mathsf{answer}(d)\,;r
\end{aligned}$$

In particular, we call *most general* answers the answers corresponding to m.g. derivations.

Example 13 (Standard SLD derivations). Consider a program P in the syntactic doctrine $\mathcal{P}_\Pi$ and a goal $p(t_1)$ of sort σ. Given a clause $p(t_2) \overset{cl}{\longleftarrow} q(t)$, and an mgu $\langle r_1, r_2\rangle$ for $p(t_1)$ and $p(t_2)$, we have a most general derivation step

$$p(t_1) \overset{\langle r_1, r_2, cl \rangle}{\leadsto}_g q(r_2; t)\ . \tag{5}$$

This strictly corresponds to a step of the standard SLD derivation procedure for binary clauses and atomic goals.

However, in the categorical derivation, it is possible to reduce w.r.t. one of the identity arrows of the fibers. Therefore, if $p(t) : \sigma$,

$$p(t) \xrightarrow{\langle id_\sigma,\, id_{p(t)} \rangle}\!\!\rightsquigarrow_g p(t) \tag{6}$$

is an identity step which does not have a counterpart in the standard resolution procedure. However, these steps have an identity answer. Therefore, fixing a goal $p(t)$, the set

$$\mathsf{answer}\{d \mid d : p(t) \rightsquigarrow_g{}^* \mathbf{G}\} \tag{7}$$

is the set of partial answers for the goal $p(t)$.

We can use categorical derivations to build several interesting models for logic programs. In particular, with the answer function we can build models which are the general counterpart of partial computed answers, correct answer and ground answers.

Example 14 (Model for ground answers). Consider a program P in $\mathcal{P}_\Pi$ and an interpretation $[\![\_]\!]$ in the LP doctrine $\mathcal{Q}$ defined in Example 6, such that

$$[\![p(t)]\!] = \{\mathsf{answer}(d) \mid d : p(t) \rightsquigarrow_g{}^* \mathbf{G} \text{ is a m.g. ground derivation}\} \ , \tag{8}$$

where a *ground derivation* is a derivation whose last goal is in the fiber $\mathcal{P}(1)$. Now, for each clause $p_1(t_1) \xleftarrow{cl} p_2(t_2)$, if d is a m.g. ground derivation of $p_2(t_2)$, then

$$d' = p_1(t_1) \xrightarrow{\langle id,\, id,\, cl \rangle}\!\!\rightsquigarrow p_2(t_2) \cdot d \tag{9}$$

is a m.g. ground derivation for $p_1(t_1)$ with $\mathsf{answer}(d') = \mathsf{answer}(d)$. Therefore, $[\![p_1(t_1)]\!] \supseteq [\![p_2(t_2)]\!]$ and this gives an obvious mapping ι from clauses to arrows in the fibers of $\mathcal{Q}$. It turns out that $([\![\_]\!], \iota)$ is a model for P.

5 Completeness

Assume given a program P over the LP doctrine $\mathcal{P} : \mathbb{C}^o \longrightarrow \mathsf{Cat}$. It is possible to use categorical derivations to obtain a free model of P. First of all, consider the following definitions:

Definition 15 (Flat derivations). *A derivation is called* flat *(on the fiber σ) when all the r fields in the labels of the two backchain rules are identities (on σ).*

Definition 16 (Simple derivations). *A derivation is called* simple *when*

- *there are no two consecutive* backchain-arrow *steps,*
- *there are no* backchain-arrow *steps with identity arrows f.*

Given a derivation $d : \mathbf{G}_1 \leadsto \mathbf{G}_2$ with $\mathsf{answer}(d) = \theta$, there is a canonical flat simple derivation $\bar{d} : \theta^\sharp \mathbf{G}_1 \leadsto \mathbf{G}_2$ obtained by collapsing consecutive backchain-arrow steps. If we define a congruence $\equiv$ on derivations such that

$$d_1 \equiv d_2 \iff \mathsf{answer}(d_1) = \mathsf{answer}(d_2) \text{ and } \bar{d_1} = \bar{d_2} \ , \tag{10}$$

it is possible to define an LP doctrine $\mathcal{F}_P$ over $\mathbb{C}$ such that $\mathcal{F}_P(\sigma)$ is the category of equivalence classes of flat simple derivations on the fiber σ.

Now, we can define an interpretation $[\![\_]\!] = (id_{\mathbb{C}}, \tau)$ from $\mathcal{P}$ to $\mathcal{F}_P$ and a function ι such that:

- $\tau_\sigma(\mathbf{G}) = \mathbf{G}$;
- $\tau_\sigma(f : \mathbf{G} \to \mathbf{G}') = \left[\mathbf{G}' \xrightarrow{\langle id_\sigma, f \rangle} \mathbf{G}\right]_\equiv$;
- $\iota(\mathbf{Hd} \xleftarrow{cl} \mathbf{Tl}) = \left[\mathbf{Hd} \xrightarrow{\langle id_\sigma, id_\sigma, cl \rangle} \mathbf{Tl}\right]_\equiv$

We obtain that $([\![\_]\!], \iota)$ is a free model of P, which we will denote by F_P. Then, we have the following corollaries:

Theorem 17 (Soundness theorem). *Assume given a program P in $\mathcal{P}$, a goal $\mathbf{G}$ and a model $M = ([\![\_]\!], \iota) : \mathcal{P} \to \mathcal{Q}$. If d is a derivation from $\mathbf{G}$ to $\mathbf{G}'$ with computed answer θ, there exists an arrow $\theta^\sharp [\![\mathbf{G}]\!] \xleftarrow{p} [\![\mathbf{G}']\!]$ in $\mathcal{Q}$, where $p = \mathsf{arrow}(d)$ is defined by induction:*

$$\begin{aligned}
\mathsf{arrow}(\epsilon_{\mathbf{G}}) &= id_{\mathbf{G}} \\
\mathsf{arrow}(d \cdot \langle r, f \rangle) &= r^\sharp(\mathsf{arrow}(d)) \,;\, f \\
\mathsf{arrow}(d \cdot \langle r, t, cl \rangle) &= r^\sharp(\mathsf{arrow}(d)) \,;\, t^\sharp(\iota(cl))
\end{aligned}$$

Theorem 18 (Completeness theorem). *Assume given a program P in $\mathcal{P}$, a free model $M : \mathcal{P} \to \mathcal{Q}$ and goals $\mathbf{G}$, $\mathbf{G}'$ of sort σ. If there is an arrow $f : M(\mathbf{G}) \to M(\mathbf{G}')$ in the fiber $M(\sigma)$ of $\mathcal{Q}$, then there is a simple flat derivation $\mathbf{G}' \overset{d}{\leadsto}{}^* \mathbf{G}$.*

6 Fixpoint Semantics

Assume we have a program $(P, \mathcal{P})$. We have just defined the notions of SLD derivations. Now, we look for a fixpoint operator, similar in spirit to the immediate consequence operator T_P of van Emden and Kowalski [25]. Starting from an interpretation $[\![\_]\!] : \mathcal{P} \to \mathcal{Q}$, our version of T_P gives as a result a new interpretation $[\![\_]\!]' : \mathcal{P} \to \mathcal{Q}$ which, in some way, can be extended to a model of P with more hopes of success than $[\![\_]\!]$.

Our long term objective is the ability to give fixpoint semantics to all of the possible programs in our framework. However, in this paper we will restrict our attention to a subclass of programs which have particular freeness properties.

Definition 19 (Goal Free logic program). *A logic program $(P, \mathcal{P})$ is called* goal free *when there is a set $\{X_1 : \sigma_1, \dots, X_n : \sigma_n\}$ of sorted* generic goals *with the following properties:*

- *$\mathcal{P}$ is obtained from an LP doctrine $\bar{\mathcal{P}}$ by freely adjoining the generic goals to the appropriate fibers of $\bar{\mathcal{P}}$;*
- *there are no clauses targeted at a goal in $\bar{\mathcal{P}}$.*

An instance of a generic goal is called *dynamic goal.* We want to stress here that only the meaning of dynamic goals is modified step after step by the fixpoint construction, while all the goals in $\bar{\mathcal{P}}$ have a fixed meaning. Note that, given $[\![\_]\!] : \mathcal{P} \longrightarrow \mathcal{Q}$, the interpretation of all the dynamic goals only depends from the interpretation of generic goals. Intuitively, dynamic goals are those defined by the program P, and which are modified incrementally by bottom-up approximation. Fixed goals are the built-in predicates contributed by the ambient theory.

Example 20. If P is a program over the syntactic doctrine $\mathcal{P}_\Pi$ of Example 3, then it is goal free. Actually, we can define $\bar{\mathcal{P}} : \mathbb{C}^o \longrightarrow \mathsf{Cat}$ such that

- for each $\sigma \in \mathrm{Obj}(\mathbb{C})$, $\bar{\mathcal{P}}(\sigma) = 0$, i.e. the empty category;
- for each $t \in \mathrm{Mor}(\mathbb{C})$, $\bar{\mathcal{P}}(t) = id_0$.

Then $\mathcal{P}_\Pi$ is obtained by $\bar{P}$ freely adjoining a goal $p(id_\sigma)$ for each $p : \sigma \in \Pi$.

However, if we consider the syntactic doctrine in Example 4, then a program P must not have any arrow targeted at p or $symp$ if it wants to be goal free.

In order to define a fixpoint operator with reasonable properties, we require a more complex categorical structure in the target doctrine $\mathcal{Q}$ than in $\mathcal{P}$.

Definition 21 (Semantic doctrine). *A semantic LP doctrine $\mathcal{Q}$ is an LP doctrine where*

- *fibers have coproducts and canonical colimits of ω-chains;*
- *each reindexing functor $\mathcal{Q}t$ has a left-adjoint $\exists^{\mathcal{Q}}_t$ and preserves on the nose canonical colimits of ω-chains.*

We will drop the superscript $\mathcal{Q}$ from $\exists^{\mathcal{Q}}_t$ when it is clear from the context. If we only work with finite programs, it is enough for fibers to have only finite coproducts.

Example 22. Given a finite product category $\mathbb{C}$, consider the indexed category $\mathcal{Q}$ as defined in Example 6. It is possible to turn $\mathcal{Q}$ into a semantic LP doctrine. Actually:

- each fiber is a complete lattice, hence it has coproducts given by intersection and canonical colimits of ω-chains given by union;
- we can define $\exists^{\mathcal{Q}}_f$, with $f : \rho \longrightarrow \sigma$ as the function which maps an $X \subseteq \mathrm{Hom}_{\mathbb{C}}(1, \rho)$ to
$$\exists^{\mathcal{Q}}_f(X) = \{t\,; f \mid t \in X\} \tag{11}$$
which is a subset of $\mathrm{Hom}_{\mathbb{C}}(1, \sigma)$.

We can prove that all the conditions for semantic doctrines are satisfied.

Now, assume we have an interpretation $[\![\_]\!] = (F, \tau)$ from $\mathcal{P}$ to $\mathcal{Q}$, where $\mathcal{Q}$ is a semantic LP doctrine. We want to build step after step a modified interpretation which is also a model of P. With a single step we move from $[\![\_]\!]$ to $\mathbf{E}_P([\![\_]\!]) = (F, \tau')$ where

$$\begin{aligned} \tau'_{\sigma_i}(X_i) &= [\![X_i]\!] \vee \bigvee_{X_i(t) \leftarrow \mathbf{Tl} \in P} \exists_{Ft} [\![\mathbf{Tl}]\!] \ , \\ \tau'_{\sigma}(X_i(t)) &= t^\sharp(\tau'_{\sigma_i}(X_i)) \ , \end{aligned} \tag{12}$$

while $\tau' = \tau$ restricted to $\bar{\mathcal{P}}$. We should define τ' on arrows but, since there are only identities between dynamic goals, the result is obvious.

In the same way, if δ is an arrow between interpretations, we have $\mathbf{E}_P(\delta) = \delta'$, where

$$\begin{aligned} \delta'_{\sigma_i, X_i} &= \delta_{\sigma_i, X_i} \vee \bigvee_{X_i(t:\rho \longrightarrow \sigma_i) \leftarrow \mathbf{Tl} \in P} \exists_{Ft} \delta_{\rho, \mathbf{Tl}} \ , \\ \delta'_{\sigma, X_i(t)} &= t^\sharp(\delta'_{\sigma_i, X_i}) \ , \\ \delta'_{\sigma, \mathbf{G}} &= \delta_{\sigma, \mathbf{G}} \text{ if } \mathbf{G} \in \mathrm{Obj}(\bar{\mathcal{P}}) \ . \end{aligned} \tag{13}$$

Since the only non-trivial arrows are in $\bar{\mathcal{P}}$ and δ_σ is a natural transformation for each σ, the same can be said of δ'_σ. It follows that $\mathbf{E}_P$ is well defined.

It is interesting to observe that there is a canonical transformation ν between $[\![\_]\!]$ and $\mathbf{E}_P([\![\_]\!])$ given by:

$$\nu_{\sigma_i, X_i} = [\![X_i]\!]_{\sigma_i} \xrightarrow{in} \mathbf{E}([\![\_]\!])_{\sigma_i}(X_i) \ , \tag{14}$$

$$\nu_{\sigma, X_i(t)} = t^\sharp(\iota_{\nu_i, X_i}) \ , \tag{15}$$

$$\nu_{\sigma, \mathbf{G}} = id_{\mathbf{G}} \text{ if } \mathbf{G} \in \mathrm{Obj}(\bar{\mathcal{P}}) \ , \tag{16}$$

where *in* is the appropriate injection. Therefore, we can build an ω-chain

$$[\![\_]\!] \xrightarrow{\nu} \mathbf{E}_P([\![\_]\!]) \xrightarrow{\mathbf{E}_P(\nu)} \mathbf{E}^2_P([\![\_]\!]) \rightarrow \ldots \mathbf{E}^n_P([\![\_]\!]) \xrightarrow{\mathbf{E}^n_P(\nu)} \ldots$$

and we can prove that the colimit $\mathbf{E}^\omega_P([\![\_]\!])$ is a fixpoint for $\mathbf{E}_P$. Finally, we have the following:

Theorem 23. *Given a program $(P, \mathcal{P})$, a semantic LP doctrine $\mathcal{Q}$ and an interpretation $[\![\_]\!] : \mathcal{P} \rightarrow \mathcal{Q}$, then $\mathbf{E}_P$ has a least fixpoint greater than $[\![\_]\!]$. Such a fixpoint can be extended to a model of P in $\mathcal{Q}$.*

Example 24. If we write the definition of $\mathbf{E}_P$ in all the details for the syntactic doctrine in Example 22, we obtain

$$\mathbf{E}_P([\![\_]\!])_{\sigma_i}(X_i) = [\![X_i]\!] \cup \bigcup_{X_i(t) \leftarrow X_j(r)} \{f\,; t \mid f\,; r \in [\![X_j]\!], \mathsf{dom}(f) = 1\} \ , \tag{17}$$

$$\mathbf{E}_P([\![\_]\!])_{\sigma_i}(X_i(t)) = \{f \mid f; t \in [\![\mathbf{Tl}]\!]\} \ . \tag{18}$$

If we work with $\mathbb{C}$ defined by the free algebraic category for a signature Σ, then $\mathbf{E}_P([\![\text{-}]\!])$ becomes equivalent to the standard T_P semantics for logic programs.

Assume $\mathbb{C} = \mathit{Set}$. Moreover, assume we have two predicate symbols $p : \mathbb{N}$ and $\mathsf{true} : 1$ and two clauses $p(\mathsf{succ}\,;\mathsf{succ}) \leftarrow p(id_{\mathbb{N}})$ and $p(0) \leftarrow \mathsf{true}$. Let $[\![\text{-}]\!]$ be the unique interpretation which maps true to $\mathrm{Hom}(1,1)$ and p to $\emptyset$. Then, we can compute successive steps of the $\mathbf{E}_P$ operator starting from $[\![\text{-}]\!]$, obtaining

$$
\begin{aligned}
&\mathbf{E}_P^0([\![\text{-}]\!])(p) = \emptyset \\
&\mathbf{E}_P^1([\![\text{-}]\!])(p) = \{0\} \\
&\mathbf{E}_P^2([\![\text{-}]\!])(p) = \{0, 2\} \\
&\quad\vdots \\
&\mathbf{E}_P^n([\![\text{-}]\!])(p) = \{0, 2, \ldots, 2(n-1)\}
\end{aligned}
\tag{19}
$$

where we identify an arrow $f : 1 \longrightarrow \mathbb{N}$ with $f(\cdot)$, i.e. f applied to the only element of its domain. If we take the colimit of this ω-chain, we have

$$\mathbf{E}_P^\omega([\![\text{-}]\!])(p) = \{f : 1 \longrightarrow \mathbb{N} \mid f(\cdot) \text{ is even }\} \ , \tag{20}$$

which is what we would expect from the intuitive meaning of the program P.

7 An Example: Binary CLP

We are going to show that our categorical framework can handle quite easily the broad class of languages known with the name of *constraint logic programming* [17]. It is evident we need a categorical counterpart of a *constraint system.* We refer to the definition which appears in [22].

Definition 25 (Constraint system). *A* constraint system *over a finite product category $\mathbb{C}$ is an indexed category over $\mathbb{C}$ such that each fiber is a meet semilattice and reindexing functors have left adjoints.*

Now, given a constraint system $\mathcal{D}$ over $\mathbb{C}$, let us denote by $\mathbb{D}$ the corresponding category we obtain by the Grothendieck construction [16]. To be more precise:

- objects of $\mathbb{D}$ are pairs $\langle \sigma, c\rangle$ where $\sigma \in \mathrm{Obj}(\mathbb{C})$ and $c \in \mathrm{Obj}(\mathcal{D}(\sigma))$;
- arrows in $\mathbb{D}$ from $\langle \sigma_1, c_1\rangle$ to $\langle \sigma_2, c_2\rangle$ are given by arrows $f : \sigma_1 \longrightarrow \sigma_2$ in $\mathbb{C}$ such that $c_1 \leq f^\sharp c_2$. We denote such an arrow with $(f, c_1 \leq c_2)$.

Given a predicate signature Π over $\mathbb{C}$, we define a new LP doctrine $\mathcal{P}_\Pi^{\mathcal{D}}$ over $\mathbb{D}$. For each $\langle \sigma, c\rangle$ in $\mathbb{D}$, the corresponding fiber is the discrete category whose objects are of the form $c \,\Box\, p(t)$ with $p : \rho$ in Π and $t : \sigma \longrightarrow \rho$. For each arrow $(f, c_1 \leq c_2)$, the reindexing functor maps $c_2 \,\Box\, p(t)$ to $c_1 \,\Box\, p(f\,; t)$.

Now, we fix a program P. For each goal $c \,\Box\, p_1(f)$ of sort $\langle \sigma, c\rangle$ and clause $c' \,\Box\, p_1(f_1) \xleftarrow{cl} c' \,\Box\, p_2(f_2)$ of sort $\langle \sigma', c'\rangle$, let $\langle r, t\rangle$ be the mgu of f and f_1 in $\mathbb{C}$, and $c'' = r^\sharp c \wedge t^\sharp c'$. Then $\langle (r, c'' \leq c), (t, c'' \leq c_1) \rangle$ is an mgu of $\mathbf{G}$ and cl in $\mathcal{P}_\Pi^{\mathcal{D}}$. We can perform a m.g. SLD step

$$\mathbf{G} \xrightarrow{\langle (r, c'' \leq c), (t, c'' \leq c'), cl \rangle} c'' \,\Box\, p_2(t\,;f_2) \ . \tag{21}$$

As a result, a clause that we typically write as $p_1(t_1) \leftarrow c \,\Box\, p_2(t_2)$, with $p_1(t_1)$, $p_2(t_2)$ and c of sort σ, behaves like a clause $c \,\Box\, p_1(t_1) \leftarrow c \,\Box\, p_2(t_2)$ of sort $\langle \sigma, c \rangle$ in our framework.

We can also build a semantic doctrine $\mathcal{Q}$ over $\mathbb{D}$ such that the fiber corresponding to $\langle \sigma, c \rangle$ is the lattice of downward closed subsets of constraints of sort σ less than c, i.e.

$$\mathcal{Q}(\sigma, c) = \wp_\downarrow \{c' \in \mathrm{Obj}(\mathcal{D}\sigma) \mid c' \leq c\}. \tag{22}$$

Moreover,

$$\mathcal{Q}(f, c_1 \leq c_2)(X) = \downarrow \{c_1 \wedge f^\sharp c \mid c \in X\} \ , \tag{23}$$

$$\exists^{\mathcal{Q}}_{(f, c_1 \leq c_2)}(X) = \downarrow \{\exists^{\mathcal{D}}_f c \mid c \in X\} \ . \tag{24}$$

where $\downarrow Y$ is the downward closure of the set of constraints Y. It is easy to check that these form a pair of adjoint functors and that $\mathcal{Q}$ is indeed a semantic LP doctrine. Therefore, we can compute a fixpoint semantics.

If $\mathbb{C}$ is the algebraic category freely generated by an empty set of function symbols and $\mathcal{D}$ is a constraint system on real numbers, consider the program

$$x^2 = y \,\Box\, p(x) \leftarrow x^2 = y \,\Box\, q(x, y)$$
$$x = 2y \,\Box\, q(x, y) \leftarrow x = 2y \,\Box\, \mathsf{true}$$

where p, q and true are predicate symbols of sort $\langle 1, \top_1 \rangle$, $\langle 2, \top_2 \rangle$ and $\langle 0, \top_0 \rangle$ respectively. Here, 0, 1 and 2 denote the sorts of all the goals of the corresponding arity. Moreover, we assume there is a constraint $\top_i$ for each arity i which is the top of $\mathcal{D}(i)$, preserved by reindexing functors. Assume we start with the interpretation $[\![\text{-}]\!]$ mapping p and q to $\emptyset$ and true to $\mathcal{D}(0)$. Then, by applying the $\mathbf{E}_P$ operator:

$$\begin{aligned} \mathbf{E}_P([\![\text{-}]\!])(q) &= [\![q]\!] \cup \exists_{(id_2, x = 2y \leq \top_2)} [\![x = 2y \,\Box\, \mathsf{true}]\!] \\ &= (!_2, x = 2y)^\sharp \, [\![\mathsf{true}]\!] \\ &= \downarrow \{x = 2y\} \end{aligned} \tag{25}$$

where $!_2$ is the unique arrow from 2 to 0. We also have $\mathbf{E}_P([\![\text{-}]\!])(p) = \emptyset$. At the second step

$$\begin{aligned} \mathbf{E}^2_P([\![\text{-}]\!])(p) &= \mathbf{E}_P([\![\text{-}]\!])(p) \cup \exists_{(\pi^2_1, x^2 = y \leq \top_1)} \mathbf{E}_P([\![\text{-}]\!])(x^2 = y \,\Box\, q(x, y)) \\ &= \exists_{(\pi^2_1, x^2 = y \leq \top_1)} (id_2, x^2 = y \leq \top_2)^\sharp \, \mathbf{E}_P([\![\text{-}]\!])([\![q]\!]) \\ &= \exists_{(\pi^2_1, x^2 = y \leq \top_1)} \downarrow \{x^2 = y \text{ and } x = 2y\} \\ &= \downarrow \{x = 0 \text{ or } x = 1/2\} \end{aligned} \tag{26}$$

where π^2_1 is the projection arrow from 2 to 1. Moreover, $\mathbf{E}^2_P([\![\text{-}]\!])(q) = \mathbf{E}_P([\![\text{-}]\!])(q)$ and we have reached the fixpoint.

8 Conclusions

We have introduced a categorical framework to handle several extensions of logic programming, based on Horn clauses, but interpreted in a context which is not necessarily the Herbrand universe. Typical examples of these languages are CLP [17] and logic programs with built-in or embedded data types [20].

With respect to the stated intentions in Section 1.1, we have not tackled the problem of programs with constraints on goals when it comes to fixpoint semantics. From this point of view, the only advantage offered by our framework is the ability to treat builtins. Goals whose semantics can be modified by clauses (i.e. dynamic goals) must be freely generated as in [13].

Our categorical structures capture pure clausal programs but require the addition of monoidal structure to handle conjunctions of categorical predicates externally. But the addition of monoidal structure is straightforward, and is described in detail in [1].

We briefly sketch the main ideas. We use monoidal LP doctrines, i.e. LP doctrine endowed with a monoidal structure for each fiber which is preserved on the nose by reindexing functors. Given monoidal LP doctrines $\mathcal{P}$ and $\mathcal{Q}$, a monoidal interpretation is an interpretation $(F, \tau) : \mathcal{P} \to \mathcal{Q}$ such that τ_σ preserves on the nose the monoidal structure. This condition means that the semantics of the conjunction is given compositionally. A monoidal model for $(P, \mathcal{P})$ is a monoidal interpretation together with a choice function ι for the clauses in P. We also define a monoidal derivation in the same way as we have done in section 4, but the backchain-clause rule is replaced with the following:

$$\mathbf{G} \xrightarrow{\langle r, t, \mathbf{G}_1, \mathbf{G}_2, cl \rangle} \mathbf{G}_1 \otimes t^\sharp \mathbf{Tl} \otimes \mathbf{G}_2 \tag{27}$$

if $\mathbf{Hd} \xleftarrow{cl} \mathbf{Tl}$ is a clause, $\otimes$ is the monoidal tensor and $r^\sharp \mathbf{G} = \mathbf{G}_1 \otimes t^\sharp \mathbf{Hd} \otimes \mathbf{G}_2$. Again, if we define an appropriate equivalence relation on monoidal derivations, we can build a free monoidal model. Finally, for the fixpoint semantics, everything proceeds as for Section 6, provided that we use monoidal semantic LP doctrines, i.e. a monoidal LP doctrines with the same properties which hold for semantic LP doctrines. We just need to add a pair of conditions to the definition of τ'_σ and δ'_σ in (12) and (13), namely,

$$\tau'_\sigma(\mathbf{G}_1 \otimes_\sigma \mathbf{G}_2) = \tau'_\sigma(\mathbf{G}_1) \otimes \tau'_\sigma(\mathbf{G}_2) \ , \tag{28}$$

$$\delta'_{\sigma, \mathbf{G}_1 \otimes \mathbf{G}_2} = \delta'_{\sigma, \mathbf{G}_1} \otimes \delta'_{\sigma, \mathbf{G}_2} \ . \tag{29}$$

Together with the goal-free condition, we also require that clauses only have atomic goals as heads. Then, all the results we have shown in this paper also hold for the monoidal case.

Finally, note that we can use weaker structure on the fibers, like premonoidal structures, to give an account of selection rules [1].

References

1. G. Amato. *Sequent Calculi and Indexed Categories as a Foundation for Logic Programming*. PhD thesis, Dipartimento di Informatica, Università di Pisa, 2000.
2. K. R. Apt. Introduction to Logic Programming. In J. van Leeuwen, editor, *Handbook of Theoretical Computer Science*, volume B: Formal Models and Semantics, pages 495–574. Elsevier and The MIT Press, 1990.
3. A. Asperti and S. Martini. Projections instead of variables. In G. Levi and M. Martelli, editors, *Proc. Sixth Int'l Conf. on Logic Programming*, pages 337–352. The MIT Press, 1989.
4. R. Barbuti, R. Giacobazzi, and G. Levi. A General Framework for Semantics-based Bottom-up Abstract Interpretation of Logic Programs. *ACM Transactions on Programming Languages and Systems*, 15(1):133–181, 1993.
5. M. Barr and C. Wells. *Category Theory for Computing Science*. Prentice Hall, New York, 1990.
6. A. Bossi, M. Gabbrielli, G. Levi, and M. C. Meo. A Compositional Semantics for Logic Programs. *Theoretical Computer Science*, 122(1–2):3–47, 1994.
7. A. Brogi. *Program Construction in Computational Logic*. PhD thesis, Dipartimento di Informatica, Università di Pisa, 1993.
8. M. Comini, G. Levi, and M. C. Meo. A Theory of Observables for Logic Programs. *Information and Computation*, 169:23–80, 2001.
9. M. Comini, G. Levi, M. C. Meo, and G. Vitiello. Abstract diagnosis. *Journal of Logic Programming*, 39(1-3):43–93, 1999.
10. A. Corradini and A. Asperti. A categorical model for logic programs: Indexed monoidal categories. In *Proceedings REX Workshop '92*. Springer Lectures Notes in Computer Science, 1992.
11. A. Corradini and U. Montanari. An algebraic semantics for structured transition systems and its application to logic programs. *Theoretical Computer Science*, 103(1):51–106, August 1992.
12. P. Cousot and R. Cousot. Abstract Interpretation and Applications to Logic Programs. *Journal of Logic Programming*, 13(2 & 3):103–179, 1992.
13. S. Finkelstein, P. Freyd, and J. Lipton. Logic programming in tau categories. In *Computer Science Logic '94*, volume 933 of *Lecture Notes in Computer Science*, pages 249–263. Springer Verlag, Berlin, 1995.
14. S. Finkelstein, P. Freyd, and J. Lipton. A new framework for declarative programming. To appear in *Theoretical Computer Science*, 2001.
15. P. J. Freyd and A. Scedrov. *Categories, Allegories*. North-Holland, Elsevier Publishers, Amsterdam, 1990.
16. B. Jacobs. *Categorical Logic and Type Theory*. Studies in Logic and the Foundations of Mathematics. North Holland, Elsevier, 1999.
17. J. Jaffar and M. J. Maher. Constraint logic programming: A survey. *Journal of Logic Programming*, 19–20:503–581, 1994.
18. Y. Kinoshita and A. J. Power. A fibrational semantics for logic programs. In R. Dyckhoff, H. Herre, and P. Schroeder-Heister, editors, *Proceedings of the Fifth International Workshop on Extensions of Logic Programming*, volume 1050 of *LNAI*, pages 177–192, Berlin, Mar. 28–30 1996. Springer.
19. A. Kock and G. E. Reyes. Doctrines in categorical logic. In J. Barwise, editor, *Handbook of Mathematical Logic*, pages 283–313. North Holland, 1977.

20. J. Lipton and R. McGrail. Encapsulating data in logic programming via categorical constraints. In C. Palamidessi, H.Glaser, and K. Meinke, editors, *Principles of Declarative Programming*, volume 1490 of *Lecture Notes in Computer Science*, pages 391–410. Springer Verlag, Berlin, 1998.
21. G. Nadathur and D. Miller. An overview of λProlog. In R. A. Kowalski and K. A. Bowen, editors, *Proc. Fifth Int'l Conf. on Logic Programming*, pages 810–827. The MIT Press, 1988.
22. P. Panangaden, V. J. Saraswat, P. J. Scott, and R. A. G. Seely. A Hyperdoctrinal View of Concurrent Constraint Programming. In J. W. de Bakker et al, editor, *Semantics: Foundations and Applications*, volume 666 of *Lecture Notes in Computer Science*, pages 457–475. Springer-Verlag, 1993.
23. D. Rydeheard and R. Burstall. A categorical unification algorithm. In *Category Theory and Computer Programming, LNCS 240*, pages 493–505, Guildford, 1985. Springer Verlag.
24. R. Seely. Hyperdoctrines, Natural Deduction and the Beck Condition. *Zeitschrift für Math. Logik Grundlagen der Math.*, 29(6):505–542, 1983.
25. M. H. van Emden and R. A. Kowalski. The semantics of predicate logic as a programming language. *Journal of the ACM*, 23(4):733–742, 1976.

Functional Logic Programming with Failure: A Set-Oriented View*

F.J. López-Fraguas and J. Sánchez-Hernández

Dep. Sistemas Informáticos y Programación, Univ. Complutense de Madrid
{fraguas,jaime}@sip.ucm.es

Abstract. Finite failure of computations plays an important role as programming construct in the logic programming paradigm, and it has been shown that this also extends to the case of the functional logic programming paradigm. In particular we have considered *CRWLF*, a previous proof-theoretic semantic framework able to deduce negative (failure) information from functional logic programs. The non-deterministic nature of functions considered in *CRWLF* leads naturally to set-valued semantic description of expressions. Here we reformulate the framework to stress that set flavour, both at syntactic and semantic levels. The given approach, for which we obtain equivalence results with respect to the previous one, increases the expressiveness for writing programs and (hopefully) clarifies the understanding of the semantics given to non-deterministic functions, since classical mathematical notions like union of sets or families of sets are used. An important step in the reformulation is a useful program transformation which is proved to be correct within the framework.

1 Introduction

Functional logic programming (*FLP* for short) [7] is a powerful programming paradigm trying to combine into a single language the nicest features of both functional and logic programming styles. Most of the proposals consider some kind of constructor-based rewrite systems as programs and use some kind of narrowing as operational mechanism. There are practical systems, like Curry [8] or $\mathcal{TOY}$ [11], supporting most of the features of functional and logic languages.

There is nevertheless a major aspect of logic programming still not incorporated to existing *FLP* proposals. It is *negation as failure*, a main topic of research in the logic programming field (see [4] for a survey), and a very useful expressive resource for writing logic programs.

There have been a few works devoted to this issue. In [13,14] the work of Stuckey [16] about *constructive negation* is adapted to *FLP*, in strict and lazy versions. A different approach has been followed in [12], where a *C*onstructor *B*ased *Re W*riting *L*ogic with *F*ailure (*CRWLF*) is proposed as a proof-theoretic

* The authors have been partially supported by the Spanish CICYT (project TIC 98-0445-C03-02 'TREND')

R. Nieuwenhuis and A. Voronkov (Eds.): LPAR 2001, LNAI 2250, pp. 455–469, 2001.

semantic framework for failure in *FLP*. Starting from *CRWL* [5,6], a well established theoretical framework for *FLP* including a deduction calculus for reduction, *CRWLF* consists of a new proof calculus able to prove (computable cases of) failure of *CRWL*-provability corresponding to 'finite failure' of reduction. The non-deterministic nature of functions considered in *CRWL* and *CRWLF* leads naturally to set-valued semantic description of expressions. In this paper we reformulate the framework to stress that set flavour, both at syntactic and semantic levels.

The organization of the paper is as follows. We first give some motivations and discuss preliminary examples to help the understanding of the paper. Section 3 presents the *CRWLF* framework. In Section 4 we define and give correctness results for a program transformation which is needed for the rest of the paper. In Section 5 we reformulate in a set-oriented manner the *CRWLF* framework: at the syntactic level we introduce set-constructs like unions or indexed unions; we present a proof calculus for the new programs; we explain how to transform *CRWLF*-programs into this new syntax, and give a strong result of semantic equivalence.

2 Preliminary Discussion

• ***CRWLF* and non-deterministic functions:** *CRWL* [5,6] models reduction by means of a relation $e \to t$, meaning operationally 'the expression e reduces to the term t' or semantically 't is an approximation of e's denotation'. The main technical insight of *CRWLF* was to replace the *CRWL*-statements $e \to t$ by the statements $e \triangleleft \mathcal{C}$, where $\mathcal{C}$ is what we call a *Sufficient Approximation Set* (*SAS*) for e, i.e., a finite set of approximations collected from all the different ways of reducing e to the extent required for the proof in turn. To prove failure of e corresponds to prove $e \triangleleft \{\mathsf{F}\}$, where F is a constant introduced in *CRWLF* to represent failure.

While each proof of *CRWL* concentrates on one particular way of reducing e, *CRWLF* obtains proofs related to all the possible ways of doing it. That the two things are not the same is because *CRWL*-programs are not required to be confluent, therefore defining functions which can be non-deterministic, i.e. yielding, for given arguments, different values coming from different possible reductions. The use of lazy non-deterministic functions is now a standard programming technique in systems like Curry or $\mathcal{TOY}$.

Non-determinism induces some kind of set-valued semantics for functions and expressions. As a simple example, assume the constructors z and s, and consider the non-confluent program:

$$\begin{array}{ll} f(X) = X & add(z, Y) \quad\;\;\; = Y \\ f(X) = s(X) & add(s(X), Y) = s(add(X, Y)) \end{array}$$

For each X, $f(X)$ can be reduced to two possible values, X and $s(X)$. The expression $add(f(z), f(z))$ can be reduced in different ways to obtain three possible values: $z, s(z)$ and $s(s(z))$. This set-valued semantics is reflected in the model semantics of *CRWL*, but not at the level of the proof calculus. *CRWL* is only able to prove separately $add(f(z), f(z)) \rightarrow z$, $add(f(z), f(z)) \rightarrow s(z)$ and $add(f(z), f(z)) \rightarrow s(s(z))$ (and partial approximations like $add(f(z), f(z)) \rightarrow s(\bot)$).

In contrast, the calculus of *CRWLF* is designed to collect sets of values. For instance, to prove failure of the expression $g(add(f(z), f(z)))$, when g is defined by $g(s(s(s(X)))) = z$, *CRWLF* needs to prove $add(f(z), f(z)) \triangleleft \{z, s(z), s(s(z))\}$. One of our main interests in the present work has been to reconsider some aspects of *CRWLF* to emphasize this set-minded view of programs.

• **Call-time choice semantics:** The semantics for non-deterministic functions adopted in *CRWL* is *call-time choice* [9]. Roughly speaking it means: to reduce $f(e_1, \ldots, e_n)$ using a rule of f, first choose one of the possible values of $e_1, \ldots, e_n$ and then apply the rule. Consider for instance the function $double(X) = add(X, X)$, and the expression $double(f(z))$, where f is the non-deterministic function defined above. The values for $double(f(z))$ come from picking a value for $f(z)$ and then applying the rule for *double*, obtaining then only two values, z and $s(s(z))$, but not $s(z)$.

To understand the fact that $double(f(z))$ and $add(f(z), f(z))$ are not the same in call-time choice, one must think that in the definition of *double* the variable X ranges over the universe of values (constructor terms), and not over the universe of expressions, which in general represent sets of values. This corresponds nicely to the classical view of functions in mathematics: if we define $double(n) = add(n, n)$ for natural numbers (values), then the equation $double(A) = add(A, A)$ is not valid for sets A of natural numbers, according to the usual definition of application of a function f to a subset of its domain: $f(A) = \{f(x) \mid x \in A\}$. In fact, we have $double(\{0,1\}) = \{double(x) \mid x \in \{0,1\}\} = \{0,2\}$, while $add(\{0,1\}, \{0,1\}) = \{add(x,y) \mid x \in \{0,1\}, y \in \{0,1\}\} = \{0,1,2\}$ That is, mathematical practice follows call-time semantics.

The use of classical set notation can clarify the reading of expressions. For instance, instead of $double(f(z))$ we can write $\bigcup_{X \in f(z)} double(X)$. These kind of set-based changes in syntax is one of our contributions.

• **Overlapping programs:** To write programs in a set-oriented style we find the problem that different values for a function application can be spread out through different rules. This is not the case of non-overlapping rules, and the case of rules with identical (or variant) heads is also not problematic, since the rules can be merged into a single one: for the function f above, we can write $f(X) = \{X\} \cup \{s(X)\}$. The problem comes with definitions like $l(z, z) = z$, $l(z, X) = s(z)$, where the heads overlap but are not variants. To avoid such situations Antoy introduces in [3] the class of *overlapping inductively sequential* programs and proposes in [1] a transformation from general programs to that format. We consider also this class of programs when switching to set-oriented syntax, and propose a transformation with a better behavior than that of [1].

3 The *CRWLF* Framework

The *CRWLF* calculus that we show here is a slightly modified version of that in [12], in two aspects. First, for the sake of simplicity we have only considered programs with unconditional rules. Second, in [12] programs were 'positive', not making use of failure inside them. Here we allow programs to use a 'primitive' function *fails*(_) intended to be *true* when its argument fails to be reduced, and *false* otherwise. This behavior of *fails* is determined explicitly in the proof calculus.

The function *fails* is quite an expressive resource. As an application we show by an example how to express *default rules* in function definitions.

Example 1. In many pure functional systems pattern matching determines *the* applicable rule for a function call, and as rules are tried from top to bottom, default rules are implicit in the definitions. In fact, the $n+1$-th rule in a definition is only applied if the first n rules are not applicable. For example, assume the following definition for the function f:

$$f(z) = z \qquad f(X) = s(z)$$

The evaluation of the expression $f(z)$ in a functional language (like Haskell [15]), will produce the value z by the first rule. The second rule is not used for evaluating $f(z)$, even if pattern matching would succeed if the rule would be considered individually. This contrasts with functional logic languages (like Curry [8] or $\mathcal{TOY}$ [11]) which try to preserve the declarative reading of each rule. In such systems the expression $f(z)$ would be reduced, by applying in a non-deterministic way any of the rules, to the values z and $s(z)$.

To achieve the effect of default rules in *FLP*, an explicit syntactical construction *'default'* can be introduced, as suggested in [13]. The function f could be defined as:

$$\begin{array}{l} f(z) = z \\ default\ f(X) = s(z) \end{array}$$

The intuitive operational meaning is: to reduce a call to f proceed with the first rule for f; if the reduction fails then try the default rule. Using the function *ifThen* (defined as $ifThen(true, X) = X$) and the predefined function *fails*, we can transform the previous definition into:

$$\begin{array}{l} f(X) = f'(X) \\ f(X) = ifThen(fails(f'(X)), s(z)) \end{array} \qquad f'(z) = z$$

This definition achieves the expected behavior for f without losing the equational meaning of rules.

3.1 Technical Preliminaries

We assume a signature $\Sigma = DC_\Sigma \cup FS_\Sigma \cup \{fails\}$ where $DC_\Sigma = \bigcup_{n \in \mathbb{N}} DC^n_\Sigma$ is a set of *constructor* symbols containing at least $true$ and $false$, $FS_\Sigma = \bigcup_{n \in \mathbb{N}} FS^n_\Sigma$

is a set of *function* symbols, all of them with associated arity and such that $DC_\Sigma \cap FS_\Sigma = \emptyset$, and *fails* $\notin DC \cup FS$ (with arity 1). We also assume a countable set $\mathcal{V}$ of *variable* symbols. We write $Term_\Sigma$ for the set of (total) *terms* (we say also *expressions*) built over Σ and $\mathcal{V}$ in the usual way, and we distinguish the subset $CTerm_\Sigma$ of (total) constructor terms or (total) *cterms*, which only make use of DC_Σ and $\mathcal{V}$. The subindex Σ will be usually omitted. Terms intend to represent possibly reducible expressions, while cterms represent data values, not further reducible.

We will need sometimes to use the signature $\Sigma_\perp$ which is the result of extending Σ with the new constant (0-arity constructor) $\perp$, that plays the role of the undefined value. Over $\Sigma_\perp$, we can build the sets $Term_\perp$ and $CTerm_\perp$ of (partial) terms and (partial) cterms respectively. Partial cterms represent the result of partially evaluated expressions; thus, they can be seen as approximations to the value of expressions. The signature $\Sigma_{\perp,\mathsf{F}}$ results of adding to $\Sigma_\perp$ a new constant F, to express failure of reduction. The sets $Term_{\perp,\mathsf{F}}$ and $CTerm_{\perp,\mathsf{F}}$ are defined in the natural way.

We will use three kind of substitutions $CSubst, CSubst_\perp$ and $CSubst_{\perp,\mathsf{F}}$ defined as applications from $\mathcal{V}$ into $CTerm, CTerm_\perp$ and $CTerm_{\perp,\mathsf{F}}$ respectively.

As usual notations we will write $X, Y, Z, ...$ for variables, c, d for constructor symbols, f, g for functions, e for terms and s, t for cterms. In all cases, primes (') and subindices can be used.

Given a set of constructor symbols D, we say that the terms t and t' have an *D-clash* if they have different constructor symbols of D at the same position.

A natural *approximation ordering* $\sqsubseteq$ over $Term_{\perp,\mathsf{F}}$ can be defined as the least partial ordering over $Term_{\perp,\mathsf{F}}$ satisfying the following properties:

- $\perp \sqsubseteq e$ for all $e \in Term_{\perp,\mathsf{F}}$,
- $h(e_1, ..., e_n) \sqsubseteq h(e'_1, ..., e'_n)$, if $e_i \sqsubseteq e'_i$ for all $i \in \{1, ..., n\}$, $h \in DC \cup FS \cup \{fails\} \cup \{\mathsf{F}\}$

The intended meaning of $e \sqsubseteq e'$ is that e is less defined or has less information than e'. Notice that according to this F is maximal. Two expressions $e, e' \in Term_{\perp,\mathsf{F}}$ are *consistent* if there exists $e'' \in Term_{\perp,\mathsf{F}}$ such that $e \sqsubseteq e''$ and $e' \sqsubseteq e''$.

We extend the order $\sqsubseteq$ and the notion of consistency to sets of terms: given $\mathcal{C}, \mathcal{C}' \in CTerm_{\perp,\mathsf{F}}$, $\mathcal{C} \sqsubseteq \mathcal{C}'$ if for all $t \in \mathcal{C}$ there exists $t' \in \mathcal{C}'$ with $t \sqsubseteq t'$ and for all $t' \in \mathcal{C}'$ there exists $t \in \mathcal{C}$ with $t \sqsubseteq t'$. The sets $\mathcal{C}, \mathcal{C}'$ are consistent if there exists $\mathcal{C}''$ such that $\mathcal{C} \sqsubseteq \mathcal{C}''$ and $\mathcal{C}' \sqsubseteq \mathcal{C}''$.

A *CRWLF*-program $\mathcal{P}$ is a set of rewrite rules of the form $f(\bar{t}) \to e$, where $f \in FS^n$; $\bar{t}$ is a linear tuple (each variable in it occurs only once) of cterms; $e \in Term$ and $var(e) \subseteq var(\bar{t})$. We say that $f(\bar{t})$ is the *head* and e is the *body* of the rule. We write $\mathcal{P}_f$ for the set of defining rules of f in $\mathcal{P}$.

To express call-time choice, the calculus of the next section uses the set of c-instances of a rule R, defined as $[R]_{\perp,\mathsf{F}} = \{R\theta \mid \theta \in CSubst_{\perp,\mathsf{F}}\}$.

3.2 The Proof Calculus *CRWLF*

The proof calculus *CRWLF* defines the relation $e \triangleleft \mathcal{C}$ where $e \in Term_{\perp,\mathsf{F}}$ and $\mathcal{C} \subseteq CTerm_{\perp,\mathsf{F}}$; we say that $\mathcal{C}$ is a *Sufficient Approximation Set* (*SAS*) for the expression e. A *SAS* is a finite approximation to the denotation of an expression. For example, if f is defined as $f(X) \to X$, $f(X) \to s(X)$, then we have the sets $\{\perp\}$, $\{z, \perp\}$, $\{z, s(\perp)\}$, $\{\perp, s(\perp)\}$, $\{\perp, s(z)\}$ and $\{z, s(z)\}$ as finite approximations to the denotation of $f(z)$.

Table 1. Rules for *CRWLF*-provability

(1) $\dfrac{}{e \triangleleft \{\perp\}}$ $\quad e \in Term_{\perp,\mathsf{F}}$

(2) $\dfrac{}{X \triangleleft \{X\}}$ $\quad X \in \mathcal{V}$

(3) $\dfrac{e_1 \triangleleft \mathcal{C}_1 \quad ... \quad e_n \triangleleft \mathcal{C}_n}{c(e_1, ..., e_n) \triangleleft \{c(\overline{t}) \mid \overline{t} \in \mathcal{C}_1 \times ... \times \mathcal{C}_n\}}$ $\quad c \in DC^n \cup \{\mathsf{F}\}$

(4) $\dfrac{e_1 \triangleleft \mathcal{C}_1 \quad ... \quad e_n \triangleleft \mathcal{C}_n \quad ... \quad f(\overline{t}) \triangleleft_R \mathcal{C}_{R,\overline{t}} \quad ...}{f(e_1, ..., e_n) \triangleleft \mu(\bigcup_{R \in \mathcal{P}_f, \overline{t} \in \mathcal{C}_1 \times ... \times \mathcal{C}_n} \mathcal{C}_{R,\overline{t}})}$ $\quad f \in FS^n$

(5) $\dfrac{}{f(\overline{t}) \triangleleft_R \{\perp\}}$

(6) $\dfrac{e \triangleleft \mathcal{C}}{f(\overline{t}) \triangleleft_R \mathcal{C}}$ $\quad (f(\overline{t}) \to e) \in [R]_{\perp,\mathsf{F}}$

(7) $\dfrac{}{f(t_1, ..., t_n) \triangleleft_R \{F\}}$ $\quad R \equiv (f(s_1, ..., s_n) \to e), t_i$ and s_i have a $DC \cup \{\mathsf{F}\}$-clash for some $i \in \{1, ..., n\}$

(8) $\dfrac{e \triangleleft \{\mathsf{F}\}}{fails(e) \triangleleft \{true\}}$

(9) $\dfrac{e \triangleleft \mathcal{C}}{fails(e) \triangleleft \{false\}}$ $\quad t \in \mathcal{C}, t \neq \perp, t \neq \mathsf{F}$

Rules for *CRWLF*-provability are shown in Table 1. Rules 1 to 7 are the restriction of the calculus in [12] to unconditional programs. Rules 8 and 9 define the function *fails* according to the specification given in Sect. 3.

The auxiliary relation $\triangleleft_R$ used in rule 4 depends on a particular program rule R, and is defined in rules 5 to 7. The function μ in rule 4 is a simplification function for *SAS*'s to delete irrelevant occurrences of F. It is defined as $\mu(\{\mathsf{F}\}) = \{\mathsf{F}\}$; $\mu(\mathcal{C}) = \mathcal{C} - \{\mathsf{F}\}$ otherwise (see [12] for a justification).

Given a program $\mathcal{P}$ and an expression e, we write $\mathcal{P} \vdash_{CRWLF} e \triangleleft \mathcal{C}$ to express that the relation $e \triangleleft \mathcal{C}$ is provable with respect to *CRWLF* and the program $\mathcal{P}$. The *denotation* of e is defined as $[\![e]\!]^{CRWLF} = \{\mathcal{C} \mid \mathcal{P} \vdash_{CRWLF} e \triangleleft \mathcal{C}\}$. Notice that the denotation of an expression is a set of sets of partial values. For the function f above we have $[\![f(z)]\!]^{CRWLF} = \{\{\perp\}, \{z, \perp\}, \{z, s(\perp)\}, \{\perp, s(\perp)\}, \{\perp, s(z)\}, \{z, s(z)\}\}$

The calculus *CRWLF* verifies the following properties:

Proposition 1. *Let $\mathcal{P}$ be a CRWLF-program. Then:*

a) **Consistency of SAS's:** $\mathcal{P} \vdash_{CRWLF} e \lhd \mathcal{C}, e \lhd \mathcal{C}' \Rightarrow \mathcal{C}$ *and* $\mathcal{C}'$ *are consistent. Moreover, there exists* $\mathcal{C}''$ *such that* $\mathcal{P} \vdash_{CRWLF} e \lhd \mathcal{C}''$, *with* $\mathcal{C} \sqsubseteq \mathcal{C}''$ *and* $\mathcal{C}' \sqsubseteq \mathcal{C}''$.
b) **Monotonicity:** $e \sqsubseteq e'$ *and* $\mathcal{P} \vdash_{CRWLF} e \lhd \mathcal{C} \Rightarrow \mathcal{P} \vdash_{CRWLF} e' \lhd \mathcal{C}$
c) **Total Substitutions:** $\mathcal{P} \vdash_{CRWLF} e \lhd \mathcal{C} \Rightarrow \mathcal{P} \vdash_{CRWLF} e\theta \lhd \mathcal{C}\theta$, *for* $\theta \in CSubst$.

These properties can be understood in terms of information. As we have seen, in general we can obtain different *SAS*'s for the same expression corresponding to different degrees of evaluation. Nevertheless, **Consistency** ensures that any two *SAS*'s for a given expression can be refined to a common one. **Monotonicity** says that the information that can be extracted from an expression can not decrease when we add information to the expression itself. And **Total Substitutions** shows that provability in *CRWLF* is closed under total substitutions.

4 Overlapping Inductively Sequential Programs

In [3], Antoy introduces the notion of *O*verlapping *I*nductively *S*equential programs (*OIS*-programs) based on the idea of definitional trees [2]. We give here an equivalent but slightly different definition.

Definition 1 (*OIS-CRWLF*-Programs). *A CRWLF-program is called* overlapping inductively sequential *if every pair of rules* $f(\overline{t}_1) \to e_1, f(\overline{t}_2) \to e_2$ *satisfies: the heads* $f(\overline{t}_1)$ *and* $f(\overline{t}_2)$ *are unifiable iff they are the same up to variable renaming.*

We next see that every *CRWLF*-program can be transformed into a semantically equivalent *OIS-CRWLF*-program.

4.1 Transformation of *CRWLF*-Programs into *OIS-CRWLF*-Programs

We need some usual terminologies about positions in terms. A position u in a term e is a sequence of positive integers $p_1 \cdot ... \cdot p_m$ that identifies the symbol of e at position u. We write $VP(e)$ for the set of positions in e occupied by variables. We say that a position u is *demanded by a rule* $f(\overline{t}) \to e$ if the head $f(\overline{t})$ has a constructor symbol of DC at position u. Given a set of rules $\mathcal{Q}$ and a position u, we say that u is *demanded* by $\mathcal{Q}$ if u is demanded by some rule of $\mathcal{Q}$, and we say that u is *uniformly demanded* by $\mathcal{Q}$ if it is demanded by all rules of $\mathcal{Q}$.

Definition 2 (Transformation of Sets of Rules). *The transformation algorithm is specified by a function* $\Delta(\mathcal{Q}, f(\overline{s}))$ *where:*

- $\mathcal{Q} = \{(f(\overline{t}_1) \to e_1), ..., (f(\overline{t}_n) \to e_n)\}$
- $f(\overline{s})$ *a* **pattern compatible with** $\mathcal{Q}$, *i.e.,* $\overline{s}$ *is a linear tuple of cterms and for all* $i \in \{1, ..., n\}$, $f(\overline{s})$ *is more general than* $f(\overline{t}_i)$ *(i.e.,* $\overline{s}\theta = \overline{t}_i$, *for some* $\theta \in CSubst$*).*

Δ is defined by the following three cases:

1. **Some position u in $VP(f(\overline{s}))$ is uniformly demanded by $\mathcal{Q}$** *(if there are several, choose any).*
   Let X be the variable at position u in $f(\overline{s})$. Let $C = \{c_1, ..., c_k\}$ be the set of constructor symbols at position u in the heads of the rules of $\mathcal{Q}$ and $\overline{s}_{c_i} = \overline{s}[X/c_i(\overline{Y})]$, where $\overline{Y}$ is a m-tuple of fresh variables (assuming $c_i \in DC^m$). For each $i \in \{1, ..., k\}$ we define the set $\mathcal{Q}_{c_i}$ as the set of rules of $\mathcal{Q}$ demanding c_i at position u.
   Return $\Delta(\mathcal{Q}_{c_1}, f(\overline{s}_{c_1})) \cup ... \cup \Delta(\mathcal{Q}_{c_k}, f(\overline{s}_{c_k}))$
2. **Some position in $VP(f(\overline{s}))$ is demanded by $\mathcal{Q}$, but none is uniformly demanded.**
   Let $u_1, ..., u_k$ be the demanded positions (ordered by any criterion). Consider the following partition (with renaming of function names in heads) over $\mathcal{Q}$:
   • *Let $\mathcal{Q}^{u_1}$ be the subset of rules of $\mathcal{Q}$ demanding position u_1, where the function symbol f of the heads has been replaced by f^{u_1}, and $\overline{\mathcal{Q}^{u_1}} = \mathcal{Q} - \mathcal{Q}^{u_1}$.*
   • *Let $\mathcal{Q}^{u_2}$ be the subset of rules of $\overline{\mathcal{Q}^{u_1}}$ demanding position u_2, where the function symbol f of the heads have been replaced by f^{u_2} and let $\overline{\mathcal{Q}^{u_2}} = \overline{\mathcal{Q}^{u_1}} - \mathcal{Q}^{u_2}$.*
   ...
   • *Let $\mathcal{Q}^{u_k}$ be the subset of rules $\overline{\mathcal{Q}^{u_{k-1}}}$ demanding position u_k, where the function symbol f of the heads have been replaced by f^{u_k}.*
   • *And let $\mathcal{Q}^0$ be the subset of rules of $\mathcal{Q}$ that do not demand any position.*
   Return $\mathcal{Q}^0 \cup \{f(\overline{s}) \to f^{u_1}(\overline{s}), ..., f(\overline{s}) \to f^{u_k}(\overline{s})\} \cup \Delta(\mathcal{Q}^{u_1}, f^{u_1}(\overline{s})) \cup ... \cup \Delta(\mathcal{Q}^{u_k}, f^{u_k}(\overline{s}))$

3. **No position in $VP(f(\overline{s}))$ is demanded by $\mathcal{Q}$,** *then* **Return** $\mathcal{Q}$

The initial call for transforming the defining rules of f will be $\Delta(\mathcal{P}_f, f(\overline{X}))$, and a generic call will have the form $\Delta(\mathcal{Q}, f^N(\overline{s}))$, where $\mathcal{Q}$ is a set of rules and $f^N(\overline{s})$ is a pattern compatible with $\mathcal{Q}$. We illustrate this transformation by an example:

Example 2. Consider the constants a, b and c and a function defined by the set of rules $\mathcal{P}_f = \{f(a, X) \to a, f(a, b) \to b, f(b, a) \to a\}$. To obtain the corresponding *OIS*-set of rules the algorithm works in this way:

$$\underbrace{\Delta(\{f(a,X) \to a, f(a,b) \to b, f(b,a) \to a\}, f(Y,Z))}_{\text{by 1}} =$$

$$\underbrace{\Delta(\{f(a,X) \to a, f(a,b) \to b\}, f(a,Z))}_{\text{by 2}} \cup \underbrace{\Delta(\{f(b,a) \to a\}, f(b,Z))}_{\text{by 1}} =$$

$$\{f(a,X) \to a\} \cup \{f(a,Z) \to f^2(a,Z)\} \cup \underbrace{\Delta(\{f^2(a,b) \to b\}, f(a,Z))}_{\text{by 1}} \cup$$

$$\underbrace{\Delta(\{f(b,a) \to a\}, f(b,a))}_{\text{by 3}} =$$

$$\{f(a,X) \to a\} \cup \{f(a,Z) \to f^2(a,Z)\} \cup \underbrace{\Delta(\{f^2(a,b) \to b\}, f(a,b))}_{\text{by 3}} \cup \{f(b,a) \to a\} =$$

$\{f(a,X) \to a\} \cup \{f(a,Z) \to f^2(a,Z)\} \cup \{f^2(a,b) \to b\} \cup \{f(b,a) \to a\} =$
$\{f(a,X) \to a, f(a,Z) \to f^2(a,Z), f(b,a) \to a, f^2(a,b) \to b\}$

Our transformation is quite related to the actual construction of the definitional tree [2,10] of a function. A different algorithm to obtain an *OIS*-set of rules from a general set of rules is described in [1]. For the example above, such algorithm provides the following set of rules:

$$f(X,Y) \to f_1(X,Y) \mid f_2(X,Y) \qquad \begin{array}{l} f_1(a,Y) \to a \\ f_2(a,b) \;\; \to b \end{array} \qquad f_2(b,a) \to a$$

where the symbol '|' stands for a choice between two alternatives. This transformed set is worse than the one obtained by our transformation: for evaluating a call to f it begins with a search with two alternatives f_1 and f_2, even when it is not needed. For example, for evaluating $f(b,a)$, it tries both alternatives, but this reduction corresponds to a deterministic computation with the original program and also with our transformed one. The situation is clearly unpleasant if instead of b, we consider an expression e with a costly reduction to b.

Definition 3 (Transformation of Programs). *Given a CRWLF-program $\mathcal{P}$ we define the transformed program $\Delta(\mathcal{P})$ as the union of the transformed sets of defining rules for the functions defined in $\mathcal{P}$.*

It is easy to check that $\Delta(\mathcal{P})$ is indeed an *OIS-CRWLF*-program, and that $\Delta(\mathcal{P}) = \mathcal{P}$ if $\mathcal{P}$ is already an *OIS-CRWLF*-program.

Theorem 1 (Correctness of the Transformation). *For every CRWLF-program $\mathcal{P}$, $\Delta(\mathcal{P})$ is an OIS-CRWLF-program satisfying: for every $e \in Term_{\perp,\mathsf{F}}$ built over the signature of $\mathcal{P}$, $\mathcal{P} \vdash_{CRWLF} e \triangleleft \mathcal{C} \Leftrightarrow \Delta(\mathcal{P}) \vdash_{CRWLF} e \triangleleft \mathcal{C}$.*

5 A Set Oriented View of *CRWLF*: $\widehat{CRWLF}$

In this section we introduce the notion of **sas-expression** as a syntactical construction, close to classical set notation, that provides a clear "intuitive semantics" for the denotation of an expression.

5.1 Sas-Expressions

A sas-expression is intended as a construction for collecting values. These values may either appear explicitly in the construction or they can be eventually obtained by reducing function calls. Formally, a sas-expression $\mathcal{S}$ is defined as:

$$\mathcal{S} ::= \{t\} \mid \bigcup_{X \in f(\bar{t})} \mathcal{S}_1 \mid \bigcup_{X \in fails(\mathcal{S}_1)} \mathcal{S}_2 \mid \bigcup_{X \in \mathcal{S}_1} \mathcal{S}_2 \mid \mathcal{S}_1 \cup \mathcal{S}_2$$

where $t \in CTerm_{\perp,\mathsf{F}}$, $\bar{t} \in CTerm_{\perp,\mathsf{F}} \times ... \times CTerm_{\perp,\mathsf{F}}$, $f \in FS^n$ and $\mathcal{S}_1, \mathcal{S}_2$ are sas-expressions.

The variable X in $\bigcup_{X \in \mathcal{S}_1} \mathcal{S}_2$ is called a produced variable. We can define formally the set $pvar(\mathcal{S})$ of **produced variables** of a sas-expression $\mathcal{S}$ as:

- $pvar(\{t\}) = \emptyset$
- $pvar(\bigcup_{X \in f(\overline{t})} \mathcal{S}) = \{X\} \cup pvar(\mathcal{S})$
- $pvar(\bigcup_{X \in fails(\mathcal{S}_1)} \mathcal{S}_2) = \{X\} \cup pvar(\mathcal{S}_1) \cup pvar(\mathcal{S}_2)$
- $pvar(\bigcup_{X \in \mathcal{S}_1} \mathcal{S}_2) = \{X\} \cup pvar(\mathcal{S}_1) \cup pvar(\mathcal{S}_2)$
- $pvar(\mathcal{S}_1 \cup \mathcal{S}_2) = pvar(\mathcal{S}_1) \cup pvar(\mathcal{S}_2)$

A sas-expression $\mathcal{S}$ is called **admissible** if it satisfies the following properties:

- if $\mathcal{S} = \mathcal{S}_1 \cup \mathcal{S}_2$ then it must be $(var(\mathcal{S}_1) - pvar(\mathcal{S}_1)) \cap pvar(\mathcal{S}_2) = \emptyset$, and conversely $(var(\mathcal{S}_2) - pvar(\mathcal{S}_2)) \cap pvar(\mathcal{S}_1) = \emptyset$. The aim of this condition is to express that a variable can not appear in both $\mathcal{S}_1$ and $\mathcal{S}_2$ as produced and as not-produced variable.
- if $\mathcal{S} = \bigcup_{X \in r} \mathcal{S}$ then $X \notin var(r) \cup pvar(\mathcal{S})$ and $var(r) \cap pvar(\mathcal{S}) = \emptyset$

In the following we write $SasExp$ for the set of admissible sas-expressions.

We now define substitutions for non-produced variables.

Definition 4 (Substitutions for Sas-Expressions). *Given $\mathcal{S} \in SasExp$, $Y \notin pvar(\mathcal{S})$ and $s \in CTerm_{\bot,\mathsf{F}}$, the* **substitution** *$\mathcal{S}[Y/s]$ is defined on the structure of $\mathcal{S}$ as:*

- $\{t\}[Y/s] = \{t[Y/s]\}$
- $(\bigcup_{X \in f(\overline{t})} \mathcal{S}_1)[Y/s] = \bigcup_{X \in f(\overline{t})[Y/s]} \mathcal{S}_1[Y/s]$
- $(\bigcup_{X \in fails(\mathcal{S}_1)} \mathcal{S}_2)[Y/s] = \bigcup_{X \in fails(\mathcal{S}_1[Y/s])} \mathcal{S}_2[Y/s]$
- $(\bigcup_{X \in \mathcal{S}_1} \mathcal{S}_2)[Y/s] = \bigcup_{X \in \mathcal{S}_1[Y/s]} \mathcal{S}_2[Y/s]$
- $(\mathcal{S}_1 \cup \mathcal{S}_2)[Y/s] = \mathcal{S}_1[Y/s] \cup \mathcal{S}_2[Y/s]$

The expression $\mathcal{S}\theta$, where $\theta = [Y_1/s_1]...[Y_k/s_k]$, stands for the successive application of the substitutions $[Y_1/s_1], ..., [Y_k/s_k]$ to $\mathcal{S}$.

We will also use **set-substitutions** *for sas-expressions: given a set $\mathcal{C} = \{s_1, ..., s_n\} \in CTerm_{\bot,\mathsf{F}}$ we will write $\mathcal{S}[Y/\mathcal{C}]$ as a shorthand for the distribution $\mathcal{S}[Y/s_1] \cup ... \cup \mathcal{S}[Y/s_n]$.*

In order to simplify some expressions, we also introduce the following notation: given $h \in DC^n \cup FS^n$ and $\mathcal{C} = \{t_1, ..., t_m\} \subseteq CTerm_{\bot,\mathsf{F}}$, we will write $h(e_1, ..., e_{i-1}, \mathcal{C}, e_{i+1}, ..., e_n) \lhd \mathcal{C}'$ as a shorthand for $\mathcal{C}' = \mathcal{C}_1 \cup ... \cup \mathcal{C}_m$, where $h(e_1, ..., e_{i-1}, t_1, e_{i+1}, ..., e_n) \lhd \mathcal{C}_1$,..., $h(e_1, ..., e_{i-1}, t_m, e_{i+1}, ..., e_n) \lhd \mathcal{C}_m$. We will also use a generalized version of this notation and write $h(\mathcal{C}_1, ..., \mathcal{C}_n) \lhd \mathcal{C}$, where $\mathcal{C}_1, ..., \mathcal{C}_n \in CTerm_{\bot,\mathsf{F}}$.

5.2 Terms as Sas-Expressions

In this section we precise how to convert expressions into the set-oriented syntax of sas-expressions.

Definition 5 (Conversion into Sas-Expressions). *The sas-expression $\widehat{e}$ corresponding to $e \in Term_{\bot,\mathsf{F}}$ is defined inductively as follows:*

- $\widehat{X} = \{X\}$
- $\widehat{c(e_1, ..., e_n)} = \bigcup_{X_1 \in \widehat{e_1}} \cdots \bigcup_{X_n \in \widehat{e_n}} \{c(X_1, ..., X_n)\}$, *for every* $c \in DC^n \cup \{\perp, \text{F}\}$, *where the variables* $X_1, ..., X_n$ *are fresh.*
- $\widehat{f(e_1, ..., e_n)} = \bigcup_{X_1 \in \widehat{e_1}} \cdots \bigcup_{X_n \in \widehat{e_n}} \bigcup_{X \in f(X_1,...,X_n)} \{X\}$, *for every* $f \in FS^n$, *where the variables* $X_1, ..., X_n$ *and* X *are fresh.*
- $\widehat{fails(e)} = \bigcup_{X \in fails(\widehat{e})} \{X\}$, *where the variable* X *is fresh.*

As an example of conversion we have

$$\widehat{double(f(X))} = \bigcup_{Y \in \widehat{f(X)}} \bigcup_{Z \in double(Y)} \{Z\} =$$
$$\bigcup_{Y \in \bigcup_{Y_1 \in \{X\}} \bigcup_{Y_2 \in f(Y_1)} \{Y_2\}} \bigcup_{Z \in double(Y)} \{Z\}$$

This expression could be simplified to the shorter one $\bigcup_{Y \in f(X)} \bigcup_{Z \in double(Y)} \{Z\}$, but this is not needed for our purposes and we do not insist in that issue.

The set-based syntax of sas-expressions results in another benefit from the point of view of expressiveness. The notation $\bigcup_{X \in \mathcal{S}} \mathcal{S}'$ is a construct that binds the variable X and generalizes the sharing-role of (non-recursive) local definitions of functional programs. For instance, an expression like $\bigcup_{Y \in f(X)} \{c(Y, Y)\}$ expresses the sharing of $f(X)$ through the two occurrences of Y in $c(Y, Y)$. The same expression using typical *let* notation would be *let* $Y = f(X)$ *in* $c(Y, Y)$.

5.3 Denotational Semantics for Sas-Expressions: $\widehat{CRWLF}$

In this section we present the proof calculus $\widehat{CRWLF}$ for sas-expressions. This calculus is defined for programs with a set oriented notation. The idea is to start with a *CRWLF*-program $\mathcal{P}$, transform it into an *OIS-CRWLF*-program $\Delta(\mathcal{P})$ and then, transform the last into a $\widehat{CRWLF}$-program $\widehat{\Delta(\mathcal{P})}$, obtained by joining the rules with identical heads into a single rule whose body is a sas-expression obtained from the bodies of the corresponding rules. We have proved in Sect. 4 that the first transformation preserves the semantics. In this section we prove the same for the last one, obtaining then a strong equivalence between *CRWLF* and $\widehat{CRWLF}$.

Definition 6 ($\widehat{CRWLF}$**-Programs).** *A* $\widehat{CRWLF}$*-Program* $\widehat{\mathcal{P}}$ *is a set of* **non-overlapping** *rules of the form:* $f(\overline{t}) \twoheadrightarrow \mathcal{S}$*, where* $f \in FS^n$*;* $\overline{t}$ *is a linear tuple (each variable occurs only once) of cterms;* $s \in SasExp$ *and* $(var(\mathcal{S}) - pvar(\mathcal{S})) \subseteq var(\overline{t})$*. Non-overlapping means that there is not any pair of rules with unifiable heads in* $\widehat{\mathcal{P}}$*.*

According to this definition, it is easy to obtain the corresponding $\widehat{CRWLF}$-program $\widehat{\mathcal{P}}$ from a given *OIS-CRWLF*-program $\mathcal{P}$:

$$\widehat{\mathcal{P}} = \{f(\overline{t}) \twoheadrightarrow \widehat{e_1} \cup ... \cup \widehat{e_n} \mid f(\overline{t}) \rightarrow e_1, ..., f(\overline{t}) \rightarrow e_n \in \mathcal{P}$$
$$\text{and there is not any other rule in } \mathcal{P} \text{ with head } f(\overline{t})\}$$

Table 2. Rules for $\widehat{CRWLF}$-provability

$$(1)\ \frac{}{\mathcal{S} \mathrel{\hat{\triangleleft}} \{\perp\}}\quad \mathcal{S} \in SasExp \qquad\qquad (2)\ \frac{}{\{X\} \mathrel{\hat{\triangleleft}} \{X\}}\quad X \in \mathcal{V}$$

$$(3)\ \frac{t_1 \mathrel{\hat{\triangleleft}} \mathcal{C}_1 \quad t_n \mathrel{\hat{\triangleleft}} \mathcal{C}_n}{\{c(t_1,...,t_n)\} \mathrel{\hat{\triangleleft}} \{c(\overline{t}') \mid \overline{t}' \in \mathcal{C}_1 \times ... \times \mathcal{C}_n\}}\quad c \in DC \cup \{\mathsf{F}\}$$

$$(4)\ \frac{\mathcal{S}' \mathrel{\hat{\triangleleft}} \mathcal{C}' \quad \mathcal{S}[X/\mathcal{C}'] \mathrel{\hat{\triangleleft}} \mathcal{C}}{\bigcup_{X \in f(\overline{t})} \mathcal{S} \mathrel{\hat{\triangleleft}} \mathcal{C}}\quad (f(\overline{t}) \twoheadrightarrow \mathcal{S}') \in [\widehat{\mathcal{P}}]_{\perp,\mathsf{F}}$$

$$(5)\ \frac{\mathcal{S}[X/\mathsf{F}] \mathrel{\hat{\triangleleft}} \mathcal{C}}{\bigcup_{X \in f(\overline{t})} \mathcal{S} \mathrel{\hat{\triangleleft}} \mathcal{C}}\quad \begin{array}{l}\text{for all } (f(s_1,...,s_n) \twoheadrightarrow \mathcal{S}') \in \widehat{\mathcal{P}},\\ t_i \text{ and } s_i \text{ have a } DC \cup \{\mathsf{F}\}\text{-clash for some } i \in \{1,...,n\}\end{array}$$

$$(6)\ \frac{\mathcal{S}_1 \mathrel{\hat{\triangleleft}} \{\mathsf{F}\} \qquad \mathcal{S}_2[X/true] \mathrel{\hat{\triangleleft}} \mathcal{C}}{\bigcup_{X \in fails(\mathcal{S}_1)} \mathcal{S}_2 \mathrel{\hat{\triangleleft}} \mathcal{C}}$$

$$(7)\ \frac{\mathcal{S}_1 \mathrel{\hat{\triangleleft}} \mathcal{C}' \qquad \mathcal{S}_2[X/false] \mathrel{\hat{\triangleleft}} \mathcal{C}}{\bigcup_{X \in fails(\mathcal{S}_1)} \mathcal{S}_2 \mathrel{\hat{\triangleleft}} \mathcal{C}}\quad \text{there is some } t \in \mathcal{C}', t \neq \perp, t \neq \mathsf{F}$$

$$(8)\ \frac{\mathcal{S}_1 \mathrel{\hat{\triangleleft}} \mathcal{C}' \qquad \mathcal{S}_2[X/\mathcal{C}'] \mathrel{\hat{\triangleleft}} \mathcal{C}}{\bigcup_{X \in \mathcal{S}_1} \mathcal{S}_2 \mathrel{\hat{\triangleleft}} \mathcal{C}} \qquad\qquad (9)\ \frac{\mathcal{S}_1 \mathrel{\hat{\triangleleft}} \mathcal{C}_1 \qquad \mathcal{S}_2 \mathrel{\hat{\triangleleft}} \mathcal{C}_2}{\mathcal{S}_1 \cup \mathcal{S}_2 \mathrel{\hat{\triangleleft}} \mathcal{C}_1 \cup \mathcal{C}_2}$$

The non-overlapping condition is guaranteed because we join all the rules with the same head (up to renaming) into a single rule.

Table 2 shows the rules for $\widehat{CRWLF}$-provability. Rules 1, 2 and 3 have a natural counterpart in *CRWLF*. For rule 4 we must define the set of c-instances of rules of the program: $[\widehat{\mathcal{P}}]_{\perp,\mathsf{F}} = \{R\theta \mid R = (f(\overline{t}) \twoheadrightarrow \mathcal{S}) \in \widehat{\mathcal{P}}$ and $\theta \in CSubst_{\perp,\mathsf{F}} \mid_{var(\overline{t})}\}$. The notation $CSubst_{\perp,\mathsf{F}} \mid_{var(\overline{t})}$ stands for the set of substitutions $CSubst_{\perp,\mathsf{F}}$ restricted to $var(\overline{t})$. As $var(\overline{t}) \cap pvar(\mathcal{S}) = \emptyset$ the substitution is well defined according to Definition 4.

Notice that rule 4 uses a c-instance of a rule, and this c-instance is unique if it exists (due to the non-overlapping condition imposed to programs). If such c-instance does not exist, then by rule 5, the corresponding expression reduces to F. Rules 6 and 7 are the counterparts of 8 and 9 of *CRWLF*. Finally, rules 8 and 9 are due to the recursive definition of sas-expressions and have a natural reading.

Given a $\widehat{CRWLF}$-program $\widehat{\mathcal{P}}$ and $\mathcal{S} \in SasExp$ we write $\widehat{\mathcal{P}} \vdash_{\widehat{CRWLF}} \mathcal{S} \mathrel{\hat{\triangleleft}} \mathcal{C}$ if the relation $\mathcal{S} \mathrel{\hat{\triangleleft}} \mathcal{C}$ is provable with respect to $\widehat{CRWLF}$ and the program $\widehat{\mathcal{P}}$. The denotation of $\mathcal{S}$ is defined as $[\![\mathcal{S}]\!]^{\widehat{CRWLF}} = \{\mathcal{C} \mid \mathcal{S} \mathrel{\hat{\triangleleft}} \mathcal{C}\}$.

Example 3. Assume the *OIS-CRWLF*-program:

$$\begin{array}{lll} add(z,Y) \rightarrow Y & & f(X) \rightarrow X \\ add(s(X),Y) \rightarrow s(add(X,Y)) & double(X) \rightarrow add(X,X) & f(X) \rightarrow s(X) \end{array}$$

The corresponding $\widehat{CRWLF}$-program $\widehat{\mathcal{P}}$ is:

$$
\begin{array}{ll}
add(z,Y) & \twoheadrightarrow \{Y\} \\
add(s(X),Y) & \twoheadrightarrow \bigcup_{A\in\bigcup_{B\in\{X\}}\bigcup_{C\in\{Y\}}\bigcup_{D\in add(B,C)}\{D\}}\{s(A)\} \\
double(X) & \twoheadrightarrow \bigcup_{A\in\{X\}}\bigcup_{B\in\{X\}}\bigcup_{C\in add(A,B)}\{C\} \\
f(X) & \twoheadrightarrow \{X\}\cup\bigcup_{A\in\{X\}}\{s(A)\}
\end{array}
$$

Within *CRWLF* we can prove $double(f(z)) \triangleleft \{z, s(s(z))\}$, and within $\widehat{CRWLF}$ we can obtain the same *SAS* by proving $\widehat{double(f(z))} \mathrel{\hat{\triangleleft}} \{z, s(s(z))\}$. Let us sketch the form in which this proof can be done. First, we have:

$$\widehat{double(f(z))} = \bigcup_{A\in\bigcup_{C\in\{z\}}\bigcup_{D\in f(C)}\{D\}}\bigcup_{B\in double(A)}\{B\}$$

By rule 8 of $\widehat{CRWLF}$ this proof is reduced to the proofs:

$$\bigcup_{C\in\{z\}}\bigcup_{D\in f(C)}\{D\} \mathrel{\hat{\triangleleft}} \{z, s(z)\} \qquad (\varphi_1)$$

$$\bigcup_{B\in double(z)}\{B\} \cup \bigcup_{B\in double(s(z))}\{B\} \mathrel{\hat{\triangleleft}} \{z, s(z)\} \qquad (\varphi_2)$$

By rule 8 (φ_1) is reduced to the proofs $\{z\} \mathrel{\hat{\triangleleft}} \{z\}$ and $\bigcup_{D\in f(z)}\{D\} \mathrel{\hat{\triangleleft}} \{z, s(z)\}$. The first is done by rule 3 and the other is reduced by rule 4. On the other hand, by rule 9 the proof (φ_2) can be reduced to the proofs:

$$\bigcup_{B\in double(z)}\{B\} \mathrel{\hat{\triangleleft}} \{z\} \qquad (\varphi_3) \qquad\qquad \bigcup_{B\in double(s(z))}\{B\} \mathrel{\hat{\triangleleft}} \{s(s(z))\} \qquad (\varphi_4)$$

Both (φ_3) and (φ_4) proceed by rule 4 in a similar way. We fix our attention in (φ_4) which, using the rule for *double*, is reduced to:

$$\bigcup_{A\in s(z)}\bigcup_{B\in s(z)}\bigcup_{C\in add(A,B)}\{C\} \mathrel{\hat{\triangleleft}} \{s(s(z))\}$$

and then, by two applications of rule 8 to: $\bigcup_{C\in add(s(z),s(z)}\{C\} \mathrel{\hat{\triangleleft}} \{s(s(z))\}$. Now, rule 4 uses the first defining rule for *add* and the proof is reduced to:

$$\bigcup_{A\in\bigcup_{B\in\{z\}}\bigcup_{C\in\{s(z)\}}\bigcup_{D\in add(B,C)}\{D\}}\{s(A)\} \mathrel{\hat{\triangleleft}} \{s(s(z))\}$$

By rule 8 it is reduced to:

$$\bigcup_{B\in\{z\}}\bigcup_{C\in\{s(z)\}}\bigcup_{D\in add(B,C)}\{D\} \mathrel{\hat{\triangleleft}} \{s(z)\} \quad (\varphi_5) \qquad\qquad \{s(s(z))\} \mathrel{\hat{\triangleleft}} \{s(s(z))\} \quad (\varphi_6)$$

The proof (φ_6) is done by successive applications of rule 3 and (φ_5) is reduced by rule 8 (twice) to $\bigcup_{D\in add(z,s(z))}\{D\} \mathrel{\hat{\triangleleft}} \{s(z)\}$. This last proceeds by applying the first defining rule of *add* by means of rule 4.

5.4 *CRWLF* & $\widehat{CRWLF}$

We show here the strong semantic equivalence between *CRWLF* and $\widehat{CRWLF}$.

Lemma 1 (Semantic Equivalence of *CRWLF* and $\widehat{CRWLF}$). *Let $\mathcal{P}$ be an OIS-CRWLF-program and $\widehat{\mathcal{P}}$ be the corresponding $\widehat{CRWLF}$-program. Let $e \in Term_{\perp,F}$ and $\widehat{e} \in SasExp$ be the corresponding sas-expression. Then*

$$\mathcal{P} \vdash_{CRWLF} e \lhd \mathcal{C} \Leftrightarrow \widehat{\mathcal{P}} \vdash_{\widehat{CRWLF}} \widehat{e} \,\widehat{\lhd}\, \mathcal{C}.$$

As a trivial consequence of this lemma, we arrive at our final result:

Theorem 2. *Let $\mathcal{P}$ be a general CRWLF-program and $\widehat{\Delta(\mathcal{P})}$ be the corresponding $\widehat{CRWLF}$-program. Let e be an expression built over the signature of $\mathcal{P}$ and $\widehat{e}$ be the corresponding sas-expression. Then: $\mathcal{P} \vdash_{CRWLF} e \lhd \mathcal{C} \Leftrightarrow \widehat{\Delta(\mathcal{P})} \vdash_{\widehat{CRWLF}} \widehat{e} \,\widehat{\lhd}\, \mathcal{C}$.*

As a consequence, denotations of expressions are preserved in the transformation process, i.e., $[\![e]\!]^{CRWLF} = [\![\widehat{e}]\!]^{\widehat{CRWLF}}$ (referred to $\mathcal{P}$ and $\widehat{\Delta(\mathcal{P})}$, respectively). So, the properties about consistency, monotonicity and substitutions of Prop. 1 are preserved in $\widehat{CRWLF}$ when considering expressions and the corresponding sas-expressions.

6 Conclusions

We have extended and reformulated *CRWLF* [12], a proof-theoretic framework designed to deduce failure information from positive functional logic programs (i.e., programs not making use of failure inside them). To allow programs the use of failure, we have introduced a built-in function *fails*(_), and extended the proof calculus to deal with it.

We have discussed the declarative meaning of functions defined in programs. Since functions can be non-deterministic, they are in general set-valued. Each rule in the program defines (partially, since there can be more rules) a function as a mapping from (tuples of) constructor terms to sets of constructor terms. If we try to re-write the defining rules of a function f to express directly which is the value (set of constructor terms) of applying f to given arguments, we face the problem that this set can be distributed among different overlapping rules. To overcome this problem we have considered the class of overlapping inductively sequential programs [3] in which overlapping rules are always variants. We have defined a transformation of general programs into such kind of programs and proved that the transformation preserves the semantics, which constitutes itself an interesting application of the developed formal framework. Our transformation behaves better than that proposed in [1], if the transformed program is going to be used in existing systems like Curry [8] or $\mathcal{TOY}$ [11].

To stress the set-theoretic reading of programs, we have introduced set-oriented syntactic constructs to be used in right hand sides of rules, like set braces, union of sets, or union of indexed families of sets. This provides a more intuitive reading of programs in terms of classical mathematical notions, close to the intended semantics. As additional interesting point of this new syntax, indexed unions are a binding construct able to express sharing at the syntactic level, playing a role similar to local (*let* or *where*) definitions. As far as we know, this is the first time that some kind of local definitions are incorporated to a formal semantic framework for functional logic programming.

Our last contributions have been a transformation of overlapping inductively sequential programs into programs with set-oriented syntax, and a specific proof calculus for the latter, by means of which we prove that the transformation preserves the semantics of programs. Apart from any other virtues, we have strong evidence that these new set-oriented syntax and proof calculus are a better basis for an ongoing development of an operational (narrowing based) semantics and subsequent implementation of a functional logic language with failure.

References

[1] S. Antoy Constructor-based Conditional Narrowing. To appear in Proc. PPDP'01, Springer LNCS.

[2] S. Antoy Definitional Trees. In Proc. ALP'92, Springer LNCS 632, pages 143-157, 1992.

[3] S. Antoy Optimal Non-Deterministic Functional Logic Computations. In Proc. ALP'97, Springer LNCS 1298, pages 16-30, 1997.

[4] K.R. Apt and R. Bol. Logic programming and negation: A survey. *Journal of Logic Programming*, 19&20:9–71, 1994.

[5] J.C. González-Moreno, T. Hortalá-González, F.J. López-Fraguas, and M. Rodríguez-Artalejo. A Rewriting Logic for Declarative Programming. In *Proc. ESOP'96*, pages 156–172. Springer LNCS 1058, 1996.

[6] J.C. González-Moreno, T. Hortalá-González, F.J. López-Fraguas, and M. Rodríguez-Artalejo. An approach to declarative programming based on a rewriting logic. *Journal of Logic Programming*, 40(1):47–87, 1999.

[7] M. Hanus. The integration of functions into logic programming: From theory to practice. *Journal of Logic Programming*, 19&20:583–628, 1994.

[8] M. Hanus (ed.). Curry: An integrated functional logic language. Available at `http://www.informatik.uni-kiel.de/ mh/curry/report.html`, June 2000.

[9] H. Hussman. Non-Determinism in Algebraic Specifications and Algebraic Programs Birkhäuser Verlag, 1993.

[10] R. Loogen, F.J. López, M. Rodríguez. A demand driven computation strategy for lazy narrowing. *Proc. PLILP'3*, Springer LNCS 714, 184–200, 1993.

[11] F.J. López-Fraguas and J. Sánchez-Hernández. $\mathcal{TOY}$: A multiparadigm declarative system. In *Proc. RTA'99, Springer LNCS* 1631, pages 244–247, 1999.

[12] F.J. López-Fraguas and J. Sánchez-Hernández. Proving Failure in Functional Logic Programs In *Proc CL'2000*, Springer LNAI 1861, pages 179–193, 2000.

[13] J.J. Moreno-Navarro. Default rules: An extension of constructive negation for narrowing-based languages. In *Proc. ICLP'95*, pages 535–549. MIT Press, 1994.

[14] J.J. Moreno-Navarro. Extending constructive negation for partial functions in lazy functional-logic languages. In *Proc. ELP'96*, pages 213–227. Springer LNAI 1050, 1996.

[15] S. Peyton Jones, J. Hughes (eds.) Haskell 98: A Non-strict, Purely Functional Language. Available at `http://www.haskell.org`, February 1999.

[16] P.J. Stuckey. Constructive negation for constraint logic programming. In *Proc. LICS'91*, pages 328–339, 1991.

Operational Semantics for Fixed-Point Logics on Constraint Databases

Stephan Kreutzer

LuFG Mathematische Grundlagen der Informatik,
RWTH Aachen, D-52056 Aachen
kreutzer@informatik.rwth-aachen.de

Abstract. In this paper we compare the expressive power of various fixed-point logics on linear or dense order constraint databases. This comparison is not done on absolute terms, i.e. by comparing their expressive power for arbitrary queries, rather for definability of partially recursive queries. The motivation for choosing this benchmark comes from fixed-point logics as query languages for constraint databases. Here, non-recursive queries are of no practical interest.
It is shown that for linear constraint databases already transitive closure logic is expressive enough to define all partially recursive queries, i.e., transitive-closure logic is expressively complete for this class of databases. It follows that transitive-closure, least, and stratified fixed-point logic are equivalent with respect to this benchmark.

1 Introduction

Logics and query languages allowing the definition of fixed-points of definable operators have a long tradition both in (finite) model theory and database theory.

In finite model theory, the interest in fixed-point logics comes from questions connected with the definability or description of computations in logical formalisms. To obtain logics strong enough to describe properties interesting from a computational point of view, extensions of first-order logic by operators to define fixed-points have been considered. Among the logics obtained in this way are *transitive-closure logic* (FO(TC)), which extends first-order logic by an operator to define the transitive closure of definable graphs, and *least fixed-point logic* (FO(LFP)), which extends first-order logic by an operator to define the least fixed-point of operators defined by positive formulae. We give precise definitions of these logics in Section 2.

Query languages incorporating fixed-point concepts have also been studied in database theory. Here, the fixed-point constructs have not been added to full first-order logic but to conjunctive queries instead. To obtain more expressive logics than this query language, called *Datalog*, database theorists incorporated negation in various ways. One of these extensions is *Stratified Datalog*, where negation is allowed in a limited way. Stratified Datalog plays a rather prominent role in database theory as it has a good balance between expressive power and complexity.

R. Nieuwenhuis and A. Voronkov (Eds.): LPAR 2001, LNAI 2250, pp. 470–484, 2001.

Once the logics and query languages had been defined, it became obvious that fixed-point logics had corresponding Datalog variants and vice versa. For instance, Datalog is a logic equivalent to existential fixed-point logic (FO(EFP)), the restriction of least fixed-point logic to existential formulae.

Generally, it is clear that FO(TC) $\subseteq$ FO(SFP) $\subseteq$ FO(LFP) and, further, that FO(EFP) $\subseteq$ FO(SFP), where FO(SFP) is equivalent to Stratified Datalog[1]. Further, FO(TC) and FO(EFP) are incomparable. Whether these inclusions are strict depends on the kind of structures under consideration. It has been shown, that on arbitrary structures all inclusions are strict. The standard example separating FO(SFP) and FO(LFP) is the property of a binary relation of being a well-ordering. See [DG] for a very recent survey on fixed-point logics.

On finite structures, the situation depends on whether an ordering is available. If the structures are ordered, FO(SFP) and FO(LFP) coincide with PTIME and, if the order is given by a successor relation, the same is true for FO(EFP). Whether FO(TC) and FO(LFP) have the same expressive power on finite ordered structures depends on whether NLOGSPACE equals PTIME. See [EF95] for an extensive study of these questions on finite structures.

In [Kol91], Kolaitis showed that on unordered finite structures FO(SFP) is strictly weaker than FO(LFP). To prove this he used so-called game trees which can be defined in FO(LFP) but not in FO(SFP).

In this paper we are mainly interested in the expressive power of transitive-closure logic, stratified Datalog, and least fixed-point logic in the context of constraint databases (See [KLP00] for a detailed overview of constraint databases.) We give a precise definition of constraint databases in the next section. These structures lie somewhere between finite and arbitrary infinite structures. They usually have an ordering on their universe available, so that the separation methods for finite structures do not work, but on the other hand the database relations often provide too much structure to use the methods that work on general infinite structures. The problem here is, that - classically - logics are separated by showing that a class of structures with certain properties is definable in one logic but not in the other. In the constraint setting, the context structure is fixed in advance, whereas the relations that vary are first-order definable and thus have a rather simple structure. However, it can still be shown that on many interesting context structures, least fixed-point logic is more expressive than, for instance, stratified Datalog.

So far, much work on fixed-point logics in the context of constraint databases has focused on syntactic variants defined with regard to certain properties of the resulting languages, as polynomial time complexity, see e.g. [GK97,Kre01], or termination, see e.g. [GK00]. Further, the logics have been considered in terms of absolute definability, i.e., the main question was whether there are relations or properties definable in one logic but not in another.

Besides this classification, the expressive power can also be measured with respect to a fixed benchmark. This approach is taken here, where we consider

[1] Actually, FO(SFP) stands for *stratified fixed-point logic*, a name that will become clear later.

constraint databases over the real ordered group $(\mathbb{R}, <, +)$. As benchmark we take the class of partially computable queries. Precisely, we investigate which portions of this class of queries are definable in each of the logics mentioned above.

The motivation for choosing the class of partially recursive queries as benchmark comes from the use of fixed-point logics as query languages. Someone using the logics to ask queries about a given database will only be interested in computable queries, i.e., those whose evaluation terminates. Thus a query language that is more expressive than another only in means of the power to define non-recursive queries will not be considered as being expressively stronger.

When speaking about logics defining partially computable queries we first have to specify what it means for a formula to define a computable query. So far we only considered the standard model-theoretical semantics of fixed-point logics. Formally, the model-theoretical semantics for a logic $\mathcal{L}$ can be seen as a function

$$\text{mod} : \varphi \in \mathcal{L} \longmapsto (\text{mod}_\varphi : (A, \sigma) \longmapsto \mathcal{P}(A^*)),$$

taking formulae $\varphi \in \mathcal{L}$ to functions that map a database $\mathfrak{B} := (A, \sigma)$ to relations over its universe. The problem is that the functions mod_φ are not required to be computable. Further, in the constraint database setting, the problem arises that the resulting relations on A are not necessarily finitely representable in the context structure. Therefore, we have to give the logics an operational semantics, i.e., a total recursive function

$$\text{op} : \varphi \in \mathcal{L} \longmapsto (\text{op}_\varphi : (A, \sigma) \longmapsto \mathcal{P}(A^*)),$$

where the functions op_φ are partially recursive and take databases to finitely representable relations.

Clearly, not every such function can sensibly be called an operational semantics. One obvious condition that should be satisfied by any operational semantics for a logic is, that it is consistent with the model-theoretical semantics, i.e., for all databases $\mathfrak{B}$ and formulae φ where $\text{op}_\varphi(\mathfrak{B})$ is defined, the two semantics should agree on the result, i.e., $\text{mod}_\varphi(\mathfrak{B}) = \text{op}_\varphi(\mathfrak{B})$.

Although the consistency condition is a necessary condition, it alone does not ensure that the semantics meets our expectations. For instance, the operational semantics mapping each formula to the everywhere undefined function would trivially satisfy the consistency requirement.

Thus, besides this consistency criterion also some kind of completeness condition is needed. Unlike for consistency, there is no canonical definition for an operational semantics to be complete. In this paper we take the view that an operational semantics for a logic is complete if it is most powerful possible, i.e. there is no other operational semantics and no partially computable query which is definable in the logic under the second but not under the first semantics.

In Section 3, we define operational semantics for the fixed-point logics mentioned above which satisfy both, the consistency and the completeness condition.

The latter condition will be proved by showing that under the operational semantics we define for transitive-closure logic, all partially computable queries on linear constraint databases become definable in FO(TC). This shows that FO(TC) is expressively complete for this class of databases.

It follows from this that also least and stratified fixed-point logic are expressively complete and thus the three logics are equivalent with respect to the class of partially computable queries. This equivalence does not hold for existential fixed-point logic, where we show that there even exist queries definable in first-order logic but not in existential fixed-point logic.

Finally, in Section 4 we will consider constraint databases over the real line. Here it will be shown that the question about the expressive power of fixed-point logics can be reduced to the question for finite ordered databases. Thus, stratified Datalog and least fixed-point logic have the same expressive power and transitive-closure logic is equal to both if, and only if, NLOGSPACE equals PTIME.

2 Preliminaries

Constraint Databases. Constraint Databases have been introduced by Kanellakis, Kuper, and Revesz [KKR90,KKR95] as a model for infinite relational databases that have a finite representation and are therefore accessible to algorithmic problems.

Let a signature τ and a τ-structure $\mathfrak{A}$ be given. *Constraint databases* are defined with respect to this fixed structure $\mathfrak{A}$. For a finite relational signature σ, a *σ-constraint database* $\mathfrak{B}$ *over* $\mathfrak{A}$, or simply *constraint database* if σ and $\mathfrak{A}$ are understood or irrelevant, is a σ-expansion of $\mathfrak{A}$ such that for all relation symbols $R \in \sigma$ there is a quantifier-free formula over $\mathfrak{A}$ defining $R^{\mathfrak{B}}$ in $\mathfrak{A}$. In these defining formulae elements of the universe may be used as parameters. The database relations in σ are called *finitely representable* or *constraint relations.*

In this paper we are specifically interested in *linear constraint databases,* i.e., constraint databases over the structure $(\mathbb{R}, <, +)$. Thus, linear constraint relations are defined by boolean combinations of linear equalities and inequalities. In this paper we only allow rational coefficients in these formulae defining database relations[2].

Fixed-point logics. As mentioned in the introduction, we are specifically interested in the expressive power of transitive-closure and least fixed-point logic as well as Datalog and stratified Datalog. We define FO(TC) and FO(LFP) first and then turn to the Datalog variants.

Definition 1 Transitive-closure logic (FO(TC)) *is defined as the extension of first-order logic by the following formula building rule. If $\varphi(\overline{x}, \overline{y})$ is a formula with free tuples of variables $\overline{x}, \overline{y}$ of equal length, then*

[2] After all, constraint databases have been defined in order to be finitely representable and it is debatable whether formulae with transcendental coefficients could sensibly be called finitely representable.

$$\psi := [\mathrm{TC}_{\overline{x},\overline{y}}\,\varphi](\overline{s},\overline{t})$$

is also a formula, where $\overline{s},\overline{t}$ *are tuples of terms of the same length as* $\overline{x}$ *and* $\overline{y}$. *The free variables of* ψ *are the variables occurring free in* $\overline{s},\overline{t}$ *and the free variables of* φ *other than* $\overline{x}$ *and* $\overline{y}$.

Given a structure $\mathfrak{A}$, *the semantics of FO(TC) is defined inductively with the meaning of the* TC*-rule being that for some tuples* $\overline{a},\overline{b}$, $\mathfrak{A} \models ([\mathrm{TC}_{\overline{x},\overline{y}}\,\varphi])[\overline{a},\overline{b}]$ *if, and only if,* $(\overline{a},\overline{b})$ *is in the transitive closure of the relation* $\{(\overline{u},\overline{v}) : \mathfrak{A} \models \varphi[\overline{u},\overline{v}]\}$.

Note that the result of a formula in FO(TC) on a linear constraint database does not have to be finitely representable anymore. For instance, the formula $\varphi(y) := [\mathrm{TC}_{x,y}\, x+1 = y](0,y)$ defines the natural numbers on any linear constraint database. But clearly, the result is not finitely representable.

Definition 2 Least fixed-point logic FO(LFP) *is defined as the extension of first-order logic by the following formula building rule. If* $\varphi(R,\overline{x})$ *is a formula with free first-order variables* $\overline{x} := x_1,\dots,x_k$ *and a free second-order variable* R *of arity* k *such that* φ *is positive in* R, *then*

$$\psi := [\mathbf{lfp}_{R,\overline{x}}\,\varphi](\overline{t})$$

is also a formula, where $\overline{t}$ *is a tuple of terms of the same length as* $\overline{x}$. *The free variables of* ψ *are the variables occurring in* $\overline{t}$ *and the free variables of* φ *other than* $\overline{x}$.

Given a structure $\mathfrak{A}$, *the semantics of* FO(LFP) *is defined inductively with the meaning of the* FO(LFP)*-rule being as follows. Define the stages* R^α *of an fixed-point induction as*

$$\begin{array}{ll} R^0 & := \varnothing \\ R^{\alpha+1} & := \{\overline{a} : \mathfrak{A} \models \varphi[R^\alpha,\overline{a}]\} \\ R^\lambda & := \bigcup_{\alpha<\lambda} R^\alpha. \end{array}$$

For a given structure $\mathfrak{A}$ *and a tuple* $\overline{a} \in A$, *the formula* $[\mathbf{lfp}_{R,\overline{x}}\,\varphi]$ *becomes true for* $\overline{a}$ *if, and only if,* $\overline{a} \in R^\alpha$, *where* α *is the least* α *such that* $R^\alpha = R^{\alpha+1}$. *As* φ *is required to be positive in* R *such a stage* α *always exists.*

We now turn to the definition of the Datalog variants. To harmonise notation, we will not deal with the Datalog variants directly but consider the corresponding fixed-point logics instead. In the case of Datalog this is the well known existential fixed-point logic.

Definition 3 Existential least fixed-point logic *is defined as the restriction of* FO(LFP) *to formulae without universal quantifiers and with negation being allowed only in front of atoms which are not built up from fixed-point variables.*

For stratified Datalog there are various syntactically different fixed-point extensions of FO equivalent to it. We follow the notation introduced by Kolaitis in [Kol91][3].

Definition 4 Stratified Fixed-Point Logic (FO(SFP)) *is defined as follows.*

- *Let* $\mathrm{FO(SFP)}_1$ *be defined as existential fixed-point logic.*
- *Define* $\mathrm{FO(SFP)}_{i+1}$ *as the class of existential fixed-point formulae which may use literals of the form* $\psi(\overline{x})$*, where* ψ *is an* $\mathrm{FO(SFP)}_l$ *formula with* $l \leq i$*. Note that these formulae may occur under the scope of negation symbols.*

Stratified Fixed-Point logic is defined as the union $\mathrm{FO(SFP)} := \bigcup_{i \in \omega} \mathrm{FO(SFP)}_i$ *of all* $\mathrm{FO(SFP)}_i$ *for* $i \in \omega$*.*

Clearly, FO(SFP) and stratified Datalog have the same expressive power and a stratified Datalog program with l strata corresponds to a formula in $\mathrm{FO(SFP)}_l$. We sometimes write $[\mathbf{sfp}_{R,\overline{x}}\,\varphi]$ instead of $[\mathbf{lfp}_{R,\overline{x}}\,\varphi]$. This happens in cases where we compare FO(SFP) and FO(LFP) and want to make it very clear in which logic we are.

It can easily be shown that a formula $[\mathrm{TC}_{\overline{x},\overline{y}}\,\varphi(\overline{x},\overline{y})](\overline{s},\overline{t})$ of FO(TC) is equivalent to the FO(SFP)-formula $[\mathbf{lfp}_{R,\overline{z}}\,(\overline{z} = \overline{s} \vee \exists \overline{z}'\,(R\overline{z}' \wedge \varphi(\overline{z}',\overline{z})))](\overline{t})$. Thus, $\mathrm{FO(TC)} \subseteq \mathrm{FO(SFP)}$. In fact, it can even be shown that every FO(SFP)-formula of the form $[\mathbf{lfp}_{R,\overline{x}}\,\varphi_0(\overline{x}) \vee \exists \overline{x}' \in R\,\varphi_1(\overline{x},\overline{x}')](\overline{t})$ such that R does not occur in φ_0 and φ_1 is equivalent to a formula in FO(TC), provided that φ_0 and φ_1 are equivalent to formulae in FO(TC).

It is also clear that $\mathrm{FO(SFP)} \subseteq \mathrm{FO(LFP)}$.

3 Finitely Representable Expansions of the Real Ordered Group

In this section we consider constraint databases over the real ordered group $(\mathbb{R},<,+)$ and show that transitive-closure, least, and stratified fixed-point logic define the same class of partially computable queries. This is proven by showing that all partially computable queries are already definable in FO(TC). For this, we first have to give the logics an operational semantics.

3.1 Operational Semantics for Fixed-Point Logics

Throughout this section, we denote by CDB the class of constraint databases over $(\mathbb{R},<,+)$ and by CRel the class of finitely representable relations over $(\mathbb{R},<,+)$. We don't distinguish between finitely representable relations and their representing formulae and denote both by CRel. It will always be clear from the context whether the relation or the formula is meant.

[3] Note that in this paper the logic was called *existential* fixed-point logic!

Definition 5 *For a given logic $\mathcal{L}$, an operational semantics $op_{\mathcal{L}}$ is defined as a total recursive function*

$$\text{op} : \varphi \in \mathcal{L} \longmapsto (\text{op}_\varphi : \text{CDB} \longrightarrow \text{CRel})$$

taking formulae $\varphi \in \mathcal{L}$ to partially computable functions op_φ which take constraint databases over $(\mathbb{R}, <, +)$ to representations of finitely representable relations over $(\mathbb{R}, <, +)$.

For $\varphi \in \mathcal{L}$ we denote by $mod_\varphi(\mathfrak{B})$ the set of elements defined by φ under the model-theoretical semantics for $\mathcal{L}$. An operational semantics op for $\mathcal{L}$ is consistent with the model-theoretical semantics *if, and only if, for all formulae φ and all databases $\mathfrak{B}$ such that $op_\varphi(\mathfrak{B})$ is defined, $mod_\varphi(\mathfrak{B}) = op_\varphi(\mathfrak{B})$.*

We now define an operational semantics for transitive-closure logic. This operational semantics closely resembles the usual definition of the model-theoretical semantics.

Definition 6 (Operational semantics for FO(TC)) *For each formula $\varphi \in$ FO(TC) we define a function op_φ : CDB $\longrightarrow$ CRel by induction on the structure of φ. Fix a quantifier elimination procedure for $(\mathbb{R}, <, +)$, i.e., an evaluation schema for first-order queries.*

- *If $\varphi \in$ FO, define $op_\varphi(\mathfrak{B}) := \varphi'$, where φ' is obtained from φ by first substituting each occurrence of a database relation symbol by the formula defining the relation in $\mathfrak{B}$ and then eliminating the quantifiers using the quantifier elimination method fixed above.*
- *If $\varphi := \varphi_1 \wedge \varphi_2$, define $op_\varphi(\mathfrak{B})$ as $((op_{\varphi_1}(\mathfrak{B})) \wedge (op_{\varphi_2}(\mathfrak{B}))$. For other boolean connectives the function op_φ is defined analogously.*
- *If $\varphi := \exists x \varphi_1$, define $op_\varphi(\mathfrak{B})$ as the result of applying the quantifier-elimination method fixed above to $op_{\varphi_1}(\mathfrak{B})$.*
- *Now suppose that φ is of the form $\varphi := [\text{TC}_{\overline{x},\overline{y}}\, \psi(\overline{x}, \overline{y})](\overline{u}, \overline{v})$. We inductively define formulae σ_i, $i \in \omega$, as follows. Recall that we allowed the use of rational numbers as parameters in the formulae. Let I be the indices of parameters among $\overline{u} := u_1, \dots, u_n$, i.e., u_i is a constant if, and only if, $i \in I$.*
  (i) $\sigma_0 := \psi(\overline{x}, \overline{y}) \wedge \bigwedge_{i \in I} u_i = x_i$.
  (ii) $\sigma_{i+1} := \exists \overline{x}'\, \sigma_i(\overline{x}, \overline{x}') \wedge \psi(\overline{x}', \overline{y})$.
  If there is no $j \in \omega$ such that σ_j and σ_{j+1} are equivalent in $\mathfrak{B}$, then $op_\varphi(\mathfrak{B})$ is undefined. Otherwise let i be the smallest such j and define

$$op_\varphi(\mathfrak{B}) := \exists \overline{x} \exists \overline{y}\, ((\overline{u} = \overline{x}) \wedge (\overline{y} = \overline{v}) \wedge \sigma_i(\overline{x}, \overline{y})).$$

Finally, we define the operational semantics op for FO(TC) as the function taking formulae φ to op_φ.

Observe the difference between this definition of an operational semantics and the standard way to define the model-theoretical semantics as outlined in Definition 1 in the way the formula σ_0 is defined. The conjunct $\bigwedge_{i \in I}(u_i = x_i)$ reduces the computation of the transitive closure to the computation of all tuples which are reachable from tuples with some fixed components. Thus, by letting constants occur in the tuple $\overline{u}$ one gets some control over the process of building up the transitive closure. However limited this control might seem, we will show below that it is enough to allow the definition of arbitrary partially computable queries over databases from CDB, whereas it seems unlikely that this is also possible without this modification.

It is now an easy observation that the model-theoretical and the operational semantics for FO(TC) are consistent.

Proposition 7 *The operational semantics of Definition 6 is consistent with the model-theoretical semantics of FO(TC).*

3.2 Expressive Completeness of Transitive Closure Logic

We now turn to the definability of partially computable queries by formulae of FO(TC).

Definition 8 *A partially computable query Q is defined by a formula $\varphi \in$ FO(TC) if for all databases $\mathfrak{B}$, $Q(\mathfrak{B})$ is defined if, and only if, $op_\varphi(\mathfrak{B})$ is defined and in this case $Q(\mathfrak{B}) = op_\varphi(\mathfrak{B})$.*

We show now that all partially computable functions on constraint databases over $(\mathbb{R}, <, +)$ can be defined in FO(TC). The proof runs along the following line. We first show that the logic PFOL as introduced by Vandeurzen et. al. [Van99] is a subset of FO(TC). This enables us to use the results on finite representations definable in PFOL. We then show that the run of Turing-machines can be simulated in FO(TC).

Recall that PFOL was defined as an extension of FO by a restricted form of multiplication. Precisely, the logic allows the use of atoms $x \cdot p = y$, where p is a so-called *product variable.* These product variables have to be bound by a quantifier $\exists p \in \varphi_p$ or $\forall p \in \varphi_p$, where $\varphi_p(x)$ must be a formula defining a finite set. The semantics of a quantifier $Qp \in \varphi_p$ is the semantics of Q relativised to the set defined by φ_p.

To show that PFOL $\subseteq$ FO(TC) it suffices to prove that atoms of the form $x \cdot p = y$ can be defined in FO(TC) by a formula whose evaluation always terminates.

We show that atoms of this form can be defined by a formula *mult* in FO(TC) provided that the formula φ_p defines a set of rational numbers. In all cases where we use PFOL formulae below this will always be true. The formula *mult* makes use of two auxiliary formulae $\varphi_{nd}(p, n, d)$, stating that n and d are the numerator and denominator of the rational number p, and $\varphi_{im}(a, b, c)$, which defines $a \cdot b = c$, provided that b is an integer.

By the discussion above, we may use quantifiers $\exists p \in \varphi_p$ in our formulae as abbreviation for $\exists p \varphi_p(p)$, where φ_p is the unique formula binding p in the PFOL formula.

The formula φ_{im} is defined as

$$\varphi_{im}^{\psi}(x,y,z) := [\mathrm{TC}_{x,y,z;x',y',z'} \begin{array}{l} x = x' \wedge y' = y-1 \wedge \\ z' = z + x \wedge 0 \leq y \wedge \psi(y) \end{array}](x,y,0,x,0,z).$$

The formula is parameterised by the formula ψ which will be replaced by a concrete formula whenever we use φ_{im} below. The idea is, that ψ bounds the possible values for y from above, whereas the conjunct $0 \leq y$ bounds y from below. Thus, if there exists a number c such that ψ is not satisfied for any $c' > c$, then the evaluation of φ_{im} is guaranteed to terminate. We abbreviate $\varphi_{im}^{\psi}(a,b,c)$ as $a \cdot_i^{\psi} b = c$.

We now give the definition of the formula *mult* and define φ_{nd} below. The formula *mult* is defined as

$$\mathrm{mult}(x,p,y) := \exists d \exists n \, \varphi_{nd}(p,n,d) \wedge (x \cdot_i^{\varphi_n} n = z \cdot_i^{\varphi_d} d),$$

where $x \cdot_i^{\varphi_n} n = y \cdot_i^{\varphi_d} d$ is an abbreviation for $\exists z(x \cdot_i^{\varphi_n} n = z \wedge z = y \cdot_i^{\varphi_d} d)$, and the formulae φ_n and φ_d are defined as $\varphi_n(x) := \exists d \exists p \, \varphi_{nd}(p,x,d)$ and $\varphi_d(x) := \exists n \exists p \, \varphi_{nd}(p,n,x)$.

Finally, to define φ_{nd} we assume a formula $\gamma(i,j,i',j')$ defining a Gödel enumeration of pairs (i,j) of natural numbers. Using this, we can set

$$\begin{aligned} \varphi_{nd}(p,n,d) := \varphi_p(p) \wedge d \cdot_i^{\varphi_p} p = n \wedge \\ [\mathrm{TC}_{x,y,x',y'} \neg x = y \cdot_i^{\varphi_p} p \wedge \gamma(x,y,x',y')\,](1,0,n,d), \end{aligned}$$

where φ_p is the formula binding p in the PFOL formula.

Recall that the operational semantics above guarantees that the evaluation of the TC operator start with the pair 0, 1. The conjunct $\neg x = y \cdot_i^{\varphi_p} p$ ensures that it terminates once a pair n, d of numerator and denominator for p is reached. Thus φ_{nd} defines exactly one pair n, d for each p. As the formula is used only for product variables p, it defines a finite set. This ensures that the formula φ_n and φ_d above define finite sets as well. Thus, for product variables p the formula $\mathrm{mult}(x,p,y)$ terminates and defines the set $\{(a,b,c) : a \cdot b = c \text{ and } b \in \varphi_p\}$.

The proof of the following lemma is now straight-forward.

Lemma 9 *Each PFOL formula where all product variables are bound by formulae defining sets of rationals only is equivalent to a formula in FO(TC) whose evaluation always terminates.*

It has been shown by Vandeurzen [Van99] that there are PFOL queries *code* and *decode*, such that for a given databases $\mathfrak{B} := ((\mathbb{R}, <, +), S^{\mathfrak{B}})$, where S is k-ary, *code* defines a finite set $S^{\mathrm{enc}} \subseteq \mathbb{R}^{k(k+1)}$ of $(k+1)$-tuples of points in $\mathbb{R}^k$, and $S^{\mathfrak{B}}$ can be recovered from this finite encoding S^{enc} by the formula *decode*, i.e., $S = \{\overline{a} : (\mathbb{R}, <, +) \models \mathrm{decode}(S^{\mathrm{enc}})\}$.

As all parameters occurring in the formulae defining the database relations are required to be rational, and therefore also all points in the encoding have rational coordinates, Lemma 9 implies that such an finite encoding of the database relation can also be defined in FO(TC).

We now turn to the simulation of the run of a Turing-machine $M := (Q, \Sigma := \{0,1\}, q_0, \delta, \{q_f\})$ computing a given query. Here, Q is the set of states of M, Σ is the alphabet, q_0 the initial state, and q_f the unique halting state. δ is a set of rules of the form $(q,a) \rightarrow (q',a',m)$, where $q,q' \in Q$, $a,a' \in \Sigma$, and $m \in \{-1,1,0\}$. Such a rule states that if M is in state q and the head scans a position labelled a then M replaces a by a', goes into state q' and moves according to m the head to the left, to the right, or not at all.

We can assume w.l.o.g. that M operates on the encoding of the input database as defined above. Further, we assume that the machine halts with the head scanning the first position on the tape.

A configuration of M will be encoded as a tuple (x_l, x_r, t, s), where x_l and x_r are natural numbers encoding the tape content, $0 \leq t \in \mathbb{N}$ denotes the step counter, and s contains the current state of the Turing-machine. A tape content $a_0 a_1 \ldots a_n$ will be encoded as follows. Let $0 \leq p \leq n$ be the current head position. The inscription $a_0 \ldots a_{p-1}$ of the tape to the left of p is coded inversely, i.e., as $a_{p-1} \ldots a_0$, in x_l by $x_l := \Sigma_{i=0}^{p-1} 2^i \cdot a_{p-1-i}$. The inscription $a_p \ldots a_n$ of the tape to the right of p is coded in x_r by $x_r := \Sigma_{i=0}^{n-p} 2^i \cdot a_{p+i}$. As the machine only uses finitely many positions on the tape and all cells which have not been visited by the machine are defined to be 0, we can also think of x_r as the infinite sum $\Sigma_{i=0}^{\infty} 2^i \cdot a_{p+i}$.

The run of M will be simulated by the formula φ_M. We use bold face letters $\mathbf{q_0}, \mathbf{q_f}, \ldots, \mathbf{a}, \mathbf{m}$ to denote fixed constants of the Turing-machine, e.g. states $\mathbf{q_0}$, symbols $\mathbf{a}$ of the alphabet, or $\mathbf{m}$.

$$\varphi_M := \exists t \exists x\ [\mathrm{TC}_{\substack{x_l,x_r,t,s;\\ x_l',x_r',t',s'}} \begin{pmatrix} (t=-1) \wedge \mathrm{init}) \vee \\ (t \geq 0 \wedge s \neq \mathbf{q_f} \wedge \mathrm{compute} \end{pmatrix}](\begin{matrix} -1,-1,-1,-1; \\ x,t,\mathbf{q_f},0 \end{matrix}).$$

The formulae *init* and *compute* are defined such that

1. $init(x_l', x_r', t', s')$ becomes true for the tuple x_l', x_r', t', s' coding the input configuration, i.e., $x_l' = 0$, x_r' codes the input, $s' = \mathbf{q_0}$, i.e., the machine is in the initial state, and, finally, $t' = 0$.
2. compute$(x_l, x_r, t, s; x_l', x_r', t', s')$ becomes true for a pair of tuples, if the x_l', x_r', t', s' codes the successor configuration of the configuration coded in x_l, x_r, t, s.

The conjunct $s \neq \mathbf{q_f}$ is needed to terminate the evaluation of the formula once the machine reaches the final state q_f.

We now turn to the definition of the formula *compute.* To define this, we first need three auxiliary formulae *move-right*$_a$, *move-left*$_a$, and *don't-move*$_a$ with free variables $\{x_l, x_r, x_l', x_r'\}$ which define the transition from the tape content coded in (x_l, x_r) to the new tape content (x_l', x_r') if the machine writes the symbol a and moves to the right, to the left or doesn't move at all.

(i) move-right is defined as

$$\textit{move-right}_{\mathbf{a}} := x_l' = 2x_l + \mathbf{a} \wedge x_r' = x_r \text{ div } 2.$$

Consider the following situation:

$$\overbrace{|\,|\,|\,|\,|\,|\,|\,|\,|\,|\,|\,|\,|\,|\,|\,|\,|\,|\,|\,|\,|\,|\,|\,|}^{x_l}\overbrace{\mathbf{b}|\,|\,|\,|\,|\,|\,|\,|\,|\,|\,|\,|\,|\,|\,|\,|\,|\,|\,|\,|\,|\,|\,|\,|\,|\,|}^{x_l}$$

where the head scans the symbol b, the tape to the left is coded in x_l, and the tape to the right containing b is coded in x_r. As the head moves to the right, the pair (x_l', x_r') must code the new tape content as follows.

$$\overbrace{|\,|\,|\,|\,|\,|\,|\,|\,|\,|\,|\,|\,|\,|\,|\,|\,|\,|\,|\,|\,|\,|\,|\,|\,\mathbf{a}|}^{x_l'}\overbrace{\,|\,|\,|\,|\,|\,|\,|\,|\,|\,|\,|\,|\,|\,|\,|\,|\,|\,|\,|\,|\,|\,|\,|\,|\,|\,|}^{x_l'}$$

Thus, the position containing the b must be removed from the right side coded in x_r and x_r' resp., it must be added to the left side coded in x_l and x_l' resp., and, the symbol $\mathbf{b}$ must be replaced by $\mathbf{a}$. This is done by setting x_r' to x_r div 2, i.e., removing the position entirely, and setting x_l' to $2x_l + \mathbf{a}$. The same ideas are used in the next two formulae taking care of the head moving to the right or not moving at all.

(ii) *don't-move* is defined as

$$\textit{don't-move}_{\mathbf{a}} := x_l' = x_l \wedge x_r' = (x_r \text{ div } 2) \cdot 2 + \mathbf{a}.$$

(iii) *move-left* is defined as

$$\textit{move-left}_{\mathbf{a}} := x_l' = x_l \text{ div } 2 \wedge x_r' = ((x_r \text{ div } 2) \cdot 2 + \mathbf{a}) \cdot 2 + (x_l \text{ mod } 2).$$

We are now ready to state the definition of the formula *compute*.

$$\begin{aligned}\text{compute} := {} & t' = t + 1 \wedge \exists c\,(c = x_r \text{ mod } 2) \wedge \\ & \textstyle\bigvee_{(q,a)\to(q',a',m)\in\delta} s = \mathbf{q} \wedge s' = \mathbf{q}' \wedge c = \mathbf{a} \wedge p' = p + \mathbf{m} \wedge \\ & \qquad ((m = 1 \wedge \textit{move-right}_{\mathbf{a}'}) \vee \\ & \qquad (m = 0 \wedge \textit{don't-move}_{\mathbf{a}'}) \vee \\ & \qquad (m = -1 \wedge \textit{move-left}_{\mathbf{a}'})).\end{aligned}$$

We now turn to the definition of the formula init. Again we first need some auxiliary formulae. Recall from above that there is a formula *enc* which defines a representation $enc(S) \subseteq \mathbb{R}^{k(k+1)}$ of the input $S \subseteq \mathbb{R}^k$ by a finite set of tuples of points. We use this to define the initial configuration by letting the Turing-tape contain this set of tuples of points. To simplify notation, we assume an encoding $S' := enc(S)$ of the input S by a finite set of natural numbers, i.e., the tuples of points reduce to 1-tuples of points in $\mathbb{R}^1$ and, further, the coordinates of this "points" are natural numbers. Observe that such an encoding does not correspond to any possible input relation S but the extension to points and tuples of higher dimension and to rational coordinates will be straight forward. We comment on this below.

The formula init is defined as

$$\text{init}(x_l', x_r', t', s') := t' = 0 \wedge s' = \mathbf{q_0} \wedge x_l' = 0 \wedge \text{start}(x_r'),$$

where the formula start is defined as

$$\text{start}(x) := \exists p = \max(S') \wedge [\text{TC}_{p,x;p',x'} \left(\begin{pmatrix} p = x = -1 \wedge p' = \min(S') \wedge \\ \text{append}(1, p', x') \end{pmatrix} \vee \begin{pmatrix} p \in S' \wedge p' \in S' \wedge p' = \text{succ}(p) \wedge \\ \text{append}(x, p', x') \end{pmatrix} \right)](-1, -1, x', p).$$

Here the formulae *max*, *min*, and *succ* are defined with respect to the lexicographical ordering of the points in the encoding S' and the formula $\text{append}(x', p, x)$ defines x' to code the tape inscription obtained from the inscription coded in x with the bit representation of p being appended at the end. It is defined as

$$\text{append} := x' = p' + x \wedge \exists c\, [\text{TC}_{x,p,x',p'} \begin{pmatrix} p' = 2 \cdot p \wedge x' = x \text{ div } 2 \wedge x > 0 \wedge \\ (\exists \hat{p} \in S'\ x \leq \hat{p}) \end{pmatrix}](x, p, 0, c).$$

The formula first shifts the bit representation of the point p as many bits to the right as the number of bits needed for representation of x and stores the result in c. Then it simply adds x to c and gets the desired bit representation in x'. The part that might cause confusion is the conjunct $(\exists \hat{p} \in S'\ x \leq \hat{p})$. This is unnecessary for the computation of x' but guarantees that the evaluation of the formula terminates. This is achieved by binding the values for x by the largest point in the encoding S'. As S' is finite, the process of building up the transitive closure must be finite as well.

As mentioned above, the case that the encoding S' is unary does not happen for any input relation. Also it is unlikely, that the points in the encoding all have natural coordinates. But the formula can easily - although with a huge overhead in notation - be extended to rational numbers and encodings of higher arity. Termination of the evaluation process is also guaranteed for the general case, as all the computations needed to encode the input can be bounded by the values of points in the finite set S'.

Finally, we have to decode the result of the computation. For this we can use the PFOL-formula *decode* mentioned above. Further, we need some preprocessing to decode the output of the machine given in one single number x into tuples of points. But the inductions involved can all be bounded by the number x coding the output of the Turing machine.

Now, the proof of the following lemma is straight forward.

Lemma 10 *Let f be a query on constraint databases over $(\mathbb{R}, <, +)$ and let M be a Turing-machine computing it. Let $f_\varphi := op_{\varphi_M}$ be the function assigned by the operational semantics to the formula φ_M as constructed above. Then, for each database $\mathfrak{B} := ((\mathbb{R}, <, +), \sigma)$,*

(i) M halts on input $\mathfrak{B}$ if, and only if, $f_\varphi(\mathfrak{B})$ is defined, and
(ii) $f_\varphi(\mathfrak{B})$ defines the same set of elements as represented by the output of M on $\mathfrak{B}$.

Thus we have shown the following theorem.

Theorem 11 *Under the operational semantics defined above, FO(TC) defines exactly the partially computable queries on constraint databases over* $(\mathbb{R}, <, +)$.

The proof of the theorem also yields a negative answer to further decidability questions. For instance, one might ask whether it is decidable for a given FO(TC)-formula φ and a first-order formula ψ if for all databases $\mathfrak{B}$ such that $\mathrm{mod}_\varphi(\mathfrak{B})$ is defined $\mathrm{op}_\psi(\mathfrak{B}) \subseteq \mathrm{op}_\varphi(\mathfrak{B})$. Using the proof given above, it is an easy exercise to reduce the halting problem for Turing machines to this question, thus proving it undecidable.

Corollary 12 *Let* φ *be a FO(TC)-formula and* $\psi \in \mathrm{FO}$. *It is undecidable, whether for all databases* $\mathfrak{B} \in \mathrm{CDB}(\mathbb{R}, <, +)$ *such that* $\mathrm{mod}_\varphi(\mathfrak{B})$ *is defined,*

$$\mathrm{op}_\psi(\mathfrak{B}) \subseteq \mathrm{op}_\varphi(\mathfrak{B}).$$

3.3 Completeness of Stratified Datalog and Least Fixed-Point Logic

Clearly, FO(SFP) is more expressive than FO(TC). Thus, Theorem 11 generalises to FO(SFP) and FO(LFP) in the sense that each partially computable query can be defined in these logics. However, a bit care has to be taken on whether the formulae terminate in the cases where the query is computable. Let $\varphi := [\mathrm{TC}_{\overline{x},\overline{y}}\psi(\overline{x},\overline{y})](\overline{u},\overline{v})$ be a FO(TC)-formula. Then φ can inductively be translated to the equivalent FO(SFP)-formula $\varphi^* := [\mathrm{FO(SFP)}_{R,\overline{x},\overline{y}}\psi^*(\overline{x},\overline{y}) \vee \exists\overline{z}\; R\overline{x}\overline{z} \wedge \psi^*(\overline{z},\overline{y})](\overline{u},\overline{v})$. However, under the standard operational semantics, this formula might not terminate although, given the operational semantics above, the FO(TC)-formula might. To avoid this we recursively translate formulae φ as above to $\varphi^* := [\mathrm{FO(SFP)}_{R,\overline{x},\overline{y}}(\overline{x} = \overline{u} \wedge \psi^*(\overline{x},\overline{y})) \vee \exists\overline{z}(R\overline{x}\overline{z} \wedge \psi^*(\overline{z},\overline{y}))](\overline{u},\overline{v})$. This closely resembles the operational semantics we used for FO(TC) and thus guarantees termination of the formulae.

3.4 Existential Fixed-Point Logic

In the previous sections we have seen that FO(TC), FO(SFP), and FO(LFP) all express the same class of partially recursive queries. Regarding existential fixed-point logic (FO(EFP)), it can easily be shown that this logic is much weaker than the other three. In fact, there are even first-order definable queries that are not expressible in existential fixed-point logic. An example is the boolean query that is true for all databases which are bounded, i.e. where there is a number c such that there is no point in the database with an coordinate greater than c. This can easily be expressed in first-order logic. As it is known that $\mathrm{FO} \cap \mathrm{FO(EFP)}$ is exactly the class of positive existential first-order formulae and that these formulae are preserved under extensions of the structure, it is an easy observation that this query cannot be expressed in existential fixed-point logic.

4 Dense Linear Orders

In this section we consider dense linear order databases, e.g. constraint databases over $(\mathbb{R}, <, +)$. Fixed-point logics on this class of databases have been studied in [BST98,GK99,Kre99] where it is shown that questions about fixed-point queries on dense order databases can be reduced to the corresponding questions on finite databases. In particular, in [GK99] it has been shown that for all dense linear order database $\mathfrak{B}$ there is a finite ordered database $\text{inv}(\mathfrak{B})$ with universe B, called the *invariant of* $\mathfrak{B}$ such that

- there is a function $\widehat{\pi}$ from finite subsets $S \subseteq B$ to FO(LFP)-formulae over $(\mathbb{R}, <, +)$ and
- for each FO(LFP)-formula φ on $\mathfrak{B}$ there is a FO(LFP)-formula φ' on $\text{inv}(\mathfrak{B})$

with the property that if $S = \varphi'(\text{inv}(\mathfrak{B}))$ is the result of the evaluation of φ' in the invariant of $\mathfrak{B}$ and $P := \{\overline{a} : (\mathbb{R}, <, +) \models \widehat{\pi}(S)\}$ is the set of elements satisfying the formula $\widehat{\pi}(S)$, then

$$R = \varphi(\mathfrak{B}),$$

where $\varphi(\mathfrak{B})$ denotes the set of tuples satisfying φ in $\mathfrak{B}$.

Now, by the results mentioned in the introduction, it follows that the formula φ' on the finite ordered database is equivalent to a formula φ^* in stratified fixed-point logic. To obtain a stratified fixed-point formula equivalent to the original query φ we have to transform φ^* back to a formula over $\mathfrak{B}$. It follows immediately from the results proved in [GK99] that there is a stratified fixed-point formula ψ over $\mathfrak{B}$ defining the relation R as defined above.

Thus we have shown the following theorem.

Theorem 13 *Stratified fixed-point logic and fixed-point logic have the same expressive power on the class of finitely representable structures over the real line* $(\mathbb{R}, <)$.

5 Conclusion

In this paper we compared various fixed-point logics with respect to the fraction of partially computable queries on linear constraint databases they define. For this, we first had to equip the logics with an operational semantics, which allowed us to speak about computability of queries defined by these logics. We then showed that already transitive-closure logic is expressive enough to define all partially recursive queries on linear constraint databases. Thus, with respect to this benchmark, transitive-closure, least, and stratified fixed-point logic are equivalent. As mentioned in the introduction, this is contrary to the relationship of the logics in terms of absolute definability, i.e., where there are no restrictions on the class of queries under consideration.

The motivation for choosing the class of partially recursive queries as benchmark comes from the usage of fixed-point logics as query languages, where non-recursive queries are of no practical interest.

Acknowledgement. I want to thank Jan Van den Bussche and Floris Geerts for the many helpful discussions we had on the topics of this paper and especially for pointing out the importance of the precise operational semantics used in the proofs. I also want to thank Dietmar Berwanger for the time he spent on the details of the proofs and the many helpful comments he made.

References

[BST98] O. Belegradek, A. Stolboushkin, and M. Taitslin. Extended order-generic queries. *Annals of Pure and Applied Logic*, 1998. To appear.

[DG] A. Dawar and Y. Gurevich. Fixed-point logics. *Bulletin of Symbolic Logic*. to appear.

[EF95] H.-D. Ebbinghaus and J. Flum. *Finite Model Theory*. Springer, 1995.

[GK97] S. Grumbach and G. M. Kuper. Tractable recursion over geometric data. In *Principles and Practice of Constraint Programming*, number 1330 in LNCS, pages 450 – 462. Springer, 1997.

[GK99] E. Grädel and S. Kreutzer. Descriptive complexity theory for constraint databases. In *Computer Science Logic*, number 1683 in LNCS, pages 67 – 82. Springer, 1999.

[GK00] F. Geerts and B. Kuijpers. Linear approximation of planar spatial databases using transitive-closure logic. In *Proceedings of the 19th ACM Symp. on Principles of Database Systems (PODS), 2000*, pages 126–135. ACM Press, 2000.

[KKR90] P. C. Kanellakis, G. M. Kuper, and P. Z. Revesz. Constraint query languages. In *Proc. 9th ACM Symp. on Principles of Database Systems*, pages 299–313, 1990.

[KKR95] P. Kanellakis, G. Kuper, and P. Revesz. Constraint query languages. *Journal of Computer and Systems Sciences*, 51:26–52, 1995. (An extended abstract appeared in the Proceedings of PODS'90).

[KLP00] G. Kuper, L. Libkin, and J. Paredaens, editors. *Constraint Databases*. Springer, 2000.

[Kol91] P. Kolaitis. The expressive power of stratified logic programs. *INFORMATION AND COMPUTATION*, 90:50–66, 1991.

[Kre99] S. Kreutzer. Descriptive complexity theory for constraint databases, 1999. Diplomarbeit an der RWTH Aachen.

[Kre01] S. Kreutzer. Query languages for constraint databases: First-order logic, fixed-points, and convex hulls. In *Proceedings of the 8th International Conference on Database Theory (ICDT)*, number 1973 in Lecture Notes in Computer Science, pages 248–262. Springer, 2001.

[Van99] L. Vandeurzen. *Logic-Based Query Languages for the Linear Constraint Database Model*. PhD thesis, Limburgs Universitair Centrum, 1999.

Efficient Negation Using Abstract Interpretation

Susana Muñoz, Juan José Moreno, and Manuel Hermenegildo

Universidad Politécnica de Madrid Dpto. LSIIS – Facultad de Informática. Campus de Montegancedo s/n, 28660, Madrid, SPAIN. susana|jjmoreno|herme@fi.upm.es, voice: +34-91-336-7455, fax: +34-91-336-7412.

Abstract. While negation has been a very active area of research in logic programming, comparatively few papers have been devoted to implementation issues. Furthermore, the negation-related capabilities of current Prolog systems are limited. We recently presented a novel method for incorporating negation in a Prolog compiler which takes a number of existing methods (some modified and improved by us) and uses them in a combined fashion. The method makes use of information provided by a global analysis of the source code. Our previous work focused on the systematic description of the techniques and the reasoning about correctness and completeness of the method, but provided no experimental evidence to evaluate the proposal. In this paper,we provide experimental data which indicates that the method is not only feasible but also quite promising from the efficiency point of view. In addition, the tests have provided new insight as to how to improve the proposal further. Abstract interpretation techniques (in particular those included in the Ciao Prolog system preprocessor) are important for the strategy to success.

Keywords: Negation in Logic Programming, Constraint Logic Programming, Program Analysis, Implementations of Logic Programming, Abstract Interpretation.

1 Introduction

The fundamental idea behind Logic Programming (LP) is to use a computable subset of logic as a programming language. Probably, negation is the most significant aspect of logic that was not included from the start due to the significant additional complexity that it involves. However, negation has an important role for example in knowledge representation, where many of its uses cannot be simulated by positive programs. The different proposals differ not only in expressivity but also in semantics. Presumably as a result of this, implementation aspects have received comparatively little attention. A search on the The Collection of Computer Science Bibliographies [12] with the keyword "negation" yields nearly 60 papers, but only 2 include implementation in the keywords, and fewer than 10 treat implementation issues at all. Perhaps because of this, the negation techniques supported by current Prolog compilers are rather limited.

R. Nieuwenhuis and A. Voronkov (Eds.): LPAR 2001, LNAI 2250, pp. 485–494, 2001.

Our objective is to design and implement a practical form of negation and incorporate it into a Prolog compiler. In [17] we studied systematically what we understood to be the most interesting existing proposals: negation as failure (*naf*) [7], use of delays to apply *naf* in a secure way [14], intensional negation [1],[2], and constructive negation [5],[6]. We could not find a single technique that offered both completeness and an efficient implementation. However, we proposed to use a combination of these techniques and that information from a static analysis of the program could be used to reduce the cost of selecting among techniques. We provided a coherent presentation of the techniques, implementation solutions, and a proof of correctness for the method, but we did not provide any experimental evidence to support the proposal. This is the purpose of this paper. One problem that we face is the lack of a good collection of benchmarks using negation to be used in the tests. One of the reasons has been discussed before: there are few papers about implementation of negation. Another fact is that negation is typically used in small parts of programs and it is very difficult to find it because it is not one of their main components. Additionally, the lack of sound implementations makes programmer avoid negations, even complicating the code or changing its semantics. We have had to collect a number of examples using negation from logic programming textbooks, research papers, and our own experience teaching Prolog.

We have tested these examples with all of our techniques in order to establish their efficiency. We have also measured the improvement of efficiency thanks to the use of the static analyzers. We have used the Ciao system [4] that is an efficient Prolog implementation and incorporates all the needed static analyses. However, it is important to point out that the techniques used are fairly standard, so they can be incorporated into almost any Prolog compiler.

In both cases the results have been very interesting. The comparison of the techniques has allowed us to improve the right order in which to apply them. Furthermore, we have learned that the impact of the use of the information from the analyzers is quite significant.

The rest of the paper is organized as follows. Section 2 presents more details on our method to handle negation and how it has been included in the Ciao system. Section 3 presents the evaluation of the techniques and how the results have helped us reformulate our strategy. The impact of the use of abstract interpretation is studied in 3.3.

2 Implementation of a Negation System

In this section we present shortly the techniques from the literature which we have integrated in a uniform framework. The techniques and the proposed combination share the following characteristics:

- We are interested in techniques with a single and simple semantics. The simplest alternative is to use the Closed Word Assumption (CWA) [7] by program completion and Kunen's 3-valued semantics [10]. These semantics will be the basis for soundness results.

- Another important issue is that they must be "constructive", i.e., program execution should produce adequate goal variable values for making a negated goal false. Chan's constructive negation [5],[6] fulfills both objectives. However, it is difficult to implement and expensive in terms of execution resources. Our idea is to use the simplest technique for each particular case.
- The formulations need to be uniform in order to allow the mixture of techniques and to establish sufficient correctness conditions to use them.
- We also provide a Prolog implementation of each of the techniques to combine them as also to obtain a portable implementation of negation.

2.1 Disequality Constraints

An instrumental step in order to manage negation in a more advanced way is to be able to handle disequalities between terms such as $t_1 \neq t_2$. Prolog implementations typically include only the built-in predicate `/== /2` which can only work with disequalities if both terms are ground and simply succeedss in the presence of free variables. A "constructive" behaviour must allow the "binding" of a variable with a disequality. On the other hand, the negation of an equation $X = t(\overline{Y})$ produces the universal quantification of the free variables in the equation, unless a more external quantification affects them. The negation of such an equation is $\forall\ \overline{Y}\ X \neq t(\overline{Y})$.

We have defined a predicate `=/= /2`, used to check disequalities, in a similar way to explicit unification (`=`). The main difference is that it incorporates negative normal form constraints instead of bindings and the decomposition step can produce disjunctions. When a universal quantification is used in a disequality (e.g., $\forall Y\ X \neq c(Y)$) the new constructor `fA/1` is used (e.g., `X / c(fA(Y))`).

2.2 Negation Techniques

- `Negation as failure and delays`
  Typical Prolog systems implementation of `naf(Q)` is unsound unless the free variables of Q are ground. The sound version ensures that the call to `naf` is made only when the variables of the negated goal are ground (although it has the risk of floundering). It replaces a call to $\neg p(\overline{X})$ by: $\ldots, when(ground(\overline{X}), naf(p(\overline{X}))), \ldots$
- `Constructive negation for finite solutions`
  We have implemented a Prolog predicate `cnegf(Q)` to implement finite constructive negation, that can be used if the number of solutions can be determined to be finite. It calculates the negation of the disjunction of all solutions of Q. It is a simple and efficient version of the constructive negation.
- `Intensional negation and universal quantification`
  Intensional negation is a novel approach to obtain the program completion by transforming the original program into a new one that introduces the "only if" part of the predicate definitions (i.e., interpreting implications as equivalences). We reformulate the transformation by using a single constraint to express the complement of a term, instead of a set of terms. The transformation is fully formalized in [17].

– `General constructive negation`
Full constructive negation is needed when all the previous techniques are not applicable. While there are several papers treating theoretical aspects of it, we have not found papers dealing with its implementation. We decided to design an implementation from scratch. Up to now, we have achieved only a very simple implementation that certainly needs to be improved. We have implemented a predicate `cneg/1` for full constructive negation.

2.3 Strategy

Our most novel proposal is a method for combining these techniques in order to get a correct, complete, and efficient system to handle negation. Our strategy tries to use the most efficient negation method for each particular case. Information from global program analysis and some heuristics are used to select among techniques and to optimize the computations involved in the processing of negation. We assume that correct and acceptably accurate analyses are available for the properties of groundness (variables that are bound to a ground term in a certain point of the program), goal delay (identification of delay literals which will not delay, possibly after reordering), and finiteness of the number of solutions.

Our first goal is to produce a (pseudo)predicate `neg/1` which will compute constructively the negation of any Prolog (sub)goal $\neg G(\overline{X})$, selecting the most appropriate technique at run-time. We would also like to generate a specialized version of `neg` for each negated literal in the program (each call to `neg`), using only the simplest technique required. This is a previous process to call the predicate `neg/1`. It is at compile-time in the following steps::

1. Groundness of $\overline{X}$ is checked before the call to G. On success, simple negation as failure is applied, i.e., it is compiled to `naf(`$G(\overline{X})$`)`.[1]
2. Otherwise, it is generated a new program replacing the goal $\neg G(\overline{X})$ by `when(ground(`$\overline{X}$`), naf(`$G(\overline{X})$`))` and the "elimination of delays" technique is applied to it. If the analysis and the program transformation are able to remove the delay (perhaps moving the goal) the resulting program is used.[2]
3. Otherwise, if the finiteness analysis over $G(\overline{X})$ successes, then finite constructive negation can be used, transforming the negated goal into `cnegf(`$G(\overline{X})$`)`.
4. Otherwise, the intensional negation approach is tried by generating the corresponding negated predicates and replacing the goal by `call_not(`$G(\overline{X})$`, S)` that will call `not__G(`$\overline{X}$`)`. During this process, new negated goals can appear and the same compiler strategy is applied to each of them. If `S` is bound to `success` or `fail` then negation is solved, otherwise we continue.
5. If everything fails, full constructive negation must be used and the executed goal is `cneg(`$G(\overline{X})$`)`.

[1] Since floundering is undecidable, the analysis only provides an approximation of the cases where negation as failure can be applied safely. This means that maybe we are avoiding to use the technique even in cases that it could work properly.

[2] Again, the approximation of the analysis could forbid us to apply the method in some cases in which it might still provide a sound result.

The strategy is complete and sound with respect to Kunen 3-valued semantics. This follows from the soundness of the negation techniques, the correctness of the analysis, and the completeness of constructive negation.
Let us illustrate the behavior of the method by using some simple examples. Consider the following program:

```
less(0, s(Y)).                       member(X, [X|L]).
less(s(X), s(Y)) :- less(X, Y).     member(X, [Y|L]) :- member(X, L).

p1(X) :- member(X, [0, s(0)]),      p3(X) :- neg(less(X, s(s(0)))).
        neg(less(X, s(0))).          p4(X) :- neg(less(s(0), X)).
p2(X) :- neg(less(X, s(0))),        p5(X) :- neg(less(X, s(X))).
        member(X, [0, s(0)]).
```

Each of the p_i predicates requires a different variant. For p1, the groundness test for variable X succeeds and naf/1 can be used, so it behaves as:

```
p1(X) :- member(X, [0, s(0)]),      ?- p1(X).
        naf(less(X, s(0))).             X = s(0)
```

Applying the "elimination of delays" analysis to program:

```
p2(X) :- when(ground(X), naf(less(X, s(0)))),
        member(X, [0, s(0)]).
```

the delay can be eliminated, reordering the goals as follows:

```
p2(X) :- member(X, [0, s(0)]),      ?- p2(X).
        naf(less(X, s(0))).             X = s(0)
```

The case for p3 is solved because the finiteness test can be proved to succeed, so the program is rewritten as:

```
p3(X) :- cnegf(less(X, s(s(0)))).   ?- p3(X).
                                        X / 0 ,  X / s(0)
```

p4 needs intensional negation, so the generated program is:

```
not__less(W, Z) :- W =/= 0,         ?- p4(X).
       fA(X, W =/= s(X)),               X = 0 ?;
       fA(Y, Z =/= s(Y)).               X = s(0)
not__less(s(X), s(Y)) :-
       not__less(X, Y).
p4(X) :-
       not__less(s(0), X).
```

Finally, p5 needs full constructive negation because the intensional approach is not able to give a result:

```
p5(X) :- cneg(less(X, s(X))).       ?- p5(X).
                                        no
```

3 Evaluating the Strategy

3.1 Example Programs

As mentioned earlier, one problem that we have faced is the lack of a good collection of benchmarks using negation to be used in the tests. We have however collected a number of examples using negation from logic programming textbooks, research papers, and our own experience teaching Prolog:

- **disjoint**: Code to verify that two lists have no common elements. Negation is used to check that elements of the first list are not in the second one.
- **jugs**: There are two jugs, one holding 3 and the other 5 gallons of water, they are both full at the beginning. Jugs can be filled, emptied, and dumped one into the other either until the poured-into jug is full or until the poured-out-of jug is empty. Devise a sequence of actions that will produce 4 gallons of water in the larger jug. Negation is used to check that the status of the jugs is not repeated during the process.
- **robot**: Simulation of the behavior of a robot. Negation is used to check that possible new positions for the robot are not dangerous.
- **trie**: It finds the list of word-FileList couples that shows the sublist of files where each word appears (from an initial list of words and files). Negation is used when reading words to find the first non alphanumeric character.
- **numbers9**: It uses negation to detect impossible cases in balanced trees.
- **closure**: Transitive closure of a network. Negation is used to avoid infinite loops (detecting repeated nodes). From [15] page 169.
- **union**: It is used `neg(member (X, L1))` to check if an element X appears in both lists (for union of two lists without repetitions). From [15] page 154.
- **include**: $include(P, Xs, Ys)$ is true when Ys is the list of the elements of Xs such that $P(X)$ is true. Negation is used to detect elements that do not satisfy the property $P(X)$. From [15] page 227.
- **flatten**: Flattening a list using difference-lists. Negation is used to consider lists that are not empty. From [11] Program 915.2, page 241.
- **lessNodd**: Returns the list of odd natural numbers that are less than a number N. Negation is used to control that a number is not even.
- **friend**: Deduces the relationship between two people using the stored information from a database. Negation is used to exclude ancestors and descendats from the category of friends of a person.

3.2 Experimental Results

We have first measured the execution times in milliseconds for the previous examples when using all the different (applicable) negation techniques that we have discussed, and also noted which technique is selected by our strategy (in boldface). A '–' in a cell means that the technique is not applicable. All measurements were made using Ciao Prolog[3] 1.5 on a Pentium II at 350 Mhz. Small programs were executed a sufficient number of times to obtain repeatable data. The results are shown in Table 1, where each column means:

- **const.** shows the time taken by general constructive negation (`cneg`).
- **naf/delay** uses either `naf` directly or within a delay directive. A 'D' is placed before the time in the second case.
- **fin.const.** is the time of the finite version of constructive negation, `cnegf`.

[3] The negation system is coded as a library module ("package"), which includes the corresponding syntactic and semantic extensions (i.e. Ciao's attributed variables). Such extensions apply locally within each module which uses this negation library.

Table 1. Comparing different negation techniques

programs	**const.**	**naf/delay**	**ratio**	**fin.const.**	**ratio**	**intens.**	**ratio**
disjoint1	7440	**780**	9.5	2740	2.7	-	-
disjoint2	3330	-	-	**1120**	2.9	-	-
jugs	8140	**859**	9.4	2175	3.7	<1	x
robot	4600	**1310**	3.5	1900	2.4	-	-
trie	8950	**1850**	4.8	2140	4.1	-	-
numbers9	286779	-	-	-	-	**25230**	11.3
closure1a	5100	**730**	6.9	1450	3.5	140	36.4
closure2a	3520	**560**	6.2	900	3.9	100	35.2
closure3a	10550	**1700**	6.2	2700	3.9	280	37.6
closure1b	26350	D**2240**	11.7	16460	1.6	8570	3.0
closure2b	17400	D**1500**	11.6	10580	1.6	5420	3.2
closure3b	16700	D**4510**	3.7	10120	1.6	16070	1.0
union1	1150	**300**	3.8	320	3.5	189	6.0
union2	20930	-	-	**9470**	2.2	2940	7.1
include1	9020	**1270**	7.1	2680	3.3	170	53.0
include2	9910	-	-	**2995**	3.3	-	-
flatten	32379	**8500**	3.8	12570	2.5	10	x
lessNodd1	58980	**4850**	12.1	17550	3.3	1270	46.4
lessNodd2	7750	**1490**	5.2	2700	2.8	-	-
lessNodd3	>3600000	-	-	-	-	**1540**	x
friend1a	16150	**2280**	7.0	-	-	39500	0.4
friend2a	17630	**<1**	x	-	-	10	x
friend3a	447200	D**4430**	100.9	-	-	43200	10.3
friend4a	>3600000	D**8750**	x	-	-	>3600000	x
friend1b	17350	**3020**	5.74	-	-	9	x
friend2b	17650	**<1**	x	-	-	10	x
friend3b	92500	D**3060**	30.2	-	-	43200	2.1
friend4b	>3600000	D**6050**	x	-	-	171290	x
average			13.0		2.9		18.3

- **intens.** uses the `not_'p'` predicate from the intensional negation program transformation.
- **ratio** columns measure the speedup of the technique to their left w.r.t. constructive negation.An 'x' means the ratio is extremely high.

It is clear that the technique chosen by our strategy is always equal to or better than general constructive negation. In many cases, it is also the best possible of the examined technique. We now study each technique separately:

- Using **naf** instead of **const.** results in speed-ups that range from 3.5 to 30.2. The average is more than 8.
- The **delay** technique, when applicable, has a considerable impact, speeding programs even 100 times.
- The **fin.const.**is around 3 times faster than **const.**.

- The **intens.** has a more random behavior. Very significant speed-ups are interleaved with more modest results and even some slow-down (*friend1a*).

The most surprising result is the efficiency of intensional negation. The transformational approach seems the most adequate in those cases provided that we restrict the use of the technique to the case where there are no universal quantifications in the resulting program. On the other hand, it is possible that the intensional program may not be able to produce a result (wasting time) and its use is a dynamic decision. Although these problems do not arise often in practice, they are a serious risk. So we decide to modify the strategy to use intensional negation as the preferable technique, but only when it can be used safely.

As conclusion, our strategy produces notable benefits. It preserves the completeness of general constructive negation but typically at a fraction of the cost.

3.3 Measuring the Impact of Abstract Interpretation

As mentioned above, the selection strategy and the program optimizations performed make use of information from global program analysis. We have obtained the information and performed the transformations using the analyzers and specializers that are part of the Ciao system's preprocessor, CiaoPP [9].

In particular, from the analysis point of view, the *groundness* analysis has been performed using the domain and algorithms described in [13]. In order to *eliminate delays* a technique is used which, given a program with delays, tries to identify those that are not needed, perhaps after some safe reordering of literals, as described in [8,16]. Finally, the upper bounds complexity and execution cost analysis [4] has been used to determine *finiteness in the number of solutions.*

The transformations have been implemented using the specializer in CiaoPP. The source programs always make calls to a version of the generic predicate similar to the `neg` predicate presented in section 2. The specializer creates specialized versions of the generic predicate for each literal calling `neg` in which tests and clauses are eliminated as determined by the information available from the analyzers. For example, if the groundness test is proven true at compile-time, the specializer will eliminate the test and the rest of the clauses of `neg` and eventually even replace the literal calling `neg` with a direct call to `naf`. This is done automatically by CiaoPP without having to write any additional code.

In order to estimate the advantages obtained by using this approach we now present some experimental results comparing the execution time of the programs that might be generated without the help of the analyzers and the versions produced automatically by the Ciao preprocessor. In the first case, the calls to `neg` always call (a slightly modified version of) the full version of the `neg` predicate. Thus, for example, the groundness test is performed at execution time. The clause to check the finiteness of the goal and then call `cnegf` is removed since such checking cannot be made safely at run-time. Moreover, the delay technique

[4] Note that an upper bound cost that is not infinity implies a finite number of solutions (an alternative is [3]

Table 2. Impact of program analysis

program	with pp.	without pp.	ratio	naf	ratio	secure naf	ratio	prep.
disjoint1	1020	1700	1.66	780	0.76	1469	1.44	78
jugs	969	8419	8.68	859	0.88	1690	1.74	227
robot	1960	3100	1.58	1310	0.66	1800	0.91	700
trie	1890	2450	1.29	1850	0.97	1900	1.00	508
union1	300	350	1.16	230	0.76	300	1.00	119
closure1a	730	2600	3.56	730	1.00	900	1.23	257
closure2a	570	1970	3.45	560	0.98	670	1.17	257
closure3a	1710	5050	2.95	1700	0.99	2010	1.17	257
include1	1099	1180	1.07	1080	0.98	1270	1.15	178
flatten	8859	9300	1.04	8500	0.95	8080	0.91	168
lessNodd1	7310	8670	1.18	4850	0.66	6300	0.86	58
lessNodd2	1780	1830	1.02	1490	0.83	1590	0.89	58
friend1b	3220	3360	1.04	3020	0.93	3180	0.98	198
friend1a	2820	2860	1.01	2280	0.80	2840	1.00	198
average			2.33		0.86		1.10	
closure1b	610	8610	14.11	-	-	-	-	257
closure2b	570	5700	10.00	-	-	-	-	257
closure3b	1800	16300	9.05	-	-	-	-	257
friend3a	3100	43350	13.98	-	-	-	-	198
friend4a	6210	>3600000	x	-	-	-	-	198
friend3b	3100	43400	14.00	-	-	-	-	198
friend4b	6210	171495	27.61	-	-	-	-	198
average			14.79					
disjoint2	1125	3700	3.28	-	-	-	-	78
union2	9590	21010	2.19	-	-	-	-	119
include2	3070	10010	3.26	-	-	-	-	178
average			5.65					
average			2.37		0.86		1.10	

is not used because, in general, it has the risk of floundering. In contrast, the version obtained with the help of the analyzers can remove the groundness check, use the reordering proposed by the elimination of delays, and use the information of the finiteness analysis to call `cnegf`.

Table 2 presents the results. We have also added for reference columns showing the execution time of using `naf` directly and a secure version of `naf`, i.e., checking groundness before. Finally, we have also added the time taken by CiaoPP to perform the analysis and transformation.

The table reveals that the impact of abstract interpretation is significant enough to justify its use. For those examples where `naf` is applicable, the analyzer is able to detect groundness statically in all the cases, so the call to `neg` is replaced by `naf`. It is worth mentioning that the implementation of the dynamic groundness test in Ciao is quite efficient (it is performed at a very low level, inherited from its &-Prolog origins). Even so, the speedup can reach a factor of over 8, and the average is 2.33. The impact of the elimination of delay is even better in general. Notice that if the delay technique is not used, intensional negation could be used instead, which in many cases is a very efficient approach. Even with this drawback, the use of abstract interpretation is helpful. When the finiteness analysis avoids the use of full constructive negation the speed-ups are greater than 3. The difference between the programs after preprocessing and the direct use of `naf` is irrelevant. The code produced by the preprocessor is better than the secure use of `naf` because of the elimination of groundness tests.

Acknowledgments. We are grateful to M. Carro and D. Cabeza for providing examples and to them, F. Bueno, and G. Puebla for their support using the Ciao system preprocessor. This work was funded in part by CICYT project EDIPIA (TIC99-1151).

References

1. R. Barbuti, D. Mancarella, D. Pedreschi, and F. Turini. Intensional negation of logic programs. *Lecture notes on Computer Science*, 250:96–110, 1987.
2. R. Barbuti, D. Mancarella, D. Pedreschi, and F. Turini. A transformational approach to negation in logic programming. *JLP*, 8(3):201–228, 1990.
3. C. Braem, B. Le Charlier, S. Modart, and P. Van Hentenryck. Cardinality analysis of Prolog. In *ILPS*, pages 457–471. The MIT Press, 1994.
4. F. Bueno. *The CIAO Multiparadigm Compiler: A User's Manual*, 1995.
5. D. Chan. Constructive negation based on the complete database. In *Proc. Int. Conference on LP'88*, pages 111–125. The MIT Press, 1988.
6. D. Chan. An extension of constructive negation and its application in coroutining. In *Proc. NACLP'89*, pages 477–493. The MIT Press, 1989.
7. K. L. Clark. Negation as failure. In J. Minker H. Gallaire, editor, *Logic and Data Bases*, pages 293–322, New York, NY, 1978.
8. M. García , K. Marriott, and P. Stuckey. Efficient analysis of constraint logic programs with dynamic scheduling. In *ILPS*, pages 417–431. MIT Press, 1995.
9. M. Hermenegildo, F. Bueno, G. Puebla, and P. López-García. Program Analysis, Debugging and Optimization Using the Ciao System Preprocessor. In *1999 ICLP*, pages 52–66, Cambridge, MA, November 1999. MIT Press.
10. K. Kunen. Negation in logic programming. *JLP*, 4:289–308, 1987.
11. E. Shapiro L. Sterling. *The Art of Prolog*. The MIT Press, 1987.
12. The Collection of Computer Science Bibliographies. `http://liinwww.ira.uka.de/bibliography/LogicProgramming/index.html`.
13. K. Muthukumar and M. Hermenegildo. Compile-time derivation of variable dependency using abstract interpretation. *JLP*, 13(2/3):315–347, July 1992.
14. L. Naish. Negation and Control in Prolog. In *LNCS*, number 238. Springe, 1985.
15. R. A. O'Keefe. *The Craft of Prolog*. The MIT Press, 1990.
16. G. Puebla, M. García , K. Marriott, and P. Stuckey. Optimization of Logic Programs with Dynamic Scheduling. In *1997 International Conference on LP*, pages 93–107, Cambridge, MA, June 1997. MIT Press.
17. J.J. Moreno S. Muñoz. How to incorporate negation in a prolog compiler. In V. Santos Costa E. Pontelli, editor, *2nd International Workshop PADL'2000*, volume 1753 of *LNCS*, pages 124–140, Boston, MA (USA), 2000. Springer.

Certifying Synchrony for Free

Sylvain Boulmé and Grégoire Hamon

Laboratoire d'Informatique de Paris 6 (LIP6),
8, rue du Capitaine Scott, 75015 Paris, France.
`Sylvain.Boulme,Gregoire.Hamon@lip6.fr`

Abstract. We express reactive programs in COQ using data-flow synchronous operators. Following LUCID-SYNCHRONE approach, synchronous static constraints are here expressed using dependent types. Hence, our analysis of synchrony is here directly performed by COQ typechecker.

1 Introduction

Synchronous languages [Hal93] have been designed to help in the conception of reactive systems, especially critical reactive systems (planes, power plants control...). *Synchrony* is a program property which ensures bounded reaction-time and memory at execution. Synchronous languages statically check this property, however, in a critical context, it may be needed to have a formal proof of this property, or more generally to prove program properties.

In this work we are internested in LUCID-SYNCHRONE [CP00a] (LS for short), a *data-flow synchronous language*. We present here a natural and *shallow* embedding of LS into the COQ proof assistant. This embedding concerns both the dynamic and the static semantics of the language, such that synchrony analysis is obtained for free. Moreover, it gives us a denotational semantics of LS in COQ and is thus a good starting point for designing a prover for LS programs in COQ, following [Fil99,Par95] approach. This semantics can also be used to experiment with the language: we have used it to propose a notion of recursive functions for LS, as a generalization of recursive streams (see [BH01]).

We are now going to quickly introduce LS and COQ. These introductions are just aiming at making this paper self-explanatory, for more details on these tools, you should consult their tutorials and reference manuals ([PCCH01][1], [BBC+00]).

1.1 LUCID-SYNCHRONE

LUCID-SYNCHRONE is a language born to bring synchronous data-flow languages like LUSTRE [HCRP91] closer to general functional languages, in particular ML. This was needed for several reasons. First, synchronous languages were in need of more mechanisms of abstraction. Second, to better understand the link between these two families of languages, and third, to use this link in a certification

[1] The LS compiler is available at: `http://www-spi.lip6.fr/lucid-synchrone/`

R. Nieuwenhuis and A. Voronkov (Eds.): LPAR 2001, LNAI 2250, pp. 495–506, 2001.

or proof context. LS has proved to bring good answers to the first need, it has inspired the next generation of the industrial tool SCADE [Tel01] [CP00b]. We are here interested in the third need, and in formally certifying or proving programs.

LS is an ML like language over streams (or *data-flow*): all values are infinite sequences. These streams can be on each instant either absent or present. They are equipped with a *clock*, a boolean information indicating on each instant whether the stream is present or absent. The clock which is always `true` is called the *basic clock* of the system. To ensure synchrony, clocks have to verify some constraints, this is done by a static analysis, the *clock calculus* [Cas92]. Previous works on LS [CP98] have shown that it could be defined as a ML type system extended with dependent types. This has allowed the LS compiler to provide clocks polymorphism and inference.

The compiler also performs other static analysis. Especially, it checks *causality* in recursive definitions. Instantaneous recursion is forbidden: the current value of a stream should not depend on itself. This property is also represented in our encoding.

1.2 Coq

Coq is a proof assistant based on the Calculus of Constructions [CH88], enriched with inductive [PM93] and co-inductive [Gim94] type definitions. Calculus of Constructions is a typed lambda-calculus, with *types* as first-class values (i.e. types are terms). Hence, *terms* may be:

- *identifiers*, defined constants or declared variables in the context.
- the *application* of a functional term `M` to a term `N`, denoted by "`(M N)`".
- the *abstraction* of a variable `x` of type `A` in a term `b`, denoted by "`[x:A]b`".
- the *product* of a type family `B` indexed by a variable `x` of type `A` (i.e. the type of functions "`[x:A]b`" where `b` is of type `B`, assuming `x` of type `A`). It is generally denoted by "`(x:A)B`" or simply "`A->B`" if `x` does not occur in `B`.

In the spirit of Curry-Howard isomorphism, types may represent programming datatypes or logical propositions. This is expressed in Coq using two special types of types, `Set` as type of datatypes, and `Prop` as type of propositions. Hence, "`(x:A)B`" may also be interpreted as "for all `x` in `A`, `B`" and "`->`" as the logical implication.

Via coinductive type definitions [Gim98], Coq provides infinite values and co-recursion[2]. We have used them to define synchronous streams in Coq.

Coq provides syntactic features, such as implicit terms (denoted by a "?") or defined constants with implicit arguments, that force the system to try some type inference *à la* ML[3]. We have heavily used these features to provide some clock inference.

---

[2] Let us note however that Coq is strongly normalizing: hence, all computations terminate, even on infinite values.

[3] with the following exceptions: there is no mechanism for polymorphic generalization and inference may fail due to undecidability of high-order unification.

1.3 Related Works

Valid LS programs check some non-trivial static properties. Some of these properties are guaranteed by static analyses performed by the compiler. Others are guaranteed by construction, i.e. by the semantics of the language. A first difficulty was to understand how to integrate these properties in our description. If we are only interested in proving properties about LS programs, then a simple approach consist in stating these properties as axioms or hypothesis in the description, relying on a compiler to check them. This approach is for instance suggested by [BCDPV99]. Here, we are more ambitious. We want to prove the existence of LS programs, and their static fundamental properties, independently of any external system. This is also the approach of [DCC00]. In this approach, a compiler could still be used to provide some Coq proofs from its static analysis, thus easing the work on Coq.

Synchronous languages have been introduced for software and hardware reliability. Thus, formalizing synchronous systems is an active research area. A lot of case studies have been done, using many formalisms [KNT00,BCDPV99,CGJ99]. There are also some axiomatizations of synchronous languages [BCDPV99, NBT98], our work lies in this latter category. Our main originality here, is to embed the clock calculus of LS as a special instance of Coq type system. LS is well-suited for this study, as its clock calculus is expressed as a dependent type system whereas other synchronous data-flow languages (Lustre, Signal [BLJ91]) use specific analysis.

2 Sampled Streams and Their Equality in Coq

We first define the type of *"sampled elements of* A*"*, to represent instantaneous values of type A in synchronous streams. On a given instant, a sampled element can be either present or absent. We also introduce an error element, which will be raised in case of instantaneous recursion (*non-causal* program).

Then, we define clocks as streams of booleans. The type of *"sampled streams"* can then be defined as a coinductive type parametrized by a type A and a clock c. Its single constructor sp_cons takes as arguments a sampled element and a sampled stream.

```
Inductive samplElt[A:Set]: bool -> Set:=
 | None: (samplElt A false)
 | Any: A -> (samplElt A true)
 | Fail: (samplElt A true).

Definition clock:=(Stream bool).

CoInductive samplStr[A:Set]: clock -> Set:=
 sp_cons: (c:clock)
          (samplElt A (hd c))->(samplStr A (tl c))->(samplStr A c).
```

We define two destructors sp_hd and sp_tl for accessing respectively the head and the tail of sampled streams. We have of course the following property:

```
Lemma unfold_samplStr:
 (c:clock; s:(samplStr A c))s=(sp_cons (sp_hd s) (sp_tl s)).
```

The equality we consider over sampled streams, denoted by `sp_eq`, is bisimulation or extensional equality. It is defined for streams that may not have *interconvertible* clocks, but only *bisimulable* clocks. We have also defined a notion of "clock coercion" compatible with bisimulation (see [BH01]).

We are actually only interested in programs producing *wellformed* sampled streams, i.e. sampled streams without `Fail` element. Hence, we have defined a logical predicate `sp_wf` indicating wellformedness of sampled streams (see [BH01]).

3 Lucid-Synchrone Data-Flow Operators in Coq

We now detail the encoding of LS data-flow operators. The language provides three kinds of operators, *point-wise* operators are classical operators like +, −, ... lifted to streams, sampling operators are streams operators allowing under or over-sampling and *delay* operators allow delaying a stream.

3.1 Point-Wise Operators

First, every object of the base language is lifted into a constant sampled stream. As in LS, these constants have polymorphic clocks. Operator `elt_const` returns a sampled element: either `Any` of its argument or `None` depending on the clock. The `sp_const` operator only iterates it on every instant. To make the following Coq code more readable, we have replaced by "· · ·" some type information needed by typechecking. By convention, `A` and `B` are variables of type `Set`.

```
Variable a: A.

Definition elt_const : (b:bool)(samplElt A b)
  := [b]<···>if b then (Any a) else (None A).

CoFixpoint sp_const : (c:clock)(samplStr A c)
  := [c](sp_cons (elt_const (hd c)) (sp_const (tl c))).
```

Lifted functions will then be applied point-wisely on streams. `sp_extend` takes a stream of functions and a stream of arguments, and returns the stream of their point-wise application. Functions and arguments are required to be on the same clock, thus, no memory is required by this function. As before, `elt_extend` is the instantaneous application on sampled elements, and `sp_extend` iterates it on every instant.

An interesting application of `sp_extend` is the definition of `sp_if`, the point-wise if-then-else (or multiplexer in circuits):

```
Definition If:= [b:bool; x,y:A]if b then x else y.

Definition sp_if:=
 [c:clock; lc:(samplStr bool c); x,y:(samplStr A c)]
  (sp_extend (sp_extend (sp_extend (sp_const If ?) lc) x) y).
```

```
Definition elt_extend:
 (b:bool)(samplElt A->B b)->(samplElt A b)->(samplElt B b)
 := [b; f]<···>Cases f of
         | None => [_](None B)
         | (Any vf) =>
             [x]Cases x of
                 | (Any vx) => (Any (vf vx))
                 | Fail => (Fail ?)
                 | ···
                 end
         | Fail => [_](Fail ?)
         end.

CoFixpoint sp_extend:
 (c:clock)(samplStr A->B c)->(samplStr A c)->(samplStr B c)
 := [c;f;x](sp_cons (elt_extend (sp_hd f) (sp_hd x))
                    (sp_extend (sp_tl f) (sp_tl x))).
```

Fig. 1. Definition of extend operator

3.2 Sampling Operators

Sampling operators are used either to filter a stream (when) or to combine several complementary streams (merge). The when operator filters a streams on a boolean condition: the result is the sub-stream of the entry only present when the boolean condition is true. Thus the clock of the result differs from the one of the entry: it is on a subclock of it, defined by the condition.

We first need an operator to dynamically build such a subclock. The clock constructor sp_on coerces a sampled boolean stream into a clock. Hence, this is the type operator introducing dependent types in the LS clock system.

As usual, elt_on defines the instantaneous behavior of the constructor, and sp_on only iterates it on every instant. With Fail as argument, elt_on returns true: the error will be diffused by the sampling operations (see elt_when below).

```
Definition elt_on: (b:bool)(samplElt bool b)->bool
 := [b;o]Cases o of
        | None => false
        | (Any x) => x
        | Fail => true
        end.

CoFixpoint sp_on: (c:clock)(samplStr bool c) -> clock
 := [c;lc](Cons (elt_on (sp_hd lc)) (sp_on (sp_tl lc))).
```

Now we can define sp_when, the sampling operator. It simply copies its input, forgetting elements when clock of the output is false.

```
Definition elt_when:
 (b:bool;o:(samplElt bool b))(samplElt A b)->(samplElt A (elt_on o))
 := [b;o]<···>Cases o of
         | None => [x](None ?)
         | (Any b0) =>
              [x:(samplElt A true)]<···>if b0 then x else (None ?)
         | Fail => [x](Fail ?)
         end.

CoFixpoint sp_when:
  (c:clock; lc:(samplStr bool c))(samplStr A c)->(samplStr A (sp_on lc))
 := [c;lc;x](sp_cons ··· (elt_when (sp_hd lc) (sp_hd x))
                         (sp_when (sp_tl lc) (sp_tl x))).
```

The sp_merge operator is defined in the same way. It is a kind of if-then-else, whose branches have exclusive clocks[4]. It allows a kind of over-sampling, since output is on faster clock than branches of the sp_merge. Its type is:

```
CoFixpoint sp_merge :
 (A:Set; c:clock; lc:(samplStr bool c))
     (samplStr A (sp_on lc))
      ->(samplStr A (sp_on (sp_not lc)))->(samplStr A c).
```

We have the following relation between sp_if, sp_merge and sp_when (where sp_eq is bisimulation over sampled streams):

```
Lemma if_equiv:
 (A:Set; c:clock; lc:(samplStr bool c); x,y:(samplStr A c))
  (sp_wf x)->  (sp_wf y) ->
    (sp_eq (sp_if lc x y)
          (sp_merge (sp_when lc x) (sp_when (sp_not lc) y))).
```

3.3 Delay Operators

Delay operators allow referring to past values, thus providing implicit memory manipulations. We consider here the *"followed by"* operator (fby) which is an initialized delay (LS also provides uninitialized delay, and initializer, their full description in Coq can be found in [BH01]).

If x and y are two streams sampled on the same clock, then x fby y is a stream sampled on this clock, whose present elements are, at first, the first present element of x, and then forever the previous present element of y. Hence, x fby y is a delay of y, initialized with the first element of x.

The fact that x and y have the same clock is fundamental here: it guarantees that only one element of y will have to be memorized before x yields its first value, i.e fby is a one place buffer. Hence, clocks provide here a simple way to express static synchronization constraints.

[4] In the type of sp_merge, sp_not is the point-wise negation defined using sp_extend.

Examples in Coq syntax. Before defining formally `fby` in Coq, we study some examples to illustrate the expressive power of delays within the rest of the language. It is also the opportunity to show inference mechanisms in Coq, very close to the inference mechanisms of LS. We use here some grammar extensions of Coq, to provide a more friendly syntax:

- lifted constants are given between back-quote as `‘(0)‘`, their clocks are inferred.
- `sp_extend` is abbreviated into `ext`.
- `when` is the infix notation corresponding to the operator `sp_when`, with permuted arguments. (Hence the condition is given on the right).
- `merge` is an abbreviation for `sp_merge`, forcing the condition to be explicit (the condition is implicit in `sp_merge`, which makes the type inference fail on most practical examples).
- `rec0` is the fixpoint operator for streams. It takes a function as argument, which introduces the bounded name for referring to recursive occurrences of the stream being built. `rec0` may be prefixed by "`<c>`" where `c` is the clock of the result. This syntactic feature is useful for binding clock variables which need to be generalized by hand. This operator will be studied in details in section 4.

The sequence of natural numbers can now be written as `Nat` below. Coq infers the type `(c:clock)(samplStr nat c)` for this definition. This stream is polymorphic on clock. This must be explicitly expressed to Coq. Here, Coq infers clocks for the constants `‘(0)‘` and `‘S‘` (natural successor function), using `fby` and `ext` clock constraints.

```
Definition Nat := [c](<c>rec0 [N](‘(0)‘ fby (ext ‘S‘ N))).
```

We can also define the Fibonacci sequence: [5]

```
Definition Fib :=
  [c](<c>rec0 [fib] (‘(1)‘ fby (ext (ext ‘plus‘ fib) (‘(0)‘ fby fib)))).
```

A delicate feature of delays is the fact that they do not permute with sampling operators. For instance, `Nat_on` and `Nat_mod`, both of the same type, differs only in their definition by the position of `when` with respect to `fby`. Their semantics are very different. The former enumerates naturals on `(sp_on lc)`, and returns zero on `(sp_on (sp_not lc))`. The latter indicates at each instant the number of passed instants since `lc` was false. Indeed, in the former case, `when` is applied before `fby`: thus, the clock of `fby` is `(sp_on lc)`. On the contrary, in the latter case, `fby` is on `c`.

```
Definition Nat_on :=
  [c; lc](<c>rec0 [N](merge lc (‘(0)‘ fby ((ext ‘S‘ N) when lc)) ‘(0)‘)).

Definition Nat_mod :=
  [c; lc](<c>rec0 [N](merge lc ((‘(0)‘ fby (ext ‘S‘ N)) when lc) ‘(0)‘)).
```

[5] In LS, this definition is compiled using only a memory size of two integers.

Formal descriptions of fby. Below, we first define an internal operator (ie not a LS operator) for delay. It takes a sampled stream and a sampled element on `true` (ie `Fail` or a value) and uses it in order to initialize the delay. It is defined by cofixpoint, and actually this last parameter is used for memorizing the last element of the stream. Then, we define `sp_fby x y`: we wait for the first present element of `x` and use it to delay `y`.

```
CoFixpoint sp_delay:
 (c:clock)(samplStr A c)->(samplElt A true)->(samplStr A c)
 := [c]<···>Cases c of (Cons hc tc) =>
        <···>if hc
             then
               [x;a](sp_cons a (sp_delay (sp_tl x) (sp_hd x)))
             else
               [x;a](sp_cons (None A) (sp_delay (sp_tl x) a))
      end.

CoFixpoint sp_fby:
 (c:clock)(samplStr A c)->(samplStr A c)->(samplStr A c)
 := [c]<···>Cases c of (Cons hc tc) =>
        <···>if hc
             then
               [x;y](sp_delay y (sp_hd x))
             else
               [x;y](sp_cons (None A) (sp_fby (sp_tl x) (sp_tl y)))
      end.
```

4 Recursive Constructions

Recursive constructions in LS can not be directly (or syntactically) translated into cofixpoints of Coq: guarded conditions of Coq are too restrictive for this purpose. However, we can build in Coq a generic recursion operator (using cofixpoint of Coq) which emulates recursive constructions of LS. This kind of trick is already used in the standard library of Coq for emulating generic wellfounded recursion with primitive recursion. However, here the computational behavior of our recursive constructions is very far from the one when compiled in LS.

LS provides two notions of recursive constructions: recursive streams and recursive functions of streams. The first are always reactive, but not the second (see [BH01]). Thus, we are especially interested in the first construction. However, we define here a unique operator of recursion, from which both constructions can be derived. As some preconditions of this recursion operator can be simplified in the particular case of recursive streams, we only present this case. We do not present here the formal encoding of this operator (see [BH01]), it is built classically as a smallest fixpoint: by successive approximations using `Fail`. Indeed, for the considered functions, there is at most one fixpoint (see `rec0_uniq` below): the smallest is also the biggest.

4.1 Basic Recursion on Streams

Recursive streams are built by iterating infinitely a function on itself, using the `rec0` operator used in previous examples. This operator is of type:

```
(A:Set; c:clock)((samplStr A c)->(samplStr A c)) -> (samplStr A c)
```

However, applying `rec0` only makes sense for functions satisfying some preconditions: length-fail-preservation (`F0_lfp`) on the basic clock, and wellformedness-increase (`F0_nfstwf_inc`).

```
Variable c: clock.
Variable F0: (samplStr A c) -> (samplStr A c).

Hypothesis F0_lfp:
  (s1,s2:(samplStr A c); n:nat)
    (sp_inf n s1 s2)->(sp_inf n (F0 s1) (F0 s2)).

Hypothesis F0_nfstwf_inc:
  (n:nat; s:(samplStr A c))(glob_nfstwf n s)->(glob_nfstwf (S n) (F0 s)).
```

We now detail the meaning of these preconditions.

Length-fail-preserving functions (on the basic clock). Length-fail-preservation on the basic clock is an invariant property satisfied by every LS programs. It deals both with synchrony (length-preservation) and with the "error semantics" of `Fail` (fail-preservation).

Length-preservation on the basic clock means that for every LS function, at every instant, the function takes one sampled element (possibly `None`) and returns one sampled element (possibly `None`). *Fail-preservation* means that functions are monotonous with respect to the flat order with `Fail` as minimum element.

Hence, we have defined `(sp_inf n)` as an order over sampled streams such that `(sp_inf n s1 s2)` means that the `n` first elements of `s1` are inferior for the flat order to their respective element in `s2` (see [BH01]). Now we informally say that a function is length-fail-preserving if for every `n`, it preserves the order `(sp_inf n)`. Length-fail-preservation has been proved for all LS operators.

Wellformedness-increase. Wellformedness-increase is related to causality: length-fail-preserving and causal functions are indeed wellformedness-increasing. First, we have defined a notion of *"partial-wellformedness"*: `(glob_nfstwf n s)` indicates whether the stream `s` has no fail element until the `n`-th instant of the basic clock (see [BH01]). And we say that a function F of type `(samplStr A c) -> (samplStr A c)` is *wellformedness-increasing*, if its input is partially wellformed until the n-th instant implies that its output is partially wellformed until the $n+1$-th instant. Thus, by iterating infinitely on F, we build a wellformed stream.

Then, we can prove that `sp_fby` is wellformedness-increasing on its second argument, and for others operators, we can prove partial-wellformedness preservation.

Correctness of `rec0`. Under the preconditions given above, `(rec0 F0)` is of type `(samplStr A c)`, and satisfies the three following properties (proven in Coq), stating that `(rec0 F0)` is wellformed, and is the unique fixpoint of `F0`.

```
Lemma rec0_wf: (sp_wf (rec0 F0)).

Theorem rec0_inv: (sp_eq (rec0 F0) (F0 (rec0 F0))).

Theorem rec0_uniq:
  (r0:(samplStr A c))(sp_eq r0 (F0 r0))->(sp_eq (rec0 F0) r0).
```

We have already seen some examples of single recursive streams using `rec0`. The satisfaction of recursive preconditions for each of these examples has been proved in Coq. Most often, these proofs have been completely discharged by the Coq prover using *à la prolog* resolution on a basis of lemmas containing properties of each LS operator with respect to length-fail-preservation and partial wellformedness.

4.2 Other Recursive Constructions

The `rec0` operator can also be used to express *mutually recursive streams* of LS, by putting each mutually recursive occurrence as a parameter of a simple recursive stream and linking mutual recursion by hand. Hence, expressing such mutual definitions of LS in Coq need some syntactic treatment, but it seems automatable. In order to prove that such "mutually recursive definitions" satisfy the preconditions of `rec0`, we have proven that `rec0` has itself a good behavior with respect to length-fail-preservation and partial wellformedness (see [BH01]).

Actually, all the previous properties of `rec0` are specialized properties of a more general operator `rec1`. This operator has type:

```
rec1: (A,B:Set; C:(B->clock))
        (((x:B)(samplStr A (C x)))->(x:B)(samplStr A (C x)))
          ->(x:B)(samplStr A (C x))
```

Thus, it allows building recursive functions of type `(x:B)(samplStr A (C x))` where `B` is any type. Motivations and formal encoding of `rec1` are given in [BH01].

5 Conclusion

We have here established an embedding of LS into Coq, preserving the semantics of strongly typed functional languages with polymorphism, dependent types, and streams:

- streams of LS are represented by sampled streams in Coq.
- functions of LS are represented by functions of Coq.
- clock concepts (polymorphism, dependent types) of LS are represented by the equivalent type concepts in Coq.

This result strengthens both LS and COQ. Indeed, it shows that LS can be derived naturally from a more general language. It also shows that COQ coinductive part is powerful enough to represent programs from the real world.

As a consequence, LS programs can be almost syntactically embedded into COQ. Actually, this embedding requires expliciting some clock and types parameters to COQ (especially because in COQ, there is no automatic generalization over polymorphic variables), but it would be easy to automate this translation, using LS typecheker. Indeed, most of the clock inference of LS is already done by the type inference of COQ. We have illustrated this point on some examples along the paper[6].

Currently, automation for building proofs of the validity of LS programs (length-fail-preserving and partial wellformedness increasing) is not very powerful: we only use *à la prolog* resolution as a good basis of lemmas. We could probably use the compiler analyses to produce these proofs more efficiently. COQ typechecker would just have then to check their correction. Hence, an application to this work, could be to certify the validity of LS programs.

Then, it would be interesting to build tools for proving general properties on LS programs into COQ. This could lead us to define a notion of *"synchronous property"*. Indeed, we may find a logic following Curry-Howard isomorphism such that proofs in this logic are synchronous functions, and then have a theorem of realizability for this logic. It would provide a good framework for synthesizing proofs from programs following Parent approach [Par95].

Another application to this work could be to prove the correction of a LS compiler. It may consist in proving that the compiler satisfies the denotational semantics presented here. In particular, it would require to prove that the operational semantics of LS (using co-iteration [CP98]) refines this denotational semantics.

Acknowledgements. We would like to thank Marc Pouzet for all the time spend discussing this work and for many useful suggestions.

References

[BBC+00] Barras B, et al. *The Coq Proof Assistant Reference Manual, version 6.3.1.* Coq Project, INRIA-Rocquencourt, May 2000.

[BCDPV99] Bensalem S, et al. A methodology for proving control programs with Lustre and PVS. In *Dependable Computing for Critical Applications, DCCA-7.* IEEE Computer Society, January 1999.

[BH01] Boulmé S and Hamon G. A clocked denotational semantics for Lucid-Synchrone in Coq. Technical report, LIP6, 2001. Available at `http://www-spi.lip6.fr/lucid-synchrone/lucid_in_coq_report.ps`.

[BLJ91] Benveniste A, et al. Synchronous programming with events and relations: The Signal language and its semantics. *Science of Computer Programming*, 16:103–149, 1991.

[6] More examples and the whole COQ code of the encoding is available at `http://www-spi.lip6.fr/lucid-synchrone/lucid_in_coq/`

[Cas92] Caspi P. Clocks in dataflow languages. *Theorical Computer Science*, 94:125–140, 1992.

[CGJ99] Coupet-Grimal S and Jakubiec L. Hardware verification using co-induction in Coq. In *TPHOLs'99*, number 1690 in LNCS. 1999.

[CH88] Coquand T and Huet G. The Calculus of Constructions. *Information and Computation*, 76:95–120, 1988.

[CP98] Caspi P and Pouzet M. A co-iterative characterization of synchronous stream functions. In *Coalgebraic Methods in Computer Science (CMCS'98)*, ENTCS. 28-29 March 1998.

[CP00a] Caspi P and Pouzet M. Lucid Synchrone, an ML extension to Lustre. In *Submited for publication*. 2000.

[CP00b] Colaco JL and Pouzet M. Prototypages. Rapport final du projet GENIE II, Verilog SA, Janvier 2000.

[DCC00] Dumas-Canovas C and Caspi P. A PVS proof obligation generator for Lustre programs. In *LPAR'2000*, number 1955 in LNAI. 2000.

[Fil99] Filliâtre JC. *Preuve de programmes impératifs en théorie des types*. Ph.D. thesis, Université Paris-Sud, July 1999.

[Gim94] Gimenez E. Codifying guarded definitions with recursive schemes. Technical Report 95-07, LIP ENS-Lyon, December 1994.

[Gim98] Gimenez E. A tutorial on recursive types in Coq. Technical Report 0221, INRIA, May 1998.

[Hal93] Halbwachs N. *Synchronous programming of reactive systems*. Kluwer Academic Pub., 1993.

[HCRP91] Halbwachs N, et al. The Synchronous dataflow programming language Lustre. *Proceedings of the IEEE*, 79(9):1305–1320, September 1991.

[KNT00] Kerboeuf M, et al. The steam-boiler problem in Signal-Coq. In *TPHOLs'2000*, number 1869 in LNCS. 2000.

[NBT98] Nowak D, et al. Co-inductive axiomatization of a synchronous language. In *TPHOLs'98*, number 1479 in LNCS. 1998.

[Par95] Parent C. Synthesizing proofs from programs in the Calculus of Inductive Constructions. In *Mathematics for Programs Constructions'95*, number 947 in LNCS. 1995.

[PCCH01] Pouzet M, et al. *Lucid Synchrone v2.0 - Tutorial and Reference manual*. LIP6, April 2001. Available at http://www-spi.lip6.fr/lucid-synchrone/lucid_synchrone_2.0_manual.ps.

[PM93] Paulin-Mohring C. Inductive Definitions in the System Coq - Rules and Properties. In *TLCA*, number 664 in LNCS. 1993.

[Tel01] Telelogic. *Telelogic Tau Scade language - Reference manual*, 2001.

A Computer Environment for Writing Ordinary Mathematical Proofs

David McMath, Marianna Rozenfeld, and Richard Sommer

Education Program for Gifted Youth
Stanford University
Stanford, California 94305-4115 {mcdave,marianna,sommer}@epgy.stanford.edu

Abstract. The EPGY Theorem-Proving Environment is designed to help students write ordinary mathematical proofs. The system, used in a selection of computer-based proof-intensive mathematics courses, allows students to easily input mathematical expressions, apply proof strategies, verify logical inference, and apply mathematical rules. Each course has its own language, database of theorems, and mathematical inference rules. The main goal of the project is to create a system that imitates standard mathematical practice in the sense that it allows for natural modes of reasoning to generate proofs that look much like ordinary textbook proofs. Additionally, the system can be applied to an unlimited number of proof exercises.

1 Introduction

The Education Program for Gifted Youth (EPGY), at Stanford University, is an ongoing research project developing computer-based courses and offering them to students via distance learning. We offer courses in mathematics and other subjects and target pre-college students of high ability. The EPGY Theorem-Proving Environment is a tool used in EPGY's proof-intensive mathematics courses. Whereas other computer tools for teaching mathematics (for example, graphing calculators and "dynamic geometry tools") emphasize experimental and inductive approaches, the EPGY theorem-proving environment aims to preserve the traditional emphasis on deductive reasoning in mathematics. In doing so, the system aims to come as close as possible to "standard mathematical practice", both in how the final proofs look and in the kinds of methods used to produce them. In particular, we expect the student to make the kinds of steps normally present in student proofs. The system works to verify the students' logical reasoning and generate and prove "obvious" side conditions that are needed for a correct formal proof but which are routinely omitted in standard practice.

Our use of the Theorem Proving Environment emphasizes teaching mathematics, and we strive to avoid, as much as possible, having to teach a complete logic course or to require lengthly tutorials in how to use a specialized tool. Also, students need to transition in and out of the mainstream curriculum as they move in and out of our program, so we want our courses to look as ordinary

R. Nieuwenhuis and A. Voronkov (Eds.): LPAR 2001, LNAI 2250, pp. 507–516, 2001.

as possible while allowing for the use of the Theorem Proving Environment. Currently the system is being used by students in courses in Euclidean geometry and linear algebra, and it is scheduled for use in courses in calculus and differential equations.

2 Background and Related Work

EPGY is an outgrowth of earlier projects at Stanford in computer-based education dating back to the 1960s. Currently, EPGY offers courses in mathematics from first grade through much of the undergraduate mathematics curriculum. All of these courses are computer-based and self-paced; they consist of multimedia lectures and interactive exercises. These courses are offered to pre-college and college students of high ability as part of a distance-learning program.

Work on interactive theorem proving at EPGY's predecessor, the Institute for Mathematical Studies in the Social Sciences, dates back to the early 1960s with the use of an interactive theorem prover for the teaching of elementary logic to elementary- and middle-school children. With the advent of more powerful automated proof-checking systems, interactive proof systems for university-level logic and set theory were created. These proof systems formed the core component of the Stanford logic course starting in 1972 and the Stanford set theory course starting in 1974 [9].

Work on derivation systems for mathematics courses began in 1985 as part of a project to develop a computer-based course in calculus. This work consisted of three parts. The first part was the formulation of a formal derivation system for differential and integral calculus [2]. The second part was an attempt to integrate the core of the set theory proof system with the symbolic mathematical program REDUCE [4,10]. The third part focused on interactive derivations of the standard problems in the first year of calculus. Because this system incorporated only a rudimentary knowledge of logic, it was not suitable for proving any fundamental theorems [6].

3 A Description of the Theorem Proving Environment

In the EPGY Theorem Proving Environment, a proof consists of a sequence of proof steps, each of which consists of a mathematical statement and a justification line. Although displayed sequentially, proof steps are represented in tree-form, according to the dependencies of proof steps that are entered as assumptions. Steps that are given initially, entered as assumptions, or taken from the course-specific database of axioms, definitions, and theorems, are immediately recognized as proved. When a newly generated step is shown to follow from already proved statements, it is marked as proved. The initial state of the proof includes a "final goal", and the proof is complete when the final goal is proved. (See the EPGY Theorem Proving Environment User Manual [3].)

The student composes a proof by selectively applying an assortment of tools for creating and justifying proof steps. He or she may apply a logical rule (Section 4.4, below), enter an assumption or apply a proof strategy (Section 3.1), apply a mathematical rule (Section 3.2), or simply type in a new statement and ask the system to verify that it follows from some other step(s) (Section 3.3).

Many of the rules and strategies can be applied in the backward as well as the forward direction. There are typically many rules that can be applied to a particular proof step, allowing for an unlimited variety of paths to a complete proof. Although the system includes a complete set of natural deduction rules, when teaching students to use the system we focus on those that are commonly used in mathematical practice and those that are generally advantageous in our logical framework.

3.1 Proof Strategies

The theorem-proving environment encourages *structured theorem proving.* In particular, students can apply a variety of common proof strategies. These strategies include conditional proof, biconditional proof, proof by contradiction, proof by cases, and proof by induction.

Students can apply these strategies in the forward and backward directions. For example, in order to develop a conditional proof in the forward direction, the student can insert an assumption, proceed to a goal, and then discharge the assumption to obtain a statement of the form "assumption implies goal." Alternatively, using the conditional proof strategy in the backward direction on a conditional statement generates a conditional proof format where the hypothesis of the conditional appears as an assumption and the conclusion of the conditional appears as the proof goal.

Proof strategies are represented using Fitch-style diagrams, so the student can easily keep track of what assumptions are available at a given location in the proof.

3.2 The EPGY Derivation System

For the application of mathematical rules, the Theorem Proving Environment uses the EPGY Derivation System [6], a tool that has been used in standard algebra and calculus derivations in EPGY courses for over six years. The EPGY Derivation System is an environment in which students can manipulate equations, inequalities, and individual terms by applying built-in mathematical inference rules or term-rewriting rules. The Derivation System is an important tool for generating new proof steps from old ones because it allows the student to flesh-out a claim like "it follows from simple computation that...."

In a typical use of the Derivation System within the Theorem Proving Environment, the student first selects a term or formula he or she would like to manipulate, possibly selects some other proof steps he or she thinks might be relevant, and finally invokes the Derivation System. Within the Derivation System, the term or formula of interest appears in the "working" area and other relevant facts appear as side-conditions.

Inside the Derivation System, the student essentially manipulates a formula by selecting a subexpression of the "working" expression and invoking one of the rules. (Available rules are determined by the student's location in the course.) Most rules provide simple algebraic manipulations of existing terms, but many involve side-conditions. For instance, the student may divide both sides of an equation by x, but only if x is a nonzero scalar. As another example, the student may left-multiply both sides of an equation by a matrix A, but only if A has the correct number of columns. Or a student may replace the matrix B by the matrix BAA^{-1}, provided A is an invertible matrix with the correct number of rows. The Derivation System keeps track of side-conditions and does some checking to decide whether a new condition follows from existing ones. Mostly, though, the System merely reports extra side-conditions back to the Theorem Proving Environment, which treats them as new proof obligations. In this regard, the Derivation System is quite different from a normal computer algebra system.

The Derivation System has only the most rudimentary capacity to deal with quantified variables, and its assumptions about terms' definedness are very restrictive (in contrast with the larger Theorem Proving Environment; see Section 4). Furthermore, a student has very little flexibility to enter brand-new terms. These simplifications are in line with the idea that the Derivation System should carry out the purely "computational" part of the proof. By virtue of these logical simplifications, though, a good student can move rapidly to transform even complicated terms to reach a desired goal.

3.3 Logical Verification

A student may enter a statement as a goal and propose that it follows from some other steps. In listing the justifications of a statement, the student may include other steps from the proof or choose from a database of axioms, definitions, and theorems. As students progress through the course and learn new axioms, definitions, and theorems, they gain the ability to apply them in their proofs.

When the Environment tries to verify the inference, it calls upon the automated reasoning program Otter [5] written by William McCune[1]. The Environment passes Otter the justifications as given statements and asks it to prove the proof step using strategies that seem appropriate. If Otter is successful, the proof step is marked as "provable" from the justifications (or "proved", if the justifications are themselves proved). If it is unsuccessful, the proof step is unchanged. In some cases, when Otter returns unsuccessfully, the student is asked whether he or she would like to "try harder". This happens when the system has identified that the goal might lend itself to some alternative Otter strategy.

[1] Given that all EPGY students use the Microsoft Windows operating system, the DOS version of Otter is the most suitable automated reasoning system to back our logical-verification tool.

We are constantly identifying and developing alternative strategies for Otter, so this feature changes frequently.

Our use of Otter is intended to mimic an intelligent tutor looking over the student's shoulder and saying "I agree that this follows simply" without the student having to explain all the painful details. The feature allows a student to make logical inferences that would perhaps involve several steps in a detailed, formal proof. To keep the system from accepting large leaps of logic, we limit Otter by allowing it only a few seconds to search for a proof (typically around five seconds). Our experience shows that very often Otter can verify reasonable inferences using our default strategy and time limit. Of course, success depends on many factors, and it is easy to find proof steps and justifications that seem reasonable but are not verified in the allotted time. We continually tinker with Otter's strategies, trying to refine its ability to verify "obvious" inferences but reject more complicated ones; we intend to use student data to help classify "obvious" statements more precisely.

As described below in Section 4, the Theorem Proving Environment presents the student with a multi-sorted logic of partial terms with some variables ranging over functions and other higher-order objects. Otter's logic, on the other hand, is single-sorted, total, and first-order. So we were forced early on to develop a translation from the students' language in the Theorem Proving Environment into statements in standard first-order logic. Some aspects of the translation are mentioned in Section 4.

A drawback to using Otter (and the incumbent translation) for our automatic verification is that the student is not given any information as to why an inference has been rejected. An inference may be rejected because it represents too big a step of logic, because the justifications do not imply the goal, or because our strategies are insufficient for Otter to complete the verification. Merely examining Otter's output, it is difficult to decide which is the reason for a failure. We will examine student data to try to classify common rejections and then program the Environment to give advice. For now, however, the expectation is that the student will study the inference, perhaps break it down into smaller steps, perhaps add some justifications, and perhaps change the statement being verified.

4 Logical Framework

Students using the EPGY Theorem Proving Environment work in a multi-sorted logic of partial terms with function variables, built-in operations on functions, and overloading of function symbols and relation symbols. Each course that uses the theorem proving environment has its own types, function and relation symbols, and conditions for definedness of functions. We have a proof that this logical framework is sound, modulo the soundness of Otter and the correctness of the other external systems that we use for the automatic verification of proof obligations, as described below.

4.1 Definedness and the Strong Interpretation

For each function symbol included in the language for a course, the system requires an author-coded definedness condition. Relations on terms are interpreted in the strong sense; in particular, the relation

$$R(\tau_1, \ldots, \tau_n)$$

as expressed in the "display language" of the students' world, is understood internally to state

$$R(\tau_1, \ldots, \tau_n) \& \ \tau_1 \downarrow \& \ \ldots \& \ \tau_n \downarrow$$

where $\tau \downarrow$ is the formula obtained by unraveling the definedness conditions of the functions in τ.

4.2 Quantifiers and Types

Since the Theorem Proving Environment uses a logic of partial terms, quantified variables range only over defined terms. Furthermore, it uses a multi-sorted language to ensure that quantified variables range only over terms of a particular type. For instance, in a linear algebra course, where "A" is a variable whose sort is "matrix", a theorem about matrices might be stated "$\forall\ A\ \phi(A)$". To instantiate such a theorem, a student would need to provide a term denoting a matrix: a term such as "$1+2$" would not be allowed at all because $1+2$ is not a matrix.

Sorts are not the only tool for describing types; there are explicit relations, too. For each type T, the Theorem Proving Environment includes a relation "is a T". The type-relations sometimes appear explicitly as proof obligations. Most type conditions are purely syntactic and are automatically either accepted or rejected by the system. Some are harder to decide and are left to the student as proof obligations (Section 4.3). An example of a "harder" type condition is deciding whether or not $(a+bi)(c+di)$ is an real number, where a, b, c, and d are reals. To justify the proof obligation "$(a+bi)(c+di)$ is a Real", the student might invoke a theorem that this is true when $ad+bc=0$.

There is one other important use of our type-relations. When theorems are passed to Otter as justifications or goals, they must be translated from the multi-sorted language of the Theorem Proving Environment into something Otter can understand. The usual translation of the theorem "$\forall\ A\ \phi(A)$" is "$\forall\ A\ (A$ is a Matrix $\rightarrow \phi'(A))$" (where ϕ' is a translation of the formula ϕ).

4.3 Proof Obligations

In enforcing the strong interpretation of relations, the Theorem Proving Environment generates many extra formulas, or "proof obligations", which the student must justify in order to complete his or her inferences. Many such formulas are simply added to the proof as new proof lines. For instance, if a student wants to instantiate "$\forall\ A\ \phi(A)$" with the matrix B^{-1}, he or she will need to prove that

B is an invertible matrix. This is simply added as a new proof goal; it is the student's responsibility to justify the statement.

Whenever a new proof obligation is generated, the Environment does some simple checking to see whether it is "obvious" before adding a new proof step. It may call Otter or do some other internal processing. The purpose of this checking is to keep the proof from becoming cluttered with simple, obvious facts. We think of such obvious facts as being the type of "hidden assumption" that is often wrapped up in a statement in an ordinary mathematics textbook.

4.4 Proof Rules

The Theorem Proving Environment provides several rules that create and justify proof steps. The student can instantiate a quantified statement, use generalization in the forward or backward direction, and substitute for equals or expand definitions in the forward or backward direction. In this section, we describe some of these rules, focusing on how they relate to our multi-sorted logic of partial terms.

Universal instantiation is a fairly simple rule. Using a statement $\forall\ x\ \phi(x)$, the student supplies a new term τ to conclude $\phi(\tau)$. As part of this action, the Theorem Proving Environment may require extra proof obligations about the definedness or type of τ.

The student may use universal generalization in either the forward or the backward direction. From a statement

$$\phi(x), \tag{1}$$

where x is a free variable, the student may conclude

$$\forall\ x\ \phi(x). \tag{2}$$

The student is working "backwards" if he or she starts with statement (2) and creates statement (1); in this case, step (2) is marked "Provable assuming (1)" and will become "Proved" when (1) is justified. The student is working "forwards" if he or she starts with statement (1) and generates statement (2) as a conclusion.

Existential generalization and existential instantiation are dual operations to universal instantiation and universal generalization, respectively. They may generate appropriate proof obligations, and existential generalization can be used in either the forward or the backward direction.

Students have two other tools for creating new proof lines from old ones. Using the "substitute" rule and a statement of the form $\gamma \to \tau = \sigma$ (or a similar statement with a quantifier), the student can create a new proof line $\phi(\sigma)$ from the line $\phi(\tau)$. The Environment will require γ as a proof obligation. The "expand definition" rule works similarly, except that it starts with a statement of the form $\forall\ \vec{x}\ \ (R(x_1, \ldots, x_n) \leftrightarrow \phi)$.

When using substitution or definition expansion from a quantified statement, we must be careful not to apply the rule to an undefined term. So, for instance, if the student tried to use the substitution rule $\forall\ x\ (x \neq 0 \rightarrow \frac{x}{x} = 1)$ to make a substitution from $\frac{\tau}{\tau}$, the Environment would generate proof obligations from both $\tau \neq 0$ (the hypothesis of the formula) and $\tau \downarrow$ (to account for the instantiation).

4.5 Higher Types

As mentioned earlier (Section 3.3), the Theorem Proving Environment uses Otter to check some verifications, and Otter uses a first-order language. The language of the Theorem Proving Environment, however, has variables ranging over functions and other higher types. Some aspects of this higher-order logic are easy to translate for Otter, but others are more difficult.

Simple function-valued variables are handled relatively easily. We simply add an "apply" function[2] to the language of the Theorem Proving Environment. The definedness condition of a term "apply(f, x)" is essentially "x is in the domain of f", so the Theorem Proving Environment has such a binary relation[3]. Given these operations, functions become first-class objects, so it is easy to translate them for Otter. Since we control the vocabulary of the Theorem Proving Environment, we can handle explicit higher-order functionals similarly.

We also handle the more complicated case where an operation on functions is applied to an open term that implicitly defines a function. For example, the simple term "$\sum_{k=1}^{n} A_{k,k}$" (defining the trace of the $n \times n$-matrix A) is interpreted as "sum$(1, n, f)$", where f is the function defined by $f(k) = A_{k,k}$. Other expressions, like "the $m \times n$-matrix whose (i, j)-th entry is $\frac{1}{i+j}$" and "$\frac{d}{dx} \sin(x)$", require functions implicitly defined by terms. As part of its translation for Otter, our system needs to extract these functions and give them explicit descriptions. As an illustration, we give the details of how summation is translated.

Example: Summation. In translating the formula $\phi\,(\sum_{k=m}^{n} \tau(k))$, we assume that the term τ does not contain any summations. We will replace the summation-term with an equivalent one without changing the rest of the formula.

We create a new function-variable f and add the axioms

$$\forall\ k\ \ (\tau(k) \downarrow\rightarrow f(k) = \tau(k))\,,$$

$$\forall\ k\ \ (\tau(k) \downarrow\rightarrow k \text{ is in the domain of } f)$$

(where "$\tau(k) \downarrow$" represents the formula obtained by unraveling all the definedness conditions for functions appearing in $\tau(k)$). Then the original formula can be replaced by $\phi\,(\text{sum}(m, n, f))$. The definedness condition for the term sum(m, n, f) function is

$$\forall\ k\ \ (m \leq k \leq n \rightarrow k \text{ is in the domain of } f)\,.$$

[2] Technically, we need a separate apply function for unary functions, binary functions, etc., because Otter does not support functions with variable numbers of arguments.

[3] Technically, binary, ternary, etc. relations.

In fact, this is an unwieldy translation, especially if the formula contains many nested summations (we work inside-out in that case). Otter can directly verify only the simplest statements about summation, so the student typically needs the Environment's other tools to write proofs about summations.

5 Student Use

Presently, the Theorem Proving Environment is being used in EPGY's geometry and linear algebra courses, and it will be incorporated into the EPGY multivariable calculus and differential equations courses later this year. The proof environment has been used by approximately 60 students in the geometry course.

In our geometry course students are able to prove theorems about incidence, parallel, betweenness and congruence (including some of the basic triangle congruence theorems) in a version of Hilbert's axioms of geometry. In the linear algebra course the system is capable of theorems in matrix algebra and theorems about eigenvalues and eigenvectors. In calculus, the system can be used for basic continuity theorems; for example, that the sum of two continuous functions is continuous.

The history of the students' actions are recorded so that we can "play back" a student's proof from start to finish, displaying all steps including those that were deleted by the student. Using this feature, we have had the opportunity to examine many students' proofs. The analysis of these proofs has influenced both the development of the system and our presentation of the material in our courses.

6 Future Directions

The main goal of the Theorem Proving Environment project is to develop a system that imitates, both in construction and final form, the proofs of "standard mathematical practice". For this reason, many of our directions of future study will focus on how to make the Theorem Proving Environment a more natural tool for students.

One clear area to target for improvement is the system's ability to automatically discharge "obvious" proof obligations. Because of the way proof obligations are generated, it is often the case that another statement within the proof would be helpful as a justification. Classifying exactly when a statement is "relevant" will be a very difficult task, but some initial experiments have shown that we can improve Otter's performance by first scanning through the proof with some very basic algorithms.

As a further aid in discharging proof obligations, we are studying more extensive use of computer algebra systems. We currently use Maple V, Release 5.1, to automatically check some obligations that appear to involve only algebraic computations. This has been a successful strategy so far, but one drawback is that most computer algebra systems (Maple included) were designed for efficient computation and not necessarily for logical soundness so we need to be very careful when we use them. Nevertheless, when used appropriately, Maple in particular can quickly decide many questions which give Otter great difficulty.

Given that proof obligations are often generated in a restricted, decidable fragment of a mathematical theory, we intend to investigate the use of decision procedures for these cases. For example, in linear algebra and analysis, it is common to generate proof obligations that are expressed as order relations on linear terms with integer coefficients. Additionally, we may incorporate such decision procedures into the verification process directly, in cases where we can automatically determine that they apply.

In a further effort to make our students' proofs more natural, we would also like to improve our treatment of higher types. At the moment, our built-in tools deal fairly well with functions and operations on functions. When we need to translate higher-order objects for Otter, however, the statements quickly become very complicated, so some seemingly simple statements are hard to verify. This will be an increasing problem as we develop our differential calculus course. We plan to continually improve and simplify our translation, but we will also consider using provers based on higher-order logic. In principle, our system can use any number of automated reasoning systems for logical verification; however, given the limitation resulting from our use of Microsoft Windows, most higher-order provers (e.g., PVS, HOL, ACL2, etc.) are not available for our immediate use.

References

1. Barwise, B. & Etchemendy, J. (1999). *Language, Proof and Logic.* Seven Bridges Press. New York.
2. Chuaqui, R. & Suppes, P., (1990). An equational deductive system for the differential and integral calculus. In P. Martin-Lof & G. Mints, (Eds.), *Lecture Notes in Computer Science, Proceedings of COLOG-88 International Conference on Computer Logic (Tallin, USSR).* Berlin and Heidelberg: Springer Verlag, pp. 25-49.
3. Education Program for Gifted Youth (EPGY). Theorem Proving Environment Overview. `http://epgy.stanford.edu/TPE`.
4. Hearn, A. (1987). Reduce user's manual, Version 3.3. (Report CP 78). The RAND Corporation. Santa Monica CA.
5. McCune, William. OTTER 3.0 reference manual and guide. Technical Report ANL-94/6. Argonne National Laboratory. January 1994.
6. Ravaglia, R. (1990). *User's Guide for the Equational Derivation System.* Education Program for Gifted Youth, Palo Alto.
7. Ravaglia R., Alper, T. M., Rozenfeld, M., & Suppes, P. (1998). Successful Applications of Symbolic Computation. In *Human Interaction with Symbolic Computation,* ed. N. Kajler. Springer-Verlag, New York, pp. 61-87.
8. Sieg, W., & Byrnes, J. (1996). Normal Natural Deduction Proofs (in classical logic). Tech-report CMU-PHIL-74. Department of Philosophy, Carnegie Mellon Univ., Pittsburgh, PA 15213.
9. Suppes, P. (Ed.). (1981). *University-level computer-assisted instruction at Stanford: 1968-1980.* Stanford, CA: Institute for Mathematical Studies of the Social Sciences, Stanford University.
10. Suppes, P. & Takahashi, S. (1989). An interactive calculus theorem-prover for continuity properties. *Journal of Symbolic Computation,* Volume 7, pp. 573-590.

On Termination of Meta-programs

Alexander Serebrenik and Danny De Schreye

Department of Computer Science, K.U. Leuven
Celestijnenlaan 200A, B-3001, Heverlee, Belgium
{Alexander.Serebrenik, Danny.DeSchreye}@cs.kuleuven.ac.be

1 Introduction

The term *meta-programming* refers to the ability of writing programs that have other programs as data and exploit their semantics [4]. The choice of logic programming as a basis for meta-programming offers a number of practical and theoretical advantages. One of them is the possibility of tackling critical foundation problems of meta-programming within a framework with a strong theoretical basis. Another is the surprising ease of programming. These reasons motivated an intensive research on meta-programming inside the logic programming community [4,16,19,22,23].

On the other hand, termination analysis is one of the most intensive research areas in logic programming as well. See [12] for the survey. More recent work on this topic can be found among others in [14,18,20,24,30].

Traditionally, termination analysis of logic programs have been done either by the "transformational" approach or by the "direct" one. A transformational approach first transforms the logic program into an "equivalent" term-rewrite system (or, in some cases, into an equivalent functional program). Here, equivalence means that, at the very least, the termination of the term-rewrite system should imply the termination of the logic program, for some predefined collection of queries[1]. Direct approaches do not include such a transformation, but prove the termination directly on the basis of the logic program. In [25] we have developed an approach that provides the best of both worlds: a means to incorporate into "direct" approaches the generality of general term-orderings.

The aim of this paper is presenting a methodology allowing us to perform a correct termination analysis for a broad class of meta-interpreters together with different classes of object programs. Unlike the previous work on compositionality of termination proofs [3] the approach presented allows a simple reuse of the termination proof of the object program for the meta-program.

This methodology is based on the "combined" approach to termination analysis mentioned above.

[1] The approach of Arts [5] is exceptional in the sense that the termination of the logic program is concluded from a weaker property of *single-redex normalisation* of the term-rewrite system.

R. Nieuwenhuis and A. Voronkov (Eds.): LPAR 2001, LNAI 2250, pp. 517–530, 2001.

Example 1. Our research has been motivated by the famous "vanilla" meta-interpreter M_0, undoubtly belonging to logic programming classics.

$$solve(true).$$
$$solve((Atom, Atoms)) \leftarrow solve(Atom), solve(Atoms).$$
$$solve(Head) \leftarrow clause(Head, Body), solve(Body).$$

Termination of this meta-interpreter, presented in Example 1, has been studied by Pedreschi and Ruggieri. They proved, that LD-termination of the goal G with respect to a program P implies LD-termination of the goal $solve(G)$ with respect to M_0 and P (Corollary 40, [23]). However, we claim more: the two statements are equivalent, i.e., the goal G LD-terminates with respect to a program P if and only if the goal $solve(G)$ LD-terminates with respect to M_0 and P. □

In order for meta-interpreters to be useful in applications they should be able to cope with a richer language than the one of the "vanilla" meta-interpreter, including, for example, negation. Moreover, typical applications of meta-interpreters, such as debuggers, will also require producing some additional output or performing some additional tasks during the execution, such as constructing proof trees or cutting "unlikely" branches for an uncertainty reasoner with cutoff. These extensions can and usually will influence termination properties of the meta-interpreter.

By extending the suggested technique [25] to normal programs, we are able to perform the correct analysis of a number of (possibly extended) meta-interpreters, performing tasks as described above. We identify popular classes of meta-interpreters, such as *extended meta-interpreters* [22], and using this technique prove that termination is usually improved. We also state more generic conditions implying preservation of termination.

The rest of this paper is organised as following. We start by some preliminary remarks and basic definitions. Then, we present the methodology developed applied to the "vanilla" meta-interpreter. Afterwards we show how the same methodology can be applied for more advanced meta-interpreters and conclude.

2 Preliminaries

A *quasi-ordering* over a set S is a reflexive and transitive relation $\geq$ defined on elements of S. If neither $s \geq t$, nor $t \geq s$ we write $s \| t$. An ordered set S is said to be *well-founded* if there are no infinite descending sequences $s_1 > s_2 > \ldots$ of elements of S. If the set S is clear from the context we will say that the ordering, defined on it, is well-founded.

We follow the standard notation for terms and atoms. A *query* is a finite sequence of atoms. Given an atom A, $rel(A)$ denotes the predicate occurring in A. $Term_P$ and $Atom_P$ denote, respectively, sets of all terms and atoms that can be constructed from the language underlying P. The extended Herbrand Universe U_P^E (the extended Herbrand base B_P^E) is a quotient set of $Term_P$ ($Atom_P$) modulo the variant relation.

We refer to an SLD-tree constructed using the left-to-right selection rule of Prolog, as an LD-tree. We will say that a goal G *LD-terminates* for a program P, if the LD-tree for (P, G) is finite.

The following definition is borrowed from [1].

Definition 1. *Let P be a program and p, q be predicates occurring in it.*

- *We say that p* refers to *q in P if there is a clause in P that uses p in its head and q in its body.*
- *We say that p* depends on *q in P and write $p \sqsupseteq q$, if (p, q) is in the transitive, reflexive closure of the relation* refers to.
- *We say that p and q are* mutually recursive *and write $p \simeq q$, if $p \sqsupseteq q$ and $q \sqsupseteq p$.*

We also abbreviate $p \sqsupseteq q$, $q \not\sqsupseteq p$ by $p \sqsupset q$.

Results for termination of meta-interpreters presented in this paper are based on notion of order-acceptability, introduced in [25]. This notion of order-acceptability generalises the notion of acceptability with respect to a set [13] in two ways: 1) it generalises it to general term orderings, 2) it generalises it to mutual recursion, using the standard notion of mutual recursion [1]—the original definition of acceptability required decrease only for calls to the predicate that appears in the head of the clause. This restriction limited the approach to programs only with direct recursion.

Before introducing the order-acceptability we need the following notion.

Definition 2. *[13] Let P be a definite program and S be a set of atomic queries. The* call set, *Call(P, S), is the set of all atoms A, such that a variant of A is a selected atom in some derivation for $P \cup \{\leftarrow Q\}$, for some $Q \in S$ and under the left-to-right selection rule.*

Definition 3. *Let S be a set of atomic queries and P a definite program. P is* order-acceptable *with respect to S if there exists a well-founded ordering $>$, such that*

- *for any $A \in$ Call(P, S)*
- *for any clause $A' \leftarrow B_1, \ldots, B_n$ in P, such that* $\mathrm{mgu}(A, A') = \theta$ *exists,*
- *for any atom B_i, such that* $\mathrm{rel}(B_i) \simeq \mathrm{rel}(A)$
- *for any computed answer substitution σ for $\leftarrow (B_1, \ldots, B_{i-1})\theta$:*

$$A > B_i\theta\sigma$$

In [25] we prove the following theorem.

Theorem 1. *Let P be a program. P is order-acceptable with respect to a set of atomic queries S if and only if P is LD-terminating for all queries in S.*

We discovered in [25] that order-acceptability is a powerful technique, able to analyse a wide variety of programs, such as *normalisation* [14], *derivative* [15], *bid* [10], and credit evaluation expert system [28] to mention a few. In this paper we will see that order-acceptability plays a key role in analysing termination of meta-programs.

3 Basic Definitions

In this section we present a number of basic definitions. We start by defining the kind of program we call a meta-program. Then we introduce two semantic notions that relate computed answers of the interpreted program and of the meta-program and conclude by discussing an appropriate notion of termination for meta-interpreters.

3.1 Interpreted Programs and Meta-programs

In this subsection we define the notion of a meta-interpreter, that is a program having another program as data. We've seen already in Example 1 that the input program is represented as a set of atoms of the predicate *clause*. We call this representation a *clause-encoding* and define it formally as following.

Definition 4. *Let P be a program. The* clause-encoding $\gamma_{ce}(P)$ *is a collection of facts of a new predicate* clause*, such that* $\mathit{clause}(H, B) \in \gamma_{ce}(P)$ *if and only if* $H \leftarrow B$ *is a clause in P.*

Example 2. Let P be the following program:

$$p(a). \quad p(X) \leftarrow q(X). \quad q(b).$$

Then, the following program is $\gamma_{ce}(P)$:

$$\mathit{clause}(p(a), \mathit{true}) \qquad \mathit{clause}(p(X), q(X)). \qquad \mathit{clause}(q(b), \mathit{true}).$$

□

A *meta-interpreter* for a language is an interpreter for the language written in the language itself. We follow [28] by using a predicate *solve* for the meta-interpreter.

Definition 5. *The program P is called a* meta-program *if it can be represented as $M \cup I$, such that:*

- *M defines a predicate solve that does not appear in I.*
- *I is a clause-encoding of some program P'.*

M is called the meta-interpreter. *P' is called the interpreted program.*

We also assume that $,/2$ and *clause*/2 do not appear in the language underlying the interpreted program. Observe, that if this assumption is violated, clear distinction between the meta-interpreter and the interpreted program is no longer possible.

3.2 Soundness and Completeness of Meta-interpreters

Now we are going to define the notions of *soundness* and *completeness* for meta-interpreters, that will relate computed answers of the interpreted program to the computed answers of the meta-program.

Definition 6. *The meta-interpreter M is called* sound *if for every program P, every goal $G_0 \in B_P^E$ and every $H_1, \ldots, H_n \in U_M^E$*

- *if $solve(t_0, t_1, \ldots, t_n)$ is a computed answer for some $\{solve(G_0, H_1, \ldots, H_n)\} \cup M \cup \gamma_{ce}(P)$*
- *then t_0 is a computed answer for $\{G_0\} \cup P$.*

Note that $H_1, \ldots, H_n$ are extra arguments of solve that support added functionality (see Example 3 below). The definition of soundness, as well as further definitions require some property to hold for *all* programs. Correctness of these definitions does not depend on the class of the programs considered. However, constructing meta-interpreters that will satisfy the properties required for all Prolog programs can be difficult. Thus, we start by restricting the class of programs considered to definite logic programs. In Section 6 we study a broader class of programs.

Definition 7. *The meta-interpreter M is called* complete *if*

- *for every program P and every goal $G_0 \in B_P^E$*
- *if t_0 is a computed answer for $\{G_0\} \cup P$, then*
  - *for every $H_1, \ldots, H_n \in U_M^E$*
  - *if there exist $s_1, \ldots, s_n$ such that $solve(s_0, s_1, \ldots, s_n)$ is a computed answer for $\{solve(G_0, H_1, \ldots, H_n)\} \cup M \cup \gamma_{ce}(P)$*
  - *then there exist $t_1, \ldots, t_n$ such that $solve(t_0, t_1, \ldots, t_n)$ is a computed answer for $\{solve(G_0, H_1, \ldots, H_n)\} \cup M \cup \gamma_{ce}(P)$.*

Example 3. The following meta-interpreter M_1 is both sound and complete: $solve(A) \leftarrow fail$. It is sound, since there are no computed answers for $\leftarrow solve(G)$. It is also complete, since $s_1, \ldots, s_n$ required in Definition 7 do not exist. The "vanilla" meta-interpreter M_0 (Example 1) is also both sound and complete, as shown by Levi and Ramundo in [19].

The following meta-interpreter M_2, mimicking the LD-refutation with bounded depth (the depth provided as the second argument) is sound, but is not complete.

$$solve(true, 0).$$
$$solve((A, B), N) \leftarrow solve(A, N), solve(B, N).$$
$$solve(A, s(N)) \leftarrow clause(A, B), solve(B, N).$$

It is intuitively clear why this meta-interpreter is sound. To see that it is not complete, let P be a program resented in Example 2, let G_0 be $p(X)$ and let t_0 be $p(b)$. Then, given $H_1 = s(0)$ there exist s_1, such that $solve(s_0, s_1)$ is a computed answer for $\{solve(G_0, H_1)\} \cup M \cup \gamma_{ce}(P)$. Namely, $s_1 = s(0)$ and $s_0 = p(a)$. However, there exists no t_1 such that $solve(p(b), t_1)$ is a computed answer for $\{solve(G_0, H_1)\} \cup M \cup \gamma_{ce}(P)$. □

3.3 Notion of Termination

Recall that our aim is to study termination of meta-interpreters, that is termination of goals of the form $solve(G_0, H_1, \ldots, H_n)$, where G_0 is a goal with respect to the interpreted program. Thus, the crucial issue is defining an appropriate *notion of termination* for meta-interpreters.

For many applications, such as debuggers, the desired behaviour of a meta-interpreter is to preserve termination. However, there are many meta-interpreters that may change termination behaviour of the interpreted program, either by improving or by violating it.

Definition 8. *(non-violating LD-termination)*

1. *Let M be a meta-interpreter defining* solve *with arity* 1. *M is called* non-violating LD-termination *if for every program P and every goal $G_0 \in B_P^E$ if the LD-tree of $\{G_0\} \cup P$ is finite, then the LD-tree of $\{solve(G_0)\} \cup (M \cup \gamma_{ce}(P))$ is finite as well.*
2. *Let M be a meta-interpreter defining* solve *with arity $n+1$, $n > 0$. M is called* non-violating LD-termination with respect to $S \subseteq (U_M^E)^n$ *if for every program P and every goal $G_0 \in B_P^E$ if the LD-tree of $\{G_0\} \cup P$ is finite, then for every sequence $(H_1, \ldots, H_n) \in S$, the LD-tree of $\{solve(G_0, H_1, \ldots, H_n)\} \cup (M \cup \gamma_{ce}(P))$ is finite as well.*

It should be noted, that traditionally this feature is called *improving termination*. However, this name is not quite successful, since by improving we do not mean that the meta-program terminates *more often* than the original one, but that it terminates *at least as often* as the original one. Thus, we chose to use more clear names.

It also follows from the definition of non-violation that every meta-interpreter defining *solve* with arity greater than 1 does not violate termination with respect to the empty set.

Example 4. Recall once more the meta-interpreters shown in Example 3. M_1 does not violate termination, and M_2 does not violate termination with respect to $(U_{M_2}^E)^1$, that is with respect to $U_{M_2}^E$. □

Definition 9. *(non-improving LD-termination)*

1. *Let M be a meta-interpreter defining* solve *with arity* 1. *M is called* non-improving LD-termination *if for every program P and every goal $solve(G_0) \in B_{M \cup \gamma_{ce}(P)}^E$, finiteness of the LD-tree of $\{solve(G_0)\} \cup (M \cup \gamma_{ce}(P))$ implies finiteness of the LD-tree of $\{G_0\} \cup P$.*
2. *Let M be a meta-interpreter defining* solve *with arity $n+1$, $n > 0$. M is called* non-improving LD-termination with respect to $S \subseteq (U_M^E)^n$ *if for every program P and every goal $solve(G_0, H_1, \ldots, H_n) \in B_{M \cup \gamma_{ce}(P)}^E$, such that $(H_1, \ldots, H_n) \in S$, finiteness of the LD-tree of $\{solve(G_0, H_1, \ldots, H_n)\} \cup (M \cup \gamma_{ce}(P))$ implies finiteness of the LD-tree of $\{G_0\} \cup P$.*

Example 5. The meta-interpreter M_1 improves termination, while the meta-interpreter M_2 does not improve it w.r.t *Vars*, where *Vars* is a set of variables. □

Finally, we will say that a meta-interpreter M defining *solve* with arity $n+1$ is *preserving termination* (*preserving termination with respect to* $S \subseteq (U_M^E)^n$, if $n > 0$), if it is non-violating LD-termination (non-violating LD-termination with respect to S) and non-improving LD-termination (non-improving LD-termination with respect to S). The meta-interpreter M_0 preserves termination and the meta-interpreter M_2 preserves termination with respect to *Vars*, that is if it is used to measure the depth of LD-refutation of a give goal, and not to bound it. In the next sections we prove these statements.

4 Termination of "Vanilla" Meta-interpreter

Termination of the "vanilla" meta-interpreter, presented in Example 1, has been studied by Pedreschi and Ruggieri. They proved, that "vanilla" does not violate termination (Corollary 40, [23]). However, we can claim more—this meta-interpreter preserves termination.

We base our proof on soundness and completeness of "vanilla", proved in [19]. Observe that in general soundness and completeness are not sufficient for the calls set to be preserved. Indeed, consider the following example, motivated by the ideas of unfolding [6].

Example 6. The following meta-interpreter M_3 eliminates calls to undefined predicates.

$$\begin{array}{l} solve(true).\\ solve((A,B)) \leftarrow solve(A), solve(B).\\ solve(A) \leftarrow clause(A,B), check(B), solve(B).\\ \\ check((A,B)) \leftarrow check(A), check(B).\\ check(A) \leftarrow clause(A,\_). \end{array}$$

This meta-interpreter is sound and complete, i.e., preserves computed answers. However, it does not preserve termination. Indeed, let P be the following program [6]:

$$p \leftarrow q, r. \quad t \leftarrow r, q. \quad q \leftarrow q.$$

and let p be the goal. Then, p with respect to P does not terminate, while $\leftarrow solve(p)$ with respect to $M_3 \cup \gamma_{ce}(P)$ terminates (finitely fails). Thus, this meta-interpreter does not preserve LD-termination. Observe, that unfolding may only improve termination [6], thus, this meta-interpreter is improving LD-termination. □

Thus, we need some additional result, claiming that the "vanilla" meta-interpreter preserves the calls.

Lemma 1. *Let P be an interpreted program, M_0 be the vanilla meta-interpreter and $G \in B_P^E$, then*

$$\{solve(A) \mid A \in Call(P, G)\} \equiv Call(M_0 \cup \gamma_{ce}(P), solve(G)) \ \cap \ \{solve(A) \mid A \in B_P^E\}$$

where $\equiv$ means equality up to variable renaming.

Proof. For all proofs we refer to [26]. ∎

Theorem 2. *Let P be a definite program, S a set of queries, and M_0 the vanilla meta-interpreter, such that $M_0 \cup \gamma_{ce}(P)$ is LD-terminating for all queries in $\{solve(G) \mid G \in S\}$. Then, P is LD-terminating for all queries in S.*

Proof. (sketch) By Theorem 1 $M_0 \cup \gamma_{ce}(P)$ is order-acceptable with respect to $\{solve(G) \mid G \in S\}$. We are going to prove order-acceptability of P with respect to S. By Theorem 1 this will imply termination.

Since $M_0 \cup \gamma_{ce}(P)$ is order-acceptable with respect to $solve(S) = \{solve(G) \mid G \in S\}$ there is a well-founded ordering $>$, satisfying requirements of Definition 3. Define a new ordering on atoms of P as following: $A \succ B$ if $solve(A) > solve(B)$.

The ordering is defined on $\{G \mid solve(G) \in Call(M_0 \cup \gamma_{ce}(P), solve(S))\}$. By Lemma 1 this set coincides with $Call(P, S)$. From the corresponding properties of $>$ follows that $\succ$ is well-defined and well-founded.

The only thing that remains to be proved is that P is order-acceptable with respect to S via $\succ$. Let $A \in Call(P, S)$ and let $A' \leftarrow B_1, \ldots, B_n$ be a clause in P, such that mgu$(A, A') = \theta$ exists. Then, θ is also mgu of $solve(A)$ and $solve(A')$.

Let σ map $B\theta$ to $(B_1, \ldots, B_n)\theta$. It is one of the computed answer substitutions for $\leftarrow clause(A\theta, B\theta)$. Thus, by order-acceptability of $M_0 \cup \gamma_{ce}(P)$ with respect to $solve(S)$ holds: $solve(A) > solve((B_1, \ldots, B_n)\theta)$.

Order-acceptability also implies $solve((B_1, \ldots, B_n)\theta) > solve(B_1\theta)$ and $solve((B_1, \ldots, B_n)\theta) > solve((B_2, \ldots, B_n)\theta\sigma_1)$, where σ_1 is a computed answer substitution for $solve(B_1\theta)$. By proceeding in this way we conclude, that for any atom B_i, $solve(A) > solve(B_i\theta\sigma_1 \ldots \sigma_{i-1})$, where σ_j is a computed answer substitution for $\leftarrow solve(B_j\theta\sigma_1 \ldots \sigma_{j-1})$. By definition of $\succ$, this means that $A \succ B_i\theta\sigma_1 \ldots \sigma_{i-1}$.

Soundness and completeness imply the order-acceptability and complete the proof. ∎

The second direction of the theorem has been proved by Pedreschi and Ruggieri [23]. It allows us to state the following corollary.

Corollary 1. *Tha "vanilla" meta-interpreter preserves LD-termination.*

The proof of Theorem 2 sketched above, suggests the following methodology for proving that some meta-interpreter improves LD-termination. First, define an ordering on the set of calls to the meta-interpreter, that reflects its behaviour.

Then, establish the relationship between a new ordering and the one that reflects order-acceptability with respect to a set of the interpreted program. Prove using this relationship that the newly defined ordering is well-defined, well-founded and reflects order-acceptability of the meta-program with respect to a corresponding set of calls. In order for the proofs to be correct one may need to assume (or to prove as a prerequisite) that the meta-interpreter is sound and that the set of calls of the interpreted program and of the meta-program correspond to each other. The opposite direction can be proved by using a similar methodology.

5 Advanced Meta-interpreters

Typical applications of meta-interpreters, such as debuggers, will also require producing some additional output or performing some additional tasks during the execution, such as constructing proof trees or cutting "unlikely" branches for an uncertainty reasoner with cutoff. As we are going to see in Example 7 these extensions can and usually will influence termination properties of the meta-interpreter.

In this section we identify an important class of meta-interpreters that are able to perform additional tasks and extend the methodology presented in the previous section to analyse them.

Definition 10. *A definite program of the following form*

$$\begin{array}{l} solve(true, t_{11}, \ldots, t_{1n}) \leftarrow C_{11}, \ldots, C_{1m_1}. \\ solve((A, B), t_{21}, \ldots, t_{2n}) \leftarrow \\ \qquad D_{11}, \ldots, D_{1k_1}, solve(A, t_{31}, \ldots, t_{3n}), \\ \qquad D_{21}, \ldots, D_{2k_2}, solve(B, t_{41}, \ldots, t_{4n}) \\ \qquad C_{21}, \ldots, C_{2m_2}. \\ solve(A, t_{51}, \ldots, t_{5n}) \leftarrow \\ \qquad D_{31}, \ldots, D_{3k_3}, clause(A, B, s_1, \ldots, s_k), \\ \qquad D_{41}, \ldots, D_{4k_4}, solve(B, t_{61}, \ldots, t_{6n}) \\ \qquad C_{31}, \ldots, C_{3m_3}. \end{array}$$

together with defining clauses for any other predicates occurring in the C_{kl} and D_{pq} (none of which contain solve or clause) is called a double extended meta-interpreter.

This class of meta-interpreters extends the class of extended meta-interpreters studied by [22]. It includes many useful meta-interpreters, such as a proof trees constructing meta-interpreter [28], that can be used as a basis for explanation facilities in expert system, meta-interpreters allowing reasoning about theories and provability [8,21] or reasoning with uncertainty [28]. Moreover, this class also describes a depth tracking tracer for Prolog, a reasoner with threshold cutoff [28] and a pure four port box execution model tracer [7]. Note, that despite the similarity with Example 6, Example 6 is not a double extended meta-interpreter due to the call to predicate *clause* in the definition of *check*.

Definition 11. *Let* $H \leftarrow B_1, \ldots, B_i, \ldots, B_n$ *be a clause, and let* v *be a variable in* B_i. *We'll say that* $\leftarrow B_1, \ldots, B_{i-1}$ *is* irrelevant *for* v *if for every computed answer substitution* σ *for* $\leftarrow B_1, \ldots, B_{i-1}$, $v\sigma = v$.

We'll call a double extended meta-interpreter *restricted* if for any i, $\leftarrow D_{i1}, \ldots, D_{ik_i}$ is irrelevant for meta-variables A and B. The following theorem states conditions on the restricted double extended meta-interpreter E that imply E to be non-violating LD-termination.

Theorem 3. *Let* P *be an interpreted program,* D *a restricted double extended meta-interpreter, and* $G \in B^E_{D\cup\gamma_{ce}(P)}$, *such that* G *is terminating with respect to* P *and* $\{A \mid A \in Call(D \cup \gamma_{ce}(P), solve(G)), solve \sqsupset rel(A)\}$ *is terminating with respect to* D *then* $solve(G)$ *terminates with respect to* $D \cup \gamma_{ce}(P)$.

In general, the second direction of the theorem does not necessary hold. Indeed, consider the following uncertainty reasoner with cutoff, motivated by [28].

Example 7.

$$
\begin{array}{ll}
solve(true, 1, T). & solve(A, C, T) \leftarrow \\
solve((A, B), C, T) \leftarrow & \quad clause(A, B, C1), \\
\quad solve(A, C1, T), & \quad C1 > T, T1 \text{ is } T/C1, \\
\quad solve(B, C2, T), & \quad solve(B, C2, T1), \\
\quad minimum(C1, C2, C). & \quad C \text{ is } C1 * C2.
\end{array}
$$

Let P be the following uncertainty-program: $clause(r, r, 0.9)$. When executed as a usual program, ignoring uncertainty coefficients, the goal $\leftarrow r$ does not terminate. However, for any specified threshold *Threshold* > 0 the goal $\leftarrow solve(r, Certainty, Threshold)$ finitely fails. □

Termination of this example followed from the fact that given some positive threshold *Threshold* there always be a natural n, such that $0.9^n <$ *Threshold*. To cause the second direction of Theorem 3 to hold this kind of termination should be eliminated. That is, termination of the meta-program shall depend only on the meta-calls. To formalise this intuition we set a requirement on the ordering used to prove termination of the meta-program. We say that an ordering $>$ *ignores* argument position i of a functor f, if for all $t_1, \ldots, t_n$, for all s_1, s_2 and for all u, if $f(t_1, \ldots, t_{i-1}, s_1, t_{i+1}, \ldots, t_n)\ \rho\ u$ then $f(t_1, \ldots, t_{i-1}, s_2, t_{i+1}, \ldots, t_n)\ \rho\ u$, for every $\rho \in \{<, >, =, \|\}$.

Theorem 4. *Let* P *be an interpreted program and* D *a double extended meta-interpreter, such that* $D \cup \gamma_{ce}(P)$ *is order-acceptable with respect to* $solve(G)$ *via an ordering* $>$, *that ignores all argument positions of* solve, *except for the first one. Then,*

1. D *terminates w.r.t.* $\{A \mid A \in Call(D \cup \gamma_{ce}(P), solve(G)), solve \sqsupset rel(A)\}$ *and*
2. P *terminates w.r.t.* G.

6 Extending the Language of the Interpreted Programs

So far we have considered only definite programs. However, in order to make our approach practical the language of the underlying object programs should be extended to include negation, frequently appearing in applications of the meta-interpreters.

In order to prove that meta-interpreters with negation preserve termination we use among others a termination analysis framework based on order-acceptability. Originally this framework was designed only for study of termination of definite programs. In [26] we extended this framework to normal programs as well. Here we present briefly some results that can be obtained for the meta-interpreters in the extended framework.

First of all, instead of LD-derivations and trees LDNF-derivations and trees should be considered. Recall, that LDNF-derivation *flounders* if there occurs in it or in any of its subsidiary LDNF-trees a goal with the first literal being non-ground and negative.

Definition 12. *The program P is called* non-floundering with respect to a set of queries S, *if all its LDNF-derivations starting in queries $G \in S$ are non-floundering.*

By extending the notion of order-acceptability to normal programs and applying the same methodology as above one can prove that the following meta-interpreter M_4, being an immediate extension of vanilla meta-interpreter to normal programs [16], preserves LDNF-termination. Soundness and completeness of M_4 are proved in Theorem 2.3.3 [17].

$$solve(true).$$
$$solve((Atom, Atoms)) \leftarrow solve(Atom), solve(Atoms).$$
$$solve(\neg Atom) \leftarrow \neg solve(Atom).$$
$$solve(Head) \leftarrow clause(Head, Body), solve(Body).$$

Theorem 5. *Let P be a normal program, S be a set of queries. Then P is LDNF-terminating w.r.t. S if and only if $M_4 \cup \gamma_{ce}(P')$ LDNF-terminates with respect to $\{solve(G) \mid G \in S\}$.*

7 Conclusion

We have presented a methodology for proving termination properties of meta-programs. The problem of termination was studied by a number of authors (see [12] for the survey, and more recent work can be found in [13,14,18,20,24, 27,30]).

Our methodology gains it power from using the integrated approach, suggested in [25], that extends the traditional notion of acceptability [2] with the wide class of term-orderings that have been studied in the context of the term-rewriting systems. In this work we have shown that this approach allows one to define relatively simple relation between the ordering that satisfies the requirements of order-acceptability for an object program and for the meta-interpreter extended by this object program and a corresponding set of goals. Thus, the methodology is useful to establish if the meta-interpreter improves or preserves termination. In particular, in the work on compositionality of termination proofs [3], level mappings for an object program cannot easily be reused for the meta-program.

Despite the intensive research on meta-programming inside the logic programming community [4,19,22] termination behaviour of meta-programs attracted less attention. Pedreschi and Ruggieri [23] use generic verification method, based on specifying preconditions and postconditions. Unfortunately, their termination results are restricted only to the "vanilla" meta-interpreter. It is not immediate how their results can be extended to alternative meta-interpreters, nor if the relationship between termination characterisation of the object program and the meta-program can be established.

We consider as a future work identifying additional classes of meta-interpreters, such as [9,11,29] and studying their termination behaviour.

Acknowledgement. Alexander Serebrenik is supported by GOA: "LP^+: a second generation logic programming language".

References

1. K. R. Apt. *From Logic Programming to Prolog.* Prentice-Hall Int. Series in Computer Science. Prentice Hall, 1997.
2. K. R. Apt and D. Pedreschi. Studies in Pure Prolog: Termination. In J. W. Lloyd, editor, *Proc. Esprit Symp. on Comp. Logic*, pages 150–176. Springer Verlag, 1990.
3. K. R. Apt and D. Pedreschi. Modular termination proofs for logic and pure prolog programs. In G. Levi, editor, *Advances in Logic Programming Theory*, pages 183–229. Oxford University Press, 1994.
4. K. R. Apt and F. Turini, editors. *Meta-Logics and Logic Programming.* Logic Programming. The MIT Press, 1995.
5. T. Arts. *Automatically proving termination and innermost normalisation of term rewriting systems.* PhD thesis, Universiteit Utrecht, 1997.
6. A. Bossi and N. Cocco. Preserving universal temination through unfold/fold. In G. Levi and M. Rodríguez-Artalejo, editors, *Algebraic and Logic Programming*, pages 269–286. Springer Verlag, 1994. LNCS 850.
7. A. Bowles and P. Wilk. Tracing requirements for multi-layered meta-programming. In H. Abramson and M. H. Rogers, editors, *Meta-Programming in Logic Programming*, pages 205–216. The MIT Press, 1989.
8. A. Brogi, P. Mancarella, D. Pedreschi, and F. Turini. Composition operators for logic theories. In J. W. Lloyd, editor, *Proc. Esprit Symp. on Comp. Logic*, pages 117–134. Springer Verlag, 1990.
9. M. Bruynooghe, D. De Schreye, and B. Martens. A general criterion for avoiding infinite unfolding during partial deduction. *New Generation Computing*, 11(1):47–79, 1992.

10. F. Bueno, M. J. García de la Banda, and M. V. Hermenegildo. Effectiveness of global analysis in strict independence-based automatic parallelization. In M. Bruynooghe, editor, *Logic Programming, Proc. of the 1994 Int. Symp.*, pages 320–336. MIT Press, 1994.
11. M. H. Cheng, M. H. van Emden, and P. A. Strooper. Complete sets of frontiers in logic-based program transformation. In H. Abramson and M. H. Rogers, editors, *Meta-Programming in Logic Programming*, pages 283–297. The MIT Press, 1989.
12. D. De Schreye and S. Decorte. Termination of logic programs: The never-ending story. *J. Logic Programming*, 19/20:199–260, May/July 1994.
13. S. Decorte and D. De Schreye. Termination analysis: some practical properties of the norm and level mapping space. In J. Jaffar, editor, *Proc. of the 1998 Joint Int. Conf. and Symp. on Logic Programming*, pages 235–249. MIT Press, June 1998.
14. S. Decorte, D. De Schreye, and H. Vandecasteele. Constraint-based termination analysis of logic programs. *ACM Transactions on Programming Languages and Systems (TOPLAS)*, 21(6):1137–1195, November 1999.
15. N. Dershowitz and Z. Manna. Proving termination with multiset orderings. *Communications of the ACM (CACM)*, 22(8):465–476, August 1979.
16. P. Hill and J. Gallagher. Meta-programming in logic programming. In D. M. Gabbay, C. Hogger, and J. Robinson, editors, *Handbook of logic in Artificial Intelligence and Logic Programming*, pages 421–498. Clarendon press, 1998. volume 5. Logic Programming.
17. P. Hill and J. Lloyd. Analysis of meta-programs. In H. Abramson and M. H. Rogers, editors, *Meta-Programming in Logic Programming*, pages 23–52. The MIT Press, 1989.
18. S. Hoarau. *Inférer et compiler la terminaison des programmes logiques avec contraintes.* PhD thesis, Université de La Réunion, 1999.
19. G. Levi and D. Ramundo. A formalization of metaprogramming for real. In D. S. Warren, editor, *Logic Programming, Proceedings of the Tenth International Conference on Logic Programming*, pages 354–373. MIT Press, 1993.
20. N. Lindenstrauss and Y. Sagiv. Automatic termination analysis of logic programs. In L. Naish, editor, *Proc. of the Fourteenth Int. Conf. on Logic Programming*, pages 63–77. MIT Press, July 1997.
21. B. Martens and D. De Schreye. Two semantics for definite meta-programs, using the non-ground representation. In K. Apt and F. Turini, editors, *Meta-Logics and Logic Programming*, pages 57–81. MIT Press, Cambridge, MA, 1995. ISBN: 0-262-01152-2.
22. B. Martens and D. De Schreye. Why untyped nonground metaprogramming is not (much of) a problem. *Journal of Logic Programming*, 22(1):47–99, January 1995.
23. D. Pedreschi and S. Ruggieri. Verification of meta-interpreters. *Journal of Logic and Computation*, 7(2):267–303, November 1997.
24. S. Ruggieri. *Verification and validation of logic programs.* PhD thesis, Universitá di Pisa, 1999.
25. A. Serebrenik and D. De Schreye. Non-transformational termination analysis of logic programs, based on general term-orderings. In K.-K. Lau, editor, *Logic Based Program Synthesis and Transformation 10th International Workshop, Selected Papers*, volume 2042 of *Lecture Notes in Computer Science*, pages 69–85. Springer Verlag, 2001.
26. A. Serebrenik and D. De Schreye. On termination of meta-programs. Technical Report CW 306, Departement Computerwetenschappen, K.U.Leuven, Leuven, Belgium, 2001. Available at
http://www.cs.kuleuven.ac.be/publicaties/rapporten/CW2001.html.

27. J.-G. Smaus. *Modes and Types in Logic Programming.* PhD thesis, University of Kent, 1999.
28. L. Sterling and E. Shapiro. *The Art of Prolog.* The MIT Press, 1994.
29. F. van Harmelen. A classification of meta-level architectures. In H. Abramson and M. H. Rogers, editors, *Meta-Programming in Logic Programming*, pages 103–122. The MIT Press, 1989.
30. S. Verbaeten. *Static verification of compositionality and termination for logic programming languages.* PhD thesis, Department of Computer Science, K.U.Leuven, Leuven, Belgium, June 2000. v+265+xxvii.

A Monotonic Higher-Order Semantic Path Ordering

Cristina Borralleras[1] and Albert Rubio[2]

[1] Universitat de Vic, Spain
cristina.borralleras@uvic.es
[2] Universitat Politècnica de Catalunya, Barcelona, SPAIN
rubio@lsi.upc.es

Abstract. There is an increasing use of (first- and higher-order) rewrite rules in many programming languages and logical systems. The *recursive path ordering* (RPO) is a well-known tool for proving termination of such rewrite rules in the first-order case. However, RPO has some weaknesses. For instance, since it is a simplification ordering, it can only handle simply terminating systems. Several techniques have been developed for overcoming these weaknesses of RPO. A very recent such technique is the *monotonic semantic path ordering* (MSPO), a simple and easily automatable ordering which generalizes other more ad-hoc methods.
Another recent extension of RPO is its higher-order version HORPO. HORPO is an ordering on terms of a typed lambda-calculus generated by a signature of higher-order function symbols. Although many interesting examples can be proved terminating using HORPO, it inherits the weaknesses of the first-order RPO.
Therefore, there is an obvious need for higher-order termination orderings without these weaknesses. Here we define the first such ordering, the *monotonic higher-order semantic path ordering* (MHOSPO), which is still automatable like MSPO. We give evidence of its power by means of several natural and non-trivial examples which cannot be handled by HORPO.

1 Introduction

There is an increasing use of higher-order rewrite rules in many programming languages and logical systems. As in the first-order case, termination is a fundamental property of most applications of higher-order rewriting. Thus, there exists a need to develop for the higher-order case the kind of semi-automated termination proof techniques that are available for the first-order case.

There have been several attempts at designing methods for proving strong normalization of higher-order rewrite rules based on ordering comparisons. These orderings are either quite weak [LSS92,JR98], or need an important user interaction [PS95]. Recently, in [JR99], the recursive path ordering (RPO) [Der82] —the most popular ordering-based termination proof method for first-order rewriting— has been extended to a higher-order setting by defining a higher-order recursive path ordering (HORPO) on terms following a typing discipline

R. Nieuwenhuis and A. Voronkov (Eds.): LPAR 2001, LNAI 2250, pp. 531–547, 2001.

including ML-like polymorphism. This ordering is powerful enough to deal with many non-trivial examples and can be automated. Besides, all aforementioned previous methods operate on terms in η-long β-normal form, hence apply only to the higher-order rewriting "à la Nipkow" [MN98], based on higher-order pattern matching modulo $\beta\eta$. HORPO is the first method which operates on arbitrary higher-order terms, therefore applying to the other kind of rewriting, based on plain pattern matching, where β-reduction is considered as any other rewrite rule. Furthermore, HORPO can operate as well on terms in η-long β-normal form, and hence it provides a termination proof method for both kinds of higher-order rewriting (see also [vR01] for a particular version of HORPO dealing η-long β-normal forms).

However, HORPO inherits the same weaknesses that RPO has in the first-order case. RPO is a *simplification ordering* (a monotonic ordering including the subterm relation), which extends a precedence on function symbols to an ordering on terms. It is simple and easy to use, but unfortunately, it turns out, in many cases, to be a weak termination proving tool. First, there are many term rewrite systems (TRSs) that are terminating but are not contained in any simplification ordering, i.e. they are not *simply terminating.* Second, in many cases the head symbol, the one that is compared with the precedence, does not provide enough information to prove the termination of the TRS. Therefore, since HORPO follows the same structure and the same use of a precedence as in RPO (in fact, it reduces to RPO when restricted to first-order terms), it is easy to expect that similar weaknesses will appear when proving termination of higher-order rewriting.

To avoid these weaknesses, in the first-order case, many different so-called *transformation methods* have been developed. By transforming the TRS into a set of ordering constraints, the *dependency pair* method [AG00] has become a successful general technique for proving termination of (non-simply terminating) TRSs.

As an alternative to transformation methods, more powerful term orderings like the *semantic path ordering* (SPO) ([KL80]) can be used. SPO generalizes RPO by replacing the precedence on function symbols by any (well-founded) underlying (quasi-)ordering involving the whole term and not only its head symbol. Although the simplicity of the presentation is kept, this makes the ordering much more powerful. Unfortunately, SPO is not so useful in practice, since, although it is well-founded, it is not, in general, monotonic. Hence, in order to ensure termination, apart from checking that the rules of the rewrite system are included in the ordering, in addition the monotonicity for contexts of the rewrite rules has to be proved.

In [BFR00], a monotonic version of SPO, called MSPO, has been presented. MSPO overcomes the weaknesses of RPO, it is automatable and it is shown to generalize other existing transformation methods.

Due to the fact that RPO and SPO share the same "path ordering nature", our aim is to obtain for SPO and MSPO the same kind of extensions to the higher-order case as it was done for RPO.

In this paper we present the *higher-order semantic path ordering* (HOSPO) which operates on terms of a typed lambda-calculus generated by a signature of higher-order function symbols. As done for HORPO in [JR99], HOSPO is proved well-founded by Tait and Girard's computability predicate proof technique. Then a monotonic version of HOSPO, called MHOSPO, is obtained, which provides an automatable powerful method for proving termination of higher-order rewriting on arbitrary higher-order terms union β-reduction. To illustrate this power several non-trivial examples are shown to be terminating.

In this work we do not consider η-reductions, although all results can be extended to include them at the expense of some easy, but technical, complications. For the same reason we have not included ML-like polymorphism.

Besides its own interest as a termination method for higher-order rewriting, the extension of HORPO to HOSPO and the definition of MHOSPO on top of HOSPO is also interesting for other reasons. On the one hand, it shows the stability of the definition of HORPO, since it extends to HOSPO in the same way as RPO extends to SPO. On the other hand, it shows the stability of the definition of MSPO, since MHOSPO is obtained from HOSPO in the same way as MSPO is obtained from SPO. This gives some intuition of why term orderings provide a more adequate framework for defining general termination proving methods than other techniques.

Formal definitions and basic tools are introduced in Section 2. In Section 3 an example motivating the need of extending HORPO is given. In Section 4 we present and study the higher-order semantic path ordering. Section 5 introduces MHOSPO. The method is applied to two examples in Section 6. Some conclusions and possible extensions are given in Section 7. The reader is expected to be familiar with the basics of term rewrite systems [DJ90] and typed lambda calculi [Bar92]. Due to the lack of room we have provided almost no proofs. All them can be found in [BR01].

2 Preliminaries

2.1 Types, Signatures, and Terms

We consider terms of a simply typed lambda-calculus generated by a signature of higher-order function symbols.

The set of types $\mathbb{T}$ is generated from the set $V_{\mathbb{T}}$ of *type variables* (considered as sorts) by the constructor $\rightarrow$ for *functional types* in the usual way. Types are called *functional* when they are headed by the $\rightarrow$ symbol, and *basic* when they are a type variable. As usual, $\rightarrow$ associates to the right. In the following, we use α, β for type variables and $\sigma, \tau, \rho, \theta$ for arbitrary types.

Let $\equiv$ be the congruence on types generated by equating all type variables in $V_{\mathbb{T}}$. Note that two types are equivalent iff they have the same arrow skeleton, i.e. $\sigma \equiv \tau$ iff replacing all type variables in σ and τ by the same type variable α we obtain two identical types.

A signature $\mathcal{F}$ is a set of function symbols which are meant to be algebraic operators, equipped with a fixed number n of arguments (called the *arity*) of respective types $\sigma_1 \in \mathbb{T}, \ldots, \sigma_n \in \mathbb{T}$, and an output type $\sigma \in \mathbb{T}$. A *type declaration* for a function symbol f will be written as $f : \sigma_1 \times \ldots \times \sigma_n \to \sigma$. Type declarations are not types, although they are used for typing purposes. Note, however, that $\sigma_1 \to \ldots \to \sigma_n \to \sigma$ is a type if $f : \sigma_1 \times \ldots \times \sigma_n \to \sigma$ is a type declaration. We will use the letters f, g, h to denote function symbols.

Given a signature $\mathcal{F}$ and a denumerable set $\mathcal{X}$ of variables, the set of *raw algebraic λ-terms* is defined by $\mathcal{T} := \mathcal{X} \mid (\lambda\mathcal{X} : \mathbb{T}.\mathcal{T}) \mid @(\mathcal{T}, \mathcal{T}) \mid \mathcal{F}(\mathcal{T}, \ldots, \mathcal{T})$. Terms of the form $\lambda x : \sigma.u$ are called *abstractions*, while the other terms are said to be *neutral*. For sake of brevity, we will often omit types. $@(u, v)$ denotes the application of u to v. The application operator is allowed to have a variable arity. We call a *partial left-flattening* of the term $@(@(\ldots @(t_1, t_2) \ldots, t_{n-1}), t_n)$, any term of the form $@(@(\ldots @(t_1, t_2) \ldots, t_i), t_{i+1}, \ldots, t_n)$. As a matter of convenience, we may write $@(u, v_1, \ldots, v_n)$ for $@(@(\ldots @(u, v_1) \ldots), v_n)$, assuming $n \geq 1$.

We denote by $\mathcal{V}ar(t)$ the set of free variables of t. We may assume for convenience (and without further notice) that bound variables in a term are all different, and are different from the free ones. The *subterm* of t at position p is denoted by $t|_p$, and we write $t \trianglerighteq t|_p$. The result of replacing $t|_p$ at position p in t by u is denoted by $t[u]_p$. We use $t[u]$ to indicate that u is a subterm of t, and simply $t[\,]_p$ for a term with a hole, also called a context. The notation $\overline{s}$ will be ambiguously used to denote a list, or a multiset, or a set of terms $s_1, \ldots, s_n$.

2.2 Typing Rules

Typing rules restrict the set of terms by constraining them to follow a precise discipline. Environments are sets of pairs written $x : \sigma$, where x is a variable and σ is a type. Our typing judgments are written as $\Gamma \vdash M : \sigma$ if the term M can be proved to have the type σ in the environment Γ:

Variables:

$$\frac{x : \sigma \in \Gamma}{\Gamma \vdash x : \sigma}$$

Functions:

$$\frac{f : \sigma_1 \times \ldots \times \sigma_n \to \sigma \in \mathcal{F} \qquad \Gamma \vdash t_1 : \sigma'_1 \equiv \sigma_1 \;\ldots\; \Gamma \vdash t_n : \sigma'_n \equiv \sigma_n}{\Gamma \vdash f(t_1, \ldots, t_n) : \sigma}$$

Abstraction:

$$\frac{\Gamma \cup \{x : \sigma\} \vdash t : \tau}{\Gamma \vdash (\lambda x : \sigma.t) : \sigma \to \tau}$$

Application:

$$\frac{\Gamma \vdash s : \sigma \to \tau \quad \Gamma \vdash t : \sigma' \equiv \sigma}{\Gamma \vdash @(s, t) : \tau}$$

A term M has type σ in the environment Γ if $\Gamma \vdash M : \sigma$ is provable in the above inference system. A term M is typable in the environment Γ if there exists a unique type σ such that M has type σ in the environment Γ. A term M is typable if it is typable in some environment Γ. Note again that function symbols are uncurried, hence must come along with all their arguments.

The reason to use $\equiv$ is that having a larger set of typable terms allow us to increase the power of the ordering we will define (see the end of the proof of example 3).

Substitutions are supposed to be well-typed. We use the letter γ for substitutions and postfix notation for their application, e.g. $t\gamma$. Substitutions behave as endomorphisms defined on free variables (avoiding captures).

2.3 Higher-Order Rewrite Rules

The rewrite relation which is considered in this paper is the union of the one induced by a set of higher-order rewrite rules and the β-reduction relation both working modulo α-conversion.

We use $\longrightarrow_\beta$ for the β-reduction rule: $@(\lambda x.v, u) \longrightarrow_\beta v\{x \mapsto u\}$. The simply typed λ-calculus is confluent and terminating with respect to β-reductions.

As said, for simplicity reasons, in this work we do not consider η-reductions, although all results can be extended to include them.

A higher-order *term rewrite system* is a set of rewrite rules $R = \{\Gamma \vdash l_i \rightarrow r_i\}_i$, where l_i and r_i are higher-order terms such that l_i and r_i have the same type σ_i in the environment Γ. Note that usually the terms l_i and r_i will be typable in the system without using the type equivalence $\equiv$, i.e. they will be typable by the system replacing $\equiv$ by syntactic equality $=$ on types.

Given a term rewriting system R, a term s rewrites to a term t at position p with the rule $\Gamma \vdash l \rightarrow r$ and the substitution γ, written $s \xrightarrow[l\rightarrow r]{p} t$, or simply $s \rightarrow_R t$, if $s|_p = l\gamma$ and $t = s[r\gamma]_p$ (modulo α-conversion). We denote by $\xrightarrow[R]{*}$ the reflexive, transitive closure of the rewrite relation $\xrightarrow[R]{}$. We are actually interested in the relation $\longrightarrow_{R\beta} = \longrightarrow_R \cup \longrightarrow_\beta$.

Given a rewrite relation $\longrightarrow$, a term s is strongly normalizing if there is no infinite sequence of rewrites issuing from s. The rewrite relation itself is *strongly normalizing*, or *terminating*, if all terms are strongly normalizing.

2.4 Orderings and Quasi-Orderings

We will make intensive use of well-founded orderings for proving strong normalization properties. We will use the vocabulary of rewrite systems for orderings and quasi-orderings (see e.g. [DJ90]). For our purpose, a *(strict) ordering*, always denoted by $>$ or $\succ$ (possibly with subscripts), is an irreflexive and transitive relation. An ordering $>$ is *monotonic* if $s > t$ implies $f(\ldots s \ldots) > f(\ldots t \ldots)$; it is *stable* if $s > t$ implies $s\gamma > t\gamma$ for all substitutions γ; and it is *well-founded* if there are no infinite sequences $t_1 > t_2 > \ldots$ An ordering is said to be higher-order when it operates on higher-order terms and is α-compatible: it does not distinguish between α-convertible terms.

A *quasi-ordering*, always denoted by $\succeq$ or $\geq$, is a transitive and reflexive binary relation. Its inverse is denoted by $\preceq$. Its *strict part* $\succ$ is the strict ordering $\succeq \setminus \preceq$ (i.e, $s \succ t$ iff $s \succeq t$ and $s \not\preceq t$). Its *equivalence* $\sim$ is $\succeq \cap \preceq$. Note that $\succeq$ is the disjoint union of $\succ$ and $\sim$.

A quasi-ordering $\succeq$ is *well-founded* if $\succ$ is. It is *stable* if $\succ$ is and $s\sigma \succeq t\sigma$ whenever $s \succeq t$. $\succeq$ is *quasi-monotonic* if $f(\ldots, s, \ldots) \succeq f(\ldots, t, \ldots)$ whenever

$s \succeq t$. A quasi-ordering is said to be higher-order when it operates on higher-order terms and its equivalence includes α-conversion. Note that if $\succ$ is a higher-order ordering $\succ \cup =_\alpha$ is a higher-order quasi-ordering whose strict part is $\succ$.

Assume $>_1, \ldots, >_n$ are orderings on sets $S_1, \ldots, S_n$. Then its *lexicographic combination* $(>_1, \ldots, >_n)_{lex}$ is an ordering on $S_1 \times \ldots \times S_n$. We write $>_{lex}$ if all sets and orderings are equal. Similarly the lexicographic combination of quasi-orderings $\succeq_1, \ldots, \succeq_n$ is denoted by $(\succeq_1, \ldots, \succeq_n)_{lex}$ and defined as $s(\succeq_1, \ldots, \succeq_n)_{lex} t$ iff either $s \succ_i t$ for some i and $s \succeq_j t$ for all $j < i$, or $s \succeq_i t$ for all i. If all $>_i$, respectively $\succeq_i$, are well-founded then its lexicographic combination also is. Same happens for stability and α-compatibility.

Assume $\succ$ is an ordering on a set S. Then its *multiset extension*, denoted by $\succ\!\succ$, is an ordering on the set of multisets of elements of S, defined as the transitive closure of: $M \cup \{s\} \succ\!\succ M \cup \{t_1, \ldots, t_n\}$ if $s \succ t_i \; \forall i \in [1..n]$ (using $\cup$ for multiset union). If $\succ$ is well-founded, stable and α-compatible then $\succ\!\succ$ also is.

Definition 1. *A higher-order reduction ordering is a well-founded, monotonic and stable higher-order ordering $>$, such that $\longrightarrow_\beta \subsetneq >$.*

A higher-order quasi-rewrite ordering is a quasi-monotonic and stable higher-order quasi-ordering $\succeq$, such that $\longrightarrow_\beta \subseteq \succeq$. A higher-order quasi-reduction ordering is in addition well-founded.

Reduction orderings allow us to show that the relation $\longrightarrow_R \cup \longrightarrow_\beta$ is terminating by simply comparing the left-hand and right-hand sides of each rule in R:

Theorem 1. *Let $R = \{\Gamma \vdash l_i \to r_i\}_{i \in I}$ be a higher-order rewrite system such that $l_i > r_i$ for every $i \in I$. Then the relation $\longrightarrow_R \cup \longrightarrow_\beta$ is strongly normalizing.*

2.5 The Higher-Order Recursive Path Ordering (HORPO)

We present here a restricted version of HORPO (with no status for function symbols) which is enough for our purposes. The HORPO is based on a quasi-ordering $\geq_\mathcal{F}$, called *precedence*, on the set of function symbols $\mathcal{F}$ whose strict part $>_\mathcal{F}$ is well-founded and whose equivalence is denoted by $=_\mathcal{F}$. HORPO compares terms of equivalent type by using the head symbol wrt. the precedence and/or the arguments recursively following a similar structure as RPO in the first-order case.

Additionally, in HORPO, in order to make the ordering more powerful, when comparing two terms s and t, when s is headed by an algebraic function symbol, we cannot only use the arguments of s but also any term in the so called *computable closure* of s, which mainly allows us to introduce abstractions in some cases. The intuition for doing so comes from the strong normalization proof. In that proof, it is crucial to show the computability (in the sense of Tait and Girard's strong normalization proof technique) of the right-hand side term t by using the left-hand side arguments of s, which are assumed to be computable, and the head function symbol. Therefore, instead of using directly the arguments of s, we can use any term obtained applying computability preserving operations to its arguments.

To ease the reading, here we give a subset of the possible computability preserving operations given in [JR99] which is enough for our purposes and gives the flavor of the method.

Definition 2. *Given a term $s = f(s_1, \ldots, s_n)$, we define its computable closure $\mathcal{CC}(s)$ as $\mathcal{CC}(s, \emptyset)$, where $\mathcal{CC}(s, \mathcal{V})$ with $\mathcal{V} \cap \mathcal{V}ar(s) = \emptyset$, is the smallest set of well-typed terms containing the arguments $s_1, \ldots, s_n$, all variables in $\mathcal{V}$ and closed under the following two operations:*

1. *precedence: $h(\overline{u}) \in \mathcal{CC}(s, \mathcal{V})$ if $f >_{\mathcal{F}} h$ and $\overline{u} \in \mathcal{CC}(s, \mathcal{V})$.*
2. *abstraction: $\lambda x.u \in \mathcal{CC}(s, \mathcal{V})$ if $x \notin \mathcal{V}ar(s) \cup \mathcal{V}$ and $u \in \mathcal{CC}(s, \mathcal{V} \cup \{x\})$.*

Now we give the definition of HORPO, denoted by $\succ_{horpo}$, adapted from [JR99], where $\succeq_{horpo}$ means the union of $\succ_{horpo}$ and α-conversion.

$$s : \sigma \underset{horpo}{\succ} t : \tau \text{ iff } \sigma \equiv \tau \text{ and}$$

1. $s = f(\overline{s})$ with $f \in \mathcal{F}$, and $u \succeq_{horpo} t$ for some $u \in \overline{s}$
2. $s = f(\overline{s})$ with $f \in \mathcal{F}$ and $t = g(\overline{t})$ with $f >_{\mathcal{F}} g$, and for all $t_i \in \overline{t}$ either $s \succ_{horpo} t_i$ or $u \succeq_{horpo} t_i$ for some $u \in \mathcal{CC}(s)$
3. $s = f(\overline{s})$ and $t = g(\overline{t})$, $f =_{\mathcal{F}} g \in \mathcal{F}$ and $\{\overline{s}\} \succ\!\succ_{horpo} \{\overline{t}\}$
4. $s = f(\overline{s})$ with $f \in \mathcal{F}$, $t = @(\overline{t})$ is some partial left-flattening of t, and for all $t_i \in \overline{t}$ either $s \succ_{horpo} t_i$ or $u \succeq_{horpo} t_i$ for some $u \in \mathcal{CC}(s)$
5. $s = @(s_1, s_2)$, $t = @(t_1, t_2)$ and $\{s_1, s_2\} \succ\!\succ_{horpo} \{t_1, t_2\}$
6. $s = \lambda x.u$ and $t = \lambda x.v$, and $u \succ_{horpo} v$
7. $s = @(\lambda x.u, v)$ and $u\{x \mapsto v\} \succeq_{horpo} t$

The definition of HORPO is used as a recursive algorithm to check whether a term s is greater than a term t. In case 6 we apply an α-conversion on the heading lambda if necessary. The following theorem states that HORPO is a higher-order reduction ordering, which means that if we show that the left hand side of each rule in a rewriting system is greater than the right hand side then we can conclude that the system is terminating for higher-order rewriting.

Theorem 2. *The transitive closure of $\succ_{horpo}$ is a higher-order reduction ordering.*

3 A Motivating Example

In this section we present an example which on the one hand will help us to show how HORPO is used, and on the other hand will exhibit its weakness, since the example cannot be proved terminating although it is, and the need to improve in the direction of semantic orderings.

The example defines the *prefix sum* of a list of natural numbers, i.e. the list with the sum of all prefixes of the given list, using the *map* function. We do not include the rules defining the + symbol.

Example 1. Prefix sum. Let $V_{\mathbb{T}} = \{Nat, List\}$,
$\mathcal{X} = \{\ x : Nat, xs : List, F : Nat \rightarrow Nat\ \}$ and
$\mathcal{F} = \{\ [] : List,\ cons : Nat \times List \rightarrow List,\ + : Nat \times Nat \rightarrow Nat,$
$\quad map : (Nat \rightarrow Nat) \times List \rightarrow List,\ ps : List \rightarrow List \qquad \}.$

$$map(F, []) \rightarrow [] \tag{1}$$
$$map(F, cons(x, xs)) \rightarrow cons(@(F, x), map(F, xs)) \tag{2}$$

$$ps([]) \rightarrow [] \tag{3}$$
$$ps(cons(x, xs)) \rightarrow cons(x, ps(map(\lambda y.x + y, xs))) \tag{4}$$

Now we try to prove that this system is included in HORPO. Rules 1 and 3 hold applying case 1 of the definition of HORPO. For the second rule we need to show that $map(F, cons(x, xs)) : List \succ_{horpo} cons(@(F, x), map(F, xs)) : List$. In this case the only possibility is to have $map >_{\mathcal{F}} cons$ and apply case 2. Then we check recursively (1) $map(F, cons(x, xs)) : List \succ_{horpo} @(F, x) : Nat$ and (2) $map(F, cons(x, xs)) : List \succ_{horpo} map(F, xs) : List$. For (1) we apply case 4, since $F \in \mathcal{CC}(map(F, cons(x, xs)))$ and $map(F, cons(x, xs)) : List \succ_{horpo} x : Nat$, applying twice case 1. Finally, to prove (2) we apply case 3 which holds since $cons(x, xs) : List \succ_{horpo} xs : List$ by case 1.

For the last rule, we can only apply case 2 taking $ps >_{\mathcal{F}} cons$. This requires that $ps(cons(x, xs)) : List \succ_{horpo} x : Nat$, which holds applying twice case 1, and also $ps(cons(x, xs)) : List \succ_{horpo} ps(map(\lambda y.x + y, xs)) : List$. For the latter we apply case 3, which requires $cons(x, xs) : List \succ_{horpo} map(\lambda y.x + y, xs) : List$. To prove this we need $cons >_{\mathcal{F}} map$ and apply case 2, showing that $\lambda y.x + y \in \mathcal{CC}(cons(x, xs))$ taking $cons >_{\mathcal{F}} +$, and $cons(x, xs) : List \succ_{horpo} xs : List$ using case 1.

Unfortunately, to show that the second rule is in HORPO we need to take $map >_{\mathcal{F}} cons$ and to show the last rule we need $cons >_{\mathcal{F}} map$, which of course cannot be the case if $>_{\mathcal{F}}$ is well-founded. Note that the considered system cannot be proved either using the definition of HORPO in [JR99], hence the problem is not due to the simplified version of HORPO we are considering here.

Now, if we look at the example, the intuition behind its termination comes from the fact that in all recursive calls the size of the list parameter decrease. This somehow means that this parameter should play an important role when comparing the terms, since the use of the head symbol is not enough. Generalizing path orderings to using more information about the term than only the head symbol is done by means of *semantic path orderings* [KL80].

4 The Higher-Order Semantic Path Ordering (HOSPO)

We present now HOSPO, which generalizes HORPO by using a well-founded stable higher-order quasi-ordering $\succeq_Q$, which does not need to include β-reduction, instead of the precedence $\geq_{\mathcal{F}}$. We also adapt in the same way the computable closure. Note that, although we can fully adapt the definition of the computable closure given in [JR99], for simplicity reasons, we will provide only an adapted version of the restricted computable closure given in section 2.5.

Definition 3. *Given a term $s = f(s_1, \ldots, s_n)$, we define its computable closure $\mathcal{CC}(s)$ as $\mathcal{CC}(s, \emptyset)$, where $\mathcal{CC}(s, \mathcal{V})$ with $\mathcal{V} \cap \mathcal{V}ar(s) = \emptyset$, is the smallest set of well-typed terms containing all variables in $\mathcal{V}$ and all terms in $\{s_1, \ldots, s_n\}$, and closed under the following operations:*

1. *quasi-ordering: $h(\overline{u}) \in \mathcal{CC}(s, \mathcal{V})$ if $f(\overline{s}) \succ_Q h(\overline{u})$ and $\overline{u} \in \mathcal{CC}(s, \mathcal{V})$.*
2. *abstraction: $\lambda x.u \in \mathcal{CC}(s, \mathcal{V})$ if $x \notin \mathcal{V}ar(s) \cup \mathcal{V}$ and $u \in \mathcal{CC}(s, \mathcal{V} \cup \{x\})$.*

Now we give the definition of HOSPO, where $\succeq_{hospo}$ means the union of $\succ_{hospo}$ and α-conversion.

Definition 4. *$s : \sigma \succ_{hospo} t : \tau$ iff $\sigma \equiv \tau$ and*

1. *$s = f(\overline{s})$ with $f \in \mathcal{F}$, $u \succeq_{hospo} t$ for some $u \in \overline{s}$.*
2. *$s = f(\overline{s})$ and $t = g(\overline{t})$ with $f, g \in \mathcal{F}$, $s \succ_Q t$, and for all $t_i \in \overline{t}$ either $s \succ_{hospo} t_i$ or $u \succeq_{hospo} t_i$ for some $u \in \mathcal{CC}(s)$.*
3. *$s = f(\overline{s})$ and $t = g(\overline{t})$ with $f, g \in \mathcal{F}$, $s \succeq_Q t$ and $\{\overline{s}\} \succ\succ_{hospo} \{\overline{t}\}$*
4. *$s = f(\overline{s})$, $f \in \mathcal{F}$, $@(\overline{t})$ is some partial left-flattening of t, and for all $t_i \in \overline{t}$ either $s \succ_{hospo} t_i$ or $u \succeq_{hospo} t_i$ for some $u \in \mathcal{CC}(s)$.*
5. *$s = @(s_1, s_2)$, $t = @(t_1, t_2)$, $\{s_1, s_2\} \succ\succ_{hospo} \{t_1, t_2\}$*
6. *$s = \lambda x.u$, $t = \lambda x.v$, $u \succ_{hospo} v$*
7. *$s = @(\lambda x.u, v)$ and $u\{x \mapsto v\} \succeq_{hospo} t$*

In case 6 we apply an α-conversion on the heading lambda if necessary. Note that $\succeq_Q$ is only used in cases 2 and 3, where the head symbol of both terms is in $\mathcal{F}$. On the other hand, case 7 captures β-reduction at top position, and since, in general, HOSPO is not monotonic, it may be the case that HOSPO does not include β-reduction at any position.

The resulting ordering is shown to be well-defined by comparing pairs of terms $\langle t, s\rangle$ in the well-founded ordering $(\rhd, \rightarrow_\beta \cup \rhd)_{lex}$.

Lemma 1. *$\succ_{hospo}$ is stable under substitutions and α-compatible.*

For stability under substitutions, first we show that $u \in \mathcal{CC}(s)$ implies that $u\gamma \in \mathcal{CC}(s\gamma)$ for every substitution γ. Then the proof is done by induction on the pair $\langle t, s\rangle$ wrt. $(\rhd, \rightarrow_\beta \cup \rhd)_{lex}$, distinguishing cases according to the definition of $\succ_{hospo}$ and using the stability of $\succeq_Q$. For α-compatibility we follow the same pattern.

To prove well-foundedness of the ordering we follow the Tait and Girard's computability predicate proof method as for HORPO in [JR99]. We denote by $[\![\sigma]\!]$ the computability predicate of type σ.

Definition 5. *The family of type interpretations $\{[\![\sigma]\!]\}_{\sigma\in\mathcal{T}_S}$ is the family of subsets of the set of typed terms whose elements are the least sets satisfying the following properties:*

1. *If σ is a basic type, then $s:\sigma \in [\![\sigma]\!]$ iff $\forall t:\tau$ s.t. $s \succ_{hospo} t$, $t \in [\![\tau]\!]$.*
2. *If $s:\sigma = \tau \to \rho$ then $s \in [\![\sigma]\!]$ iff $@(s,t) \in [\![\rho]\!]$ for every $t \in [\![\tau']\!]$, with $\tau' \equiv \tau$.*

The above definition is based on a lexicographic combination of an induction on the size of the type and a fixpoint computation for basic types. The existence of a least fixpoint is ensured by the monotonicity of the underlying family of functionals (indexed by the set of basic types) with respect to set inclusion (for each basic type). Note that for basic types this definition can be seen as a closure wrt. case 1, taking as initial set for each basic type the set of minimal, wrt. $\succ_{hospo}$, terms (which includes the variables). A typed term s of type σ is said to be computable if $s \in [\![\sigma]\!]$. A vector $\overline{s}$ of terms is computable iff so are all its components.

Property 1 *Computability properties.*

1. *Every computable term is strongly normalizable.*
2. *If s is computable and $s \succ_{hospo} t$ then t is computable.*
3. *A neutral term s is computable iff t is computable for every t s.t. $s \succ_{hospo} t$.*
4. *If $\overline{t}$ is a vector of at least two computable terms s.t. $@(\overline{t})$ is a typed term, then $@(\overline{t})$ is computable.*
5. *$\lambda x:\sigma.u$ is computable iff $u\{x \mapsto w\}$ is computable for every computable term $w:\alpha \equiv \sigma$.*

Note that variables are computable as a consequence of Property 1.3. The precise assumption of the following property comes from the ordering used in the proof by induction of Lemma 2 and gives some intuition about the definition of the computable closure.

Property 2 *Assume $\overline{s}:\overline{\tau}$ is computable, as well as every term $h(\overline{u})$ with $\overline{u}$ computable and $f(\overline{s}) \succ_Q h(\overline{u})$. Then every term in $\mathcal{CC}(f(\overline{s})$ is computable.*

Lemma 2. *Let $f:\overline{\sigma} \to \tau \ \in \mathcal{F}$ and $\overline{t}:\overline{\tau} \equiv \overline{\sigma}$ be a set of terms. If $\overline{t}$ is computable, then $f(\overline{t})$ is computable.*

The proof is done by induction on the ordering $\langle \succ_Q, \succ\!\!\succ_{hospo}\rangle$ operating on pairs $\langle f(\overline{t}), \overline{t}\rangle$. This ordering is well-founded since we are assuming that $\overline{t}$ is computable and hence strongly normalizing by Property 1.1. Note that in the assumption of Property 2 we are only using the first component of the induction ordering. By using both components, we can improve the computable closure, as done in [JR99], adding new cases (see [BR01] for details).

Lemma 3. *$\succ_{hospo}$ is well-founded.*

The proof is done by showing that $t\gamma$ is computable for every typed term t and computable substitution γ, by induction on the size of t and using Property 1.5 and Lemma 2. Note that for the empty substitution γ we have that all typed terms are computable and hence strongly normalizable by Property 1. 1.

5 A Monotonic Higher Order Semantic Path Ordering

In this section we present a monotonic version of HOSPO, called MHOSPO, and show how it can be used in practice.

To define MHOSPO we need an additional quasi-ordering $\succeq_I$ as ingredient. This quasi-ordering is used to ensure monotonicity, and due to this we need to require some properties on it.

Definition 6. *We say that $\succeq_I$ is* quasi-monotonic on $\succeq_Q$ *(or $\succeq_Q$ is* quasi-monotonic wrt. *$\succeq_I$) if*

$$s \succeq_I t \quad \textit{implies} \quad f(\ldots s \ldots) \succeq_Q f(\ldots t \ldots)$$

for all terms s and t and all function symbols f.

A pair $\langle \succeq_I, \succeq_Q \rangle$ is called a higher-order quasi-reduction pair *if $\succeq_I$ is a higher-order quasi-rewrite ordering, $\succeq_Q$ is a well-founded stable higher-order quasi-ordering, and $\succeq_I$ is quasi-monotonic on $\succeq_Q$.*

Now we give the definition of MHOSPO.

Definition 7. *Let $\langle \succeq_I, \succeq_Q \rangle$ be a higher-order quasi-reduction pair.*

$$s \succ_{mhospo} t \textit{ iff } s \succeq_I t \textit{ and } s \succ_{hospo} t.$$

Theorem 3. *The transitive closure of $\succ_{mhospo}$ is a higher-order reduction ordering.*

Well-foundedness follows from the fact that $\succ_{mhospo} \subseteq \succ_{hospo}$ and $\succ_{hospo}$ is well-founded. Stability and α-compatibility follow respectively from the stability and α-compatibility of $\succeq_I$ and $\succ_{hospo}$. Monotonicity follows directly from the fact that $\succeq_I$ is quasi-monotonic on $\succeq_Q$ and includes β-reduction, and cases 3, 5 and 6 of $\succ_{hospo}$. Finally, to prove that $\longrightarrow_\beta \; \subseteq \; \succ_{mhospo}$, we use monotonicity, case 7 of HOSPO and the fact that $\succeq_I$ includes β-reduction.

Note that HORPO is a particular case of MHOSPO, which is obtained by taking $\succeq_I$ as $s \succeq_I t$ for all s and t, which has an empty strict part (and trivially fulfils all required properties), and $\succeq_Q$ as a precedence.

In order to make MHOSPO useful in practice we need general methods to obtain quasi-reduction pairs $\langle \succeq_I, \succeq_Q \rangle$. We will first provide possible candidates for the quasi-ordering $\succeq_I$ and then show how to obtain a $\succeq_Q$ forming a pair.

5.1 Building $\succeq_I$

We consider $\succeq_I$ obtained by combining an interpretation I on terms with some higher-order quasi-reduction ordering $\succeq_B$, called the *basic* quasi-ordering, i.e. $s : \sigma \succeq_I t : \tau$ if and only if $I(s : \sigma) \succeq_B I(t : \tau)$ (note that hence we also have that $s : \sigma \succ_I t : \tau$ if and only if $I(s : \sigma) \succ_B I(t : \tau)$). An obvious candidate for $\succeq_B$ is (the transitive closure of) HORPO union α-conversion. For the interpretation I, as a general property, we require the preservation of the typability of terms and the quasi-monotonicity, stability, α-compatibility and the inclusion of β-reduction of the basic quasi-ordering $\succeq_B$. Note that, since $\succeq_B$ is well-founded, the obtained $\succeq_I$ is also well-founded and hence it is a quasi-reduction ordering, although $\succeq_I$ is only required to be a quasi-rewrite ordering. The reason for adding the well-foundedness property to $\succeq_I$ in this construction will become clear later when building the quasi-reduction pairs $\langle \succeq_I, \succeq_Q \rangle$.

Below some suitable such interpretations obtained by adapting usual interpretations for the first-order case are provided. We consider interpretations that are mappings from typed terms to typed terms. As a matter of simplicity we have considered only interpretations to terms in the same given signature and set of types. Note that we can enlarge our signature (or the set of types) if new symbols (or types) are needed in the interpretation. On the other hand if we consider interpretations to terms in a new signature and set of types then we not only need to interpret the terms but also the types.

Each symbol $f : \sigma_1 \times ... \times \sigma_n \to \sigma$ can be interpreted either by (1) a projection on a single argument of an equivalent type to the output type of f, denoted by the pair $(f(x_1, \ldots, x_n), x_i)$ with $x_i : \tau$ and $\sigma \equiv \tau$, or else by (2) a function symbol f_I, with an equivalent output type to f, applied to a sequence obtained from the arguments of f preserving the typability of the term, denoted by the pair $(f(x_1, \ldots, x_n), f_I(x_{i_1}, \ldots, x_{i_k}))$, for some $k \geq 0$, $i_1, \ldots, i_k \in \{1, ..., n\}$ and $f_I : \sigma'_{i_1} \times ... \times \sigma'_{i_k} \to \sigma'$, with $\sigma'_{i_j} \equiv \sigma_{i_j}$ for all $j \in \{1, ..., k\}$ and $\sigma' \equiv \sigma$. In order to include β-reduction we consider I to be the identity for λ and @. Additionally, we consider I to be the identity for variables (although it can be any bijection). We assume that there is only one pair for each symbol. Usually the identity pairs will be omitted. Thus the interpretation I of a term is obtained, as usual, by using the pairs on the top symbol once the arguments have been recursively interpreted.

It is easy to show that this interpretations preserve typability and the quasi-monotonicity, stability, α-compatibility and the inclusion of the β-reduction of $\succeq_B$.

Example 2. Following the example 1, consider the interpretation I defined by the pairs $(map(x_1, x_2), x_2)$ and $(cons(x_1, x_2), cons_I(x_2))$, where $cons_I : List \to List$, then we have that:

1. $I(map(F, cons(x, xs))) = cons_I(xs)$
2. $I(cons(@(F, x), map(F, xs))) = cons_I(xs)$
3. $I(ps(cons(x, xs))) = ps(cons_I(xs))$
4. $I(cons(x, ps(map(\lambda y.x + y, xs)))) = cons_I(ps(xs))$
5. $I(@(F, x)) = @(F, x)$ and $I(\lambda y.x + y) = \lambda y.x + y$

5.2 Building $\succeq_Q$

Now we show how higher-order quasi-reduction pairs $\langle \succeq_I, \succeq_Q \rangle$ can be obtained. This can be done in a general way, as for MSPO in [BFR00], but for simplicity reasons we will just provide the most usual examples of quasi-orderings $\succeq_Q$ that work in practice.

The simplest case is consider that $\succeq_Q$ and $\succeq_I$ coincide, provided that $\succeq_I$ is a quasi-reduction ordering (which is the case with the $\succeq_I$ we have defined in the previous section).

A more elaborated case for $\succeq_Q$ is to combine lexicographically a precedence and the quasi-ordering $\succeq_I$, that is $\succeq_Q$ is defined as

$$(\succeq_{\mathcal{P}}, \succeq_I)_{lex}$$

where $\succeq_{\mathcal{P}}$ is a (well-founded) precedence, which can be completely different from the precedence used in the HORPO inside $\succeq_I$. Note that the precedence is used on terms by just comparing their head symbols. We can also add another precedence as third component. Since $\succeq_I$ has been built to be well-founded and the precedences are well-founded, its lexicographic combination also is. Quasi-monotonicity of $\succeq_I$ on $\succeq_Q$ can be easily shown using the quasi-monotonicity of $\succeq_I$.

Finally, using an idea coming from the dependency pair method [AG00], instead of using directly $\succeq_I$ inside $\succeq_Q$, we can apply first a *renaming* of the head symbol, in case it is a function symbol, before using $\succeq_I$. This renaming allow us to apply different interpretations when a function symbol occurs on the head than when it occurs inside the term. Therefore thanks to the renaming sometimes the proof can be easier. Since this renaming is not needed in our examples we refer to [BR01] for details.

6 Examples

Let us illustrate the use and the power of MHOSPO, by means of several examples. Due to the lack of room, only in the first example we will give some details of the checking (see [BR01] for further details).

Example 3. We recall example 1.

$$map(F, []) \to [] \tag{1}$$
$$map(F, cons(x, xs)) \to cons(@(F, x), map(F, xs)) \tag{2}$$

$$ps([]) \to [] \tag{3}$$
$$ps(cons(x, xs)) \to cons(x, ps(map(\lambda y.x + y, xs))) \tag{4}$$

Termination of this TRS can be proved with $\succ_{mhospo}$ taking $\succeq_Q$ as $(\succeq_{\mathcal{P}}, \succeq_I)_{lex}$. The precedence $\succeq_{\mathcal{P}}$ is defined by $ps \succ_{\mathcal{P}} map \succ_{\mathcal{P}} cons$ and $ps \succ_{\mathcal{P}} +$; and we define $\succeq_I$ by combining $\succ_{horpo}$, with the precedence $ps \succ_{\mathcal{F}} cons_I$, as basic quasi-ordering and the interpretation function I defined by the pairs $(map(x_1, x_2), x_2)$ and $(cons(x_1, x_2), cons_I(x_2))$, where $cons_I : List \to List$. Note that with this interpretation for the *map* function only the List parameter is considered and the List is interpreted as the amount of *cons* it has, which represents its size.

In order to prove that all rules are included in the obtained MHOSPO, we need to check both that $l \succeq_I r$ and $l \succ_{hospo} r$ for all rules $l \to r$ in the system. Fist of all recall that, since *List* and *Nat* are type variables (considered as sorts) we have $List \equiv Nat$, which will be used many times along the checking.

We start showing that all rules are included in $\succeq_I$. Rules 1 and 2 have the same interpretation for both sides. For rule 3 we trivially have $I(ps([])) = ps([]) \succ_{horpo} [] = I([])$. For rule 4, $I(ps(cons(x, xs))) = ps(cons_I(xs)) \succ_{horpo} cons_I(ps(xs)) = I(cons(x, ps(map(\lambda y.x + y, xs))))$, using $ps \succ_{\mathcal{F}} cons_I$.

Rules 1 and 3 are included in HOSPO by case 1. For rule 2 we show that $map(F, cons(x, xs)) \succ_{hospo} cons(@(F, x), map(F, xs))$. We apply first case 2, since $map(F, cons(x, xs)) \succ_Q cons(@(F, x), map(F, xs))$ by the first component of $\succeq_Q$ as $map \succ_{\mathcal{P}} cons$. Then we need to check recursively that (1) $map(F, cons(x, xs)) \succ_{hospo} @(F, x)$ and that (2) $map(F, cons(x, xs)) \succ_{hospo} map(F, xs)$. For (1) we apply case 4 since $F \in \mathcal{CC}(map(F, cons(x, xs)))$ and $map(F, cons(x, xs)) \succ_{hospo} x$ applying case 1 twice. For (2) we apply again case 2 since $map(F, cons(x, xs)) \succ_Q map(F, xs)$, by the second component of $\succeq_Q$ as $I(map(F, cons(x, xs))) = cons_I(xs) \succ_{horpo} xs = I(map(F, xs))$, and the recursive checking hold in the same way as before.

For the last rule we need $ps(cons(x, xs)) \succ_{hospo} cons(x, ps(map(\lambda y.x + y, xs)))$. We apply case 2 using the precedence component. For the recursive checking we only develop $ps(cons(x, xs)) \succ_{hospo} ps(map(\lambda y.x + y, xs))$. Then we apply again case 2 twice in the first case using the second component of $\succeq_Q$ and in the second case using the precedence. Finally we show (apart from the easy checking for xs) that $\lambda y.cons(x, xs) + y \in \mathcal{CC}(ps(cons(x, xs)))$ using the closure with case 2 and then case 1 with the precedence, and conclude with $\lambda y.cons(x, xs) + y \succ_{hospo} \lambda y.x + y$, which holds easily (note that $\lambda y.cons(x, xs) + y$ is well-typed since $Nat \equiv List$).

The last part of the proof of the previous example may look hard to automate, since we have to pick a term from the computable closure of $ps(cons(x, xs))$ and then check that it is greater than or equal to $\lambda y.x + y$. In practice, we look for such a term in the computable closure in a goal-directed way: since $\lambda y.x + y$ is headed by lambda and then $+$ we apply case 2 and case 1, and then, when we reach x, we check whether some argument of $ps(cons(x, xs))$ (which belongs to the computable closure by definition) is greater than or equal to x. Therefore, since $cons(x, xs) \succ_{hospo} x$, by monotonicity we conclude, without any additional checking, that $\lambda y.cons(x, xs) + y \succ_{hospo} \lambda y.x + y$

Let us present another example which can be proved by MHOSPO and not by HORPO. We only provide the ingredients of MHOSPO which are needed to prove that the rules are included in the ordering.

Example 4. Quick sort. Let $\mathcal{V}_{\mathbb{T}} = \{Bool, Nat, List\}$,
$\mathcal{X} = \{x, y : Nat; xs, ys : List; p : Nat \to Bool\}$ and
$\mathcal{F} = \{\ 0 : Nat,\ s : Nat \to Nat,\ le, gr : Nat \times Nat \to Bool,$
$True, False : Bool,\ if : Bool \times List \times List \to List,$
$[] : List,\ cons : Nat \times List \to List,\ ++ : List \times List \to List,$
$filter : (Nat \to Bool) \times List \to List,\ qsort : List \to List \quad \}$

$$\begin{array}{ll} if(True, xs, ys) \rightarrow xs & [] +\!\!+ xs \rightarrow xs \\ if(False, xs, ys) \rightarrow ys & cons(x, xs) +\!\!+ ys \rightarrow cons(x, xs +\!\!+ ys) \end{array}$$

$$\begin{array}{ll} le(0, y) \rightarrow True & gr(0, y) \rightarrow False \\ le(s(x), 0) \rightarrow False & gr(s(x), 0) \rightarrow True \\ le(s(x), s(y)) \rightarrow le(x, y) & gr(s(x), s(y)) \rightarrow gr(x, y) \end{array}$$

$$\begin{array}{l} filter(p, []) \rightarrow [] \\ filter(p, cons(x, xs)) \rightarrow if(@(p, x), cons(x, filter(p, xs)), filter(p, xs)) \end{array}$$

$$\begin{array}{l} qsort([]) \rightarrow [] \\ qsort(cons(x, xs)) \rightarrow qsort(filter(\lambda z.le(z, x), xs)) +\!\!+ cons(x, []) +\!\!+ \\ \qquad qsort(filter(\lambda z.gr(z, x), xs)) \end{array}$$

Termination of this TRS can be proved with $\succ_{mhospo}$ taking $\succeq_Q$ as $(\succeq_{\mathcal{P}}, \succeq_I)_{lex}$. The precedence $\succeq_{\mathcal{P}}$ is defined by $0 \succ_{\mathcal{P}} True, False$; $+\!\!+ \succ_{\mathcal{P}} cons =_{\mathcal{P}} filter \succ_{\mathcal{P}} if$ and $qsort \succ_{\mathcal{P}} filter, +\!\!+, cons, le, gr, []$, and we define $\succeq_I$ by combining $\succ_{horpo}$ as basic ordering and the interpretation I defined by the pairs $(filter(x_1, x_2), filter_I(x_2))$ and $(if(x_1, x_2, x_3), if_I(x_2, x_3))$ where $filter_I : List \rightarrow List$ and $if_I : List \times List \rightarrow List$. As precedence for $\succ_{horpo}$ we take $0 \succ_{\mathcal{F}} True, False$; $qsort \succ_{\mathcal{F}} +\!\!+, cons, []$ and $+\!\!+ \succ_{\mathcal{F}} cons =_{\mathcal{F}} filter_I \succ_{\mathcal{F}} if_I$.

Let us finally mention that there are also some natural examples that come from the disjoint union of a first-order TRS, which can be proved terminating by MSPO (or by the dependency pair method), and a higher-order TRS, which can be proved terminating by HORPO. Although its components can be proved terminating separately, no method can ensure the termination of the whole system. Using MHOSPO, we can somehow combine the proofs (used in MSPO and HORPO) and show its termination.

7 Conclusions

In this paper we have presented a new ordering-based method for proving termination of higher-order rewriting. The method properly extends both MSPO (in the first-order case) and HORPO (in the higher-order case). The method can be automated and its power has been shown by means of several examples which could not be handled by the previous methods.

Finally let us mention some work already in progress and some future work we plan to do.

1. We are currently working on a constraint-based termination proof method, in the light of the dependency pair method [AG00], for the higher-order case. Using the ideas of [BFR00], the constraints are extracted from the definition of MHOSPO. Here we show the result of applying this method to Example 1:

$$\begin{array}{l} \mathcal{I} : map(F, []) \succeq_I [] \;\wedge\; map(F, cons(x, xs)) \succeq_I cons(@(F, x), map(F, xs)) \;\wedge \\ \quad ps([]) \succeq_I [] \;\wedge\; ps(cons(x, xs)) \succeq_I cons(x, ps(map(\lambda y.x + y, xs))) \end{array}$$

$$\begin{array}{l} \mathcal{Q} : MAP(F, cons(x, xs)) \succ_I MAP(F, xs) \;\wedge \\ \quad PS(cons(x, xs)) \succ_I PS(map(\lambda y.x + y, xs)) \end{array}$$

where $\mathcal{I}$ is the constraint coming from $\succeq_I$ and $\mathcal{Q}$ the constraint coming from $\succeq_Q$, considering that $\succeq_Q$ is defined as the lexicographic combination of a precedence (obtained by a simple cycle analysis) and $\succeq_I$ after applying a renaming of head symbols.
Solving these constraints requires on the one hand, as in the first-order case, to automatically generate the adequate quasi-ordering $\succeq_I$ (note that we are using the same kind of interpretations as in the first-order case) and on the other hand to adapt the notion of dependency graph for the higher-order case.

2. We can adapt, in the same way as it can be done for HORPO [JR01], the method to be applicable to higher-order rewriting "à la Nipkow" [MN98], i.e. rewriting on terms in η-long β-normal form.
3. We will study other possible interpretations to build $\succeq_I$ using functionals in a similar way as in [Pol96], but with two relevant differences. First due to the fact that we are building a quasi-ordering we can use *weakly monotonic functionals* instead of *strict functionals*. Second, since we are not working on terms in η-long β-normal forms, we have to study whether we need to define $\succeq_I$ by first obtaining η-long β-normal form and then interpreting the normalized terms by using functionals. Note that if we normalize first, $\succeq_I$ will include trivially β-reduction.
4. We want to add to HOSPO more powerful cases to deal with terms headed by lambdas, which is, by now, the main weakness of the ordering, as well as some other improvements that have already been added to the initial version of HORPO [JR01].
5. We want to analyze the relationship between our method and a recent constraint-based method developed in [Pie01] for proving termination of higher-order logic programs.

References

[AG00] T. Arts and J. Giesl. Termination of term rewriting using dependency pairs. *Theoretical Computer Science*, 236:133–178, 2000.

[Bar92] H. P. Barendregt. Lambda calculi with types. In S. Abramsky, D. M. Gabbay and T. S. E. Maibaum, eds., *Handbook of Logic in Computer Science.* Oxford University Press, 1992.

[BFR00] C. Borralleras, M. Ferreira, and A. Rubio. Complete monotonic semantic path orderings. *Proc. of the 17th International Conference on Automated Deduction, LNAI* 1831, pp. 346–364, Pittsburgh, USA, 2000. Springer-Verlag.

[BR01] C. Borralleras and A. Rubio. A monotonic higher-order semantic path ordering (Long version). Available at `www.lsi.upc.es/ albert/papers.html`, 2001.

[Der82] N. Dershowitz. Orderings for term-rewriting systems. *Theoretical Computer Science*, 17(3):279–301, 1982.

[DJ90] N. Dershowitz and J.-P. Jouannaud. Rewrite systems. In Jan van Leeuwen, ed., *Handbook of Theoretical Computer Science*, vol. B: Formal Models and Semantics, chap. 6, pp. 244–320. Elsevier Science Publishers B.V., 1990.

[JR98] J-P. Jouannaud and A. Rubio. Rewite orderings for higher-order terms in η-long β-normal form and the recursive path ordering. *Theoretical Computer Science*, 208:33–58, 1998.

[JR99] J-P. Jouannaud and A. Rubio. The higher-order recursive path ordering. In *14th IEEE Symposium on Logic in Computer Science (LICS)*, pp. 402–411, 1999.

[JR01] J.-P. Jouannaud and A. Rubio. Higher-order Recursive Path Orderings à la carte (draft), 2001.

[KL80] S. Kamin and J.-J. Lévy. Two generalizations of the recursive path ordering. Unpublished note, Dept. of Computer Science, Univ. of Illinois, Urbana, IL, 1980.

[LSS92] C. Loría-Sáenz and J. Steinbach. Termination of combined (rewrite and λ-calculus) systems. In *Proc. 3rd Int. Workshop on Conditional Term Rewriting Systems*, LNCS 656, pp. 143–147, 1992. Springer-Verlag.

[MN98] Richard Mayr and Tobias Nipkow. Higher-order rewrite systems and their confluence. *Theoretical Computer Science*, 192(1):3–29, 1998.

[Pie01] Brigitte Pientka. Termination and reduction checking for higher-order logic programs. *Proc. First International Joint Conference on Automated Reasoning*, volume 2083 of *LNAI*, pp. 402–415, 2001. Springer-Verlag.

[Pol96] J. van de Pol. *Termination of Higher-Order Rewrite Systems.* PhD thesis, Departament of Philosophy–Utrecht University, 1996.

[PS95] J. van de Pol and H. Schwichtenberg. Strict functional for termination proofs. In *Proc. of the International Conference on Typed Lambda Calculi and Applications*, 1995.

[vR01] Femke van Raamsdonk. On termination of higher-order rewriting. *12th Int. Conf. on Rewriting Techniques and Applications*, LNCS 2051, pp. 261–275, 2001.

The Elog Web Extraction Language*

Robert Baumgartner[1], Sergio Flesca[2], and Georg Gottlob[1]

[1] DBAI, TU Wien, Vienna, Austria
{baumgart,gottlob}@dbai.tuwien.ac.at
[2] DEIS, Università della Calabria, Rende (CS), Italy
flesca@si.deis.unical.it

Abstract. This paper illustrates some aspects of the visual wrapper generation tool *Lixto* and describes its internal declarative logic-based language *Elog*. In particular, it gives an example scenario and contains a detailed description of predicates including their input/output behavior and introduces several new conditions. Additionally, entity relationship diagrams of filters and patterns are depicted and some words on the implementation are issued. Finally, some possible ramifications are discussed.

1 Introduction and System Architecture

Almost every kind of information is available on the Web, however one cannot query this information in a convenient way. The task of a *wrapper* is to identify and isolate the relevant parts of Web documents, and to automatically extract those relevant parts even though the documents may continually change contents and even (to a certain extent) structure. The wrapper transforms the extracted parts into XML (or a relational database) to make them available for querying and further processing. The idea of *Lixto* is to visually and interactively assist a developer in creating and using wrapper programs able to perform these tasks.

Lixto [3,4] is a visual and interactive wrapper generation and data extraction tool which can be used to create *XML companions* of HTML pages. It can extract relevant information of an HTML page and pages which are linked to it. Information about related approaches on wrapper generation can be found in [1, 6,7,8,9,10,11]. In this paper we give an overview of the internal language used by *Lixto*, the logic-based declarative *Elog* web extraction language, in particular of its extraction predicates. The architecture of *Lixto* is as follows. The *Extraction Pattern Builder* guides a wrapper designer through the process of generating a wrapper. The extracted data of the sample page she works on is stored in an internal format called the *Pattern Instance Base*. As output, an *Extraction Program* is generated which can be applied onto structurally similar pages. The *Extractor* module is the interpreter of the internal language *Elog* (which is invisible to the wrapper designer), and can be used as stand-alone module on an

* All methods and algorithms of the *Lixto* system are covered by a pending patent. For papers on *Lixto* and further developments see www.lixto.com.

R. Nieuwenhuis and A. Voronkov (Eds.): LPAR 2001, LNAI 2250, pp. 548–560, 2001.

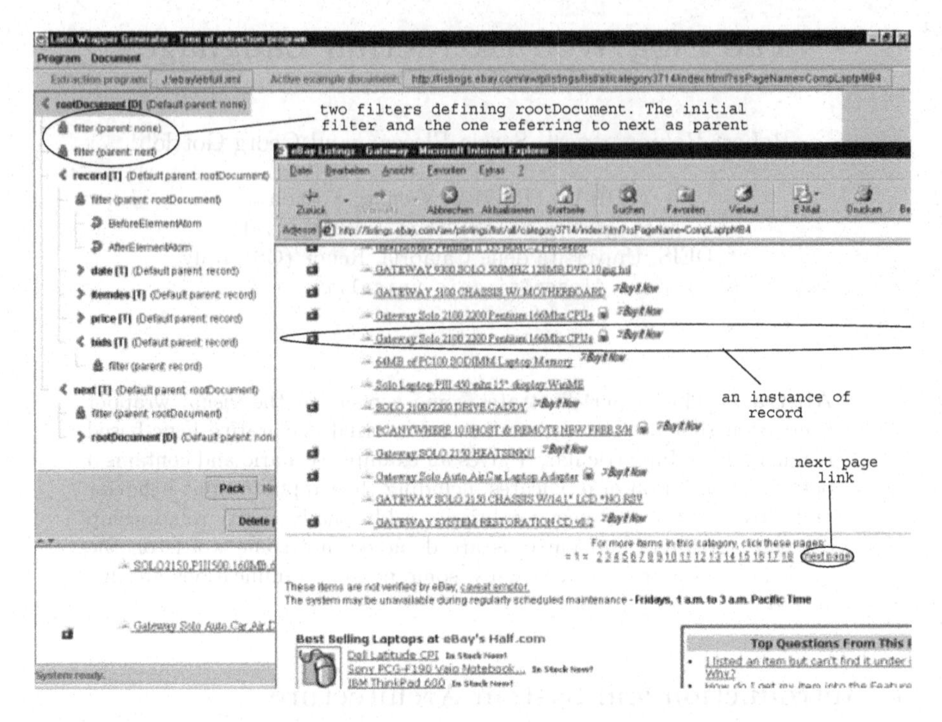

Fig. 1. Pattern hierarchy of a recursive *eBay* program and a sample *eBay* page

extraction program and an HTML page to generate an XML companion. To this end, the internal data format of the pattern instance base can be selectively mapped to XML by using the visual *XML Translation Builder* to generate an *XML Translation Scheme* which can be accessed by the *Extractor*.

This paper is organized as follows. In Section 2, the visual wrapper generation of *Lixto* is explained in an example-based way, whereas Section 3 is devoted to a description of the syntax and semantics of *Elog*, in particular its predicates, and a description of filters and patterns and their relationships. Section 8 gives an outline of the actual *Lixto* implementation. The final section describes some current and future work. For a general overview of *Lixto*, empirical results, and some comparison with competing tools we refer to [4]. For the details of one example, we refer to [3]. For further discussion of some advanced features of *Lixto* such as recursive aspects, we refer to [2].

2 User View

We briefly describe how to work with the *Extraction Pattern Builder*. In particular, the following screenshots (Figs. 1, 2, 9) are taken from the new release of the current *Lixto* beta version. With *Lixto*, a wrapper designer can create a wrapper program in a fully visual and interactive way by teaching the system what to extract based on one (or more) example pages. Each such program consists of a

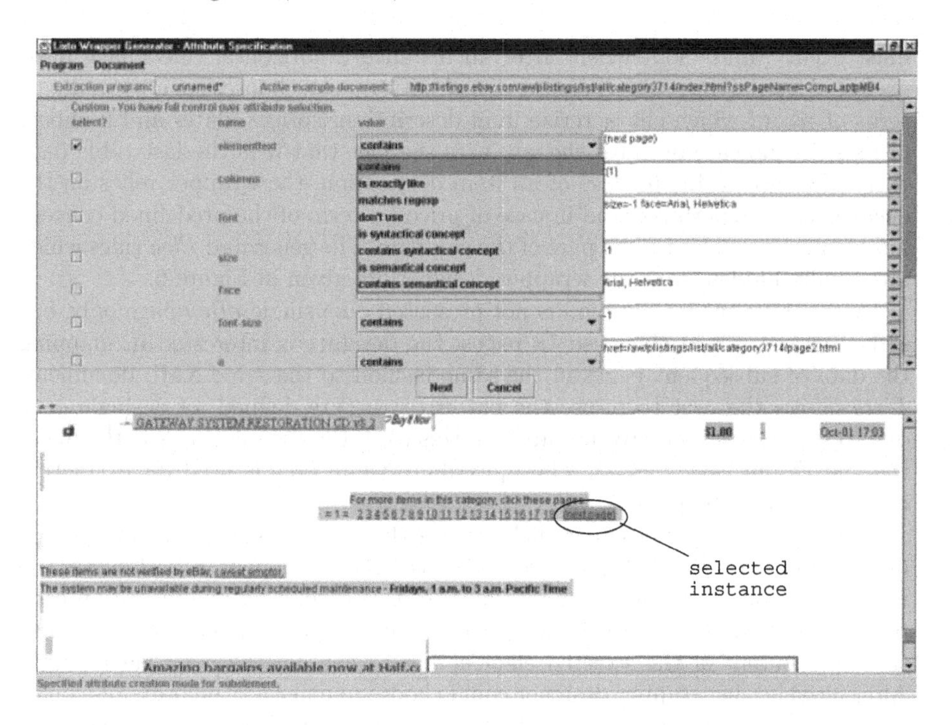

Fig. 2. Adding a filter extracting the tree region containing "next page"

number of *patterns*. Each pattern characterizes one kind of information, e.g. all prices.

After creating a new program and opening a sample document, the designer can start to define patterns. She selects a pattern type (tree, string or document pattern) and a pattern name. Patterns carry user-defined names which are also used as default XML tags. To each pattern one or more filters can be added. A pattern extracts the instances matched by all its filters. In our implementation, when defining a filter, the designer selects an example instance and an attribute selection mechanism, and in the background the system generates a basic *Elog* rule representing this filter by choosing a suited element path and some attributes. Then the designer can test which instances are matched by the current filter.

If undesired targets are matched, she has the choice to refine the filter by adding conditions to it. Filters are added as long as some desired pattern instances are not yet matched. Alternately imposing conditions and adding new filters the desired information can be perfectly characterized.

Assume an example scenario in which a developer wishes to create a wrapper program for *eBay*. First, the wrapper designer chooses a relevant example page, e.g. a page on notebooks of a particular brand (Fig. 1). Next, the designer adds a pattern which identifies records by simply choosing one example record, and adding additional conditions such as "somewhere before an instance a headline must occur", and "somewhere after an instance a horizontal rule image must occur". After having constructed a *record* pattern, she chooses to add child patterns of *record* which characterize item descriptions, prices, dates and numbers of bids. In the case of dates she e.g. uses the fact that it is the last table data entry of a record. In the case of an item description, the wrapper relies on the occurrence of hyperlinks, and in case of prices, a term of the predefined concept *isCurrency* is required to be part of the contents. The generated *Elog* rules which are usually hidden from the wrapper designer are given in Figure 6.

As the relevant information is not presented on a single *eBay* page only, but split over several, in this case 18 pages, the designer is interested in mapping the data of subsequent pages in the same fashion to the same XML document. *Lixto* allows the user to re-use the pattern structure defined for a single page due to support of recursive features. In this case, the designer uses the value of the "next" link (see Fig. 2), whose attribute value *href* is used for extracting further *eBay* documents.

First, the wrapper designer clicks selects the "(next page)" element through two consecutive mouse-clicks directly in the browser display. Fig. 2 shows the manual attribute selection user interface. In this case, a unique match on each page is required. Therefore the wrapper designer imposes strict criteria such as that the content of the selected element has to contain the text "next page". Alternatively, the wrapper designer could choose to enter a regular expression or predefined concepts. In this case, the filter matches exactly the desired instance, so there is no need to impose additional conditions. As next step, the wrapper designer adds a filter to *ebaydocument* which points to the parent *next*. In this way, the pattern structure is altered from a plain tree to a cyclic pattern graph, and extracted instances of *next* are used as input instances to extract further instances of *ebaydocument*. The resulting pattern graph is visualized in *Lixto* as partially expanded infinite tree (see Fig. 1).

With the *XML Translation Builder*, a wrapper designer can define which patterns shall be mapped to XML and in which way. One can for instance define that all *eBay* records are treated on the same level, and that the *next* pattern is not written to XML. A part of the resulting XML companion is depicted in Figure 3. It can be used for further information processing. If the page structure does not change significantly, the *Extractor* will continue to work correctly on new pages, especially if rather stable conditions had been chosen by the wrapper designer. Even designers neither familiar with HTML nor capable of script programming can create complex *Lixto* wrappers.

3 *Elog* Language Definition

3.1 Document Model and Extraction Mechanisms

As explained in [2,4], *Elog* operates on a tree representation of an HTML document. The nodes of the HTML tree are referred to as elements. Each element is associated with an attribute graph which stores pairs of attribute-designators and corresponding attribute-values, a node number, and a start and end character offset. The extraction objects over which variables range are *tree regions* and *string sources* of a given HTML document. A tree region characterizes lists of elements (e.g. a list of three table rows) or single elements (e.g. a paragraph). A filter is internally represented as a "datalog like" rule. Conditions are reflected by additional body atoms.

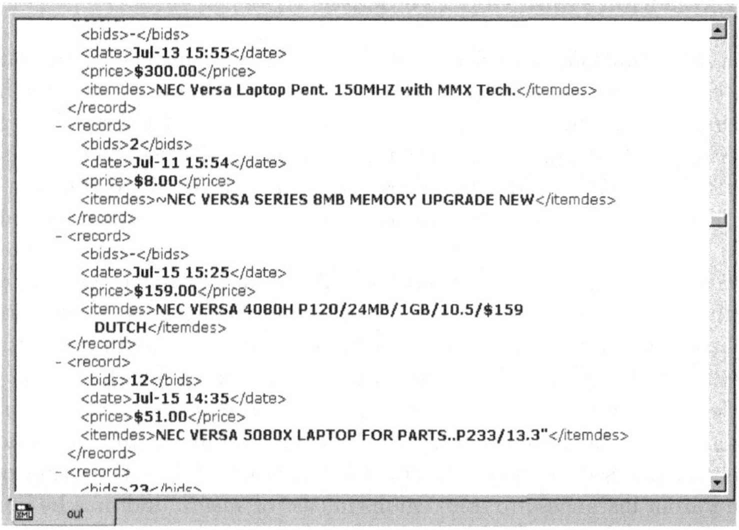

```
    <bids>-</bids>
    <date>Jul-13 15:55</date>
    <price>$300.00</price>
    <itemdes>NEC Versa Laptop Pent. 150MHZ with MMX Tech.</itemdes>
  </record>
- <record>
    <bids>2</bids>
    <date>Jul-11 15:54</date>
    <price>$8.00</price>
    <itemdes>~NEC VERSA SERIES 8MB MEMORY UPGRADE NEW</itemdes>
  </record>
- <record>
    <bids>-</bids>
    <date>Jul-15 15:25</date>
    <price>$159.00</price>
    <itemdes>NEC VERSA 4080H P120/24MB/1GB/10.5/$159
      DUTCH</itemdes>
  </record>
- <record>
    <bids>12</bids>
    <date>Jul-15 14:35</date>
    <price>$51.00</price>
    <itemdes>NEC VERSA 5080X LAPTOP FOR PARTS..P233/13.3"</itemdes>
  </record>
- <record>
out
```


Fig. 3. XML output of *eBay* example

W.r.t. tree extraction, as defined in [4], an *element path definition* characterizes a path with some additional attribute requirements and is hence very similar to an *XPath* query. As an example, consider $(.\star.hr, [(size, 3), (width, .*)])$. This element path definition identifies horizontal rules (the star acts as a wildcard) of size 3 with some specified width attribute (regardless of the attribute value due to ".*"). Observe that for a simpler language definition we recently introduced the *hasProperty* predicate to express the required attributes independently, in this example e.g. with *hasProperty(X,size,3)* where X ranges over instances of $.\star.hr$. Additionally, an attribute condition might refer to a variable (see Fig. 6 in *price*) on which additional constraints are posed by some predicate.

The second extraction method, string extraction is usually applied to the decompose the content value of a leaf element. A *string definition* is characterized as regular expression in which additionally some variable references to e.g. predefined concepts might occur. As an example consider the string definitions occurring as second parameter of the *subtext* predicate in the rules defining *currency* and *amount* in Figure 6. Additionally, attribute values can be extracted using an *attribute definition*, which is simply a particular attribute designator.

The built-in predicates of the *Elog* language implement basic extraction tasks. *Elog* predicates are atoms of the form $P(t_1, ..., t_n)$ where P is a predicate name and $t_1 \ldots t_n$ are either variables or constants whose values range over tree regions, string sources, constant path definition objects, and numerical arguments (such as distance parameters). The union of these classes is referred to as the *Herbrand universe* on which an *Elog* program operates.

3.2 Extraction Definition Predicates

Extraction definition predicates contain a variable which is instantiated with instances of a parent-pattern of the rule in which they occur, and based on the element path definition return instances of the new pattern. They form the basic body predicate of an extraction rule. Each *Elog* rule exactly contains one extraction definition predicate. These predicates form three different groups, depending if they extract a tree region, a string source, or a new document.

- $subelem(S, epd, X)$, $subsq(S, epd, X)$: A ground instance $subelem(s, epd, x)$ evaluates to true iff s is a tree region, epd an element path definition, x is a subtree in s and $root(x)$ matches epd. *subsq* operates similarly, but extracts tree regions (a list of elements as one extraction instance).
- $subatt(S, ad, X)$, $subtext(S, sd, X)$: The first predicate extracts from a tree region S attribute values of a given attribute definition ad as instances of X, whereas the second one extracts substrings which fulfill a string definition sd. Parent instances are tree regions in case of *subatt*, and may be both string or tree regions in case of *subtext*.
- $getDocument(S, X)$, $getDocumentOfHref(S, X)$ extract from a given URL as instance of S (a string source in the first case, and in the second case, an instance of a tree region whose *href* attribute is considered) a new document as a tree region.

3.3 *Elog* Rules and Patterns

Filters are represented using *Elog* extraction rules. Rules contain condition atoms which are explained in the next section.

A *standard rule* defines a component pattern X of a pattern S (thus, aggregation hierarchies can be defined). Standard rules are of the form: $New(S, X) \leftarrow Par(\_, S), Ex(S, X), Cd(S, X, \ldots)[a, b], ..., [c, d]$, where *New* and *Par* are pattern predicates referring to the pattern defined by this rule and its parent pattern. S is the parent variable to be instantiated with a parent-pattern instance, X is the target variable to be instantiated with an extracted pattern instance, $Ex(S, X)$ is a tree (string) extraction definition atom, and the optional $Cd(S, X, \ldots)$ is a number of further imposed conditions on the target pattern. The extracted instances of a rule can be restricted to several intervals where $[a, b]$ expresses that the instance number a up to instance number b is considered. Additionally, a rule extracts minimal instances only.

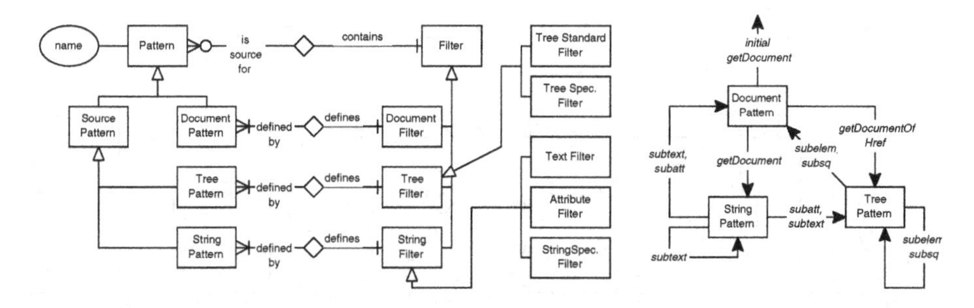

Fig. 4. Pattern Extended Entity Relationship Diagram

A *specialization rule* specializes a pattern *Old* to a pattern *New*: $New(S,X) \leftarrow Old(S,X), Cd(S,X,\ldots)[a,b],...,[c,d]$. A *document rule* extracts new documents from given URLs. It can use below mentioned document conditions *DocCd* as restrictions: $New(S,X) \leftarrow Par(\_,S), getDocument(S,X), DocCd(S,X,\ldots)$. Document filters can also refer to relative URLs by accessing the information stored in the previous URL.

An *Elog pattern (definition) p* is a set of *Elog* rules with the same head predicate symbol. An *Elog* pattern is called homogeneous, if all its filters refer to the same parent pattern, otherwise heterogeneous. In case of a homogeneous pattern, the notion of "parent pattern" can be associated with a pattern rather than with its filters. It is forbidden to combine tree, string or document filters with each other within one pattern. The head predicate is an IDB predicate; it is visually defined with *Lixto* and named by the wrapper designer. This name is also used as default XML tag in the XML mapping [4]. Also the extracted instances of a pattern are minimized. In our current implementation, we chose to consider only those instances not contained in any other instance of the same parent-pattern instance.

Patterns (and their filters) are restricted in their use of parent patterns and pattern references as depicted on the right-hand part of Figure 4. An arc from pattern a to b indicates that the filters of a pattern of kind a can refer to patterns of kind b as parents with using the mentioned extraction definition predicate. An EER diagram illustrating relationships between patterns and filters is given in Figure 4 on the left side, and Figure 5 shows an EER diagram which illustrates filter and condition relationships in detail.

The semantics of extraction rules is very similar to the semantics of standard datalog rules. There are two possibilities to assign a semantics to an *Elog* program. The first is to define an own semantics (which exploits many similarities to Datalog), the second is to rewrite an *Elog* program (see [2]) as Datalog program and apply the standard Datalog semantics. An *Elog* program differs from Datalog in the following aspects:

- *Built-In Predicates.* In *Elog* several built-in predicates (e.g. *subelem*) are used which are restricted to a fixed input/output behavior. Moreover, constants for navigating tree regions and string sources are used.

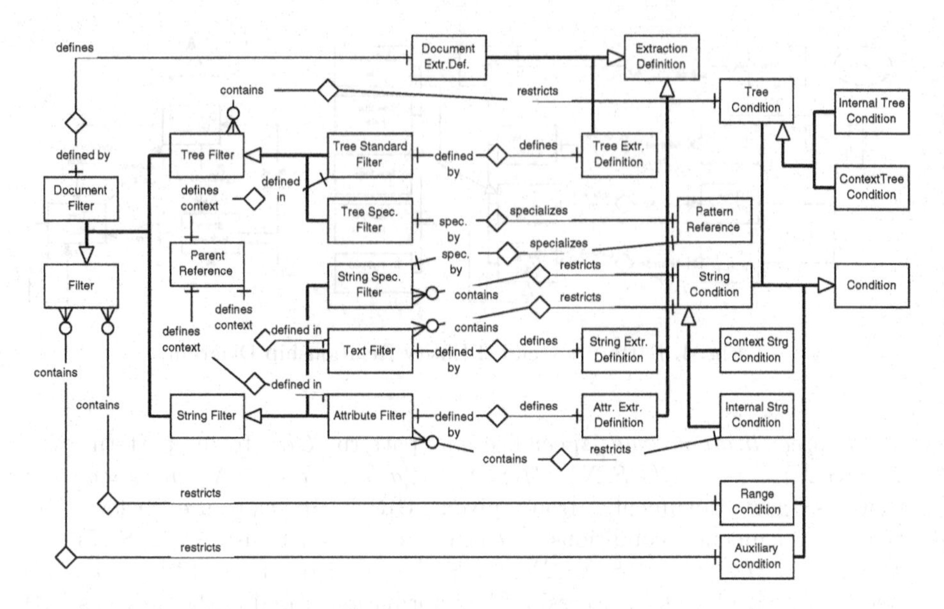

Fig. 5. Filter Extended Entity Relationship Diagram

- *Range conditions.* A rewriting of range conditions introduces new rules containing negation and generates a stratified Datalog program. In *Elog*, range conditions are applied after evaluating the rule and by removing all instances not within the range intervals. In case an *Elog* program uses ranges and arbitrary pattern references, this intuitive meaning gets lost, and in the Datalog rewriting, the program is no longer stratified.
- *Minimizations.* By default, in *Elog* both the instances extracted by a single rule, and by a pattern are minimized, i.e. just the minimal tree regions or strings are considered. Representing this in Datalog requires additional rules and further built-in predicates such as *containedIn*.

In the current implementation of *Lixto*, full *Elog* is not yet supported, as some syntactic restrictions are made. For example, use of pattern references is limited.

3.4 Extraction Program and Pattern Instance Base

An *Elog extraction program* P is a collection of *Elog* patterns. A program can be represented via its pattern graph [2]. A directed arc is drawn from one pattern to another one, if there is at least one filter referring to the first pattern as parent. The pattern graph is a tree in case of homogeneous programs. We denote by $P(H)$ the *pattern instance base* created by evaluating all patterns of P over an HTML document H and storing them in their hierarchical order. The vertices of $P(H)$ are all pattern instances extracted from P with start document H. There is an arc from vertex a to vertex b in $P(H)$ if and only if b is the parent-pattern instance of a. Each pattern instance is associated with a pattern name.

```
ebaydocument(S, X) ← getDocument(S = $1, X)
ebaydocument(S, X) ← next( , S), getDocumentOfHref(S, X)
        next(S, X) ← ebaydocument( , S), subelem(S, (⋆.content, [(href, .*),
                     (elementtext, (next page))]), X)
      record(S, X) ← ebaydocument( , S), subelem(S, .table, X)
                     before(S, X, (⋆.tr, [(elementtext, . * Current.*)]), 0, 100, , )
                     after(S, X, (⋆.img, [(src, . * spacer.gif)]), 0, 100, , )
     itemdes(S, X) ← record( , S), subelem(S, (⋆.td. ⋆.content, [(href, .*)], X)
       price(S, X) ← record( , S), subelem(S, (⋆.td, [(elementtext, \var[Y].*)]), X),
                     isCurrency(Y)
        bids(S, X) ← record( , S), subelem(S, ⋆.td, X), before(S, X, .td, 0, 30, Y, ),
                     price( , Y)
        date(S, X) ← record( , S), subelem(S, ⋆.td, X), notafter(S, X, .td, 100)
    currency(S, X) ← price( , S), subtext(S, \var[Y], X), isCurrency(Y)
      amount(S, X) ← price( , S), subtext(S, [0 − 9]+\.[0 − 9]+, X)
```

Fig. 6. *Elog* Extraction Program for linked *eBay* pages

The pattern instance base is a forest of hierarchically ordered pattern instances. Each tree corresponds to the extracted values from one particular HTML document. The pattern instance base is an intermediate data representation used by the XML translation builder to create an XML translation scheme and a corresponding XML companion.

As an example program, consider the *eBay* program in Figure 6. The pattern *ebaydocument* is a document pattern consisting of two filters with different parents. The first one refers to the starting document, which is in this case, fixed, whereas the second on follows the "next" link on each page. "$1" is interpreted as a constant whose value is the URL of the start document of a *Lixto* session. The used condition predicates are explained below.

3.5 Context and Internal Condition Predicates

Context condition predicates further restrain the instances matching an extraction definition atom based on surroundings. In Figure 7, we illustrate based on an example tree region, which nodes can be referred by context and internal conditions. By default, context conditions operate only within the current parent-pattern instance. Context conditions express that something must or must not occur before or after an instance. They can operate on tree regions or string sources, hence they use a string definition or an element path definition.

In our actual implementation, the before and after conditions are further qualified by an interval *(start,end)* of relative distance parameters expressing how far the external element may occur from the desired pattern instance to be extracted. For an example of condition predicates, see the rule defining *record* in Figure 6. There, an after and a before condition are used. The first two parameters are parent-instance and target-instance variable followed by an element path

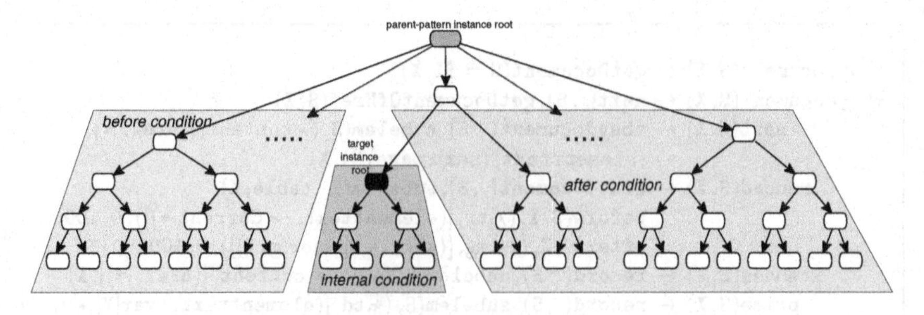

Fig. 7. Conditions

definition; the next arguments indicate a minimum and a maximum distance, and the two final parameters are output variables. These are instantiated with the actual instance and the actual distance, and could be referred by further predicates.

Further supported contextual condition predicates are *above* and *below*, which make use of an additionally defined attribute designator *colno* which expresses column numbers. A ground instance $below(s, x, epd, y)$ evaluates to true iff s and x are tree regions, *epd* is an element path definition and y is a subtree of s such that $root(y)$ is matched by *epd*, and y occurs before x and has the same value for the attribute *colno*. If a designer wants to extract the third column of a table, but only starting with the fifth line, then she first defines to use *colno=3*, and then imposes the condition that it occurs under the contents as given in the fifth entry (or some attribute information of the fifth entry). *below* is similar to *after* where *epd* contains "colpos=[value]" with the difference that the value depends on the *colno* value of the target instance and vice versa. Moreover, we offer the possibility of contextual conditions which refer to elements outside the parent-pattern instance, e.g. within the "grandparent", i.e. etc. Such an extended concept is very useful together with *below/above* predicates in hierarchical extraction.

Internal condition predicates include *contains*, which is used for restricting extracted pattern instances based on properties contained in the instances themselves, i.e. in the tree regions that constitute those instances. The *firstsubtree* condition states that the first child of a tree region must contain a particular element – this is very useful for defining lists of elements, as it gives the possibility to express that the first and last child must contain some elements with specific properties.

3.6 Auxiliary Conditions and Conditions on Document Filters

Concept predicates are unary or binary relations. They refer to semantic concepts such as *isCity(X)*, expressing that the string is a city name, or syntactic ones like *isDate(X,Y)*. Predicates like $isDate(X, Y)$ can create an output variable – e.g. for an input date x, the system returns a date in normal form y. Some predicates are built-in, however more concepts can be added to the system using the convenient *Lixto concept editor*. Moreover, for several concepts, *comparison predicates* allow to compare values (e.g. dates) such as $<(X,Y)$.

Pattern predicates of the head are the IDB predicates defined by the wrapper designer. Those of the body refer to previously created patterns. Each matched pattern instance is element of one designated pattern; for example, *price* may be a pattern name and the matched targets are its instances. Each aggregation filter contains a reference to its parent pattern. Additionally, as discussed above, further pattern references are possible. For instance, a price pattern can be constructed by imposing the constraint that immediately before a target of pattern *item* needs to occur, which is expressed in *Elog* as $before(S, X, .\star.content, 0, 1, Y, \_), item(\_, Y)$.

Range conditions do not correspond to predicates in the usual sense. They allow a designer to express conditions on the cardinality of the set of targets extracted with a filter based on their order of appearance in the parent-pattern instance. Such restriction intervals need not to be contiguous, as a set of intervals can be used. Negative numbers reflect counting from the opposite side.

On document filters the following conditions can be imposed: $smaller(X, v)$ requires that the size of a Web page as instance of X is smaller than some given value v in KB. $samedomain(X, Y)$ evaluates to true iff instances of X and Y (where Y is usually a constant) are URLs of the same domain. Moreover, one can specify a number v for each document pattern: If the pattern has been evaluated already for v times, then no further evaluation occurs.

3.7 Input-Output Behavior of Elog Predicates

As already mentioned, one additional feature of *Elog* is that built-in predicates have an input-output behavior (adornments) that prevents them from being freely used in *Elog* rules. An extraction definition predicate for instance uses a parent-pattern variable as input, and a pattern variable as output which is used as input variable in condition predicates. An atom can be evaluated only after all its input variables are bound to effective values. The following list specifies for each argument position of each built-in predicate the type, input (i) or output (o) of variables that occur within these position. An underscore indicates that the type (input/output) is irrelevant.

$subelem(i,i,o)$	$subsq(i,i,o)$	$subtext(i,i,o)$	$subatt(i,i,o)$
$getDocument(i,o)$	$before(i,i,i,i,i,o,o)$	$notbefore(i,i,i,i)$	$below(i,i,i,o)$
$contains(i,i,o)$	$notcontains(i,i)$	$firstsubtree(i,i)$	$parentpattern(\_,o)$
$isPattern(i,i)$	$isConcept(i)$	$isConcept(i,o)$	$compare(i,i)$

As an example of a unary concept, consider *isCity(i)*, and of a binary concept, consider *isDate(i,o)*. An example of a pattern reference is *price(i,i)*, and an example of a comparison condition is $<(i,i)$.

The element path definition (string definition) is usually a constant input, but can additionally contain variables. These variables are treated as output variables. They occur in case of a reference to some concept atom (e.g. see the

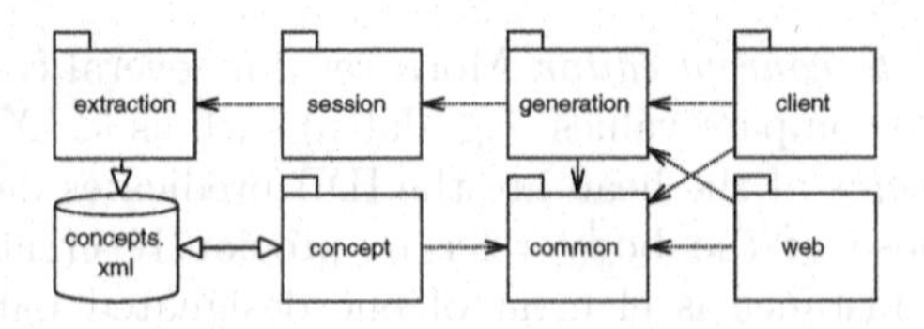

Fig. 8. Sketch of Lixto's package structure

above example rule defining *price*). The instances of each variable that occurs in an element path definition are as usual all possible matches.

Consider the following example: $price(S, X) \leftarrow record(\_, S), subelem(S, (.\star .td, [(elementtext, \backslash var[Y].*)]), X), isCurrency(Y)$. The predicate *record* is evaluated and all instances s of S are generated; they are used to evaluate the extraction definition predicate. *subelem* computes possible instances x and y of X and Y based on the given tree path. All possible substitution instances (s, x, y) are stored. After y is bound, *isCurrency(Y)*, is evaluated.

4 Implementation and Package Structure

Lixto is implemented entirely in Java. We chose to implement our own *Elog* interpreter instead of using an existing Datalog interpreter and rewriting rules into Datalog. Figure 4 gives an overview of *Lixto*'s package structure: *extraction* is the *Elog* interpreter. It is accessed by *session*, where the actual rule and condition creation is carried out. *generation* handles the pattern generation algorithm, which decides which action is followed by which step in the interactive creation process. Currently, two frontends are supported: A local *client* and a servlet frontend (*web*). The latter offers the wrapper designer the possibility to mark relevant data areas in her favorite browser, e.g. *Netscape* or *Internet Explorer*. *common* contains shared objects and message files, whereas in *concept* the syntactic and semantic concept editors (for a sample screenshot see Fig. 9) are located.

5 Ramifications, Current and Future Work

Various extensions of *Elog* are obvious such as using various forms of negation. Current theoretical research investigates the expressive power of *Elog* wrappers over unranked labeled trees. Further ramifications of *Elog* include universally quantified conditions and complement extraction, e.g. to remove advertisments of Web pages. Additionally, the framework of document navigation is being extended to also give the possibility to issue post requests. Moreover, current work is devoted to implementing consistency check alerts that can be defined in the XML translation builder: The user is given the choice to impose a required multiplicity of an element. Based on this, an XML document type definition can be created, and moreover, warnings are given if a criterion is not satisfied

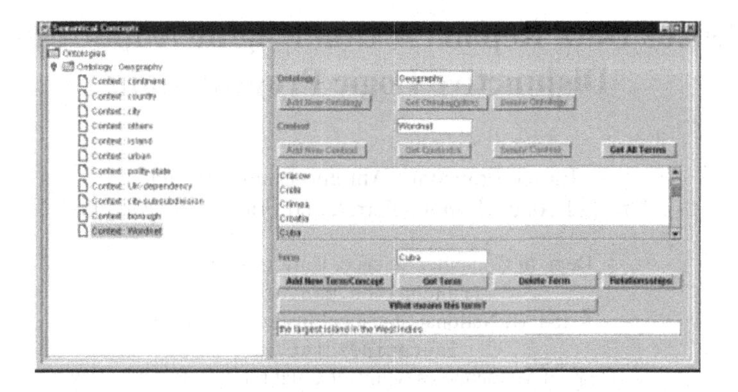

Fig. 9. Lixto's semantic concepts editor

on some input Web page. A *Pattern Description Language* is being developed which translates *Elog* rules into colloquial expressions. A conversion tool that transforms a subset of *Elog* programs into XSLT will be developed, hence, for a limited class of programs, simply a stylesheet and an HTML page can be used to produce an XML companion. Finally, some AI methods will be added to support the user, and *Lixto* will be embedded into the *InfoPipes* framework [5].

References

1. P. Atzeni and G. Mecca. Cut and paste. In *Proc. of PODS*, 1997.
2. R. Baumgartner, S. Flesca, and G. Gottlob. Declarative information extraction, web crawling and recursive wrapping with Lixto. In *Proc. of LPNMR*, 2001.
3. R. Baumgartner, S. Flesca, and G. Gottlob. Supervised wrapper generation with Lixto. In *Proc. of VLDB (Demonstration Session)*, 2001.
4. R. Baumgartner, S. Flesca, and G. Gottlob. Visual web information extraction with Lixto. In *Proc. of VLDB*, 2001.
5. M. Herzog and G. Gottlob. InfoPipes: A flexible framework for M-commerce applications. In *Proc. of TES*, 2001.
6. C-N. Hsu and M.T. Dung. Generating finite-state transducers for semistructured data extraction from the web. *Information Systems*, 23/8, 1998.
7. N. Kushmerick, D. Weld, and R. Doorenbos. Wrapper induction for information extraction. In *Proc. of IJCAI*, 1997.
8. L. Liu, C. Pu, and W. Han. XWrap: An extensible wrapper construction system for internet information. In *Proc. of ICDE*, 2000.
9. I. Muslea, S. Minton, and C. Knoblock. A hierarchical approach to wrapper induction. In *Proc. of 3rd Intern. Conf. on Autonomous Agents*, 1999.
10. B. Ribeiro-Neto, A. H. F. Laender, and A. S. da Silva. Extracting semi-structured data through examples. In *Proc. of CIKM*, 1999.
11. A. Sahuguet and F. Azavant. Building light-weight wrappers for legacy web datasources using W4F. In *Proc. of VLDB*, 1999.

Census Data Repair: A Challenging Application of Disjunctive Logic Programming

Enrico Franconi[1], Antonio Laureti Palma[2],
Nicola Leone[3], Simona Perri[3], and Francesco Scarcello[4]

[1] Dept. of Computer Science, Univ. of Manchester, UK
franconi@cs.man.ac.uk
[2] ISTAT, National Statistical Institute, Roma, Italy
lauretip@istat.it
[3] Dept. of Mathematics, Univ. of Calabria, Rende (CS), Italy
leone@unical.it, sperri@si.deis.unical.it
[4] DEIS, Univ. of Calabria, Rende (CS), Italy
scarcello@deis.unical.it

Abstract. Census data provide valuable insights on the economic, social and demographic conditions and trends occurring in a country. Census data is collected by means of millions of questionnaires, each one including the details of the persons living together in the same house. Before the data from the questionnaires is sent to the statisticians to be analysed, a cleaning phase (called "imputation") is performed, in order to eliminate consistency problems, missing answers, or errors. It is important that the imputation step is done without altering the statistical validity of the collected data. The contribution of this paper is twofold. On the one hand, it provides a clear and well-founded declarative semantics to questionnaires and to the imputation problem. On the other hand, a correct modular encoding of the problem in the disjunctive logic programming language DLP^w, supported by the **DLV** system, is shown. It turns out that DLP^w is very well-suited for this goal. Census data repair appears to be a challenging application area for disjunctive logic programming.

1 Introduction

In most countries, a census of population is hold every five or ten years. The census consistently updates the most fundamental source of information about a country. The collected information provides a statistical portrait of the country and its people. The census is the only reliable source of detailed data for small population groups such as the very elderly or specific industrial and occupational categories, and for small geographic areas such as, for example, a city neighbourhood. Census data can be used in many ways such as providing the boundaries for federal electoral districts, helping businesses to select new manufacturing sites, analysing markets for products and services, and to develop employment policies and programs.

Each family compiles a questionnaire, which includes the details of the head of the household (householder) together with the other persons living in the house. The forms are collected and then analysed by statistical agencies in order to modify and update the population household statistics. Questionnaires may be incomplete and/or may contain

R. Nieuwenhuis and A. Voronkov (Eds.): LPAR 2001, LNAI 2250, pp. 561–578, 2001.

inconsistent information. It turns out that a significant proportion of the forms have problems of this kind, which if not corrected could severely alter the updated statistics. There are millions of questionnaires to be processed each time, and it is desirable to employ methodologies to detect (*edit*) and automatically resolve (*impute*) errors in the forms. All the methodologies currently employed by the census agencies – including the most popular Fellegi and Holt methodology [7] – are based on statistical principles, which do not have a clear semantics with respect to the complexity of the various errors that may happen, so that their behaviour while imputing the data is often unpredictable. Moreover, it is difficult to compare the various methodologies, since they are defined only on a procedural basis.

The first contribution of this paper is to define in a pure classical logic setting the semantics of the edit and imputation problems. The approach is very general and very expressive, since it makes use of full First Order Logic. In Section 4, the framework is defined in its generality, while making use of a simplified basic questionnaire as a running example. The advantage of this approach is the ability to specify in a declarative fashion the characteristics of the census questionnaire, the intra- and inter-questions constraints, and the additional statistical information required to guide the corrections. This is the first proposal in the literature making use of Logic at all the stages of the definition of the problem.

The second important contribution of the paper is to provide a correct encoding of the edit and imputation problems in an executable specification using an extension of disjunctive logic programming. In Section 6, we provide the rationale of the modular encoding, together with partial translations of the running example. For this purpose, disjunctive logic programming extended with two kinds of constraints has been used (see Section 5). The idea is that the preferred models of the logic program encoding the problem correspond to the repairs of a given questionnaire. It turns out that the solution of this challenging problem requires most of the expressive capabilities of disjunctive logic programming with constraints. Importantly, this disjunctive logic programming language is supported by **DLV** [5,6], a system which is freely available on the web, and can therefore be used to obtain an immediate implementation. Preliminary results of an experimentation activity carried out at the Italian National Statistical Institute show that the approach is viable also from the viewpoint of performance.

2 The Census Questionnaire

A *household* is a group of persons who occupy the whole or part of a housing unit and provide themselves with food and possibly other essentials for living. It is customary that, during the census of population periodically carried out by every country, a single questionnaire is associated to each household, involving questions about each member of the household. The notion of household may vary from country to country and it is in general to be distinguished from the notion of family. In the context of this paper we will not consider all the subtleties which make each census different from each other, but we will maintain an abstract level which could be adapted to the different situations, and nonetheless it will be in agreement with the recommendations for the 2000 European censuses of population [9]. In this Section, a basic questionnaire will be introduced, including all the core attributes (also called *variables*) considered in most censuses; the semantic definitions and the methodology presented in this paper can be easily extended to handle all the variables of a complete questionnaire.

Each questionnaire is centred around the notion of *reference person*. For statistical purposes, all persons living in private households are identified from their relationship to the reference member of the household. It is outside the scope of this paper to understand how the various administrations define and select the one reference person in a household to whom all other persons in the household report or designate their relationship. In order to identify members of the household, an integer number is assigned to each person, with the number "1" reserved to identify the reference person. The following classification of persons living in a private household by `relationship` to the household's reference person is adopted in a basic questionnaire: Spouse; Partner; Child; Parent; Other relative of reference person, spouse or partner; Non-relative of reference person, spouse, or partner.

The other *structural* attributes – to be specified for each member of the household – considered to be part of a basic questionnaire are: `Sex`: Male, Female; `Age`: integer number; `Marital Status`: Single, Married, Divorced, Widowed.

A census form to be compiled by the members of a household will then contain, for each member, questions for at least each of the above attributes.

3 Dealing with Missing and Inconsistent Data

When the millions of compiled forms are returned to the national central statistical agency to be analysed, they may contain many errors, such as *missing* or *inconsistent data*. For example, it is possible that a person declared to be the spouse of the reference person, but at the same time he/she forgot to declare a marital status, or he/she declared to be single, or to be 6 years old. Before the data from the questionnaires is sent to the statisticians to be analysed, a cleaning phase is performed, in order to eliminate missing values or inconsistencies. It is very important that this step is done *without altering the (statistical) validity* of the collected data. For example, if the spouse declared to be 6 years old, and if there are other arguments to *enforce* that he/she is actually the spouse of the reference person (for example, he/she may have additionally declared to be married), then his/her age should be changed to make the data consistent: any age, say, greater than 16 years would be fine if only absolute validity of the data is taken into account. However, the age should be changed to an age in agreement with the average age for a spouse in his/her conditions, and not with a value which may alter the statistics. In this case, it would be more sensible to change the age to, say, 36 years, rather than to 96 years (there are very few people of that age, and this would alter the statistics of old people) or to 16 years (there are very few people who are married at that age). Other corrections can be done *deterministically* – in the sense that there is only one valid change, which is also a statistically valid change – for example for a spouse who forgot to specify the marital status, and for which asserting that he/she is married does not introduce any other inconsistency.

For these reasons, a collection of *edit* rules is introduced by the statistical agencies for each questionnaire class, in order to understand whether a questionnaire is consistent, and to guide the repair of inconsistent questionnaires. The process of automatically producing a set of statistically consistent questionnaires from the raw ones is called *imputation*.

4 Formalisation of the Imputation Problem

We define a questionnaire $\mathcal{Q}$ as a pair $\langle r, E\rangle$, where r is a relation (i.e., a finite set of tuples) over the schema

$$sch : \mathtt{R}(\underline{\mathtt{PersonId}}, \mathtt{Relationship}, \mathtt{Sex}, \mathtt{Age}, \mathtt{MaritalStatus})$$

that encodes the answers of a household to the questionnaire, and E is a finite set of first order (short: FO) formulas encoding the edit rules that r should satisfy. Note that, in this paper, we will only use relations with the above schema *sch*. Thus, hereafter, we will always omit to specify the schema of a relation. Hence, e.g., by "all relations" we will mean "all relations over schema *sch*". Note also that the imputation problem is defined with respect single questionnaires only. Therefore, the edit rules are associated to each single questionnaire. Of course, the edit rules are the same for all questionnaires.

The `PersonId` attribute is key for any relation r over *sch*, and the domain of each attribute is the finite set of values specified in Section 2, with in addition the special *null* value. Null values encode missing answers in the questionnaire. The edit rules, encoded through the FO sentences E, play the role of integrity constraints over the relation R. In these formulas the predicate R, additional comparison predicates over the domains, and constants for domain values may occur. We say that $\mathcal{Q}$ is a *complete questionnaire* if no null value occur in the tuples of r, and that Q is a *consistent questionnaire* if it is complete and r is model for the theory E, i.e., $r \models E$.

Example 1 Consider a questionnaire $\mathcal{Q}_1 = \langle r_1, E_1\rangle$, where r_1 is the following relation:

PersonId	Relationship	Sex	Age	Marital Status
1	reference	F	31	married
2	spouse	M	39	married

and where E_1 is the following set of edit rules:

1. a spouse of the reference person should be married (but not necessarily vice versa):
$\forall x.\ \exists y\ v_1\ v_2.\ R(x, \text{spouse}, v_1, v_2, y) \rightarrow y = \text{married};$
2. (formal) cohabitant partners of the reference person can not be married with somebody else (i.e., they should be either single, or divorced, or widowed):
$\forall x.\ \exists y\ v_1\ v_2.\ R(x, \text{partner}, v_1, v_2, y) \rightarrow y \neq \text{married};$
3. the reference person cannot be married with more than one person:
$\forall x\, y.\, \exists v_1\, v_2\, v_3\, v_4\, v_5\, v_6.\, R(x, spouse, v_1, v_2, v_3) \wedge R(y, spouse, v_4, v_5, v_6) \rightarrow x = y$
4. the reference person and its spouse should have a different sex:
$\forall x.\ \exists y\ v_1\ v_2\ v_3\ z\ v_4\ v_5.\ R(x, spouse, y, v_1, v_2) \wedge R(1, v_3, z, v_4, v_5) \rightarrow y \neq z;$
5. any married person should be at least 16 years old:
$\forall x.\ \exists y\ v_1\ v_2.\ R(x, v_1, v_2, y, \text{married}) \rightarrow y \geq 16;$
6. the difference in age between a parent and a child should be bigger than 12 years:
$\forall x.\ \exists y\ z\ v_1\ v_2\ v_3\ v_4\ v_5.\, R(x, \text{child}, v_1, y, v_2) \rightarrow (R(1, v_3, v_4, z, v_5) \wedge (z - y) \geq 12),$
and
$\forall x.\ \exists y\ z\ v_1\ v_2\ v_3\ v_4\ v_5.\ R(x, \text{parent}, v_1, y, v_2) \rightarrow (R(1, v_3, v_4, z, v_5) \wedge (y - z) \geq 12).$

The questionnaire $\mathcal{Q}_1$ is consistent and complete, as no null value occur in r_1 and all the edit rules are satisfied by r_1.

If a questionnaire $\mathcal{Q} = \langle r, E \rangle$ is not complete and/or not consistent, then we should repair it, providing some new corrected relation denoting a complete and consistent questionnaire.

Definition 1 (Admissible Repair). Let $\mathcal{Q} = \langle r, E \rangle$ be a questionnaire and ρ a mapping from tuples over *sch* to tuples over *sch*. We say that such a mapping is a *repair* for $\mathcal{Q}$. For a relation $\bar{r}$, denote by $\rho(\bar{r})$ the relation $\{\rho(t) \mid t \in \bar{r}\}$. ρ is an *admissible repair* for $\mathcal{Q}$ if $\langle \rho(r), E \rangle$ is a complete and consistent questionnaire.

Example 2 Consider the questionnaire $Q_2 = \langle r_2, E_1 \rangle$, where E_1 is the set of edit rules in Example 1, and r_2 is the following relation:

PersonId	Relationship	Sex	Age	Marital Status
1	reference	F	31	married
2	spouse	M	39	null

An admissible repair for this questionnaire is the mapping ρ_2 saying that the reference person has an unmarried partner, i.e., the mapping that changes the second tuple to $\langle 2, \text{partner}, M, 39, \text{single} \rangle$ and leaves untouched the first tuple.

Starting from the observation that the errors in the compilation of a form are exceptions, we make our best guess for a corrected questionnaire by minimising the changes to the original relation leading to a complete and consistent questionnaire. For this purpose, we introduce a measure of the number of changes that a repair makes to the relation of a questionnaire. For two tuples $t = \langle v_1, \ldots, v_m \rangle$ and $t' = \langle v'_1, \ldots, v'_m \rangle$, let $dist(t, t')$ be the number of values v_j occurring in t that differ from the corresponding values in t', i.e., such that $v_j \neq v'_j$. Let $\mathcal{Q} = \langle r, E \rangle$ be a questionnaire and ρ a repair for it; we define $changes(\rho, \mathcal{Q}) = \sum_{t \in r} dist(t, \rho(t))$.

Definition 2 (Minimal Repair). An admissible repair ρ for a questionnaire $\mathcal{Q}$ is *minimal* if $changes(\rho, \mathcal{Q})$ is the minimum number of changes over all possible admissible repairs for $\mathcal{Q}$.

Example 3 Consider again the questionnaire $Q_2 = \langle r_2, E_1 \rangle$ in Example 2. The questionnaire has only a minimal repair, ρ'_2, namely the one where the null value is replaced by the 'married' marital status for the spouse of the reference person:

PersonId	Relationship	Sex	Age	Marital Status
1	reference	F	31	married
2	spouse	M	39	married

Note that the repair ρ_2 in the previous example is not minimal. Indeed, it changes both the relationship and the marital status for person 2 and hence $changes(\rho_2, \mathcal{Q}_2) = 2$, while $changes(\rho'_2, \mathcal{Q}_2) = 1$.

In general, there are many possible minimal repairs for an inconsistent and/or incomplete questionnaire. We should then choose one of the minimal repairs without altering the statistical properties of the census. This can be obtained by exploiting some extra information about the census domain, possibly old statistics concerning the same population. Such information can be encoded through a set of FO formulas P that we call *preference rules*, used for expressing some preferences over the repaired relation r', defined as $r' = \rho(r)$, given r. To distinguish the two relations within the same formula, we use a different predicate symbol R' for the repaired relation r': therefore, formulas in P refer to both the predicates R and R'. Intuitively, a preference rule specifies a preferred way to repair the data of a person under some circumstances. The preference rules should be satisfied by as many persons in the household as possible. In order to introduce such a measure, we exploit that each person is uniquely identified by her/his PersonId, and we define preference rules as open formulas ϕ_x, with one free variable x ranging over the domain of the key attribute PersonId. Therefore, these rules are in fact FO queries, telling how many tuples (i.e., how many persons) do actually satisfy them.

Given a substitution θ for the variable x in the domain of the key attribute, $\phi_{\theta x}$ denotes the FO sentence obtained by replacing the variable x according to θ. For a preference rule ϕ_x and the relations r and r', we define

$$\phi_x(r, r') = \{ \theta x \mid [r, r'] \models \phi_{\theta x} \}.$$

where $[r, r']$ denotes the interpretation induced by the two relation instances r and r' over predicates R and R', respectively. Intuitively, the relation $\phi_x(r, r')$ contains the members of the household whose repair r' satisfies the preference rule ϕ. If $|\phi_x(r, r')|$ denotes the number of tuples in $\phi_x(r, r')$, for a set of preference rules P we define $|P(r, r')| = \sum_{\phi \in P} \phi(r, r')$.

Example 4 Consider the following preference rule ϕ_x:

$$\forall s_1, a_1, s_2, a_2 . R(1, \text{reference}, s_1, a_1, \text{married}) \wedge R(x, \mathsf{null}, s_2, a_2, \text{married}) \rightarrow R'(x, \text{spouse}, s_2, a_2, \text{married})$$

This rule expresses that it is likely for a married person living in the household, whose relationship with the reference person is unknown, to be his/her spouse.

Preference rules are used to establish an ordering within the minimal repairs of a questionnaire. Intuitively, when we change some value in order to repair inconsistencies and/or to replace null values, we want to satisfy as many preference rules as possible.

Now we are ready to give a formal definition of the imputation problem.

Definition 3 (Preferred Repair). A *preferred repair* ρ for a questionnaire $\mathcal{Q}$ is a minimal repair such that the number of satisfied preference rules $|P(r, \rho(r))|$ is the greatest over all minimal repairs for $\mathcal{Q}$.

Definition 4 (Imputation Problem). Let $\mathcal{Q} = \langle r, E \rangle$ be a questionnaire and P a set of preference rules, expressed as open FO formulas over predicates R and R'. The *imputation problem* for $\mathcal{Q}$ with respect to P is the problem of finding a preferred repair ρ for $\mathcal{Q}$.

Please note that each imputation problem involves only the data of a single household – i.e., it should be computed for each census form at a time without considered the rest of the data. Thus, the size of the problem is relatively small. This includes the number of family members, the number of the attributes defining a questionnaire and the size of their domains, and the number of the edit and preference rules which are in total usually less between 50 and 100 for a standard complete census questionnaire. A crucial parameter is the size of the domains; as we have seen, these sizes are not usually large, with the exception of the domain of the age attribute. To overcome this problem, usually the domain of the age attribute is partitioned into age intervals. According to our experience, edit rules are also not a source of complexity: they tend to have a rather standard structure.

Example 5 Consider the questionnaire $Q_3 = \langle r_3, E_1 \rangle$, where E_1 is the set of edit rules in Example 1, and r_3 is the following relation:

PersonId	Relationship	Sex	Age	Marital Status
1	reference	F	31	married
2	null	M	39	married

Note that there is no unique way to provide the missing 'relationship' value for the second tuple of r_3. The person identified by 2 may be another relative or a non-relative belonging to the household, or the spouse of the reference person (but not a partner, child, or parent). All these alternative belong to the set of the minimal repairs for Q_3. However, as specified by the preference rule stated above, most married couples live together, and hence we should probably prefer the "spouse" repair. Let ρ_3 be the minimal repair that leaves untouched the first tuple of r_3 and maps its second tuple to $\langle 2, \text{spouse}, M, 39, \text{married} \rangle$. Moreover, let $r'_3 = \rho_3(r_3)$. Then, $\phi_x(r_3, r'_3) = \{1, 2\}$, because ϕ_x is satisfied by $[r_3, r'_3]$ both substituting x with 1 and substituting x with 2. Consider a repair ρ'_3 where the second tuple is mapped to $\langle 2, \text{relative}, M, 39, \text{married} \rangle$. In this case, $\phi_x(r_3, \rho'_3(r_3)) = \{1\}$, because the tuple for person 2 does not satisfy ϕ_x.

Thus, as expected, the unique solution of the imputation problem for Q_3 w.r.t. P is the repair ρ_3 giving the following relation $r'_3 = \rho_3(r_3)$.

PersonId	Relationship	Sex	Age	Marital Status
1	reference	F	31	married
2	spouse	M	39	married

Example 6 Consider the questionnaire $Q_4 = \langle r_4, E_1 \rangle$, where E_1 is the set of edit rules in Example 1, and r_4 is the following relation:

PersonId	Relationship	Sex	Age	Marital Status
1	reference	F	31	married
2	parent	M	6	widowed

It is easy to see that the set of minimal repairs of Q_4 includes any questionnaire which is obtained by Q_4 by substituting the age of the parent with any value between 47 and 120 (the maximum age). We should not prefer a too big or a too small age difference for average parent-child pairs. This can be expressed through the following preference rule ϕ'_x, stating that we prefer age differences in the range $(25, 35)$:

$$\begin{aligned}&\forall s'_1, s_2, s'_2, a'_1, a_2, a'_2, m'_1, m_2, m'_2.\\ &\quad R(x, \text{parent}, s_2, a_2, m_2) \ \wedge\ R'(1, \text{reference}, s'_1, a'_1, m'_1) \ \rightarrow\\ &\qquad R'(x, \text{parent}, s'_2, a'_2, m'_2) \ \wedge\ 25 \leq (a'_2 - a'_1) \leq 35\end{aligned}$$

The following is not among the minimal repairs of Q_4, since it does not involve a minimal number of changes:

PersonId	Relationship	Sex	Age	Marital Status
1	reference	F	31	married
2	child	M	6	single

5 Disjunctive Logic Programming with Constraints

In this section we describe disjunctive logic programming language with constraints (DLP^w) [4], which is supported by the **DLV** system [5,6]. We will use DLP^w in Section 6 to implement our approach to repair inconsistent census data. We first provide an informal description of the DLP^w language by examples, and we then supply a formal definition of the syntax and semantics of DLP^w.

5.1 DLP^w by Examples

Consider the problem SCHEDULING, consisting in the scheduling of course examinations. We want to assign course exams to time slots in such a way that no two exams are assigned to the same time slot if the corresponding courses have some student in common – we call such courses "incompatible". Supposing that there are three time slots available, ts_1, ts_2 and ts_3, we express the problem in DLP^w by the following program $\mathcal{P}_{sch}$:

$$\begin{aligned}&r_1 : \ assign(X, ts_1) \vee assign(X, ts_2) \vee assign(X, ts_3) \text{ :- } course(X)\\ &s_1 : \ \text{ :- } assign(X, S), assign(Y, S), incompatible(X, Y)\end{aligned}$$

Here we assumed that the courses and the pair of incompatible courses are specified by input facts with predicate *course* and *incompatible*, respectively. Rule r_1 says that each course is assigned to either one of the three time slots ts_1, ts_2 or ts_3; the strong constraint s_1 (a rule with empty head) expresses that no two incompatible courses can be assigned to the same time slot. In general, the presence of strong constraints modifies the semantics of a program by discarding all models which do not satisfy some of them. Clearly, it may happen that no model satisfies all constraints. For instance, in a specific instance of above problem, there could be no way to assign courses to time slots without having some overlapping between incompatible courses. In this case, the problem does not admit any solution. However, in real life, one is often satisfied with an approximate solution, in which constraints are satisfied as much as possible. In this light, the problem at hand can be restated as follows (APPROX SCHEDULING): "assign courses to time slots trying not to overlap incompatible courses". In order to express this problem we introduce the notion of *weak* constraint, as shown by the following program $\mathcal{P}_{a\_sch}$:

$$r_1: \ assign(X, ts_1) \vee assign(X, ts_2) \vee assign(X, ts_3) :- course(X)$$
$$w_1: \ :\sim assign(X, S), assign(Y, S), incompatible(X, Y)$$

From a syntactical point of view, a weak constraint is like a strong one where the implication symbol :– is replaced by :~ . The semantics of weak constraints minimises the number of violated instances of constraints. An informal reading of the above weak constraint w_1 is: "preferably, do not assign the courses X and Y to the same time slot if they are incompatible". Note that the above two programs $\mathcal{P}_{sch}$ and $\mathcal{P}_{a\_sch}$ have exactly the same preferred models if all incompatible courses can be assigned to different time slots (i.e., if the problem admits an "exact" solution).

In general, the informal meaning of a weak constraint, say, :~ B, is "try to falsify B" or "B is preferably false", etc. Weak constraints are very powerful for capturing the concept of "preference" in commonsense reasoning.

Since preferences may have, in real life, different priorities, weak constraints in DLP^w can be assigned different priorities as well, according to their "importance"[1]. For example, consider the case when incompatibilities among courses have different defeasibility degree – e.g., basic courses with common students should be considered with a higher degree of incompatibility than advanced courses. Consider the following problem (SCHEDULING WITH PRIORITIES): "schedule courses by trying to avoid overlapping between basic incompatible courses first, and then by trying to avoid overlapping between advanced incompatible courses" (i.e., privilege the elimination of overlapping between basic incompatible courses). If incompatibilities are specified through input facts with predicates *basic_incompatible* and *advanced_incompatible*, we can represent SCHEDULING WITH PRIORITIES by the following program $\mathcal{P}_{p\_sch}$:

$$r_1: \ assign(X, ts_1) \vee assign(X, ts_2) \vee assign(X, ts_3) :- course(X)$$
$$w_2: \ :\sim assign(X, S), assign(Y, S), basic\_incompatible(X, Y) \quad [:2]$$
$$w_3: \ :\sim assign(X, S), assign(Y, S), advanced\_incompatible(X, Y) \quad [:1]$$

The weak constraint w_2 is defined "stronger than" w_3, since w_2 has a higher priority (2) than w_3 (1). The preferred models (called *best models*) of the above program are the assignments of courses to time slots that minimise the number of overlappings between basic incompatible courses and, among these, the assignments which minimise the number of overlappings between advanced incompatible courses.

5.2 Syntax

A *term* is either a constant or a variable[2]. An *atom* is of the form `a(t1, ..., tn)`, where `a` is a *predicate* of arity *n* and `t1, ..., tn` are terms. A *literal* is either a *positive* literal *p* or a *negative* literal `not` *p*, where *p* is an atom.

[1] Note that priorities are meaningless for strong constraints, since all of them *must* be satisfied.
[2] Note that function symbols are not part of datalog.

A *(disjunctive) rule* r is a clause of the form

$$\mathtt{a_1} \vee \cdots \vee \mathtt{a_n} \text{ :- } \mathtt{b_1}, \cdots, \mathtt{b_k}, \mathtt{not}\ \mathtt{b_{k+1}}, \cdots, \mathtt{not}\ \mathtt{b_m}. \qquad \mathtt{n} \geq 1,\ \mathtt{m} \geq 0$$

where $\mathtt{a_1}, \cdots, \mathtt{a_n}, \mathtt{b_1}, \cdots, \mathtt{b_m}$ are atoms. The disjunction $a_1 \vee \cdots \vee a_n$ is the *head* of r, while the conjunction $b_1, ..., b_k, \mathtt{not}\ b_{k+1}, ..., \mathtt{not}\ b_m$ is the *body* of r. If $n = 1$ (i.e., the head is $\vee$-free), then r is *normal*; if $m = k$ (the body is not -free), then r is *positive*.

A *strong constraint* (integrity constraint) has the form $\text{:- } \mathtt{L_1}, \cdots, \mathtt{L_m}.$, where each $\mathtt{L_i}, 1 \leq i \leq m$, is a literal; it is a rule with empty head.

A *weak constraint* has the form $:\sim \mathtt{L_1}, \cdots, \mathtt{L_m}.[: \mathtt{1}]$, where each L_i, $1 \leq i \leq m$, is a literal and l is a term. l denotes the *priority layer*, once the weak constraint has been instantiated l should be a positive integer[3]. If the priority level l is omitted, then it defaults to 1.

The language DLP^w include all possible rules and constraints (weak and strong). A DLP^w program $\mathcal{P}$ is a finite subset of the language DLP^w.

5.3 Semantics

Informally, the semantics of a DLP^w program $\mathcal{P}$ is given by the stable models of the set of the rules of $\mathcal{P}$ satisfying all strong constraints and minimising the number of violated weak constraints according to the prioritisation.

The Herbrand Universe, the Herbrand Base, and the ground instantiation $ground(\mathcal{P})$ of a DLP^w program $\mathcal{P}$ are defined in the usual way. Let P, S, and W be, respectively, the set of ground instances of the rules, the strong constraints, and the weak constraints of a DLP^w program $\mathcal{P}$. An interpretation I for $\mathcal{P}$ is a subset of the Herbrand Base of $\mathcal{P}$ (i.e., it is a set of ground atoms). A positive ground literal A is true w.r.t. I if $A \in I$; otherwise it is false w.r.t. I. A negative ground literal not A is true w.r.t. I if $A \notin I$; otherwise it is false w.r.t. I. A ground rule $r \in P$ is satisfied in I if some head literal of r is true or some body literal of r is false w.r.t. I. A constraint (strong or weak) c is satisfied in I, if some literal of c is false w.r.t. I. An interpretation satisfying all rules of P is a model of P. The *Gelfond-Lifschitz transformation* of P with respect to I, denoted by P^I, is the positive program defined as follows:

$$\begin{aligned} P^I = \{\ & a_1 \vee \cdots \vee a_n \text{ :- } b_1, \cdots, b_k | \\ & a_1 \vee \cdots \vee a_n \text{ :- } b_1, \cdots, b_k, \neg b_{k+1}, \cdots, \neg b_m \in P \ \ and \ \ b_i \notin I,\ k < i \leq m\} \end{aligned}$$

I is a *stable model* for P if I is a subset-minimal model of P^I. A *candidate model* of $\mathcal{P}$ is a stable model of P which satisfies each strong constraint in S.

For the weak constraints, only those candidate models are considered which minimise the number of the violated (weak) constraints in the greatest priority layer, and among them those which minimise the number of the violated constraints in the previous layer, etc. This can be expressed by an objective function for $\mathcal{P}$ and a candidate model M:

$$\begin{aligned} & f(1) = 1 \\ & f(n) = f(n-1) \cdot WC + 1, \qquad \text{if } n > 1 \\ & H_M = \textstyle\sum_{i=1}^{max_l} (f(i) \cdot ||violated(M, i)||) \end{aligned}$$

[3] Note that the language of **DLV** supports also weights besides layers. Since we do not use them in our application, we omit the weights to simplify the presentation.

where WC denotes the total number of weak constraints in $\mathcal{P}$, max_l denotes the maximum priority layer in $\mathcal{P}$, $\|violated(M,i)\|$ denotes the number of weak constraints in layer i which are violated w.r.t. M. A candidate model of $\mathcal{P}$ for which H_M is minimal among all candidate models of $\mathcal{P}$ is a *best model* of $\mathcal{P}$.

As an example, consider the following program $\mathcal{P}_s$

$$a \vee b :\!-\ c. \qquad :\sim a, c. \quad [:2]$$
$$c. \qquad :\sim b. \quad [:1]$$

The stable models for the set $\{\ c.\ a \vee b :\!-\ c.\}$ of ground rules of this example are $M_1 = \{\mathtt{a},\mathtt{c}\}$ and $M_2 = \{\mathtt{b},\mathtt{c}\}$, they are also the candidate models, since there is no strong constraint. In this case, $WC = 2$, and $max_l = 2$. Thus, $f(1) = 1$, $f(2) = 3$, $H_{M_1} = 3$, and $H_{M_2} = 1$. So M_2 is preferred over M_1 (M_2 is a best model of $\mathcal{P}_s$). Indeed, M_1 violates the more important weak constraint having level 2; while M_2 violates only a weak constraint of level 1.

6 Solving the Imputation Problem

In this section we show how to solve the imputation problem using a disjunctive logic program with weak constraints [4] whose best models correspond to the preferred repairs of a given questionnaire. This program first verifies if the input data satisfies the edit rules or contains null values, i.e., if the questionnaire is consistent and complete. If this is the case, then the program has a unique best model corresponding to the given questionnaire, unmodified. Otherwise, the program corrects automatically the data, and each of its best models encodes a preferred repair, i.e., it maximises the number of satisfied preference rules).

6.1 Running Example

As a running example we consider the questionnaire $Q_5 = \langle r_5, E_1 \rangle$ and the preference rules ϕ_x of Example 4 and ϕ'_x of Example 6 . E_1 is the set of edit rules in Example 1, and r_5 is the following relation:

PersonId	Relationship	Sex	Age	Marital Status
1	reference	F	31	single
2	parent	null	12	widowed

The questionnaire is incomplete (it is not specified the sex for the person "2") and inconsistent with respect to the edit rule 6 from E_1 (the person "2" is a parent of the reference person and she/he is 12 years old).

6.2 Data Representation

Each component of a household is identified by an integer number. The number "1" identifies the reference person. The questionnaire relation is encoded by the following

EDB binary predicates: `relationship, age, maritalstatus`, and `sex`. For each atom over these predicates, the first argument corresponds to the identification number of a person, while the domain for the second argument depends on the predicate, as described below:

- `relationship`: reference, spouse, partner, son, parent, otherRelative, nonRelative,
- `sex`: male, female,
- `marital status`: single, married, divorced, widowed,
- `age`: integer number.

For instance, an atom `relationship(2,spouse)` indicates that the household component with identification number "2" is the spouse of the reference person. In our running example the relation r_5 is represented by the following set of facts:

```
{relationship(1,reference), sex(1,female), age(1,31),
 maritalstatus(1,single)
 relationship(2,parent), age(2,12), maritalstatus(2,widowed)}
```

The relation corresponding to a preferred repair for the given questionnaire is encoded through a set of facts with the same name as the predicates encoding the input relation, but capitalised. For instance, `Age(1,33)` means that the reference person is aged 33 in the preferred repair. Therefore, the "output" relation corresponding to a preferred repair is represented by the following IDB predicates: `Relationship, Age, MaritalStatus`, and `Sex`.

6.3 Description of the DLP^w Program

The DLP^w program consists of the following five modules automatically generated from the edit rules:

- detection of errors and missing data;
- generation of possible correction of data values;
- admissible repairs check;
- minimal repairs generation;
- preferred repairs generation.

Next, we describe the five modules. To help the intuition, we carry out an informal description by referring to the running example.

Detection of Errors and Missing Data. This module verifies that the input data is correct (i.e., there is no inconsistency w.r.t some edit rule) and that there is no missing information about the components of the household (i.e., for each person, there exists a tuple for each of the predicates). If either some null value or some error is detected in any input atom, this module derives a corresponding atom over the predicates `wrongRelationship, wrongAge, wrongMaritalStatus`, and `wrongSex`. Missing values are identified by using negation. For instance, consider the input predicate `relationship`. The following rules detect if we miss the relationship information for some member of the household:

```
specifiedRelationship(X) :- relationship(X,Y).
wrongRelationship(X,missing) :- not specifiedRelationship(X),
                                person(X).
```

If a relationship of a person X is not specified, the wrongRelationship(X,missing) atom is derived. This means that it is necessary to complete the data. In the running example, since the sex of the person "2" is not specified , the module derives the atom wrongSex(2,missing).

In order to detect errors, the DLP^w program includes rules corresponding to the edit rules of the questionnaire, that single out inconsistencies. If an edit rule is violated, then the corresponding rule of the module detects this situation and provides some atoms, which may be responsible for this violation. For instance, consider the edit rule 5 in the running example, which says that any married person should be at least 16 years old. The following rule suggests that, in the case of violation for a person X, either the age or the marital status of X is wrong:

```
wrongMaritalStatus(X,married) v wrongAge(X,Z):-
    maritalstatus(X,married),age(X,Z),Z<16.
```

Note that, for presentation clarity, we made a simplifying assumption. We assume that a violated edit rule does not need to change more than one atom to be satisfied (e.g. either marital status or age can be changed in the above rule, but we assume that we do not need to change both). Even if this assumption is plausible we can easily relax it by modifying the encoding.

Generation of Possible Corrections of Data Values. The previous module derives atoms of the form wrongSomething corresponding to wrong values that caused the violation of some edit rule. For each of them, we should provide a new value for the repaired questionnaire. This is accomplished by disjunctive rules whose heads contain an atom for each domain value, representing a candidate change for the guilty atom.

For instance, the following rule guesses a value for the (output) sex predicate Sex, if the sex is wrong:

```
Sex(X,male) v Sex(X,female) :- wrongSex(X,_).
```

In the previous module, since we derived wrongSex(2,missing), a new value for the output predicate Sex is guessed.

Admissible Repairs Check. Once we have guessed a repair for the given questionnaire, we have to check if the repair is admissible. This is accomplished by integrity constraints over the output predicates that encode the edit rules of the questionnaire. Thus, the output atoms occurring in the candidate models of the program so far correspond to admissible repairs for the questionnaire.

For instance, consider the edit rule 1 stating that the spouse of the reference person should be married, and the edit rule 5 stating that any non single person should be at least 16 years old. They are encoded by the following constraints:

```
:- Relationship(X,spouse), MaritalStatus(X,Y), Y<>married.
:- MaritalStatus(X,Y), Y<>single, Age(X,Z), Z<16.
```

A candidate model for the program of the running example is[4]:

```
A={wrongSex(2,missing), wrongAge(2,12), Relationship(1,reference),
   Sex(1,female), Age(1,31), MaritalStatus(1,single),
   Relationship(2,parent), Sex(2,female), Age(2,70),
   MaritalStatus(2,widowed)}
```

corresponding to the following repair:

PersonId	Relationship	Sex	Age	Marital Status
1	reference	F	31	single
2	parent	F	70	widowed

Another candidate model for this program is

```
A'={wrongSex(2,missing), wrongRelationship(2,parent),
    Relationship(1,reference), Sex(1,female), Age(1,31),
    MaritalStatus(1,single) Relationship(2,child), Sex(2,male),
    Age(2,12), MaritalStatus(2,single)}
```

corresponding to the following repair:

PersonId	Relationship	Sex	Age	Marital Status
1	reference	F	31	single
2	child	M	12	single

Minimal Repairs Generation. To enforce the computation of the only candidate models corresponding to minimal repairs of the questionnaire, we exploit the weak constraints extension of disjunctive logic programming. Using weak constraints, we can assign a penalty to each value change we make to the input questionnaire. This is accomplished by the following constraints:

```
:  relationship(X,Y), Relationship(X,Z), Z<>Y. [:2]
:  age(X,Y), Age(X,Z), Z<>Y. [:2]
:  sex(X,Y), Sex(X,Z), Z<>Y. [:2]
:  maritalstatus(X,Y), MaritalStatus(X,Z), Z<>Y. [:2]
```

Note that we use level 2 priority for the weak constraints above, because minimisation of changes has the highest priority in the imputation problem (as defined in Section 4), and we will use level 1 priority for specifying less important properties below.

The candidate model `A'` above violates three weak constraints, while the candidate model `A` violates two weak constraints. Thus, `A` is a best model of the program, and it corresponds to a minimal repair for Q_5.

[4] We omit to specify the input facts again in the models.

Preferred-Repairs Generation. To maximise the number of satisfied preference rules (Definition 3), we use again weak constraints. The module contains a weak constraint for each preference rule. This constraint assigns a penalty for each violation of the corresponding preference rule. These weak constraints have level 1 priority, since they have a lower priority than the weak constraints enforcing minimisations of changes. Indeed, by definition of the imputation problem, the preferred repairs should be chosen among the minimal repairs for the questionnaire. Thus, the candidate model of the program minimising the cost of weak constraints encodes the preferred repair for the questionnaire.

For instance, the following weak constraint corresponds to the preference rule of the running example stating that, if the reference person is married and some other married person is in the household, then we prefer the situation in which they are married each other:

```
:  MaritalStatus(1,married), MaritalStatus(X,married),
   Relationship(X,Y), Y <> spouse, X <> 1.     [:1]
```

The candidate model A is a minimal repair but it is not the preferred repair for Q_5. Indeed, it does not satisfy the preference rule stating that the age difference between a parent and a child should be in the range (25,35), on average.

The following candidate model is a best model of the program and corresponds to a preferred repair of the questionnaire.

```
A''={wrongSex(2,missing), wrongAge(2,12), Relationship(1,reference),
     Sex(1,female), Age(1,31), MaritalStatus(1,single),
     Relationship(2,parent), Sex(2,female), Age(2,60),
     MaritalStatus(2,widowed)}
```

Remark 1. To show the feasibility of our approach, we used the executable specification language DLP^w, supported by the **DLV** system. It is worthwhile noting that disjunction is not strictly necessary in our program, and could be replaced by unstratified negation (with a polynomial blow up of the program size). Weak constraints, on the contrary, are strictly needed to implement the semantics of preferred repairs, and cannot be rewritten into normal logic rules. Thus, normal logic programs cannot be used to implement our semantics, while DLP^w provides a natural and elegant support for the implementation.

7 Related Work

There are various methodologies available to statisticians for dealing with the millions of records that have to be cleaned [10]. The most widely used for census data is the Fellegi and Holt methodology (FH [7]). More recently, the New Imputation Methodology (NIM [2]) has been introduced as an improvement over FH.

In both FH and NIM edit rules are written in a declarative fashion, and they are used to check the consistency of a household questionnaire; the consistency check is usually implemented with active rules in a relational database. When a questionnaire fails to satisfy the edit rules, the information needed for the imputation phase is borrowed from a similar questionnaire that passed the edit rules (which is called a *donor* form). NIM initially searches for donors that match the failed record on as many as possible of the involved attribute values. It then analyses the edit rules to determine the *minimum* number of non-matching attributes between the failed record and that particular donor, such that the imputed record will eventually pass the edits. Various subsets of the attributes are imputed to determine which is the optimum imputation for a failed edit household. It is crucial that in the imputed record the joint distribution of attributes is maintained. In contrast to NIM, FH first determines the minimum number of attributes to impute and then performs the imputation, possibly by searching for donors. According to the experiments, changing the order of these operations allows NIM to efficiently solve larger and more complex imputation problems.

Both the above methods do not have a declarative semantics. In particular, various implementations slightly differ in the imputation phase, making it impossible to understand what gets repaired and why. In addition, they are computationally expensive, since both rely inherently on donors, which have to be found in the large database of size of the entire census.

Our proposal has two clear advantages over FH and derivative methods. First of all, it is equipped with formal declarative semantics, which unambiguously specifies the meaning and the behaviour of the imputation task. Surprisingly, there has been no previous attempt in the field to devise explicitly a formal semantics to the imputation task. This semantics is not in contrast with what in principle should be the behaviour of the FH and NIM procedures. However, we have noticed that the various algorithms currently used do produce different results which are hard to interpret and compare given the absence of a declarative semantics. We hope that our clear semantics will help in understanding and possibly fixing those differences. Secondly, we have clearly separated the consistency check phase, the abstract imputation phase, and the preference selection phase. While we give precise and complete definition for the former phases, we have defined the latter preference selection phase up to the choice of a mechanism behind the preference rules. We leave open the definition of them to the statisticians, who may choose their own preferred strategy, such as a donor strategy – with possibly different similarity measures, and with global or local comparisons – or a strategy based on statistical histories, or others.

Our approach is highly modular. In principle, each questionnaire is processed and corrected alone, independently on all other census data. This modularity property allows for a high degree of parallelism (several questionnaires can be processed in parallel on different machines) and ensures a higher computational load. Indeed, even if the correction of a questionnaire may require an exponential time, this time is exponential in the size of a single questionnaire and in the number of edit rules. This is true up to the computation of the preference rules, which – depending on the strategy chosen by the statisticians – may again look at the whole set of questionnaires. The advantage of our proposal is to single out this latter phase and to have a principled way of relating it with the abstract imputation problem. We also propose a provably correct implementation of the abstract imputation problem in DLP^w. We have implemented our approach on the disjunctive logic programming system **DLV**, and we have started an experimentation activity at the Italian Statistical Agency (ISTAT). The results of the experiments show the feasibility of this approach with realistic questionnaires (composed by the edit rules and the form data), if only the abstract imputation problem is taken into account, i.e., if the preference rules are given.

To our knowledge, there has been in the literature only a proposal using a logic-based approach to the edit and the imputation problems [3]. However, this approach does not explicitly define a declarative semantics of the imputation problem, and most importantly it suffers from a combinatorial explosion of the encoding of the problem in propositional logic. Moreover, the main focus of [3] is on the problems of consistency and redundancy of edit rules. The imputation problem is solved – again in a propositional setting – still in an ad-hoc manner by using donors taken from correct questionnaires.

The problem of correcting collection of data with missing or inconsistent values also arises in the context of integration of knowledge from multiple sources, e.g., in data warehouses. Some recent logical approaches to querying and repairing inconsistent databases have been proposed in [1,8]. Such approaches are based on *subset-minimal* repairs, and it is possible to specify some preference on the possible corrections. The use of subset-minimal repairs is more coarse grained than our approach based on *minimal change* followed by a *preference* criterion. In fact, our notion of minimality is based on the finer grained measure of the number of changes within tuples. For example, let us consider two admissible repairs of a questionnaire, each one having only one tuple changed with respect to the original questionnaire; this is the case of the two admissible repairs for Q_2 proposed in example 2 (ρ_2) and example 3 (ρ'_2). These two repairs are ranked equal according to a subset-minimal criterion, while our minimal change criterion selects only the repair(s) where the least number of attributes was changed, namely ρ'_2. In addition, we further allow general preference rules among the set of minimal repairs, expressed in a declarative way, with the goal of producing a single preferred repair.

We believe that our minimal change criterion could be applied as a basic selection criterion also for the problems in [1,8], since it leads to more sensible choices. Moreover, even if it is hard to precisely compare the complexity of the approaches pursued by [1,8] with ours – since the problems are different (computation of a consistent answer in all minimal repairs versus the computation of the minimal repairs) – a general complexity argument applies as follows. First note that the imputation problem is a search problem, and that we refer here to the complexity of the problem to decide whether a value of a tuple gets a certain value in some minimal repair of the questionnaire. In this context, choices among different solutions based on weights or cardinalities of the solutions are typically feasible in a more efficient way, compared with choices based on the subset-minimality criterion. More specifically, in our case, the adoption of a general subset-minimal criterion would raise the complexity from Δ_2^p (our upper bound, given by the fragment we use of DLP^w with a limited – head-cycle-free – disjunction [4]) to Σ_2^p.

8 Conclusions

In this paper we have formally defined the semantics of the edit and imputation problems for census data, and we have provided a correct encoding in disjunctive logic programming with constraints. We believe that our framework is quite general and can be applied to contexts other than census data repair.

We have implemented our approach on the disjunctive logic programming system **DLV**, and we have started an experimentation activity at the Italian Statistical Agency (ISTAT). Preliminary results of experiments show the feasibility of this approach with realistic data.

We plan to have an extensive experimentation with real census data provided by the Italian Statistical Agency – including their donor-based strategy for computing the preference rules – and to compare the outcome of our approach with the well established imputation methodologies based on statistics. We also want to devise a methodology for edit and preference rule design, and to precisely characterise the computational properties of the abstract imputation problem.

References

1. M. Arenas, L. Bertossi, and J. Chomicki. Specifying and Querying Database repairs using Logic Programs with Exceptions. In *Proceedings International Conference on Flexible Query Answering*, pages 27–41, 2000.
2. Michael Bankier. Experience with the new imputation methodology used in the 1996 canadian censuses with extensions for future censuses. In *Statistical Commission and Economic Commission for Europe, Conference of European statisticians, UN/ECE work session on statistical Data Editing*, Rome, Italy, 1999.
3. Renato Bruni and Antonio Sassano. Errors detection and correction in large scale data collecting. In F. Hoffmann et al., editor, *Proc. of the Fourth International Symposium on Intelligent Data Analysis (IDA-2001)*, volume 2189 of *LNCS*, pages 84–94. Springer-Verlag, 2001.
4. Francesco Buccafurri, Nicola Leone, and Pasquale Rullo. Enhancing Disjunctive Datalog by Constraints. *IEEE Transactions on Knowledge and Data Engineering*, 12(5):845–860, 2000.
5. Thomas Eiter, Nicola Leone, Cristinel Mateis, Gerald Pfeifer, and Francesco Scarcello. The KR System `dlv`: Progress Report, Comparisons and Benchmarks. In Anthony G. Cohn, Lenhart Schubert, and Stuart C. Shapiro, editors, *Proceedings Sixth International Conference on Principles of Knowledge Representation and Reasoning (KR'98)*, pages 406–417. Morgan Kaufmann Publishers, 1998.
6. Wolfgang Faber, Nicola Leone, and Gerald Pfeifer. Experimenting with heuristics for answer set programming. In *Proceedings of the Seventeenth International Joint Conference on Artificial Intelligence (IJCAI) 2001*, Washington, USA, August 2001. To appear.
7. I. P. Fellegi and D. Holt. A systematic approach to automatic edit and imputation. *Journal of the American Statistical Association*, 71(353):17–35, March 1976.
8. G. Greco, S. Greco, and E. Zumpano. A Logic Programming Approach to the Integration, Repairing and Queriyng of Inconsistent Databases. In *Proceedings International Conference on Logic Programming*, 2001.
9. United Nations Economic Commission for Europe and the Statistical Office of the European Communities. Recommendations for the 2000 censuses of population and housing in the ECE region. Technical Report Statistical Standards And Studies – No. 49, UN/ECE Statistical Division, 1998.
10. William E. Winkler. State of statistical data editing and current research problems. In *Statistical Commission and Economic Commission for Europe, Conference of European statisticians, UN/ECE work session on statistical Data Editing*, Rome, Italy, 1999.

Boolean Functions for Finite-Tree Dependencies*

Roberto Bagnara[1], Enea Zaffanella[1], Roberta Gori[2], and Patricia M. Hill[3]

[1] Department of Mathematics, University of Parma, Italy.
{bagnara,zaffanella}@cs.unipr.it

[2] Department of Computer Science, University of Pisa, Italy.
gori@di.unipi.it

[3] School of Computing, University of Leeds, United Kingdom.
hill@comp.leeds.ac.uk

Abstract. Several logic-based languages, such as Prolog II and its successors, SICStus Prolog and Oz, offer a computation domain including *rational trees* that allow for increased expressivity and faster unification. Unfortunately, the use of infinite rational trees has problems. For instance, many of the built-in and library predicates are ill-defined for such trees and need to be supplemented by run-time checks whose cost may be significant. In a recent paper [3], we have proposed a data-flow analysis called *finite-tree analysis* aimed at identifying those program variables (the *finite variables*) that are not currently bound to infinite terms. Here we present a domain of Boolean functions, called *finite-tree dependencies* that precisely captures how the finiteness of some variables influences the finiteness of other variables. We also summarize our experimental results showing how finite-tree analysis, enhanced with finite-tree dependencies is a practical means of obtaining precise finiteness information.

1 Introduction

Many logic-based languages refer to a computation domain of *rational trees.* While rational trees allow for increased expressivity, they also have a surprising number of problems. (See [4] for a survey of known applications of rational trees and a detailed account of many of the problems caused by their use.) Some of these problems are so serious that rational trees must be used in a very controlled way, disallowing infinite trees in any context where they are "dangerous". This, in turn, causes a secondary problem: in order to disallow infinite trees in selected contexts, one must first detect them, an operation that may be expensive.

In [4], we have introduced a composite abstract domain, $H \times P$, for finite-tree analysis. The H domain, written with the initial of *Herbrand* and called the *finiteness* component, is the direct representation of the property of interest: a set of variables guaranteed to be bound to finite terms. The generic domain P (the *parameter* of the construction) provides sharing information that can include,

* The MURST project, "Certificazione automatica di programmi mediante interpretazione astratta", partly supported the work of the first two authors and EPSRC grant M05645 partly supported the work of the second and fourth authors.

R. Nieuwenhuis and A. Voronkov (Eds.): LPAR 2001, LNAI 2250, pp. 579–594, 2001.

apart from variable aliasing, groundness, linearity, freeness and any other kind of information that can improve the precision on these components, such as explicit structural information. Sharing information is exploited in $H \times P$ for two purposes: detecting when new infinite terms are possibly created (this is done along the lines of [22]) and confining the propagation of those terms as much as possible. As shown in [3,4], by giving a generic specification for this parameter component in terms of the *abstract queries* it supports (in the style of the *open product* construct [12]), it is possible to define and establish the correctness of the abstract operators on the finite-tree domain independently from any particular domain for sharing analysis.

The domain $H \times P$ captures the negative aspect of term-finiteness, that is, the circumstances under which finiteness can be lost. However, term-finiteness has also a positive aspect: there are cases where a variable is granted to be bound to a finite term and this knowledge can be propagated to other variables. Guarantees of finiteness are provided by several built-ins like `unify_with_occurs_check/2`, `var/1`, `name/2`, all the arithmetic predicates, besides those explicitly provided to test for term-finiteness such as the `acyclic_term/1` predicate of SICStus Prolog. The information encoded by H is *attribute independent* [14], which means that each variable is considered in isolation. What is missing is information concerning how finiteness of one variable affects the finiteness of other variables. This kind of information, usually called *relational information*, is not captured at all by H and is only partially captured by the composite domain $H \times P$ of [4].

Here we present a domain of Boolean functions that precisely captures how the finiteness of some variables influences the finiteness of other variables. This domain of *finite-tree dependencies* provides relational information that is important for the precision of the overall finite-tree analysis. It also combines obvious similarities, interesting differences and somewhat unexpected connections with classical domains for *groundness dependencies*.

Finite-tree and groundness dependencies are similar in that they both track *covering* information (a term s covers t if all the variables in t also occur in s) and share several abstract operations. However, they are different because covering does not tell the whole story. Suppose x and y are free variables before either the unification $x = f(y)$ or the unification $x = f(x, y)$ are executed. In both cases, x will be ground if and only if y will be so. However, when $x = f(y)$ is the performed unification, this equivalence will also carry over to finiteness. In contrast, when the unification is $x = f(x, y)$, x will never be finite and will be totally independent, as far as finiteness is concerned, from y. Among the unexpected connections is the fact that finite-tree dependencies can improve the groundness information obtained by the usual approaches to groundness analysis.

The paper is structured as follows: the required notations and preliminary concepts are given in Section 2; the concrete domain for the analysis is presented in Section 3; Section 4 introduces the use of Boolean functions for tracking finite-tree dependencies, whereas Section 5 illustrates the interaction between groundness and finite-tree dependencies. Our experimental results are presented in Section 6. The paper concludes in Section 7.

2 Preliminaries

2.1 Infinite Terms and Substitutions

For a set S, $\wp(S)$ is the powerset of S, $\wp_f(S)$ is the set of all the *finite* subsets of S, whereas $\# S$ denotes the cardinality of S. Let *Sig* denote a possibly infinite set of function symbols, ranked over the set of natural numbers and *Vars* a denumerable set of variable symbols, disjoint from *Sig*. Then *Terms* denotes the free algebra of all (possibly infinite) terms in the signature *Sig* having variables in *Vars*. It is assumed that *Sig* contains at least two distinct function symbols, one having rank 0 and one with rank greater than 0 (so that there exist finite and infinite terms both with and without variables). If $t \in \mathit{Terms}$ then $\mathrm{vars}(t)$ denotes the set of variables occurring in t. If $\mathrm{vars}(t) = \varnothing$ then t is said to be *ground*; t is a *finite term* (or *Herbrand term*) if it contains a finite number of occurrences of function symbols. The sets of all ground and finite terms are denoted by *GTerms* and *HTerms*, respectively.

A *substitution* is a total function $\sigma \colon \mathit{Vars} \to \mathit{HTerms}$ that is the identity almost everywhere; in other words, the *domain of* σ, which is defined as $\mathrm{dom}(\sigma) \stackrel{\mathrm{def}}{=} \{\, x \in \mathit{Vars} \mid \sigma(x) \neq x \,\}$, is a finite set of variables. If $x \in \mathit{Vars}$ and $t \in \mathit{HTerms} \setminus \{x\}$, then $x \mapsto t$ is called a *binding*. The set of all bindings is denoted by *Bind*. Substitutions are conveniently denoted by the set of their bindings. Accordingly, a substitution σ is identified with the (finite) set $\{\, x \mapsto \sigma(x) \mid x \in \mathrm{dom}(\sigma) \,\}$. We denote by $\mathrm{vars}(\sigma)$ the set of all variables occurring in the bindings of σ.

A substitution of the form $\{x_1 \mapsto x_2, \ldots, x_{n-1} \mapsto x_n, x_n \mapsto x_1\}$ is *circular* if and only if $n > 1$ and $x_1, \ldots, x_n$ are distinct variables. A substitution is in *rational solved form* if it has no circular subset. The set of all substitutions in rational solved form is denoted by *RSubst*.

Given a substitution $\sigma \colon \mathit{Vars} \to \mathit{HTerms}$, the symbol '$\sigma$' also denotes the function $\sigma \colon \mathit{HTerms} \to \mathit{HTerms}$ defined as usual. That is, for each $t \in \mathit{HTerms}$, $\sigma(t)$ is the term obtained by replacing each occurrence of each variable x in t by the term $\sigma(x)$. If $t \in \mathit{HTerms}$, we write $t\sigma$ to denote $\sigma(t)$. Let $s \in \mathit{HTerms}$ and $\sigma \in \mathit{RSubst}$. Then $\sigma^0(s) \stackrel{\mathrm{def}}{=} s$ and $\sigma^i(s) \stackrel{\mathrm{def}}{=} \sigma\bigl(\sigma^{i-1}(s)\bigr)$ for all $i \in \mathbb{N}$, $i > 0$. Thus the sequence of finite terms $\sigma^0(s), \sigma^1(s), \ldots$ converges to a (possibly infinite) term, denoted by $\sigma^\infty(s)$ [17,18].

2.2 Equations

An *equation* has the form $s = t$ where $s, t \in \mathit{HTerms}$. *Eqs* denotes the set of all equations. A substitution σ may be regarded as a finite set of equations, that is, as the set $\{\, x = t \mid x \mapsto t \in \sigma \,\}$. We say that a set of equations e is in *rational solved form* if $\{\, s \mapsto t \mid (s = t) \in e \,\} \in \mathit{RSubst}$. In the rest of the paper, we will often write a substitution $\sigma \in \mathit{RSubst}$ to denote a set of equations in rational solved form (and vice versa).

Some logic-based languages, such as Prolog II, SICStus and Oz, are based on $\mathcal{RT}$, the theory of rational trees [9,10]. This is a syntactic equality theory (i.e., a theory where the function symbols are uninterpreted), augmented with a *uniqueness axiom* for each substitution in rational solved form. It is worth noting that any set of equations in rational solved form is, by definition, satisfiable in $\mathcal{RT}$.

Given a set of equations $e \in \wp_{\mathrm{f}}(Eqs)$ that is satisfiable in $\mathcal{RT}$, a substitution $\sigma \in RSubst$ is called a *solution for* e *in* $\mathcal{RT}$ if $\mathcal{RT} \vdash \forall(\sigma \rightarrow e)$, i.e., if every model of the theory $\mathcal{RT}$ is also a model of the first order formula $\forall(\sigma \rightarrow e)$. If in addition $\mathrm{vars}(\sigma) \subseteq \mathrm{vars}(e)$, then σ is said to be a *relevant* solution for e. If $\mathcal{RT} \vdash \forall(\sigma \leftrightarrow e)$, then σ is a *most general solution for* e *in* $\mathcal{RT}$. The set of all the relevant most general solution for e in $\mathcal{RT}$ will be denoted by $\mathrm{mgs}(e)$.

The function $\downarrow(\cdot)\colon RSubst \rightarrow \wp(RSubst)$ is defined, for each $\sigma \in RSubst$, by $\downarrow\sigma \stackrel{\mathrm{def}}{=} \bigl\{\, \tau \in RSubst \bigm| \exists \sigma' \in RSubst \,.\, \tau \in \mathrm{mgs}(\sigma \cup \sigma') \,\bigr\}$. The next result shows that $\downarrow(\cdot)$ corresponds to the closure by entailment in $\mathcal{RT}$.

Proposition 1. *Let* $\sigma \in RSubst$. *Then* $\downarrow\sigma = \bigl\{\, \tau \in RSubst \bigm| \mathcal{RT} \vdash \forall(\tau \rightarrow \sigma) \,\bigr\}$.

2.3 Boolean Functions

Boolean functions have already been extensively used for data-flow analysis of logic-based languages. An important class of these functions used for tracking groundness dependencies is *Pos* [1]. This domain was introduced in [19] under the name *Prop* and further refined and studied in [11,20].

Boolean functions are based on the notion of Boolean valuation.

Definition 2. (Boolean valuations.) *Let* $VI \in \wp_{\mathrm{f}}(Vars)$ *and* $\mathbb{B} \stackrel{\mathrm{def}}{=} \{0,1\}$. *The set of* Boolean valuations over VI *is* $Bval \stackrel{\mathrm{def}}{=} VI \rightarrow \mathbb{B}$. *For each* $a \in Bval$, *each* $x \in VI$, *and each* $c \in \mathbb{B}$ *the valuation* $a[c/x] \in Bval$ *is given, for each* $y \in VI$, *by*

$$a[c/x](y) \stackrel{\mathrm{def}}{=} \begin{cases} c, & \text{if } x = y; \\ a(y), & \text{otherwise.} \end{cases}$$

If $X = \{x_1, \ldots, x_k\} \subseteq VI$, *then* $a[c/X]$ *denotes* $a[c/x_1] \cdots [c/x_k]$.

Bval contains the distinguished elements $\mathbf{0} \stackrel{\mathrm{def}}{=} \lambda x \in VI \,.\, 0$ and $\mathbf{1} \stackrel{\mathrm{def}}{=} \lambda x \in VI \,.\, 1$.

Definition 3. (Boolean functions.) *The set of* Boolean functions over VI *is* $Bfun \stackrel{\mathrm{def}}{=} Bval \rightarrow \mathbb{B}$. *Bfun is partially ordered by the relation* $\models$ *where, for each* $\phi, \psi \in Bfun$,

$$\phi \models \psi \quad \stackrel{\mathrm{def}}{\iff} \quad \bigl(\forall a \in Bval : \phi(a) = 1 \implies \psi(a) = 1\bigr).$$

The distinguished elements $\top, \bot \in Bfun$ are defined by $\bot \stackrel{\mathrm{def}}{=} \lambda a \in Bval \,.\, 0$ and $\top \stackrel{\mathrm{def}}{=} \lambda a \in Bval \,.\, 1$. respectively. For each $\phi \in Bfun$, $x \in VI$, and $c \in \mathbb{B}$, the function $\phi[c/x] \in Bfun$ is given, for each $a \in Bval$, by $\phi[c/x](a) \stackrel{\mathrm{def}}{=} \phi\bigl(a[c/x]\bigr)$. When $X \subseteq VI$, $\phi[c/X]$ is defined in the expected way. If $\phi \in Bfun$ and $x, y \in VI$ the function $\phi[y/x] \in Bfun$ is given by $\phi[y/x](a) \stackrel{\mathrm{def}}{=} \phi\bigl(a\bigl[a(y)/x\bigr]\bigr)$, for each

$a \in Bval$. Boolean functions are constructed from the elementary functions corresponding to variables and by means of the usual logical connectives. Thus x denotes the Boolean function ϕ such that, for each $a \in Bval$, $\phi(a) = 1$ if and only if $a(x) = 1$. For $\phi_1, \phi_2 \in Bfun$, we write $\phi_1 \wedge \phi_2$ to denote the function ϕ such that, for each $a \in Bval$, $\phi(a) = 1$ if and only if both $\phi_1(a) = 1$ and $\phi_2(a) = 1$. A variable is restricted away using Schröder's elimination principle [21]: $\exists x \,.\, \phi \stackrel{\text{def}}{=} \phi[1/x] \vee \phi[0/x]$. Note that existential quantification is both monotonic and extensive on *Bfun*. The other Boolean connectives and quantifiers are handled similarly.

$Pos \subset Bfun$ consists precisely of those functions assuming the true value under the *everything-is-true* assignment, i.e., $Pos \stackrel{\text{def}}{=} \{ \phi \in Bfun \mid \phi(\mathbf{1}) = 1 \}$. For each $\phi \in Bfun$, the *positive part of* ϕ, denoted $\operatorname{pos}(\phi)$, is the strongest *Pos* formula that is entailed by ϕ. Formally, $\operatorname{pos}(\phi) \stackrel{\text{def}}{=} \phi \vee \bigwedge VI$.

For each $\phi \in Bfun$, the set of *variables necessarily true for* ϕ and the set of *variables necessarily false for* ϕ are given, respectively, by

$$\operatorname{true}(\phi) \stackrel{\text{def}}{=} \{ x \in VI \mid \forall a \in Bval : \phi(a) = 1 \implies a(x) = 1 \},$$

$$\operatorname{false}(\phi) \stackrel{\text{def}}{=} \{ x \in VI \mid \forall a \in Bval : \phi(a) = 1 \implies a(x) = 0 \}.$$

3 The Concrete Domain

A knowledge of the basic concepts of abstract interpretation theory [13,15] is assumed. In this paper, the concrete domain consists of pairs of the form (Σ, V), where V is a finite set of *variables of interest* and Σ is a (possibly infinite) set of substitutions in rational solved form.

Definition 4. (The concrete domain.) *Let* $\mathcal{D}^\flat \stackrel{\text{def}}{=} \wp(RSubst) \times \wp_f(Vars)$. *If* $(\Sigma, V) \in \mathcal{D}^\flat$, *then* (Σ, V) *represents the (possibly infinite) set of first-order formulas* $\{ \exists \Delta \,.\, \sigma \mid \sigma \in \Sigma, \Delta = \operatorname{vars}(\sigma) \setminus V \}$ *where* σ *is interpreted as the logical conjunction of the equations corresponding to its bindings. The operation of projecting* $x \in Vars$ *away from* $(\Sigma, V) \in \mathcal{D}^\flat$ *is defined as follows:*

$$\exists x \,.\, (\Sigma, V) \stackrel{\text{def}}{=} \left\{ \sigma' \in RSubst \;\middle|\; \begin{array}{l} \sigma \in \Sigma, \overline{V} = Vars \setminus V, \\ \mathcal{RT} \vdash \forall(\exists \overline{V} \,.\, (\sigma' \leftrightarrow \exists x \,.\, \sigma)) \end{array} \right\}.$$

The concrete element $(\{\{x \mapsto f(y)\}\}, \{x, y\})$ expresses a dependency between x and y. In contrast, $(\{\{x \mapsto f(y)\}\}, \{x\})$ only constrains x. The same concept can be expressed by saying that the variable name 'y' matters in the first case but not in the second. Thus the set of variables of interest is crucial for defining the meaning of the concrete and abstract descriptions. Despite this, always specifying the set of variables of interest would significantly clutter the presentation. Moreover, most of the needed functions on concrete and abstract descriptions preserve the set of variables of interest. For these reasons, we assume there exists a set $VI \in \wp_f(Vars)$ containing, at each stage of the analysis, the current variables of interest. As a consequence, when the context makes it clear, we will write $\Sigma \in \mathcal{D}^\flat$ as a shorthand for $(\Sigma, VI) \in \mathcal{D}^\flat$.

3.1 Operators on Substitutions in Rational Solved Form

There are cases when an analysis tries to capture properties of the particular substitutions computed by a specific rational unification algorithm. This is the case, for example, when the analysis needs to track structure sharing for the purpose of compile-time garbage collection, or provide upper bounds to the amount of memory needed to perform a given computation. More often the interest is on properties of the rational trees themselves. In these cases it is possible to define abstraction and concretization functions that are independent from the finite representations actually considered. Moreover, it is important that these functions precisely capture the properties under investigation so as to avoid any unnecessary precision loss.

Pursuing this goal requires the ability to observe properties of (infinite) rational trees while just dealing with one of their finite representations. This is not always an easy task since even simple properties can be "hidden" when using non-idempotent substitutions. For instance, when $\sigma^\infty(x) \in \mathit{GTerms} \setminus \mathit{HTerms}$ is an infinite and ground rational tree, all of its finite representations in *RSubst* will map the variable x into a finite term that is not ground.

These are the motivations behind the introduction of two computable operators on substitutions that will be used later to define the concretization functions for the considered abstract domains. First, the groundness operator 'gvars' captures the set of variables that are mapped to ground rational trees by 'σ^∞'. We define it by means of the *occurrence operator* 'occ' introduced in [16].

Definition 5. (Occurrence and groundness operators.) *For each* $n \in \mathbb{N}$, *the* occurrence function $\mathrm{occ}_n \colon \mathit{RSubst} \times \mathit{Vars} \to \wp_\mathrm{f}(\mathit{Vars})$ *is defined, for each* $\sigma \in \mathit{RSubst}$ *and each* $v \in \mathit{Vars}$, *by*

$$\mathrm{occ}_n(\sigma, v) \stackrel{\mathrm{def}}{=} \begin{cases} \{v\} \setminus \mathrm{dom}(\sigma), & \text{if } n = 0; \\ \{\, y \in \mathit{Vars} \mid \mathrm{vars}(y\sigma) \cap \mathrm{occ}_{n-1}(\sigma, v) \neq \varnothing \,\}, & \text{if } n > 0. \end{cases}$$

The occurrence operator $\mathrm{occ} \colon \mathit{RSubst} \times \mathit{Vars} \to \wp_\mathrm{f}(\mathit{Vars})$ *is given, for each substitution* $\sigma \in \mathit{RSubst}$ *and* $v \in \mathit{Vars}$, *by* $\mathrm{occ}(\sigma, v) \stackrel{\mathrm{def}}{=} \mathrm{occ}_\ell(\sigma, v)$, *where* $\ell = \#\sigma$.

The groundness operator $\mathrm{gvars} \colon \mathit{RSubst} \to \wp_\mathrm{f}(\mathit{Vars})$ *is given, for each substitution* $\sigma \in \mathit{RSubst}$, *by*

$$\mathrm{gvars}(\sigma) \stackrel{\mathrm{def}}{=} \{\, y \in \mathrm{dom}(\sigma) \mid \forall v \in \mathrm{vars}(\sigma) : y \notin \mathrm{occ}(\sigma, v) \,\}.$$

The finiteness operator 'hvars', introduced in [4], captures the set of variables that 'σ^∞' maps to finite terms.

Definition 6. (Finiteness operator.) *For each* $n \in \mathbb{N}$, *the* finiteness function $\mathrm{hvars}_n \colon \mathit{RSubst} \to \wp(\mathit{Vars})$ *is defined, for each* $\sigma \in \mathit{RSubst}$, *by*

$$\mathrm{hvars}_n(\sigma) \stackrel{\mathrm{def}}{=} \begin{cases} \mathit{Vars} \setminus \mathrm{dom}(\sigma), & \text{if } n = 0; \\ \mathrm{hvars}_{n-1}(\sigma) \cup \{\, y \in \mathrm{dom}(\sigma) \mid \mathrm{vars}(y\sigma) \subseteq \mathrm{hvars}_{n-1}(\sigma) \,\}, & \text{if } n > 0. \end{cases}$$

The finiteness operator hvars: *RSubst* $\rightarrow \wp(\mathit{Vars})$ *is given, for each substitution* $\sigma \in \mathit{RSubst}$*, by* $\mathrm{hvars}(\sigma) \stackrel{\mathrm{def}}{=} \mathrm{hvars}_\ell(\sigma)$*, where* $\ell \stackrel{\mathrm{def}}{=} \# \sigma$.

Example 7. Let

$$\sigma = \bigl\{x \mapsto f(y,z), y \mapsto g(z,x), z \mapsto f(a)\bigr\},$$
$$\tau = \bigl\{v \mapsto g(z,w), x \mapsto f(y), y \mapsto g(w), z \mapsto f(v)\bigr\},$$

where $\mathrm{vars}(\sigma) \cup \mathrm{vars}(\tau) = \{v,w,x,y,z\}$. Then $\mathrm{gvars}(\sigma) \cap \mathrm{vars}(\sigma) = \{x,y,z\}$ and $\mathrm{hvars}(\tau) \cap \mathrm{vars}(\tau) = \{w,x,y\}$.

The following proposition states how 'gvars' and 'hvars' behave with respect to the further instantiation of variables.

Proposition 8. *Let* $\sigma, \tau \in \mathit{RSubst}$*, where* $\tau \in \downarrow \sigma$*. Then*

$$\mathrm{hvars}(\sigma) \supseteq \mathrm{hvars}(\tau), \tag{8a}$$
$$\mathrm{gvars}(\sigma) \cap \mathrm{hvars}(\sigma) \subseteq \mathrm{gvars}(\tau) \cap \mathrm{hvars}(\tau). \tag{8b}$$

4 Finite-Tree Dependencies

Any finite-tree domain must keep track of those variables that are definitely bound to finite terms, since this is the final information delivered by the analysis. In [4] we have introduced the composite abstract domain $H \times P$, where the set of such variables is explicitly represented in the *finiteness component* H.

Definition 9. (The finiteness component H.**)** *The set* $H \stackrel{\mathrm{def}}{=} \wp(\mathit{VI})$*, partially ordered by reverse subset inclusion, is called* finiteness component. *The concretization function* $\gamma_H \colon H \rightarrow \wp(\mathit{RSubst})$ *is given, for each* $h \in H$*, by*

$$\gamma_H(h) \stackrel{\mathrm{def}}{=} \bigl\{\, \sigma \in \mathit{RSubst} \bigm| \mathrm{hvars}(\sigma) \supseteq h \,\bigr\}.$$

As proven in [3], equivalent substitutions in rational solved form have the same finiteness abstraction.

Proposition 10. *Let* $\sigma, \tau \in \mathit{RSubst}$*, where* $\sigma \in \gamma_H(h)$ *and* $\mathcal{RT} \vdash \forall(\sigma \leftrightarrow \tau)$*. Then* $\tau \in \gamma_H(h)$.

The precision of the finite-tree analysis of [4] is highly dependent on the precision of the generic component P. As explained before, the information provided by P on groundness, freeness, linearity, and sharing of variables is exploited, in the combination $H \times P$, to circumscribe as much as possible the creation and propagation of cyclic terms. However, finite-tree analysis can also benefit from other kinds of relational information. In particular, we now show how *finite-tree dependencies* allow to obtain a positive propagation of finiteness information.

Let us consider the finite terms $t_1 = f(x)$, $t_2 = g(y)$, and $t_3 = h(x,y)$: it is clear that, for each assignment of rational terms to x and y, t_3 is finite if and only if t_1 and t_2 are so. We can capture this by the Boolean formula $t_3 \leftrightarrow (t_1 \wedge t_2)$. The important point to notice is that this dependency will keep holding for any further simultaneous instantiation of t_1, t_2, and t_3. In other words, such dependencies are preserved by forward computations (which proceed by consistently instantiating program variables).

Consider $x \mapsto t \in \mathit{Bind}$ where $t \in \mathit{HTerms}$ and $\mathrm{vars}(t) = \{y_1, \ldots, y_n\}$. After this binding has been successfully applied, the destinies of x and t concerning term-finiteness are tied together: forever. This tie can be described by the dependency formula

$$x \leftrightarrow (y_1 \wedge \cdots \wedge y_n), \tag{2}$$

meaning that x will be bound to a finite term if and only if y_i is bound to a finite term, for each $i = 1, \ldots, n$. While the dependency expressed by (2) is a correct description of any computation state following the application of the binding $x \mapsto t$, it is not as precise as it could be. Suppose that x and y_k are indeed the same variable. Then (2) is logically equivalent to

$$x \rightarrow (y_1 \wedge \cdots \wedge y_{k-1} \wedge y_{k+1} \wedge \cdots \wedge y_n). \tag{3}$$

Correct: whenever x is bound to a finite term, all the other variables will be bound to finite terms. The point is that x has just been bound to a non-finite term, irrevocably: no forward computation can change this. Thus, the implication (3) holds vacuously. A more precise and correct description for the state of affairs caused by the cyclic binding is, instead, the negated atom $\neg x$, whose intuitive reading is "x is not (and never will be) finite."

We are building an abstract domain for finite-tree dependencies where we are making the deliberate choice of including only information that cannot be withdrawn by forward computations. The reason for this choice is that we want the concrete constraint accumulation process to be paralleled, at the abstract level, by another constraint accumulation process: logical conjunction of Boolean formulas. For this reason, it is important to distinguish between *permanent* and *contingent* information. Permanent information, once established for a program point p, maintains its validity in all points that follow p in any forward computation. Contingent information, instead, does not carry its validity beyond the point where it is established. An example of contingent information is given by the h component of $H \times P$: having $x \in h$ in the description of some program point means that x is definitely bound to a finite term *at that point*; nothing is claimed about the finiteness of x at later program points and, in fact, unless x is ground, x can still be bound to a non-finite term. However, if at some program point x is finite and ground, then x will remain finite. In this case we will ensure our Boolean dependency formula entails the positive atom x.

At this stage, we already know something about the abstract domain we are designing. In particular, we have positive and negated atoms, the requirement of describing program predicates of any arity implies that arbitrary conjunctions of these atomic formulas must be allowed and, finally, it is not difficult to observe that the merge-over-all-paths operations [13] will be logical disjunction, so that the domain will have to be closed under this operation. This means that the carrier of our domain must be able to express any Boolean function: *Bfun* is the carrier.

Definition 11. ($\gamma_F \colon \mathit{Bfun} \to \wp(\mathit{RSubst})$.) *The function* $\mathrm{hval} \colon \mathit{RSubst} \to \mathit{Bval}$ *is defined, for each* $\sigma \in \mathit{RSubst}$ *and each* $x \in \mathit{VI}$, *by*

$$\mathrm{hval}(\sigma)(x) = 1 \quad \stackrel{\mathrm{def}}{\iff} \quad x \in \mathrm{hvars}(\sigma).$$

The concretization function $\gamma_F \colon \mathit{Bfun} \to \wp(\mathit{RSubst})$ *is defined, for* $\phi \in \mathit{Bfun}$, *by*

$$\gamma_F(\phi) \stackrel{\mathrm{def}}{=} \bigl\{\, \sigma \in \mathit{RSubst} \bigm| \forall \tau \in {\downarrow}\sigma : \phi\bigl(\mathrm{hval}(\tau)\bigr) = 1 \,\bigr\}.$$

The following theorem shows how most of the operators needed to compute the concrete semantics of a logic program can be correctly approximated on the abstract domain *Bfun*.

Theorem 12. *Let* $\Sigma, \Sigma_1, \Sigma_2 \in \wp(\mathit{RSubst})$ *and* $\phi, \phi_1, \phi_2 \in \mathit{Bfun}$ *be such that* $\gamma_F(\phi) \supseteq \Sigma$, $\gamma_F(\phi_1) \supseteq \Sigma_1$, *and* $\gamma_F(\phi_2) \supseteq \Sigma_2$. *Let also* $(x \mapsto t) \in \mathit{Bind}$, *where* $\{x\} \cup \mathrm{vars}(t) \subseteq \mathit{VI}$. *Then the following hold:*

$$\gamma_F\Bigl(x \leftrightarrow \bigwedge \mathrm{vars}(t)\Bigr) \supseteq \bigl\{\{x \mapsto t\}\bigr\}; \tag{12a}$$

$$\gamma_F(\neg x) \supseteq \bigl\{\{x \mapsto t\}\bigr\}, \text{ if } x \in \mathrm{vars}(t); \tag{12b}$$

$$\gamma_F(x) \supseteq \bigl\{\, \sigma \in \mathit{RSubst} \bigm| x \in \mathrm{gvars}(\sigma) \cap \mathrm{hvars}(\sigma) \,\bigr\}; \tag{12c}$$

$$\gamma_F(\phi_1 \wedge \phi_2) \supseteq \bigl\{\, \mathrm{mgs}(\sigma_1 \cup \sigma_2) \bigm| \sigma_1 \in \Sigma_1, \sigma_2 \in \Sigma_2 \,\bigr\}; \tag{12d}$$

$$\gamma_F(\phi_1 \vee \phi_2) \supseteq \Sigma_1 \cup \Sigma_2; \tag{12e}$$

$$\gamma_F(\exists x \,.\, \phi) \supseteq \exists\!\!\!\exists x \,.\, \Sigma. \tag{12f}$$

Cases (12a), (12b), and (12d) of Theorem 12 ensure that the following definition of amgu_F provides a correct approximation on *Bfun* of the concrete unification of rational trees.

Definition 13. *The function* $\mathrm{amgu}_F \colon \mathit{Bfun} \times \mathit{Bind} \to \mathit{Bfun}$ *captures the effects of a binding on a finite-tree dependency formula. Let* $\phi \in \mathit{Bfun}$ *and* $(x \mapsto t) \in \mathit{Bind}$ *be such that* $\{x\} \cup \mathrm{vars}(t) \subseteq \mathit{VI}$. *Then*

$$\mathrm{amgu}_F(\phi, x \mapsto t) \stackrel{\mathrm{def}}{=} \begin{cases} \phi \wedge \bigl(x \leftrightarrow \bigwedge \mathrm{vars}(t)\bigr), & \text{if } x \notin \mathrm{vars}(t); \\ \phi \wedge \neg x, & \text{otherwise.} \end{cases}$$

Other semantic operators, such as the consistent renaming of variables, are very simple and, as usual, their approximation does not pose any problem.

The next result shows how finite-tree dependencies may improve the finiteness information encoded in the h component of the domain $H \times P$.

Theorem 14. *Let* $h \in H$ *and* $\phi \in \mathit{Bfun}$. *Let also* $h' \stackrel{\mathrm{def}}{=} \mathrm{true}\Bigl(\phi \wedge \bigwedge h\Bigr)$. *Then*

$$\gamma_H(h) \cap \gamma_F(\phi) = \gamma_H(h') \cap \gamma_F(\phi).$$

Example 15. Consider the following program, where it is assumed that the only "external" query is '?- r(X, Y)':

```
p(X, Y) :- X = f(Y, _).
q(X, Y) :- X = f(_, Y).
r(X, Y) :- p(X, Y), q(X, Y), acyclic_term(X).
```

Then the predicate p/2 in the clause defining r/2 will called with X and Y both unbound. Computing on the abstract domain $H \times P$ gives us the finiteness description $h_p = \{x, y\}$, expressing the fact that both X and Y are bound to finite terms. Computing on the finite-tree dependencies domain *Bfun*, gives us the Boolean formula $\phi_p = x \rightarrow y$ (Y is finite if X is so).

Considering now the call to the predicate q/2, we note that, since variable X is already bound to a non-variable term sharing with Y, all the finiteness information encoded by H will be lost (i.e., $h_q = \varnothing$). So, both X and Y are detected as possibly cyclic. However, the finite-tree dependency information is preserved, because $\phi_q = (x \rightarrow y) \wedge (x \rightarrow y) = x \rightarrow y$.

Finally, consider the effect of the abstract evaluation of acyclic_term(X). On the $H \times P$ domain we can only infer that variable X cannot be bound to an infinite term, while Y will be still considered as possibly cyclic, so that $h_r = \{x\}$. On the domain *Bfun* we can just confirm that the finite-tree dependency computed so far still holds, so that $\phi_r = x \rightarrow y$ (no stronger finite-tree dependency can be inferred, since the finiteness of X is only contingent). Thus, by applying the result of Theorem 14, we can recover the finiteness of Y:

$$h'_r = \mathrm{true}\Bigl(\phi_r \wedge \bigwedge h_r\Bigr) = \mathrm{true}\bigl((x \rightarrow y) \wedge x\bigr) = \{x, y\}.$$

Information encoded in $H \times P$ and *Bfun* is not completely orthogonal and the following result provides a kind of consistency check.

Theorem 16. *Let $h \in H$ and $\phi \in$ Bfun. Then*

$$\gamma_H(h) \cap \gamma_F(\phi) \neq \varnothing \quad \Longrightarrow \quad h \cap \mathrm{false}(\phi) = \varnothing.$$

Note however that, provided the abstract operators are correct, the computed descriptions will always be mutually consistent, unless $\phi = \bot$.

5 Groundness Dependencies

Since information about the groundness of variables is crucial for many applications, it is natural to consider a static analysis domain including both a finite-tree and a groundness component. In fact, any reasonably precise implementation of the parameter component P of the abstract domain specified in [4] will include some kind of groundness information. We highlight similarities, differences and connections relating the domain *Bfun* for finite-tree dependencies to the abstract domain *Pos* for groundness dependencies. Note that these results also hold when considering a combination of *Bfun* with the groundness domain *Def* [1].

Definition 17. ($\gamma_G\colon Pos \to \wp(RSubst)$.) *The function* gval: $RSubst \to Bval$ *is defined as follows, for each* $\sigma \in RSubst$ *and each* $x \in VI$:

$$\mathrm{gval}(\sigma)(x) = 1 \quad \stackrel{\mathrm{def}}{\iff} \quad x \in \mathrm{gvars}(\sigma).$$

The concretization function $\gamma_G\colon Pos \to \wp(RSubst)$ *is defined, for each* $\psi \in Pos$,

$$\gamma_G(\psi) \stackrel{\mathrm{def}}{=} \bigl\{\, \sigma \in RSubst \bigm| \forall \tau \in {\downarrow}\sigma : \psi\bigl(\mathrm{gval}(\tau)\bigr) = 1 \,\bigr\}.$$

Definition 18. *The function* $\mathrm{amgu}_G\colon Pos \times Bind \to Pos$ *captures the effects of a binding on a groundness dependency formula. Let* $\psi \in Pos$ *and* $(x \mapsto t) \in Bind$ *be such that* $\{x\} \cup \mathrm{vars}(t) \subseteq VI$. *Then*

$$\mathrm{amgu}_G(\psi, x \mapsto t) \stackrel{\mathrm{def}}{=} \psi \wedge \Bigl(x \leftrightarrow \bigwedge\bigl(\mathrm{vars}(t) \setminus \{x\}\bigr)\Bigr).$$

Note that this is a simple variant of the standard abstract unification operator for groundness analysis over finite-tree domains: the only difference concerns the case of cyclic bindings [2].

The next result shows how, by exploiting the finiteness component H, the finite-tree dependencies ($Bfun$) component and the groundness dependencies (Pos) component can improve each other.

Theorem 19. *Let* $h \in H$, $\phi \in Bfun$ *and* $\psi \in Pos$. *Let also* $\phi' \in Bfun$ *and* $\psi' \in Pos$ *be defined as* $\phi' = \exists VI \setminus h \,.\, \psi$ *and* $\psi' = \exists VI \setminus h \,.\, \mathrm{pos}(\phi)$. *Then*

$$\gamma_H(h) \cap \gamma_F(\phi) \cap \gamma_G(\psi) = \gamma_H(h) \cap \gamma_F(\phi) \cap \gamma_G(\psi \wedge \psi'); \tag{19a}$$

$$\gamma_H(h) \cap \gamma_F(\phi) \cap \gamma_G(\psi) = \gamma_H(h) \cap \gamma_F(\phi \wedge \phi') \cap \gamma_G(\psi). \tag{19b}$$

Moreover, even without any knowledge of the H component, combining Theorem 14 and Eq. (19a), the groundness dependencies component can be improved.

Corollary 20. *Let* $\phi \in Bfun$ *and* $\psi \in Pos$. *Then*

$$\gamma_F(\phi) \cap \gamma_G(\psi) = \gamma_F(\phi) \cap \gamma_G\bigl(\psi \wedge \mathrm{true}(\phi)\bigr).$$

The following example shows that, when computing on rational trees, finite-tree dependencies may provide groundness information that is not captured by the usual approaches.

Example 21. Consider the program:

```
p(a, Y).
p(X, a).
q(X, Y) :- p(X, Y), X = f(X, Z).
```

The abstract semantics of p/2, for both finite-tree and groundness dependencies, is $\phi_p = \psi_p = x \vee y$. The finite-tree dependency for q/2 is $\phi_q = (x \vee y) \wedge \neg x = \neg x \wedge y$. Using Definition 18, the groundness dependency for q/2 is

$$\psi_q = \exists z \,.\, \bigl((x \vee y) \wedge (x \leftrightarrow z)\bigr) = x \vee y.$$

This can be improved, using Corollary 20, to

$$\psi_q' = \psi_q \wedge \bigwedge \mathrm{true}(\phi_q) = y.$$

Since better groundness information, besides being useful in itself, may also improve the precision of many other analyses such as sharing [7,8], the reduction steps given by Theorem 19 and Corollary 20 can trigger improvements to the precision of other components. Theorem 19 can also be exploited to recover precision after the application of a widening operator on either the groundness dependencies or the finite-tree dependencies component.

6 Experimental Results

The work described here and in [4] has been experimentally evaluated in the framework provided by the CHINA analyzer [2]. We implemented and compared the three domains Pattern(P), Pattern($H \times P$) and Pattern($\mathit{Bfun} \times H \times P$),[1] where the parameter component P has been instantiated to the domain $\mathit{Pos} \times \mathit{SFL}$ [7] for tracking groundness, freeness, linearity and (non-redundant) set-sharing information. The Pattern($\cdot$) operator [5] further upgrades the precision of its argument by adding explicit structural information.

Concerning the *Bfun* component, the implementation was straightforward, since all the techniques described in [6] (and almost all the code, including the widenings) has been reused unchanged, obtaining comparable efficiency. As a consequence, most of the implementation effort was in the coding of the abstract operators on the H component and of the reduction processes between the different components. A key choice, in this sense, is 'when' the reduction steps given in Theorems 14 and 19 should be applied. When striving for maximum precision, a trivial strategy is to immediately perform reductions after any application of any abstract operator. For instance, this is how predicates like `acyclic_term/1` should be handled: after adding the variables of the argument to the H component, the reduction process is applied to propagate the new information to all domain components. However, such an approach turns out to be unnecessarily inefficient. In fact, the next result shows that Theorems 14 and 19 cannot lead to a precision improvement if applied just after the abstract evaluation of the merge-over-all-paths or the existential quantification operations (provided the initial descriptions are already reduced).

---

[1] For ease of notation, the domain names are shortened to P, H and Bfun, respectively.

Table 1. The precision on finite variables when using P, H and Bfun.

Prec. class	P	H	Bfun
$p = 100$	2	84	86
$80 \le p < 100$	1	31	36
$60 \le p < 80$	7	26	23
$40 \le p < 60$	6	41	40
$20 \le p < 40$	47	47	46
$0 \le p < 20$	185	19	17

Prec. improvement	P $\rightarrow$ H	H $\rightarrow$ Bfun
$i > 20$	185	4
$10 < i \le 20$	31	3
$5 < i \le 10$	11	6
$2 < i \le 5$	4	10
$0 < i \le 2$	2	24
no improvement	15	201

Theorem 22. *Let $x \in VI$, $h, h' \in H$ $\phi, \phi' \in Bfun$ and $\psi, \psi' \in Pos$. Let*

$$h_1 \stackrel{\text{def}}{=} h \cap h', \qquad \phi_1 \stackrel{\text{def}}{=} \phi \vee \phi', \qquad \psi_1 \stackrel{\text{def}}{=} \psi \vee \psi',$$
$$h_2 \stackrel{\text{def}}{=} h \cup \{x\}, \qquad \phi_2 \stackrel{\text{def}}{=} \exists x \,.\, \phi, \qquad \psi_2 \stackrel{\text{def}}{=} \exists x \,.\, \psi.$$

Let also

$$h \supseteq \operatorname{true}(\phi \wedge \bigwedge h), \qquad \phi \models (\exists VI \setminus h \,.\, \psi), \qquad \psi \models (\exists VI \setminus h \,.\, \operatorname{pos}(\phi)),$$
$$h' \supseteq \operatorname{true}(\phi' \wedge \bigwedge h'), \qquad \phi' \models (\exists VI \setminus h' \,.\, \psi'), \qquad \psi' \models (\exists VI \setminus h' \,.\, \operatorname{pos}(\phi')).$$

Then, for $i = 1, 2$,

$$h_i \supseteq \operatorname{true}(\phi_i \wedge \bigwedge h_i), \qquad \phi_i \models (\exists VI \setminus h_i \,.\, \psi_i), \qquad \psi_i \models (\exists VI \setminus h_i \,.\, \operatorname{pos}(\phi_i)).$$

We conjecture that Theorem 22 can be strengthened: the reduction process affecting the *Bfun* component, corresponding to Eq. (19b) of Theorem 19, seems to be useless also after the application of an abstract unification. In any case, this reduction process can be usefully exploited to recover precision after the application of a widening operator on the *Bfun* component.

A goal-dependent analysis was run for all the programs in our benchmark suite and the results (with respect to the precision) are summarized in Table 1. Here, the precision is measured as the percentage of the total number of variables that the analyser can show to be Herbrand. Two alternative views are provided.

In the first view, each column is labeled by an analysis domain and each row is labeled by a precision interval. For instance, the value '31' at the intersection of column 'H' and row '$80 \le p < 100$' is to be read as "*for 31 benchmarks, the percentage p of the total number of variables that the analyser can show to be Herbrand using the domain* H *is between 80% and 100%.*"

The second view provides a better picture of the precision *improvements* obtained when moving from P to H (in the column 'P $\rightarrow$ H') and from H to Bfun (in the column 'H $\rightarrow$ Bfun'). For instance, the value '10' at the intersection of column 'H $\rightarrow$ Bfun' and row '$2 < i \le 5$' is to be read as "*when moving from* H *to* Bfun, *for 10 benchmarks the improvement i in the percentage of the total number of variables shown to be Herbrand was between 2% and 5%.*"

It can be seen from Table 1 that, even though the H domain is remarkably precise, the inclusion of the *Bfun* component allows for a further, and sometimes significant, precision improvement for a number of benchmarks. It is worth noting that the current implementation of CHINA does not yet fully exploit the finite-tree dependencies arising when evaluating many of the built-in predicates, therefore incurring an avoidable precision loss. We are working on this issue and we expect that the specialised implementation of the abstract evaluation of some built-ins will result in more and better precision improvements. The experimentation has also shown that, in practice, the Bfun domain does not improve the groundness information.

7 Conclusion

Several modern logic-based languages offer a computation domain based on rational trees. On the one hand, the use of such trees is encouraged by the possibility of using efficient and correct unification algorithms and by an increase in expressivity. On the other hand, these gains are countered by the extra problems rational trees bring with themselves As a consequence, those applications that exploit rational trees tend to do so in a very controlled way, that is, most program variables can only be bound to finite terms. By detecting the program variables that may be bound to infinite terms with a good degree of accuracy, we can significantly reduce the disadvantages of using rational trees.

In [4], an initial solution to the problem was proposed where the composite abstract domain $H \times P$ allows to track the creation and propagation of infinite terms. Even though this information is crucial to any finite-tree analysis, propagating the guarantees of finiteness that come from several built-ins (including those that are explicitly provided to test term-finiteness) is also important. Therefore, in this paper we have introduced a domain of Boolean functions *Bfun* for finite-tree dependencies which, when coupled to the domain $H \times P$, can enhance its expressive power. Since *Bfun* has many similarities with the domain *Pos* used for groundness analysis, we have investigated how these two domains relate to each other and, in particular, the synergy arising from their combination in the "global" domain of analysis.

References

1. T. Armstrong, K. Marriott, P. Schachte, and H. Søndergaard. Two classes of Boolean functions for dependency analysis. *Science of Computer Programming*, 31(1):3–45, 1998.
2. R. Bagnara. *Data-Flow Analysis for Constraint Logic-Based Languages.* PhD thesis, Dipartimento di Informatica, Università di Pisa, Pisa, Italy, 1997. Printed as Report TD-1/97.
3. R. Bagnara, R. Gori, P. M. Hill, and E. Zaffanella. Finite-tree analysis for constraint logic-based languages. Quaderno 251, Dipartimento di Matematica, Università di Parma, 2001. Available at `http://www.cs.unipr.it/ bagnara/`.

4. R. Bagnara, R. Gori, P. M. Hill, and E. Zaffanella. Finite-tree analysis for constraint logic-based languages. In P. Cousot, editor, *Static Analysis: 8th International Symposium, SAS 2001*, volume 2126 of *Lecture Notes in Computer Science*, pages 165–184, Paris, France, 2001. Springer-Verlag, Berlin.
5. R. Bagnara, P. M. Hill, and E. Zaffanella. Efficient structural information analysis for real CLP languages. In M. Parigot and A. Voronkov, editors, *Proceedings of the 7th International Conference on Logic for Programming and Automated Reasoning (LPAR 2000)*, volume 1955 of *Lecture Notes in Computer Science*, pages 189–206, Réunion Island, France, 2000. Springer-Verlag, Berlin.
6. R. Bagnara and P. Schachte. Factorizing equivalent variable pairs in ROBDD-based implementations of *Pos*. In A. M. Haeberer, editor, *Proceedings of the "Seventh International Conference on Algebraic Methodology and Software Technology (AMAST'98)"*, volume 1548 of *Lecture Notes in Computer Science*, pages 471–485, Amazonia, Brazil, 1999. Springer-Verlag, Berlin.
7. R. Bagnara, E. Zaffanella, and P. M. Hill. Enhanced sharing analysis techniques: A comprehensive evaluation. In M. Gabbrielli and F. Pfenning, editors, *Proceedings of the 2nd International ACM SIGPLAN Conference on Principles and Practice of Declarative Programming*, pages 103–114, Montreal, Canada, 2000. Association for Computing Machinery.
8. M. Codish, H. Søndergaard, and P. J. Stuckey. Sharing and groundness dependencies in logic programs. *ACM Transactions on Programming Languages and Systems*, 21(5):948–976, 1999.
9. A. Colmerauer. Prolog and infinite trees. In K. L. Clark and S. Å. Tärnlund, editors, *Logic Programming, APIC Studies in Data Processing*, volume 16, pages 231–251. Academic Press, New York, 1982.
10. A. Colmerauer. Equations and inequations on finite and infinite trees. In *Proceedings of the International Conference on Fifth Generation Computer Systems (FGCS'84)*, pages 85–99, Tokyo, Japan, 1984. ICOT.
11. A. Cortesi, G. Filé, and W. Winsborough. *Prop* revisited: Propositional formula as abstract domain for groundness analysis. In *Proceedings, Sixth Annual IEEE Symposium on Logic in Computer Science*, pages 322–327, Amsterdam, The Netherlands, 1991. IEEE Computer Society Press.
12. A. Cortesi, B. Le Charlier, and P. Van Hentenryck. Combinations of abstract domains for logic programming: Open product and generic pattern construction. *Science of Computer Programming*, 38(1–3), 2000.
13. P. Cousot and R. Cousot. Abstract interpretation: A unified lattice model for static analysis of programs by construction or approximation of fixpoints. In *Proceedings of the Fourth Annual ACM Symposium on Principles of Programming Languages*, pages 238–252, 1977.
14. P. Cousot and R. Cousot. Abstract interpretation and applications to logic programs. *Journal of Logic Programming*, 13(2&3):103–179, 1992.
15. P. Cousot and R. Cousot. Abstract interpretation frameworks. *Journal of Logic and Computation*, 2(4):511–547, 1992.
16. P. M. Hill, R. Bagnara, and E. Zaffanella. Soundness, idempotence and commutativity of set-sharing. *Theory and Practice of Logic Programming*, 2001. To appear. Available at `http://arXiv.org/abs/cs.PL/0102030`.
17. B. Intrigila and M. Venturini Zilli. A remark on infinite matching vs infinite unification. *Journal of Symbolic Computation*, 21(3):2289–2292, 1996.
18. A. King. Pair-sharing over rational trees. *Journal of Logic Programming*, 46(1–2):139–155, 2000.

19. K. Marriott and H. Søndergaard. Notes for a tutorial on abstract interpretation of logic programs. North American Conference on Logic Programming, Cleveland, Ohio, USA, 1989.
20. K. Marriott and H. Søndergaard. Precise and efficient groundness analysis for logic programs. *ACM Letters on Programming Languages and Systems*, 2(1–4):181–196, 1993.
21. E. Schröder. *Der Operationskreis des Logikkalkuls.* B. G. Teubner, Leibzig, 1877.
22. H. Søndergaard. An application of abstract interpretation of logic programs: Occur check reduction. In B. Robinet and R. Wilhelm, editors, *Proceedings of the 1986 European Symposium on Programming*, volume 213 of *Lecture Notes in Computer Science*, pages 327–338. Springer-Verlag, Berlin, 1986.

How to Transform an Analyzer into a Verifier

Marco Comini[1], Roberta Gori[2], and Giorgio Levi[2]

[1] Dipartimento di Matematica e Informatica, Università di Udine, Udine, Italy.
[2] Dipartimento di Informatica, Università di Pisa, Pisa, Italy.

Abstract. In this paper we push forward the idea of applying the abstract interpretation concepts to the problem of verification of programs. We consider the theory of abstract verification as proposed in [5] and we show how it is possible to transform static analyzers with some suitable properties to obtain automatic verification tools based on sufficient verification conditions. We prove that the approach is general and flexible by showing three different verification tools based on different domains of types for functional, logic and *CLP* programming. The verifier for functional programs is obtained from a static analyzer which implements one of the polymorphic type domains introduced by Cousot [8]. The one for logic programs is obtained from a static analyzer on a type domain designed by Codish and Lagoon [3], while the verifier for *CLP* programs is obtained from the type analyzer described in [15].

1 Abstract Interpretation and Verification

Abstract interpretation [9,10] is a general theory for approximating the semantics of discrete dynamic systems, originally developed by Patrick and Radhia Cousot, in the late 70's, as a unifying framework for specifying and validating static program analyses. The *abstract semantics* is an approximation of the concrete one, where exact (concrete) properties are replaced by approximated properties, modeled by an abstract domain. The framework of abstract interpretation can be useful to study hierarchies of semantics and to reconstruct data-flow analysis methods. It can be used to prove the safety of an analysis algorithm. However, it can also be used to systematically derive "optimal" abstract semantics from the abstract domain.

From the very beginning, abstract interpretation was shown to be useful for the automatic generation of program invariants. More recently [11,13,7], it was shown to be very useful to understand, organize and synthesize proof methods for *program verification*. In particular, we are interested in one specific approach to the generation of abstract interpretation-based partial correctness conditions [19,22], which is used also in abstract debugging [1,6,2].

The aim of verification is to define conditions which allow us to formally prove that a program behaves as expected, i.e., that the program is correct w.r.t. a given specification, a description of the program's expected behavior. In order to formally prove that a program behaves as expected, we can use a semantic approach based on abstract interpretation techniques. This approach allows us

R. Nieuwenhuis and A. Voronkov (Eds.): LPAR 2001, LNAI 2250, pp. 595–609, 2001.

to derive in a uniform way sufficient conditions for proving partial correctness w.r.t. different properties.

Assume we have a semantic evaluation function $\mathcal{T}_P$ on a concrete domain $(\mathbb{C}, \sqsubseteq)$, whose least fixpoint $\mathrm{lfp}_{\mathbb{C}}(\mathcal{T}_P)$ is the semantics of the program P. The ideas behind this approach are the following.

- As in standard abstract interpretation based program analysis, the class of properties we want to verify is formalized as an abstract domain $(\mathbb{A}, \leq)$, related to $(\mathbb{C}, \sqsubseteq)$ by the usual Galois connection $\alpha : \mathbb{C} \to \mathbb{A}$ and $\gamma : \mathbb{A} \to \mathbb{C}$ (abstraction and concretization functions). The corresponding *abstract semantic evaluation function* $\mathcal{T}_P^{\alpha}$ is systematically derived from $\mathcal{T}_P$, α and γ. The resulting abstract semantics $\mathrm{lfp}_{\mathbb{A}}(\mathcal{T}_P^{\alpha})$ is a correct approximation of the concrete semantics by construction, i.e., $\alpha(\mathrm{lfp}_{\mathbb{C}}(\mathcal{T}_P)) \leq \mathrm{lfp}_{\mathbb{A}}(\mathcal{T}_P^{\alpha})$, and no additional "correctness" theorems need to be proved.
- An element $\mathcal{S}_\alpha$ of the domain $(\mathbb{A}, \leq)$ is the specification, i.e., the abstraction of the intended concrete semantics.
- The *partial correctness* of a program P w.r.t. a specification $\mathcal{S}_\alpha$ can be expressed as

$$\alpha(\mathrm{lfp}_{\mathbb{C}}(\mathcal{T}_P)) \leq \mathcal{S}_\alpha. \tag{1}$$

- Since condition (1) requires the computation of the concrete fixpoint semantics, this condition is not effectively computable. Then, we can prove instead the condition

$$\mathrm{lfp}_{\mathbb{A}}(\mathcal{T}_P^{\alpha}) \leq \mathcal{S}_\alpha \tag{2}$$

  which implies partial correctness. Note that the new verification condition does not require the computation of the concrete fixpoint semantics. However an abstract fixpoint computation is still needed.
- A simpler condition, which is the abstract version of the Park's *fixpoint induction* condition [20], is *sufficient* for (2) and, therefore, for partial correctness to hold,

$$\mathcal{T}_P^{\alpha}(\mathcal{S}_\alpha) \leq \mathcal{S}_\alpha. \tag{3}$$

Following the above approach, we can define a verification framework parametric with respect to the (abstract) property we want to model. Given a specific property, the corresponding verification conditions are systematically derived from the framework and guaranteed to be indeed sufficient partial correctness conditions.

An important result is that, following our abstract interpretation approach, the issue of completeness of a verification method can be addressed in terms of properties of the chosen abstract interpretation. In general, in fact, given an inductive proof method, if a program is correct with respect to a specification $\mathcal{S}$ (i.e., if (1) is satisfied) the sufficient condition (3) might not hold for $\mathcal{S}$. However, if the method is *complete*, then when the program is correct with respect to $\mathcal{S}$,

```
let rec f f1 g n x = if n=0 then g(x)
       else f(f1)(function x -> (function h -> g(h(x)))) (n-1)
```

Fig. 1. The recursive function f.

there exists a property $\mathcal{X}$, stronger than $\mathcal{S}$, which verifies the sufficient condition. [19,22] proved that the method is complete if and only if the abstraction is *precise* with respect to $\mathcal{T}_P$, that is if $\alpha(\text{lfp}_{\mathbb{C}}(\mathcal{T}_P)) = \text{lfp}_{\mathbb{A}}(\mathcal{T}_P^{\alpha})$. This approach allows us to use some standard methods (see for example [18]), which allow us to systematically enrich a domain of properties so as to obtain an abstraction which is *fully precise* ($\alpha \cdot F = F^{\alpha} \cdot \alpha$) w.r.t. a given function F. Since full precision w.r.t. the semantic function $\mathcal{T}_P$ implies precision with respect to $\mathcal{T}_P$, these methods can be viewed as the basis for the systematic development of complete proof methods.

2 Sufficient Verification Conditions

As we have already pointed out, trying to prove condition (1) leads to a non-effective verification method. This is due to the fact that (1) requires the computation of the concrete fixpoint semantics, which, in general, is not effective. A verification method based on condition (2) is effective only if the abstract domain is Noetherian or otherwise if we use widening operators to ensure the termination of the computation of the abstract fixpoint semantics. This is the approach adopted, for example, in the verifier of the Ciao Prolog Development System [1].

Even if the methods based on condition (2) may seem stronger than the methods based on condition (3), this is not always the case. When the domain is non-Noetherian the use of widening operators leads to an unavoidable loss of precision, which, in some case, makes condition (2) weaker than condition (3). We will show an example of this in the case of the polymorphic type domain for functional languages considered in Section 3.2. In particular we will show that, using a verification method based on condition (2) with the ML widening, it is not possible to prove that the function in Figure 1 has type $(\text{`}a \to \text{`}a) \to (\text{`}a \to \text{`}b) \to int \to \text{`}a \to \text{`}b$ while it is possible using condition (3). Moreover, even when the abstract domain is Noetherian, the computation of the abstract fixpoint semantics may be very expensive.

On the contrary, the inductive verification method based on (sufficient) condition (3) does not require the computation of fixpoints. Therefore proving $\mathcal{T}_P^{\alpha}(\mathcal{S}_\alpha) \leq \mathcal{S}_\alpha$ is, in general, not expensive even for complex abstract domains. Moreover, when the function $\mathcal{T}_P^{\alpha}$ can be viewed as the union of functions $\mathcal{T}_c^{\alpha}$ defined on the primitive components of a program, using condition (3) has another advantage. Proving condition $\mathcal{T}_P^{\alpha}(\mathcal{S}_\alpha) \leq \mathcal{S}_\alpha$ boils down to verifying $\mathcal{T}_c^{\alpha}(\mathcal{S}_\alpha) \leq \mathcal{S}_\alpha$

[1] Available at URL: ⟨`http://www.clip.dia.fi.upm.es/Software/Ciao/`⟩.

for every c of P. In this case, this allows us to prove (3) *compositionally*. For example, in logic programming the condition $\mathcal{T}_P^\alpha(\mathcal{S}_\alpha) \leq \mathcal{S}_\alpha$ can be verified by proving for each clause $c \in P$, $\mathcal{T}_{\{c\}}^\alpha(\mathcal{S}_\alpha) \leq \mathcal{S}_\alpha$. This approach is also useful for abstract debugging [6]. If, in the compositional proof of $\mathcal{T}_P^\alpha(\mathcal{S}_\alpha) \leq \mathcal{S}_\alpha$ we fail in the program component c, there is a possible bug in c.

For all the above reasons, we consider verification methods based on condition (3). Therefore, in order to derive effective verification methods we need to choose an abstract domain $(\mathbb{A}, \leq)$ where

- the intended abstract behavior (specification) $\mathcal{S}_\alpha \in \mathbb{A}$ has a finite representation;
- $\leq$ is a decidable relation.

This allows us to use, in addition to all the Noetherian abstract domains used in static analysis, non-Noetherian domains (such as polymorphic type domains for functional languages), which lead to finite abstract semantics, and finite representations of properties.

Hence, every time we have a static analysis computed by a fixpoint abstract semantics operator, we can systematically realize a verifier based on conditions (3). We only need to realize the $\leq$ operation on the abstract domain $\mathbb{A}$. The verifier is a tool which applies once the abstract fixpoint semantic operator to the user specification $\mathcal{S}_\alpha \in \mathbb{A}$ and verifies that the result is indeed $\leq \mathcal{S}_\alpha$.

In this paper we show how easy this process can be by showing three different examples. All verification tools we will present here are obtained by starting from static analyzers defined on type domains. We prove that our approach is very general and flexible by defining verifications tools for three different paradigms: Functional, Logic and Constraint Logic Programming. In particular, the verification tool for functional programming, presented in Section 3, is obtained from a static analyzer which implements one of the polymorphic type domains introduced by Cousot in [8]. The verification tool for logic programming, presented in Section 4, is obtained from a static analyzer on a type domain designed by Codish and Lagoon [3]. Finally, the verifier for *CLP* programs, presented in Section 5, is obtained starting from the type analyzer described in [15].

3 Type Inference in Higher Order Functional Languages

As we will show in the following, the "higher-order types" abstract domain is non-Noetherian. This is therefore a typical case of application of our approach based on the effective sufficient condition (3), which does not require fixpoint computations.

Our language is a small variation of untyped λ-calculus as considered in [8]. [8] shows that several known type systems and corresponding type inference algorithms can systematically be derived from (the collecting version of) a concrete denotational semantics. The main advantage of the abstract interpretation approach to type inference is that the type abstract interpreters are correct, by construction, w.r.t. the concrete semantics. This means that "the type of the concrete value computed by the concrete semantics is in general more precise than the type computed by the type abstract interpreter". As it is often the case with abstract interpretation, approximation is introduced by abstract computations. By looking at the relation between the concrete semantics and the abstract interpreters, we can reason about the relative precision of different type inference algorithms.

The traditional point of view of type systems is quite different, since type inference is viewed as an extension of syntactic analysis. Namely, the (concrete) semantics is only defined for those programs which can be typed. Traditional type inference algorithms do also introduce approximation. However this cannot be directly related to a concrete semantics, because the latter is based on the result of type inference. The result is that there exist programs which cannot be typed, yet would have a well-defined concrete semantics, i.e., there exist non-typable programs which would never go wrong, if provided with a concrete semantics with " dynamic" type checking. Let us look at a couple of examples, where we use the ML syntax. The ML expression (taken from [8])

```
let rec f f1 g n x = if n=0 then g(x)
     else f(f1)(function x -> (function h -> g(h(x)))) (n-1) x f1
          in f (function x -> x+1) (function x -> x+1) 10 5;;
This expression has type ('a -> 'a) -> 'b but is here used with type 'b.
```

which is an application of the function f of Figure 1, cannot be typed by the Damas-Milner's algorithm [8]. By using a concrete semantics with "dynamic" type checking, we would obtain a correct concrete result (`-: int=16`).

The expression is indeed a type correct application of the function $f\ f_1\ g\ n\ x = g(f_1^n(x))$ which has the type $(`a \rightarrow `a) \rightarrow (`a \rightarrow `b) \rightarrow int \rightarrow `a \rightarrow `b$. As we will see in the following, the function cannot be typed by the Damas-Milner's algorithm, because of an approximation related to recursive functions. The same approximation does not allow the Damas-Milner's algorithm to type the expression

```
# let rec f x = x and g x = f (1+x) in f f 2;;
This expression has type int -> int but is here used with type int
```

Because of the approximation related to the "syntactic" mutual recursion, the type assigned to f is $int \rightarrow int$ rather than $`a \rightarrow `a$. Again a concrete semantics with dynamic type checking, would compute a correct concrete result (`-: int=2`). The abstract interpreter considered in the next section, succeeds in correctly typing the above expressions and is, therefore, more precise than the Damas-Milner's algorithm.

3.1 A Type Abstract Interpreter

Following the approach in [8], we have developed (and implemented in OCAML [21]) several abstract interpreters for inferring principal types, represented as Herbrand terms with variables, for various notions of types (monomorphic types à la Hindley, let polymorphism and polymorphic recursion).

For the current presentation we will represent programs using the syntax of ML. Since we will sometimes compare our results with those obtained by the Damas-Milner's algorithm, we will just consider the let-polymorphic abstract interpreter [2], which corresponds to the ML type system.

The language has one basic type only: *int*. Types are Herbrand terms, built with the basic type *int*, variables and the (functional) type constructor $\rightarrow$.

The actual domain of the abstract interpreter is more complex, and contains explicitly quantified terms and constraints. For the sake of our discussion, abstract values will simply be (equivalence classes under variable renaming of) terms. The partial order relation is the usual instantiation relation, i.e., $t_1 \leq t_2$ if t_2 is an instance of t_1. Note that the resulting abstract domain is non-Noetherian since there exist infinite ascending chains.

Our let-polymorphic type interpreter turns out to be essentially equivalent to the Damas-Milner's algorithm, with one important difference, related to the abstract semantics of recursive functions. Such a semantics should in principle require a least fixpoint computation. However since the domain is non-Noetherian, the fixpoint cannot, in general, be reached in finitely many iterations. The problem is solved in the Damas-Milner's algorithm, by using a widening operator (based on unification) after the first iteration. Widening operators [12] give an upper approximation of the least fixpoint and guarantee termination by introducing further approximation. We apply the same widening operator after k iterations. This allows us to get often the least fixpoint and, in any case, to achieve a better precision.

The "let" and "let rec" constructs are handled as "declarations"; the abstract semantic evaluation function for declarations has the following type $semd : declaration \rightarrow env \rightarrow int \rightarrow env$, where *env* is the domain of abstract environments, which associates types to identifiers and the integer parameter is used to control the approximation of the widening operator.

We now show the analysis of a recursive function *pi* which computes $\prod_{n=a}^{n=b} f(n)$. The result is an environment where the function identifier *pi* is bound to its inferred type.

```
# semd (let rec pi f a b =
     if (a - (b +1) = 0) then 1 else (f a) * (pi f (a +1) b))[] 0;;
 - : env = [ pi <- (int -> int) -> int -> int -> int ]
```

Consider now the recursive function f in Figure 1. The evaluation of the abstract semantic evaluation function *semd* with the control parameter set to 0, gives us the result of the Damas-Milner's algorithm, i.e., f cannot be typed.

```
# semd(let rec f f1 g n x = if n=0 then g(x)
    else f(f1)(function x -> (function h ->g(h(x)))) (n-1) x f1) [] 0;;
- : env = [ f <- Notype ]
```

[2] The abstract syntax of the language, together with the concrete semantics, the implementation of the abstract domain and the resulting abstract interpreter can be found at ⟨`http://www.di.unipi.it/ levi/typesav/pagina1.html`⟩.

However, the application of *semd* with the control parameter set to 3 computes the (following) right type for f, which is indeed the least fixpoint.

```
# semd(let rec f f1 g n x = if n=0 then g(x)
    else f(f1)(function x -> (function h -> g(h(x)))) (n-1) x f1)[] 3;;
- : env = [ f <- ('a -> 'a) -> ('a -> 'b) -> int -> 'a -> 'b ]
```

When the control parameter to -1, the system will try to compute the least fixpoint without using the widening operator.

3.2 From the Type Interpreter to the Type Verifier

Once we have the abstract semantic evaluation function *semd*, we can easily use it for program verification, by taking an abstract environment as specification (abstraction of the intended semantics). Assume we want to verify a declaration d w.r.t. a specification S, by "implementing" the sufficient condition (3) ($\mathcal{T}_P^\alpha(\mathcal{S}_\alpha) \leq \mathcal{S}_\alpha$) where, $\leq$ is the lifting to abstract environments of the partial order relation on terms. The application of the abstract semantic evaluation to the specification can be implemented as follows:

1. if $d = (let\ f = e)$ is the declaration of a non recursive function f, *semd d s k* returns a new environment S', where f is bound to the type computed by assuming that all the global names have the types given in the specification.
2. if $d = (let\ rec\ f = e)$ is a declaration of a recursive function f, *semd* $(let\ f = e)\ s\ k$ returns a new environment S', where f is bound to the type computed, by assuming that all the global names *and* f have the types given in the specification. In other words, we take the type for f given in the specification and we evaluate once the body of the recursive function, to get a new type for f. Note that we abstractly execute the recursive function body just once and we do not compute the fixpoint. Note also that the control parameter is possibly used only for approximating fixpoints corresponding to recursive functions occurring within e.

We are then left with the problem of establishing whether $S' \leq S$. Since S' can only be different from S in the denotation of f, we can just show that $S(f)$ is an instance of $S'(f)$. The verification method can then be implemented by a function *checkd* : *declaration* $\rightarrow$ *specification* $\rightarrow$ *int* $\rightarrow$ *bool* consisting of three lines of ML code.

It is worth noting that *checkd* allow us to verify a program consisting of a list of function declarations in a modular way. Each declaration is verified in a separate step, by using the specification for determining the types of global identifiers.

We have also implemented the verification condition (2) ($\mathrm{lfp}_{\mathbb{A}}(\mathcal{T}_P^\alpha) \leq \mathcal{S}_\alpha$) by an even simpler ML function *checkdf* : *declarationlist* $\rightarrow$ *type* $\rightarrow$ *int* $\rightarrow$ *bool*, which requires the computation of the abstract semantics (and therefore needs a closed program, i.e., a list of declarations). The specification $\mathcal{S}_\alpha$ is now the intended type of the last identifier in the list. In the following section we show and discuss some examples.

3.3 Examples

We show now two examples of verification (through *checkd*) of *pi*: in the second example, the verification fails since the type given in the specification is too general.

```
# checkd (let rec pi f a b =  if (a - (b +1) = 0) then 1 else
  (f a) * (pi f (a +1) b))[ pi <- (int -> int) -> int -> int -> int ] 0;;
- : bool = true
# checkd (let rec pi f a b = if (a - (b +1) = 0) then 1 else
  (f a) * (pi f (a +1) b))[ pi <- ('a -> 'a) -> 'a -> 'a -> 'a ] 0;;
- : bool = false
```

We can consider also the verification of the traditional identity function *id*. Note that *id* is also correct w.r.t. a specification which is an instance of the correct principal type.

```
# checkd (let id x = x)[ id <- 'a -> 'a ] 0;;
- : bool = true
# checkd (let id x = x)[ id <- int -> int ] 0;;
- : bool = true
```

Now we verify a function, which is intended to compute the factorial and which is defined by a suitable composition of *pi* and *id*. In the verification, we use the specification rather than the semantics for *pi* and *id*.

```
# checkd (let fact = pi id 1)  [ pi <- (int->int)->int->int->int;
    id <- 'a -> 'a; fact <- int -> int ] 0;;
- : bool = true
```

If we use *checkdf* rather than *checkd*, we need to provide the complete set of declarations. Note that if we use a wrong definition for *id*, this turns out as an error in *fact*.

```
# checkdf [let id x = x; let rec pi f a b = if (a - (b +1) = 0) then 1
  else (f a) * (pi f (a +1) b));let rec fact = pi id 1] (int-> int) 0;;
- : bool = true
# checkdf [let id x y= x; let rec pi f a b =  if (a - (b +1) = 0) then 1
  else (f a) * (pi f (a +1) b)); let rec fact = pi id 1] (int-> int) 0;;
- : bool = false
```

Now we show an example involving polymorphism, where two occurrences of the polymorphic function *id* take different instances of the type in the specification.

```
# checkd (let g = id id)  [ id <- 'a -> 'a; g <- 'b -> 'b ] 0;;
- : bool = true
# checkd (let g = id id) [ id <- 'a -> 'a; g <- ('b->'b)->('b->'b) ] 0;;
- : bool = true
```

In Figure 2 we consider again the recursive function f of Figure 1. We now show that if we use the verification condition defined by *checkdf* (with widening

```
# checkdf[let rec f f1 g n x = if n=0 then g(x)
    else f(f1)(function x -> (function h -> g(h(x)))) (n-1)  x f1]
        ( ('a -> 'a) -> ('a -> 'b) -> int -> 'a -> 'b ) 0;;
- : bool = false
# checkd(let rec f f1 g n x = if n=0 then g(x)
    else f(f1)(function x -> (function h -> g(h(x)))) (n-1) x f1)
          [ f <- ('a -> 'a) -> ('a -> 'b) -> int -> 'a -> 'b ] 0;;
- : bool = true
```

Fig. 2. Verification of the recursive function f.

```
# checkd(let rec f f1 g n x = if n=0 then g(x)
    else f(f1)(function x -> (function h -> g(h(x)))) (n-1) x f1)
       [ f <- (int -> int) -> (int -> int) -> int -> int -> int ] 0;;
- : bool = false
# checkdf[let rec f f1 g n x = if n=0 then g(x)
    else f(f1)(function x -> (function h -> g(h(x)))) (n-1) x f1]
       ((int -> int) -> (int -> int) -> int -> int -> int ) (-1);;
- : bool = true
# checkd(let g = (let rec f f1 g n x = if n=0 then g(x)
    else f(f1)(function x -> (function h -> g(h(x)))) (n-1) x f1
       in f)(function x -> x + 1))
          [ g <- (int -> int) -> int -> int -> int ] (-1);;
- : bool = true
```

Fig. 3. Verification of the recursive function f.

control parameter set to 0), we fail in establishing the correctness w.r.t. the principal type (since, as we have already shown, the Damas-Milner's algorithm fails). On the contrary, the verification condition defined by *checkd* succeeds.

In Figure 3, we show some aspects related to the incompleteness of the verification method defined by *checkd*, still in the case of the function f of Figure 2. In fact, *checkd* fails to establishing the correctness of f w.r.t. a specification in which all the variables in the principal type are instantiated to *int*. If we use the stronger verification method, based on the computation of the fixpoint (condition (2), without widening), we succeed. The last example shows that if we verify a specific application of f, we succeed again even with *checkd*, because the recursive definition, being inside a declaration, leads anyway to a fixpoint computation.

Let us finally consider the issue of termination. The recursive function in the first example of Figure 4 is not typed by ML. If we try to verify it w.r.t. a specification assigning to it the type $`a \rightarrow `a$, we correctly fail by using both the verification method based on condition (3) and the verification method based on condition (2) with widening. If we apply the condition (2) without widening, the verification process does not terminate.

```
# let rec f x = f;;
This expression has type 'a -> 'b but is here used with type 'b
# checkd (let rec f x = f) [ f <- 'a -> 'a ] 0;;
- : bool = false
# checkdf [let rec f x = f] ('a -> 'a ) 10;;
- : bool = false
# checkdf [let rec f x = f] ('a -> 'a ) (-1);;
Interrupted.
```

Fig. 4. Verification of the non terminating function f.

4 Type Verification in Logic Languages

In this section we will show an example of transformation of an analyzer for logic programming into a verifier. As in the case of functional programming we will consider an abstract domain of types. This domain of types for logic programming was introduced in [3]. In order to formally introduce it, we have first to define the abstraction from concrete terms to type terms. Type terms in this domain are associative, commutative and idempotent. They are built using a binary set constructor + and a collection of *monomorphic* and *polymorphic* description symbols. The monomorphic symbols are constants (e.g. $num/0$, $nil/0$) and the polymorphic symbols are unary (e.g. $list/1$). Intuitively, the description symbols represent sets of function symbols in the corresponding concrete alphabet. For example, the description symbol *list* might be defined to represent the $cons/2$ symbol in the concrete alphabet and the description symbol *num* might represent the symbols 0, 1, etc. The abstraction function is defined by induction on terms:

$$\tau(t) := \begin{cases} X & \text{if } t \text{ is the variable } X \\ num & \text{if } t \text{ is a number} \\ nil & \text{if } t = [\,] \\ list(\tau(t_1)) + \tau(t_2) & \text{if } t = [t_1|t_2] \\ other & \text{otherwise} \end{cases}$$

Thus, the abstractions of terms $[-3, 0, 7]$, $[X, Y]$ and $[X|Y]$ are $list(num) + nil$, $list(X) + list(Y) + nil$ and $list(X) + Y$ respectively.

Abstract atoms are simply built with abstract terms, and $\tau(p(t_1, \dots, t_n)) := p(\tau(t_1), \dots, \tau(t_n))$. Our abstract domain will be the types domain $\mathcal{D}_\tau$, which is the power-set of abstract atoms ordered by set inclusion.

4.1 From the Type Analyzer to the Type Verifier

We have already discussed how, once we have the abstract semantic evaluation function $\mathcal{T}_P^\alpha$, we can easily define a verification method based on condition (3). Actually, depending on the chosen evaluation function $\mathcal{T}_P^\alpha$, we can prove partial correctness of a program w.r.t. different properties. For example, we can prove that a program P is correct w.r.t. the intended types of the successful atoms or w.r.t. the intended types of the computed answers and so on. More concrete the semantic evaluation functions lead to stronger verification methods. Here, in order to show some interesting examples we consider a very strong method: the *I/O and call correctness* method *over the type domain.* It is obtained by instantiating the $\mathcal{T}_P^\alpha$ semantic evaluation function of condition (3) with an abstract semantic operator which is able to model the functional type dependencies between the initial and the resulting bindings for the variables of the goal *plus* information on call patterns. Specifications are therefore pairs of pre and post conditions, which describe the intended input-output type dependencies. They are formalized as partial functions from *GAtoms* (the set of all generic atoms) to the domain $\mathcal{D}_\tau$ (denoted by $\mathbb{A}_\tau := [GAtoms \rightharpoonup \mathcal{D}_\tau]$) and are ordered by $\sqsubseteq$, the pointwise extension of $\subseteq$ on $\mathbb{A}_\tau$.

Proving condition (3) guarantees that for every procedure the post condition holds whenever the pre conditions are satisfied and that the pre conditions are satisfied by all the procedure calls. It is worth noting that the verification conditions, obtained in this case from condition (3) are a slight generalization of the ones defined by the Drabent-Maluszynski method [14].

We have developed a prototype verifier [3] which is able to test our verification conditions on the types domain. The verifier is obtained by using the existing abstract operations defined in the type analyzer implemented by Lagoon [4]. The verification method can then be implemented by a function *verifyIOcall* : *clause* $\rightarrow$ *InputSpec* $\rightarrow$ *OutputSpec* $\rightarrow$ *bool* consisting in several Prolog predicates which implement condition (3) in case of a $\mathcal{T}_P^\alpha$ function which models the type dependencies of *I/O and call pattern* [5]. The code turns out to essentially compute ACI-unification between the abstractions of the atoms of a clause and all the matching items of the specification. Since the $\sqsubseteq$ operation on $\mathbb{A}_\tau$ is the pointwise extension of subset inclusion, the resulting set (which is necessarily finite) is then checked to be a subset of the specification.

In the following section we show and discuss some examples.

4.2 Examples

The `queens` program of Figure 5 is proved to be correct w.r.t. the following intended specification w.r.t. the type domain $\mathbb{A}_\tau$.

As we have already pointed out, the verification method based on condition (3) is *compositional.* Therefore, in order to perform the I/O and call correctness verification, we apply the predicate *verifyIOcall* to the clause to be verified and to the pre-post program specifications (both given as lists of type atoms). In this way, if the predicate *verifyIOcall* returns *false* we can have a hint

[3] Available at URL:
⟨`http://www.dimi.uniud.it/ comini/ Projects/PolyTypesVerifier/`⟩.

[4] Available at URL:
⟨`http://www.cs.bgu.ac.il/ mcodish/ Software/aci-types-poly.tgz`⟩.

```
c1:     queens(X,Y) :- perm(X,Y), safe(Y).
c2: perm([],[]).
c3: perm([X|Y],[V|Res]) :- delete(V,[X|Y],Rest), perm(Rest,Res).
c4: delete(X,[X|Y],Y).
c5: delete(X,[F|T],[F|R]) :- delete(X,T,R).
c6: safe([]).
c7: safe([X|Y]) :- noattack(X,Y,1), safe(Y).
c8: noattack(X,[],N).
c9: noattack(X,[F|T],N) :- X =\= F, X =\= F + N, F =\= X + N,
                           N1 is N + 1, noattack(X,T,N1).
```

Fig. 5. The queens program

$$\mathcal{S}^I_\tau := \begin{cases} queens(X,Y) & \mapsto \{queens(nil + list(num), T), queens(nil, T)\} \\ perm(X,Y) & \mapsto \{perm(nil + list(num), T), perm(nil, T)\} \\ delete(X,Y) & \mapsto \{delete(T, nil + list(num), U), delete(T, nil, U)\} \\ safe(X,Y) & \mapsto \{safe(nil + list(num)), safe(nil)\} \\ noattack(X,Y,Z) & \mapsto \left\{ \begin{array}{l} noattack(num, nil, num), \\ noattack(num, nil + list(num), num) \end{array} \right\} \end{cases}$$

$$\mathcal{S}^O_\tau := \begin{cases} queens(X,Y) & \mapsto \left\{ \begin{array}{l} queens(nil, nil), \\ queens(nil + list(num), nil + list(num)) \end{array} \right\} \\ perm(X,Y) & \mapsto \left\{ \begin{array}{l} perm(nil, nil), \\ perm(nil + list(num), nil + list(num)) \end{array} \right\} \\ delete(X,Y) & \mapsto \left\{ \begin{array}{l} delete(num, nil + list(num), nil), \\ delete(num, nil + list(num), nil + list(num)) \end{array} \right\} \\ safe(X,Y) & \mapsto \{safe(nil + list(num)), safe(nil)\} \\ noattack(X,Y,Z) & \mapsto \left\{ \begin{array}{l} noattack(num, nil, num), \\ noattack(num, nil + list(num), num) \end{array} \right\} \end{cases}$$

on the clause that may be wrong. In the following, for the sake of readability, we have chosen to skip the specification arguments in the calls to the tool (except for the first). We can now prove that the queens program is correct w.r.t. the I/O and call correctness conditions.

```
| ?- verifyIOcall( (queens(X,Y) :- perm(X,Y), safe(Y)),
   [queens(nil+list(num),U), queens(nil,U),
    perm(nil+list(num),U), perm(nil,U), safe(nil+list(num)), safe(nil),
    delete(T,nil+list(num),U), delete(T,nil,U),
    noattack(num,nil,num), noattack(num,nil+list(num),num)],
   [queens(nil+list(num),nil+list(num)), queens(nil,nil),
    perm(nil+list(num),nil+list(num)), perm(nil,nil),
    delete(num,nil+list(num),nil+list(num)),
    delete(num,nil+list(num),nil), safe(nil+list(num)), safe(nil),
    noattack(num,nil,num), noattack(num,nil+list(num),num)]).
Clause is OK.
```

```
:-entry nqueens(int,any).

nqueens(N,List):- length(List,N), List::1..N, constraint_queens(List),
                  labeling(List,0,most_constrained,indomain).
constraint_queens([X|Y]):- safe(X,Y,1), constraint_queens(Y).
constraint_queens([]).
safe(X,[Y|T],K):- noattack(X,Y,K), K1 is K+1, safe(T,Y,K1).
safe(_,[],_).
noattack(X,Y,K):- X #\= Y, Y #\= X+K, X #\= Y+K.
```

Fig. 6. The CHIP queens program

The same answer is given for all the other clauses of the program.

Note that if we change the order of the atoms in the body of clause `c1` we obtain the clause `c1': queens(X,Y) :- safe(Y), perm(X,Y)` which can no longer be proved correct w.r.t. the considered specification. Indeed, now Y in the call *safe*(Y) is not assured to be a list of numbers. The tool detects that there is something potentially wrong

```
| ?- verifyIOcall((queens(X,Y):-safe(Y),perm(X,Y)), [...],[...]).
Clause may be wrong because call safe(U) (atom number 1 of body) is not
 in the call-specification.
```

5 Type Verification in Constraint Logic Languages

Another example of the transformation methodology of an analyzer is [4], where the resulting tool is employed to diagnose CHIP programs w.r.t. type information. Types are over-approximations of program semantics. This is the *descriptive* approach to types. The abstract domain is a space of types, described by a restricted class of *CLP* programs called *regular unary constraint logic* (RULC) programs [15]. This class is a generalization to constraint logic programming of regular unary programs (used by [17,16]). Thus, the specification S is a RULC program and the abstract immediate consequence operator is the one operating on RULC programs of [15]. If the type generated for the head of a clause c by $\mathcal{T}^{\alpha}_{\{c\}}(S)$ is not a subtype of the corresponding predicate in S, then the clause is responsible of generating wrong type information. S is given "by need" by querying the user about the correctness of the actual semantics (which is computed by the analyzer) and (in case is needed) about the intended types.

A prototype [5] of the type diagnoser has been implemented as an extension of the type analyzer of CHIP programs of [15]. Consider the *wrong* CHIP version of the `queens` program of Figure 6. The call `safe(X,T,K1)` in the recursive definition of `safe` has been replaced by the wrong call `safe(T,Y,K1)`. The interaction with the call-success diagnoser is as in the following.

[5] Available at URL: ⟨`http://www.ida.liu.se/ pawpi/Diagnoser/diagnoser.html`⟩.

```
Do you like Call-Type constraint_queens(list(anyfd))? YES
Do you like Call-Type safe(list(anyfd),list(anyfd),int)?  NO
What should it be?  anyfd, list(anyfd), int.
Do you like Succ-Type safe(list(anyfd),[],int)? NO
What should it be?  anyfd, list(anyfd), int.
Do you like Succ-type constraint_queens( ([]|[anyfd]) )? NO
what should it be?  list(anyfd).
Do you like Succ-Type noattack(anyfd,anyfd,int)?  YES

Diagnoser WARNING: Clause "safe(X,[Y|T],K) :- noattack(X,Y,K), K1 is K+1,
                   safe(T,Y,K1)" suspiciuos because of atom safe(T, Y, K1).

Do you like Call-Type noattack(list(anyfd),anyfd,int)?  NO
What should it be?  anyfd, anyfd, int.
Do you like Succ-Type nqueens(nnegint, ([]|[anyfd]) )?  NO
What should it be?  int, list(int).
End of diagnosis, no (more) warnings.
```

Thus we are warned about the (only) incorrect clause of the program.

6 Conclusions

Based on the theory of abstract verification, as proposed in [5], we have shown how it is possible and "easy" to transform static analyzers (with suitable properties) into automatic verifiers. In this paper we have presented three different verification tools based on different type domains for functional, logic and *CLP* programming. However, our abstract verification approach is general and flexible. Existing static analyzers can be transformed into verification tools dealing with different abstract domains for different programming paradigms, provided the analyzers are defined as construction of abstract fixpoint semantics.

References

1. F. Bourdoncle. Abstract Debugging of Higher-Order Imperative Languages. In *Programming Languages Design and Implementation '93*, pages 46–55, 1993.
2. F. Bueno, P. Deransart, W. Drabent, G. Ferrand, M. Hermenegildo, J. Maluszynski, and G. Puebla. On the Role of Semantic Approximations in Validation and Diagnosis of Constraint Logic Programs. In M. Kamkar, editor, *Proceedings of the AADEBUG'97*, pages 155–169. Linköping University, 1997.
3. M. Codish and V. Lagoon. Type Dependencies for Logic Programs using ACI-unification. *Journal of Theoretical Computer Science*, 238:131–159, 2000.
4. M. Comini, W. Drabent, and P. Pietrzak. Diagnosis of CHIP Programs Using Type Information. In M. C. Meo and M. Vilares Ferro, editors, *Appia-Gulp-Prode'99, Joint Conference on Declarative Programming*, pages 337–349, 1999.
5. M. Comini, R. Gori, G. Levi, and P. Volpe. Abstract Interpretation based Verification of Logic Programs. In S. Etalle and J.-G. Smaus, editors, *Proceedings of the Workshop on Verification of Logic Programs*, volume 30 of *Electronic Notes in Theoretical Computer Science*. Elsevier Science Publishers, 2000. Available at URL: ⟨http://www.elsevier.nl/locate/entcs/volume30.html⟩.

6. M. Comini, G. Levi, M. C. Meo, and G. Vitiello. Abstract Diagnosis. *Journal of Logic Programming*, 39(1-3):43–93, 1999.
7. P. Cousot. Constructive Design of a Hierarchy of Semantics of a Transition System by Abstract Interpretation. In S. Brookes and M. Mislove, editors, *Proceedings of MFPS'97*, volume 6 of *Electronic Notes in Theoretical Computer Science*. Elsevier Science Publishers, 1997. Available at URL: ⟨`http://www.elsevier.nl/locate/entcs/volume6.html`⟩.
8. P. Cousot. Types as abstract interpretations (Invited Paper). In *Conference Record of the 24th ACM Symp. on Principles of Programming Languages (POPL'97)*, pages 316–331. ACM Press, 1997.
9. P. Cousot and R. Cousot. Abstract Interpretation: A Unified Lattice Model for Static Analysis of Programs by Construction or Approximation of Fixpoints. In *Proceedings of Fourth ACM Symp. Principles of Programming Languages*, pages 238–252, 1977.
10. P. Cousot and R. Cousot. Systematic Design of Program Analysis Frameworks. In *Proceedings of Sixth ACM Symp. Principles of Programming Languages*, pages 269–282, 1979.
11. P. Cousot and R. Cousot. Abstract Interpretation Frameworks. *Journal of Logic and Computation*, 2(4):511–549, 1992.
12. P. Cousot and R. Cousot. Comparing the Galois Connection and Widening/Narrowing Approaches to Abstract Interpretation. In M. Bruynooghe and M. Wirsing, editors, *Proceedings of PLILP'92*, volume 631 of *Lecture Notes in Computer Science*, pages 269–295. Springer-Verlag, 1992.
13. P. Cousot and R. Cousot. Inductive Definitions, Semantics and Abstract Interpretation. In *Proceedings of Nineteenth Annual ACM Symp. on Principles of Programming Languages*, pages 83–94. ACM Press, 1992.
14. W. Drabent and J. Maluszynski. Inductive Assertion Method for Logic Programs. *Theoretical Computer Science*, 59(1):133–155, 1988.
15. W. Drabent and P. Pietrzak. Type Analysis for CHIP. In *proceedings of Types for Constraint Logic Programming, post-conference workshop of JICSLP'98*, 1998.
16. J. Gallagher and D. A. de Waal. Regular Approximations of Logic Programs and Their Uses. Technical Report CSTR-92-06, Department of Computer Science, University of Bristol, 1992.
17. J. Gallagher and D. A. de Waal. Fast and Precise Regular Approximations of Logic Programs. In P. Van Hentenryck, editor, *Proceedings of the Eleventh International Conference on Logic Programming*, pages 599–613, Cambridge, Mass., 1994. MIT Press.
18. R. Giacobazzi and F. Ranzato. Completeness in abstract interpretation: A domain perspective. In M. Johnson, editor, *Proceedings of the 6th International Conference on Algebraic Methodology and Software Technology (AMAST'97)*, Lecture Notes in Computer Science. Springer-Verlag, 1997.
19. G. Levi and P. Volpe. Derivation of Proof Methods by Abstract Interpretation. In C. Palamidessi, H. Glaser, and K. Meinke, editors, *Principles of Declarative Programming. 10th International Symposium, PLILP'98*, volume 1490 of *Lecture Notes in Computer Science*, pages 102–117. Springer-Verlag, 1998.
20. D. Park. Fixpoint Induction and Proofs of Program Properties. *Machine Intelligence*, 5:59–78, 1969.
21. D. Rémy and J. Vouillon. Objective ML:An effective object-oriented extension to ML. *Theory and Practice of Object-Systems*, 4(1):27–50, 1998.
22. P. Volpe. *Derivation of proof methods for logic programs by abstract interpretation.* PhD thesis, Dipartimento di Matematica, Università di Napoli Federico II, 1999.

Andorra Model Revised: Introducing Nested Domain Variables and a Targeted Search

Rong Yang[1] and Steve Gregory[2]

[1] School of Computer Science
University of the West of England, UK
Rong.Yang@uwe.ac.uk
[2] Department of Computer Science
University of Bristol, UK
steve@cs.bris.ac.uk

Abstract. The Andorra Model is a computation model to improve the efficiency of Prolog programs as well as to exploit parallelism. The model was designed in two stages: the basic model and the extended model. The major difference between the two is that a binding determinacy principle replaced the original clause determinacy principle, and an and-or box rewriting computation replaced the traditional resolution.
This work aims to tackle some unsolved problems left in the Extended Andorra Model. We propose to replace the original and-or box rewriting method by a *targeted* search. The search is called targeted because we only look for possible solutions of certain specified variables. The variables shared between different local computations can be dynamically changed to finite domain variables after the targeted search, and their consistency checked eagerly. Therefore, many unnecessary or-branches can be pruned at an early stage. A special feature of our domain variable is that we allow a domain to contain non-ground compound terms, i.e., open structures. Variables within these open structures can also become domain variables, leading to *nested domain variables.*
We have tested our idea by an experimental implementation under SICStus Prolog, and obtained very encouraging results.

1 Introduction

The Andorra model is a computation model designed to exploit both *and*- and *or*-parallelism in logic programs. It is also an execution model to improve the efficiency of Prolog programs by introducing new control strategies. The model was designed in two phases: the basic model and the extended model. The Basic Andorra Model is based on clause determinacy. That is, goals which do not create a choice point (i.e., determinate goals) are always eagerly executed. The Andorra-I system [3,9,10,14], a prototype of the Basic Andorra Model, was successfully developed by a research group led by David Warren at Bristol University. Although the Basic Andorra Model can reduce search space for many types of

R. Nieuwenhuis and A. Voronkov (Eds.): LPAR 2001, LNAI 2250, pp. 610–623, 2001.

application, it is powerless for applications with so-called *independent and-* parallelism. In the Extended Andorra Model [13], a binding determinacy principle replaced the original clause determinacy principle, and an and-or box rewriting computation replaced traditional resolution. This was regarded as an interesting and promising idea, but it needed more study and investigation. Meanwhile, a team of researchers at SICS was working on a similar idea but with explicit control. The outcome of this was a powerful new logic programming language, Andorra Kernel Language [6]. However, creating a new language was not a major focus for the Bristol team. David Warren's interest was to explore the model with implicit control. Unfortunately, the Extended Andorra Model with implicit control was not able to be put into practice because of lack of funding.

In this paper, we present our recent work on the Extended Andorra Model. The work aims to tackle some unsolved problems left in the model. The focus is not parallelization of logic programs. The focus is to investigate efficient control strategies and data structures. We propose to replace the original and-or box rewriting method by a targeted search. The search is called targeted search because we only look for possible solutions of certain specified variables. The variables shared between different local computations can be dynamically changed to finite domain variables after the local search. The consistency of these domain variables is checked eagerly. Therefore, many unnecessary or-branches can be pruned at an early stage. A special feature of our domain variable is that we allow a domain to contain non-ground compound terms, i.e., open structures. Variables within these open structures can also become domain variables, leading to *nested domain variables.*

We have tested our idea by an experimental implementation under SICStus Prolog. The result is encouraging.

The rest of the paper is organized as follows. Section 2 summarizes the Andorra Model to make the paper self-contained. Section 3 presents our revised model. A large proportion of this section is to explain the idea of nested domain variables. In Section 4, implementation issues are discussed. Section 5 presents some test results. Related work is discussed in the following section, while the final section gives some conclusions.

2 Andorra Model

In the Basic Andorra Model, all determinate goals (i.e., goals which do not create choicepoints) are first executed concurrently. When no determinate goals are left, one goal is selected to fork or-branches, on each of which some goals may become determinate. The computation switches between these two phases.

The Extended Andorra Model aimed to improve on the basic model by allowing some non-determinate goals to run concurrently and eagerly, provided that these non-determinate goals do not bind external variables. In order to manipulate multiple local non-determinate computations, an and-or box rewriting scheme was designed. From the implementation point of view, the system would no longer be stack based, but would be a breadth-first tree based system with some intelligent control.

The Andorra Kernel Language [6] uses the Andorra principle as the computational model but the programming language is a guarded committed-choice one, rather than Prolog. The language introduces non-determinate deep guards, by which the user can explicitly define which goals can be searched locally. Although the work on AKL has been overtaken by the Oz project [5], AKL's core idea remains.

3 Our Revised Model

3.1 A General Description of the Model

The revised Andorra model has three computation phases: determinate execution, targeted search, and global forking. The computation flow is as shown in Figure 1.

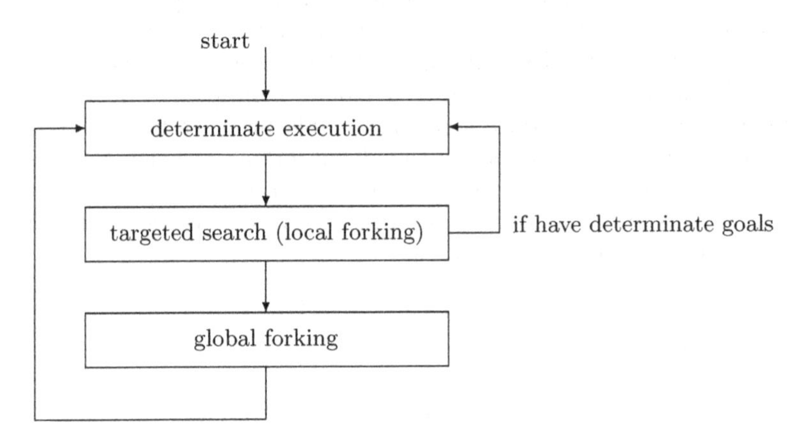

Fig. 1. Three phases in our model

The determinate phase is exactly the same as that of the Basic Andorra Model. When there is no determinate goal left, we enter the targeted search phase. The purpose of this phase is to eagerly collect solutions or partial solutions where it is beneficial and not too expensive. The idea is similar to the lookahead technique [7,12] except that lookahead is used to reduce existing domains for a variable while our target search can also generate a domain for an unbound variable.

We impose some conditions on which goals are eligible for targeted search. Taking the classic Prolog program `member/2` as an example,

```
member(X,[X|_]).
member(X,[_|T]):- member(X,T).
```

the condition for member/2 to perform targeted search could be that the second argument is a ground list. We assume that this kind of condition may be obtained by compile-time analysis or by a user declaration. During the targeted search phase, all goals satisfying the targeted search condition are executed.

To illustrate our model, we use a very simple query which finds common numbers that belong to both the primes list and the fibonacci list (the size of both lists is 1000).

```
?- primes(1000,L1), member(X,L1), fib(1000,L2), member(X,L2)
```

If the above query is run under Prolog, all goals are executed left-to-right and depth-first. As it is not a well-ordered query, the computation for fib(1000,L2) is repeated unnecessarily.

Under the Basic Andorra Model, the two determinate goals, primes(1000,L1) and fib(1000,L2), are executed first. Then the value of X is obtained through backtracking, avoiding the problem caused by badly ordered queries. Our new model executes the two determinate goals in exactly the same way as the Basic Andorra Model, but after this we enter the targeted search phase instead of making a global choicepoint. We evaluate the two member goals and produce a set of possible bindings for the variable X. Note that for this example although the global forking is avoid, the targeted search does not save computation effort. That is, it needs the same computation steps as the Basic Andorra Model does. In the next subsection, we will show the real advantages of the targeted search.

3.2 Targeted Search

Why is targeted search necessary? When is it necessary? The simple example given in the last subsection does not show a great deal of its advantages. The following is a more convincing example taken from [4]. Assume that we have a world geometry database and suppose that we need to find two countries, one in Africa and one in Asia, such that both countries are situated on the coast of the same ocean. This can be expressed by the following Prolog query:

```
?- ocean(X), borders(X,C1), country(C1), in(C1,africa),
     borders(X,C2), country(C2), in(C2,asia).
```

When the query is executed by Prolog, much unnecessary backtracking takes place. For instance, when ocean(X) returns a solution atlantic to variable X, the computation eventually fails at the last goal in(C2,asia). Ideally, at this point, we would hope to retry ocean(X). However, Prolog has to backtrack to the latest choicepoint, borders(X,C1). Therefore, all computation to produce many new countries bordering atlantic is actually wasted. This is a typical example of independent and-parallelism, where Prolog's chronological backtracking faces a real defeat and so does the Basic Andorra Model.

The Extended Andorra Model was partly motivated by the need to tackle this kind of problem. The actual approach proposed [13,6] was to construct an and-or tree and allow some local non-determinate computations to execute simultaneously provided that they do not create non-determinate bindings to external variables. One concern with this approach was the cost of rewriting the and-or tree. Moreover, under Warren's implicit control, it was not clear how to identify whether a local search can eventually stop or at what point a local search should be stopped.

In our revised model, we apply a local computation to collect the possible bindings for some specified variables. After the local computation, these variables are changed to finite domain variables. Assigning an unbound variable to a finite domain is a determinate binding, so it can be performed without any delay.

Through program analysis, user annotation, or both, we can determine for which programs, with which condition, it is worth performing this kind of local computation. Most importantly, we need to make sure the search can be terminated. For example, in the world geography database, the borders/2 relation consists of nearly 1000 pairs. One possible criterion is to perform local computation for a goal only if at least one of its arguments is bound. Alternatively, we might decide to allow local computation for any relation defined only by clauses with no body goals, such as borders/2, because local computation would always terminate.

Now we make some concrete decisions. Assume that borders/2 and in/2 can perform local computation when one of their arguments is a constant, while ocean/1 and country/1 can perform local computation when their argument is either a constant or a finite domain variable. Then, under our model the above query is executed in the following way:

```
?- ocean(X), borders(X,C1), country(C1), in(C1,africa),
   borders(X,C2), country(C2), in(C2,asia).
                |
                | targeted search for in(C1,africa) and
                | in(C2,asia)
                |
                | C1 and C2 become domain variables
                V
?- ocean(X), borders(X,C1), country(C1),
          borders(X,C2), country(C2).
                |                                    cont.

(cont. from the last page)
```

```
                          |
                          |
                          | targeted search for country(C1) and
                          | country(C2)
                          |
                          | the domain of C1 and C2 are reduced
                          V
     ?- ocean(X), borders(X,C1), borders(X,C2).
          |
          |
          | using ocean(X) to make non-determinate forking
          |
         / \---------------------------------------
        /        .....  |           ......  \ X =
       / X=             | X=indian_ocean      \ souther_ocean
      /  arctic_ocean   | C1=dvar([djibouti,...])  \
     /                  | C2=dvar([bangladesh,...]) \
     |                  |                            |
    fail            solutions found                 fail
```

Alternatively, if an eager search strategy is used, we can apply targeted search to all goals in the query. Then we can enter the non-determinate forking by labelling the domain variable X. In either case, we can avoid unnecessary backtracking.

3.3 Nested Domain Variables

The above example only demonstrates the simple case where the targeted search can return a set of constants. There are many other cases where the possible bindings of a variable are not constants, but compound terms with unbound variables.

The following is an example given by David Warren [13] and also studied by other researchers [6].

```
sublist([],[]).
sublist([X|L],[X|L1]):- sublist(L,L1).
sublist(L,[_|L1]):- sublist(L,L1).

?- sublist(L,[c,a,t,s]), sublist(L,[l,a,s,t]).
```

Under Prolog's left-right and depth-first execution order, the first goal generates a sublist of a given list, and the second goal tests whether the sublist is also a sublist of another given list. The number of possible sublists of a given list L is 2^n where n is the length of L. Therefore, the time complexity of the above query is $O(2^n)$ under Prolog's control strategy. A classical question is: can we improve the efficiency of an algorithm by changing only the control but not the logic? In the above example, if two goals can be executed concurrently (or in a coroutined way), then the test goal (i.e., the second `sublist`) can run eagerly to prevent unwanted sublists at an early stage.

It would be no use if our targeted search on `sublist` returned all possible sublists. We should only search sublists with the first element filled as the first step, then search for the rest of the elements, one by one. This can be achieved by a "shallow" local search which only looks for possible bindings to the head of the sublist. That is, for instance, the shallow search on goal `sublist(L,[c,a,t,s])` returns

```
L = dvar([],[c|_],[a|_],[t|_],[s|_])
```

During the search, the computation on the second clause

(i.e., `sublist([X|L],[X|L1]):- sublist(L,L1)`)

stops after the head unification because the body goal no longer contributes to the first element of the list.

Now we have a domain which contains some open-ended lists. This is a good place to explain our notion of nested domain variables. A nested domain variable has incomplete structures in its domain and these incomplete structures may contain domain variables. Going back to the example, all tail variables in the domain can become domain variables. This happens if targeted search is applied again, but this time it targets on the next element of the list. The domain of `L` would be updated to

```
L = dvar([],[c|dvar([],[a|_],[t|_],[s|_])],
            [a|dvar([],[t|_],[s|_])],
            [t|dvar([],[s|_])],
            [s])
```

So far, we have ignored the second `sublist` goal in the query. Its targeted search should be performed simultaneously with the first goal. Assuming that the targeted searches switch between the two goals, the solution for the variable `L` is produced in the following steps:

Step 1. search on the first goal targeted on the first element

```
L = dvar([],[c|_],[a|_],[t|_],[s|_])
```

Step 2. search on the second goal targeted on the first element

`L`'s domain obtained from step 1 is immediately visible from the second goal. Thus, this local search is actually to test existing domain values and remove inconsistent ones, if any. The following is `L`'s newly reduced domain:

```
L = dvar([],[a|_],[t|_],[s|_])
```

Step 3. search on the first goal targeted on the second element

```
L = dvar([], [a|dvar([],[t|_],[s|_])], [t|dvar([],[s|_])], [s])
```

Step 4. search on the second goal targeted on the second element

```
L = dvar([], [a|dvar([],[t|_],[s|_])], [t], [s])
```

Step 5. search on the first goal targeted on the third element

```
L = dvar([], [a|dvar([],[t|dvar([],[s|_])],[s])], [t], [s])
```

Step 6. search on the second goal targeted on the third element

```
L = dvar([], [a|dvar([],[t],[s])], [t], [s])
```

This represents the final solution for `L`. That is,

`L` can be either `[]`, `[a]`, `[a,t]`, `[a,s]`, `[t]`, or `[s]`.

From this example, we have shown how a nested domain variable is used as a communication channel between non-determinate computations.

We believe that the nested domain variable is a useful data structure not only for Prolog-type programs but also for finite domain constraint programs. We use a simple job scheduling example to explain this in more detail.

Suppose that two jobs need to be scheduled. Finite domain variables `St1` and `St2` represent the start times (non-negative integers) of job1 and job2. We know that job1's duration is 5 hours and job2's duration is 2 hours. Assume that the two jobs have to be done within a maximum duration of 7 hours. These can be expressed by the inequalities:

`St1+5 =< 7` and `St2+2 =< 7`.

At this point, after evaluating these inequalities, we have two reduced domains:

`St1` $\in$ `{0,1,2}` and `St2` $\in$ `{0,1,2,3,4,5}`.

If we further assume that the two jobs have to share the same resource, this can be expressed by a `non_overlap` constraint:

```
non_overlap(St1, St2):- St1+5 =< St2; St2+2 =< St1.
```

That is, we either do not start job2 until job1 has finished or do not start job1 until job2 has finished.

The `non_overlap` constraint consists of two disjunctive inequalities, so it cannot be checked determinately. With current constraint programming techniques, this can be handled by a lookahead algorithm [7,12], which enumerates the domain values of `St1` and `St2` and removes impossible values from the two domains. In our example, after we test `non_overlap` constraints using lookahead, we can discover that there are only two possible pairs:

`(St1 = 0, St2 = 5)`, or

`(St1 = 2, St2 = 0)`.

In current constraint programming systems, the result from the lookahead algorithm reduces each domain individually. Therefore, we now have

`St1` $\in$ {`0,2`} and `St2` $\in$ {`0,5`}.

Although this has greatly reduced both domains, a much tighter constraint,

`(St1,St2)` $\in$ {`(0,5), (2,0)`}

has been lost.

By introducing nested domain variables, we can represent several domains together as a tuple; `St1` and `St2` can be paired as `S = (St1,St2)`. Then, after the targeted search on the `non_overlap` constraint, we will obtain:

`S = dvar((0,5),(2,0))`.

No information is lost. `non_overlap(St1,St2)` will terminate, whereas with two separate domains the goal `non_overlap(St1,St2)` would have to suspend.

One might question whether it is really necessary to maintain this kind of relation between several domains. To further demonstrate its advantage, let us assume that in the above example a new constraint, `St1 =< St2`, is imposed later on. If the system knows

`St1` $\in$ {`0,2`} and `St2` $\in$ {`0,5`},

the constraint `St1 =< St2` cannot discover any impossible values. However, if the system knows

`(St1,St2)` $\in$ {`(0,5), (2,0)`}

it can immediately remove the impossible pair `(2,0)` and produce determinate bindings for `St1` and `St2`.

Another question is whether it is practical to use a nested domain variable combining many variables together. A nested domain might grow exponentially. During our experiment (Section 5), we tested a program which produces a deeply nested domain whose size is greater than 2^{16}. It did increase the running time, but did not run of memory.

4 Implementation

We are interested to see whether our model is feasible. As a first experiment, we decided to use SICStus Prolog, a well established Prolog system, rather than develop a low-level implementation. SICStus Prolog has a powerful coroutine facility and provides a special library, the attribute variable library [11], which allows us to define destructively assigned variables.

4.1 Program Transformation

We need to transform an ordinary Prolog program into different code such that the program will be executed as if it is run under our model. This is not a problem because goal suspension can be easily implemented in SICStus Prolog.

We discuss how to compile a program into its targeted search form. For "shallow" programs (e.g., database-type programs), this is very straightforward. All we need to do is check whether the targeted search condition is met and, if so, we check whether the targeted variable is already a domain variable or still a free variable. This leads to two different types of code: in the first case we do forward checking, while in the second case we simply use `findall` or `bagof` to collect all solutions and return them as a domain.

For recursive programs, we need to generate special code which performs targeted search incrementally. This requires some program analysis and maybe some user annotations. Going back to our `sublist` example, provided the compiler knows that the first element in the first argument is the target, it can identify that the body goal in the second clause should be stopped. Similarly, it can also identify that the recursive goal in the third clause must be carried on because the head unification does not produce any output on the first argument.

The following is the transformed `sublist` used for targeted search:

```
sublist_local_search([],[], true).
sublist_local_search([X|L],[X|L1], sublist_local_search(L,L1,_)).
sublist_local_search(L,[_|L1], SusGoal):-
        sublist_local_search(L,L1, SusGoal).
```

Comparing this code with the original code, we can see that they are almost identical except for the following two changes. First, we added an extra argument (the third argument) which returns the suspended goals, if any. In other words, the new argument indicates where the computation should continue when the next local search is performed. Another change is that the recursion in the second clause is removed but is returned as a suspended goal.

4.2 Implementing Domain Variables

Domain variables are implemented by using attributed variables [11] provided in SICStus Prolog. An attributed variable can be associated with arbitrary attributes. Moreover, these attributes can not only be updated but also are backtrackable.

We have already shown how nested domain variables are structured in the `sublist` example. As well as a set of values, our domain variable can also be associated with some suspended goals, so we have an extra slot to store this. The actual domain variable in our implementation has the following structure:

```
dvar((Value1,GoalList1),(Value2,GoalList1), ...)
```

Another issue is how to deal with unification after introducing nested domain variables. Unification between two nested domain variables is carried out by performing an intersect operation recursively along the nested structure. Unification between a nested domain variable and a ground term is also very easy. We simply follow the ground term to trim out all incorrect values in the nested domain. The tedious part is to unify a nested domain with a non-ground structure. For example, consider a domain variable

`L = dvar([2+dvar([4,5]),3+dvar([6,7])])`,

which represents four possible expressions:

`2+4, 2+5, 3+6,` and `3+7`

When `L` is unified with `X+Y`, we can produce

`X = dvar([2,3])` and `Y = dvar([4,5,6,7])`.

but we cannot terminate this unification at this point because, if either `X`, `Y`, or `L` changes its domain, we need to check it again. That is, we have to keep `L=X+Y` suspended and resume it when the domain of any of the variables is reduced.

5 Some Results

We have developed code to support nested domain variables, and tested our model with a few simple programs: three database examples and three string comparison examples. The results are summarized in Figure 2.

The database examples are from the world geography database. `database1` is the query discussed in Section 3.2, and the other two are similar queries to `database1`. `protein_seq` takes three protein sequences and searches for common subsequences between them. `reverse_list` is to find common sublists between two reversed list, while `same_list` is a query which looks for all common sublists between two identical lists.

The machine used for testing is a Pentium II PC. All programs were compiled and run under SICStus 3.6 (Linux version). As database queries are quite fast, we tested them by repeating 10 runs as well as by a single run.

As the above table shows, apart from the last one, all transformed programs are much faster under our model than the original programs. We know that for the first five programs the search space (i.e., the number of inferences) is greatly reduced under our model. However, we were not sure whether the overhead for supporting the model is too big to make the model feasible. The above results are very encouraging.

We deliberately chose the last example, `same_list`, because it is a special case where our model cannot provide any advantage. In its original program, all

	under Prolog's control	under our model
database1	110	30
same prog. 10-run	580	150
database2	20	10
same prog. 10-run	120	55
database3	50	20
same prog. 10-run	310	135
protein_seq	13510	1910
reversed_list	2780	20
same_list	10370	29500

Fig. 2. Test Results (time in millisecond)

possible sublists (a total of 2^{16}) are generated and tested one by one through backtracking. In our model, a nested domain variable has to be constructed, comprising a tree with 2^{16} nodes. This requires huge memory space, which is why its run time ends up about 3 times slower. Programs like `same_list` are very rare, so we believe that the result here does not really represent a drawback of the model.

6 Related Work

The idea of using local computation has a long history and has been applied in many areas. Within the logic (and constraint) programming discipline, a well known form of local computation is *lookahead* [12], based on the classic idea of arc consistency [7]. Our targeted search is similar to lookahead in all but a few respects. Under constraint programming, lookahead is used to reduce existing domains. In our case, we also use it to generate a domain for an unbound logical variable as well as to restrict a domain. Most importantly, in our targeted local search, we aim to achieve a general form of lookahead which can not only check arc consistency but also incrementally check path consistency.

In AKL implementations [6,8], a form of local search is provided, which is similar to our proposed targeted search in many respects. Perhaps the main difference is at the language level: AKL's local search has to be explicitly defined by using deep guards, while we aimed to make it more flexible.

In our model, a variable can be dynamically changed to a domain variable. A similar idea has also been proposed in the past [1,8]. However, our domain variables have the unique feature that a domain can be nested inside another domain. Another difference from [1] is that the domain information is extracted from the head unification in [1], while we also extract domains from local computation.

7 Conclusion and Future Work

This work has investigated issues in how to provide better control for logic programs such that the efficiency of programs can be improved. Our starting point was the Extended Andorra Model. By revising the model, we proposed a targeted search, so called because we only look for possible solutions of certain specified variables. This targeted search can be simply achieved by Prolog's `bagof`, so we do not need to use the original and-or box rewriting method, which is quite expensive. It is hoped that this revised model can be easily implemented in a stack-based system.

In our model, variables shared between different computations can be dynamically changed to finite domain variables after the local search, and their consistency can be checked eagerly.

One important outcome from this work is the notion of nested domain variables. We introduced a special domain which can contains non-ground compound terms, i.e., open structures. Variables within these open structure can become domain variables. A nested domain can keep information on the Cartesian product of several domains. With our current implementation, the Cartesian product is represented as a tree structure. Nested domains can be exploited not only in Prolog-type programs but also in finite domain constraint programs.

We have tested our idea by an experimental implementation under SICStus Prolog. Nested domain variables are implemented by using the attributed variables of SICStus Prolog. The experimental results confirm the expected benefits.

As future work, we would like to investigate the following issues:

- We need to study in more detail how nested domain variables can be applied to finite domain constraint programs. For instance, we may need some clear rules to select which variables should be grouped as a tuple, i.e., represented as a nested domain.
- We are interested in designing some kind of user declarations for specifying the targeted search condition. We will study the language HAL [2], which has introduced various user annotations.

Acknowledgements. We would like to thank all anonymous reviewers for their useful and encouraging comments.

References

1. R. Bahgat, V. Santos Costa, and R. Yang. ARCH: A Parallel Execution Model that Minimises the Search Space of Logic Programs. *Egyptian Computer Journal*, 23(2), 1996.

2. B. Demoen, M. Garcia de la Banda, W. Harvey, K. Marriott, and P. Stuckey. Herbrand constraint solving in HAL. In *Proceedings of the International Conference on Logic Programming*, pages 260–274. MIT Press, December 1999.
3. I. Dutra. A Flexible Scheduler for Andorra-I. In A. Beaumont and G. Gupta, editors, *Lecture Notes in Computer Science 569, Parallel Execution of Logic Programs*, pages 70–82. Springer-Verlag, June 1991.
4. G. Gupta and D. H. D. Warren. An Interpreter for the Extended Andorra Model. Presented at ICLP'90 Workshop on Parallel Logic Programming, Eilat, Israel, June 1990.
5. S. Haridi, P. V. Roy, P. Brand, and C. Schulte. Programming Languages for Distributed Applications. *New Generation Computing*, 16(3), 1998.
6. S. Janson and S. Haridi. Programming Paradigms of the Andorra Kernel Language. In *Logic Programming: Proceedings of the International Logic Programming Symposium*, pages 167–186. MIT Press, October 1991.
7. A. K. Mackworth. Consistency in Networks of Relations. *Artificial Intelligence*, 8(1):99–118, 1977.
8. R. Moolenaar and B. Demoen. Hybrid Tree Search in the Andorra Model. In *Proceedings of the 8th International Conference on Logic Programming*, pages 110–123. MIT Press, June 1994.
9. V. Santos Costa, D. H. D. Warren, and R. Yang. The Andorra-I Engine: A parallel implementation of the Basic Andorra model. In *Logic Programming: Proceedings of the 8th International Conference.* MIT Press, 1991.
10. V. Santos Costa, D. H. D. Warren, and R. Yang. The Andorra-I Preprocessor: Supporting full Prolog on the Basic Andorra model. In *Logic Programming: Proceedings of the 8th International Conference.* MIT Press, 1991.
11. The Intelligent Systems Laboratory, Swedish Institute of Computer Science. SICStus Prolog User's Manual. www.sics.se/sicstus/docs/3.7.1/html/sicstus_toc.html, 1998.
12. P. Van Hentenryck. *Constraint Satisfaction in Logic Programming.* MIT Press, 1989.
13. D. H. D. Warren. The Extended Andorra Model with Implicit Control. Presented at ICLP'90 Workshop on Parallel Logic Programming, Eilat, Israel, June 1990.
14. R. Yang et al. Performance of the Compiler-based Andorra-I System. In *Logic Programming: Proceedings of the 10th International Conference.* MIT Press, 1993.

Coherent Composition of Distributed Knowledge-Bases through Abduction

Ofer Arieli, Bert Van Nuffelen, Marc Denecker, and Maurice Bruynooghe

Department of Computer Science, University of Leuven
Celestijnenlaan 200A, B-3001 Heverlee, Belgium

Abstract. We introduce an abductive method for coherent composition of distributed data. Our approach is based on an abductive inference procedure that is applied on a meta-theory that relates different, possibly inconsistent, input databases. Repairs of the integrated data are computed, resulting in a consistent output database that satisfies the meta-theory. Our framework is based on the $\mathcal{A}$-system, which is an abductive system that implements SLDNFA-resolution. The outcome is a robust application that, to the best of our knowledge, is more expressive (thus more general) than any other existing application for coherent data integration.

1 Introduction

In many cases complex reasoning tasks have to integrate knowledge from multiple sources. A major challenge in this context is to compose contradicting sources of information such that what is obtained would properly reflect the combination of the distributed data on one hand[1], and would still be *coherent* (in terms of consistency) on the other hand.

Coherent integration and proper representation of amalgamated data is extensively studied in the literature (see, e.g., [1,3,7,13,14,20,21,22,23,26,29]). Common approaches for dealing with this task are based on techniques of belief revision [20], methods of resolving contradictions by quantitative considerations (such as "majority vote" [21]) or qualitative ones (e.g., defining priorities on different sources of information or preferring certain data over another [2,4,5]). Other approaches are based on rewriting rules for representing the information in a specific form [14], or use multiple-valued semantics (e.g., annotated logic programs [28,29] and bilattice-based formalisms [12,22]) together with non-classical refutation procedures [11,19,28] that allow to decode within the language itself some "meta-information" such as confidence factors, amount of belief for/against a specific assertion, etc.

Each one of the techniques mentioned above has its own limitations and/or drawbacks. For instance, in order to properly translate the underlying data to a specific form, formalisms that are based on rewriting techniques must assume

[1] This property is sometimes called *compositionality*; see, e.g., [30].

R. Nieuwenhuis and A. Voronkov (Eds.): LPAR 2001, LNAI 2250, pp. 624–638, 2001.

that the underlying data (or some part of it, such as the set of integrity constraints) has a specific syntactical structure. Other formalisms (e.g., that of [20]) are based on propositional languages, and so in both cases the expressiveness is limited. In some of the non-classical formalisms mentioned above (e.g., those that are based on annotated logics and several probabilistic formalisms), semantical notions interfere with the syntax. Moreover, in many of these frameworks syntactical embeddings of first-order formulae into non-classical languages are needed. Such translations may damage or bias the intuitive meaning of the original formulae. Finally, some of the approaches mentioned above are not capable of resolving contradictions unless the reasoner specifies his/her preferences. In other approaches, the mechanism of resolving contradictions is determined in advance, or is ad-hoc (thus it is oriented towards specific kinds of problems). This interference necessarily reduces the flexibility and the generality of the corresponding mediative engine.

In this paper we start from the perspective of a pure declarative representation of the composition of distributed data. This approach is based on a meta-theory relating a number of different (possibly inconsistent) input databases with a consistent output database. The underlying language is that of ID-logic [9], which can be embedded in an abductive logic program. Our composing system is implemented by the abductive solver the, $\mathcal{A}$-system [18]. In the context of this work, we extended this system with an optimizing component that will allow us to compute preferred coherent solutions to restore the consistency of the database.

Our approach is related to other work on the use of abduction in the context of databases. [16] proposed to use abduction for database updating. [15,27] developed a framework for explaining or unexplaining observations by an extended form of abduction in which arbitrary formulas may be added or formulas of the theory may be removed. In this paper, the focus is on a different application of abduction, namely composition and integrity restoration of multiple databases.

By this declarative approach we are able to overcome some of the shortcomings of the amalgamating techniques mentioned above. In particular, our system has the following capabilities:

1. *Any* first-order formula may be specified for describing the domain of discourse (as part of the integrity constraints). Thus, to the best of our knowledge, our approach is more general and expressive than any other available application for coherent data integration.
2. No syntactical embeddings of first-order formulae into different languages nor any extensions of two-valued semantics are necessary. Our approach is based on a pure generalization of classical refutation procedures.
3. The way of keeping the data coherent is encapsulated in the component that integrates the data. This means, in particular, that no reasoner's input nor any other external policy for making preferences among conflicting sources is compulsory in order to resolve contradictions.

In the sequel we show that our system is sound, complete, and supports various types of special information, such as timestamps and source tracing. We also discuss implementation issues and provide some experimental results.

2 Coherent Composition of Knowledge-Bases

2.1 Problem Description

Definition 1. A *knowledge-base* $\mathcal{KB}$ is a pair $(\mathcal{D}, \mathcal{IC})$, where $\mathcal{D}$ (the *database*) is a set of atomic formulae, and $\mathcal{IC}$ (the set of *integrity constraints*) is a finite set of first order formulae.

As usual in such cases, we apply the closed world assumption on databases, i.e., every atom that is not mentioned in the database is considered false. The underlying semantics corresponds, therefore, to minimal Herbrand interpretations.

Definition 2. A formula ψ *follows* from a database $\mathcal{D}$ if the minimal Herbrand model of $\mathcal{D}$ is also a model of ψ.

Definition 3. A knowledge-base $\mathcal{KB} = (\mathcal{D}, \mathcal{IC})$ is *consistent* if all the integrity constraints are consistent, and each one follows from $\mathcal{D}$.

Our goal is to integrate n consistent knowledge-bases, $\mathcal{KB}_i = (\mathcal{D}_i, \mathcal{IC}_i)$, $i = 1, \ldots n$, to a single knowledge-base in such a way that the data in this knowledge-base will contain everything that can be deduced from one of the sources of information, without violating any integrity constraint of another source. The idea is to consider the union of the distributed data, and then to restore its consistency. A key notion in this respect is the following:

Definition 4. [14] A *repair* of $\mathcal{KB} = (\mathcal{D}, \mathcal{IC})$ is a pair $(\mathsf{Insert}, \mathsf{Retract})$ such that $\mathsf{Insert} \cap \mathsf{Retract} = \emptyset$, $\mathsf{Insert} \cap \mathcal{D} = \emptyset$, $\mathsf{Retract} \subseteq \mathcal{D}$, and every integrity constraint follows from $\mathcal{D} \cup \mathsf{Insert} \setminus \mathsf{Retract}$. [2]
$(\mathcal{D} \cup \mathsf{Insert} \setminus \mathsf{Retract}, \mathcal{IC})$ is called a *repaired knowledge-base* of $\mathcal{KB}$.

As there may be many ways to repair an inconsistent knowledge-base, it is often convenient to make preferences among the repairs and to consider only the most preferred ones. Below are two common preference criteria.

Definition 5. Let $(\mathsf{Insert}, \mathsf{Retract})$ and $(\mathsf{Insert}', \mathsf{Retract}')$ be two repairs of a given knowledge-base.

- *set inclusion preference criterion* :
  $(\mathsf{Insert}', \mathsf{Retract}') \leq_i (\mathsf{Insert}, \mathsf{Retract})$ if $\mathsf{Insert} \subseteq \mathsf{Insert}'$ and $\mathsf{Retract} \subseteq \mathsf{Retract}'$.

[2] I.e., Insert are elements that should be inserted into $\mathcal{D}$ and $\mathsf{Retract}$ are elements that should be removed from $\mathcal{D}$ in order to obtain a consistent knowledge-base.

– *cardinality preference criterion*:
$(\mathsf{Insert}', \mathsf{Retract}') \leq_c (\mathsf{Insert}, \mathsf{Retract})$ if $|\mathsf{Insert}|+|\mathsf{Retract}| \leq |\mathsf{Insert}'|+|\mathsf{Retract}'|$.

Let $\leq$ be a semi-order on the set of repairs, expressing a preference criterium.

Definition 6. [14] A *$\leq$-preferred repair* of a knowledge-base $\mathcal{KB}$ is a repair $(\mathsf{Insert}, \mathsf{Retract})$ of $\mathcal{KB}$ s.t. there is no other repair $(\mathsf{Insert}', \mathsf{Retract}')$ of $\mathcal{KB}$ for which $(\mathsf{Insert}, \mathsf{Retract}) \leq (\mathsf{Insert}', \mathsf{Retract}')$. [3]

Definition 7. The set of all the $\leq$-preferred repairs of a knowledge-base $\mathcal{KB}$ is denoted by $!(\mathcal{KB}, \leq)$.

Definition 8. A *$\leq$-repaired knowledge-base* of $\mathcal{KB}$ is a repaired knowledge-base of $\mathcal{KB}$, constructed from a $\leq$-preferred repair of $\mathcal{KB}$. The set of all the $\leq$-repaired knowledge-bases of $\mathcal{KB}$ is denoted by

$$\mathcal{R}(\mathcal{KB}, \leq) = \{\, (\mathcal{D} \cup \mathsf{Insert} \setminus \mathsf{Retract}\,,\, \mathcal{IC}) \mid (\mathsf{Insert}, \mathsf{Retract}) \in\, !(\mathcal{KB}, \leq) \,\}.$$

Note that if $\mathcal{KB}$ is consistent and the preference criterion is a partial order and monotonic in the size of the repairs (as in Definition 5), then $\mathcal{R}(\mathcal{KB}, \leq) = \{\mathcal{KB}\}$, i.e., $\mathcal{KB}$ is the (only) $\leq$-repaired knowledge-base of itself, and so there is nothing to repair in this case, as expected.

Definition 9. For $\mathcal{KB}_i = (\mathcal{D}_i, \mathcal{IC}_i)$, $i = 1, \ldots n$, let $\mathcal{UKB} = (\bigcup_{i=1}^{n} \mathcal{D}_i, \bigcup_{i=1}^{n} \mathcal{IC}_i)$.

In the rest of this paper we describe a system that, given n distributed knowledge-bases and a preference criterion $\leq$, computes the set $\mathcal{R}(\mathcal{UKB}, \leq)$ of the $\leq$-repaired knowledge-bases of $\mathcal{UKB}$. The reasoner may use different strategies to determine the consequences of this set. Among the common approaches are the skeptical (conservative) one, that it is based on a "consensus" among all the elements of $\mathcal{R}(\mathcal{UKB}, \leq)$ (see [14]), a "credulous" approach in which entailments are decided by any element in $\mathcal{R}(\mathcal{UKB}, \leq)$, an approach that is based on a "majority vote", etc. A detailed discussion on these methods and ways of assuring the consistency of the composed data in each method, will be presented elsewhere.

We conclude this section by noting that in the sequel we shall assume that $\mathcal{IC} = \bigcup_{i=1}^{n} \mathcal{IC}_i$ is consistent. This is a usual assumption in the literature and it is justified by the nature of the integrity constrains as describing statements that are widely accepted. Thus, it is less likely that integrity constraints would contradict each other. Contradictions between the data in the different $\mathcal{KB}$'s and integrity constraints are more frequent, and may occur due to many different reasons. In the next section we consider some common cases.

[3] In [14] this notion is defined for the specific case where the preference condition is taken w.r.t. set inclusion.

2.2 Examples

In all the following examples we use set inclusion as the preference criterion.[4]

Example 1. [14, Example 1] Consider a distributed knowledge-base with relations of the form $teaches(\texttt{course\_name}, \texttt{teacher\_name})$. Suppose also that each knowledge-base contains a single integrity constraint, stating that the same course cannot be taught by two different teachers:

$$\mathcal{IC} = \{ \forall X \forall Y \forall Z\, (teaches(X,Y) \wedge teaches(X,Z) \rightarrow Y = Z) \}.$$

Consider now the following two knowledge-bases:

$$\mathcal{KB}_1 = (\{teaches(c_1,n_1),\ teaches(c_2,n_2)\},\ \mathcal{IC}),$$
$$\mathcal{KB}_2 = (\{teaches(c_2,n_3)\},\ \mathcal{IC})$$

Clearly, $\mathcal{KB}_1 \cup \mathcal{KB}_2$ is inconsistent. Its preferred repairs are $(\emptyset,\ \{teaches(c_2,n_2)\})$ and $(\emptyset,\ \{teaches(c_2,n_3)\})$. Hence, the two repaired knowledge-bases are:

$$\mathcal{R}_1 = (\{teaches(c_1,n_1),\ teaches(c_2,n_2)\},\ \mathcal{IC}), \text{ and}$$
$$\mathcal{R}_2 = (\{teaches(c_1,n_1),\ teaches(c_2,n_3)\},\ \mathcal{IC}).$$

Example 2. [14, Example 2] Consider a distributed knowledge-base with relations of the form $supply(\texttt{supplier}, \texttt{department}, \texttt{item})$ and $class(\texttt{item}, \texttt{type})$. Let

$$\mathcal{KB}_1 = (\{supply(c_1,d_1,i_1),\ class(i_1,t_1)\},\ \mathcal{IC}), \text{ and}$$
$$\mathcal{KB}_2 = (\{supply(c_2,d_2,i_2),\ class(i_2,t_1)\},\ \emptyset), \text{ where}$$
$$\mathcal{IC} = \{ \forall X \forall Y \forall Z\, (supply(X,Y,Z) \wedge class(Z,t_1) \rightarrow X = c_1) \}$$

states that only supplier c_1 can supply items of type t_1.
$\mathcal{KB}_1 \cup \mathcal{KB}_2$ is inconsistent and has two preferred repairs: $(\emptyset,\ \{supply(c_2,d_2,i_2)\})$ and $(\emptyset,\ \{class(i_2,t_1)\})$. Hence, there are two ways to repair it:

$$\mathcal{R}_1 = (\{supply(c_1,d_1,i_1),\ class(i_1,t_1),\ class(i_2,t_1)\},\ \mathcal{IC}),$$
$$\mathcal{R}_2 = (\{supply(c_1,d_1,i_1),\ supply(c_2,d_2,i_2),\ class(i_1,t_1)\},\ \mathcal{IC}).$$

Example 3. [14, Example 4] Let $\mathcal{D}_1 = \{p(a),\ p(b)\}, \mathcal{D}_2 = \{q(a),\ q(c)\}$, and $\mathcal{IC} = \{\forall X (p(X) \rightarrow q(X))\}$. Again, $(\mathcal{D}_1, \emptyset) \cup (\mathcal{D}_2, \mathcal{IC})$ is inconsistent. The corresponding preferred repairs are $(\{q(b)\},\ \emptyset)$ and $(\emptyset,\ \{p(b)\})$. The repaired knowledge-bases are therefore the following:

$$\mathcal{R}_1 = (\{p(a),\ p(b),\ q(a),\ q(b),\ q(c)\},\ \mathcal{IC}),$$
$$\mathcal{R}_2 = (\{p(a),\ q(a),\ q(c)\},\ \mathcal{IC}).$$

[4] Generally, in what follows we shall fix a preference criterion for choosing the "best" repairs and omit its notation whenever possible.

3 Knowledge Integration through Abduction

In this section we introduce an abductive method for a coherent integration of knowledge-bases. Our framework is composed of a language for describing the problem domain (ID-logic, [9]), an abductive solver that is based on an abductive refutation procedure (SLDNFA, [10]), and a computational model for controlling the search ($\mathcal{A}$-system [18]).

3.1 ID-Logic and Abductive Logic Programming

ID-logic [9] is a framework for declarative knowledge representation that extends classical logic with inductive definitions. This logic incorporates two types of knowledge: definitional and assertional. Assertional knowledge is a set of first order statements, representing a general truth about the domain of discourse. Definitional knowledge is a set of rules of the form $p \leftarrow \mathcal{B}$, in which the head p is a predicate and the body $\mathcal{B}$ is a first order formula. A predicate that does not occur in any head is called *open* (sometimes called *abducible*).

Below we present an ID-logic meta-theory describing the composition of databases in terms of open predicates `insert` and *retract*. The key property of this theory is that its *abductive* solutions describe the coherent compositions. Abductive reasoning on an ID-logic theory can be performed by mapping it into an abductive logic program [8] under the extended well-founded semantics [24] and applying an abductive inference procedure to it. An *abductive logic program* (ALP)) is a triple $\mathcal{T} = (\mathcal{P}, \mathcal{A}, \mathcal{IC})$, such that

- $\mathcal{P}$ is a logic program, the clauses of which are interpreted as definitions for the predicates in their head,
- $\mathcal{A}$ is a set of predicates, none of which occurs in the head of a clause in $\mathcal{P}$. The elements in $\mathcal{A}$ are called the *abducible predicates*.
- $\mathcal{IC}$ is a set of first-order formulae, called the *integrity constraints*.

Constants, functors and predicate symbols are defined as usual in logic programs.

Definition 10. An (abductive) *solution* for a theory $(\mathcal{P}, \mathcal{A}, \mathcal{IC})$ and a query $\mathcal{Q}$ is a set Δ of ground abducible atoms, all having a predicate symbols in $\mathcal{A}$, together with an answer substitution θ, such that: (a) $\mathcal{P} \cup \Delta$ is consistent, (b) $\mathcal{P} \cup \Delta \models \mathcal{IC}$, and (c) $\mathcal{P} \cup \Delta \models \forall \mathcal{Q}\theta$.

In what follows we use ID-logic to specify the knowledge integration, and implement the reasoning process by an abductive refutation procedure. For this we represent any data in some distributed database by a predicate `db`, and denote the elements in the composed database by the predicate `fact`. The latter predicate is defined as follows:

```
fact(X) :- db(X), not retract(X).
fact(X) :- insert(X).
```

In particular, in order to restore consistency, some facts may be removed and some other facts may be introduced. These facts are represented by the (abducible) predicates `retract` and `insert`, respectively. To assure proper computations of the solutions, the following integrity constraints are also specified:[5]

- An element cannot be retracted and inserted at the same time:
  `ic :- insert(X), retract(X).`
- An inserted element should not belong to a given database:
  `ic :- insert(X), db(X).`

Assuming that all the integrity constraints of the distributed knowledge-bases are compatible and that no distinctions are made among the origins of the composed facts, the following steps are performed:

1. Each database fact X is represented by an atom db(X).
2. Every occurrence of an atom P in some integrity constraint is replaced by fact(P). This is done in order to assure that every integrity constraint would hold for the composed data as well.
3. A solution is computed in terms of the abducible predicates `insert` and `retract`.

3.2 The $\mathcal{A}$-System

The reasoning process of our revision system is performed by the $\mathcal{A}$-system, introduced in [18]. The basic idea of this system is a reduction of a high level specification into a lower level constraint store, which is managed by a constraint solver. The system is a synthesis of the refutation procedures SLDNFA [10] and ACLP [17], together with an improved control strategy. The latest version of the system can be obtained from `http://www.cs.kuleuven.ac.be/~dtai/kt/`. It runs on top of Sicstus Prolog 3.8.5. Below we sketch the theoretical background as well as some practical considerations behind this system. For more information, see [10] and [18].

Abductive inferences. Given an abductive theory $(\mathcal{P}, \mathcal{A}, \mathcal{IC})$ as defined above, the logical reduction of a query $\mathcal{Q}$ can be described as a derivation for $\mathcal{Q}$ through a rewriting state process. A state $\mathcal{S}$ consists of two types of elements: a set Pos($\mathcal{S}$) of literals (possibly with free variables), called *positive goals*, and a set Neg($\mathcal{S}$) of denials, called *negative goals*. The set $\Delta(\mathcal{S})$ denotes the abducible atoms in $\mathcal{S}$, i.e. positive goal atoms whose predicate is an abducible. $\mathcal{C}(\mathcal{S})$ denotes the set of constraint atoms in $\mathcal{S}$.

A rewriting derivation proceeds from state $\mathcal{S}_i$ by selecting a literal of $\mathcal{S}_i$ and applying a suitable inference rule, yielding a new state $\mathcal{S}_{i+1}$. The main inference rules are given by the following rewrite rules. In the list below we denote by A and B some literals, and by C a constraint literal. $\mathcal{P}$ denotes the theory under consideration. For readability, we do not mention cases in which Pos($\mathcal{S}$) or Neg($\mathcal{S}$) is the same in states number i and $i+1$.

- *Rules for defined predicates:*

[5] In what follows we use the notation "`ic :- B`" to denote the denial "`false` ← `B`".

- if $A(\overline{X}) \leftarrow B_j[\overline{X}] \in \mathcal{P}$ and $A(\overline{t}) \in \texttt{Pos}(\mathcal{S}_i)$, then $\texttt{Pos}(\mathcal{S}_{i+1}) = \texttt{Pos}(\mathcal{S}_i) \setminus \{A(\overline{t})\} \cup \{B_j[\overline{t}]\}$.
- if $\leftarrow A(\overline{t}), Q \in \texttt{Neg}(\mathcal{S}_i)$, then $\texttt{Neg}(\mathcal{S}_{i+1}) = \texttt{Neg}(\mathcal{S}_i) \setminus \{\leftarrow A(\overline{t}), Q\} \cup U$, where $U = \{\leftarrow B_j[\overline{t}], Q \mid A(\overline{t}) \leftarrow B_j[\overline{t}] \in \mathcal{P}\}$.

– *Rules for open predicates:*
- if $\leftarrow A(\overline{t}), Q \in \texttt{Neg}(\mathcal{S}_i)$ and $p(\overline{s}) \in \Delta(\mathcal{S}_i)$ then $\texttt{Neg}(\mathcal{S}_{i+1}) = \texttt{Neg}(\mathcal{S}_i) \setminus \{\leftarrow A(\overline{t}), Q\} \cup \{U\} \cup \{R\}$, where $U = \leftarrow \overline{t} = \overline{s}, Q$, and $R = \leftarrow A(\overline{t}), \overline{t} \neq \overline{s}, Q$.

– *Rules for negations:* Assume that A is not a constraint literal.
- if $\neg A \in \texttt{Pos}(\mathcal{S}_i)$ then $\texttt{Pos}(\mathcal{S}_{i+1}) = \texttt{Pos}(\mathcal{S}_i) \setminus \{\neg A\}$ and $\texttt{Neg}(\mathcal{S}_{i+1}) = \texttt{Neg}(\mathcal{S}_i) \cup \{\leftarrow A\}$.
- if $\leftarrow \neg A, Q \in \texttt{Neg}(\mathcal{S}_i)$ then one of the following branches is taken:
  1. $\texttt{Pos}(\mathcal{S}_{i+1}) = \texttt{Pos}(\mathcal{S}_i) \cup \{A\}$ and $\texttt{Neg}(\mathcal{S}_{i+1}) = \texttt{Neg}(\mathcal{S}_i) \setminus \{\leftarrow \neg A, Q\}$.
  2. $\texttt{Neg}(\mathcal{S}_{i+1}) = \texttt{Neg}(\mathcal{S}_i) \setminus \{\leftarrow \neg A, Q\} \cup \{\leftarrow A, \leftarrow Q\}$.

– *Rules for constraint literals:*
- if $\leftarrow C, Q \in \texttt{Neg}(\mathcal{S}_i)$ then one of the following branches is taken:
  1. $\texttt{Pos}(\mathcal{S}_{i+1}) = \texttt{Pos}(\mathcal{S}_i) \cup \{\neg C\}$, $\texttt{Neg}(\mathcal{S}_{i+1}) = \texttt{Neg}(\mathcal{S}_i) \setminus \{\leftarrow C, Q\}$.
  2. $\texttt{Pos}(\mathcal{S}_{i+1}) = \texttt{Pos}(\mathcal{S}_i) \cup \{C\}$, $\texttt{Neg}(\mathcal{S}_{i+1}) = \texttt{Neg}(\mathcal{S}_i) \setminus \{\leftarrow C, Q\} \cup \{\leftarrow Q\}$.

  Remark: It is important here to assume that the underlying constraint solver is capable of handling negated constraint literals. This is indeed the case with the constraint solver used by our system (Sicstus).

The *initial state* $\mathcal{S}_0$ for a theory $\mathcal{P}$ and a query $\mathcal{Q}$ consists of the query $\mathcal{Q}$ as a positive goal and the set of all denials in $\mathcal{P}$ as negative goals. A *successful state* $\mathcal{S}$ fulfills the following conditions:

1. $\mathcal{S}$ contains positive goals only of the form of abducible atoms or constraint atoms,
2. negative goals in $\mathcal{S}$ are denials containing some open atom $p(\overline{t})$ which has already been selected and resolved with each abduced atom $p(\overline{s}) \in \mathcal{S}$, and
3. the constraint store $\mathcal{C}(\mathcal{S})$ of $\mathcal{S}$ is satisfiable.

Definition 11. A *successful abductive derivation* of a query $\mathcal{Q}$ w.r.t. $\mathcal{P}$ is a sequence of states $\mathcal{S}_0, \mathcal{S}_1, \ldots, \mathcal{S}_n$, where: (a) $\mathcal{S}_0$ is an initial state for $\mathcal{P}$ and $\mathcal{Q}$, (b) For every $0 \leq i \leq n-1$, $\mathcal{S}_{i+1}$ is obtained from $\mathcal{S}_i$ by applying one of the transition rules, and (c) $\mathcal{S}_n$ is a successful state.

Whenever `false` is derived (in one of the constraint domains) the derivation backtracks. A derivation *flounders* when universally quantified variables appear in a selected negated literal in a denial.

Let $\mathcal{S}_n$ be a final state of a successful derivation. Then any substitution θ that assigns a ground term to each free variable of $\mathcal{S}_n$ and which satisfies the constraint store $\mathcal{C}(\mathcal{S}_n)$ is called a *solution substitution* of $\mathcal{S}_n$. Such a substitution always exists since $\mathcal{C}(\mathcal{S}_n)$ is satisfiable for a successful derivation.

Theorem 1. [18] *Let $\mathcal{T} = (\mathcal{P}, \mathcal{A}, \mathcal{IC})$ be an abductive theory s.t. $\mathcal{P} \models \mathcal{IC}$, $\mathcal{Q}$ a query, $\mathcal{S}$ the final state of a successful derivation for $\mathcal{Q}$, and θ a solution substitution of $\mathcal{S}$. Then the pair $\theta(\Delta(\mathcal{S}))$ and θ is an abductive solution for $\mathcal{T}$ and $\mathcal{Q}$.*

Control strategy. The selection strategy applied during the derivation process is crucial. A Prolog-like selection strategy (left first, depth first) often leads to trashing, because it is blind to other choices and it does not result in a global overview of the current state of the computation. In the development of the $\mathcal{A}$-system the main focus was on the improvement of the control strategy. The idea is to apply first those rules that have a deterministic change of the state, and so information is propagated. If none of such rules are applicable, then one of the left over choices is selected and a choice is made. This resembles a CLP-solver, in which the constraints propagate their information as soon a choice is made. This propagation yields less amount of choices and thus often dramatically increases the performance.

3.3 Implementation and Experiments

In this section we present the structure of our system, discuss a few implementation issues, and give some experimental results.

The structure of the system. Figure 1 shows a layered description of the implemented system. The upper most level consists of the data to be integrated, i.e., the database information and the integrity constrains. This layer together with the composer form an ID-Logic theory that is processed by the $\mathcal{A}$-system.

The *composer* consists of the meta-theory for integrating the distributed data in a coherent way. It is interpreted here as an abductive theory, in which the abducible predicates provide the information on how to restore the consistency of the amalgamated data.

The abductive system (enclosed by dotted lines in Figure 1) consists of three main components: A finite domain constraint solver (the one of Sicstus Prolog), an abductive meta-interpreter (described above), and an optimizer.

The *optimizer* is a component that, given a preference criterion on the space of the solutions, computes only the most-preferred (abductive) solutions. Given such a preference criterion, this component prunes "on the fly" those branches of the search tree that lead to worse solutions than what we have already computed. This is actually a branch and bound "filter" on the solutions space that speeds-up execution and makes sure that only the desired solutions will be obtained. If the preference criterion is monotonic (in the sense that from a partial solution it can be determined whether it potentially leads to a solution that is not worse than a current one), then the optimizer is *complete*, that is, it can compute all the optimal solutions (see also Section 3.4).

Note that the optimizer is a general component added to the $\mathcal{A}$-system. Not only this domain benefits, but it is useable in other application domains like e.g. planning.

Experimental study. Figure 2 contains the code (data section + composer) for implementing Example 1 (The codes for Examples 2 and 3 are similar). We have executed this code as well as other examples from the literature in our

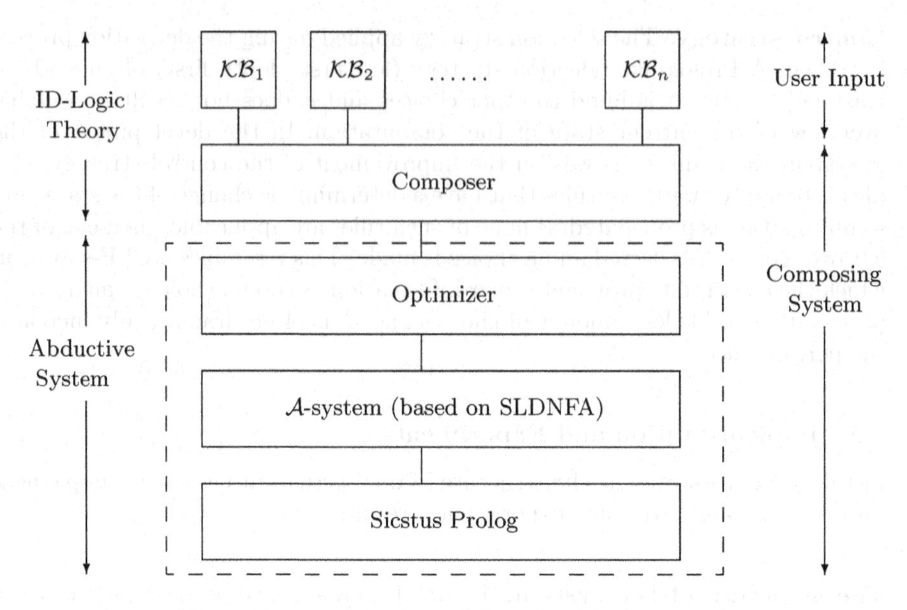

Fig. 1. A schematic view of the system components.

system. As Theorem 3 below guarantees, the output in each case was the set of the most preferred solutions of the corresponding problem.

3.4 Soundness and Completeness

In this section we give some soundness and completeness results for our system. In what follows we denote by $\mathcal{T}$ an abductive theory in ID-logic, constructed as describe above for composing n given knowledge-bases $\mathcal{KB}_1, \ldots, \mathcal{KB}_n$. Also, $\texttt{Proc}_{\texttt{ALP}}$ denotes some sound abductive proof procedure (e.g., SLDNFA [10]).

Proposition 1. *Every abductive solution that is obtained by* $\texttt{Proc}_{\texttt{ALP}}$ *for a theory* $\mathcal{T}$ *is a repair of* $\mathcal{UKB}$.

Proof: By the construction of $\mathcal{T}$ it is easy to see that all the conditions specified in Definition 4 are met: the first two conditions are assured by the integrity constraints of the composer. The third condition immediately follows from the composer's rules. The last condition is satisfied since by the soundness of $\texttt{Proc}_{\texttt{ALP}}$ it produces abductive solutions Δ_i for $\mathcal{T}$, thus by the second property in Definition 10, for every such solution $\Delta_i = (\mathsf{Insert}_i, \mathsf{Retract}_i)$ we have that $\mathcal{P} \cup \Delta_i \models \mathcal{IC}$. Since $\mathcal{P}$ contains a data section with all the facts, it follows that $\mathcal{D} \cup \Delta_i \models \mathcal{IC}$, i.e. every integrity constraints follows from $\mathcal{D} \cup \mathsf{Insert}_i \setminus \mathsf{Retract}_i$. □

Theorem 2. (Soundness) *Every output that is obtained by running* $\mathcal{T}$ *in the* $\mathcal{A}$*-system together with a* $\leq_c$*-optimizer [respectively, together with an* $\leq_i$*-optimizer] is a* $\leq_c$*-preferred repair [respectively, an* $\leq_i$*-preferred repair] of* $\mathcal{UKB}$.

```
/* ------- Composer: -------
:- dynamic ic/0, fact/1, db/1.

abducible(insert(_)).
abducible(retract(_)).

fact(X) :- db(X), not(retract(X)).
fact(X) :- insert(X).
ic :- insert(X), db(X).
ic :- insert(X), retract(X).

/* ------- Example 1: -------
db(teaches(1,1)).  db(teaches(2,2)).                    % D1
db(teaches(2,3)).                                       % D2
ic :- fact(teaches(X,Y)), fact(teaches(X,Z)), Y\=Z.     % IC
```

Fig. 2. Code for Example 1

Proof: Follows from Proposition 1 (since the $\mathcal{A}$-system is based on SLDNFA that is a sound abductive proof procedure), and the fact that the $\leq_c$-optimizer prunes paths that lead to solutions which are not $\leq_c$-preferable. Similar arguments hold for systems with an $\leq_i$-optimizer. □

Proposition 2. *Suppose that the query '*$\leftarrow$ `true`*' has a finite SLDNFA-tree w.r.t.* $\mathcal{T}$*. Then every* $\leq_c$*-preferred repair and every* $\leq_i$*-preferred repair of* $\mathcal{UKB}$ *is obtained by running* $\mathcal{T}$ *in the* $\mathcal{A}$*-system.*

Outline of proof: The proof that all the abductive solutions with minimal cardinality are obtained by the system is based on [10, Theorem 10.1], where it is shown that SLDNFA^o, which is an extension of SLDNFA, aimed for computing solutions with minimal cardinality, is complete (see [10, Section 10.1] for further details). Similarly, the proof that all the abductive solutions which are minimal w.r.t. set inclusion are obtained by the system is based on [10, Theorem 10.2] that shows that SLDNFA$_+$, which is another extension of SLDNFA, aimed for computing minimal solutions w.r.t. set inclusion, is also complete (see [10, Section 10.2] for further details).

Now, $\mathcal{A}$-system is based on the combination of SLDNFA^o and SLDNFA$_+$. Moreover, as this system does not change the refutation tree (but only controls the way rules are selected), Theorems 10.1 and 10.2 in [10] are applicable in our case as well. Thus, all the $\leq_c$- and the $\leq_i$-minimal solutions are produced. This in particular means that every $\leq_c$-preferred repair as well as every $\leq_i$-preferred repair of $\mathcal{UKB}$ is produced by our system. □

Theorem 3. (Completeness) *In the notations of Proposition 2 and under its assumptions, the output of the execution of* $\mathcal{T}$ *in the* $\mathcal{A}$*-system together with a* $\leq_c$*-optimizer [respectively, together with an* $\leq_i$*-optimizer] is exactly* $!(\mathcal{UKB}, \leq_c)$ *[respectively,* $!(\mathcal{UKB}, \leq_i)$*].*

Proof: We shall show the claim for the case of $\leq_c$; the proof w.r.t. $\leq_i$ is similar.

Let (Insert, Retract) $\in$!($\mathcal{UKB}, \leq_c$). By Proposition 2, Δ = (Insert, Retract) is one of the solutions produced by the $\mathcal{A}$-system for $\mathcal{T}$. Now, during the execution of our system together with the $\leq_c$-optimizer, the path that corresponds to Δ cannot be pruned from the refutation tree, since by our assumption (Insert, Retract) has a minimal cardinality among the possible solutions, so the pruning condition is not satisfied. Thus Δ will be produced by the $\leq_c$-optimized system. For the converse, suppose that (Insert, Retract) is some repair of $\mathcal{UKB}$ that is produced by the $\leq_c$-optimized system. Suppose for a contradiction that (Insert, Retract) $\notin$!($\mathcal{UKB}, \leq_c$). By the proof of Proposition 2, there is some Δ' = (Insert′, Retract′) $\in$!($\mathcal{UKB}, \leq_c$) that is constructed by the $\mathcal{A}$-system for $\mathcal{T}$, and (Insert′, Retract′) $<_c$ (Insert, Retract). But $|\Delta'| < |\Delta|$, and so the $\leq_c$-optimizer would prone the path of the Δ solution once its cardinality becomes bigger than $|\Delta'|$. This contradicts our assumption that (Insert, Retract) is produced by the $\leq_c$-optimized system. □

4 Handling Specialized Information

4.1 Timestamped Information

Many database applications contain temporal information. This kind of data may be divided to two types: time information that is part of the data itself, and time information that is related to database operations (e.g., records on when the database was updated). Consider, for instance, $\texttt{birth\_day(John,15/05/2001)}_{16/05/2001}$. Here, John's date of birth is an instance of the former type of time information, and the subscripted data that describes the time in which this fact was added to the database, is an instance of the latter type of time information.

In our approach, timestamp information can be integrated by adding a temporal theory describing the state of the database at any particular time point. One way of doing so is by using *situation calculus*. In this approach a database is described by initial information and a history of events performed during the database lifetime (see [25]). Here we use a different approach, which is based on *event calculus*. The idea is to make a distinction between two kinds of events: `add_db` and `del_db` that describe the database modifications, and the composer-driven events `insert` and `retract` that are used for constructing database repairs. In this view, the extended composer has the following form:

```
holds_at(P,T) :- initially(P), not clipped(0,P,T).
holds_at(P,T) :- add(P,E), E<T, not clipped(E,P,T).
clipped(E,P,T) :- del(P,C), E≤C, C<T.

add(P,T) :- add_db(P,T).        add(P,T) :- insert(P,T).
del(P,T) :- del_db(P,T).        del(P,T) :- retract(P,T).
ic :- insert(P,T), retract(P,T).
ic :- insert(P,T), add_db(P,T).
ic :- retract(P,T), del_db(P,T).
```

In this extended context the integrity constrains must be carefully specified. Consider, e.g. the statement that a person can be born only on one date:
`ic :- holds_at(birth_day(P,D1),T), holds_at(birth_day(P,D2),T), D1≠D2.`
The problem here is that to ensure consistency this constraint must be checked at every point in time. This may be avoided by a simple rewriting that ensures that the constraint will be verified only when an event occurs:

```
ic(birth,T) :- holds_at(birth_day(P,D1),T),
               holds_at(birth_day(P,D2),T), D1\=D2.
ic :- add_db(birth_day(_,_),T), NT = T+1, ic(birth,NT).
ic :- del_db(birth_day(_,_),T), NT = T+1, ic(birth,NT).
```

4.2 Keeping Track of Source Identities

There are cases in which it is important to preserve the identity of the database from which a specific piece of information was originated. This is useful, for instance, when one wants to make preferences among different sources, or when some specific source should be filtered out (e.g, when the corresponding database is not available or becomes unreliable). This kind of information may be decoded by adding another argument to every fact, which denotes the identity of its origin. This requires minor modifications in the basic composer, since the composer controls the way in which the data is integrated. As such, it is the only component that can keep track to the source of the information.

Suppose, then, that for every database fact we add another argument that identifies its source. I.e., `db(X,S)` denotes that `X` is a fact originated from a database `S`. The composer then has the following form:

```
fact(X,S) :- db(X,S), not retract(X)
fact(X,composer) :- insert(X)
ic :- insert(X), db(X,S)
ic :- insert(X), retract(X)
```

Note that the composer considers itself as an extra source that inserts brand new data facts. Now it is possible, e.g., to trace information that comes from a specific source, make preferences among different sources (by specifying appropriate integrity constraints), and filter data that comes from certain sources. The last property is demonstrated by the following rule:

```
validFact(X) :- fact(X,S), trusted_source(S)
```

where `trusted_source` enumerates all reliable sources of the data.

4.3 Handling Quantitative Information

Next we consider a potential way of decoding in the integrated data some quantitative information, such as certainty factors or probabilities.

Suppose that `db(X,i)` denotes that fact `X` holds with probability `i`. One can define a strategy on how to reason with this kind of information, and decode it in the composer. For instance, the composer below uses a conservative policy that takes for each fact its lowest probability:

```
fact(X,i) :- db(X,_), not retract(X), i = min{j | db(X,j)}
fact(X,1) :- insert(X,1)
ic :- insert(X,1), db(X,_)
ic :- insert(X,1), retract(X)
```

For implementing this kind of program the underlying system should be able to compute aggregations (possibly together with recursion). Adding this capability to our system is one of the subjects for a future work.

5 Conclusion and Further Work

In this paper we have developed a formal declarative foundation for rendering coherent data, provided by different knowledge-bases, and presented an application that implements this approach. Like other systems (e.g., [6,14,20,29]), our system mediates among the sources of information and between the reasoner and the underlying data.

Composing distributed data by a meta-theory in ID-logic yields a robust and easily extendable system. Extra meta information about the data facts, such as time stamps and source, are easily dealt with by extending the meta-theory properly. Due the inherent modularity of the chosen approach, each part is independent and can be adapted according to the needs.

It is important to note that our composing system inherits the functionality of the underlying solver. This implies, in particular, flexibility, modularity, easy interaction with different sources of information, and the ability to reason with *any* set of first order integrity constraints.[6] As such, our system may be easily modified and extended with addition background knowledge.

Among the directions for further exploration are dealing with more general forms of databases, in which views (or rules) are allowed, and lifting the condition that all the integrity constraints are compatible with each other. Another important challenge is to extend the capabilities of the abductive system with aggregation. This would allow us to integrate different types of databases, and would provide means of solving new kinds of problems.

References

1. M.Arenas, L.E.Bertossi, J.Chomicki. Consistent query answers in inconsistent databases. *Proc. PODS'99*, 68–79, 1999.
2. O.Arieli. Four-valued logics for reasoning with uncertainty in prioritized data. In: *Information, Uncertainty, Fusion*, 263–309, Kluwer, 1999.
3. C.Baral, S.Kraus, J Minker. Combining Multiple Knowledge Bases. *IEEE Trans. on Knowledge and Data Enginnering* 3(2), 208–220, 1991.
4. S.Benferhat, C.Cayrol, D.Dubois, J.Lang, H.Prade. Inconsistency management and prioritized syntax-based entailment. *Proc. IJCAI'93*, 640–645, 1993.

[6] Provided that the constraints do not lead to floundering. To the best of our knowledge no other application of data integration has this ability.

5. S.Benferhat, D.Dubois, H.Prade. How to infer from inconsistent beliefs without revising? *Proc. IJCAI'95*, 1449–1455, 1995.
6. L.Bertossi, M.Arenas, C.Ferretti. SCDBR: An automated reasoner for specifications of database updates. *Intelligent information Systems* 10(3), 253–280, 1998.
7. F.Bry. Query Answering in Information Systems with Integrity Constraints. *Proc. IICIS'97*, 113–130, 1997.
8. M. Denecker, A.C. Kakas. Abductive Logic Programming, *Special issue of Journal of Logic Programming*, 44 (1-3), 2000.
9. M.Denecker. Extending classical logic with inductive definitions. *Proc. CL'2000*, J. Lloyd et al., editors, LNAI 1861, Springer, 703–717, 2000.
10. M.Denecker, D.De Schreye. SLDNFA an abductive procedure for abductive logic programs. *Journal of Logic Programming* 34(2), 111–167, 1998.
11. M.Fitting. Negation as refutation. *Proc. LICS'89*, IEEE Press, 63–70, 1989.
12. M.Fitting. Bilattices and the semantics of logic programming. *Journal of Logic Programming* 11(2), 91–116, 1991.
13. M.Gertz, U.W.Lipeck. An extensible framework for repairing constraint violations. *Proc. IICIS'97*, 89–111, 1997.
14. S.Greco, E.Zumpano. Querying inconsistent databases. *Proc. LPAR'2000*, M.Parigot and A.Voronokov, editors, LNAI 1955, 308–325, Springer, 2000.
15. K.Inoue, C.Sakama. Abductive framework for nonmonotonic theory change. *Proc. IJCAI'95*, 204-210, 1995.
16. T.Kakas, P.Mancarella. Database updates through abduction. *Proc VLDB'90*, 650–661, 1990.
17. T.Kakas, A.Michael, C.Mourlas. ACLP: Abductive constraint logic programming. *Journal of Logic Programming* 44(1–3), 129–177, 2000.
18. T.Kakas, B.Van Nuffelen, M.Denecker. $\mathcal{A}$-System: Problem solving through abduction. Proc. IJCAI'01, 2001.
19. M.Kifer, E.L.Lozinskii. A logic for reasoning with inconsistency. *Journal of Automated Reasoning* 9(2), 179–215, 1992.
20. P.Liberatore, M.Schaerf. BReLS: a system for the integration of knowledge bases. *Proc KR'2000*, 145–152, 2000.
21. J.Lin, A.O.Mendelzon. Merging databases under constraints. *Int. Journal of Cooperative Information Systems* 7(1), 55–76, 1998.
22. B.Messing. Combining knowledge with many-valued logics. *Data and Knowledge Engineering* 23, 297–315, 1997.
23. A.Olivé. Integrity checking in deductive databases. *Proc VLBD'91*, 513–523, 1991.
24. L.M. Pereira, J.N. Aparicio, J.J. Alferes. , Hypothetical Reasoning with Well Founded Semantics , *Proc. of the 3th Scandinavian Conference on AI* , B. Mayoh, IOS Press, 289-300, 1991
25. R. Reiter. On specifying database updates. *Journal of Logic Programming*, 25(1), 53–91, 1995.
26. P.Z.Revesz. On the semantics of theory change: Arbitration between old and new information. *Proc. PODS'93*, 71–82, 1993.
27. C.Sakama, K.Inoue. Updating extended logic programs through abduction. *Proc LPNMR'99*, 147–161, 1999.
28. V.S.Subrahmanian. Mechanical proof procedures for many valued lattice-based logic programming. *Journal of Non-Classical Logic* 7, 7–41, 1990.
29. V.S.Subrahmanian. Amalgamating knowledge-bases. *ACM Trans. on Database Systems* 19(2), 291–331, 1994.
30. S.Verbaeten, M.Denecker, D.De Schreye. Compositionality of normal open logic programs. *Journal of Logic Programming* 41(3), 151–183, 2000.

Tableaux for Reasoning about Atomic Updates

Christian G. Fermüller, Georg Moser, and Richard Zach

Technische Universität Wien, Austria
{chrisf,moser,zach}@logic.at

Abstract. A simple model of dynamic databases is studied from a modal logic perspecitve. A state α of a database is an atomic update of a state β if at most one atomic statement is evaluated differently in α compared to β. The corresponding restriction on Kripke-like structures yields so-called update logics. These logics are studied also in a many-valued context. Adequate tableau calculi are given.

1 Introduction

Various approaches employing modal logics for the representation of knowledge and for (mechanized) reasoning about data have been investigated. See, e.g., [3,15,6,10,9] for some recent work of relevance to database theory.

Here we investigate a particularly simple model of (dynamic) databases. The states of a database are identified with assignments of truth values to basic propositions. Some states are considered as results of *updating* other states of the database. In other words, a binary *update relation* is defined over the set of possible states. This amounts to defining usual Kripke interpretations. Standard normal modal logics arise if we augment classical propositional logic (over the signature of basic propositions of the database) with the modalities $\Box$ and $\Diamond$, interpreted as "in all updated states" and "in some updated state", respectively. However, as we shall see below, interesting deviations from standard modal logics are needed to model atomic, i.e. stepwise, updates instead of arbitrary ones.

Literature on the so-called "update problem" usually aims at formalizing changes in databases triggered by *arbitrary complex* changes in the environment to which the database refers. Here however, we want to model only *atomic* or *"single-step" updates*[1]. More exactly, each update operation is assumed to change the truth value of at most one basic proposition at a time. In general, atomic updates reflect adaption to a changing environment (or improved knowledge) only via *sequences* of such atomic update operations. However, we think that considering *atomic* updates leads to a more realistic model of the actual computational behavior of dynamic databases. At a fundamental level the evolution of any database proceeds in basic steps, each of which corresponds to some well defined atomic action that can be performed on a database entry. We aim at a conceptually clear as well as technically simple logical model of this aspect of dynamic databases.

[1] What we call "atomic update" here was called "single-step updates" in a previous — unpublished — version of this paper by the first author. This preliminary version of the paper is accessible at `http://www.cin.ufpe.br/~wollic/wollic2000/proceedings/`.

R. Nieuwenhuis and A. Voronkov (Eds.): LPAR 2001, LNAI 2250, pp. 639–653, 2001.

The subtle constraint on the update relation seems to have dramatic effects for the corresponding modal logics: the set of formulas valid in all corresponding Kripke interpretations is not closed under substitution. In response to this fact we propose to use a *two-sorted* propositional language that allows us to distinguish between "atoms" (basic propositions of the database) and genuine propositional variables; and consequently between "concrete" and "schematic" statements about data. We define a corresponding semantics and provide complete and sound *tableau calculi* for the resulting logics.

We generalize this model of atomic dynamic databases to scenarios allowing for incomplete and inconsistent information. Replacing classical logic by Belnap's well-known four-valued logic [4] opens the space for new types of modal operators over corresponding update models. Some examples of such *distribution modalities* expressing properties of updates will be investigated. We claim that in general the concept of distribution modalities is a versatile tool to model a broad range of updates in (dynamic) databases. A variant of tableaux for finite-valued logics with distribution modalities introduced in [7] turns out to be adequate for formalizing reasoning in corresponding logics.

We emphasize that the concepts and results presented here should be considered only as a first step in exploring the scope and limits of many-valued Kripke structures and distribution modalities in the context of reasoning about dynamic databases. Accordingly, we conclude with a list of future topics of research.

2 Atomic Databases and Kripke Interpretations

Our first object of investigation is arguably the simplest logical model of a database. It refers to a fixed set of atomic units of information (propositions, called atoms) and presumes that the only information explicitly contained in the database is which of those atomic propositions hold and which do not hold.

More formally, by a *(classical) state (of a database)* we mean a total function of type $\mathsf{atoms} \mapsto \{\mathbf{t},\mathbf{f}\}$, where atoms is a non-empty, countable set of propositional atoms. Obviously we can evaluate classical propositional formulas over the signature atoms (and standard connectives) with respect to a state α as usual:

- $v_\alpha(p) = \alpha(p)$, for $p \in \mathsf{atoms}$
- $v_\alpha(\top) = \mathbf{t}$ and $v_\alpha(\bot) = \mathbf{f}$
- $v_\alpha(\neg A) = \mathbf{t}$ iff $v_\alpha(A) = \mathbf{f}$
- $v_\alpha(A \circ B) = \widetilde{\circ}(v_\alpha(A), v_\alpha(B))$

where $\circ \in \{\wedge, \vee, \supset, \equiv\}$ and $\widetilde{\circ}$ is the classical boolean function associated with the binary connective $\circ$. In other words, a *query* is an arbitrary propositional formula A over atoms, which receives the answer $v_\alpha(A)$ if the database is in state α.

We are interested in the dynamic structure of a database; i.e., the possible transitions from states to states triggered by update operations. As explained above, we focus on the—arguably—most elementary type of an update operation: A single application of such an update operation changes the truth status of at most one atomic unit of information. Correspondingly, state α' is called an *atomic update* of a state α if the following condition is satisfied:

(au) $\alpha(p) \neq \alpha'(p)$ for *at most one* $p \in \mathsf{atoms}$.

Throughout the paper we will consider *atomic* updates *only*, and therefore often drop the adjective "atomic."

Definition 1. *An* (atomic-)update model *is a pair* $\mathcal{D} = (\Sigma, U)$ *where*

- Σ *is a set of states of a database over (a fixed set)* atoms, *i.e., a set of functions of type* atoms $\mapsto \{\mathbf{t}, \mathbf{f}\}$, *and*
- U *is a binary relation over* Σ, *subject to the restriction that* $\forall \alpha, \alpha' \in \Sigma : \alpha U \alpha'$ *implies that* α' *is an atomic update of* α.

We extend the expressibility of the query language by adding to it the modal operators $\Box$ and $\Diamond$, with the intended meaning "in all (reachable) updates" and "in some (reachable) update", respectively. More exactly—referring to states α of a atomic-update model $\mathcal{D} = (\Sigma, U)$—we extend the definition of v_α as follows:

- $v_\alpha^{\mathcal{D}}(\Box A) = \mathbf{t}$ iff $\forall \beta \in \Sigma$: if $\alpha U \beta$, then $v_\beta^{\mathcal{D}}(A) = \mathbf{t}$, and
- $v_\alpha^{\mathcal{D}}(\Diamond A) = \mathbf{t}$ iff $\exists \beta \in \Sigma : \alpha U \beta$ and $v_\beta^{\mathcal{D}}(A) = \mathbf{t}$.

This simple logical machinery allows for the expression of statements that refer not only to the current state of a database but also to possible updates of a states.

Example 1. The formula $A \supset \Box A$ may be paraphrased as "If the statement A is currently validated by the database, then all possible (atomic) updates will still validate A". Similarly $\Diamond A \wedge \Diamond \neg A$ expresses that A is contingent, i.e., a statement that will be evaluated differently in different possible updates of the current state of the database. Likewise we can express the fact that there is no possible update of the current state by "$\neg \Diamond \top$". The statement that for every possible update (of the current state) a further update is possible is expressed by "$\Box \Diamond \top$."

There is a close connection between states of a database and worlds of a Kripke structure where a world β is accessible from a world α iff β is an atomic update of α.

Definition 2. *A* (Kripke) interpretation *is a triple* $\mathcal{M} = (W, R, V)$ *where*

- W *is a non-empty* set of worlds,
- R *is a binary* accessibility relation *on* W,
- $V : \mathsf{PV} \times W \mapsto \{\mathbf{t}, \mathbf{f}\}$ *is a* truth value assignment *to the infinite set* PV *of* propositional variables.

The corresponding evaluation function $v^{\mathcal{M}}$ *that assigns a truth value to each formula* A *in each world* $w \in W$ *is defined as usual.* $\mathcal{M}$ *is a* (counter-)interpretation *for a formula* A *if* $v^{\mathcal{M}}(A, w) = \mathbf{t}$ $(\mathbf{f})$ *for some* $w \in W$. A *is* valid *in* $\mathcal{M}$ *if* $\mathcal{M}$ *is not a counter-interpretation for* A*; i.e., if* $v^{\mathcal{M}}(A, w) = \mathbf{t}$ *for all* $w \in W$.

Definition 3. *The* skeleton $T(\mathcal{M})$ *of an interpretation* $\mathcal{M} = (W, R, V)$ *is the undirected graph with* W *as set of nodes and an edge between* $v, w \in W$ *iff* $v \neq w$ *and either* vRw *or* wRv. *We call an interpretation* $\mathcal{M}$ tree-like *if its skeleton* $T(\mathcal{M})$ *is a tree (i.e., a connected acyclic graph).*

Clearly, condition (**au**) corresponds to condition

(**au′**) wRv implies $V(p,v) \neq V(p,w)$ for *at most one* $p \in \mathsf{PV}$.

for Kripke interpretations. We say that an interpretation $\mathcal{M} = (W, R, V)$ fulfills condition (**au′**) *on a subset* $P \subseteq \mathsf{PV}$ if for all $v, w \in W$: if wRv then $V(p,v) = V(p,w)$ for all except at most one $p \in P$.

If a Kripke interpretation $\mathcal{M} = (W, R, V)$ satisfies (**au′**) for all its worlds then it corresponds to a (unique) update model $\mathcal{D}_{\mathcal{M}} = (\Sigma, U)$, where atoms is identified with PV, $\Sigma = \{\lambda p[V(p,w)] \mid w \in W\}$, and $\alpha U \beta \iff vRw$ where $\alpha = \lambda p[V(p,v)]$ and $\beta = \lambda p[V(p,w)]$. Conversely, every update model $\mathcal{D}$ corresponds to Kripke interpretation $\mathcal{M}_{\mathcal{D}}$ that satisfies (**au′**).

By requiring the update relation in a model to fulfill simple properties we can adapt our model to databases which obey certain dynamic constraints. For instance, requiring the update relation U to be *symmetric* corresponds to modeling databases for which every update is reversible. Similarly in many applications it will be useful to require U to be *reflexive* (corresponding to: the "empty" update operation is always applicable) or *serial* (corresponding to: every state can be updated). Observe however that, e.g., *transitivity* does not in general make sense for atomic updates: the atomic update of an atomic update is not expected to be atomic itself.

Definition 4. *The class of all update models is called* update K-models. *An update model is called an* update KB-, D-, T-, *or* TB-model *if its update relation is symmetric, serial, reflexive, or symmetric and reflexive, respectively.*

3 Concrete versus Schematic Statements

It might seem as if—so far—we have only described just another view of normal modal logic. However, by insisting that the truth value of at most *one* atom can be changed in one update operation we ensured that, e.g., the formula

$$F = (p \wedge q) \supset \Box(p \vee q)$$

is evaluated true in all states of all models, if p and q are different atoms. By contrast, substituting (in F) p for q results in a formula which is false in all states in which p is $\mathbf{t}$ and where there is an atomic update in which p is $\mathbf{f}$. In other words, the set of formulas true in all states of an update model is in general *not closed under substitution.*

There is a simple way of recovering closure under substitution:

Definition 5. *A formula A is* schematically valid *in an (atomic-)update model $\mathcal{D} = (\Sigma, U)$ if $v^{\mathcal{D}}_{\alpha}(A') = \mathbf{t}$ for all substitution instances A' of A and all $\alpha \in \Sigma$.*

The set of formulas that are schematically valid in all update Λ-models is called update-Λ *(for $\Lambda \in \{\mathsf{K}, \mathsf{KB}, \mathsf{D}, \mathsf{T}, \mathsf{TB}\}$).*

By definition, each update-Λ is closed under substitution. It is easy to see that they are also closed under modus ponens and the necessity rule. Therefore they can be considered as ordinary modal logics and can be directly compared to the corresponding standard logics (which we identify with the sets of formulas valid in all corresponding Kripke interpretations).

Our first main result is the following

Theorem 1. *For $\Lambda \in \{\mathsf{K}, \mathsf{KB}, \mathsf{D}, \mathsf{T}, \mathsf{TB}\}$, update-$\Lambda$ and (ordinary) Λ coincide.*

Proof. If a formula is valid in all Λ-interpretations then, in particular, it is valid in all Λ-interpretations satisfying condition (**au**$'$) for all worlds. Since such interpretations correspond to update models it follows that $\Lambda \subseteq$ update-Λ.

For the converse we prove the following:

Claim. Every tree-like Λ-interpretation $\mathcal{M} = (W, R, V)$ can be transformed into a Λ-interpretation $\mathcal{M}' = (W, R, V')$ such that condition (**au**$'$) is satisfied and for all $w \in W$: $v^{\mathcal{M}}(A, w) = v^{\mathcal{M}'}(A\theta, w)$ for all formulas A and some substitution θ.

The claim implies that if $\mathcal{M}$ is a counter-interpretation for A then $\mathcal{D}_{\mathcal{M}'}$ is a counter-update-model for $A\theta$. It is a consequence of the usual tableau-based completeness proofs for $\Lambda \in \{\mathsf{K}, \mathsf{B}, \mathsf{D}, \mathsf{T}, \mathsf{TB}\}$, that without loss of generality a (counter)-Λ-interpretation for any formula A may be assumed to be tree-like (Recall Definition 3 and see, e.g., [8], but also Theorem 3 below.) Therefore update-$\Lambda \subseteq \Lambda$ follows from the claim.

To establish the claim, consider the skeleton $T(\mathcal{M})$ of $\mathcal{M}$ and define

$$\mathrm{diff}_V^P(v, w) = |\{p \in P \mid V(p, v) \neq V(p, w)\}|$$

for each edge (v, w) in $T(\mathcal{M})$. Obviously, if $\mathrm{diff}_V^{\mathsf{PV}}(v, w) \leq 1$ for all edges (v, w) then $\mathcal{M}$ satisfies the atomic update condition and nothing is left to prove. Since only finitely many propositional variables can occur in a single formula A we restrict our attention to the assignments in $\mathcal{M}$ of a finite subset P of PV; more exactly we assume that—at the beginning of our construction—$V(p, w) = \mathbf{t}$ for all $w \in W$ and all $p \in \mathsf{PV} - P$.

Let $\mathrm{diff}_V^P(v, w) > 1$; then there are two different propositional variables $p, q \in P$ such that $V(p, v) \neq V(p, w)$ and $V(q, v) \neq V(p, w)$. We set

$$\theta = \{p \leftarrow (e \equiv f), q \leftarrow (f \equiv g)\}$$

for pairwise different variables $e, f, g \notin P$. We now update the truth value assignment V of $\mathcal{M}$ to an assignment V' such that the following three conditions are satisfied:

1. $\mathrm{diff}_V^{P'}(v, w) < \mathrm{diff}_{V'}^{P'}(v, w)$, where $P' = P \cup \{e, f, g\}$,
2. $\mathrm{diff}_V^{\mathsf{PV}}(u, u') \leq \mathrm{diff}_{V'}^{\mathsf{PV}}(u, u')$ for all edges (u, u') in $T(\mathcal{M})$,
3. $v_{\mathcal{M}'}(A\theta, u) = v_{\mathcal{M}}(A, u)$ for all $u \in W$ and all formulas A built up from variables in P, where $\mathcal{M}' = (W, R, V')$.

We start by assigning appropriate truth values to e, f, g in v and w. Without loss of generality, we may assume that either

(a) $V(p, v) = V(q, v) = \mathbf{t}$ and $V(p, w) = V(q, w) = \mathbf{f}$, or
(b) $V(p, v) = V(q, w) = \mathbf{t}$ and $V(p, w) = V(q, v) = \mathbf{f}$.

In case (a) we set $V'(e, v) = V'(f, v) = V'(g, v) = V'(e, w) = V'(g, w) = \mathbf{t}$ and $V'(f, w) = \mathbf{f}$. In case (b) we set $V'(e, v) = V'(f, v) = V('e, w) = \mathbf{t}$ and $V'(g, v) = V'(f, w) = V'(g, w) = \mathbf{f}$. In both cases condition 1 is satisfied and $v_{\mathcal{M}'}(A\theta, u) = v_{\mathcal{M}}(A, u)$ for $u \in \{v, w\}$.

Observe that p and q are not relevant for evaluating $A\theta$; we may thus set $V'(p,u) = V'(q,u) = \mathbf{t}$ in all worlds $u \in W$.

The assignment of truth values to e, f, g in worlds u distinct from v and w is defined by induction on the distance $d(u)$ to the world v in $T(\mathcal{M})$; where $d(u)$ is defined as the minimal number of edges in a sequence $u, u_1, \ldots, u_k, v$ of adjacent nodes. The induction hypothesis is:

(IH) Conditions 2 and 3, above, are satisfied if we only consider the worlds $u \in W$ for which $d(u) \leq n$.

(IH) trivially holds for $n = 1$.

Let u' be a world with $d(u') = n+1$. Since $T(\mathcal{M})$ is a tree there is a unique u with (u', u) in $T(\mathcal{M})$ and $d(u) = n$. By induction hypothesis, we have already defined an appropriate assignment to e, f, g in u. To find the appropriate truth values for e, f, g in u' we distinguish the following cases.

(1) $V(p,u) = V(q,u) = \mathbf{t}$. (IH) leaves two possibilities for V' with respect to e, f, g in u:
  (1.1) $V'(e,u) = V'(f,u) = V'(g,u) = \mathbf{t}$. We set $V'(e,u') = V(p,u')$ and $V'(f,u') = \mathbf{t}$ and $V'(g,u') = V(q,u')$.
  (1.2) $V'(e,u) = V'(f,u) = V'(g,u) = \mathbf{f}$. We set $V'(e,u') = \tilde{\neg} V(p,u')$ and $V'(f,u') = \mathbf{f}$ and $V'(g,u') = \tilde{\neg} V(q,u')$.
(2) $V(p,u) = \mathbf{t}$ and $V(q,u) = \mathbf{f}$. Again, (IH) leaves two possibilities:
  (2.1) $V'(e,u) = V'(f,u) = \mathbf{t}$ and $V'(g,u) = \mathbf{f}$. V' is like in case (1.1).
  (2.2) $V'(e,u) = V'(f,u) = \mathbf{f}$ and $V'(g,u) = \mathbf{t}$. V' is like in case (1.2).
(3) $V(p,u) = \mathbf{f}$ and $V(q,u) = \mathbf{t}$. Like case (2), except for swapping $\mathbf{t}$ and $\mathbf{f}$ in the assignments to f in u'.
(4) $V(p,u) = \mathbf{f}$ and $V(q,u) = \mathbf{f}$. Like case (1), except for swapping $\mathbf{t}$ and $\mathbf{f}$ in the assignments to f in u'.

In all cases it easy to check that (IH) holds for $n+1$ after the described adjustments. Therefore the construction eliminates the particular counter-example to (**au**$'$) without introducing a new one. The whole construction is repeated for each pair (x,y) of adjacent worlds where $\mathrm{diff}^{\mathsf{PV}}_{V^*}(x,y) > 1$ until (**au**$'$) is satisfied. (V^* is the respective valuation from the previous step.) □

Remark 1. As is to be expected from the intended semantics of *atomic* updates update-Λ=Λ *does not hold* in general if Λ is a logic for which the accessibility relation is *transitive*. E.g., one can check that the formula

$$F = (p \wedge q) \supset [\Diamond\Box\bot \vee \Box(\neg p \vee q) \vee \Diamond\Diamond(p \vee q)]$$

is schematically valid in all atomic-update models with transitive update relation. However, it is easy to construct a (Kripke) counter-interpretation with transitive accessibility relation for F. (Modulo obvious augmentations of Definitions 4 and 5) this fact can be expressed as update-$\mathsf{K4} \neq \mathsf{K4}$. Similarly, the "update counterparts" of $\mathsf{K5}$, $\mathsf{S4}$, $\mathsf{S5}$, etc. do *not* coincide with the respective standard logics.

Remark 2. Independently of any considerations on update models, Theorem 1 can be viewed as a *strengthening of the completeness theorem* for the *standard* normal logics K, KB, D, T, and TB. It states that for every non-valid formula F there is a counter-interpretation of an instance of F that obeys the atomic-update restriction (**au**$'$). Indeed, the proof of the theorem consists in an explicit construction of such a substitution instance and its corresponding update counter-model.

We are interested in reasoning about dynamic databases both at the level of "schematic" statements and by evaluating statements referring to concrete atoms of a database. Theorem 1 tells us that we remain within standard normal modal logics as long as only schematic validity is considered. In order to be able to refer to the schematic as well as the concrete level simultaneously we define the language $\mathcal{UL}$ over a *two-sorted* propositional signature:

- An *atomic formula* of $\mathcal{UL}$ is either an element $p \in \mathsf{atoms}$ or a schematic variable or $\top$ or $\bot$. (The set of propositional variables and atoms are disjoint.)
- *Complex formulas* of $\mathcal{UL}$ are built up as usual from the atomic formulas using the connectives $\neg, \wedge, \vee, \supset$ and the modalities $\Box$, $\Diamond$.

A formula of our extended language is called *concrete* if it does not contain propositional variables. Otherwise, it is called *schematic*. For concrete formulas F, $v_\alpha^{\mathcal{M}}(F)$ is defined as in Section 2. An arbitrary (possibly schematic) formula F is called *valid* in $\mathcal{M}$ if for all concrete formulas F' that arise by substituting the propositional variables of F with concrete formulas we have $v_\alpha^{\mathcal{M}}(F') = \mathbf{t}$ for all states α of $\mathcal{M}$.

Notation. We use lower case letters for atoms. Different letters always denote different atoms. Propositional variables are denoted by upper case letters from the end of the alphabet.

Example 2. The concrete formula $(a \wedge \neg b) \supset \Box(b \supset a)$ is valid in all update models. However the schematic formula $(X \wedge \neg b) \supset \Box(b \supset X)$ is not valid in most update models.

The concrete formula $\phi = \Diamond(a \wedge b) \wedge \Diamond(a \wedge \neg b) \wedge \Diamond(\neg a \wedge b) \wedge \Diamond(\neg a \wedge \neg b)$ can never evaluate to $\mathbf{t}$, since this would mean that in at least one of the accessible updates both atoms, a and b, are evaluated differently than in the current state. In other words $\neg\phi$ is valid in all update models. In contrast, it is easy to find counter models for $\Box(X \vee Y) \vee \Box(X \vee \neg Y) \vee \Box(\neg X \vee Y) \vee \Box(\neg X \vee \neg Y)$.

4 Prefixed Tableaux Adapted to Update Models

We have defined adequate syntax and semantics of a language that allows to express various statements with respect to changing databases (of a particularly simple type). To substantiate the claim that this formalism provides a basis for *reasoning* we have to define sound and complete calculi, suitable for automated proof search. Fortunately, Fitting's analytic *prefixed tableaux* [8] for standard normal logics turn out to be adaptable to our scenario. (See also [12] for an overview and history of related methods.)

We assume familiarity with tableaux but review the relevant terminology.

A *prefix* is a finite sequence of natural numbers (separated by dots). A prefix τ is a *simple extension* of a prefix σ if $\tau = \sigma.n$ for some $n \in \mathbb{N}$. A *prefixed formula* is a pair consisting of a prefix σ and formula F written as $\sigma :: F$. (Kripke-) interpretations are extended to prefixed formulas by referring to an *assignment* ϕ of worlds to prefixes. More formally, we define $v_\phi^{\mathcal{M}}(\sigma :: F) = v^{\mathcal{M}}(F, \phi(\sigma))$. If S is a set of prefixed formulas, then Pre(S) is the set of prefixes in S..

Prefixed tableaux are downward rooted trees of prefixed formulas, generated by appending new prefixed formula to a branch according to three types of rules.

Non-modal rules:

The rules for negation and disjunction are as follows:

$$(\neg\neg)\,\frac{\sigma :: \neg\neg F}{\sigma :: F} \qquad (\vee)\,\frac{\sigma :: F \vee G}{\sigma :: F \mid \sigma :: G} \qquad (\neg\vee)\,\frac{\sigma :: \neg(F \vee G)}{\begin{array}{c}\sigma :: \neg F\\ \sigma :: \neg G\end{array}}$$

We refer to $\sigma :: F$ and $\sigma :: G$ in $(\vee)$ as the two *sides* of the conclusion. The rules for conjunction and implication are similar.

Modal rules:

The rules for analyzing the modality $\Box$ in the basic modal logic K are

$$(\mathrm{K})\,\frac{\sigma :: \Box F}{\sigma.n :: F} \qquad (\pi)\,\frac{\sigma :: \neg\Box F}{\sigma.n :: \neg F}$$

where for (π) n is such that the prefix $\sigma.n$ is new to the current branch and for (K) $\sigma.n$ has been already used in the current branch. $\Diamond$ is treated as $\neg\Box\neg$. For serial, reflexive, and symmetric models we have to add the following rules, respectively:

$$(\mathrm{D})\,\frac{\sigma :: \Box F}{\sigma :: \Diamond F} \qquad (\mathrm{T})\,\frac{\sigma :: \Box F}{\sigma :: F} \qquad (\mathrm{KB})\,\frac{\sigma.n :: \Box F}{\sigma :: F}$$

Closure rules:

The closure rules for standard modal logics are

$$\frac{\begin{array}{c}\sigma :: \neg F\\ \sigma :: F\end{array}}{\mathtt{closed}} \qquad \frac{\sigma :: \neg\top}{\mathtt{closed}}$$

To accommodate the difference between atoms and schematic variables in the language $\mathcal{UL}$ as well as for the atomic update condition in update models it suffices to extend the standard tableau calculi by additional closure rules.

(Atomic) update closure rules:

$$\frac{\begin{array}{c}\sigma :: a\\ \sigma.n :: \neg a\\ \sigma :: b\\ \sigma.n :: \neg b\end{array}}{\mathtt{closed}} \qquad \frac{\begin{array}{c}\sigma :: \neg a\\ \sigma.n :: a\\ \sigma :: b\\ \sigma.n :: \neg b\end{array}}{\mathtt{closed}} \qquad \frac{\begin{array}{c}\sigma :: a\\ \sigma.n :: \neg a\\ \sigma :: \neg b\\ \sigma.n :: b\end{array}}{\mathtt{closed}} \qquad \frac{\begin{array}{c}\sigma :: \neg a\\ \sigma.n :: a\\ \sigma :: \neg b\\ \sigma.n :: b\end{array}}{\mathtt{closed}}$$

where a and b are different atoms.

If Λ is one of the logics K, KB, D, T, or TB, then a tableau constructed according to the above rules and the corresponding modal rules is called an *update Λ-tableau*.

A branch B of a tableau is *closed* if one of the above closure rules is applicable; otherwise B is called *open*. Let B be an open branch; the result B' of applying a rule ρ to one of the prefixed formulas in B and adding the prefixed formula(s) of (one side of) the conclusion of ρ to B is called an *extension of B*, as usual.

If all branches in a tableau **T** are *closed*, then **T** is called *closed*.

A closed update Λ-tableau with root $1 :: \neg F$ is a *tableau proof* of F. We will establish soundness and completeness of the presented tableau calculi, following essentially the proofs for standard normal logics as presented, e.g., in [8,14,12].

Let Π be a set of prefixes. Let $\sigma \rhd \tau$, $(\sigma, \tau \in \Pi)$ denote that τ is *Λ-accessible* from σ. The definition of $\rhd$ is given in the following table. (We call a prefix σ a *Λ-deadend* if Λ is non-serial and if there is no τ accessible from σ. In the case of the serial counterpart of Λ we demand that any Λ-deadend is made reflexive.)

Λ	$\sigma \rhd \tau$ iff
K	$\tau = \sigma.n$ for some $n \geq 1$
KB	$\tau = \sigma.n$ or $\sigma = \tau.m$
D	K-condition or (σ is a K-deadend and $\sigma = \tau$)
T	$\tau = \sigma.n$ or $\tau = \sigma$
TB	$\tau = \sigma$ or $\tau = \sigma.n$ or $\sigma = \tau.m$

This definition implies that $\langle \Pi, \rhd \rangle$ is a Λ-frame for $\Lambda \in \{\mathsf{K}, \mathsf{KB}, \mathsf{D}, \mathsf{T}, \mathsf{TB}\}$. In the following, we identify the set of propositional atoms atoms with a subset of PV (this subset is again denoted as atoms), thus treating our two-sorted (prefixed) $\mathcal{UL}$-formulas as a ordinary (prefixed) formula of modal logic.

A branch B of an update Λ-tableau is *satisfied* by a Λ-interpretation $\mathcal{M} = (W, R, V)$ if there is an assignment ϕ such that $v_\phi^{\mathcal{M}}(\sigma :: F) = \mathbf{t}$ for all $\sigma :: F$ in B.

Observe that open branches of update tableaux are, by definition, also branches of ordinary (modal) tableaux. Hence the following lemma is standard.

Lemma 1. *Let B be an open branch in an update Λ-tableau. Assume that B is satisfied by an Λ-interpretation $\mathcal{M}$ such that for all $w \in W$, condition* (**au**$'$) *is fulfilled. Then every extension B' of B is also satisfied by $\mathcal{M}$.*

Theorem 2 (Soundness). *Let $\Lambda \in \{\mathsf{K}, \mathsf{KB}, \mathsf{D}, \mathsf{T}, \mathsf{TB}\}$. If F has an update Λ-tableau proof then F is valid in all update Λ-models.*

Proof. (Indirectly.) Suppose that F is not valid in all update Λ-models. Then some instance F' of F has a counter-Λ-interpretation $\mathcal{M} = (W, R, V)$, which fulfills condition (**au**$'$) for all $w \in W$.

Now assume that there exists a tableau proof **T** of F. We can instantiate **T** to obtain a closed tableau **T**$'$ with root $1 :: \neg F'$. By the first assumption $v_\phi^{\mathcal{M}}(\neg F') = \mathbf{t}$. Using Lemma 1 inductively, if follows that there exists a branch in **T**' satisfied by $\mathcal{M}$. This contradicts the assumption that **T** and hence also **T**' is closed. □

A set S of prefix $\mathcal{UL}$-formulas is *atomically closed* if

1. There is a formula A such that both $\sigma :: A$ and $\sigma :: \neg A$ occur in S, or
2. $\sigma :: \neg\top$ occurs in S, or
3. one of the following cases holds, where a, b are different atoms:

$$\begin{array}{llll}\{\,\sigma :: a, & \sigma.n :: \neg a, & \sigma :: b, & \sigma.n :: \neg b\,\} \subseteq S\\ \{\,\sigma :: \neg a, & \sigma.n :: a, & \sigma :: b, & \sigma.n :: \neg b\,\} \subseteq S\\ \{\,\sigma :: a, & \sigma.n :: \neg a, & \sigma :: \neg b, & \sigma.n :: b\,\} \subseteq S\\ \{\,\sigma :: \neg a, & \sigma.n :: a, & \sigma :: \neg b, & \sigma.n :: b\,\} \subseteq S\end{array}$$

A set S of prefix $\mathcal{UL}$-formulas is *Λ-downward saturated* if it is *not* atomically closed and the usual conditions for downward saturatedness are satisfied by composite formulas F. (See, e.g., [12,8].) We recall only the case where $F = \sigma :: \Box A$: Let $\Pi = \mathrm{Pre}(S)$, if $\sigma :: \Box A$ occurs in S, then $\tau :: A \in S$ for every $\tau \in \Pi$ such that $\sigma \rhd \tau$.

We use the following corollary, extracted from the proof of Theorem 1.

Corollary 1. *Let $\mathcal{M} = (W, R, V)$ be a tree-like Λ-interpretation that, for all $w \in W$ fulfills the atomic update condition (**au′**) on some subset P of* PV*. Then there exists an Λ-interpretation $\mathcal{M}' = (W, R, V)$ such that for all $w \in W$: w fulfills the atomic update condition (**au′**) on all* PV *and $v^{\mathcal{M}}(A, w) = v^{\mathcal{M}'}(A\theta, w)$ for all formulas A and some substitution θ with domain* $\mathsf{PV} - P$.

Theorem 3 (Completeness). *For $\Lambda \in \{\mathsf{K}, \mathsf{KB}, \mathsf{D}, \mathsf{T}, \mathsf{TB}\}$, if an $\mathcal{UL}$-formula F is valid in all update Λ-models, then there exists a tableau proof of F.*

Proof. (Indirectly.) Suppose that all tableaux with root $1 :: \neg F$ have an open branch. Then a systematic tableau construction, as described in [12] or [8], yields an open branch B that is downward saturated. As in the standard completeness proofs, one can show that B is satisfied by a tree-like Λ-interpretation $\mathcal{M} = (W, R, V)$. In particular, we have $v^{\mathcal{M}}_{\phi}(1 :: F) = \mathbf{f}$ for some assignment ϕ. Moreover, since B is Λ-downward saturated, (**au′**) is fulfilled on (the subset of PV called) atoms (because of clause 3 in the definition of atomical closure, above.) By Corollary 1 we obtain a counter-Λ-interpretation $\mathcal{M}' = (W, R, V')$ for F' that fulfills (**au′**) on all variables, where in F' only variables that are not in atoms have been instantiated. But this implies that F cannot be valid in all Λ-update models. □

Remark on Integrity Constraints

In reasoning about changing states of a database, *integrity constraints* are of central importance. By an integrity constraint we simply mean a condition, referring to specific atoms and/or schematic variables, that has to be fulfilled in all states of a given database. Assuming that, in reference to single state, those conditions are expressible in $\mathcal{UL}$, the framework of prefixed tableaux allows the inclusion of integrity constraints in reasoning about databases by simply treating the corresponding formulas of $\mathcal{UL}$ as *global axioms* (in the sense of [8,14]).

5 Incomplete and Inconsistent Data

Our model of the dynamic behavior of a database is yet too simple to capture phenomena like possibly incomplete and inconsistent data. However, we claim that the basic formalism of atomic update models and corresponding tableaux is easily adapted to such scenarios.

Belnap's four-valued logic [4] has been suggested repeatedly as a tool for reasoning about (possibly) inconsistent and incomplete information. The main intuition in this context is that a database may not only contain information implying that a statement is *false* or *true*, but such information may also be absent or inconsistent. The four possible states of knowledge are represented by the four truth values **f** (*false*), **u** (*undetermined*), $\bot$(*inconsistent*), and **t** (*true*), respectively. This intended interpretation induces the following truth functions for the connectives $\neg$, $\wedge$, and $\vee$:

	$\neg$
f	**t**
u	**u**
$\bot$	$\bot$
t	**f**

$\wedge$	**f**	**u**	$\bot$	**t**
f	**f**	**f**	**f**	**f**
u	**f**	**u**	**f**	**u**
$\bot$	**f**	**f**	$\bot$	$\bot$
t	**f**	**u**	$\bot$	**t**

$\vee$	**f**	**u**	$\bot$	**t**
f	**f**	**u**	$\bot$	**t**
u	**u**	**u**	**t**	**t**
$\bot$	$\bot$	**t**	$\bot$	**t**
t	**t**	**t**	**t**	**t**

For the definition of other connectives (in particular forms of implication) and the choice of designated truth values we refer to the extensive investigations of Avron and Arieli (see, e.g., [2,1]).

The many-valued context allows to extend the classical universal and existential modalities to the more general concept of *distribution modalities*, introduced in [7]. Let $\mathcal{V}$ be the set of truth values; and, correspondingly, let a state of a database be an assignment $\alpha : \mathsf{atoms} \mapsto \mathcal{V}$. Then any function $\widetilde{\mu}$ of type $2^{\mathcal{V}} \mapsto \mathcal{V}$ induces a truth function of a distribution modality μ by:

$$v^{\mathcal{D}}_{\alpha}(\mu F) = \widetilde{\mu}(\{v^{\mathcal{D}}_{\beta}(F) \mid \beta \in \Sigma{:}\,\alpha U \beta\}).$$

Here Σ are the states of the update model $\mathcal{D}$ and U is its accessibility relation. $\{v^{\mathcal{D}}_{\beta}(F) \mid \beta \in \Sigma{:}\,\alpha U \beta\}$ is called the *distribution* of F in $\mathcal{D}$ at α. Again, a (many-valued) update model corresponds to a (many-valued) Kripke interpretation. In particular, we call the update models in which the states of the database consist in assignments of type $\mathsf{atoms} \mapsto \{\mathbf{t}, \mathbf{u}, \mathbf{f}, \bot\}$ *Belnap update structures*. This context allows us to define modalities like

- *det*(F) with the intended meaning: "No update renders information on F incomplete or inconsistent", and
- *unif*(F) with the intended meaning: "F is evaluated uniformly in all updates".

Since *det*(F) is intended to express a meta-linguistic (and therefore classical) property of F within the object language itself, it always evaluates to **t** or **f**. More exactly, its semantics is fixed by:

$$\widetilde{det}(W) = \begin{cases} \mathbf{t} & \text{if } W = \emptyset, \{\mathbf{f}\}, \{\mathbf{t}\}, \text{or } \{\mathbf{t}, \mathbf{f}\} \\ \mathbf{f} & \text{otherwise} \end{cases}$$

On the other hand "uniform evaluation" admittedly is an ambiguous concept. Certainly, we want *unif*(F) to be *true* if either F evaluates to **t** in all updates, or to **f** in all updates. Likewise, it is clear that *unif*(F) is *false* if the distribution contains **t** *and* **f** (i.e., if there is an update evaluating the formula to **t**, but also another update that evaluates it to **f**.) But we want *unif*(F) to be *undetermined* if the distribution of F contains **u**. One way to round off and formalize these intuitions is to define the truth function for *unif* as follows:

$W \subseteq \mathcal{V}$	$\widetilde{unif}(W)$
$\emptyset, \{\mathbf{f}\}, \{\mathbf{t}\}$	$\mathbf{t}$
$\{\mathbf{u}\}, \{\mathbf{u},\mathbf{f}\}, \{\mathbf{u},\mathbf{t}\}$	$\mathbf{u}$
$\{\mathbf{f},\mathbf{t}\}, \{\mathbf{f},\mathbf{u},\mathbf{t}\}, \{\mathbf{f},\bot,\mathbf{t}\}, \{\mathbf{f},\mathbf{u},\bot,\mathbf{t}\}$	$\mathbf{f}$
$\{\bot\}, \{\mathbf{f},\bot\}, \{\bot,\mathbf{t}\}, \{\mathbf{u},\bot\}, \{\mathbf{f},\mathbf{u},\bot\}, \{\mathbf{u},\bot\,\mathbf{t}\}$	$\bot$

Of course, *det* and *unif* are just two simple examples. Observe that there are 4^{2^4} possible distribution modalities definable over Belnap update structures. All of them refer to properties of the "truth status" of statements with respect to the class of possible stepwise evolutions of the database. We also remind the reader that Belnap update models come in different variants according to different constraining properties of the update relation.

To define a particular *Belnap update logic* with respect to a class of Belnap update models we therefore have to fix three independent parameters (in addition to the set of atoms and propositional variables):

(1) a set of designated truth values $\mathcal{V}_D \subseteq \mathcal{V}$; usually $\{\mathbf{t}\}$ or $\{\mathbf{t},\bot\}$
(2) a set of $\{\mu_1,\ldots,\mu_n\}$ of distribution modalities (with associated truth functions $\widetilde{\mu_1},\ldots,\widetilde{\mu_n}$ and four-valued connectives (specified by their truth tables)
(3) properties like symmetry or reflexivity, which we want the update relation to observe.

We call a concrete formula F *valid* in such a logic if $v_\alpha^{\mathcal{D}}(F) \in \mathcal{V}_D$ for all states α of all corresponding atomic update models $\mathcal{D}$. This is extended to schematic formulas in the obvious way. (See Section 3.)

6 Prefixed Signed Tableaux for Belnap Update Models

It is well known that appropriate analytic calculi for all (truth functional) finite valued logics can be defined using *signed* versions of tableaux (see, e.g., [13]). These can be extended to finite valued modal logics by combining prefixes (denoting worlds) and signs (denoting truth values) as was shown in [7]. We describe a simplified example of the latter calculi, adapted for update structures, for the special case of Belnap update models with serial (but otherwise general) update relation and (only) modality *det*.[2]

A *prefixed signed formula* is a triple consisting of a finite sequence of natural numbers σ (prefix), a truth value v, and a formula F, written as $\sigma\colon[v]\colon F$.

Remark 3. In classical logic the prefixed signed formulas $\sigma\colon[\mathbf{t}]\colon F$ and $\sigma\colon[\mathbf{f}]\colon F$ are just notational variants of the prefixed formulas $\sigma :: F$ and $\sigma :: \neg F$, respectively. For many-valued logics truth value signs are not only an elegant way to make semantic information explicit but are, in general, *needed* to obtain complete tableau calculi.

[2] Other properties of the update relation result in simple technical variations of some modal rules. The corresponding calculi are omitted here for space reasons.

Again, a *(prefixed signed)* tableau is a downward rooted tree of prefixed signed formulas, constructed using the following rules.

Non-modal rules: can directly be read off from the truth tables of connectives. We refer to [13,16] for general methods and results about constructing optimal rules.

Closure rules: The standard closure rule is

$$\frac{\sigma\colon[v]\colon F \quad \sigma\colon[w]\colon F}{\texttt{closed}}$$

where v and w are different truth values. (F need not be atomic.)

A modal operator μ induces an additional closure rules if a formula μF never evaluates to a particular truth value. For instance, the modality *det* triggers the following two closure rules:

$$\frac{\sigma\colon[\mathbf{u}]\colon \mathit{det}(F)}{\texttt{closed}} \qquad \frac{\sigma\colon[\bot]\colon \mathit{det}(F)}{\texttt{closed}}$$

Modal rules:

A general method for constructing modal rules from associated truth functions is described in [7]. We present greatly simplified[3] versions for the remaining cases of *det*-modalized formulae:

$$\frac{\sigma\colon[\mathbf{t}]\colon \mathit{det}(F)}{\sigma.n\colon[\mathbf{t}]\colon F \mid \sigma.n\colon[\mathbf{f}]\colon F} \qquad \frac{\sigma\colon[\mathbf{f}]\colon \mathit{det}(F)}{\sigma.n\colon[\mathbf{u}]\colon F \mid \sigma.n\colon[\bot]\colon F}$$

where $\sigma.n$ already occurs on the branch.

(Atomic) update closure rule:

$$\frac{\sigma\colon[u_1]\colon a \quad \sigma.n\colon[v_1]\colon a \quad \sigma\colon[u_2]\colon b \quad \sigma.n\colon[v_2]\colon b}{\texttt{closed}}$$

where a and b are different atoms and $v_i \neq u_i$ for $i = 1$ and $i = 2$.

The results of [7] and Theorems 2 and 3 can be combined straightforwardly to obtain

Theorem 4. *A formula F is valid in a Belnap update logic if and only if for all non-designated truth values v there exists a corresponding update tableaux with root $1\colon[v]\colon F$ that is closed.*

Remark 4. For all mentioned variants of update logics, systematic and terminating tableau construction procedures can be defined as usual. This, in particular, implies the *decidability* of these logics.

[3] The simplification makes essential use of the fact that *det* is the only modal operator and that the update relation is serial, but otherwise unrestricted.

7 Open Ends

Other types of update operations. Obviously atomic updates as defined by condition (**au**) are only a special case.[4] One might, e.g., study multiple update relations that are indexed by the "new information" that triggers the update. This information is often represented by a boolean combination of atoms and thus naturally induces a corresponding algebra of update relations (similar to the algebra of programs in dynamic logic).

Different underlying many-valued logics. Update models can be defined over all kinds of truth functional logics as mechanism for "local" evaluation. As an interesting example we mention the bi-lattice based logics suggested by M.L. Ginsberg [11] for modeling default reasoning. Also dynamic *fuzzy* databases can be modeled by building on an appropriate fuzzy logic (e.g., some finite-valued Lukasiewicz logic).

Other useful distribution modalities. As explained above, every function of type $2^{\mathcal{V}} \mapsto \mathcal{V}$ induces a distribution modality. A systematic investigation of expressibility, complexity of corresponding rules and functional dependency between different sets of modalities is still lacking.

Modeling global update constraints. As a simple example consider the condition—for Belnap update models—that updates can only *increase knowledge* about data. Technically this corresponds to requiring $\alpha(a) \leq_k \beta(a)$ if $\alpha U \beta$, where $\leq_k$ is the partial "knowledge order" defined by $\mathbf{u} \leq_k \mathbf{t} \leq_k \bot$ and $\mathbf{u} \leq_k \mathbf{f} \leq_k \bot$.

First-order reasoning. Both, update models and corresponding tableau, are readily generalized to the first-order level. This move, of course, vastly improves the expressibility and complexity of the corresponding logics. Their strength and limits should also be explored.

References

1. Ofer Arieli and Arnon Avron. The logical role of the four-valued bilattice. In *13th Annual IEEE Symposium on Logic in Computer Science (LICS)*, pages 118–126, Indianapolis (USA), 1998. IEEE Computer Society.
2. Ofer Arieli and Arnon Avron. The value of the four values. *Artificial Intelligence*, 102(1):97–141, 1998.
3. Philippe Balbiani. A modal logic for data analysis. In Wojciech Penczek and Andrzej Szalas, editors, *Proc. Mathematical Foundations of Computer Science, 21st MFCS*, volume 1115 of *Lecture Notes in Computer Science*, pages 167–179, Cracow, Poland, 1996. Springer-Verlag.
4. Nuel D. Belnap. A useful four-valued logic. In J.M. Dunn and G. Epstein, editors, *Modern Uses of Multiple-Valued Logic*, pages 8–37. D. Reidel Publishing Co., 1977.
5. Thomas Eiter and Georg Gottlob. On the complexity of propositional knowledge base revision, updates, and counterfactuals. *Artificial Intelligence*, 57:227–270, 1992.
6. Dieter Fensel, Rix Groenboom, and G.R.Renardel de Lavalette. Modal change logic (MCL): Specifying the reasoning of knowledge-based systems. *Data Knowl. Eng.*, 25(1-2):243–269, 1998.

[4] For a thorough computational analysis of different related concepts see [5].

7. Christian G. Fermüller and Herbert Langsteiner. Tableaux for finite-valued logics with arbitrary distribution modalities. In Harrie de Swart, editor, *Proc. Automated Reasoning with Analytic Tableaux and Related Methods (TABLEAUX'98)*, volume 1397 of *Lecture Notes in Computer Science*, pages 156–171, Oisterwijk (Netherlands), 1998. Springer-Verlag.
8. Melvin C. Fitting. *Proof Methods for Modal and Intuitionistic Logics*. D. Reidel Publishing Co., Dordrecht, 1983.
9. Melvin C. Fitting. Modality and databases. In Roy Dyckhoff, editor, *Proc. Automated Reasoning with Analytic Tableaux and Related Methods (TABLEAUX 2000)*, pages 19–39, Lecture Notes in Computer Science 1847, St. Andrews, Scotland, 2000. Springer-Verlag.
10. Nir Friedman and Joseph Y. Halpern. Modeling belief in dynamic systems. II: Revision and update. *J. Artif. Intell. Res. (JAIR)*, 10:17–167, 1999.
11. Matthew L. Ginsberg. Multi-valued logics. *Computational Intelligence*, 4(3), 1988.
12. Rajeev Goré. Tableau methods for modal and temporal logics. In M. D'Agostino, D. Gabbay, R. Hähnle, and J. Posegga, editors, *Handbook of Tableau Methods*, pages 297–396. Kluwer Academic Publishers, 1999.
13. Reiner Hähnle. *Automated Deduction in Multiple-valued Logics*. Clarendon Press, Oxford, 1993.
14. Fabio Massacci. Single Step Tableaux for Modal Logics. *J. Automated Reasoning*, 24(3):319–364, 2000.
15. Mark Ryan and Pierre-Yves Schobbens. Counterfactuals and updates as inverse modalities. *J. Logic Lang. Inf.*, 6(2):123–146, 1997.
16. Gernot Salzer. Optimal axiomatizations for multiple-valued operators and quantifiers based on semilattices. In Michael McRobbie and John Slaney, editors, *Proc. 13th Conference on Automated Deduction, New Brunswick/NJ, USA*, volume 1104 of *Lecture Notes in Computer Science*, pages 688–702. Springer-Verlag, 1996.

Inference of Termination Conditions for Numerical Loops in Prolog

Alexander Serebrenik* and Danny De Schreye

Department of Computer Science, K.U. Leuven
Celestijnenlaan 200A, B-3001, Heverlee, Belgium
{Alexander.Serebrenik, Danny.DeSchreye}@cs.kuleuven.ac.be

1 Introduction

Numerical computations form an essential part of almost any real-world program. Clearly, in order for a termination analyser to be of practical use it should contain a mechanism for inferring termination of such computations. However, this topic attracted less attention of the research community. In this work we concentrate on automatic termination inference for logic programs depending on numerical computations. Dershowitz *et al.* [8] showed that termination of general numerical computations, for instance on floating point numbers, may be counter-intuitive, i.e., the observed behaviour does not necessarily coincide with the theoretically expected one. Thus, we restrict ourselves to integer computations only.

While discussing termination of integer computations the following question should be asked: what conditions on the queries should be assumed, such that the queries will terminate. We refer to this question as the *termination inference problem.*

Example 1. $p(X) \leftarrow X < 7, X1$ *is* $X + 1, p(X1)$. This program terminates for queries $p(X)$, for all integer values of X. Thus, the answer for the termination inference problem is the condition "*true*". □

This example also hints at why the traditional approaches to termination analysis fail to prove termination of this example. These approaches are mostly based on the notion of *level mapping*, that is, a function from the set of all possible atoms to the natural numbers, which should decrease while traversing the rules. In our case, such a level mapping should depend on X, but X can be negative as well!

Two approaches for solving this problem are possible. First, one can change the definition of the level mapping to map atoms to integers. However, integers are, in general, not well-founded. To prove termination one should prove that the mapping is to some well-founded subset of integers. In the example above $(-\infty, 7)$ forms such a subset with an ordering $\succ$, such that $x \succ y$ if $x < y$, with respect to the usual ordering on integers.

* supported by GOA: "LP^+: a second generation logic programming language".

R. Nieuwenhuis and A. Voronkov (Eds.): LPAR 2001, LNAI 2250, pp. 654–669, 2001.

The second approach that we present in the paper does not require changing the definition of level mapping. Indeed, the level mapping as required exists. It maps $p(X)$ to $7 - X$ if $X < 7$ and to 0 otherwise. This level mapping decreases while traversing the rule, i.e., the size of $p(X)$, $7 - X$, is greater than the size of $p(X1)$, $6 - X$, thus, proving termination. We present a transformation that allows us to define such a level mappings in an automatic way by incorporating techniques of [8], such as level mapping inference, in the well-known framework of the acceptability with respect to a set [5,6]. This integration provides not only a better understanding of termination behaviour of integer computations, but also the possibility to perform the analysis automatically as in Decorte *et al.* [7].

The rest of the paper is organised as follows. After making some preliminary remarks, we present in Section 3 our transformation—first by means of an example, then more formally. In Section 4 we discuss more practical issues and present the algorithm implementing the termination inference. In Section 5 we discuss further extensions, such as proving termination of programs depending in numerical computations as well as symbolic ones. Then we review related work and conclude.

2 Preliminaries

We follow the standard notation for terms and atoms. A *query* is a finite sequence of atoms. Given an atom A, *rel*(A) denotes the predicate occuring in A. $Atom_P$ denotes a set of all atoms that can be constructed from the language underlying P. The extended base B_P^E is a quotient set of $Atom_P$ modulo the variant relation. An SLD-tree constructed using the left-to-right selection rule of Prolog is called an LD-tree. A goal G *LD-terminates* for a program P, if the LD-tree for (P, G) is finite.

Definition 1. *[1] Let P be a program and p, q be predicates occuring in it. We say that p* refers to *q* in *P if there is a clause in P that uses p in its head and q in its body; that p* depends on *q* in *P and write $p \sqsupseteq q$, if (p, q) is in the transitive, reflexive closure of the relation* refers to*; and that p* and *q* are mutually recursive *and write $p \simeq q$, if $p \sqsupseteq q$ and $q \sqsupseteq p$.*

We recall some basic notions, related to termination analysis. A *level mapping* is a function $|\cdot|: B_P^E \to \mathcal{N}$, where $\mathcal{N}$ is the set of the naturals.

We study termination of programs with respect to sets of queries. The following notion is one of the most basic notions in this framework.

Definition 2. *[6] Let P be a definite program and S be a set of atomic queries. The* call set*, Call(P, S), is the set of all atoms A, such that a variant of A is a selected atom in some derivation for $P \cup \{\leftarrow Q\}$, for some $Q \in S$ and under the left-to-right selection rule.*

The following definition [14] generalises the notion of acceptability with respect to a set [5,6] by extending it to mutual recursion.

Definition 3. *Let S be a set of atomic queries and P a definite program. P is* acceptable with respect to S *if there exists a level mapping $|\cdot|$ such that for any $A \in Call(P,S)$, for any $A' \leftarrow B_1,\ldots,B_n$ in P, such that* $\mathrm{mgu}(A,A') = \theta$ *exists, for any B_i, such that $rel(B_i) \simeq rel(A)$ and for any c.a.s. σ for $\leftarrow (B_1,\ldots,B_{i-1})\theta$ holds that $|A| > |B_i\theta\sigma|$.*

De Schreye *et al.* [5] characterise LD-termination in terms of acceptability.

Theorem 1. *(cf. [5]) Let P be a program. P is acceptable with respect to a set S if and only if P is LD-terminating for all queries in S.*

We also need to introduce the notion of interargument relations.

Definition 4. *[7] Let P be a definite program, p/n a predicate in P. An* interargument relation *for p/n is $R_p \subseteq \mathcal{N}^n$. R_p is a* valid interargument relation for p/n with respect to a norm $\|\cdot\|$ *if and only if for every $p(t_1,\ldots,t_n) \in Atom_P$ if $P \models p(t_1,\ldots,t_n)$ then $(\|t_1\|,\ldots,\|t_n\|) \in R_p$.*

To characterise program transformations Bossi and Cocco [3] introduced the following notion for a program P and a query Q: $\mathcal{M}[\![P]\!](Q) = \{\sigma \mid$ there is a successful LD-derivation of Q and P with c.a.s. $\sigma\} \cup \{\perp \mid$ there is an infinite LD-derivation of Q and $P\}$.

3 Methodology

In this section we introduce our methodology using a simple example. In the subsequent sections, we formalise it and discuss different extensions.

The following example generates an oscillating sequence and stops if the generated value is greater than 1000 or smaller than -1000.

Example 2. We are interested in proving termination of the set of queries $S = \{p(z) \mid z \text{ is an integer}\}$ with respect to the following program:
$p(X) \leftarrow X > 1, X < 1000, X1 \textit{ is } -X * X, p(X1).$
$p(X) \leftarrow X < -1, X > -1000, X1 \textit{ is } X * X, p(X1).$
The direct attempt to define the level mapping of $p(X)$ as X fails, since X can be positive as well as negative. Thus, a more complex level mapping should be defined. We start with some observations.

The first clause is applicable if $1 < X < 1000$, the second one, if $-1000 < X < -1$. Thus, termination of $p(X)$ for $X \le -1000$, $-1 \le X \le 1$ or $X \ge 1000$ is trivial. Moreover, if an infinite sequence is obtained by applying the first clause at the first step, then for the recursive call $p(X1)$, it holds that $-1000 < X1 < -1$ and if the second clause was applied at the first step of the infinite sequence, then for the recursive call $p(X1)$, it holds that $1 < X1 < 1000$. We use this observation and replace a predicate p with two new predicates $p^{1<X<1000}$ and $p^{-1000<X<-1}$, such that $p^{1<X<1000}$ is called if $p(X)$ is called and $1 < X < 1000$ holds and $p^{-1000<X<-1}$ is called if $p(X)$ is called and $-1000 < X < -1$ holds. The following program is obtained:

$p^{1<X<1000}(X) \leftarrow X > 1, X < 1000, X1 \text{ is } -X * X, p^{-1000<X<-1}(X1).$
$p^{-1000<X<-1}(X) \leftarrow X < -1, X > -1000, X1 \text{ is } X * X, p^{1<X<1000}(X1).$
Now we define two *different* level mappings, one for atoms of $p^{1<X<1000}$ and another one for atoms of $p^{-1000<X<-1}$. Let $\mid p^{1<X<1000}(n) \mid = 1000 - n$ if $1 < n < 1000$ and 0 otherwise and let $\mid p^{-1000<X<-1}(n) \mid = 1000 + n$ if $-1000 < n < -1$ and 0 otherwise. We verify acceptability of the transformed program with respect to $\{p^{1<X<1000}(n) \mid 1 < n < 1000\} \cup \{p^{-1000<X<-1}(n) \mid -1000 < n < -1\}$. This implies termination of the transformed program with respect to these queries, and thus, termination of the original program with respect to S.

Due to the lack of space we discuss only queries of the form $p^{1<X<1000}(n)$ for $1 < n < 1000$. The only clause that its head can be unified with this query is the first clause. The only atom of a predicate mutually recursive with $p^{1<X<1000}$ is $p^{-1000<X<-1}(m)$. Then, $\mid p^{1<X<1000}(n) \mid > \mid p^{-1000<X<-1}(m) \mid$ should hold[1], i.e., $1000 - n > 1000 + m$, that is $1000 - n > 1000 - n^2$ ($n > 1$ and $m = -n^2$), which is true for $n > 1$. □

The intuitive presentation above hints at the major issues to be discussed in the following sections: how the cases such as those above can be extracted from the program, and how the program should be transformed.

3.1 Basic Notions

In this section we formally introduce some notions that further analysis will be based on. Recall that the aim of our analysis is to find, given a predicate and a query, a sufficient condition for termination of this query with respect to this program. Thus, we need to define a notion of a termination condition. We start with a number of auxiliary definitions.

Definition 5. *Let p be a predicate of arity n. Then,* $\$1^p, \ldots, \$n^p$ *are called* argument position denominators.

If the predicate is clear from the context the superscripts will be omitted.

Definition 6. *Let P be a program, S be a set of queries. An argument position i of a predicate p is called* integer argument position, *if for every* $p(t_1, \ldots, t_n) \in$ *Call*(P, S), t_i *is an integer.*

Argument position denominators corresponding to integer argument positions will be called integer argument position denominators.

An *integer inequality* is an atom of one of the following forms *Exp1* > *Exp2*, *Exp1* < *Exp2*,*Exp1* ≥ *Exp2* or *Exp1* ≤ *Exp2*, where *Exp1* and *Exp2* are constructed from integers, variables and the four operations of arithmetics. A *symbolic inequality over the arguments of a predicate p* is constructed similarly to an integer inequality. However, instead of variables, integer argument positions denominators are used.

Example 3. $X > 0$ and $Y \leq X + 5$ are integer inequalities. Given a predicate p of arity 3, having only integer argument positions $\$1^p > 0$ and $\$2^p \leq \$1^p + \$3^p$ are symbolic inequalities over the arguments of p. □

[1] The clause is applicable only if $1 < n < 1000$. Thus, $\mid p^{-1000<X<-1}(n) \mid = 1000 + n$.

Disjunctions of conjunctions based on integer inequalities are called *integer conditions*. Similarly, propositional calculus formulae based on symbolic inequalities over the arguments of the same predicate are called *symbolic conditions over the integer arguments of this predicate.*

Definition 7. *Let $p(t_1,\dots,t_n)$ be an atom and let c_p be a symbolic condition over the arguments of p. An* instance of the condition with respect to an atom, *$c_p(p(t_1,\dots,t_n))$, is obtained by replacing the argument positions denominators with the corresponding arguments, i.e., $\$i^p$ with t_i.*

Example 4. Let $p(X,Y,5)$ be an atom and let c_p be $(\$1^p > 0) \wedge (\$2^p \leq \$1^p + \$3^p)$. Then, $c_p(p(X,Y,5))$ is $(X > 0) \wedge (Y \leq X + 5)$. □

Now we are ready to define *termination condition* formally.

Definition 8. *Let P be a program, and Q be an atomic query. A symbolic condition $c_{\mathrm{rel}(Q)}$ is a* termination condition *for Q if given that $c_{\mathrm{rel}(Q)}(Q)$ holds, Q left-terminates with respect to P.*

A termination condition for Example 2 is *true*, i.e., $p(X)$ terminates for every integer X. We'll see further that this is not always the case.

We discuss now inferring what values integer arguments can take during traversal of the rules, i.e., the "case analysis" performed in Example 2. It provides already the underlying intuition—calls of the predicate p^c are identical to the calls of the predicate p, where c holds for its arguments. More formally, we define a notion of *set of adornments*. Later we specify when it is *guard-tuned* and we show how such a guard-tuned set of adornments can be constructed.

Definition 9. *Let p be a predicate. The set $\mathcal{A}_p = \{c_1,\dots,c_n\}$ of symbolic conditions over the integer arguments of p is called* set of adornments for p *if for all i,j such that $1 \leq i < j \leq n$, $c_i \wedge c_j = \mathit{false}$ and $\bigvee_{i=1}^{n} c_i = \mathit{true}$.*

Example 5. Example 2, continued. The following are examples of sets of adornments: $\{\$1 \leq 100, \$1 > 100\}$ and $\{(\$1 \leq -1000) \vee (-1 \leq \$1 \leq 1) \vee (\$1 \geq 1000), -1000 < \$1 < -1, 1 < \$1 < 1000\}$. □

3.2 Program Transformation

The next question that should be answered is how the program should be transformed given a set of adornments. After this transformation $p^c(X_1,\dots,X_n)$ will behave with respect to the transformed program exactly as $p(X_1,\dots,X_n)$ does, for all calls that satisfy the condition c. To define a transformation formally we introduce the following definition:

Let $H \leftarrow B_1,\dots,B_n$ be a rule. $B_1,\dots,B_i$, is called *prefix of the rule*, if for all j, $1 \leq j \leq i \leq n$, B_j is an integer inequality and the only variables in its arguments are variables of H. $B_1,\dots,B_i$ is called *the maximal prefix* of the rule, if it is a prefix and $B_1,\dots,B_i,B_{i+1}$ is not a prefix.

Since a prefix constrains only variables appearing in the head of a clause there exists a symbolic condition over the arguments of the predicate of the head, such that the prefix is its instance with respect to the head. In general, this symbolic condition is not necessarily unique. The following notion guarantees uniqueness of such symbolic conditions. In this case we say that the symbolic condition *corresponds* to the prefix.

Definition 10. *[8] A rule $H \leftarrow B_1, \ldots, B_n$ is called* partially normalised *if all integer argument positions in H are occupied by distinct variables*[2].

We will also say that a program P is partially normalised if all the rules in P are partially normalised. After integer argument positions are identified a program can be easily rewritten to partially normalised form.

Now we are ready to present the transformation formally.

Definition 11. *Let P be a program and let p be a predicate in it. Let $\mathcal{A} = \bigcup_{q \in P} \mathcal{A}_q$ be a set of possible adornments for P. Then, the program P^a, called* adorned with respect to p, *is obtained in two steps as following:*

1. *For every rule r in P, for every subgoal $q(t_1, \ldots, t_n)$ in the body of r, s.t. $p \simeq q$ and for every $A \in \mathcal{A}_q$ replace $q(t_1, \ldots, t_n)$ by $q^A(t_1, \ldots, t_n)$.*
2. *For every rule r*
   Are adornments and inequalities in the body of r consistent? $*$
   If not—reject the rule.
   If r defines some q, such that $q \simeq p$
   Get as adornments of the head of r all $A \in \mathcal{A}_q$, that are consistent with comparisons of the maximal prefix of r and adornments of the body of r.

Example 6. Example 2, continued. The sets of adornments presented in Example 5 are used. With the first set of adornments we obtain P^{a_1}:
$p^{\$1 \leq 100}(X) \leftarrow X > 1, X < 1000, X1 \text{ is } -X * X, p^{\$1 \leq 100}(X1).$
$p^{\$1 > 100}(X) \leftarrow X > 1, X < 1000, X1 \text{ is } -X * X, p^{\$1 \leq 100}(X1).$
$p^{\$1 \leq 100}(X) \leftarrow X < -1, X > -1000, X1 \text{ is } X * X, p^{\$1 \leq 100}(X1).$
$p^{\$1 \leq 100}(X) \leftarrow X < -1, X > -1000, X1 \text{ is } X * X, p^{\$1 > 100}(X1).$
If the second set of adornments is used, the program P^{a_2} is obtained:

$$p^{1<\$1<1000}(X) \leftarrow X > 1, X < 1000, X1 \text{ is } -X * X, p^{-1000<\$1<-1}(X1). \tag{1}$$

$$p^{1<\$1<1000}(X) \leftarrow X > 1, X < 1000, X1 \text{ is } -X * X, p^{(\$1 \leq -1000) \vee (-1 \leq \$1 \leq 1) \vee (\$1 \geq 1000)}(X1). \tag{2}$$

$$p^{-1000<\$1<-1}(X) \leftarrow X < -1, X > -1000, X1 \text{ is } X * X, p^{1<\$1<1000}(X1). \tag{3}$$

$$p^{-1000<\$1<-1}(X) \leftarrow X < -1, X > -1000, X1 \text{ is } X * X, p^{(\$1 \leq -1000) \vee (-1 \leq \$1 \leq 1) \vee (\$1 \geq 1000)}(X1). \tag{4}$$

□

[2] If such a rule has only integer arguments Apt *et al.* [2] call it *homogeneous*.

Correctness of the transformation should be proved. Finiteness of the number of clauses, the number of subgoals in a clause and the number of elements in an adornment ensure that the transformation terminates. Next we need to prove that the transformation preserves termination.

Adorning clauses introduces new predicates. This means that the query Q gives rise to a number of different queries. Clearly, termination of all of these queries with respect to P^a is equivalent to termination of Q with respect to P^a augmented by a set of the clauses, such that for every $p \simeq rel(Q)$ and for every $A \in \mathcal{A}_p$ the clause $p(X_1, \ldots, X_n) \leftarrow p^A(X_1, \ldots, X_n)$ is added. We call this extended program P^{ag}.

Lemma 1. *Let P be a program, and let Q be a query. Let P^{ag} be a program obtained as described above. Then,* $\mathcal{M}[\![P^{ag}]\!](Q) \subseteq \mathcal{M}[\![P]\!](Q)$.

Proof. For all proofs we refer to [13]. ■

The second direction of the containment depends on the consistency check strategy applied at the point marked by $*$ in the definition of P^a.

Example 7. Let Q be $p(X)$ and let P be the following program:
$p(X) \leftarrow X > 0, q(X), X < 0.$ $\qquad$ $q(X) \leftarrow X > 0, p(X).$
Predicates p and q are mutually recursive. Thus, both of them should be adorned. Let $\mathcal{A}_p$ be $\{\$1 > 0, \$1 \leq 0\}$ and $\mathcal{A}_q$ be $\{\$1 > 0, \$1 \leq 0\}$. The following program is obtained after the first step of the adorning process.
$p(X) \leftarrow X > 0, q^{\$1>0}(X), X < 0.$ $\qquad$ $q(X) \leftarrow X > 0, p^{\$1>0}(X).$
$p(X) \leftarrow X > 0, q^{\$1\leq 0}(X), X < 0.$ $\qquad$ $q(X) \leftarrow X > 0, p^{\$1\leq 0}(X).$
The second step of the adorning process infers adornments for the heads of the clauses, possibly rejecting the inconsistent ones. If the inference technique tries to use all the information it has in the body constraints and adornments of body subgoals, a program $\{q^{\$1>0}(X) \leftarrow X > 0, p^{\$1>0}(X)\}$ is obtained. Other clauses are rejected because of the inconsistency. The query $p(X)$ terminates with respect to the extended program while it does not terminate with respect to the original one. Thus, such an inference technique can actually improve termination.

In order for termination to be preserved a weaker inference engine should be used, for example, considering inequalities only of the maximal prefix. Then the following is obtained: $p^{\$1>0}(X) \leftarrow X > 0, q^{\$1>0}(X), X < 0.$ $q^{\$1>0}(X) \leftarrow X > 0, p^{\$1>0}(X)$. The query $p(X)$ does not terminate with respect to the extended program as expected. The following lemma shows that if this weaker inference is used, termination is preserved. □

Lemma 2. *Let P be a program, and let Q be a query. Let P^{ag} be a program obtained as described above. Then,* $\mathcal{M}[\![P]\!](Q) \subseteq \mathcal{M}[\![P^{ag}]\!](Q)$.

For the case of maximal prefixes the following summarises the results.

Theorem 2. *Let P be a program, let Q be a query and let $\mathcal{A}$ be a set of adornments. Let P^{ag} be a program obtained as described above with respect to $\mathcal{A}$. Then,* $\mathcal{M}[\![P]\!](Q) = \mathcal{M}[\![P^{ag}]\!](Q)$.

This theorem has two important corollaries.

Corollary 1. *Let P be a program, let Q be a query and let $\mathcal{A}$ be a set of adornments. Let $A = \{a \mid a \in \mathcal{A}, \text{for all } q \text{ such that } rel(Q)^a \sqsupseteq q : q \text{ is not recursive in } P^a\}$. Then $\bigvee_{a \in A}$ is a termination condition for P.*

Example 8. Example 6, continued. In P^{a_2} $p^{(\$1 \leq -1000) \vee (-1 \leq \$1 \leq 1) \vee (\$1 \geq 1000)}$ does not depend on recursive predicates. By the corollary, $(\$1 \leq -1000) \vee (-1 \leq \$1 \leq 1) \vee (\$1 \geq 1000)$ is a termination condition for $p(X)$. □

Theorem 2 implies that a program P is LD-terminating with respect to all queries in a set of atomic queries S if and only if P^{ag}, constructed as above, is acceptable with respect to S. The latter is equivalent to acceptability of P^a with respect to $\{q^A(t_1, \ldots, t_n) \mid q(t_1, \ldots, t_n) \in S, A \in \mathcal{A}_q\}$.

Corollary 2. *Let P be a program, S be a set of atomic queries and $\mathcal{A} = \bigcup_{Q \in S, q \simeq rel(Q)} \mathcal{A}_q$ be a set of adornments. Let P^a be obtained with respect to $\mathcal{A}$. P is LD-terminating with respect to all queries in S if and only if P^a is acceptable with respect to $\{q^A(t_1, \ldots, t_n) \mid q(t_1, \ldots, t_n) \in S, A \in \mathcal{A}_q\}$.*

This corollary allows us to complete the termination proof for Example 2.

Example 9. We show that P^{a_2} is acceptable with respect to the set $S = \{p^{(\$1 \leq -1000) \vee (-1 \leq \$1 \leq 1) \vee (\$1 \geq 1000)}(X), p^{1 < \$1 < 1000}(X), p^{-1000 < \$1 < -1}(X)\}$. Then, $S = Call(P^{a_2}, S)$. Let $|\cdot|$ be defined as: $|\, p^{-1000 < \$1 < -1}(X)\, | = 1000 + X$, if $-1000 < X < -1$ and 0 otherwise; $|\, p^{1 < \$1 < 1000}(X)\, | = 1000 - X$ if $1 < X < 1000$ and 0 otherwise; $|\, p^{(\$1 \leq -1000) \vee (-1 \leq \$1 \leq 1) \vee (\$1 \geq 1000)}(X)\, | = 0$.

We do not prove completely that P^{a_2} is acceptable with respect to S via $|\cdot|$, but analyse only one call, $p^{1 < \$1 < 1000}(X)$. There are two clauses, (1) and (2), such that their heads can be unified with it. (2) is not recursive and the condition holds vacuously. (1) is recursive and acceptability requires $|\, p^{1 < \$1 < 1000}(X)\, | > |\, p^{-1000 < \$1 < -1}(-X^2)\, |$, where $1 < X < 1000$. If $-X^2 \leq -1000$ then $|\, p^{-1000 < \$1 < -1}(-X^2)\, | = 0$ and descent is clear. Otherwise, $|\, p^{-1000 < \$1 < -1}(-X^2)\, | = 1000 - X^2$, where $0 < 1000 - X^2 < 1000 - X$, since $X > 1$. As before, there is descent in the level mapping. The other calls are proved similarly. □

4 Practical Issues

In the previous section we have shown the transformation that allows reasoning on termination of the numerical computations. In this section we discuss a number of practical issues to be considered for automation.

4.1 Guard-Tuned Sets of Adornments

In Example 5 we have seen two different sets of adornments. Both of them are valid according to Definition 9. However, $\{-1000 < \$1 < -1, 1 < \$1 <$

$1000, (\$1 \leq -1000) \vee (-1 \leq \$1 \leq 1) \vee (\$1 \geq 1000)\}$ is in some sense preferable to $\{\$1 \leq 100, \$1 > 100\}$. First of all, it has *a declarative reading*: the sets that are constructed express conditions that, when satisfied, allow traversing the rule. Second, observe that P^{a_1} has not only two mutually recursive predicates, as P^{a_2} does, but also self-loop on one of the predicates. To distinguish between "better" and "worse" sets of adornments we define *guard-tuned* sets of adornments.

Definition 12. *Let P be a partially normalised program, let p be a predicate in P. A set of adornments $\mathcal{A}_p$ is called* guard-tuned *if for every $A \in \mathcal{A}_p$ and for every rule $r \in P$ with the symbolic condition c corresponding to its maximal prefix, either $c \wedge A =$ false or $c \wedge A = A$ holds.*

Example 10. The first set of adornments, presented in Example 5, is not guard-tuned while the second one is guard-tuned. □

Examples 5 and 10 suggest two ways of constructing a guard-tuned set of adornments. Given a program P one might collect the symbolic conditions, corresponding to the maximal prefixes of the rules defining a predicate p (we denote this set $\mathcal{C}_p$) and add the completion of the constructed disjunction. Unfortunately, this set is not necessarily a set of adornments and if so, it is not necessary guard-tuned.

Example 11. $r(X) \leftarrow X > 5.\ \ r(X) \leftarrow X > 10, r(X)$. Two sets of symbolic conditions can be constructed: $\{r^{\$1 \leq 5}, r^{\$1>5}, r^{\$1>10}\}$ which is not a set of adornments and $\{r^{\$1 \leq 5}, r^{\$1>5}\}$ which is not guard-tuned. □

We use a different approach. First, we find $\mathcal{C}_p = \{c_1, \ldots, c_n\}$. Then we define $\mathcal{A}_p$ to be the set of conjunctions of c_i's and their negations. We claim that the constructed set is always a guard-tuned set of adornments.

Example 12. As above, $\mathcal{C}_p = \{\$1 > 5, \$1 > 10\}$. After simplifying and removing inconsistencies $\mathcal{A}_p = \{\$1 > 10, \$1 > 5 \wedge \$1 \leq 10, \$1 \leq 5\}$. □

Lemma 3. *Let P be a program, p be a predicate in P and $\mathcal{A}_p$ be constructed as described. Then $\mathcal{A}_p$ is a guard-tuned set of adornments.*

4.2 How to Define a Level Mapping?

The problem with defining level mappings is that they should reflect changes on possibly negative arguments and remain non-negative at the same time. We also like to remain in the framework of level mappings on atoms defined as linear combinations of sizes of their arguments.

Definition 13. *Let $p^{E_1\, \rho\, E_2}$ be an adorned predicate, where E_1 and E_2 are expressions and $\rho \in \{>, \geq\}$. The* primitive level mapping *is defined as:*
$p^{E_1\, \rho\, E_2}(t_1, \ldots, t_n)\ |^{\mathrm{pr}} = (E_1 - E_2)(t_1, \ldots, t_n)$
if $E_1(t_1, \ldots, t_n)\ \rho\ E_2(t_1, \ldots, t_n)$ and 0 otherwise.

If more than one conjunct appears in the adornment, the level mapping is defined as a linear combination of primitive level mappings corresponding to the conjuncts. If a conjunct is a disjunction, it is ignored, since disjunctions are introduced only if some rule *cannot* be applied.

Definition 14. *Let p^c be an adorned predicate, The* natural level mapping *is:* $\mid p^c(t_1,\ldots,t_n) \mid \ = \sum_{E_1\ \rho\ E_2 \in c} c_{E_1\ \rho\ E_2} \mid p^{E_1\ \rho\ E_2}(t_1,\ldots,t_n) \mid^{\mathrm{pr}}$, *where the c's are natural number coefficients, E_1, E_2 and ρ are as above.*

Example 13. The level mappings used in Example 9 are natural level mappings such that $c_{\$1>1} = c_{\$1<-1} = 0$, $c_{\$1<1000} = c_{\$1>-1000} = 1$. For $p^{(\$1\leq-1000)\vee(-1\leq\$1\leq1)\vee(\$1\geq1000)}$ the definition holds trivially. □

The approach of [7] defines symbolic counterparts of the level mappings and infers the values of the coefficients by solving a system of constraints.

4.3 Inferring Termination Constraints

In this section, we combine the steps studied so far to an algorithm that infers termination conditions. The termination condition is constructed as a disjunction of two: c_1 for non-recursive cases, according to Corollary 1, and c_2, for recursive cases, incrementally refined by adding to conjunction constraints on the integer variables, obtained from the acceptability condition, as in [7][3]. The algorithm is presented in Figure 1.

Example 14. $q(X,Y) \leftarrow X > Y, Z \text{ is } X - Y, q(Z,Y)$.
We look for values of X and Y such that $q(X,Y)$ terminates. First, the algorithm infers adornments. In our case $\{\$1 > \$2, \$1 \leq \$2\}$ are inferred.

The adorned version of this program is
$q^{\$1>\$2}(X,Y) \leftarrow X > Y, Z \text{ is } X - Y, q^{\$1>\$2}(Z,Y)$.
$q^{\$1>\$2}(X,Y) \leftarrow X > Y, Z \text{ is } X - Y, q^{\$1\leq\$2}(Z,Y)$.

There is no clause defining $q^{\$1\leq\$2}$. By Corollary 1, $\$1 \leq \$2$ is a termination condition. This is the one we denoted c_1. The termination condition for $q^{\$1>\$2}$, denoted c_2 is initialised to be $\$1 > \$2$. The level mapping is $\mid q^{\$1>\$2}(X,Y) \mid = c_{\$1>\$2}(X-Y)$ if $X > Y$ and 0 otherwise. The acceptability decrease implies (see [7]): $c_{\$1>\$2}(X-Y) > c_{\$1>\$2}((X-Y)-Y)$, that is $c_{\$1>\$2}Y > 0$. Since $c_{\$1>\$2} \geq 0$, $Y > 0$ and $c_{\$1>\$2} > 0$ should hold. We update c_2 to be $(\$1 > \$2) \wedge (\$2 > 0)$. Now we restart the whole process with respect to $Y > 0$. The following adorned program is obtained:
$q^{\$1>\$2,\$2>0}(X,Y) \leftarrow X > Y, Z \text{ is } X - Y, q^{\$1>\$2,\$2>0}(Z,Y)$.
$q^{\$1>\$2,\$2\leq0}(X,Y) \leftarrow X > Y, Z \text{ is } X - Y, q^{\$1>\$2,\$2\leq0}(Z,Y)$.
$q^{\$1>\$2,\$2\leq0}(X,Y) \leftarrow X > Y, Z \text{ is } X - Y, q^{\$1\leq\$2,\$2\leq0}(Z,Y)$.

[3] Any other technique proving termination and able provide some constraint that, if satisfied, implies termination can be used instead of [7].

Let P be a partially normalised program, let Q be a query and let q be $rel(Q)$.

1. For each $p \simeq q$ construct $\mathcal{A}_p$.
2. Adorn P with respect to q and $\bigcup_{p \simeq q} \mathcal{A}_p$.
3. Let $A = \{a \mid a \in \mathcal{A}_q, \textit{for all } p \textit{ such that } q^a \sqsupseteq p : p \textit{ is not recursive in } P^a\}$. Let $c_1 = \bigvee_{a \in A}$. Let $c_2 = \bigvee_{a \in \mathcal{A}_q, a \notin A}$.
4. Remove "irrelevant clauses"
   Let $A_1, \ldots, A_n \in \mathcal{A}_q$ be the only consistent with c_2 adornments of q.
   For every rule r in P^a
   If for all i, $q^{A_i} \not\sqsupseteq rel(Head(r))$ remove r from P^a
5. Define a symbolic counterparts of norms, level mappings and interargument relations.
6. Construct constraints on the symbolic variables. Obtain S.
7. Solve S.
   a) Solution of S doesn't produce extra constraints on variables.
      Report termination for $c_1 \vee c_2$.
   b) Solution of S produces extra constraints involving new integer variables.
      Conjunct these constraints to termination condition c_2.
      Go back to step 2.
   c) Otherwise report termination for c_1.

Fig. 1. Termination Inference Algorithm

The second and the third clauses are removed, since they are "irrelevant" with respect to $\$2 > 0$. The level mapping is redefined as

$$\mid q^{\$1>\$2}(X,Y) \mid = c_{\$1>\$2} * \begin{cases} X - Y \text{ if } X > Y \\ 0 \qquad\quad \text{otherwise} \end{cases} + c_{\$2>0} * \begin{cases} Y \text{ if } Y > 0 \\ 0 \text{ otherwise} \end{cases}$$

Acceptability decreases imply $c_{\$1>\$2}(X - Y) + c_{\$2>0}Y > c_{\$1>\$2}((X - Y) - Y) + c_{\$2>0}Y$, i.e., $0 > -c_{\$1>\$2}Y$. The inequality holds, since $Y > 0$ and $c_{\$1>\$2} > 0$ are assumed to hold. This solution does not impose additional constraints on integer variables. Thus, the analysis terminates reporting $\$1 \leq \$2 \vee (\$1 > \$2 \wedge \$2 > 0)$ as a termination condition. □

In order to prove correctness of this algorithm we have to prove its termination and partial correctness. Termination follows from termination of its steps and from the finiteness of the number of integer variables, restricting a number of backwards steps from 7(b) to 2. Partial correctness follows from the correctness of transformations and [7].

5 Further Extensions

In this section we discuss possible extensions of the algorithm presented above. First of all, we re-consider inference of adornments, then we discuss integrating termination analysis of numerical and symbolic computations.

5.1 Once More about the Inference of Adornments

The set of adornments $\mathcal{A}_p$, inferred in Subsection 4.1 may sometimes be too weak for inferring precise termination conditions.

Example 15. $p(X, Y) \leftarrow X < 0, Y1$ *is* $Y + 1, X1$ *is* $X - 1, p(Y1, X1)$. The maximal prefix of the rule above is $X < 0$, thus, $\mathcal{C}_p = \{\$1 < 0\}$ and $\mathcal{A}_p = \{\$1 < 0, \$1 \geq 0\}$. The only termination condition found is $\$1 \geq 0$, while the precise termination condition is $\$1 \geq 0 \vee (\$1 < 0 \wedge \$2 \geq -1)$. □

The problem occured due to the fact that $\mathcal{A}_p$ restricts only *some* subset of integer argument positions, while for the termination proof information on integer arguments outside of this subset may be needed.

Definition 15. *Let P be a program, let p be a predicate in P, let C_q be a set of symbolic conditions over the integer argument positions of q, and $C = \cup_{q \in P} C_q$. A symbolic condition c over the integer argument positions of p is called an* extension of C *if there exists $r \in P$, defining p, such that some integer argument position denominator appearing in c does not appear in C_p, and c is implied by some $c_q \in C_q$ for the recursive subgoals and some interargument relations for the non-recursive ones.*

Let C be a set of symbolic conditions over the integer argument positions of p and let $\varphi(C)$ be $C \cup \{c \mid c$ is an extension of $C\}$. Define the set of adornments for p as $\{c'_1 \wedge \ldots \wedge c'_n \mid c'_i \in \varphi^*(\mathcal{C}_p)$ or $\neg c'_i \in \varphi^*(\mathcal{C}_p)\}$, where φ^* is a fixpoint of powers of φ and $\mathcal{C}_p$ is defined as in Subsection 4.1.

Example 16. Example 15, continued. The only extension of $\mathcal{C}_p$ is $\$1 < 0 \wedge \$2 < -1$, i.e., $\varphi(\mathcal{C}_p) = \{\$1 < 0, \$1 < 0 \wedge \$2 < -1\}$. Thus, $\varphi^*(\mathcal{C}_p) = \varphi(\mathcal{C}_p)$ and $\mathcal{A}_p = \{\$1 < 0 \wedge \$2 < -1, (\$1 < 0 \wedge \$2 \geq -1) \vee \$1 \geq 0\}$. □

An alternative approach to propagating such an information was suggested in [8]. It allows one to propagate the existing adornments but not to infer the new ones and thus, is less precise than our approach.

5.2 Integrating Numerical and Symbolic Computation

In the real-world programs numerical computations are sometimes interleaved with symbolic ones, as illustrated by the following example [11].

Example 17.

```
collect(X, [X|L], L) ← atomic(X).
collect(T, L0, L) ←
    compound(T), functor(T, _, A),
    process(T, 0, A, L0, L).

process(_, A, A, L, L).
process(T, I, A, L0, L2) ←
    I < A, I1 is I + 1, arg(I1, T, Arg),
    collect(Arg, L0, L1),
    process(T, I1, A, L1, L2).
```

To prove termination of $\{collect(\text{tree}, \text{variable}, [])\}$ three decreases should be shown: between a call to *collect* and a call to *process* between a call to *process* and a call to *collect* and between two calls to *process*. The first two can be shown only by a symbolic level mapping, the third one—only by the numerical approach. □

Thus, our goal is to *combine* the existing symbolic approaches with the numerical one presented so far. One of the possible ways to do so is to combine two level mappings, $|\cdot|_1$ and $|\cdot|_2$ by mapping each atom $A \in B_P^E$ to a pair of natural numbers $(|A|_1, |A|_2)$ and prove termination by establishing decreases on orderings of such pairs [14].

Example 18. Example 17, continued. Define $\varphi : B_P^E \to (\mathcal{N} \cup \mathcal{N}^2)$ as: $\varphi(collect(t, l0, l)) = \|t\|$, $\varphi(process(t, i, a, l0, l)) = (\|t\|, a-i)$ where $\|\cdot\|$ is a term-size norm. The decreases are satisfied with respect to $>$, such that $A_1 > A_2$ if and only if $\varphi(A_1) \succ \varphi(A_2)$, where $\succ$ is defined as: $n \succ m$, if $n >_{\mathcal{N}} m$, $n \succ (n, m)$, if *true*, $(n, m_1) \succ (n, m_2)$, if $m_1 >_{\mathcal{N}} m_2$ and $(n_1, m) \succ n_2$, if $n_1 >_{\mathcal{N}} n_2$ and $>_{\mathcal{N}}$ is the usual order on the naturals. □

This integrated approach allows one to analyse correctly examples such as *ground*, *unify*, *numbervars* [15] and Example 6.12 in [8].

6 Conclusion

Termination of numerical computations was studied by a number of authors [1,2, 8]. Apt *et al.* [2] provided a declarative semantics, so called Θ-semantics, for Prolog programs with first-order built-in predicates, including arithmetic operations. In this framework the property of strong termination, i.e., finiteness of all LD-trees for all possible goals, was completely characterised based on appropriately tuned notion of acceptability. This approach provides important theoretical results, but seems to be difficult to integrate in automatic tools. In [1] it is claimed that an unchanged acceptability condition can be applied to programs in pure Prolog with arithmetic by defining the level mappings on ground atoms with the arithmetic relation to be zero. This approach ignores the actual computation, and thus, its applicability is restricted to programs using some arithmetic but not really relaying on them, such as *quicksort*. Moreover, as Example 14 illustrates, there are many programs that terminate only for *some* queries. Alternatively, Dershowitz *et al.* [8] extended the query-mapping pairs formalism of [9] to deal with numerical computations. However, this approach inherited the disadvantages of [9], such as high computational price.

More research has been done on termination analysis for constraint logic programs [4,10,12]. Since numerical computations in Prolog should be written in a way that allows a system to verify their satisfiability we can see numerical computations of Prolog as an *ideal constraint system*. Thus, all the results obtained for ideal constraints systems can be applied. Unfortunately, the research was either oriented towards theoretical characterisations [12] or restricted to domains isomorphic to $\mathcal{N}$ [10].

In a contrast to the approach of [8] that was restricted to verifying termination, we presented a methodology for *inferring* termination conditions. It is not clear whether and how [8] can be extended to infer such conditions. A main contribution of this work to the theoretical understanding of termination of numerical computations is in situating them in the well-known framework of acceptability and allowing integration with the existing approaches to termination of symbolic computations. The methodology presented can be integrated in automatic termination analysers, such as [7].

The kernel technique is powerful enough to analyse correctly examples such as *gcd* and *mod* [8] and all examples appearing in Chapter 8 of [15], which is dedicated to arithmetic. These examples include the examples appearing in [1]. Moreover, our approach gains its power from the underlying framework of [7] and thus, allows one to prove termination of some examples that cannot be analysed correctly by [8], similar to *confused delete* [7]. The extended technique, presented in Section 5, allows one to analyse correctly examples such as Ackermann's function, *ground*, *unify*, *numbervars* [15] and Example 6.12 in [8].

As future work we consider a complete implementation of the algorithm. Due to the use of the constraint solving techniques we expect it both to be powerful and highly efficient.

References

1. K. R. Apt. *From Logic Programming to Prolog.* Prentice-Hall Int. Series in Computer Science. Prentice Hall, 1997.
2. K. R. Apt, E. Marchiori, and C. Palamidessi. A declarative approach for first-order built-in's in prolog. *Applicable Algebra in Engineering, Communication and Computation*, 5(3/4):159–191, 1994.
3. A. Bossi and N. Cocco. Preserving universal temination through unfold/fold. In G. Levi and M. Rodríguez-Artalejo, editors, *Algebraic and Logic Programming*, pages 269–286. Springer Verlag, 1994. LNCS 850.
4. L. Colussi, E. Marchiori, and M. Marchiori. On termination of constraint logic programs. In U. Montanari and F. Rossi, editors, *Principles and Practice of Constraint Programming - CP'95,*, pages 431–448. Springer Verlag, 1995. LNCS 976.
5. D. De Schreye, K. Verschaetse, and M. Bruynooghe. A framework for analyzing the termination of definite logic programs with respect to call patterns. In I. Staff, editor, *Proc. of the Int. Conf. on Fifth Generation Computer Systems.*, pages 481–488. IOS Press, 1992.
6. S. Decorte and D. De Schreye. Termination analysis: some practical properties of the norm and level mapping space. In J. Jaffar, editor, *Proc. of the 1998 Joint Int. Conf. and Symp. on Logic Programming*, pages 235–249. MIT Press, June 1998.
7. S. Decorte, D. De Schreye, and H. Vandecasteele. Constraint-based termination analysis of logic programs. *ACM Transactions on Programming Languages and Systems (TOPLAS)*, 21(6):1137–1195, November 1999.
8. N. Dershowitz, N. Lindenstrauss, Y. Sagiv, and A. Serebrenik. A general framework for automatic termination analysis of logic programs. *Applicable Algebra in Engineering, Communication and Computing*, 12(1-2):117–156, 2001.
9. N. Lindenstrauss and Y. Sagiv. Automatic termination analysis of logic programs. In L. Naish, editor, *Proc. of the Fourteenth Int. Conf. on Logic Programming*, pages 63–77. MIT Press, July 1997.

10. F. Mesnard. Inferring left-terminating classes of queries for constraint logic programs. In M. Maher, editor, *Proc. JICSLP'96*, pages 7–21. The MIT Press, 1996.
11. C. Pollard and I. A. Sag. *Head-driven Phrase Structure Grammar*. The University of Chicago Press, 1994.
12. S. Ruggieri. *Verification and validation of logic programs*. PhD thesis, Universitá di Pisa, 1999.
13. A. Serebrenik and D. De Schreye. Inference of termination conditions for numerical loops. Technical Report CW 308, Departement Computerwetenschappen, K.U.Leuven, Leuven, Belgium, 2001.
14. A. Serebrenik and D. De Schreye. Non-transformational termination analysis of logic programs, based on general term-orderings. In K.-K. Lau, editor, *Logic Based Program Synthesis and Transformation 10th International Workshop, Selected Papers*, volume 2042 of *Lecture Notes in Computer Science*, pages 69–85. Springer Verlag, 2001.
15. L. Sterling and E. Shapiro. *The Art of Prolog*. The MIT Press, 1994.

Termination of Rewriting with Strategy Annotations*

Salvador Lucas

DSIC, Universidad Politécnica de Valencia
Camino de Vera s/n, E-46022 Valencia, Spain
e.mail: slucas@dsic.upv.es

Abstract. We investigate termination of rewriting computations guided by strategy annotations. We show that proofs of termination can be obtained by proving (innermost) termination of context-sensitive rewriting (*CSR*). Hence, we investigate how to prove innermost termination of *CSR* using existing methods for proving termination of *CSR*.

Keywords: Rewriting strategies, termination.

1 Introduction

Strategy annotations (e.g., lists of integers that are associated to the symbols of the signature) are used in programming languages such as OBJ2 [FGJM85], OBJ3 [GWMFJ00], CafeOBJ [FN97], and Maude [CELM96] to introduce *replacement restrictions* aimed at improving *termination* ([GWMFJ00], Section 2.4.4).

Example 1. The following OBJ3 program (borrowed from [OF97]):

```
obj EXAMPLE is
  sorts Sort .
  op 0    : -> Sort .
  op s    : Sort -> Sort .
  op _::_ : Sort Sort -> Sort [strat: (1 0)] .
  op inf  : Sort -> Sort .
  op nth  : Sort Sort -> Sort .
  var X Y L : Sort .
  eq nth(s(X),Y::L) = nth(X,L) .
  eq nth(0,X::L) = X .
  eq inf(X) = X::inf(s(X)) .
endo
```

specifies an *explicit* strategy annotation for the list constructor '::' which disables replacements on the second argument. In this way, the evaluation of the expression nth(s(0),inf(0)) always finishes and produces the term s(0), even though the 'infinite list' inf(0) is a part of the expression.

* Work partially supported by Acción Integrada Hispano-Italiana HI2000-0161, Spanish CICYT, and Conselleria de Cultura i Educació de la Generalitat Valenciana.

R. Nieuwenhuis and A. Voronkov (Eds.): LPAR 2001, LNAI 2250, pp. 669–684, 2001.

Unfortunately, there is a lack of formal techniques to analyze how a particular choice of strategy annotations modifies the termination of programs. Since term rewriting systems (TRSs [BN98,DP01]) provide a suitable computational model for programs written in these programming languages, in this paper, we investigate termination of rewriting computations controlled by strategy annotations. Strategy annotations can be given different shapes and computational interpretations. Following Visser's recent classification [Vis01], we consider the following *computational* strategies which are associated to strategy annotations:

1. *E-strategy* [FGJM85,Eke98], which permits us to completely avoid the evaluation of some arguments of function symbols (in an ordered way).
2. *Just-in-time* (by van de Pol [Pol01]), which is designed to *delay* the evaluation of arguments as much as possible.

We show that context-sensitive rewriting (*CSR*, a simple restriction of rewriting that forbids reductions on selected arguments of functions [Luc98]) provides a suitable framework for describing and analyzing computations with programs using such kind of strategy annotations. We focus on the innermost character of these computational models and show that the analysis of *innermost* termination of *CSR* provides a more accurate (even complete, for the E-strategy) characterization of termination of rewriting under strategy annotations. Termination of *CSR* has been studied in [GM99,Luc96,Zan97]. In these works, termination of *CSR* for a given TRS is demonstrated by proving termination of a *transformed* TRS. In this way, with *CSR* we can use the standard methods for proving termination of rewriting (see [Der87] for a survey). We prove that the (two) transformations of [GM99] are *correct* for proving the *innermost* termination of *CSR*. The transformation of [Luc96] is correct in the cases that we characterize below. Zantema's transformation [Zan97] does *not* provide correct proofs of innermost termination of *CSR*. On the other hand, we found that transformations of [GM99] (even the second one, which is complete for proving termination of *CSR*) are *not* complete for proving innermost termination of *CSR*. The transformation of [Luc96] is complete under the same assumptions that make it sound for proving innermost termination of *CSR*.

Section 2 gives some preliminaries. Section 3 introduces *CSR*. Sections 4 and 5 connect (innermost) termination of *CSR* with termination of rewriting under E- and van de Pol strategies. Section 6 investigates how to prove innermost termination of *CSR*. Section 7 discusses related work. Section 8 concludes.

2 Preliminaries

Given a set A, $\mathcal{P}(A)$ denotes the set of all subsets of A. Given a binary relation R on a set A, we denote the reflexive closure of R by $R^=$, its transitive closure by R^+, and its reflexive and transitive closure by R^*. An element $a \in A$ is an R-normal form, if there exists no b such that $a\ R\ b$; NF_R is the set of R-normal forms. We say that b is an R-normal form of a, if b is an R-normal form and $a\ R^* b$. We say that R is *terminating* iff there is no infinite sequence $a_1\ R\ a_2\ R\ a_3 \cdots$.

Throughout the paper, $\mathcal{X}$ denotes a countable set of variables and Σ denotes a signature, i.e., a set of function symbols $\{\mathtt{f},\mathtt{g},\ldots\}$, each having a fixed arity given by a mapping $ar : \Sigma \to \mathbb{N}$. The set of terms built from Σ and $\mathcal{X}$ is $\mathcal{T}(\Sigma,\mathcal{X})$. A term is said to be linear if it has no multiple occurrences of a single variable. Terms are viewed as labelled trees in the usual way. Positions $p, q, \ldots$ are represented by chains of positive natural numbers used to address subterms of t. Given positions p, q, we denote its concatenation by $p.q$. Positions are ordered by the standard prefix ordering $\leq$. Given a set of positions P, $maximal_{\leq}(P)$ is the set of maximal positions of P w.r.t. $\leq$. If p is a position, and Q is a set of positions, $p.Q = \{p.q \mid q \in Q\}$. We denote the empty chain by Λ. The set of positions of a term t is $\mathcal{P}os(t)$. Positions of non-variable symbols in t are denoted as $\mathcal{P}os_{\Sigma}(t)$, and $\mathcal{P}os_{\mathcal{X}}(t)$ are the positions of variables. The subterm at position p of t is denoted as $t|_p$, and $t[s]_p$ is the term t with the subterm at position p replaced by s. The symbol labelling the root of t is denoted as $root(t)$.

A rewrite rule is an ordered pair (l, r), written $l \to r$, with $l, r \in \mathcal{T}(\Sigma,\mathcal{X})$, $l \notin \mathcal{X}$ and $\mathcal{V}ar(r) \subseteq \mathcal{V}ar(l)$. The left-hand side (*lhs*) of the rule is l and the right-hand side (*rhs*) is r. A TRS is a pair $\mathcal{R} = (\Sigma, R)$ where R is a set of rewrite rules. $L(\mathcal{R})$ denotes the set of *lhs*'s of $\mathcal{R}$. An instance $\sigma(l)$ of a *lhs* l of a rule is a redex. The set of redex positions in t is $\mathcal{P}os_{\mathcal{R}}(t)$. A TRS $\mathcal{R}$ is left-linear if for all $l \in L(\mathcal{R})$, l is a linear term. A term $t \in \mathcal{T}(\Sigma,\mathcal{X})$ rewrites to s (at position p), written $t \stackrel{p}{\to}_{\mathcal{R}} s$ (or just $t \to s$), if $t|_p = \sigma(l)$ and $s = t[\sigma(r)]_p$, for some rule $\rho : l \to r \in R$, $p \in \mathcal{P}os(t)$ and substitution σ. A TRS is terminating if $\to$ is terminating. We say that t *innermost* rewrites to s, written $t \to_i s$, if $t \stackrel{p}{\to} s$ and $p \in maximal_{\leq}(\mathcal{P}os_{\mathcal{R}}(t))$. A TRS is *innermost* terminating if $\to_i$ is terminating.

3 Rewriting with Syntactic Replacement Restrictions

A mapping $\mu : \Sigma \to \mathcal{P}(\mathbb{N})$ is a *replacement map* (or Σ-map) if $\forall f \in \Sigma,\ \mu(f) \subseteq \{1,\ldots,ar(f)\}$ [Luc98]. The ordering $\sqsubseteq$ on M_{Σ}, the set of all Σ-maps, is: $\mu \sqsubseteq \mu'$ if for all $f \in \Sigma$, $\mu(f) \subseteq \mu'(f)$. Thus, $\mu \sqsubseteq \mu'$ means that μ considers less positions than μ' (for reduction), i.e., μ is more restrictive than μ'.

A replacement map μ specifies the *argument* positions which can be reduced for each *symbol* in Σ. Accordingly, the set of μ*-replacing positions* $\mathcal{P}os^{\mu}(t)$ of $t \in \mathcal{T}(\Sigma,\mathcal{X})$ is: $\mathcal{P}os^{\mu}(t) = \{\Lambda\}$, if $t \in \mathcal{X}$ and $\mathcal{P}os^{\mu}(t) = \{\Lambda\} \cup \bigcup_{i \in \mu(root(t))} i.\mathcal{P}os^{\mu}(t|_i)$, if $t \notin \mathcal{X}$. The set of positions of replacing redexes in t is $\mathcal{P}os^{\mu}_{\mathcal{R}}(t) = \mathcal{P}os_{\mathcal{R}}(t) \cap \mathcal{P}os^{\mu}(t)$. In *context-sensitive rewriting* (*CSR* [Luc98]), we (only) contract *replacing* redexes: t μ-rewrites to s, written $t \hookrightarrow_{\mu} s$, if $t \stackrel{p}{\to}_{\mathcal{R}} s$ and $p \in \mathcal{P}os^{\mu}(t)$.

Example 2. Consider the TRS

```
nth(0,x:y)    → x                inf(x) → x:inf(s(x))
nth(s(x),y:z) → nth(x,z)
```

with $\mu(\mathtt{:}) = \mu(\mathtt{inf}) = \mu(\mathtt{s}) = \{1\}$ and $\mu(\mathtt{nth}) = \{1, 2\}$. Then, we have:

$\mathtt{nth(\underline{inf(0)})} \hookrightarrow_{\mu} \mathtt{nth(0:inf(s(0)))}$

Since $1.2 \notin \mathcal{P}os^{\mu}(\texttt{nth(0:inf(s(0)))})$, redex `inf(s(0))` cannot be μ-rewritten.

The $\hookrightarrow_{\mu}$-normal forms are called μ-normal forms. A TRS $\mathcal{R}$ is μ-terminating if $\hookrightarrow_{\mu}$ is terminating. With *innermost CSR*, $\hookrightarrow_{\mu}$, we only contract *maximal* positions of replacing redexes: $t \hookrightarrow_{\mu} s$ if $t \xrightarrow{p}_{\mathcal{R}} s$ and $p \in maximal_{\leq}(\mathcal{P}os^{\mu}_{\mathcal{R}}(t))$. We say that $\mathcal{R}$ is *innermost* μ-terminating if $\hookrightarrow_{\mu}$ is terminating.

Strategy annotations are simple mechanisms for specifying rewriting strategies. They are *associated to symbols f of the signature Σ* and mainly concern: (1) the possibility of reducing the *arguments* of f (indexed by $1, \ldots, k$, if f is a k-ary symbol), and (2) the possibility of applying the (different) rules defining f (i.e., rules $l \to r \in R$ such that $root(l) = f$) to redexes rooted by symbol f. We investigate two kinds of strategy annotations.

4 Termination of Rewriting under the E-Strategy

A *positive* local strategy (or E-strategy [FGJM85,Eke98,Nag99,NO01]) for a k-ary symbol $f \in \Sigma$ is a sequence $\varphi(f)$ of integers taken from $\{0, 1, \ldots, k\}$ which are given in parentheses[1] (see Example 1). A mapping φ that associates a local strategy $\varphi(f)$ to every $f \in \Sigma$ is called a E-strategy map [NO01]. Roughly speaking, when considering a function call $f(t_1, \ldots, t_k)$, only the arguments whose indices are present as *positive* integers in the local strategy for f are evaluated (following the specified ordering). If 0 is found, then the evaluation of f is attempted. Nagaya describes the operational semantics of term rewriting under E-strategy maps as follows [Nag99]: Let $\mathcal{L}$ be the set of all lists consisting of natural numbers. By $\mathcal{L}_n$ we denote the set of all lists of natural numbers not exceding $n \in \mathbb{N}$. We use the signature $\Sigma_{\mathcal{L}} = \{f_L \mid f \in \Sigma \wedge L \in \mathcal{L}_{ar(f)}\}$ and labelled variables $\mathcal{X}_{\mathcal{L}} = \{x_{nil} \mid x \in \mathcal{X}\}$. An E-strategy map φ for Σ is extended to a mapping from $\mathcal{T}(\Sigma, \mathcal{X})$ to $\mathcal{T}(\Sigma_{\mathcal{L}}, \mathcal{X}_{\mathcal{L}})$ as follows:

$$\varphi(t) = \begin{cases} x_{nil} & \text{if } t = x \in \mathcal{X} \\ f_{\varphi(f)}(\varphi(t_1), \ldots, \varphi(t_k)) & \text{if } t = f(t_1, \ldots, t_k) \end{cases}$$

The mapping $erase : \mathcal{T}(\Sigma_{\mathcal{L}}, \mathcal{X}_{\mathcal{L}}) \to \mathcal{T}(\Sigma, \mathcal{X})$ removes labellings from symbols. The relation $\to_{\varphi}$ on $\mathcal{T}(\Sigma_{\mathcal{L}}, \mathcal{X}_{\mathcal{L}}) \times \mathbb{N}^*_+$ (i.e., pairs $\langle t, p\rangle$ of labelled terms t and positions p) is [NO01,Nag99]: $\langle t, p\rangle \to_{\varphi} \langle s, q\rangle$ if and only if $p \in \mathcal{P}os(t)$ and either

1. $root(t|_p) = f_{nil}$, $s = t$ and $p = q.i$ for some i; or
2. $t|_p = f_{i:L}(t_1, \ldots, t_k)$ with $i > 0$, $s = t[f_L(t_1, \ldots, t_k)]_p$ and $q = p.i$; or
3. $t|_p = f_{0:L}(t_1, \ldots, t_k)$, $erase(t|_p)$ is not a redex, $s = t[f_L(t_1, \ldots, t_k)]_p$, $q = p$; or
4. $t|_p = f_{0:L}(t_1, \ldots, t_k) = \sigma(l')$, $erase(l') = l$, $s = t[\sigma(\varphi(r))]_p$ for some $l \to r \in R$ and substitution σ, $q = p$.

[1] Apart from this, we use the standard notation of lists which is also used in [NO01]: *nil* is the empty list and $i : L$ is the list whose first element is i and whose tail is L.

We write $e \in L$ to denote that item e appears somewhere within the list L. Algebraic languages OBJ2, OBJ3, CafeOBJ, and Maude admit the specification of E-strategies. Symbols without an explicit local strategy are given a *default* one whose concrete shape depends on the considered language[2]. Given an E-strategy map φ for Σ, we let $\mu^\varphi \in M_\Sigma$ be $\mu^\varphi(f) = \{i > 0 \mid i \in \varphi(f)\}$ for each $f \in \Sigma$. We drop superscript φ if no confusion arises. We have the following.

Theorem 1. [Luc01] *Let $\mathcal{R}$ be a TRS and φ be a positive E-strategy map. Let $t \in \mathcal{T}(\Sigma_\mathcal{L}, \mathcal{X}_\mathcal{L})$, and $p \in \mathcal{P}os^\mu(erase(t))$ be s.t. $root(t|_p) = f_L$ for some suffix L of $\varphi(f)$. If $\langle t, p\rangle \to_\varphi \langle s, q\rangle$, then $q \in \mathcal{P}os^\mu(erase(s))$ and $erase(t) \hookrightarrow_\mu^= erase(s)$.*

Semantics of OBJ programs[3] under a given E-evaluation map φ is usually given by means of an evaluation function $eval_\varphi : \mathcal{T}(\Sigma, \mathcal{X}) \to \mathcal{P}(\mathcal{T}(\Sigma, \mathcal{X}))$ (from terms to their sets of 'computed values') rather than specifying the concrete rewrite steps leading to computed values [Eke98]. Nakamura and Ogata define [NO01]: $eval_\varphi(t) = \{erase(s) \in \mathcal{T}(\Sigma, \mathcal{X}) \mid \langle \varphi(t), \Lambda\rangle \to_\varphi^* \langle s, \Lambda\rangle \wedge \langle s, \Lambda\rangle \in \mathsf{NF}_{\to_\varphi}\}$.

Example 3. Consider the following TRS $\mathcal{R}$ [Eke98]:

$$\begin{array}{llll} \mathtt{f(b)} & \to \mathtt{c} & \mathtt{h(c)} & \to \mathtt{g(f(a))} \\ \mathtt{g(x)} & \to \mathtt{h(x)} & \mathtt{a} & \to \mathtt{b} \end{array}$$

and φ given by $\varphi(\mathtt{f}) = \mathtt{(0\ 1)}$, $\varphi(\mathtt{g}) = \varphi(\mathtt{h}) = \mathtt{(1\ 0)}$, $\varphi(\mathtt{a}) = \mathtt{(0)}$, and $\varphi(\mathtt{b}) = nil$. Term $t = \mathtt{g(f(a))}$ is evaluated using $\to_\varphi$ on $\varphi(t) = \mathtt{g_{(1\ 0)}(f_{(0\ 1)}(a_{(0)}))}$(we underline contracted redexes in the 'term' component of pairs):

$$\begin{array}{l} \langle \mathtt{g_{(1\ 0)}(f_{(0\ 1)}(a_{(0)}))}, \Lambda\rangle \to_\varphi \langle \mathtt{g_{(0)}(f_{(0\ 1)}(a_{(0)}))}, 1\rangle \\ \quad \to_\varphi \langle \mathtt{g_{(0)}(f_{(1)}(a_{(0)}))}, 1\rangle \to_\varphi \langle \mathtt{g_{(0)}(f_{\mathit{nil}}(\underline{a_{(0)}}))}, 1.1\rangle \\ \quad \to_\varphi \langle \mathtt{g_{(0)}(f_{\mathit{nil}}(b_{\mathit{nil}}))}, 1.1\rangle \to_\varphi \langle \mathtt{g_{(0)}(f_{\mathit{nil}}(b_{\mathit{nil}}))}, 1\rangle \\ \quad \to_\varphi \langle \underline{\mathtt{g_{(0)}(f_{\mathit{nil}}(b_{\mathit{nil}}))}}, \Lambda\rangle \to_\varphi \langle \mathtt{h_{(1\ 0)}(f_{\mathit{nil}}(b_{\mathit{nil}}))}, \Lambda\rangle \\ \quad \to_\varphi \langle \mathtt{h_{(0)}(f_{\mathit{nil}}(b_{\mathit{nil}}))}, 1\rangle \to_\varphi \langle \mathtt{h_{(0)}(f_{\mathit{nil}}(b_{\mathit{nil}}))}, \Lambda\rangle \\ \quad \to_\varphi \langle \mathtt{h_{\mathit{nil}}(f_{\mathit{nil}}(b_{\mathit{nil}}))}, \Lambda\rangle \end{array}$$

where $\langle \mathtt{h_{\mathit{nil}}(f_{\mathit{nil}}(b_{\mathit{nil}}))}, \Lambda\rangle$ is a $\to_\varphi$-normal form. Then, $\mathtt{h(f(b))} \in eval_\varphi(t)$.

According to the previous definition of $eval_\varphi$, we can say that

> A TRS $\mathcal{R}$ is *φ-terminating* if, for all $t \in \mathcal{T}(\Sigma, \mathcal{X})$, there is no infinite $\to_\varphi$-rewrite sequence starting from $\langle \varphi(t), \Lambda\rangle$.

Since local strategies are finite lists, the number of $\to_\varphi$-reduction steps that corresponds to items (1) to (3) of the definition of $\to_\varphi$ (and that keep unchanged the *erased* terms) is finite. Thus, according to Theorem 1, we have the following.

Theorem 2. [Luc01] *Let $\mathcal{R}$ be a TRS and φ be a positive E-strategy map. If $\mathcal{R}$ is μ-terminating, then $\mathcal{R}$ is φ-terminating.*

---

[2] For instance, in Maude, the default local strategy associated to a k-ary symbol f, is $\mathtt{(1\ 2\ \cdots\ k\ 0)}$, see [Eke98].

[3] As in [GWMFJ00], by OBJ we mean OBJ2, OBJ3, CafeOBJ, or Maude.

Theorem 2 connects termination of *CSR* and φ-termination for positive *E*-strategy maps φ. Termination of *CSR* has been studied in [GM99,Luc96,Zan97]. For instance, the (TRS which represents the) OBJ program of Example 1 can be proved (μ-)terminating by using Zantema's techniques (see Examples 2 and 3 of [Zan97]). However, termination of *CSR* only *approximates* φ-termination.

Example 4. Consider the TRS [Gra96]:

$$\texttt{f(a)} \to \texttt{f(a)} \qquad \texttt{a} \to \texttt{b}$$

and let $\varphi(\texttt{f}) = \texttt{(1 0)}$ and $\varphi(\texttt{a}) = \texttt{(0)}$. This TRS is φ-terminating, but it is *not* μ-terminating, since we have: $\underline{\texttt{f(a)}} \hookrightarrow_\mu \underline{\texttt{f(a)}} \hookrightarrow_\mu \cdots$.

The point here is that computations under the *E*-strategy are 'basically' innermost. Innermost rewriting computations can be terminating even for nonterminating TRSs. This gives rise to the topic of *innermost* termination of rewriting which has been studied in e.g., [AG97,Gra96]. For instance, the TRS of Example 4 is nonterminating, but innermost terminating [Gra96].

Given a TRS $\mathcal{R} = (\Sigma, R)$, we consider Σ as the disjoint union $\Sigma = \mathcal{C} \uplus \mathcal{D}$ of symbols $c \in \mathcal{C}$, called *constructors* and symbols $f \in \mathcal{D}$, called *defined functions*, where $\mathcal{D} = \{root(l) \mid l \to r \in R\}$ and $\mathcal{C} = \Sigma - \mathcal{D}$. We say that an *E*-strategy map φ is *elementary* if for all $f \in \mathcal{D}$, $\varphi(f) = (i_1 \cdots i_n\ \texttt{0})$ and $i_j > 0$ for $1 \leq j \leq n$.

Remark 1. Consecutive occurrences of zero can be simplified into a single one (Corollary 3.3 in [Eke98]). Since [Eke98,Nag99] discuss why in interesting cases 0 is the last index of local strategies associated to defined symbols, the only critical requirement which is introduced with elementary strategies is that 0 occurs *only at the end* of the local strategy.

Theorem 3. *Let $\mathcal{R} = (\mathcal{C} \uplus \mathcal{D}, R)$ be a TRS and φ be a positive elementary E-strategy map. Let $t \in \mathcal{T}(\Sigma, \mathcal{X})$. If $\langle \varphi(t), \Lambda \rangle \to_\varphi^* \langle s, p \rangle$, then $p \in \mathcal{P}os^\mu(erase(s))$ and $t \overset{i}{\hookrightarrow}{}_\mu^* erase(s)$.*

Theorem 3 does not hold without requiring elementarity of φ.

Example 5. Consider $\mathcal{R}$, φ, and t as in Example 3. According to Theorem 1, the μ-rewriting steps associated to the evaluation of t are:

$$\texttt{g(f(}\underline{\texttt{a}}\texttt{))} \overset{i}{\hookrightarrow}_\mu \underline{\texttt{g(f(b))}} \hookrightarrow_\mu \texttt{h(f(b))}$$

Due to redex f(b), the second μ-rewriting step is *not* innermost,

Reasoning in a way similar to Theorem 1 and Theorem 2, Theorem 3 entails the following.

Theorem 4. *Let $\mathcal{R} = (\mathcal{C} \uplus \mathcal{D}, R)$ be a TRS and φ be a positive elementary E-strategy map. If $\mathcal{R}$ is innermost μ-terminating, then $\mathcal{R}$ is φ-terminating.*

For nonelementary *E*-strategies, Theorem 4 can fail to hold.

Example 6. Consider the TRS $\mathcal{R}$ of Example 4 and φ given by $\varphi(\mathtt{f}) = \mathtt{(0\ 1\ 0)}$, $\varphi(\mathtt{a}) = \mathtt{(0)}$, and $\varphi(\mathtt{b}) = nil$. Note that $\mathcal{R}$ is innermost μ-terminating. However, $\mathcal{R}$ is not φ-terminating, since we have:

$$\underline{\langle \mathtt{f}_{\mathtt{(0\ 1\ 0)}}(\mathtt{a}_{\mathtt{(0)}}), \Lambda\rangle} \to_\varphi \underline{\langle \mathtt{f}_{\mathtt{(0\ 1\ 0)}}(\mathtt{a}_{\mathtt{(0)}}), \Lambda\rangle} \to_\varphi \cdots$$

Since μ-termination implies innermost μ-termination (but not vice versa), analyzing innermost termination of *CSR* provides a more accurate framework for proving termination of TRSs under positive, elementary E-strategies. In fact, we obtain a *complete* proof method.

Theorem 5. *Let $\mathcal{R} = (\mathcal{C} \uplus \mathcal{D}, R)$ be a TRS and φ be a positive elementary E-strategy map. If $\mathcal{R}$ is φ-terminating, then $\mathcal{R}$ is innermost μ-terminating.*

Without elementarity, φ-termination may not imply innermost μ-termination.

Example 7. Consider $\mathcal{R}$ and φ as in Example 3. Note that $\mathcal{R}$ is not innermost μ-terminating:

$$\underline{\mathtt{h(c)}} \hookrightarrow_\mu \mathtt{g(f(\underline{a}))} \hookrightarrow_\mu \mathtt{g(\underline{f(b)})} \hookrightarrow_\mu \underline{\mathtt{g(c)}} \hookrightarrow_\mu \underline{\mathtt{h(c)}} \hookrightarrow_\mu \cdots$$

However, $\mathcal{R}$ is φ-terminating, since whenever (the labelled version of) the term `g(f(a))` is reached the derivation stops in `h(f(b))` without producing `h(c)` which is needed to generate the cycle (see Example 3).

5 Termination of Rewriting under van de Pol's Strategy Annotations

Let $\mathcal{R} = (\Sigma, R)$ be a TRS. According to van de Pol [Pol01], a strategy annotation associated to a given symbol $f \in \Sigma$ is a list $\varsigma(f)$ whose elements can be either a number $i \in \{1, \ldots, ar(f)\}$ or a rule $l \to r \in R$ such that $root(t) = f$. In principle, strategy annotations contain no duplicated items [Pol01].

Example 8. Consider the TRS [Pol01]:

$$\begin{array}{llll} \alpha: \mathtt{if(true,x,y)} & \to \mathtt{x} \qquad & \gamma: \mathtt{if(x,y,y)} & \to \mathtt{y} \\ \beta: \mathtt{if(false,x,y)} & \to \mathtt{y} & & \end{array}$$

Then, a possible strategy annotation for `if` is $\varsigma(\mathtt{if}) = \mathtt{[1,}\alpha\mathtt{,}\beta\mathtt{,2,3,}\gamma\mathtt{]}$.

We say that ς is *full regarding rules* (or just *r-full*) if for all $l \to r \in R$, $l \to r \in \varsigma(root(l))$. Given a strategy annotation, van de Pol describes the *rewriting strategy* that it specifies. A rewriting strategy is seen as a function that given a term t yields either some rewrite of t, i.e., a pair (p, s) such that $t \xrightarrow{p} s$, or $\perp$ if no rewrite step has been selected. Given a term t and a strategy annotation ς, $rewr_\varsigma$ indicates the (unique, if any) rewrite step that can be performed on t.

Definition 1. [Pol01] *Let $\mathcal{R} = (\Sigma, R)$ be a TRS, ς be a strategy annotation, and $t \in \mathcal{T}(\Sigma, \mathcal{X})$. Then, $rewr_\varsigma(t) = rewr_\varsigma(t, \varsigma(root(t)))$, where*

$$
\begin{aligned}
rewr_\varsigma(t, nil) &= \bot \\
rewr_\varsigma(t, (l \to r : L)) &= \begin{cases} (\Lambda, \sigma(r)) & \text{if } t = \sigma(l) \text{ for some } \sigma \\ rewr_\varsigma(t, L) & \text{otherwise} \end{cases} \\
rewr_\varsigma(t, (i : L)) &= \begin{cases} (i.p, t[s]_i) & \text{if } rewr_\varsigma(t|_i) = (p, s) \text{ for some } p, s \\ rewr_\varsigma(t, L) & \text{otherwise} \end{cases}
\end{aligned}
$$

We write $t \xrightarrow{p}_\varsigma s$ (or just $t \to_\varsigma s$) if $(p, s) = rewr_\varsigma(t) \neq \bot$. Thus, t is a $\to_\varsigma$-normal form (or just a ς-normal form) if and only if $rewr_\varsigma(t) = \bot$.

Remark 2. Van de Pol's strategy annotations include not only indices of arguments of function symbols but also rules defining function symbols. Occurrences of 0 in E-strategies can be thought of as abstractions of these items. Given a strategy annotation ς, it is immediate to obtain a 'corresponding' E-strategy map φ by replacing rule items $l \to r$ in $\varsigma(f)$ by 0, for each $f \in \Sigma$ (and removing consecutive occurrences of 0, see Remark 1 above).

Given a strategy annotation ς for Σ, we let $\mu^\varsigma \in M_\Sigma$ be $\mu^\varsigma(f) = \{i \in \mathbb{N} \mid i \in \varsigma(f)\}$ for each $f \in \Sigma$. We drop superscript ς if no confusion arises. The following theorem establishes a very close connection between $\to_\varsigma$ and $\hookrightarrow_\mu$.

Theorem 6. *Let $\mathcal{R}$ be a TRS, ς be a strategy annotation, and $t, s \in \mathcal{T}(\Sigma, \mathcal{X})$. If $t \to_\varsigma s$, then $t \hookrightarrow_\mu s$.*

We say that a TRS is ς-terminating if $\to_\varsigma$ is terminating. According to Theorem 6, we have the following immediate consequence.

Theorem 7. *Let $\mathcal{R}$ be a TRS and ς be a strategy annotation. If $\mathcal{R}$ is μ-terminating, then $\mathcal{R}$ is ς-terminating.*

Termination of $\to_\varsigma$ can also be characterized as innermost μ-termination: A strategy annotation ς is elementary for a TRS $\mathcal{R} = (\mathcal{C} \uplus \mathcal{D}, R)$ if there are no $f \in \mathcal{D}, \alpha \in R$, and $i \in \mathbb{N}$ such that $\alpha : i : L$ is a suffix of $\varsigma(f)$.

Theorem 8. *Let $\mathcal{R}$ be a TRS, ς be an r-full, elementary strategy annotation, and $t, s \in \mathcal{T}(\Sigma, \mathcal{X})$. If $t \to_\varsigma s$, then $t \,\dot{\hookrightarrow}_\mu\, s$.*

Note that r-fullness is necessary in Theorem 8 to ensure that the step $t \to_\varsigma s$ does not forget any inner redex due to the lack of the corresponding rule in the strategy annotations. Hence, we have the following.

Theorem 9. *Let $\mathcal{R}$ be a TRS and ς be an r-full, elementary strategy annotation. If $\mathcal{R}$ is innermost μ-terminating, then $\mathcal{R}$ is ς-terminating.*

In general, ς-termination does not imply (innermost) μ-termination.

Example 9. Consider the TRS $\mathcal{R}$:

$$\alpha : \texttt{b} \to \texttt{a} \qquad \beta : \texttt{b} \to \texttt{c(b)}$$

and ς given by $\varsigma(\texttt{b}) = [\alpha,\beta]$ and $\varsigma(\texttt{c}) = [1]$. Then, $\mathcal{R}$ is clearly ς-terminating, but it is *not* (innermost) μ-terminating.

Example 9 also shows that ς-termination of a TRS does *not* imply φ-termination for the corresponding E-strategy map (see Remark 2), since a local strategy (0) for b and (1) for c in Example 9 would lead to nonterminating computations with the E-strategy. Moreover, φ-termination does not imply ς-termination either.

Example 10. Consider the following TRS (based on that of Example 8)

$$\alpha : \texttt{if(true,x,y)} \to \texttt{x} \qquad \gamma : \texttt{if(x,y,y)} \to \texttt{a}$$
$$\beta : \texttt{if(false,x,y)} \to \texttt{y} \qquad \delta : \texttt{b} \to \texttt{if(a,b,b)}$$

and $\varsigma(\texttt{if}) = [1,\alpha,\beta,2,3,\gamma]$, $\varsigma(\texttt{b}) = [\delta]$. The corresponding E-strategy map φ is $\varphi(\texttt{f}) = (1\ 0\ 2\ 3\ 0)$, $\varphi(\texttt{b}) = (0)$. Note that $\mathcal{R}$ is not ς-terminating:

$$\underline{\texttt{b}} \to_\varsigma \texttt{if(a,}\underline{\texttt{b}}\texttt{,b)} \to_\varsigma \texttt{if(a,if(a,}\underline{\texttt{b}}\texttt{,b),b)} \to_\varsigma \cdots$$

However, $\mathcal{R}$ is φ-terminating, since we have:

$$\underline{\langle \texttt{b}_{(0)}, \Lambda\rangle} \to_\varphi \langle \texttt{if}_{(1\ 0\ 2\ 3\ 0)}(\texttt{a}_{nil},\texttt{b}_{(0)},\texttt{b}_{(0)}), \Lambda\rangle$$
$$\to_\varphi^+ \underline{\langle \texttt{if}_{(0\ 2\ 3\ 0)}(\texttt{a}_{nil},\texttt{b}_{(0)},\texttt{b}_{(0)}), \Lambda\rangle} \to_\varphi \langle \texttt{a}_{nil}, \Lambda\rangle$$

6 Proving Innermost Termination of *CSR*

Innermost termination of *CSR* has been related to termination of elementary local and van de Pol's strategies. How can innermost termination of *CSR* be proven? Since proving μ-termination of a TRS $\mathcal{R}$ is usually achieved by proving *termination* of a transformed TRS (e.g., [GM99,Luc96,Zan97]), the question naturally arises of whether *innermost* μ-termination is detected by these transformations. In this section, we investigate this problem.

The first correct transformation for proving termination of *CSR* was described in [Luc96]. The basic idea is very simple: since non-μ-replacing arguments cannot be rewritten with *CSR*, it makes sense to *remove* them (by appropriately reducing the *arity* of symbols): Given a signature Σ, the *μ-contracted signature* Σ^μ is obtained by renaming each $f \in \Sigma$ as $f_\mu \in \Sigma^\mu$ and giving it the arity $ar(f_\mu) = |\mu(f)|$. Terms from the signatures Σ and Σ^μ are related by a *μ-contracting* function $\tau_\mu : \mathcal{T}(\Sigma,\mathcal{X}) \to \mathcal{T}(\Sigma^\mu,\mathcal{X})$. This function *drops* the non-replacing immediate subterms of a term t and constructs a 'μ-contracted' term by joining the (also transformed) replacing arguments below the corresponding operator of the μ-contracted signature. Transformation τ_μ can be used to transform TRSs. Let $\mathcal{R} = (\Sigma, R)$ be a TRS and $\mu \in M_\Sigma$. The set of rules R^μ of the μ-contraction $\mathcal{R}^\mu = (\Sigma^\mu, R^\mu)$ of $\mathcal{R}$ is $R^\mu = \{\tau_\mu(l) \to \tau_\mu(r) \mid l \to r \in R\}$. The following example illustrates μ-contraction and shows that, in general, the transformation is *not* correct for proving innermost μ-termination.

Example 11. Consider the TRS

```
f(a(b)) → f(a(b))          a(c) → b
```

and $\mu(\mathtt{a}) = \varnothing$, $\mu(\mathtt{f}) = \{1\}$. Then, $\mathcal{R}^\mu$ is (we use the same symbols; the arities may decrease due to removing non-μ-replacing arguments)

```
f(a) → f(a)          a → b
```

which is innermost terminating. However, $\mathcal{R}$ is *not* innermost μ-terminating, since we have: $\mathtt{f(a(b))} \overset{i}{\hookrightarrow}_\mu \mathtt{f(a(b))} \overset{i}{\hookrightarrow}_\mu \cdots$.

However, when considering the *canonical* replacement map $\mu^{can}_{\mathcal{R}}$, which is the most restrictive replacement map (in M_Σ) ensuring that the non-variable subterms of the left-hand sides of the rules of $\mathcal{R}$ are replacing, i.e., the minimum Σ-map μ such that $\forall l \in L(\mathcal{R}), \mathcal{P}os_\Sigma(l) \subseteq \mathcal{P}os^\mu(l)$ [Luc98], we have the following.

Theorem 10. *Let $\mathcal{R} = (\Sigma, R)$ be a left-linear TRS and $\mu \in M_\Sigma$ be such that $\mu^{can}_{\mathcal{R}} \sqsubseteq \mu$. If $\mathcal{R}^\mu$ is innermost terminating, then $\mathcal{R}$ is innermost μ-terminating.*

The main problem with the contractive transformation is that it is only useful to prove μ-termination of *μ-conservative* TRSs. A TRS $\mathcal{R}$ is μ-conservative if $\mathcal{R}^\mu$ has no rule with extra variables in the right-hand side [Luc96]. An extra variable x can appear in a rule of $\mathcal{R}^\mu$ if all occurrences of x are non-μ-replacing in the left-hand side l of the corresponding rule $l \to r$ of $\mathcal{R}$, but x is μ-replacing in r.

In order to overcome this problem, given $\mathcal{R}$ and μ, Zantema [Zan97] defines a new transformed TRS $\mathcal{R}^\mu_Z$ which is obtained by *marking* the *non-replacing arguments* of function symbols (disregarding their positions, see [Zan97] for a detailed description of the transformation). Unfortunately, Zantema's transformation is *not* correct for proving innermost μ-termination.

Example 12. Consider the TRS $\mathcal{R}$:

```
f(b,a(x)) → f(b,a(b))
```

and $\mu(\mathtt{a}) = \varnothing$, $\mu(\mathtt{f}) = \{1,2\}$ (note that $\mu^{can}_{\mathcal{R}} \sqsubseteq \mu$). Then, $\mathcal{R}^Z_\mu$ is:

```
f(b,a(x)) → f(b,a(b'))          activate(b') → b
b         → b'                  activate(x)  → x
```

where `b'` and `activate` are new symbols. It is not difficult to see that $\mathcal{R}^Z_\mu$ is innermost terminating. However, $\mathcal{R}$ is *not* innermost μ-terminating.

Recently, Giesl and Middeldorp have introduced a transformation which can be used to prove termination of *CSR* [GM99] and that (at least from the theoretical point of view) is strictly more powerful than the contractive transformation and Zantema's transformation[4]. They *mark* the replacing positions of a term (by using a new symbol `active`), since these positions are the only ones where

[4] The first statement is proved in [GM99]; the second one has been demonstrated recently [GM01].

CSR may take place. Given a TRS $\mathcal{R} = (\Sigma, R)$ and $\mu \in M_\Sigma$, the TRS $\mathcal{R}^1_\mu = (\Sigma \cup \{\mathtt{active}, \mathtt{mark}\}, R^1_\mu)$ consists of the rules (for all $l \to r \in R$ and $f \in \Sigma$):

$$\begin{aligned}\mathtt{active}(l) &\to \mathtt{mark}(r)\\ \mathtt{mark}(f(x_1,\ldots,x_k)) &\to \mathtt{active}(f([x_1]_f,\ldots,[x_k]_f))\\ \mathtt{active}(x) &\to x\end{aligned}$$

where $[x_i]_f = \mathtt{mark}(x_i)$ if $i \in \mu(f)$, otherwise $[x_i]_f = x_i$. Concerning this transformation, we have the following result.

Theorem 11. *Let $\mathcal{R} = (\Sigma, R)$ be a TRS and $\mu \in M_\Sigma$. If $\mathcal{R}^1_\mu$ is innermost terminating, then $\mathcal{R}$ is innermost μ-terminating.*

Giesl and Middeldorp noticed that this transformation is incomplete for proving termination of *CSR*, i.e., there exist TRSs $\mathcal{R}$ and replacement maps μ such that $\mathcal{R}$ is μ-terminating but $\mathcal{R}^1_\mu$ is not terminating (see Example 1 in [GM99]). The transformation remains incomplete for proving innermost μ-termination.

Example 13. Consider the TRS $\mathcal{R}$ of Example 4. If $\mu = \mu_\top$, then $\mathcal{R}^1_\mu$ is:

$$\begin{aligned}\mathtt{active(f(a))} &\to \mathtt{mark(f(a))} & \mathtt{mark(f(x))} &\to \mathtt{active(f(mark(x)))}\\ \mathtt{active(a)} &\to \mathtt{mark(b)} & \mathtt{mark(a)} &\to \mathtt{active(a)}\\ \mathtt{active(x)} &\to \mathtt{x} & \mathtt{mark(b)} &\to \mathtt{active(b)}\end{aligned}$$

$\mathcal{R}$ is innermost μ-terminating, but with $\mathcal{R}^1_\mu$ we have the following infinite innermost derivation:

$$\begin{aligned}\underline{\mathtt{active(f(a))}} &\to_i \underline{\mathtt{mark(f(a))}} \to_i \mathtt{active(f(}\underline{\mathtt{mark(a)}}\mathtt{))}\\ &\to_i \mathtt{active(f(}\underline{\mathtt{active(a)}}\mathtt{))} \to_i \mathtt{active(f(a))} \to_i \cdots\end{aligned}$$

Giesl and Middeldorp also provided a correct and complete transformation to deal with termination of *CSR*. Basically their idea is to permit *a single* (context-sensitive) reduction step each time. They achieve this by using new symbols f' for each (non-constant) symbol $f \in \Sigma$ and shifting a single symbol `active` to (non-deterministically) reach the replacing position where the redex is placed. The application of a rewrite rule changes `active` into `mark` which is propagated upwards through the term, in order to be replaced by a new symbol `active` that enables new reduction steps. After checking that no 'strange' symbols remain uncontrolled (using a symbol `proper` such that $\mathtt{proper}(t)$ reduces to $\mathtt{ok}(t)$ if and only if t is a ground term of the original signature), a rule $\mathtt{top(ok}(x)\mathtt{))} \to \mathtt{top(active}(x)\mathtt{))}$ enables a new reduction step (see [GM99] for a more detailed explanation). Given a TRS $\mathcal{R} = (\Sigma, R)$ and $\mu \in M_\Sigma$, the TRS $\mathcal{R}^2_\mu = (\Sigma \cup \{f' \mid f \in \Sigma \wedge ar(f) > 0\} \cup \{\mathtt{active}, \mathtt{mark}, \mathtt{ok}, \mathtt{proper}, \mathtt{top}\}, R^2_\mu)$ consists of the following rules: for all $l \to r \in R$, $f \in \Sigma$ such that $k = ar(f) > 0$, $i \in \mu(f)$, and constants $c \in \Sigma$,

$$\begin{aligned}
\mathtt{active}(l) &\to \mathtt{mark}(r)\\
\mathtt{active}(f(x_1,\ldots,x_i,\ldots,x_k)) &\to f'(x_1,\ldots,\mathtt{active}(x_i),\ldots,x_k)\\
f'(x_1,\ldots,\mathtt{mark}(x_i),\ldots,x_k) &\to \mathtt{mark}(f(x_1,\ldots,x_i,\ldots,x_k))\\
\mathtt{proper}(c) &\to \mathtt{ok}(c)\\
\mathtt{proper}(f(x_1,\ldots,x_k)) &\to f(\mathtt{proper}(x_1),\ldots,\mathtt{proper}(x_k))\\
f(\mathtt{ok}(x_1),\ldots,\mathtt{ok}(x_k)) &\to \mathtt{ok}(f(x_1,\ldots,x_k))\\
\mathtt{top}(\mathtt{mark}(x)) &\to \mathtt{top}(\mathtt{proper}(x))\\
\mathtt{top}(\mathtt{ok}(x)) &\to \mathtt{top}(\mathtt{active}(x))
\end{aligned}$$

The transformation is also correct for proving innermost termination of *CSR*.

Theorem 12. *Let $\mathcal{R} = (\Sigma, R)$ be a TRS and $\mu \in M_\Sigma$. If $\mathcal{R}^2_\mu$ is innermost terminating, then $\mathcal{R}$ is innermost μ-terminating.*

But now the transformation is *not* complete for proving innermost μ-termination.

Example 14. Consider again the TRS $\mathcal{R}$ in Example 4 and $\mu = \mu_\top$. We obtain the following $\mathcal{R}^2_\mu$ system:

$$\begin{array}{llllll}
\mathtt{active(f(a))} & \to & \mathtt{mark(f(a))} & \mathtt{proper(b)} & \to & \mathtt{ok(b)}\\
\mathtt{active(a)} & \to & \mathtt{mark(b)} & \mathtt{proper(f(x))} & \to & \mathtt{f(proper(x))}\\
\mathtt{active(f(x))} & \to & \mathtt{f'(active(x))} & \mathtt{f(ok(x))} & \to & \mathtt{ok(f(x))}\\
\mathtt{f'(mark(x))} & \to & \mathtt{mark(f(x))} & \mathtt{top(mark(x))} & \to & \mathtt{top(proper(x))}\\
\mathtt{proper(a)} & \to & \mathtt{ok(a)} & \mathtt{top(ok(x))} & \to & \mathtt{top(active(x))}
\end{array}$$

In this case, we have the following infinite innermost derivation:

$$\begin{aligned}
\mathtt{top}(\underline{\mathtt{active(f(a))}}) &\to_i \underline{\mathtt{top(mark(f(a))}} \to_i \mathtt{top(proper(f(a)))}\\
&\to_i^* \underline{\mathtt{top(ok(f(a)))}} \to_i \mathtt{top}(\underline{\mathtt{active(f(a))}}) \to_i
\end{aligned}$$

...

Surprisingly, for the μ-contractive transformation, we have a completeness result.

Theorem 13. *Let $\mathcal{R} = (\Sigma, R)$ be a left-linear TRS and $\mu \in M_\Sigma$ be such that $\mu^{can}_\mathcal{R} \sqsubseteq \mu$ and $\mathcal{R}$ is μ-conservative. If $\mathcal{R}$ is innermost μ-terminating, then $\mathcal{R}^\mu$ is innermost terminating.*

Note that μ-conservativeness is necessary to ensure that $\mathcal{R}^\mu$ is a TRS. Since TRSs with extra variables cannot be innermost terminating, without this requirement, the theorem would be incorrect.

7 Related Work

Syntactic annotations have been used in the OBJ family of languages for many years (as local strategies). However, only recently (but quite intensively) has the formal analysis of computations with OBJ's local strategies been addressed (e.g., [Eke98,FGK01,Luc01,Nag99,NO01,OF97,Pol01]). As far as the author knows, only [FGK01,Luc01] have investigated the problem of proving termination of rewriting under positive local strategies. Termination of van de Pol's strategy annotations has not been studied before. In [FGK01], an inductive method is proposed to directly prove (ground) termination of rewriting with positive local strategies without applying any transformation. We have checked that the two examples used in [FGK01] to illustrate their technique can easily be proved terminating by using Zantema's transformation [Zan97] and an *automatic* tool such as Contejean and Marché's C*i*ME 2.0 system (see `http://cime.lri.fr`). Moreover, we note that only proofs of termination of *CSR* (and Theorem 2) are necessary to deal with these examples. On the other hand, in order to be able to use their methods, it is necessary to use a different technique to ensure that the constant symbols are terminating (w.r.t. computations guided by the strategies). This is easy if there is no rewrite rule $c \to r$ asociated to any constant symbol c. Note that φ-termination of (a TRS containing) the TRS $\mathcal{R}$:

$$\mathtt{a} \to \mathtt{f(a)}$$

with $\varphi(\mathtt{f}) = nil$, could not be proven in this way. However, φ-termination of $\mathcal{R}$ is easily proved by using the μ-contractive transformation of [Luc96], since $\mathcal{R}^\mu$:

$$\mathtt{a} \to \mathtt{f}$$

is clearly terminating. Nevertheless, Fissore et al.'s technique can work when our techniques do not. For instance, the TRS [GF01]

$$\mathtt{f(a,g(x))} \to \mathtt{f(a,h(x))} \qquad \mathtt{h(x)} \to \mathtt{g(x)}$$

terminates with the strategy φ_1 such that $\varphi_1(\mathtt{f}) = \mathtt{(0\ 1\ 2)}$ but it does not terminate with $\varphi_2(\mathtt{f}) = \mathtt{(1\ 2\ 0)}$ (let $\varphi_1(\mathtt{h}) = \varphi_2(\mathtt{h}) = \mathtt{(0)}$). In both cases $\mu(\mathtt{f}) = \{1, 2\}$. Thus, we are not able to distinguish them (note that φ_1 is not elementary), whereas their technique seems to work [GF01].

8 Conclusions and Future Work

We have investigated how to prove termination of rewriting under local and van de Pol's strategy annotations. We have also shown that, in general, these problems are not comparable (see Examples 9 and 10). We have shown that the analysis of (innermost) termination of *CSR* provides a suitable characterization of termination of rewriting under positive local and van de Pol's strategy annotations (it is even complete for local strategies, see Theorems 4 and 5). We have investigated the use of transformations that are correct to prove termination of *CSR* [GM99,Luc96,Zan97] as formal tools for proving innermost termination of *CSR*. Transformations of [GM99] are *correct* for proving *innermost* termination of *CSR*. The transformation of [Luc96] is correct for left-linear TRSs and replacement maps that are less restrictive than the canonical replacement map. Zantema's transformation is not correct in the general case.

Concerning future work, we note that framework aimed at modelling computations under strategy annotations mucst take into account:

1. The presence of *replacement restrictions* on the arguments of symbols (i.e., the absence of some indices, as in Example 1).
2. The (possible) *innermost* character of computations (as in OBJ programs).

3. The *position of the occurrences of* 0 in strategy annotations (as exemplified by Gnaedig et al.'s previous example).
4. The *priority* of applying some rules according to (some) strategy annotations (as in van de Pol's approach, see Example 9).
5. The presence of *special classes* of symbols (e.g., AC operators).
6. The presence of *sorts* and *modules* as done in OBJ.

In this paper, we have (partially) covered the first two characteristics. This has proven to be sufficient for completely characterizing termination of rewriting under elementary E-strategies. By also considering other subfields of rewriting such as *priority* rewriting [Pol98], *AC*-rewriting [DP01], etc., we would obtain a more accurate characterization of the problem in more general cases[5]. Strategy annotations can also be simulated in programming languages that provide for more powerful mechanisms for defining strategies such as ELAN [BKKMR98]. Our results also apply to ensure termination of programs written in such languages when such kinds of strategies are used. The analysis of termination of ELAN programs controlled by arbitrary strategies is also a subject for future work.

Innermost termination of *CSR* should also be further investigated. It can be very different from termination of *CSR*. For instance, terminating TRSs are, of course, μ-terminating. However, the innermost terminating TRS of Example 4 is not innermost μ-terminating, if $\mu = \mu_\bot$. Thus, in contrast to μ-termination, in general, it is not possible to prove innermost μ-termination using proofs of innermost termination. On the other hand, it is well-known that innermost termination implies termination for, e.g., nonoverlapping TRSs (see [Gra96]). Since innermost termination can be easier to prove than termination (see [AG97,Gra96], this is used for obtaining indirect proofs of termination. If this remains true for *CSR*, then we could obtain new methods for proving termination of *CSR*.

Acknowledgements. I thank Jürgen Giesl, Isabelle Gnaedig, Olivier Fissore, Aart Middeldorp, and the anonymous referees for their helpful remarks. I also thank O. Fissore for sending me a copy of [FGK01].

References

[AG97] T. Arts and J. Giesl. Proving Innermost Normalisation Automatically. In H. Comon, editor, *Proc. of 8th International Conference on Rewriting Techniques and Applications, RTA'97*, LNCS 1232:157-171, Springer-Verlag, Berlin, 1997.

[BKKMR98] P. Borovanský, C. Kirchner, H. Kirchner, P.-E. Moreau, and C. Ringeissen. An Overview of ELAN. In C. Kirchner and H. Kirchner, editors, *Proc. of 2nd International Workshop on Rewriting Logic and its Applications, WRLA'98*, Electronic Notes in Computer Science, 15(1998):1-16, 1998.

[5] Termination of AC-*CSR* has already been studied in [FR99].

[BN98] F. Baader and T. Nipkow. Term Rewriting and All That. Cambridge University Press, 1998.

[CELM96] M. Clavel, S. Eker, P. Lincoln, and J. Meseguer. Principles of Maude. In J. Meseguer, editor, *Proc. 1st International Workshop on Rewriting Logic and its Applications*, Electronic Notes in Theoretical Computer Science, volume 4, 25 pages, Elsevier Sciences, 1996.

[Der87] N. Dershowitz. Termination of rewriting. *Journal of Symbolic Computation*, 3:69-115, 1987.

[DP01] N. Dershowitz and D.A. Plaisted. Rewriting. In A. Robinson and A. Voronkov, editors. *Handbook of Automated Reasoning*, volume 1, chapter 9, Elsevier, 2001.

[Eke98] S. Eker. Term Rewriting with Operator Evaluation Strategies. In C. Kirchner and H. Kirchner, editors, *Proc. of 2nd International Workshop on Rewriting Logic and its Applications, WRLA'98*, Electronic Notes in Computer Science, 15(1998):1-20, 1998.

[FGJM85] K. Futatsugi, J. Goguen, J.-P. Jouannaud, and J. Meseguer. Principles of OBJ2. In *Conference Record of the 12th Annual ACM Symposium on Principles of Programming Languages, POPL'85*, pages 52-66, ACM Press, 1985.

[FGK01] O. Fissore, I. Gnaedig, and H. Kirchner. Termination of rewriting with local strategies. In M.P. Bonacina and B. Gramlich, editors, *Proc. of 4th International Workshop on Strategies in Automated Deduction, STRATEGIES'01*, pages 35-54, 2001.

[FN97] K. Futatsugi and A. Nakagawa. An Overview of CAFE Specification Environment – An algebraic approach for creating, verifying, and maintaining formal specification over networks –. In *Proc. of 1st International Conference on Formal Engineering Methods*, 1997.

[FR99] M.C.F. Ferreira and A.L. Ribeiro. Context-Sensitive AC-Rewriting. In P. Narendran and M. Rusinowitch, editors, *Proc. of 10th International Conference on Rewriting Techniques and Applications, RTA'99*, LNCS 1631:286-300, Springer-Verlag, Berlin, 1999.

[GF01] I. Gnaedig and O. Fissore. Personal communication. July 2001.

[GL01] B. Gramlich and S. Lucas (editors). 1st International Workshop on Reduction Strategies in Rewriting and Programming, WRS'01. *Proceedings*, volume 2359, Servicio de Publicaciones de la Universidad Politécnica de Valencia, 2001. See also: volume 57 of ENTCS, Elsevier, *to appear.*

[GM99] J. Giesl and A. Middeldorp. Transforming Context-Sensitive Rewrite Systems. In P. Narendran and M. Rusinowitch, editors, *Proc. of 10th International Conference on Rewriting Techniques and Applications, RTA'99*, LNCS 1631:271-285, Springer-Verlag, Berlin, 1999.

[GM01] J. Giesl and A. Middeldorp. Personal communication. May 2001.

[Gra96] B. Gramlich. On Proving Termination by Innermost Termination. In H. Ganzinger, editor, *Proc. of 7th International Conference on Rewriting Techniques and Applications, RTA'96*, LNCS 1103:97-107, Springer-Verlag, Berlin, 1996.

[GWMFJ00] J.A. Goguen, T. Winkler, J. Meseguer, K. Futatsugi, and J.-P. Jouannaud. Introducing OBJ. In J. Goguen and G. Malcolm, editors, *Software Engineering with OBJ: algebraic specification in action*, Kluwer, 2000.

[Luc96] S. Lucas. Termination of context-sensitive rewriting by rewriting. In F. Meyer auf der Heide and B. Monien, editors, *Proc. of 23rd. International Colloquium on Automata, Languages and Programming, ICALP'96*, LNCS 1099:122-133, Springer-Verlag, Berlin, 1996.

[Luc98] S. Lucas. Context-sensitive computations in functional and functional logic programs. *Journal of Functional and Logic Programming*, 1998(1):1-61, January 1998.

[Luc01] S. Lucas. Termination of on-demand rewriting and termination of OBJ programs. In *Proc. of 3rd International Conference on Principles and Practice of Declarative Programming, PPDP'01*, pages 82-93, ACM Press, 2001.

[Nag99] T. Nagaya. Reduction Strategies for Term Rewriting Systems. PhD Thesis, School of Information Science, Japan Advanced Institute of Science and Technology, March 1999.

[NO01] M. Nakamura and K. Ogata. The evaluation strategy for head normal form with and without on-demand flags. In K. Futatsugi, editor, *Proc. of 3rd International Workshop on Rewriting Logic and its Applications, WRLA'00, Electronic Notes in Theoretical Computer Science*, volume 36, 17 pages, 2001.

[OF97] K. Ogata and K. Futatsugi. Implementation of Term Rewritings with the Evaluation Strategy. In H. Glaser and P. Hartel, editors, *Proc of 9th International Symposium on Programming Languages, Implementations, Logics and Programs, PLILP'97*, LNCS 1292:225-239, Springer-Verlag, Berlin, 1997.

[Pol98] J. van de Pol. Operational semantics of rewriting with priorities. *Theoretical Computer Science*, 200:289-312, 1998.

[Pol01] J. van de Pol. Just-in-time: on Strategy Annotations. In [GL01], pages 39-58.

[Vis01] E. Visser. A Survey of Strategies in Program Transformation Systems. In [GL01], pages 97-128.

[Zan97] H. Zantema. Termination of Context-Sensitive Rewriting. In H. Comon, editor, *Proc. of 8th International Conference on Rewriting Techniques and Applications, RTA'97*, LNCS 1232:172-186, Springer-Verlag, Berlin, 1997.

Inferring Termination Conditions for Logic Programs Using Backwards Analysis

Samir Genaim and Michael Codish

The Department of Computer Science
Ben-Gurion University of the Negev
Beer-Sheva, Israel
{genaim,mcodish}@cs.bgu.ac.il

Abstract. This paper focuses on the inference of modes for which a logic program is guaranteed to terminate. This generalizes traditional termination analysis where an analyzer tries to verify termination for a specified mode. The contribution is a methodology which combines traditional termination analysis and backwards analysis to obtain termination inference. This leads to a better understanding of termination inference, simplifies its formal justification, and facilitates implementation. We evaluate the application of this approach to enhance an existing termination analyzer to perform also termination inference.

1 Introduction

This paper focuses on the inference of modes for which a logic program is guaranteed to terminate. This generalizes traditional termination analysis where an analyzer tries to verify termination for a specified mode. For example, for the classic *append*/3 relation, a standard analyzer will determine that a query of the form $append(x, y, z)$ with x bound to a closed list terminates and likewise for the query in which z is bound to a closed list. In contrast, termination inference provides the result $append(x, y, z) \leftarrow x \vee z$ with the interpretation that the query $append(x, y, z)$ terminates if x or z are bound to closed lists. We refer to the first type of analysis as performing *termination checking* and to the second as *termination inference* and we make the observation that the (missing) link between the two is a technique called *backwards analysis.*

Backwards analysis addresses the following type of question: Given a program and an assertion at a given program point, what are the weakest requirements on the inputs to the program which guarantee that the assertion will hold whenever execution reaches that point. In a recent paper, King and Lu [12] describe a framework for backwards analysis for logic programs set in the context of abstract interpretation. In their approach, the underlying abstract domain is required to be condensing or equivalently, a complete Heyting algebra. This ensures that when working backwards from an assertion in the program, at each step we can find a best approximation (weakest requirement) to eventually provide a condition on the inputs which guarantees that the assertion will hold.

R. Nieuwenhuis and A. Voronkov (Eds.): LPAR 2001, LNAI 2250, pp. 685–694, 2001.

To demonstrate this link between termination checking and termination inference, we apply backwards analysis as described by King and Lu [12] to enhance the termination (checking) analyzer described in [4] so that it will perform also termination inference. Our focus is on universal termination using Prolog's left-most selection rule and we assume that unifications do not violate the occurs check.

Termination inference is considered previously by Mesnard and coauthors in [15,16,17] (with a tool accessible at `http://www.complang.tuwien.ac.at/cti`). Our observation is that the link with backwards analysis provides a straightforward justification and also leads to a better implementation design.

2 Preliminaries and Motivating Example

We assume a familiarity with the standard logic program terminology [13,1] as with the basics of abstract interpretation [5,6]. This section reviews the program analyses upon which we build in the rest of the paper. For notation, in brief: Variables in logic programs are denoted using the upper case as in Prolog; while in relations, Boolean formula, and other mathematical context we use the lower case. We let $\bar{x}$ denote a tuple of distinct variables $x_1, \ldots, x_n$. To highlight a specific point in a program we use labels of the form ⓐ.

Size relations and instantiation dependencies rest at the heart of termination analysis: size information to infer that some measure on program states decreases as computation progresses; and instantiation information, to infer that the underlying domain is well founded. Consider the recursive clause of the *append*/3 relation: $append([X|Xs], Ys, [X|Zs]) \leftarrow append(Xs, Ys, Zs)$. It does not suffice to observe that the size of the first and third arguments decrease in the recursive call. To guarantee termination one must also ensure that one of these arguments is sufficiently instantiated in order to argue that this recursion can be activated only a finite number of times.

Instantiation information is obtained through abstract interpretation over the domain Pos which consists of the positive Boolean functions augmented with a bottom element (representing the formula *false*). The elements of the domain are ordered by implication and represent equivalence classes of propositional formula. This domain is usually associated with its use to infer groundness dependencies where a formula of the form $x \wedge (y \rightarrow z)$ is interpreted to describe a program state in which x is definitely bound to a ground term and there exists an instantiation dependency such that whenever y becomes bound to a ground term then so does z. Similar analyses can be applied to infer dependencies with respect to other notions of instantiation. For details on Pos see [14].

Size relations express linear information about the sizes of terms (with respect to a given norm function) [2,3,7,11]. For example, the relation $x \leq z \ \wedge \ y \leq z$ describes a program state in which the sizes of the terms associated with x and y are less or equal to the size of the term associated with z. Similarly, $z = x + y$ describes a state in which the sum of the sizes of the terms associated with x and y is equal to the size of the term associated with z. Several methods for inferring size relations are described in the literature [2,3,7,8]. They differ primarily in their approach to obtaining a finite analysis as the abstract domain of size relations contains infinite chains.

Throughout this paper we will use the so-called term-size norm for size relations for which the corresponding notion of instantiation is groundness. We base our presentation on the termination analyzer described in [4] although we could use as well almost any of the alternatives described in the literature. This analyzer is based on a bottom-up semantics which makes loops observable in the form of binary clauses. This provides a convenient starting point for termination inference as derived in this paper. Each element in the abstraction of this semantics represents a loop and is of the form $p(\bar{x}) \leftarrow \pi, p(\bar{y})$ where π is a conjunction of linear constraints.

For the full picture, we note that the analyzer of [4] involves two phases: First, the user provides a program and the analyzer approximates its loops over two domains: size relations and instantiation dependencies. Then, the user specifies the input modes of an initial goal and the analyzer performs a termination check. For termination inference, it is the first part of the first phase of the termination analysis which is useful. From the descriptions of the loops with size information we extract the intitial Boolean assertions from which backwards analysis then proceeds. We demonstrate our approach by example in four steps:

The first step: Consider the *append*/3 relation.

```
append([X|Xs],Ys,[X|Zs]) :- append(Xs,Ys,Zs).
append([],Ys,Ys).
```

The termination checker [4] reports a single loop (abstract binary clause):

```
append(A,B,C) :- [D<A, F<C, B=E], append(D,E,F).
```

indicating that subsequent calls to *append* in a computation, involve a decrease in size for the first and third arguments ($D < A$ and $F < C$) and maintain the size of the second argument ($B = E$). To guarantee that this loop may be traversed only a finite number of times, it is sufficient to require that A or C be sufficiently instantiated. This is expressed as a Boolean condition: $append(x, y, z) \leftarrow (x \vee z)$.

Backwards analysis is now applied to infer the weakest conditions on the program's predicates which guarantee this condition. For this example the inference is complete and we have derived the result: $terminates(append(x, y, z)) \leftarrow x \vee z$.

The second step: Consider the use of *append*/3 to define list membership. Adding the clause:

```
member(X,Xs) :- append(A,[X|B],Xs).
```

to the program introduces no additional loops. Backwards analysis should specify the weakest condition on $member(X, Xs)$ which guarantees the termination condition $A \vee Xs$ for $append(A, [X|B], Xs)$. This is obtained through projection which for backwards analysis is defined in terms of universal quantification as $\forall_A.(A \vee Xs)$. The resulting Boolean precondition for $member/2$ is: $terminates(member(x, y)) \leftarrow y$.

The third step: We now add to the program a definition for the subset/2 relation:

```
subset([X|Xs],Ys) :- member(X,Ys), subset(Xs,Ys).
subset([],Ys).
```

Termination checking reports an additional loop:

```
subset(A,B) :- [B=D,C<A], subset(C,D).
```

which will be traversed a finite number of times if the first argument (A) is sufficiently instantiated. However, for the program to terminate both of its loops must terminate — also the one for *append*/3 in the call to $member(X, Ys)$. So, drawing on the result of the previous step, also the second argument for *subset*/2 must be instantiated. To sum up, we have $terminates(subset(x, y)) \leftarrow x \wedge y$.

The fourth step: This step demonstrates that the precondition on a call in a clause body may be (partially) satisfied by answers to calls which precede it. Consider adding to the program a clause:

```
s(X,Y,Z) :- ⓐ append(X,Y,T), ⓑ subset(T,Z).
```

which defines a relation $s(x, y, z)$ such that the set z contains the union of sets x and y. The preconditions for termination derived in the previous steps specify the conditions $x \vee t$ and $t \wedge z$ at points ⓐ and ⓑ respectively. In addition, from a standard groundness analysis we know that on success $append(x, y, t)$ satisfies $(x \wedge y) \leftrightarrow t$ (intuitively: indicating the flow of data either from x and y to t or vice versa). So, instead of imposing on the clause head the conditions from both calls in its body, as we did in the previous step, we may weaken the second condition in view of the results from the first call. Namely, the termination condition inferred for $s(x, y, z)$ is $\forall_t.((x \vee t) \wedge (((x \wedge y) \leftrightarrow t) \rightarrow t \wedge z)) \equiv x \wedge y \wedge z$.

In general, the steps illustrated above need to be applied in iteration. Though what we have shown works correctly for our example. In the next section we describe more formally the steps required for backwards analysis.

3 Backward Analysis

This section presents an abstract interpretation for backwards analysis using the domain Pos distilled from the general presentation given in [12]. Clauses are assumed to be normalized and contain assertions so that they are of the form $h(\bar{x}) \leftarrow \mu \diamond b_1, \ldots, b_n$ where μ is a Pos formula, interpreted as an instantiation condition which must be satisfied when the clause is called, and b_i is either an atom, or a unification operation.

The analysis associates pre- and post- instantiation conditions, specified in Pos, with the predicates of the program. The postcondition ψ_p for predicate p is the result of the standard instantiation dependency analysis. It reflects the instantiations generated by p. The precondition φ_p for p is a condition which guarantees the termination of calls to p. Preconditions are initialized to *true* (the top element in *Pos*) and become more restrictive (move down in Pos) through iteration until they stabilize. At each iteration, clauses are processed from right to left using the current aproximations for preconditions on the calls together with the postconditions to infer new approximations for the preconditions.

For the basic step, consider a clause of the form: $p \leftarrow \ldots$ ⓐ$, q,$ ⓑ $\ldots$ Denote the current approximation of the precondition for q by φ_q and its postcondition by ψ_q. Assume that processing the clause from right to left has already propagated a condition e_b at the point ⓑ. Then, to insure that e_b will hold after the success of q, it suffices to require at ⓐ the conjunction of φ_q with the weakest condition σ such that $(\sigma \wedge \psi_q) \rightarrow e_b$. This σ is precisely the pseudo-complement [10] of ψ_q with respect to e_b which for Pos is obtained as $\psi_q \rightarrow e_b$. So propagating one step to the left gives the condition $e_a = \varphi_q \wedge (\psi_q \rightarrow \varphi_b)$.

Now consider a clause $h(\bar{x}) \leftarrow \mu \diamond b_1, \ldots, b_n$ with an assertion $\mu \in$ Pos. Denote the current approximation of the precondition for b_i by φ_i and its postcondition by ψ_i $(1 \leq i \leq n)$. Assume that the current approximation of the precondition for $h(\bar{x})$ is φ. Backwards analysis infers a new approximation φ' on $h(\bar{x})$ by consecutive application of the basic step described above. We start with $e_{n+1} = \mathit{true}$ and through n steps (with i going from n to 1) compute a condition $e_i = \varphi_i \wedge (\psi_i \rightarrow e_{i+1})$ which should hold just before the call to b_i. After computing e_1 we take $e_0 = \mu \wedge e_1$ and project e_0 on the variables $\bar{x}$ of the head by means of universal quantification. The new condition is finally obtained through conjunction with the previous condition φ.

To be precise, as Pos is not closed under universal quantification, projection of x from φ is defined as the largest element in Pos which implies $\forall_x.\varphi$. This is well-defined as the bottom element in Pos (*false*) is always a candidate.

Example 1. Consider the clause

```
subset(A,B) :- ⓔ0 A ◇ ⓔ1 A=[X|Xs], ⓔ2 B=Ys,
        ⓔ3 member(X,Ys), ⓔ4 subset(Xs,Ys) ⓔ5.
```

(the assertion A states that the first argument must be ground) and assume that the postconditions and current approximation of the preconditions are (respectively):

$$post = \left\{ \begin{array}{l} member(x,y) \leftarrow (y \rightarrow x) \\ subset(x,y) \leftarrow (y \rightarrow x) \end{array} \right\} \qquad pre = \left\{ \begin{array}{l} member(x,y) \leftarrow y \\ subset(x,y) \leftarrow x \end{array} \right\}.$$

The conditions $e_5, \ldots, e_0$ are obtained as follows:

$$\begin{array}{ll} e_5 = \mathit{true} & e_2 = \mathit{true} \wedge ((B \leftrightarrow Ys) \rightarrow e_3) \\ e_4 = Xs \wedge ((Ys \rightarrow Xs) \rightarrow e_5) & e_1 = \mathit{true} \wedge ((A \leftrightarrow (X \wedge Xs) \rightarrow e_2) \\ e_3 = Ys \wedge ((Ys \rightarrow X) \rightarrow e_4) & e_0 = A \wedge e_1 \end{array}$$

Projecting e_0 to the variables in the head gives $\forall_{Xs,Ys,X}.(e_0) = A \wedge B$. Which leads to the new precondition $subset(x,y) \leftarrow x \wedge y$. Note that the preconditions for unifications in the clause body are *true* and their postconditions, the usual groundness dependences.

Backwards analysis is formalized in [12] as the greatest fixed point of an operator over Pos. Our implementation is described in [9].

4 Termination Inference

Termination inference proceeds as follows: **(a)** apply the initial phase of the termination analysis described in [4] to obtain a set of abstract binary clauses which approximate the loops in the program (with size relations); **(b)** extract Boolean conditions on the instantiation of variables to guarantee that each of the identified loops can be executed only a finite number of times; and **(c)** apply backwards analysis as defined in [12] to infer modes for initial goals which guarantee that these Boolean conditions will hold.

The following definition specifies how to extract from the results of the initial phase of the termination analysis those assertions from which backwards analysis starts. The idea is that: (1) in each loop, at least one set of arguments I, the sum of the sizes of which decreases, should all be instantiated enough (so that is a disjunction); and (2) all of the loops must satisfy the previous point (so that is a conjunction).

Definition 1. *The termination assertion $\mu(p(\bar{x}))$ for the predicate p/n in the program P is determined as follows:*

1. *The condition for a single binary clause is*
   $\mu(p(\bar{x}) \leftarrow \pi, p(\bar{y})) = \bigvee \left\{ \bigwedge_{i \in I} x_i \,\middle|\, I \subseteq \{1, \ldots, n\},\ \pi \models (\sum_{i \in I} x_i > \sum_{i \in I} y_i\ ) \right\}$
2. *and the assertion for $p(\bar{x})$ is:*
   $\mu(p(\bar{x})) = \bigwedge \{\ \mu(\ell) \mid \ell = p(\bar{x}) \leftarrow \pi, p(\bar{y}) \in [\![P]\!]^{bin}_{size}\ \}$

In theory we could obtain a stronger assertion by considering arbitrary linear combinations of the arguments of $p(\bar{x})$ instead of restricting coefficients to 0 and 1 as we do in the definition by taking subsets I of the argument positions. In practice, in the implementation, we impose a weaker assertion which does not consider all subsets $I \subseteq \{1, \ldots, n\}$, but rather only the singletons (to detect argument positions which decrease in size) and the set of arguments which do not decrease in size (in case their sum does). This simplistic approach works well in practice. A more elaborate approach is described in [18].

Example 2. Consider as P the *split*/3 relation (from merge sort):

```
split([],[],[]).
split([X|Xs],[X|Ys],Zs) :- split(Xs,Zs,Ys).
```

The binary clauses obtained by the analyzer of [4] are:

$$\begin{aligned}
\ell_1 &= \ split(x_1, x_2, x_3) \leftarrow [y_1 < x_1, y_3 < x_2, x_3 = y_2], split(y_1, y_2, y_3).\\
\ell_2 &= \ split(x_1, x_2, x_3) \leftarrow [y_1 < x_1, y_2 < x_2, y_3 < x_3], split(y_1, y_2, y_3).\\
\ell_3 &= \ split(x_1, x_2, x_3) \leftarrow [y_1 < x_1, y_3 < x_2, y_2 < x_3], split(y_1, y_2, y_3).
\end{aligned}$$

We have $\mu(\ell_1) = \mu(\ell_3) = x_1 \vee (x_2 \wedge x_3)$, because $y_1 < x_1$ and $y_2 + y_3 < x_2 + x_3$; and $\mu(\ell_2) = x_1 \vee x_2 \vee x_3$ because $y_1 < x_1, y_2 < x_2, y_3 < x_3$. The assertion for *split*/3 is $\mu(split(x_1, x_2, x_3)) = (x_1 \vee (x_2 \wedge x_3)) \wedge (x_1 \vee x_2 \vee x_3) = x_1 \vee (x_2 \wedge x_3)$.

Definition 2. *A mode is a tuple of the form* $p(m_1, \ldots, m_n)$ *where* m_i $(1 \leq i \leq n)$ *is either* **b** *('bound') or* **f** *('free'). We say that* $p(m_1, \ldots, m_n)$ *is safe for* $p(x_1, \ldots, x_n)$ *if the conjunction* $\wedge\{x_i \mid m_i = b\}$ *implies the termination condition inferred by backwards analysis for* $p(\bar{x})$.

Example 3. In the previous example we inferred $\mu(split(x_1, x_2, x_3)) = \varphi$ with $\varphi = x_1 \vee (x_2 \wedge x_3)$. Hence $p(b, f, f)$ and $p(f, b, b)$ are safe modes for $split/3$ because $x_1 \rightarrow \varphi$ and $(x_2 \wedge x_3) \rightarrow \varphi$.

The correctness of the method follows from the results of [4] and [12].

Theorem 1. *Let P be a logic program and* $p(\bar{m})$ *a safe mode for* $p(\bar{x})$. *Then P terminates for* $p(\bar{m})$.

Proof (sketch). Let $p(\bar{m})$ be a safe mode for p/n, let G be an initial query of this mode and let Q be a call to a predicate q/k which loops in an SLD derivation for G. Let μ be the Boolean assertion imposed on q/k by termination inference and φ be the termination condition for p/n. From the correctness of backwards analysis [12] it follows that μ must hold for Q because $\wedge\{x_i|m_i = b\} \Rightarrow \varphi$ and φ guarantee μ. From the construction of μ which considers the binary clauses for q and the correctness of the termination analysis [4] it follows that the loop on q/k must terminate.

5 Experimental Results

We have implemented an analyzer for termination inference and it is accessible at `http://www.cs.bgu.ac.il/ mcodish/TerminWeb`. Basically, we combine the first phase of the termination analysis described in [4] (which describes the programs loops using size information) with an implementation of the backwards analysis algorithm described in [12] (for the Pos domain).

To evaluate our analyzer, we use the same benchmarks as used in [16]. The experimentation is set up to use the same parameters (choice of norm and widening steps) as reported in [16]. Our analyzer runs SICStus 3.7.1 on a Pentium III 500MHZ machine with 128MB RAM under Linux RedHat 7.1 (kernel 2.4.2-2). Timings for cTI are reported for a faster machine (Athlon 750MHz, 256Mb, SICStus 3.8.4). Table 1 indicates analysis times (in seconds). The columns indicate the costs for: **Size**: approximating loops with size information; **Pos**: approximating answers with instantiation dependencies; **Ass**: computing initial instantiation assertions (from the size information); **BA**: backwards analysis; **Total**: total analysis time (including preprocessing - not itemized on its own). **cTI**: total analysis time using cTI (as reported in [16]).

The two blocks of programs in Table 1 correspond respectively to those from Tables 2 and 5 in [16]. For the first block we infer exactly the same termination conditions as cTI. For the second block (of larger programs), Mesnard and Neumerkel report precision in terms of the percentage of the programs predicates for which some (non false) termination condition is inferred. We obtain the same percentages, except for the last three programs where a "$\oplus$" indicates that we infer more terminating predicates than does cTI and a "$\ominus$" vice-versa.

The results indicate that the precision of the two analyzers is quite similar and that (given that cTI is running on a faster machine) ours is in most cases more efficient. The interesting aspects of the experimental results come from a closer comparison with previous work: First, in comparison with termination checking as reported in [4], we observe that in most cases termination inference is not only more general but also faster than termination checking. Note that the two columns labelled by **Size**, and **Pos** correspond to tasks which are performed anyway during (the first phase of) termination checking. The next two columns (labelled **Ass** and **BA**) concern tasks specific to termination inference which are very fast and in general less expensive than the cost of the second phase (checking a given mode) of the analysis described in [4].

Table 1. Experimental Results

program	Size	Pos	Ass	BA	Total	cTI
permute	0.12	.00	.01	.00	0.14	0.15
duplicate	0.03	.00	.00	.00	0.03	0.05
sum1	0.05	.00	.01	.00	0.06	0.18
merge	0.19	.00	.02	.00	0.21	0.26
dis-con	0.09	.00	.00	.01	0.10	0.24
reverse	0.05	.00	.01	.00	0.08	0.08
append	0.05	.01	.00	.00	0.06	0.09
list	0.01	.01	.00	.00	0.03	0.01
fold	0.05	.00	.01	.00	0.06	0.10
lte	0.06	.01	.00	.00	0.07	0.13
map	0.05	.00	.00	.00	0.05	0.09
member	0.04	.01	.00	.00	0.05	0.03
msort	0.44	.00	.02	.00	0.46	0.43
msort⋆	0.98	.01	.01	.01	1.02	0.57
msort_ap	0.63	.00	.04	.00	0.67	0.79
msort_ap⋆	1.29	.03	.03	.00	1.35	0.92
naive_rev	0.08	.01	.00	.00	0.10	0.12
ordered	0.03	.00	.00	.00	0.03	0.04
overlap	0.05	.01	.00	.00	0.06	0.05
permute	0.10	.00	.01	.00	0.13	0.15
quicksort	0.38	.01	.04	.00	0.43	0.39
sum2	0.08	.00	.01	.00	0.09	0.08
select	0.09	.01	.00	.00	0.10	0.09
subset	0.09	.01	.00	.00	0.11	0.12
ann	4.46	.07	.30	.03	5.02	5.01
bid	0.62	.02	.05	.01	0.74	0.79
boyer	2.55	.05	.04	.01	2.75	3.53
browse	0.96	.01	.15	.00	1.16	1.81
credit	0.43	.02	.04	.01	0.54	0.61
peep	4.46	.04	.07	.02	4.68	12.08
plan	1.03	.02	.03	.01	1.12	0.71
qplan	10.86	.05	.51	.03	11.58	7.30
rdtok ⊕	2.86	.02	.16	.01	3.10	2.92
read ⊖	4.43	.03	.04	.03	4.65	6.87
warplan ⊕	2.54	.04	.14	.03	2.83	3.18

Second, in comparison with the termination inference described in [16], note that while the total analysis times are similar, our backwards analysis phase is 5-6 times faster (on a slower machine) than the corresponding phase in cTI (based on the comparison of our Table 1 with Table 5 from [16]). This is due to the application of a carefully designed backwards analysis algorithm which propagates information (backwards) through the clause bodies. In contrast, the corresponding phase in cTI sets up the entire collection of recursive equations specifying the constraints that hold at each program point and then solves these simultaneously.

6 Related Work

Backwards reasoning for imperative programs dates back to the early days of static analysis and has been applied extensively in functional programming. Applications of backwards analysis in the context of logic programming are few. For details concerning other applications of backwards analysis, see [12]. The application described in [12] is similar to ours. There, the authors infer modes for a logic program which guarantee that Prolog builtins do not report instantiation errors. The authors note that when trying to figure out how to run programs written by a third party (for instance when collecting and testing that benchmark programs for program analysis actually work) they typically start from builtins and work backwards to infer the intended modes of use for the program.

In fact, our work can also be applied to the same task as it is natural to assume that the intended mode of use results in terminating computations. So for example where King and Lu infer the mode $x \vee y$ for the predicate $permutation\_sort(x, y)$, termination inference gives the more restrictive mode x; and where they infer for $partition(x_1, x_2, x_3, x_4)$ (in the quicksort program) the mode $x_2 \wedge (x_1 \vee (x_3 \wedge x_4))$, to guarantee termination we infer the mode x_1. The conjunction of the two (as the intended mode of use should be both terminating and not lead to instantiation errors) gives the mode $x_1 \wedge x_2$ (which is the intended mode of use). It is interesting to note that the two backwards analyses can be performed together. We simply start from the conjunction of the initial assertions from the two applications.

The only other work on termination inference that we are aware of is that of Mesnard and coauthors. The implementation of Mesnard's analyzer is described in [16] and its formal justification is given in [17]. Their cTI analyzer is very similar to ours. The main difference is in the design. Our approach is "black box", combining existing components from a standard termination checker and a generic backwards analysis technique. There are two main technical differences between the analysers: (1) when inferring the initial Boolean assertions from the results of the size analysis, cTI uses a more sophisticated, albeit more costly, technique (to detect level mappings) adapted from [18]. In practice, for the benchmark collection this makes almost no difference for precision but it is in general more powerful; and (2) In the phase where we apply backwards analysis implemented as a simple Prolog meta-interpreter, cTI invokes a μ-calculus solver to compute the greatest fixed point of a system of equations which seems more complex (though equivalent) to what backwards analysis is solving.

7 Conclusion

We have demonstrated that backwards analysis provides a useful link between termination checking and termination inference. This leads to a better understanding of termination inference and simplifies the formal justification and the implementation of termination inference. We demonstrate how putting the components together enables us to enhance the termination analyzer described in [4] to perform also termination inference.

Acknowledgement. We acknowledge the many discussions, as well as the exchange of code and benchmarks, with Andy King, Fred Mesnard and Cohavit Taboch.

References

1. K. R. Apt. Introduction to logic programming. In J. van Leeuwen, editor, *Handbook of Theoretical Computer Science*, volume B: Formal Models and Semantics, pages 495–574. Elsevier, Amsterdam and The MIT Press, Cambridge, 1990.
2. F. Benoy and A. King. Inferring argument size relationships with CLP(R). In *Sixth International Workshop on Logic Program Synthesis and Transformation (LOPSTR'96)*, pages 204–223, 1996.
3. A. Brodsky and Y. Sagiv. Inference of monotonicity constraints in Datalog programs. In *Proceedings of the Eighth ACM SIGACT-SIGART-SIGMOD Symposium on Principles of Database Systems*, pages 190–199, 1989.
4. M. Codish and C. Taboch. A semantic basis for the termination analysis of logic programs. *The Journal of Logic Programming*, 41(1):103–123, 1999.
5. P. Cousot and R. Cousot. Abstract interpretation: A unified lattice model for static analysis of programs by construction or approximation of fixpoints. In *Proc. 4th ACM Symp. Principles of Programming Languages*, pages 238–252, New York, 1977. ACM Press.
6. P. Cousot and R. Cousot. Abstract interpretation and application to logic programs. *The Journal of Logic Programming*, 13(2–3):103–179, 1992.
7. Patrick Cousot and Nicholas Halbwachs. Automatic discovery of linear restraints among variables of a program. In *Proceedings of the Fifth Annual ACM Symposium on Principles of Programming Languages*, pages 84–96, January 1978.
8. D. De Schreye and K. Verschaetse. Deriving linear size relations for logic programs by abstract interpretation. *New Generation Computing*, 13(02):117–154, 1995.
9. S. Genaim and M. Codish. Inferring termination conditions for logic programs using backwards analysis. Technical report, Ben-Gurion University of the Negev, 2001. `http://www.cs.bgu.ac.il/ mcodish/Papers`.
10. R. Giacobazzi and F. Scozzari. A logical model for relational abstract domains. *ACM Transactions on Programming Languages and Systems*, 20(5):1067–1109, 1998.
11. M. Karr. Affine relationships among variables of a program. *Acta Informatica*, 6:133–151, 1976.
12. A. King and L. Lu. A backward analysis for constraint logic programs. Technical report, Kent University, 2001.
13. J. W. Lloyd. *Foundations of Logic Programming*. Springer-Verlag, Berlin, second edition, 1987.
14. K. Marriott and H. Søndergaard. Precise and efficient groundness analysis for logic programs. *ACM Letters on Programming Languages and Systems*, 2(1–4):181–196, 1993.
15. F. Mesnard. Inferring left-terminating classes of queries for constraint logic programs. *Proc. of JICSLP'96*, pages 7–21, 1996.
16. F. Mesnard and U. Neumerkel. Applying statsic analysis techniques for inferring termination conditions of logi programs. In *Static Analysis Symposium*, 2001.
17. F. Mesnard and S. Ruggieri. On proving left termination of constraint logic programs. Technical report, Universite de La Reunion, 2001.
18. K. Sohn and A. van Gelder. Termination dedection in logic programs using argument sizes. In *Intl. Symp. on Principles of Database Systems*, pages 216–226. ACM Press, 1991.

Reachability Analysis of Term Rewriting Systems with Timbuk

Thomas Genet and Valérie Viet Triem Tong

IRISA / Université de Rennes 1
Campus de Beaulieu
F-35042 Rennes Cedex
{genet,viettrie}@irisa.fr

Abstract. We present Timbuk – a tree automata library – which implements usual operations on tree automata as well as a completion algorithm used to compute an over-approximation of the set of descendants $\mathcal{R}^*(E)$ for a regular set E and a term rewriting system $\mathcal{R}$, possibly non linear and non terminating. On several examples of term rewriting systems representing programs and systems to verify, we show how to use Timbuk to construct their approximations and then prove unreachability properties of these systems.

1 Introduction

Term Rewriting Systems (TRSs for short) are a very simple way to describe functions as well as parallel processes or state transition systems where rewriting models respectively evaluation, progression or transitions.

In [6], we proposed a technique for approximating the set of descendants: given a TRS $\mathcal{R}$ and two regular sets of terms E and F both recognized by tree automata, approximation of the set of descendants $\mathcal{R}^*(E)$ permits, in particular, to show the non $\mathcal{R}$-reachability of terms of F from terms of E. One of the main difference with other existing proof techniques on TRSs is that approximations can be computed on TRSs even if they are non terminating (and non confluent). With regards to regular approximations used in abstract interpretation, our method does not focus on automation but, instead, it lets the user adapt its approximation rules to the TRS and the property he wants to verify. Thus, regular approximations can be more precise at the price of requiring user interaction. These aspects turns out to be of interest and have some practical applications like for the verification of cryptographic protocols [7].

The approximation technique, initially prototyped with ELAN [2], is now implemented in the Timbuk library [8], written in Ocaml [13]. This library provides basic primitives on non deterministic tree automata like intersection, union, complement of languages, determinisation of tree automata, as well as a *completion* algorithm for computing approximations.

In this paper, we briefly recall the basic definitions of TRSs and tree automata in section 2. Then, in section 3, we recall what approximations are. The

R. Nieuwenhuis and A. Voronkov (Eds.): LPAR 2001, LNAI 2250, pp. 695–706, 2001.

construction of approximation in practice with Timbuk is detailed in section 4. And finally, we conclude on some comparisons with other works and systems in section 5.

2 Preliminaries

Comprehensive surveys can be found in [5,1] for term rewriting systems, in [3,9] for tree automata and tree language theory.

Let $\mathcal{F}$ be a finite set of symbols, each associated with an arity function, and let $\mathcal{X}$ be a countable set of variables. $\mathcal{T}(\mathcal{F},\mathcal{X})$ denotes the set of terms, and $\mathcal{T}(\mathcal{F})$ denotes the set of ground terms (terms without variables). The set of variables of a term t is denoted by $\mathcal{V}ar(t)$. A substitution is a mapping σ from $\mathcal{X}$ into $\mathcal{T}(\mathcal{F},\mathcal{X})$, which can uniquely be extended to an endomorphism of $\mathcal{T}(\mathcal{F},\mathcal{X})$. Its domain $\mathcal{D}om(\sigma)$ is $\{x \in X \mid x\sigma \neq x\}$.

A term rewriting system $\mathcal{R}$ is a set of *rewrite rules* $l \to r$, where $l, r \in \mathcal{T}(\mathcal{F},\mathcal{X})$, $l \notin \mathcal{X}$, and $\mathcal{V}ar(l) \supseteq \mathcal{V}ar(r)$. A rewrite rule $l \to r$ is *left-linear* (resp. *right-linear*) if each variable of l (resp. r) occurs only once. A rule is linear if it is both left and right-linear. A TRS $\mathcal{R}$ is linear (resp. left-linear, right-linear) if every rewrite rule $l \to r$ of $\mathcal{R}$ is linear (resp. left-linear, right-linear). The TRS $\mathcal{R}$ induce a rewriting relation $\to_{\mathcal{R}}$ on terms whose reflexive transitive closure is denoted by $\to^*_{\mathcal{R}}$. The set of $\mathcal{R}$-descendants of a set of ground terms E is $\mathcal{R}^*(E) = \{t \in \mathcal{T}(\mathcal{F}) \mid \exists s \in E \text{ s.t. } s \to^*_{\mathcal{R}} t\}$.

Let $\mathcal{Q}$ be a finite set of symbols, with arity 0, called *states*. $\mathcal{T}(\mathcal{F} \cup \mathcal{Q})$ is called the set of *configurations*. A *transition* is a rewrite rule $c \to q$, where $c \in \mathcal{T}(\mathcal{F} \cup \mathcal{Q})$ and $q \in \mathcal{Q}$. A *normalized transition* is a transition $c \to q$ where $c = q' \in \mathcal{Q}$ or $c = f(q_1, \ldots, q_n)$, $f \in \mathcal{F}$, $ar(f) = n$, and $q_1, \ldots, q_n \in \mathcal{Q}$. A bottom-up non-deterministic finite tree automaton (tree automaton for short) is a quadruple $\mathcal{A} = \langle \mathcal{F}, \mathcal{Q}, \mathcal{Q}_f, \Delta \rangle$, where $\mathcal{Q}_f \subseteq \mathcal{Q}$ and Δ is a set of normalized transitions. A tree automaton is *deterministic* if there are no two rules with the same left-hand side. The rewriting relation induced by the transitions of $\mathcal{A}$ (the set Δ) is denoted by $\to_{\mathcal{A}}$. The tree language recognized by $\mathcal{A}$ is $\mathcal{L}(\mathcal{A}) = \{t \in \mathcal{T}(\mathcal{F}) \mid \exists q \in \mathcal{Q}_f \text{ s.t. } t \to^*_{\mathcal{A}} q\}$.

3 Approximations

Starting from a tree automaton $\mathcal{A}_0 = \langle \mathcal{F}, \mathcal{Q}_0, \mathcal{Q}_f, \Delta_0 \rangle$ and a left-linear[1] TRS $\mathcal{R}$, the aim of the approximation algorithm is to compute a tree automaton $\mathcal{A}_k$ such that $\mathcal{L}(\mathcal{A}_k) \supseteq \mathcal{R}^*(\mathcal{L}(\mathcal{A}_0))$. Approximations are used to show that terms recognized by a tree automaton $\mathcal{A}_{bad}$ are not reachable by rewriting terms of $\mathcal{L}(\mathcal{A}_0)$ with $\mathcal{R}$. For this, it is enough to show that $\mathcal{L}(\mathcal{A}_k) \cap \mathcal{L}(\mathcal{A}_{bad}) = \emptyset$ i.e., compute the automaton recognizing the intersection and show that the recognized language is empty.

[1] Approximations can also be computed for non left-linear systems with some restrictions on the automaton we consider, see section 4.3.

The technique consists in successively computing tree automata $\mathcal{A}_1, \mathcal{A}_2, \ldots$ such that $\forall i \geq 0 : \mathcal{L}(\mathcal{A}_i) \subseteq \mathcal{L}(\mathcal{A}_{i+1})$ and if $s \in \mathcal{L}(\mathcal{A}_i)$, such that $s \rightarrow_{\mathcal{R}} t$ then $t \in \mathcal{L}(\mathcal{A}_{i+1})$, until we get an automaton $\mathcal{A}_k$ with $k \in \mathbb{N}$ such that $\mathcal{L}(\mathcal{A}_k) = \mathcal{L}(\mathcal{A}_{k+1})$. Thus, $\mathcal{A}_k$ also verifies $\mathcal{L}(\mathcal{A}_k) \supseteq \mathcal{R}^*(\mathcal{L}(\mathcal{A}_0))$. More precisely, to construct $\mathcal{A}_{i+1}$ from $\mathcal{A}_i$, we achieve a *completion step* which consists in finding *critical pairs* between $\rightarrow_{\mathcal{R}}$ and $\rightarrow_{\mathcal{A}_i}$. For a substitution σ and a rule $l \rightarrow r \in \mathcal{R}$, a critical pair is an instance $l\sigma$ of l such that there exists $q \in \mathcal{Q}$ satisfying $l\sigma \rightarrow^*_{\mathcal{A}_i} q$ and $r\sigma \not\rightarrow^*_{\mathcal{A}_i} q$. For $r\sigma$ to be recognized as the same state, it is enough to join the critical pair:

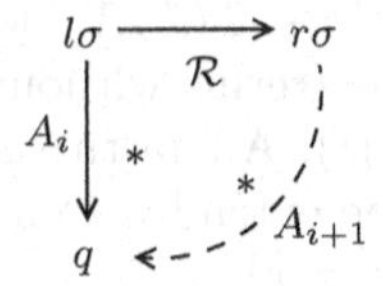

and add the new transition $r\sigma \rightarrow q$ to $\mathcal{A}_{i+1}$. However, the transition $r\sigma \rightarrow q$ is not necessarily of the form $f(q_1, \ldots, q_n) \rightarrow q'$ and so has to be normalized first. For example, to normalize a transition of the form $f(g(a), h(q')) \rightarrow q$, we need to find some states q_1, q_2, q_3 and replace the previous transition by a set of normalized transitions: $\{a \rightarrow q_1, g(q_1) \rightarrow q_2, h(q') \rightarrow q_3, f(q_2, q_3) \rightarrow q\}$.

Assume that q_1, q_2, q_3 are new states, then adding the transition itself or its normalized form does not make any difference. Now, assume that $q_1 = q_2$, the normalized form becomes $\{a \rightarrow q_1, g(q_1) \rightarrow q_1, h(q') \rightarrow q_3, f(q_1, q_3) \rightarrow q\}$. This set of normalized transitions represents the regular set of non normalized transitions of the form $f(g^*(a), h(q')) \rightarrow q$ which contains the transition we wanted to add initially but also many others. Hence, this is an approximation. We could have made an even more drastic approximation by identifying q_1, q_2, q_3 with q, for instance.

Timbuk provides several techniques to automatise the normalization process. We detail only two of them:

• One is a set of *priority transitions*: these are specific transitions of the automaton which are systematically used to simplify the new transitions before any user normalization is performed. For example, assume that $a \rightarrow q_a$ and $g(q_a) \rightarrow q_0$ are priority transitions of the automaton, then the transition of the previous example would be simplified into $f(q_0, h(q')) \rightarrow q$ before requiring new states to end the normalization. Note that the set of priority transitions has to be defined by the user because using such 'deterministic' transitions (always normalizing the same configuration by the same state) leads to approximation in general[2].

[2] For example, using the set of priority transitions $\{a \rightarrow q', b \rightarrow q'\}$ to normalize the transition $f(a) \rightarrow q$ will give the transition $f(q') \rightarrow q$ which is an approximation of the initial transition since it represents the set of non normalized transitions $\{f(a) \rightarrow q, f(b) \rightarrow q\}$.

• A second tool for normalizing automatically new transitions are *approximation rules.* Approximation rules are strictly more expressive[3] than priority transitions since they are not only tree automata transitions but rewrite rules with variables. The approximation rules are applied on the new transitions to normalize. The general form for approximation rules is the following: $[s \to x] \to [l_1 \to x_1, \dots, l_n \to x_n]$ where $[s \to x]$ with $s \in \mathcal{T}(\mathcal{F} \cup \mathcal{Q}, \mathcal{X})$ and $x \in \mathcal{X} \cup \mathcal{Q}$ is a pattern to be matched over the transition to normalize and $[l_1 \to x_1, \dots, l_n \to x_n]$ are rules used to normalize the left hand side of the new transition. The syntactical constraint for those rules is the following: $l_i \in \mathcal{T}(\mathcal{F} \cup \mathcal{Q}, \mathcal{X})$ and either $x_i \in \mathcal{Q}$ or $x_i \in \mathcal{V}ar(l_i) \cup \mathcal{V}ar(s) \cup \{x\}$. To normalize a transition of the form $t \to q'$, we match s on t and x on q', obtain a given substitution σ and then we normalize t with the rewrite rules $l_1\sigma \to r_1\sigma, \dots, l_n\sigma \to r_n\sigma$ where $r_1\sigma, \dots, r_n\sigma$ should be some states. For example, normalizing a transition $f(h(q_1), g(q_2)) \to q_3$ with approximation rule $[f(x, g(y)) \to z] \to [g(u) \to z]$ will give a substitution $\sigma = \{x \mapsto h(q_1), y \mapsto q_2, z \mapsto q_3\}$, an instantiated set of rewrite rules $[g(u) \to q_3]$. Thus, $f(h(q_1), g(q_2)) \to q_3$ will be normalized into a normalized transition $g(q_2) \to q_3$ and a partially normalized transition $f(h(q_1), q_3) \to q_3$.

Note that, whatever the normalization may be, a safety theorem of [6] ensures that when the completion terminates on a tree automaton $\mathcal{A}_k$, it is such that $\mathcal{L}(\mathcal{A}_k) \supseteq \mathcal{R}^*(\mathcal{L}(\mathcal{A}_0))$.

4 Computing Approximations with Timbuk

A completion step i with Timbuk, constructing automaton $\mathcal{A}_i$ from automaton $\mathcal{A}_{i-1}$, can be divided into 5 phases: (1) automatically find some new critical pairs between the TRS and $\mathcal{A}_{i-1}$, (2) automatically construct the corresponding new transitions, (3) automatically normalize the new transitions by priority transitions and approximation rules, (4) ask the user to provide some rules and possibly new states to normalize what remains to be normalized in the new transitions, (5) automatically construct $\mathcal{A}_i$ by adding the normalized new transitions to $\mathcal{A}_{i-1}$.

After each completion step i, the user can choose between several actions (in a menu) like displaying the current automaton $\mathcal{A}_i$, checking the intersection between $\mathcal{A}_i$ and some other automata recognizing the terms which should be proven unreachable, and an undo action to come back to the automaton $\mathcal{A}_{i-1}$ corresponding to the previous completion step.

4.1 Interactive Approximation

In the following introductory example, we compute an approximation of the reverse function (symbol `rev` defined by TRS `R1`) on the regular language of

[3] One may use approximation rules to simulate priority transitions but the interest of priority transitions lies in the fact they can be added during completion, see section 4.1.

terms recognized by automaton `A0` i.e., `rev` applied to any flat lists of `a`'s and `b`'s where all `a`'s are before `b`'s in the list. The second automaton called `Problems` recognize a regular language of terms that should be unreachable from `A0` by rewriting with `R1`: flat lists where there is at least one '`a`' before a '`b`' in the list. Here is the complete specification file:

```
Ops nil:0 cons:2 app:2 rev:1 a:0 b:0
Vars x y z
TRS R1
   app(x, nil) -> x
   app(cons(x, y), z) -> cons(x, app(y, z))
   rev(nil) -> nil
   rev(cons(x, y)) -> app(rev(y), cons(x, nil))

Automaton A0
States qrev qlab qlb qa qb
Description  qrev: "rev applied to lists where a are before b"
             qlab: "lists where a are before b (possibly empty)"
             qlb : "lists of b (poss. empty)"    qa  : "symbol a"   qb  : "symbol b"
Final States qrev
Transitions
       rev(qlab) -> qrev           nil -> qlab cons(qa, qlab) -> qlab
       cons(qa, qlb) -> qlab       nil -> qlb          cons(qb, qlb) -> qlb
       a -> qa                     b -> qb

Automaton Problems
States qlabl qlbl ql qa qb
Final States qlabl
Transitions
       cons(qa, qlabl) -> qlabl    cons(qb, qlabl) -> qlabl
       cons(qa, qlbl) -> qlabl     cons(qb, ql) -> qlbl
       cons(qa, ql) -> ql          cons(qb, ql) -> ql
       a -> qa                     b -> qb
       nil -> ql
```

The first completion step gives some new transitions and the following output:

```
Adding transition: nil -> qrev ... already normalized!
Adding transition: app(rev(qlab),cons(qa,nil)) -> qrev
Do you want to give by hand some rules to normalize the transition? (y/n)?
```

The first transition is already normalized and automatically added, however the second one has to be normalized. First, we have to find states to place configurations `rev(qlab)` and `nil`. Since the state `qlab` recognizes a list of `a`'s followed by some `b`'s, we intend `rev(qlab)` to be a list of `b`'s followed by some `a`'s, so let us normalize it by a new state called `qlba`. In fact, we define two new states, say `qlba` to normalize `rev(qlab)` and `qnil` to normalize `nil`, by typing the following commands:

```
New States qlba qnil.
* rev(qlab) -> qlba             * nil -> qnil.
```

where the * symbol preceding the transitions means that we want to install the following transition in the set of priority transitions. Hence, in the next completion steps, if a new configuration of the form `rev(qlab)` appears, it will be automatically normalized into the state `qlba`. After giving these normalization rules, the transition is still not normalized. Timbuk shows the result of the normalization process so far:

```
Normalization simplifies the transition into: app(qlba,cons(qa,qnil)) -> qrev
Adding transition: app(qlba,cons(qa,qnil)) -> qrev
```

Once more, we are asked to give some rules for normalizing this transition. Since `cons(qa, qnil)` represents a list with one `a`, we can create a new state `qla` to normalize it, and this terminates the normalization of the first transition. There remains a transition to normalize:

```
Adding transition: app(rev(qlb),qla) -> qrev
```

Since we intend that the `rev` function applied to any list of `b`'s should give a list of `b`'s we do not need to introduce any new state but simply normalize it by proposing the following priority transition: `* rev(qlb) -> qlb`.

This terminates the first completion step. In the following six completion steps it is enough to successively introduce the following priority transitions to normalize the new transitions we are proposed and thus terminate the completion:

```
* app(qlb, qla) -> qlba       * cons(qb, qnil) -> qlb      * app(qnil, qlb) -> qlb
* app(qnil, qla) -> qla       * rev(qnil) -> qnil          * app(qla, qla) -> qla.
```

Finally, from the menu it is possible to see the completed automaton which now contains 30 transitions and to compute the intersection with the automaton `Problems`, which gives an empty automaton meaning that applying `rev` to a list of `a`'s followed by some `b`'s cannot result into any list where there is an '`a`' before a '`b`'.

4.2 Debugging Term Rewriting Systems with Timbuk

For linear TRS[4], by normalizing every new transition with new states, we can perform some *exact completion steps* without approximation i.e. we can compute a subset of reachable terms. More precisely, after the i-th completion step the automaton $\mathcal{A}_i$ is such that $\forall t \in \mathcal{L}(\mathcal{A}_i) : \exists s \in \mathcal{L}(\mathcal{A}_0)$ s.t. $s \rightarrow_{\mathcal{R}}{}^* t$.

The second example describes the behavior of a system of two processes that is supposed to count '+'and '−' symbols in a list. Initially, the list is divided into two parts and each part is given to a single process. One process, let us call it P_+ is supposed to count the '+' symbols and the other one, P_- is supposed to count the '−' symbols. Each process have an incoming message queue. The process P_+ counts '+' symbol in its list, it sends a message to process P_- each time that it finds a '−' symbol, and reads messages in its message queue to take into account the '+' symbols found by process P_-. The behavior of process 'P_- is symmetrical. This behavior can be described by the following TRS, where a term of the form `S(p1, p2, s1, s2)` represent a state of the system where process P_+ is in a configuration described by term `p1`, P_- is in a configuration described by term `p2`, and the message queues for processes P_+ and P_- are respectively `s1` and `s2`. A term of the form `Proc(l, c)` is a process configuration where its current list of symbols is `l` and its local counter is `c`. The terms `o`, `s(o)`, ... represent the naturals $0, 1, \ldots$. Queues are represented by lists where the `add` symbol adds a message in the queue i.e., at the end of the list.

[4] Left-linearity restriction on the TRS can even be weakened, see section 4.3

```
TRS R1
add(x, nil) -> cons(x, nil)                                        (* add in queue *)
add(x, cons(y, z)) -> cons(y, add(x, z))

S(Proc(cons(plus, y), c), z, m, n) -> S(Proc(y, s(c)), z, m, n)              (* P+ counts + *)
S(Proc(cons(minus, y), c), u, m, n) -> S(Proc(y, c), u, m, add(minus, n))
S(Proc(x, c), z, cons(plus,m), n) -> S(Proc(x, s(c)), z, m, n) (* P+ reads a mesg *)

S(x, Proc(cons(minus, y), c), m, n) -> S(x, Proc(y, s(c)), m, n)             (* P- counts - *)
S(x, Proc(cons(plus, y), c), m, n) -> S(x, Proc(y, c), add(plus, m), n)
S(x, Proc(z, c), m, cons(minus,n)) -> S(x, Proc(z, s(c)), m, n) (* P- reads a mesg *)
```

The initial configuration of the system is described by the following tree automaton recognizing every configuration where the two processes have a counter initialized to zero, any non empty list of symbols to count and an empty message queue.

```
Automaton A0
States q0 qinit qzero qlist qsymb
Description
        q0        : "initial configuration"                    qzero      : "zero"
        qinit     : "a process in an initial state"
        qlist     : "any non empty list of plus and minus symbols"
        qnil      : "the empty list"                           qsymb      : "any symbol"
Final States q0
Transitions
      o -> qzero                              nil -> qnil
      plus -> qsymb                           minus -> qsymb
      cons(qsymb, qnil) ->qlist               cons(qsymb, qlist) -> qlist
      Proc(qlist, qzero) -> qinit             S(qinit, qinit, qnil, qnil) -> q0
```

Assume that we want to find the proper conditions for process P_+ (resp. P_-) to terminate without leaving any uncounted '+' symbol (resp. '−' symbol). When the process ends, it returns the value of its counter: the term `Stop(c)` represents a terminated process returning the value `c`. An automaton `Bad_state`, representing the incorrect states of the system, recognizes all the terms of the form `S(Stop(i), p, full, m)` and `S(p, Stop(i), m, full)` where `i` is any natural, `p` is a process in any configuration (terminated or not), `full` is a non empty message queue and `m` is any message queue (empty or not).

Assume that we naively choose to stop a process as soon as its list is empty. This can be done by adding the following rewrite rule to the previous TRS: `Proc(nil, c) -> Stop(c)`. Since the whole TRS is linear, we can achieve some *exact completion steps* by normalizing every new transition with new states. After the third completion step, if we compute an intersection with the `Bad_state` automaton, we obtain a non empty intersection meaning that such a bad configuration is reachable. To avoid this bad behavior, it is necessary that each process additionally check that its message queue is empty before terminating. This can be encoded by the following rules, replacing `Proc(nil, c) -> Stop(c)`:

```
S(Proc(nil, c), z, nil, n) -> S(Stop(c), z, nil, n)
S(x, Proc(nil, c), m, nil) -> S(x, Stop(c), m, nil)
```

Similarly we can achieve some exact completion steps and check that the intersection is empty. It is the case for the three first steps but the intersection is no longer empty after the fourth exact completion step. This is due to the fact that a process P_+, for example, may have an empty list, an empty queue and then stops while process P_- has some + in its list, and thus may send later some messages to P_+ that is already stopped. A solution consists in using a synchronizing message `end` sent by P_- to P_+ when P_- has reached the end of its list. Then, P_+ stops only if its list is empty and the head of its queue contains the `end` message sent by P_-. The behavior of P_- is symmetrical. The set of rules controlling the process termination becomes:

```
S(Proc(nil, c), z, m, n) -> S(Proc(nil, c), z, m, add(end,n))    (* P+ ends its list *)
S(x, Proc(nil, c), m, n) -> S(x, Proc(nil, c), add(end,m), n)    (* P- ends its list *)

S(Proc(nil, c), z, cons(end,m), n)  -> S(Stop(c), z, m, n)       (* P+ stops *)
S(x, Proc(nil, c), m, cons(end, n)) -> S(x, Stop(c), m, n)       (* P- stops *)
```

Note that that the two first rewrite rules are non terminating. We also have to modify the tree automaton `Bad_states` such that it recognizes the states where a process is stopped but its message queue contains *at least one* uncounted symbol '+' or '−' and possibly some `end` messages. Then, starting from `A0`, we can perform some exact completion steps and check that the intersection is empty. After the fourth exact completion step, the completed automaton has more than 6000 states and more than 8000 transitions, and intersection with `Bad_state` still results in an empty automaton. Thus, it is worth trying to approximate in order to *prove* that this solution is finally a correct one. Here is a possible approximation to add to the specification:

```
Approximation Procapp
States qlist qnil qsymb qzero qnat qrunproc qemptyproc qterminated qend qnil_end qlist_end
Rules [x -> y] -> [                    Proc(qlist, z) -> qrunproc
    o -> qzero                             Proc(qnil, z) -> qemptyproc
    s(qzero) -> qnat                       Stop(z) -> qterminated
    s(qnat) -> qnat                        cons(qend, qnil) -> qnil_end
    plus -> qsymb                          cons(qend, qnil_end) -> qnil_end
    minus -> qsymb                         add(qend, qnil) -> qnil_end
    end -> qend                            add(qend, qnil_end) -> qnil_end
    nil -> qnil                            add(qend, qlist) -> qlist_end
    cons(qsymb, qnil) ->qlist              add(qend, qlist_end) -> qlist_end
    cons(qsymb, qlist) -> qlist            add(qsymb, qnil) -> qlist
                                           add(qsymb, qlist) -> qlist ]
```

In this approximation named `Procapp` we define a set of states (new or in common with `A0`) and a set of approximation rules. Note that the left-hand side `[x -> y]` of the rule of `Procapp` matches every new transition to normalize. In the right-hand side of the rule, we simply give all configurations or all configuration patterns that should be normalized into distinct states in order to be able to prove the property. For instance, it is important to distinguish between empty lists (`qnil`), lists with at least a symbol (`qlist`), empty lists with at least an `end` message (`qnil_end`) and lists with at least a symbol and at least an `end` message (`qlist_end`). Similarly, it is important to distinguish between running processes (`qrunproc`), processes with an empty list (`qemptyproc`) and terminated processes (`qterminated`). Thanks to this approximation, the completion process does not require any other normalization from the user and terminate on a tree automaton with 13 states and 95 transitions. The intersection between this automaton and the automaton `Bad_state` is empty and thus we have proved that all bad states are unreachable from the initial configurations.

4.3 More Expressiveness and More Detailed Approximations

In this section, we show how to design more precise approximations to verify more complex rewrite specifications with Associative and Commutative (AC) symbols and non left-linear TRSs. Such an extended specification formalism is useful, for instance, to model and verify cryptographic protocols [7]. Those protocols are supposed to be secure in an hostile environment where an intruder stores every message and every key he sees, decrypts some parts, forges new messages with the parts he has and sends every possible message in its store in order to attack some agents. We can model the intruder store using a term built with an Associative Commutative (AC) symbol `store`, where for example the term `store(a, store(store(b, a), c))` represents the multiset $\{\!\{a, a, b, c\}\!\}$. The terms `pubkey(x)`, `privkey(x)`, `encr(k, c)`, and `cons(x, y)` represent respectively the public and private key of an agent `x`, the encryption of `c` using the key `k` and a message composed of two parts `x` and `y`. We can model some of the message constructions that an intruder can do on its store, like it is done for example in [15]:

```
(* The intruder can encrypt any stored component with any stored key *)
store(z, pubkey(x)) -> store(encr(pubkey(x), z), store(z, pubkey(x)))
store(z, privkey(x)) -> store(encr(privkey(x), z), store(z, privkey(x)))

(* The intruder can decompose or compose any component he has *)
store(cons(x,y), m) -> store(store(cons(x,y), m),store(x, y))
store(x, y) -> store(cons(x, y), store(x,y))
```

The rules encoding the AC behavior of the `store` symbol are also necessary:

```
store(x, y) -> store(y, x)
store(store(x, y), z) -> store(x, store(y, z))
store(x, store(y, z)) -> store(store(x, y), z)
```

Note that those rules are highly non terminating, we thus have to define strong approximation rules. When using AC symbols are simply used for representing sets of objects, a quite natural approximation rule for the `store` symbol is the following: `[store(x, y) -> z] -> [x -> z        y -> z]`. This rule normalizes every new configuration of the form `store(s, t) -> q` (where `s` and `t` are not states) into configurations `s -> q`, `t -> q` and `store(q, q) -> q`. The intuition behind this rule is that every 'subset' `x` and `y` of the store `store(x, y)` should be recognized by the same state as `store(x, y)`.

We have represented some of the intruder manipulations but our specification still lacks decryption of encrypted components for which the intruder has the decryption key. To describe this behavior, we need non left-linear rules in order to check the correspondence between stored keys and the key that was used to encrypt the message:

```
store(encr(privkey(x),z), pubkey(x)) -> store(encr(privkey(x),z), store(pubkey(x),z))
store(encr(pubkey(x),z), privkey(x)) -> store(encr(pubkey(x),z), store(privkey(x),z))
```

This encodes the fact that to decrypt a message encoded with the *private* key of an agent x, the intruder should have in its store the *public* key of x, and vice versa. In [7], we have defined a sufficient constraint on the automaton such that completion with non left-linear rules still gives an over-approximation of reachable terms. Roughly, the constraint on the automaton $\mathcal{A}_i$ is the following:

for every rule $l \to r$ whose left-hand side has a non linear variable x, for every substitution σ and every state q such that $l\sigma \to_{\mathcal{A}}^{*} q$ there exists a unique q' such that $x\sigma \to_{\mathcal{A}}^{*} q'$. The state q' is called a *deterministic state*. Going back to the two rewrite rules of our example, this means that we have to ensure that terms matched by the variable `x` are recognized by deterministic states. Since terms matched by `x` should be agents, all we have to ensure is that during completion all terms representing agents are recognized by deterministic states: this can be ensured by the choice of appropriate approximation rules or priority transitions. For example assume, that we represent agents by terms of the form `agent(i)` where `i` is a natural. Then the following approximation rules should make the state `qagt` deterministic[5]:

```
[x -> y] -> [o -> qnat      s(qnat) -> qnat      agent(qnat) -> qagt]
```

The state `qagt` is deterministic but it contains all agents. However, using the same technique it is possible to have any variety of regular categorization of agents, for example: two distinct agents A and B, a server S, an unbounded number of other honest agents and an unbounded number of dishonest agents:

```
[x -> y] -> [o -> zero              s(zero) -> one              s(one) -> two
             s(two) -> qodd         s(qodd) -> qeven            s(qeven) -> qodd
             agent(zero) -> qA      agent(one)  -> qB           agent(two)  -> qS
             agent(qodd) -> qHonnest  agent(qeven) -> qDishonnest ]
```

In the context of cryptographic protocols, deterministic states are also useful for a precise normalization of all the new transitions generated by the protocol specification. For instance, assume that the intruder obtains a new piece of information: let `encr(pubkey(qA), cons(m1, cons(m2, m3))) -> qstore` be the new transition to be added, where `qA` is the deterministic state recognizing only the agent A and `qstore` the state recognizing all the store of the intruder. If we use a too drastic normalization rule of the form: `[x -> y] -> [z -> qstore]` then messages components `m1`, `m2`, `m3` are likely to be normalized into state `qstore` and thus available to the intruder in spite of their encryption by `pubkey(qA)`. A normalization rule of the form: `[encr(x, y) -> z] -> [y -> qprotected]` avoids this problem but normalizes the content of every encrypted component by the same state `qprotected`, and thus makes no difference between a secret known by A, B or any other agent. A correct solution is for example: `[encr(pubkey(qA), y) -> z] -> [y -> qAsecret]` which produces the normalized transitions `encr(pubkey(qA), qAsecret) -> qstore` and `cons(m1, cons(m2, m3)) -> qAsecret`. If order and number of messages `m1`, `m2` and `m3` are not important for the verification of the property, it is either possible to collapse the structure of the message by adding the following approximation rule: `[x -> qAsecret] -> [y -> qAsecret]` which normalizes every subterm of the configuration matched by `x` with the unique state `qAsecret`, for every new transition matching `[x -> qAsecret]`. Thus, every message component remains secret but the message structure has been lost. More details about proving cryptographic protocols properties with our approximation technique are given in [7].

[5] For safety, this can also be checked during completion by computing intersections between the states matched by non linear variables. This is another action proposed by the user menu.

5 Conclusion

In this article we presented the Timbuk tool and its completion algorithm to construct approximations of the sets of descendants. Whereas many tools prove some properties on TRS under strong restrictions on the TRSs, approximations permit to prove some unreachability properties on non linear TRSs that are non terminating and may contain some AC symbols. Properties that can be proved are only 'regular' properties but are of practical interest for instance in the case of cryptographic protocols. Furthermore, we have presented here some new tools – priority transitions and approximation rules – in order to make approximation construction more intuitive and more automatic.

Although we focus on approximation, for some classes of TRSs and regular languages E, $\mathcal{R}^*(E)$ is regular and can be exactly recognized [9,10]. But those classes are very restrictive if we intend to use TRS for specification in general. In spite of this, D. Monniaux [14] has shown that even some simple decidable classes can be used to model some intruder knowledge for cryptographic protocol verification. A more recent regular class was found by P. Réty [16] where restrictions are weker on the TRS and stronger on the regular language E which is restricted to data terms. Nevertheless, the restriction on the TRS is still strong w.r.t. a specification language since it forbids, in particular, nested function symbols. As a result, all the examples of this paper, are still out of the scope of an exact computation of $\mathcal{R}^*(E)$. However, we think that it is worth integrating results of [16] in Timbuk for proving reachability in addition to unreachability.

In [11,4], some approximations based on tree languages are proposed: for higher order functional programs transformed into term rewriting systems in [11] and for imperative and functional first order programs in [4]. In both, the aim is to achieve static analysis and thus the priority is given to automation: for ensuring termination, the approximation methodology is fixed and there is no user control over the approximation rules. Moreover, the approximation of [11] and the widening of [4, section 6.1] could not be used in our context since they loose relational information. In particular, if many new transitions with left-hand side of the form `encr(pubkey(A), m1)`, `encr(pubkey(B), m2)`, ... are produced by the same rewrite rule, they are all normalized using the same states. Then `m1` will share a common state with `m2` and thus `m1` will be no longer secret for `B` and vice versa.

As far as we know, two other distributed tools also implement tree automata: Mona & Fido [12] and RX [17]. In Mona & Fido, tree automata are essentially an internal data structure (deterministic binary tree automata optimized with BDDs) used to decide WS1S and WS2S logics. In RX[6] like in Timbuk, the user can describe regular languages in the usual way using deterministic or non-deterministic grammars, and then compute some intersections, unions, differences between those languages. However, like Mona & Fido, RX was designed for a purpose very different from Timbuk and thus does not implement approximations.

[6] which was designed to prove some termination theorems in combinatory logic.

References

1. F. Baader and T. Nipkow. *Term Rewriting and All That.* Cambridge University Press, 1998.
2. P. Borovanský, C. Kirchner, H. Kirchner, P.-E. Moreau, and M. Vittek. ELAN: A logical framework based on computational systems. In *Proc. 1st WRLA*, volume 4 of *ENTCS*, Asilomar (California), 1996.
3. H. Comon, M. Dauchet, R. Gilleron, F. Jacquemard, D. Lugiez, S. Tison, and M. Tommasi. Tree automata techniques and applications. `http://www.grappa.univ-lille3.fr/tata/`, 1997.
4. P. Cousot and R. Cousot. Formal Language, Grammar and Set-Constraint-Based Program Analysis by Abstract Interpretation. In *Conference Record of FPCA'95 SIGPLAN/SIGARCH/WG2.8*, pages 170–181. ACM Press, 1995.
5. N. Dershowitz and J.-P. Jouannaud. *Handbook of Theoretical Computer Science*, volume B, chapter 6: Rewrite Systems, pages 244–320. Elsevier Science Publishers B. V. (North-Holland), 1990. Also as: Research report 478, LRI.
6. T. Genet. Decidable approximations of sets of descendants and sets of normal forms. In *Proc. 9th RTA Conf., Tsukuba (Japan)*, volume 1379 of *LNCS*, pages 151–165. Springer-Verlag, 1998.
7. T. Genet and F. Klay. Rewriting for Cryptographic Protocol Verification. In *Proc. 17th CADE Conf., Pittsburgh (Pen., USA)*, volume 1831 of *LNAI*. Springer-Verlag, 2000.
8. T. Genet and V. Viet Triem Tong. Timbuk Documentation. IRISA / Université de Rennes 1, 2001. `http://www.irisa.fr/lande/genet/timbuk/`.
9. R. Gilleron and S. Tison. Regular tree languages and rewrite systems. *Fundamenta Informaticae*, 24:157–175, 1995.
10. F. Jacquemard. Decidable approximations of term rewriting systems. In H. Ganzinger, editor, *Proc. 7th RTA Conf., New Brunswick (New Jersey, USA)*, pages 362–376. Springer-Verlag, 1996.
11. N. Jones. Flow analysis of lazy higher-order functional programs. In S. Abramsky and C. Hankin, editors, *Abstract Interpretation of Declarative Languages*, pages 103–122. Ellis Horwood, Chichester, England, 1987.
12. N. Klarlund and A. Møller. MONA Version 1.4 User Manual, January 2001.
13. X. Leroy, D. Doligez, J. Garrigue, D. Rémy, and J. Vouillon. The Objective Caml system release 3.00 – Documentation and user's manual. INRIA, 2000. `http://caml.inria.fr/ocaml/htmlman/`.
14. D. Monniaux. Abstracting Cryptographic Protocols with Tree Automata. In *Proc. 6th SAS, Venezia (Italy)*, 1999.
15. L. Paulson. Proving Properties of Security Protocols by Induction. In *10th Computer Security Foundations Workshop*. IEEE Computer Society Press, 1997.
16. P. Réty. Regular Sets of Descendants for Constructor-based Rewrite Systems. In *Proc. 6th LPAR Conf., Tbilisi (Georgia)*, volume 1705 of *LNAI*. Springer-Verlag, 1999.
17. J. Waldmann. RX: an interpreter for Rational Tree Languages, 1998. `http://www.informatik.uni-leipzig.de/ joe/rx/`.

Binding-Time Annotations without Binding-Time Analysis

Wim Vanhoof and Maurice Bruynooghe

Department of Computer Science, K.U.Leuven, Belgium
{wimvh,maurice}@cs.kuleuven.ac.be

Abstract. The basic task of binding-time analysis (BTA) is to compute annotations that guide the unfolding decisions of a specialiser. The main problem is to guarantee that the specialisation will terminate. In the context of logic programming, only few automatic such analyses have been developed, the most sophisticated among them relying on the result of a separate termination analysis. In this work, we devise an analysis that generates the annotations *during* termination analysis, which allows much more liberal unfoldings than earlier approaches.

1 Introduction

Partial evaluation is a well-studied source-to-source transformation, capable of specialising a program P with respect to a part s of its input. The result is a program P_s that computes, when provided with the remaining part d of the input, the same result as the original program P on the complete input s and d. The general effect of partial evaluation is that the computations performed by a program are *staged*: some (ideally all) operations in P that depend only on s are performed by the specialiser; the remaining computations (those depending on d) by the residual program P_s. Partial evaluation can be used to speed up the computation of a program, in particular when the program must be run a number of times while part of its input (the part denoted by s) remains constant. Indeed, using partial evaluation, the computations depending on s need to be performed only once to construct P_s, which can then be run any number of times with different inputs d. The heart of any partial evaluator is an evaluation mechanism for the language under consideration. In a logic programming setting, "evaluation" of a program corresponds to building an SLD-tree for a program/query pair $\langle P, Q\rangle$. If the program terminates, the corresponding SLD-tree is finite. In this setting, *partially available* input corresponds to a query Q' that is less instantiated than Q. Due to the nature of logic programming, the program could, in principle, simply be evaluated with respect to Q'. Most likely, however, the SLD-tree built for $\langle P, Q'\rangle$ will be infinite. Indeed, if the control flow is determined by a value that is unknown in $\langle P, Q'\rangle$, SLD-derivations of infinite length may be created resulting in a non-terminating specialisation process. Instead of building such a possibly infinite SLD-tree, a partial evaluator for logic programs builds a finite number of *finite* SLD-trees that together cover the

R. Nieuwenhuis and A. Voronkov (Eds.): LPAR 2001, LNAI 2250, pp. 707–722, 2001.

complete computation for $\langle P, Q' \rangle$ [14]. The resulting SLD-trees are *partial*, in the sense that, while building the SLD-tree, the partial evaluator unfolds some predicate calls whereas it does not unfold others. The predicate calls that are not unfolded are said to be *residualised* – they will appear as code in the residual program.

Most work on partial evaluation in logic programming concentrates on the so-called *on-line* approach [11]: during the construction of a partial SLD-tree, the partial evaluator selects each call occurring in an SLD-derivation and decides whether or not to unfold it; usually basing its decision on the structure of the SLD-tree built so far. In the *off-line* approach on the other hand, the program is first analysed by a so-called binding-time analysis (BTA). Binding-time analysis is a global analysis that takes a program and (an abstraction of) the query and generates an *annotated* version of the original program, in which every predicate call is accompanied by an instruction stating whether or not instances of this call must be unfolded. The actual specialiser builds the partial SLD-trees simply by following the instructions generated by BTA. While in general an on-line partial deduction system can achieve better results than an off-line system, the off-line approach also offers a number of advantages. First of all, the separation of the process in a binding-time analysis followed by a specialisation phase makes the process conceptually easier to reason about, and results in a fairly simple (and efficient!) specialiser from which the burden of continuously monitoring the evaluation process has been removed. Also, the analysis output can be represented by annotations on the original source program, and provides as such excellent feedback to the user providing clues to why an optimisation was (not) performed. In spite of these advantages, only few efforts have been made to construct an off-line partial evaluator for logic programming, in particular [16] and [9]. Both approaches require, however, the binding-time analysis to be performed by hand. In previous work [18], we have developed a binding-time analysis for the strongly moded logic programming language Mercury. Adapting such an analysis to an unmoded language is far from trivial. To the best of our knowledge, the first serious attempt to create an automatic binding-time analysis for pure logic programs is [3]. The analysis advocates the use of termination conditions to decide what predicate calls can safely be unfolded. These conditions must, however, be created by hand or be derived by a separate termination analysis which imposes some serious restrictions on the unfolding possibilities as we will demonstrate further on. In this work, we generate the necessary annotations *during* termination analysis, which will allow for much more liberal unfoldings during specialisation.

The remainder of this paper is organised as follows: in Section 2 we motivate our work by demonstrating the need for a more refined control mechanism than the use of termination conditions alone. In Section 3 we adapt an existing termination analysis to our needs and develop the actual binding-time analysis. Section 4 reports on a prototype implementation of the analysis and we conclude in Section 5.

2 The Role of Termination in Binding-Time Analysis

The basic task of binding-time analysis is to annotate every predicate call in a program as either *static* or *dynamic* such that constructing an SLD-derivation by unfolding the statically annotated calls – leaving the dynamically annotated ones as they are – terminates for every call that may occur during specialisation. As was suggested before in the literature [3,7], it seems natural to base the decision whether or not to unfold a predicate call on the *termination properties* of the particular call. The motivation is obvious: if it can be shown that the (specialisation-time instance of the) call terminates under normal evaluation, the call can safely be annotated as *static*, since unfolding it during specialisation will terminate. First, we take a closer look at how the termination properties of a call can be expressed; next, we discuss the use of such properties for binding-time analysis.

The condition under which a call is guaranteed to terminate is usually expressed in terms of the degree of instantiatedness of the call's arguments, measured with respect to a given *norm*. Such a norm is a function that maps a term to an expression that approximates the "size" of the term. Two examples of frequently used norms are the *termsize* norm, denoted by $\|.\|_{ts}$, which counts the number of functors in a term, and the *listlength* norm, denoted by $\|.\|_{ll}$ which counts the number of elements in a list.

$$\|t\|_{ts} = \begin{cases} 1 + \sum_{i=1}^{n} \|t_i\|_{ts} & \text{if } t = f(t_1, \ldots, t_n) \\ t & \text{if } t \text{ is a variable} \end{cases} \qquad \|t\|_{ll} = \begin{cases} 1 + \|Xs\|_{ll} & \text{if } t = [X|Xs] \\ t & \text{if } t \text{ is a variable} \\ 0 & \text{otherwise} \end{cases}$$

Note that the norms are *symbolic* as they map a term to a value that can possibly include variables. An occurrence of a variable X in a symbolic norm means the "size" of X with respect to the given norm.

Example 1.

$$\begin{array}{ll} \| f(a,b,g(c)) \|_{ts} = 5 & \| f(a,b,g(c)) \|_{ll} = 0 \\ \| [X_1, X_2, X_3] \|_{ts} = 4 + X_1 + X_2 + X_3 & \| [X_1, X_2, X_3] \|_{ll} = 3 \\ \| [X_1, X_2|X_3] \|_{ts} = 2 + X_1 + X_2 + X_3 & \| [X_1, X_2|X_3] \|_{ll} = 2 + X_3 \end{array}$$

If a norm maps a term to an expression that does not contain variables, the term is said to be *instantiated enough*:

Definition 1. *(From [13]) A term t is* instantiated enough *with respect to a symbolic norm $\|.\|$ if $\|t\|$ is a ground term.*

In Example 1, the term $[X_1, X_2, X_3]$ is instantiated enough with respect to the listlength norm (since $\| [X_1, X_2, X_3] \|_{ll} = 3$), but not with respect to the termsize norm (since $\| [X_1, X_2, X_3] \|_{ts} = 4 + X_1 + X_2 + X_3$, the latter expression still containing variables). This characteristic can be used to define the conditions under which a call to a predicate terminates. For example, a call to the well-known `append/3` predicate can be shown to terminate when either its first or its third argument is instantiated enough with respect to the *listlength* norm.

To the best of our knowledge, the only automatic binding-time analysis for unmoded logic programs that incorporates termination conditions is [3]. It uses a Pos-based analysis to compute a safe approximation of what arguments in a predicate call will be instantiated enough during specialisation and combines this information with the termination condition of the called predicate in order to annotate the call as either *static* or *dynamic*. The approach is appealing as it separates the actual analysis from the construction of termination conditions, which can be given by the user or automatically derived by a separate termination analysis (like e.g. [15]). However, basing the decision to unfold a call on the termination characteristics of the call imposes considerable restrictions on the unfolding possibilities. The fact that a call is marked *static* only in case it terminates implies that only calls that can be *completely* unfolded to *true* or *fail* are unfolded. While this approach might be appropriate for some applications, it is not for general logic programs. Consider the following example, implementing a simple Vanilla meta interpreter.

Example 2. Consider the meta interpreter depicted in Fig. 1. The interpreter has the `member/2` and `append/3` predicates as object program. The clauses are numbered for later reference.

```
1:solve([]).
2:solve([A|Gs]):- solve_atom(A), solve(Gs).
3:solve_atom(A):-clause(A,Body), solve(Body).

4:clause(member(X,Xs), [append(_,[X|_],Xs)]).
5:clause(append([],L,L), []).
6:clause(append([X|Xs],Y,[X|Zs]),[append(Xs,Y,Zs)]).
```

Fig. 1. Vanilla meta interpreter

Assume we want to specialise the meta interpreter from Example 2 with respect to the query `solve([member(X,Xs)])` in order to remove the interpretation overhead and to obtain the object-level definitions of `member/2` and `append/3`. Any sensible termination analysis will indicate possible non-termination for this query, the reason being of course that, since an object level call `member(X,Xs)` does not terminate, neither will the meta call `solve([member(X,Xs)])`. Hence, if we take termination of a call as its unfolding condition, no call to `solve/1` will be annotated *static* by the analysis and consequently no such call will be unfolded during specialisation, resulting in a program that is far from optimally specialised.

Intuitively, however, we can see that it is perfectly safe to unfold all calls to the `solve/1` predicate as long as the intermediate calls to `solve_atom/1` are residualised. The idea is that the `solve/1` predicate in a sense only performs the parsing of an object goal (deconstructing a list of object atoms), which is terminating in Example 2 and could hence be performed during specialisation. Thus, residualising the calls to `solve_atom/2` and unfolding the others results in the specialised program depicted in the left-hand side of Fig. 2. Applying a standard structuring filtering transformation [8] results in the program depicted in the right-hand side which corresponds with (a renaming of) the traditional

```
solve([member(X,Xs)]):-
    solve_atom(member(X,Xs)).

solve_atom(member(X,Xs)):-
    solve_atom(append(A,[X|_], Xs)).
solve_atom(append([],[X|B],[X|B])).
solve_atom(append([E|Es],[X|B],[Z|Zs])):-
    solve_atom(append(Es, [X|B], Zs)).
```

```
solve([member(X,Xs)]):-
    sa_mem(X,Xs).

sa_mem(X,Xs) :-
    sa_app(A,[X|_],Xs).

sa_app([],[X|B],[X|B]).
sa_app([E|Es],[X|B],[Z|Zs]):-
    sa_app(Es, [X|B], Zs).
```

Fig. 2. Specialised Vanilla

member/2 and append/3 predicates. This example illustrates the need to be able to *partially* unfold a call: building a derivation in which some of the selected atoms are unfolded while others are residualised.

The question remains how to derive annotations that imply such behaviour during specialisation. Clearly, using the results of a separate termination analysis is insufficient, since these analyses assume that *all* intermediate calls are unfolded. Yet termination of such partial unfolding remains an important issue. In what follows, we try to merge these observations, and develop a binding-time analysis that does not incorporate the results of a separate termination analysis, but is rather constructed by modifying a termination analysis, such that it takes the effect of residualising calls into account *during the termination analysis.* Consequently, the resulting analysis no longer proves termination of plain evaluation of a call, but rather termination of *partial* evaluation of the call.

3 From Termination Analysis to Binding-Time Analysis

The general idea behind our binding-time analysis is as follows: assume that we want to annotate a program P for specialisation with respect to a query Q. If termination of Q with respect to P can be proven, then every call in the program can safely be annotated *static* and specialisation boils down to plain evaluation. If, on the other hand, termination could not be proven, we use the termination analysis to indicate due to what call in the program termination could not be proven and mark the call *dynamic*. Next, we rerun the termination analysis, now taking the fact that the dynamically annotated call is *not* unfolded into account. The process is repeated until enough calls are annotated *dynamic* such that termination *of the specialisation* is proven. In what follows, we first adapt an existing termination analysis such that, if it is unable to prove termination, it pinpoints a call in the program due to which termination could not be proven; next we develop the actual binding-time analysis.

3.1 Enhancing Termination Analysis

We assume some familiarity with the basic issues in (automatic) termination analysis of logic programs. See [5] for an overview. As usual, we refer with the notion of "termination" of program to its termination with respect to the left-to-right selection rule. In what follows, we focus in particular on the concepts and terminology of [4], as this work provides the necessary foundations for our binding-time analysis. Given a symbolic norm $\|.\|$, we define the *abstraction* of a program with respect to $\|.\|$ as the program that is obtained by replacing each term t in the program by $\|t\|$.

Example 3. Consider the append/3 predicate and its abstraction with respect to the list-length norm $\|.\|_{ll}$ in Figure 3.

append	abstract append/3 w.r.t. $\|.\|_{ll}$
`append(X,Y,Z):- X=[], Y=Z.`	`append(X,Y,Z):- X=0, Y=Z.`
`append(X,Y,Z):- X=[E|Xs], Z=[E|Zs],` `append(Xs,Y,Zs).`	`append(X,Y,Z):- X=1+Xs, Z=1+Zs,` `append(Xs,Y,Zs).`

Fig. 3. The listlength abstraction of append/3

For simplicity, we assume a normalised representation of clauses in which the head of a clause contains only distinct variables; all unifications are thus explicit in the body of the clause. An abstract program is formally defined over a first order constraint logic programming language denoted CLP($\mathcal{N}$). Constraints in CLP($\mathcal{N}$) are conjunctions of the relations $\{=, \leq, \geq, <, >\}$ on terms $\mathcal{T}$ constructed from the program's variables and the set of function symbols $\mathbb{N} \cup \{+/2\}$. For two atoms $A = p(t_1, \ldots, t_n)$ and $B = p(t'_1, \ldots, t'_n)$, we use $A = B$ as an abbreviation for the constraint $\bigwedge_{i=1}^{n}(t_i = t'_i)$. A clause in CLP($\mathcal{N}$) is of the form $H \leftarrow \mu, B_1, \ldots, B_n$ where μ is a constraint and $H, B_1, \ldots, B_n$ are atoms constructed from the program's predicate symbols and $\mathcal{T}$. For a program P, we denote its abstraction with respect to the norm $\|.\|$ by $P_{\|.\|}$. We assume that each clause in $P_{\|.\|}$ has a unique number associated with it and where appropriate, we denote with $i : C$ the clause C with number i. Computations in CLP($\mathcal{N}$) are performed over $\mathbb{N}$ with the standard interpretations for $\{=, \leq, \geq, <, >\}$.

We follow the approach of [4], and compute a finite approximation of the *abstract binary unfoldings semantics* of a program P. The abstract binary unfoldings semantics of P consists of a (possibly infinite) set of abstract binary clauses. Where the abstract program expresses existing relations on the size of the arguments in the program, the associated abstract binary clauses express relations on the sizes of the arguments in *subsequent calls* that can occur in $P_{\|.\|}$. We slightly adapt some definitions of [4] to enable the analysis to produce the more detailed information required for our binding-time analysis. A first definition is that of a binary clause, which we generalise to the notion of a *labelled* abstract binary clause.

Definition 2. *A* labelled abstract binary clause *is a clause in CLP($\mathcal{N}$) that is either of the form $H \overset{i,j}{\leftarrow} \mu$, or $H \overset{i,j}{\leftarrow} \mu, B$ where $i, j \in \mathbb{N}$. The set of all such binary* *clauses is denoted by $\mathcal{BC}$. A clause of the first form, $H \overset{i,j}{\leftarrow} \mu$ is also referred to as a labelled constrained atom.*

The set of labelled abstract binary clauses of a program $P_{\|.\|}$ is defined as the least fixed point of the operator $T_P^{\|.\|}$ defined in Definition 3. The $T_P^{\|.\|}$ operator is adapted from [4] such that it associates a label to each constructed binary clause, referring to how the binary clause was constructed. In what follows, we will often simply refer to "binary clauses" when we mean effectively "abstract labelled binary clauses". Also, we will drop the label from a binary clause when it is unimportant. In Definition 3, $\overline{\exists}_V(\mu_0)$ denotes the projection of a constraint μ_0 onto a set of variables V and Id denotes the set of *identity* binary clauses, these are clauses of the form $p(X_1, \ldots, X_n) \leftarrow p(X_1, \ldots, X_n)$. Unfolding an atom with respect to an identity clause results in the atom itself. We furthermore assume that clauses are renamed apart wherever appropriate.

Definition 3. $T_P^{\|.\|} : \wp(\mathcal{BC}) \mapsto \wp(\mathcal{BC})$ *is defined as*

$$T_P^{\|.\|}(I) = \left\{ H \overset{i,j}{\leftarrow} \mu, B \left| \begin{array}{l} C = i : H \leftarrow \mu_0, B_1, \ldots, B_m \in P_{\|.\|}, 1 \leq j \leq m, \\ \langle A_k \leftarrow \mu_k \rangle_{k=1}^{j-1} \in I, \\ A_j \leftarrow \mu_j, B \in I \cup Id, j < m \Rightarrow B \neq true \\ \mu' = \mu_0 \wedge \bigwedge_{k=1}^{j} (\mu_j \wedge \{B_k = A_k\}) \\ \mu = \overline{\exists}_{vars(\langle H,B \rangle)}(\mu') \end{array} \right. \right\}$$

Given a set of binary clauses I, $T_P^{\|.\|}(I)$ is a new set of binary clauses constructed by unfolding prefixes of clauses in $P_{\|.\|}$. If $H \leftarrow \mu, B_1, \ldots, B_m$ is a clause in $P_{\|.\|}$, for each $1 \leq j \leq m$, the body atoms $B_1, \ldots, B_{j-1}$ are unfolded with respect to constrained atoms in I and the corresponding instance of B_j is unfolded with respect to a binary clause $H_j \leftarrow \mu_j, B$ ($B \neq true$) from $I \cup Id$. Note that the use of the identity clause to "unfold" B_j results in a binary clause of the form $H \leftarrow \mu, B_j$ (which expresses that a call unifying with μ, H results in a call unifying with μ, B_j). Constrained atoms are allowed to unfold B_j only in case $j = m$; indeed, an answer is obtained only in case all body atoms are unfolded by a constrained fact. Note that the label associated to a clause constructed by $T_P^{\|.\|}$ carries information on how the clause was constructed: a clause $H \overset{i,j}{\leftarrow} \mu, B$ is created by resolving the $j-1$ leftmost body atoms of the i'th clause of $P_{\|.\|}$ with constrained atoms and the j'th atom with a binary clause.

In general, the least fixed point of $T_P^{\|.\|}$, lfp($T_P^{\|.\|}$) is an infinite set of binary clauses, as illustrated in the next example (from [4]).

Example 4. Reconsider the `append/3` predicate from Example 3. The abstract binary unfoldings are computed as in Fig. 4.

To obtain a finitary analysis, different approaches exist to further approximate the abstract domain.

$$(1)\ (T_P^{\|\cdot\|})^1(\emptyset) = \left\{ \begin{array}{l} append(X,Y,Z) \overset{1,1}{\leftarrow} X = 0, Z = Y. \\ append(X,Y,Z) \overset{2,1}{\leftarrow} \\ \quad X = 1 + Xs, Z = 1 + Zs, \\ \quad append(Xs,Y,Zs). \end{array} \right\}$$

$$(2)\ (T_P^{\|\cdot\|})^2(\emptyset) = \left\{ \begin{array}{l} append(X,Y,Z) \overset{2,1}{\leftarrow} X = 1, Z = 1 + Y. \\ append(X,Y,Z) \overset{2,1}{\leftarrow} \\ \quad X = 2 + Xs, Z = 2 + Zs, \\ \quad append(Xs,Y,Zs). \end{array} \right\} \cup (T_P^{\|\cdot\|})^1(\emptyset)$$

$$(3)\ (T_P^{\|\cdot\|})^3(\emptyset) = \left\{ \begin{array}{l} append(X,Y,Z) \overset{2,1}{\leftarrow} X = 2, Z = 2 + Y. \\ append(X,Y,Z) \overset{2,1}{\leftarrow} \\ \quad X = 3 + Xs, Z = 3 + Zs, \\ \quad append(Xs,Y,Zs). \end{array} \right\} \cup (T_P^{\|\cdot\|})^2(\emptyset)$$

$$\ldots$$

Fig. 4. Computing the abstract binary unfoldings.

Example 5. Reconsider the abstract binary unfoldings of append/3 from Example 4. Further abstracting using polyhedral approximations [2] (thereby arbitrarily keeping one of the involved labels) results in the set

$$\mathrm{lfp}(T_P^{\|\cdot\|}) = \left\{ \begin{array}{l} append(X,Y,Z) \overset{1,1}{\leftarrow} Z = Y + X. \\ append(X,Y,Z) \overset{2,1}{\leftarrow} \\ \quad Xs < X, Zs < Z, Ys = Y, \\ \quad append(Xs,Ys,Zs). \end{array} \right\}$$

The binary clauses capture size relations that exist between the arguments of subsequent predicate calls. In order to be useful for termination analysis, these size relations must be combined with instantiation information, that specifies which of the arguments are instantiated enough with respect to the norm under consideration. Such instantiation information is obtained by a standard groundness analysis on the abstracted program. In what follows we consider, as in [4], an abstract domain that combines size relations and instantiation information. We denote with mgu^α the abstract most general unifier over this domain, and denote with $\approx$ the equivalence of syntactic objects. For a program P, we denote with $\mathcal{B}_P$ the finite set of abstract binary clauses which approximates, with respect to some given abstraction, $\mathrm{lfp}(T_P^{\|\cdot\|})$ over the combined abstract domain.

In termination analysis, one is interested in the termination behaviour of a specific call with respect to the given program. First, we define the abstraction of a call $p(t_1,\ldots,t_n)$ with respect to a norm $\|.\|$ as $\|p(t_1,\ldots,t_n)\| = p(\|t_1\|,\ldots,\|t_n\|)$. The (possibly infinite) set of calls that arise during computation of an initial call Q in P can be approximated by a finite set of abstract calls, $calls_P^\alpha(Q)$, which is determined as follows:

Definition 4. *Given a program P, an abstract initial call Q and a finite set of abstract binary clauses $\mathcal{B}_P$ approximating lfp($T_P^{\|\cdot\|}$).*

$$calls_P^{\alpha}(Q) = \left\{ B\theta \middle| \begin{array}{l} H \leftarrow B \in \mathcal{B}_P, \\ \theta = mgu^{\alpha}(Q,H) \end{array} \right\}$$

The work of [4] defines a sufficient condition to show termination of a call Q with respect to a program P. Given a finite approximation $\mathcal{B}_P$ of lfp($T_P^{\|\cdot\|}$), it is sufficient to show for each call $C \in calls_P^{\alpha}(Q)$ a strict decrease in size from the head to the single body atom for all recursive clauses of $\mathcal{B}_P$ that unify with the call C. Adding labels to the abstract binary clauses enables one to reformulate the termination condition of [4] at the level of the *original* clauses of P. To that end, we introduce the notion of a clause being *loop safe* in one of its body atoms. Intuitively, if we say that a clause $H \leftarrow B_1, \ldots, B_n$ is loop safe in its i'th body atom with respect to a set of (abstract) calls S, this means that none of the calls in S unifying with H will spawn an infinite derivation through (instances of) this body atom.

Definition 5. *Given a program P, a set of abstract calls S and a finite approximation $\mathcal{B}_P$ of lfp($T_P^{\|\cdot\|}$). Assume there exist a binary clause $\beta = H \overset{i,j}{\leftarrow} \mu, B \in \mathcal{B}_P$ and a call $C \in S$ such that $\theta = mgu^{\alpha}(H,C)$ and $B\theta \approx C$. Let $i_1, \ldots, i_k$ be the argument positions that are instantiated enough both in $H\theta$ and $B\theta$. We denote these arguments by $(H\theta)_{i_1}, \ldots, (H\theta)_{i_k}$ and $(B\theta)_{i_1}, \ldots, (B\theta)_{i_k}$. We say that the clause i of P is* loop safe *with respect to S in body atom j if for each such $\beta \in \mathcal{B}_P$ and $C \in S$ there exists a function f such that*

$$\mu \models f((H\theta)_{i_1}, \ldots, (H\theta)_{i_k}) > f((B\theta)_{i_1}, \ldots, (B\theta)_{i_k}).$$

Note that Definition 5 takes only those (abstract) calls and binary clauses into account such that applying the most general unifier of the head of the clause and the call on the body atom results in a recursive call with an equivalent call pattern. See [4] for details on why this is sufficient. Given Definition 5 from above, we define for a clause i of P and a set of abstract calls S,

$$LS_{P,S}^{i} = \{ j | \text{the clause } i \text{ is loop safe w.r.t. } S \text{ in body atom } j \}$$

Example 6. Let P denote the program consisting of the `append/3` predicate with the abstract binary unfoldings from Example 5 and let Q denote the abstracted initial call `append(0,Y,Z)`. This call unifies (through mgu$^{\alpha}$) only with the head of the binary clause labelled $(1,1)$, since unification of `append(0,Y,Z)` with the other clause, labelled $(2,1)$, fails due to the fact that the size constraints are not satisfied since no $Xs < 0$. Hence, we have that both clauses of `append/3` are loop safe with respect to $S = calls_P^{\alpha}(append(0,Y,Z)) = \{append(0,Y,Z)\}$. Or, we have that $ls_{P,S}^{1} = \emptyset$ and $LS_{P,S}^{2} = \{1\}$.

An important result from [4] can now be reformulated as follows: Given a program P and initial goal Q, if each clause of P is loop safe with respect tot $calls_P^{\alpha}(Q)$ in each of its body atoms, then Q terminates with respect to P.

3.2 From Termination Analysis to Binding-Time Analysis

Recall that we want to enable the termination analysis to indicate *why* termination of a program cannot be proven. We therefore define the notion of the *leftmost possibly looping atom* of a clause as the leftmost atom of the clause for which the termination analysis cannot prove that it is loop safe.

Definition 6. *Consider a program P, a set of abstract calls S and a finite approximation $\mathcal{B}_P$ of $lfp(T_P^{\|\cdot\|})$. Let $H \leftarrow B_1, \ldots, B_n$ be the i'th clause of P. We define its* leftmost possibly looping body *atom as follows*

$$LLA^i_{P,S} = \begin{cases} min(\{1,\ldots,n\} \setminus LS^i_{P,S}) & if\ (\{1,\ldots,n\} \setminus LS^i_{P,S}) \neq \emptyset \\ undefined & otherwise \end{cases}$$

Example 7. Let P denote the program consisting of the `append/3` predicate with the abstract binary unfoldings from Example 5 and let Q denote the abstracted initial call `append(X,0,Z)` and $S = calls^{\alpha}_P(Q)$. Although we still have that $LS^1_{P,S} = \emptyset$, we also have that $LS^2_{P,S} = \emptyset$. Indeed, the second clause in the **append** program is not loop safe with respect to S in its only body atom, due to the existence of the binary clause labelled $(2,1)$ (see Example 5). Unifying this clause with the call `append(X,0,Z)` results in the binary clause

$$append(X,0,Z) \leftarrow append(Xs,0,Zs).$$

Only the second argument of both atoms is instantiated enough, and there does not exist a function f such that $X > Xs, Z > Zs \models f(0) > f(0)$. Hence, we have that $LLA^2_{P,S} = 1$.

In general, finding the leftmost looping atom of a clause (if it exists) is an undecidable problem. In practical systems, however, the function f in Definition 5 is fixed, and is usually defined as a linear combination of the involved arguments. When f is fixed, the test of Definition 5 can be evaluated, and consequently the sets $LS^i_{P,Q}$ and $LLA^i_{P,Q}$ can be computed. For any clause i in P, $LLA^i_{P,S}$ provides a safe approximation of the leftmost looping atom in the clause, since it is guaranteed that no atom to its left can be looping, when the program is evaluated with respect to an initial call Q and $S = calls^{\alpha}_P(Q)$.

Now, we have developed the necessary machinery to define the binding-time analysis, which requires annotating the atoms in each of the program's clauses. Annotating the body atoms of a clause usually consists of adding a label to each atom, specifying whether the atom is unfolded during specialisation, or residualised. In this work, however, we focus on the termination aspects of the unfolding, and hence employ a slightly different notion of annotations. In what follows, we simply replace atoms that should be residualised by *true*. Doing so permits one to study the termination behaviour of a specialiser that simply unfolds the *static* atoms (and generates code for those that are residualised) by studying the termination behaviour of the annotated program under normal evaluation.

Definition 7. *Given a clause* $H \leftarrow B_1, \ldots, B_n$*, an* annotated version of *the clause is a clause* $H \leftarrow B'_1, \ldots, B'_n$*, where for each* i *such that* $1 \leq i \leq n$*, it holds that either* $B'_i = B_i$ *or* $B'_i =$ *true. An annotated version of a program* $P = \bigcup_i C_i$ *is a program* $P' = \bigcup_i C'_i$ *such that for every such clause* C_i*, it holds that* C'_i *is an annotated version of* C_i*.*

Note that, according to Definition 7, every clause is an annotated version of itself. When annotating a program, one generally wants to mark as many atoms *static* as possible, while guaranteeing termination of the unfolding. This is the main idea behind the analysis presented in this work. Suppose we have to annotate a program P with respect to an initial call Q. If we can prove that Q terminates with respect to P, the annotated version of P is simply P itself (every atom is annotated *static*). Hence, during specialisation, the goal Q will be completely unfolded, and specialisation of Q boils down to plain evaluation of Q in P. If, on the other hand, termination of Q with respect to P can not be proven by our analysis, at least one of P's clauses must have a leftmost looping atom, and we mark this atom *dynamic* (by replacing it by *true* in P). This process is repeated until the annotated program is loop safe. This is the main intuition behind the algorithm for binding-time analysis which is depicted in Fig. 5. Note

> Given a program P and initial call Q.
> Let $P_0 = P$, $S_0 = calls^{\alpha}_{P}(Q)$, $k = 0$.
> **repeat**
>   if there exist a clause i in P_k such that $LLA^{i}_{P_k,S_k} = j$
>   then
>   let P_{k+1} be the program obtained by replacing the j'th
>   body atom in the i'th clause in P_k by *true* and
>   let $S_{k+1} = S_k \cup calls^{\alpha}_{P_{k+1}}(Q)$
>   else
> $P_{k+1} = P_k$
> $k = k + 1$
> **until** $P_k = P_{k-1}$
> $P' = P_k$, $S' = S_k$

Fig. 5. The BTA algorithm.

that the algorithm is non deterministic: if several clauses i exist in P_k for which $LLA^{i}_{P_k,S_k}$ is defined, one of these atoms must be selected for replacement by *true*. Also note the construction of the set S': starting from the program's initial abstract callset S_0, the abstract callset of the annotated program is added in each round of the algorithm. Doing so guarantees that the calls that are unfolded are correctly represented by an abstract call in S', but it also ensures that S' contains abstractions of the (concrete instances of the) calls that were replaced by *true* during the process. In other words, the set S' contains an abstraction of every call that is encountered (unfolded or residualised) during specialisation of P with respect to the initial call Q.

Termination of the BTA algorithm is straightforward, since in every iteration an atom in a clause is replaced by *true*, and the program only has a finite number of atoms. The result of the algorithm includes a logic program P' with respect to which evaluation of any call that is abstracted by a call in the set S' terminates. This is an important result, as it implies termination of *specialisation* of such a call when the specialisation is performed by following the annotations corresponding to P'. More formally, we can define such an unfolding rule as follows:

Definition 8. *An atom A in a goal at the leaf of an SLD-tree is* selectable *unless it is an instance of an atom in P that is replaced by true in P'. The unfolding rule U_{bta} unfolds the leftmost selectable atom in each goal of the SLD-tree under construction. If no atom is selectable, no further unfolding is performed.*

Now, the SLD-tree built by U_{bta} for $P \cup \{Q\}$ is finite since U_{bta} unfolds – apart from Q – only atoms that are instances of an atom in P'. Moreover, every atom A that is *not* unfolded by U_{bta} – and hence present in the residual program – is a concretisation of a call in S'. Hence, building an SLD-tree for $P \cup \{A\}$ again terminates. This kind of termination is often referred to as *local* termination: building a *finite* SLD-tree for each atom that is specialised. Constructing a *finite* set of atoms that are specialised involves a second kind of termination, often referred to as *global* termination. Global termination is not guaranteed by BTA alone. Indeed, the abstract callset S' is a finite set, but an infinite number of concretisations of the calls in S' may be constructed during specialisation.

4 Experimental Evaluation

Table 1 summarises a number of experiments that were run with an implementation of the described binding-time analysis. The second column (*Round1*) presents the timings for termination analysis of the original program (in which all calls are annotated *static*). In case the outcome of the analysis is possible non-termination, the third column (*Round2*) presents the timings for termination analysis of the program in which the problematic call is annotated *dynamic*. None of the benchmarks, which are taken from the DPPD library [12], required more than two rounds of the termination analysis to derive a terminating annotated program. The benchmarks were run under SICStus Prolog 3.7.1 on a Sun Ultra E450 server with 256Mb RAM operating under SunOS 5.6. The fourth column in Table 1 contains the time needed to produce the specialised program using the LOGEN system [9]. The final column contains the specialisation time of MIXTUS [17] – a well-known on-line specialiser for Prolog – as a reference point. Table 1 shows that binding-time analysis is the most expensive operation in the specialisation process. However, recall that the results of binding-time analysis can be used to perform *several* specialisations (with respect to values approximated by the binding-times from the partial deduction query). For the considered benchmarks, the cost of binding-time analysis will be recovered after a few specialisations compared with MIXTUS. Typical speedups obtained by the specialisation range from 1.15 to 2.23 for these benchmarks.

Table 1. Timings (in ms) for the binding-time analysis and full specialisation.

Benchmark	Round 1	Round 2	LOGEN	Total	MIXTUS
ex_depth	240.0	230.0	4.4	474	200
match	470.0	180.0	2.4	652	50
map.rev/reduce	200.0	–	4.3	204	100
parser	100.0	50.0	–	150	–
regexp1-3	740.0	280.0	15.1	1035	670
transpose	210.0	150.0	7.0	367	290

5 Discussion

In this work, we have taken a rather unusual approach towards binding-time analysis. Well-known techniques from termination analysis are adapted and used to annotate a program in successive steps, until it can be proven that specialisation – rather than full evaluation – of a call terminates. Preliminary experiments show that the approach is feasible and results in more liberal unfoldings than with earlier known approaches that use separately generated (or hand crafted) termination conditions like [3]. Examples are the `solve` example and the `regexp` benchmark from above, since in these programs, the ability to partially unfold a predicate call is crucial to achieve a fair amount of specialisation. In the `solve` example from Section 2, our analysis is able to compute that the call to `solve_atom` is the leftmost looping atom in the program's second clause and that annotating this call *dynamic* suffices to obtain termination, and hence the results devised in Section 2. The `regexp` benchmark is depicted in Fig. 6. Assume we want to specialise this program for a query in which the first argument (the regular expression that needs to be matched) is ground. Termination is not guaranteed, hence a binding-time analysis based on termination conditions would not be able to unfold *any* call to `gen/3`. Still, our binding-time analysis is able to spot the only problematic call sequence from head to body atom (underlined in Fig. 6), marking the other calls *static* such that all calls except for the underlined one can be unfolded during specialisation.

```
gen(empty,T,T).
gen(char(X),[X|T],T).
gen(or(X,Y),H,T) :- gen(X,H,T).
gen(or(X,Y),H,T) :- gen(Y,H,T).
gen(cat(X,Y),H,T) :- gen(X,H,T1), gen(Y,T1,T).
gen(star(X),T,T).
gen(star(X),H,T) :- gen(X,H,T1), gen(star(X),T1,T).
```

Fig. 6. The `regexp` benchmark

In contrast with [3] – being a polyvariant analysis – our binding-time analysis is *monovariant*: it creates only a single annotated version of every predicate. This is not an issue in the benchmarks presented above, but for more involved programs, the resulting annotations are likely to be suboptimal, since calls in which different arguments are instantiated enough are likely to expose a different termination behaviour, and hence they might profit from being unfolded differently. Another characteristic of the analysis that might be an issue when analysing larger programs, is that the binding-time analysis basically deals with boolean binding-times: either a value is instantiated enough with respect to a norm, or it is not. Although some work exists towards automating the process of choosing a suitable norm, most systems require the norm to be selected by the user. The particular norm that is used by the system determines the granularity of a term that is considered *static* for binding-time analysis. The use of the *termsize* norm, for example, corresponds to distinguishing, during binding-time analysis, between definitely ground terms and possibly non ground terms. The use of the *listlength* norm, on the other hand, enables one to consider a term *static* when it is instantiated up to a list skeleton. Even if the norm is provided manually, finding a suitable norm might not be trivial or might even be impossible – in particular for programs that employ values of different types. These issues are not due to the binding-time analysis itself, but are rather connected with the termination analysis. We expect better (more precise) termination analyses to lead to better (more precise) binding-time analysis.

In this work, we have used termination analysis to ensure – in an off-line setting – *local* termination of the specialisation process. A topic for further research is the use of termination analysis towards *globally* controlling the specialisation process as well. A possible approach towards ensuring (global) termination in off-line partial evaluation of functional programs is presented in [1]. In this work, the output of a termination analysis is used to make enough values *dynamic* such that the program enters – during specialisation – only a finite number of different configurations (where a configuration is defined as a program point together with values for the variables at that program point). If this is the case, the program is said to *quasi-terminate* and termination of partial evaluation is ensured by memoizing the configurations. A weakness of the approach of [1] is that its termination analysis only recognises "in-situ" decreases, i.e. a decrease in the size of a single argument between recursive calls. A more general termination analysis is developed in [10], capable of dealing with indirect function calls and permuted arguments (lifting the in-situ criterion). Developing an analogous analysis for binding-time analysis is mentioned as an important issue in [10]. The notion of quasi-termination for logic programs has also been explored [6] in the context of termination analysis of *tabled* logic programs. In [3], it is noted that global termination of the process is ensured if quasi-termination of the program with the residualised predicates tabulated can be established. Precisely how to integrate such a technique with a suitable and refined abstraction mechanism is an interesting topic for further research.

Acknowledgements. We thank Michael Codish for stimulating discussions and for making the source code of the TerminWeb termination analyser publically available, Michael Leuschel for his interest and for performing some tests with LOGEN and the result of BTA, and anonymous referees for their valuable comments.

References

1. Peter Holst Andersen and Carsten Kehler Holst. Termination analysis for offline partial evaluation of a higher order functional language. In *Proceedings of the Third International Static Analysis Symposium (SAS)*, pages 67 – 82, 1996.
2. F. Benoy and A. King. Inferring argument size relationships with CLP(R). In *Proceedings of LOPSTR'96*, volume 1207 of *Lecture Notes in Computer Science*, pages 204–223, 1997.
3. Maurice Bruynooghe, Michael Leuschel, and Kostis Sagonas. A polyvariant binding-time analysis for off-line partial deduction. In C. Hankin, editor, *Programming Languages and Systems, Proc. of ESOP'98, part of ETAPS'98*, pages 27–41, Lisbon, Portugal, 1998. Springer-Verlag. LNCS 1381.
4. M. Codish and C. Taboch. A semantic basis for the termination analysis of logic programs. *Journal of Logic Programming*, 41(1):103–123, 1999.
5. D. De Schreye and S. Decorte. Termination of logic programs: the never-ending story. *Journal of Logic Programming*, 19/20:199–260, 1994.
6. S. Decorte, D. De Schreye, M. Leuschel, and B. Martens. Termination analysis for tabled logic programming. In N. Fuchs, editor, *Proceedings of LOPSTR'97*, number 1463 in Lecture Notes in Computer Science, pages 107–123, 1998.
7. S. Decorte and D. De Schreye. Termination analysis: Some practical properties of the norm and level mapping space. In Joxan Jaffar, editor, *Proceedings of the 1998 Joint International Conference and Symposium on Logic Programming (JICSLP-98)*, pages 235–249, Cambridge, 1998. MIT Press.
8. J. Gallagher and M. Bruynooghe. Some low-level source transformations for logic programs. In M. Bruynooghe, editor, *Proceedings Meta'90*, pages 229–244, Leuven, 1990.
9. J. Jørgensen and M. Leuschel. Efficiently generating efficient generating extensions in Prolog. In O. Danvy, R. Glück, and P. Thiemann, editors, *Proceedings Dagstuhl Seminar on Partial Evaluation*, pages 238–262, Schloss Dagstuhl, Germany, 1996. Springer-Verlag, LNCS 1110.
10. Chin Soon Lee, Neil D. Jones, and Amir M. Ben-Amram. The size-change principle for program termination. In *ACM Symposium on Principles of Programming Languages*, volume 28, pages 81–92. ACM press, 2001.
11. M. Leuschel, B. Martens, and D. De Schreye. Controlling generalisation and polyvariance in partial deduction of normal logic programs. *ACM Transactions on Programming Languages and Systems*, 20(1):208 – 258, 1998.
12. Michael Leuschel. The ECCE partial deduction system and the DPPD library of benchmarks. Obtainable via `http://www.cs.kuleuven.ac.be/ lpai`, 1996.
13. Naomi Lindenstrauss and Yehoshua Sagiv. Automatic termination analysis of logic programs. In Lee Naish, editor, *Proceedings of the 14th International Conference on Logic Programming*, pages 63–77, Cambridge, 1997. MIT Press.
14. J. W. Lloyd and J. C. Shepherdson. Partial evaluation in logic programming. *Journal of Logic Programming*, 11(3&4):217–242, 1991.

15. Fred Mesnard. Inferring left-terminating classes of queries for constraint logic programs. In Michael Maher, editor, *Proceedings of the 1996 Joint International Conference and Symposium on Logic Programming*, pages 7–21, Cambridge, 1996. MIT Press.
16. T. Mogensen and A. Bondorf. Logimix: A self-applicable partial evaluator for Prolog. In K.-K. Lau and T. Clement, editors, *Proceedings LOPSTR'92*, pages 214–227. Springer-Verlag, Workshops in Computing Series, 1993.
17. D. Sahlin. Mixtus: An automatic partial evaluator for full Prolog. *New Generation Computing*, 12(1):7–51, 1993.
18. W. Vanhoof and M. Bruynooghe. Binding-time analysis for Mercury. In D. De Schreye, editor, *16th International Conference on Logic Programming*, pages 500 – 514. MIT Press, 1999.

Concept Formation via Proof Planning Failure*

Raúl Monroy

Departamento de ciencias computacionales
Tecnológico de Monterrey, Campus Estado de México
Carretera al Lago de Guadalupe, Km. 3.5, Atizapán, México
raulm@campus.cem.itesm.mx

Abstract. The analysis of failed proof attempts is central to concept formation. This process essentially makes use of abduction, a form of reasoning that identifies explanations for an observed phenomenon. The main problem with abduction is the combinatorial explosion: the search space originated from a failed proof attempt is often unmanageable. A careful proof search guidance is thus required to enable a successful analysis of failure. Fortunately, the search space generated by proof planning [6] is moderately small. Using an abduction mechanism built upon proof planning [18], we have successfully patched 40 faulty conjectures about the HOL theory of lists [3]. On each faulty conjecture, our mechanism was able to synthesise a condition that turns the conjecture into a theorem. Each condition proved to be a concept that is known to be useful and interesting. This process is a form of *concept formation*. Concept formation was done *automatically*. Once refined, the conjectures can then be used to write a fast, uniform proof procedure for proving properties of list constants without effort.

1 Introduction

Understanding mal-formulations is central to both concept formation and theory refinement. Mal-formulations often become evident by the appearance of either a faulty proof, or a failed proof attempt. Experience has shown that fault analysis often holds the key for the completion of proofs, the discovery of lemmas, the generalisation of theories and for the invention of new mathematical concepts [15].

We are interested in the analysis and correction of failed proof attempts, especially where that correction involves the synthesis of new concepts. To approach fault correction, we use *abduction*. Abduction is a form of logical inference that can be used to uncover the causes of observed phenomena [20]. We use abduction when no further deduction is possible, exploring the associated partial proof tree. These trees are usually huge and might well be infinite. Thus, a careful search guidance is required if a combinatorial explosion is to be avoided.

* The author is grateful to Simon Colton and the anonymous referees for providing invaluable, useful suggestions on an earlier version of this paper. This research was supported by CONACYT grants SEP-REDII and 33337-A.

R. Nieuwenhuis and A. Voronkov (Eds.): LPAR 2001, LNAI 2250, pp. 723–736, 2001.

Proof planning [6] is used to automate control of proof search. It makes use of heuristics that capture the way in which proof search should go while yielding mathematically natural proofs. Proof planning dramatically restricts the proof search space making it possible to exploit any failure or partial success. Thus it is a means of carefully guiding the use of abduction for the correction of faults, as shown in [17,18].

This paper reports on using abduction to develop a theory based on higher-order functions. The target theory is the list theory of HOL [11], reported in [23] and based on the work of [3,2]. The motivation behind this decision is, amongst other things, of practical matters: Theorems about the higher-order functions of a theory can often be used to establish lots of theorems about user-defined constants with little effort. Thus we ultimately aim to suggest guidelines for building general proof procedures in the list theory of HOL. Thus, while the concepts we form might be for mathematicians, they are primarily intended to be employed by tools, such as HOL, to improve their performance.

Concept formation in HOL's list theory was done automatically. Human intervention was required only to speculate 40 conjectures, all related with the theory higher-order functions. Each conjecture was proof planned separately; upon failure, an abduction mechanism [18] was used to automatically identify a condition, if any, that turns the conjecture into a theorem. These conditions turned out to be properties that are known to be useful, e.g., associativity, commutativity, monoid, etc.

1.1 Paper Overview

The rest of this paper is organised as follows: §2 provides a short description of HOL's list theory, while §3 and §4 respectively discuss proof planning and the abduction mechanism that we have built in it. Our approach to concept formation using abduction on proof planning failure is then presented in §5. Then we recapitulate experimental results found throughout our investigation §6. §7 briefly discusses related work. Conclusions drawn from our experiments, as well as indications for further work appear in §8.

2 A Theory of Lists Based on Higher-Order Functions

The HOL theory of lists is based largely on the higher-order functions 'fold left' (foldl) and 'fold right' (foldr.) It involves proof methods that can prove theorems about many inductively defined constants, without using induction. The deduction power of these methods originates in the use of conditional, higher-order rewrite-rules, extracted from theorems about foldl and foldr.

Fold left and fold right are schematically specified as follows:[1]

$$\mathsf{foldl}\ F\ E\ X_0 :: X_1 :: \cdots :: X_n = F\ (\ldots(F\ (F\ E\ X_0)\ X_1)\ldots)\ X_n$$
$$\mathsf{foldr}\ F\ E\ X_0 :: X_1 :: \cdots :: X_n = F\ X_0\ (F\ X_1\ (\ldots(F\ X_n\ E)\ldots))$$

[1] $H :: T$ denotes the list of head H and tail T; nil denotes the empty list. :: is the list constructor function.

where E and F respectively denote the base element and the step function. Formally, foldr and foldl are given by [23]:

$$\text{foldr } F\ E \text{ nil} = E$$
$$\text{foldr } F\ E\ (H :: L) = F\ H\ (\text{foldr } F\ E\ L)$$
$$\text{foldl } F\ E \text{ nil} = E$$
$$\text{foldl } F\ E\ (H :: L) = \text{foldl } F\ (F\ E\ H)\ L$$

The fold functions provide a template with which we can conveniently define most list operations. A couple of examples would be illustrating. Let a natural number be represented as a list of booleans with the most significant bit at the head of the list.[2] Then to define a function, list2nat, that converts any one such a list to its corresponding natural number, we simply write:

$$\text{list2nat } L = \text{foldl } (\lambda\, E\, X.(2 \times E) + X)\ 0\ L$$

The second example is about an ordinary system operation, namely: list concatenation, which is given by:

$$\forall L_1, L_2.\ \text{app } L_1\ L_2 = \text{foldr } ::\ L_2\ L_1$$

From these definitions, we can derive the equations that are commonly associated with the recursive definition of both list2nat and app, namely:

$$\text{list2nat nil} = 0$$
$$\text{list2nat } (X :: L) = ((\text{boolval } X) \times (2 \text{ exp}(\text{length } L))) + (\text{list2nat } L)$$

$$\text{app nil } L = L$$
$$\text{app } H :: M\ L = H :: (\text{app } M\ L)$$

where length and exp have their natural interpretation, returning the number of elements in a list and the result of multiplying the quantity base by itself a quantity exponent number of times, and where `boolval` converts a boolean into an integer number.

Thus, using theorems about higher-order functions, we can write proof procedures that can prove a number of theorems with little effort.

This paper was prompted by the following observation: The more theorems about higher-order functions a proof procedure knows, the more powerful it is. We suggest that the abduction mechanism introduced in [18] can be used to automate the discovery of new theorems in the HOL theory of lists, while possibly yielding new concepts.

As mentioned earlier in the text, our abduction mechanism is built within an existing proof plan for inductive theorem proving (described in [6] and implemented in the *CLAM* [5] proof planning system). While the proof plan for induction carefully guides the search for a proof, the abduction mechanism exploits any failure or partial success attained along the way. We discuss these techniques below.

[2] This representation, called *big-endian*, is typical in applications of formal methods to hardware development.

3 Proof Planning

Proof planning is a meta-level reasoning technique to automate control of proof search. A proof plan is a high-level representation of the general structure of the members of a proof family, and is used to guide the search for more proofs in that family. Proof planning works in the context of a tactical style of reasoning, building large, complex tactics out of simpler ones. It splits theorem proving into two tasks, one in which a proper tactic is assembled, and other in which the tactic is executed yielding an actual proof.[3]

Methods are the building-blocks of proof planning. A *method* is a high-level description of a tactic. It specifies the preconditions under which the tactic is applicable and the effects of its application. The application of a method to a given goal consists in checking the preconditions against the goal and then determining the output new goals by computing the effects.

Proof planning is the recursive process that reasons about and composes tactics. It returns a customised tactic together with its justification, called a *proof plan*. In the normal case of success, proof plan execution guarantees correctness of the final proof. Proof planning is cheaper than searching for a proof in the underlying object theory. This is for two reasons: First, each plan step covers a lot of object-level theorem proving steps: proof planning emphasises proof structure, filling in direct but tedious, onerous reasoning. Second, the method preconditions dramatically restrict the search space: backtracking hardly occurs.

Given that it emphasises key steps and structure, proof planning makes it easy to guide the synthesis of programs while proving a specification statement [1]. This observation has been extensively elaborated, especially in the context of inductive theorem proving.

3.1 The Proof Plan for Induction and Rippling

Inductive proof planning is the application of proof planning to inductive theorem proving. It is characterised by a collection of methods, defined as follows: The *induction* method selects the most promising induction scheme via a process called *rippling analysis*. The base case(s) of proofs by induction are dealt with by the *elementary* and *sym_eval* methods. Elementary is a tautology checker for propositional logic and has limited knowledge of intuitionistic propositional sequents, type structures and properties of equality. Sym_eval simplifies the goal by means of exhaustive symbolic evaluation and other routine reasoning.

Similarly, the step case(s) of proofs by induction are dealt with by the *ripple* and *fertilise* methods. Ripple applies *rippling* [4], a heuristic that guides transformations in the induction conclusion to enable the use of an hypothesis, called *fertilisation*. The proof plan for induction also involves *generalise*, a method that generalises away common sub-terms in an expression, such as an identity, an implication, etc.

[3] Sometimes, however, object-level steps need to be interleaved whilst assembling a tactic: In some cases, some of the later planning steps cannot be made without the detail provided by the earlier object-level ones.

Rippling exploits the observation that an initial induction conclusion is a copy of one of the hypotheses, except for extra terms, e.g., the successor function, wrapping the induction variables. By marking such differences explicitly, rippling can attempt to place them at positions where they no longer prevent the conclusion and hypothesis from matching. Rippling is therefore an annotated term-rewriting system. It applies a special kind of rewrite rule, called a *wave-rule*, which manipulates the differences between two terms while keeping their common structure intact.

Our abduction mechanism [18] is built within the inductive proof plan. It makes use of the plan's heuristics so as to identify the restricted way in which the search for a proof can fail. Proof failure and its analysis is captured via a proof critic.

3.2 Proof Planning with Critics

The incorporation of an exception handler to proof planning is called *proof planning with critics* [13]. The exception handler is invoked whenever the applicability preconditions of a method partially hold. Then, it will try the proof critics associated to such a method, if any, one at a time, in the order of appearance.

Proof Critics are the building blocks of the exception handler. A *proof critic* specifies the conditions in which the search for a proof plan breaks down as well as providing the associated corrective action or patch. A critic is *applicable* if the current goal matches the input formula, the critic preconditions hold, and if the applicability preconditions of the method to which the critic is associated partially hold.

Unlike the application of a method, the application of a proof critic does not refine the proof plan under construction. It just enables further proof planning by means of a side effect. Critics effects may include a modification to the input formulae, e.g., generalisation or fault correction, or to the working theory, e.g., lemma discovery. Proof planning with critics has been successfully used for lemma discovery [14], formula generalisation [14] and faulty formula correction [17,18].

With this, we complete our revision of proof planning. We now describe the abduction mechanism used to concept formation.

4 The Abduction Mechanism

Our abduction mechanism [18] is used to exploit proof planning failure so as to correct faulty conjectures. Let $\boldsymbol{X}$ denote a tuple of distinct variables; then, given a theory, Γ, and a faulty conjecture, $\forall \boldsymbol{X}.\, G(\boldsymbol{X})$, the method builds a definition for a *corrective predicate*, $P(\boldsymbol{X})$, such that:

- $P(\boldsymbol{X})$ is *correct*: $\Gamma \vdash \forall \boldsymbol{X}.\, P(\boldsymbol{X}) \rightarrow G(\boldsymbol{X})$;
- $P(\boldsymbol{X})$ is *consistent*: $\Gamma \cup \{P(\boldsymbol{X})\} \nvdash \bot$;
- $P(\boldsymbol{X})$ is *nontrivial*: $\{P(\boldsymbol{X})\} \nvdash G$; and
- $P(\boldsymbol{X})$ is both *terminating* and *well-defined*.

The synthesis of a corrective predicate is driven by the proofs-as-programs principle [12], which relates inference with computation. So a recursive predicate relates to an inductive proof attempt; likewise, a conditional predicate relates to the use of case analysis. The synthesis of a corrective predicate is taken as a program transformation task. Accordingly the abduction mechanism consists of a collection of *construction commands*, each of which is associated with a proof planning method and automatically executed upon plan formation. Thus, the abduction mechanism relies upon the proof planning paradigm: the careful search guidance used in proof plan formation drives the synthesis of, possibly recursive, corrective predicates.

A construction command is a small program written in a meta-language. The meta-language consists, among other things, of a handful *editing commands*, geared towards the construction of conditional, recursive, equational procedures. An editing commands performs a low-level task, typical of a program editor, such as adding an argument, imposing a recursive structure, expanding a case into several sub-cases and so on.

The abduction mechanism is built within *CLAM* and it operates during proof plan formation. Each goal is labelled with an equation that contains one or more predicate meta-variables. The input goal, $\forall \boldsymbol{X}.\, G(\boldsymbol{X})$, is labelled with $\mathrm{P}(\boldsymbol{X}) = P_0$ and the aim of the abduction method is to instantiate P_0, the current predicate meta-variable, along a proof planning attempt of $\forall \boldsymbol{X}.\, G(\boldsymbol{X})$.

If $\Gamma \cup \{G(\boldsymbol{X})\} \vdash \bot$, P_0 will be set to false. Conversely, if $\Gamma \vdash \forall \boldsymbol{X}.\, G(\boldsymbol{X})$, P_0 will be trivially set to true. If $\forall \boldsymbol{X}.\, G(\boldsymbol{X})$ is faulty, P_0 will be other than true or false and an algorithm for it will be constructed or identified.

The construction commands are defined as follows:

induction instantiates the current predicate meta-variable with an actual fresh predicate. The fresh predicate is so that it potentially has a recursive structure that is dual to the inductive principle being applied. Each base or step case of the induction principle is pairwise associated with a predicate case, which it instantiates;

elementary instantiates the current predicate meta-variable with the proposition true;

fertilise instantiates the current predicate variable so that it makes the current corrective predicate recursive;

casesplit expands the current equation case into a number of cases, one for each case the proof is being split into;

generalise instantiates the current predicate meta-variable with an actual fresh predicate that takes as argument the compound term that is being generalised away; and

deadend does either of two things: If the dead end goal is inconsistent with the working theory, then deadend instantiates the current predicate meta-variable with the proposition false. Otherwise, dead end will abduct the dead end goal, adding it to the working theory.

Except for deadend, each construction command is associated with the proof planning method carrying its name. Deadend is associated with the base_case proof critic. It is invoked whenever no further proof planning is possible, with the proviso that symbolic evaluation was expected to establish the goal.

To register predicate relations, the abduction method maintains a graph, in which each node is labelled with a predicate and the (outward) arcs of it point at the symbols in terms of which the predicate is defined. This so-called *dependency graph* is used to ensure that the corrective predicate is well-defined. Whenever the structure of a predicate changes, the mechanism runs a sort of garbage-collection algorithm which, using the dependency graph, updates the structure of all of the predicates.

In the section that follows, we aim to illustrate the way in which *CLAM*, once it has been extended with the abduction mechanism, can be used to develop a theory via concept formation.

5 Concept Formation via Abduction on Proof Planning Failure

To attain concept formation in the HOL theory of lists, we follow the methodology outlined below:

1. Build a set of example faulty conjectures, each of which models an 'attractive' property about the fold higher-order functions. An example property of this kind is as follows: "folding the concatenation of two lists amounts to manipulating the result of folding each list separately"; in symbols:

$$\vdash \quad \forall F, E, L_1, L_2.\, \mathsf{foldr}\ F\ E\ (\mathsf{app}\ L_1\ L_2) = F\ (\mathsf{foldr}\ F\ E\ L_1)(\mathsf{foldr}\ F\ E\ L_2) \quad (1)$$

   where app stands for list concatenation.
2. For each faulty conjecture of the test set, run the following experiment: take the conjecture, make *CLAM* try to proof plan it, simplify the output corrective predicate and then collect the concepts that have been formed. The steps of this experiment are all automated.

On every run, our abduction mechanism identified a corrective predicate, turning the associated conjecture into a theorem. Each corrective predicate proved to specify a property that is known to be useful, such as associativity, commutativity and so on.

To illustrate our methodology, we work by example. Consider (1) again. By running *CLAM*, the partial proof plan associated to this conjecture was generated automatically. It consisted of 8 applications of the induction method, yielding the corrective predicate shown below:

$$\begin{aligned}
\mathrm{P}\,\mathrm{nil}\,L_2\,F\,E\,X\,Y\,Z &\leftrightarrow \mathrm{Q}\,L_2\,F\,E\,X\,Y\,Z\\
\mathrm{P}\,(H_1 :: L_1)\,L_2\,F\,E\,X\,Y\,Z &\leftrightarrow (\mathrm{P}\,L_1\,L_2\,F\,E\,X\,Y\,Z) \wedge (\mathrm{R}\,L_1\,L_2\,F\,E\,X\,Y\,Z)\\
\mathrm{Q}\,\mathrm{nil}\,F\,E\,X\,Y\,Z &\leftrightarrow I_1
\end{aligned}$$

$$\mathrm{Q}\,(H_2 :: L_2)\, F\, E\, X\, Y\, Z \leftrightarrow (\mathrm{Q}\, L\, F\, E\, X\, Y\, Z) \wedge (\mathrm{Q}'\, L\, F\, E\, X\, Y\, Z)$$

$$\begin{aligned} \mathrm{Q}'\,\mathrm{nil}\, F\, E\, X\, Y\, Z &\leftrightarrow I_2 \\ \mathrm{Q}'\,(H_2 :: L_2)\, F\, E\, X\, Y\, Z &\leftrightarrow \top \end{aligned}$$

$$\begin{aligned} \mathrm{R}(L_1\,\mathrm{nil}\, F\, E\, X\, Y\, Z &\leftrightarrow \mathrm{R}'\, L_1\, F\, E\, X\, Y\, Z \\ \mathrm{R}\, L_1\,(H_2 :: L_2)\, F\, E\, X\, Y\, Z &\leftrightarrow \mathrm{R}''\, L_1\, L_2\, F\, E\, X\, Y\, Z \end{aligned}$$

$$\begin{aligned} \mathrm{R}'\,\mathrm{nil}\, F\, E\, X\, Y\, Z &\leftrightarrow I_3 \\ \mathrm{R}'\,(H_2 :: L_2)\, F\, E\, X\, Y\, Z &\leftrightarrow \top \end{aligned}$$

$$\begin{aligned} \mathrm{R}''\, L_1\,\mathrm{nil}\, F\, E\, X\, Y\, Z &\leftrightarrow \top \\ \mathrm{R}''\, L_1\,(H_2 :: L_2)\, F\, E\, X\, Y\, Z &\leftrightarrow \mathrm{S}\, L_1\, L_2\, F\, E\, X\, Y\, Z \end{aligned}$$

$$\begin{aligned} \mathrm{S}\,\mathrm{nil}\, L_2\, F\, E\, X\, Y\, Z &\leftrightarrow \top \\ \mathrm{S}\,(H_1 :: L_1)\, L_2\, F\, E\, X\, Y\, Z &\leftrightarrow \mathrm{S}'\, L_2\, F\, E\, X\, Y\, Z \end{aligned}$$

$$\begin{aligned} \mathrm{S}'\,\mathrm{nil}\, F\, E\, X\, Y\, Z &\leftrightarrow I_4 \\ \mathrm{S}'\,(H_2 :: L_2)\, F\, E\, X\, Y\, Z &\leftrightarrow \top \end{aligned}$$

Where the terms I_1, I_2, I_3 and I_4 respectively stand for:

$$\begin{array}{lrcl} I_1 & F\ E\ E & = & E \\ I_2 & F\ E\ X & = & X \\ I_3 & F\ X\ E & = & X \\ I_4 & F\ X\ (F\ Y\ Z) & = & F\ (F\ X\ Y)\ Z \end{array}$$

And where the term variables X, Y and Z are either Skolem constants, as introduced by the induction method, or replace compound terms that appeared in both sides of the identity.

At first, P seems to be meaningless, but a few, intuitive manoeuvres disclosed interesting bits. First, P is unnecessarily recursive; it can be proven to be equivalent to the conjunction of I_i ($i \in \{1, \ldots, 4\}$). To get rid of redundancies, we use Walther's simplification procedure [22]. Second, identity I_1 is irrelevant, as can be subsumed by I_2 or I_3. These transformations return the conjunction of I_2, I_3 and I_4. Together, these identities convey that F and E form a *monoid*: F is associative and E is both the left and right identity of F.

In the next section, we summarise the results obtained throughout our investigations.

6 Experimental Results

This section summarises the experimental results produced by a test, run on our abduction mechanism.

Table 1 provides a description of the concepts that were discovered through our experimentation. Both concepts and their associated definition have straightforward interpretation. Each concept captures a property that has proven to be useful. Concept formation is *fully automatic.*

Table 1. Concept Definitions

Concept	Definition
left_id $F\ E$	$F\ E\ X\ =\ X$
right_id $F\ E$	$F\ X\ E\ =\ X$
comm F	$F\ X\ Y = F\ Y\ X$
assoc F	$F\ X\ (F\ Y\ Z)\ =\ F\ (F\ X\ Y)\ Z$
fcomm $F\ G$	$F\ X\ (G\ Y\ Z)\ =\ G\ (F\ X\ Y)\ Z$
fcomm+ $F\ G$	$F\ X\ (G\ Y\ Z)\ =\ G\ Y\ (F\ X\ Z)$
fcomm++ $F\ G\ H$	$F\ (G\ X)\ Y\ =\ H\ X\ Y$
eqc $F\ G\ E$	$G\ E\ X\ =\ F\ X\ E$
eqd $F\ G\ E$	$F\ X\ Y\ =\ G\ X\ (F\ E\ Y)$
flip H	$H\ A\ B\ =\ \mathsf{foldr}\ F\ B\ A$
dist H	$H\ A\ (H\ B\ C)\ =\ H\ (\mathsf{app}\ A\ B)\ C$

Table 2 shows some of the example faulty conjectures against which we tested our mechanism.[4] For each faulty conjecture, we provide the concepts formed by our method and the total elapsed planning time (PT), given in seconds. Most symbols in Table 2 have direct meaning, so we draw attention only to the symbols below:

flatten: returns the result of concatenating the elements of a list of lists;
map: applies a function to every element of a list;
sort: sorts the elements of a list; and
reverse: reverses a list.

As shown by the worked example of §5, fault correction sometimes yields uninteresting formulae, e.g. $F\ E\ E\ =\ E$. Often, these formulae can be automatically eliminated using the simplest subsumption condition, term matching. Sometimes, however, term matching is not enough. Then, we found out that the associated formula constitutes an intermediate result. Though it does not contribute to the concept being formed, the lemma might be interesting in its own right. Table 3 shows the lemmas we formed; each lemma appeared in only one experiment.

The whole test set included 40 experiments. Each faulty conjecture was successfully patched. Failure in plan formation occurred occasionally. Often, failure had its root in the absence of a bridging lemma. By contrast, changing the configuration of the inductive proof plan was almost unnecessary (1 out of 40). This took the form of adding an unusual method to the standard method data base. The method, called *apply_lemma*, is used to apply a lemma that cannot be oriented as a reduction rule without running the risk of non-termination, e.g. commutativity. It is expensive in general and, so, a more elegant solution is, for example, to include symmetry of equality in symbolic evaluation.

[4] Due to space constrains, the symmetric results for foldl have been omitted from display.

Table 2. Example faulty conjectures

Faulty Conjecture	New Concept	PT (secs)
foldr F E (app L M) $=F$ (foldr$F$ E L) (foldr F E M)	left_id F E right_id F E assoc F	161.54
foldr F E (app L M) $=G$ (foldr$F$ E L) (foldr F E M)	left_id G E right_id G E fcomm F G	326.26
foldr F E (app L M) $=F$ (foldr$F$ E M) (foldr F E L)	right_id F E assoc F comm F	403.98
foldr F E (app L M) $=G$ (foldr$F$ E M) (foldr F E L)	left_id G E right_id G E fcomm+ F G	996.7
foldr F E (flat L) $=$ foldr F E (map L ($\lambda z.$ foldr F E Z))	right_id F E assoc F	181.87
foldr F E (flat L) $=$ foldr G E (map L ($\lambda Z.$foldr F E Z))	left_id G E right_id G E fcomm F G	346.31
foldr F $(F\ X\ Y)$ $Z=G\ X$ (foldr F $(F\ E\ Y)$ Z)	fcomm+ F G eqd F G E	148.14
foldr F E (rev L) $=$ foldr F E L	assoc F comm F	107.23
foldr ($\lambda X, M. F\ (G\ X)\ M$) E (rev L) $=$ foldr ($\lambda X, M. F\ (G\ X)\ M$) E L	assoc F comm F	318.56
foldr F E (rev L) $=$ foldr G E L	fcomm+ F G	128.33
foldr F E (sort L) $=$ foldr F E L	assoc F comm F	29.5
foldr F E $L=$ foldl G E L	equc F G E assoc F comm F	109.95
foldr F A (map L G) $=$ foldr H B L	$A=B$ fcomm++ F G H	46.46
foldr F A (flat L) $=$ foldr H B L	$A=B$ flip H dist H	22.13
F X (foldr F E M) $=$ foldr F L M	comm F assoc F left_id F E	29.25
foldl F $(F\ X\ Y)$ $L=F\ X$ (foldl F Y L)	assoc F	40.55

Table 3. Formed lemmas

Formed lemma	Root Concepts
$F\,X\,(F\,Y\,Z) = F\,(F\,Y\,X)\,Z$	assoc F comm F
$G\,X\,(F\,Y\,(F\,E\,Z)) = F\,Y\,(F\,X\,Z)$	eqd $F\ G\ E$ fcomm+ $F\ G$
$G\,X\,(F\,(F\,E\,Y)\,Z) = F\,(F\,X\,Y)\,Z$	eqd $F\ G\ E$ fcomm+ $F\ G$
$G\,(F\,X\,E)\,Y = F\,X\,Y$	left_id $G\ E$ right_id $G\ E$ fcomm+ $F\ G$

The example faulty conjectures used in the test were gathered basically from four sources: Bird's books [3,2], the HOL98 corpus and Curzon and Wong's paper [23]. Some theorems reported in these sources were artificially turned into a faulty formula. We also considered slight variations of them.

A hand proof attempt tends to be shorter than a mechanical one. So a human mathematician might spend lesser time spotting a fault—and sometimes its associated mend—specially when she knows what she is looking for. By contrast, a mechanical proof is both long and tedious, since dead ends are found deeper in a proof attempt. In return, mechanical concept formation can be automated and might find concepts that could have been missed otherwise. This is because an automated system explores branches that a human might close untimely, without worrying any further.

The average total elapsed proof planning time was 253.6 sec, with a standard deviation of 253.5. Thus, the examples are done automatically within a few hundred seconds. The test was run on a 270MHz Ultra 5, a SuperSPARC machine with 64Mb of RAM running solaris 7. The full test, as well as the abduction method, is available upon request, by sending electronic-mail to the author. Alternatively, readers may as well visit the following URL:

`http://research.cem.itesm.mx/raulm/pub/code/fault-correction`

7 Related Work

Concept formation has been an active area of research for many years. AM [16], Graffiti [9,8] and HR [7] are amongst the most popular computer programs that automate theory discovery. These systems build on both an explicit representation and a set of production rules. The rules exploit current knowledge, while associating to the results a level of interestingness. AM and HR are designed to invent and assess mathematical definitions. Both provide support to sustain why certain concepts that have been formed are taken as interesting. Then, they use the most interesting ones to build a theory that includes definitions, computations, models, theorems and open conjectures.

Graffiti is a conjecture discovery system developed to work in graph theory and chemistry. It has been successfully used to speculate a number of interesting conjectures, documented in over 60 manuscripts, including published papers, preprints, Ph.D. theses and technical reports. Only HR and Graffiti are still being used and only HR and Graffiti have added to Mathematics. AM never did invent anything new to mathematicians and has not been used for over 15 years.

Correcting a faulty conjecture, via building a predicate, is not new. The first attempt at automatic fault correction was reported by [19]. In a similar vein, [10] first pioneered the use of proofs-as-programs for the construction of a corrective condition. Franova and Kodratoff never formalised their approach, they call *predicate synthesis*, and described it only by example, hence, making it difficult for readers to reproduce their results.

Protezen has also investigated the application of proofs-as-programs for fixing faulty conjectures [21]. He investigated the use of predicate synthesis in several interesting faulty conjectures, yielding conditional, recursive corrective predicates. However, like Franova and Kodratoff, Protzen did not provide a procedural account of his method, introducing it by example only.

Monroy [18] gave a formal means of mechanisation for predicate synthesis and other fault correction techniques found in the literature [17]. He has shown that an abduction framework, together with a methodology based on editing and construction commands, is helpful in constructing patching conditions for faulty conjectures.

8 Conclusions and Indications for Further Work

Abduction can be used to explore the tree associated to a failed proof attempt. This returns a collection of formulae, each of which represents a dead end formula, which the proof method could not develop any longer. Using both the dead end formulae and the structure of the partial proof tree, we can build a corrective predicate. Any one of these predicates amounts to a concept not present in the working theory; sometimes it involves a bridging lemma. The level of interestingness associated with the corrective predicates provides evidence for using abduction as a concept formation process.

Using abduction blindly, however, could be a hopeless process. This is because the tree associated to a failed proof attempt is huge and possibly infinite. Proof planning has made our experimental results possible. This is both because it provides a significant level of automation in inductive theorem proving, and because, working at a meta-level, it dramatically restricts the abduction search space.

Our results are promising; *CI^AM* together with the abduction mechanism could be used to explore open conjectures in a theory. This might result in a proof or the production of a patching condition, that might well encompass an unknown, but interesting concept.

Our method is just an experiment in concept formation, leaving plenty of room for improvements. For example, by choosing a set of faulty conjectures with an 'attractive' property, we are in a way choosing the concept our method should find. Thus ongoing work is concerned with extending the method (or coupling it) with (exploratory) techniques that make use of interestingness to formulate open conjectures. What is more, a combined system would improve the level of automation, since our method would not require the open conjectures to be supplied by hand.

Ongoing work is also concerned with exploring other application domains. While our method may not work as well where the underlying proofs have a less predictable structure, we reckon planning failure provides a means to concept formation that is worth exploring.

References

[1] Alessandro Armando, Alan Smaill, and Ian Green. Automatic synthesis of recursive programs: The proof-planning paradigm. *Automated Software Engineering*, 6(4):329–356, 1999.

[2] Richard Bird. *Introduction to Functional Programming Using Haskell.* Prentice Hall Europe, 1998. Second Edition.

[3] Richard S. Bird and Philip Wadler. *Introduction to Functional Programming.* Prentice-Hall, 1988.

[4] A. Bundy, A. Stevens, F. van Harmelen, A. Ireland, and A. Smaill. Rippling: A heuristic for guiding inductive proofs. *Artificial Intelligence*, 62:185–253, 1993. Also available from Edinburgh as DAI Research Paper No. 567.

[5] A. Bundy, F. van Harmelen, C. Horn, and A. Smaill. The Oyster-Clam system. In M. E. Stickel, editor, *Proceedings of the 10th International Conference on Automated Deduction*, Lecture Notes in Artificial Intelligence, Vol. 449, pages 647–648. Springer-Verlag, 1990. Also available from Edinburgh as DAI Research Paper No. 507.

[6] Alan Bundy. The use of explicit plans to guide inductive proofs. In R. Lusk and R. Overbeek, editors, *Proceedings of the 9th Conference on Automated Deduction*, Lecture Notes in Computer Science, Vol. 310, pages 111–120, Argonne, Illinois, USA, 1988. Springer-Verlag. Also available from Edinburgh as DAI Research Paper No. 349.

[7] S. Colton, A. Bundy, and T. Walsh. Automatic concept formation in pure mathematics. In *Proceedings of IJCAI99*, volume vol 2, pages 786–791. Morgan Kaufmann, 1999.

[8] E. DeLaVina and S. Fajtlowicz. Ramseyian properties of graphs. *Electronic Journal of Combinatorics*, 3, 1996.

[9] S. Fajtlowicz. On conjectures of graffiti. *Discrete Mathematics*, 72(23):113–118, 1988.

[10] M. Franova and Y. Kodratoff. Predicate synthesis from formal specifications. In B. Neumann, editor, *Proceedings of the 10th European Conference on Artificial Intelligence, ECAI'92*, pages 87–91, Chichester, England, 1992. John Wiley and Sons.

[11] M. J. C. Gordon and T. F. Melham, editors. *Introduction to HOL: A theorem proving environment for higher order logic.* Cambridge University Press, 1993.

[12] W. A. Howard. The formulae-as-types notion of construction. In J. P. Seldin and J. R. Hindley, editors, *To H. B. Curry; Essays on Combinatory Logic, Lambda Calculus and Formalism*, pages 479–490. Academic Press, 1980.

[13] A. Ireland. The Use of Planning Critics in Mechanizing Inductive Proofs. In A. Voronkov, editor, *International Conference on Logic Programming and Automated Reasoning – LPAR 92, St. Petersburg*, Lecture Notes in Artificial Intelligence No. 624, pages 178–89. Springer-Verlag, 1992. Lecture Notes in Artificial Intelligence Vol. 624. Also available from Edinburgh as DAI Research Paper No. 592.

[14] A. Ireland and A. Bundy. Productive use of failure in inductive proof. *Journal of Automated Reasoning*, 16(1–2):79–111, 1996. Also available from Edinburgh as DAI Research Paper No 716.

[15] I. Lakatos. *Proofs and refutations: The logic of Mathematical discovery.* Cambridge University Press, 1976.

[16] D. B. Lenat. AM: An artificial intelligence approach to discovery in mathematics as heuristic search. In *Knowledge-based systems in artificial intelligence.* McGraw Hill, 1982. Also available from Stanford as TechReport AIM 286.

[17] R. Monroy, A. Bundy, and A. Ireland. Proof plans for the correction of false conjectures. In F. Pfenning, editor, *Proceedings of the 5th International Conference on Logic Programming and Automated Reasoning, LPAR'94*, Lecture Notes in Artificial Intelligence, Vol. 822, pages 54–68, Kiev, Ukraine, 1994. Springer-Verlag. Also available from Edinburgh as DAI Research Paper No. 681.

[18] Raúl Monroy. The use of abduction and recursion-editor techniques for the correction of faulty conjectures. In P. Flenner and P. Alexander, editors, *Proceedings of the 15th Conference on Automated Software Engineering*, pages 91–99, Grenoble, France, 2000. IEEE Computer Society Press. Celebrated on September 11-15, 2000.

[19] J S. Moore. *Computational Logic: Structure Sharing and Proof of Program Properties, Part II.* PhD thesis, University of Edinburgh, 1974. Available from Edinburgh as DCL memo No. 68 and from Xerox PARC, Palo Alto as CSL 75-2.

[20] C. S. Peirce. *Collected papers of Charles Sanders Peirce*, volume 2. Harvard University Press, 1959. edited by Harston, C. and Weiss, P.

[21] M. Protzen. Patching faulty conjectures. In M.A. McRobbie and J.K. Slaney, editors, *13th Conference on Automated Deduction*, Lecture Notes in Artificial Intelligence, Vol. 1104, pages 77–91, New Brunswick, NJ, USA, 1996. Springer-Verlag. Lecture Notes in Artificial Intelligence, Vol. 1104.

[22] C. Walther. On proving termination of algorithms by machine. *Artificial Intelligence*, 71(1):101–157, 1994.

[23] Wai Wong and Paul Curzon. A theory of lists for HOL based on higher-order functions. In T. Melham and J. Camilleri, editors, *the Supplementary Proceedings of the 7th International Workshop on Higher Order Logic Theorem Proving and its Applications.* University of Malta, 1994.

Author Index

Lecture Notes in Artificial Intelligence (LNAI)

Lecture Notes in Computer Science

Vol. 2201: G.D. Abowd, B. Brumitt, S. Shafer (Eds.), Ubicomp 2001: Ubiquitous Computing. Proceedings, 2001. XIII, 372 pages. 2001.

Vol. 2202: A. Restivo, S. Ronchi Della Rocca, L. Roversi (Eds.), Theoretical Computer Science. Proceedings, 2001. XI, 440 pages. 2001.

Vol. 2204: A. Brandstädt, V.B. Le (Eds.), Graph-Theoretic Concepts in Computer Science. Proceedings, 2001. X, 329 pages. 2001.

Vol. 2205: D.R. Montello (Ed.), Spatial Information Theory. Proceedings, 2001. XIV, 503 pages. 2001.

Vol. 2206: B. Reusch (Ed.), Computational Intelligence. Proceedings, 2001. XVII, 1003 pages. 2001.

Vol. 2207: I.W. Marshall, S. Nettles, N. Wakamiya (Eds.), Active Networks. Proceedings, 2001. IX, 165 pages. 2001.

Vol. 2208: W.J. Niessen, M.A. Viergever (Eds.), Medical Image Computing and Computer-Assisted Intervention – MICCAI 2001. Proceedings, 2001. XXXV, 1446 pages. 2001.

Vol. 2209: W. Jonker (Ed.), Databases in Telecommunications II. Proceedings, 2001. VII, 179 pages. 2001.

Vol. 2210: Y. Liu, K. Tanaka, M. Iwata, T. Higuchi, M. Yasunaga (Eds.), Evolvable Systems: From Biology to Hardware. Proceedings, 2001. XI, 341 pages. 2001.

Vol. 2211: T.A. Henzinger, C.M. Kirsch (Eds.), Embedded Software. Proceedings, 2001. IX, 504 pages. 2001.

Vol. 2212: W. Lee, L. Mé, A. Wespi (Eds.), Recent Advances in Intrusion Detection. Proceedings, 2001. X, 205 pages. 2001.

Vol. 2213: M.J. van Sinderen, L.J.M. Nieuwenhuis (Eds.), Protocols for Multimedia Systems. Proceedings, 2001. XII, 239 pages. 2001.

Vol. 2214: O. Boldt, H. Jürgensen (Eds.), Automata Implementation. Proceedings, 1999. VIII, 183 pages. 2001.

Vol. 2215: N. Kobayashi, B.C. Pierce (Eds.), Theoretical Aspects of Computer Software. Proceedings, 2001. XV, 561 pages. 2001.

Vol. 2216: E.S. Al-Shaer, G. Pacifici (Eds.), Management of Multimedia on the Internet. Proceedings, 2001. XIV, 373 pages. 2001.

Vol. 2217: T. Gomi (Ed.), Evolutionary Robotics. Proceedings, 2001. XI, 139 pages. 2001.

Vol. 2218: R. Guerraoui (Ed.), Middleware 2001. Proceedings, 2001. XIII, 395 pages. 2001.

Vol. 2220: C. Johnson (Ed.), Interactive Systems. Proceedings, 2001. XII, 219 pages. 2001.

Vol. 2221: D.G. Feitelson, L. Rudolph (Eds.), Job Scheduling Strategies for Parallel Processing. Proceedings, 2001. VII, 207 pages. 2001.

Vol. 2224: H.S. Kunii, S. Jajodia, A. Sølvberg (Eds.), Conceptual Modeling – ER 2001. Proceedings, 2001. XIX, 614 pages. 2001.

Vol. 2225: N. Abe, R. Khardon, T. Zeugmann (Eds.), Algorithmic Learning Theory. Proceedings, 2001. XI, 379 pages. 2001. (Subseries LNAI).

Vol. 2226: K.P. Jantke, A. Shinohara (Eds.), Discovery Science. Proceedings, 2001. XII, 494 pages. 2001. (Subseries LNAI).

Vol. 2227: S. Boztaş, I.E. Shparlinski (Eds.), Applied Algebra, Algebraic Algorithms and Error-Correcting Codes. Proceedings, 2001. XII, 398 pages. 2001.

Vol. 2229: S. Qing, T. Okamoto, J. Zhou (Eds.), Information and Communications Security. Proceedings, 2001. XIV, 504 pages. 2001.

Vol. 2230: T. Katila, I.E. Magnin, P. Clarysse, J. Montagnat, J. Nenonen (Eds.), Functional Imaging and Modeling of the Heart. Proceedings, 2001. XI, 158 pages. 2001.

Vol. 2232: L. Fiege, G. Mühl, U. Wilhelm (Eds.), Electronic Commerce. Proceedings, 2001. X, 233 pages. 2001.

Vol. 2233: J. Crowcroft, M. Hofmann (Eds.), Networked Group Communication. Proceedings, 2001. X, 205 pages. 2001.

Vol. 2234: L. Pacholski, P. Ružička (Eds.), SOFSEM 2001: Theory and Practice of Informatics. Proceedings, 2001. XI, 347 pages. 2001.

Vol. 2237: P. Codognet (Ed.), Logic Programming. Proceedings, 2001. XI, 365 pages. 2001.

Vol. 2239: T. Walsh (Ed.), Principles and Practice of Constraint Programming – CP 2001. Proceedings, 2001. XIV, 788 pages. 2001.

Vol. 2240: G.P. Picco (Ed.), Mobile Agents. Proceedings, 2001. XIII, 277 pages. 2001.

Vol. 2241: M. Jünger, D. Naddef (Eds.), Computational Combinatorial Optimization. IX, 305 pages. 2001.

Vol. 2242: C.A. Lee (Ed.), Grid Computing – GRID 2001. Proceedings, 2001. XII, 185 pages. 2001.

Vol. 2250: R. Nieuwenhuis, A. Voronkov (Eds.), Logic for Programming, Artificial Intelligence, and Reasoning. Proceedings, 2001. XV, 738 pages. 2001. (Subseries LNAI).

Vol. 2248: C. Boyd (Ed.), Advances in Cryptology – ASIACRYPT 2001. Proceedings, 2001. XI, 603 pages. 2001.

Vol. 2256: M. Brooks, D. Corbett, M. Stumptner (Eds.), AI 2001: Advances in Artificial Intelligence. Proceedings, 2001. XII, 666 pages. 2001. (Subseries LNAI).